The Complete Book of 1970s Broadway Musicals

The Complete Book of 1970s Broadway Musicals

Dan Dietz

ROWMAN & LITTLEFIELD
Lanham • Boulder • New York • London

Published by Rowman & Littlefield
A wholly owned subsidiary of The Rowman & Littlefield Publishing Group, Inc.
4501 Forbes Boulevard, Suite 200, Lanham, Maryland 20706
www.rowman.com

Unit A, Whitacre Mews, 26-34 Stannary Street, London SE11 4AB

British Library Cataloguing in Publication Information Available

Library of Congress Cataloging-in-Publication Data

Dietz, Dan, 1945– author.
The complete book of 1970s Broadway musicals / Dan Dietz.
pages cm
Includes bibliographical references and index.
ISBN 978-1-4422-5165-6 (hardback : alk. paper) — ISBN 978-1-4422-5166-3 (ebook) 1. Musicals—New York (State)—New York—20th century—History and criticism. I. Title.
ML1711.8.N3D532 2015
792.6'45097471—dc23

2015007993

∞™ The paper used in this publication meets the minimum requirements of American National Standard for Information Sciences—Permanence of Paper for Printed Library Materials, ANSI/NISO Z39.48-1992. Printed in the United States of America

To the memory of my aunt,
Amelia Cioffi Symonette

Contents

Acknowledgments

I want to take this opportunity to thank my friends Mike Baskin and Ken DePew for their helpful comments and suggestions in the writing of this book.

Introduction

The Complete Book of 1970s Broadway Musicals examines in detail all 285 musicals that opened between January 1, 1970, and December 31, 1979. The musicals discussed are: eighty-four book musicals with new music; three with preexisting music; one opera; six plays with incidental songs; twenty-six fairly traditional revues; thirty-two personality revues; two ice revues; three dance musicals and revues; twenty musicals and revues that originated either Off- or Off-Off-Broadway; twenty-two imports; fifty-six revivals; one return engagement; and twenty-nine pre-Broadway closings (including one musical that closed during Broadway previews). For a quick rundown of these shows, see the Alphabetical List of Shows, Appendix A: Chronology (by Season), and Appendix B: Chronology (by Classification).

The purpose of this book is to present a complete picture of each musical, including technical information and commentary. My goal is to provide a handy reference source that examines technical aspects (cast and song lists, for example) as well as information that sheds new light on both familiar and forgotten musicals of the era. I've included obscure details about the productions because so often this kind of information personalizes a show and brings it to life. I've also examined the books and song structures of the musicals, and have noted occasional curious choices made by a musical's creative team (for example, see entries for *70, Girls, 70* and *A Little Night Music*).

The decade of the 1970s is important in the history of musical theatre because it institutionalized the concept musical as a viable means of presenting a story in which mood and atmosphere are more important than the traditional linear means of telling a story with a well-defined beginning, middle, and end. For the concept musical, the story and characters are less important than the overall viewpoint of the production, and to that end the pattern of the book, lyrics, music, direction, choreography, visual design, and performance style tell an often abstract story that avoids traditional narrative styles and clear-cut conclusions.

To be sure, the concept musical had been around for decades, from W. H. Auden and Benjamin Britten's 1941 opera *Paul Bunyan*, Richard Rodgers and Oscar Hammerstein II's *Allegro* (1947), Alan Jay Lerner and Kurt Weill's *Love Life* (1948), and Galt MacDermot, Gerome Ragni, and James Rado's *Hair* (Off-Broadway, 1967; Broadway, 1968). But it was in the 1970s when the concept musical flowered with a stunning series of ambitious productions, among them Stephen Sondheim's quintet of groundbreaking musicals as well as *Chicago* and *A Chorus Line*.

Sondheim's *Company* was the decade's first concept musical. Its somewhat circular story was bookended by a birthday party and it included a series of staccato-like glimpses into the lives of contemporary New Yorkers who seek company and communication, but for all their phone calls to one another all they seem to get is a busy signal.

And it was Sondheim who defined and owned the decade. Besides *Company*, his *Follies, A Little Night Music, Pacific Overtures*, and *Sweeney Todd, The Demon Barber of Fleet Street* opened, and these works stretched the boundaries of musical theatre with their unique approaches in utilizing music to tell their stories.

In regard to technical information, the entries in this book include: name of theatre (and transfers, if applicable); opening and closing dates of production; number of performances (for consistency, I've used the performance numbers reported in *Best Plays*); the show's advertising tag (including variations of the tag as used in a show's program, flyer, script, and other source materials); and names of book writers, sketch writers, lyricists, composers, directors, choreographers, musical directors, producers, and scenic, costume, and lighting designers. All cast members are included, and each performer's name is followed by the name of the character portrayed (performers' names in italics reflect those billed above the show's title).

Also included are the number of acts; for book musicals, the time and locale of the show; and the titles of musical numbers are given by act (following each song's title is the name of the performer, not the character, who introduced the song). If a musical is based on source material, such information is cited. Occasionally programs didn't include every musical number, but the song lists in this book reflect every musical sequence that was performed in a show, whether or not it was listed in the program. Also, if a song is known by a variant title, the alternate title is given in parentheses.

The commentary for each musical includes a brief plot summary (in the case of revues or revue-like musicals, representative sketches and plot sequences are discussed); brief quotes from the critics; informative trivia; details about London and other international productions as well as New York revivals; and data about recordings, published scripts, and film, radio, television, and video versions. In most cases, the commentary also includes information regarding the show's gestation and pre-Broadway tryout history. Tony Award winners and nominees are listed (the names of the winners are bolded), and the winners of the New York Drama Critics' Circle Award and Pulitzer Prize are also cited. Throughout the book, bolded titles refer to productions that are discussed elsewhere in the text.

The book includes eleven appendixes: black revues and musicals, chronology by season, chronology by classification, a discography, a filmography, a list of Gilbert and Sullivan revivals, Jewish revues and musicals, a chronology of selected (mostly nonmusical) productions that included songs, dances, or background music, a list of published scripts, a list of Radio City Music Hall productions, and a list of theatres where the musicals were performed.

The book also includes a bibliography. Virtually all the information in the book is drawn from such original source materials as programs, souvenir programs, window cards (posters), flyers, recordings (including demonstration recordings), scripts (both published and unpublished), and contemporary reviews.

Alphabetical List of Shows

The following is an alphabetical list of all 285 musicals discussed in this book. There are multiple listings for those musicals produced more than once during the decade, and those entries are followed by the year of the production.

1970 Season

CHARLES AZNAVOUR

Theatre: Music Box Theatre
Opening Date: February 4, 1970; *Closing Date*: February 22, 1970
Performances: 23
Lyrics and *Music*: Unless otherwise noted, all lyrics and music by Charles Aznavour
Production Supervisor: Leon Sanossian; *Producers*: Norman Twain in association with Albert I. Fill; *Musical Direction*: Henry Byrs
Cast: *Charles Aznavour*
The one-man show (with orchestra) was presented in two acts.

Musical Numbers

All songs performed by Charles Aznavour.
Act One: "Le tamos" (lyric by J. Davis); "I Will Give to You" (English lyric by B. Morrisson); "Happy Anniversary" (English lyric by Herbert Kretzmer); "We'll Drift Away" (lyric by George Garvarentz, English lyric by B. Kaye); "Le toreador"; "Sunday's Not My Day" (lyric by T. Veran; English lyric by B. Morrisson); "Apaga la luz" (English lyric by R. Deleon); "Isabelle"; "I Will Warm Your Heart" (English lyric by Gene Lees); "To My Daughter" (English lyric by B. Morrisson); "Et pourtant" (English lyric by George Garvarentz); "The Wine of Youth" (English lyric by B. Morrisson); "Yesterday When I Was Young" (English lyric by Herbert Kretzmer); "Emmenez-moi"; "It Will Be My Day" (English lyric by B. Morrisson)
Act Two: "All Those Pretty Girls" (English lyric by B. Kaye); "De t'avoir aimer"; "My Hand Needs Your Hand" (lyric by P. Roche, English lyric by B. Kaye); "You've Let Yourself Go" (English lyric by Marcel Stellman); "Desormais" (lyric by George Garvarentz); "Who" (English lyric by Herbert Kretzmer); "Reste" (lyric by Bachelor); "Venice Dressed in Blue" (English lyric by B. Kaye, music by F. Dorin); "August Days in Paree" (lyric by George Garvarentz, English lyric by D. Newburg); "Les comediens" (music by Jacques Plante); "And I in My Chair" (English lyric by D. Newburg); "You've Got to Learn" (English lyric by Marcel Stellman); "Les bons moments"

Broadway's first musical event of the decade was *Charles Aznavour*, a one-man concert of songs by the popular French singer, lyricist, and composer, who was accompanied by an eleven-member orchestra. Among the selections were his hit songs "Yesterday When I Was Young" and "You've Let Yourself Go."

Mel Gussow in the *New York Times* likened Aznavour to a male Edith Piaf, and noted the singer's persona was that of a "waif" and a "wounded bird" whose "hurts show in the lines of his face and of his songs." The critic mentioned that with this production Aznavour revealed a new command of English, which allowed him to communicate "clearly and unhaltingly." As a result, he was now a "stronger" singer and was "quite simply at the top of his form."

Aznavour had first appeared in New York in concert at Carnegie Hall in 1963. He then played on Broadway in his one-man show *The World of Charles Aznavour*, which opened at the Ambassador Theatre on October 14, 1965, for twenty-nine performances, and after the current engagement he was seen on Broadway three more times: ***Charles Aznavour on Broadway*** (October 15, 1974, for sixteen performances at the Minskoff Theatre); *Charles Aznavour* (March 14, 1983, for fourteen performances at the Lunt-Fontanne Theatre); and *Aznavour on Broadway* (October 20, 1998, for twenty-four performances at the Marquis Theatre).

GANTRY

"The New Musical"

Theatre: George Abbott Theatre
Opening Date: February 12, 1970; *Closing Date*: February 12, 1970
Performances: 1
Book: Peter Bellwood
Lyrics: Fred Tobias
Music: Stanley Lebowsky
Based on the 1927 novel *Elmer Gantry* by Sinclair Lewis.
Direction: Onna White (production supervised by Robert Weiner); *Producers*: Joseph Cates and Jerry Schlossberg (Fred Menowitz, Associate Producer); *Choreography*: Onna White (Patrick Cummings, Assistant Choreographer); *Scenery*: Robin Wagner; *Costumes*: Ann Roth; *Lighting*: Jules Fisher; *Musical Direction*: Arthur Rubenstein
Cast: Tom Batten (Bill Morgan), Dorothea Freitag (Sister Dorothea), Gloria Hodes (Adelberta Shoup), Rita Moreno (Sharon Falconer), *Robert Shaw* (Elmer Gantry), Wayne Tippit (Jim Lefferts), Ted Thurston (George F. Babbitt), Kenneth Bridges (Reverend Garrison), Bob Gorman (Trosper), David Sabin (Gunch), Zale Kessler (Prout), David Hooks (Reverend Toomis), Robert Donahue (Architect), James N. Maher (Photographer), J. Michael Bloom (Deaf Man), Beth Fowler (Deaf Man's Wife); Townspeople, Revival Troupe, Students, Workmen: Chuck Beard, J. Michael Bloom, Kenneth Bridges, Patrick Cummings, Robert Donahue, Sandy Ellen, Carol Estey, Beth Fowler, Gloria Hodes, Keith Kaldenberg, Clyde Laurents, Robert Lenn, James N. Maher, Kathleen Robey, Dixie Stewart, Diane Tarleton, Maralyn Thoma, Terry Violino, Mimi Wallace
The musical was presented in two acts.
The action takes place during the 1920s, mostly in Chicago, but also in North Dakota and Kansas.

Musical Numbers

Act One: "Wave a Hand" (Tom Batten, Revival Troupe); Gantry Gets the Call: (1) "He Was There" and (2) "Play Ball with the Lord" (Robert Shaw, Revival Troupe, Townspeople); "Katie Jonas" (Rita Moreno); "Thanks, Sweet Jesus!" (Robert Shaw, Townspeople); "Someone I've Already Found" (Robert Shaw); "He's Never Too Busy" (Rita Moreno, Robert Shaw, Tom Batten, Gloria Hodes, Revival Troupe); "We're Sharin' Sharon" (Robert Shaw)
Act Two: "We Can All Give Love" (Rita Moreno, Gloria Hodes, Townspeople); "Foresight" (Ted Thurston, David Sabin, Bob Gorman, Zale Kessler); "These Four Walls" (Rita Moreno); "Show Him the Way" (Robert Shaw, Townspeople); "The Promise of What I Could Be" (Robert Shaw); "Gantry's Reaction" (Robert Shaw); "We're Sharin' Sharon" (reprise) (Robert Shaw)

Gantry was the first new book musical of the decade and one of the season's three musicals to play for just one performance (the others were *La Strada*, which had opened two months earlier, and ***Blood Red Roses***). *Gantry* ushered in a string of musical flops that opened throughout the remaining months of the season: six more new book musicals (***Georgy***, ***Blood Red Roses***, ***Minnie's Boys***, ***Look to the Lilies***, ***Cry for Us All***, and ***Park***) opened and quickly closed. Further, a seventh (***Purlie***) enjoyed a long run but nonetheless failed to return a profit; the play-with-music ***Operation Sidewinder*** closed at Lincoln Center after its limited engagement and didn't risk a commercial transfer to a regular Broadway house; and a revival of ***The Boy Friend*** lost money. But there were two hits: the long-running but extremely disappointing ***Applause*** (which became the season's longest-running musical) and Stephen Sondheim's iconic and groundbreaking ***Company***.

Based on Sinclair Lewis's popular novel *Elmer Gantry*, the musical *Gantry* focused on the titular con artist (played by Robert Shaw) who adopts the pious posture of a God-fearing minister and later promotes evangelist Sharon Falconer (Rita Moreno) in her rise to fame and fortune as one of the country's leading religious figures. The successful film version of the novel earned Oscars for Burt Lancaster (Best Actor) in the title role and Shirley Jones (Best Supporting Actress) as the prostitute Lulu Baines with whom he's involved, but the musical eliminated the Lulu Baines subplot and instead concentrated on Gantry and Sharon's relationship, which evolves from one of business to one of both business and pleasure. When Sharon dies in a fire and her tabernacle is destroyed, Gantry is left with nothing, but one assumes he'll soon be searching for green pastures of the monetary kind. Like the movie, the musical also included the character of George F. Babbitt, the title character of Lewis's 1922 novel *Babbitt*.

The musical received uniformly negative notices, but the critics were divided on the merits of Robert Shaw's performance. The British actor and writer was here making his Broadway musical debut, and while most of the reviewers agreed that his singing voice was at best passable, they were in disagreement over his interpretation of the role. Clive Barnes in the *New York Times* said his performance was "blazing, corrupt, evil and yet malignantly persuasive" and it "could have shattered the theatre and satisfied literature." But Douglas Watt in the *New York Daily News* found him "miscast" and noted he came across as a "dim echo" of Harold Hill in *The Music Man*. Richard Watts in the *New York Post* said he was "virtually the whole show" and brought his "personal zest" to the role, and Martin Gottfried in *Women's Wear Daily* found him "almost miraculous." But Edwin Newman on WNBC4TV said he was "grossly miscast," and John J. O'Connor in the *Wall Street Journal* noted his performance lacked a "central spark" and a "fire-and-brimstone fanaticism." Perhaps as written the leading role was too watered-down; as Watts noted, in the novel Elmer Gantry is a "scoundrel" and a "Tartuffe-like hypocrite with no redeeming qualities," but for the musical he was a "flawed hero" instead of a "downright villain."

As for Rita Moreno, she too received mixed notices. Barnes said she made her character "surprisingly real," but Watt found her "surprisingly bland"; Watts said she was "quietly appealing," but Leonard Harris on WCBSTV2 said she couldn't manage the charisma required of the character, and Gottfried said she had "stage absence."

The critics were also sharply divided on the merits of Onna White's direction and choreography. Barnes said she brought "electricity" to the production and created "exciting" staging in which "dance and movement" were an "integral part" of her creative vision, and O'Connor also praised her "superb" direction. But Gottfried suggested White was so "intimidated" by her directorial and choreographic responsibilities that she "failed to fulfill" them.

Gottfried also took the chorus to task, complaining that they had given up on the musical; he suggested that such "unprofessional conduct" should sentence them all "to a year of bus-and-truck company work." Robin Wagner's scenic design also came in for criticism. Watt said it was the "dingiest" he'd ever seen for a musical, and Gottfried noted the set sometimes gave no hint of what it was supposed to depict, and thus the normally "inventive" Wagner wasn't "particularly inventive" this time around. (The critic mentioned that perhaps the designer had been constrained by a small budget, and it's noteworthy that the musical opted for a four-week preview period instead of a traditional, and expensive, out-of-town tryout.)

As for Stanley Lebowsky's music and Fred Tobias's lyrics, the critics were less than impressed, and noted the score drew heavily on the style of gospel music. Barnes said the songs were strictly "Bible-belt" with "sanctimonious" harmony and "watery fervor"; Watts noted the songs added little to the evening; and O'Connor said the numbers were only "hand-clappingly adequate." Gottfried mentioned that while Lebowsky had a "nice sense of melody," his songs were "catchily forgettable"; he also noted that while the composer had written a series of "separate" songs for the musical, he hadn't composed a coherent and unified score. Watt singled out the barbershop quartet "Foresight," which was "commonplace" but nonetheless a show-stopper in its delivery by Ted Thurston, David Sabin, Bob Gorman, and Zale Kessler.

The cast album of *Gantry* was to have been recorded by RCA Victor Records (and was assigned release # LSOD-2010), but the recording was canceled due to the musical's brief run. However, a demo recording of the score (released on an unnumbered CD by an unnamed company which also includes demo and cover recordings of the scores for *Something More!* [1964] and *Pleasures and Palaces* [1965]), offers seven songs heard in the Broadway production ("The Promise of What I Could Be," "These Four Walls," "Someone I've

Already Found," "Foresight," "He's Never Too Busy," "Show Him the Way," and "We Can All Give Love"); one number not heard on Broadway ("She Was a Woman"); and two cover versions ("He's Never Too Busy" by Jane Morgan and "Foresight" by Roslyn Kind).

There have been two other lyric adaptations of Lewis's novel, both titled *Elmer Gantry*. In 1988, one version with book by John Bishop, lyrics by Robert Satuloff and Bishop, and music by Mel Marvin played at Ford's Theatre in Washington, D.C., with a cast that included Casey Biggs (Elmer Gantry) and Sharon Scruggs (Sharon Falconer). (Like the Broadway version, the character of Lulu Baines was eliminated from the adaptation.) This version resurfaced twenty-six years later in a revised production that still credited Bishop with the book and Marvin for the music; but this time around only Satuloff was cited as lyricist, and Lisa Bishop was credited for additional book material. The new version opened at Signature Theatre in Arlington, Virginia, on October 17, 2014, and Peter Marks in the *Washington Post* commented that despite its "narrative wrinkles" the musical was "a smooth and confident ride" with a score "absolutely worthy of a listen."

An operatic adaptation premiered at the Nashville Opera in November 2007; the libretto was by Herschel Garfein and the music by Robert Aldridge. The opera was recorded by Naxos Records (two-CD set # 8.669032-33), and the cast included Keith Phares (Elmer Gantry), Patricia Risley (Sharon Falconer), and Heather Buck (Lulu Baines).

Musicals about religious charlatans bookended the decade. As mentioned, *Gantry* was the first book musical of the 1970s, and in the fall of 1979 ***Daddy Goodness*** closed during its pre-Broadway tryout.

Gantry was the final production to play at the luckless Adelphi Theatre, which had opened in 1928 as the Craig, was later named the 54th Street Theatre, and then finally the George Abbott. The theatre's slightly out-of-the-way location was probably a mitigating factor in its lack of success, but it would also appear that doomed-to-fail musicals were fatalistically drawn to the venue. The theatre hosted an inordinate number of flop musicals, including *Jonica* (1930), *The Well of Romance* (1930), *Swing It* (1937), *Allah Be Praised!* (1944), *The Girl from Nantucket* (1945), *Nellie Bly* (1946), *The Duchess Misbehaves* (1946), *Around the World in Eighty Days* (1946), *Portofino* (1958), *Happy Town* (1959), *13 Daughters* (1961), *La Grosse Valise* (1965), *Darling of the Day* (1968), and *Buck White* (1969), and when an occasional hit opened there (such as *On the Town* [1944] and *No Strings* [1962]), those shows quickly transferred to a more centrally located theatre.

GEORGY

"A NEW MUSICAL"

Theatre: Winter Garden Theatre
Opening Date: February 26, 1970; *Closing Date*: February 28, 1970
Performances: 4
Book: Tom Mankiewicz
Lyrics: Carole Bayer (Sager)
Music: George Fischoff
Based on the 1965 novel *Georgy Girl* by Margaret Forster and the screenplay of the 1966 film *Georgy Girl* by Margaret Forster and Peter Nichols.
Direction: Peter Hunt; *Producers*: Fred Coe in association with Joseph P. Harris and Ira Bernstein; *Choreography*: Howard Jeffrey; *Scenery* and *Lighting*: Jo Mielziner; *Costumes*: Patricia Zipprodt; *Musical Direction*: Elliot Lawrence
Cast: Dilys Watling (Georgy), Stephen Elliott (James Leamington), Louis Beachner (Ted), Melissa Hart (Meredith), Helena Carroll (Peg), John Castle (Jos), Richard Quarry (Peter), Cynthia Latham (Health Officer); Party Guests, Londoners, Others: Kathryn Doby, Sherry Durham, Patricia Garland, Margot Head, Mary Jane Houdina, Jane Karel, Barbara Monte-Britton, Michon Peacock, Mary Zahn, Rick Atwell, Pi Douglass, Arthur Faria, Charlie Goeddertz, Neil Jones, Sal Pernice, Richard Quarry, Allan Sobek, Tony Stevens; Children: Kelley Boa, Mona Daleo, Jackie Paris, Donna Sands, Jill Streisant, Dewey Golkin, Jeffrey Golkin, Anthony Marciona, Roger Morgan, Johnny Welch; Singers: Susan Goeppinger, Del Horstmann, Don Jay, Geoff Leon, Regina Lynn
The musical was presented in two acts.
The action takes place during the present time in London.

Musical Numbers

Act One: "Howdjadoo" (Dilys Watling, Children); "Make It Happen Now" (Dilys Watling); "Ol' Pease Puddin'" (John Castle, Dilys Watling); "Just for the Ride" (Melissa Hart, Men); "So What?" (Dilys Watling); "Georgy" (Stephen Elliott); "A Baby" and "Howdjadoo" (reprise) (Dilys Watling, John Castle, Melissa Hart); "That's How It Is" (Dilys Watling, Stephen Elliott); "There's a Comin' Together" (John Castle, Dilys Watling, Chorus)
Act Two: "Something Special" (Dilys Watling, John Castle); "Half of Me" (Dilys Watling); "Gettin' Back to Me" (Melissa Hart); "Sweet Memory" (Louis Beachner, Stephen Elliott, Chorus); "Georgy" (reprise) (Stephen Elliott); "Life's a Holiday" (John Castle, Dilys Watling); "Make It Happen Now" (reprise) (Dilys Watling); "There's a Comin' Together" (reprise/finale) (Company)

In many respects, the 1966 film version of the 1965 novel *Georgy Girl* helped to create the myth of the mid-1960s swinging London scene of casual attitudes toward sex, relationships, and responsibility. And it was set to the bouncy beat of its irresistible title song (lyric by performer Jim Dale and music by Tom Springfield). But for all its "mod" trappings, the plot of the novel, film, and musical was essentially a Cinderella story about ungainly duckling Georgy (Dilys Watling) whose life revolves around her glamorous if superficial roommate Meredith (Melissa Hart), Meredith's cute but irresponsible boyfriend (and later husband) Jos (John Castle), and Georgy's family friend James (Stephen Elliott), a rich man twice her age who is genuinely attracted to her. Meredith and Jos have a baby, and because children and domesticity are really all that Georgy wants, she becomes the baby's surrogate mother. On the other hand, Meredith detests domestic life and soon abandons both Jos and the child. Although Georgy, Jos, and the baby become a tentative family, Jos soon drops out of Georgy's life when he realizes she loves the child more than she loves him. But stalwart James is always in the background, and he proposes to her. They marry, and then Georgy has all she's ever wanted: a baby, a home, and a husband (and their importance is probably in that order).

Because the plot offered modern adult situations and attitudes that were tied to the familiar old-fashioned Cinderella story, because its characters were generally complex and colorful, and because the story was set against the atmosphere and mood of mid-1960s London, it's easy to see why a musical version seemed promising. But despite both a production that genuinely tried to create a thoughtful and touching musical and four solid and well-cast leading performers, the musical never quite came together.

More than anything, it was probably the score that doomed the show. It offered a pleasant if mild collection of songs, but none of them really stood out and they couldn't match the charm of the film's well-known title song. Three critics singled out "Sweet Memory," but overall they were disappointed with the score. Richard Watts in the *New York Post* found the songs "fairly routine"; Clive Barnes in the *New York Times* said the score "rarely rose above the hopefully anonymous"; and Martin Gottfried in *Women's Wear Daily* found the music "mediocre." But while Douglas Watt in the *New York Daily News* said the score wasn't "particularly distinguished" he nonetheless found it "lively and cheerful," and Edwin Newman on WNBC4TV noted the score had an "insistent and sometimes infectious drive."

John O'Connor in the *Wall Street Journal* commented that the film's "episodic" plot was "dazzlingly" edited with short sequences, but the musical's book was "disastrously bogged down," and Watts found the musical's narrative "serviceable" but ineffective. However, Gottfried mused on what might have been. He explained that choreographer Howard Jeffrey approached all the musical numbers as if they were "constructed [as] a series of mini-musicals." He staged each song "as a complete musical within itself" and his choreography was "excellent." However, these sequences weren't related to one another, and Gottfried suggested if Jeffrey had also been the musical's director and had staged the book scenes in the same manner as the musical numbers, the complete "unit" of song, dance, and story might have been "quite marvelous."

Jeffrey seems to have held great promise as a choreographer, but after *Georgy* he never again created dances for a Broadway musical. For that matter, despite the good reviews for the four leads, *Georgy* was in many ways their swan song. The musical marked Watling and Castle's only Broadway appearances; Elliott was later seen in other Broadway productions, but didn't appear in another musical; and Hart was seen just twice more on Broadway (as a replacement in the 1997 revival of *Candide* and as a member of the ensemble in *The Scarlet Pimpernel* [also 1997]).

During the tryout and New York preview period, the following songs were dropped: "Frickered Fling," "Mrs. Jones," "Toy Balloon," "This Time Tomorrow," "And She Would Smile," "Party Dance," and "Birthdays." During preproduction, the songs "For You (I Will Live)" and "Electric Windows" were cut.

The cast album was scheduled to be recorded by Bell Records but was canceled due to the production's quick closing. The song "Something Special" was included in *The Golddiggers . . . Today!* released by RCA Victor Records (LP # LSP-4643). The musical's demo recording includes seven songs heard in the Broadway production ("There's a Comin' Together," "Howdjadoo," "Ol' Pease Puddin'," "Something Special," "Gettin' Back to Me," "So What?," and the title song), two deleted numbers ("Toy Balloon" and "This Time Tomorrow"); and two unused songs ("For You [I Will Live]" and "Electric Windows").

During the 2000s, it was announced that a studio cast recording of *Georgy* was in the offing, along with two other musicals of the era, *A Mother's Kisses*, which closed during its 1968 pre-Broadway tryout, and ***Lovely Ladies, Kind Gentlemen***. But as of this writing the recordings haven't been released.

In the early 1990s, the Wings Theatre Company and City Stock presented a limited-run revival of the musical. The production retained eleven songs from the original ("Make It Happen Now," "Ol' Pease Puddin'," "Just for the Ride," "So What?," "Georgy," "A Baby," "That's How It Is," "There's a Comin' Together," "Half of Me," "Gettin' Back to Me," and "Sweet Memory") and two dropped numbers ("Mrs. Jones" and "Toy Balloon"). Not used in the revival were "Howdjadoo," "Something Special," and "Life's a Holiday."

Awards

Tony Award Nominations: Best Leading Actress in a Musical (Dilys Watling); Best Featured Actress in a Musical (Melissa Hart)

OPERATION SIDEWINDER

Theatre: Vivian Beaumont Theatre
Opening Date: March 12, 1970; *Closing Date*: April 25, 1970
Performances: 52
Play: Sam Shepard
Lyrics: Sam Shepard, Robin Remaily, Peter Stampfel, Antonia, Tuli Kupferberg, and Steve Weber
Music: The Holy Modal Rounders; electronic music by Phil Smiley Delson
Direction: Michael A. Schultz; *Producer*: The Repertory Theatre of Lincoln Center (Jules Irving, Director); *Movement Consultant*: Rhoda Levine; *Scenery*: Douglas W. Schmidt (snake design by Jean Delasser); *Costumes*: Willa Kim (Mariana Torres, Additional Costumes); *Lighting*: John Gleason (strobe lighting designed by Michael O'Keefe); *Film Sequence*: Dudley Dickenson and Dean Evanson
Cast: Robert Phalen (Dukie, Captain, Second Desert Tactical Troop), Barbara Eda-Young (Honey), Michael Miller (Mechanic, Third Desert Tactical Troop), Andy Robinson (Young Man), Robert Riggs (Forest Ranger, First Desert Tactical Troop), Roberts Blossom (Billy), Joseph Mascolo (Colonel Warner), Gus Fleming (Cadet), Don Plumley (Mickey Free), Ralph Drischell (First Cohort to Mickey Free), Arthur Sellers (Second Cohort to Mickey Free), Catherine Burns (Carhop), Garrett Morris (Blood), Paul Benjamin (Blade), Charles Pegues (Dude), Paul Sparer (General Browser), Ray Fry (Doctor Victor), Michael Levin (Spider Lady), Joan Pringle (Edith), Philip Bosco (Captain Bovine); Indians: Jose Barrera, Paul Benjamin, Gregory Borst, Gus Fleming, Robert Keesler, Michael Levin, Clark Luis, Richard Mason, Muriel Miguel, Louise Mofsie, Santos Morales, Garrett Morris, Jean-Daniel Noland, Joan Pringle, and Barbara Spiegel; the songs were performed by The Holy Modal Rounders (Marvin Sylvor and Jeff Cutler, Musical Directors)
The play with music was presented in two acts.
The action takes place during the present time in an American desert.

Musical Numbers

Note: All songs were performed by The Holy Modal Rounders.
Act One: "Do It Girl" (lyric by Peter Stampfel and Antonia); "Float Me Down Your Pipeline" (lyric by Antonia); "Generalonely" (lyric by Steve Weber); "Catch Me" (lyric by Sam Shepard); "Euphoria" (lyric by

Robin Remaily); "Synergy" (lyric by Peter Stampfel and Antonia); "Dusty Fustchuns" (aka "Don't Leave Me Dangling in the Dust") (lyric by Robin Remaily); "Alien Song" (lyric by Sam Shepard)
Act Two: "Bad Karma" (lyric by Peter Stampfel and Antonia); "I Disremember Quite Well" (lyric by Antonia); "C.I.A. Man" (lyric by Peter Stampfel, Tuli Kupferburg, and Antonia); "Hopi Chants" (traditional)

Sam Shepard's *Operation Sidewinder* was a play with music that probably would have been more at home downtown at Joseph Papp's Public Theatre than at Lincoln Center. It was somewhat similar to the free-form, antiestablishment diatribes that frequently popped up at the Public, and no doubt uptown audiences were less receptive to Shepard's nonlinear scattershot criticisms of American society, the military, the CIA, and other traditional targets of the left. Perhaps the work was meant to be satiric, but if so the satire was heavy-handed. If the work had been more focused it might have been somewhat interesting, but it was so diffuse and muddled in plot, so lacking in characterization, and so watery in its satire that it now comes across as a parody of the protest plays of the late 1960s and early 1970s.

The episodic evening dealt with a hippie and his girlfriend; he's a more-sensitive-than-thou type who detests capitalism, materialism, and the establishment, and to this end reveals himself to be a terrorist who plans to subvert a nearby military establishment with the introduction of hallucinatory drugs into its water supply. He also nonchalantly murders two innocent strangers at a gas station. Meanwhile, a government computer in the shape of a huge snake has broken loose and is rampaging across the desert, where it so excites the hippie's girlfriend that she has an orgasm. Further, there's a black convertible racing around the desert full of Black Panthers who are in cahoots with the hippie; one of them murders a park ranger, who, like the other establishment figures of the military and the CIA, is depicted as a fool.

To top it off, a Spider Woman predicts that the material world will be destroyed and the spiritual one will emerge, and she oh-so-helpfully explains that the world is full of either snake people (of the spiritual realm) or lizard people (those of the earth). And there are also desert Indians who treat the computer-snake as a sacred icon. And then (apparently) the desert (or maybe most of the world) blows up, perhaps leaving everyone (except the Indians) dead. Or maybe not. Shepard's play was clearly all over the map, and his dialogue didn't help matters. Walter Kerr in the *New York Times* noted that in a key scene the hippie screams out "I am!" eleven times, and Kerr suggested that such repetitive insistence "does not become language" and "is the communicative gambit of a 4-year-old."

And all of the above was set to music. Between the scenes, a six-man folk group, The Holy Modal Rounders (who also wrote the music), performed eleven mostly extraneous songs.

Clive Barnes in the *New York Times* was gentle in his criticism, but nonetheless noted that Shepard had written "a rather bad play about a rather good subject" and "was so busy making his points that he has almost forgotten to write his play." Richard Watts in the *New York Post* said the evening had "provocative ideas" but was confusing and unclear; ultimately, the play and its "heavy-handed" humor was "disappointing, cluttered and confused" even if it couldn't be "ignored." James Davis in the *New York Daily News* found the production itself "spectacular" with its moving cars and fireworks (and there were strobe lighting effects and the pop-art conception of the computer snake). But the plot itself was uninteresting and "quite dull and weak."

Martin Gottfried in *Women's Wear Daily* found the play "relevant" and thus "important." But he felt the production never quite came together, and although "everything" was "right" about the play, it nonetheless fell apart. The director Michael A. Schultz was "utterly lost"; the performances were "disastrous"; and the music "irrelevant." He noted that the work was "conceived as a pop comic strip" which superimposed American Indian ritualism into its story (and he commented that Indians were now the "new heroes" for hippies and Broadway playwrights). Shepard's vision was "great and true," and it was "terribly disappointing" that he couldn't pull it off.

Perhaps the most fascinating aspect of the play is that Lincoln Center actually produced it. The theatre company might have better served its subscribers by offering a revival of *East Lynne*.

The script was first published in a Spring 1969 issue of *Esquire* magazine, and then in hardback by Bobbs-Merrill, in 1970. The cast album was scheduled to be recorded by United Artists, but perhaps because of the mostly dismissive reviews the recording was canceled. The Holy Modal Rounders recorded at least three songs from *Operation Sidewinder* on various albums: "Euphoria" first appeared six years earlier on their album *The Holy Modal Rounders* (Prestige Records), and was later recorded for *The Last Round* (Adelphi Records) and *Too Much Fun!* (Rounder Records); "Generalonely" was included in *Good Taste Is Timeless* (Metromedia Records); and "Synergy" was recorded for *Alleged in Their Own Time* (Rounder Records).

The song "Hathor" (lyric by Peter Stampfel) may also have been heard in the production.

As one or two critics noted, the play was similar in theme and style to the out-of-control 1970 film *Zabriskie Point*, which had been released four weeks before *Operation Sidewinder* premiered. The Michelangelo Antonioni film was coscripted by Shepard, and it too took place mostly in a desert and also centered around a hippie (who may have murdered a policeman) and a girl he meets. They spend their time making love, smoking pot, and painting in psychedelic patterns and colors a plane he has stolen. Like *Operation Sidewinder* the film ends in an apocalyptic explosion.

PURLIE

"A New Musical Comedy"

Theatre: Broadway Theater (during run, the musical transferred to the Winter Garden and ANTA Theatres)
Opening Date: March 15, 1970; *Closing Date*: November 7, 1971
Performances: 689
Book: Ossie Davis, Philip Rose, and Peter Udell
Lyrics: Peter Udell
Music: Gary Geld
Based on the 1961 play *Purlie Victorious* by Ossie Davis.
Direction: Philip Rose; *Producer*: Philip Rose; *Choreography*: Louis Johnson; *Scenery*: Ben Edwards; *Costumes*: Ann Roth; *Lighting*: Thomas Skelton; *Musical Direction*: Joyce Brown
Cast: Cleavon Little (Purlie), Linda Hopkins (Church Soloist), Melba Moore (Lutiebelle), Novella Nelson (Missy), Sherman Hemsley (Gitlow), C. David Colson (Charlie), Helen Martin (Idella), John Heffernan (Ol' Cap'n); Dancers: Loretta Abbott, Hope Clark, Judy Gibson, Lavinia Hamilton, Arlene Rolant, Ella Thompson, Myrna White, Morris Donaldson, George Faison, Al Perryman, Harold Pierson, William Taylor, Larry Vickers; Singers: Carolyn Bird, Barbara Christopher, Denise Elliott, Synthia Jackson, Mildred Lane, Alyce Webb, Mildred Pratcher, Peter Colly, Milt Grayson, Tony Middleton, Ray Pollard
The musical was presented in two acts.
The action takes place "not too long ago" in south Georgia.

Musical Numbers

Act One: "Walk Him Up the Stairs" (Entire Company); "New-Fangled Preacher Man" (Cleavon Little); "Skinnin' a Cat" (Sherman Hemsley, The Field Hands); "Purlie" (Melba Moore); "The Harder They Fall" (aka "Ten Feet Tall") (Cleavon Little, Melba Moore); "The Barrels of War" (C. David Colson); "The Unborn Love" (C. David Colson); "Big Fish, Little Fish" (John Heffernan, C. David Colson); "I Got Love" (Melba Moore); "God's Alive" (C. David Colson); "Great White Father" (aka "The Great White Father of the Year") (The Cotton Pickers); "Skinnin' a Cat" (reprise) (Sherman Hemsley, C. David Colson); "Down Home" (Cleavon Little, Novella Nelson)
Act Two: "The First Thing Monday Morning" (The Cotton Pickers); "He Can Do It" (Novella Nelson, Melba Moore); "The Harder They Fall" (reprise) (Sherman Hemsley, Melba Moore, Novella Nelson); "The World Is Comin' to a Start" (C. David Colson, Company); "Walk Him Up the Stairs" (reprise) (Entire Company)

Purlie was based on Ossie Davis's 1961 play *Purlie Victorious*, which played for 261 performances on Broadway and was filmed in 1963 as *Gone Are the Days*. The likeable musical's fable-like story was set "not too long ago" in south Georgia where the title hero (Cleavon Little) lays claim to a piece of property where his ancestors once preached and where he now hopes to build his own church. But the specter of rich, never-say-surrender Confederate Ol' Cap'n (John Heffernan) is a stumbling block to progress because of his influence in the backwater community. Of course, all ends well (except for Ol' Cap'n, who manages to drop dead while standing up).

Like its source, the often amusing musical failed to recoup its investment. The story kidded black militants, white liberals, and white racists, but never went quite far enough in its satire. Perhaps the era wasn't ready for such an across-the-board spoof: ridiculing white racists was acceptable, but white liberals and black militants were no doubt sacrosanct and above caricature. If the musical had followed through with its tongue-in-cheek look at all sides of the racial issue, it might have been really something: a unique, witty, and sardonic look at a touchy subject set in an almost timeless never-never land of backwoods Georgia.

If the libretto didn't fully explore its marvelous potential, the amiable score was also something of a letdown. It often settled for easy choices; although excitingly orchestrated and performed, the pleasant "I Got Love" and the title number were overly simplistic and somewhat generic, and a few others (such as "The Harder They Fall" and "Skinnin' a Cat") seemed to say it all in their titles. And there were long dialogue sections in the script without a note of music, particularly a very long period in the second act which played like a straight drama. In fact, the second act included just three new songs (along with two reprises).

If the lyrics and music had matched the depth and brilliance of "Down Home," an outwardly simple blues with an achingly haunting melody and a surprisingly complex lyric (which contrasted black life in both city and country), the score might have been one of the finest of its era. Another problem with the production was that it often played like a chamber musical. There were only seven major speaking roles, and one suspected the evening might have been more satisfying (and financially successful) in an intimate Off-Broadway house. As it was, the show looked too small for the cavernous stage of the Broadway Theatre. Further, there were choreographic possibilities in the story that were never developed. Dance was utilized just once, in the dazzling opening number ("Walk Him Up the Stairs"). If the musical had been conceived for Off Broadway, it could have gotten by with modest production values; but for Broadway the somewhat underpopulated show required more inventive sets, a more imaginative use of its chorus, and a vision that utilized more choreography in its storytelling.

The critics were generally kind to the show. Clive Barnes in the *New York Times* found the story "thin" and said the "admirable enough" lyrics and music "never raise the roof or even inflame the spirit." But even so the songs were "superior" (but not "brilliant") and the show was "the most successful and richest of all black musicals." John J. O'Connor in the *Wall Street Journal* said the lyrics were "cliché-ridden" but the music was "serviceable" and "sometimes downright explosive." Martin Gottfried in *Women's Wear Daily* found the story "uneventful" and "conventional," and stated that while Ossie Davis was "an intelligent black man," his "affectionate" attitude toward race relations was now "impossible." As a result, Davis's supposedly naive beliefs were proof of how "disastrously white America has tied its black people up in conditioned thought."

Richard Watts in the *New York Post* said the show was "highly disappointing" and noted he'd rarely seen a musical begin "so promisingly in both acts" and then lose "its momentum so quickly." Walter Kerr in the *New York Times* felt the musical had lost the "spit-in-the-eye zaniness" of the original play, and noted this was no doubt because the political and social climate had changed so radically during the nine years between the premieres of the play and the musical. As for John Chapman in the *New York Daily News*, the musical was "robust, tuneful and thoroughly enjoyable."

The critics praised the cast, but it was Melba Moore (as Purlie's love interest) who walked off with the best reviews. She was compared to no less than Fannie Brice, Pearl Bailey, Dionne Warwick, Aretha Franklin, Barbra Streisand, and Billie Holiday. But despite the critical accolades and a Tony Award for Best Featured Actress in a Musical, she unfortunately never had much of a Broadway career and appeared in just one more full-fledged musical (***Timbuktu!***). Cleavon Little won the Tony for Best Actor in a Musical, and while his performance was solid enough, it was the fire and intensity of Robert Guillaume's performance in the touring production that made him the definitive Purlie.

The script was published in softcover by Samuel French in 1971, and the cast album was released by Ampex Records (LP # A40101); the CD was issued by RCA Victor (# 60229-2-RG). The musical's demo recording includes the unused song "Easy Goin' Man."

There was talk of a film version, and in the October 17, 1979, issue of *Variety* a full-page advertisement exclaimed that "Muhammed Ali Is *Purlie*." Using Mozelle's Broadway poster artwork, the ad touted a forthcoming film version by Hush Production Inc. and the Seidelman/Nice Company. The ad noted that along with Ali (aka Cassius Clay) in the title role, the other members of the cast would include Sherman Hemsley, Patti LaBelle, Melba Moore, Dionne Warwick, "and more to come." But along with the names of the performers came a caveat: "Billing Not Contractually Binding." Of course, the film never materialized, but in 1981 a regional production of the musical was filmed and released on videocassette by MGM/CBS Home Video (# CV700087). Melba Moore, Sherman Hemsley, and Linda Hopkins reprised their original Broadway roles, and others in the cast were Robert Guillaume (Purlie), Don Scardino (Charlie), Rhetta Hughes (Missy), Clarice Taylor (Idella), and Brandon Maggart (Ol Cap'n).

A brief return engagement by the musical's touring company played at the Billy Rose Theatre on December 27, 1972, for fourteen performances (for more information, see entry).

Tony Awards and Nominations

Best Musical (*Purlie*); Best Leading Actor in a Musical (**Cleavon Little**); Best Featured Actress in a Musical (**Melba Moore**); Best Director of a Musical (Philip Rose); Best Choreographer (Louis Johnson)

BLOOD RED ROSES

"A PLAY WITH SONGS"

Theatre: John Golden Theatre
Opening Date: March 22, 1970; *Closing Date*: March 22, 1970
Performances: 1
Book and *Lyrics*: John Lewin
Music: Michael Valenti
Direction: Alan Schneider; *Producers*: Seymour Vall and Louis S. Goldman in association with Rick Mandell and Bjorn I. Swanstrom; *Choreography*: Larry Fuller; *Scenery*: Ed Wittstein; *Costumes*: Deidre Cartier; *Lighting*: Tharon Musser; *Musical Direction*: Milton Setzer
Cast: William Tost (Grenadier Guard), Bill Gibbens (Grenadier Guard), Sydney Walker (Fitzroy Somerset, Lord Raglan, Commander-in-Chief Her Majesty's Forces, The Crimea), Ronald Drake (Prince Albert), Jeanie Carson (Queen Victoria, Alice Crabbe, Florence Nightingale), Jess Richards (Private William Cockcroft), Philip Bruns (Private John Smalls), Jay Gregory (W. H. Russell), Charles Abbott (A Russian Soldier), Lowell Harris (Cornet Edwin May)
The musical was presented in two acts.
The action takes place in England and in the Crimean Peninsula during the Crimean War of 1854–1855.

Musical Numbers

Act One: "The Cream of English Youth" (Entire British Army); "A Garden in the Sun" (Jeanie Carson, Ronald Drake, Sydney Walker); "Song of How Mucked (Fucked) Up Things Are" (Philip Bruns, Jess Richards); "The Cream of English Youth" (reprise) (Philip Bruns, Jess Richards); "Song of Greater Britain" (Jeanie Carson); "Black Dog Rum" (Sydney Walker, The Fusiliers); "In the Country Where I Come From" (Jess Richards); "The English Rose" (Philip Bruns, Jess Richards); "Soldiers' Prayer" (The Fusiliers)
Act Two: "Blood Red Roses" (Jess Richards); "The Fourth Light Dragoons" (Lowell Harris); "The English Rose" (reprise) (Philip Bruns); "Song of the Fair Dissenter Lass" (Jeanie Carson); Finale (Entire Company)

Best Plays reported *Blood Red Roses* had originally been intended as an Off-Broadway production with a capitalization of $65,000, but producer Seymour Vall decided to instead open on Broadway, where the musical cost $175,000 to mount. The production was an antiwar diatribe with a small cast of ten, and perhaps it might have had a chance Off Broadway. But when it opened on Broadway, its first performance was also its last and so it joined the earlier *La Strada* and ***Gantry*** as one of the season's three single-performance musicals.

The revue-like antiwar musical used the Crimean War as an example of what the program noted was the "triumph of futility and brutalization" in war. The musical was also unhappy with the Industrial Age, and complained that the period created "wealth, power, smugness." In case anyone didn't get it, the program then compared the Crimean War to the then current Vietnam War (which the program notes referred to as "America's Vietnam adventure"). The musical trod the same ground as the earlier *Oh What a Lovely War* (London, 1963; New York, 1964), which had been a smug and obvious antiwar piece set during World War I (in one sequence, a news panel showed the number of war dead while a Pierrot chorus sang the title song). The London musical managed a few months on Broadway, but like *Blood Red Roses* lost money.

The main problem with these shows was their smug, obvious irony and their holier-than-thou sensitivity. But antiwar and antiestablishment musicals were definitely part of the zeitgeist, and *Hair* (Off Broadway, 1967; Broadway, 1968) led the pack. Other Broadway musicals of the era flirted with antiwar sentiments, but these attitudes were usually relegated to one song per musical. The World War I setting of the Broadway-bound *Mata Hari* (1967) included a soldier's lament to his "Maman" about war and killing; *Her First Roman* (1968) had Roman soldiers singing "What Are We Doing in Egypt?"; the Civil War setting of *Maggie Flynn* (1968) offered draft dissenters singing "Never Gonna Make Me Fight"; the 1796 era of *Billy* (1969) included a male chorus chanting "It Ain't Us Who Make the Wars" ("but it's us that's gotta fight 'em"); and *1776* (1969) offered "Momma, Look Sharp," the last words of a dying soldier to his mother.

Blood Red Roses received some of the worst reviews of the season, and the critics complained of its lack of subtlety, its penchant for moralizing, its depiction of establishment figures as dolts, its pale imitations of Brechttian attitudes, and its songs in the style of Kurt Weill. And like *Mata Hari* (and to an extent *1776*), the musical used a soldier (actually two soldiers) who weaved in and out of the action as symbols of the little men who are forced to fight the rich man's wars. One soldier (Jess Richards) is an innocent and the other (Philip Bruns) a former pimp, and of course it's the former who dies in the war. Like *Oh What a Lovely War*, the musical was presented in the manner of British music hall. Here, Ed Wittstein's inventive decor utilized a presentational look of miniature, toy theatre with two-dimensional cardboard pen-and-ink and water-colored pop-ups and cut-outs.

Martin Gottfried in *Women's Wear Daily* complained there were so many derivative antiwar productions that now there were ones that were "derivative of the derivations." Queen Victoria and Prince Albert were depicted as "idiots" and British aristocrats were "clumsily mocked as insensitive." Lampoons of British colonialism were old-hat, and Gottfried wondered why the material was presented in such a "trite" manner (he concluded it was due to "creative inhibition"). Richard Watts in the *New York Post* found the first act "incredibly tiresome," and while the second was sometimes "real" and "deeply moving," it was by then "too late" to rescue the "disappointing" musical. Clive Barnes in the *New York Times* noted the evening was "too contemporary in feeling and language" and was more in the spirit of "Carnaby Street than mid-Victorian England" (Watts had mentioned the use of four-letter words, and indeed while the program listed one number as "Song of How Mucked Up Things Are," "mucked" wasn't the word that was actually heard on stage).

John J. O'Connor in the *Wall Street Journal* said the evening lacked "theatrical spark"; Leonard Probst on WNBC4TV found the musical "surprisingly dull" with "second-rate" dialogue, lyrics, and music; and Leonard Harris on WCBSTV2 said the show was "terribly earnest and terrible" with a staging that reminded him of high school pageants.

A few years after the closing of *Blood Red Roses*, two of its songs ("Song of the Fair Dissenter Lass" [as "The Fair Dissenter Lass"] and the title number) surfaced in Michael Valenti's revue *Lovesong*, which was first performed in Toronto, then Off Off Broadway at The Showplace on July 8, 1976, and later Off-Broadway at the Top of the Village Gate on October 5, 1976, for twenty-four performances. Jess Richards, who had appeared in *Blood Red Roses* and introduced the title song, again performed the number in *Lovesong*. The revue was recorded in 1980 by Original Cast Records (LP # OC-8022) and the album included "Blood Red Roses" and "Song of the Fair Dissenter Lass"; Richards was among the performers, but curiously Robert Manzari was the lead singer for "Blood Red Roses."

Blood Red Roses continued the trend of musicals that opened cold in New York for a series of preview performances without benefit of pre-Broadway tryouts. Shows of this nature were rare in earlier years, but the current season offered no less than six (besides *Blood Red Roses*, there were *Coco*, ***Gantry***, ***Purlie***, ***Minnie's Boys***, and ***Look to the Lilies***). All of them closed in the red, although *Coco* recouped during its post-Broadway tour, which starred Katharine Hepburn.

MINNIE'S BOYS

"A Rollicking New Marx Brothers Musical"

Theatre: Imperial Theatre
Opening Date: March 26, 1970; *Closing Date*: May 31, 1970
Performances: 76
Book: Arthur Marx and Robert Fisher

Lyrics: Hal Hackady
Music: Larry Grossman; incidental music by Marvin Hamlisch and Peter Howard
Direction: Stanley Prager; *Producers*: Arthur Whitelaw, Max J. Brown, and Byron Goldman (Peter N. Grad, Associate Producer); *Choreography*: Marc Breaux; *Scenery*: Peter Wexler; *Costumes*: Donald Winters; *Lighting*: Jules Fisher; *Musical Direction*: John Berkman
Cast: Lewis J. Stadlen (Julie [Groucho] Marx), Irwin Pearl (Leonard [Chico] Marx), Daniel Fortus (Adolph [Harpo] Marx), Alvin Kupperman (Herbie [Zeppo] Marx), Gary Raucher (Milton [Gummo] Marx), Jean Bruno (Mrs. Flanagan, Harpist), Jacqueline Britt (Mrs. Krupnik, Murdock), *Shelley Winters* (Minnie Marx), Arny Freeman (Sam [Frenchie] Marx), Merwin Goldsmith (Hochmeister), Mort Marshall (Al Shean), Doug Spingler (Cop), Ronn Hansen (Sidebark), Evelyn Taylor (Acrobat), David Vaughan (Acrobat), George Bunt (Acrobat), Marjory Edson (Cindy, Miss White House), Richard B. Shull (Maxie, Sandow), Stephen Reinhardt (Telegraph Boy), Casper Roos (Robwell), Gene Ross (Theatre Manager), Roland Winters (E. F. Albee), Julie Kurnitz (Mrs. McNish), Lynne Gannaway (Miss Taj Mahal), Vicki Frederick (Miss Eiffel Tower); Ensemble: Jacqueline Britt, Jean Bruno, Bjarne Buchtrup, George Bunt, Dennis Cole, Deede Darnell, Joan B. Duffin, Marjory Edson, Vicki Frederick, Marcelo Gamboa, Lynne Gannaway, Ronn Hansen, Elaine Manzel, Stephen Reinhardt, Casper Roos, Gene Ross, Carole Schweid, William W. Sean, Doug Spingler, Evelyn Taylor, David Vaughan, Toodie Witmer. Mary Zahn
The musical was presented in two acts.
The action takes place during the early years of the twentieth century in various cities such as New York, Chicago, Philadelphia, and Nagadoches, Texas.

Musical Numbers

Act One: "Five Growing Boys" (Shelley Winters, Neighbors); "Rich Is" (Mort Marshall, The Marx Family); "More Precious Far" (Lewis J. Stadlen, Alvin Kupperman, Daniel Fortus, Shelley Winters); "Four Nightingales" (Lewis J. Stadlen, Alvin Kupperman, Daniel Fortus); "Underneath It All" (Richard B. Shull, Girls); "Mama, a Rainbow" (Daniel Fortus, Shelley Winters); "You Don't Have to Do It for Me" (Shelley Winters, Lewis J. Stadlen, Irwin Pearl, Daniel Fortus, Alvin Kupperman); "If You Wind Me Up" (Shelley Winters, Lewis J. Stadlen, Alvin Kupperman, Daniel Fortus, Irwin Pearl); "Where Was I When They Passed Out the Luck?" (Lewis J. Stadlen, Alvin Kupperman, Daniel Fortus, Irwin Pearl)
Act Two: "The Smell of Christmas" (Lewis J. Stadlen, Daniel Fortus, Alvin Kupperman, Irwin Pearl); "You Remind Me of You" (Lewis J. Stadlen, Julie Kurnitz); "Minnie's Boys" (Shelley Winters, Company); "Be Happy" (Shelley Winters, Daniel Fortus, Irwin Pearl, Alvin Kupperman, Gary Raucher); "The Act" (Lewis J. Stadlen, Alvin Kupperman, Daniel Fortus, Irwin Pearl, Shelley Winters); Finale (Company)

Minnie's Boys was about the early lives of the five Marx Brothers, and like many of the musicals that opened during the season, it opted for an extended series of New York previews rather than a traditional pre-Broadway tryout. But an insert in a preview program signed by Groucho Marx suggested that the audience should imagine itself at a Philadelphia tryout performance, and he noted that any "rough spots" should be overlooked "out of gratitude for not having to live in Philadelphia."

The musical did indeed have rough spots, but the main problem was that the audience had seen it all before. We'd been through Mama Rose and Baby June and Gypsy Rose Louise, and we'd been through Fannie Brice and the mother who taught her everything she knows. And a few in the audience had even been there for the show-biz trials and travails of Sophie Tucker and Laurette Taylor. So a musical about the Marx Brothers was sure to hold little or no suspense because we knew how it would turn out. June and Gypsy and Fannie and Sophie and Laurette might not have been all that well remembered when their biographical musicals opened because they hadn't left behind classic films and their personas were perhaps not all that familiar to modern Broadway audiences. But the Marx Brothers' classic series of surreal comedies never went away, and so the musical was under the further handicap of presenting actors who had to impersonate freshly remembered comic film performers.

If Hal Hackady's lyrics and Larry Grossman's music had been of the caliber for the scores of *Gypsy* and *Funny Girl*, the musical might have gotten by. But their contributions were only average; there was an amusing number in the typical Groucho manner when he sings to the Margaret Dumont character that "You Remind Me of You"; "Where Was I When They Passed Out the Luck" was a rather nice, quirky number; and the sweet if generic "Mama, a Rainbow" was a pleasant and solid Broadway ballad. But otherwise the songs were on the bland and unimaginative side.

To compound the evening's problems, star Shelley Winters as the mother of the Marx Brothers seemed uncomfortable on the musical stage. Clive Barnes in the *New York Times* noted her role wasn't much and that she was "in search of a part to play"; further, hers was an "ungrateful" job because the musical was clearly about the brothers and not their mother. John J. O'Connor in the *Wall Street Journal* admitted her role wasn't the "meatiest," but said she seemed "incapable of even latching on to the bare bones." Instead of creating a pushy and driving stage mother, she projected a certain "hostile shyness" as a "pathetic victim." Martin Gottfried in *Women's Wear Daily* said she had the stage presence of a "vacuum cleaner and seems to suck in rather than let out any performing"; she was more "spectator" than "participant" and was a "terribly insecure performer." But Richard Watts in the *New York Post* said she gave a "warm-hearted portrayal" and Leonard Harris on WCBSTV2 commented that hers was a "nice, warm, Freudian performance."

Overall, Watts found the show "pleasant and refreshing," but Barnes felt it lacked a "genuine story." Walter Kerr in the *New York Times* gave special praise to the writers for not allowing the familiar Marx Brothers' shtick to take over in the early scenes. He noted this would have been an understandable temptation, but the creators allowed the familiar mannerisms to "grow casually, almost absent-mindedly." Although the show was "partly patchwork," he nonetheless had a "perfectly good time" because the on-stage brothers "were not trying too hard to become" their eventual show-business personas.

As Groucho, Lewis J. Stadlen received good notices. Kerr said he was a performer of "intelligence" and "instinct"; Watts said he was "simply wonderful"; Barnes found him "remarkably good"; and O'Connor said he was especially delightful and gave "the closest thing in the show to a high-fidelity impersonation." But Gottfried was generally unimpressed and said Stadlen "did a standard Groucho Marx."

The book was cowritten by Arthur Marx (Groucho's son), and Groucho himself was billed as "production consultant." For the opening-night curtain calls, Groucho joined the cast on the stage, and Barnes reported that he made the "generous suggestion" that Lewis J. Stadlen was "more talented than he was himself." Barnes said Groucho might have been right, but he suspected that in the future no one would ever be doing Lewis J. Stadlen impersonations.

Librettists Arthur Marx and Robert Fisher revisited Groucho when their *Groucho: A Life in Revue* opened Off Broadway on October 8, 1986, for 254 performances at the Lucille Lortel Theatre. The show included songs and shtick associated with the comedian's career, and Groucho was played by Frank Ferrante, who reprised the role when the production was seen in London the following year. The Off-Broadway cast album was released by Original Cast Records (CD # OCR-9498), and the script was published in paperback by Samuel French in 1988.

Although the brothers were not mentioned specifically, they were for all purposes seen in the 1980 Broadway musical *A Day in Hollywood/A Night in the Ukraine*, two one-act musicals that opened on May 1 at the John Golden Theatre for 588 performances; directed and choreographed by Tommy Tune, the book and lyrics were by Dick Vosburgh and the music by Frank Lazarus. *A Night in the Ukraine* was in the mode of a typical Marx Brothers' movie and the characters included Serge B. Samovar (a lawyer), Carlo (an Italian footman), Gino (a gardener), and Mrs. Pavlenko (a rich widow).

During previews of *Minnie's Boys*, "Stage Door Johnny" was cut. The musical's demo recording includes two unused songs, "Theme from *Minnie's Boys*" (aka "92nd Street") and "Empty."

The cast album had been scheduled to be recorded by RCA Victor (the preview programs included a full-page ad for the RCA album), but the musical was instead recorded and issued by Project Three Records (LP # TS-6002-SD), which also released the CD. The recording includes "Empty," "Nacogdoches Vaudeville Sequence," and "They Give Me Love," none of which were listed in the opening-night program and seem to have been added to the show sometime during the Broadway run. Omitted from the recording were "More Precious Far," "If You Wind Me Up," and "The Smell of Christmas." The script was published in softcover by Metromedia-On-Stage in 1971, and didn't include "The Smell of Christmas."

LOOK TO THE LILIES

Theatre: Lunt-Fontanne Theatre
Opening Date: March 29, 1970; *Closing Date*: April 19, 1970
Performances: 25

Book: Leonard Spigelgass
Lyrics: Sammy Cahn
Music: Jule Styne
Based on the 1962 novel *Lilies of the Field* by William E. Barrett.
Direction: Joshua Logan; *Producers*: Edgar Lansbury, Max J. Brown, Richard Lewine, and Ralph Nelson; *Choreography*: Uncredited; *Scenery* and *Lighting*: Jo Mielziner; *Costumes*: Carrie F. Robbins; *Musical Direction*: Milton Rosenstock
Cast: *Al Freeman Jr.* (Homer Smith), Maggie Task (Sister Gertrude), Virginia Craig (Sister Elizabeth), Linda Andrews (Sister Agnes), *Shirley Booth* (Mother Maria), Taina Elg (Sister Albertine), Anita Sheer (Lady Guitarist), Patti Karr (Juanita), Carmen Alvarez (Rosita), Titos Vandis (Juan Archuleta), Marc Allen III (Bartender), Joe Benjamin (First Policeman, Judge, Monsignor O'Hara), Richard Graham (Second Policeman), Paul Eichel (Courtroom Guard, Poker Player), Michael Davis (Courtroom Guard, Poker Player), Don Prieur (District Attorney, Poker Player), Ben Laney (Defense Attorney); Townspeople: Singers—Marian Haraldson, Sherri Huff, Suzanne Horn, Maggie Worth, Marc Allen III, Michael Davis, Paul Eichel, Tony Falco, Ben Laney, Don Prieur; Dancers—Carol Conte, Maria DiDia, Tina Faye, Ravah Malmuth, Glenn Brooks, Harry Endicott, Gary Gendell, Steven Ross; Children—Lisa Bellaran, Lori Bellaran, Ray Bellaran
The musical was presented in two acts.
The action takes place in a small town in New Mexico during the present time.

Musical Numbers

Act One: Overture (Orchestra); "Gott Is Gut" (Shirley Booth, Taina Elg, Virginia Craig, Maggie Task, Linda Andrews); "First Class Number One Bum" (Al Freeman Jr.); "Himmlisher Vater" (Shirley Booth, Taina Elg, Virginia Craig, Maggie Task, Linda Andrews); "Follow the Lamb" (Al Freeman Jr., Shirley Booth, Taina Elg, Virginia Craig, Maggie Task, Linda Andrews); "Meet My Seester" (Patti Karr, Carmen Alvarez); "Don't Talk about God" (Al Freeman Jr.); "When I Was Young" (Shirley Booth); "On That Day of Days" (Patti Karr, Carmen Alvarez, Children, Townspeople); "You're a Rock" (Al Freeman Jr.); "I Am What I Am" (Shirley Booth); "I'd Sure Like to Give It a Shot" (Al Freeman Jr.); "I'd Sure Like to Give It a Shot" (dance) (Al Freeman Jr., Patti Karr, Carmen Alvarez, Customers)
Act Two: Entr'Acte (Orchestra); "I Admire You Very Much, Mr. Schmidt" (Taina Elg); "Look to the Lilies" (Shirley Booth, Taina Elg, Virginia Craig, Maggie Task, Linda Andrews); "Some Kind of Man" (Al Freeman Jr.); "Homer's Pitch" (Al Freeman Jr., Townspeople); "Casamagordo, New Mexico" (Taina Elg, Virginia Craig, Maggie Task, Linda Andrews); "Follow the Lamb" (reprise) and "One Little Brick at a Time" (Al Freeman Jr., Townspeople); "I, Yes Me, That's Who" (Shirley Booth); "Prayer" (Townspeople); "I, Yes Me, That's Who" (reprise) (Al Freeman Jr.)

Look to the Lilies was a short-lived failure based on William E. Barrett's 1962 novel *Lilies of the Field*, which during the following year was adapted into the popular film of the same name that starred Lilia Skala and Sydney Poitier. For the musical adaptation, almost everything that could have gone wrong did go wrong. The story's outcome was numbingly predictable. As soon as the strong-willed German nun Mother Maria (Shirley Booth) and the strong-willed black fugitive Homer Smith (Al Freeman Jr.) meet, we know their edgy and tentative relationship will eventually blossom into mutual respect and admiration. Mother Maria and her group of immigrant German nuns live in New Mexico in the hope that a chapel will be built for the poor Mexicans and Indians in their small community, and when Homer appears on the scene Mother Maria feels that he was directed by God to come to their town and build it. But Homer doesn't see it that way, considering he's on the lam for car theft and resisting arrest and is about to make his way to Mexico (Martin Gottfried in *Women's Wear Daily* noted the writers ensured that Homer's crimes were of the "forgivable variety"). But despite the contest of wills, there's of course absolutely no doubt that Homer will build the chapel. As a result, the evening lacked tension and surprise because you knew exactly where the characters were going and how the story would play out.

If Jule Styne and Sammy Cahn's score had been stronger, the musical might have had a chance. But the songs were mostly bland and derivative, and only once (in the haunting "I, Yes Me, That's Who") was the score truly inspired. Otherwise, the nuns' "Follow the Lamb" was jubilant if predictable, the kind of song that in spirit and mood could have comfortably found itself as part of the score for *Sister Act*; and Homer's slick "First Class Number One Bum" and "I'd Sure Like to Give It a Shot" indicated he had perhaps spent too much time in Las Vegas.

As for the leads, Booth, in her last Broadway musical, was uncomfortable; there was little humor and warmth in her characterization, and she came across as overly rigid and stern (and her German accent became a bit tiresome: *Yook to the Yillyees*, anyone?); and Freeman, who seemed to be channeling Sammy Davis Jr., was awkward and out of his element in a musical role. Joshua Logan's direction was uninspired, the choreography was nil, and the plot was knee-deep in sweet nuns, sweet blacks, sweet Mexicans, sweet Indians, sweet children, and sweet prostitutes (the latter's big number was "Meet My Seester"); perhaps there was even a sweet dog or two around. The show was all sugar and no salsa.

Disappointing, too, was Jo Mielziner's plain and often skeletal décor. It seems a given that the musical's climax would have shown the raising of the chapel as the audience watched; but this potentially show-stopping scenic effect never took place (perhaps budgetary constraints prevented it, because the show looked cheap and despite its thirty-four member cast looked somewhat underpopulated against the scrim-like scenery).

Richard Watts in the *New York Post* said the musical was "slender" and "not very sturdy," but was still "pleasant" and "likeable"; and he noted the "agreeable" score was not one of Styne's "most distinguished"; John J. O'Connor in the *Wall Street Journal* found the music "relentlessly circa 1940" and the lyrics often "merely simpleminded"; and Gottfried said the score was in Styne's "usual urbane style" but never attempted to relate to the characters, the story, and the setting (he found Cahn's lyrics at best "workmanlike" and at worst "silly," and quoted part of one song: "What else can we say/Except Ole"). On the other hand, John Schubeck on WABCTV7 found the score "magnificent" (he also noted that Freeman gave a "towering performance").

Douglas Watt in the *New York Daily News* said the musical was a "leaden affair" with a "sluggish pace" that "stops dead in its tracks time and again." Clive Barnes in the *New York Times* found the direction "poor" and the plot "static"; and while the story was "all heart," it might cause "heartburn." But he concluded that *Look to the Lilies* was a "family" musical appropriate for "diamond wedding anniversaries" and "Catholic weddings."

Gottfried complained that the "only occasionally annoying" musical failed to create a real relationship between the two leading characters and thus the evening was "ruined" by "insensitive" direction and actor "problems." Thus Booth and Freeman spent the evening as "strangers" in a show that was about their relationship. Although Logan's direction was "not tidy," it wasn't "messy," and the critic concluded that overall the show's source material wasn't "inherently musical."

In preproduction, the musical was known as *Some Kind of Man*. During previews, the following songs were cut: "To Do a Little Good," "Why Can't He See," "Them and They," "Does It Really Matter," and "There Comes a Time." Joyce Trisler was listed as choreographer during previews, but by the opening no one was credited (one critic mentioned that Peter Gennaro had unofficially stepped in as choreographer once Trisler had left the musical).

Look to the Lilies was scheduled to be recorded by Warner Brothers Records, and was one of five of the season's musicals whose recordings were canceled due to their short runs (the others were *Buck White*, ***Gantry***, ***Georgy***, and ***Operation Sidewinder***). But a demo recording of the score was released by Blue Pear Records (LP # BP-1010) and later issued on CD by Déjà Vu Records (# 1010) with a pairing of Frank Loesser's *Pleasures and Palaces*, which closed during its pre-Broadway tryout in 1965. The recording includes eight songs from *Look to the Lilies*: six used songs ("Follow the Lamb," "I, Yes Me, That's Who," "I'd Sure Like to Give It a Shot," "One Little Brick at a Time," "Some Kind of Man," and the title number); one deleted song ("There Comes a Time"); and an unused one ("Kick the Door"). The recording *I'm the Greatest Star! The Overtures of Jule Styne Volume Two* (Jay Records CD # CDJAY-1335) by the National Symphony Orchestra and conducted by Jack Everly includes the overture to *Look to the Lilies*, and the collection *18 Interesting Songs from Unfortunate Shows* (Take Home Tunes LP # THT-777) includes "First Class Number One Bum" and the title number.

Styne recycled two songs from the score for later musicals. The unused "Kick the Door" surfaced as "For You" in *One Night Stand* (1980), which closed during Broadway previews (the song is included on the cast album of *One Night Stand*). First written as "My Reason for Being" and then later in its final version as "Am I to Wish Her Love," "I, Yes Me, That's Who" was heard in Styne's final Broadway musical *The Red Shoes*, an ambitious and lavish musical version of the 1948 classic film, which opened on Broadway for just five performances in 1993. As "Melody from *The Red Shoes*," the instrumental version of the number is included in *Michael Feinstein Sings the Jule Styne Songbook* (Elektra Nonesuch CD # 9-79274-2); the recording was released two years before the premiere of *The Red Shoes*, and the liner notes indicate the music for the song was "written a number of years ago" and that the lyric was currently being written by Barbara Schottenfeld (it's unclear who wrote the final lyric: the lyricists of record were Marsha Norman and Paul Stryker, the latter a pseudonym for Bob Merrill).

APPLAUSE

"A New Musical"

Theatre: Palace Theatre
Opening Date: March 30, 1970; *Closing Date*: May 27, 1972
Performances: 896
Book: Betty Comden and Adolph Green
Lyrics: Lee Adams
Music: Charles Strouse
Based on the short story "The Wisdom of Eve" by Mary Orr (which was first published in the May 1946 issue of *Cosmopolitan* magazine); the 1950 film *All about Eve* (screenplay by Joseph L. Mankiewicz) was based on the story.
Direction and *Choreography*: Ron Field; *Producers*: Joseph Kipness and Lawrence Kasha in association with Nederlander Productions and George M. Steinbrenner III; *Scenery*: Robert Randolph; *Costumes*: Ray Aghayan; *Lighting*: Tharon Musser; *Musical Direction*: Donald Pippin
Cast: John Anania (Tony Announcer, Peter), Alan King (Tony Host), *Lauren Bacall* (Margo Channing), Penny Fuller (Eve Harrington), Robert Mandan (Howard Benedict), Tom Urich (Bert), Brandon Maggart (Buzz Richards), Len Cariou (Bill Sampson), Lee Roy Reams (Duane Fox), Ann Williams (Karen Richards), Jerry Wyatt (Bartender), Howard Kahl (Bob), Orrin Reiley (Piano Player, TV Director), Ray Becker (Stan Harding), Bill Allsbrook (Danny), Bonnie Franklin (Bonnie), Carol Petri (Carol, Autograph Seeker), Mike Misita (Joey), Gene Kelton (Musician), Nat Horne (Musician), David Anderson (Musician); Singers: Laurie Franks, Ernestine Jackson, Sheilah Ryan, Jeannette Seibert, Henrietta Valor, Howard Kahl, Orrin Reiley, Jerry Wyatt; Dancers: Renee Baughman, Joan Bell, Debi Carpenter, Patti D'Beck, Marilyn D'Honau, Marybeth Kurdock, Carol Petri, Bill Allsbrook, David Anderson, John Cashman, Don Daenen, Nikolas (Nicholas) Dante, Gene Foote, Gene Kelton, Nat Horne, Mike Misita, Ed Nolfi, Sammy Williams
The musical was presented in two acts.
The action takes place during the present time in and around New York City.

Musical Numbers

Act One: "Backstage Babble" (First-Nighters); "Think How It's Gonna Be" (Len Cariou); "But Alive" (Lauren Bacall, Boys); "The Best Night of My Life" (Penny Fuller); "Who's That Girl?" (Lauren Bacall); "Applause" (Bonnie Franklin, Gypsies); "Hurry Back" (Lauren Bacall); "Fasten Your Seat Belts" (Brandon Maggart, Ann Williams, Robert Mandan, Lee Roy Reams, Len Cariou, Guests); "Welcome to the Theatre" (Lauren Bacall)
Act Two: "Inner Thoughts" (Ann Williams, Brandon Maggart, Lauren Bacall); "Good Friends" (Lauren Bacall, Ann Williams, Brandon Maggart); "The Best Night of My Life" (reprise) (Penny Fuller); "She's No Longer a Gypsy" (Bonnie Franklin, Lee Roy Reams, Gypsies); "One of a Kind" (Len Cariou, Lauren Bacall); "One Hallowe'en" (Penny Fuller); "Something Greater" (Lauren Bacall); Finale (Lauren Bacall, Company)

Applause was based on Mary Orr's 1946 short story "The Wisdom of Eve." The story had been filmed as *All about Eve* in 1950, but for legal reasons the musical adaptation couldn't use any material—dialogue, characters, and plot situations—that had been specifically created for the film; as a result, Betty Comden and

Adolph Green's libretto had to be exclusively based on the short story itself and on new characters and incidents that they themselves created.

The story focused on the world of New York theatre, and centered on famous if somewhat insecure stage star Margo Channing (Bette Davis in the film, Lauren Bacall in the musical) and aspiring actress Eve Harrington (Anne Baxter/Penny Fuller) whose iron will ensures there will be no detours on her road to stardom. The film was immediately recognized as a classic and won six Academy Awards, including Best Picture, Best Screenplay, and Best Direction. Joseph L. Mankiewicz's incisive direction and witty screenplay provided an unflinching look at the world of cut-throat show business with its carefully wrought plot, memorable dialogue, and sharply etched characters; and Davis and Baxter gave the performances of their careers.

Unfortunately, the musical adaptation was tiresome and never matched the spectacularly entertaining film. Almost every aspect of the production (book, lyrics, music, performances, direction, choreography, and even the décor) was strictly by the numbers. With the notable exception of Penny Fuller, there was nothing inspired about the evening, and the creative team seemed content with a safe and predictable product that never explored the possibilities inherent in a musical adaptation. For all the evening's attempts at speed and excitement, the show seemed to be conceived and carried out in slow motion.

But at least the disappointing musical offered a few compensations: as Eve, Penny Fuller gave a blistering performance, and her "One Hallowe'en" was a tantalizing promise of what the entire musical should have been like; and "Good Friends," a trio with an ironic lyric and an insinuating melody, was another truly original musical moment.

Like *Hello, Dolly!* and *Mame*, the musical provided an opportunity for many theatergoers to see former film favorites on the musical stage. Lauren Bacall was succeeded by the inspired casting of Anne Baxter, the film's original Eve who now played the role of Margo Channing. With her sense of movement and timing, Baxter seemed a natural on the musical stage; hers was a deeply heartfelt performance. She was later succeeded by Arlene Dahl, and then for the national tour Eleanor Parker gave a finely wrought characterization. In 1973, Alexis Smith appeared in a regional production of the musical. (When it came to Bacall's successor, there was a virtual who's who of yesterday's stars mentioned: Ginger Rogers, Rita Hayworth, Susan Hayward, Melina Mercouri, Cyd Charisse, Ann Miller, Dolores Gray, Anne Baxter, and Eleanor Parker; of course, Baxter took over for New York, and Parker appeared in the national tour).

For all its mediocrity, *Applause* had the good fortune to open during a lean season in which eight musicals had opened and quickly closed (*Jimmy*, *Buck White*, *La Strada*, ***Gantry***, ***Georgy***, ***Blood Red Roses***, ***Minnie's Boys***, and ***Look to the Lilies***). The season's "event" musical ***Coco*** had proven disappointing, and without Katharine Hepburn in the title role, it too might have quickly shuttered (it finally closed in the black after Hepburn took it on the road). As for ***Purlie***, it was somewhat popular but was never a sell-out hit; and despite its run of 689 performances it too closed without returning its investment. After *Applause*, ***Cry for Us All*** and ***Park*** were fast flops, and the revival of ***The Boy Friend*** had a short run of just three months.

The only competition for *Applause* was ***Company***, and the two musicals made interesting contrasts between a conventional and uninspired Broadway adaptation and an original, groundbreaking musical. But because ***Company*** opened after the Tony Award cut-off date, *Applause* found itself in the enviable position of having no real Tony competition (there were just two other shows up for Best Musical, *Coco* and ***Purlie***), and it won four awards (Best Musical, Best Leading Actress in a Musical, Best Direction, and Best Choreography). (For the next award season, ***Company*** won six Tony Awards, including Best Musical.) *Applause* was the longest-running musical of the season, and outlasted ***Company*** by almost two-hundred performances.

The critics showered praise on the musical and on Lauren Bacall. Clive Barnes in the *New York Times* said Bacall was a "sensation," and while the book was "among the best in years," he noted the score was "second-rate." Martin Gottfried in *Women's Wear Daily* agreed with Barnes about Bacall ("a great star performance"), but for him the book was the "weakest" aspect of the show (however, he found the score "excellent"). John Chapman in the *New York Daily News* suggested Bacall could even make a hit out of *Coco*, and said the musical was a "beautifully coordinated work"; while Richard Watts in the *New York Post* predicted the show would be a "gigantic hit," and praised the "splendid" Bacall and the "pleasant" score.

John J. O'Connor in the *Wall Street Journal* found Bacall "smashing," but said the score was "sometimes merely competent" though often "first-rate." He thought "She's No Longer a Gypsy" could be cut without damaging the show (incidentally, that song incorporated musical nods to recent and currently running New York musicals, such as *Cabaret* and *Oh! Calcutta!*).

Walter Kerr in the *New York Times* felt the show was a "rock-solid success" and described Bacall as "Medea, Medusa, and Theda Bara combined." He noted that he could "fuss" about certain aspects of the production, such as when the musical employed the "parallel use of a sound track when Miss Bacall's singing voice is already being miked, making it seem twice as miked." He also felt that when "She's No Longer a Gypsy" quoted "hit bits" from other musicals, it was in order to "help" the number "along."

Leonard Harris on WCBSTV2 said Bacall's singing "barely gets by" and her dancing was "more energetic than graceful," but for all that "she's a star." Leonard Probst on WNBC4TV said the show was the season's best, that Bacall gave the "best single performance this year," and that Penny Fuller was superb. He found the score "listenable" but not "memorable," and noted that while the book was "smart" it wasn't "really funny."

The musical was titled *Tell Your Friends* in preproduction, and the book was by Sidney Michaels before it was readapted by Betty Comden and Adolph Green; songs dropped during this period were: "Tell Your Friends," "I Want—," "How Does It Feel to Have Everything?," "God Bless," "The Loneliest Man in Town," "Nothing Can Get to Me Now," "Fairfield County, USA," and "Get Her Away from Me." During the tryout, Diane McAfee was succeeded by Penny Fuller, and the following songs were deleted: "It Was Always You," "Disco" (also titled "Disco for Margo"), "'Smashing'—*New York Times*," and "Love Comes First." ("'Smashing'—*New York Times*" surfaced briefly in the 1978 flop ***A Broadway Musical***.)

The script was published in hardback by Random House in 1971, and is also included in the 1976 hardback collection *Great Musicals of the Broadway Theatre/Volume Two* (published by the Chilton Book Company and edited by Stanley Richards). The original cast album was released by ABC Records (LP # ABC-OCS-11); the CD was issued by Decca Broadway (# 012-159-404-2) and includes four bonus tracks: the title song (played by Charles Strouse at the piano), the unused "God Bless" and "The Loneliest Man in Town," and the cut "'Smashing'—*New York Times*." The collection *Lost in Boston II* (Varese Sarabande CD # VSD-5485) includes the deleted "It Was Always You," and *Charles Sings Strouse* (PS Classics Records CD # PS-646) includes the unused "Fairfield County, USA" and the cut "'Smashing'—*New York Times*." The latter is also performed in *Unsung Musicals II* (Varese Sarabande CD # VSD-5564). *Jason Graae Sings Charles Strouse* (Varese Sarabande CD # VSD-5711) includes "One of a Kind" and the title song.

The London production opened at Her Majesty's Theatre on November 16, 1972, with Bacall; others in the cast were Angela Richards (Eve), Eric Flynn (Bill), Rod McLennan (Buzz), and Sarah Marshall (Karen). It was followed by a dreary CBS television adaptation on March 13, 1973, which starred three members of the Broadway cast: Bacall, Penny Fuller, and Robert Mandan; the production was directed and choreographed by Ron Field and Bill Foster, and others in the cast included Larry Hagman (Bill), Harvey Evans (Duane), Debbie Bowen (Bonnie), and, from the London cast, Rod McLennan (Buzz) and Sarah Marshall (Karen). The television version omitted the following numbers: "Think How It's Gonna Be," "Inner Thoughts," "Good Friends," and "She's No Longer a Gypsy."

In 1996, the musical was revived with Stephanie Powers for a brief tour. The role of the gypsy chorus member was eliminated (traditionally, the character's first name is always that of the performer who plays the part); the title song was now the opening number (sung by Margo and the company); four songs were eliminated ("Backstage Babble," "Hurry Back," "She's No Longer a Gypsy," and "Something Greater"); and three were added ("Margo," "She Killed Them!," and "I Don't Want to Grow Old").

The musical was revived in concert format by Encores! for five performances beginning on February 7, 2008, with Christine Ebersole (Margot), Erin Davie (Eve), Kate Burton (Karen), Chip Zien (Buzz), and Mario Cantone (Duane).

Awards

Tony Awards and Nominations: Best Musical (***Applause***); Best Leading Actor in a Musical (Len Cariou); Best Leading Actress in a Musical (**Lauren Bacall**); Best Featured Actor in a Musical (Brandon Maggart); Best Featured Actress in a Musical (Bonnie Franklin); Best Featured Actress in a Musical (Penny Fuller); Best Director of a Musical (**Ron Field**); Best Scenic Designer (Robert Randolph); Best Costume Designer (Ray Aghayan); Best Lighting Designer (Tharon Musser); Best Choreographer (**Ron Field**)

CRY FOR US ALL

"A New Musical"

Theatre: Broadhurst Theatre
Opening Date: April 8, 1970; *Closing Date*: April 15, 1970
Performances: 9
Book: William Alfred and Albert Marre
Lyrics: William Alfred and Phyllis Robinson
Music: Mitch Leigh
Based on the 1965 play *Hogan's Goat* by William Alfred.
Direction: Albert Marre; *Producers*: Mitch Leigh in association with C. Gerald Goldsmith; *Choreography*: Todd Bolender; *Scenery* and *Lighting*: Howard Bay; *Costumes*: Robert Fletcher; *Musical Direction*: Herbert Grossman
Cast: Scott Jacoby (Miggsy), Darel Glaser (Flylegs), Todd Jones (Cabbage), *Steve Arlen* (Matthew Stanton), *Joan Diener* (Kathleen Stanton), *Robert Weede* (Edward Quinn), Tommy Rall (Petey Boyle), Helen Gallagher (Bessie Legg), Dolores Wilson (Maria Haggerty), Paul Ukena (John "Black Jack" Haggerty), Edwin Steffe (James "Palsy" Murphy), William Griffis (Father Stanislaus Coyne), Jay Stuart (State Senator Thomas Walsh), Charles Rule (Mortyeen O'Brien), John Ferrante (Peter Mulligan), Elliott Savage (Father Maloney), Taylor Reed (The Cruelty Man), Fran Stevens (Mrs. Teresa Tuohy), Elaine Cancilla (Fiona Quigley), Jack Trussel (Jack O'Banion), Dora Rinehart (Mrs. Mortyeen O'Brien), Bill Dance (Aloysius "Wishy" Doyle), Ronnie Douglas (Mutton Egan)
The musical was presented in one act.
The action takes place in Brooklyn during a five-day period in early May 1890.

Musical Numbers

"See No Evil" (Scott Jacoby, Darel Glaser, Todd Jones); "The End of My Race" (Steve Arlen); "How Are Ya Since?" (Joan Diener, Steve Arlen, The Constituents); "The Mayor's Chair" (Robert Weede); "The Cruelty Man" (Scott Jacoby, Darel Glaser, Todd Jones); "The Verandah Waltz" (Joan Diener, Steve Arlen); "Home Free All" (Steve Arlen, The Constituents); "The Broken Heart or The Wages of Sin" (Scott Jacoby, Darel Glaser, Todd Jones); "The Confessional" (Steve Arlen, Elliott Savage); "Who to Love If Not a Stranger?" (Joan Diener); "Cry for Us All" (Tommy Rall, The Mourners); "Swing Your Bag" (Helen Gallagher); "Call in to Her" (Joan Diener, Steve Arlen); "That Slavery Is Love" (Joan Diener); "I Lost It" (Scott Jacoby, Darel Glaser, Todd Jones); "Aggie, Oh Aggie" (Robert Weede); "The Leg of the Duck" (Tommy Rall); "This Cornucopian Land" (Steve Arlen, The Constituents); "How Are Ya Since?" (reprise) (Joan Diener, Robert Weede); "The Broken Heart or the Wages of Sin" (reprise) (Scott Jacoby, Darel Glaser, Todd Jones); "Cry for Us All" (reprise) (The Constituents)

Cry for Us All was based on William Alfred's successful 1965 Off-Broadway drama *Hogan's Goat*, which played for 607 performances (for the lyric adaptation, Alfred was the co-librettist and co-lyricist). Like the play, the musical took place in the Brooklyn of 1890, where the city's powerful, old-guard Mayor Quinn (Robert Weede) and Sixth Ward leader immigrant Matthew Stanton (Steve Arlen) are in a fierce battle for political power. They have also been rivals for the unseen and now dying Aggie Hogan, whom they both loved. Stanton is happily married to Kathleen (Joan Diener), but Quinn ferrets out a secret: Stanton was once married to Aggie, and they were never divorced. When Quinn gives the marriage certificate to Kathleen, she prepares to leave Stanton; but Stanton and Kathleen argue, and in their struggle at the top of the stairs of their veranda, she falls to her death. Stanton has now lost everything: the two women he has loved, his political career, and his freedom, as he'll be charged with criminal negligence or perhaps even murder.

The gripping if melodramatic story with its colorful characters and the atmosphere of Irish Brooklyn in the 1890s had plenty of potential for a powerful musical, and *Cry for Us All* came tantalizingly close in finding a lyric voice for the breadth and scope of its story. Mitch Leigh's score was melodic and often right on target, but he was working within the constraints of the era, and his score didn't go far enough. The show might have succeeded had it utilized more music and perhaps been sung-through. The plot was operatic, and

Broadway opera is what the musical should have been. The musical adaptation had one particularly inspired notion in the clever decision to use three "street-rats" (that is, a chorus of three street urchins) to pepper the musical as a Greek chorus with their sardonic comments in song about the plot and the characters.

Leigh's score deserved better lyrics. Some were inspired, but others were lacking in wit and power. Further, the score emphasized Kathleen, when it should have focused more on Stanton and Quinn. And as written the musical had too many extraneous characters who came across as walk-ons. Quinn's political crony Petey Boyle (Tommy Rall) and street walker Bessie Legg (Helen Gallagher) didn't have much to do (the latter had just one song), and for that matter neither did the other supporting players. Because the story was set in the bar and backroom of a café, in various Brooklyn homes, and on various city streets, the music could have utilized choral numbers and dance sequences in order to flesh out the story and create a sweeping dramatic musical in operatic tradition. There were so many missed opportunities, and the somewhat intimate approach to story and song made the plot seem smaller and less tragic than it was. Rall was given just one opportunity to dance, and Gallagher was given none at all.

A fascinating if perhaps fatal aspect of the musical was Howard Bay's magnificent revolving set. It was an impressive wonder as it depicted the world of the story, including a high stretch of steps going up to Stanton's brownstone and its surrounding veranda. But unfortunately the technical marvel of the decor was all wrong for the small stage of the Broadhurst. The turntable dominated the musical and so the staging and the scenes sometimes felt cramped. Moreover, the set all but precluded much in the way of dance.

Leigh's score was often melodic and ingratiating. "How Are Ya Since?" had a nice Irish lilt, and "The Leg of the Duck" was a randy Irish jig; "This Cornucopian Land" was a rich patriotic salute to America that could have come out of a John Philip Sousa operetta or a George M. Cohan musical; "The Verandah Waltz" was a sweet turn-of-the-century waltz; the title song was a powerful dirge; and there were two outstanding character-establishing songs for Matt and Quinn: Matt's "The End of My Race" was an exciting exposition of his background (and its title foreshadowed his doom) and Quinn's tough and sly "The Mayor's Chair" showed his backbone of political steel. The aria "Aggie, Oh Aggie" was another intensely personal moment for Quinn, and the various songs for the street urchins were crowd pleasers. But otherwise the score was often heavy in bombastic and somewhat generic ballads (too many of them for Kathleen) which never really defined her character.

Martin Gottfried in *Women's Wear Daily* felt the score didn't jell and wasn't reflective of its time and place, but he noted Leigh's "very substantial" music was "inventive, rhythmically interesting and very singable." As for Joan Diener, her character's demise was "the worse falling-down-a-flight-of-stairs-and-dying scene" he'd ever watched. Further, the story had been "tilted" to make Diener the central character: she also had "many" costume changes, her expression was "best described as pancake make-up," she sang "from the neck up," and she looked "exclusively" at the audience.

John J. O'Connor in the *Wall Street Journal* reported that the musical lost approximately $750,000 during its brief run; he found the score "ponderous," the lyrics "grammatically mangled," and the scenic design "cumbersome." John Bartholomew on WABCTV7 said the musical was a "noble effort" that was "very strange" because it was written well and yet never "really took off" and touched the audience. Leonard Harris on WCBSTV2 felt the musical really wanted to be an opera, and he missed the "freshness and poetry" of the source material (as for Joan Diener, she "thoroughly" overacted and sang with an "exaggerated, unpleasant tremolo"); and Edwin Newman on WNBC4TV found the score "ambitious" but sometimes "pretentious," and summed up the evening as "peculiarly lifeless and lugubrious."

John Chapman in the *New York Daily News* felt the "earnest" musical wasn't able to "find its way through the ins and outs" of the turntable décor. Richard Watts in the *New York Post* said the "ambitious" evening was "little short of disastrous," and noted that the "striking atmospheric setting" featured staircases that whirled around "more vigorously than the plot does." And Clive Barnes in the *New York Times* said the evening was an "inflated bore" that "collapses in compromise" as both drama and musical (but he found Joan Diener "outstanding," liked the "Irish flamboyance" of newcomer Steve Arlen, praised the "vigorous" singing of Robert Weede, noted that Tommy Rall and Helen Gallagher added their talents to the "fine" company, and said Scott Jacoby, Darel Glaser, and Todd Jones were full of "verve and charm" as the street urchins).

During the troublesome tryout in New Haven and Boston, fifth-billed Margot Moser left the show when her character of Josephine Finn was eliminated. As the tryout progressed, Joan Diener's role was enlarged (Diener was the wife of Albert Marre, the show's director and co-librettist). And in the middle of the tryout the musical's title was changed from *Cry for Us All* to *Who to Love* and then reverted to *Cry for Us All*. During the tryout and New York preview period, the show was presented in two acts, but by opening night the show was performed without an intermission. During the tryout and previews, a total of eight songs were cut: "Where Are All the Good Times Gone?," "Macula non est in te," "I'm My Own Woman," "The Splendor of Her Gaze," "I Was Her Slave," "Take My Hand," "Throw the Rascals Out," and "The Fatal Game, or I Win and You Lose." After the musical opened on Broadway, "Search Your Heart" (for the character of Matthew Stanton) was added to the score.

The cast album was recorded by Project Three Records (LP # TS-1000SD); the CD was issued by Kritzerland Records (# KR-20013-6). Of the musical's eighteen songs, thirteen were recorded (omitted were "See No Evil," "Home Free All," "The Confessional," "Call in to Her," and "I Lost It"). The recording also included "Search Your Heart," which was added after the New York opening.

Awards

Tony Award Nominations: Best Leading Actor in a Musical (Robert Weede); Best Scenic Designer (Howard Bay)

THE BOY FRIEND

"A MUSICAL COMEDY OF THE 1920'S"

Theatre: Ambassador Theatre
Opening Date: April 14, 1970; *Closing Date*: July 18, 1970
Performances: 119
Book, Lyrics, and *Music*: Sandy Wilson
Direction: Gus Schirmer; *Producers*: John Yorke, Don Saxon, and Michael Hellerman (Robert Saxon, Associate Producer); *Choreography*: Buddy Schwab; *Scenery* and *Costumes*: Andrew and Margaret Brownfoot (Stanley Simmons, Costume Supervisor); *Lighting*: Tharon Musser; *Musical Direction*: Jerry Goldberg
Cast: Barbara Andres (Hortense), Lesley Secombe (Nancy), Sandy Duncan (Maisie), Mary Zahn (Fay, Lolita), Simon McQueen (Dulcie), *Judy Carne* (Polly), Marcelo Gamboa (Marcel, Pepe), Ken Mitchell (Alphonse), Arthur Faria (Pierre), Jeanne Beauvais (Madame Dubonnet), Harvey Evans (Bobby Van Heusen), Leon Shaw (Percival Browne), Ronald Young (Tony), Tony Stevens (Phillipe, Waiter), Carol Culver (Monica), David Vaughan (Lord Brockhurst), Marie Paxton (Lady Brockhurst), Jeff Richards (Gendarme)
The musical was presented in three acts.
The action takes place in Nice, France, in 1926.

Musical Numbers

Act One: "Perfect Young Ladies" (Barbara Andres, Lesley Secombe, Sandy Duncan, Mary Zahn, Simon McQueen); "The Boy Friend" (Judy Carne, Sandy Duncan, Simon McQueen, Mary Zahn, Lesley Secombe, Marcelo Gamboa, Arthur Faria, Ken Mitchell, Tony Stevens); "Won't You Charleston with Me?" (Sandy Duncan, Harvey Evans); "Fancy Forgetting" (Jeanne Beauvais, Leon Shaw); "I Could Be Happy with You" (Judy Carne, Roland Young); "The Boy Friend" (reprise) (Company)
Act Two: "Sur la plage" ("On the Beach") (Sandy Duncan, Harvey Evans, Mary Zahn, Marcelo Gamboa, Simon McQueen, Ken Mitchell, Lesley Secombe, Arthur Faria, Carol Culver, Tony Stevens); "A Room in Bloomsbury" (Judy Carne, Ronald Young); "It's Nicer in Nice" (Barbara Andres, Simon McQueen, Mary Zahn, Lesley Secombe, Marcelo Gamboa, Arthur Faria, Ken Mitchell); "The 'You-Don't-Want-to-Play-with-Me' Blues" (Jeanne Beauvais, Leon Shaw, Simon McQueen, Mary Zahn, Lesley Secombe, Carol Culver); "Safety in Numbers" (Sandy Duncan, Harvey Evans, Marcelo Gamboa, Arthur Faria, Ken Mitchell); Finale (Company)
Act Three: "The Riviera" (Sandy Duncan, Harvey Evans, Mary Zahn, Marcel Gamboa, Simon McQueen, Ken Mitchell, Lesley Secombe, Arthur Faria, Carol Culver, Tony Stevens); "It's Never Too Late to Fall in

Love" (David Vaughan, Simon McQueen); "Carnival Tango" (Marcelo Gamboa, Mary Zahn); "Poor Little Pierrette" (Jeanne Beauvais, Judy Carne); Finale (Company)

Sandy Wilson's *The Boy Friend* premiered in London on April 14, 1953, for a brief engagement at the Players Theatre; it returned there on October 13, and then in December opened at the Embassy Theatre (both venues were essentially small "Off–West End" venues). The West End production opened on January 14, 1954, at Wyndham's Theatre for a marathon run of 2,084 performances (Anne Rogers played the leading role of Polly). The first New York production opened at the Royale Theatre on September 30, 1954, for 485 performances (a nineteen-year-old Julie Andrews was Polly), and on January 25, 1958, an Off-Broadway revival was presented at the Cherry Lane Theatre for 763 performances. For the latter, Gus Schirmer directed, Buddy Schwab choreographed, and the cast included Jeanne Beauvais (Madame DuBonnet), David Vaughn (Lord Brockhurst), and Leon Shaw (Percival Brown), all of whom reprised their assignments for the current Broadway revival, which met with generally cool notices and played for only 119 showings.

The Boy Friend was an amusing tongue-in-cheek salute to the frothy musicals of the 1920s; it may have winked at, but never condescended to, the conventions of the period's musicals (in reviewing the original Broadway production, William Hawkins in the *New York World-Telegram and Sun* noted that the flappers' "classic walk" included "elbows in, hand out and pinkies up," and Walter Kerr in the *New York Herald Tribune* commented that just before a face-to-face couple went into their dance, they swirled to opposite sides of the stage "in great flowing swoops" and then quickly rejoined one another in hand-held bliss before starting to dance).

The musical focused on heroine Polly (Judy Carne) and hero Tony (Ronald Young), both rich but thinking the other poor; there was of course the requisite happy ending when lowly messenger-boy Tony is revealed to be the son and heir of Lord Brockhurst and that Polly is the daughter of that well-known millionaire Percival Brown. The revival also included Sandy Duncan as Maisie, Polly's sidekick.

Many of the critics felt the revival lacked charm. John Chapman in the *New York Daily News* found the production "terribly cute" and "solemnly staged," and said he just couldn't get into the spirit of the evening. John J. O'Connor in the *Wall Street Journal* said the revival was "soggy" and "woefully weak"; and Martin Gottfried in *Women's Wear Daily* noted the "unimaginative" production was "heavy-handed" with "small-scale" direction and acted with a certain amount of "sloppiness" by the company.

Clive Barnes in the *New York Times* said the "harmless enough" evening had "skittish" direction, and suggested the revival might have been more at home in a cabaret setting or an Off-Broadway theatre. The choreography had a "well-worn" look, and the production was "frenetically hysterical" and "unhappily obvious."

But Richard Watts in the *New York Post* liked the "entirely beguiling" evening and Edwin Newman on WNBC4TV said the musical had "improved with age." He noted that Sandy Duncan twice stopped the show, John Bartholomew Tucker on WABCTV7 said she stole it, and Barnes found her "delicious." Gottfried praised Judy Carne (who was then a popular television personality with her weekly appearances on the hit variety show *Laugh-In*), whom he found "marvelous" and "entirely delightful"; Watts liked her "great sweetness," and Barnes found her "precisely right" and "very pleasant."

The 1954 Broadway production omitted "It's Nicer in Nice," but the current revival included the song, which was also recorded for its cast album (the number was also performed in the 1958 Off-Broadway revival).

The script was published in hardback by Andre Deutsch (London) and by E.P. Dutton (New York), both in 1955; a softcover edition was issued by Samuel French (London) in 1960.

The original London cast album was released by HMV Records (LP # DLP-1078); the CD was issued by Sepia (# 1042); the original Broadway production was released by RCA Victor Records (LP # LOC-1018; CD # 60056-2-RG); and the current revival was issued by Decca Records (LP # DL-79177); the CD was released by Broadway Decca Records (# B0004736-02). Other recordings of the score include both 1967 and 1984 London revivals as well as a 1996 German production.

A very misguided and radically revised film version was directed by Ken Russell and released by MGM in 1971 (Twiggy portrayed Polly, and other cast members included Christopher Gable, Max Adrian, Glenda Jackson, and Tommy Tune). The film may well define the word *charmless*. The soundtrack was issued by MGM Records (LP # 1SE-32ST).

Sandy Wilson wrote a sequel to *The Boy Friend*. Set in the 1930s, *Divorce Me, Darling!* looked at *The Boy Friend*'s characters from the perspective of a decade later, and like most musical sequels it didn't live up to the original. It opened in London at the Globe Theatre on February 1, 1965, for ninety-one performances and was recorded by Decca Records (LP # LK/SLK-4675); the CD was issued by Must Close Saturday Records (# MCSR-3013). A 1997 revival of a revised version of the sequel was recorded by That's Entertainment Records (# CD-CDTER-1245). *Divorce Me, Darling!* was never produced on Broadway, but a notable production took place in 1984 when Houston's Theatre Under the Stars paired it with a revival of *The Boy Friend*.

Awards

Tony Award Nomination: Best Leading Actress in a Musical (Sandy Duncan)

PARK

"A Musical"

Theatre: John Golden Theatre
Opening Date: April 22, 1970; *Closing Date*: April 25, 1970
Performances: 5
Book and *Lyrics*: Paul Cherry
Music: Lance Mulcahy
Direction: John Stix; *Producers*: Edward Padula and A Division of Eddie Bracken Ventures, Inc.; *Choreography*: Lee Theodore; *Scenery* and *Costumes*: Peter Harvey; *Lighting*: Martin Aronstein; *Musical Direction*: Oscar Kosarin
Cast: Don Scardino (Young Man [Jamie]), Joan Hackett (Young Woman [Sara]), David Brooks (Man [Austin]), Julie Wilson (Woman [Elizabeth])
The musical was presented in two acts.
The action takes place during the present time in a park.

Musical Numbers

Act One: "All the Little Things in the World Are Waiting" (Don Scardino); "Hello Is the Way Things Begin" (Joan Hackett); "Bein' a Kid" (Don Scardino, Joan Hackett); "Elizabeth" (David Brooks); "He Talks to Me" (Julie Wilson, David Brooks); "Tomorrow Will Be the Same" (Don Scardino, Joan Hackett, David Brooks, Julie Wilson); "One Man" (Julie Wilson); "Park" (Don Scardino)
Act Two: "I Want It Just to Happen" (Joan Hackett); "I Can See" (Julie Wilson); "Compromise" (Don Scardino); "Jamie" (Don Scardino, David Brooks); "Tomorrow Will Be the Same" (reprise) (Don Scardino, Joan Hackett, David Brooks, Julie Wilson); "I'd Marry You Again" (Julie Wilson, David Brooks); "Bein' a Kid" (reprise) (Don Scardino, Joan Hackett, David Brooks, Julie Wilson); "Park" (reprise) (Don Scardino, Joan Hackett, David Brooks, Julie Wilson)

Park, a tiny one-set musical with four cast members and an orchestra of six, should never have attempted a Broadway run. It lasted just five performances, and although it was obvious the show belonged in an intimate Off-Broadway venue, it probably would have failed there, too. The coy and pretentious plot dealt with four ostensible strangers (who are identified as "Man," "Woman," "Young Man," and "Young Woman," and who were respectively played by David Brooks, Julie Wilson, Don Scardino, and Joan Hackett) who suffer from such trendy ailments as alienation and generationgapitis. They meet in a park and attempt to "relate" to one another by playing truth games. It turns out they are indeed related (mother, father, and two young adult children) and the quartet has decided to undergo a kind of group therapy by at first pretending not to know one another. The last half of the 1960s was enamored with generation-gap comedies, but *Park* got on the bandwagon rather late in the game and had little to offer but clichés (for example, father was too busy a businessman, and if only he'd taken Junior for walks when he was a tyke maybe the young man wouldn't be so mixed up today). It was that kind of show, and the critics would have none of it.

Richard Watts in the *New York Post* said the "curiously flat and aimless" *Park* was "an evening of virtual nothingness" which never got "beyond well-meaning mediocrity." John J. O'Connor in the *Wall Street*

Journal found the production "too fragile," and Douglas Watt in the *New York Daily News* said it induced "fatigue." He pounced on the "basic dishonesty of the writing" and noted the book and lyrics abounded in "pseudo-profundities" that "glaze the mind, spirit and eyes"; he quoted a line from the script ("Love has no shame") and one line from a lyric ("Time is a promise that is never spoken").

Leonard Harris on WCBSTV2 also mentioned the line about time being an unspoken promise and suggested that the "bad whimsy that litters *Park* is irreversible artistic pollution." Edwin Newman on WNBC4TV noted that the production used an amplifier when it actually needed a "silencer," and John Bartholomew on WABCTV7 said the "small, warm, fragile and fey" musical "should've stood off-Broadway."

Like most of the critics, Clive Barnes in the *New York Times* liked the cast (Joan Hackett walked away with the best notices) and felt the music itself was "pleasant" enough despite never making his heart "jump"; and Martin Gottfried in *Women's Wear Daily* wrote a valentine to Hackett (she was a "great star"), but noted the score was reminiscent of *The Fantasticks*. He commented that the four performers seemed to come "from different stage worlds" with Julie Wilson playing in a "Fifties book musical," David Brooks in a "Thirties operetta," and Don Scardino on a "Sunday afternoon television rock musical." Thus the performers' musical styles caused the songs to sound as if they came from different shows, and all the cast members acted "completely disinterested" in one another. (But perhaps Gottfried was on to something. Maybe the score should have been consciously written in four distinct musical vernaculars which defined the characters and reflected their separate identities.)

For all their therapy in the park with Freud, did the foursome come together as a family? Not really, because by the finale all four characters take off separately and seem as lonely as when he or she had arrived. But one character suggests that "maybe we'll meet again."

The script was published in paperback by Samuel French in 1970. In preproduction, the musical was titled both *A Park Is 4 People* and *Park Is Four People*.

The musical had first been performed in regional theatre at Baltimore's Center Stage. Brooks, Wilson, and Hackett appeared in this production, and the Young Man was performed by Ted Leplat. For Baltimore, the scenery was designed by Jason Phillips, the costumes by Ritchie M. Spencer, and the lighting by C. Mitch Rogers.

COMPANY

"A Musical Comedy"

Theatre: Alvin Theatre
Opening Date: April 26, 1970; *Closing Date*: January 1, 1972
Performances: 705
Book: George Furth
Lyrics and *Music*: Stephen Sondheim
Direction: Harold Prince; *Producers*: Harold Prince in association with Ruth Mitchell; *Choreography*: Michael Bennett; *Scenery* and *Projections*: Boris Aronson; *Costumes*: D. D. Ryan; *Lighting*: Robert Ornbo; *Musical Direction*: Harold Hastings
Cast: *Dean Jones* (Robert), *Barbara Barrie* (Sarah), *Charles Kimbrough* (Harry), *Merle Louise* (Susan), *John Cunningham* (Peter), *Teri Ralston* (Jenny), *George Coe* (David), *Beth Howland* (Amy), *Steve Elmore* (Paul), *Elaine Stritch* (Joanne), *Charles Braswell* (Larry), *Pamela Myers* (Marta), *Donna McKechnie* (Kathy), *Susan Browning* (April); The Vocal Minority: Cathy Corkill, Carol Gelfand, Marilyn Saunders, Dona D. Vaughn
The musical was presented in two acts.
The action takes place during the present time in New York City.

Musical Numbers

Act One: "Company" (Dean Jones, Company); "The Little Things You Do Together" (Elaine Stritch, Company); "Sorry-Grateful" (Charles Kimbrough, George Coe, Charles Braswell); "You Could Drive a Person Crazy" (Donna McKechnie, Susan Browning, Pamela Myers); "Have I Got a Girl for You" (Charles Braswell, John Cunningham, Steve Elmore, George Coe, Charles Kimbrough); "Someone Is Waiting" (Dean

Jones); "Another Hundred People" (Pamela Myers); "Getting Married Today" (Beth Howland, Steve Elmore, Teri Ralston, Company)

Act Two: "Side by Side by Side" (Dean Jones, Company); "What Would We Do without You?" (Dean Jones, Company); "Poor Baby" (Barbara Barrie, Teri Ralston, Merle Louise, Beth Howland, Elaine Stritch); "Tick Tock" (dance) (Donna McKechnie); "Barcelona" (Dean Jones, Susan Browning); "The Ladies Who Lunch" (Elaine Stritch); "Being Alive" (Dean Jones)

The musical theatre of the 1970s belonged to Stephen Sondheim, who defined the decade with five groundbreaking musicals that forever changed the face of musical theatre: *Company*, ***Follies*** (1971; Sondheim's masterwork and arguably the greatest of all Broadway musicals), ***A Little Night Music*** (1973), ***Pacific Overtures*** (1976), and ***Sweeney Todd, The Demon Barber of Fleet Street*** (1979). During the decade, Sondheim also wrote one song for George Furth's 1971 Broadway comedy *Twigs*; the background music for Arthur Laurents's 1973 Off-Broadway drama *The Enclave*; some new lyrics for the 1973 Off-Broadway revival of ***Candide*** (which transferred to Broadway the following year); and with Anthony Perkins cowrote the screenplay for the 1973 mystery film *The Last of Sheila*. In 1974, he wrote the musical *The Frogs* (which premiered at Yale University that year and was later produced by Lincoln Center in 2004); composed the background score for the 1974 film *Stavisky*; and in 1976 contributed a song for the film *The Seven-Per-Cent Solution*. The decade also saw Broadway revivals of two of his earlier musicals, first *A Funny Thing Happened on the Way to the Forum* in 1972 (which included new songs) and then *Gypsy* in 1974 (for which of course he wrote the lyrics, not the music). The 1978 film version of ***A Little Night Music*** included new material by Sondheim.

Sondheim's staggering output brought him more and more recognition, and he was recognized as a living institution, the giant of musical theatre who had no peers. He stood alone and defined the boundaries of musical theatre by proving there were no boundaries. As a result, there were two important tributes to him during the decade, which institutionalized him as an icon whose position as the master of modern musical theatre was solidified. On the night of Sunday, March 11, 1973, at the Shubert Theatre when ***A Little Night Music*** was dark, the theatre world saluted Sondheim in a special one-performance evening in which dozens of performers sang his familiar and his unknown songs. *SONDHEIM: A Musical Tribute* instantly became one of those legendary nights in the theatre, an evening when such luminaries as Len Cariou, Jack Cassidy, Glynis Johns, Larry Kert, Angela Lansbury, Mary McCarty, Chita Rivera, Ethel Shutta, Alexis Smith, and Nancy Walker sang in honor of the reigning genius of musical theatre. Then in 1976, the tribute revue ***Side by Side by Sondheim*** opened to critical acclaim and a long run in London, and the next year was followed by a Broadway production that ran for 384 performances. (Incidentally, Anthony Shaffer even titled his new mystery *Who's Afraid of Stephen Sondheim*, but withdrew the title at Sondheim's request; when the thriller opened in London in 1970, and then later that same year on Broadway, it was retitled *Sleuth*.) All the abovementioned works of Sondheim were recorded, including the incidental songs and background music for the plays, films, and tribute revues.

Company was one of the earliest concept musicals. Benjamin Britten and W. H. Auden's 1941 opera *Paul Bunyan* may well be the first lyric work that could be termed thus, and late in the decade Richard Rodgers and Oscar Hammerstein II's *Allegro* (1947) and Alan Jay Lerner and Kurt Weill's *Love Life* (1948) were the first concept musicals to be produced on Broadway (to be sure, they weren't characterized as such back then, although it's interesting to note that in his opening night review of the latter John Chapman in the *New York Daily News* said that in "conception" the musical was "superb"). *Allegro* analyzed a man's life from his birth through his thirty-fifth year, and focused on his relationships and career; and *Love Life* was a sardonic look at marriage in the United States from the colonial era through the present day. In the late 1960s, Jule Styne's *Hallelujah, Baby!* was in structure a concept musical with its look at race relations through the decades, but it never quite got beyond its clichéd making-it-in-show-business saga, and Galt MacDermot's *Hair* (Off-Broadway, 1967; Broadway, 1968) was an ambitious but disappointing look at American drop-outs with a sophomoric book and lyrics that never really held together; only the melodic and ingratiating score saved the evening.

Like *Love Life* (and to an extent *Allegro*), *Company* looked askew at marriage. It examined contemporary relationships in modern-day Manhattan, in this case from the perspective of bachelor Robert (otherwise known as Bobby, played by Dean Jones), his five married-couple friends, Sarah and Harry (Barbara Barrie and Charles Kimbrough), Susan and Peter (Merle Louise and John Cunningham), Jenny and David (Teri Ralston and George Coe), Amy and Paul (Beth Howland and Steve Elmore), and Joanne and Larry (Elaine Stritch and

Charles Braswell), and his three girlfriends, Marta (Pamela Myers), Kathy (Donna McKechnie), and April (Susan Browning). The cynical and sour view of commitment (and the lack of it) struck a raw nerve for many, who were also startled by the musical's nonlinear plot, for which George Furth provided staccato-like glimpses into Bobby's various relationships.

The story was presented against a magnificent set by Boris Aronson, a dark and somewhat menacing jungle-gym of chrome, Plexiglas, and steel that included moving elevators as well as isolated spaces that depicted apartment interiors, parks, and private clubs. In the background were a series of blurred black-and-white photographs of New York City, and the musical not only looked ice-cold, it was. It was unflinching in its almost detached view of life in the big city, and even a traditional vaudeville-styled production number ("Side by Side by Side") was somewhat threatening as it showed the five couples and Bobby celebrating friendship: the number took on the look of old-time Broadway when the couples donned straw hats and canes, but they wielded their canes like weapons and the song and its staging suggested that perhaps Bobby was not all that important to them.

Sondheim's score was the most magnificent heard on Broadway in years. It was sometimes a pastiche of traditional Broadway razzmatazz ("Side by Side by Side"), the Andrews Sisters (the trio "You Could Drive a Person Crazy" for Robert's girlfriends), and a general blend of easy-listening contemporary music (the bossa-nova-inflected "The Ladies Who Lunch," Joanne's blistering attack on herself and the rich women in her set who have nothing much to do in their pampered lives and so attempt to stay frantically busy with empty endeavors). The score also offered a unique "sound" that soon came to define the character and flavor of the typical Sondheim song: the jangly and jagged title number used the busy signals of a telephone to depict characters who try but fail to connect with one another (at one point, a character observes that the true pulse of New York City is the busy signal, and it's noteworthy that three songs in the musical refer in one way or another to telephone calls); the verbal pyrotechnics of the swirling "Getting Married Today" showed Amy's dilemma of whether or not to walk down the aisle with Paul; the conversational, flamenco-inflected "Barcelona" found Bobby and April barely connecting, she with hopeful earnestness and he with general disinterestedness; and Marta's "Another Hundred People" served as the musical's theme song in its précis of disconnected, dangling, and unfulfilled relationships.

The husbands joked with Bobby about his love life and revealed a certain amount of jealousy about his bachelorhood ("Have I Got a Girl for You") and they also ruefully showed their ambivalence toward marriage ("Sorry-Grateful"); the wives are also ambivalent about Bobby's single status (the fugue "Poor Baby" in which they tell him "no one wants you to be happy more than I do" . . . but they pause between the words "happy" and "more," and Joanne warns Bobby that his current girlfriend is "tall enough to be your mother"); and the husbands and wives join together with their dissonant praise of marriage ("The Little Things You Do Together" describes how a couple can "enjoy" concerts, "annoy" neighbors, and "destroy" their children). Finally, there was Bobby's breakthrough moment in the touching and elegiac "Being Alive" when he realizes he needs more in life than just the casual company of friends and girlfriends.

For the concept musical, the story and characters are less important than the mood, atmosphere, and viewpoint of the production. A linear storyline with a defined beginning, middle, and end is less important than the overall pattern in which book, lyrics, music, direction, choreography, visual design, and performance style tell an essentially abstract story that avoids a traditional narrative and a clear-cut conclusion. Sondheim's new musical was all this in its depiction of the restless and discontented singles and married couples seeking *Company* in contemporary Manhattan. In the era's concept musicals, we also regret the ***Follies*** of lost youth, ideals, and innocence; we witness a priest's loss of faith while celebrating ***Mass***; and we discover that long *Hair* is a means of protesting the status quo. At the end of *Oklahoma!*, Jud Fry dies, Curly and Laurey get married, and the country has a brand new state. But what happens to Ben and Phyllis at the end of ***Follies***? Will they reconcile and reluctantly accept their essentially loveless marriage for what it is? And is it too late for Sally and Buddy to repair their unhappy lives? The musical didn't offer answers to these questions.

As for Bobby, just what happens to the birthday boy when his friends throw another surprise party for him at the end of the show? Or is the party a kind of surreal extension of the earlier one that began the first act? Was everything in between his introspective review of his relationships? Why has he decided to skip his own party? And what about an earlier scene when he visits one of the couples and witnesses a contentious moment between them? Oddly enough, when he's left them and they're alone, they embrace. Was Bobby seeing something negative that wasn't there? The concept musical presented situations and asked questions for which there were perhaps no neat resolutions and clear-cut answers.

Company received many rave reviews, but a few critics were perplexed by it.

Martin Gottfried in *Women's Wear Daily* said it was in "a league by itself"; here was a "tremendous," "magnificent," and "sleekly professional" musical. Harold Prince's "superb" direction was the "best he's ever done" and Sondheim's score was "so superior" to what passed for music in the current Broadway theatre that "comparisons are absurd." His rave review had one caveat: Donna McKechnie's solo dance "Tick Tock" was "embarrassing and dated" and should be cut. Gottfried was correct: the number seemed like a parody of pretentious interpretative dancing, and the voice-overs of Bobby and April that accompanied it were often unclear and confusing.

According to Douglas Watt in the *New York Daily News*, *Company* was "Broadway's first musical treatment of nerve ends"; Furth's book was "diamond-sharp" and Sondheim's score was "equally scintillating" with "welcome and essential warmth." John J. O'Connor in the *Wall Street Journal* said the new show was the season's best musical and noted the score was also one of the "best" on Broadway (he also liked Joanne's comment that smoking "may be the only thing that separates us from the lower forms"). And Leonard Harris on WCBSTV2 said *Company* was a "knockout" with its "sharp" and "valid" book and Sondheim's "simple, yet extraordinarily complex and interesting" score.

Edwin Newman on WNBC4TV said the "extremely impressive achievement" offered a "splendid" set design and he praised the "thought and intelligence" that were obvious in the casting choices. But he felt the musical was "saddled" with the misguided notion that it had "something significant" to say about marriage. He felt the show's aims were in "conflict" and thus at times it was a "good" show and at other times wasn't. Richard Watts in the *New York Post* found the musical "disappointing" and "surprisingly uningratiating," and said the score was "pleasant but not particularly interesting."

Clive Barnes in the *New York Times* said he was "antagonized" by the musical's "slickness" and "obviousness," and stated the evening had two flaws: most of the characters were "trivial, shallow, worthless and horrid" and the evening's structure was basically a "series of linked scenes." But there was "lyrical suppleness" in the "elegant wit" and sparseness of Sondheim's lyrics, and his music was "academically very interesting." He predicted that many would love *Company* and said it deserved to be a hit. In the same newspaper, Walter Kerr said the production was "brilliantly designed, beautifully staged, sizzlingly performed, inventively scored"; and the evening's "misanthropic" mood was "highly original" for a Broadway musical (and he noted that "misery loves *Company*"), and everything else about it was "equally original, equally uncompromising." He also mentioned that Sondheim had never before written a "more sophisticated, more pertinent" and "more melodious" score. He "admired" the musical, but he didn't really like it because ultimately all the characters were disagreeable and at the show's center, Bobby was more an "eavesdropper" than a full participant in the proceedings.

During the tryout, "Happily Ever After" was replaced by "Being Alive," and "The Ladies Who Lunch" was titled "Drinking Song." One month after the production opened on Broadway, Dean Jones left the musical and was replaced by Larry Kert, his standby. When the Tony Award nominations rolled around, the nominating committee included Kert as one of the contenders for Best Leading Actor in a Musical, a highly unusual move because the acting nominations had always been exclusively reserved for those performers who originated a role on opening night, and not for those who succeeded the opening-night leads. Like many musicals of the era, the production included a role that became a favorite for former film and stage stars. During the Broadway run, Jane Russell succeeded Elaine Stritch, and others who played the role of Joanne on Broadway and on tour were Julie Wilson and Vivian Blaine. For one of the national tours, George Chakiris played Bobby.

Songs dropped during preproduction include "Multitudes of Amys," "Marry Me a Little," and "The Wedding Is Off."

The musical has been revived in New York a number of times. The first major revival was presented by The York Theatre Company on October 23, 1987, for 20 performances ("Tick Tock" was titled "Love Dance"); the next was seen at the Harold Clurman Theatre on November 5, 1991, for 14 performances; The Roundabout Theatre Company's production opened at Criterion Center Stage Right on October 5, 1995, for 68 performances ("Marry Me a Little" was included in the score, and among the cast members were Boyd Gaines as Bobby, Kate Burton as Sarah, Debra Monk as Joanne, and Charlotte d'Amboise as Kathy). The most recent revival opened on November 29, 2006, at the Ethel Barrymore Theatre for 246 performances with Raul Esparza (Bobby) and Barbara Walsh (Joanne); this version also included "Marry Me a Little," and utilized the unfortunate conceit of having the performers also play musical instruments (the director John Doyle also used this gimmick for his Broadway revival of ***Sweeney Todd, The Demon Barber of Fleet Street***). The musical was also performed in concert at Avery Fisher Hall by the New York Philharmonic on April 7, 2011, for four performances; it too offered "Marry Me a Little," and the cast members included Neil Patrick Harris (Bobby), Craig Bierko (Peter), and Patti LuPone (Joanne).

The London production opened at Her Majesty's Theatre on January 18, 1972, for 344 performances with many of the Broadway cast members (Larry Kert, Elaine Stritch, Beth Howland, Teri Ralston, and Steve Elmore).

The script was published in hardback by Random House in 1970 and was also included in the 1973 hardback collection *Ten Great Musicals of the American Theatre*, edited by Stanley Green (Chilton Book Company) (although the collection isn't notated as volume one, there was a second volume in the series). In 1996, The Theatre Communications Group published both hardback and paperback editions of the script, which included various additions and revisions for various productions, including the interpolation of the unused "Marry Me a Little" for Bobby at the end of the first act; at least one politically corrected lyric (for "You Could Drive a Person Crazy," "gay" was substituted for "fag"); and in one scene Peter makes a pass at Bobby (which the latter chooses to interpret as a joke).

The lyrics for *Company* (including "Happily Ever After," "Marry Me a Little," "Multitudes of Amys," and "The Wedding Is Off") are included in Sondheim's collection *Finishing the Hat/Collected Lyrics (1954–1981) with Attendant Comments, Principles, Heresies, Grudges, Whines and Anecdotes*.

The brilliant cast recording was released by Columbia Records (LP # OS-3550); the most recent CD edition was issued by Sony Classical/Columbia/Legacy (# SK-65283) and includes a bonus track of "Being Alive" sung by Larry Kert; the so-called London cast recording (CBS Records LP # 70108; later issued by Sony West End Records CD # SMK-53496) is actually the Broadway cast album for which newly recorded tracks by Larry Kert were substituted for those of Dean Jones. The production's demo recording includes "Happily Ever After" and both a regular and a "rock" version of the title song. Columbia released a private promotional recording of the musical (# AS-6/XLP-153168) that includes interviews by Lee Jordan with Stephen Sondheim, Harold Prince, Dean Jones, Elaine Stritch, and Barbara Barrie; the recording also includes selections from the original cast album (the title song as well as "Someone Is Waiting," "Side by Side by Side," "Sorry-Grateful," "You Could Drive a Person Crazy," and "Another Hundred People").

The 1995 revival was recorded by Broadway Angel (CD # 7243-5-55608-2-7) and the 2006 revival by Nonesuch/PS Classics (CD # 106876-2); both include the interpolated "Marry Me a Little." A 1996 London revival was recorded by First Night Records (CD # CASTCD-57) and it too includes "Marry Me a Little"; a 2001 German cast recording titled *Company* (unnamed and unnumbered CD) includes eight selections from the Prinzregententheatre production as well as four songs from other Sondheim musicals; and a 2001 Brazilian cast album was issued on CD (VSCD # 0001 and includes "Marry Me a Little."

Company . . . in Jazz (Varese Sarabande CD # VSD-5673) by the Trotter Trio includes nine songs from the musical. The cut "Happily Ever After" was heard in *SONDHEIM: A Musical Tribute* where it was sung by Larry Kert (the evening was recorded on a two-LP set by Warner Brothers Records and was later released on a two-CD set by RCA Victor Records # 60515-2-RC); and "Multitudes of Amys" is included in the collection *Unsung Sondheim* (Varese Sarabande CD # VSD-5433). The 1981 Off-Broadway song-cycle-like musical *Marry Me a Little* (which used little-known songs by Sondheim) included two songs from *Company* ("Marry Me a Little" and "Happily Ever After") and was recorded by RCA Victor Records (LP # ABL1-4159; later issued on CD # 7142-2-RG).

The recording session for the original Broadway cast album was the subject of D. A. Pennebaker's fascinating documentary film *Company*, which was issued on DVD by DocuRama (# NVG-9457); the 2006 Broadway revival was shown on public television on February 20, 2008, and was released on DVD by Image Entertainment (# ID448OEKDVD); and the 2011 concert by the New York Philharmonic was shown on public television and released on DVD.

George Furth's book was originally written as an evening of short one-act playlets titled *Threes* in which Kim Stanley was to star and Anthony Perkins was to direct. The project never materialized, and eventually Furth's script evolved into the book for *Company*. An unused short playlet was later reworked by Furth for his play *Twigs* in 1971.

Awards

Tony Awards and Nominations: Best Musical (***Company***); Best Leading Actor in a Musical (Larry Kert); Best Leading Actress in a Musical (Susan Browning); Best Leading Actress in a Musical (Elaine Stritch); Best

Featured Actor in a Musical (Charles Kimbrough); Best Featured Actress in a Musical (Barbara Barrie); Best Featured Actress in a Musical (Pamela Myers); Best Director of a Musical (**Harold Prince**); Best Book of a Musical (**George Furth**); Best Lyrics (**Stephen Sondheim**); Best Music (**Stephen Sondheim**); Best Scenic Designer (**Boris Aronson**); Best Lighting Designer (Robert Ornbo); Best Choreographer (Michael Bennett)

New York Drama Critics' Circle Award: Best Musical 1969–1970 (***Company***)

1970–1971 Season

BOB AND RAY: THE TWO AND ONLY

Theatre: John Golden Theatre
Opening Date: September 24, 1970; *Closing Date*: February 13, 1971
Performances: 158
Sketches: Bob Elliott and Ray Goulding
Direction: Joseph Hardy; *Producers*: Joseph I. and Johnna Levine in association with Hy Saporta (Ben Gerard, Associate Producer); *Scenery*: William Ritman; *Lighting*: Thomas Skelton
Cast: *Bob Elliott, Ray Goulding*
The revue was presented in two acts.
The action takes place in a setting that is "quite cluttered" and the time is "the following Tuesday."
Note: The program indicated that many of the following characters created by Bob Elliott and Ray Goulding (all of whom were performed by Bob and Ray) would appear in the production (however, some were missing or had quit; some were committed, confined, or in the pound; and one was an accidental transplant donor). The program also stated the intermission would be "in its usual place."

Character Sketches

Hector Lassie; Wally Ballou, Ward Smith, Captain Larson, Dr. Derek Dexter, Edgar G. Fanshaw, Martin LeSoeur, Gabe Preston, Charlies (a poet), Mary McGoon, Harlow P. Whitcomb, Maitland W. Montmorency, Good Professor Groggins, McBeebee Twins, Mayor Ralph Moody Thayer, John W. Norbis, Larry Lovebreath, Leonard Bonfiglio, Clinton Snidely, David Chetley, T. Wilson Messy, Neil A. Starbush, Stuffy Hodgson, Thomas E. Rote, Barry Campbell, Biff Burns, Fielding Backstayge, Fahnstock P. Bodry, T. Wilson Messy Jr., O. Leo Lahey, Word Carr, Wolfman, Dean Archer Armstead, Clyde L. "Hap" Whartney, Arthur Schermerhorn, Gregg Marlowe, Mr. Trace, Mister Science, Komodo Dragon Expert

Bob Elliott and Ray Goulding were popular radio and television personalities who created quirky characters with bizarre backstories. Most of the humor was derived from interviews with these highly unique folk who, like their interviewers, don't see the inherent madness of their situations. The twosome performed the roles of both the interviewers and the interviewees.

The revue-like series of comic caricatures didn't include any music, and so *Bob and Ray: The Two and Only* was one of those theatrical offerings that didn't fall into the neat category of a musical or of a straight play. Since the evening was in the nature of a revue, it's included in this volume (but again with the caveat that it didn't offer any music).

Bob and Ray performed their character sketches in a setting that represented a crowded attic filled with old furniture and bric-a-brac. In fact, one critic noted the cast of Arthur Miller's recent drama *The Price* could move right in and feel at home (Miller's play also took place in an attic filled with clutter). But for all the comfy, down-home look of the set, the evening utilized closed-circuit television in order for the humorists to add a touch of verisimilitude to their interviews.

There was a bit of critical grumbling that the evening's humor was completely centered on the broadcasting industry, but for all that, Martin Gottfried in *Women's Wear Daily* found the production "harmless" but "charming," and he liked the "dry, extremely likable comedians." Walter Kerr in the *New York Times* said Bob and Ray were "very, very, very funny," and John J. O'Connor in the *Wall Street Journal* noted their brand of humor had "malice toward none" and "pinpricks for all." Clive Barnes in the *New York Times* found the "richly amusing" evening a "heartwarming theatrical entertainment."

Among the highlights were interviews in which a television host introduces his guest, "The Corrupt Mayor of Skunkhaven, New Jersey"; a man who boasts he never forgets punch lines (but unfortunately can't recall the jokes leading up to them); and a clueless interviewer on Times Square who misses the big news stories going on all around him (such as murder, rape, and arson) while he single-mindedly asks bland questions of his guest, a cranberry grower.

Another sketch dealt with a hapless fellow in South Dakota who finds himself the prize winner of a television give-away program. When an interviewer asks him when he realized he was the winner, he replies, "Two days ago when the trucks came in with the cables." There was also an interview with a parakeet trainer who uses whips and chairs to keep the birds in line, and another one with a very hostile and defensive apartment dweller who keeps a herd of wild boar in his apartment because in New York just where else can you keep them?

The cast recording was issued by Columbia Records (LP # S-30412).

THE ROTHSCHILDS

"A Musical Legend"/"A Musical"

Theatre: Lunt-Fontanne Theatre
Opening Date: October 19, 1970; *Closing Date*: January 2, 1972
Performances: 507
Book: Sherman Yellen
Lyrics: Sheldon Harnick
Music: Jerry Bock
Based on the 1962 book *The Rothschilds: Portrait of a Dynasty* by Frederic Morton.
Direction and *Choreography*: Michael Kidd; *Producers*: Lester Osterman (A Hillard Elkins Production); *Scenery* and *Costumes*: John Bury; *Lighting*: Richard Pilbrow; *Musical Direction*: Herbert Greene
Cast: Keene Curtis (Prince William of Hesse, Joseph Fouche, Herries, Prince Metternich), Roger Hamilton (Guard, Banker), Hal Linden (Mayer Rothschild), Michael Maitland (First Urchin, Young Nathan Rothschild), Kim Michels (Second Urchin), Robby Benson (Third Urchin, Young Solomon Rothschild), Leila Martin (Gutele [Mama] Rothschild), Thomas Trelfa (First Vendor), Kenneth Bridges (Second Vendor), Jon Peck (Third Vendor), Paul Tracey (General, Skeptic), Leo Leyden (Budurus), Elliott Savage (First Banker), Carl Nicholas (Second Banker), Lee Franklin (Young Amshel Rothschild), Mitchell Spera (Young Jacob Rothschild), Howard Honig (Blum), Nina Dova (Mrs. Kaufman), Peggy Cooper (Mrs. Segal), Christopher Chadman (Peasant), Timothy Jerome (Amshel Rothschild), David Garfield (Solomon Rothschild), Chris Sarandon (Jacob Rothschild), Paul Hecht (Nathan Rothschild), Allan Gruet (Kalman Rothschild), Jill Clayburgh (Hannah Cohen); Members of the Hessian Court, People of the Frankfort Ghetto, Members of the Austrian Court, Grenadiers, Couriers, Crowned Heads of Europe, Banker-Brokers: Rick Atwell, Steve Boockvor, Kenneth Bridges, Henry Brunges, Christopher Chadman, Peggy Cooper, Patrick Cummings, Nina Dova, Vicki Frederick, Penny Guerard, Roger Hamilton, Ann Hodges, Howard Honig, Del Lewis, John Mineo, Carl Nicholas, Jon Peck, Ted Pejovich, Denise Pence, Jean Richards, Elliott Savage, Wilfred Schuman, Lani Sundsten, Paul Tracey, Thomas Trelfa
The musical was presented in two acts.
The action takes place between 1772 and 1818 in Hesse, Frankfort, London, and various European capitals.

Musical Numbers

Act One: "Pleasure and Privilege" (Keene Curtis, Ensemble); "One Room" (Hal Linden, Leila Martin); "He Tossed a Coin" (Hal Linden, Thomas Trelfa, Kenneth Bridges, Jon Peck, Ensemble); "Sons" (Hal Linden, Leila Martin, Lee Franklin, Robby Benson, Michael Maitland, Mitchell Spera); "Everything" (Paul Hecht, Leila Martin, David Garfield, Allan Gruet, Timothy Jerome, Chris Sarandon); "Rothschild and Sons" (Hal Linden, Paul Hecht, David Garfield, Allan Gruet, Timothy Jerome, Chris Sarandon); "Allons" (Keene Curtis, Male Ensemble); "Rothschild and Sons" (reprise) (Hal Linden, Paul Hecht, David Garfield, Allan Gruet, Timothy Jerome, Chris Sarandon); "Sons" (reprise) (Leila Martin, Hal Linden)

Act Two: Hymn: "Give England Strength" (Keene Curtis, Male Ensemble); "This Amazing London Town" (Paul Hecht); "They Say" (Paul Tracey, Male Ensemble); "I'm in Love! I'm in Love!" (Paul Hecht); "I'm in Love! I'm in Love!" (reprise) (Jill Clayburgh); "In My Own Lifetime" (Hal Linden); "Have You Ever Seen a Prettier Little Congress?" (Keene Curtis); "Stability" (Keene Curtis, Ensemble); "Bonds" (Paul Hecht, David Garfield, Allan Gruet, Timothy Jerome, Chris Sarandon, Keene Curtis, Ensemble)

Based on Frederic Morton's book of the same name about the Rothschilds' dynasty, Jerry Bock and Sheldon Harnick's *The Rothschilds* was a mostly predictable rags-to-riches story with generally generic characters and an often ponderous by-the-numbers approach to a saga that should have been compelling and exciting. Perhaps it was unfair to call it an inversion of Bock and Harnick's *Fiddler on the Roof*, but comparisons with the team's earlier hit were inevitable, and so instead of the poor and eternally downtrodden Jewish family of Tevye, his wife, and five daughters, we now had the poor but upwardly mobile Jewish family of Mayer (Hal Linden), his wife Gutele (Leila Martin), and their five sons. The story trod over well-worn territory and there was little in the way of suspense and surprise.

Bock and Harnick's score was too often vapid and colorless, and "One Room," "Sons," and "This Amazing London Town" seemed like early drafts of final versions still to come. Particularly grating was "I'm in Love! I'm in Love!," which could have been a reject from the team's *She Loves Me*. Some made a case for Mayer's "big" wanting song "In My Own Lifetime," but it too was tired and overly familiar in its wish for a better life and it could easily have been sung by Tevye during *Fiddler*'s tryout. And a throwaway number like "Allons" was almost laughable and came across as a choral interlude from an operetta of *The Vagabond King* variety.

But when *The Rothschilds* got things right, it took wings; these high spots revealed just how earthbound and uninspired was the rest of the show. One brilliant conceit which held the sprawling story together was the use of the same actor (Keene Curtis) to portray all the authority figures (and stumbling blocks) on the road to the Rothschilds' success; Curtis played Prince William, Fouche, Herries, and Metternich, and his smooth, charming, and yet threatening interpretations won him a Tony Award for Best Featured Actor in a Musical. And part of the score was brilliant, specifically those songs that dealt with money, social status, and court and stock exchange intrigues ("Everything," "Pleasure and Privilege," "He Tossed a Coin," "They Say," "Have You Ever Seen a Prettier Little Congress?," "Stability," and "Bonds"). These numbers were clever and imaginative, and had the rest of the score been as inventive the musical might have been truly unique, a witty financial operetta instead of a rich man's *Fiddler on the Roof*.

The musical also offered an ingenious *Gypsy*-like moment that depicted the passing of time (in that musical, the vaudeville number "Baby June and Her Newsboys" began with the children going through their musical paces, but through stage magic the youngsters suddenly vanished and were replaced by older players who have now taken over their roles; years have gone by and the children are older, but Mama Rose's brood is still performing the same old act). During an early scene in *The Rothschilds*, Meyer and his family descend through a trap door in the floor of their shop to hide in the cellar from a frenzied mob during a pogrom. When we see the sons descend, they are children, but soon they emerge from the cellar as young men. In a few stage moments, sixteen years have gone by: the boys have grown, Meyer and his wife are older, and despite the passing of years the pogroms still continue.

Although the reviews were mixed, the critics were definitely in a kind and generous mood, but despite its generally positive reception, its Bock and Harnick pedigree, and two major Tony Awards, the musical lost money.

Richard Watts in the *New York Post* noted the musical had its "difficulties" and lacked suspense but otherwise was a "striking, interesting and certainly highly unusual" production. And Clive Barnes in the *New*

York Times said the evening had "geniality" rather than "incandescence," "show-stopping" performances rather than numbers, and a weak structure that lacked the sweeping action necessary for a big Broadway musical; but *The Rothschilds* was nonetheless a "good" musical that got the new season off to a "solid start."

John Chapman in the *New York Daily News* found the book "troublesome" but liked the musical's early scenes and especially "He Tossed a Coin." He noted that Michael Kidd had directed "the whole, big lumbering" musical and he supposed Kidd "did the best he could with what he had to work with." Martin Gottfried in *Women's Wear Daily* said the "lead-footed and overstuffed" evening was a "vulgarization" of musical theatre that represented a "depressing step backward" for Bock and Harnick. Edwin Newman on WNBC4TV commented that the show was formulaic and "there was no point at which it came to life"; and Leonard Harris on WCBSTV2 liked the evening, "warts and all" (there was too much "Jewish chauvinism" and the second act lacked "musical and dramatic qualities," but much of the story's drama was effective and the score was "always good and often touching"). As for John Schubeck on WABCTV7, the show was "not a great musical or a great comedy but a great play with satisfactory music," and the first act was "one of the finest" he'd ever seen.

The musical's window card (poster) and opening night program were highly unusual. The window card was covered in red felt with a gold leaf design, and the program itself had its own "dust jacket" which was also in red felt with gold leaf design.

The production's tryout was tumultuous, and apparently the unpleasant experience is the reason Bock never again composed another Broadway musical. It was the theatre's loss, because for almost fifteen years he and Harnick had provided delightful scores for a series of highly individual shows; but after *The Rothschilds* there was never again another new Bock and Harnick musical.

During the tryout, the musical was extensively rewritten, and the show's choreographer, Michael Kidd, succeeded Derek Goldby as director. So many songs were dropped on the way to Broadway that the programs for the first tryout stop (in Detroit) and the New York opening night read like two different musicals. Bock and Harnick literally threw out most of their score and wrote a completely new one. As a result, over a dozen musical numbers were cut: "The Royal Hessian Auction," "Jew, Do Your Duty," "I Will Bow," "William's Fine Troops," "My Cousin Christian," "The French Imperial Auction," "The British Free Enterprise Auction," "Messenger Ballet," "You're a Fraud, Sir," "Gold Smugglers' Gavotte," "The Grand Alliance Auction," "Never Again" (aka "Valse de Rothschild"), "Money," and "Just a Map" (which had been based on the unused song "Meyer's Lullaby"); another song, "Meyer's Fine Coins," may have been an early title for "He Tossed a Coin."

The Rothschilds all but ignored dance, which was surprising for a musical with Michael Kidd at the helm. The tryout programs indicate the show was originally conceived with more choreography in mind ("Messenger Ballet" and "Gold Smugglers' Gavotte" were deleted during the pre-Broadway run), but by opening night what little choreography remained was negligible.

The script was published in softcover by Metromedia-on-Stage in an undated edition; the cast album was recorded by Columbia Records (LP # S-30337; issued on CD by Sony Broadway # SK-30337). For a S.T.A.G.E. tribute to Jerry Adler, Jerry Bock, and Cy Coleman, "In My Own Lifetime" was performed by Hal Linden (the concert was recorded on a two-CD set by LML Music # 201). The collection *Lost in Boston II* (Varese Sarabande CD # VSD-5485) includes the cut song "Just a Map."

In late 1972, Twentieth Century-Fox announced in *Variety* that it would produce an "exciting musical motion picture" adaptation of the stage production, but of course a film version never materialized.

The musical was revived Off Off Broadway by the American Jewish Theatre for approximately 64 performances beginning on February 25, 1990; the production transferred to Off Broadway, where it opened on April 27, 1990, at the Circle in the Square (Downtown) for 379 showings.

Of the eighteen musicals that opened on Broadway during the season, five dealt with specifically Jewish themes: after *The Rothschilds*, the following premiered during the next three months: ***Light, Lively and Yiddish***, ***The President's Daughter***, ***Two by Two***, and ***Ari***.

Awards

Tony Awards and Nominations: Best Musical (*The Rothschilds*); Best Leading Actor in a Musical (**Hal Linden**); Best Featured Actor in a Musical (**Keene Curtis**); Best Director of a Musical (Michael Kidd); Best Book

(Sherman Yellen); Best Lyrics (Sheldon Harnick); Best Score (Jerry Bock); Best Scenic Designer (John Bury); Best Choreographer (Michael Kidd)

STORY THEATRE

Theatre: Ambassador Theatre
Opening Date: October 26, 1970; *Closing Date*: July 3, 1971
Performances: 243
Adaptation: Paul Sills
Lyrics and *Music*: Various lyricists and composers (for more information, see list of *Sketches and Musical Numbers*, below)
Based on various stories by the Grimm Brothers and a few of Aesop's fables.
Direction: Paul Sills; *Producer*: Zev Bufman; *Scenery* and *Projections*: Michael Devine; *Costumes*: Stephanie Kline; *Lighting*: H. R. Poindexter
Cast: Peter Bonerz, Hamid Hamilton Camp, Melinda Dillon, Mary Frann, Valerie Harper, Richard Libertini, Paul Sand, Richard Schaal; Music performed by The True Brethren (aka The True Brothers: Raphael Grinage, Hamid Hamilton Camp, Lauren Karapetian, Lewis Ross, Loren Pickford)
The revue was presented in two acts.

Sketches and Musical Numbers

Act One: "A Lot Can Happen in a Day" (lyric and music by Hamid Hamilton Camp) (Hamid Hamilton Camp); *The Little Peasant* (Little Peasant: Hamid Hamilton Camp; Peasant's Wife: Melinda Dillon; Cowherd: Paul Sand; Judge: Peter Bonerz; Farmer's Wife: Valerie Harper; Parson: Richard Libertini; Farmer: Richard Schaal; Rich Peasants: Melinda Dillon, Mary Frann, Paul Sand, Valerie Harper); *The Bremen Town Musicians* (Ass: Richard Schaal; Hound: Paul Sand; Cat: Peter Bonerz; Cock: Richard Libertini; Robbers: Valerie Harper, Hamid Hamilton Camp); *Is He Fat* (Man # 1: Hamid Hamilton Camp; Man # 2: Richard Schaal; Sexton: Richard Libertini; Parson: Peter Bonerz); *The Robber Bridegroom* (Miller: Richard Schaal; Daughter: Melinda Dillon; Robber Bridegroom: Paul Sand; Old Woman: Valerie Harper; Maiden: Mary Frann; Robbers: Peter Bonerz, Richard Schaal, Richard Libertini); the segment included "I'll Be Your Baby Tonight" (aka "Dwarf Music"); lyric and music by Bob Dylan; sung by Hamid Hamilton Camp; *Henny Penny* (Henny Penny: Valerie Harper; Cocky Locky: Richard Schaal; Ducky Daddles: Hamid Hamilton Camp; Goosey Poosey: Melinda Dillon; Turkey Lurkey: Paul Sand; Foxy Woxy: Richard Libertini); the segment included "(I Feel Like I'm) Fixin' to Die Rag" (aka "Tradition Music"); lyric and music by Joe McDonald; sung by Lewis Ross
Act Two: "About Time" (lyric and music by Hamid Hamilton Camp) (Hamid Hamilton Camp); *The Master Thief* (Old Man: Richard Schaal; Wife: Melinda Dillon; Master Thief: Peter Bonerz; Count: Richard Libertini; Soldiers: Hamid Hamilton Camp, Paul Sand, Richard Schaal; Countess: Valerie Harper; Parson: Richard Schaal; Clerk: Paul Sand); the segment included "Dear Landlord; lyric and music by Bob Dylan; sung by Hamid Hamilton Camp; *Venus and the Cat* (Man: Richard Schaal; Cat: Mary Frann; Venus: Valerie Harper); *The Fisherman and His Wife* (Narrator: Hamid Hamilton Camp; Fisherman: Richard Libertini; Flounder: Peter Bonerz; Wife: Melinda Dillon); *Two Crows* (Crow # 1: Peter Bonerz; Crow # 2: Hamid Hamilton Camp); *The Golden Goose* (Mother: Valerie Harper; Simpleton: Paul Sand; Eldest Son: Richard Schaal; Little Gray Man: Hamid Hamilton Camp; Second Son: Richard Libertini; Eldest Daughter: Valerie Harper; Second Daughter: Mary Frann; Parson: Richard Libertini; Sexton: Peter Bonerz; Peasant: Richard Schaal; King: Hamid Hamilton Camp; Princess: Melinda Dillon); this segment included "Here Comes the Sun"; lyric and music by George Harrison; sung by Lewis Ross

Story Theatre was a revue-like evening of sketches by Paul Sills that were mostly adapted from fairy tales by the Grimm Brothers (there were also a few sketches taken from Aesop's fables); the production was sometimes accompanied by original and standard popular songs. The show was slightly improvisational in feel, and occasionally the cast members exchanged roles at some performances. The production had first been presented in Los Angeles at the Mark Taper Forum, and the New York version ran out the season; late in the run, Sills's ***Metamorphoses*** (based on Ovid's work) opened and was performed in repertory with *Story Theatre*.

The revue included eight cast members and five musicians, and the production values were modest. While the evening worked reasonably well on the Ambassador Theatre's stage, it might have been more effective in an intimate Off-Broadway venue where it probably would have enjoyed a much longer run. But to the credit of Sills and his company, the delightful production never took on the belt and brass of an overproduced revue; it stayed within the confines of its concept and never pushed too hard. In fact, while the performers played the child-like characters of the traditional fairy tales, they themselves were never childish and never condescended to the material. They had fun in the show, but they took their roles seriously and never played for obvious camp effect.

Clive Barnes in the *New York Times* said he had a "great" time at the "great, unequivocally great" show in which "happily and evenly matched" performances had clearly been rehearsed "to a sharp knife-edge of perfection"; Richard Watts in the *New York Post* liked the "imaginative and unpretentious delight" of both the familiar and unfamiliar fables; and Martin Gottfried in *Women's Wear Daily* said the production worked well because of Sills's "personal inspiration" and his unique understanding of "the essence of storytelling."

But John Chapman in the *New York Daily News* was not amused, and suggested he might have enjoyed the "whimsical" evening if he "had been a bit more than a half century younger."

The script was published in paperback by Samuel French in 1971, and the cast album was recorded on a two-LP set by Columbia Records (LP # SG-30415). In 1971, public television showed a series of Sills's *Story Theatre* adaptations, and five were issued on two DVDs by Kultur Video (unfortunately, these fairy-tale adaptations weren't any of the ones seen in the Broadway production).

Later in the decade, Sills offered *More from Story Theatre*, which presented folk and fairy tales by the Grimm Brothers as well as ones from the *Arabian Nights* and from European, Celtic, and American sources. The evening was produced at the Kennedy Center's Eisenhower Theatre in September 1979; again, Sills directed and adapted the material, and three members from *Story Theatre*'s original Broadway cast (Hamid Hamilton Camp, Richard Libertini, and Richard Schaal) performed in the production. The new version was never seen in New York, and it's unclear if it played beyond Washington, D.C.

Sills was one of the driving forces behind Chicago's theatre scene of the late 1950s and 1960s, and his brand of improvisational theatre blossomed with the legendary Second City troupe, which introduced the concept of sketches that were improvisational in nature but were rehearsed and edited and sometimes drew inspiration from suggestions by the audience. *From the Second City* opened on Broadway in 1961 with a cast that included Barbara Harris, and was followed by eleven Second City revues that were produced Off Broadway between 1962 and 1984; the first was *Seacoast of Bohemia*, which opened in early 1962 for 258 performances and whose cast members included Barbara Harris and Alan Arkin; the final offering was 1984's appropriately titled *Orwell That Ends Well*, which played for 110 showings; and the longest- running revue in the series was *Alarums and Excursions*, which opened in mid-1962 and played for 619 performances. Of the twelve Second City offerings seen in New York, Sills directed three productions and codirected two others. He returned to Off Broadway in 1986 when he directed the improvisational revue *Sills & Company*, which played for 118 performances.

An Off-Broadway musical titled *Aesop's Fables* presented the familiar tales in *Story Theatre* fashion; the rock musical had originally been produced in Chicago, and then opened at the Mercer Arts Center on August 17, 1972, where it played for fifty-eight performances.

Awards

Tony Awards and Nominations: Best Play (*Story Theatre*); Best Featured Actor in a Play (**Paul Sand**); Best Lighting Designer (**H. R. Poindexter**)

LIGHT, LIVELY AND YIDDISH

"A New Musical"

Theatre: Belasco Theatre

Opening Date: October 27, 1970; *Closing Date*: January 10, 1971

Performances: 88

Book: Adaptation by Ben Bonus, text by A. Shulman and Wolf and Sylvia Younin, and additional texts by M. Gershenson, Ch. N. Bialik, Ch. Cheffer, and Mina Bern

Lyrics: A. Shulman, and Wolf and Sylvia Younin

Music: Eli Rubenstein

Direction: Mina Bern; *Producer*: Sol Dickstein; *Choreography*: Felix Fibich; *Scenery*: Josef Ijaky; *Costumes*: Sylvia Friedlander; *Musical Direction*: Renee Solomon

Cast: David Ellin (English Narrator), Mina Bern (Zelde), Leon Liebgold (Rag Seller, Kalmen), Reizl Bozyk (Dumpling Woman, Innkeeper), Lili Liliana (Bagel Woman), Miriam Kressyn (Sosye), Seymour Rexite (Nokhem), David Carey (Kvas Seller), Diane Cypkin (Gitele), *Ben Bonus* (Hershele); Dancers: Marcia Brooks, Helen Butleroff, Jack Dyville, Harry Endicott, Robyn Kessler, Tony Masullo, Maggie Masullo, Eileen McCabe, Joseph Tripolino

The musical was presented in two acts.

The first act takes place in a shtetl (a little village), and the second in New York City and Tel Aviv.

Musical Numbers

Note: The program didn't identify the singers who performed the numbers.

Act One: "A yarid" ("A Fair"); "Yiddish"; "Shver tsu zyin a Yidene" ("It's Hard to Be a Jewish Woman"); "Dus hut mir keyner nit gezugt" ("Nobody Told Me This"); "Tsen azeyger" ("Ten O'Clock"); "Tfile tsu Got" ("Prayer to God"); "Vu lz yoysher?" ("Where Is Justice?"); "A freylekhs" ("A Joyful Song")

Act Two: "Light, Lively and Yiddish" (music based on traditional Yiddish folk music); "Khavertes" ("Girl Friends"); "Tsu mayn dor" ("The Song of My Generation"); "Israel"; "A shukh putser" ("Shoe Shine Boy"); "A briv" ("A Letter"); "S'vet kumen der tog" ("The Day Will Come")

Light, Lively and Yiddish was a revue-like musical that contrasted Jewish life in a small European town (or *shtetl*) with life in New York and Tel Aviv. The musical was performed in Yiddish, but an English narrator explained the story to those who didn't understand the language.

The virtually plot-free first act focused on a fair in the shtetl in which various townspeople are introduced, including a rag seller, vendors of bagels and dumplings, and an innkeeper. A young man and woman want to marry, but can't afford it; but the town's rich man is tricked into financing the wedding. In the second act, two elderly women in a retirement home reminisce about life in the shtetl; a neighborhood boy returns home from college; and a group from the neighborhood fly to Tel Aviv for a vacation and while there discuss life in Israel, including their belief that "peace must and will come."

Lewis Funke in the *New York Times* found the evening "engaging and diverting," and while it wouldn't "spark a renaissance in the American-Yiddish theatre," it was "nice" for a diversion. He noted that although the musical employed a narrator to explain the action and utilized an English synopsis in the program, a knowledge of Yiddish was "essential" to "reap the show's full flavor," and he praised the "melodic, spirited and, where needed, properly sentimental" score.

A slight brouhaha resulted when the revue's producer (identified as Max Eisen in the *New York Times*) and star Ben Bonus charged NBC and its theatre critic Edwin Newman with "discrimination" for not reviewing the musical and filed a complaint with the New York City Commission on Human Rights. The *Times* reported that Newman stated he didn't understand Yiddish and thus as a critic "there is no service I can perform" for those who understand the language. He further noted that "I really hate to dignify this nonsense."

Many of the creators of *Light, Lively and Yiddish* (such as Ben Bonus, Mina Bern, and Felix Fibich) had been represented on Broadway in 1966 with *Let's Sing Yiddish*, another musical that also contrasted life in the shtetl with that of the large city (and it too included a wedding in its plot).

THE PRESIDENT'S DAUGHTER

"Murray Rumshinsky's New Yiddish-American Musical Comedy"
Theatre: Billy Rose Theatre
Opening Date: November 3, 1970; *Closing Date*: January 3, 1971
Performances: 72

Book: H. Kalmanov
Lyrics: Jacob Jacobs
Music: Murray Rumshinsky
Direction: Jacob Jacobs; *Producer*: Jacob Jacobs; *Choreography*: Henrietta Jacobson; *Scenery* and *Costumes*: Barry Arnold; *Lighting*: Uncredited; *Musical Direction*: Murray Rumshinsky
Cast: Michele Burke (Frances), Charlotte Cooper (Esther), Jack Rechtzeit (Yanek), Diana Goldberg (Minke), *Chayele Rosenthal* (Freidel), Jacob Jacobs (Nathan), George Guidall (Sam Golden), Jaime Lewin (Reb Yosel), Thelma Mintz (Bertha), Rachela Relis (Miriam)
The musical was presented in two acts.
The action takes place during the present time in Flatbush.

Musical Numbers

Act One: Overture (Orchestra); "Women's Liberation" (Diana Goldberg, Thelma Mintz, Charlotte Cooper, Rachela Relis); "The President's Daughter" (Chayele Rosenthal); "I Have What You Want!" (Diana Goldberg, Jacob Jacobs); "A Lesson in Yiddish" (Jack Rechtzeit); "Everything Is Possible in Life" (Chayele Rosenthal, George Guidall); "Welcome, Mr. Golden!" (Chayele Rosenthal, Jacob Jacobs, Diana Goldberg, Charlotte Cooper, Jaime Lewin, Michele Burke)
Act Two: "Stiochket" (Jack Rechtzeit); "Without a Mother" (Chayele Rosenthal); "Love at Golden Years" (Rachela Relis, Jaime Lewin); "If Only I Could Be a Kid Again" (Chayele Rosenthal); "An Old Man Shouldn't Be Born" (Jacob Jacobs); "We Two" (Diana Goldberg, Jack Rechtzeit); "What More Do I Need?" (George Guidall); "What Would You Do?" (Chayele Rosenthal, Jacob Jacobs)

Despite its title, *The President's Daughter* wasn't a political revue or musical. It was a Yiddish-American situation comedy with songs, and was partially performed in Yiddish. The slight plot dealt with widower Sam Golden (George Guidall) who seeks a wife (and a mother for his seven-year-old daughter Frances, played by Michele Burke). He soon becomes involved with Freidel (Chayele Rosenthal), a visitor from Poland, but his scheming mother-in-law, Miriam (Rachela Relis), and his sister-in-law, Esther (Charlotte Cooper), resent the relationship because Esther has hoped to succeed her late sister as Sam's new wife. Upon his return from a trip to Atlantic City, Sam introduces his new girlfriend, Bertha (Thelma Mintz), to his surprised circle of friends and relatives. But once it's revealed that Bertha has a mean streak, Sam decides to let Frances choose who his new wife should be, and Frances chooses Freidel.

Thomas Lask in the *New York Times* wrote that he didn't know why he bothered to summarize the plot because the story had "nothing" to do with the evening, which in truth was "a series of sketches, patter, songs and dances stretched along two acts." He noted that the dialogue weaved back and forth between Yiddish and English ("like the ingredients of a seven-layer cake"), and the "best jokes" were in Yiddish. The "spirited, sentimental, saucy" songs were "sweet and serviceable" and the music was "cool—Jewish wedding cool that is." The performances were "broad and right up front" and the direction and choreography were "energetic, not to say boisterous." And he tantalized the reader by noting that the first-act curtain line was "a beauty" and "absolutely great"; in fact, "it may be the best curtain on Broadway between now and next June."

TWO BY TWO

"A New Musical"

Theatre: Imperial Theatre
Opening Date: November 10, 1970; *Closing Date*: September 11, 1971
Performances: 351
Book: Peter Stone
Lyrics: Martin Charnin
Music: Richard Rodgers
Based on the 1954 play *The Flowering Peach* by Clifford Odets.

Direction: Joe Layton; *Producer*: Richard Rodgers; *Scenery*: David Hays; *Projections*: Cris Alexander; *Costumes*: Fred Voelpel; *Lighting*: John Gleason; *Musical Direction*: Jay Blackton

Cast: *Danny Kaye* (Noah), Joan Copeland (Esther), Walter Willison (Japheth), Harry Goz (Shem), Marilyn Cooper (Leah), Michael Karm (Ham), Tricia O'Neil (Rachel), Madeline Kahn (Goldie)

The musical was presented in two acts.

The action takes place "before, during and after the Flood" in and around Noah's home, on the ark, and atop Mt. Ararat.

Musical Numbers

Act One: "Why Me?" (Danny Kaye); "Put Him Away" (Harry Goz, Michael Karm, Marilyn Cooper); "The Gitka's Song" (Danny Kaye, Family, The Gitka); "Something, Somewhere" (Walter Willison); "You Have Got to Have a Rudder on the Ark" (Danny Kaye, Harry Goz, Michael Karm, Walter Willison); "Something Doesn't Happen" (Tricia O'Neil, Joan Copeland); "An Old Man" (Joan Copeland); "Ninety Again!" (Danny Kaye); "Two by Two" (Danny Kaye, Family); "I Do Not Know a Day I Did Not Love You" (Walter Willison); "Something, Somewhere" (reprise) (Danny Kaye)

Act Two: "When It Dries" (Danny Kaye, Family); "Two by Two" (reprise) (Danny Kaye, Joan Copeland); "You" (Danny Kaye); "The Golden Ram" (Madeline Kahn); "Poppa Knows Best" (Danny Kaye, Walter Willison); "I Do Not Know a Day I Did Not Love You" (reprise) (Tricia O'Neil, Walter Willison); "As Far as I'm Concerned" (Harry Goz, Marilyn Cooper); "Hey, Girlie" (Danny Kaye); "The Covenant" (Danny Kaye)

Clifford Odets's 1954 comedy *The Flowering Peach* dealt with Noah, his family, and the Flood, and told the familiar story from the perspective of Borscht Belt humor with beloved Yiddish star Menasha Skulnik in the leading role. At least the play had a point of view, something that Richard Rodgers's musical version, *Two by Two*, completely lacked. The "Jewish" element of the story was leavened out, and the puny-looking new musical plopped down on the huge stage of the Imperial with a lack of freshness and imagination.

The musical consisted of just eight performers, unattractive costumes, and cheap-looking scenery (***Look to the Lilies***, ***Ari***, and *Two by Two* seemed to be in competition for the decade's Worst Scenic Design Tony Award). Peter Stone's script was workmanlike but uninspired, Joe Layton's direction was at best serviceable, and there was no choreography to speak of. The musical talked about the flood of floods, the world's largest menagerie, and the construction of a huge ark. But for all the inherent promise of clever and memorable scenic effects, the musical had none (the era was fascinated with architecture: ***Look to the Lilies*** with the building of a chapel; *Two by Two* with an ark; and ***Lovely Ladies, Kind Gentlemen*** with a teahouse).

The only really inspired device was the use of projections that depicted paintings of the Old Masters, such as the appearance of a panel from the Sistine Chapel when Noah (Danny Kaye) talked to God (yes, like Tevye, Noah chats it up with the Almighty, who responds with the sound of thunderclaps). In fact, sometimes Noah and his wife, Esther (Joan Copeland), seemed ready to go into a scene or song from *Fiddler on the Roof*, and their family members borrowed popular cultural attitudes and situations from the late 1960s and early 1970s. There was some trendy generation gap business when Japheth (Walter Willison) rebels against Noah, God, and the notion that most of the world's inhabitants must drown in order to redeem mankind; further, Japheth is attracted to Rachel (Tricia O'Neil), who is unhappily married to his brother Ham (Michael Karm); and Noah's son Shem (Harry Goz) and his wife, Leah (Marilyn Cooper), trade put-downs in the proud tradition of television sitcoms. Coming along for the cruise of cruises is Goldie (Madeline Kahn), who seems a good prospect for the unmarried Japheth. But the romantic entanglements of almost soap-opera proportion sort themselves out when Rachel and Ham get the First Divorce, which allows Rachel to marry her former brother-in-law Japheth, and for Ham to take up with Japheth's intended, Goldie.

The score (with lyrics by Martin Charnin) was one of Rodgers's least attractive, and only Japheth's haunting ballad "I Do Not Know a Day I Did Not Love You" and his explosive cry of bewilderment "Something, Somewhere" stood out. Various songs were serviceable enough, but others such as "Put Him Away," "You Have Got to Have a Rudder on the Ark," "When It Dries," and "Poppa Knows Best" were numbingly ordinary; "Hey, Girlie" could have easily been interpolated into *Fiddler on the Roof*; and the bizarre "The Golden Ram" might have been the big song from some very strange unproduced musical based on Lana Turner's 1955 biblical epic *The Prodigal.* Harry Goz and Marilyn Cooper's obvious but nonetheless amusing insult duet "As Far as I'm Concerned" was one of the show's guilty pleasures (and follows in the Rodgers tradition of such put-down numbers as "I Feel at Home with You" [*A Connecticut Yankee*; 1927] and "Ev'rything I've Got" [*By Jupiter*; 1942]); the title song had a pleasant lilt; and others such as "Something Doesn't Happen" were sincere but rather tentative.

And then there was Danny Kaye's performance. Most of the critics adored him and said they were glad he was back on Broadway after three decades (apparently his vaudeville-like visits to the Palace in 1953 and the Ziegfeld in 1963 didn't count as Broadway appearances). Except for Martin Gottfried in *Women's Wear Daily*, who said Kaye had "no charisma," was "so without presence you hardly remember whether he is on or off stage," and had a "weak" singing voice (but could act and was an "unusually credible Noah"), the other critics wrote valentines to him. He was "magnificent" (John Chapman in the *New York Daily News*); he was "great" (Clive Barnes in the *New York Times*); he was "brilliant" (Richard Watts in the *New York Post*); and he was "thoroughly charming and ingratiating" (John J. O'Connor in the *Wall Street Journal*).

As for the musical itself, Barnes said it was so long it should have been titled *Three by Three.* Gottfried noted that the show was a "product" and Rodgers's score was "typical of his corporate work of this period" and so "unmemorable" it was a "wonder" the orchestra members "didn't forget" the score between the time they referred to their sheet music and turned to their instruments. Edwin Newman on WNBC4TV said the show was "soft and sticky" and its treatment of religion was "gruesomely pietistic." Leonard Harris on WCBSTV2 said the work was formulaic; and John Schubeck on WABCTV7 noted the performances were "quite good" but not good enough to keep *Two by Two* from being a "bad evening."

But O'Connor said the show moved along "quite agreeably"; Chapman said the "lovely" musical "profoundly" moved him and he was "enthralled" by the "absorbing" book, "splendid" cast, and "beguiling" music; and although Watts said the work was "ambitious" and had "many virtues," he found it "a bit disappointing" and noted that the score was "appealing" if not "brilliant."

According to the street rumors, as the musical evolved it became more and more *The Danny Kaye Show*, and because the musical itself had little to offer and Kaye's name was selling tickets, he was allowed to pretty much do what he wanted. Apparently life was not pretty backstage, and most of the cast reportedly detested Kaye. Midway through the run he hurt his leg, and for a while performed in a wheelchair. In his *More Opening Nights on Broadway*, Steven Suskin reports that Kaye was soon "running down the other actors in his wheelchair" and "goosing the girls with his crutch" (and when ***On the Twentieth Century*** was set to go into production later in the decade, Madeline Kahn "vociferously vetoed" Kaye for the role of Oscar Jaffe). At one performance in the waning months of the run, Kaye seemed more animated during the curtain calls than in the previous two acts.

During the tryout, the following songs were deleted: "Everything That's Gonna Be Has Been," "Forty Nights," "The Death of Me," "I Can't Complain," "Without My Money" "Getting Married to a Person" (later reworked as "Mama Always Makes It Better" for ***I Remember Mama***), and "The Brother Department" (revised as "As Far as I'm Concerned"). During the Broadway run, "When It Dries" was cut from the show, but not before it was recorded for the cast album (Columbia Records LP # S-30338), later issued on CD by Sony Broadway (# SK-30338).

Awards

Tony Award Nomination: Best Featured Actor in a Musical (Walter Willison)

THE ME NOBODY KNOWS

Theatre: Helen Hayes Theatre (during run, the musical transferred to the Lyceum Theatre)
Opening Date: December 18, 1970; *Closing Date*: November 28, 1971
Performances: 378
Text: Adapted by Robert H. Livingston and Herb Schapiro
Lyrics: Will Holt
Music: Gary William Friedman; additional lyrics by Herb Schapiro

Based on the 1969 collection *The Me Nobody Knows: Children's Voices from the Ghetto* (edited by Stephen M. Joseph).

Direction: Robert H. Livingston; *Producers*: Jeff Britton in association with Sagittarius Productions, Inc.; *Choreography*: Patricia Birch; *Scenery* and *Lighting*: Clarke Dunham; *Media Designs* and *Photography*: Stan Goldberg and Mopsy; *Costumes*: Patricia Quinn Stuart; *Musical Direction*: Edward Strauss

Cast: Melanie Henderson (Rhoda), Laura Michaels (Lillian), Jose Fernandez (Carlos), Irene Cara (Lillie Mae), Douglas Grant (Benjamin), Beverly (Ann) Bremers (Catherine), Gerri Dean (Melba), Northern J. Calloway (Lloyd), Paul Mace (Donald), Carl Thoma (Clorox), Kevin Lindsay (William), Hattie Winston (Nell)

The revue was presented in two acts.

Musical Numbers

Act One: "Dream Babies" (Gerri Dean); "Light Sings" (Kevin Lindsay, Company); "This World" (Company); "Numbers" (Company); "What Happens to Life" (Laura Michaels, Northern J. Calloway); "Take Hold the Crutch" (Hattie Winston, Company); "Flying Milk and Runaway Plates" (Douglas Grant, Company); "I Love What the Girls Have" (Paul Mace); "How I Feel" (Beverly Bremers, Jose Fernandez); "If I Had a Million Dollars" (Company)

Act Two: "Fugue for Four Girls" (Irene Cara, Laura Michaels, Beverly Bremers, Hattie Winston); "Rejoice" (Carl Thoma); "Sounds" (Hattie Winston, Beverly Bremers); "The Tree" (Jose Fernandez); "Robert, Alvin, Wendell and Jo Jo" (Melanie Henderson, Laura Michaels, Irene Cara, Kevin Lindsay); "Jail-Life Walk" (Paul Mace, Northern J. Calloway, Carl Thoma); "Something Beautiful" (Melanie Henderson); "Black" (Douglas Grant, Carl Thoma, Irene Cara, Northern J. Calloway, Gerri Dean, Hattie Winston, Melanie Henderson, Kevin Lindsay); "The Horse" (Northern J. Calloway); "Let Me Come In" (Company); "War Babies" (Northern J. Calloway)

The Me Nobody Knows: Children's Voices from the Ghetto was a collection of various writings (such as letters, poems, and essays) by inner-city school children that was edited by Stephen M. Joseph; its musical version opened Off Broadway, and then later transferred to Broadway. Although a program note stated that the spoken text of *The Me Nobody Knows* was written by children between the ages of seven and eighteen who attended New York City public schools in Bedford-Stuyvesant, Harlem, Jamaica, Manhattan, and the Youth House in the Bronx, only four of the musical's twenty-one lyrics were actually penned by them ("Fugue for Four Girls," "Rejoice," "The Horse," and "War Babies"). The lyrics of three songs ("Dream Babies," "This World," and "Something Beautiful") were by Herb Schapiro, and the lyrics for the remaining fourteen numbers were by Will Holt; and all the music was by Gary William Friedman. If the show had been created entirely by school children, it might have been more effective; although the sheen of Broadway professionalism added a certain gloss to the production, a calculated knowingness and eagerness to please worked against the material.

As for the performers, they were hardly show business novices. Their program bios indicated that all but one of them had extensive backgrounds in theatre (some had appeared in the Broadway runs of *The Sound of Music, A Time for Singing, Hair, Maggie Flynn,* and other shows), film (*The French Connection*), television (including soap operas), recordings, the Metropolitan Opera, USO shows, and even modeling. They were certainly talented, but unfortunately their showbiz know-how mitigated against the effectiveness of the musical's message. And because the material was too often self-aware, it seemed slightly dishonest about its seemingly innocent and untouched cries of hope and despair from the ghetto streets.

Perhaps the show should have been written, composed, and performed by non-professionals and toured as part of New York's summer park programs; it might also have done well playing on the college circuit. There would have been an authenticity about a short, small-scale musical written and performed by school children, and a restructured and rewritten production in this manner might have been successful and certainly more satisfying.

The song cycle originally opened Off Broadway at the Orpheum Theatre on May 18, 1970, for 208 performances, and at the end of the year transferred to Broadway at the Helen Hayes Theatre (and then later to the Lyceum).

In reviewing the Off-Broadway production, Martin Gottfried in *Women's Wear Daily* said the musical was a "bummer" that had been "haphazardly strung together" with "shallow" music, often "dumb" lyrics, and a setting that depicted a "pretty version" of a ghetto backed by somewhat "irrelevant" projections (incidentally, slide and film projections were fast becoming a cliché for the era's musicals and were part of the designs for such shows as *The Happy Time, Coco,* ***Company***, ***Two by Two***, and ***Soon***). Gottfried was appalled that the ghetto was presented as "cheer time in middle class suburbia" and that the evening depicted racial oppression with the use of "adorable" children. As such, the evening was handled in the manner of a "left wing Art Linkletter."

Walter Kerr in the *New York Times* said the "collage" offered sentiments that weren't necessarily deep or original; James Davis in the *New York Daily News* felt the evening of "elementary rock" was a "grammar-school rock-protest musical of the *Hair* family"; Jerry Tallmer in the *New York Post* noted the evening's message was no longer "new" or "dramatic" and suggested that "a little of this kind of thing goes a long way"; and while Edwin Newman on WNBC4TV found the musical "unusual and commendable," it was "something of a jumble" and didn't mesh into a "complete" show.

But Leonard Harris on WCBSTV2 pronounced the evening a "clear success," and John J. O'Connor in the *Wall Street Journal* praised the "excellent" music, expert lyrics, and the "astonishingly talented" cast.

The script was published in paperback by Metromedia on Stage in an undated edition, and the cast album was released by Atlantic Records (LP # 1566). "Light Sings" is included in the collection *The Golddiggers . . . Today!* (RCA Victor Records LP # LSP-4643). A London production was mounted during the 1972–1973 season, and in the early 1980s a version of the musical was seen on the Showtime Channel. An Off-Off-Broadway revival opened at the South Street Theatre on April 5, 1984, for sixteen performances, and in his review Alvin Klein in the *New York Times* said the "tepid" musical wasn't "all it used to be" because it offered a "rather insulated, almost quaint view" of teenagers who live in the ghetto.

One of the revue's songs ("Light Sings") inspired a ballet of the same name that premiered in 1978. Patricia Birch choreographed *Light Sings*, which used the music of eight songs from *The Me Nobody Knows* (besides "Light Sings," the others were "Dream Babies," "This World," "Something Beautiful," "I Love What the Girls Have," "How I Feel," "If I Had a Million Dollars," and "Let Me Come In").

Gary William Friedman and Herb Schapiro's 1994 Off-Broadway revue *Bring in the Morning* was another excursion into the writings of young people, but it lasted for just fifty-one performances. In 1980 Friedman and Will Holt explored old age with their showcase production of *Turns*, which in its revised version was seen Off Broadway in 1983 as *Taking My Turn*.

In regard to the length of the Broadway run of *The Me Nobody Knows*, reference sources such as *Best Plays* have curiously inflated the number of its Broadway performances and thus cite 586 showings. *Best Plays* normally differentiates between the runs of Broadway and Off-Broadway performances in its *Facts and Figures* section, but for some reason the Broadway annual insists that *The Me Nobody Knows* had a Broadway run of 586 showings. However, the musical actually played on Broadway for 378 performances (and its Off-Broadway run was 208).

Awards

Tony Award Nominations: Best Musical (*The Me Nobody Knows*); Best Director (Robert H. Livingston); Best Book (Robert H. Livingston and Herb Schapiro); Best Lyrics (Will Holt); Best Score (Gary William Friedman)

LOVELY LADIES, KIND GENTLEMEN

"A New Musical Comedy" / "A New Musical"

Theatre: Majestic Theatre
Opening Date: December 28, 1970; *Closing Date*: January 9, 1971
Performances: 16
Book: John Patrick
Lyrics and *Music*: Stan Freeman and Franklin Underwood

Based on the 1951 novel *The Teahouse of the August Moon* by Vern J. Sneider and the 1953 play of the same name by John Patrick.

Direction: Lawrence Kasha; *Producer*: Herman Levin; *Choreography*: Marx Breaux; *Scenery*: Oliver Smith; *Costumes*: Freddy Wittop; *Lighting*: Thomas Skelton; *Musical Direction*: Theodore Saidenberg

Cast: *Kenneth Nelson* (Sakini), David Steele (Missionary), *David Burns* (Colonel Wainwright Purdy III), Lou Wills (Sergeant Gregovich), *Ron Husmann* (Captain Fisby), Sachi Shimizu (Old Lady), Tisa Chang (The Daughter), June Angela (Child), Gene Profanato (Child), Dana Shimizu (Child), Lady Astor (a goat who played herself), Sab Shimono (Ancient Man, Mr. Keora), Alvin Lum (Mr. Seiko), Lori Chinn (Miss Higa Jiga), David Thomas (Mr. Oshira), Big Lee (Mr. Hokaida), *Eleanor Calbes* (Lotus Blossom), Remak Ramsay (Captain McLean), David Steele (Logan), Jim Weston (Miller), Stephen Bolster (O'Malley), Stuart Craig Wood (Cabot), James B. Spann (Stock), Kirk Norman (Lipshitz), James Hobson (Swenson), Dennis Roth (Cardone), Richard Nieves (Mancini), Charlie J. Rodriguez (Colombo); Okinawans and Americans: Barbara Coggin, Catherine Dando, Joan Nelson, Sumiko, Tisa Chang, Lori Chinn, Christi Curtis, Marjory Edson, Rosalie King, Sylvia Nolan, Jo Ann Ogawa, Sachi Shimizu, Susan Sigrist, Stephen Bolster, James Hobson, Alvin Lum, Richard Nieves, Kirk Norman, Charlie J. Rodriguez, Dennis Roth, Sab Shimono, James B. Spann, David Steele, Jim Weston, Stuart Craig Wood, Henry Boyer, Paul Charles, Charlie Goeddertz, J. J. Jepson, Tim Ramirez, Steven Ross, Joe Milan, Ken Urmston

The musical was presented in two acts.

The action takes place during 1946 in Okinawa.

Musical Numbers

Act One: "With a Snap of My Finger" (Kenneth Nelson, Okinawans, GIs); "Right-Hand Man" (David Burns, Kenneth Nelson, Ron Husmann, GIs); "Find Your Own Cricket" (Kenneth Nelson, David Thomas, Lori Chinn, Villagers); "One Side of World" (Kenneth Nelson); "Geisha" (Eleanor Calbes); "You Say—They Say" (Kenneth Nelson, Villagers); "This Time" (Ron Husmann); "Simple Words" (Eleanor Calbes); "Garden Guaracha" (Remak Ramsay); "If It's Good Enough for Lady Astor" (Ron Husmann, Remak Ramsay, Kenneth Nelson, Villagers)

Act Two: "Chaya" (aka "Teahouse") (Kenneth Nelson, Villagers); "Call Me Back" (Ron Husmann, Remak Ramsay, Kenneth Nelson); "Lovely Ladies, Kind Gentlemen" (Kenneth Nelson); "You've Broken a Fine Woman's Heart" (David Burns); "One More for the Last One" (Kenneth Nelson, Lou Wills, GIs, Villagers)

Lovely Ladies, Kind Gentlemen was based on Vern J. Sneider's 1951 novel *The Teahouse of the August Moon* and its subsequent 1953 stage version by John Patrick. The play was one of the biggest hits of the 1950s: it ran for 1,027 performances and won Broadway's triple crown: the Pulitzer Prize for drama, the New York Drama Critics' Circle Award for Best Play, and the Tony Award for Best Play. It also won a Tony for David Wayne (Sakini) as Best Leading Actor in a Play, and others in the original cast were John Forsythe (Captain Fisby) and Paul Ford (Colonel Purdy). The London production opened in 1954 with Eli Wallach as Sakini and played for 964 performances, and in 1956 the MGM film version was released with Marlon Brando (Sakini), Glenn Ford (Fisby), and Paul Ford, who reprised his Broadway role. The play was revived for a limited engagement at City Center in 1956, and in an unusual casting choice the actress Rosita Diaz portrayed Sakini.

But for all the comedy's popularity during the era, it's now a forgotten hit. By 1970, the general consensus was that the story had not worn well and that its view of Okinawans was naive and condescending. If the musical had opened in the latter part of the 1950s or early 1960s, it might have had a chance. But in 1970 the nation was embroiled in the Vietnam War, and if racial politics didn't do in the musical (see below), then the idea of a merry musical about American servicemen in the Far East surely did.

The lighthearted plot dealt with well-meaning but inept army personnel assigned to Okinawa in 1946 in order to help the island recover from World War II and to introduce democracy (whether the Okinawans want it or not). But it's the Okinawans who teach the Americans a thing or two. Instead of marketing useless cricket cages, they learn how to brew and sell a potent brandy made from sweet potatoes, and instead of building a five-sided schoolhouse (modeled after the Pentagon), they insist on a teahouse (or *chaya*). The Americans nominally in charge are the blustery Colonel Purdy (David Burns), who helpfully explains that "a communications system is meant to communicate," and the well-meaning if befuddled Captain Fisby (Ron Husmann). But it's really the Okinawan Sakini (Kenneth Nelson) who runs the show.

There were opposing critical reactions to the treatment of the Okinawans. Richard Watts in the *New York Post* felt that "any suspicion" that the musical was "patronizing" was "fantastically unfounded," and noted that if anyone was mocked it was the Americans, who came across as "naïve but well-meaning." But Martin Gottfried in *Women's Wear Daily* said the musical was an example of "classic 40's liberalism" which was actually "prejudice." The "natives" are "cute" and haven't any need for "schoolhouses (education)" and a geisha is full of "obedience and subservience." He also mentioned that Sakini was the "ultimate Oriental" who spoke in "childlike poetry-prose the way movie-Indians do." Gottfried condemned this "rubbish," and was disappointed with the score; but he liked David Burns and said the choreography "seemed almost interesting" (but since there was so little of it, he really couldn't tell one way or the other).

Clive Barnes in the *New York Times* found the evening too "cute," too "coy," and too "patronizing," and said the score was a "chop-suey of almost compelling unoriginality." He noted that Burns stormed through the musical in "friendly contempt" and stopped the show with "You've Broken a Fine Woman's Heart." Edwin Newman on WNBC4TV suggested that if the musical was supposed to be a "family entertainment" it was "misconceived." Except for "two good music hall numbers" (probably "You've Broken a Fine Woman's Heart" and "One More for the Last One"), the score was "largely without distinction"; moreover, the production was "uncomfortably patronizing" toward Okinawans. But he praised the "admirable" David Burns, and said Kenneth Nelson, Ron Husmann, and Remak Ramsay did the best they could with their material.

Douglas Watt in the *New York Daily News* found the musical "lively, colorful and generally engaging," and said Burns was "superb" in "You've Broken a Fine Woman's Heart"; he also said Nelson and Husmann were "delightful" in "Call Me Back," a number about hammy performers. Although Watts felt the evening wasn't as brilliant as the original play, he nonetheless said its "imaginative charm" added up to a "reasonably entertaining" show. It was a "cheerful and friendly" and "modestly agreeable" musical with "pleasant if not especially stimulating" songs.

During the tryout, Bernie West was replaced by David Burns, Judy Knaiz by Lori Chinn, and the following numbers were cut: "Suddenly Now," "I'll Grow a Garden for You," "Miracle," "Batata," "Very, Very Lucky Lady," "All That Has Happened," and "Very Simple." Unused songs in an early draft of the script include "Spread the Word" and "Red Stuff."

Perhaps the most dramatic aspects of *Lovely Ladies, Kind Gentlemen* took place offstage. White-American Kenneth Nelson was cast as the Okinawan Sakini, and almost immediately producer Herman Levin was criticized for not casting an Asian American in the part. Flyers distributed by the Brotherhood of Artists proclaimed: "No more white actors in 'yellow face'! Would any sane sensitive producer—today—consider a white actor in 'black face'? Why then this affront to the Asian-American community? . . . But you can help stamp out this indignity. Boycott *Lovely Ladies, Kind Gentlemen*!" And there were further protests that with so many Okinawan characters in the story, only twelve Asian-Americans were cast. (But there were no protests when ***Aint Supposed to Die a Natural Death*** included black actors in white face.)

And pretty soon it was the producer and the performers themselves who were protesting. Barnes began his review by announcing that he "came to bury" the "literal and heavy-handed" musical, "not to praise it"; and said the "strangely dated" show "modestly opened" with "clumsy" direction and music that was "as expressionless as an egg." The cast took out an advertisement in the *Times* that stated, "Well, Mr. Barnes, we refuse to be buried!" But buried they were, and the production closed after sixteen performances. *Best Plays* reported the show cost over $600,000 to produce, and lost more than that due to poor ticket sales during its tryout and Broadway run.

The script was published in paperback by Samuel French in 1971; it includes the complete lyrics for about half the songs, and the others are referenced by title only. There was no cast recording, but in the mid-2000s Original Cast Records announced it would produce a studio/cast album, and as of this writing an Internet cast album website indicates that all the vocal tracks have been completed (the album's cast includes Lou Diamond Phillips, Robert Morse, original cast member Eleanor Calbes, and the late Mickey Rooney and Charles Nelson Reilly). The collection *Unsung Musicals III* (Varese Sarabande CD # VSD-5769) includes the song "Simple Words" (aka "Simple Word").

Awards

Tony Award Nominations: Best Leading Actor in a Musical (David Burns); Best Costume Designer (Freddy Wittop)

SOON

"A Rock Opera"

Theatre: Ritz Theatre
Opening Date: January 12, 1971; *Closing Date*: January 13, 1971
Performances: 3
Book: Adaptation by Martin Duberman
Lyrics: Scott Fagan
Music: Joseph Martinez Kookoolis and Scott Fagan
Based on an original story by Joseph Martinez Kookoolis and Scott Fagan.
Direction: Uncredited, with "additional staging" by Gerald Freedman; *Producers*: Bruce W. Stark and Sagittarius Productions, Inc.; *Choreography*: Fred Benjamin; *Scenery*: Kert Lundell; *Costumes*: David Chapman; *Lighting*: Jules Fisher; *Musical Direction*: Louis St. Louis
Cast: Barry Bostwick (Kelly), Marta Heflin (Annie), Dennis Belline (Wilson Wilson), Joseph Campbell Butler (Neil), Richard Gere (Michael), Peter Allen (Henry), Marion Ramsey (Hope), Leata Galloway (Faith), Vicki Sue Robinson (Charity), Pamela Pentony (Rita), Nell Carter (Sharon); Friends of Henry: Singer Williams, Michael Jason, John C. Nelson; Record Company Executives: Del Hinkley, Angus Cairns, Larry Spinelli, Paul Eichel; Tony Middleton (Songwriter); Pendleton Brown (Psychedelic Necktie)
The musical was presented in two acts.
The action takes place during the present time "on the road" and in the city.

Musical Numbers

Note: The program didn't identify performers of songs.
Act One: "Let the World Begin Again"; "In Your Hands"; "I See the Light"/"Gentle Sighs"; "Roll Out the Morning"; "Everybody's Running"; "Henry Is Where It's At"; "Music, Music"; "Glad to Know Ya"; "Rita Cheeta"; "Henry's Dream Theme"; "To Touch the Sky"; The Chase: "Everybody's Running" (reprise); "Marketing, Marketing"; "Sweet Henry Loves You"; "One More Time"; "Straight"; and "Wait"
Act Two: "Faces, Names and Places"; "Annie's Thing"; "Doing the High"; "Soon"; "Country Store Living"; "What's Gonna Happen to Me"; "On the Charts"; "Molecules"; "So Much That I Know"; "Child of Sympathy"; "Frustration"; "Doing the High" (reprise); "It Won't Be Long"

With the opening of *Soon*, the Ritz Theatre was back in business as a legitimate Broadway house. The venue first opened its doors in 1921, but from 1943 to 1965 it was a radio and then television studio. It went dark in the mid-1960s but was refurbished and reclaimed for Broadway in 1971, and in 1990 it was again refurbished and reopened as the Walter Kerr Theatre.

Unfortunately, the "new" Ritz got off to an undistinguished start when the dreary so-called "rock opera" *Soon* opened on January 12, 1971, and closed the next day.

The plot dealt with the members of a rock group and their communal angst when they achieve fame, success, and money but discover what so many show-business sagas have taught us: It's Lonely at the Top, especially when you've Sold Out. It seems the group wants to write message and protest songs (this was the early 1970s, after all), but the business executives of their record company insist they write and record popular bubble-gum music. And so they do, to their sadness and consternation. Fame is theirs, and the money rolls in, but they're no longer happy because they've rejected their ideals.

The plot was hardly original or compelling (see Clifford Odets's 1949 play *The Big Knife*, which was a dramatic variation of the old story and dealt with a Broadway actor who sells his artistic soul to Hollywood), and the critics were less than impressed.

It's noteworthy that John Schubeck on WABCTV7 was especially struck by the audience and its applause when the musical lectured them on the horrors of "avarice, hatreds and shabby values" as well as "profit and possessions." But the critic wryly noted that when the first-nighters left the theatre they were met by a waiting row of limousines to spirit them away. However, Schubeck said he had a "great time" and mentioned the evening was like a combination of *Hair* and ***Company***, "but more up to date than both."

Douglas Watt in the *New York Daily News* felt there was a certain validity to the musical's story, but it was unfortunately filled with "dime-store idealism" and had the "air of an embarrassing school entertainment." Martin Gottfried in *Women's Wear Daily* said the book was a "disaster," the acting "embarrassing," and the overall evening "boring" and "saddening." And Edwin Newman on WNBC4TV found the book "weak" and the show more in the nature of a rock concert than a rock opera.

Clive Barnes in the *New York Times* noted that the writers had created "a commercial musical" about "the horrors of musical commercialism." It might have been helpful had they employed "a strong satiric approach" to the material, but unfortunately "much of the music is as feeble and as cheap as the writers say it is." But he praised the "uniformly good" cast with their "distinctive personalities" and their "zest and honestly projected pop voices" (and he singled out Barry Bostwick and Marta Helflin).

A few critics had mild praise for the score. Newman said it was "pleasant and sometimes more" than that; Gottfried suggested the songs weren't "especially distinctive" but nonetheless captured the essence of "rock's energy and lyricism"; Richard Watts said the score was "pleasant and certainly lively"; and the songs weren't "at all bad," according to Douglas Watt.

The reviewers also noted that the evening was replete with four-letter words, and at one point a female character was gang-raped. To add to the coarseness of the production, the five-piece orchestra was identified in the program as "Pit-Shit."

Soon is best remembered today for the number of its cast members who went on to fame on television, Broadway, film, concerts, and recordings: the musical represented either the Broadway debuts or early Broadway appearances by Barry Bostwick, Peter Allen, Richard Gere, Nell Carter, and Marta Heflin.

Soon and ***Frank Merriwell***, or ***Honor Challenged*** were mistakenly assumed to be among the first of the so-called "Middle Theatre"/"Limited Gross Broadway"/"Limited Broadway" productions, a financial experiment that lasted for a few seasons in the early 1970s. But according to *Best Plays*, ***Johnny Johnson*** was the only musical of the season to open under the new experiment.

For the record, under the new contractual arrangements, Broadway theatres were limited in the number of tickets they could sell (between 299 and 500 seats, depending on the size of the theatre); the remaining seats were roped off and tickets for these were not for sale. Because the profits for these productions were limited, so were the contracts for the cast, stagehands, and (for musicals) orchestra members, and thus the weekly nut for a given Limited Broadway production was kept low. *Best Plays* reported that weekly ticket sales for such productions couldn't exceed $25,000 and that the highest-priced tickets were set at a $5 top. The definitions of Limited Broadway were somewhat confusing, and the rules were subject to change. Some reference sources consider shows under Limited Broadway contracts as Off-Broadway productions, while others classify them as Broadway offerings. (To be as inclusive as possible, this book considers musicals under Limited Broadway contracts as Broadway shows.)

Further, there wasn't always a clear distinction between the traditional turfs of Broadway and Off Broadway. ***Grease*** opened at the Off-Broadway Eden Theatre, and four months later transferred to Broadway. There was the assumption that the show's tenure at the Eden was under an Off-Broadway contract, but it turned out that from its first performance at the Eden the musical was under a standard Broadway contract. As a result, ***Grease*** was an Off-Broadway musical in location only. And when the Broadway capitalization for ***Smith*** fell through, the producers opted for an Off-Broadway mounting and opened at the Eden. But *Variety* reported the performers had already signed Broadway contracts and thus while the show was under mostly Off-Broadway contracts (apparently in regard to stagehands, orchestra members, and theatre rental), the performers themselves were paid under Broadway contracts.

ARI

"A NEW MUSICAL"

Theatre: Mark Hellinger Theatre
Opening Date: January 15, 1971; *Closing Date*: January 30, 1971

Performances: 19
Book and *Lyrics*: Leon Uris
Music: Walt Smith; additional music by William Fisher
Based on the 1958 novel *Exodus* by Leon Uris.
Direction: Lucia Victor; *Producers*: Ken Gaston and Leonard Goldberg (Ronald Reckseit and Lisa Lipsky, Associate Producers); *Choreography*: Talley Beatty; *Scenery*: Robert Randolph; *Costumes*: Sara Brook; *Lighting*: Nananne Porcher; *Musical Direction*: Stanley Lebowsky
Cast: Joseph Della Sorte (Joab), Mark Zeller (Zev), Martin Ross (David), C. K. Alexander (Mandria), Jack Gwillim (General Sutherland), Jamie Ross (Major Caldwell), David Cryer (Ari Ben Canaan), Norwood Smith (Mark Parker), Constance Towers (Kitty Fremont), John Savage (Dov), Jacqueline Mayro (Karen), Roger Morgan (Benjy), Alexander Orfaly (Armeteau), Edward Becker (Friend of Armeteau), Casper Roos (Captain Henley): Refugee Children: Tracey Eman, Kelley Boa, Mona Daleo, Toni Lund, Lynn Reynolds, Timmy Ousey, Todd Jones, Johnny Welch, Tony Dean; Refugees and British Soldiers: Dancers—Bryant Baker, Bjarne Buchtrup, Ron Crofoot, Richard Dodd, Pi Douglass, Richard Maxon, Ronn Steinman, Carol Estey, Reggie Israel, Karen L. Jablons, Joanna Mendl, Gayle Pines, Deborah Strauss; Singers—Edward Becker, Ted Bloecher, Bennett Hill, Henry Lawrence, Art Matthews, Casper Roos, D. Brian Wallach, Bonnie Marcus, Patricia Noal, Susan Schevers, Suzanne Horn
The musical was presented in two acts.
The action takes place during 1946 on the island of Cyprus.

Musical Numbers

Act One: "Children's Lament" (Children); "Yerushaliam" (David Cryer); "The Saga of the Haganah" (Martin Ross, Mark Zeller, Joseph Della Sorte, C. K. Alexander); "The Saga of the Haganah" (reprise) (C. K. Alexander); "Give Me One Good Reason" (Constance Towers); "Dov's Nightmare" (John Savage, Victims of the Holocaust); "Karen's Lullaby" (Jacqueline Mayro); "Aphrodite" (C. K. Alexander, Alexander Orfaly); "My Galilee" (David Cryer, Palestinians); "The Lord Helps Those Who Help Themselves" (Martin Ross, Palestinians); "The Alphabet Song" (Jacqueline Mayro, Children); "Tactics" (performers uncredited; probably a rifle dance by the male dancers); "Give Me One Good Reason" (reprise) (Constance Towers); "My Brother's Keeper" (David Cryer)
Act Two: "The Exodus" (Martin Ross, Ensemble); "He'll Never Be Mine" (Constance Towers); "One Flag" (Jacqueline Mayro, Children); "The Lord Helps Those Who Help Themselves" (reprise) (C. K. Alexander); "I See What I Choose to See" (Jacqueline Mayro, John Savage); "Hora-Galilee" (dance) (Jacqueline Mayro, John Savage, Children, Palestinians); "Ari's Promise" (David Cryer); "Ari's Promise" (reprise) (Company); "The Exodus" (reprise) (Company)

Leon Uris wrote the book and lyrics for *Ari*, which he adapted from his 1958 best-selling novel *Exodus*. The book was filmed in 1960 and enjoyed a hit theme song composed by Ernest Gold, who didn't compose the music for the stage production (Gold's single Broadway effort, 1968's *I'm Solomon*, was a "Jewish" musical set in biblical times). *Ari* focused on the efforts of the title character (David Cryer) and his supporters to ensure that a ship (the *Exodus*) with refugee Jewish children leaves Cyprus for the new Jewish homeland of Israel despite resistance from the British who are stationed on the island. Added to the mix are Kitty (Constance Ford), a Gentile nurse who falls in love with Ari, the emotionally scarred Dov (John Savage) who has nightmares about his experience in a concentration camp, and Karen (Jacqueline Mayro), who loves him.

The musical was serious, earnest, stolid, grave, sober, straightforward . . . and stupefyingly tedious. The book, lyrics, and music were lifeless in their by-the-numbers approach to the potentially epic and dramatic story, and the evening lacked surprise and inspiration. The performers did what they could, but their material was hopeless, the scenery unattractive, and the musical's idea of an elaborate dance number was jaw-droppingly tasteless (see below). The characters of the tragic Dov and Karen were particularly annoying in their tear-stained, heart-on-the-sleeve manner, and their "I See What I Choose to See" was the lowest point in an evening of lows. Kitty's "Give Me One Good Reason" ("why I should get involved") was a tiresome ballad out of the Broadway cookie-cutter; and "The Lord Helps Those Who Help Themselves" and "The Exodus" tried for spine-tingling choral effect but failed to make an impression. The musical seemed to sleepwalk its way through the plot, everything was on automatic pilot, and there was never a moment of genuine musical theatre magic.

Richard Watts in the *New York Post* found *Ari* a "serious disappointment"; it was "dramatically ineffective" and the "agreeable" score was "not very interesting." Douglas Watt in the *New York Daily News* said the production was "humorless and numbingly dull" and had a score that "would have sounded tired and even dated in the days of *The Desert Song*." The headline in T. E. Kalem's review in *Time* was "D.O.A."; he found the musical "pitiable" and noted that the Broadway season had offered so many Jewish shows it seemed like a "secular synagogue," and he pleaded "shalom and enough already."

Edwin Newman on WNBC4TV said the material was "obvious" in its "sheer banality," the music was "mechanical," and the dialogue the "most stilted" of the season; Leonard Harris on WCBSTV2 found the musical "dreadful" and said the music, décor, orchestrations, and choreography ranged "from mediocre on down." But although John Schubeck on WABCTV7 had reservations about the musical (such as the sluggish opening sequence), he felt the evening eventually boiled with "action, suspense and feeling" and was "spellbinding."

Martin Gottfried in *Women's Wear Daily* said *Ari* was a "disgrace" to "the name of Broadway." It was "incompetent" and was just about "the last straw" with its "primitive" production values, which offered "abysmally designed and shabbily executed" settings, "sluggish and ragged" direction, and songs that would be "rejected" by a summer resort for its weekend show. He noted that the musical "actually" included a concentration camp ballet, which was "nearly matched" by a rifle dance ("Tactics").

During the tryout, the following songs were cut: "Let the Good Book Lead the Way," "A Time to Love," "H.M.J.F.C.," "Falling Too Far," and "When He Is Broken"; "Learning Hebrew" was probably an early title for "The Alphabet Song," and "Ari's Soliloquy" may have been an early title for "Ari's Promise." Other numbers that may have been performed during the tryout were: "Come and Spend Your Life with Me," "Don't Be Afraid to Love," "Don't I Know You from Somewhere," "A Time to Love," "I'm Alone," and "Love Is for the Birds." In his book *American Song*, Ken Bloom reports that at least two unspecified songs from the musical were written by lyricist Lyn Duddy and composer Jerry Bresler (who were represented later in the decade with the huge flop ***Spotlight***, which played for less than one week of its scheduled four-week tryout in Washington, D.C.).

Gottfried said the concentration camp ballet was "nearly matched" by the rifle dance, and noted the ballet "was all I could bear and I couldn't bear that." The elaborate "Dov's Nightmare" had the character reliving the horrors of the Holocaust when he was imprisoned in a concentration camp (at one point, either in rehearsals or during part of the tryout, the dance was also titled "Ballet of the Warsaw Ghetto"), and it was but one of a number of the era's bizarre ballet sequences, including "The Cookie Chase" (*Anyone Can Whistle*, 1964); "King Lear Ballet" (*Café Crown*, 1964); "Bear Hunt" (*The Yearling*, 1965); "Interrogation Ballet" (*Mata Hari*, 1967); and the untitled but usually referenced "Lettuce Harvest Ballet" (*Here's Where I Belong*, 1968).

Ari's cast album was scheduled to be recorded by Steady Records, but was canceled due to the musical's brief run. The musical's demo recording includes eight untitled songs, and the lead male singer is likewise unidentified (but is certainly David Cryer). Five songs from the Broadway production are included: "Yerushaliam," "The Exodus," "My Brother's Keeper," "The Alphabet Song"/"Learning Hebrew," and "Ari's Soliloquy"/"Ari's Promise"; and the unused or cut "Come and Spend Your Life with Me," "A Time to Love," and "I'm Alone."

In his review, Watt referred to *The Desert Song* (by indicating that the score for *Ari* would have been "tired" and "dated" during the era of that 1920s operetta), and two years later David Cryer actually played the male lead in the short-lived revival of that venerable operetta by Sigmund Romberg. Cryer was a good-looking singer of the stalwart variety, and in the 1940s and 1950s would have probably enjoyed a busy and successful career. Despite his strong presence in three major Broadway musical appearances, the shows themselves were all failures (besides the short-running *Ari* and the revival of ***The Desert Song***, he was also in *Come Summer*). As a result, he never again created a leading role in a Broadway musical.

NO, NO, NANETTE

"THE NEW 1925 MUSICAL"

Theatre: 46th Street Theatre
Opening Date: January 19, 1971; *Closing Date*: February 4, 1973

Performances: 861
Book: Otto Harbach and Frank Mandel; book adapted by Burt Shevelove
Lyrics: Irving Caesar and Otto Harbach
Music: Vincent Youmans; incidental music by Luther Henderson
Based on the 1919 play *My Lady Friends* by Emil Nyitray and Frank Mandel (which in turn had been adapted from the novel *Oh James!* by May Edgington).
Direction: Burt Shevelove (production supervised by Busby Berkeley); *Producers*: Pyxidium Ltd.; *Choreography*: Donald Saddler; *Scenery* and *Costumes*: Raoul Pene du Bois; *Lighting*: Jules Fisher; *Musical Direction*: Buster Davis
Cast: *Patsy Kelly* (Pauline), *Helen Gallagher* (Lucille Early), *Ruby Keeler* (Sue Smith), *Jack Gilford* (Jimmy Smith), *Bobby Van* (Billy Early), Roger Rathburn (Tom Trainor), *Susan Watson* (Nanette), K. C. Townsend (Flora Latham aka Flora from Frisco), Loni Zoe Ackerman (Betty Brown aka Betty from Boston), Pat Lysinger (Winnie Winslow aka Winnie from Washington); Nanette's Friends: Bob Becker, John Beecher, Joretta Bohannon, Roger Braun, Marcia Brushingham, Kenneth Carr, Jennie Chandler, Kathy Conry, Christine Cox, Kevin Daly, Ed Dixon, Ellen Elias, Mercedes Ellington, Jon Engstrom, Marian Haraldson, Gregg Harlan, Jamie Haskins, Gwen Hillier, Sayra Hummel, Scott Hunter, Dottie Lester, Cheryl Locke, Joanne Lotsko, Mary Ann Niles, Kate O'Brady, Sue Ohman, Jill Owens, Ken Ploss, John Roach, Linda Rose, Ron Schwinn, Sonja Stuart, Monica Tiller, Pat Trott, Phyllis Wallach
The musical was presented in three acts.
The action takes place during a weekend in early Summer 1925 in New York City and Atlantic City.

Musical Numbers

Act One: "Too Many Rings around Rosie" (lyric by Irving Caesar) (Helen Gallagher, Boys, Girls); "I've Confessed to the Breeze" (lyric by Otto Harbach) (Susan Watson, Roger Rathburn); "The Call of the Sea" (lyric by Irving Caesar) (Bobby Van, Girls); "I Want to Be Happy" (lyric by Irving Caesar) (Jack Gilford, Susan Watson, Ruby Keeler, Boys, Girls); "No, No, Nanette" (lyric by Otto Harbach) (Susan Watson, Roger Rathburn); Finaletto Act One (Susan Watson, Boys, Girls)
Act Two: "Peach on the Beach" (aka "The Deep Blue Sea") (lyric by Otto Harbach) (Susan Watson, Boys, Girls); "Tea for Two" (lyric by Irving Caesar) (Susan Watson, Roger Rathburn, Boys, Girls); "You Can Dance with Any Girl at All" (lyric by Irving Caesar) (Helen Gallagher, Bobby Van); Finaletto Act Two (Entire Company)
Act Three: "Telephone Girlie" (lyric by Otto Harbach) (Bobby Van, Loni Zoe Ackerman, K. C. Townsend, Pat Lysinger); "'Where-Has-My-Hubby-Gone' Blues" (aka "Who's the Who") (lyric by Irving Caesar) (Helen Gallagher, Boys); "Waiting for You" (lyric by Otto Harbach) (Susan Watson, Roger Rathburn); "Take a Little One-Step" (lyric by Zelda Sears) (Ruby Keeler, Bobby Van, Helen Gallagher, Patsy Kelly, Boys, Girls); Finale (Entire Company)

The delightful revival of Vincent Youmans's 1925 musical *No, No, Nanette* was perhaps the season's biggest surprise. Here was an old-fashioned birthday cake of a musical with nothing on its mind but the most lighthearted of stories, an array of fetching songs, a clutch of knockout dance routines, a lavish production of eye-popping and colorful décor and costumes, and, there in the midst of the festivities, was iconic 1930s movie star Ruby Keeler herself, as Sue Smith, a society matron not above joining her ward Nanette's friends for a little toe-tapping. There were few moments in 1970s musicals as spine-tingling as "I Want to Be Happy": after two of the principals finished the number, the chorus boys stepped in and softly crooned the song to the accompaniment of plunking ukuleles, and then Keeler suddenly appeared at the top of a staircase, drawn by the music. And as soon as she and the dancing chorus went into their show-stopping shuffle, all hell broke loose in the 46th Street Theatre. You never dreamed that one day you'd see this legendary performer in a Broadway show, she the awkward chorus-girl kid in *42nd Street* who went on in the star's place and came back a star; and yet there she was, going into her dance with all the ease and aplomb of a seasoned trouper and as if she'd never been away from Broadway for forty-two years.

If all these goodies weren't enough, the cast also included old-timer Patsy Kelly (as Sue's maid Pauline) with her gags and her welcome over-the-top grimaces and shticks, not to mention her battle of wills with an independent-minded vacuum cleaner; endearing comedian Jack Gilford (as Jimmy, Sue's eternally befuddled husband); Broadway song-and-dance veteran Helen Gallagher (Sue's best friend Lucille Early); and MGM musical dancer Bobby Van (Lucille's husband and Jimmy's lawyer Billy). Susan Watson played the title role, and since a pretty 1920s ingenue can't live without a handsome boyfriend, Roger Rathburn (Tom) filled the requirement quite nicely.

The action took place in 1925 at the Smiths' Manhattan townhouse and at the playground of old Atlantic City. There were the usual complications, especially when it turns out that millionaire Bible publisher Jimmy has innocently been providing generous allowances to three gold diggers, Flora from Frisco (K. C. Townsend), Betty from Boston (Loni Zoe Ackerman), and Winnie from Washington (Pat Lysinger). And, lo and behold, all three vamps turn up in Atlantic City where they're on the prowl for more simoleons from their sugar-daddy. When Sue mistakenly assumes that it's Billy and not Jimmy who is romantically involved with the threesome she of course has no other recourse but to tell best friend Lucille about Billy's apparent shenanigans. But the mix-ups and misunderstandings are happily resolved by the final curtain.

Besides "I Want to Be Happy," Keeler and the chorus kids whooped it up with an eleven o'clock dance number "Take a Little One-Step"; Watson and Rathburn sang the praises of "Tea for Two," which then morphed into a breezy soft-shoe production number; the lavish, carnival-like "Peach on the Beach" was replete with Japanese lanterns and Easter-egg-colored beach balls; Gallagher and Van stopped the show with "You Can Dance with Any Girl at All," one of the era's finest dance sequences, which was an exhilarating and breathtaking seven-minute compendium of almost every dance style of the era, including the maxixe, the turkey trot, the tango, and the Castle Walk; and Gallagher, drenched in blue lighting and swathed in a midnight-blue gown, belted out the smoky torch song "'Where-Has-My-Hubby-Gone' Blues" as a quartet of would-be swains in swank dinner clothes made it clear they'd willingly substitute for hubby. The score was musical comedy nirvana, and it was sung and danced to perfection.

One or two critics felt the musical didn't quite make up its mind if it should be played straight, as camp, or as outright satire; and there was a bit of grumbling that the evening's pace could have been swifter, a strange complaint considering that the show moved with lightning speed. Douglas Watt in the *New York Daily News* said the revival worked "beautifully" with a "fine sense of style." Richard Watts in the *New York Post* found the evening "excellent, richly tuneful fun" and a "happy addition to the season." Jack Kroll in *Newsweek* said that to see and hear such "great" songs as "Tea for Two" and "I Want to Be Happy" was "to feel a flush of something near to lunacy, a crazy patriotism for the dream-country of one's own blessed fantasies." And T. E. Kalem in *Time* found the musical a "copious delight" and noted that Keeler was "warmly appealing," Kelly a "comic howitzer of maid with hilarious delayed-fuse timing," and Gallagher a "smolderingly authentic Fitzgerald heroine" come to life.

John J. O'Connor in the *Wall Street Journal* praised the "sparkling" revival; John Schubeck on WABCTV7 found the cast "sensational" with the kind of style he hadn't seen on Broadway for years; Leonard Harris on WCBSTV2 felt some of the "cuteness" was "too too," but the revival was nonetheless "yes, yes"; and Leonard Probst on WNBC4TV praised the "superb" revival and said "there hasn't been a night like this on Broadway in years."

Martin Gottfried in *Women's Wear Daily* felt that director and adaptor Burt Shevelove had settled for a "rather charming" and "vacantly agreeable" approach when he could have created a "marvelously funny" evening that should have played straight with the material and allowed it to "mock itself" and thus create a "double reality." But the show offered "genuinely thrilling" dances that were "absolutely fantastic," and the production was "very easy to look at."

When the production closed, it was the longest-running revival in Broadway history and ushered in what was then known as the nostalgia craze. During the following seasons, there were a number of revivals of such old-time favorites as ***On the Town***, ***Irene***, ***Good News***, ***The Desert Song***, ***Very Good Eddie***, ***Going Up!***, and ***Oh, Kay!*** as well as tributes to the Broadway of yesteryear (***Rodgers and Hart***, ***Music! Music!***, ***Ain't Misbehavin'***, and ***Eubie!***).

To be sure, the tryout was not a smooth one, and its trials are well documented in Don Dunn's *The Making of 'No, No, Nanette'*, which was published by The Citadel Press in 1972. But when the show opened on Broadway it was as smooth and sweet as icing on a cake, a dream of a musical that offered nonstop enchantment.

During the tryout, Tom Tiller and then Hiram Sherman played the role of Jimmy, which was eventually assumed by Jack Gilford; and in the title role Carol Demas was succeeded by Susan Watson (in 1976, Demas was replaced by Patti LuPone in ***The Baker's Wife***, but in 1972 she created the role of Sandy Dumbrowski in ***Grease***). Although the musical was technically helmed by Busby Berkeley, it was Shevelove and Donald Saddler who were the architects of the evening, and Berkeley received "production supervised" credit. The song "Always You" (for Sue and Jimmy) was dropped, as was "Only a Moment Ago," which briefly replaced it.

The original production of *No, No, Nanette* premiered in Detroit on April 20, 1924, and its engagement in Chicago played for almost a full year. In the meantime, another version toured the country and a London production opened at the Palace Theatre on March 11, 1925, where it chalked up 665 performances. And, oh, yes, the producers finally got around to opening the musical on Broadway: it premiered on September 16, 1925, at the Globe (now Lunt-Fontanne) Theatre for 321 showings. A 1930 film version by First National included just two numbers from the Broadway production ("Tea for Two" and "I Want to Be Happy"), and an RKO adaptation was released in 1940 with Anna Neagle as Nanette (for the 1973 London revival, Neagle played Sue). In 1950, Warner Brothers' *Tea for Two* borrowed the musical's title and three songs ("Tea for Two," "I Want to Be Happy," and "The Call of the Sea") and wove them into a completely new story line.

Except for "My Doctor," "Fight Over Me," and "Pay Day Pauline," the current revival retained the entire score, which was supplemented by "I've Confessed to the Breeze" (lyric by Otto Harbach), which had been cut during the tryout of the original production, and "Take a Little One-Step" (first heard in 1924's *Lollipop* with a lyric by Zelda Sears, the song was later interpolated into *Nanette*'s 1925 London production). "Only a Moment Ago," which was dropped during the revival's tryout, utilized music from an unpublished song by Youmans and had a new lyric by Shevelove, and "Always You" (lyric and music by Charles Gaynor) was also cut. The title song was a new version of "My Boy and I" (lyric by Oscar Hammerstein II and William Cary Duncan) from *Mary Jane McKane* (1923) and "Waiting for You" was a revised version of "You Started Something" (lyric by Arthur Francis aka Ira Gershwin) from *Two Little Girls in Blue* (1921).

The revival's cast album was released by Columbia Records (LP # S-30563), which also issued the private promotional recording *Backstage at 'No, No, Nanette'* (LP # AS-2-1023) in which radio and television interviewer Lee Jordan talked with cast members (the recording also included songs from the original cast album). The CD of the cast album was released by Sony Classical/Columbia/Legacy (# SK-60890) and includes the deleted "Only a Moment Ago" (with Keeler and Gilford), some of the interviews on the Lee Jordan promotional recording, and the previously recorded but unreleased second act opening and "Peach on the Beach."

The musical was first revived in London at the Hippodrome in 1936, where it had 115 showings, and the second revival opened at the Drury Lane on May 15, 1973, for 277 performances with Anna Neagle (Sue), Anne Rogers (Lucille), Thora Hird (Pauline), and Tony Britton (Jimmy). Eight songs from the 1936 revival were recorded and later released on a pairing with Jerome Kern's *Sunny* by Stanyan Records (LP # 10035), and the cast album of the 1973 revival was issued by CBS Records (LP # 70126).

In the early 1960s, *Reader's Digest* in conjunction with RCA Custom Records released a boxed set of operettas that offered selections from *No, No, Nanette* (LP # RDM-40-10) conducted by Lehman Engel (the recording included "Take a Little One-Step"); in 1969, EMI/Odeon (LP # TWO-278) released a studio cast recording of the score with Vivienne Martin, Ann Beach, and Tony Adams (the album included "Take a Little One-Step," "I've Confessed to the Breeze," and "Fight Over Me"); and in conjunction with the 1971 Broadway revival RCA Victor Records (LP # LSP-4504) released *Music from the Broadway Musical 'No, No, Nanette'* by The RCA Broadway Strings and Velvet Voices.

On April 2, 1986, the musical was presented in concert at Carnegie Hall for five performances. John McGlinn conducted, and among the cast members were Leigh Berry (Sue), Jane Connell (Pauline), Rebecca Luker (Nanette), Cris Groenendaal (Billy), Judy Kaye (Lucille), Robert Nichols (Jimmy), and George Dvorsky (Tom). The concert included "My Doctor," "Fight Over Me," and "Pay Day Pauline."

The musical was next seen in New York on May 12, 1988, when it was revived by the Equity Library Theatre for thirty-two performances; the production included "Love Me, Lulu" (the program credited Irving Caesar with lyric and music, and noted the song was copyrighted in 1988). The most recent revival was presented at City Center by Encores! on May 8, 2008, for six performances; the cast included Sandy Duncan (Sue) and Charles Kimbrough (Jimmy).

Awards

Tony Awards and Nominations: Best Leading Actor in a Musical (Bobby Van); Best Leading Actress in a Musical (**Helen Gallagher**); Best Featured Actress in a Musical (**Patsy Kelly**); Best Direction (Burt Shevelove); Best Costume Designer (**Raoul Pene du Bois**); Best Choreography (**Donald Saddler**)

OH! CALCUTTA!

"A MUSICAL ENTERTAINMENT"

Theatre: Belasco Theatre
Opening Date: February 26, 1971; *Closing Date*: August 12, 1972
Performances: 610
Sketch Writers and *Contributors*: Samuel Beckett, Jules Feiffer, Dan Greenburg, John Lennon, Jacques Levy, Leonard Melfi, David Newman and Robert Benton, Sam Shepard, Clovis Trouille, Kenneth Tynan, and Sherman Yellen
Lyrics and *Music*: The Open Window (Robert Dennis, Peter Schickele, and Stanley Walden)
Direction: Jacques Levy; *Producer*: Hillard Elkins (An E.P.I.C. Production); *Choreography*: Margo Sappington; *Scenery*: James Tilton; *Projections*: Gardner Compton and Emile Ardolino; *Photographs*: Michael Childers; *Costumes*: Fred Voelpel; *Lighting*: David F. Segal; *Musical Direction*: Norman Bergen
Cast: Mel Auston, Raina Barrett, Ray Edelstein, Samantha Harper, Patricia Hawkins, William Knight, Mitchell McGuire, Pamela Pilkenton, Gary Rethmeier, Nancy Tribush
The revue was presented in two acts.

Sketches and Musical Numbers

Act One: Prologue; "Taking Off the Robe"/"Oh! Calcutta!" (Company); "Dick & Jane" (Raina Barrett, Gary Rethmeier); "Suite for Five Letters" (Mel Auston, Samantha Harper, Patricia Hawkins, William Knight, Pamela Pilkenton); "Will Answer All Sincere Replies" (Nancy Tribush, Samantha Howard, Gary Rethmeier, and unknown male performer); "Paintings of Clovis Trouille" (The Open Window); "Jack & Jill" (Patricia Hawkins and unknown male performer); "Delicious Indignities" (Samantha Harper, William Knight); "Was It Good for You, Too?"/"Green Pants"/"I Like the Look" (Raina Barrett, Nancy Tribush, William Knight, Pamela Pilkenton, Gary Rethmeier, and possibly Mitchell McGuire)
Act Two: "Much Too Soon" (Company, The Open Window); "One on One" (Mel Auston, Pamela Pilkenton); "Rock Garden" (William Knight and unknown male performer); "Four in Hand" (Mel Auston, Gary Rethmeier, and two other male performers); "Coming Together, Going Together" (Company)

The sex revue *Oh! Calcutta!* was "devised" by critic Kenneth Tynan, who had once memorably described *Flower Drum Song* as "the world of woozy song." The revue originally opened Off Broadway at the Eden Theatre on June 17, 1969, where it played for 704 performances; the current Broadway transfer played for 610 showings. Four years after it closed, the show was revived at the Edison Theatre on September 24, 1976, for 5,959 performances (according to *Best Plays*, the Edison run was sometimes under a Middle or Limited Broadway contract, and occasionally the production gave ten performances weekly instead of the regular eight performances mandated by the standard Broadway contract). (For more information about the 1976 revival, see entry.)

The revue gained instant notoriety because the cast performed in the nude and because the evening's theme was sex in solo, duo, and multiple varieties. So the total number of 7,273 New York performances isn't all that surprising. But what *is* surprising is that many who should have known better took the revue seriously. It was often pretentious, almost always puerile, and it lacked wit and sexiness. Surely the era's pornographic movies were more honest in their depictions of sex, and were probably more entertaining. The sketches and score of *Oh! Calcutta!* were unmemorable, and only the melody of the title song stayed in the memory because it seemed to define the sound of instrumental elevator music.

The revue didn't credit the specific sketches, and so instead the writers were lumped together on the program's title page (perhaps the creators were too shamefaced to own up to their material). During Off-Broadway previews, some of the contributors credited in the program were Maria Irene Fornes, Bruce Jay Friedman, David Mercer, Edna O'Brien, and Tennessee Williams; their specific sketches might have been dropped before opening night, or perhaps they later requested no official program credit. Among the sequences deleted during Off-Broadway previews were "I'll Shoot Your Dog If You Don't" and "Anybody Out There Want It?"

In reviewing the Off-Broadway production, James Davis in the *New York Daily News* said the "stag show" proved that "simulated sex acts can be pretty dull without wit," and Richard P. Cooke in the *Wall*

Street Journal noted that after the cast abandoned their clothing the show was little more than the "matter-of-fact realm of the nudist camp"; he also mentioned that the evening was a "letdown" with "singularly flat" sketches. Jerry Tallmer in the *New York Post* said he'd seen better skits in the old days of burlesque, and Clive Barnes in the *New York Times* said *Oh! Calcutta!* "is the kind of show to give pornography a dirty name." Barnes said that "disappointment" was the operative word to describe the revue with its "prissy and silly" jokes and its "doggedly sophomoric and soporific" humor.

Marya Manne on WCBSTV2 suggested that those in search of an "erotic evening" should seek out "old-fashioned burlesque"; the revue lacked "wit and lusty joy" and soon degenerated into "plain crudity"; and John Bartholomew Tucker on WABCTV7 said the evening was "about as sophisticated as the dull daydreams of Sinclair Lewis' Babbitt."

The Off-Broadway cast album was released by Aidart Records (LP # AID-9903), and other recordings include the Australian cast (RCA Camden Records LP # INTS-1178) and the collection *'Oh! Calcutta!' and the Best of 'Salvation'* (Polydor Records LP # 2371-103). The script was published in hardback by Grove Press, Inc., in 1969. A closed-circuit film version was released in 1972 by Tigon Films and was directed by Jacques Levy (and was later issued on DVD). A successful London production opened during the 1970–1971 season.

FOLLIES

"A New Musical"

Theatre: Winter Garden Theatre
Opening Date: April 4, 1971; *Closing Date*: July 1, 1972
Performances: 522
Book: James Goldman
Lyrics and *Music*: Stephen Sondheim
Direction: Harold Prince and Michael Bennett; *Producers*: Harold Prince in association with Ruth Mitchell; *Scenery*: Boris Aronson; *Costumes*: Florence Klotz; *Lighting*: Tharon Musser; *Musical Direction*: Harold Hastings
Cast: Dick Latessa (Major-Domo), *Dorothy Collins* (Sally Durant Plummer), Marti Rolph (Young Sally), Ethel Barrymore Colt (Christine Crane), Fred Kelly (Willy Wheeler), Mary McCarty (Stella Deems), John J. Martin (Max Deems), Justine Johnston (Heidi Schiller), John Grigas (Chauffer), Sheila Smith (Meredith Lane), Peter Walker (Chet Richards), Michael Bartlett (Roscoe), Helon Blount (Deedee West), Sonja Levkova (Sandra Donovan), Ethel Shutta (Hattie Walker), Mary Jane Houdina (Young Hattie), Marcie Stringer (Emily Whitman), Charles Welch (Theodore Whitman), Victor Griffin (Vincent), Jayne Turner (Vanessa), Michael Misita (Young Vincent), Graciela Daniele (Young Vanessa), Fifi D'Orsay (Solange LaFitte), Yvonne De Carlo (Carlotta Campion), *Alexis Smith* (Phyllis Rogers Stone), *John McMartin* (Benjamin Stone), Virginia Sandifur (Young Phyllis), Kurt Peterson (Young Ben), *Gene Nelson* (Buddy Plummer), Harvey Evans (Young Buddy), Arnold Moss (Dimitri Weismann), Ralph Nelson (Kevin), Victoria Mallory (Young Heidi); Party Musicians: Taft Jordan, Aaron Bell, Charles Spies, Robert Curtis; Showgirls: Suzanne Briggs, Trudy Carson, Kathie Dalton, Ursula Maschmeyer, Linda Perkins, Margot Travers; Singers and Dancers: Graciela Daniele, Mary Jane Houdina, Rita O'Connor, Julie Pars, Suzanne Rogers, Roy Barry, Steve Boockvor, Michael Misita, Joseph Nelson, Ralph Nelson, Ken Urmston, Donald Weissmuller

The musical was presented in one act.

The action takes place tonight on the stage of the Weismann Theatre.

Musical Numbers

"Beautiful Girls" (Michael Bartlett, Company); "Don't Look at Me" (Dorothy Collins, John McMartin); "Waiting for the Girls Upstairs" (Gene Nelson, John McMartin, Alexis Smith, Dorothy Collins, Harvey Evans, Kurt Peterson, Virginia Sandifur, Marti Rolph); "Rain on the Roof" (Marcie Stringer, Charles Welch); "Ah, Paris!" (Fifi D'Orsay); "Broadway Baby" (Ethel Shutta); "The Road You Didn't Take" (John McMartin); "Bolero d'amour" (dance) (Victor Griffin, Jayne Turner); "In Buddy's Eyes" (Dorothy Collins); "Who's That Woman?" (Mary McCarty, Company); "I'm Still Here" (Yvonne De Carlo); "Too Many

Mornings" (John McMartin, Dorothy Collins); "The Right Girl" (Gene Nelson); "One More Kiss" (Justine Johnston, Victoria Mallory); "Could I Leave You?" (Alexis Smith); *Loveland—The Folly of Love*: "Loveland" (Ensemble; The Spirit of First Love: Kathie Dalton; The Spirit of Young Love: Margot Travers; The Spirit of True Love: Suzanne Briggs; The Spirit of Pure Love: Trudy Carson; The Spirit of Romantic Love: Linda Perkins; The Spirit of Eternal Love: Ursula Maschmeyer); *The Folly of Youth*: "You're Gonna Love Tomorrow" (Kurt Peterson, Virginia Sandifur); "Love Will See Us Through" (Harvey Evans, Marti Rolph); *Buddy's Folly*: "The God-Why-Don't-You-Love-Me Blues" (aka "Buddy's Blues") (Gene Nelson, with Suzanne Rogers and Rita O'Connor); *Sally's Folly*: "Losing My Mind" (Dorothy Collins); *Phyllis's Folly*: "The Story of Lucy and Jessie" (Alexis Smith, Dancing Ensemble); *Ben's Folly*: "Live, Laugh, Love" (John McMartin, Dancing Ensemble)

There were always the ghosts.

It's the end for the fabled Weismann Theatre, where producer Dimitri Weismann (Arnold Moss) once presented his annual series of *Follies* revues. Later, the once lavish theatre hosted ballet companies, repertory theatre, and film, and then deteriorated into porn movies. Now it's to be demolished to make way for a brand new parking lot, and so tonight's the last time the ghosts of its former show girls will haunt their old theatre. They are impossibly tall and regal, impossibly beautiful, and all are wearing fabulous costumes from musicals of times past. They slowly promenade about the semi-darkened stage in a kind of reverie, perhaps in a state of shock with the realization that youth and beauty and fame and even their lives are long over. And now the very theatre that housed their former glory will soon vanish. Over the decades they've heard spectral applause from long-ago audiences and heard distant music from half-forgotten shows, but after tonight all of it will be gone forever.

And so for the theatre's last night, Weismann is holding the first and last reunion party for the performers who once appeared in his revues. The guests soon arrive, but they can't see the ghosts, some of them shades of their youth which watch them in bewildered fascination. Among the invited are former chorus girls Phyllis (Alexis Smith) and Sally (Dorothy Collins) and the stage door Johnnies they eventually married, Ben (John McMartin) and Buddy (Gene Nelson). Phyllis and Ben are now the consummate Upper East Side New Yorkers, she sleek and sophisticated, and he rich and powerful, formerly an appointee with the United Nations and now the head of a foundation. Sally and Buddy's lives took different roads, and they settled in a middle-class suburb in Phoenix where he's a traveling salesman and she seems to be constantly suffering from depression. Both couples are unhappily married, and during the intervening years have been caught in an unending web of regrets, recriminations, and what-might-have-beens. The ghosts of their youth watch them and see the festering resentments that will soon erupt into a surreal *Follies*, a musical time warp where past and present will collide.

Up to now, the party has meandered along in the crumbling, dimly lit theatre, and the partygoers have performed some of their old *Follies* routines. But when Phyllis, Ben, Sally, Buddy, and their ghosts Young Phyllis (Virginia Sandifur), Young Ben (Kurt Peterson), Young Sally (Marti Rolph), and Young Buddy (Harvey Evans) engage in an across-the-decades confrontation with the past and the wrong choices they made, the argument explodes and Buddy, Sally, Phyllis, and Ben are each thrust into starring roles in their personal *Follies*. Each one is given a double-edged *Follies*-like song, each number a musical breakdown that simultaneously mirrors old-time Broadway and the follies of their lives.

And with the explosion into the dream world of the *Follies* came the greatest scenic effect in the history of musical theatre: within split seconds, the dark and gloomy Weismann stage was magically transformed into the arcadia of fairy-tale Loveland. From the flies and wings came acres of lacy pink Valentine drops, and a chorus of Fragonard-like cavaliers, swains, and Dresden-doll ladies extolling the eternally happy world of Loveland where "everybody lives to love." And then the main characters go into their follies, and each sequence flows from one to the other as Buddy, Sally, Phyllis, and Ben are seen in various locales of Loveland.

On a thoroughfare in Loveland, traveling salesman Buddy sings "The God-Why-Don't-You-Love-Me Blues" in which he's torn between Sally and his girlfriend Margie; in a boudoir in Loveland, Sally appears in a glamorous silver-beaded gown and sings the torch song "Losing My Mind"; in a honky-tonk in Loveland Phyllis describes her dual personality in "The Story of Lucy and Jessie"; and in a supper club in Loveland Ben in Fred Astaire mode celebrates the debonair philosophy of "Live, Laugh, Love." But love and laughter are alien to Ben, and he forgets the words to the song. The conductor shouts the lyrics to him, but he's collapsing inside and ruins the number. The irked members of the chorus line glare at him but nonetheless continue on as if he didn't exist.

And then there is another surreal explosion, and this time the entire evening's action is compressed into two or three minutes of nightmarish activity (the script describes it as a "terrible cacophony" in which "the night's experience is being vomited").

And just as suddenly the party is over. The sun breaks through a wall that has been demolished by the wrecker's ball, and Phyllis, Ben, Sally, and Buddy are left with the detritus of their lives. There's probably not much hope for any of them, and their empty and unhappy present is no doubt prologue to an equally bleak and meaningless future.

And then as always there are the ghosts, left alone in the rubble of the theatre with nowhere to go.

The nonlinear story line of *Follies* emphasized mood instead of plot, and never before or since has a musical so brilliantly presented such a fluid depiction of time and space with the intermingling of past and present into a single dimension. James Goldman's masterful book was spare and incisive in its look at the loss of youth, ideals, and innocence. His Proustian remembrance of things from an unrecoverable past did its work with brittle wit and achingly sad insight. His book is one of the most compact in all musical theatre, and it proved to be the perfect framework to tell the story and create moody portraits of some of the most complex and complicated characters ever seen on the musical stage.

Moreover, Goldman and director Harold Prince created short film-like sequences that zoomed in and then quickly faded as they briefly but succinctly viewed the party guests. The script's stage directions note that at times the stage seems "huge and empty," and at others "closed in and intimate." Further, the "material is free to be now here, now there or, on occasion, different places all at once." Even some of the songs flashed forward out of nowhere and then quickly disappeared, such as the sequence that included "Rain on the Roof," "Ah, Paris!," and "Broadway Baby." The intermission-less evening never broke its stride and the action flowed continuously as it steadily built to the climactic Loveland sequence.

Sondheim's score may well be the finest in all musical theatre. He actually wrote two scores. The first consisted of brilliant pastiche numbers performed at the party or in Loveland which conjured up Irving Berlin, Jerome Kern, George Gershwin, Cole Porter, Harold Arlen, Kurt Weill, and the team of Buddy De Sylva, Lew Brown, and Ray Henderson, and he even created a sequence ("You're Gonna Love Tomorrow" and "Love Will See Us Through") that managed to suggest Richard Rodgers with both Oscar Hammerstein II and Lorenz Hart. In some cases, Sondheim surpassed the past masters of the musical: Kern, Gershwin, and Arlen wrote memorable torch songs, but there's probably never been a better one than "Losing My Mind." Another brilliant pastiche was "Who's That Woman?" (referred to as the "mirror number"), a song from the *Follies* that the girls perform at the party (one of them remarks that the number even "winded" her when she was nineteen). But the girls are game and give it their all; and as they sing and dance, their youthful ghosts appear in scanty outfits sewn together with thousands of pieces of mirrors, and as the two generations danced the past and the present dazzlingly came together.

The second score was "pure" Sondheim, and all the book songs found him at the peak of his powers: Ben's introspective and self-loathing "The Road You Didn't Take"; Phyllis's blistering attack "Could I Leave You?"; Buddy's bewilderment over who might be "The Right Girl"; and Sally's self-effacing "Don't Look at Me" and her self-deceptive "In Buddy's Eyes." And there was the ultimate show-business I've-seen-it-all anthem "I'm Still Here," sung by Carlotta (Yvonne DeCarlo), perhaps the only character in the musical who accepts the vagaries of existence and knows that life owes you absolutely nothing.

Here then was the greatest of all musicals. Some critics were confused by it (and the clueless headline of Frank Getlein's review in the Washington *Evening Star* stated, "Middle Age Can Be Fun: *Follies* Is Fine and Frisky") and others entirely missed the point (Clive Barnes in the *New York Times*, in a reference to ***No, No, Nanette*** and maybe the upcoming ***70, Girls, 70***, said that "perhaps too many little old ladies are passing by just lately," and suggested *Follies* was a musical whose cast album should be released on the old 78 RPM format). But many knew they were seeing the production of a lifetime, and the cognoscenti returned to see it over and over again. Perhaps Martin Gottfried (here writing in the *New York Times*) said it best: "*Follies* is monumental theatre. Not because I say so but because it is there for anybody to see."

Despite many rave reviews and numerous awards, the musical lost money on Broadway. Upon its closing after 522 performances, *Variety* reported its deficit at $640,000 on a $700,000 capitalization. After New York, the musical played in St. Louis and Los Angeles (where ironically it was the inaugural production of the Shubert Theatre), and when it permanently closed there *Variety* reported it had actually cost $792,596 to open in New York, and that after the Broadway production and the two subsequent road engagements the musical's losses amounted to over $700,000.

During its long-gestating preproduction phase, the musical was titled *The Girls Upstairs* and its straightforward plot focused on a reunion of two show girls and their husbands, all of them with a reason to murder one of the others. In a *Newsweek* preview of the upcoming 1969–1970 season, the magazine referred to *The Girls Upstairs* both as a comedy and a musical about "a reunion of former Ziegfeld girls in a condemned theatre" and noted the show was scheduled to open in mid-February 1970 at an as yet unspecified theatre. When Harold Prince became associated with the production, the musical took a different course. In an interview with Mel Gussow in the *New York Times*, he said that instead of a "naturalistic" story he wanted a more "abstract" one with a "gauzy feeling," and Sondheim described the new version as "a dream play, a memory piece." During the tryout, Edwin Steffe was succeeded by Arnold Moss, and "Can That Boy Foxtrot!" and "Uptown, Downtown" were replaced by "I'm Still Here" and "The Story of Lucy and Jessie." During the tryout and New York previews, the musical was sometimes presented in two acts, with the break coming after "Too Many Mornings."

The script was published in hardback by Random House in 1971, and the abridged cast album was issued by Capitol Records (LP # S0-761). The CD has been released three times, by Capitol Records (# CDP-7-92094-2), Broadway Angel (# ZDM-7-64666-2-0), and Kritzerland (# KR-20023-3); all three CDs include "One More Kiss," which had been recorded during the cast album session but had been eliminated from the LP release due to lack of space. If any cast album deserved a two-LP set, it was *Follies*. Besides "One More Kiss," "Rain on the Roof," "Loveland," and "Bolero d'amour" were omitted, and many numbers were condensed. Later recordings were more complete, but the performances on the original cast recording remain definitive and the only other one that comes close to capturing the essence of the original is the 1998 Paper Mill Playhouse production (see below).

The musical has been revived four times in New York, two fully staged productions and two concert versions. A limited-engagement concert version of two performances was presented at Avery Fisher Hall at Lincoln Center on September 6 and September 7, 1985, by the New York Philharmonic and an array of guest performers. It was recorded live on a two-LP (# HBC2-7128) and two-CD set (# RCD2-7128) by RCA Victor Records, and was presented on public television in 1986. A DVD of the concert is included in *The Stephen Sondheim* collection, a boxed set issued by Image Entertainment (# ID-17531MDVD).

Next was a mostly disappointing revival that opened at the Belasco Theatre on April 5, 2001, for 116 showings (Polly Bergen as Carlotta and Betty Garrett as Hattie were the production's standouts) and went unrecorded. The slightly revised script was published in paperback by the Theatre Communications Group in 2001, and a later edition was released in 2011.

A second concert version was presented by Encores! at City Center on February 8, 2007, for six performances, and the most recent fully staged revival opened at the Marquis Theatre on September 12, 2011, for 152 performances; the cast album was released by PS Classics (CD # PS-1105).

Virtually all productions since the original have been slightly revised, and a few memorable lines in Goldman's original book have been deleted and a more hopeful ending has been added. The London version premiered at the Shaftesbury Theatre on July 21, 1987, for 644 performances. "The Road You Didn't Take," "Bolero d'amour," "Love Will See Us Through," "Loveland," "The Story of Lucy and Jessie," and "Live, Laugh, Love" were dropped; and added to the revival were "Country House," "Social Dancing," a completely new version of "Loveland," "Ah, but Underneath," and "Make the Most of Your Music," the latter two substituting for "The Story of Lucy and Jessie" and "Live, Laugh, Love." The cast recording was released on 2-LP (# 3) and 2-CD (# CD-3) sets by First Night Records.

The production by the Paper Mill Playhouse, Millburn, New Jersey, opened on April 15, 1998, and as noted above its two-CD recording TVT soundtrax (# TVT-1030-2) remains the second-most-satisfying recording of the score. Although it substituted "Ah, but Underneath" for "The Story of Lucy and Jessie," it happily included the latter along with eight songs written for but not used in the Broadway production: "Bring on the Girls," "Can That Boy Foxtrot!," "Pleasant Little Kingdom," "All Things Bright and Beautiful," "That Old Piano Roll," "Who Could Be Blue?," "Little White House," and "Uptown, Downtown." Other unused songs written for the original production were "The World's Full of Boys"/"The World's Full of Girls," "Cheri," and "It Wasn't Meant to Happen."

The Trotter Trio's *Follies: Themes from the Legendary Musical* is an instrumental album released by Varese Sarabande (CD # VSD-5934).

In 1974, Sondheim wrote the background music for the film *Stavisky*, and three unused songs from *Follies* were part of the score: "Bring on the Girls," "The World's Full of Boys (Girls)," and "Who Could Be Blue?"

The music of "All Things Bright and Beautiful" accompanied the promenade of ghosts in the opening minutes of the first act of the original Broadway production, and "That Old Piano Roll" was also heard as underscoring. Various Sondheim collections have included the cut and unused songs from the production.

Ted Chapin's *Everything Was Possible: The Birth of the Musical 'Follies'* is a firsthand account of the making of the original production; it was published in hardback by Alfred A. Knopf in 2003. The used, cut, unused, and updated lyrics for *Follies* are included in Sondheim's collection *Finishing the Hat: Collected Lyrics (1954–1981) with Attendant Comments, Principles, Heresies, Grudges, Whines and Anecdotes* (Alfred A. Knopf, 2010).

There was a tantalizing moment when it appeared Twentieth Century-Fox was going forward with a film version. On April 15, 1973, A. H. Weiler in the *New York Times* reported that Jean-Claude van Itallie would write the screenplay and that the locale would be changed from a soon-to-be-demolished Broadway theatre to a movie studio that is being razed. Weiler reported that old Fox movie sets as well as snippets of Fox musicals would be used in the projected film.

Awards

Tony Awards and Nominations: Best Musical (*Follies*); Best Leading Actress in a Musical (Dorothy Collins); Best Leading Actress in a Musical (**Alexis Smith**); Best Featured Actor in a Musical (Gene Nelson); Best Director of a Musical (Harold Prince); Best Book of a Musical (James Goldman); Best Score (**Stephen Sondheim**); Best Scenic Designer (**Boris Aronson**); Best Costume Designer (**Florence Klotz**); Best Lighting Designer (**Tharon Musser**); Best Choreographer (**Michael Bennett**)
New York Drama Critics' Circle Award: **Best Musical** (1970–1971)

JOHNNY JOHNSON

Theatre: Edison Theatre
Opening Date: April 11, 1971; *Closing Date*: April 11, 1971
Performances: 1
Book and *Lyrics*: Paul Green
Music: Kurt Weill
Direction: Jose Quintero; *Producers*: Timothy Gray and Robert Fletcher in association with Midge La Guardia; *Choreography*: Bertram Ross; *Scenery*: Peter Harvey; *Costumes*: Robert Fletcher; *Lighting*: Roger Morgan; *Musical Direction*: Joseph Klein
Cast: Ralph Williams (Johnny Johnson), Alice Cannon (Minny Belle Tompkins), Paul Michael (Mayor, Wounded French Soldier, Private Fairfax, American Commander, Brother Thomas), June Helmers (Miz Smith, French Nurse), Bob Lydiard (Photographer, Johann Lang), Christopher Klein (Messenger, Anguish Howington Jr.), James Billings (Grandpa Joe, Wounded French Soldier, Private Goldberger, Chief, Doctor Mahodan), Gordon Minard (Anguish Howington, Private Harwood), Charlotte Jones (Aggie, Sister of the Organization for the Delight of Soldiers Disabled in the Line of Duty, Miss Newro), Norman Chase (Captain Valentine), Wayne Sherwood (Doctor McBray, Wounded French Soldier, Private O'Day, Scottish Commander, German Priest, Secretary), Clay Johns (Private Jessell, Wounded French Soldier, Private Svenson, Orderly, British Commander, Lieutenant, Military Police, Brother George), Alexander Orfaly (Recruiting Sergeant, Wounded French Soldier, Corporal George, Belgian Major General, Captain, Doctor Frewd), Nadine Lewis (Goddess of Liberty), Norman Riggins (English Sergeant, Doctor, French Major General, American Priest, Brother William)
The musical was presented in two acts.
The action takes place during the period of World War I in an American small town, New York City, France, and in an American city.

Musical Numbers

Act One: Introduction (Orchestra); "Over in Europe" (Paul Michael); "Democracy's Call" (Alice Cannon, Paul Michael, Company); "Up Chickamauga Hill" (James Billings); "Johnny's Melody" (Ralph Williams); "Aggie's Song" (Charlotte Jones); "Oh, Heart of Love" (Alice Cannon); "Farewell, Goodbye" (Alice Cannon); "The Sergeant's Chant" (Alexander Orfaly); "Valentine's Tango" (Norman Chase); Interlude: "You're in the Army Now" (Orchestra); "Johnny's Oath" (Orchestra); "Song of the Goddess of Liberty" (Nadine Lewis); "Song of the Wounded Frenchmen" (Wayne Sherwood, Clay Johns, Alexander Orfaly, James Billings, Paul Michael); "Tea Song"(Norman Riggins, Soldiers); "Cowboy Song" (aka "Oh, the Rio Grande") (Gordon Minard); "Johnny's Dream" (Alice Cannon); "Song of the Guns" (Male Chorus); "Music of the Stricken Redeemer" (Orchestra)

Act Two: Entr'acte: "Army Song" (Orchestra); "Mon Ami, My Friend" (June Helmers); "Allied High Command" (Officers); "The Laughing Generals" (Orchestra); "The Battle" (Orchestra); "Prayer in Times of War and Tumults" (Norman Riggins, Wayne Sherwood); "No Man's Land" (Orchestra); "Song of the Goddess of Liberty" (reprise) (Nadine Lewis); "The Psychiatry Song" (James Billings); "Hymn to Peace" (Asylum Inmates); "Johnny Johnson's Song" (Ralph Williams); "How Sweetly Friendship Binds" (performer[s] unknown); "Oh, Heart of Love" (reprise) (Alice Cannon); "Johnny's Melody" (aka "When Man Was First Created") (reprise) (Ralph Williams)

Because the United States was enmeshed in the unpopular Vietnam War, the antiwar musical *Johnny Johnson* must have seemed a natural for the Broadway of the early 1970s. Paul Green and Kurt Weill's musical focused on the title character, an innocent and naive young American who finds himself drafted into World War I and soon fighting on the battlefields of France. When the young pacifist sprays laughing gas at high-ranking officers, he's committed to an insane asylum where he and other inmates fantasize they're representatives of the League of Nations. Johnny is eventually released and returns to the United States where he crafts nonaggressive toys for children. And meanwhile the world gets ready for the next war.

Johnny Johnson was Weill's first Broadway musical, and the score included a number of melodic songs, such as "Oh, Heart of Love," "Cowboy Song" (better known as "Oh, the Rio Grande"), and "Mon Ami, My Friend." Although the original production lasted just two months, Weill soon found his stride and his next three musicals were hits: *Knickerbocker Holiday* (1938), *Lady in the Dark* (1941), and *One Touch of Venus* (1943).

Richard Watts in the *New York Post* felt the original production had been "disturbingly uneven," and in reviewing the revival said the score was "as fresh and beautiful as ever" but Green's book was "heavy-handed" and "unequal" to its ambition. Douglas Watt in the *New York Daily News* found Weill's "sardonic and lyrical" contributions among his "best," but noted the book's humor was often "terribly obvious and downright mawkish." Henry Popkin in the *Wall Street Journal* also found the book "heavy-handed" and said it was so "artificial" that it risked "simple-mindedness" (but Weill's songs stood out as "brilliant but solitary jewels against a notably less sparkling background").

Like most of the reviewers, Leonard Probst on WNBC4TV praised Ralph Williams, who in the title role was "deeply sincere, believable and a fine actor"; he also enjoyed the "wonderfully bitter and romantic" music. John Schubeck on WABCTV7 praised the "quite suitable" Williams, and while he enjoyed the "delightful" songs he felt the evening was "one of the dullest" because the book was "sadly overwritten."

Martin Gottfried in *Women's Wear Daily* found Green's book a "pathetic imitation" of Bertolt Brecht's style, and said the script was "obvious, awkward and dated," and in need of revision. But he reported that Green wouldn't permit any changes to the script, and as a result the revival was doomed. Its failure was compounded by the "sheer inadequacy" of Jose Quintero's direction, and thus the production couldn't survive such "lifelessness and unimagination." But Weill's "magnificent" score was "well served" and the balance between the orchestra and the singers "was just right" and "musically" the evening was "impeccable."

The musical originally opened at the 44th Street Theatre on November 19, 1936, for a short run of sixty-eight performances (Russell Collins played the title role, and other cast members included Elia Kazan, John Garfield, and Lee J. Cobb). It was briefly revived Off Broadway during the 1940–1941 season, and then again had a short run Off Broadway when it opened at the Carnegie Hall Playhouse on October 21, 1956 (James Broderick was Johnny Johnson). Like the earlier versions, the current production was a failure and it joined ***Frank Merriwell*, or *Honor Challenged*** as one of the season's two single-performance musicals.

As discussed in the entry for ***Soon***, the 1970–1971 season inaugurated the Limited (or Middle) Broadway contract, and although ***Soon*** and ***Frank Merriwell*** were rumored to be Limited productions, *Johnny Johnson* was the season's only musical to open under the new experiment.

The script for the musical was published in hardback by Samuel French in 1937. There have been two recordings of the score. A studio cast album conducted by Samuel Matlowsky with Burgess Meredith, Lotte Lenya, Evelyn Lear, and Jane Connell was released by MGM Records (LP # E-3447) and then later by Heliodor Records (LP # H/HS-25024). *Music from 'Johnny Johnson'* was released by Erato Records (CD # 0630-17870-2).

70, GIRLS, 70

Theatre: Broadhurst Theatre
Opening Date: April 15, 1971; *Closing Date*: May 15, 1971
Performances: 36
Book: Fred Ebb and Norman L. Martin
Lyrics: Fred Ebb
Music: John Kander; dance music by Dorothea Freitag
Based on the 1958 play *Breath of Spring* by Peter Coke (which was adapted as the film *Make Mine Mink* in 1960).
Direction: Paul Aaron ("entire production supervised" by Stanley Prager); *Producers*: Arthur Whitelaw in association with Seth Harrison; *Choreography*: Onna White (Martin Allen, Assistant Choreographer); *Scenery* and *Lighting*: Robert Randolph; *Costumes*: Jane Greenwood; *Musical Direction*: Oscar Kosarin
Cast: Thomas Anderson, Tommy Breslin, Hans Conried, Robert G. Dare, Sally De May, Joey Faye, Dorothea Freitag, Ruth Gillette, Lloyd Harris, Lillian Hayman, Henrietta Jacobson, Gil Lamb, Lucie Lancaster, Marjorie Leach, Abby Lewis, Steve Mills, Mildred Natwick, Naomi Price, Lillian Roth, Goldye Shaw, Beau Tilden, Bobbi Tremain, Jay Velie, Coley Worth
The musical was presented in two acts.
The action takes place during the present time on the stage of the Broadhurst Theatre.

Musical Numbers

Act One: "Old Folks" (Company); "Home" (Mildred Natwick, Lillian Roth, Lucie Lancaster, Gil Lamb, Hans Conried, Lillian Hayman, Goldye Shaw); "Broadway, My Street" (Lillian Hayman, Goldye Shaw, Thomas Anderson, Joey Faye, Lloyd Harris, Henrietta Jacobson, Beau Tilden, Bobbi Tremain, Jay Velie, Coley Worth); "The Caper" (Hans Conried); "Coffee in a Cardboard Cup" (Lillian Hayman, Goldye Shaw); "You and I, Love" (Steve Mills, Abby Lewis, Thomas Anderson, Ruth Gillette, Lloyd Harris, Bobbi Tremain, Jay Velie, Coley Worth); "Do We?" (Lucie Lancaster, Gil Lamb); "Hit It, Lorraine" (Mildred Natwick, Hans Conried, Lillian Roth, Lucie Lancaster, Dorothea Freitag); "See the Light" (Lillian Roth, Joey Faye, Coley Worth, Thomas Anderson, Jay Velie)
Act Two: Entr'Acte (Ruth Gillette, Joey Faye, Lloyd Harris, Jay Velie); "Boom Ditty Boom" (Mildred Natwick, Hans Conried, Lillian Roth, Gil Lamb, Lillian Hayman, Lucie Lancaster, Goldye Shaw); "Believe" (Lillian Hayman, Mildred Natwick, Hans Conried, Lillian Roth, Gil Lamb, Lucie Lancaster, Goldye Shaw); "Go Visit (Your Grandmother)" (Tommy Breslin, Henrietta Jacobson); "70, Girls, 70" (Company); "The Elephant Song" (Mildred Natwick, Lillian Hayman, Goldye Shaw); "Yes" (Mildred Natwick, Company)

With its needlessly confusing and often irrelevant plot details *70, Girls, 70* seemed to purposely trip itself up. The essential story dealt with a group of elderly folks who live in a shabby retirement hotel in Manhattan. Although the unpublished script provided names for the characters, the program confusedly identified them as "The Ensemble Characters" and only the names of the performers themselves were listed. Hence, the Mildred Natwick character (identified as Ida in the script) finds a profitable way to pass her days: she shoplifts. But not on small-scale items such as hairpins or tubes of toothpaste; she goes after furs and jewels. She encourages her fellow seniors to join her, and before long their dreary lives are full of excitement and their seedy hotel is luxuriously refurbished with gleaming chandeliers, new furniture, and vases of flowers. But in Robin Hood fashion, they share their spoils by subsidizing indigent seniors and inviting them to move into the hotel. The merry gang never gets caught in their capers because no one suspects elderly people of being criminals. But when one heist goes wrong, the Natwick character takes full blame, and thus saves her cohorts from trouble with the law. And even she is "saved": "Mildred Natwick" tells us that "Ida" has suddenly died (offstage) and has escaped the indignities of a trial and incarceration. But this being a musical comedy, Ida (in the person of Mildred Natwick) returns from the afterlife and in *Mame* fashion appears in the sky, sitting on a glittery crescent moon where in song she exhorts her friends to always say "Yes" to life.

But wait. Maybe all this wasn't the real plot. Because the actual setting for the musical was the stage of the Broadhurst Theatre itself, where *70, Girls, 70* is playing. There are no characters who live in a retirement hotel, there are no characters who go out and help themselves to jewels and furs, and instead the group of performers on the stage are supposed to be retired actors who in some way have managed to get access to the Broadhurst and its stage where they act out a *play* about seniors living in a retirement hotel who shoplift in order to add excitement and luxury to their lives and to help out the less fortunate.

To add to the general confusion, sometimes the performers who acted in the play about seniors paused and entered into a kind of theatrical limbo for an occasional musical number in which they commented about such topics as Broadway ("Broadway, My Street"), family relationships ("Go Visit Your Grandmother"), and the state of the world ("Coffee in a Cardboard Cup"). And once in a while they would break the fourth wall and directly address the audience.

The head-scratching plot and the lack of star names in the cast (albeit a welcome company of old favorites such as Natwick, Lillian Roth, Hans Conried, Lillian Hayman, Joey Faye, and Gil Lamb) worked against the musical, and the score was a generally disappointing one by the usually reliable team of lyricist Fred Ebb and composer John Kander. The show clearly needed rave reviews to survive, but none were forthcoming and the production shuttered after a month.

To be sure, Kander and Ebb came up with some pleasant songs; "Broadway, My Street," "Go Visit Your Grandmother," "Coffee in a Cardboard Cup," "Yes," and the score's best number "The Elephant Song" (which according to the script is "not your *ordinary* death song"). Incidentally, "Yes" became part of Liza Minnelli's repertoire and was most famously featured in her memorable 1972 television special *Liza with a "Z."* Minnelli also performed the song in her 1974 Broadway concert ***Liza***.

Douglas Watt in the *New York Daily News* found the "jumble of a show" as "enlivening" as a New Year's Eve party "thrown by the members of the St. Petersburg shuffleboard club"; the "simple" book was awash in "awful jokes and puns" and the score was "pleasant" but "mindless" and "wearing." Richard Watts in the *New York Post* said the musical was "less than exciting" and offered "agreeable" if "hardly memorable" songs; but he liked the "talented" cast and said the "ageless" Mildred Natwick was "wonderful."

Edwin Newman on WNBC4TV said the show sagged between songs but musically was "hard to resist" with its "strong music hall flavor." John Schubeck on WABCTV7 said the first act was "lethargic" but picked up in the second half with a series of "show-stopping" songs. On the other hand, Leonard Harris on WCBSTV2 felt the musical ran out of steam in the second half but otherwise was "pleasant and professional" (and he cautioned that the script's "touch of Pirandello" shouldn't "scare" off anyone).

Martin Gottfried in *Women's Wear Daily* said it took a while to "figure out" what was going on, and the scenery was "so vague" the show could have taken place in Afghanistan. He felt Kander and Ebb's talents were not just "wasted" but "degraded" within the confines of the show's "primitive Broadwayism" and "trashy vernacular," and *70, Girls, 70* was "probably the sloppiest" musical he'd ever seen. He found the plot "rather condescending" to the aged, but he asked his readers to "be kind" to the "good actress" Mildred Natwick, and suggested this would be the only kindness that the "degrading production" deserved.

Clive Barnes in the *New York Times* found the evening "mixed" with some "bright" songs and a "sveltely amusing star performance" by Mildred Natwick. Otherwise, the "dual level" of the basic story line's action as well as the part of the plot that is supposedly being "performed" by actors on the stage of a theatre was confusing. It seemed as if two shows were being offered simultaneously, and if so, this was "no bargain package." He noted that director Stanley Prager had "done his best" to "make sense of the split-level book" but unfortunately when the show morphed from "one level to the other" it creaked at the joints.

During the Philadelphia tryout, "Go Visit Your Grandmother" was a "guy" duet for David Burns and Tommy Breslin (the latter was the only young member of the cast, and in the musical-within-a-musical he played the role of the hotel's bellhop). At one tryout performance, Burns and Breslin were performing the number on the stage of the Forrest Theatre when Burns had a heart attack (which apparently some in the audience thought was part of the script) and within an hour or two he was dead. The legendary two-time Tony

Award winner who created the roles of Banjo in *The Man Who Came to Dinner*, Mayor Shinn in *The Music Man*, Senex in *A Funny Thing Happened on the Way to the Forum*, and Horace Vandergelder in *Hello, Dolly!* ended his days in perhaps the manner every performer dreams of: as a star on the stage in a new show with the sound of applause ringing in his ears.

Burns was replaced by Hans Conried, but "Go Visit Your Grandmother" was reassigned to Henrietta Jacobson (who was joined by Breslin). Violet Carlson left the cast, and the number "Folk Song" was cut. Director Paul Aaron continued to receive credit as director, but by New York Stanley Prager was listed as the supervisor for the entire production. The musical was based on Peter Coke's 1958 London play *Breath of Spring*, which in turn had been filmed in 1960 as *Make Mine Mink*. Joe Masteroff, who had written the book of *She Loves Me* and Kander and Ebb's *Cabaret*, adapted the material for the musical version, but by the time the show was produced it was Ebb and Norman L. Martin who received book credit (although Masteroff was cited in the program as the adaptor).

The Broadway cast album was recorded by Columbia Records (LP # S-30589); the CD was issued by Sony Broadway (# SK-30589).

A revised Chicago production in 1989 was scripted by Martin and David Thompson and was later presented in Great Britain at the Chichester Festival on June 27, 1990. It then opened in London at the Vaudeville Theatre on June 17, 1991. The London production's cast included Dora Bryan, Pip Hinton, Shezwae Powell, and Stephanie Voss; this version included three new songs ("Well Laid Plans," "Emma Finch," and "I Can't Do That Anymore") and omitted four ("The Caper," "You and I, Love," "See the Light," and "The Elephant Song"). The London cast album was released by That's Entertainment Records (CD # CDTER-1186).

Awards

Tony Award Nomination: Best Leading Actress in a Musical (Mildred Natwick)

METAMORPHOSES

Theatre: Ambassador Theatre
Opening Date: April 22, 1971; *Closing Date*: July 3, 1971
Performances: 35
Adaptation and *Lyrics*: Arnold Weinstein
Music: The True Brethren
Based on Ovid's series of over 250 narrative poems collectively titled *Metamorphoses* (Ovid completed the epic work in 8 CE).
Direction: Paul Sills; *Producers*: Story Theatre Productions; *Scenery*: James Trittipo; *Costumes*: Noel Taylor; *Lighting*: H. R. Poindexter
Cast: Lewis Arquette, Regina Baff, Charles Bartlett, Hamid Hamilton Camp, Melinda Dillon, MacIntyre Dixon, Mary Frann, Valerie Harper, Paula Kelly, Richard Libertini, Paul Sand, Richard Schaal, Avery Schreiber, Penny White; The True Brethren (Hamid Hamilton Camp, Lewis Ross, Raphael Grinage, Lauren Karapetian, and Loren Pickford)
The production was presented in two acts.

Musical Numbers

Note: The program listed the titles of Ovid's tales, but didn't provide the names of the musical numbers, which were written and performed by the group The True Brethren.

Act One: "The Creation" (Company); "Io" (Io: Mary Frann; Io's Sister: Regina Baff; Jove: Hamid Hamilton Camp and Charles Bartlett; Juno: Valerie Harper; Argos: Richard Schaal; Io's Father: Avery Schreiber; Mercury: Paul Sand; Syrinx: Penny White); "Europa" (Europa: Paula Kelly; Jove: Hamid Hamilton Camp and Charles Bartlett); "Vulcan and Venus and Mars" (Vulcan: Avery Schreiber; Juno: Valerie Harper; Thetis: Paula Kelly; Venus: Penny White; Vulcan's Girls: Mary Frann, Regina Baff; Mars: Richard Schaal;

Mercury: Paul Sand); "Phaethon" (Phaethon: Paul Sand; Clymene: Valerie Harper; Sun: Hamid Hamilton Camp; Horses: Charles Bartlett, Richard Schaal, and Avery Schreiber); "Callisto" (Jove: Hamid Hamilton Camp; Callisto: Regina Baff; Diana: Penny White; Nymphs: Mary Frann, Paula Kelly; Juno: Valerie Harper; Orion: Paul Sand)

Act Two: "Picus and Canens" (Picus: Paul Sand; Canens: Penny White; Circe: Paula Kelly; Hunters: Avery Schreiber, Charles Bartlett, and Richard Schaal); "Procris and Cephalus" (Cephalus: Richard Schaal; Hunters: Avery Schreiber, Hamid Hamilton Camp; Aurora: Mary Frann; Procris: Valerie Harper; Diana: Penny White; Diana's Girls: Paula Kelly, Regina Baff); "Pygmalion" (Pygmalion: Avery Schreiber; Statue: Mary Frann); "Peleus and Thetis" (Thetis: Paula Kelly; Jove: Hamid Hamilton Camp; Peleus: Charles Bartlett; Proteus, God of Changes: Avery Schreiber and Richard Schaal); "Baucis and Philemon" (Baucis: Valerie Harper; Philemon: Avery Schreiber; Jove: Hamid Hamilton Camp; Mercury: Paul Sand)

Paul Sills's concurrently running ***Story Theatre*** presented stories and fables by the Brothers Grimm and by Aesop, and his new work *Metamorphoses*, which offered tales from Ovid, joined ***Story Theatre*** in repertory. At first, both were given four times weekly by the same cast members, but the new work didn't prove as popular as its predecessor and soon *Metamorphoses* was presented three times weekly and ***Story Theatre*** five times. When the productions closed, the former had played for 243 performances while the latter had tallied up just 35 showings. For a time, there was hope that Sills's innovative approach to theatre by depicting short stories and poems through dialogue, songs, dance, and mime might pave the way for more such productions, but as far as Broadway was concerned ***Story Theatre*** and *Metamorphoses* both began and ended the short-lived experiment.

Martin Gottfried in *Women's Wear Daily* said the evening was "pleasant" and "enjoyable" but "nothing to write Homer about." He liked Sills's "superior" dialogue, but felt the narratives themselves were "too detailed" and thus grew "too complicated to follow." He praised Sills's skills as a director as "enchanting and precise," and said Paul Sand was able to "walk right up to the edge of cuteness without slipping over." Edwin Newman on WNBC4TV echoed Gottfried and noted there were "too many words" along with too much matching of words to action, and all this was topped with explanations by the performers as to what they were doing. As a result, the barrage of wordage made the evening "tedious."

Peter J. Rosenwald in the *Wall Street Journal* found *Metamorphoses* a "thoroughly engaging and often hilarious entertainment." He wryly noted that his search of six midtown Manhattan bookstores failed to yield even a single copy of Ovid's *Metamorphoses*, and he hoped Sills's production would revive interest in the classical poet.

For many of the critics, Avery Schreiber was the evening's star, and he shined as Pygmalion and Vulcan. T. E. Kalem in *Time* found him a "comic treasure," Douglas Watt in the *New York Daily News* said the "junior Zero Mostel" was a "chunky and expert comedian," and John Schubeck on WABCTV7 crowned him the production's "stand-out."

Columbia released the cast album of ***Story Theatre***, but *Metamorphoses* wasn't recorded.

FRANK MERRIWELL, OR HONOR CHALLENGED

"A New Musical"

Theatre: Longacre Theatre
Opening Date: April 24, 1971; *Closing Date*: April 24, 1971
Performances: 1
Book: Skip Redwine, Larry Frank, and Heywood Gould
Lyrics and *Music*: Skip Redwine and Larry Frank
Based on the character of Frank Merriwell, the hero of a series of stories by William George Gilbert Patten (aka Burt L. Standish) which first appeared as a short story in the magazine *Tip Top Weekly* in 1896; the musical was based on the very first *Frank Merriwell* story, "Frank Merriwell's School Days."
Direction and *Choreography*: Neal Kenyon (Bonnie Ano, Assistant Choreographer); *Producers*: Sandy Farber and Stanley Barnett in association with Nate Friedman (Aaron Ziegelman, Associate Producer); *Scenery*: Tom John; *Costumes*: Frank Thompson; *Lighting*: John Gleason; *Musical Direction*: Jack Holmes
Cast: J. J. Jepson (Clyde), Larry Ross (Ned), Walter Bobbie (Hugh), Neva Small (Belinda Belle Snodd), Lori Cesar (Snella Jean), Ellie Smith (Una Marie), Thomas Ruisinger (Professor Burrage), Liz Sheridan (Mrs. Snodd),

Jennifer Williams (Esther Carmichael), Peter Shawn (Bart Hodge), Gary Keith Steven (Tad Jones), Larry Ellis (Frank Merriwell), Linda Donovan (Inza Burrage), Bill Hinnant (Manuel)
The musical was presented in two acts.
The action takes place during 1897 and 1898 in Fardale, a small American town.

Musical Numbers

Act One: "There's No School Like Our School" (Students, Local Girls); "Howdy, Mr. Sunshine" (Larry Ellis, Gary Keith Steven); "Prim and Proper" (Students, Local Girls); "Inza" (Larry Ellis); "Look for the Happiness Ahead" (Larry Ellis, Company); "I'd Be Crazy to Be Crazy over You" (Neva Small, Peter Shawn); "Now It's Fall" (Students); "The Fallin'-Out-of-Love Rag" (Neva Small, Students, Local Girls, Larry Ellis)
Act Two: "Frank, Frank, Frank" (Company); "In Real Life" (Larry Ellis); "The Broadway of My Heart" (Thomas Ruisinger, Liz Sheridan); "Winter's Here" (Students); "The Pure in Heart" (Larry Ellis, Company); "I Must Be Crazy to Be Crazy over You" (reprise) (Neva Small); "Don't Turn His Picture to the Wall" (Gary Keith Steven, Students, Local Girls); "Manuel, Your Friend" (Bill Hinnant); "The Pure in Heart" (reprise) (Larry Ellis, Company); "Look for the Happiness Ahead" (reprise) (Company)

Frank Merriwell, or *Honor Challenged* and the revival of *Johnny Johnson* were the shortest-running musicals of the season, and both Frankie and Johnny couldn't muster more than one performance apiece. *Frank Merriwell* was based on a decades-long series of short stories, dime novels, comic books, and comic strips by William George Gilbert Patten (aka Burt A. Standish) that depicted the adventures of the small-town hero; as the program noted, Frank is an "honest, handsome, healthy, high-minded" college boy who is "always on the side of honor and right" and who outwits "scalawags with ingenuity, prowess, and an unshakable code of ethics."

The musical took place at Frank's college where the hero (Larry Ellis) battles wits with the evil Manuel (Bill Hinnant), a spy who hopes to blow up the college's science laboratory and thus destroy American military secrets. The dastardly deed will ensure that the country loses the Spanish-American War.

Martin Gottfried in *Women's Wear Daily* said the musical looked chintzy, had "static" staging, and offered "little" music and "few" dances. Moreover, there was a "second-rate campiness" about it with a "homosexual underbelly" that was more "flagrant" considering the stalwart hero, his college buddies, and an "occasional woman in caricature." As a result, the show was "lavendered over with boyishness." Douglas Watt in the *New York Daily News* said the musical was a "dog" with "empty-headed songs" and "perfunctory" direction and choreography. It had the "pathetic appearance of a stunted little show," and was "incredibly silly from start to finish." But he singled out the talented Bill Hinnant and Neva Small and suggested they would soon be better employed.

Richard Watts in the *New York Post* found the musical an "embarrassingly amateurish concoction"; Leonard Harris on WCBSTV2 said the book was "unfunny" and the score "dreadful"; and Leonard Probst on WNBC4TV felt the evening was "mostly tiresome." But John Schubeck on WABCTV7 liked the "clever spoof" with its "clever" songs and swiftly moving plot. He suggested that *Frank Merriwell* wasn't for "straights or stiffs, and if you don't know or can't imagine what that means, forget about seeing it."

Clive Barnes in the *New York Times* said the "modestly deplorable" musical had a "distinctively undistinguished" score and a "wrong-headed" book. It was clearly from the "camp-fire" school of musicals in the *Little Mary Sunshine* (1959) and *Dames at Sea* (1968) mode, but here the satire of dime-store novels required, but was denied, "total sincerity" from its writers and thus the evening couldn't "be taken seriously."

The script was published in paperback by Samuel French in 1971.

EARL OF RUSTON

"A Country Rocker"

Theatre: Billy Rose Theatre
Opening Date: May 5, 1971; *Closing Date*: May 8, 1971
Performances: 5
Book: C. C. Courtney and Ragan Courtney

Music: Peter Link
Direction: C. C. Courtney; *Producer*: David Black; *Scenery, Costumes*, and *Lighting*: Neil Peter Jampolis; *Musical Direction*: Uncredited (probably John Bergeron)
Cast: C. C. Courtney and Ragan Courtney (Earl), Jean Waldo Beck (Leda Pearl Crump), Leecy R. Woods Moore (Herself), Leon Medica (The Sheriff, Bass Guitar), Bootsie Normand (Mr. Turner, Lead Guitar), Chip McDonald (Reverend Reynolds, Rhythm Guitar), Bobby Thomas (The Doctor, Drums), Lynda Lawley (Ernestine), Bonnie Guidry (Mary Lee Woods), John Bergeron (Piano); *Note*: Some of the performers were also members of the musical's five-piece band, which was called Goatleg.
The musical was presented in one act.
The action takes place during the recent past, mostly in Ruston, Louisiana.

Musical Numbers

Note: The program didn't list individual singers; * = Denotes music by C. C. Courtney and ** = Denotes music by C. C. Courtney and Raglan Courtney.
"Just Your Old Friend"; "Earl Is Crazy"; "Guitar Song"; "Easy to Be Lonely"; "Standing"; "Der Blues" (traditional music); "Probably" (**); "Mama, Earl Done Ate the Tooth Paste Again" (*); "Silvers Theme"; "Mama, Mama, Mama"; "I've Been Sent Back to the First Grade" (*); "The Revival"; "My Name Is Leda Pearl" (*); "Insane Poontang" (*); "You Still Love Me" (*); "Earl Was Ahead"

The quirky *Earl of Ruston* never had a chance on Broadway and lasted for just five performances; as with so many musicals of the era, it probably would have worked better Off Broadway where it might have found its target audience and could have been seen to better advantage in an intimate playing space. Within the confines of the Billy Rose Theatre (albeit one of the smaller Broadway venues but still a large theatre about four or five times the size of the typical Off-Broadway house), the small cast *and* orchestra of *Earl of Ruston* totaled just eleven performers and they were backed by scenery that was little more than wooden platforms on an otherwise bare stage.

The true story dealt with Earl D. Woods of Ruston, Louisiana, a young man who was mentally ill, spent time in an institution, and died on June 5, 1969. Besides his occasional forays into asylums, Earl likes to playfully help himself to his neighbors' welfare checks, spend time ruminating on Hitler, occasionally indulge in a vocabulary all his own, and court the equally eccentric Leda Pearl Crump (Jean Waldo Beck), whom he eventually marries.

The musical was a family affair in which Earl's cousins C. C. Courtney and Raglan Courtney wrote the book, lyrics, and some of the music; C. C. also directed; and both Courtneys portrayed the title character, sometimes playing two versions of Earl at the same moment. Further, Earl's mother, Leecy R. Woods Moore, played herself; she sat on the side of the stage, watched the proceedings, and occasionally joined in the action.

Martin Gottfried in *Women's Wear Daily* said the "unorganized" evening was more in the nature of a rock concert that told Earl's story in a series of "rambling" anecdotes set to "mediocre" music; Richard Watts in the *New York Post* stated the evening could "at best be dismissed as lamentable" and felt its "chief sin" was that of "persistent dullness"; and Douglas Watt in the *New York Daily News* said the "ill-advised" musical tried for a "folksy and charming" approach that instead came across as "merely idiotic" (but he noted the songs were sometimes "attractive").

Leonard Probst on WNBC4TV found the evening "tasteless and depressing" and said the rock music was "rock quarried from an endless pile of rock"; he noted *Earl of Ruston* was a "marvelous" musical for those who were related to Earl, but otherwise outsiders would find little of interest. Leonard Harris on WCBSTV2 said the evening's "infantile meanderings" proved that "out of the mouths of babes comes mostly baby talk."

Clive Barnes in the *New York Times* said the musical attempted to cross *Our Town* with *Hair*, but unfortunately its book took "garrulity to insane lengths" and the score was a "disappointment." Once the musical established its premise, it was "off and away," but unfortunately the show and the audience never went "anywhere."

But *Best Plays* had a completely different take on the musical. It was an "imaginative, stimulating," and "arrogantly daring effort to push out the frontiers of the musical stage," and those who saw it could "congratulate themselves on having witnessed a stage in the progress" of the gifted C. C. Courtney, Raglan Courtney, and Peter Link.

There was no cast album, but Capitol released *Earl of Ruston* (LP # ST-465), a studio recording credited to The Salvation Company which included eight songs, seven of which were heard in the Broadway production: "Just Your Old Friend" (two versions), "(The) Guitar Song," "Silver's (Silvers) Theme," "(It's) Easy to Be Lonely," "The Revival," "Earl Is Crazy," and "Earl Is Ahead," and the unused "R.U.S.T.O.N." The album credits Peter Link, Raglan Courtney, and L. Moore (presumably Leecy R. Woods Moore) as the creators of "Just Your Old Friend."

The recording gives almost no clue that the songs are from a musical and thus is similar to a few other "show" albums of the era that were recorded as perhaps concept albums and chose to downplay any theatrical association, such as the Off-Broadway musicals *House of Leather* and *Exchange* (the latter was released as *Tamalpais Exchange*).

Peter Link and C. C. Courtney had enjoyed a minor success with their 1969 Off-Broadway musical *Salvation*; there were two recordings (the cast album as well as a collection of songs from the score) and the musical even enjoyed a hit song ("If You Let Me Make Love to You Then Why Can't I Touch You"). In 1972, Link wrote some lovely bandstand-in-the-park music for the Broadway revival of *Much Ado about Nothing* (see Appendix H) and the unmemorable songs for the dreadful musical adaptation of ***Lysistrata***, which might well be the all-time low of 1970s musicals. In 1978, Link's ***King of Hearts*** was briefly seen on Broadway (and was recorded), and his Off-Broadway song-cycle *The River* was produced in 1988.

Link and *Earl of Ruston*'s band, Goatleg, teamed up again later in 1971 for the Off-Broadway musical *The Wedding of Iphigenia* and *Iphigenia in Concert*. One of the clichés of the rock musical was that it seemed vitally essential for the members of the orchestra to be called by a group name. As a result, Goatleg for *Earl of Ruston* and the *Iphigenia* bill; Pitshit for ***Soon***; Zeitgeist for *The Last Sweet Days of Isaac* (1970); Hugo for *House of Leather* (1970); The Wet Clam for *I Dreamt I Dwelt in Bloomingdale's* (1970); Touchstone for *Tarot* (1971); Bandana for *The Ballad of Johnny Pot* (1971); Pure Love and Pleasure (which was succeeded by another band, Shaker) for *Earthlight*; and for *The Survival of St. Joan* (1971), the band changed its name: during the tryout they were known as Ruffin but then adopted the more appropriately titled Smoke Rise.

LOLITA, MY LOVE

"A New Musical"

The musical opened on February 15, 1971, at the Shubert Theatre, Philadelphia, Pennsylvania, and closed there on February 27. After a brief hiatus, the musical then opened on March 18 at the Shubert Theatre, Boston, Massachusetts, where it permanently closed on March 27.

Book and *Lyrics*: Alan Jay Lerner

Music: John Barry

Based on the 1955 novel *Lolita* by Vladimir Nabokov.

Direction: Tito Capobianco; *Producer*: Norman Twain (Stone Widney, Associate Producer); *Choreography*: Danny Daniels; *Scenery*: Ming Cho Lee; *Costumes*: Jose Varona; *Lighting*: Jules Fisher; *Musical Direction*: Herbert Grossman

Cast: *John Neville* (Humbert Humbert), Kendall March (Mona Dahl), Leonard Frey (Claire Quilty), Valerie Camille (Vivian Darkbloom), Dorothy Loudon (Charlotte Haze), Annette Ferra (Lolita), Josh Wheeler (Reverend Doctor Neiling), Lance Westergard (Young Man), David Thomas (Neighbor), Fran Stevens (Mrs. Thornbush), Jacqueline Johnson (Camp Counsellor), Jacqueline Britt (Camp Counsellor), Jacque Dean (Camp Counsellor), Neil McNelis (Mr. Bliss), John Mineo (First Bellboy), Irwin Pearl (Second Bellboy), Gretel Cummings (Miss Amy Pratt), John Witham (Dick Schiller), Gretel Cummings (Miss Amy Pratt), Daniel Walsh (Bill Crest), Adam Petroski (Patrolman Power), Frank Bouley (Patrolman Steel); Singers: Frank Bouley, Jacqueline Britt, Walter P. Brown, Rhoda Butler, Jacque Dean, Lynn East, Linda Ellis, Robert Hultman, Jacqueline Johnson, Neil McNelis, Irwin Pearl, Adam Petroski, Meg Scanlan, Fran Stevens, David Thomas, Trudy Wallace, Daniel Walsh, Josh Wheeler, John Witham; Dancers: Velerie Camille, Carol Conte, Larry Grenier, Mickey Gunnerson, Carolin Kirsch, John Mineo, Jo Anne Ogawa, Pamela Peadon, Don Percassi, Rosalin Ricci, Dan Siretta, Patrick Spohn, Jill Streisant, Lance Westergard, Lee Wilson

The musical was presented in two acts.

The action takes place during the present time throughout the United States, but mostly in Vermont, Arizona, and Kansas City.

Musical Numbers

Act One: "Lolita" (John Neville); "Going Going Gone" (Leonard Frey, Friends); "In the Broken Promise Land of Fifteen" (John Neville); "The Same Old Song" (Dorothy Loudon, Annette Ferra); "Mother Needs a Boyfriend" (Annette Ferra); "Lolita" (reprise) (John Neville); "Dante, Petrarch and Poe" (John Neville, Dorothy Loudon, Leonard Frey, Friends); "Sur Les Quais" (Dorothy Loudon); "Charlotte's Letter" (John Neville, Dorothy Loudon, Choir); "Farewell, Little Dream" (John Neville); "Have You Got What You Came With?" (Fran Stevens, Jacqueline Johnson, Jacqueline Britt, Jacque Dean); "At the Bed-D By Motel" (Neil McNelis, Leonard Frey, Guests); "Tell Me, Tell Me" (John Neville)

Act Two: "Buckin' for Beardsley" (Beardsley Students); "Beardsley School for Girls" (Beardsley Girl Students); "It's a Bad, Bad World" (Leonard Frey, Students); "The Same Old Song" (reprise) (Annette Ferra, John Neville); "How Far Is It to the Next Town?" (John Neville); "How Far It It to the Next Town?" (reprise) (John Neville, Annette Ferra, Ensemble); "Lolita" (reprise) (Ensemble)

Lolita, My Love and ***Prettybelle*** were the only musicals of the season that shuttered prior to their scheduled Broadway openings. They were truly daring, politically incorrect works that dealt with verboten themes, and today would stand no chance of production, on Broadway or elsewhere; but these two musicals pushed the boundaries of lyric theatre with their controversial stories and characters. One admires the courage of their creators for bringing to the musical stage an array of complicated characters who single-mindedly embrace what society condemns. Much of today's musical theatre is pietistic and trendy in its catering to the politically correct attitudes of audiences who demand stories that reflect and reinforce their own beliefs. They support a new kind of censorship that discourages complex and socially alienated characters, and the New Censorship is particularly intolerant of revivals and thus insist that songs, plots, and characters of earlier musicals must be altered in order to follow the party line of current thinking.

Lolita, My Love told the daring story of college professor Humbert Humbert (John Neville) and his obsessive love for Lolita (Annette Ferra, who was replaced by Denise Nickerson), a twelve-year-old girl wise beyond her years and who in nymphet fashion willingly beds older men. In order to get closer to her, Humbert marries her widowed mother, Charlotte (Dorothy Loudon), who soon realizes his intentions (she accuses him of being a "detestable, abominable, criminal, European monster"). In horror, she runs into the street and is hit and killed by a car. Lolita has also become sexually involved with playwright Claire Quilty (Leonard Frey), who follows her and Humbert as they travel across country. Unlike Humbert, who truly loves Lolita, Quilty is only interested in her as a kinky sexual conquest. Nonetheless, Lolita eventually dumps Humbert for Quilty, and later ends up as an ordinary (and pregnant) housewife living in a trailer park in Kansas City with her doltish young husband. Humbert blames Quilty for destroying Lolita's innocence, and murders him.

Vladimir Nabokov's novel was scandalous in 1955, and to this day it continues to shock in its unflinching depiction of a pedophile and the child who is depicted as more seductress than victim (when the two first have sex together, Humbert realizes he's not her first lover). A brilliant 1962 film version by Stanley Kubrick sidestepped some of the controversy by casting Sue Lyon in the title role; although she was fourteen at the time of the filming, she looked much older and thus her Lolita came across as an eighteen-year-old rather than as a little girl. The black comedy included memorable performances by James Mason (Humbert), Peter Sellers (Quilty), and Shelley Winters (Charlotte). A second film version in 1997 was much franker in its depiction of the story, and the cast included Jeremy Irons (Humbert), Frank Langella (Quilty), Dominique Swain (Lolita), and Melanie Griffith (Charlotte). An unsuccessful nonmusical version of the novel was adapted by Edward Albee with Donald Sutherland as Humbert; the production opened at the Brooks Atkinson Theatre on March 19, 1981, for twelve performances.

Because of the nature of the story, the 1997 film version reportedly had trouble finding wide distribution. And in 2005 composer John Harbison abandoned his operatic adaptation because of the controversial nature of the story (in an interview with the *New York Times*, he said "certain material" was "untenable on our present-day stage").

About midway through its chaotic tryout, *Lolita, My Love* suddenly closed in Philadelphia for revisions and recasting, and then reopened in Boston. But it was all for naught, and the musical permanently closed there without risking New York. With its demise went one of the finest scores of the era: Alan Jay Lerner's lyrics were among his most brilliant and John Barry's score was richly melodic and theatrically effective.

The score's highlights include gorgeous ballads ("In the Broken Promise Land of Fifteen," "Tell Me, Tell Me," and the title song); Lolita's musical gripe to Humbert that "All You Can Do Is Tell Me You Love Me";

and three expansive musical sequences that blew out the walls of the theatre with their sheer theatricality. The first was Charlotte's "Sur le quais," a shimmering fantasy in which she pathetically describes her life in small-town Vermont in terms of chic and sophisticated high life in Paris; the lecture "Dante, Petrarch and Poe" in which Humbert catalogs writers who were obsessed by young girls; and the hallucinatory "How Far Is It to the Next Town." The latter's irresistible and driving music and Lerner's both poetic and conversational lyric (which was peppered like a roadmap with the names of towns and cities) depicted a limbo in which Humbert and Lolita drive across country as they're eternally pursued by a mysterious car (which is "never farther and never nearer" and seems "painted . . . on the mirror").

During the tryout, Annette Ferra (Lolita) was replaced by Denise Nickerson; director Tito Capobianco was succeeded by Noel Willman, and choreographer Danny Daniels by Dan Siretta. Laurence Guittard was the understudy for both John Neville and Leonard Frey. During the run, many songs were deleted and others ("If It Ain't Fun," "Saturday," "I Always Believe in Me," and "All You Can Do Is Tell Me You Love Me") were added.

Ernest Schier in the Philadelphia *Evening Bulletin* called the musical a "disaster," and William Collins in the *Philadelphia Inquirer* said the adaptation was a "ghost" of the classic novel. Gagh in *Variety* complained about the "interminable" two-hour first act and the fact that the novel didn't readily adapt to lyric treatment; he singled out three "melodically memorable" songs (the title number, "Farewell, Little Dream," and the "song rouser" with "a Piaf-style lilt," "Sur les quais"). *Variety* reported that the musical would cut short its scheduled five-week engagement in Philadelphia, would undergo revisions in New York, and then reopen on March 15 for a three-week tryout at Boston's Wilbur Theatre. Instead, the work opened at Boston's Shubert Theatre where it played for one week before permanently closing with losses in the range of $800,000.

The musical had been scheduled to open on Broadway at the Mark Hellinger Theatre, clearly Lerner's favorite venue and where his *My Fair Lady* (1956), *On a Clear Day You Can See Forever* (1965), *Coco* (1969), and ***1600 Pennsylvania Avenue*** (1976) opened. The cast album of *Lolita, My Love* was scheduled to be recorded by Columbia Records, but was canceled due to the musical's out-of-town closing. Happily, a live performance tape made through the sound system of Boston's Shubert Theatre was preserved, and many years later was transferred to LP by Blue Pear Records (# BP-1009). Brent Barrett's collection *The Alan Jay Lerner Album* (Fynsworth Alley CD # 302-062-161-2) includes "In the Broken Promise Land of Fifteen" and "Tell Me, Tell Me."

PRETTYBELLE

"A New Musical"

The musical opened on February 1, 1971, at the Shubert Theatre, Boston, Massachusetts, and permanently closed there on March 6.

Book and *Lyrics*: Bob Merrill

Music: Jule Styne

Based on the 1970 novel *Prettybelle/A Lively Tale of Rape and Resurrection* by Jean Arnold.

Direction and *Choreography*: Gower Champion; *Producers*: Alexander H. Cohen (Hildy Parks, Associate Producer; A Gower Champion Production); *Scenery*: Oliver Smith; *Costumes*: Ann Roth; *Lighting*: Nananne Porcher; *Musical Direction*: Peter Howard

Cast: William Larsen (Henry Baines), Barbara Ann Walters (Sybil Mae Asch), *Angela Lansbury* (Prettybelle Sweet), Susan Plantt (Nurse, First GoGo Girl, Baby Doll), Linda Lubera (Nurse, Second GoGo Girl, Waitress), Richard Kuss (Doctor Dimmer, Magistrate), Chad Block (Mayor, Pool Hall Mexican, Sheriff, First TV Interviewer), Charlotte Rae (Mother Sweet), Renee Lippin (Lovey Sweet), Dean Crane, Jr. (John Sweet), Jon Cypher (Ray Schaeffer), Joe Morton (Willy Thomas), Igors Gavon (Cully Hart), Robert Karl (Huey Lipscomb, Sheriff), Jan Leighton (Bubba Rawlings), Brian Hall (Boy Scout), Michael Jason (Folksinger), Mark Dawson (Leroy Sweet), Christine Cooper (Third GoGo Girl, Marie, Waitress), Joe Milan (Bouncer, Japanese Gardens Waiter, Sheriff, Second TV Interviewer), Peter Lombard (Mason Miller), Bert Michaels (Jesus), George Blackwell (Motel Clerk), Bobby Lee (Juan Lopez), Sean Walsh (Bud Michaels), Maggie Task (Rose Anson), Howard Porter (Pickett Webster)

The musical was presented in two acts.

The action takes place during the present and recent past, mostly in Piciyumi and New Orleans, Louisiana.

Musical Numbers

Act One: "(The Twice-Weekly) Piciyumi Gazette" (Angela Lansbury, William Larsen, Barbara Ann Walters); "Manic Depressives" (Angela Lansbury); "Policeman's Hymn" (Police Band); "Prettybelle" (Michael Jason); "You Ain't Hurtin' Your Ole Lady None" (Mark Dawson, Jon Cypher, Igors Gavon, Jan Leighton, and Robert Karl); "To a Small Degree" (Angela Lansbury); "Back from the Great Beyond" (Mark Dawson); "How Could I Know What Was Goin' On?" (Angela Lansbury); "I Never Did Imagine" (Angela Lansbury, Bert Michaels); "New Orleans Poon" (Charlotte Rae); "In the Japanese Gardens (of Shreveport, Louisiana)" (Angela Lansbury); "An Individual Thing" (Peter Lombard); "I Met a Man" (Angela Lansbury); "Prettybelle" (reprise) (Michael Jason)
Act Two: "The No-Tell Motel" (Angela Lansbury, Company); "I'm in a Tree" (Angela Lansbury); "When I'm Drunk (I'm Beautiful)" (Angela Lansbury); "Give Me a Share in America" (Joe Morton); "Prettybelle" (reprise) (Angela Lansbury, Michael Jason)

Like ***Lolita, My Love***, *Prettybelle* was a controversial musical that closed during its Broadway tryout. The two musicals were fresh and daring in their vision of complicated characters who were devoid of vanilla-flavored personalities with well-regulated, cookie-cutter outlooks. These characters heartily embraced what society condemns, and didn't mouth the politically correct and pious liberal platitudes of the day. But their creators paid dearly for their daringly original conceptions: both musicals received poor reviews and scant attendance and each lost a fortune, making them among the most expensive failures in Broadway history.

Prettybelle was based on Jean Arnold's 1970 novel of the same name, which was subtitled "A Lively Tale of Rape and Resurrection," and for the musical Angela Lansbury starred as the title character, a manic-depressive nymphomaniac alcoholic who is confined to a mental institution where she writes her memoirs as a form of therapy. As she writes, her past comes to life and she re-lives the sordid events of her days in Piciyumi, Louisiana, where she learned that her racist sheriff husband Leroy Sweet (Mark Dawson) was responsible for the deaths of innocent blacks and other minorities. In order to atone for his sins, Prettybelle decides she must sacrifice herself by being raped by as many minority men as possible, including a Mexican named Jesus (Bert Michaels), a half-Jewish psychiatrist, a black, and a Sioux Indian. Of course, she voluntarily participates in these sexual encounters, and so the word "rape" isn't quite precise. (And today the word itself would be forbidden; for decades, the Off-Broadway hit *The Fantasticks* included the number "The Rape Ballet," but a politically correct sea-change occurred and now the sequence is titled "The Seduction Ballet.")

Prettybelle's memories also include the incident when her teenage son John (Dean Crane Jr.) murdered four men because of their resemblance to his father; the time when Leroy was beaten to death and returned from the beyond in order to identify the "radicals" who killed him; her decision to leave her money to the NAACP; her sex-on-the-brain mother-in-law (Charlotte Rae); her hateful two-hundred-pound daughter Lovey (Renee Lippen) who eventually heads off to New York City and Greenwich Village in order to become a hippie; the more-liberal-than-thou lawyer Mason Miller, who has sex only with blacks, Asians, and other minorities (Prettybelle considers this "reverse discrimination"); and local school teacher Ray Schaeffer (Jon Cypher) who leads the local branch of the Ku Klux Klan and enjoys raping and mutilating women.

Considering what Prettybelle encountered in the world, her life in the sanitarium seems normal by comparison. One of the era's favorite themes was that inmates in sanitariums are saner and happier than those on the outside, and musical theatre explored this notion in Stephen Sondheim's *Anyone Can Whistle* (1964, which also starred Lansbury) and the 1966 film and its later musical adaptation ***King of Hearts***; and of course the novel, play, and film *One Flew Over the Cuckoo's Nest* was also a variation of the theme.

Certainly the musical's story was off-putting to many in the audience. With a title like *Prettybelle*, playgoers no doubt expected to see Lansbury in full Mame-mode, a *Hello, Dolly!*–styled evening of frolicsome direction and choreography by Gower Champion, and a take-home score on the order of Bob Merrill and Jule Styne's previous Broadway collaboration *Funny Girl*. Instead they witnessed what may have been the strangest musical seen in Boston since 1955, when Marc Blitzstein's *Reuben Reuben* (which also played at the Shubert Theatre) so upset audiences that one irate ticket-holder physically threatened the composer for concocting the confusing story about an aphoniac who wanders through the *film noir* night streets of Manhattan in his search for truth, self-identity, and other such abstractions while he contemplates suicide.

Elliot Norton in the *Boston Herald-American* said *Prettybelle* would "offend," "irritate," and "bewilder" audiences, but praised the "absolutely magnificent" Lansbury in what was "the most extraordinary performance she has ever given." Samuel Hirsch in the *Boston Herald Traveler* noted the evening wavered between "parody and fantasy," and that its two assets were Lansbury's "enchanting" performance and Gower Champion's "tasteful, imaginative staging." He mentioned that Styne's score had "energy and character."

Star in *Variety* said producer Alexander Cohen would have "major problems" with Bob Merrill's "choppy, aimless, vulgar and unfunny" book and lyrics, and noted the "foul plot" included four-letter words as well as three "nearly naked" dancers "for the voyeur trade." Styne's score was "solid" and "professional" but "undistinguished," but he noted Lansbury was a "game trouper" with her memorable "When I'm Drunk" (which just about everyone agreed was the score's highlight).

The musical had been scheduled to open in New York at the Majestic Theatre on March 15, 1971, and the cast album was set to be recorded by Metromedia Records; when the show closed in Boston, the album was canceled. Songs dropped during preproduction were "Not Bad for an Alcoholic Schizophrenic!," "Take This Servant Back to Your Bosom, Jesus," "Rape and Resurrection," "A Daddy, a Son, and a Gun," "Willy Boy," and "In the Wild Adirondacks." One song in the musical ("An Individual Thing") had earlier been considered for Merrill and Styne's *Funny Girl*.

Eleven years after *Prettybelle* folded, the production was recorded and released by Original Cast Records (LP # OC-8238) which included original cast members Angela Lansbury, Mark Dawson, Igors Gavon, Bert Michaels, Bobby Lee, Peter Lombard, and Michael Jason (now Michael Stein). The CD was issued by Varese Sarabande Records (# VSD-5439).

Prettybelle and ***Lolita, My Love*** shared more than just bizarre plots and pre-Broadway closings. Both also sang the praises of motels: the former with "The No-Tell Motel" and the latter with "At the Bed-D-By Motel."

1971–1972 Season

YOU'RE A GOOD MAN, CHARLIE BROWN

"A New Musical Entertainment"

Theatre: John Golden Theatre
Opening Date: June 1, 1971; *Closing Date*: June 27, 1971
Performances: 32
Book: John Gordon (a *nom de plume* for Clark Gesner)
Lyrics and *Music*: Clark Gesner; additional material by Joseph Raposo
Based on the comic strip *Peanuts* by Charles M. Schulz
Direction: Joseph Hardy; *Producers*: Arthur Whitelaw and Gene Persson (Warren Lockhart, Associate Producer); *Musical Staging*: Patricia Birch; *Scenery* and *Costumes*: Alan Kimmel; *Lighting*: Jules Fisher; *Musical Direction*: Jack Holmes
Cast: Stephen Fenning (Linus), Dean Stolber (Charlie Brown), Lee Wilson (Patty), Carter Cole (Schroeder), Grant Cowan (Snoopy), Liz O'Neal (Lucy)
The musical was presented in two acts.
The action takes place during an average day in the life of Charlie Brown.

Musical Numbers

Act One: "You're a Good Man, Charlie Brown" (Company); "Schroeder" (Liz O'Neal, Carter Cole); "Snoopy" (Grant Cowan, Dean Stolber); "My Blanket and Me" (Stephen Fenning); "Kite" (Dean Stolber); "Dr. Lucy" ("The Doctor Is In") (Liz O'Neal, Dean Stolber); "Book Report" (Dean Stolber, Liz O'Neal, Stephen Fenning, Carter Cole)
Act Two: "The Red Baron" (Grant Cowan); "T.E.A.M." ("The Baseball Game") (Company); "Glee Club Rehearsal" (Company); "Little Known Facts" (Liz O'Neal, Stephen Fenning, Dean Stolber); "Suppertime" (Grant Cowan); "Happiness" (Company)

You're a Good Man, Charlie Brown originally opened Off Broadway on March 7, 1967, at Theatre 80 St. Marks for a marathon run of 1,597 performances. The small revue-like musical featured a cast of six performers, a five-piece combo, and modest scenery, and it was a major miscalculation to revive it on Broadway. Even the somewhat intimate John Golden Theatre was too large for it, and the musical played for just one month.

The Off-Broadway production was tiresome in its overly cute and twee manner and its out-of-the-mouths-of-babes-and-dog wisdom. The adaptation seemed obvious and predictable, and only once did the evening take off, when Snoopy went into a one-pooch vaudeville routine celebrating the highlight of a dog's day in "Suppertime." This show-stopper was truly inspired and made the rest of the production look routine. But the musical was popular with critics and audiences and it enjoyed a four-year run.

The critics also praised the revival. Douglas Watt in the *New York Daily News* said the musical had a "strange enchantment" and he hoped it would "prosper" in its "new career" on Broadway. Richard Watts in the *New York Post* noted the show had an "enchanting loveableness" about it, while John Schubeck on WABCTV7 found it "clever and cute and truly worth seeing." And although Leonard Probst on WNBC4TV said it was "amusing in a mild way, charming and well done," he felt the "peanut-sized show" worked better in a "peanut-sized theatre."

There are numerous recordings of the score. A concept album was released by MGM Records on its Leo the Lion Records/King Leo Series (LP # LE-900) in 1966, a year before the original Off-Broadway production opened; the album's cast includes Orson Bean (Charlie Brown), Clark Gesner (Linus), Barbara Minkus (Lucy), and Bill Hinnant (Snoopy). There were then two recordings of the 1967 original cast, both released by MGM Records. The first (LP # SIE-9-0C) was recorded live from an early performance at the Theatre 80 St. Marks, and the second (LP # SIE-9-0C-X) in a studio. A television version seen on NBC's *Hallmark Hall of Fame* on February 9, 1973, starred Wendell Burton in the title role and Bill Hinnant from the original cast; the soundtrack was released by Atlantic Records (LP # SD-7252), and it marks the fourth recording in which Hinnant sings the role of Snoopy. A later cartoon version of the musical was telecast by CBS on November 6, 1985, and was released on DVD by Warner Home Video. A studio cast album of the score was released by Pickwick Records (LP # PC-3069 and # SPC-3069).

The script of the musical was published in hardback by Random House in 1968. The London production opened on February 1, 1968, at the Fortune Theatre for 116 performances.

The musical was revived on Broadway for a second time on February 4, 1999, at the Ambassador Theatre for 150 performances; Andrew Lippa wrote two new songs for the production, "Beethoven Day" and the delightful "My New Philosophy," which was sung by Kristin Chenoweth, who won the Tony Award for Best Featured Actress in a Musical (Roger Bart played Snoopy, and he won a Tony for Best Featured Actor in a Musical). The revival was recorded by RCA Victor Records (CD # 09026-63384-2).

The original Off-Broadway production included two songs that were dropped in preproduction or during rehearsals; these were "Queen Lucy" and "Peanuts' Potpourri," and they were replaced by "Glee Club Rehearsal."

There was a musical about Snoopy, but not by Clark Gesner. With lyrics by Hal Hackady and music by Larry Grossman, it premiered in Los Angeles as *Snoopy!!!* in 1976 with Don Potter in the title role (he had also played Snoopy in the 1968 London production of *You're a Good Man, Charlie Brown*). As *Snoopy*, the musical opened Off Broadway at the Lamb's Theatre on December 20, 1982, for 152 performances with David Garrison in the title role. The Off-Broadway production and its 1983 London version were recorded; the Los Angeles production was released on LP and CD by DRG Records (# 6103), and the London version by Polydor (CD # 820247).

JESUS CHRIST SUPERSTAR

Theatre: Mark Hellinger Theatre
Opening Date: October 12, 1971; *Closing Date*: June 30, 1973
Performances: 720
Lyrics: Tim Rice
Music: Andrew Lloyd Webber
Direction: Tom O'Horgan; *Producers*: Robert Stigwood in association with MCA, Inc., and by arrangement with David Land (R. Tyler Gatchell Jr., and Peter Neufeld, Associate Producers); *Scenery*: Robin Wagner; *Costumes*: Randy Barcelo; *Lighting*: Jules Fisher; *Musical Direction*: Marc Pressel
Cast: Ben Vereen (Judas Iscariot), Jeff Fenholt (Jesus of Nazareth), Yvonne Elliman (Mary Magdalene), Alan Braunstein (First Priest), Michael Meadows (Second Priest). Bob Bingham (Caiaphas), Phil Jethro (Annas), Steven Bell (Third Priest), Dennis Buckley (Simon Zealotes, Merchant, Leper), Barry Dennen (Pontius Pilate), Michael Jason (Peter, Merchant, Leper), Linda Rios (Maid by the Fire, Leper), Tom Stovall (Soldier, Judas' Tormentor), Peter Schlosser (Old Man, Apostle, Leper), Paul Sylvan (Soldier, Judas' Tormentor), Paul Ainsley (King Herod, Merchant, Leper), Robin Grean (Cured Leper, Temple Lady), James Sbano (Cured Leper, Apostle, Merchant, Tormentor ["Judas' Death"]), Laura Michaels (Cured Leper, Temple Lady), Clifford Lipson (Cured Leper, Apostle, Merchant, Tormentor ["Judas' Death"]), Bonnie Schon (Cured Leper,

Temple Lady, Reporter), Pi Douglass (Cured Leper, Apostle, Reporter), Celia Brin (Cured Leper, Apostle Woman, Temple Lady), Dennis Cooley (Cured Leper, Apostle, Tormentor ["Judas' Death"]), Anita Morris (Reporter, Apostle Woman, Temple Lady, Leper), Ted Neeley (Reporter, Leper), Kay Cole (Reporter, Apostle Woman, Temple Lady, Leper), Kurt Yaghjian (Reporter, Leper), Margaret Warncke (Reporter, Leper), Willie Windsor (Reporter, Apostle, Leper), Ferne Bork (Reporter, Apostle Woman, Temple Lady, Leper), Samuel E. Wright (Reporter, Apostle, Leper), Denise Delapenha (Apostle Woman, Temple Lady, Leper), Robalee Barnes (Apostle, Merchant, Leper, Reporter), Doug Lucas (Apostle, Leper, Reporter, Tormentor ["Judas' Death"]), Charlotte Crossley (Soul Girl, Leper), Cecelia Norfleet (Soul Girl, Leper), Janet Powell (Soul Girl, Leper), Edward Barton (Judas' Tormentor, Soldier), Tony Gardner (Judas' Tormentor, Soldier); Randall's Island (musicians: Elliott Randall, Guitar, Drums, and Bass; Paul Fleisher, Flute, Saxophone, and Clarinet; Len Herman, Drums, Vibes, and Tympani; Gary King, Bass Guitar; and Pot, All Keyboard Instruments and Flute); Palm Sunday Attendants, Alabaster Monsters, The Mob, and Members of the Crowd: Performed by various members of the cast.

The musical was presented in two acts.

The action takes place during a seven-day period in 33 AD in Bethany, Jerusalem, The Garden of Gethsemane, and on Golgotha.

Musical Numbers

Act One: Overture (Company); "Heaven on Their Minds" (Ben Vereen); "What's the Buzz" (Jeff Fenholt, Yvonne Elliman, Apostles, Apostles' Women); "Strange Thing Mystifying" (Ben Vereen, Jeff Fenholt, Apostles, Apostles' Women); "Everything's Alright" (Yvonne Elliman, Ben Vereen, Jeff Fenholt, Apostles, Apostles' Women); "This Jesus Must Die" (Bob Bingham, Phil Jethro, Priests, Company); "Hosanna" (Bob Bingham, Jeff Fenholt, Company); "Simon Zealotes" (Dennis Buckley, Company); "Poor Jerusalem" (Jeff Fenholt); "Pilate's Dream" (Barry Dennen); "The Temple" (Jeff Fenholt, Company); "I Don't Know How to Love Him" (Yvonne Elliman, Jeff Fenholt); "Damned for All Time" (Ben Vereen, Phil Jethro, Bob Bingham, Priests)

Act Two: "The Last Supper" (Jeff Fenholt, Ben Vereen, Apostles); "Gethsemane" (Jeff Fenholt); "The Arrest" (Michael Jason, Jeff Fenholt, Apostles, Reporters, Bob Bingham, Phil Jethro); "Peter's Denial" (Linda Rios, Michael Jason, Paul Sylvan, Peter Schlosser, Yvonne Elliman); "Pilate and Christ" (Barry Dennen, Paul Sylvan, Jeff Fenholt, Company); "King Herod's Song" (Paul Ainsley); "Could We Start Again, Please" (Yvonne Elliman, Michael Jason); "Judas' Death" (Ben Vereen, Phil Jethro, Bob Bingham); "Trial before Pilate" (Barry Dennen, Bob Bingham, Jeff Fenholt, The Mob); "Superstar" (Ben Vereen, Company); "The Crucifixion" (Jeff Fenholt, Company); "John 19:41" (Orchestra)

Jesus Christ Superstar began as a self-described "rock opera" released by Decca Records on a two-LP set in October 1970, with lyrics by Tim Rice and music by Andrew Lloyd Webber (a year earlier, a single release of the title song had been a hit). Following the sensational success of the single record and the later LP recording (the latter reportedly sold over two-and-a-half-million copies by the time of the musical's Broadway premiere), the score was successfully performed in concert venues, and so a fully staged presentation was almost a given. When the production opened at the Mark Hellinger Theatre (in his program biography, Ben Vereen perhaps presciently noted that "theatre is church," and indeed the Mark Hellinger is now a church), it was a media event with all the attendant hype and hoopla, including a *Time* cover story. But for all its name recognition, the musical had a surprisingly modest run on Broadway, and topped out at 720 performances (musicals of the era that certainly had much less publicity managed to run longer, including ***No, No, Nanette*** with 861 performances and ***Raisin*** with 847).

Jesus Christ Superstar was apparently well-intended in its depiction of "the last seven days in the life of Jesus of Nazareth." Of course, for believers these were not the last seven days of Christ's life, because three days later he arose from the dead and lived on Earth for forty more days before ascending into heaven for eternal life. But the musical wasn't about to get into such fine theological points. As it was, the work was criticized by both Christian and Jewish groups (and both factions picketed the production). The former felt the musical was too flippant in its approach to Christ and too sympathetic to Judas, and the latter regarded the musical as anti-Semitic because it seemed to blame Jews for Christ's crucifixion. And in some quarters there was even criticism because the role of Judas was performed by a black actor (Vereen).

The album was overproduced with grandiose orchestrations and large choral effects, and no doubt the bombastic pomposity of its presentation made the work seem "important" to many listeners. To be sure, some of the music was effective, and it was clever if not slightly cynical of Rice and Lloyd Webber to write a generic boy-and-girl ballad like "I Don't Know How to Love Him" and have it function as a song for Mary Magdalene to sing about Christ. If the music itself bespoke what non-operagoers interpreted as opera-like music, the lyrics adroitly managed to be "relevant," one of the era's favorite words. As a result, the characters sang in anachronistic colloquialisms ("Was that just PR?"; "Walk across my swimming pool"; "You'll escape in the final reel") which no doubt many listeners could "relate" to.

If the album could succeed so well despite (or because of) all its musical frills and furbelows, it's no surprise that the stage version followed its lead with equivalent visual effects to match the musical ones. Director Tom O'Horgan perhaps didn't trust the intrinsic material, and so he and the musical's designers created an over-the-top spectacle, a lavish display for its own sake that also foreshadowed many of the pretentious Euro-pop and Disney-inspired musicals that followed in later years. But in 1971, the Broadway-musical-as-Disneyland-spectacular was something new, and so one must credit (or blame) O'Horgan for starting a trend that exists to this day and that defines what the Broadway musical has become for many, a showcase for special effects with feel-good and familiar material.

The special effects may have had nothing to do with Christ and the days leading up to his crucifixion, but the gimmicks dazzled the public. Christ is first seen as he emerges from a huge chalice-like object; he later ascends from beneath the stage floor on a hidden elevator that propels him high above the stage as a special-effects magical robe unfolds around him and swirls down to the stage floor; and for the crucifixion scene, he and a huge golden cross are projected from the stage and over the audience. The high priests wore monstrous bobble-headed hat wear; Roman soldiers wore masks resembling the robot Gort in the 1951 film *The Day the Earth Stood Still*; and Herod was depicted as a kind of Carmen Miranda drag queen replete with a fancy headdress and the requisite platform shoes. If all this weren't enough, Pontius Pilate made his grand entrance through a giant-sized doorway that resembled the profile of Caesar and contained six sets of eyes (*Time* noted the design had a "throbbing resemblance" to an advertisement for Excedrin headache pills) and above the stage the high priests appeared on a catwalk that seemed to be constructed of dinosaur bones.

The musical was also a rarity in that it was completely sung-through. Although *The Golden Apple* (1954) was completely sung, most such musicals as *Carmen Jones* (1943) and *The Most Happy Fella* (1956) included occasional lines of dialogue. But *Jesus Christ Superstar* institutionalized the Broadway musical as both a spectacle and as a sung-through presentation.

Much was made of the fact that the musical was the first produced on Broadway that had been inspired by a record album (everyone seemed to forget, or didn't know, that 1957's *Shinbone Alley* had been based on the 1955 album *archy and mehitabel* and that 1960s *Beg, Borrow or Steal* had first been conceived as the 1959 album *Clara*; and that Off-Broadway's 1967 ***You're a Good Man, Charlie Brown*** had originated as a concept recording in 1966). A few critics noted that Yvonne Elliman (as Mary Magdalene) was the only carry-over from the album, but the Broadway cast also included Barry Dennen, who had created the role of Pontius Pilate for the recording.

Martin Gottfried in *Women's Wear Daily* said the musical had no "feeling" and "no sense of anything happening in a theatre": it was "simply there." And when Christ arose on the huge elevator in his gargantuan robe, the musical "for all the world" looked as if it belonged in the Easter show at Radio City Music Hall. Leonard Probst on WNBC4TV found the "tasteless" and "tiresome" evening "part put-on, part camp, part passion play and part silly" and suggested Jeff Fenholt's Christ came across as "bored and petulant." Richard Watts in the *New York Post* felt the evening was "commonplace," was never "exciting or moving," and the lyrics "somehow didn't seem an improvement over the King James version."

Time noted the evening's "vulgarity" was "less in the realm of religion than of theatrical taste," but felt that at least audiences who attended the musical were confronted with ideas such as whether Christ is a man or the Son of God rather than wonder "whether Lauren Bacall will lose her boy friend" (this of course a reference to ***Applause***). The review concluded that "things might easily have been worse" because at one point O'Horgan had contemplated a "vinyl-clad, hip Christ crucified on the handle bars of a Harley Davidson" (a variation of this image was used for the artwork of Lloyd Webber's 1996 musical *Whistle Down the Wind*, which closed during its tryout in Washington, D.C., and dealt with a group of children who believe an itinerant man on the lam from the police is actually Christ).

Kevin Sanders on WABCTV7 said *Jesus Christ Superstar* was "possibly the most magnificently staged show ever assembled"; Douglas Watt in the *New York Daily News* found the show a "triumph" and a "stunningly effective theatrical experience"; and George Melloan in the *Wall Street Journal* said the musical was like a "string of exploding firecrackers, each with different sparks," and the evening was a "remarkably fresh retelling" of the familiar story.

The script is included in the 1979 hardback collection *Great Rock Musicals* published by Stein and Day and edited by Stanley Richards and is also included in the releases of the numerous recordings of the score, including the original Decca album, which offered an oversized script in the LP package. Of all the recordings, probably the best is the original 1970 Decca album release (# DXSA-7206).

The London production opened at the Palace Theatre on August 9, 1972, with Paul Nicholas in the title role, and played for 3,358 performances.

The sometimes visually impressive but otherwise tedious film version was released by Universal in 1973; directed by Norman Jewison, the cast included Ted Neeley (Jesus Christ); Carl Anderson (Judas); Joshua Mostel (Herod); and, from the original album and Broadway cast, Yvonne Elliman and Barry Dennen. Neeley had played two small roles in the Broadway production and had been one of Jeff Fenholt's two understudies.

There have been four New York revivals: the first opened at the Longacre Theatre on November 23, 1977, for ninety-six performances (see entry); the next at Madison Square Garden on January 17, 1995, for sixteen performances (Ted Neeley and Carl Anderson reprised their film roles); the third at the Ford Center for the Performing Arts on April 16, 2000, for 161 showings; and the most recent at the Neil Simon Theatre on March 22, 2012, for 116 performances.

Awards

Tony Award Nominations: Best Featured Actor in a Musical (Ben Vereen); Best Score (lyrics by Tim Rice, music by Andrew Lloyd Webber); Best Scenic Designer (Robin Wagner); Best Costume Designer (Randy Barcelo); Best Lighting Designer (Jules Fisher)

AINT SUPPOSED TO DIE A NATURAL DEATH

"TUNES FROM BLACKNESS"

Theatre: Ethel Barrymore Theater (during the run, the musical transferred to the Ambassador Theatre)
Opening Date: October 20, 1971; *Closing Date*: July 30, 1972
Performances: 325
Book, Lyrics, and *Music*: Melvin Van Peebles
Direction: Gilbert Moses; *Producers*: Eugene V. Wolsk, Charles Blackwell, Emanuel Azenberg, and Robert Malina (Howard Friedman, Associate Producer); *Scenery*: Kert Lundell; *Costumes*: Bernard Johnson; *Lighting*: Martin Aronstein; *Musical Direction*: Arthur Jenkins
Cast: Gloria Edwards, Dick Williams, Ralph Wilcox, Barbara Alston, Joe Fields, Marilyn B. Coleman, Arthur French, Carl Gordon, Madge Wells, Lauren Jones, Clebert Ford, Sati Jamal, Jimmy Hayeson, Tony Brealond, Beatrice Winde, Albert Hall, Garrett Morris, Bill Duke, Minnie Gentry; Musicians: Harold Wheeler, Arthur Jenkins, Richard Pratt, Bill Salter, Lloyd Davis, Charles Sullivan, and Robert Corten
The musical was presented in two acts.
The action takes place here and now.

Musical Numbers

Act One: "Just Dont Make No Sense" (Arthur French); "Coolest Place in Town" (Gloria Edwards); "You Can Get Up Before Noon without Being a Square" (Ralph Wilcox); "Mirror Mirror on the Wall" (Joe Fields); "Come Raising Your Leg on Me" (Marilyn B. Coleman); "You Gotta Be Holdin Out Five Dollars on Me" (Carl Gordon, Madge Wells); "Sera Sera Jim" (Lauren Jones); "Catch That on the Corner" (Clebert Ford); "The Dozens" (Jimmy Hayeson); "Funky Girl on Motherless Broadway" (Toney Brealond)

Act Two: "Tenth and Greenwich" (Beatrice Winde); "Heh Heh (Chuckle) Good Mornin Sunshine" (Arthur French); "You Aint No Astronaut" (Jimmy Hayeson); "Three Boxes of Long Please" (Albert Hall); "Lily Done the Zampoughi Every Time I Pulled Her Coattail" (Garrett Morris, Barbara Alston); "I Got the Blood" (Bill Duke); "Salamaggis Birthday" (Dick Williams); "Come on Feet Do Your Thing" (Sati Jamal); "Put a Curse on You" (Minnie Gentry); "Just Don't Make No Sense" (reprise) (Company)

The critics didn't quite know what to make of the apostrophe-challenged *Aint Supposed to Die a Natural Death*, Melvin Van Peebles's self-described "Tunes from Blackness." The revue-like evening consisted of a series of vignettes in monologue style in which the performers mostly spoke or chanted (and only occasionally sang) their numbers to the accompaniment of seven musicians (in some ways, the presentation of the songs was an early version of rap).

Like the earlier ***The Me Nobody Knows*** and the later ***Inner City*** (which opened two months after Van Peebles's revue), the production purportedly depicted life in the ghetto of an inner city slum. Van Peebles's world was filled with pimps, prostitutes, panhandlers, Black Panther types, drug pushers, drunks, lesbians, male hustlers, drag queens, bag ladies, corrupt cops, and convicted murderers. Today, the vignettes verge on parody, and the stories seem awkward and contrived.

The critics were mixed in their assessment of the musical. Douglas Watt in the *New York Daily News* noted there was some "saving humor" to the evening, but otherwise the writing was often "clumsy, repetitious and obscure" and Gilbert Moses's direction was in the manner of "catch-as-catch-can." Richard Watts in the *New York Post* said the production had "agreeable if undistinguished" songs but otherwise "chaos chiefly reigned" and the show was a "confused, confusing and ineffectual black musical drama." T. E. Kalem in *Time* said Van Peebles brought his "bile" to the theatre and left his "craft" at the stage door. The musical was a "jumbled-up" version of Elmer Rice's *Street Scene* with a "torpid" book and "undistinguished" music, and had Van Peebles's ghetto characters been created by a white playwright they'd have been "promptly denounced as racist stereotypes." Kalem said black writers like Van Peebles believe they are "raising welts" on "The Man's conscience" but were in fact simply catering to "assorted liberal breast beaters."

But other critics gushed. Martin Gottfried in *Women's Wear Daily* said the "magnificent" and "tremendously innovative" musical showed the "unmistakable truth" of "something you knew all along." The evening was of the "highest artistic level," one solo dance was "the most fabulous" he'd ever seen, and a rape scene was "nearly unbearable" to watch. For Jack Kroll in *Newsweek*, the show was "one of the most brilliant and significant theatrical explosions that Broadway has seen in years," and Peter J. Rosenwald in the *Wall Street Journal* found the evening an "often compelling and moving theatrical experience." Clive Barnes in the *New York Times* noted that the overall musical effect was sometimes "monotonous" like "an opera with recitative and no arias," but the evening nonetheless had "the power to shock and excite." But he perhaps gave his readers an eye-rolling *oh please!* moment when he concluded that he could "forgive" the musical's "faults" if "it can forgive mine."

A few white critics seemed to suggest they weren't qualified to review the musical. Watts wondered if white critics were "properly equipped" to review "certain" black theatre works, and while Kevin Sanders on WABCTV7 liked the musical, he noted it gave him an "uneasy feeling" and he wondered if that was because he was white. (It may be unfair to overanalyze these comments, but one wonders: Should a non-Jewish critic exempt himself from reviewing *Fiddler on the Roof*? Should a black critic excuse himself from a revival of *The Three Sisters*? Is a male critic unqualified to review *How I Learned to Drive*? Is a female critic unqualified to assess *That Championship Season*?)

The revue came across as a diatribe against white America, most clearly in the final sequence "Put a Curse on You" in which a bag lady (Minnie Gentry) excoriates the audience for being complicit in allowing racism to exist. The character chants her hope that the audience's children will undergo damnation and become junkies and prostitutes, and she hopes rats will climb into their babies' cradles. As she chanted her hateful curses, the lights went up in the theatre and shone on the audience. (The number was performed on the season's Tony Award show, and many television viewers must have reeled in bewilderment over its viperous curses.)

But perhaps a curse on white America is an unfair interpretation of what Van Peebles was trying to convey, because in some ways he seemed to blame everyone, blacks as well as whites. In the opening number

"Just Dont Make No Sense," a character complains that "the man" is there to shoot him (and even city buses won't stop for him), but also notes that his "brothers" are quick to "fat mouth" him down; in fact, "everybody" is "in the race" to keep him in his place. Further, in a seemingly lighthearted sequence ("Lily Done the Zampoughi Every Time I Pulled Her Coattail"), a man remembers how his girlfriend Lily danced herself into a frenzy after they had sex, and as he described their relationship she appeared on a platform and proceeded to dance the Zampoughi. But then we discover he had murdered her and is now facing the chair. And in "Salamaggis Birthday," a black woman is raped by both a white *and* a black cop (the whites in the musical were portrayed by black actors wearing white masks). So Van Peebles seemed to say no one was exempt from the state of the world as he saw it.

The cast album was recorded on a two-LP set by A & M Records (LP # SP-3510), and the script was published in paperback by Bantam Books in 1972.

An early version of the musical was first presented at Sacramento State College, Sacramento, California, in 1970. And like the first two offerings of the season (***You're a Good Man, Charlie Brown*** and ***Jesus Christ Superstar***), the musical had first been introduced on a concept album (in Van Peebles's case, the songs had been heard in, or were inspired by, material in his solo albums *Aint Supposed to Die a Natural Death*, *Brer Soul*, and *As Serious as a Heart-Attack*).

Later in the season, Van Peebles did a complete about-face, and instead of a bitter work like *Aint Supposed to Die a Natural Death* he offered the sunny lark ***Dont Play Us Cheap***. In 1982, his lighthearted musical *Waltz of the Stork* played on Broadway for a few months, apparently under a variation of the Middle or Limited contracts of the 1970s, and two years later as *Waltz of the Stork Boogie* it was briefly revived Off Off Broadway. *Champeen!*, his Off-Off-Broadway musical about Bessie Smith, played for a limited engagement in 1983. During the era, Van Peebles was associated with a musical adaptation of William Makepeace Thackeray's *Vanity Fair*; the work never materialized, but the *New York Times* reported Glenda Jackson was to have starred and that Van Peebles had written the book and had cowritten the lyrics with Mildred Kayden, who had composed the music.

Awards

Tony Award Nominations: Best Musical (*Aint Supposed to Die a Natural Death*); Best Featured Actress in a Musical (Beatrice Winde); Best Director of a Musical (Gilbert Moses); Best Book (Melvin Van Peebles); Best Score (Melvin Van Peebles); Best Scenic Designer (Kert Lundell); Best Lighting Designer (Martin Aronstein)

TO LIVE ANOTHER SUMMER, TO PASS ANOTHER WINTER

"A New Musical from Israel"

Theatre: Helen Hayes Theatre
Opening Date: October 21, 1971; *Closing Date*: March 19, 1972
Performances: 173
Text and *Lyrics*: Hayim Hefer; additional lyrics by Naomi Shemer; lyrics translated mostly by David Paulsen
Music: Dov Seltzer; additional music by David Krivoshei, Alexander Argov, and Naomi Shemer
Direction and *Choreography*: Jonatan (aka Jonathan) Karmon; *Producer*: Leonard Soloway; *Scenery* and *Lighting*: Neil Peter Jampolis; *Costumes*: Lydia Pincus Gany; *Musical Direction*: David Krivoshei
Cast: Rivka Raz, Aric Lavie, Yona Atari, Ili Gorlizki, Hanan Goldblatt; Singers: Abigail Atarri, Lisa Butbul, David Devon, Rafi Ginat, Sarah Golan, Ronit Goldblatt, Moses Goldstein, Lenore Grant, Mordechai Hamer, Yochai Hazani, Judith Rosenberg, Tslila Steren, Hillik Zadok; Dancers: Zvulum Cohen, Constantin Dolgicer, Katya Dror, David Glazer, Nava Harari, Yuval Harat, Hana Kiviti, Ruth Lerman, Joseph Maimon, Ita Oren, Adam Pasternak, Hadassa Shachar, Ofira Tishler, Tuvia Tishler, Efraim Zamir, Miriam Zamir
The revue was presented in two acts.

Musical Numbers

Act One: "Son of Man" (lyric by Hayim Hefer and translated by David Axelrod, music by Dov Seltzer) (Rivka Raz, Aric Lavie, Company); "The Sacrifice" (aka "Come, Angel Come") (lyric by Havim Hefer, music by Dov Seltzer) (Aric Lavie, Yochai Hazani, Company); "What Are the Basic Things?" (translated by Lillian Burstein) (Ili Gorlizki, Company); "The Grove of Eucalyptus" (lyric and music by Naomi Shemer; translated by George Sherman) (Rivka Raz, Company); "The Tradition That Was Destroyed: Hasidic Medley" (the sequence included "Yevurachacha," "Yedid nefesh," "Vehuhair lebenue," and "Dance") (music by Sarah and Ehud Zweig, David Weinkranz, and Rabbi Carlibach) (Hanan Goldblatt, Ili Gorlizki, Rivka Raz, Yona Atari, Company); "The Boy with the Fiddle" (lyric by Hayim Hefer, music by Alexander Argov) (Aric Lavie); "Can You Hear My Voice?" (lyric by Rachel and translated by George Sherman, music by Samuel Kraus) (Yona Atari, Company); "Mediteranee" (lyric by Hayim Hefer, music by Dov Seltzer) (Company); "When My Man Returns" (lyric by Hayim Hefer, music by George Moustaki) (Rivka Raz); "Better Days" (lyric by Hayim Hefer, music by Dov Seltzer) (Yona Atari, Company); "Tha'am Haze" (lyric by Hayim Hefer, music by Dov Seltzer) (Company)

Act Two: "To Live Another Summer, to Pass Another Winter" (lyric by Hayim Hefer, music by Dov Seltzer) (Yona Atari, Aric Lavie, Hanan Goldblatt, Rivka Raz, Company); "Hora Hora" (music by Alexander Argov) (Company); "Noah's Ark" (music by Naomi Shemer) (Ili Gorlizki); "Don't Destroy the World" (lyric by Hayim Hefer in collaboration with Hayim Guri, music by Dov Seltzer) (Aric Lavie); "Give Shalom and Sabbath to Jerusalem" (lyric by Hayim Hefer, music by Dov Seltzer) (Company); "Sorry We Won It" (lyric by Hayim Hefer, music by David Krivoshei) (Ili Gorlizki, Yona Atari, Hanan Goldblatt); "I'm Alive" (lyric by Hayim Hefer, music by David Krivoshei) (Rivka Raz, Company); "Give Me a Star" (lyric by Hayim Hefer, music by David Krivoshei) (Rivka Raz, Aric Lavie, Company); Finale (Company)

Jonatan (aka Jonathan) Karmon's Israeli revue *To Live Another Summer, to Pass Another Winter* was soon followed by ***Only Fools Are Sad***. Both productions originated in Tel Aviv, both ran for a few months in New York, and both dealt with various aspects of the Jewish experience. The former looked mostly at life in modern Israel, while the latter concentrated on the Hassidic movement of the eighteenth century. And while the former had a large cast of singers and dancers, all of whom were from Israel, the latter was a small production with six performers.

The *New York Times* reported that *To Live Another Summer* was "designed for export" to the United States, and when it "previewed" in English in Tel Aviv it became a "foreign language production in its own country" in anticipation of the U.S. engagement. The revue had in fact "been written in Hebrew, but was translated into English before it was ever performed." Karmon noted that one number ("Hora Hora," which had originally been titled "Hora Schnora") looked at American financial contributions to Israel: Americans say they never tire of giving, and the Israelis reply they never get tired of asking. The song went over well in Tel Aviv, but the word "schnorrer" caused a problem in New York because in the United States the word had pejorative connotations (see ***King of Schnorrers***). As a result, the title was changed but the words of the song remained the same.

The critics were divided on the merits of the revue, but it nonetheless managed a five-month run, and like ***Aint Supposed to Die a Natural Death***, ***Dont Play Us Cheap***, and ***Two Gentlemen of Verona*** it was recorded on a two-LP cast album. The recording was released by Buddah Records (LP # BDS-95004) and included all the lyrics. During the run, the song "I Wanted to Be a Hero" (music by David Krivoshei) was added to the score and was performed by Hanan Goldblatt and David Devon; it wasn't included on the cast album.

Douglas Watt in the *New York Daily News* said the "semi-rock" revue flowed "smoothly with artful simplicity and unpretentiousness." The "cheering entertainment" included the sorrowful "The Boy with a Fiddle," who was forced to play while his family was taken away to a concentration camp, and the tongue-in-cheek "Sorry We Won It" apologized for Israel's victory in the Six-Day War. Richard Watts in the *New York Post* liked the "moving and enthralling" production, and was impressed by its "joy, humor and zestfulness." Watt had mentioned how impressed he was by a "lovely" unidentified blonde dancer who held his "attention every moment she's on the stage," and Watts too described her as "the loveliest young woman I've seen on the stage in a long time" and noted that he discovered her name was Ruth Lerman. George Melloan in the *Wall Street Journal* found the evening "specialized fare," but said it was "delightful" and "pleasant," and Louis Botto on WNBC4TV found the revue "entertaining."

Leonard Harris on WCBSTV2 said the production was "disappointing" because it didn't seem "distinctively Israeli" or "distinctively anything." In fact, much of the music was reminiscent of "Las Vegas International rock," a style to be "avoided in nightclubs all over the world." Kevin Sanders on WABCTV7 found the revue "uneven" and suggested that at times its title could have been *The Gold Diggers Visit the Kibbutz*. He liked the "upbeat" songs and dances but otherwise felt there was a "repetitive sameness" to much of the material. Martin Gottfried in *Women's Wear Daily* supposed the revue was "perfectly harmless" but its appeal to its target audience was "crude" and "insulting." He resented the evening's "cheap sentiment" and noted it was "inadequate entertainment at Broadway price levels."

Clive Barnes in the *New York Times* felt the revue had "an endearing vitality and an enduring spirit." The production was "wry" and "sentimental," and even its "propaganda" had "a certain self-mockery to it that only an Arab could hate." The staging and dancing were "bright and energetic," the design was 'imaginative," and while the show wasn't meant to be a "slam-bang musical extravaganza" it was nonetheless "a pleasant" and "beguiling" work.

Director and choreographer Jonatan Karmon brought a total of six Jewish-oriented revues to New York over a period of fourteen years. The 1962 dance revue *Karmon Israeli Dancers* was followed by *The Grand Music Hall of Israel* (1968) and *The New Grand Music Hall of Israel* (1969), and after *To Live Another Summer, to Pass Another Winter* he offered a new version of ***The Grand Music Hall of Israel*** in 1973 as well as the revue ***Don't Step on My Olive Branch*** (1976).

ON THE TOWN

Theatre: Imperial Theatre
Opening Date: October 31, 1971; *Closing Date*: January 1, 1972
Performances: 73
Book and *Lyrics*: Betty Comden and Adolph Green
Music: Leonard Bernstein
Based on an idea by Jerome Robbins (and by his and Leonard Bernstein's 1944 ballet *Fancy Free*).
Direction and *Choreography*: Ron Field (Michael Shawn, Assistant Choreographer); *Producers*: Jerry Schlossberg-Vista Productions (A Ron Field Production) (Rick Mandell and Allen Litke, Associate Producers); *Scenery*: James Trittipo; *Costumes*: Ray Aghayan and Bob Mackie; *Lighting*: Tharon Musser; *Musical Direction*: Milton Rosenstock
Cast: David Wilder (Workman, S. Uperman), Jess Richards (Chip), Remak Ramsay (Ozzie), Ron Husmann (Gabey), Carol Petri (Flossie), Marybeth Kurdock (Flossie's Friend), Don Croll (Bill Poster, MC at Congacabana, MC at Congo Cabana), Zoya Leporska (Little Old Lady), Orrin Reiley (Announcer, Figment), Donna McKechnie (Ivy Smith), Bernadette Peters (Hildy), Phyllis Newman (Claire), Fran Stevens (Maude P. Dilly), Tom Avera (Pitkin), Marilyn Cooper (Lucy Schmeeler), Gina Paglia (Gina Henie), Sandra Dorsey (Diana Dream), Laura Kenyon (Senorita Dolores), Larry Merritt (Bimmy), John Mineo (Coney Island Zoot Suit Dancer), Tony Stevens (Coney Island Zoot Suit Dancer): Singers: Martha Danielle, Sandra Dorsey, Bobbi Franklin, Laura Kenyon, Gail Nelson, Marie Santell, Don Croll, Richard Marr, Orrin Reiley, Dennis Roth, Luke Stover, David Wilder, Craig Yates; Dancers: Carole (Kelly) Bishop, Eileen Casey, Jill Cook, Nancy Dalton, Marybeth Kurdock, Nancy Lynch, Gina Paglia, Pamela Peadon, Carol Petri, Andy Bew, Paul Charles, Larry Merritt, John Mineo, Jeff Phillips, Ken Scalice, Doug Spingler, Tony Stevens, Chester Walker
The musical was presented in two acts.
The entire action takes place in New York City during twenty-four hours on a June day in 1944.

Musical Numbers

Act One: "I Feel Like I'm Not Out of Bed Yet" (David Wilder, Male Singers); "New York, New York" (Jess Richards, Remak Ramsay, Ron Husmann); "Miss Turnstiles Ballet" (Contestants, Donna McKechnie, Manhattanites); "Come Up to My Place" (Bernadette Peters, Jess Richards); "(I Get) Carried Away" (Phyllis Newman, Remak Ramsay); "Lonely Town" (Ron Husmann, New Yorkers); "Do-Do-Re-Do" (Donna

McKechnie, Fran Stevens, Teachers, Students); "I Can Cook, Too" (Bernadette Peters, Jess Richards); "Lucky to Be Me" (Ron Husmann, New Yorkers); "Times Square Ballet" (Entire Company)

Act Two: "*So Long, Baby* Ice Revue" (Gina Paglia, Skaters); "Nightclub Song" (aka "I'm Blue" and "I Wish I Was Dead") (Sandra Dorsey); "Nightclub Song" (Spanish version) (Laura Kenyon); "You Got Me" (Phyllis Newman, Remak Ramsay, Bernadette Peters, Jess Richards); "I Understand" (Tom Avera, Marilyn Cooper); "Playground of the Rich Ballet" (Ron Husmann, Donna McKechnie, High Society Dancers); "Some Other Time" (Phyllis Newman, Bernadette Peters, Jess Richards, Remak Ramsay); "Coney Island Hep Cats" (Carol Petri, Friends, Zoot Suit Dancers); "New York, New York" (reprise) (Entire Company)

The revival of *On the Town* came along as the so-called nostalgia craze was in full swing. The critics were generally kind, but for some reason the production didn't go over well with audiences and was gone in two months. Despite its richly melodic score by Leonard Bernstein, its ample opportunities for comedy, and its emphasis on a wide range of dance styles, the public has never viewed the musical as a classic, must-see title. Maybe a big-name star would have helped the current production; although the talented cast boasted many established as well as up-and-coming names (there was one Tony Award winner in the company, and four future Tony winners), they weren't big enough to attract the ticket-buyers.

Although the musical was a long-running hit in 1944, its revivals have been problematic. Most of them, including the current one, topped out at about seventy performances. The national tour that followed the original production met with indifferent business; an Off-Broadway revival at the Carnegie Hall Playhouse opened on January 15, 1959, and played for seventy performances; the current revival lasted for seventy-three showings; a November 19, 1998, revival at the Gershwin Theatre ran for sixty-five; and the belated London premiere opened at the Prince of Wales Theatre on May 30, 1963, for fifty-three performances.

A third Broadway revival opened on October 16, 2014, at the Lyric Theatre (Ben Brantley in the *New York Times* praised the "jubilant" production and noted its "jelly bean hues" made "vintage Technicolor look pallid"). As of this writing, the revival is still running and perhaps will break the jinx (it's already the longest-running revival of the show).

On the Town was inspired by the ballet *Fancy Free* (choreography by Jerome Robbins and music by Leonard Bernstein), which premiered at the Metropolitan Opera House on April 18, 1944. The Broadway production opened later in the year; Robbins choreographed, and the book and lyrics were by Betty Comden and Adolph Green.

The musical took place in New York during a twenty-four-hour period in which three sailors on shore leave prowl about the town for romantic adventure (one lyric noted "there's just one thing that's important in Manhattan / When you have just one day"). Chip (Jess Richards) becomes entangled with man-eating taxi-driver Hildy (Bernadette Peters), and Ozzie (Remak Ramsay) hooks up with wacky anthropologist Claire (Phyllis Newman), but Gabey (Ron Husmann) has fallen in love with the photograph of Miss (Subway) Turnstiles of the Month Ivy Smith (Donna McKechnie). Much of the evening was devoted to Gabey, his pals, and their gals in search of the elusive Ivy, whom they finally track down in Coney Island. By dawn, the three couples must part, and the unspoken background of the war hovers over the proceedings. But they all hope they'll meet again "Some Other Time," which was a lovely, understated ballad performed at the end of the musical.

The score also offered two spectacular ballads for Gabey, the blues "Lonely Town" and the joyous "Lucky to Be Me"; amusing comedy songs for Hildy, "Come Up to My Place" and "I Can Cook, Too"; a mock-operetta spoof for Claire and Ozzie, "I Get Carried Away"; and a satire of nightclub songs ("I'm Blue"). The musical's most famous number is "New York, New York" ("it's a helluva town") in which the gobs salute the city and its promise of adventure and romance. Bernstein also created sinuously bluesy and swinging dance music; one depicted an evening in Times Square ("Times Square Ballet"), another a subway trip to Coney Island, and two dances contrasted an imaginary and a real Coney Island, the former a so-called playground of the rich (the script described a "dreamy void of blue" in which sophisticated men and "unattainable" women dance "easily and coldly"), the latter a "gaudy honky-tonk sort of place."

When the revival opened, New York City was at its nadir, and some of the critics were in a sour mood as they compared the cheery and optimistic city of the past with the blighted one of the present. Jack Kroll in *Newsweek* noted the revival played to a city "reeling in a slow vertigo of decay" in which the old "helluva town" now felt "a lot like hell"; Martin Gottfried in *Women's Wear Daily* said the original production reflected a time of national confidence and "security," but the present-day country was one of "insecurity" and

Broadway itself was "inactive and stumbling"; and George Melloan in the *Wall Street Journal* warned that the musical evoked "the memory of another and better New York" and "any evocation of the past always risks the danger of being mismatched with the mood of the present."

But many of the critics noted the evening captured the lighthearted mood of the 1940s with its zoot suits, reet pleats, shoulder pads, upswept hairdos, wedgies, platforms, and snoods, and they praised the rich music and sparkling lyrics. Gottfried liked the "show business vernacular" and "technical depth" of Bernstein's music and the "affecting" book and lyrics by Comden and Green, and while T. E. Kalem in *Time* thought the revival was a "dud," he enjoyed the "peppy dissonances and romantic melodic line" of Bernstein's score.

According to Gottfried, Ron Field's choreography had "agreeable stretches" and occasionally reached "moments of real interest," but he just wasn't "fertile enough" to create inventive dances that added up to thirty minutes of playing time. Kalem said Field "enlarged the definition of chutzpah by re-choreographing Jerome Robbins's dance numbers," and Kroll noted the choreography was "safe and acceptable" and sometimes "pleasant and rousing" but nonetheless lacked "the galvanic freshness of real style." He also felt Field failed to utilize the skills of Donna McKechnie, whom he hailed as "the most electrifying dancer in show business."

Kroll also complained that the three male leads were bland "like interchangeable vanilla popsicles" in their Navy whites, and Richard Watts in the *New York Post* suggested Bernadette Peters would have been more effective had she "calmed down a bit." Walter Kerr in the *New York Times* criticized Peters's lipstick, makeup, and hairdo, noting "she doesn't look period, she looks terrible" and that she resembled Mae Murray, a silent film star of the 1920s. He also mentioned that Phyllis Newman was forced to wear a tailored suit that "should be sent directly back to the tailor."

During the tryout, Kurt Peterson (Gabey) and Bill Gerber (Ozzie) were replaced by Ron Husmann and Remak Ramsay.

The original production opened at the Adelphi Theatre on December 28, 1944, for 463 performances. Decca Records released a sort-of cast album (issued on a 78 RPM set, and then later on LP # DL-8030) that was a combination of original cast members (Betty Comden, Adolph Green, and Nancy Walker) and Mary Martin (who sang Gabey's songs!); the album was paired with selections from *Lute Song*, which opened in 1946 and starred Martin. The London cast album (which included Elliott Gould as Ozzie) was issued on LP by CBS Records (# SAPG-60005) and on CD by Sony/Masterworks Broadway/Arkiv (# 500728); a studio cast by Stet Records (LP # DS-150129) included many songs written for the film version (see below); a 1993 concert production was released by Deutsche Grammophon (CD # 437-516-2) in the horrid era of "crossover" recordings (in this case, everyone in the world from opera singers Samuel Ramey and Evelyn Lear to Broadway Baby David Garrison to jazz song stylist Cleo Laine to actress Tyne Daly); a complete two-CD 1996 studio cast album issued by Jay Records (CDJAY2-1231) includes the almost-forgotten "I Understand" (aka "Pitkin's Song"); and the 2014 revival was released on a two-CD set by PS Classics (# PS-1525). The unused "Ain't Got No Tears Left" is included in the collection *Leonard Bernstein's New York* (Nonesuch CD #79400-2), and another unused number "Dream with Me" has surfaced in at least two collections, including *Leonard Bernstein: Arias and Barcarolles, Songs and Duets* (Koch CD # 3-7000-2).

The best recording of the score is a 1960 release by Columbia Records (LP # OL-5540/# OS-2028; issued by Sony Classical/Columbia/Legacy on CD # SK-60538) that includes original Broadway cast members Betty Comden, Adolph Green, Nancy Walker, and Cris Alexander as well as John Reardon and Michael Kermoyan; Leonard Bernstein conducts.

The script was published in hardback in 1997 as part of the collection *The New York Musicals of Comden and Green* (Applause Books) which also includes the scripts of *Wonderful Town* (1953) and *Bells Are Ringing* (1956) but sadly ignores *Subways Are for Sleeping* (1961). The script was also published in 2014 by the Library of Congress in the hardback collection *American Musicals*, which includes the scripts of fifteen other shows. Carol J. Oja's *Bernstein Meets Broadway: Collaborative Art in a Time of War* (Oxford University Press, 2014) provides information about the musical's background.

The 1949 film version by MGM was notable for its lively cast, which included Gene Kelly (Gabey), Frank Sinatra (Chip), Jules Munshin (Ozzie), Vera-Ellen (Ivy), Ann Miller (Claire), Betty Garrett (Hildy), and, reprising her Broadway role, Alice Pearce as Lucy Schmeeler. In a major departure from sound-stage-bound filming, some scenes were filmed in New York, and the real and studio New York locations blend well together and look like a Technicolor dream. Unfortunately, only three songs were retained from the stage production ("New York, New York," "Come Up to My Place," and, surprisingly, "I Feel Like I'm Not Out of Bed Yet") along with some of Bernstein's dance music. Comden and Green supplied new lyrics for new songs by Roger

Edens, and while pleasant enough they're not particularly distinguished. The soundtrack album was released by Show Biz Records (LP # 5603).

Awards

Tony Award Nomination: Best Featured Actress in a Musical (Bernadette Peters)

THE GRASS HARP

"A New Musical"

Theatre: Martin Beck Theatre
Opening Date: November 2, 1971; *Closing Date*: November 6, 1971
Performances: 6
Book and *Lyrics*: Kenward Elmslie
Music: Claibe Richardson; dance and incidental music by John Berkman
Based on the 1951 novella by Truman Capote (which he adapted for the stage in 1952).
Direction: Ellis Rabb; *Producers*: Theatre 1972 (Richard Barr, Charles Woodward, and Michael Harvey; Michael Kasdan, Associate Producer) (A University of Michigan Professional Theatre Program Production); *Choreography*: Rhoda Levine; *Scenery* and *Lighting*: James Tilton; *Costumes*: Nancy Potts; *Musical Direction*: Theodore Saidenberg
Cast: *Barbara Cook* (Dolly Talbo), Russ (Rusty) Thacker (Collin Talbo), *Carol Brice* (Catherine Creek), *Ruth Ford* (Verena Talbo), Christine Stabile (Maude Riordan), *Max Showalter* (Doctor Morris Ritz), John Baragrey (Judge Cool), *Karen Morrow* (Babylove); The Heavenly Pride and Joys: Kelly Boa, Trudy Bordoff, Colin Duffy, Eva Grant, and David Craig Moskin; Harvey Vernon (Sheriff Amos Legrand)
The musical was presented in one act.
The action takes place in the past, at the Talbo House in Joy City, and in River Woods.

Musical Numbers

"Dropsy Cure Weather" (Barbara Cook, Carol Brice, Russ Thacker); "This One Day" (Russ Thacker); "This One Day" Dance (Russ Thacker, Christine Stabile); "Think Big Rich" (Max Showalter); "If There's Love Enough" (Carol Brice); "Yellow Drum" (Barbara Cook, Carol Brice, Russ Thacker); "Marry with Me" (Carol Brice); "I'll Always Be in Love" (aka "Chain of Love") (Barbara Cook); "Floozies" (Russ Thacker); *The Babylove Miracle Show*: (a) "Call Me Babylove" (Karen Morrow); (b) "Walk into Heaven" (Karen Morrow); (c) "Hang a Little Moolah on the Washline" (Karen Morrow, The Heavenly Pride and Joys); (d) "Talkin' in Tongues" (Karen Morrow, Carol Brice); and (e) "Whooshin' through My Flesh" (Karen Morrow, Carol Brice, Barbara Cook, Russ Thacker, Company); "Walk into Heaven" (reprise) (Karen Morrow); "Something for Nothing" (Max Showalter); "(The) Indian Blues" (Carol Brice, Company); "Take a Little Sip" (Russ Thacker, Barbara Cook, Carol Brice, Christine Stabile, Company); "Yellow Drum" (reprise) (Company); "What Do I Do Now (He's Gone)" (Ruth Ford); "Pick Yourself a Flower" (Karen Morrow, Company); "The Flower Fortune Dance" (Company); "Reach Out" (Barbara Cook, Company)

The wispy plot of Truman Capote's 1951 novella *The Grass Harp*, his 1952 stage adaptation, and its current musical version was a fey one about two quaint Southern sisters, the childlike and fanciful Dolly Talbo (Barbara Cook) and the somewhat avaricious but essentially kind Verena Talbo (Ruth Ford). Gypsies once gave Dolly a secret recipe for the dropsy, and so she carefully guards it from prying eyes. But Verena and her con-man suitor Doctor Ritz (Max Showalter) see commercial possibilities in the potion, which could make them all rich. Dolly refuses to give up the recipe and moves into a tree house with the Talbo's black house servant Catherine (Carol Brice), who believes she's an Indian princess, and Dolly's cousin Collin (Russ Thacker), a young man whom the sisters adopted when he was a boy. When Verena realizes Doctor Ritz is a fraud, she reconciles with Dolly and joins the clan in the tree house. It was *that* kind of story, and for many its eccentricities were too twee, too precious, and too calculated for comfort.

Many have made the case for Kenward Elmslie and Claibe Richardson's score. The songs are pleasant, and the lovely ballad "Chain of Love" (aka "I'll Always Be in Love") and the stirring march "Yellow Drum" are outstanding; the "Indian Blues" is genuinely quirky; and the extended musical sequence "The Babylove Miracle Show" is ambitious. But the score never quite captured the necessary magic required of what is essentially a delicate fable, and it was sometimes too obvious, such as the lively if generic "Floozies."

The critics were generally unimpressed, and the musical closed after its first week. The headline of Douglas Watt's review in the *New York Daily News* proclaimed, "Good Cast Climbs Goo-Goo Tree to Play Stringless *Grass Harp*." The "cloying nonsense," was "so soft and sweet you could poke your finger through it" and was "just a lopsided ball of cotton candy." Richard Watts in the *New York Post* found the work "tasteful and pleasantly unpretentious," but noted it was also unexciting and soon became "tiresome" in its lack of "dramatic vividness." Martin Gottfried in *Women's Wear Daily* noted the evening lasted for ninety minutes, which was short for a musical but "nowhere near short enough." The adaptation was "clumsy," the direction only added "lethargy and uncertainty" to the proceedings, and the score was "trite." But the tree house setting was "marvelously striking," and Barbara Cook had "the most beautiful voice in all of theatre" but "shamed it in application to this tripe."

Clive Barnes in the *New York Times* said the musical was as difficult to like as to dislike, and the evening generally suffered from "mawkish sentimentality." Although the score wasn't "memorable," it wasn't "entirely forgettable"; at its best it had a "country-and-banjo jauntiness" and at its worst was similar to "the background music to an agrarian documentary on educational television."

But Louis Botto on WNBC4TV found the show "magical" and the score "enchanting," and felt it was "offbeat" in its "originality." Kevin Sanders on WABCTV7 said the "great" evening was the "most delightful" musical to open during the season; it was a "sheer delight" and "Yellow Drum" was "destined to be a big hit."

Perhaps Steven Suskin in *More Opening Nights on Broadway* said it best: in the opening sequence the musical "covered itself in weeds" when Barbara Cook announced it was "dropsy-cure weather." Suskin noted there was "something sublimely ridiculous" about the very word *dropsy* and so whether the show was good or bad the sound of the word immediately "lost the audience" and "everything that followed seemed just plain silly."

Like the musical version, the nonmusical stage adaptation also opened at the Martin Beck Theatre, where it premiered on March 27, 1952, and played for thirty-six performances; the cast included Mildred Natwick (Dolly), Ruth Nelson (Verena), Johnny Stewart (Collin), George Burke (Catherine), Jonathan Harris (Doctor Ritz), Russell Collins (Judge Cool), and Alice Pearce (as Babylove, the eccentric evangelist). The play included incidental music by Virgil Thomson.

The musical's world premiere took place on December 26, 1967, at the Trinity Square Repertory Theatre's Rhode Island School of Design Theatre in Providence, Rhode Island. The cast included Barbara Baxley (Dollyheart, as the character was then called), Skip Hinnant (Collin), Carol Brice (Catherine), David Doyle (Doctor Ritz), Elaine Stritch (Babylove), and Carol Bruce (Verena). The production was directed by Adrian Hall and was presented in three acts. Numbers heard in this version that were not used in the Broadway production were: "Spit 'n' Whittle," "Miss Got Rocks," "A Genteel Sufficiency of Abundance," "Them as Has Gits," "Cool, Cool Elbow," "One Thing in Particular," "It Takes All Kinds," "Brazil," "I Trust the Wrong People," "Yoofry," "Pink," "Where's My Sister?," and "I Want to Go Home." The song "Dollyheart's Genuine Gypsy Drop Cure" seems to have been an early title for "Dropsy Cure Weather."

The musical was next produced in October 1971 by the University of Michigan's Professional Theatre Program at the Power Center for the Performing Arts in Ann Arbor; the song "The One and Only Person in the World" was cut, and Celeste Holm, who played the role of Babylove, was succeeded by Karen Morrow for New York.

Between the Rhode Island and Michigan productions, *Newsweek*'s preview of the 1969–1970 theatre season noted that the musical would open on Broadway in January 1970 as *The Yellow Drum* with Barbara Cook in the cast and Ellis Rabb as director. The article mentioned that "pop singer Mama Cass Elliot may make her acting debut as an unorthodox lady evangelist."

The script was published in softcover by Samuel French in an undated but probably 1972 edition. The cast album was recorded by Painted Smiles Records (LP # PS-1354), and later released on CD (# PSCD-102). *Kenward Elmslie Revisited* (Painted Smiles Records LP # PS-1339) includes three cut songs from *The Grass Harp*: "The One and Only Person in the World" (Max Showalter), "Brazil" (George Rose), and "I Trust the Wrong People" (Elaine Stritch). The cast album of the Painted Smiles CD includes the *Revisited* track of Showalter's number as well as five songs from Elmslie and Claibe Richardson's *Lola*, which was produced Off

Off Broadway by the York Theatre Company in 1982. The cast album of *The Grass Harp* was later reissued by Varese Sarabande Records (# VSD-6010) and includes as bonus tracks the songs performed by Rose and Stritch on the *Revisited* recording.

On June 19, 1977, CBS presented a thirty-minute segment about the musical on *Camera Three*, which included interviews with cast members (including Barbara Cook, Carol Brice, and Ruth Ford) and a few songs from the production.

The musical was revived Off Broadway at the York Playhouse on November 16, 1979, for a limited engagement of sixteen performances and included "The One and Only Person in the World" for Judge Cool. The musical was later revived Off Off Broadway by the Apple Corps Theatre in the early 1980s in a showcase production (which also included "The One and Only Person in the World").

There were three nonmusical adaptations of the original play for television. The first was produced by NBC on the *Kraft Television Theatre* on September 17, 1952, a few months after the play had closed; the cast included Broadway members Mildred Natwick (Dolly) and Russell Collins (Doctor Ritz); another version (which at least one source erroneously attributes to the *Play of the Week* series) was telecast on December 11, 1957; and a *Play of the Week* version was seen on March 28, 1960; the latter's direction was by Word Baker a few weeks before he directed the original production of *The Fantasticks*, and Lillian Gish (Dolly), Carmen Matthews (Verena), and original 1952 cast members Russell Collins (Doctor Ritz) and Georgia Burke (Catherine) were among the performers. A nonmusical theatrical film was released by Fine Line Features in 1996 with Piper Laurie (Dolly), Sissy Spacek (Verena), Walter Matthau (Judge Cool), Nell Carter (Catherine), Jack Lemmon (Doctor Ritz), Edward Furlong (Collin), and Mary Steenbergen in the Babylove role.

Perhaps a successful musical version of a Capote work is not to be. Despite its glorious score, *House of Flowers* (1954) played for just a few months on Broadway (and its 1968 Broadway revival lasted a few weeks), and David Merrick abruptly closed *Holly Golightly/Breakfast at Tiffany's* (1966) during its New York preview period. There have been three lyric versions of Capote's 1956 short story "A Christmas Memory" (two musicals, and one opera), but they don't seem to have made much of an impression. However, the story's 1966 nonmusical television adaptation on *ABC Stage 67* was touching, and its main characters were those depicted in *The Grass Harp* (that is, two sisters and the young boy). Geraldine Page was memorable as the simple, loving sister who announces that it's "fruitcake weather," and so she and the boy proceed to gather the necessary ingredients to make their annual fruitcakes to send to President Roosevelt and others on their fruitcake list. Fruitcake weather was clearly more welcome than dropsy-cure weather.

ONLY FOOLS ARE SAD

"ISRAEL'S PRIZE-WINNING MUSICAL"

Theatre: Edison Theatre
Opening Date: November 22, 1971; *Closing Date*: March 26, 1972
Performances: 144
Text: Dan Almagor; translated by Shimon Wincelberg and Valerie Arnon
Lyrics: Translated by Robert Friend
Music: Derived from Hassidic songs and arranged by Yohanan Zarai and Gil Aldema
Direction: Yossi Yzraely; *Producer*: Yaacov Agmon; *Scenery*: Dani Karavan (scenery supervised by Herbert Senn); *Costumes*: Ruth Dar (costumes supervised by Helen Pond); *Lighting*: Yehiel Orgal (lighting supervised by Robert Brand); *Musical Direction*: Not credited
Cast: Galia Ishay, Danny Litanny, Don Maseng, Shlomo Nitzan, Michal Noy, Aviva Schwarz
The revue was presented in two acts.

Sketches and Musical Numbers

Act One: "Once There Was a Melody . . ." (Company); "Isaac, The Baker" ("The Treasure") (Narrators: Danny Litanny, Michal Noy; Isaac: Galia Ishay); "A Merry Melody" (Company); "Berl, The Tailor" ("Opening a New Account") (Berl: Don Maseng; Rabbi Levy Itzhak: Shlomo Nitzan); "The Promise That Was Kept" (Narrator: Danny Litanny); "Don't Suck the Bones" (Narrator: Shlomo Nitzan); "Eat, Lord, and Enjoy"

(Narrator: Michal Noy); "Tell Me What the Rain Is Saying" (Soloist: Aviva Schwarz); "Don't Sell It Cheap" (Narrator: Shlomo Nitzan); "A Drinking Song" (Soloist: Don Maseng); "The Ten Ruble Note" (Narrator: Shlomo Nitzan); "Kol rinah vishu'ah" (Company); "Gedaliah, The Tar Maker" (Narrator: Aviva Schwarz; Rabbi Israel Ba'al Shem Tov: Shlomo Nitzan; Gedeliah: Danny Litanny)

Act Two: "The Goat" (Narrators: Don Maseng, Michal Noy; The Son: Galia Ishay); "Forest, Forest" (Soloist: Michal Noy); "Smoking on the Sabbath" (Narrator: Shlomo Nitzan); "Bim-Bam-Bom" (Company); "Waiting for the Messiah" (Narrator: Michael Noy; Rabbi Moshe Teitelbaum: Don Maseng); "Haim, The Goose-Herder" (Galia Ishay); "Getzl, The Shoemaker (Aleph . . . Beth)" (Danny Litanny); "The Rabbi Who Promised to Wait" (Narrator: Shlomo Nitzan); "A Letter to the Rabbi" (Soloist: Don Maseng); "Angel, Angel . . ." (Galia Ishay); "Only Fools Are Sad" (Soloist: Aviva Schwarz); "Avreymele Melamed" (Soloists: Danny Litanny, Shlomo Nitzan, and Don Maseng); "A Sabbath Song" (Soloist: Shlomo Nitzan); "And God Said Unto Jacob" (Soloist: Danny Litanny)

Like ***To Live Another Summer, to Pass Another Winter***, which had opened a month earlier, *Only Fools Are Sad* was a revue that consisted of songs and stories about Jewish life. The former emphasized Jewish life in modern-day Israel while the latter looked at the Hassidic population in Europe during the eighteenth century. It was performed by a six-member cast who spoke almost entirely in English but with a smattering of Yiddish, and was based on Hassidic songs, stories, fables, and parables. Both revues played for about half the season.

Only Fools Are Sad first premiered in Tel Aviv in October 1968 as *Ish Hassid haya* (*Once There Was a Hassid*), and according to the program notes it was performed in cities throughout Israel for a total of 650 performances. The Israeli cast recording was issued by AP Records (LP # AP-332).

James Davis in the *New York Daily News* suggested the "pleasant" but "placid" evening would have been better served in the concert hall because the "lightweight" material wasn't particularly theatrical. (In fact, if photos from the Tel Aviv and New York productions are any indication, the cast members had the look of the era's hippies, and so perhaps the Broadway production might have been better suited to a Village cabaret setting.)

Kevin Sanders on WABCTV7 found the material "mildly pleasant" but "thin and dry," and said it was reminiscent of children's television shows "before *Sesame Street*." He noted the production was like hearing a full evening of Irish folk songs about the potato revolution and thus it didn't seem to "have enough general relevance." Clive Barnes in the *New York Times* remarked that the "gentle celebration" was "endearing and happy," and while non-Jewish audiences would enjoy it, "a touch of Jewish blood" wouldn't hurt (particularly in a sequence that joked about the differences between citrons and lemons).

Richard Watts in the *New York Post* said the production was a "disarming little entertainment," but the folk tales told in ***Story Theatre*** fashion were a "little monotonous" and he suspected the evening would be most enjoyed by those familiar with Hassidic tradition. Martin Gottfried in *Women's Wear Daily* said the revue was "remarkably reminiscent" of the "Greenwich Village hootenannies of the '50s" with "the same pretentious guitar strumming, the same dead-ahead, dead-serious stares, and the same ethnic consciousness" which Theodore Bikel had brought to Town Hall "100-some years ago."

TWO GENTLEMEN OF VERONA

"A Grand New Musical"

Theatre: St. James Theatre
Opening Date: December 1, 1971; *Closing Date*: May 20, 1973
Performances: 613
Book: John Guare and Mel Shapiro
Lyrics: John Guare
Music: Galt MacDermot
Based on the play *The Two Gentlemen of Verona* by William Shakespeare (written circa 1598).
Direction: Mel Shapiro; *Producer*: The New York Shakespeare Festival (Joseph Papp, Producer; Bernard Gersten, Associate Producer); *Choreography*: Jean Erdman; *Scenery*: Ming Cho Lee; *Costumes*: Theoni V. Aldredge; *Lighting*: Lawrence Metzler; *Musical Direction*: Harold Wheeler

Cast: Frank O'Brien (Thurio), Jose Perez (Speed), Clifton Davis (Valentine), Raul Julia (Proteus), Diana Davila (Julia), Alix Elias (Lucetta), John Bottoms (Launce), Frederic Warriner (Antonio, Tavern Host), Phineas (a canine performer who played the role of Crab), Norman Matlock (Duke of Milan), Jonelle Allen (Silvia), Alvin Lum (Eglamour); Citizens of Verona and Milan: Loretta Abbott, Christopher Alden, Roger Briant, Douglas Brickhouse, Stockard Channing, Paul DeJohn, Nancy Denning, Richard De Russo, Arthur Erickson, Georgyn Geetlein, Sheila Gibbs, Jeff Goldblum, Edward Henkel, Albert Insinnia, Jane Jaffe, Signa Joy, Kenneth Lowry, Sakinah Mahammud, Otis Salid, Madeleine Swift; Black Passion Quartet: Sheila Gibbs, Signa Joy, Kenneth Lowry, and Sakinah Mahammud

The musical was presented in two acts.

The action takes place in Verona, Milan, and in the forest.

Musical Numbers

Note: The program didn't list musical numbers; the following is taken from the published script and the cast album.

Act One: "Summer, Summer" (Ensemble); "I Love My Father" (Ensemble); "That's a Very Interesting Question" (Raul Julia, Clifton Davis); "I'd Like to Be a Rose" (Raul Julia, Clifton Davis); "Thou, Julia, Thou Has Metamorphosed Me" (Raul Julia); "Symphony" (Raul Julia, Ensemble); "I Am Not Interested in Love" (Diana Davila); "Love, Is That You?" (Frank O'Brien, Georgyn Geetlein); "Thou, Proteus, Thou Has Metamorphosed Me" (Diana Davila); "What Does a Lover Pack?" (Diana Davila, Raul Julia, Ensemble); "Pearls" (John Bottoms); "I Love My Father" (reprise) (Raul Julia, Ensemble); "Two Gentlemen of Verona" (Diana Davila, Alix Elias, Ensemble); "Follow the Rainbow" (Clifton Davis, Jose Perez, Raul Julia, John Bottoms, Diana Davila, Alix Elias); "Where's North?" (Clifton Davis, Jose Perez, Norman Matlock, Jonelle Allen, Frank O'Brien, Ensemble); "Bring All the Boys Back Home" (Norman Matlock, Ensemble); "Love's Revenge" (Clifton Davis); "To Whom It May Concern Me" (Jonelle Allen, Clifton Davis); "Night Letter" (Jonelle Allen, Clifton Davis); "Love's Revenge" (reprise) (Clifton Davis, Raul Julia, Jose Perez, John Bottoms); "Calla Lily Lady" (Raul Julia)

Act Two: "Land of Betrayal" (Alix Elias); "Thurio's Samba" (Frank O'Brien, Norman Matlock, Ensemble); "Hot Lover" (John Bottoms, Jose Perez); "What a Nice Idea" (Diana Davila); "Who Is Silvia?" (Raul Julia, The Black Passion Quartet, Ensemble); "Love Me" (Jonelle Allen, The Black Passion Quartet, Ensemble); "Eglamour" (Alvin Lum, Jonelle Allen); "Kidnapped" (Diana Davila, Norman Matlock, Raul Julia, Frank O'Brien, Ensemble); "Mansion" (Clifton Davis); "Eglamour" (reprise) (Jonelle Allen, Alvin Lum); "What's a Nice Girl Like Her" (Raul Julia); "Dragon Fight" (aka "Land of Betrayal)" (Alvin Lum, Raul Julia, Clifton Davis); "Don't Have the Baby" (Alix Elias, Jose Perez, John Bottoms, Diana Davila); "Love, Is That You?" (reprise) (Frank O'Brien, Alix Elias); "Milkmaid" (John Bottoms, Sheila Gibbs); Finale: "I Love My Father" (reprise) and "Love Has Driven Me Sane" (Company)

Two Gentlemen of Verona opened to almost unanimously rapturous reviews, and won the Tony Award for Best Musical, beating out ***Follies***. But for all its acclaim, the musical had a relatively modest run on Broadway and has for all purposes disappeared. The evening was a self-indulgent, overly cute, and more-trendy-than-thou adaptation that condescended to the audience with its dumbed-down antics and its politically correct sensibility.

Because Shakespeare's comedy is one of his weakest, here was an opportunity to create a witty and potentially Marx Brothers–styled approach to the story's familiar themes of star-crossed lovers, misunderstandings, disguises, kidnappings, and impersonations. Cupid's arrows have struck Proteus (Raul Julia) and Valentine (Clifton Davis), and so the former is in love with local girl Julia (Diana Davila) and the latter with Silvia (Jonelle Allen) from Milan. But Mel Shapiro and John Guare's book missed the mark, which was especially disappointing because Guare's 1971 dark, brooding, and yet screamingly funny Off-Broadway play *The House of Blue Leaves* is one of the finest of the era, a surreal, black comedy-drama told with insight and imagination.

What made *Two Gentlemen of Verona* bearable were some of its performances and Galt MacDermot's richly melodic score, an extended merry-go-round of some three-dozen songs (including reprises) that gaily poured forth from his music box. One wishes a full-length instrumental recording of the score with the Broadway orchestrations had been recorded; it would have been a pleasure to hear the lush music without the lyrics, which ran from the trite ("you can't love another without loving yourself") to the vulgar (the melodic delight of "Thurio's Samba" was almost obliterated by an unending litany of four-letter words). Among MacDermot's other inspirations were "Summer, Summer," "I Love My Father," and the explosive "Night Letter."

But the production itself was awash in silly shtick: red tissue-paper hearts and confetti were tossed about the stage and into the audience, and during one number the cast blew soap bubbles at the spectators; later, the performers played with yo-yos and Frisbees; they juggled, they did hand-stands, they performed cartwheels, and they made entrances on pogo sticks and gold Baroque scooters. (The musical indulged in the same kind of childish sensibility that ruined the revival of ***Candide*** two seasons later, and was a precursor of the free-for-all approach for such productions as the 2013 revival of ***Pippin***.)

Because this was the early 1970s, and because the show emanated from the Public, there was a hip political slant to the proceedings: the Duke of Milan, who dresses in Che-like attire with beret and sunglasses, is a war-monger; the company sings the antiwar "Bring All the Boys Back Home"; and many of the principal characters from Old Italy's towns of Verona and Milan are either black or Puerto Rican. Everything was too much: the stage business was determinedly wacky and the would-be high spirits came across as self-indulgent varsity show low-jinks.

But the critics adored the musical. Clive Barnes in the *New York Times* said it was "lovely fun" with "a strangely New York feel" and "a very New York sense of irreverence"; in the same newspaper, Walter Kerr noted the evening was "an improvisation with no malice in it," with "a kink of its own" and a "certain mirth of mind." Martin Gottfried in *Women's Wear Daily* said the work was "playful and bright and very grand fun" with "energy, wit and originality." Irma Pascal Heldman in the *Wall Street Journal* said the show was "the most delicious" one in New York, and she praised MacDermot's "vibrant" music and Guare's "witty" and "original" lyrics. Jack Kroll in *Newsweek* enjoyed the evening's "joyous skylarking."

Douglas Watt in the *New York Daily News* liked the "charming" songs and "cheerfully nutty" lyrics; Richard Watts in the *New York Post* noted that MacDermot had composed "the best rock score" he'd ever heard; and Leonard Harris on WCBSTV2 said the evening was a "a rocking, dancing, supersensational" show "with at least a dozen hit tunes."

An unidentified reviewer on WABCTV7 said Jonelle Allen was "the most exciting thing" in the show, but noted the lyrics were "pretty lousy." The critic also mentioned that one of the funniest moments in the evening was a purely impromptu one in which the canine performer Phineas (who played the role of Crab) made his entrance, sat on the stage, listened to the dialogue, and "then looked straight at the audience and yawned mightily."

The most negative review came from T. E. Kalem in *Time* who said the musical rode the current vogue of taking a work from the past and playing it for "cute," "camp," and "snide" effects, but never playing it "straight." He noted the trivial rendering of Shakespeare's play perfectly captured a comment by T. S. Eliot, who had once written that some audiences want to be "distracted from distraction by distraction."

The production's best performances were by Diana Davila, who created an amusingly tentative and charmingly confused Julia, and Jonelle Allen, who was a show-stopping Silvia. Allen was a sizzling presence who walked away with the reviews, and her beauty, her roof-raising voice, and her lithe and graceful dancing gave the promise of a long Broadway career. But as of this writing, *Two Gentlemen of Verona* sadly marks her most recent Broadway appearance. For the record, here are some of the critics' comments about her: "radiant and magnetic" (Heldman); "flamethrowing" (Kroll); "stops the show cold" with her "bundle of sensuous joy" and "controlled ferocity" (Watt); "likely to wipe out the very floor of the St. James" (Kerr); and a "one-woman heat wave" (Kalem).

The script was published by Holt, Rinehart & Winston in 1973 in a lavish hardback that included photographs, drawings, and sheet music for some of the songs. The script was also included in the hardback collection *Great Rock Musicals*, published by Stein and Day in 1979 and edited by Stanley Richards. The cast album was released on a two-LP set by ABC-Dunhill Records (# BCSY-1001) and on CD by Decca Broadway Records (# 440-017-565-2). Kilmarnock Records (LP # KIL-72004) issued a selection of songs from the musical, which was conducted by Galt MacDermot and performed by Sheila Gibbs and Ken (Kenneth) Lowry, both of whom appeared in the Off Broadway and Broadway productions.

The London production opened at the Phoenix Theatre on April 26, 1973, for 237 performances and was recorded by RSO Records on a one-LP set (# RSO-SUPER-2394-110).

The musical first opened Off-Broadway (as *The Two Gentlemen of Verona*) on July 27, 1971, at the Delacorte Theatre in a free production by the Public Theatre where it played for fourteen performances; following this limited engagement, a "mobile tour" version played throughout New York City for twenty-three more showings. The summer mounting included Carla Pinza (Julia) and Jerry Stiller (Launce), who were succeeded by Diana Davila and John Bottoms for Broadway.

In the chorus of the Off-Broadway and Broadway productions was Jeff Goldblum; and for the Broadway edition Stockard Channing performed in the chorus. She soon became perhaps the foremost interpreter of John Guare, and appeared in three more productions of his works. She starred in the 1986 revival of *The House of Blue Leaves*; created the role of Ouisa Kittredge in the original *Six Degrees of Separation* (1990), and reprised her role for the 1993 film version; and appeared in *Four Baboons Adoring the Sun* (1992).

Awards

Tony Awards and *Nominations*: Best Musical (***Two Gentlemen of Verona***); Best Leading Actor in a Musical (Clifton Davis and Raul Julia); Best Leading Actress in a Musical (Jonelle Allen); Best Director of a Musical (Mel Shapiro); Best Book (**John Guare** and **Mel Shapiro**); Best Score (lyrics by John Guare, music by Galt MacDermot); Best Costume Designer (Theoni V. Aldredge); Best Choreographer (Jean Erdman)

WILD AND WONDERFUL

"A 'Big-City' Fable"

Theatre: Lyceum Theatre
Opening Date: December 7, 1971; *Closing Date*: December 7, 1971
Performances: 1
Book: Phil Phillips
Lyrics and *Music*: Bob Goodman; dance music by Thom Janusz
Based on an original work by Bob Brotherson and Bob Miller.
Direction: Burry Fredrik; *Producers*: Rick Hobard in association with Raymonde Weil (John C. O'Regan, Associate Producer); *Choreography*: Ronn Forella; *Scenery*: Stephen Hendrickson; *Costumes*: Frank Thompson; *Lighting*: Neil Peter Jampolis; *Musical Direction*: Thom Janusz
Cast: Laura McDuffie (Jenny), Walter Willison (Charlie), Robert Burr (Lionel Masters), Larry Small (Brother John), Ted Thurston (Father Desmond); Ensemble: Yveline Baudez, Pam (Pamela) Blair, Mary Ann Bruning, Carol Conte, Bob Daley, Anna Maria Fanizzi, Marcelo Gamboa, Adam Grammis, Patti Haine, Ann Reinking, Jimmy Roddy, Steven Vincent, Eddie Wright Jr.
The musical was presented in two acts.
The action takes place during the present time "in the big city."

Musical Numbers

Act One: "Wild and Wonderful" and Dance (Company); "My First Moment" (Laura McDuffie); "I Spy" (Walter Willison); "Desmond's Dilemma" (Ted Thurston, Larry Small); "(The) Moment Is Now" (Ensemble); "Something Wonderful (Can Happen)" (Laura McDuffie); "Chances" (Laura McDuffie, Models); "She Should Have Me" (Robert Burr); "Jenny" (Walter Willison); "Fallen Angels" (Larry Small, Company); Dance (Company)

Act Two: "Petty Crime" (Laura McDuffie, Judge [singer unidentified in program], Company); "Come a Little Closer" (Laura McDuffie, Walter Willison); "Little Bits and Pieces" (Robert Burr, Models); "Is This My Town" (Laura McDuffie); "You Can Reach the Sun" (Larry Small, Company); "Wild and Wonderful" (reprise) (Company)

Notes for the unpublished script of an early version of *Wild and Wonderful* state that the musical's book is a "façade" for "the acting out of the games the characters play with each other" and the characters' songs "represent the truth of themselves that they are unable to see." But "the audience sees both sides." The notes indicate the score is "a mixture of modified rock, mock-opera, and standard show type numbers."

By the time of the Broadway production, the musical seems to have changed focus and hit upon the amusing conceit in which its heroine Jenny (Laura McDuffie) views the episodes of her life as variations on old movies (in a 1940s-styled courtroom scene, she's accused of "premeditated littering"). But the critics didn't find her visions all that interesting, and the Limited Broadway production shuttered after one performance; along with ***Heathen!***, *Wild and Wonderful* was the season's shortest-running musical.

The plot dealt with middle-class college student Jenny who decides to drop out and enjoy a life of adventure in the East Village. She meets the seemingly radical Charlie (Walter Willison), who is actually a CIA agent who suspects her of being a domestic terrorist. In order to observe her movements, he pretends to fall in love with her as they hang out in a Catholic Church shelter that caters to runaways, hippie types, and, who knows, possible anarchists. The shelter is run by progressive Brother John (Larry Small) who his superior Father Desmond (Ted Thurston) thinks is perhaps too easy on the youthful flock. In the meantime, Father Desmond worries how he'll be able to continue funding both the church and the shelter. But all ends well: Charlie discovers Jenny isn't a terrorist, comes to realize that he loves her, and reveals that he's actually a millionaire and so will be able to help Father Desmond.

Richard Watts in the *New York Post* found the show a "little tame" for Broadway. It wasn't "at all wild" and was "considerably less than wonderful," but at its best was a "nice, modest little entertainment" with "pleasant" songs, "lively" dances, and "excellent" performances by the two leads.

Douglas Watt in the *New York Daily News* suggested the musical should have been titled *Tame and Terrible*, and complained that the book "defied" description and the dialogue when "not just plain dumb" didn't "hold together." But he noted the courtroom scene and the "One O'Clock Jump"–styled number "Petty Crime" was so "entertaining" that he briefly hoped the evening had finally found its stride. But Martin Gottfried in *Women's Wear Daily* said the musical didn't "even have the heart to be terrible." It was "shameless" because it never developed its concept and became "an industrial show without the car or soap commercials."

Leonard Harris on WCBSTV2 found the book "miniscule" and "dreadful," and noted that a Broadway musical "doesn't have to be big to be bad." Kevin Sanders on WABCTV7 found the direction "limp" and the book "strangely humorless and long-winded"; but there were "pleasant" songs and two "big, exciting dance numbers." Otherwise, the musical celebrated youth but "seemed prematurely middle-aged."

Clive Barnes in the *New York Times* found the "terrible and witless" show "wet, windy and wretched," and suggested it would send you back to television, or even back to television commercials. The show provided "a new dimension to flatness" with "bad" music, "bad" lyrics, a "worse than bad" book, "unsupportable" choreography, and "singularly hideous" and "spectacularly unflattering" costumes. He noted that he'd always try to remember *Wild and Wonderful* "as a yardstick to measure the future."

Songs cut in preproduction were: "Love Your Country," "Let's Keep It Clean," "Thou Shalt Not," "Dying to Live," "Thinking of Me," "Our Reigning Day," and "The Proper Time to Be Around."

INNER CITY

"A Street Cantata"

Theatre: Ethel Barrymore Theatre
Opening Date: December 19, 1971; *Closing Date*: March 11, 1972
Performances: 97
Lyrics: Eve Merriam
Music: Helen Miller
Based on Eve Merriam's 1969 book *The Inner City Mother Goose.*
Direction: Tom O'Horgan; *Producers*: Joseph Kipness, Lawrence Kasha, and Tom O'Horgan in association with RCA Records (Harvey Milk and John M. Nagel, Associate Producers); *Scenery*: Robin Wagner; *Costumes*: Joseph G. Aulisi; *Lighting*: John Dodd in association with Jane Reisman; *Musical Direction*: Clay Fullum
Cast: Joy Garrett, Carl Hall, Delores Hall, Fluffer Hirsch, Linda Hopkins, Paulette Ellen Jones, Larry Marshall, Allan Nicholls, Florence Tarlow
The revue was presented in two acts.

Musical Numbers

Act One: (I) *Nub of the Nation*: "Fee Fi Fo Fum" (Linda Hopkins); "Now I Lay Me" (Carl Hall, Delores Hall, Allan Nicholls); "Locks" and "I Had a Little Teevee" (Fluffer Hirsch); "Hushabye Baby" and "My Mother Said" (Paulette Ellen Jones); "Diddle Diddle Dumpling" and "Rub a Dub Dub" (Larry Marshall); "You'll Find Mice" (Linda Hopkins); "Ding Dong Bell" (Carl Hall, Company); "The Brave Old City of New York" (Joy Garrett); "Urban Renewal" (Linda Hopkins); "The Nub of the Nation" (Company); (II) *Urban Mary*: "Mary, Mary" (Company); "City Life" (Florence Tarlow); "One Misty Moisty Morning" (Larry Marshall); "Jack Be Nimble" (Carl Hall, Fluffer Hirsch, Larry Marshall); "If Wishes Were Horses" (Delores Hall); (III) *Deep in the Night*: "One Man" and "Deep in the Night" (Linda Hopkins); (IV) *Take-a-Tour, Congressman*: "Statistics" (Company); "Twelve Rooftops Leaping" (Company); "Take-a-Tour, Congressman" (Company); "Simple Simon" (Larry Marshall, Allan Nicholls, Company); "Poverty Program" (Company); "One, Two" (Carl Hall, Company); "Tom, Tom" (Allan Nicholls); "Hickety, Pickety" (Company); "Half Alive" (Delores Hall); (V) *The Spirit of Education*: "This Is the Way to Go to School" (Company); "The Spirit of Education" (Florence Tarlow); "Little Jack Horner" (Company); "Subway Dream" (Larry Marshall); "Christmas Is Coming" (Fluffer Hirsch); "I'm Sorry Says the Machine" (Larry Marshall, Company); "Jeremiah Obadiah" (Larry Marshall); "Riddle Song" (Company); "Shadow of the Sun" (Company)

Act Two: (I) *Wisdom*: "Boys and Girls Come Out to Play" (Company); "Summer Nights" (Joy Garrett, Delores Hall, Paulette Ellen Jones); "Lucy Locket" (Fluffer Hirsch); "Winter Nights" (Linda Hopkins, Florence Tarlow); "Wisdom" (Larry Marshall); "The Hooker" (Joy Garrett); (II) *Starlight*: "Wino Will" and "Man in the Doorway" (Paulette Ellen Jones); "Starlight Starbright" (Delores Hall); "The Cow Jumped over the Moon" (Larry Marshall); "The Dealer" (Allan Nicholls); (III) *Crooked Man*: "Taffy" (Carl Hall, Fluffer Hirsch, Company); "Numbers" (Larry Marshall, Company);"The Pickpocket" (Carl Hall); "Law and Order" (Delores Hall, Company); (IV) *Kindness*: "Kindness" (Allan Nicholls, Company); "As I Went Over" (Allan Nicholls); "There Was a Little Man" (Company); "Who Killed Nobody" (Company); (V) *If*: "It's My Belief" (Linda Hopkins); "Street Sermon" (Carl Hall); "The Great If" (Carl Hall); "On This Rock" (Company); "The Great If" (Company)

During the 1971–1972 season, everything seemed to come in twos: two Jewish revues (***To Live Another Summer, to Pass Another Winter*** and ***Only Fools Are Sad***), two religious musicals (***Jesus Christ Superstar*** and ***Hard Job Being God***), two musicals aimed at the family trade (the revival of ***You're a Good Man, Charlie Brown*** and ***Anne of Green Gables***), two that contrasted different periods of time (***Different Times*** and ***Heathen!***), and two revivals from the 1940s (***On the Town*** and ***Lost in the Stars***).

And with the opening of *Inner City*, Broadway now had its second look at life in the ghettoes of New York (***Aint Supposed to Die a Natural Death*** had opened two months earlier). While many critics had endorsed Melvin Van Peebles's venomous look at the culture of inner city life, most were not so indulgent with *Inner City*, which they deemed somewhat unrealistic in its lighthearted look at issues which were anything but frivolous. There was also some grousing that a few white performers but no Puerto Ricans had been included in the primarily black cast (Martin Gottfried in *Women's Wear Daily* noted "inner cities are black and Puerto Rican" and "liberal notions cannot change that fact").

In her 1969 book *The Inner City Mother Goose*, Eve Merriam had modernized classic nursery rhymes and presented them with a skewed and somewhat bemused look at life in the inner city. And so the revue-like musical was a series of haphazard gripes about decaying schools, poor housing conditions, rampant crime, corrupt police and city officials, and prevalent drug use. But Gottfried noted the songs had little to say about the litany of big-city problems except that they existed; he also mentioned that while the evening was divided into ten sections, their titles made no "sense" in the program or in fact. He found Helen Miller's score "nearly atrocious" and criticized some of Tom O'Horgan's directorial choices (such as placing some of the performers in the boxes of the balcony in order for them to offer supposedly "spontaneous outbursts" of cheering and shouting during and after a musical number).

Richard Watts in the *New York Post* noted the evening's purpose was to show "how terrible it is to be a New Yorker," and felt the production had a "singular lack of wit in the satirical thrusts." Douglas Watt in the *New York Daily News* said the revue was a "big mistake" because Merriam didn't have "anything new" to say about the well-worn catalog of New York's ills. He also felt the grim content was at odds with the "musical comedy treatment" it was given; as a result, the music was often "flip or sentimental" and sometimes "too glossy" for the show's context. O'Horgan's "busy" staging was full of "meaningless activity" and the "liberal" use of four-letter words was "embarrassing" if not "dishonest" in view of the musical's determination to be "light-hearted and sentimental at all costs." Leonard Harris on WCBSTV2 said the musical was a "sharp, entertaining" show provided you could laugh at murder, muggings, "and kindred rib ticklers." But he liked the "good" songs and praised the cast (and singled out "gospel shouter" Linda Hopkins).

Clive Barnes in the *New York Times* assessed the musical as "more concerned with being a cantata than it is with the streets" and therefore the evening had a "certain smartness" but lacked "humanity." As for the music, it was "so unmemorable that you cannot remember it" and thus the "quality" of the score made the description "cantata" seem "pretentious." The show had some "good things" in it, but they were "not enough" to carry the evening.

But Kevin Sanders on WABCTV7 (wrongly) predicted the musical was "another hit, another big one." The "exciting" evening was the "fastest moving show ever on Broadway," the music had "verve and drive," and the lyrics were "exuberant" with "refreshing frankness."

The cast album was released by RCA Victor (LP # LSO-1171), and was later issued on CD by ArkivMusic/RCA (# 83212).

Inner City was another distressing example of writers who didn't bother to create book musicals with plots and characters. Instead, too many fell into the rut of creating song cycles (which they sometimes identified as cantatas or collages or tapestries) or in some cases weak stories with revue-like characteristics, and often it was difficult for an audience to take a vested interest in the stage proceedings because sometimes watching these shows in a theatre was tantamount to listening to their cast albums. The 1971–1972 season offered six such shows (***Aint Supposed to Die a Natural Death***, *Inner City*, ***The Selling of the President***, ***Dont Bother Me I Cant Cope***, ***Different Times***, and ***Hard Job Being God***). It's telling that the only musicals of the season that are revived with any kind of regularity (on Broadway, in regional theatre, or in major foreign productions) are ones with more or less traditional books (***Sugar*** and ***Jesus Christ Superstar***).

Inner City also brought Tom O'Horgan's brief heyday as Broadway's hottest director to an abrupt end. He had enjoyed three hits in a row with *Hair* (1968; 1,750 performances), the drama *Lenny* (1971; 453 performances), and ***Jesus Christ Superstar*** (1971; 711 performances). But it all went immediately downhill: *Inner City* lasted for just ninety-seven performances; ***Mary C. Brown and the Hollywood Sign*** closed during its pre-Broadway tryout; ***Dude*** played for sixteen performances; the "rock spectacle" ***Sgt. Pepper's Lonely Hearts Club Band on the Road*** faltered after sixty-six showings; the drama *The Leaf People* (1975) ran for eight; the comedy *I Won't Dance* (1981) closed on opening night and was the last production to play the Helen Hayes Theatre before it was demolished; the 1984 revival of ***The Three Musketeers*** lasted for nine performances; and *Senator Joe* (1989) closed after three Broadway previews.

Awards

Tony Award: Best Featured Actress in a Musical (**Linda Hopkins**)

ANNE OF GREEN GABLES

"A Musical"

Theatre: City Center 55th Street Theatre
Opening Date: December 21, 1971; *Closing Date*: January 2, 1972
Performances: 16
Book: Donald (Don) Harron
Lyrics: Donald (Don) Harron and Norman Campbell; additional lyrics by Mavor Moore and Elaine Campbell
Music: Norman Campbell
Based on the 1908 novel *Anne of Green Gables* by Lucy Maud Montgomery.
Direction and *Choreography*: Alan Lund; *Producers*: City Center of Music and Drama, Inc. (Norman Singer, Executive Director) in association with The Charlottetown Festival (of Prince Edward Island, Canada) (A Canadian National Musical Theatre Production); *Scenery*: Murray Laufer; *Costumes*: Marie Day; *Lighting*: Ronald Montgomery; *Musical Direction*: John Fenwick

Cast: Maud Whitmore (Mrs. Rachel Lynde), Cleone Duncan (Mrs. MacPherson, Lucilla), Nancy Kerr (Mrs. Barry), Flora MacKenzie (Mrs. Sloane, Mrs. Spencer), Kathryn Watt (Mrs. Pye), Lloyd Malenfant (The Minister), Bill Hosie (Earl, Stationmaster), George Merner (Cecil), *Elizabeth Mawson* (Marilla Cuthbert), *Peter Mews* (Matthew Cuthbert), *Gracie Finley* (Anne Shirley), Roma Hearn (Mrs. Blewett, Miss Stacy), Glenda Landry (Diana Barry), Sharlene McLean (Prissy Andrews), Barbara Barsky (Josie Pye), Patti Toms (Ruby Gillis), Lynn Marsh (Tillie Boulter), Deborah Millar (Gertie Pye), *Jeff Hyslop* (Gilbert Blythe), George Juriga (Charlie Sloane), Dan Costain (Moody McPherson), Andre Denis (Gerry Buote), John Powell (Tommy Sloane), Calvin McRae (Malcolm Andrews), Jack Northmore (Mr. Phillips)

The musical was presented in two acts.

The action takes place at the turn of the twentieth century in Avonlea, a tiny village located on Prince Edward Island, Canada.

Musical Numbers

Act One: "Great Workers for the Cause" (Maud Whitmore, Ladies); "Where Is Matthew Going?" (Townspeople); "Gee, I'm Glad I'm No One Else but Me" (Gracie Finley); "The Facts" (Gracie Finley, Flora MacKenzie, Roma Hearn, Elizabeth Mawson); "Where'd Marilla Come From?" (Bill Hosie, George Merner, Ladies); "Humble Pie" (Peter Mews, Gracie Finley); "Oh, Mrs. Lynde!" (Gracie Finley); "Back to School Ballet" (Pupils); "Avonlea, We Love Thee" (Jack Northmore, Pupils); "Wondrin'" (Jeff Hyslop); "Did You Hear?" (Barbara Barsky, Kathryn Watt, Cleone Duncan, Nancy Kerr, Bill Hosie, George Merner, Maud Whitmore); "Ice Cream" (Glenda Landry, Company); "The Picnic" (Company)

Act Two: "Where Did the Summer Go To?" (Pupils); "Kindred Spirits" (Gracie Finley, Glenda Landry); "Open the Window!" (Roma Hearn, Pupils); "The Words" (Peter Mews); "Open the Window" (reprise) (Roma Hearn, Pupils); "Nature Hunt Ballet" (Pupils); "I'll Show Him" (Gracie Finley, Jeff Hyslop); "General Store" (Cleone Duncan, Peter Mews, Townspeople); "Pageant Song" (Pupils); "If It Hadn't Been for Me" (Pupils); "Where Did the Summer Go To?" (reprise) (Gracie Finley, Jeff Hyslop); "Anne of Green Gables" (Peter Mews); "The Words" (reprise) (Elizabeth Mawson); "Wond'rin'" (reprise) (Gracie Finley, Jeff Hyslop)

Anne of Green Gables was based on Lucy Maud Montgomery's popular novel of the same name about orphan Anne Shirley, who finds a home in the small village of Avonlea when she's adopted by a sister and brother.

The musical played at City Center over the holidays for a limited engagement of two weeks, and was probably presented under a special contract for a visiting production. For classification purposes, the musical rests in a middle ground of not quite being a regular Broadway or Off-Broadway offering. To be as inclusive as possible, it's included in this book (but with the caveat that it wasn't a regular commercial Broadway production).

Clive Barnes in the *New York Times* said the "undemanding" and "unpretentious" musical had a "folksy air" and "a certain special charm." The music was "agreeable" but "quite unmemorable," the dances were a pleasurable reminder "of the days when choreography was back in style on the Broadway stage," and the production looked "cheerfully old-fashioned." Although the musical seemed "a little lost in the prairie spaces" of City Center, "its mixture of corn and maple syrup" made it an "attractive enough" show for children during the Christmas holiday season.

The work had been first presented on Canadian television in 1955 and 1958, and a revised and expanded version for the stage premiered at the Charlottetown Festival on Prince Edward Island, Canada, during Summer 1965 where it soon became a staple in the company's repertoire (as of this writing, the musical is scheduled for performances at the festival for the entire summer of 2015). On April 16, 1969, a London production opened at the New Theatre for 300 performances with Polly James in the title role. It offered a new song ("When I Say My Say"), which wasn't included in the later published script.

The Charlottetown production was recorded by Ready Records (LP # LR-045), and the London cast album was released by CBS Records (LP # 70053). The script was published in paperback by Samuel French in 1972.

Another musical version of the story opened Off Broadway on March 29, 2007, for forty-one performances, and the cast recording was issued by Jay Records (CD # CDJAY-1404). Piper Goodeve played the title role, the book and lyrics were by Gretchen Cryer, and the music was by Nancy Ford.

THE SIGN IN SIDNEY BRUSTEIN'S WINDOW

Theatre: Longacre Theatre
Opening Date: January 26, 1972; *Closing Date*: January 29, 1972
Performances: 5
Adaptation: Robert Nemiroff and Charlotte Zaltzburg
Lyrics: Ray Errol Fox
Music: Gary William Friedman
Based on the 1964 play *The Sign in Sidney Brustein's Window* by Lorraine Hansberry.
Direction: Alan Schneider; *Producer*: Robert Renfield (Robert Nemiroff, Associate Producer); *Musical Staging*: Rhoda Levine; *Scenery*: William Ritman; *Costumes*: Theoni V. Aldredge; *Lighting*: Richard Nelson; *Musical Direction*: Mack Schlefer
Cast: The Singers: Pendleton Brown, Richard Cox, John Lansing, and Arnetia Walker; *Hal Linden* (Sidney Brustein), John Danelle (Alton Scales), *Zohra Lampert* (Iris Parodus Brustein), Mason Adams (Wally O'Hara), Dolph Sweet (Max), Frances Sternhagen (Mavis Parodus Bryson), William Atherton (David Ragin), Kelly Wood (Gloria Parodus)
The play with music was presented in three acts.
The action takes place during the early 1960s in New York City.

Musical Numbers

Note: The following songs, which the program didn't identify by act, were performed by Pendleton Brown, Richard Cox, John Lansing, and Arnetia Walker: "Can a Flower Think?"; "In Another Life"; "Mountain Girl"; "To the People"; "While There's Still Time"; "Things as They Are"; and "Sweet Evenin'"

The original 1964 production of Lorraine Hansberry's play *The Sign in Sidney Brustein's Window* failed on Broadway, where it closed at the Longacre Theatre after 101 showings (sadly, Hansberry died at the age of thirty-four, two days after the play gave its final performance). The current revised version by Robert Nemiroff and Charlotte Zaltzburg also opened at the Longacre but couldn't manage a full week of performances. The production added seven songs that were performed by an onstage quartet between scenes and commented on the action.

Hansberry's 1959 play *A Raisin in the Sun* about a black family living in Chicago was a long-running hit, but *The Sign in Sidney Brustein's Window* had little to do with race and racism. Of its nine characters (eight for the current version), only one was black. And while the earlier play was a tightly woven drama that examined the members of a black family at a critical juncture in their lives, the new drama was hard to take seriously because it was so scattershot in a story overrun with melodramatic situations and attitudes.

The title character (Hal Linden) is a Jewish man who runs a small progressive Village newspaper that has backed congressional candidate Wally O'Hara (Mason Adams) for office. Brustein believes O'Hara shares his liberal ideals and standards (hence, the sign of endorsement in his window), but to his dismay he realizes O'Hara is just another political hack who toes his political party's line, lacks values, and just wants to get elected. Brustein's Greek-Irish-Cherokee wife Iris (Zohra Lampert) has little talent but nonetheless dreams of becoming a great actress, and jumps at the chance to appear in television commercials; her older sister Mavis (Frances Sternhagen) is a conservative matron with major marital problems, including a philandering husband and his out-of-wedlock child; and her younger sister Gloria (Kelly Wood) is a prostitute who intends to give up her profession when she marries black man Alton Scales (John Danelle).

But Scales rejects Gloria when he learns about her past, and so she commits suicide. Added to the mix are David Ragin (William Atherton), a gay playwright who uses everyone he knows, and Max (Dolph Sweet), a Village painter. It was all very New York, and all of it was the stuff of trendy soap opera. And to top off the plot-heavy evening, the new version of the play had the extra baggage of a singing quartet, a kind of Greek chorus who between the scenes punctuated the action with musical commentary.

Richard Watts in the *New York Post* said that like its source the revised play was "too cluttered," and the addition of songs was an "interruption." Martin Gottfried in *Women's Wear Daily* noted the play was "clumsy then and clumsier now," and felt Hansberry was more interested in abstract "argument" than in a full-blooded story. Further, the characters were "stereotypes" and the overly long evening clocked in at almost three hours. He felt the production was a "disaster" and mentioned that Hal Linden occasionally lapsed into a "left over" accent from ***The Rothschilds*** and Zohra Lampert's performance was "deep in the heart of her Jewish mannerisms."

Betty Rollin on WNBC4TV found the play "rambling, sophomoric," and "out of date." And while Leonard Harris on WCBSTV2 enjoyed the first act, he felt the remaining ones didn't go anywhere; he liked the play "well enough" but wished it were "better"; and Irma Pascal Heldman in the *Wall Street Journal* noted that the play tried "to get too much said in too short a time."

Like Heldman, Douglas Watt in the *New York Daily News* also had reservations about the drama. It was one of the "better evenings" of the current Broadway scene, but there was "too much of it." The final scene was "somewhat superfluous in a play already overburdened with situations," and there was a certain "cold calculation" in the writing that attempted to give the impression of "real persons with real problems" but that never quite created believable characters.

Clive Barnes in the *New York Times* said the "flawed" work sometimes sank into "melodrama" and its "individual scenes" were "better than the play itself," but this time around the short-running 1964 drama had "the good red blood of a Broadway success running through it." But he was "not at all happy" with the "clumsy device" of using songs to make "portentous and unnecessary comments on the action." While the play wasn't "particularly profound" and was "far from perfect," he predicted many playgoers would "find it an entertaining play that is at times even provocative."

Watt found the soft-rock-styled music "attractive" and the lyrics "appealing and well-constructed," and Watts said the score was "pleasant." But Gottfried noted the music was of the "stage rock genre," which was "no genre at all"; and the lyrics ranged from "silly to satisfactory."

As Brustein's suburban sister-in-law, Frances Sternhagen walked off with the best reviews. Watt found her "first-rate" and Rollin said she was "brilliant." Watts said her character was a "mass" of prejudices and bigotry; but instead of being "disagreeable" Sternhagen created a "thoroughly well-meaning and likable" woman and she dominated the evening.

The adaptors Robert Nemiroff and Charlotte Zaltzberg later wrote the book of the long-running ***Raisin***, a musical adaptation of *A Raisin in the Sun*. Nemiroff was Hansberry's husband and the literary executor of her estate; he had adapted Hansberry's writings about her life into the 1969 Off-Broadway reading *To Be Young, Gifted and Black*, and in 1970 his adaptation of Hansberry's play *Les Blancs* played briefly on Broadway. Zaltzberg was Nemiroff's associate, and according to the program notes she was currently in the process of preparing Hansberry's papers and posthumous works for publication.

Awards

Tony Award Nomination: Best Featured Actress in a Play (Frances Sternhagen)

GREASE

"A New 50's Rock 'n' Roll Musical"

Theatre: Eden Theatre (during run, the musical transferred to the Broadhurst, Royale, and Majestic Theatres)
Opening Date: February 14, 1972; *Closing Date*: April 13, 1980
Performances: 3,388
Book, Lyrics, and *Music*: Jim Jacobs and Warren Casey
Direction: Tom Moore; *Producers*: Kenneth Waissman and Maxine Fox in association with Anthony D'Amato; *Choreography*: Patricia Birch; *Scenery*: Douglas W. Schmidt; *Costumes*: Carrie F. Robbins; *Lighting*: Karl Eigsti; *Musical Direction*: Louis St. Louis
Cast: Dorothy Leon (Miss Lynch), Ilene Kristen (Patty Simcox), Tom Harris (Eugene Florczyk), Garn Stephens (Jan), Katie Hanley (Marty), Adrienne Barbeau (Betty Rizzo), James Canning (Doody), Walter Bobbie (Roger), Timothy Meyers (Kenickie), Jim Borrelli (Sonny LaTierri), Marya Small (Frenchy), Carole Demas (Sandy Dumbrowski), Barry Bostwick (Danny Zuko), Don Billett (Vince Fontaine), Alan Paul (Johnny Casino, Teen Angel), Kathi Moss (Cha-Cha Di Gregorio)

The musical was presented in two acts.
The action begins at Rydell High School's class reunion for the graduates of 1959, and then goes back in time to depict the graduates' high school years.

Musical Numbers

Act One: "Alma Mater" (Dorothy Leon, Ilene Kristen, Tom Harris); "Alma Mater" (parody) (The Pink Ladies, The Burger Palace Boys); "Summer Nights" (Carole Demas, Barry Bostwick, The Pink Ladies, The Burger Palace Boys); "Those Magic Changes" (James Canning, The Burger Palace Boys, The Pink Ladies); "Freddy, My Love" (Katie Hanley, Garn Stephens, Marya Small, Adrienne Barbeau); "Greased Lightnin'" (Timothy Meyers, The Burger Palace Boys); "Mooning" (Walter Bobbie, Garn Stephens); "Look at Me, I'm Sandra Dee" (Adrienne Barbeau); "We Go Together" (The Pink Ladies, The Burger Palace Boys)
Act Two: "Shakin' at the High School Hop" (Company); "It's Raining on Prom Night" (Carole Demas, Kathi Moss [Radio Voice]); "Shakin' at the High School Hop" (reprise) (Company); "Born to Hand-Jive" (Alan Paul); "Beauty School Dropout" (Alan Paul, Marya Small, Choir); "Alone at a Drive-In Movie" (Barry Bostwick, The Burger Palace Boys); "Rock 'n' Roll Party Queen" (James Canning, Walter Bobbie); "There Are Worst Things I Could Do" (Adrienne Barbeau); "Look at Me, I'm Sandra Dee" (reprise) (Carole Demas); "All Choked Up" (Carole Demas, Barry Bostwick, Company); "We Go Together" (reprise) (Company)

Grease was a broad but affectionate glimpse at high school life in the late 1950s where there were the Pat Boone types and the Elvis Presley types. (Guess which group emerged the victors.) The musical was mostly a flashback in which the members of the Class of 1959 look back on their years at Rydell High (is the school's name an homage to Bobby?). Danny Zuko (Barry Bostwick) is a beyond-cool tough guy with a ducktail haircut and leather jacket, and he and innocent Sandy Dumbrowski (Carole Demas) were an item over the summer. But come September it's back to school and the romance is seemingly over. So Sandy reinvents herself as a tough motorcycle babe who spouts four-letter words and wears tight slacks, gold hoop earrings, and, yes, a leather jacket. So how can there be anything but true love for Danny and Sandy?

The musical included an array of high school archetypes, including tough Italian "fast" girl Betty Rizzo (Adrienne Barbeau); class clown Roger (Walter Bobbie) who's "the mooning champ of Rydell High"; Cha-Cha Di Gregorio (Kathi Moss), an overweight wallflower who prides herself as being a really great dancer; and confused "Beauty School Dropout" Frenchy (Marya Small), who is cautioned by a heavenly Teen Angel (Alan Paul) that she's a "teenage ne'er-do-well."

The songs were in the style of the era's popular hits, and did their job well: "Summer Nights," "Freddy, My Love," "Shakin' at the High School Hop," and "All Choked Up" might easily have turned up on Dick Clark's *American Bandstand*. Sandy contemplated the horror of "It's Raining on Prom Night"; Danny sang the lament of being "Alone at a Drive-In Movie" where he's reduced to "watchin' werewolves without you"; and Rizzo suggested in "Look at Me, I'm Sandra Dee" that she could play it coy and sweet and "lousy with virginity."

The game cast, Tom Moore's fast-paced direction, and Patricia Birch's lively choreography were enhanced by Douglas W. Schmidt's nostalgic set, which was a collage of advertisement posters (for hair tonics and blackheads) and photos from the era, including a huge one of a sulky James Dean looking down on the proceedings from high above center stage.

Clive Barnes in the *New York Times* seemed uncertain of the musical's chance for success. The show amounted to a "thin joke," but he supposed "if" there was a place for a spoof of the rock-and-roll years of the 1950s, then "*Grease* might well slide into it." But only he reiterated, "If there is a place."

Douglas Watt in the *New York Daily News* found the musical "lively and funny" and noted the songs were "dandies" and "wonderfully evocative of the period"; Jack Kroll in *Newsweek* said the show was "hugely entertaining" and the performers "terrific"; and Betty Rollin on WNBC4TV said she had a "really good time" and liked the "thoroughly wonderful" book and score.

Leonard Harris on WCBSTV2 suggested the "cute idea" of parodying high school life in the 1950s couldn't "sustain itself," and the material was "just not interesting." While Martin Gottfried in *Women's Wear Daily* felt the story was "thin" and "repetitious" and the characters "too shallow and stupid," he said the production itself was "superb" and the cast gave "energetic" performances.

The script was published in hardback by Winter House, Ltd., in 1972, and was also included in the hardback collection *Great Rock Musicals*, edited by Stanley Richards and published by Stein and Day in 1979.

The original cast album was released by MGM Records (LP # 1SE-34-0C) and the CD was issued by Polydor Records (# 827-548-2); the soundtrack was released by RSO Records on a two-LP set (# RS-2-4002; CD # 825-096-2); the film's sequel (see below) was issued by Polydor (CD # 42282-5096-2); the 1994 Broadway revival was released by RCA Victor Records (CD # 09026-62703-2), and when Brooke Shields joined the cast the CD was rereleased with her tracks (# 09026-68179-2). The 2007 Broadway revival was recorded by Sony BMG Music Entertainment/Masterworks Broadway (CD # 88697-16398-2). A 1993 London revival was released by Epic Records (LP # 474632-1) and on CD by Sony (# 474632-2), and a studio cast recording by That's Entertainment Records (CD # CDTER-1220) includes John Barrowman in the cast. There have been a number of foreign cast recordings, including a South African album released by MFP Records (LP # SRSJ-8079); a 1991–1992 season Norwegian cast recording issued by Polydor Records (CD # 513-367-2); and a Hungarian album released by Polygram Records (CD # 521520-2).

The musical was first seen at the intimate Kingston Mines Theatre in Chicago a year earlier in February 1971, and it opened in New York at Off-Broadway's Eden Theatre (once the Phoenix Theatre, the original home of *The Golden Apple*, and, as of this writing, a movie complex). But despite playing in a traditional Off-Broadway house, *Best Plays* reported the production was always under a full-fledged Broadway contract. When the musical transferred to the Broadhurst Theatre four months after opening at the Eden, the "Broadway" transfer was in location only. But the modest little musical wasn't fated for a run of just a year or two in New York. It became a phenomenon and ran out the decade; when it closed in 1980 it was for a time the longest-running musical in the history of Broadway.

The 1978 film version released by Paramount Pictures was that rarity, a hit film based on a hit stage show; John Travolta was Danny Zuko and Olivia Newton-John was Sandy, and others in the cast were Stockard Channing, Edd Byrnes, Lorenzo Lamas, Eve Arden, Joan Blondell, Sid Caesar, Dody Goodman, and Alice Ghostley; and from the stage production Patricia Birch created the film's dances. Four songs were written for the movie: a title song with an irresistibly catchy melody (lyric and music by Barry Gibb); the creamy ballad "Hopelessly Devoted to You" and the lively duet "You're the One That I Want" (both with lyrics and music by John Farrar); and "Sandy" (lyric and music by Louis St. Louis and Scott Simon). Besides becoming a mega-hit movie, the film managed another rarity: it was the first in decades to boast three hit songs (the first three noted above), and later stage revivals sometimes interpolated these numbers into the score. In 1982, Birch directed the film's sequel *Grease 2*, which was produced by Paramount and starred Maxwell Caulfield, Michelle Pfeiffer, Lorna Luft, Tab Hunter, Connie Stevens, and, from the 1978 film, Arden, Caesar, and Goodman. Except for the imaginative and bouncy opening number, "Back to School Again," the film was dreary and charmless.

The first Broadway revival opened on May 11, 1994, at the Eugene O'Neill Theatre and played for 1,505 performances, and a second opened at the Brooks Atkinson Theatre on August 19, 2007, for 554 showings. As of this writing, Fox Network has announced that a three-hour adaptation will be televised live in 2016.

The London production opened on June 26, 1973, at the New London Theatre and played for 236 performances (some sources cite 258 showings), and the cast included Richard Gere as Danny Zuko.

The Broadway production included a number of up-and-coming performers: Barry Bostwick later won the Tony Award for Best Leading Actor in a Musical for ***The Robber Bridegroom***; Walter Bobbie directed the smash hit 1996 revival of ***Chicago***, which as of this writing is still playing and is the longest-running American musical in Broadway history; Alan Paul became one of the vocalists of the Manhattan Transfer singing group; and Adrienne Barbeau was in the cast of the long-running CBS television series *Maude*. The musical's first national tour included more performers who later enjoyed great successes: John Travolta (Doody) became a major television and film star, and as noted above played the leading role of Danny Zuko in the film version of *Grease*; Jerry Zaks (Kenickie) went on to direct a number of Broadway hits, including the long-running revivals of *Anything Goes* (1987), *Guys and Dolls* (1992), and *A Funny Thing Happened on the Way to the Forum* (1996) as well as the long-running composer/lyricist tribute revue *Smokey Joe's Café* (1995); Judy Kaye (Rizzo) enjoyed a long career on Broadway and in recordings, and had major roles in the original New York productions of *The Phantom of the Opera* (1988) and *Mamma Mia!* (2001); and Marilu Henner appeared on the hit ABC television series *Taxi*.

As for Jim Jacobs and Warren Casey, they were never again represented on Broadway with a new musical, but their *Island of Lost Co-eds* ("A New Jungle Musical") opened in Chicago at the 11th Street Theatre under the sponsorship of Columbia College Theatre's Music Center on May 27, 1981 (the team collaborated on the book, and the lyrics and music were by Casey). The musical was a spoof of the Dorothy Lamour South Sea Islands and jungle epics of the late 1930s and early 1940s, and Glenna Syse in the *Chicago Sun-Times* suggested that "if properly honed, there is just a possibility that this musical may have more appeal than did *Grease*." She noted the evening was filled to the brim with sarong-laden maidens, an evil queen, a mad scientist, a rampaging gorilla, a typhoon, a volcano, and even an Ann Miller–styled tap dance. Sounds amusing, but unfortunately the show never found its way to New York.

Awards

Tony Award Nominations: Best Musical (*Grease*); Best Leading Actor in a Musical (Barry Bostwick); Best Featured Actor in a Musical (Timothy Meyers); Best Featured Actress in a Musical (Adrienne Barbeau); Best Book (Jim Jacobs and Warren Casey); Best Costume Designer (Carrie F. Robbins); Best Choreography (Patricia Birch)

THE SELLING OF THE PRESIDENT

"A New Musical!"

Theatre: Shubert Theatre
Opening Date: March 22, 1972; *Closing Date*: March 25, 1972
Performances: 5
Book: Jack O'Brien and Stuart Hample
Lyrics: Jack O'Brien
Music: Bob James
Based on the 1969 book *The Selling of the President* by Joe McGinniss.
Direction: Not credited; *Producers*: John Flaxman in association with Harold Hastings and Franklin Roberts; *Musical Staging*: Ethel Martin; *Scenery*: Tom John; *Multi-Media Designs*: William Claxton, Mort Kasman, Gary Youngman, and Jim Sant'Andrea; *Costumes*: Nancy Potts; *Lighting*: Thomas Skelton; *Musical Direction*: Harold Hastings
Cast: *Pat Hingle* (Senator George W. Mason), Barbara Barrie (Grace Mason), Richard Goode (Senator Hiram Robinson), Robert Fitzsimmons (Sydney Wales), Karen Morrow (Irene Jantzen), Robert Darnell (Ted Bacon), John Glover (Ward Nichols), Johnny Olson (Johnny Olson), John Bentley (Arthur Hayes); Television's Top Singers and Dancers: Tim Noble (Minister, Davey, Ralph Reeder), Steve Shochet (Captain Terror, Barney Zawicki), Sheilah Rae (Timmy, Molly Kilgallen), Philip M. Thomas (Creepy, Randall Phillips), Pi Douglass (Ghoulie, Franklin Douglass Pierce), Rick Atwell (Van Denisovich), Jamie Carr (Casey Steele), Suellen Estey (Bonnie Sue Tyler), Delores Hall (Gloria Miller), Pamela Myers (Linda Allington), Trina Parks (Burgundy Moore), Deborah St. Darr (Inga Brand), Bill Rienecke (Doctor Lloyd Bienheim), Lurlu Lindsay (Mrs. Pearline Gibbons), Peter Grounds (Mr. Warren Stevenson), Vilma Vaccaro (Fleetwing Horn), Pam Zarit (Julie Milano); And: George Andrew Robinson and Michael Serrecchia
The musical was presented in two acts.
The action takes place in 1976.

Musical Numbers

Act One: "Something Holy" (Delores Hall, Company); "If You Like People" (Suellen Estey, Tim Noble); "Sunset" (Pi Douglass, Tim Noble, George Andrew Robinson, Steve Schochet); "If You Like People" (reprise) (Sheilah Rae, Pam Zarit, Rick Atwell, Steve Schochet, Deborah St. Darr); "Little Moon" (Jamie Carr, Vilma Vaccaro); "Come-on-a-Good-Life" (Pi Douglass, Trina Parks, Philip Thomas, Delores Hall); "I've Got to Trust You" (Pamela Myers); "If You Like People" (reprise) (Company); "Mason Cares" (Suellen Estey, Sheilah Rae, Deborah St. Darr, Pam Zarit); "On the Winning Side" (Pamela Myers); "Captain Terror" (Sheilah Rae, Steve Schochet, Pi Douglass, Philip Thomas); "He's a Man" (Trina Parks, Pam Zarit, Delores Hall)

Act Two: "Stars of Glory" (Tim Noble); "Terminix" (Steve Schochet, Deborah St. Darr, Suellen Estey, Pamela Myers); "Take My Hand" (Jamie Carr, Delores Hall, Steve Schochet, Vilma Vaccaro); "A Passacaglia" (Company); "We're Gonna Live It Together" (Company); "America" (Company)

The Selling of the President was based on Joe McGinniss's 1969 best seller about the television marketing campaign for Richard Nixon's successful 1968 presidential run. By the time of the musical's opening night on Broadway, McGinniss had disowned the production; the producers had already gone ahead and posted a closing notice; and there was no director credited in the program. None of these were good signs.

The musical used only the title of McGinniss's book, and instead a completely new story line was created about bland Senator George W. Mason (Pat Hingle) and his equally bland wife Grace (Barbara Barrie). Mason wants to be president, and thus media expert Irene Jantzen (Karen Morrow) takes over his campaign by using television to sell a potential U.S. president as a product. And so Mason wins the election and thus proves that Madison Avenue's marketing is more important than the man.

Like ***The Sign in Sidney Brustein's Window***, none of the characters sang a note of music, a somewhat unwise decision when the cast included Karen Morrow, one of Broadway's most splendid belters. Imagine casting Merman in a musical and not giving her a chance to sing! And so the musical seemed wrong-headed from the very beginning. The chorus performed all the numbers, none of which were book songs and instead were scattered throughout the evening to represent television commercials about the presidential candidate. Like the later ***Shelter***, the entire production took place in a television studio, and was crammed with banks of cameras, monitors, and lighting equipment. There was even a professional warm-up host in the person of Johnny Olson, who played himself and chatted up the audience. The evening was meant to be satirical, but the satire was heavy-handed, particularly in a scene that found the triumphant new president and first lady encased in a container of plastic emblazoned with the words "made in the U.S.A."

The show received dreadful reviews, and didn't last a full week. Douglas Watt in the *New York Daily News* said the musical "lacks the humor, thrust and point of view to make it salable," while Richard Watts in the *New York Post* found it "completely uninspired, lacking in anything faintly approaching stimulation," adding that it failed as both satire and musical comedy. George Melloan in the *Wall Street Journal* said the evening's greatest flaw was its "lack of any sense of humanity" and thus it was almost impossible for the audience to identify with the "caricatured figures" depicted on stage.

According to Kevin Sanders on WABCTV7, the musical seldom rose "above the level of a not very stylish or subtle college revue," and if marketing was what the musical was all about, then it was "going to need a very good advertising campaign." Betty Rollin on WNBC4TV said the evening was a "great big, expensive, super-produced bomb."

Martin Gottfried in *Women's Wear Daily* noted that the musical alternated between being a "nuisance" and a "shambles," and said he found "the prospect of returning for the second act unbearable." He concluded by saying the "degradation" by "primitives" of Broadway's "once-proud" musical theatre was "insufferable." Clive Barnes in the *New York Times* said the production had a "great idea for a musical" and "someone should have written book, lyrics and music for it." But the "great idea got lost on the way to the theatre" and its "main chance is timorously missed in a Sargasso Sea of mediocrity." The book was "too weak, emasculated and inane to draw the political blood needed for it to survive," and the music was "so unmemorable that you have forgotten it before you have even heard it." In the same newspaper, Walter Kerr said *The Selling of the President* was a musical of "staggering ineptitude" with dialogue that seemed to have been taken from *The Little Golden Book of the World of Politics* "by a child short on reading skills."

Although the score was generally ignored by the critics, both Watt and Watts singled out the patriotic "Take My Hand" and Sanders liked "He's a Man," a big "rah rah" production number "full of organic frenzy," which "rescued" the show.

During the tryout, Robert H. Livingston was the director; as noted, by the time the musical reached New York there was no director of record listed in the program. Talley Beatty was the choreographer, but by New York he was no longer with the show and Ethel Martin received "musical staging" credit. Howard St. John was in the cast, and was succeeded by Robert Fitzsimmons. The following songs were dropped: "Accupressure," "Cap Game," and "Minority Ticket."

During the period of the Philadelphia tryout, Donald Janson in the *New York Times* reported that McGinniss was unhappy that "a business executive associated with Terminix" (a pest-control company) had provided "substantial backing" for the production and that the script included commercial ads for the product.

As a result, McGinniss filed a complaint about the use of the commercials with the New York Dramatists Guild and the American Arbitration Association. Producer John Flaxman said he would go to court over his stand to retain the commercials, and noted that Terminix didn't have any money in the production although someone "connected with Terminix" did. In the meantime, McGinniss canceled his appearances to promote the musical. The opening night program included a song titled "Terminix," but presumably the legal issues surrounding the matter became moot when the musical closed on Broadway after five performances.

A FUNNY THING HAPPENED ON THE WAY TO THE FORUM

Theatre: Lunt-Fontanne Theatre
Opening Date: March 30, 1972; *Closing Date*: August 12, 1972
Performances: 156
Book: Burt Shevelove and Larry Gelbart
Lyrics and *Music*: Stephen Sondheim
Based on the "style and spirit" of the twenty-six surviving plays by the third-century Roman playwright Titus Maccius Plautus, including his comedy *Mostellaria*.
Direction: Burt Shevelove; *Producers*: David Black in association with Seymour Vall and Henry Honeckman, and Larry Blyden; *Choreography*: Ralph Beaumont; *Scenery*: James Trittipo; *Costumes*: Noel Taylor; *Lighting*: H. R. Poindexter; *Musical Direction*: Milton Rosenstock
Cast: *Phil Silvers* (Prologus, Pseudolus), Jack Collins (Senex), Lizabeth Pritchett (Domina), John Hansen (Hero), Larry Blyden (Hysterium), Carl Ballantine (Marcus Lycus), Reginald Owen (Erronius), Carl Lindstrom (Miles Gloriosus), Lauren Lucas (Tintinabula), Gloria Mills (Panacea), Trish Mahoney and Sonja Haney (The Geminae), Keita Keita (Vibrata), Charlene Ryan (Gymnasia), Pamela Hall (Philia), Joe Ross (Protean), Bill Starr (Protean), Chad Block (Protean)
The musical was presented in two acts.
The action takes place in Rome during a day in spring two hundred years before the Christian era.

Musical Numbers

Act One: "Comedy Tonight" (Phil Silvers, The Proteans, Company); "Farewell" (Lizabeth Pritchett); "Love, I Hear" (John Hansen); "Free" (Phil Silvers, John Hansen); "The House of Marcus Lycus" (Carl Ballantine); "Lovely" (John Hansen, Pamela Hall); "Everybody Ought to Have a Maid" (Jack Collins, Phil Silvers, Larry Blyden, Carl Ballantine); "I'm Calm" (Larry Blyden); "Impossible" (Jack Collins, John Hansen); "Bring Me My Bride" (Carl Lindstrom, Phil Silvers, The Proteans, The Courtesans)
Act Two: "That Dirty Old Man" (Lizabeth Pritchett); "Echo Song" (Pamela Hall, John Hansen); "Lovely" (reprise) (Phil Silvers, Larry Blyden); "Dirge" (Carl Lindstrom, Phil Silvers, Mourners); "Comedy Tonight" (Company)

The current revival of *A Funny Thing Happened on the Way to the Forum* opened just eight years after the original production had closed on Broadway, but perhaps eight years was too long a wait. Along with *How to Succeed in Business without Really Trying* (1961), *Forum* is one of the most comic of all musicals and perhaps should be revived regularly every three or four seasons. The current carnival was a particular delight, because the roles of Prologus and the slave Pseudolus were played by Phil Silvers, for whom the musical had originally been written (when Silvers wasn't available to appear in the original production, Zero Mostel was signed). Mostel won the Tony Award for Best Actor in a Musical, and for the revival Silvers won a Tony for himself; and when Nathan Lane starred in the 1996 revival, he too won a Tony. It is a musical-comedy dream role, one of the grandest ever written for the stage.

As the curtain rises, Prologus (Silvers) announces there'll be a "comedy tonight" (and "tragedy tomorrow"), and soon the musical was neck-deep in a free-for-all, nonstop farce of one-liners, eccentric characters, amusing songs, and Marx Brothers–styled plot complications. A eunuch is warned, "Don't you lower your voice to me!" and is told he's so incompetent he'll be a eunuch all his life; an egotistical warrior modestly sings, "I am a parade"; a slave states, "I live to grovel"; two lovers who fear happiness will never be theirs decide they'll just have "to learn to be happy without it"; and when someone asks if a plague is contagious, the response is, "Did you ever see a plague that wasn't?"

The hero (named Hero, of course, and played by John Hansen) is in love with Philia (Pamela Hall), the virgin next door. Trouble is, "next door" is a bawdy house run by Marcus Lycus (Carl Ballantine), which includes such kinky courtesans as Vibrata and Gymnasia, and Philia is scheduled to be sold to celebrity warrior Miles Gloriosus (Carl Lindstrom). It's later discovered that Philia and Miles are brother and sister, and the revelation couldn't have come soon enough or there would have indeed been a tragedy tomorrow. To make matters worse, Hero's father, Senex (Jack Collins), has his eye on Philia (an "impossible" situation filled with "horrible, impossible possibilities" in a father-and-son duet). But Senex is kept under a tight leash by his wife, the dominating Domina (Lizabeth Pritchard).

Hero promises to free his slave Pseudolus (Silvers) if the latter can secure Philia from Lycus, whom Pseudolus salutes as "a gentleman and a procurer." The opening song "Comedy Tonight" promised "a happy ending, of course," but not before the hysterical slave Hysterium (Larry Blyden) must don Philia drag and impersonate her. The original cast album's liner notes explained that the resolution of the plot was worked out by the authors "on an IBM machine."

Burt Shevelove and Larry Gelbart's breathlessly funny book was a masterpiece of mad comedy, and the book was splendidly supported by the carefree and merry songs of Stephen Sondheim, who here for the first time was represented as both lyricist and composer for a Broadway musical. The delicious score included the expansive opening number "Comedy Tonight," in which practically the entire plot is described and all the characters are introduced; the leering quartet "Everybody Ought to Have a Maid"; the loopy yet lovely ballad "Lovely" (in which Philia sings that "lovely is the one thing I can do"); and Domina's red-hot lament for Senex, "That Dirty Old Man" ("of mine").

The revival received great notices, and Martin Gottfried in *Women's Wear Daily* stated that Shevelove and Gelbart's "marvelous" book was "tremendously funny." It was "literary, consistent and impeccably structured," and was perhaps "the best book in all our musical theatre." He felt the original production had never been truly recognized as the "masterwork" it was, and he hoped the revival would clearly demonstrate that here was a "true classic."

Clive Barnes in the *New York Times* praised the "funniest, bawdiest and most enchanting Broadway musical," noted few shows were "so well-crafted," and said Silvers was a "total delight." Douglas Watt in the *New York Daily News* told his readers if they couldn't remember the last time they laughed "without letup," then they should hasten to the Lunt-Fontanne Theatre where "joy" awaited them. Richard Watts in the *New York Post* loved the "uproarious" and "excellent" revival, praised Sondheim's "melodious" score, and said Silvers had "never been in better comic form." T. E. Kalem in *Time* noted that Mostel had been "gloriously funny" in the original production, and now Silvers proved he was "every wit his equal." And Kevin Sanders on WABCTV7 praised the "first-class Broadway musical" with its "beautifully timed slapstick comedy" and Silvers's "flawless sense of stage comedy."

Despite the critical raves and Tony Awards to Silvers and Blyden, the revival closed after less than five months because of Silvers's health, and he even missed the entire final week of performances (during part of the run, John Bentley and then Tom Poston spelled him). *Variety* reported the revival lost $330,000 on its $280,000 capitalization.

The current production had first opened in Los Angeles at the Ahmanson Theatre on October 13, 1971, for forty-seven performances, and Nancy Walker played Domina (this was the third pairing of Walker and Silvers: they had appeared together in Jule Styne's 1954 musical film *Lucky Me*, and in 1960 starred on Broadway in Styne's musical *Do Re Mi*). For Walker, Sondheim wrote a new song ("Farewell"), but because of other commitments she wasn't able to appear in the New York production.

After Los Angeles, the musical played in Chicago, where Peg Murray replaced Walker (Murray was in turn succeeded by Lizabeth Pritchett). Lew Parker played Senex, but poor health resulted in his quick departure from the revival just days before the New York opening (Parker died a few months later). *Variety* reported that although Jack Collins wasn't Parker's understudy and had played the role just four times prior to the New York opening night, Collins went on for the premiere. Mort Marshall later joined the cast, and played Senex for the remainder of the run.

The revival included the "Echo Song" (which had been written for the original production but was cut during the tryout) for Philia and Hero, and dropped their trio with Pseudolus, the tongue-twisting "Pretty Little Picture." Also cut was Philia's wonderfully illogical "That'll Show Him" in which she describes how she'll get even with Miles Gloriosus: she and Miles will make mad, passionate love, but *all the while* she'll be thinking of Hero.

The original production opened at the Alvin (now Neil Simon) Theatre on May 8, 1962, for 964 performances and won Tony Awards for Best Musical, Best Book, Best Producer of a Musical (Harold Prince), Best Director of a Musical (George Abbott), Best Leading Actor in a Musical (Mostel), and Best Featured Actor in a Musical (David Burns, who played Senex). The 1996 revival opened at the St. James Theatre on April 18, 1996, for 715 performances, and like Mostel and Silvers before him, Nathan Lane won the Tony Award for Best Leading Actor in a Musical. This revival omitted "Pretty Little Picture" as well as "Farewell" and "Echo Song," but included "That'll Show Him."

The original London production opened on October 3, 1963, at the Strand Theatre for 762 performances; the cast included Frankie Howerd (Pseudolus) and Leon Greene (Miles Gloriosus), and the two later appeared in the same roles for the 1986 revival, which opened on November 14 at the Piccadilly Theatre for forty-nine performances.

The 1966 film version was directed by Richard Lester and included Zero Mostel and Jack Gilford from the original cast; here, Phil Silvers played Marcus Lycus, and others in the film were Michael Crawford (Hero), Buster Keaton (Erronius), and, from the British production, Leon Greene as Miles Gloriosus. The film was too busy, but on its own terms as a comedy was amusing; however, too little of Sondheim's score was retained (only "Comedy Tonight," "Lovely," "Everybody Ought to Have a Maid," and "The Dirge" aka "Funeral Sequence") "Free" seems to have been filmed because a scene between Mostel and Crawford leads right up to the song and then there's a quick cut to the next scene.

The script was published in hardback by Dodd, Mead in 1963, and the publisher included the script in a 1983 paperback, which also offered Sondheim's 1973 musical *The Frogs*. A paperback edition of the script was published in London by Frank Music Co. in 1963, and in 1991 Applause Theatre Book Publishers issued both hardback and paperback editions. Both the 1983 and 1991 publications include the lyrics for a number of deleted songs, some of which were cut during the 1962 tryout ("Love Is in the Air" and "Your Eyes Are Blue"); others cut in preproduction ("Invocation," "There's Something about a War," and "The Gaggle of Geese," the latter only in the 1991 edition); one dropped during rehearsals ("I Do Like You"); one written for the current revival ("Farewell"); and a complete version of "The House of Marcus Lycus."

The script is also included in the 2014 Library of Congress hardback collection *American Musicals*, which also offers the scripts of fifteen other musicals. All the lyrics are included in Sondheim's collection *Finishing the Hat: Collected Lyrics (1954–1981) with Attendant Comments, Principles, Heresies, Grudges, Whines and Anecdotes* (published by Alfred A. Knopf in 2010). Hero's "What Do You Do with a Woman?" appears to have been dropped during rehearsals, and "Love Story" was dropped during the original tryout.

The private demo recording of the score played and sung by Sondheim includes songs dropped in preproduction as well as ones dropped during rehearsals or the tryout ("Invocation," "Love Is in the Air," "Your Eyes Are Blue," "I Do Like You," "Miles Gloriosus," "Echo Song," "The Gaggle of Geese," "The Window across the Way," and "There's Something about a War") and also includes songs heard in the original Broadway production ("Love, I Hear," "Free," "The House of Marcus Lycus," "Pretty Little Picture," "Everybody Ought to Have a Maid," "That'll Show Him," "That Dirty Old Man," "Lovely," and "Impossible").

The 1962 original cast album was recorded by Capitol Records (LP # S/WAO-1717), and later issued on CD by Bay Cities Records (# BCD-3002) and Broadway Angel Records (# ZDM-0777-7-64770-2-2). The 1996 revival was issued by Angel Records (CD # 7243-8-52223-2-0), and the 1963 London cast recording was released by His Master's Voice/EMI Records (LP # CLP-1685), reissued on LP by Stet Records (# DS-15028), and later issued on CD by EMI Records (# 0777-7-89060-2). The soundtrack album was released by United Artists Records (LP # UAS-5144 and # UAL-4144) and then on CD by Ryko Records (# RCD-10727).

Other recordings of the score are an EP (extended play) recording of the Mexico City cast (titled *Amor al reves es Roma*, it was released by CBS Records # EPC-274 and includes "Comedy Tonight," "Love, I Hear," "Lovely," and "Pretty Little Picture") and an instrumental version by The Trotter Trio (CD # VSD-5707) titled *A Funny Thing Happened on the Way to the Forum . . . in Jazz* (the selections include "Your Eyes Are Blue").

The film version is available on two DVD collections, and most recently was released on DVD by Kino Lober Films.

In a preface to the 1991 edition of the script, co-librettist Larry Gelbart noted that he and Burt Shevelove's goal had been to create a musical in the "style and spirit" of the twenty-six surviving comedies by third-century Roman playwright Titus Maccius Plautus. Their working title was *A Roman Comedy*, and, believe it or not, one of Plautus's comedies was titled *Mostellaria*.

Awards

Tony Awards and Nominations: Best Leading Actor in a Musical (**Phil Silvers**); Best Featured Actor in a Musical (**Larry Blyden**); Best Director of a Musical (Burt Shevelove)

SUGAR

"A New Musical Comedy"

Theatre: Majestic Theatre
Opening Date: April 9, 1972; *Closing Date*: June 23, 1973
Performances: 505
Book: Peter Stone
Lyrics: Bob Merrill
Music: Jule Styne
Based on the screenplay by Billy Wilder and I. A. L. Diamond for the 1959 film *Some Like It Hot* and on a story by Robert Thoeren.
Direction and *Choreography*: Gower Champion (Bert Michaels, Associate Choreographer); *Producer*: David Merrick; *Scenery*: Robin Wagner; *Costumes*: Alvin Colt; *Lighting*: Martin Aronstein; *Musical Direction*: Elliot Lawrence
Cast: Sheila Smith (Sweet Sue); The Society Syncopaters: Harriett Conrad (Piano), Linda Gandell (Drums), Nicole Barth (Bass), Leslie Latham (Trumpet), Marylou Sirinek (Trumpet), Terry Cullen (Trombone), Kathleen Witmer (Trombone), Pam (Pamela) Blair (Saxophone), Eileen Casey (Saxophone), Debra Lynn (Saxophone), Sally Neal (Saxophone), and Mary Zahn (Saxophone); Alan Kass (Bienstock), Tony Roberts (Joe, and later Geraldine), Robert Morse (Jerry, and later Daphne), Steve Condos (Spats Palazzo), Gerard Brentte (Dude); Spats's Gang: Andy Bew, Roger Bigelow, Gene Cooper, Arthur Faria, Gene GeBauer, John Mineo, and Don Percassi; Dick Bonelle (Knuckles Norton), Igors Gavon (First Poker Player); Knuckles's Gang: Ken Ayers, Richard Maxon, Dale Muchmore, and Alexander Orfaly; Elaine Joyce (Sugar Kane), Ken Ayers (Cabdriver), Eileen Casey (Olga); Sunbathers: Nicole Barth, Pam Blair, Eileen Casey, Robin Hoctor, Debra Lynn, Peggy Lyman, Sally Neal, and Pamela Sousa; George Blackwell (Train Conductor), Andy Bew (Bellboy), Cyril Ritchard (Osgood Fielding Jr.); "Chicago" Singers: Ken Ayers, George Blackwell, Dick Bonelle, Igors Gavon, Hal Norman
The musical was presented in two acts.
The action takes place in 1931 in Chicago, Miami, and "in between."

Musical Numbers

Act One: Overture (Orchestra); "Windy City Marmalade" (Sheila Smith, The Society Syncopaters); "Penniless Bums" (Robert Morse, Tony Roberts, Unemployed Musicians); "Tear the Town Apart" (dance) (Steve Condos, Spats's Gang); "The Beauty That Drives Men Mad" (Robert Morse, Tony Roberts); "We Could Be Close" (Robert Morse, Elaine Joyce); "Sun on My Face" (Robert Morse, Tony Roberts, Elaine Joyce, Sheila Smith, Alan Kass, Ensemble); "The November Song" (Cyril Ritchard, The Millionaires); "(Doin' It for) Sugar" (Robert Morse, Tony Roberts)
Act Two: Entr'acte (Orchestra); "Hey, Why Not!" (Elaine Joyce, Ensemble); "Beautiful Through and Through" (Cyril Ritchard, Robert Morse); "What Do You Give to a Man Who's Had Everything?" (Tony Roberts, Elaine Joyce); "Magic Nights" (Robert Morse); "It's Always Love" (Tony Roberts); "When You Meet a Man in Chicago" (Robert Morse, Tony Roberts, Elaine Joyce, Sheila Smith, The Society Syncopaters, The Chorus Line)

Sugar was a generally uninspired adaptation of Billy Wilder's legendary farce *Some Like It Hot*. The movie was perfection, and a musical version had to match it in every respect in order to compete with the film's memorable performances, its hilarious screenplay with madcap situations and nonstop one-liners, and Billy Wilder's smooth and ingenious direction. The musical had the cream of Broadway behind it, including Gower Champion (choreography and direction), Jule Styne (music), Peter Stone (book), Robin Wagner (scenery), Alvin Colt (costumes), David Merrick (producer), and, last but not least, Robert Morse in the role of Jerry (and Daphne). But not everyone was at the top of their game, and so *Sugar* was a disappointment. Maybe it was impossible to duplicate the film: every moment is screamingly funny, the upper-berth train scene is one of the screen's classic comical moments, and Marilyn Monroe and Jack Lemmon's performances are the pinnacles of their careers.

Titled *All for Sugar* in preproduction, the musical was in trouble from its very first preview at the Kennedy Center's Opera House in Washington, D.C. Its long and arduous tryout (with one city added almost at the last moment) increased its budget, and the middling reviews weren't helpful at the box office. But despite its relatively short run of 505 performances, the musical managed to show a profit.

The familiar story began in the Chicago of 1931 (the film's action occurred in 1929) when down-and-out musicians Joe (Tony Roberts) and Jerry (Robert Morse) have the bad luck to be the only witnesses of the St. Valentine's Day massacre. In order to throw Spats Palazzo (Steve Condos) and his guns off their trail, the boys don drag as Geraldine and Daphne and join an all-girl band on its way to Miami. One of the band members is Sugar Kane (Elaine Joyce), and in Miami Joe dons playboy drag and pretends to be a millionaire in order to romance her. In the meantime, Jerry-as-Daphne is pursued by Osgood Fielding Jr. (Cyril Ritchard), a genuinely dirty-old-man and a genuine millionaire. All hell breaks loose when Spats and his gang arrive at the very hotel where the band is booked, but all ends well: the boys escape from the gangsters, and Sugar loves Joe despite the fact he's just a poor saxophone player. But the relationship between Jerry/Daphne and Osgood purposely leaves us up in the air because Osgood doesn't seem surprised or concerned that Daphne is really a man.

Stone's script and Styne and Bob Merrill's score were mostly perfunctory, and generally told the story in by-the-numbers fashion. But there were occasional good things in the show, the best being Robert Morse's truly hysterical performance as Jerry/Daphne. Jack Lemmon would seem to have no equal in the role, but Morse's performance was deliriously demented, and the sequence when he realizes he's the subject of Osgood's affection was one of memorable insanity. He flounced about the stage like a moonstruck school girl in the throes of first romance, and came to the happy realization that diamonds can be a boy's best friend, too. Another delight had Spats tap dancing his dialogue, a notion that was truly inspired.

As for the score, it was pleasant but had just two stand-out numbers. Joe and Jerry made their first appearance in drag with "The Beauty That Drives Men Mad," a rousing old-fashioned show-tune which they sang with the gusto of old-time Broadway. And "When You Meet a Man in Chicago" was a quirky off-the-wall admonition to "never ask what business he's in" because, after all, this was the Prohibition era. Many made the case for Joe's "It's Always Love," but it was overwrought and bombastic and was wisely dropped during the major 1974 regional production that toured with Morse (see below).

The critics were generally unhappy with the musical. Douglas Watt in the *New York Daily News* said *Sugar* "spends two hours trying to catch up" with *Some Like It Hot* but never does. Instead, "it just winds up breathless" and was a show of "unswerving mediocrity." Clive Barnes in the *New York Times* noted that "rarely in show-business history has so much been done by so many for so little," for here was music that "scarcely leaves the ground" with "oddly graceless and uninteresting" lyrics. Everything had been done for the show ("short of closing it out of town"), but at least Broadway had the "positive treat" of seeing an "absolutely brilliant" performance by Morse. Further, Champion had directed the musical with "demonic energy and verve" and so "for what it is" the evening was "in perfect shape" and couldn't "have been done better."

George Melloan in the *Wall Street Journal* found the evening a "pale imitation" of the film and noted the audience had "been there before" and "before" was "better." T. E. Kalem in *Time* said *Sugar* wasn't "organic" and instead was "thoroughly processed, refined and filtered" to the point where it lost its "natural energy" and became a "sterile display of high-gloss techniques." Martin Gottfried in *Women's Wear Daily* found the book "listless, humorless and dreary" but noted parts of the score "included some of Styne's best work in years." He concluded that *Sugar* had been written and produced for "no reason" other "than to work" . . . and "it didn't." Kevin Sanders on WABCTV7 admitted the musical had "dash and precision," but he wished "all this talent" had instead been "lavished on more original material."

But Leonard Harris on WCBSTV2 liked the "socko" musical, and Betty Rollin on WNBC4TV said the "big, slick fabulous" evening was "just swell." Richard Watts in the *New York Post* found the show "funny," and praised the "handsome and inventive" production.

As for Morse, Gottfried liked his "genuinely comic" performance, and when Jerry-as-Daphne finds himself in the throes of courtship and romance the musical reached its "most comic and affecting peak." Kalem said Morse lent a "touch of genius" to the production; Harris said he was "simply superb"; and Barnes found his "slyly irrepressible," "funny," and "moving" performance full of "sharp insight."

The chaotic tryout lasted three months, during which time Merrick ditched all of Jo Mielziner's scenery and had it replaced with new décor by Robin Wagner. Singer Johnny Desmond as Spats was succeeded by Steve Condos when it became clear the role would be an all-dancing one. Bert Michaels's role of Joker Gomez was eliminated, but he remained with the production as associate choreographer; and when the roles of Poliakoff and Little Bonaparte (both played by Ted Beniades) and Nellie (Connie Day) were eliminated, the two performers left the production.

The following songs were cut during the tryout: "The Girls in the Band," "Wish We Could Turn Back the Clock," "The Speakeasy," "All You Gotta Do Is Tell Me," "The Massacre," "The People in My Life," "My Nice Ways," "Spats-s-s Palazzo," "The Kooka Rooki Bongo," "Sun on Your Face" (which was different from "Sun on My Face"), and "These Eyes Have Seen Too Much." "Jerry's Ecstasy" was probably the tryout title of "Magic Nights." "(Doin' It for) Sugar" and "Sugar" were different songs heard during the tryout, and the latter was eventually cut. "The People in My Life" was a touching torch song for Sugar, but was sung during the train sequence and slowed up the action. It was reinstated for the 1974 revival, but was unwisely assigned to Joe: his character was clearly all wrong for such a plaintive blues number (with a lyric by Frank Loesser, the number was originally sung as "Look at You, Look at Me" in the 1941 film *Sis Hopkins* and can be heard on the collection *Micahael Feinstein Sings/The Jule Styne Songbook* released by Elektra Nonesuch CD # 9-79274-2). "The Kooka Rooki Bongo" was a lively production number and Morse was dazzling in Carmen Miranda-styled drag, but the song's South American rhythms were about a decade too early for a show set in 1931. "My Nice Ways" appears to be the same song that earlier had been heard during the pre-Broadway tryout of *Holly Golightly* (1966) with lyric and music by Bob Merrill. (When the musical previewed on Broadway as *Breakfast at Tiffany's*, "My Nice Ways" was no longer part of the score.)

The cast album was released by United Artists (LP # UAS-9905), and was issued twice on CD. The first was by Ryko Records (# RCD-10760) and the second by Kritzerland (CD # KR-20016-7); the latter includes the original album mix as well as a newly remixed version. The cast recording omitted three numbers ("Windy City Marmalade," "Tear the Town Apart," and "Magic Nights"), but as noted below the two latter numbers were included on the cast albums of foreign productions. The demo recording (Chappell Records # C-102-A) includes the cut songs "The People in My Life," "All You Gotta Do Is Tell Me," "Sun on Your Face," and "My Nice Ways."

In 1974, the musical briefly toured with Robert Morse and Steve Condos reprising their Broadway roles; others in the cast were Larry Kert (Joe), Leland Palmer (Sugar), Gale Gordon (Osgood), and Virginia Martin (Sweet Sue). The revival omitted "Windy City Marmalade," "Sun on My Face," "What Do You Give to a Man Who's Had Everything?," and "It's Always Love." Reinstated from the tryout were "My Nice Ways" and "The People in My Life" (as noted, the latter was unfortunately assigned to Joe). The production also included three new songs, "See You Around" (for Sugar), "Don't Be Afraid" (for Joe and Sugar), and "I'm Engaged" (for Jerry).

As *Some Like It Hot*, the musical premiered in London at the Prince Edward Theatre on March 2, 1992; Tommy Steele was Jerry. The production retained nine songs from the Broadway production and added "I'm Naive," from Styne and Merrill's 1965 television musical *The Dangerous Christmas of Red Riding Hood*, and "Dirty Old Men" (aka "Lament for Ten Men") from Merrill's *Breakfast at Tiffany's*, which closed during Broadway previews in 1966. The production also included the standard "Maple Leaf Rag" and a new title song (by Styne and Merrill). The cast recording was issued by First Night Records (CD # CD-28). "I'm Naive" is included in the collection *Lost in Boston IV* (Varese Sarabande CD # VSD-5768).

There are a number of cast albums from foreign productions. A 1999 Norwegian version (titled *Sugar*) was issued by Tylden Records (CD # GTACD-8121) and includes "Pengelens boms," "Novembersang," "Hva kan du gi til en mann som har provet alt," and "Magisk natt"; the 2000 Italian cast album *A qualcuno piace caldo* (Compagnia della Rancia Records CD # 3C) includes a number of songs from the Broadway production as well as two 1920s numbers heard in the original film ("Running Wild" and "I Wanna Be Loved by You"); and a 2003 Polish version *Sugar: Nekdo to rad horke* (unnumbered CD by CSOB) offers seven numbers from the musical (including "Tear the Town Apart"), a number of standards that were performed in the film, and a few popular songs (such as "Blue Moon," "Bei mir bist du schon" and "Beat Me Daddy Eight to the Bar"). An undated Mexico City cast album (titled *Sugar*) was recorded by Raff (LP # RF-9011) and includes nine songs from the score.

In 2002, a revised version of the musical (now titled *Some Like It Hot*) toured with Tony Curtis (who had played Joe in the original film and was now Osgood). The production wisely avoided New York, and most of its leads were generally insipid. But James Leonard Joy's décor was fanciful, with black and white settings for Chicago and Technicolor carnival sets for Miami, and Dan Siretta's choreography was surprisingly delightful with fine old-fashioned Broadway dances. The production omitted one song from the Broadway version ("Windy City Marmalade"); reinstated "The People in My Life," which had been cut from the tryout (the song was now Sugar's again); included the title song, which had been written for the London version; added a new song, "Shell Oil"; and "We Play in the Band" was probably a reworked version of "The Girls in the Band," which had been cut during the tryout. From the original film, the standard "Running Wild" was included, and "I Fall in Love Too Easily" (lyric by Sammy Cahn, music by Styne) from the 1947 MGM musical *It Happened in Brooklyn* was interpolated into the score.

Awards

Tony Award Nominations: Best Musical (*Sugar*); Best Leading Actor in a Musical (Robert Morse); Best Director of a Musical (Gower Champion); Best Choreographer (Gower Champion)

THAT'S ENTERTAINMENT

"A Musical"

Theatre: Edison Theatre
Opening Date: April 14, 1972; *Closing Date*: April 16, 1972
Performances: 4
Lyrics: Howard Dietz
Music: Arthur Schwartz
Direction: Paul Aaron; *Producers*: Gordon Crowe in association with J. Robert Breton; *Choreography*: Larry Fuller (Merry Lynn Katis, Assistant Choreographer); *Scenery* and *Lighting*: David F. Segal; *Costumes*: Jane Greenwood; *Musical Direction*: Luther Henderson
Cast: David Chaney (Greg), Jered Holmes (Richard), Judith Knaiz (Carol), Michon Peacock (Adele), Vivian Reed (Lena), Scott Salmon (Jack), Bonnie Schon (Lucille), Michael Vita (Donald), Alan Weeks (Sam)
The revue was presented in two acts.

Musical Numbers

Act One: "The Overture" (Company); Medley: "We Won't Take It Back" (*Inside U.S.A.*, 1948), "Hammacher Schlemmer, I Love You" (*The Little Show*, 1929), and "Come, Oh, Come (to Pittsburgh)" (*Inside U.S.A.*, 1948) (Michon Peacock, Bonnie Schon, Scott Salmon, David Chaney); "I'm Glad I'm Single" (*The Gay Life*, 1961) (Jared Holmes); "You're Not the Type" (*The Gay Life*, 1961) and "(What's the Use of Being) Miserable with You" (*The Band Wagon*, 1931) (Judith Knaiz, Jared Holmes); "Something to Remember You By" (*Three's a Crowd*, 1930) (Judith Knaiz); "Hottentot Potentate" (*At Home Abroad*, 1935) (Vivian Reed, Alan Weeks); "Day after Day" (*Flying Colors*, 1932) and "Fly by Night" (*Between the Devil*, 1937) (Company); "Everything" (possibly "You Have Everything" from *Between the Devil*, 1937) (Jared Holmes); "Blue Grass (of Kentucky)" (*Inside U.S.A.*, 1948) (Alan Weeks); "Fatal Fascination" (*Flying Colors*, 1932) and "White Heat" (*The Band Wagon*, 1931) (Bonnie Schon); "Right at the Start of It" (*Three's a Crowd*, 1930) (Alan Weeks); "Confession" (*The Band Wagon*, 1931) (Judith Knaiz, Michael Vita); "Smoking Reefers" (*Flying Colors*, 1932) (Vivian Reed); "How High Can a Little Bird Fly?" (1936 London musical *Follow the Sun*) (Scott Salmon); "Keep Off the Grass" (source unknown) (David Chaney); "I See Your Face before Me" (*Between the Devil*, 1937) (Michael Vita, Michon Peacock); "Experience" (*Between the Devil*, 1937)

(David Chaney); "Two-Faced Woman" (*Flying Colors*, 1932) (Alan Weeks); "Foolish Face" (*The Second Little Show*, 1930) (Scott Salmon); "By Myself" (*Between the Devil*, 1937) (Vivian Reed); "That's Entertainment" (1953 film *The Band Wagon*) (Michael Vita)

Act Two: Dance Medley: "You and the Night and the Music" (*Revenge with Music*, 1934), "Louisiana Hayride" (*Flying Colors*, 1932), and "Dancing in the Dark" (*The Band Wagon*, 1931) (Company); "Triplets" (*Between the Devil*, 1937) (Bonnie Schon, David Chaney, Jered Holmes); "High and Low" (*The Band Wagon*, 1931) (Scott Salmon); "How Low Can a Little Worm Go?" (possibly a version of How High Can a Little Bird Fly?" from the 1936 London production *Follow the Sun*) (Judith Knaiz); "Absent Minded" (source unknown) (Jared Holmes); "High Is Better Than Low" (*Jennie*, 1963) (Judith Knaiz, Scott Salmon); "If There Is Someone Lovelier Than You" (*Revenge with Music*, 1934) (David Chaney); "I've Made a Habit of You" (*The Little Show*, 1929) (Bonnie Schon); "I Guess I'll Have to Change My Plan" (*The Little Show*, 1929) (Alan Weeks); "New Sun in the Sky" (*The Band Wagon*, 1931) (Vivian Reed); "Farewell, My Lovely" (*At Home Abroad*, 1935) (Michon Peacock); "Alone Together" (*Flying Colors*, 1932) (Michael Vita); "A Shine on Your Shoes" (*Flying Colors*, 1932) (Company)

On the night of June 6, 1963, something truly terrible happened to musical theatre. This was the night of the first so-called composer/lyricist tribute revue when *The World of Kurt Weill in Song* opened Off Broadway. One always welcomes a chance to hear the music of Kurt Weill and other Broadway composers, and an overview of their music is best savored in a cabaret setting, at a concert, or on a recording. But a full evening of Greatest Hits comes across like an overblown medley tribute on a television variety show. (Incidentally, a variation of the revue resurfaced years later as ***A Kurt Weill Cabaret***.)

After the success of the Weill revue, the flood started, and within the next forty-five years Off Broadway and Off Off Broadway offered an astounding number of similar tributes, almost one-hundred in all. These included *Leonard Bernstein's Theatre Songs* (1965), *Blitzstein!* (1966), and *The Harold Arlen Songbook* (1967). Most were superfluous, and only a few, such as *The Decline and Fall of the Entire World as Seen Through the Eyes of Cole Porter Revisited* (two different editions, both 1965), were genuinely fresh. The *Decline* revues concentrated on Porter esoterica, and *Taking a Chance on Love* (2000) explored the relatively obscure work of lyricist John LaTouche.

Eventually, the composer/lyricist tributes made their way north, and the Middle/Limited Broadway production *That's Entertainment* was the first to jump on the Broadway bandwagon. It faltered after just four performances, ***Rodgers and Hart*** stumbled along for three months, and other similar tributes (to Johnny Burke, George Gershwin, Jerry Herman, Jerome Kern, Johnny Mercer, Mitchell Parrish, and others) opened and then quickly disappeared. But a few were successful, including the London import ***Side by Side by Sondheim*** (London, 1976; New York, 1977) and Off-Off-Broadway's ***Ain't Misbehavin'***, a 1978 salute to Thomas "Fats" Waller which transferred to Broadway that year and played for 1,604 performances.

The genre flourished and was soon joined by what might be classified as the singer or singing-group tributes, such as ***Beatlemania*** (1977), ***Elvis The Legend Lives*** (1978), *Elvis: A Rockin' Remembrance* (1989), and *Truly Blessed* (1990; Mahalia Jackson), or general pop-music salutes of the *Street Corner Symphony* (1997) and *It Ain't Nothin' but the Blues* (1999) variety.

And then came the truly evil jukebox musical, which appropriated popular non-theatre songs and forced them into the format and framework of the traditional book musical. These songs had to bear the burden of plot, character, and atmosphere, none of which they could comfortably handle. Perhaps the most obvious example of this genre is *Mamma Mia!* (London, 1999; New York, 2001) which grafted independently written songs by the pop group ABBA into a newly concocted story line (which was reminiscent of ***Carmelina***).

That's Entertainment was a small-scale revue that honored lyricist Howard Dietz and composer Arthur Schwartz, but for some reason it created character names for all the singers and utilized snatches of dialogue in an awkward attempt to place the songs in a fabricated story context. None of it worked, and the critics were merciless.

Richard Watts in the *New York Post* praised the "wonderful" songs, but felt the production itself was "staged rather amateurishly and without much imagination." However, the "weak and unsatisfactory" evening had one redeeming quality, and that was the "striking personality" of the "perky and attractive" Vivian Reed. Douglas Watt in the *New York Daily News* also praised Reed (she was the revue's "best performer"), but when the "strained" evening worked in bits of dialogue between the songs in order to create a plot of sorts all the characters became "a pain in the neck."

Martin Gottfried in *Women's Wear Daily* said the "wonderful" songs were presented in the manner of "a second rate Las Vegas hotel's floor show," but he enjoyed Vivian Reed's "By Myself." Betty Rollin on WNBC4TV found the evening "agreeable" and "pleasant" if not particularly "dazzling"; and Leonard Harris on WCBSTV2 said the attempt to create a running story line was "cutesy," and he suggested the revue would have been better had Vivian Reed performed every number.

The show included "Triplets," Dietz and Schwartz's merry song about three babies who hate one another. It has a long history, which began when it was first introduced during the pre-Broadway tryout of *Flying Colors* in 1932, where it was sung by Clifton Webb, Patsy Kelly, and Imogene Coca. It was cut from the production, but was recycled for the 1935 revue *At Home Abroad* as a solo for Beatrice Lillie; again, it was dropped during the tryout. The number finally made its Broadway debut two years later in *Between the Devil*, where it was introduced by The Tune Twisters (Andy Love, Jack Lathrop, and Bob Wacker) who during the show's tryout were known as The Savoy Club Boys. The song was later memorably performed by Fred Astaire, Jack Buchanan, and Nanette Fabray in the 1953 MGM film musical *The Band Wagon*.

LOST IN THE STARS

"The Memorable Musical"

Theatre: Imperial Theatre
Opening Date: April 18, 1972; *Closing Date*: May 21, 1972
Performances: 39
Book and *Lyrics*: Maxwell Anderson
Music: Kurt Weill
Based on the 1948 novel *Cry, the Beloved Country* by Alan Paton.
Direction: Gene Frankel; *Producer*: The John F. Kennedy Center for the Performing Arts; *Choreography*: Louis Johnson; *Scenery*: Oliver Smith; *Costumes*: Patricia Quinn Stuart; *Lighting*: Paul Sullivan; *Musical Direction*: Karen Gustafson
Cast: Lee Hooper (Answerer), Harold Pierson (Dancer), Rod Perry (Leader), Babafumi Akunyun (Drummer), *Brock Peters* (Stephen Kumalo), Rosetta Le Noire (Grace Kumalo), Adam Petroski (Stationmaster), Sid Marshall (The Young Man), Ruby Greene Aspinall (The Woman), Don Fenwick (Arthur Jarvis), Jack Gwillim (James Jarvis), David Jay (Edward Jarvis), Karen Ford (Mrs. Jarvis), Leonard Jackson (John Kumalo), Leonard Hayward (Paulus, McRae), Giancarlo Esposito (Alex), Mark Dempsey (Foreman, First Policeman), Alyce Elizabeth Webb (Mrs. Mkize), Garrett Saunders (Hlabeni), Peter Bailey-Britton (Eland), Marki Bey (Linda), Autris Paige (Johannes Pafuri), Damon Evans (Matthew Kumalo), Gilbert Price (Absalom Kumalo), Judy Gibson (Rose), Margaret Cowie (Irina), Roy Hausen (Second Policeman, Guard), Richard Triggs (Servant), Alexander Reed (Burton), Staats Cotsworth (Judge); Singers: Lana Caradimas, Suzanne Cogan, Karen Ford, Aleesaa Foster, Ruby Greene Aspinall, Amelia Haas, Edna Husband, Urylee Leonardos, Rona Leslie Pervil, Therman Bailey, Donald Coleman, Raymond Frith, Leonard Hayward, Autris Paige, Mandingo Shaka, Richard Triggs; Dancers: Michael Harrison, Wayne Stevenson Hayes, Oba-Ya, Michael Oiwake
The musical was presented in two acts.
The action takes place during the late 1940s in South Africa, in the small village of Ndotsheni and in Johannesburg.

Musical Numbers

Act One: Opening: "The Hills of Ixopo" (Rod Perry, Lee Hooper, Singers); "Thousands of Miles" (Brock Peters); "Train to Johannesburg" (Rod Perry, Singers); "The Search" (Brock Peters, Rod Perry, Singers); "The Little Grey House" (Brock Peters, Singers); "Stay Well" (Gilbert Price), "Trouble Man" (Margaret Cowie); "Murder in Parkwold" (Singers); "Fear" (Singers); "Lost in the Stars" (Brock Peters, Singers)
Act Two: Opening: "The Wild Justice" (Rod Perry, Singers); "O Tixo, Tixo, Help Me" (Brock Peters); "Cry, the Beloved Country" (Rod Perry, Singers); "Big Mole" (Giancarlo Esposito); "Thousands of Miles" (reprise) (Singers)

Lost in the Stars takes place during the apartheid era of South Africa, and centers on village preacher Stephen Kumalo (Brock Peters), who travels to Johannesburg and discovers that his son Absalom (Gilbert Price) has been arrested for the murder of a white man named Arthur Jarvis (Don Fenwick) during a robbery.

Ironically, Arthur was an activist for the civil rights of blacks. Absalom admits his guilt and is executed, and when Stephen meets Arthur's father James Jarvis (Jack Gwillum) the two men who are separated by the law of apartheid are united in the bond of personal tragedy that has claimed the lives of their sons.

Based on Alan Paton's 1948 novel *Cry, the Beloved Country*, the musical was curiously dry and remote. Maxwell Anderson's book and lyrics never quite captured the personal tragedies of the main characters and the national disgrace of apartheid, and Kurt Weill's music was too often emotionally detached from the characters and the action. This is arguably his weakest and most uninteresting Broadway score, although some have made a case for the title song.

A major failing of the adaptation is that two of the three main characters are given nothing to sing, and thus James Jarvis and Absalom are musical bystanders in their own musical. Stephen is given five songs, and the remaining eleven numbers are divided among amorphous singing groups and minor characters, of which six are performed by a generic Greek chorus (which includes an anonymous "Leader" and an "Answerer") and various choral groups, and five are sung by relatively minor characters (and one or two of the numbers are time-fillers almost completely extraneous to the action). The use of the abstract Greek chorus with its leader and answerer further contributed to the emotional detachment of the narrative.

During the early performances of the revival's tryout, "Stay Well" was performed by the character of Irina (who also sang it during the original 1949 production), but in order to give Absalom a musical number the song was reassigned to him. The revival's tryout also included "Who'll Buy?," which was dropped prior to New York; and "A Bird of Passage" was completely eliminated for this production.

Although a few critics noted that time had passed by some of the musical's liberal notions, the work received mostly glowing notices, and so the short run of five weeks is somewhat surprising.

Richard Watts in the *New York Post* praised the "brilliant" revival and said it retained all its "power" and "timeliness," and Jack Kroll in *Newsweek* went all out and hailed it as "probably the best show of the Broadway season." Alan T. Otten in the *Wall Street Journal* found the adaptation "stunning" and the score "magnificent" and concluded his review by asking, "What more can theatre offer?" (He also noted that *Lost in the Stars* was one of three revivals that the Kennedy Center would produce during the year; but the other two, *Of Thee I Sing* and *Kiss Me, Kate*, never materialized.)

Douglas Watt in the *New York Daily News* said the story became "increasingly naïve," and the once "glowing" musical was now "dated, contrived and a bit quaint." Martin Gottfried in *Women's Wear Daily* noted, "You don't have to be black to dislike" *Lost in the Stars*. The musical's message seemed to approve the notion of a "benevolent-segregationist" attitude in which whites and blacks played the respective roles of parent and child, and while this theory was "outdated" it didn't mean that a work of the past should be relegated to theatrical limbo. However, only Weill's score was "worthy"; otherwise, Anderson's book was "bad" and the evening was a "sluggish, clumsy blackfolks' show." He also noted the Kennedy Center revival had the "pompous, sluggish feel typical of the institutional musical."

The original production opened at the Music Box Theatre on October 30, 1949, for 273 performances. The script was published in hardback by Anderson House/William Sloane Associates in 1950, and is also included in the 1976 hardback collection *Great Musicals of the American Theatre, Volume Two* (published by the Chilton Book Company and edited by Stanley Richards). The script was also published in the December 1950 issue of *Theatre Arts*.

The original cast album was released by Decca Records (LP # DL-8028). A 1968 revival produced by Tougaloo College (Toogaloo, Mississippi) was recorded by Word Records (LP # CS-5117), and a 1992 studio cast recording (issued by MusicMasters Classics CD # 01612-67100-2) by the Orchestra of St. Luke's and the Concert Chorale of New York was conducted by Julius Rudel (the release includes "Little Tin God," which was dropped prior to the 1949 New York opening).

The musical was revived by the New York City Opera Company at City Center on April 10, 1958, for fourteen performances, and the cast included Lawrence Winters, Patti Austen, Rosetta Le Noire, Nicholas Joy, John Irving, Frederick O'Neal, Louis Gossett, Eve Jessye, Olga James, Conrad Bain, Godfrey Cambridge, and Douglas Turner.

A belated film version was released in 1974 as part of the short-lived American Film Series; directed by Daniel Mann, the cast included Brock Peters, Raymond St. Jacques, Clifton Davis, Melba Moore, and Paula Kelly. The complete AFS collection of fourteen filmed plays and musicals was released on a fourteen-DVD set by Kino (besides *Lost in the Stars*, the set includes one other musical, the 1968 Off-Broadway revue *Jacques*

Brel Is Alive and Well and Living in Paris, which was revived on Broadway in 1972 and is discussed in this book).

Awards

Tony Award Nominations: Best Leading Actor in a Musical (Brock Peters); Best Featured Actor in a Musical (Gilbert Price)

DONT BOTHER ME, I CANT COPE

"A New Musical Entertainment"

Theatre: Playhouse Theatre (during run, the revue transferred to the Edison Theatre)
Opening Date: April 19, 1972; *Closing Date*: October 17, 1974
Performances: 1,065
Lyrics and *Music*: Micki Grant
Direction: Vinnette Carroll; *Producers*: Edward Padula and Arch Lustberg (An Urban Arts Corps Production) (Gordon Gray Jr., Associate Producer) (production presented in association with Ford's Theatre Society, Washington, D.C.); *Choreography*: George Faison; *Scenery*: Richard A. Miller (scenery supervised by Neil Peter Jampolis); *Costumes*: Edna Watson (costumes supervised by Sara Brook); *Lighting*: B. J. Sammler (lighting supervised by Ken Billington); *Musical Direction*: Danny Holgate
Cast: Alex Bradford, Hope Clarke, Micki Grant, Bobby Hill, Arnold Wilkerson; Other Singers: Alberta Bradford, Charles Campbell, Marie Thomas; Dancers: Thommie Bush, Gerald G. Francis, Ben Harney, Leona Johnson; Musicians: Danny Holgate, Herb Lovell (Drums), Rudy Stevenson (Guitar, Flute), John Lucieu (Bass)
The revue was presented in two acts.

Musical Numbers

Act One: "I Gotta Keep Movin'" (Alex Bradford, Alberta Bradford, Charles Campbell, Bobby Hill; danced by Ben Harney); "Harlem Streets" (Dancers); "Lookin' over from Your Side" (Bobby Hill); "Don't Bother Me, I Can't Cope" (Company); "When I Feel Like Moving" (Hope Clarke, Dancers); "Help" (Hope Clarke); "Fighting for Pharoah" (Alex Bradford, Bobby Hill, Charles Campbell, Alberta Bradford); "Good Vibrations" (Alex Bradford, Company); "Love Power" (Bobby Hill, Hope Clarke, Company); "You Think I Got Rhythm?" (Dancers); "They Keep Coming" (Company); "My Name Is Man" (Arnold Wilkerson)
Act Two: "Questions" (Micki Grant); "It Takes a Whole Lot of Human Feeling" (Micki Grant); "You Think I Got Rhythm?" (reprise) (Arnold Wilkerson, Micki Grant); "Time Brings About a Change" (Thommie Bush, Ben Harney, Arnold Wilkerson, Micki Grant, Leona Johnson, Marie Thomas); "So Little Time" (Micki Grant); "Thank Heaven for You" (Bobby Hill, Micki Grant); "So Long Sammy" (Bobby Hill, Hope Clarke, Dancers); "All I Need" (Alberta Bradford, Company); "I Gotta Keep Movin'" (reprise) (Micki Grant, Alex Bradford, Company)

Well, it was all so confusing. The revue's title as it appeared in the program was apostrophe but not comma challenged, but the title song as listed in the program braved both a comma *and* a set of apostrophes. It all must have meant something quite subtle, but if so the revue's lyricist and composer Micki Grant never let on. As such, the evening was a mildly pleasant one of middle-of-the-road, elevator-styled music, each song flowing rather gently into the other. Grant herself appeared in the second act and dominated it with her smooth voice and cool and soothing presence. But the evening never had a clear, underlying theme, and there was no thread to hold it together. In many ways, listening to the revue's cast album was more enjoyable than watching the show itself. The easy-listening background music truly worked well as a recording.

Martin Gottfried in *Women's Wear Daily* said the revue was better suited to a cabaret setting. Moreover, he felt the evening kept selling the idea that "black people are human," and this "rather commercial,

Madison Avenue style" approach suited the "slickly liberal lyrics," which were "more than a little patronizing" to "both blacks and whites."

Richard Watts in the *New York Post* found the revue "likeable" and "refreshing," and while the evening seemed to be concerned with racial issues it did so with a "firmness" that was all the more "impressive" with its "moderation." He also noted the revue laughed at itself, particularly when two black men resent being called "black" and equally resent being called "Negro." Douglas Watt in the *New York Daily News* liked the "brightly polished, enormously spirited" show, and Edwin Wilson in the *Wall Street Journal* suggested the evening was an adult version of ***The Me Nobody Knows*** and while the material was somewhat "familiar" and there was an occasional "air of predictability" about the show, it was nonetheless agreeable.

T. E. Kalem in *Time* praised the "witty and intelligent" lyrics and the "melodiously winning" music, and Betty Rollin on WNBC4TV noted the revue's themes were "somewhat predictable and over-generalized," but the songs were "splendid" and the evening "friendly."

The script was published in paperback by Samuel French in 1975, and the cast album was released by Polydor Records (LP # PD-6013). During the Broadway run, the song "Show Me That Special Gene" was added for the second act.

The revue had first been presented Off Off Broadway by the Urban Arts Corps during the 1970–1971 season, and from there it was performed in regional theatre. The production then opened at Ford's Theatre in Washington, D.C., in September 1971, and a program note indicated that "'coping' is a basic commitment of a mature, purposeful, involved human being, that we sometimes laugh to keep from crying, that life is not necessarily fair, that happiness is a by-product not an end product, and that the ways we are similar are far greater than the ways we are different." These comments clearly defined the intentions and the nature of the revue, but in actual performance the evening was more a pleasant collection of musical numbers and less a coherent and thematic piece with a unifying concept.

During the period when the revue was playing in regional theatre, it was divided into four parts, a framework that was dropped for the New York production: *Resurrection City* (which included a section titled "Poetry Sequence by Langston Hughes & Micki Grant"), *Harlem Streets*, *Micki Sings Micki*, and *Elegy for Bessie, Billie & Jim*. During the Washington engagement, the following songs were cut: "Resurrection City," "Universe in Mourning," "My Love's So Good," "Liberated Woman," "So Now You Come," "Miss Bessie," and "Jimi." Another song heard during the tryout was "My Name Is Man," and although the program indicated the song was by Langston Hughes and Grant, the New York engagement credited the song only to Grant.

During the revue's national tour, the following songs were added: "Lock Up the Doors," "Children's Rhymes," "Billie Holiday Song," "Billie Holiday Ballet," "Ghetto Life," "Men's Dance," "Love Mississippi," "Prayer," and "Sermon." For the tour, "Fighting for Pharoah" was titled "Do a Little Living for Peace (Fighting for Pharoah)." "Universe in Mourning" had been dropped prior to New York, but was reinstated for the tour, and "Show Me That Special Gene," which had been added to the revue during the New York run, was also heard during the tour.

The revue played under a Middle (or Limited) Broadway contract, and its long run of 1,065 performances made it the longest-running musical of the season.

Awards

Tony Award Nominations: Best Musical (*Dont Bother Me, I Cant Cope*); Best Director of a Musical (Vinnette Carroll); Best Book (Micki Grant); Best Score (Micki Grant)

DIFFERENT TIMES

Theatre: ANTA Theatre
Opening Date: May 1, 1972; *Closing Date*: May 20, 1972
Performances: 24
Book, Lyrics, and *Music*: Michael Brown

Direction: Michael Brown; *Producers*: Bowman Productions, Inc., in association with William L. Witt and William J. Gumperz; *Choreography*: Tod Jackson; *Scenery* and *Costumes*: David Guthrie; *Lighting*: Martin Aronstein; *Musical Direction*: Rene Wiegert

Cast: Sam Stoneburner (Stephen Adams Levy), Barbara Williams (Margaret Adams), Jamie Ross (Gregory Adams), Mary Jo Catlett (Mrs. Daniel Webster Hepplewhite, The Kaiser, Hazel Hughes, Lady Ffenger, Mrs. Callahan, Josie), Patti Karr (Mrs. Hepplewhite's Mother, Kimberly Langley), Joyce Nolen (Nelle Harper, Hazelnut), Joe Masiell (Larry Lawrence Levy, Stan), Candace Cooke (Angela Adams, Hazelnut, Pauline), Terry Nicholson (Doughboy, Keynoter, Joe), Ronnie DeMarco (Doughboy, Mel), David K. Thome (Doughboy, Keynoter, Don), Ronald Young (Officer, Bobby, Keynoter, Frank, Frank Gonzales), Dorothy Frank (Marianne, Hazelnut, Hattie, Linda), Karin Baker (Columbia, Hazelnut, Mae Verne), Mary Bracken Phillips (Elsie, Keynoter, Abigail), Dorothy Frank (Marilyn)

The musical was presented in two acts.

The action takes place during the period 1905–1970 in Portland, Oregon; Boston; Bayonne, New Jersey; London; New York City; and Mt. Kisco, New York.

Musical Numbers

Act One: "Different Times" (Sam Stoneburner); "Seeing the Sights" (People of 1905); "The Spirit Is Moving" (Barbara Williams, People of 1905); "Here's Momma" (Barbara Williams); "Everything in the World Has a Place" (Jamie Ross, Barbara Williams); "I Wish I Didn't Love Him" (Barbara Williams); "Forward into Tomorrow" (Mary Jo Catlett, Suffragettes); "You're Perfect" (Candace Cooke); "Marianne" (Ronald Young, Terry Nicholson, Ronnie DeMarco, David K. Thome, Dorothy Frank, Karin Baker, Mary Jo Catlett); "Daddy, Daddy" (Candace Cooke, Dorothy Frank, Karin Baker, Joyce Nolen); "I Feel Grand" (Mary Jo Catlett, Candace Cooke, Dorothy Frank, Karin Baker, Joyce Nolen); "Sock Life in the Eye" (Joe Maisell); "I'm Not Through" (Joe Maisell, Marathon Dancers)

Act Two: "I Miss Him" (Dorothy Frank, Candace Cooke, Karin Baker); "One More Time" (Patti Karr, Terry Nicholson, Mary Bracken Phillips, David K. Thome, Ronald Young); "Here's Momma" (reprise) (Sam Stoneburner); "I Dreamed about Roses" (Sam Stoneburner, Patti Karr, U.S.O. Guests); "I Wish I Didn't Love Her" (reprise) (Jamie Ross); "The Words I Never Said" (Sam Stoneburner, Patti Karr); "The Life of a Woman" (Patti Karr); "Here's Momma" (reprise) (performers not identified in program); "He Smiles" (Mary Bracken Phillips, Mary Jo Catlett); "Genuine Plastic" (Sam Stoneburner, Gallery Guests); "Thanks a Lot" (Ronald Young, Mary Bracken Phillips, Friends); "When They Start Again" (Mary Bracken Phillips, Ronald Young); "Different Times" (reprise) (Sam Stoneburner); "The Spirit Is Moving" (reprise) (Company)

Michael Brown's *Different Times* followed the members of a Boston family and their descendants from 1905 to 1970. But this was no *Love Life* (1948) or ***Follies*** in its use of time and space, and there wasn't an overriding concept to the evening, except perhaps the message that the more things change the more they remain the same (the early scenes depict protests by suffragettes, and later ones protests by activists of the late 1960s). Instead, Brown's lighthearted revue-like musical was mostly a gentle spoof of popular musical styles as it followed the Adams family through the ragtime era of World War I, the Roaring Twenties, the Depression Thirties, the War Forties, the rock-and-roll era, and then right up to the protests of 1970. Nothing was taken too seriously, but it took a few scenes for the show to find its bearings. Martin Gottfried in *Women's Wear Daily* noted there didn't seem to be any particular point of view until late in the first act when a group of doughboys sang "Marianne." It was then that the evening somewhat came together and revealed itself to be a tongue-in-cheek salute to the various styles of popular American music.

The critics singled out two sequences. In "I Feel Grand," Mary Jo Catlett made quite an impression as an over-the-hill and in-her-cups speakeasy singer who can't cut the mustard anymore; and in a marathon dance sequence Joe Maisell excelled with the anthem "I'm Not Through," a salute to the never-say-die Broadway song perhaps best exemplified by "Some People" (*Gypsy*, 1959) and "Don't Rain on My Parade" (*Funny Girl*, 1964).

Richard Watts in the *New York Post* found the "unpretentious" musical "harmless" and "well-meaning." It wasn't "very stimulating," but the evening's attitudes (such as the introduction of a character named "Lady Ffenger") were "presented likeably enough" without much in the way of "wit and wisdom." The musical never rose "above the level of mediocrity," but the score was nonetheless "rather pleasant" and "I'm Not Through" was "particularly good." Douglas Watt in the *New York Daily News* said the musical was so "unassuming" it risked being unnoticeable; but he praised the "galvanic" singing of Joe Maisell, who made "I'm Not Through" a show-stopper.

Edwin Wilson in the *Wall Street Journal* noted there should be a place on Broadway for "pleasant" if not "perfect" musicals, and he felt *Different Times* deserved a chance: it might not have been a "banquet," but it was a "buffet" with "some tasty dishes." He said Mary Jo Catlett's "I Feel Grand" was a "superb comic number," and Maisell's "I'm Not Through" brought "unexpected excitement" and "ranks with the best."

Betty Rollin on WNBC4TV said many of the songs had a "certain slick attractiveness," but the musical lacked a concept; as a result, the show was little more than "mindless frivolity." And Leonard Harris on WCBSTV2 noted that if "ideas" are the "lifeblood of a musical," then *Different Times* suffered from "tired blood."

Gottfried felt the show had the "potential" to satirize and kid its targets and still "work as if it were straight." But the elements failed to jell, and he concluded that the show "probably wasn't worth the effort" it took to produce. But "I'm Not Through" was the musical's "most successful moment" and as a result the first act ended "tremendously."

Clive Barnes in the *New York Times* said the book was "terrible" and the score wasn't "memorable." Brown's score offered the kind of "undemanding music that would go pleasantly enough in revues and industrial shows or elevators" (and he noted Brown's "chief experience" had been as a contributor to revues and industrial shows). Otherwise, the score didn't "seem to have the sound of Broadway to it."

One or two critics noted that directly across the street from *Different Times* the drama *Promenade, All!* was playing at the Alvin Theatre, and it too was an overview of the life of an American family, in this case from 1895 to the present. David V. Robison's play had opened two weeks before the premiere of *Different Times*, and like the musical it didn't manage to last out the season, in this case closing after forty-eight performances.

RCA Victor Records was scheduled to record the cast album, which was canceled due to the musical's brief run. But fifteen years later the original cast members recorded the score for Painted Smiles Records (LP # PS-1332). Except for "The Life of a Woman" and "Genuine Plastic," the entire score was preserved. Unfortunately, Joe Maisell died during the preproduction phases of the recording, and so Michael Brown substituted for him; but a fragment of an early demo of Maisell's "I'm Not Through" was discovered and was included on the recording as a tribute to him.

Michael Brown was a regular contributor to Broadway and Off-Broadway revues, and he also wrote a number of industrial shows. Perhaps his most memorable song is "Lizzie Borden" from *New Faces of 1952* in which the lady is scolded because you just can't chop your poppa up in Massachusetts.

TOMMY

Theatre: City Center 55th Street Theatre
Opening Date: May 3, 1972; *Closing Date*: May 28, 1972
Performances: 31
Lyrics and *Music*: Pete Townshend; additional lyrics and music by John Entwistle, Keith Moon, and Sonny Boy Williamson
Based on the 1969 Decca album *Tommy* by the Who.
Producer: Les Grands Ballets Canadiens (Ludmilla Chiriaeff, Founder and Director; Fernand Nault, Associate Artistic Director); *Choreography*: Fernand Nault; *Scenery*: David Jenkins; *Costumes*: Francois Barbeau; *Lighting*: Nicholas Cernovitch; *Film Sequences*: Luc-Michel Hannaux, Denys Morisset, and Paul Vezina
Cast (*Note*: The dancers alternated in the roles, and the following list includes the names of those who performed during the run.): Alexandre Belin, Mannie Rowe, Vincent Warren (Tommy), Hae Shik Kim, Manon Larin, Janet Snyder, Sonia Taverner (Acid Queen), Leslie-May Downs, Reva Pincusoff, Barbara Withey (Mother), William Josef, Laszlo Tamasik (Father), Richard Beaty, William Josef, Renald Rabu (The Hawker), James Boyd, David Drummond, Lorne Toumine (The Lover), Maurice Lemay, Guillermo Gonzalez, Andris Toppe (Cousin Kevin), James Bates, Maurice Lemay, Andris Toppe (Pinball Wizard), John Stanzel (Uncle Ernie), Eileen Heath, Carole Landry (Sally Simpson); Dancers: Richard Bouchard, Francine

Boucher, James Boyd, Lorna Cameron, Robert Dicello, Louise Dore, David Drummond, Gerry Gilbert, Guillermo Gonzalez, Eileen Heath, Barbara Jacobs, Carole Landry, Melinda Lawrence, Maurice Lemay, Helen McKergow, Conrad Peterson, Reva Pincusoff, Renald Rabu, Cathy Sharp, Richard Sugarman, Susan Taylor, Michael Thomas, Andris Toppe, Lorne Tomine, Laeleen Winchu, Barbara Withey

The ballet was performed in one act.

Musical Numbers

Note: The program didn't list individual musical numbers; the ballet didn't include singers and orchestra, and instead the 1969 recording with vocals by Roger Daltry was played through the theatre's sound system. Unless otherwise noted, all lyrics and music are by Pete Townshend.

Overture; "It's a Boy"; "You Didn't Hear It" (aka "1921"); "Amazing Journey"; "Sparks"; "Eyesight to the Blind" (lyric and music by Sonny Boy Williamson); "Christmas"; "Cousin Kevin" (lyric and music by John Entwistle); "The Acid Queen"; "Underture"; "Do You Think It's Alright?"; "Fiddle About" (lyric and music by John Entwistle); "Pinball Wizard"; "There's a Doctor"; "Go to the Mirror!"; "Tommy Can You Hear Me?"; "Smash the Mirror"; "Sensation"; "Miracle Cure"; "Sally Simpson"; "I'm Free"; "Welcome"; "Tommy's Holiday Camp" (lyric and music by Keith Moon); "We're Not Gonna Take It"

Tommy was first a highly successful two-LP concept album released in 1969, written, composed, and performed by the Who (Roger Daltry, John Entwistle, Keith Moon, and Pete Townshend). The title character is a boy who witnesses the murder of his mother's lover and immediately becomes deaf, mute, and blind. Since his sense of touch remains, he becomes a world-champion "pinball wizard," but not before he undergoes various torments by family members, including sexual molestation by an uncle. In order to attempt communication with him, Tommy's mother smashes a mirror, an action that miraculously cures him. He soon creates his own religion, which draws millions of followers, but his unbending rules lead to the destruction of the church and his power. By the end of the album, he's almost in the same state as he was at the beginning, and he cries out for communication with someone. All this claptrap was taken seriously by many, who apparently were dazed by the message that lack of communication is a Problem. Or perhaps the work was really a subtle satire on such jejune reflections. Better still, maybe the musical was meant to satirize the lionization of celebrities.

The current production was a ballet version of the material by Les Grands Ballets Canadiens that originated in Canada and toured the United States in such venues as Washington, D.C.'s Kennedy Center before playing a one-month engagement in New York. The mounting was probably exempt from the standard Broadway contract because it was a visiting production booked for a limited engagement.

The ballet version didn't include live singers or musicians, and instead the Who's original recording of *Tommy* was played over the theatre's sound system as the dancers performed the ballet, which was the evening's third act; the first two acts were comprised of short ballets: *Hip and Straight* (music by Paul Duplessis, choreography by Fernand Nault) and *Ceremony* (an "environmental mass" with music by Pierre Henry and Gary Wright, choreography by Fernand Nault).

In 1975, Ken Russell directed an overwrought and undisciplined film version of *Tommy* that unaccountably impressed a lot of people; the cast included Roger Daltry, Eric Clapton, Keith Moon, Tina Turner, Elton John, Jack Nicholson, Ann-Margret, and Oliver Reed.

As *The Who's Tommy*, the work opened at the St. James Theatre on April 22, 1993, for 900 performances; the cast included Michael Cerveris in the title role. The musical received Tony Award nominations for Best Musical, Best Book, Best Costume Designer, Best Featured Actress in a Musical (Marcia Mitzman), and two for Best Featured Actor in a Musical (Michael Cerveris and Paul Kandel); and won Tonys for Best Director of a Musical (Des McAnuff), Best Score, Best Scenic Designer, Best Lighting Designer, and Best Choreographer.

The original 1969 album of *Tommy* was released by Decca Records on a two-LP set (# DXSW-7205); the CD was issued by MCA Records (# MCAD-11417). The soundtrack album was also issued on a two-LP set (by Polydor Records # PD-29502); and the two-CD Broadway cast album of the 1993 production was released by RCA Victor Records (# 09026-61874-2). The script was included in the hardback edition *Great Rock Musicals*, which was published by Stein and Day in 1979 and was edited by Stanley Richards.

HARD JOB BEING GOD

"A New Rock Musical"

Theatre: Edison Theatre
Opening Date: May 15, 1972; *Closing Date*: May 20, 1972
Performances: 6
Book: Not credited
Lyrics and *Music*: Tom Martel
Based on the Book of Genesis as well as other books of the Old Testament.
Direction: Bob Yde; *Producers*: Bob Yde in association with Andy Wiswell; *Scenery*: Ray Wilke; *Costumes*: Mary Whitehead; *Lighting*: Patrika Brown; *Musical Direction*: Roy Bittan
Cast: Gini Eastwood (Sarah, Jacob's Wife, Slave, Pharaoh's Soldier, Moabite, Judean, Susanna), Stu Freeman (Jacob's Son, Moses, Moabite, David), Tom Martel (God), Anne Sarofeen (Slave, Pharaoh's Soldier, Ruth, Judean, Shepherd), John Twomey (Abraham, Jacob, Pharoah, Moabite, Judean, Amos)
The musical was presented in one act.
The time is the period of the Old Testament.

Musical Numbers

"Hard Job Being God" (Tom Martel, Company); "Wherever You Go" (Gini Eastwood, John Twomey); "Famine" (John Twomey, Gini Eastwood, Stu Freeman); "Buy a Slave" (Egyptian Slave Merchants); "Prayer" (Gini Eastwood, Anne Sarofeen); "Moses' Song" (Stu Freeman, John Twomey); "The Ten Plagues" (John Twomey, Gini Eastwood, Anne Sarofeen, Stu Freeman); "Passover" (Gini Eastwood, Anne Sarofeen, John Twomey, Stu Freeman; "The Eleven Commandments" (Stu Freeman, Gini Eastwood, Anne Sarofeen); "Tribes" (Hebrew Woman, Tribes); "Ruth" (Gini Eastwood, Stu Freeman, John Twomey, Anne Sarofeen); "Festival" (Gini Eastwood, Anne Sarofeen, John Twomey); "Hail, David" (Gini Eastwood, Anne Sarofeen, Stu Freeman); "A Very Lonely King" (Stu Freeman); "Battle" (performers unidentified in program); "You're on Your Own" (Hebrews, Tom Martel); "A Psalm of Peace" (Gini Eastwood, Hebrews); "I'm Countin' on You" (Tom Martel, John Twomey); "Shalom l'chaim!" (Hebrews); "Amos Gonna Give You Hell" (Anne Sarofeen); "What Do I Have to Do?" (Tom Martel, Company)

Hard Job Being God was a revue-like song-cycle that depicted various events and characters of the Old Testament. Earlier in the season, ***Jesus Christ Superstar*** had opened on Broadway and Leonard Bernstein's ***Mass*** had been seen in Washington, D.C., as the inaugural production for the new Kennedy Center. And a year earlier Stephen Schwartz's *Godspell* had opened Off Broadway and was now beginning the second year of its marathon run. The era was ripe for religious-themed musicals, but perhaps *Hard Job Being God* got on the bandwagon a little too late; the Middle/Limited Broadway production managed no more than six performances.

Clive Barnes in the *New York Times* said the evening offered a "quick run-through" of the Old Testament that was "simplistic, naïve and distasteful"; and although the lyrics were "bathetic" and "puerile," the music was "unmemorable but attractive" (at least, when he "noticed" the music he "liked" it).

A 1971 recording of the score was issued by GWP Records (LP # ST-2036), and while it was identified as "the original cast album," the only singer on the recording who was also in the later 1972 New York production was Tom Martel, the show's lyricist and composer. The album included ten songs (along with their printed lyrics), all of which were heard in the Broadway production. The Broadway program itself included the lyrics for three numbers.

DONT PLAY US CHEAP

"A Comedy Musical"

Theatre: Ethel Barrymore Theatre
Opening Date: May 16, 1972; *Closing Date*: October 1, 1972
Performances: 164

Book, Lyrics, and *Music*: Melvin Van Peebles
Direction: Melvin Van Peebles; *Producer*: Melvin Van Peebles; *Scenery*: Kurt Lundell; *Costumes*: Bernard Johnson; *Lighting*: Martin Aronstein; *Musical Direction*: Not credited (probably Harold Wheeler)
Cast: Thomas Anderson (Mr. Percy), Joshie Jo Armstead (Mrs. Washington), Nate Barnett (Harold Johnson [Rat]), Frank Carey (Mr. Johnson [Cockroach]), Robert Dunn (Mr. Bowser), Rhetta Hughes (Earnestine), Joe Keyes Jr. (Trinity), Mabel King (Mrs. Bowser), Avon Long (David), George "Oopee" McCurn (Mr. Washington), Esther Rolle (Miss Maybell), Jay Vanleer (Mrs. Johnson); Musicians: Harold Wheeler (Piano), Bob Bushnell (Bass), George Davis (Guitar), Earl Williams (Drums), Bobby Thomas (Contractor)
The musical was presented in two acts.
The action takes place "here" and the time is "a coupla days before tomorrow."

Musical Numbers

Act One: "Some Days It Seems That It Don't Even Pay to Get Out of Bed" (Harold Johnson, Frank Carey); "Break That Party" (Avon Long, Joe Keyes Jr.); "8 Day Week" (Thomas Anderson, Company); "Saturday Night" (Company); "I'm a Bad Character" (Joe Keyes Jr., Company); "You Cut Up the Clothes in the Closet of My Dreams" (Joshie Jo Armstead); "It Makes No Difference" (Esther Rolle, Company); "Quittin Time" (George "Oopee" McCurn, Company)
Act Two: "Aint Love Grand" (Rhetta Hughes, Company);"The Book of Life" (Mr. Bowser, Company); Quartet: "Aint Love Grand" (reprise) (Rhetta Hughes); "Know Your Business" (Esther Rolle); "Big Future" (Nat Barnett, Frank Carey); and "Break That Party" (reprise) (Avon Long, Joe Keyes Jr.); "Feast on Me" (Mabel King, Company); "The Phoney Game" (Avon Long, Company); "Smash Him" (Company)

Melvin Van Peebles's *Dont Play Us Cheap* was his second apostrophe-challenged musical of the season, but unlike the grim and vituperative ***Aint Supposed to Die a Natural Death*** the new work was a sunny and fanciful look at what happens when two devils (or imps) invade a Saturday-night Harlem party. Miss Maybell (Esther Rolle) is throwing a birthday party for her niece Earnestine (Rhetta Hughes), and all their friends are invited. The imps, a rat named Harold Johnson (Nate Barnett) and a cockroach named Mr. Johnson (Frank Carey), must pass a party-pooping test for the devil himself, and so they're soon transformed into the humans Trinity (Joe Keyes Jr.) and David (Avon Long) for the express purpose of breaking up the evening's festivities. The handsome Trinity finds himself enjoying the party, liking the guests, and, most importantly, falling in love with Earnestine. So hell almost breaks loose with David's futile attempts to get the party-pooping in full gear. But nothing works, and Trinity remains on Earth as a human and teams up with Earnestine. As for David, he returns to his cockroachian state and is almost immediately squashed when someone steps on him; but before he fades away, he reminds Trinity (in perhaps an homage to the curse-on-you finale of Van Peebles's earlier musical) that while Trinity may now be a man, he's also a "colored" one.

Douglas Watt in the *New York Daily News* found the musical "endearing" but "loose-jointed" and suggested Van Peebles had spread himself too thin as producer, director, book writer, lyricist, and composer. Richard Watt in the *New York Post* said the "slender" but "imaginative" musical might not be a "sensational" show, but it was an "extremely engaging one" (but he couldn't figure out how the title came into play).

Edwin Wilson in the *Wall Street Journal* felt the musical fell short in its book and direction, and noted the evening sent mixed messages: some of the characters were straightforward while others were caricatures. He also mentioned that when Trinity immediately forgoes his order to disrupt the party and instead embraces it as one of the guests the "whole plot line" went "down the drain." Leonard Harris on WCBSTV2 said the show was a "knockout" and a "marvel," but Kevin Sanders on WABCTV7 noted the "very thin and disappointingly clumsy story" belonged in a "children's comic book"; and while Betty Rollin on WNBC4TV found the music "terrific" and the cast "sensational," she complained that the book was a "mess" with its "hopeless" structure and "elusive" story line.

Martin Gottfried in *Women's Wear Daily* said Van Peebles's direction was "raggedly and amateurishly" conceived with a "dumb" story, and suggested the musical's appeal was "on the level of a lowest common denominator." However, the music was "good" and "singable" and he praised Joshie Jo Armstead's showstopping "You Cut Up the Clothes in the Closet of My Dreams." But he made one curious comment, saying that the celebration of "ghetto culture as rich, joyous fun" that makes life there "livable" and "acceptable" violated the spirit and the message of ***Aint Supposed to Die a Natural Death***.

Clive Barnes in the *New York Times* noted the musical's story was weak and had "flaws of construction," but otherwise he gushed over the production and the "liberated man" Van Peebles. The "great-hearted" show had "fizz, guts and honesty" with "the joyous air of a Saturday night block party." The score was "more like a flamenco concert" and he confusedly explained that the music had a "vertical linear pattern rather than horizontal" and it "always develops upward to a climax." He also praised the "great" cast, many of whom provided "show-stopping renditions of show-stopping numbers." In the same newspaper, Walter Kerr found the book "feeble," "confused," and not "especially funny." It was "a strangely amateurish" excuse to put some musical numbers together, and Van Peebles directed in a "singularly hesitant and wandering fashion." But Kerr singled out three songs that were "knockouts" ("You Cut Up the Clothes in the Closet of My Dreams," "Quittin' Time," and "Ain't Love Grand").

The self-described "original cast and soundtrack album" was released by Stax Records on a two-LP set (# STS-2-3006) that didn't follow the running order of the songs as performed in the show and that included instrumental interludes. According to Jack Kroll in *Newsweek*, the musical was a stage version of the already completed movie (which starred the Broadway cast). The film had a limited distribution and was released in 1972 by Xenon Pictures and Yeah Inc.; it was advertised as "a hilarious hit musical direct from Broadway" in "funky" color (it was later released on DVD by Xenon Pictures # XE-XX-1062DVD).

Many sources cite the title with an exclamation point, but the Broadway program, the cast album, and the DVD omit the exclamation point (as well as the apostrophe for the word *don't*).

Awards

Tony Award Nominations: Best Featured Actor in a Musical (Avon Long); Best Book (Melvin Van Peebles)

HEATHEN!

"A NEW MUSICAL"

Theatre: Billy Rose Theatre
Opening Date: May 21, 1972; *Closing Date*: May 21, 1972
Performances: 1
Book: Sir Robert Helpmann and Eaton Magoon Jr.
Lyrics and *Music*: Eaton Magoon Jr.; dance and incidental music by Mel Marvin
Direction: Lucia Victor; *Producers*: Leonard J. Goldberg and Ken Gaston in association with R. Paul Woodville; *Choreography*: Sammy Bayes (Dan Siretta, Associate Choreographer); *Scenery*: Jack Brown; *Costumes*: Bruce Harrow; *Lighting*: Paul Sullivan; *Musical Direction*: Clay Fullum
Cast: Russ (Rusty) Thacker (Reverend Jonathan Beacon, Jonathan), Yolande Bavan (Kalialani, Kalia), Edward Rambeau (Mano'Ula, Mano), Dennis Dennehy (Mugge, Kaha Kai [The Chanter]), Justis Skae (Mugger), Sal Pernice (Mugger), Dan Merriman (Reverend Hiram Burnham, Tourist), Ann Hodges (Hepsibah Burnham, Tourist), Christopher Barrett (Church Elder, Policeman), Mary Walling (Church Elder), Michael Serrecchia (Church Elder), Mokihana (Alika), Charles Goeddertz (Hawaiian Boy), Honey Sanders (Pueo), Tina Santiago (Momona-Nui); Boys in Jail: Charles Goeddertz, Michael Serrecchia, Quitman Fludd; The Girls and Boys of Past and Present: Nancy Dafgek, Jaclynn Villamil, Mary Walling, Karen Kristin, Dennis Dennehy, Randy DiGrazio, Quitman Fludd, Charles Goeddertz, Sal Pernice, Michael Serrecchia, Justis Skae
The musical was presented in two acts.
The action takes place in the Hawaii of 1819 and 1972.

Musical Numbers

Act One: "Paradise" (Russ Thacker, Beach People); "The Word of the Lord" (Dan Merriman, Ann Hodges, Christopher Barrett, Mary Walling, Michael Serrecchia); "My Sweet Tomorrow" (Russ Thacker); "A Man among Men" (Edward Rambeau, Rowers); "Aloha" (Company); "Kalialani" (Yolande Bavan); "No Way in Hell" (Russ Thacker, Yolande Bavan, Edward Rambeau); "Battle Cry" (Yolande Bavan); "This Is Someone I Could Love" (Edward Rambeau); "House of Grass" (Edward Rambeau); "Kava Ceremony" (Company)

Act Two: "For You Brother" (Russ Thacker, Charles Goeddertz, Michael Serrecchia, Quitman Fludd); "Spear Games" (Company); "Christianity" (Company); "This Is Someone I Could Love" (reprise) (Yolande Bavan); "Heathen" (Russ Thacker); "Heathen" (reprise) (Russ Thacker, Edward Rambeau); "More Better Go Easy" (Mokihana); "Eighth Day" (Company)

Heathen! joined ***Wild and Wonderful*** as the season's shortest-running musical; both played for just one performance (and were joined by three nonmusicals that also chalked up one showing apiece, the thriller *Children! Children!*, the drama *Ring 'Round the Bathtub*, and the comedy *Tough to Get Help*).

Eaton Magoon Jr. and Sir Robert Helpmann's *Heathen!* uneasily bounced back and forth between the Hawaii of 1819 and 1972, and for the first and second act finales the two periods intermingled. But this folly was no ***Follies***, and the critics were unforgiving in the confused tale that depicted missionary Reverend Jonathan Beacon (Russ Thacker) in his attempts to bring Christianity to the island in 1819 and his dealings with resentful powerful islander chieftain Mano'ula (Edward Rambeau). (It seems that the reverend's idea of religion was to encourage the islanders to wear more clothes.) There's also a pretty girl named Kalialani (Yolande Bavan) who attracts both men. In 1972, the performers play the descendants of their forebears, and now Jonathan is a hippie and Mano'ula is Mano, a proud citizen of the United States. And Kalialani is now Kalia, and both guys are still after her.

Douglas Watt in the *New York Daily News* said *Heathen!* was "so bad that it could put a blight on tourist trade throughout the entire Pacific." He noted that the islanders were painted as "brave, happy and rather stupid," including a Bloody Mary type (Alika, played by one Mokihana) who was "full of happy talk"; the score was "dreadful"; the costumes seemed to have been "rented in Philadelphia"; and the setting resembled "three pieces of a huge diaper hung out to dry above a couple of bleached dog bones."

Richard Watts in the *New York Post* found the evening "hopelessly clumsy, inept and amateurish to an extent that is nothing short of complete disaster." Martin Gottfried in *Women's Wear Daily* said that watching the musical led him to believe that it couldn't possibly be happening and was therefore "some sort of terrible joke." Leonard Harris on WCBSTV2 lamented the book's "essential silliness" and the "banality" of the direction and choreography, while Betty Rollin on WNBC4TV said the musical's "hackneyed" message was that "heathens aren't such heathens, and that we should all love each other more."

Clive Barnes in the *New York Times* stated that "for our sins" we were given *Heathen!*, and halfway through the evening he realized "with a stab of pain" that he would have preferred to be in Las Vegas. He noted that the plot took place on "two levels, just like Grand Central Terminal," and the show itself had "a terminal look to it." The producers were the "wonderful people" who had given us ***Ari***, and thus were maintaining "their level of producing excellence." But to call *Heathen!* "the worst" musical of the season "would run the risk of overpraising its virtues" which included a "vestigial and ludicrous" book, "stilted" lyrics, and music that sometimes reached the level of "some kind of Wakiki-beach-party, all-luaus-together festivity" (but the festivity was "drab").

Kevin Sanders on WABCTV7 said the musical about Hawaiian history would make James Michener weep with its "almost incomprehensible" story; moreover, the direction caused the evening to look and sound "like a high school concert." He could hardly believe that ballet legend Sir Robert Helpmann had cowritten the book, and decided Helpmann did so "while a victim of some kind of tropical fever."

Some years later the writers revised the musical as *Aloha* (subtitled "The Spectacular New Musical," the new version seems to have been produced in Hawaii and New Zealand) and kept all the action in 1819. In this version, Bloody Mary (that is, Alika) talks directly to both the audience and the local neighborhood volcano; and when it (the volcano, not the audience) decides to erupt and spew lava, Alika gives it a good talking-to and the eruption meekly subsides.

Aloha was recorded with members of the revival cast as well as studio cast singers (Hamilton Operatic Society LP # HOS-101), and the album's artwork might understandably lead one to assume the recording is the cast album of a Hawaiian production of *Barnum*. Nine songs were retained from *Heathen!* ("My Sweet Tomorrow," "Heathen," "This Is Someone I Could Love," "No Way in Hell," "House of Grass," "Christianity," "Better More Go Easy," "Eighth Day," and "Aloha Lord," which may have been a variation of the Broadway production's "Aloha"); five new ones were added ("Suffer," "Sometimes It Rains," "Fire and Brimstone," "I

Hear Hawaii," and "Glory Be"); and one number ("Lei of Memories") was an interpolation that originally had been written by Magoon for his 1961 Broadway musical *13 Daughters* but dropped during that show's tryout engagement.

In the small but rarified genre of Hawaiian and South Sea Island musicals, *13 Daughters* was a major bomb of the 1960–1961 theatre season. The show took place in the Hawaii of the late nineteenth century and dealt with Chun, a Chinese who marries a Hawaiian princess and thus incurs the wrath of those always angry island gods (the musical is today best remembered by show buffs for its irresistibly cheesy song "Puka Puka Pants"). The same season also offered *Aloha Hawaii,* which closed during its pre-Broadway tryout. An early version of the story line for *Aloha Hawaii* reveals that like *Heathen!* it offered a boisterous island woman (who this time is a cross between Bloody Mary and Sophie Tucker). A menacing volcano also figured into the plot, but apparently no angry island gods were around.

Gian-Carlo Menotti's opera was actually titled *The Island God,* and was briefly produced by the Metropolitan Opera Company in 1942; and Leonard Bernstein's satiric opera *Trouble in Tahiti* (first produced in 1952, the work premiered on Broadway in 1955 as one-third of the revue *All in One*) offered a title song that describes a Hollywood musical in which a native girl and an American "Navy boy" tempt angry island gods by daring to fall in love (and thus promptly cause a weather event "like nothing on earth" which includes tidal waves, siroccos, hurricanes, and, yes, an erupting volcano). There was also *Paradise Island,* which was seen at the Jones Beach Marine Theatre in 1961 and 1962 and contrasted the lives of "natives" and mainland Americans (and there was a touch of perhaps verboten romance between a stuffy businessman's son and a Hawaiian princess). The 1962 Off-Broadway musical *Sweet Miani* satirized South Sea Island epics with a plot that centered on the title character (played by Broadway Baby Sheila Smith), a virgin princess in danger of being sacrificed to those angry island gods.

The ultimate show-tune tribute to Hawaii is Tom Jones and Harvey Schmidt's zany "Statehood Hula" from the 1958 Off-Broadway revue *Demi-Dozen.* Arguably the funniest song in the history of the American musical, the number was devastatingly sung by Ceil Cabot and told the tale of a supposedly simple and naive native girl who just adores Lester Lanin's society orchestra music. She tells us she makes a "marvelous lei," and knows of a beach "where people naked go/Like Joshua Logan show."

CANDIDE

The musical opened at the Curran Theatre in San Francisco, California, on July 6, 1971; at the Dorothy Chandler Pavilion in Los Angeles, California, on August 24, 1971; and at the Opera House at the Kennedy Center, Washington, D.C., on October 27, 1971, where it permanently closed on November 13, 1971.

Book: Adaptation by Sheldon Patinkin (from Lillian Hellman's original book)

Lyrics: Richard Wilbur, John LaTouche, Lillian Hellman, Dorothy Parker, Leonard Bernstein, and Felicia Cohn Montealegre Bernstein (*Note*: See song list for specific credits.)

Music: Leonard Bernstein

Based on the 1759 novel *Candide,* or *Optimism* by Voltaire (Francois-Marie Arouet).

Direction: Sheldon Patinkin; *Producers*: The Los Angeles and San Francisco Civic Light Opera Associations (Edwin Lester, General Director) in association with the John F. Kennedy Center for the Performing Arts; *Choreography*: Michael Smuin; *Scenery*: Oliver Smith; *Costumes*: Freddy Wittop; *Lighting*: Peggy Clark; *Musical Director*: Ross Reimueller

Cast: *Douglas Campbell* (Narrator, Pangloss, Martin), *Frank Porretta* (Candide), *Mary Costa* (Cunegonde), Barbara Meister (Cunegonde for all matinee performances), William Lewis (Baron, Inquistor, Marquis, Ship Captain, Governor, Ferone), Annette Cardona (Baroness, Princess, Lady of Paris, Pilgrim Mother, Governor's Mistress, Lady Frilly), Robert Ito (Body Guard, Herald, Major Domo, First Mate, Page, Keeper of Masks), Joshua Hecht (King of Hesse, Inquisitor, Sultan, Pilgrim Father, Maximillian, Chief of Police), Howard Brown (Hessian General, Conjurer, Gentleman of Paris, Pilgrim, Senor, Croupier), Eugene Green (Herman, Inquisitor, Guest, Pilgrim, Senor, Gambler), Howard Chitjian (Barker), Juleste Salve (Soldier of Lisbon, Lisbonian Gentleman), Garold Gardiner (Soldier of Lisbon), Danny Villa (Assistant to Second Inquisitor, Buenos Airian Gentleman), Rae Allen (The Old Lady), Lucy Andonian (Beggar), Marvin Samuels (Beggar), James L. Cutlip (Beggar), Cecile Wilson (Lady Silly), Tina Blandy (Lady Willy Nilly), Maris O'Neill (Lady Lightly), Damita Freeman (Lady Brightly), Marie Patrice (Lady Fly-by-Nightly), Georgelton

McClain (Venetian Gentleman), Robert Bakanic (Parisian Gentleman); Citizens, Soldiers, Beggars: Dana Alexis, Lucy Andonian, Lonna Arklin, Tina Blandy, Catherine Drew, Susan Gayle, Damita Freeman, De Maris Gordon, Anne Kaye, Brenda Lynn, Daphne Payne, Maris O'Neill, Marie Patrice, Kelly Maxwell, Anne Turner, Cecile Wilson, Karen Yarmat, Robert Bakanic, David Bender, Howard Chitjan, James L. Cutlip, Clifford Fearl, Garold Gardner, Georgelton McClain, Autris Paige, Casper Roos, Marvin Samuels, Juleste Salve, Paul Veglia, Danny Villa

The musical was presented in two acts.

The action takes place during the eighteenth century in Westphalia, Paris, Buenos Aires, on the Atlantic Ocean, and in Venice.

Musical Numbers

Act One: Overture (Orchestra); "The Best of All Possible Worlds" ("War and Peace") and "The Best of All Possible Worlds" ("Marriage") (lyric by John LaTouche) (Douglas Campbell, Mary Costa, Frank Porretta, Westphalians); "Oh, Happy We" (lyric by Richard Wilbur) (Frank Porretta, Mary Costa); "Wedding Procession" (lyric by Richard Wilbur); "Candide's Lament" (possibly "This World," lyric by John LaTouche) (Frank Porretta, Joshua Hecht); "It Must Be So" (lyric by Richard Wilbur) (Frank Porretta); "The Paris Waltz" (Ensemble); "Glitter and Be Gay" (lyric by Richard Wilbur) (Mary Costa); "You Were Dead, You Know" (lyric by John LaTouche and Richard Wilbur) (Frank Porretta, Mary Costa); "The Pilgrims' Procession" (lyric by Richard Wilbur) (Joshua Hecht, Pilgrims); "My Love" (aka "The Governor's Serenade") (lyric by John LaTouche and Richard Wilbur) (William Lewis, Rae Allen, Mary Costa); "I Am Easily Assimilated" (aka "The Old Lady's Tango") (English lyric by Leonard Bernstein, Spanish lyric by Felicia Cohn Montealegre Bernstein) (Rae Allen, Mary Costa, Harold Brown, Eugene Green); "The Quintet Finale" (lyric by Richard Wilbur) (Frank Porretta, Mary Costa, William Lewis, Rae Allen, Joshua Hecht; with comment by Douglas Campbell)

Act Two: "Words, Words, Words" (lyric by Richard Wilbur) (Douglas Campbell); "Ballad of Eldorado" (lyric by Lillian Hellman) (Frank Porretta, Buenos Airians); "Quiet" (lyric by Richard Wilbur) (Rae Allen, William Lewis, Mary Costa, Joshua Hecht); "It Must Be Me" (lyric by Richard Wilbur) (Frank Porretta); "Barcarolle: The Simple Life" (lyric by Richard Wilbur) (William Lewis, Frank Porretta, Eugene Green, Douglas Campbell, Harold Brown, Joshua Hecht, Robert Ito); "Pickpocket Ballet"; "What's the Use?" (lyric by Richard Wilbur) (Rae Allen, William Lewis, Joshua Hecht, Mary Costa, Harold Brown, Venetians); "The Venice Gavotte" (lyric by Dorothy Parker) (Rae Allen, Frank Porretta, Mary Costa, Douglas Campbell, Ensemble); "No More Than This" (possibly "Nothing More Than This," lyric by Leonard Bernstein) (Frank Porretta); "Make Our Garden Grow" (lyric by Richard Wilbur) (Ensemble)

The 1956 musical *Candide* has broken many hearts during its existence. Leonard Bernstein's brilliant score is one of the greatest ever written, Lillian Hellman's book is witty and incisive, and by all accounts the physical production was overwhelmingly magnificent. But the production lasted just seventy-three performances, and it was the scintillating cast album that kept the show alive (and for the almost sixty years following its release, the album has never gone out of print).

The musical resurfaced in a touring concert version in 1958 (which was adapted by Michael Stewart); in a 1959 London production (the book was credited to Hellman with a notation that Stewart "assisted" with the script); in a brief U.S. tour in 1967 (which was adapted by Sheldon Patinkin); and in a special one-night 1968 concert in New York at Philharmonic Hall in an adaptation that utilized the versions by Hellman, Stewart, and Patinkin.

Patinkin adapted and directed the current revival, which marked Mary Costa's third appearance as Cunegonde (she had been in the 1958 touring concert version and in the 1959 London production); and William Lewis, who had appeared as Candide in the 1968 concert, played various roles in the new version, including that of the Governor.

The current revival was the work's first major staged American production since the original closed. The four-month tryout played in San Francisco, Los Angeles, and Washington, D.C., but permanently closed after the Washington run without risking New York, and so again hearts were broken that a successful *Candide* was not in the Broadway cards. But the 1974 version reversed the musical's fortunes; it played on Broadway for over two years and won the New York Drama Critics' Circle Award for Best Musical of the 1973–1974 season (though the production didn't turn a profit). However, this was a kindergarten *Candide* for the *Laugh-In* set, and so appalled purists had their hearts broken yet again. (For more information, see entry for the 1974 revival.)

In reviewing the current production, Harv in *Variety* complained that it proceeded in "clumsy, episodic steps," the staging and the dialogue were obvious, and the "dreary" evening lasted almost three hours.

Richard Coe in the *Washington Post* noted that an uncredited Michael Kidd had been working on the revival. In comparing the Washington booking to the one that had opened a few months earlier in San Francisco, Coe now found the musical "far shorter, more headlong, and furnished with more 'fresh lines.'" He said it would "be impossible to find a tenor who so nearly suggests Candide" as Frank Porretta, who gave "a jewel of a performance," and he noted that Mary Costa's "Glitter and Be Gay" was "a show-stopper in the greatest tradition." Harry MacArthur in the *Washington Star* felt the musical's mounting was "spectacular," but said that as the evening wound down the show "creaked" and the second act boiled down to the question of "whatever-happened-to-*The-Student-Prince*?" He praised Oliver Smith's "superior" décor (Smith had designed the sets for the original 1956 production), noted the evening had everything an "opulent" musical should have, and said Porretta "won rousing applause on several occasions."

Tom Donnelly in the *Washington Daily News* had reviewed the 1956 production for the *New York World-Telegram and Sun* where he stated the musical was "charged with the excitement that arises when gifted artists come close to achieving the all but impossible." Bernstein's "ravishing" score was "lush, lovely, and voluptuous"; was "as frostily pretty as a diamond bell"; and was "easily the best score" Bernstein had ever composed. The evening may have had some structural problems and perhaps was "an example of reach exceeding grasp, but what a reach is there!" But this time around, he was less than happy, and the headline of his review proclaimed "It's Bomb Time on the Operetta Front." He stated that "any potentially splendid musical that has Mr. Patinkin for a friend doesn't need an enemy" and he criticized the emphasis on "burlesquing" the conventions of operetta and the tendency of the cast to "camp it up like crazy, in a style that might seem excessive for *Little Mary Sunshine*." (If Donnelly witnessed the nonstop silliness of the 1974 production, he must have recoiled in horror.)

The above cast and song lists reflect the opening night of the revival in San Francisco. During the course of the tryout, "Wedding Procession" and "Pickpocket Ballet" were deleted; and "The Lisbon Sequence," "The Inquisition," "Plain Words," "Bon Voyage," "The Venice Gambling Scene," and an orchestral interlude titled "Return to Westphalia" were added.

During the tryout, Douglas Campbell (as the narrator as well as Pangloss and Martin) was succeeded by Robert Klein, and for Washington Rae Allen (The Old Lady) was given star status, and so her name was placed above the title, along with those of Porretta, Costa, and Klein. Among the minor roles, Cecile Wilson (Lady Silly) was succeeded by Mickie Pollak; Tina Blandy (Lady Willy Nilly) by Pamela Sousa; Marie Patrice (Lady Fly-by-Nightly) by Carol Perea; and Annette Cardona (Lady Frilly) by Brenda Lynn. The roles of the Gentlemen from Venice, Lisbon, Buenos Aires, and Paris were eliminated, and when Annette Cardona left the production, her six roles were either eliminated or assumed by Brenda Lynn.

The original production of *Candide* opened at the Martin Beck (now Al Hirschfeld) Theatre on December 1, 1956. One of the myths surrounding the musical is that it wasn't appreciated by the critics. As noted, Donnelly raved about the score and admired the ambitious adaptation. John Chapman in the *New York Daily News* said the "artistic triumph" was the best light opera since Richard Strauss's *Der Rosenkavalier*, and noted that sixty seconds after conductor Samuel Krachmalnick brought down his baton for the overture "one sensed that here was going to be an evening of uncommon quality." Although Robert Coleman in the *New York Daily Mirror* found fault with the musical (but didn't specify his concerns), he noted the work was "distinguished" and "towers heads and shoulders above most of the song-and-dancers you'll get this or any other season"; Richard Watts in the *New York Post* felt the libretto often lacked "bite and pungency" but nonetheless he admired the often "brilliant" work which had "so much in the way of musical excellence, visual beauty, grace of style and boldness of design"; and John McClain in the *New York Journal American* said Hellman's book was bright, the music delightful, the scenery "imaginative and exciting," and the overall evening was "ambitious and brilliant."

Brooks Atkinson in the *New York Times* praised the "brilliant musical satire," which was a "triumph of stage arts molded into a symmetrical whole"; he noted that nothing in Bernstein's previous theatre music had the "joyous variety, humor and richness" of this "wonderful" score. He also mentioned that Oliver Smith's "fabulous" décor and Irene Sharaff's "vigorous" costumes made *Candide* "the most stunning production of the season."

But lone naysayer Walter Kerr in the *New York Herald Tribune* felt *Candide* was a "great ghostly wreck that sails like a Flying Dutchman across the fogbound stage of the Martin Beck." The irony was "thumped out with a crushing hand," the direction seemed "unsure," and the staging and even the performances lacked shape and definition. But if anyone emerged unscathed by "this singularly ill-conceived venture" it was Bernstein.

In his *American Drama since World War II*, Gerald Weales wrote that *Candide* was "not only the most sophisticated product of the American musical stage," it was "probably the most imaginative American play to reach Broadway since the war."

The script was published in hardback by Random House in 1957, and the cast album was recorded by Columbia (LP # OS-2350); the CD was issued by Sony Classical/Columbia/Legacy Records (# SK-86859).

Besides the 1974 revival, the musical returned on April 29, 1997, at the Gershwin Theatre for 103 performances (the cast album was released by RCA Victor Records CD # 09026-68835-2). The work was also presented by the New York City Opera Company in 1982, 1983, 1984, 1986, 1989, and 2008.

Besides the three Broadway cast albums (from 1956, 1974, and 1997), there are a number of recordings that include songs dropped during the tryout of the original production or in preproduction, including a "final, revised version, 1989" conducted by Bernstein and released by Deutsche Grammophon (LP # 429-734-1; CD # 429-734-2).

A 1989 concert version that preceded the Deutsche Grammophon recording was released by that company on DVD (# B0006905-09) and an Avery Fisher Hall/Lincoln Center concert version presented on May 5, 2005, was shown on public television and then later released on DVD by Image Entertainment (# ID2762EMDVD).

CLOWNAROUND

"A Funny Kind of Musical for the Entire Family"

The musical opened on April 27, 1972, at the Oakland Coliseum, Oakland, California, where it played for fourteen performances, and then was performed at the Cow Palace, San Francisco, California, where it permanently closed.

Text and *Lyrics*: Alvin Cooperman

Music: Moose Charlap

Direction: Gene Kelly; *Producers*: Theatre Now, Inc., in association with Harry Lashinsky and Franklin Roberts; *Choreography*: Howard Jeffrey; *Scenery, Costumes*, and *Lighting*: Sean Kenny; *Musical Direction*: Boris Kogan

Cast: *Ruth Buzzi, Dennis Allen*, The Burgers (Frank Burger, Janet [Jeanette] Burger), The Columbines (Diana Buchanan, Janet Chovan, Kathey Coburn, Jean Gorman, Joan Gorman, Sandra Gray, Catherine Groetzinger, Benita Lynn, Tara Montgomery, Pam Patka, Joann Selden, Teresa Jane Soay, Madeline Svet, Barbara Ann Verbenec, Marcie Whitney, and Vernie Whitney), Chrys Holt, The Carillo Brothers (Daniel Acosta, Pedro Carrillo), The Zamperla Family (Napoleone Zamperla, Kitty [Katty] Zamperla, Ermes Zamperla, Jany [Jane] Zamperla, Atos Zamperla, Mafalda Zamperla, and Ernestina [Ernestine] Zamperla), Ray Zecca, Maria Berisini (Berosini) (aka Miss Damorra), Don Conner; Clowns: Chuck Barnett, Maria Berisoni, Jim Betters, Frank Burger, Jeanette Burger, Balford Carr, Joe Chavez, Rise Clemmer, Teresa Cozad, Joanne DeVaronna, Debbie Doyle, Vickie Dunn, Bob Einfrank, Sidney Fish, Stephen Frye, Troy Garza, Debra Gray, Gerald Haston, Chrys Holt, Judy Johnson, Bob Keller, Paul Lubera, Bert May, Paulette Martin, Jim McEachern, Myron Meljie, Arlene Nelson, Ralph O'Neill, Joel Polis, Jason Roberts, Lisa Russell, Steve Short, Jerry Smith, Lorraine Thul, Arthur Whitfield, Artos Zamperla, Ermes Zamperla, Ernestina (Ernestine) Zamperla, Jany (Jane) Zamperla, Kitty (Katty) Zamperla, Mafalda Zamperla, Napoleone Zamperla, Ray Zecca

The revue was presented in two acts.

Musical Numbers

Act One: *Prologue* (Ruth Buzzi, Dennis Allen); *I See a Clown*: "Clowns" (The Clown Ensemble); *The Fun Fair*: "You're a Clown" and "Here Are Your Children" (Ruth Buzzi, Dennis Allen, The Burgers, Children from the Audience); *Silhouette*: "Silhouette" (aka "Paper Heart") (The Columbines); *The Animal Band*: "Animal Band" (The Clown Ensemble); *Balloon*: "Balloon" (Chrys Holt, Ensemble)

Act Two: *Thing-a-ma-jig*: "Thing-a-ma-jig" (The Clown Ensemble); *The Flickers*: "The Laugh Song" (The Carillo Brothers); *Sunny Day*: "Sunny Day" (Ensemble); *Wheels*: The Zamperlas; *I Need a Ship*: "I Need a Ship" (Ruth Buzzi, Dennis Allen, Ray Zecca, Maria Berisini, Ensemble); *Clownaround*: "Clown Alley" (Entire Company); *Clowns Say Goodnight (but Not Goodbye)*: "Clowns Say Goodnight (but Not Goodbye)" (Ruth Buzzi, Entire Company)

ClownAround was a $650,000 spectacular that celebrated clowns and clowndom, and its gargantuan setting and large cast were designed to play at arena-styled venues throughout the country. Directed by Gene Kelly, the revue opened at the Oakland Arena in Oakland, California, on April 27, 1972, for fourteen performances and then played at the Cow Palace in San Francisco, California, where it permanently closed.

British scenic designer Sean Kenny, who had created the huge turntable set for the British and Broadway productions of *Oliver!*, conjured up the spectacular setting for *ClownAround*. This was a huge skeletal flying saucer–like contraption that the show's souvenir program described as 52 feet high, 134 feet long, and 50 feet wide. The program noted that the "clown machine" consisted of six hundred individual pieces that weighed forty-four thousand pounds and could be dismantled and then reassembled for each stop on the revue's projected tour (it took twenty hours to reassemble the machine). The device consisted of twelve different performing levels as well as elevators and three turntables, and had its own self-contained lighting and sound-effects systems. The machine also included hidden props, and so for the depiction of a ship, the clown machine could be magically transformed into a sailing vessel replete with sails.

Besides dozens of clowns, the revue offered the Burgers, an animal act that consisted of twenty dogs, two ponies, four chimpanzees, and one ape; Miss Damorra and her fifty-six trained doves; and The Zamperlas, a family who entertained with their unicycles and trampolines. Perhaps the evening's most thrilling moment occurred when a young woman named Chrys Holt flew high above the stage attached to a huge helium-filled, clown-faced balloon that floated above her; the gimmick was that she was attached to the balloon only by her long hair. There was also some audience participation for the children in attendance, who were invited to come on stage during "The Fun Fair" sequence. And television comedians Ruth Buzzi and Dennis Allen served as general masters of ceremonies.

ClownAround received a negative notice from *Variety* (it was "unready" for prime time), and the weekly reported that because of its "terrific" losses the show shuttered after two weeks of performances.

RCA Victor Records recorded the cast album (LP # LSP-4741) prior to production so that it could be sold at the venues where the revue played (in a fascinating article about the cast album, Richard Thompson in the January 1979 issue of *Stereo Review* reported that the album was also sold in record stores in a few cities such as New York and Boston, but that most of the albums were later recalled and their vinyl recycled for other recordings; as a result, the cast album became one of the rarest of show albums). In 2013, the album was issued on CD by Masterworks Broadway/Sony/ArkivMusic (# 88765-49320-2).

W.C.

"A New Musical"

The musical opened in early June 1971 and played in summer stock venues throughout the summer before permanently closing. Among the theatres where the production played are: Painters Mill Music Fair (Towson, Maryland), Valley Forge Music Fair (Devon, Pennsylvania), Westbury Music Fair (Westbury, Long Island, New York), Storrowton Theatre (West Springfield, Massachusetts), and Colonie Coliseum Summer Theatre (Albany, New York).

Book: Milton Sperling and Sam Locke

Lyrics and *Music*: Al Carmines

Based on the 1949 biography *W.C. Fields: His Follies and Fortunes* by Robert Lewis Taylor.

Direction: Richard Altman; *Producer*: Ann Corio and Michael P. Iannucci (A David Black Production); *Choreography*: Bob Herget; *Scenery*: Peter Larkin; *Costumes*: Sara Brooks; *Lighting*: Lester Tapper; *Musical Direction*: Susan Romann

Cast: *Mickey Rooney* (W. C. Fields), Clark James (First Bellhop, Orso), Barry Preston (Second Bellhop, Studio Cop), Sid Marshall (Doorman, Studio Cop), David Vaughan (Desk Clerk, Rodney), Marie Anderson (Lady in Wheelchair), David McCorkle (Elevator Man), Jaclynn Villamil (First Girl), Linda Jorgens (Second Girl), Pip Sarser (Benjy), Bernice Martell (Benjy's Mother), Sam Stoneburner (Ron Kirkland), Martin J. Cassidy (Smitty), Cornel Richie (Cameraman, Hospital Doctor), Cindy Roberts (Script Girl), Essie Borden (Benjy's Nurse), Rudy Tronto (Paddy O'Hara), Bernadette Peters (Carlotta Monti), Jack Bittner (K.G.), Gary Oakes (Ben Ross), Dick Colacino (Cauliflower, Chinese Laundryman), Charlotte Povia (Mrs. Walowski), Louis Garcia (Alberto), Virginia Martin (Blondie); Girls: Essie Borden, Linda Jorgens, Bernice Martell, Cindy Roberts, and Jaclynn Villamil; Dennis Britten (Studio Doctor), Diana Barone (Mrs. Grissom); for the "Philadelphia 1890" Sequence: Freddie James Ebert (Claude [W. C. Fields as a boy]), Dennis Britten (Sausage Vendor), Marie Anderson (Cake Vendor), Sam Stoneburner (James Dukinfield), Diana Barone (Nurse), Pip Sarser (Baby), Charlotte Povia (Matron), Dick Colacino (Keystone Cop), Louis Garcia (Keystone Cop), David McCorkle (Keystone Cop), Essie Borden (Window Shopper), Fred Benjamin (Card Shark), Clark James (Card Shark), Sid Marshall (Card Shark), Barry Preston (Card Shark, Chinaman), Dennis Britten (Black Beard), Bernice Martell (Madame), Linda Jorgens (Agnes), Cindy Roberts (Bessie), Jaclynn Villamil (Emma), Fred Benjamin (Customer), David Vaughan (Customer), Cornel Richie (Piano Player)

The musical was presented in two acts.

The action takes place in Hollywood during the 1930s as well as in Philadelphia in 1890.

Musical Numbers

Act One: "Never Trust Anyone under Three" (Mickey Rooney, Company); "I'll Follow My Star" (Bernadette Peters); "There's a Little Boy in Every Man" (Freddie James Ebert, Mickey Rooney); "Why Do Women Always Choose the Wrong Man?" (Gary Oakes); "I Knew It All The Time" (Bernadette Peters); "Philadelphia 1890" (Freddie James Ebert, Company); "You Could" (Mickey Rooney, Bernadette Peters); "Never Give a Sucker an Even Break" (Virginia Martin, Essie Borden, Linda Jorgens, Bernice Martell, Cindy Roberts, Jaclynn Villamil); "Being a Pal" (Rudy Tronto, Bernadette Peters, Gary Oakes); "I'll Still Be Here" (Bernadette Peters); "You've Gotta Leave Them" (Mickey Rooney)

Act Two: "The Greatest Comic of Them All" (Company); "The Old Days" (Mickey Rooney); "You Come After Me" (Virginia Martin); "I'm Through with Men" (Bernadette Peters); "Why Do Women Always Choose the Wrong Man?" (reprise) (Gary Oakes); "Serenade" (Gary Oakes); "Bring on the Booze" (Mickey Rooney, Company); "Don't Leave Me" (Freddie James Ebert); "You Could" (reprise) (Mickey Rooney, Bernadette Peters)

Al Carmines' *W.C.* told the story of comic W. C. Fields (1880–1946), and like so many show business sagas it flopped. For every *Gypsy* (1959; Gypsy Rose Lee and June Havoc) and *Funny Girl* (1964; Fannie Brice), there were many short-running musicals, such as *Sophie* (1963; Sophie Tucker), *Jennie* (1963; Laurette Taylor), *Hello, Sucker!* (1969; Texas Guinan), ***Minnie's Boys*** (The Marx Brothers), ***Mack & Mabel*** (Mack Sennett and Mabel Normand), two different 1983 musicals about Marilyn Monroe (*Marilyn* opened in London and *Marilyn: An American Fable* on Broadway), and two different musicals titled *Chaplin* (1983 and 2012; Charlie Chaplin). And in London, *Dean* 'n' *Jean* were fast flops; the former was a 1977 musical about James Dean, and *Jean Seberg* opened in 1983 with a score by Marvin Hamlisch.

Incidentally, there were also operas about various celebrities, including Dominick Argento's *The Dream of Valentino* (1994) and three about Marilyn Monroe, Lorenzo Ferrero's *Marilyn* (*Scenes from the '50s in Two Acts*) (1980), Ezra Laderman's *Marilyn* (1983), and Gavin Bryars's *Marilyn Forever* (2010); Laderman's opera received its world premiere when it was produced in New York by the New York City Opera Company.

W.C. played in summer stock venues during the summer of 1971, and although it was scheduled for a fall production at the Fisher Theatre in Detroit before opening on Broadway it never made it beyond its summer bookings. *Variety* praised Mickey Rooney in the title role, but otherwise found the score "weak" and the choreography "mediocre."

The musical concentrated on Fields's long-term relationship with Carlotta Monti, who was played by Bernadette Peters. In 1971, Monti (with Cy Rice) wrote the memoir *W. C. Fields and Me: Memories of the Great One—by the Woman Who Lived with Him for 14 Years*, which was filmed as *W. C. Fields and Me* in 1976 with Rod Steiger and Valerie Perrine (among the film's supporting players was Bernadette Peters).

As the summer tour progressed, songs were deleted from and added to the production; among the latter were "Love Can Get You Down," "The Chickadee Girls," and "Fifty Years of Making People Laugh."

The collection *"W.C." and Other Theatre Songs of Al Carmines* (Original Cast Records CD # OC-9483) includes nine numbers from the production ("Fifty Years of Making People Laugh," "I'll Still Be Here," "You Could," "Never Give a Sucker an Even Break," "Why Do Women Always Choose the Wrong Man?," "Bring on the Booze," "I'll Follow My Star," "Serenade," and "Love Can Get You Down"); one ("You Come First") that probably was heard during the run as "You Come After Me"; and two ("Give Me an Old Tune" and "Dummy Juggler") that may or may not have been included in the tour. The album's singers are Carmines, Alice Playten, Bill Daugherty, and Debbie Damp.

If *W.C.* had made it to New York, it would have marked Mickey Rooney's Broadway debut; but if *W.C.* caused him any disappointment, the revue ***Sugar Babies*** more than made up for it (the show played for almost three years and provided a second act to Rooney's legendary career). At the time of *W.C.*'s production, Bernadette Peters's career was at a temporary low with *A Mother's Kisses* (1968; the show closed during its pre-Broadway tryout, and Peters's role was eliminated during rehearsals), the one-performance debacle of *La Strada* (1969), and the short-running 1971 Broadway revival of ***On the Town***. Also in the cast of *W.C.* was Virginia Martin, who had made memorable impressions in the original productions of *How to Succeed in Business without Really Trying* (1961; in which she created the role of Hedy LaRue) and *Little Me* (1962; in which she played the title role of Belle Poitrine), but she never again matched her early successes and made her final Broadway appearance in a minor role in the fast-folding ***Carmelina***.

Al Carmines was the ultimate Off-Broadway composer and lyricist, and over the years more than forty of his musicals were produced Off Off Broadway and Off Broadway. A few were recorded, and his masterpiece is *Promenade* (1969), a dadaesque concept musical that abounded in his rich hurdy-gurdy pastiche-driven style. In the cast of *W.C.* was Essie Borden, who appeared in a number of Carmines's musicals, such as *The Journey of Snow White* (1971), *The Faggot* (1973), *The Future* (1974), and *Someone's in the Kitchen with Dinah* (1979).

1972–1973 Season

MAN OF LA MANCHA

"A Musical Play"

Theatre: Vivian Beaumont Theatre
Opening Date: June 22, 1972; *Closing Date*: October 21, 1972
Performances: 140
Book: Dale Wasserman
Lyrics: Joe Darion
Music: Mitch Leigh
Based on the novel *Don Quixote* by Miguel de Cervantes (volume 1 of the novel was published in 1605, and volume 2 in 1615); also based on the 1959 telefilm *I, Don Quixote* by Dale Wasserman.
Direction: Albert Marre; *Producers*: Albert W. Selden and Hal James by arrangement with Lincoln Center; *Choreography*: Jack Cole; *Scenery* and *Lighting*: Howard Bay; *Costumes*: Howard Bay and Patton Campbell; *Musical Direction*: Joseph Klein
Cast: *Richard Kiley* (Don Quixote, Cervantes), *Joan Diener* (Aldonza), Irving Jacobson (Sancho), Jack Dabdoub (Innkeeper), Robert Rounseville (Padre), Lee Bergere (Dr. Carrasco), Dianne Barton (Antonia), Edmond Varrato (Barber, Horse), Shev Rodgers (Pedro, Horse), Ted Forlow (Anselmo), Eleanore Knapp (Housekeeper), John Aristides (Juan), Fernando Grahal (Tenorio, Dancing Horse), Bill Stanton (Paco), Hector (Jaime) Mercado (Jose, Dancing Horse), Rita Metzger (Maria), Laura Kenyon (Fermina), Renato Cibelli (Captain of the Inquisition), Stephen Sahlein (Guitarist); Guards and Men of the Inquisition: Jeff Killion, David Wasson, and Robert Cromwell (*Note*: For the first two performances of the revival, Edmond Varrato performed the role of Sancho.)
The musical was presented in one act.
The action takes place at the end of the sixteenth century in a dungeon in Seville and in the imagination of Cervantes.

Musical Numbers

"Man of La Mancha" ("I, Don Quixote") (Richard Kiley, Irving Jacobson, Edmond Varrato, Shev Rodgers); "It's All the Same" (Joan Diener, Shev Rodgers, Ted Forlow, John Aristides, Fernando Grahal, Bill Stanton, Hector Mercado); "Dulcinea" (Richard Kiley; then, Shev Rodgers, Ted Forlow, John Aristides, Fernando Grahal, Bill Stanton, Hector Mercado); "I'm Only Thinking of Him" (Robert Rounesville, Dianne Barton, Eleanore Knapp; then, Lee Bergere); "I Really Like Him" (Irving Jacobson); "What Does He Want of Me" (Joan Diener); "Little Bird, Little Bird" (Ted Forlow, Shev Rodgers, John Aristides, Fernando Grahal, Bill Stanton, Hector Mercado); "Barber's Song" (Edmond Varrato); "Golden Helmet of Mambrino" (Richard Kiley, Irving Jacobson, Edmond Varrato, Shev Rodgers, Ted Forlow, John Aristides, Fernando Grahal, Bill Stanton, Hector Mercado); "To Each His Dulcinea" (Robert Rounseville); "The Quest" ("The Impossible

Dream") (Richard Kiley); "The Combat" (Richard Kiley, Joan Diener, Irving Jacobson, Shev Rodgers, Ted Forlow, John Aristides, Fernando Grahal, Bill Stanton, Hector Mercado); "The Dubbing" (Jack Dabdoub, Joan Diener, Irving Jacobson); "Moorish Dance" (Ensemble); "Aldonza" (Joan Diener); "The Knight of the Mirrors" (Richard Kiley, Renato Cibelli, Jeff Killion, David Wasson, Robert Cromwell); "A Little Gossip" (Irving Jacobson); "Dulcinea" (reprise) (Joan Diener); "Man of La Mancha" (reprise) (Richard Kiley, Joan Diener, Irving Jacobson); "The Psalm" (Robert Rounseville); "The Quest" (reprise) (Company)

The original production of *Man of La Mancha* had closed a year earlier, but for the current four-month revival at Lincoln Center many of the original cast members returned, including Richard Kiley, Joan Diener, Irving Jacobson, and Robert Rounseville. The musical had first premiered in New York at Lincoln Center's original (and temporary) home, the ANTA Washington Square Theatre, and here the revival was "returning" to Lincoln Center at the Vivian Beaumont, the Center's main stage for dramatic and musical productions.

The story was framed around the imprisonment of Miguel de Cervantes (Kiley) for foreclosing on property owned by the Catholic Church. His fellow prisoners hold a mock trial, charging Cervantes with being an "idealist, a bad poet, and an honest man." For his defense, Cervantes offers to enact a "charade" to plead his case and he asks the prisoners to portray various characters in his narrative. The charade is of course Cervantes's story about Don Quixote and his manservant Sancho (Jacobson) and their quixotic adventures of tilting at windmills and fighting monsters. Along the way, they meet among others a padre (Rounseville), a scholar (Lee Bergere), an innkeeper (Jack Dabdoub), and a harlot (Diener). Quixote's innate innocence affects those he encounters, and his death leaves them ennobled and hopeful for the future. At the end of the charade, Cervantes is summoned by the Inquisition for trial and he leaves the prison cell to meet his fate.

Mitch Leigh's score was often flavored with Spanish and flamenco-styled rhythms, and his pulsating music was a perfect fit for the characters and situations. Only the character and songs of Sancho were out of place: as written, Sancho's Borscht Belt humor and weak songs reeked of the worst kind of unimaginative Broadway shtick. Otherwise, such numbers as "I, Don Quixote" ("Man of La Mancha"), "Golden Helmet of Mambrino," "Barber's Song," and "The Quest" ("The Impossible Dream") were full-blooded theatre songs, and the latter became one of the biggest hits of the era. Perhaps the shimmering and haunting "Dulcinea" was the score's finest moment, and with the exception of Sancho's songs Leigh's score was a richly textured and unified whole in the manner of a song cycle.

Douglas Watt in the *New York Daily News* was glad to see the "splendid" Kiley back in his signature role, and said the reunion of Kiley and *Man of La Mancha* was a "grand" one and his only regret was that the production was a limited engagement that couldn't run through the winter. Betty Rollin on WNBC4TV said the musical had "originality and stature" as well as "majesty," and wryly noted "we don't get much of that nowadays, and when we do, it's usually pretentious."

But Jerry Talmer in the *New York Post* found the musical's popularity a "riddle wrapped within an enigma wrapped within a mystery" and he couldn't remember "ever having sat so long between songs dying for a song to come along" and then during the songs "dying for the end of the song to come along." As for Joan Diener, she was a "very strange type—a sort of Raquel Welch on the less talented and somehow smudgier side." During the run of the original production, the musical's advertising campaign had relentlessly asked the question, "What? You've seen *Man of La Mancha* only once?," and Tallmer concluded his review by noting he'd now seen the show once and "once has been sufficient."

Dale Wasserman's adaptation was first seen as the nonmusical *I, Don Quixote,* which was presented on the CBS series *Dupont Show of the Month* on November 9, 1959, with Lee J. Cobb (Cervantes), Colleen Dewhurst (Aldonza), Eli Wallach (Sancho), and Hurd Hatfield (Carrasco). The musical version was first produced at Goodspeed Opera House, East Haddam, Connecticut, during summer 1965, and most of the cast members and creative team transferred to New York when the musical opened on November 22, 1965, for a marathon run of 2,328 performances (for New York, cast member Eddie Roll's dances for Goodspeed were replaced by Jack Cole's choreography). The Goodspeed production was presented in two acts and included two deleted songs (Aldonza's "What Kind of Animal Am I?" and Quixote's "Mask of Evil"). "Look, Look in the Mirror" was probably an early title for the sequence "The Knight of the Mirrors."

Besides the current production, the musical has been revived in New York three more times, at the Palace Theatre on September 15, 1977, for 124 performances (Kiley reprised his original role and others in the cast were Emily Yancy as Aldonza and Bob Wright as the Innkeeper; see entry); at the Marquis Theatre on April 24, 1992, for 108 performances with Raul Julia (Cervantes), Sheena Easton (Aldonza), and David Holliday (The

Innkeeper); and at the Martin Beck (now Al Hirschfeld) Theatre on December 5, 2002, for 304 performances with Brian Stokes Mitchell (Cervantes) and Mary Elizabeth Mastrantonio (Aldonza).

The original London production opened at the Piccadilly Theatre on April 24, 1968, for 253 performances with Keith Mitchell (Cervantes) and Diener.

The overblown, tiresome, and lifeless 1972 film version was released by United Artists; directed by Arthur Hiller, Peter O'Toole (Cervantes) and Sophia Loren (Aldonza) were the leads, and others in the cast were James Coco, Harry Andrews, John Castle, and, from the original stage production, Gino Conforti reprised his role of the barber.

The script was published in hardback by Random House in 1966, and is also included in the 1976 hardback collection *Great Musicals of the American Theatre, Volume Two* (published by the Chilton Book Company and edited by Stanley Richards). The original cast album was issued by Kapp Records (LP # KRL-4505), and the CD by Decca Broadway Records (# 012-159-387-2) includes a bonus track of the previously unreleased instrumental sequence "The Combat." Kiley also recorded a version of the musical for children on Golden Records (LP # 265) which includes Gerrianne Raphael, Eddie Roll, and Shev Rodgers, all members of the original Broadway company. The London cast album (issued by Decca Records # DXSA-7203) was released on a two-LP set and includes dialogue, the soundtrack album was released by United Artists (LP # UAS-9906), and the 2002 revival was recorded by RCA Victor Records (CD # 09026-64007-2).

There have been other recordings of the score, including some of those unfortunate "crossover" adaptations that seem to include the entire entertainment industry: the "All-Star Cast from Broadway, Hollywood and Opera" (released by Columbia Records LP # S-31237) includes Jim Nabors, Marilyn Horne, Jack Gilford, Richard Tucker, Madeline Kahn, and Ron Husmann but not Minnie Pearl and Spike Jones, and Sony Classical Records (CD # SK-46436) offers Placido Domingo, Julia Migenes, Mandy Patinkin, Samuel Ramey, Jerry Hadley, and Rosalind Ellis. Jay Records released a two-CD set (which includes Ron Raines, Kim Criswell, and Avery Saltzman) with dialogue, bows, and exit music (as well as a bonus track of a "popular" interpretation of "Little Bird, Little Bird").

For the current revival's opening night and second performance, Edmond Varrato substituted for Irving Jacobson because the latter suffered an accident during a rehearsal, but Jacobson rejoined the company for the third and following performances (for the two performances in which Varrato spelled Jacobson, Varrato's usual role of the barber was played by Ted Forlow). For matinees, David Atkinson performed the role of Cervantes and Gerrianne Raphael was Aldonza.

MASS

"A Theatre Piece for Singers, Players and Dancers"

Theatre: Metropolitan Opera House
Opening Date: June 28, 1972; *Closing Date*: July 22, 1972
Performances: 22
Text: The Liturgy of the Roman Catholic Mass; other English texts by Stephen Schwartz and Leonard Bernstein
Music: Leonard Bernstein
Direction: Gordon Davidson (with "staged by" credits to Davidson and Alvin Ailey); *Producers*: The John F. Kennedy Center for the Performing Arts and S. Hurok (Roger L. Stevens and Martin Fenstein, Producers; Schuyler C. Chapin, Associate Producer); *Choreography*: Alvin Ailey; *Scenery*: Oliver Smith; *Costumes*: Frank Thompson; *Lighting*: Gilbert Hemsley Jr.; *Musical Direction*: Maurice Peress
Cast: Alan Titus (Celebrant); Soloists: Gary Lipps, Neva Small, Ed Dixon, Eugene Edwards, Linda Lloyd, David Spangler, Lee Hooper, Larry Marshall, John Bennett Perry, Gina Penn, Mary Bracken Phillips, Thom Ellis, Margaret Cowie, Gary Lipps, John D. Anthony, Leigh Dodson; Singers: John D. Anthony, Cheryl Barnes, Jacqueline Britt, Jane Coleman, David Cryer, Margaret Cowie, Ed Dixon, Leigh Dodson, Eugene Edwards, Thom Ellis, Lowell Harris, Lee Hooper, Gary Lipps, Linda Lloyd, Linda Marks, Larry Marshall, Gina Penn, John Bennett Perry, Mary Bracken Phillips, Neva Small, David Spangler, Alan Titus; The Alvin Ailey Dance Theatre: Acolytes—Judith Jamison and Dudley Williams, Clive Thompson, Linda Kent, Kenneth Pearl, Sylvia Waters, Estelle E. Spurlock; Dancers—Kevin Rotardier, Sara Yarborough, Mari Kajiwara, John Parks, Hector (Jamie) Mercado, Leland Schwantes, Clover Mathis, Lynne Dell Walker; The

Norman Scribner Choir: Sopranos—Juanita Brown, Carol Gericke, Diane Higginbotham, Vicki Johnstone, Janet Kenney, Katherine Ray, Cynthia Richards, Diana Rothman, Sandra Willetts; Altos—Barbara Boller, Catherine Rounds, Alicia Kopfstein-Penk, Patricia George, Suzanne Grant, Raina Mann, Anne Miller, Janet Sooy, Joy Wood; Tenors—Barry Butts, David Coon, Robert Dorsey, Michael Hume, William Jones, Robert Kimball, John Madden, Robert Stevenson, Robert Whitney; Basses—Earl Baker, Glenn Cunningham, Albert diRuiter, Richard Frisch, Arphelius Paul Gatling, Charles Greenwell, Walter Richardson, Ronald Roxbury, Michael Tronzo; The Berkshire Boys' Choir: David Abell, Ben Borsch, Timothy Brown, Chris Cole, Sammy Coleman, Peter Coulianos, Thomas Ettinghausen, Liam Fennelly, Tim Ferrell, Jonathan Gram, Bruce Haynes, Richard Michael, Michael Miller, Chris Negus, Edward Rosen, Robert Rough, Miles Smith, Richard Swan, David Voorhees (*Note*: During the run, Alan Titus and David Cryer alternated in the role of the Celebrant.)

The musical was presented in one act.

Musical Numbers

(I) *Devotions Before Mass*: (1) "Antiphon" (Tape); (2) Hymn and Psalm—"A Simple Song" (Alan Titus); and (3) "Responsory" (Tape); (II) *First Introit* (Rondo): (1) "Prefatory Prayers" (Company); (III) *Second Introit*: (1) "In Nomine Patris" (Alan Titus, Tape); (2) "Prayer for the Congregation" (Chorale: "Almighty Father") (Choir); and (3) "Epiphany" (Oboe Solo); (IV) *Confession*: (1) "Confiteor" (Choir); (2) Trope—"I Don't Know" (Gary Lipps, Neva Small, Ed Dixon); and (3) "Easy" (Eugene Edwards, Linda Lloyd, David Spangler); (V) *Meditation # 1* (Orchestra); (VI) *Gloria*—(1) "Gloria Tibi" (Alan Titus, Boy Choir); (2) "Gloria in Excelsis" (Choir); (3) Trope—"Half of the People" (Street Chorus, Choir); and (4) Trope—"Thank You" (Lee Hooper); (VII) *Meditation # 2* (Orchestra); (VIII) *Epistle*: "The Word of the Lord" (Alan Titus, Street Chorus, Soloists, Choir); (IX) *Gospel-Sermon*: "God Said" (Street Chorus Leader: Larry Marshall, with Street Chorus); (X) *Credo*: (1) "Credo in Unum Deum" (Tape); (2) "Non Credo" (John Bennett Perry); (3) Trope—"Hurry" (Gina Penn); (4) Trope: "World without End" (Mary Bracken Phillips); and (5) Trope—"I Believe in God" (Thom Ellis, Singers); (XI) *Meditation # 3* (*De Profundis*, Part One) (Choir); (XII) *Offertory* (*De Profundis*, Part Two) (Boy Choir, Choir); (XIII) *The Lord's Prayer*: (1) "Our Father" (Alan Titus) and (2) Trope—"I Go On" (Alan Titus); (XIV) *Sanctus* (Alan Titus, Choir); (XV) *Agnus Dei* (Alan Titus, Street Chorus, Choir); (XVI) *Fraction*—"Things Get Broken" (Alan Titus); (XVII) *Pax*: *Communion*: "Secret Songs" (Margaret Cowie, Gary Lipps, John D. Anthony, Leigh Dodson, Ed Dixon, Singers)

At the request of Jacqueline Kennedy, Leonard Bernstein created *Mass* for the opening of the John F. Kennedy Center for the Performing Arts in Washington, D.C. It premiered at the Center's Opera House on September 8, 1971, for thirteen performances, and was revived there on June 1, 1972, for twenty more showings.

Bernstein's rich cornucopia of music for *Mass* is best described as eclectic because it embraces a number of styles such as traditional choir music, liturgical-styled music, songs in the Broadway show-tune vernacular, blues, and band music. He utilized the Roman Catholic Mass as a framework to create what is in many respects a concept musical, and so the ritualistic and abstract form of the Mass is one "plot" upon which is superimposed the story of a priest who celebrates the Mass. The priest finds that he's lost his faith and can no longer connect with his flock, and in a moment of sacrilege he hurls the chalice and monstrance to the floor where they shatter, and then he rips off the altar cloths. Because of the work's essentially shallow nature, which perfectly captures the touchy-feely attitude of the era, the priest and the flock are somehow instantly united in the bonds of brotherhood, love, peace, and religion. Everyone joins hands, and the audience (many perhaps in a hurry to get to their cars) is asked to join hands as well and give one another the sign of peace.

Bernstein couldn't let well enough alone and just set the Mass to music; instead he had to use the Mass as a mouthpiece for his trendier-than-thou and more-leftish-than-thou beliefs, and so parts of the evening were tirades against the Catholic Church, the government, big business, and even science. He also worked in a song about the environment ("World without End") that would have been right at home in ***Mother Earth***. The lyrics were of little help, and offered such trite thoughts as "I believe in God, but does God believe in me?" Further, Alvin Ailey's pretentious choreography brought to mind the worst aspects of interpretive dancing.

Bernstein seemed painfully sophomoric in his efforts to be hip as he thumbed his nose at the establishment, and while he was certainly entitled to his beliefs, one found it somewhat presumptuous of him to use the Mass as a means to criticize a church of which he was not a member and to create a sequence in which the most sacred objects of the Mass were used in an offensive manner to believers.

If one could rid *Mass* of its non-liturgical text, or perhaps even abandon all the text and relegate the work to continuous music, the piece would undoubtedly be a satisfying listening experience. Unfortunately, an orchestral edition of the score hasn't been recorded.

Donald Henahan in the *New York Times* noted the music itself was not the main problem with the work. The new text was "determinedly shallow" and yet "insistent" in being taken seriously, and thus the production had the "earnestness of an interfaith conference at a freshwater university," which resulted in an evening of "spiritual pabulum." Harriet Johnson in the *New York Post* noted there were "a few mild boos" in the audience, and she mentioned the work was "too naïve in its attitudes." She suggested the piece might be more effective if it were cut to half its length.

At the work's world premiere in Washington, D.C., Harold Schonberg in the *New York Times* said *Mass* was "a combination of superficiality and pretentiousness, and the greatest mélange of styles since the ladies' magazine recipe for steak fried in peanut butter and marshmallow sauce."

There are various recordings of the score, but probably the definitive one is the cast album of the Washington, D.C., production which was conducted by Bernstein and released on a two-LP set by Columbia Records (# M2-31008); a two-CD set was issued by Sony Classical (# SM2K-63089). The script was published in paperback by G. Schirmer (undated, but probably 1972). The work has been occasionally televised (including a version for public television), and an Italian production has been released on Kultur Video.

For a self-celebration of the tenth anniversary of the Kennedy Center's opening, *Mass* was revived on a smaller scale (Joseph Kolinksi was the Celebrant, and alternated with Michael Hume, who sang the role for a total of eight performances; the production was directed by Tom O'Horgan). The work was still pretentious, and its outdated message from 1971 was now even more tiresome. Bernstein's exciting music would have been better served as an orchestral piece by the National Symphony Orchestra in the Concert Hall, which is down the hall from the Opera House.

It is duly noted that for the Kennedy Center's twentieth, thirtieth, and fortieth anniversaries, *Mass* was not celebrated.

JACQUES BREL IS ALIVE AND WELL AND LIVING IN PARIS

Theatre: Royale Theatre
Opening Date: September 15, 1972; *Closing Date*: October 28, 1972
Performances: 51
Lyrics, Commentary, and *Music*: Jacques Brel (English lyrics and additional material by Eric Blau and Mort Shuman)
Direction: Moni Yakim; *Producer*: Bill Levine; *Scenery*: Les Lawrence; *Musical Direction*: Wolfgang Knittel
Cast: *Elly Stone*, *Joe Masiell*, George Ball, Henrietta Valor; Janet McCall and Joseph Neal, Alternates
The revue was presented in two acts.

Musical Numbers

Act One: "Marathon" ("Les flamandes") (Company); "Alone" ("Seul") (George Ball); "Madeleine" (Company); "I Loved" ("J'aimais") (Elly Stone); "Mathilde" (Joe Masiell); "Bachelor's Dance" ("La bouree du celibataire") (George Ball); "Timid Frieda" ("Les timides") (Henrietta Valor); "My Death" ("La mort") (Elly Stone); "Girls and Dogs" ("Les filles et les chiens") (Joe Masiell, George Ball); "Jackie" ("La chanson de Jacky") (Joe Masiell); "The Statue" ("La statue") (George Ball); "Desperate Ones" ("Les desesperes") (Company); "Sons of . . ." ("Fils de . . .") (Elly Stone); "Amsterdam" (Joe Masiell)

Act Two: "The Bulls" ("Les toros") (George Ball); "Old Folks" ("Les vieux") (Elly Stone); "Marieke" (Elly Stone); "Brussels" ("Bruxelles") (Henrietta Valor); "Fanette" ("La fanette") (George Ball); "Funeral Tango" ("Tango funebre") (Joe Masiell); "The Middle Class" ("Les bourgeois") (Joe Masiell, George Ball); "You're Not Alone" ("Jef") (Elly Stone); "Next" ("Au suivant") (Joe Masiell); "Carousel" ("La valse a mille temps") (Elly Stone); "If We Only Have Love" ("Quand on a que l'amour") (Company)

Jacques Brel Is Alive and Well and Living in Paris was a tiresome tribute to the French songwriter and performer. It inexplicably ran for 1,847 performances Off Broadway at the Village Gate where it opened on January 28, 1968, and closed on July 2, 1972. Ten weeks after its closing, the Broadway production was mounted for a limited run of six weeks.

Brel's songs were of the breathless, heart-on-the-sleeve variety, a sort of Gallic Hallmark card collection of soupy sentiment and feel-good philosophy. The evening's final song "If We Only Have Love" assured the listener that love will see us through, and unlike Stephen Sondheim's sardonic "Love Will See Us Through" from ***Follies***, Brel's simpering outlook was in alignment with such similar inspirational songs of the era as "People" (*Funny Girl* [1964]), "If I Ruled the World" (*Pickwick* [1965]), "If I Had a Hammer," and "What the World Needs Now" ("is love sweet love").

If the revue provided any amusement it was in Nat Shapiro's gushing program notes for the Off-Broadway production: he informed us that Brel is the conscience of "his people"; that his humanism consists of a "fierce" integrity and a disdain for hypocrisy; and that he is unflinchingly "honest about himself."

In his review of the revival, Anthony Mancini in the *New York Post* said Brel "at his best" was no more than "the Rod McKuen of French songwriting," his "poetic edifices" were made of "papier-mâché," and as for the revue's title, "euthanasia is recommended." Martin Gottfried in *Women's Wear Daily* noted "the engagement is limited and so is the show"; and Leonard Harris on WCBSTV2 found the evening "thoroughly over staged and over acted" with "hypnotic stares," "pregnant pauses," and "meaningful gestures." The songs were "fine" but the revue was pretentious, and he suggested the production would have been better served in a cabaret setting.

But Douglas Watt in the *New York Daily News* praised the "unique and polished entertainment"; and while Kevin Sanders on WABCTV7 suggested the work was "starting to look a little dated around the edges," he said "its heart is in the right place" and the company's teamwork was "flawless."

Following the current revival, the revue as of this writing has made nine return visits to Off Broadway and Off Off Broadway: in 1974 (Astor Place Theatre, 125 performances); 1977 (Queens Theatre in the Park/ Playwrights Horizons, 13 performances); 1978 (Town Hall, number of performances unknown); 1978 (Park Royal Cabaret Theatre, 4 performances); 1981 (Town Hall, 21 performances); 1983 (First City Theatre, 48 performances); 1985 (Equity Library Theatre, 30 performances); 1988 (Town Hall, 7 performances); 1992 (Village Gate, 131 performances); and 2006 (Zipper Theatre, 384 performances).

Elly Stone was in the original production, and returned for the current revival as well as the Town Hall visit in 1978; Joe Masiell was a replacement during the original run, and like Stone was in the current version (he also appeared in the 1978 Town Hall and 1981 revivals); and Henrietta Valor later appeared in the 1974 production (like George Ball, she too had appeared in the revue during its original run at the Village Gate). Besides Stone, the members of the original 1968 cast were Mort Shuman, Shawn Elliott, and Alice Whitfield.

A film version (with Elly Stone, Joe Masiell, Mort Shuman, and JB himself) was released in 1975 under the auspices of the short-lived American Film Theatre series and is available on DVD by Kino.

The script was published in hardback by E.P. Dutton in 1974 and in softback by The Dramatists Play Service in 2000.

The original Off-Broadway cast album was recorded on a two-LP set by Columbia Records (# D2S-779) that omitted three numbers ("Girls and Dogs," "The Statue," and "The Middle Class"). The latter was recorded during the cast album session and was added to the CD release by Sony Classical/Columbia/Legacy Records (# SK-89998). A 1974 production in Cleveland was recorded on a two-LP set by Playhouse Square Records, Inc. (# PHS-CLE-2S-101) and includes "Girls and Dogs." A Vancouver production (circa 1985) was titled *Jacques Brel Lives . . .* and the cast included Leon Bibb (who had appeared in the 1983 New York revival); the production was recorded by Jabula Records (LP # JR-38). The 2006 Off-Broadway revival was released by Ghostlight Records (CD # 7915584416-2).

The soundtrack album was released on a two-LP set by Atlantic Records (# SD-2-1000-0998). The film omitted four songs ("My Death," "Girls and Dogs," "Fanette," and "You're Not Alone") and added four, "My Childhood" ("Mon enfance") (lyric and music by Brel), "The Taxicab" ("Le gaz") (lyric and music by Brel and Gerard Jouannest), "Ne me quitte pas" (lyric and music by Brel), and "The Last Supper" ("Le dernier repas") (lyric and music by Brel).

In 1961, Elly Stone had appeared in the Off-Broadway revue *O, Oysters!!!* where she sang two songs by Brel, "Ne me quitte pas" and "Carousels and Cotton Candy" (the latter was rewritten as "Carousel" for

Jacques Brel Is Alive . . .). The song was also included in Lawrence Roman's 1964 Broadway comedy *P.S. I Love You*, where it was heard as "Days of the Waltz" (lyric by Will Holt).

Other contributors to *Jacques Brel Is Alive . . .* are the composers Francois Rauber, Jean Cortinovis (aka Corti), and the above-cited Gerard Jouannest, all of whom sold their music to Brel with the understanding they'd receive no official program credit. However, five years before his death Brel requested that all future productions of the revue acknowledge the three and their contributions. Along with Brel, the three are credited with the following: Rauber and Jouannest for "I Loved"; Cortinovis and Jouannest for "Madeleine," "The Bulls," and "Old Folks"; and Jouannest for "Mathilde," "Jackie," "Desperate Ones," "Sons of . . . ," "Marieke," "Brussels," "Funeral Tango," and "Next."

In his review of the original 1968 production, Dan Sullivan in the *New York Times* noted that Brel's songs were often an "unconscious parody" of French *chanteurs* in general. He commented that Elly Stone's efforts to emulate Edith Piaf reminded him of "a salesgirl measuring yard goods" (Piaf's shtick was to end a song with arms outstretched in crucifixtion fashion); Alice Whitfield's "blank-eyed stare of Marcel Marceau imitating a mannequin" only managed to look "like a mannequin imitating Marcel Marceau"; and Shawn Elliott tried for a Folies Bergeres effect which came across as "Times Square at midnight." Sullivan decided only Mort Shuman was comfortable with the material.

FROM ISRAEL WITH LOVE

Theatre: Palace Theatre
Opening Date: October 2, 1972; *Closing Date*: October 8, 1972
Performances: 8
Direction: Avi David; *Producers*: Pageant Productions P.T.Y. Ltd. and Colonel Saul Biber; *Choreography*: Yakov Kallusky; *Musical Direction*: Rafi Ben-Moshe
Cast: Micha Adir, Dani Amihud, Chaya Arad, Itzik Barak, Shara Badishy, Eti Brechner, David Dardashi, Irith Esched, Tami Gall, Israel Klugman, Elis Menahemi, Malli Noy, Yacov Noy, Nathan Okev, Gadi Oron, Varda Sagy, Reuven Shenar, Yonnith Shoham, Nurit Zeevi; Musicians: David Rosenthal, Izhack Lichtenfeld, Juda Asher Shkolnik, Oded Pintus, Shmyel Aroukh, Ilan Gilboa
The revue was presented in two acts.

Musical Numbers

Note: The program didn't credit individual performers for the musical sequences.
Act One: "Israel Israel"; "From the South Good Will Come"; "Call for Freedom"; "Three Legs"; "We Take Whatever Comes"; Ballet; "Jerusalem of Gold"; "Natasha"
Act Two: "A Beach Song"; "Night, Night" (Lullaby); "From Across the River" ("Coffee Song"); "The Parachutist"; "My Dear Son"; Potpourri, Israel Style: "Hava nagila," "Again, the Night Falls," and "Debka" (dance); "I Am Dying"; "A Song of Peace"

The import *From Israel with Love* was the first of two limited-run Jewish-oriented revues that opened during the season; three months later, Jonathan (aka Jonatan) Karmon's ***The Grand Music Hall of Israel*** paid a return visit at the Felt Forum for fifteen showings.

Unlike many such Israeli imports and New York homegrown Jewish revues of the period, *From Israel with Love* didn't divide its musical sequences between glimpses of Jewish life in the shtetls of Old Europe and modern life in the cities of Tel Aviv and New York. Instead, the revue was a compilation of mostly modern songs and dances, a few of which touched upon the political realities of the era.

Mel Gussow in the *New York Times* found the revue a "pleasant surprise" that was "full of vitality and exuberance." He mentioned that all the lyrics were in Hebrew and the music had a "modern beat," including "a rock Hassidic number." Although the cast had served in the Israeli army and their costumes were inspired by military uniforms, Gussow said the revue was "not the least martial" and the final number was "A Song of Peace." He noted that the humor was sometimes "heavy-handed," the evening went on too long, the staging and choreography lacked "variety," and the evening was more in the nature of a concert than a revue. Nonetheless, the work communicated "goodwill" and was even "somewhat sentimental."

DUDE, or THE HIGHWAY LIFE

Theatre: Broadway Theatre
Opening Date: October 9, 1972; *Closing Date*: October 21, 1972
Performances: 16
Book and *Lyrics*: Gerome Ragni
Music: Galt MacDermot
Direction: Tom O'Horgan; *Direction*: Adela and Peter Holzer; *Scenery*: Eugene Lee, Roger Morgan, and Franne Lee; *Costumes*: Randy Barcelo; *Lighting*: Not credited; *Musical Direction*: Thomas Pierson
Cast: *The Theatre Stars*: Allan Nicholls (# 33), Ralph Carter (Dude [as a child]), Salome Bey (Mother Earth), Delores Hall (Bread); *The Shubert Angels*: Karen-Maria Faatz, Katie Field, Helen Jennings, David Kruger, Cary Mark, Mark Perman, Aida Random (possibly Kandom), and Lynn Reynolds; *The Theatre Wings*: Alan Braunstein (Hero), Sandra Loys Toder (Halo), Dawn Johnson (Echo), Michael Jason (Solo), Rae Allen (Reba), William Redfield (Harold), Nell Carter (Suzie Moon), James Patrick Farrell III (Zero), Leata Galloway (Nero), David Lasley (Sissy), Jim Turner (Electric Bill), Dale Soules (Shadow), Barbara Monte-Britton (Shade), Bobby Alessi (Esso), Billy Alessi (Extra), Michael Meadows (Meadow), Georgianna Holmes (World War Too), Carol Estey (Noname), Dennis Simpson (Texaco), Nat Morris (Dude [as an adult])
The musical was presented in two acts.

Musical Numbers

Act One: Overture (Allan Nicholls, Company); "Theatre/Theatre" (Allan Nicholls, The Theatre Wings, The Shubert Angels); "A-Stage" (Allan Nicholls); "The Mountains" (Salome Bey); "Pears and Peaches" (The Shubert Angels); "Eat It" (The Pioneers); "Wah Wah Wah" (Nell Carter); "Suzie Moon" (Nell Carter); "Y.O.U." (Nat Morris); "I Love My Boo Boo" (Allan Nicholls, Nell Carter, Delores Hall, Salome Bey); "Hum Drum Life" (Sandra Loys Toder, Alan Braunstein, Dale Soules, Michael Meadows); "Who's It?" (Nat Morris, The Shubert Angels, The Theatre Wings); "Talk to Me about Love" (Nat Morris, James Patrick Farrell III); "Goodbyes" (Rae Allen); "I'm Small" (Alan Braunstein); "You Can Do Nothing about It" (Leata Galloway); "The Handsomest Man" (David Lasley); "Electric Prophet" (Jim Turner); "No-One" (Salome Bey)
Act Two: "Who Will Be the Children?" (The Shubert Angels); "Go Holy Ghost" (The Shubert Angels); "A Song to Sing" (Nat Morris, Delores Hall, Leata Galloway, David Lasley, The Theatre Wings, The Shubert Angels); "A Dawn" (Alan Braunstein, Sandra Loys Toder, The Theatre Wings); "The Days of This Life" (Bobby Alessi, Billy Alessi, Nat Morris, James Patrick Farrell III); "I Never Knew" (Salome Bey); "Air Male" (The Theatre Wings); "Undo" (Delores Hall); "The Earth" (William Redfield, Rae Allen); "My Darling, I Love You March" (The Theatre Wings, The Shubert Angels); "So Long, Dude" (The Theatre Wings); "Dude, All Dude" (The Theatre Wings, The Shubert Angels); "Peace, Peace" (The Shubert Angels); "Jesus Hi" (The Shubert Angels); "Baby Breath" (Salome Bey, Delores Hall, Allan Nicholls, The Shubert Angels); "Sweet Dreams" (Allan Nicholls, Company)

Dude, or *The Highway Life* was a dud, and marked Galt MacDermot's first of two gargantuan flops during the season; a few weeks after *Dude* disappeared down the old highway, ***Via Galactica*** opened and quickly closed (talk about lost in the stars), and the two shows dropped a combined total of almost $2 million. *Dude* was a reunion for two-thirds of the creators of *Hair*, with MacDermot composing the score for the new musical and Gerome Ragni contributing the book and lyrics.

Prior to the opening of *Dude*, Kilmarnock Records (# KIL-72003) released *Salome Bey Sings Songs from "Dude"* (Bey later created the role of Mother Earth in the musical, and Kilmarnock Records was MacDermot's own record company), and the liner notes explained that the story dealt with "a young man's run-in with evil, what it does to him and how he handles it." Oh, so *that's* what the show was about. Because the goings-on were so murky, the critics couldn't quite explain the plot, but they seemed to agree with the liner notes when they described how the wispy story line centered on Dude, a young man who tries to find himself on life's highway. Along the way, he attempts to understand his place in the big, wide world and the Meaning of It All. (But whoever could? Even the heroes of ***Pippin*** and ***Candide*** decide to pack it in and live out their lives in a quiet and ordinary manner.)

In preproduction, Kevin Geer played the title role, but by the first preview he'd been replaced by two actors, Ralph Carter and Nat Morris, who played the respective roles of Dude as a child and Dude as a man. (But Geer didn't quite disappear, and his photo continued to adorn the musical's program and poster; but since he's facing away from the camera, his face seems lost to posterity and only his posterior remains immortal.)

Throughout the evening, a theatrical metaphor permeated the proceedings: all the cast members were divided into three categories (The Theatre Stars, The Shubert Angels, and The Theatre Wings) and two songs were titled "Theatre/Theatre" and "A-Stage" (but the interestingly titled "Brooks Atkinson" and "A Musical Version of World War Too" were dropped during previews). The characters sported generic names (Mother Earth); wispy ones (Shadow, Shade, Echo, Zero, and Solo); and cutesy ones (Esso, Extra, Texaco, World War Too, and Electric Bill). Perhaps the most appropriately named character was Meadow, which was performed by Michael Meadows.

The abstract plot, the generic characters, and the thirty-five musical numbers were all presented in an environmental space in which the poor Broadway Theatre was gutted. The seating area of the orchestra section became the stage, and much of the action was performed in the center of this space with the audience seated around it in arena fashion. Along with a variety of ramps, there were also various little playing areas here and there, and some of the spectators were seated on what had once been the traditional stage, the very stage where Momma Rose had once taken her turn in her blistering bare-stage aria and where elegant nineteenth-century dancers had swirled to the haunting strains of the waltz "Mayfair Affair" in *Kean* (1961). Now we had an undisciplined rock-styled musical in which one character complains in song that a "big fucking guy like me" has just one small "big inch," and another sings that she "can fuck who what when where why I fuck."

The tickets advised the audience members where they would be seated; there were four main sections called Foothills, Mountains, Valleys, and Trees. All this must have meant something, but no one seemed sure what the message was. (Less than two years later, the Broadway Theatre underwent further indignity when Harold Prince's new interpretation of ***Candide*** again turned the venerable house into a series of small playing areas in honor of the then trendy notion of environmental staging.)

Richard Watts in the *New York Post* said that for all the occasional "ingenious" staging devices by Tom O'Horgan and for all the accoutrements of the environmental setting, the creators "forgot to include a play" and the philosophical points made during the evening were "more bewildering than illuminating." Walter Kerr in the *New York Times* noted that even rock musicals had "to meet the obligations earlier musicals have accepted," and thus the songs "must have something to stand on" and need "something in the way of wit" to keep them company. In the same newspaper, Clive Barnes said the musical was a "brave try" on the part of its creators, and suggested that perhaps the show hadn't been on the highway "long enough" and a couple more weeks "might have made a vital difference to a musical that aspired high but fell short." He felt the book had "primitive naiveté," the music was often "effectively powerful," and the evening's "inchoate energy" had a certain attractiveness.

In commenting on how the theatre had been gutted, Martin Gottfried in *Women's Wear Daily* asked, "What did the Broadway Theatre do to *Dude* to deserve this?" But he found it "refreshing" to see a story told with a different theatrical perspective which eliminated the traditional proscenium stage, and for all the "second- rate" music there was "still an excellent score remaining."

During previews, director Rocco Bufano and choreographer Louis Falco were succeeded by O'Horgan, who received credit for directing and staging. When their respective roles of Rags and World War Won were eliminated, Michael Dunn and Juan Antonio left the production. During the preview period, the following songs were cut: "Weeping," "I Don't Care," "If It Doesn't Belong to You," "You Should Be," "Brooks Atkinson," "All the World," "The Lone Ranger," "Jazz Bridge," "Heavens Angels," "Boo on You," "Eielo-Eielo," "Germ War," "Only a Few More Years," "Everyman," "Sad," "Children/Children," "Birds of the Air," "New York Lies," "A Thousand Repetitions," "A Musical Version of World War Too," and "Dude."

Besides the referenced album by Salome Bey, a second recording (*The Highway Life: Songs from 'Dude'*) was released by Kilmarnock Records (LP # KIL-72007) that includes numbers performed by cast members Nell Carter, Nat Morris, Jim Farrell (aka James Patrick Farrell III), Leata Galloway, Alan Braunstein, Salome Bey, and David Lasley and conducted by Thomas Pierson, who also conducted the Broadway production. The recording includes ten songs heard in the musical, "So Long, Dude," "The Days of This Life," "I Am Who I Am" (titled "You Can Do Nothing about It" for Broadway), "I'm Small," "Pears and Apples," "Wa Wa Wa" ("Wah Wah Wah" for Broadway), "Suzie Moon," "Hum Drum Life," "Air Male," and "Undo" as well as one number dropped during previews ("Weeping") and an opening instrumental sequence titled "The Highway Life: Going." The recording with Salome Bey includes five songs from the Broadway production, "Boo Boo" ("I

Love My Boo Boo" for Broadway), "No One," "I Never Knew," "Baby Breath," and "Sweet Dreams" ("Sweet Dreams Blossom" for Broadway); two of which were dropped in previews ("Only a Few More Years" and "Jazz Bridge"); and five dropped in preproduction ("I Know Your Name," "A Garden for Two," "Say What You Want to Say," "Happy Song," and "At Home").

Columbia Records had been set to record the cast album, which was canceled due to the short run of the production.

Hair had been a spectacular success for its creators, composer MacDermot and book writers and lyricists James Rado and Ragni. Although MacDermot enjoyed just one more Broadway success (***Two Gentlemen of Verona***), Ragni and Rado never had another hit. *Dude* was Ragni's last Broadway effort, and Rado's Off-Broadway *Rainbow* shuttered after forty-eight performances in 1972.

HURRY, HARRY

"A Musical Comedy"

Theatre: Ritz Theatre
Opening Date: October 12, 1972; *Closing Date*: October 13, 1972
Performances: 2
Book: Jeremiah Morris, Lee Kalcheim, and Susan Perkis
Lyrics: David Finkle
Music: Bill Weeden
Direction: Jeremiah Morris; *Producer*: Peter Grad (Ed Lewis, Associate Producer); *Choreography*: Gerald Teijelo; *Scenery*: Fred Voelpel; *Costumes*: Sara Brook; *Lighting*: Martin Aronstein; *Musical Direction*: Arthur Azenzer
Cast: Samuel D. Ratcliffe (Harrison Fairchild IV aka Harry), Phil Leeds (Harrison Fairchild III, Town Drunk, Doctor Krauss, Chief, Chorus Boy, Not-So-Grand Lama, Uncle Harry, Congregation Member), Liz Sheridan (Patience Fairchild, Mama, Writer, Native No. 3, Star, Not-So-Grand Lama, Congregation Member), Mary Bracken Phillips (Muffy Weatherford), Louis Criscuolo (Nick, Deuteronomy, Writer, Witch Doctor, Chorus Boy, Not-So-Grand Lama, Congregation Member), Jack Landron (Marco, Genesis, Writer, Native No. 5, Chorus Boy, Not-So-Grand Lama, Congregation Member), Robert Darnell (Stavos, Exodus, Writer, Native No. 1, Chorus Boy, Grand Lama, Winston, Congregation Member), Randee Heller (Helena, Writer, Native No. 4, Not-So-Grand Lama, Gypsy, Congregation Member), Donna Liggitt Forbes (Melina, Starlet, Native No. 2, Not-So-Grand Lama, Congregation Member)
The musical was presented in two acts.
The action takes place during the present time.

Musical Numbers

Act One: Overture (Orchestra); "I'm Gonna" (Samuel D. Ratcliffe); "When a Man Cries" (Louis Criscuolo, Liz Sheridan, Randee Heller, Jack Landron, Robert Darnell, Phil Leeds, Donna Liggitt Forbes); "A Trip Through My Mind" (Mary Bracken Phillips, The Dead Sea Scrolls); "Life" (Samuel D. Ratcliffe, Louis Criscuolo, Robert Darnell, Randee Heller, Jack Landron, Liz Sheridan); "Love Can" (Mary Bracken Phillips); "Africa Speaks" (Robert Darnell, Donna Liggitt Forbes, Liz Sheridan, Randee Heller, Jack Landron, Louis Criscuolo); "Somewhere in the Past" (Samuel D. Ratcliffe)
Act Two: "Hurry, Harry" (Liz Sheridan, Louis Criscuolo, Robert Darnell, Jack Landron, Phil Leeds); "Goodbye" (Mary Bracken Phillips); "You Won't Be Happy" (Samuel D. Ratcliffe, Phil Leeds); "He Is My Bag" (Samuel D. Ratcliffe, Louis Criscuolo, Robert Darnell, Donna Liggitt Forbes, Randee Heller, Jack Landron, Phil Leeds, Liz Sheridan); "Somewhere in the Past" (reprise) (Samuel D. Ratcliffe, Mary Bracken Phillips); Finale

Although the undistinguished *Hurry, Harry* was one of the season's many flops (such as ***Dude***, ***Lysistrata***, ***Ambassador***, ***Via Galactica***, ***Tricks***, ***Shelter***, ***Cyrano***, and ***Nash at Nine***), it had one distinction: it was the shortest running of them all. Like those truth-seekers ***Dude***, ***Pippin***, and ***Candide***, poor Harry was just trying to find himself and discover the meaning of life. But he had to really hurry because he had just two performances to do so.

The musical received unanimously unfavorable reviews. Martin Gottfried in *Women's Wear Daily* said the "peculiar disaster" went through "several distinct stages of trouble before settling into catastrophe," but thankfully the song list in the program provided a guideline as to how long he had to sit until the final curtain. Clive Barnes in the *New York Times* became almost immediately bored with the rich but miserable young man who travels all over the world in search of himself, and ten minutes after the curtain went up Barnes found himself thinking, "Hurry, Harry, hurry, hurry, hurry!" The book was "so flat" it made Holland seem like the Himalayas; the music had a "built-in amnesiac factor that makes it self-destruct in memory instantaneously"; and the lyrics were "possibly the worst part of the show." He noted that the set looked as if it were intended as the background for a new television quiz show, possibly called *The Hating Game*. But for all its faults, Barnes saluted the musical for having the "courage and effrontery" to actually open.

Prior to the opening, Bill Hinnant had been scheduled to play the title role, but was succeeded by Samuel D. Ratcliffe. During previews, Peter Grad and David Seltzer were credited as producers, but by opening night the latter's name was no longer associated with the show. But Seltzer was represented on Broadway the following month as coproducer of one of the decade's all-time lows, the staggeringly insufferable ***Lysistrata***.

The following songs were cut during the previews of *Hurry, Harry*: "I'd Like to Introduce Myself," "Hats," "In the Garden," "Grandpa Said," and a second-act montage sequence where Harry looked for himself in London, Madrid, Paris, New York, and on Mount Everest.

PACIFIC PARADISE

Theatre: Palace Theatre
Opening Date: October 16, 1972; *Closing Date*: October 21, 1972
Performances: 7
Opening Narration: Compiled and edited by Kit Regas
Direction: Jack Regas; *Producer*: Irving Sudrow and The New Zealand Maori Company Ltd.; *Maori Choral Direction*: Kelly Harris
Cast: Faule Bryant, Huri Callaghan, Matekino Callaghan, Sera Chase, Tiramate Dennis, Karen Donaghy, Cecilia Eparaima, Richard Eparaima, Kuini Farthing, Joshua Gardiner, Dawn Heperi, Lena Hiha, Christine Hikuroa, Eva Hona, Te Kani Horsefall, Bernadette Huata, Paraire Huata, Hemi Huata, Ngamoni Huata, Rongo Kahu, Sonny Keepa, Rachel Kewene, Tangiwai Kingi, Karu Kukutai, Josephine Loader, Putiputi Mackey, Gabrielle Mareikura, Rose Maxwell, Terry Maxwell, Kipa Morehu, Gordon Moses, Helen Moses, Philip Munro, Betty Nathan, James Nathan, Brenda Nepe, Dianne Nukutarwhiti, Ita Paenga, Tomaurangi Paki, Thomas Ratima, Kuini Reedy, Percy Reedy, Rimupae Rennie, Derna Richardson, Karen Ricka, Barbara Ringiao, Noroa Ringiao, James Robert, Pauline Ruru, Abie Scott, Roberta Smiler, Josephine Smiler, Hineawe Smith, Nagatai Stockman, Raana Tangira, Wiremu Tangira, Irirangi Tahuriorangi, Reverend Anaru Takurua, Putiputi Tonihi, Rongo Tuhura, Atareta Waerea, Royal Walker, Tom Ward, Vicky Ward, Leona Watene, Muriel Wehi, Ngapo Wehi, Tui Yates, Arapata Whaanga
The revue was presented in two acts.

Musical Numbers

Act One: *Maori Welcome Ceremony*: "Wero"; "Karanga"; "Utaina"; "Te Urunga tu" (dance); "Karanga tia"; *Legend of the Great Maori Migration*: "Poroporoaki"; "Whakaara"; "Whaikorero"; "E oho e te whanau"; "Tohi waka"; "Uia mai koia"; "Ma tangi"; "Poi waka"; "Kura ti waka"; "Ti tiro mai"; *Village Life in the New Land*: "Taku patu"; "Karu"; "He manuhiri"; "Po karekare ana"; "Tu mara mara"; "Paki kini" (dance)

Act Two: *Maori Festival*: Poi Dances—"Short Single Poi"; "Short Double Poi"; "Long Single Poi"; "Long Double Poi"; and Combination Dances; "Tangi hia"; "Pana pana/rua moko" (dance); "Tititoria"; "Koroki"; "Peru-peru"; "Ti rakau"; "Three and Four Poi Competitions"; "Pa aki kini"; "E pare ra"; "Po ata ro"

The revue *Pacific Paradise* was a limited-engagement import from New Zealand that celebrated the country's native Maori culture. Don McDonagh in the *New York Times* praised the "melodious low-key production," which included songs, chants, and dances as well as stick games, exercises, and a spear ceremony. He noted that the first act emphasized Maori history and was "obscure in its particulars," but the second half of the evening was "most effective" because it was devoted to songs and dances of the Maori.

Note to program collectors: if you're looking for one of *Pacific Paradise*, be advised there's no program cover for a revue with that title. Instead, the cover is for the New Zealand Maori Company, and only inside on the program's title page is a notation that the company is presenting a revue titled *Pacific Paradise*.

MOTHER EARTH

"A New Musical"

Theatre: Belasco Theatre
Opening Date: October 19, 1972; *Closing Date*: October 28, 1972
Performances: 12
Sketches and *Lyrics*: Ron Thronson
Music: Toni Shearer
Direction: Ray Golden (Kermit Bloomgarden, Consultant); *Producers*: Roger Ailes (A Ray Golden Production) (Howard Butcher IV and Graeme Howard, Associate Producers); *Choreography*: Lynne Morris; *Scenery*: Alan Kimmel; *Visuals*: Kenneth Shearer; *Costumes*: Mary McKinley; *Lighting*: Paul Sullivan; *Musical Direction*: Larry White
Cast: Kelly Garrett, Gail Boggs, Frank T. Coombs, Kimberly Farr, Will Jacobs, Carol Kristy, Laura Michaels, John Bennett Perry, Rick Podell, Charlie J. Rodriguez
The revue was presented in two acts.

Sketches and Musical Numbers

Act One: *Out of Space*: "Mother Earth" (Kelly Garrett, Company); *The Client*: "The Time of Our Life" (Laura Michaels, Charlie J. Rodriguez); "Corn on the Macabre" (all "Corn on the Macabre" sequences written by Ron Thronson, Roger Ailes, and Ray Golden) (Carol Kristy, Rick Podell, Gail Boggs); *The Mask Parade*: "Too Many Old Ideas" (Kelly Garrett); *The Cheerleader* (by Jerry Patch, William Black, and Ray Golden)/ *Uneasy Rider/Landscape with Figures*: "Room to be Free" (Rick Podell); *Model Wife*: "Rent a Robot" (Will Jacobs); *A Hike in the Woods* (by Jerry Patch and William Black)/*Flash Gordon*: "Plow It All Under" (Carol Kristy, Company); *Ewe Turn* (by Ray Golden)/*The Offal Truth* (by Jack Marlowe and Ray Golden)/ *The Killathon* (by Ron Thronson, Roger Ailes, and Ray Golden): "Ozymandias" (John Bennett Perry); "Talons of Time" (Kelly Garrett); "Corn on the Macabre" (reprise) (Laura Michaels, Kimberly Farr, Frank T. Coombs); *The Nursery*: "Save the World for Children" (Gail Boggs); "Sail On, Sweet Universe" (Kelly Garrett, Company)

Act Two: "Mater Terra" (Company); "Xanadu" (Carol Kristy, Company); *Breathe-Out*: "The Ecology Waltz" (lyric by Ray Golden) (Kimberly Farr, Rick Podell); *Chic Diners*: "Corn on the Macabre" (Carol Kristy, Charlie J. Rodriguez, Gail Boggs); *Women Shoppers* (by Ron Thronson and Ray Golden)/*The Swan*: "Good Morning, World" (John Bennett Perry); *The Last Redwoods/The Animals* (by Ray Golden): "Tiger! Tiger!" (Kelly Garrett); *Concrete Proposal*: "Happy Mother's Day, Mother Earth" (Charlie J. Rodriguez); *Radioactive Terminate*: "Pills" (lyric and music by Ray Golden) (Kelly Garrett, Gail Boggs, Carol Kristy, Company); *The Billboards* (by Jack Marlowe and Ray Golden): "Corn on the Macabre" (reprise) (Kelly Garrett, Rick Podell, Frank T. Coombs); "Total Recall" (by Ray Golden) (Company)

There probably wasn't much of a target audience for a revue about the environment, and so perhaps *Mother Earth* would have worked better on the college circuit or as a special on public television (but if the latter, then "that is what is wrong with public television," according to Martin Gottfried in *Women's Wear Daily*). The reviews were generally unenthusiastic, and the best Leonard Harris on WCBSTV2 could say was that "I've seen worse." The revue's preachy tone undoubtedly turned off ticket buyers, and since the notices were generally middling, the production shuttered after less than two weeks on Broadway.

Mother Earth was the kind of show that came out in favor of animals and the Redwoods and against pollution and overpopulation. (Well, yes.) As a result, it was drearily predictable. In one sketch about a dog show, the winning canines are rewarded with a spot of clean asphalt (and hopefully a convenient fire hydrant) to do their business; a fashion show reveals the latest in chic gas masks; a "killathon" offers clever ways to commit suicide in order to relieve overpopulation; a ballerina dancing *Swan Lake* keels over because the water is polluted; a restaurant offers a menu of food substitutes; and when the last Redwood is no more, a plastic monument is erected in its memory.

Laurence I. Barrett in *Time* said the revue was written "with an instrument rather more blunt than a skywriter's chisel," and he noted the evening was a "bit collegiate" and offered a "superficial non-appeal"; Gottfried found the show "too slick to be amateur and too amateur for professional theatre" and suggested "you can put up with well-intentioned energy for only so long"; and Kevin Sanders on WABCTV7 said the evening was "ablaze with anti-government, anti-Vietnam, anti-big business sentiments" and despite its "good intentions" it offered at best "some glorious moments" (but at its worst it was "terrible").

Richard Watts in the *New York Post* said the revue was "more amateurish than professional" and had "stretches of dullness"; but Douglas Watt in the *New York Daily News* praised the "amiable and fast-moving" evening and suggested the "modest entertainment" might be more effective on public television.

The program notes assured the public that all leather clothing worn by the cast was synthetic, and Clive Barnes in the *New York Times*, who felt he was stealing "wheat germ lollipops from kids," noted that the revue itself was "a man-made-fiber show that is pretending to be a daffodil." The revue's "humorless humor" was "a form of aural pollution" and the show made its subject matter "as uninteresting as cold spaghetti without the sauce." The sketches were "terrible" and some of the songs "might have been rejected by *Dude*."

There was no Broadway cast album, but Environmental Records (LP # SP-1001) released *"Mother Earth": Music from the Musical*, which included twelve songs, eight of which were heard in the New York production ("Too Many Old Ideas," "Tiger! Tiger!," "Good Morning, World,""Sail On, Sweet Universe," "The Time of Our Life," "The Talons of Time," "Happy Mother's Day, Mother Earth," and "Xanadu") and four which were dropped prior to Broadway ("Chemicals," "Who Cares If the World Is Round?," "Room to Live Prayer," and "What Color Is the Sky?"). Among the singers on the recording are Patti Austin and Carol Kristy (aka Christy), who toured with the revue during its pre-Broadway engagements (the latter was also seen in the Broadway production).

The revue premiered on January 8, 1971, at the South Coast Repertory Theatre in Costa Mesa, California, and later played in such cities as Philadelphia and Washington, D.C. Among the numbers cut prior to the Broadway production were: "Dirge for the Earth," "The Talking Lady," "The Nursing Home," "Operation Deathwatch," "Chemicals," "Population Police," "Room to Live Prayer," "Turn of the Century," "Chic Williams," "What Color Is the Sky?," and "Who Cares If the World Is Round?" At some point during the revue's road to Broadway, *Sail On, Sweet Universe* was considered for the show's title.

PIPPIN

"A Musical Comedy"

Theatre: Imperial Theatre (during run, the musical transferred to the Minskoff Theatre)
Opening Date: October 23, 1972; *Closing Date*: June 12, 1977
Performances: 1,944
Book: Roger O. Hirson
Lyrics and *Music*: Stephen Schwartz
Direction and *Choreography*: Bob Fosse; *Producer*: Stuart Ostrow; *Scenery*: Tony Walton; *Costumes*: Patricia Zipprodt; *Lighting*: Jules Fisher; *Musical Direction*: Stanley Lebowsky
Cast: Ben Vereen (Leading Player), John Rubinstein (Pippin), Eric Berry (Charles), Christopher Chadman (Lewis), Leland Palmer (Fastrada), John Mineo (Musician), Roger Hamilton (The Head, Field Marshall), Irene Ryan (Berthe), Richard Korthaze (Beggar), Paul Solen (Peasant), Gene Foote (Noble), Jill Clayburgh (Catherine), Shane Nickerson (Theo); Players: Candy Brown, Ann Reinking, Jennifer Nairn-Smith, Kathryn Doby, Pamela Sousa
The musical was presented in one act.
The action takes place during the year 780 ("and thereabouts") in the Holy Roman Empire ("and thereabouts").

Musical Numbers

"Magic to Do" (Ben Vereen, Company); "Corner of the Sky" (John Rubinstein); "Welcome Home" (Eric Berry, John Rubinstein); "War Is a Science" (Eric Berry, John Rubinstein); "Glory" (Ben Vereen) and "The Manson Trio" (dance) (Ben Vereen, Candy Brown, Pamela Sousa); "Simple Joys" (Ben Vereen); "No Time at All" (Irene Ryan, Boys); "With You" (John Rubinstein, Girls); "Spread a Little Sunshine" (Leland Palmer); "Morning Glow" (John Rubinstein); "On the Right Track" (Ben Vereen, John Rubinstein); "Kind of Woman" (Jill Clayburgh, Girls); "Extraordinary" (John Rubinstein); "The Duck Song" (John Rubinstein); "Love Song" (John Rubinstein, Jill Clayburgh); "I Guess I'll Miss the Man" (Jill Clayburgh); Finale ("Think About Your Life, Pippin") (Ben Vereen, Company)

Bob Fosse's *Pippin* was one of the most stylish and entertaining musicals of the decade. It was the story of a young man who just wants to find himself, but this dreary, old-hat cliché (which was also the subject of ***Dude*** and ***Hurry, Harry***, both of which had opened earlier in the month) was dressed up in a sleek package that used the framework of a circus and magic show to depict the adventures of the title character. Pippin (John Rubinstein) is in fact the son of Charlemagne (Eric Berry), and all Pippin wants to do is find his place in the world. He goes to war (but doesn't like it), has many a sexual fling (which nonetheless leaves him unfulfilled), and then finally comes to the realization that he's not a particularly extraordinary person and that his destiny is to settle down into an ordinary life with the widow Catherine (Jill Clayburgh) and her young son.

Fosse's staging turned the evening into a stunning series of set pieces that took an ironic view of the proceedings, and he was supported by Roger O. Hirson's unappreciated revue-like book, which provided short sketch-like designed to emphasize Fosse's sardonic vision and his show-stopping dances and musical staging. And despite the famous stories of the feud between Fosse and Stephen Schwartz, the fact is that the lyricist-composer yielded a melodic, old-fashioned score that served the story well. Among the highlights were the insinuating opening number "Magic to Do" (which described the evening as an "anecdotic revue"); the old-time sing-along "No Time at All"; the sincerely insincere "Spread a Little Sunshine" for Pippin's wicked step-mother Fastrada (who seeks to ensure that her son Lewis [Christopher Chadman] inherits the throne); the irresistible vamp of "The Manson Trio"; and the expansive splendor of the finale, "Think About Your Life, Pippin."

The evening began with thrilling visual effects: the dark and smoky bare stage suddenly revealed pairs of sinuously moving hands clad in white gloves, and soon the lights came up and the Leading Player (Ben Vereen) and the company went into the serpentine wails of "Magic to Do," a glorious opening number that like Stephen Sondheim's "Comedy Tonight" from ***A Funny Thing Happened on the Way to the Forum*** introduced the cast of characters and provided a précis of the plot to follow. The brilliant sequence ended in a splendid bit of stagecraft in which the Leading Player shows the audience a small piece of red scarf in his hand that magically vanishes. Then suddenly what appears to be the same scarf materializes on another part of the stage, and when the Leading Player pulls it from the floor it becomes larger and larger as (per the script) it "magically and majestically" sweeps the full length and height of the stage and provides the skeletal framework of Charlemagne's palace.

And Fosse and company had more tricks up their sleeves. Pippin's grandmother Berthe (Irene Ryan) advises him to live for the moment in "No Time at All," which suddenly morphed into an audience sing-along replete with a giant-sized song sheet and a bouncing ball of light. Tony Walton's stained-glass décor revealed moving eyes that spied on the action when court intrigues were afoot, and Leland Palmer's Fastrada and her "Spread a Little Sunshine" was a startling homage to Gwen Verdon in both her looks and voice as well as in her movements and dancing style (and she repeatedly informs the audience that she's "just an ordinary housewife and mother, just like all you housewives and mothers out there" as she bumps-and-grinds her way through the number). The "Glory" sequence contrasted a limbo world where soldiers die in bloody combat while the Leading Player and two other soldiers obliviously dance to the joyous ragtime vamp of the so-called "Manson Trio" (which wasn't listed in the program or on the cast album). And when one scene ends, Catherine (Jill Clayburgh) asks the theatre's electricians to keep the lights on her because she wants to sing another number ("I Guess I'll Miss the Man"), and because the song is supposedly impromptu and not part of the script, it isn't listed in the program (but is on the cast album).

The critics generally liked the musical, but a few felt the second half was a letdown after the spectacular early scenes. Martin Gottfried in *Women's Wear Daily* said the first forty-five minutes found the work "at peak energy, creativity, confidence and maturity," and "every facet" was "timed, meshed and coordinated into a colorful, magical, musical, rhythmic body." But when the plot got underway, the "tremendously imaginative entertainment" stopped "dead in its tracks" by a book that had "no story to tell." Clive Barnes in the *New York Times* said Fosse gave the production "one of the best musical stagings to be seen on Broadway in years," and although the book was "feeble" and the music "bland," the evening ran "like a racehorse." In the same newspaper, Walter Kerr said that as he watched the opening sequence he knew "unimpeded imagination will be at work tonight," but he noted the musical's material was "less exhilarating" than its method. The evening was "an exercise in style" and "as such, recommended."

Douglas Watt in the *New York Daily News* praised the "droll" book and "charming" songs, and said Fosse's "superlative" staging made *Pippin* "extraordinary" musical theatre. Richard Watts in the *New York Post* predicted that the "brilliant" show couldn't fail, and mentioned there were so many "exciting dances" and "show-stopping interludes" that he found it difficult to single out any specific one. T. E. Kalem in *Time* noted that the "splendiferous theatricality" of the musical had the "kick of a lightning bolt" with its "firecracker dance numbers," and Fosse used his "sixth sense of dance" with "undeviating intelligence." And Jack Kroll in *Newsweek* said Hirson's "self-deprecating" book qualified "as the new Broadway irony," the score was "high-octane and quick-evaporating," and the "brilliant" Fosse "programmed everyone right down to their toe-wiggles" in order to provide a "first-rate entertainment."

Edwin Wilson in the *Wall Street Journal* said the opening sequence was "theatre magic" that hadn't been seen "for a long time," and "The Manson Trio" was "quite possibly the most original and telling antiwar number the American musical has produced." For him, *Pippin* had "taste, imagination, and discipline" and was "often brilliant." Leonard Harris on WCBSTV2 said the musical was loaded with "magic," and the "chief magician" was Fosse; and while Kevin Sanders on WABCTV7 found the show "dazzling" to watch and noted Fosse had devised "flawlessly crisp and exuberant routines," the evening nonetheless reminded him of "a kind of Las Vegas night club version of *Camelot*."

Pippin became the longest-running musical of the season with a total of 1,944 performances, and it made history when it became the first musical to successfully explore the possibilities of television advertising. A brief clip of "The Mansion Trio" was enough to send customers running to the box office.

In its first advertisements, the musical was known as *The Adventures of Pippin*; during the tryout, Patrick Hines was succeeded by Roger Hamilton, and the songs "Marking Time" (for Pippin) and "Just Between the Two of Us" (for Pippin and Catherine) were cut. Part of the music for the unused "The Goodtime Ladies' Rag" was recycled for "The Manson Trio."

An early draft of the musical was in two acts and included an extended second-act opening sequence in Pippin's "anecdotic revue" where he spends time in a monastery that is more concerned with making money than praising God. The monastery's abbott states there's an order on his desk for four hundred miraculous medals that must be filled by Thursday, and Pippin duly notes that God isn't dead, he's in business (the sequence included the song "Sing Hallelujah").

The script was published in hardback by Drama Book Specialists in 1975. The cast album was released by Motown Records (LP # M76OL), and the CD was issued by Decca Broadway (# 012-159-613-2) and includes bonus tracks of "I Guess I'll Miss the Man" (sung by the Supremes), "Corner of the Sky" (The Jackson 5), and "Morning Glow" (Michael Jackson). The Mexico City cast album was released by Discos Gas Records (LP # 4064), and a Los Angeles Harbor College production was recorded by Audio Engineering Associates (LP # AEA-1317). The collection *Lost in Boston IV* (Varese Sarabande CD # VSD-5768) includes "Marking Time" (performed by Michael Rupert, who had succeeded John Rubinstein during the run of the Broadway production and who also played the role during the musical's national tour). "The Goodtime Ladies' Rag" is included in Ben Vereen's *Here I Am* (Accord Records LP # SN-7186).

The musical was filmed for Canadian television and was later shown on American cable channels, and the DVD was released by VCI Video; the company includes original cast members Ben Vereen and Christopher Chadman, and others in the production are William Katt (Pippin), Chita Rivera (Fastrada), and Martha Raye (Berthe).

The London version opened at Her Majesty's Theatre on October 30, 1973, for eighty-five performances; the cast included Paul Jones (Pippin), Northern (J.) Callaway (Leading Player), Diane Langton (Fastrada), and Elisabeth Welch (Berthe).

The musical was revived on Broadway at the Music Box Theatre on April 25, 2013, for 709 performances. Directed by Diane Paulus, the revival emphasized the circus atmosphere and magic tricks of the original production, and the choreography by Chet Walker was described as "in the style" of Bob Fosse. The show won the Tony Award for Best Revival, and the cast album was released by Ghostlight Records.

Awards

Tony Awards and Nominations: Best Musical (*Pippin*); Best Leading Actor in a Musical (**Ben Vereen**); Best Leading Actress in a Musical (Leland Palmer); Best Featured Actress in a Musical (Irene Ryan); Best Director of a Musical (**Bob Fosse**); Best Book (Roger O. Hirson); Best Score (Stephen Schwartz); Best Scenic Designer (**Tony Walton**); Best Costume Designer (Patricia Zipprodt); Best Lighting Designer (**Jules Fisher**); Best Choreographer (**Bob Fosse**)

LYSISTRATA

Theatre: Brooks Atkinson Theatre
Opening Date: November 13, 1972; *Closing Date*: November 18, 1972
Performances: 8
Book and *Lyrics*: Michael Cacoyannis
Music: Peter Link
Based on the 411 BC play *Lysistrata* by Aristophanes.
Direction: Michael Cacoyannis; *Producers*: David Black and David Seltzer (Ira Resnick, Associate Producer); *Scenery*: Robin Wagner; *Costumes*: Willa Kim; *Lighting*: Jules Fisher; *Musical Direction*: Henry "Bootsie" Normand
Cast: *Melina Mercouri* (Lysistrata), Evelyn Russell (Kalonike), Priscilla Lopez (Myrrhine), Madeline Le Roux (Lampito), Lynda Sue Marks (Corinthian Woman), Nai Bonet (Boeotian Woman), Marilou Sirinek (Policewoman), Emory Bass (Omicron), Gordon Connell (Phi-Chi), Joseph Palmieri (Omega), David Thomas (Upsilon), Jack Fletcher (Epsilon), Jane Connell (Gamma), Avril Gentles (Alphabeta), Mary Jo Catlett (Deltazeta), Patti Karr (Theta), Gayla Osbourne (Iota), Philip Bruns (Commissioner), Stephen Macht (Policeman, Spartan Herald), Charles E. Siegel (Policeman), Cynthia Bullens (Woman A), Joanne Nail (Woman B), Judith Drake (Woman C), Richard Dmitri (Kinesias), John Bentley (Spartan Delegate)
The musical was presented in one act.
The action takes place in Greece during ancient times.

Musical Numbers

"A Woman's Hands" (Melina Mercouri); "On, On, On" (Melina Mercouri, Women); "Many the Beasts" (Men); "Are We Strong?" (Melina Mercouri, Women); "And We Are In" (Melina Mercouri, Women); "Lysistrata" (Melina Mercouri, Women); "I Miss My Man" (Priscilla Lopez); "To Touch the Sky" (Melina Mercouri); "A Woman's Hands" (reprise) (Melina Mercouri); "Eels Are a Girl's Best Friend" (Women); "Let Me Tell You a Little Story" (Men and Women); "Kalimera" (Melina Mercouri, Company)

Lysistrata was one of the excrescences of the era, one of the most useless, tasteless, and tiresome musicals one could ever hope to avoid. In fact, it was so bad it made such also-rans as ***Ari***, ***Tricks***, and ***Rainbow Jones*** look like models of great musical theatre. Based on Aristophanes's satire about women who deny sex to men if the latter continue to wage war, the musical was an obvious attempt to capitalize on the unrest of the Vietnam era. But with lackluster performances, unimaginative direction, crude book and lyrics, and dreary décor, the musical was a completely hopeless enterprise. If the evening had one redeeming quality, it was probably Peter Link's score; it was by no means all that distinguished, but some of the songs, such as "Kalimera," might have served as pleasant background music on the phonograph.

Martin Gottfried in *Women's Wear Daily* said director Michael Cacoyannis was the country's "crudest" director, but with *Lysistrata* he outdid himself with "vulgarity" as he spread himself into the areas of libretto and lyric writing. In fact, the dialogue and lyrics were so tasteless that Cacoyannis became "a convincing argument against freedom of speech." As for Melina Mercouri, she did "little more than just be there," and the only "good" thing about the evening was that it lasted for little more than an hour.

Leonard Probst on NBC Radio said the "tasteless" and "muddle-headed, embarrassingly bad" musical was "Cockamamee Cacoyannis" and the mixture of ancient Greece and rock music was "like mixing souvlaki and bagels." Kevin Sanders on WABCTV7 said the "bad, very bad" and disappointing musical had "just about everything" going against it with a "crass and embarrassingly juvenile" production seeped in "gross heavy-handedness." Cacoyannis offered "no real style or concept to the evening," and Mercouri couldn't sing well and spoke in an accent that was "difficult to make out" and "out of key" with the other performers.

Clive Barnes in the *New York Times* found Cacoyannis's "frankly abominable" adaptation "one of the worst-written shows Broadway has seen in some time." Douglas Watt in the *New York Daily News* said the musical had "the breath of failure about it from start to finish"; Robin Wagner's décor was "muddy-looking," Willa Kim's costumes were "mostly dowdy," and Cacoyannis vulgarized the original play. And Richard Watts in the *New York Post* was thankful that the "disastrous clumsiness and ineffectuality" of the proceedings were "mercifully brief." Like many of the critics, Watts complained about the awkwardly updated references to "effete snobs" and the "un-Hellenic Activities Committee." (There was also an impersonation of President Nixon and references to the Iron Curtain.)

During previews, the musical was presented in two acts, and the following songs were cut: "Oh, What a Siege That Was," "As I Choose," "A Cavalry Capital," and "You Out There."

There have been numerous musical adaptations of *Lysistrata*, and almost as soon as they were produced they disappeared. *The Happiest Girl in the World* opened at the Martin Beck (now Al Hirschfeld) Theatre on April 3, 1961, for just ninety-six performances (Dran Seitz played the role of Lysistrata). The book by Fred Saidy and Henry Myers was based on a "story" by E. Y. Harburg ("with a bow to Aristophanes and Bulfinch"), the lyrics were by Harburg, and the music by Jacques Offenbach was adapted by Jay Gorney; others in the cast were Cyril Ritchard (who also directed), Janice Rule, Bruce Yarnell, Michael Kermoyan, Lainie Kazan, and David Canary.

In 1972, there were two adaptations of the play, both titled *Lysistrata*. Besides the current Broadway version, the other opened on August 27 of that year at the Murray Theatre in Chicago, Illinois, and permanently closed there on September 17. Barbara Rush played the title role, the music was by Arthur Rubinstein, the adaptation was by John Lewin, and the score was performed by the Electric Moussaka.

The Off-Off-Broadway *Lyz!* opened at the Samuel Beckett Theatre on January 10, 1999, for thirteen performances and seems to have completely vanished after the brief engagement (the book and lyrics were by Joe Lauinger, the music by Jim Crowdery, and Jill Paxton played the title role). The Broadway production *Lysistrata Jones* opened at the Walter Kerr Theatre on December 14, 2011, and played for just thirty performances; the book was by Douglas Carter Beane, the lyrics and music by Lewis Finn, and Patti Murin played the leading role. Here the plot took place at Athens University where the members of the college's losing basketball team are denied sex until they win a game.

Even the mere mention of *Lysistrata* seems to doom a production. The Off-Broadway musical *The Athenian Touch* opened at the Jan Hus Playhouse on January 14, 1964, with a book by Arthur Goodman and J. Albert Fracht, lyrics by David Eddy, and music by Willard Straight. Although it wasn't based on *Lysistrata*, it dared to reference the play in its plot, offered a song titled "Lysistrata," and even included Aristophanes as a minor character. For such sins, it closed after just one performance.

DEAR OSCAR

"A Musical Based on the Life of Oscar Wilde"

Theatre: Playhouse Theatre
Opening Date: November 16, 1972; *Closing Date*: November 19, 1972
Performances: 5
Book and *Lyrics*: Caryl Gabrielle Young
Music: Addy O. Fieger
Direction: John Allen; *Producer*: Mary W. John; *Choreography*: Margery Beddow; *Scenery*: William Pitkin; *Costumes*: Mary McKinley; *Lighting*: David F. Segal; *Musical Direction*: Arnold Gross

Cast: Richard Kneeland (Oscar Wilde), Nancy Cushman (Speranza [Lady Wilde]), Jane Hoffman (Lady Mount-Temple), Len Gochman (Frank Harris), Garnett Smith (Charles Brookfield, Al Taylor), Edward Penn (Charles Hawtry, Alfred Wood), Tinker Gillespie (Bootles), Sylvia O'Brien (Comtesse), Roger Leonard (Comtesse's Son, Sidney Mavor, Scotland Yard Detective), Jack Hoffman (Frederick), Kimberly Vaughn (Constance Lloyd), Grant Walden (Lord de Grey, Sir Edward Carson), Gary Krawford (Robert [Robbie] Ross), Richard Marr (Vicar, Sir Edward Clark), Jack Bittner (The Marquess of Queensbury), Edward McPhillips (Arthur, Theatre Attendant), Lynn Brinker (Nellie), Tommy Breslin (Clibburn), Bruce Heighley (Atkins), James Hosbein (Edward Shelly), Russ Thacker (Bosie [Lord Alfred Douglas])

The musical was presented in two acts.

The action takes place in London during 1883 and 1894.

Musical Numbers

Act One: "We Like Things the Way They Are" (Richard Kneeland, Company); "Tite Street" (Richard Kneeland, Jane Hoffman, Kimberly Vaughn); "Oscar Wilde Has Said It" (Company); "Wot's 'Is Name" (Lynn Brinker, Boys); "Poor Bosie" (Russ Thacker); "The Perfect Understanding" (Richard Kneeland, Russ Thacker); "Swan and Edgar's" (Kimberly Vaughn, Nancy Cushman); "We're Only Lovers" (Gary Krawford); "If I Could" (Richard Kneeland)

Act Two: "How Dare He" (Company); "We'll Have a Party" (Russ Thacker, Lynn Brinker, Boys); "The Actor" (Richard Kneeland); "When Did You Leave Me?" (Kimberly Vaughn, Richard Kneeland); "Good, Good Times" (Lynn Brinker); "There Where the Young Men Go" (Richard Kneeland)

Dear Oscar was a Limited or Middle Broadway production, and as with so many shows in this category there was a certain amount of confusion as to how it should be classified. *Theatre World* considered it an Off-Broadway musical, but *Best Plays* included it as a Broadway production. The *New York Theatre Critics' Reviews* divided its reviews between Off-Broadway and Broadway productions, and the annual placed *Dear Oscar* in its Broadway section. But like most of the plays and musicals that fell under Limited or Middle Broadway contract status, *Dear Oscar* was a quick failure and closed within the week.

The musical dealt with Wilde (Richard Kneeland) and his relationships with his wife Speranza (Nancy Cushman) and his young lover Bosie (aka Lord Alfred Douglas; played by Russ Thacker). When Bosie's father the Marquess of Queensberry (Jack Bittner) learns of the relationship between Wilde and his son, Wilde's stubbornness and the Marquess's hatred begin a chain of events that leads to scandal and Wilde's eventual arrest, trial, and incarceration.

Douglas Watt in the *New York Daily News* noted that while the musical had a certain "taste and style," it didn't have "originality or verve" and was therefore "rather dull" and had a "musty air." Richard Watts in the *New York Post* found the work "intelligent" but only "mildly interesting," and said the score was "pleasant" but undistinguished. Leonard Harris on WCBSTV2 said the "inept" and "dreadful" evening had a "totally lost" book, "strained" lyrics, and musical notes "meandering around in search of a melody" (and he suggested that following the words *Dear Oscar* there "should be a letter of apology").

Kevin Sanders on WABCTV7 noted the "lumbering" musical had one "dubious but considerable achievement": it managed to make Oscar Wilde "dull." The story came across as soap opera, the "effortlessly forgettable" score was "repetitive" and "undistinguished," and the show went astray with "ridiculous" songs such as one ("Swan and Edgar's") between Wilde's wife and mother in which the two sang about shopping. He concluded that the "mawkish and sentimental" musical would have sent Wilde "racing off in a desperate search for heterosexual obscurity."

During previews, two songs were dropped ("If I 'Ad 'Alf" and "For Woman") and one underwent a title change (from "We Dare You" to "How Dare He").

The musical was revived Off Off Broadway in 1980 at the Perry Street Theatre. "If I 'Ad 'Alf" was reinstated; three songs ("You Ought to Meet My Mother," "Drinkin' Nights and Sleepin' Days," and "My Dear Oscar") were added; and four ("We Like Things the Way They Are," "Wot's 'Is Name," "Poor Bosie," and "How Dare He") were omitted. For this production, Patrick Farrelly was Oscar Wilde and Rex Thompson was Bosie (in 1956, the latter had played Anna Leonowens's son Louis in the film version of *The King and I* and Peter Duchin in *The Eddy Duchin Story*).

Dear Oscar was yet another failed musical in Russ (Rusty) Thacker's career. He created the role of Sebastian in the long-running 1968 Off-Broadway hit musical *Your Own Thing*, but from there everything went downhill with six fast flops: ***The Grass Harp*** (1971; six performances), ***Heathen!*** (1972; one performance), *Dear Oscar* (1973; five performances), ***Music! Music!*** (1974; thirty-seven performances), ***Home Sweet Homer*** (1976; one performance), and *Do Black Patent Leather Shoes Really Reflect Up?* (1982; five performances). He also appeared in the 1974 Off-Broadway drama-with-songs *Once I Saw a Boy Laughing . . .* , which played for five performances, and he coproduced the 1988 Off-Broadway musical *The Wonder Years*, which ran for twenty-three showings. He was also in the 1976 Broadway drama *Me Jack, You Jill*, which, depending on the source, shuttered after fourteen previews or closed after its second official performance.

There have been at least two other musicals about Wilde. *It's Wilde!* opened Off Broadway on May 21, 1980, for seven performances; Ross Petty played the title role, the lyrics and book were by Burton Wolfe, and the music by Randy Klein. The musical was about both Wilde's life and afterlife, and John Corry in the *New York Times* noted that for the scenes in heaven everyone wore white outfits and thus came across like a "convention of vanilla ice-cream sodas." *Utterly Wilde!!!* opened at the Next Stage Company on March 22, 1995, for five performances and was a one-man musical in which Marc H. Glick portrayed Wilde; Glick adapted the text from Wilde's writings, and the lyrics and music were by John Franceschina.

AMBASSADOR

"A New Musical"

Theatre: Lunt-Fontanne Theatre
Opening Date: November 19, 1972; *Closing Date*: November 25, 1972
Performances: 19
Book: Don Ettlinger and Anna Marie Barlow
Lyrics: Hal Hackady
Music: Don Gohman
Based on the 1903 novel *The Ambassadors* by Henry James.
Direction: Stone Widney; *Producers*: Gene Dingenary, Miranda d'Ancona, and Nancy Levering (Dan Rodden, Associate Producer); *Choreography*: Joyce Tristler; *Scenery* and *Costumes*: Peter Rice (scenery supervised by Robert Guerra and costumes supervised by Sara Brook); *Lighting*: Martin Aronstein; *Musical Direction*: Herbert Grossman
Cast: Patricia Arnell (Flower Girl, Germaine), *Howard Keel* (Lewis Lambert Strether), David Sabin (Waymarsh), *Danielle Darrieux* (Marie de Vionnet), Carmen Mathews (Gloriani), Dwight Arno (Waiter), Michael Goodwin (Bilham), Michael Shannon (Chad), Andrea Marcovicci (Jeanne de Vionnet), Larry Giroux (Dancing Master, Artist, Cabaret Dancer), Jack Trussel (Guide, Hotel Manager), Robert L. Hultman (Waiter, Headwaiter), Marsha Tamaroff (Innkeeper's Wife), Nikolas Dante (Bellboy), Dixie Stewart (Lady in Park), M'el Dowd (Amelia Newsome), Alexis Hoff (Cabaret Dancer), Phillip Filiato (Cabaret Dancer), Suzanne Sponsler (Cabaret Dancer); People of Paris: Janis Ansley, Patricia Arnell, Dwight Arno, Marcia Brooks, Nikolas Dante, Richard Dodd, Vito Durante, Philip Filiato, Lynn Fitzpatrick, Larry Giroux, Charlie Goeddertz, Gerald Haston, Alexis Hoff, Robert L. Hultman, Douglas E. Hunnikin, Genette Lane, Betsy Ann Leadbetter, Nancy Lynch, Linda-Lee MacArthur, Adam Petroski, Dean Russell, Salicia Saree, Ellie Smith, Suzanne Sponsler, Dixie Stewart, Marsha Tamaroff, Jack Trussel, Chester Walker
The musical was presented in two acts.
The action takes place in Paris during 1906.

Musical Numbers

Act One: "Lilas" (Patricia Arnell); "Lambert's Quandary" (Howard Keel); "I Know the Man" (Danielle Darrieux); "The Right Time, The Right Place" (Gloriani's Guests); "She Passed My Way" (Danielle Darrieux, Gloriani's Guests); "Valse" (Gloriani's Guests); "Something More" (Howard Keel); "Love Finds the Lonely" (Andrea Marcovicci); "Kyrie Eleison" (Choir); "Surprise" (Danielle Darrieux, Howard Keel, The People of the Left Bank); "Happy Man" (Howard Keel)

Act Two: "Lilas" (reprise) and "What Happened to Paris?" (Howard Keel, Patricia Arnell); "Young with Him" (Danielle Darrieux); "Too Much to Forgive" (Howard Keel); "Why Do Women Have to Call It Love" (Carmen Mathews, David Sabin); "Mama" (Andrea Marcovicci); "That's What I Need Tonight" (Danielle Darrieux, Howard Keel); "Maxixe-Habanera" (dance) (Alexis Hoff, Phillip Filiato, Suzanne Sponsler, Larry Giroux, The People of Paris); "That's What I Need Tonight" (reprise) (Howard Keel, Danielle Darrieux, The People of Paris); "Gossip" (The Ladies of Paris); "Not Tomorrow" (Andrea Marcovicci); "All of My Life" (Howard Keel); "Thank You, No" (Howard Keel)

The London import *Ambassador* was based on Henry James's 1903 novel *The Ambassadors*, and like so much of James's work it centered on an austere, somewhat unimaginative American (in this case, Lewis Lambert Strether, played by Howard Keel) who undergoes a transformation when he visits Europe. At the request of Amelia Newsome (Me'l Dowd), Strether goes to Paris as her ambassador in order to extricate her young son Chad (Michael Shannon) from an affair with older woman Marie de Vionnet (Danielle Darrieux). Mission accomplished, but Strether finds himself falling in love with Marie when she opens his eyes to the romantic possibilities of life.

The musical hadn't been successful in London, where it had opened a year earlier, and neither was it popular in New York where it lasted little more than two weeks. It received mild rather than negative notices, and probably a decade earlier would have run out the season. But Broadway economics had changed, and there wasn't much room for a bland but pleasant musical anymore.

Douglas Watt in the *New York Daily News* said he felt like a "churl" to "dismiss" such an "inoffensive and uneventful" musical that never rose above the "placid," and while the score lacked "true invention" it was nonetheless "literate." Richard Watts in the *New York Post* also used the "P" word, noting the evening suffered from "excessive placidity." It wasn't "terrible," but it just never came to "interesting dramatic life." Leonard Harris on WCBSTV2 said the "big, lavish, traditional" musical was "bland" and never quite left the ground, and so he could only offer the "faint praise" of saying the evening was "thoroughly bearable."

Joseph H. Mazo in *Women's Wear Daily* said *Ambassador* wasn't "absolutely awful" but just "awfully banal." He felt the clichéd evening might suit the proverbial tired businessman, but in this case the businessman might fall asleep. Clive Barnes in the *New York Times* noted that despite the "considerable efforts" of the "lively" Keel and Darrieux, the work's "wan listlessness" was "effete and pallid." The musical was "not a disgrace" but "merely a pity," and he mentioned that the work had failed in London and would likely do so in New York because *Ambassador* had no "diplomatic immunity" (ultimately, the reported losses on both productions totaled $600,000).

During New York previews, "A Boy Like That" was cut (it may have been an early title for "Lambert's Quandary").

The London production had opened on October 19, 1971, at Her Majesty's Theatre for eighty-six performances. Keel and Darrieux were the stars, and for London the book was credited to Don Ettingler (for New York, both he and Anna Marie Barslow shared writing credits). The London version, which was set in 1908 instead of 1906, included an early scene which took place in Woolett, Massachusetts. For New York, the entire musical took place in Paris. Songs heard in London but deleted for Broadway were: "A Man You Can Set Your Watch By," "It's a Woman," "Charming," "What Can You Do with a Nude?," "Tell Her," "La Femme," "I Thought I Knew You," "La nuit d'amour," "Am I Wrong?," "You Can Tell a Lady by Her Hat," and "This Utterly Ridiculous Affair."

The London cast album was released by RCA Victor (LP # SER-5618).

VIA GALACTICA

"A Musical of the Future"

Theatre: Uris Theatre
Opening Date: November 28, 1972; *Closing Date*: December 2, 1972
Performances: 7
Book: Christopher Gore and Judith Ross
Lyrics: Christopher Gore
Music: Galt MacDermot

Direction: Peter Hall; *Producers*: George W. George and Bernard S. Straus in association with Nat Shapiro; *Ensemble Movement*: George Faison; *Scenery* and *Costumes*: John Bury; *Lighting*: Lloyd Burlingame; *Musical Direction*: Thomas Pierson

Cast: Irene Cara (Storyteller), Raul Julia (Gabriel Finn), Damon Evans (Hels), Edloe (April), Virginia Vestoff (Omaha), Keene Curtis (Doctor Isaacs), Bill Starr (Provo), James Dybas (Spokesman, Entertainer), Chuck Cissel (Old Man); The Blue People: Mark Baker, Jacqueline Britt, Melanie Chartoff, Richard DeRusso, Sylvia DiGiorgio, Livia Genise, Marion Killinger, Toni Lund, Bob Spencer, and Bonnie Walker; Livia Genise (Diane, Writer), Peter Nissen (Nicklas), Alex Ander (Roustabout), Mark Baker (Cook), Robert Blankshine (The Mute's Friend), Jacqueline Britt (Gypsy), Ralph Carter (Boy), Melanie Chartoff (Geologist), Chuck Cissel (Student), Lili Cockerille (Mute), Lorrie Davis (Lady), Richard DeRusso (Mechanic), Sylvia DiGiorgio (Teacher), Marion Killinger (Politician), Toni Lund (Child), Veronica Redd (Cripple), James Rivers (Tailor), Richard Ryder (Carpenter), Stan Shaw (Doctor), Leon Spelman (Gambler), Bob Spencer (Janitor), Bonnie Walker (Nurse), J. H. Washington (Grandmother)

The musical was presented in two acts.

The action takes place in 2972 on Earth and on the asteroid Ithaca.

Musical Numbers

Act One: "Via Galactica" (Irene Cara); "We Are One" (The Blue People); "Helen of Troy" (Raul Julia); "Oysters" (Damon Evans, Edloe); "The Other Side of the Sky" (Damon Evans); "Children of the Sun" (Virginia Vestoff); "Different" (Edloe, Company); "Take Your Hat Off" (Virginia Vestoff, Company); "Ilmar's Tomb" (Virginia Vestoff); "Shall We Friend?" (Raul Julia); "The Lady Isn't Looking" (Virginia Vestoff); "Hush" (Raul Julia); "Cross on Over" (Keene Curtis, Virginia Vestoff, Company); "The Gospel of Gabriel Finn" (Raul Julia)

Act Two: "Terre Haute High" (Edloe); "Life Wins" (Virginia Vestoff); "The Worm Germ" (Bill Starr); "Isaacs' Equation" (Keene Curtis); "Dance the Dark Away!" (Irene Cara, Company): "Four Hundred Girls Ago" (Raul Julia); "All My Good Mornings" (Virginia Vestoff); "Isaacs' Equation" (reprise) (Keene Curtis); "Children of the Sun" (reprise) (Virginia Vestoff, Raul Julia); "New Jerusalem" (Company)

Via Galactica was Galt MacDermot's second mega-musical disaster of the season. A few weeks earlier, ***Dude*** had disappeared down the highway after sixteen performances, and now the outer-space musical folded on the astral highway after seven showings. The two musicals lost a combined total of almost $2 million, a staggering amount for the era. After these debacles, MacDermot's main stem career was all but over and he was represented with just one more new Broadway musical, *The Human Comedy*, which transferred from Off Broadway in 1984 and lasted for just thirteen unlucky performances. His ***Two Gentlemen of Verona*** was a modest success that has now fallen into the forgotten-hit category, but *Hair* has outgrown the awkward stage of being old hat and passé and is now a genuine period piece that will undoubtedly enjoy periodic revivals.

Titled *Up!* in preproduction, *Via Galactica* was the premiere production to play at the new Uris (now Gershwin) Theatre. (In *Opening Nights*, Steven Suskin notes the original title was quickly dropped when the producers realized the advertisements for the musical would for all purposes read "Up Uris.") The inauspicious opening was a bad omen for the house, and for years it struggled to find a hit. ***Seesaw*** was a flop, and a string of failed adaptations of MGM musicals played there (***Gigi***, *Singin' in the Rain* [1985], and *Meet Me in St. Louis* [1989]), various prestige productions such as ***Treemonisha*** stumbled, revivals of ***The Desert Song***, *1776* (1997), and *On the Town* (1998) had brief runs, and *The Red Shoes* (1993) was one of the biggest flops in Broadway history when it opened and closed there after five performances. But the venue also enjoyed a few long-running productions, such as the hit revival of ***The King and I*** with Yul Brynner in 1977 (719 performances), the world premiere of Stephen Sondheim's ***Sweeney Todd, The Demon Barber of Fleet Street*** in 1979, and the long-running 1994 revival of *Show Boat* (946 performances). And in 2003, one of the biggest hits of them all opened, and as of this writing the theatre is still hosting Stephen Schwarz's ***Wicked***.

Part of the theatre's problem is that it's very large and thus requires a "big" production to both comfortably fill its stage and yet also draw some 2,000 spectators into the proceedings. Intimate shows don't work there, but spectacles do, and so *Via Galactica* certainly seemed to fill the bill with its lavish scenery, huge cast, and its broad scope of futuristic interplanetary goings-on. But the show's flyer lied when it said the work was "the most wondrous musical of our times" because director Peter Hall could never pull the evening together: the plot was almost incomprehensible and the special effects and coy staging devices overwhelmed the performers. As a result, critics and audiences were at a loss to understand the almost completely sung-through show, and the doomed vehicle couldn't survive beyond its first week.

The plot was so difficult to follow that at least two separate program inserts were required in an attempt to explain the action. The story took place in 2972 when man has explored and conquered the universe. But apparently the old axiom of "East, west, home's best" is still in fashion because everyone's decided the solar system is a nice place to visit *but*. However, things are now different on Earth: racism has been obliterated because everyone is the same color (blue); everyone wears spinning cone-shaped hats that control all emotions; everyone says "We" because the word "I" has been banished; and babies are conceived in test tubes. Because only conformity is tolerated, elderly scientist Dr. Isaacs (Keene Curtis) and his lovely young wife Omaha (Virginia Vestoff), who live on an asteroid called Ithaca, decide to escape Earth's influence by traveling via galactica to a distant star where mankind can begin all over again. Ithaca's populace prepares for the journey, but there's one problem: Dr. Isaacs has lost his body, and so only his head and brain remain, and they live in a box. Since reproduction with Omaha is impossible, the doctor invites earthling and garbage man by profession Gabriel Finn (Raul Julia) to join the travelers on their journey and to father a child for Omaha. Gabriel dies in the final battle with Earth, but not before he and Omaha have spent a night together.

The musical employed six trampolines on which the cast jumped up and down in order to simulate weightlessness. But there was no consistency to the concept, and when the performers walked on the stage itself they were clearly not weightless. There were also a couple of space ships, the Ark to take the people of Ithaca to a distant star as well as a ship from Earth that fails in its attempt to stop the exodus; moreover, there was an elaborate folding metal stairway, flashing lights, smoke screens, projections that depicted starscapes, and Helen of Troy, which was Gabriel's garbage truck, a contraption something on the order of a space-age hydraulic cherry picker that ejects garbage into orbit. The musical also employed a narrator (Irene Cara) who swung high in the air on a trapeze; perhaps along with the program inserts she was able to somewhat clarify the plot for the bewildered audience.

The critics were numb. Jack Kroll in *Newsweek* said the "bad show" was an "unappealing kind of *Babes in Spaceland.*" Clive Barnes in the *New York Times* suggested the "banality" of the book had "no interest and no point of contact with the audience" with its "appallingly weak" story and "flat and platitudinous" writing (as for all the hoopla attending the musical's well-publicized trampolines, Barnes decided they suggested "nothing more than people pointlessly bouncing up and down on trampolines"). In the same newspaper, Walter Kerr said the production was "entirely, quite staggeringly, static," and noted much of the scenery consisted of tiny white dots, which he compared to the dots sprinkled on nonpareil candy, and thus he spent the evening looking "at what seemed a steady rainfall of tapioca." Douglas Watt in the *New York Daily News* said he kept waiting for the feature film to begin, and suspected with judicious trimming the "grand mess" might entertain the audience at Radio City Music Hall between movie showings. Kevin Sanders on WABCTV7 found the musical "desperate and chaotic and grossly untidy," the score "monotonously repetitive," and, after trying to explain the plot to his viewers, said, "I know. I don't understand it, either"; and Leonard Harris on WCBSTV2 said the musical was "probably Broadway's first interplanetary disaster" and noted, "I have seen the future and it has no future."

Martin Gottfried in *Women's Wear Daily* noted the new theatre offered a Theatre Hall of Fame in its lobby and a "bomb" on its stage. There was no excuse for the "lumbering, incomprehensible, unmusical, and absolute disaster," and he said that "while you know it must end sometime, you have to wonder whether you'll make it there yourself." He hoped the theatre wouldn't end up as just another empty playhouse, and concluded there wasn't "much point in laying wall-to-wall carpeting in a garbage-dump."

Richard Watts in the *New York Post* didn't understand the plot, but said the "remarkable" musical was a "curiosity that should be seen" because it was a "stunning piece of showmanship" with "fascinating" and "elaborate" mechanical effects.

There were two opening night programs, one for the original opening of November 21 and one for the eventual official opening of November 28, and each one boasted a different insert that explained the story. One of the programs also included pages that attempted to explain the plot in conjunction with the song listing.

There was no cast recording, but *Billy Butler Plays "Via Galactica"* was released by Kilmarnock Records (LP # KIL-72009); Butler was a guitarist in the musical's orchestra, and for the album MacDermot conducted.

The album includes nine songs from the Broadway production ("Via Galactica," "400 Girls Ago," "Hush," "Life Wins," "All My Good Mornings," "New Jerusalem," "Helen of Troy," "Dance the Dark Away," "The Other Side of the Sky") and three that weren't used ("I Believe in Butterflies," "Home," and "Up").

Ralph Carter had played the title role of ***Dude*** a month earlier, and now he was in the chorus of *Via Galactica*. But he was destined to appear in a long-running, critically acclaimed, if not overwhelmingly profitable musical. And so in ***Raisin*** he was nominated for a Tony Award (as Best Featured Actor in a Musical) and introduced "Sidewalk Tree," one of the most affecting theatre songs of the era.

PURLIE

"A New Musical Comedy"

Theatre: Billy Rose Theatre
Opening Date: December 27, 1972; *Closing Date*: January 7, 1973
Performances: 14
Book: Ossie Davis, Philip Rose, and Peter Udell
Lyrics: Peter Udell
Music: Gary Geld
Based on the 1961 play *Purlie Victorious* by Ossie Davis.
Direction: Philip Rose; *Producer*: Philip Rose; *Choreography*: Louis Johnson; *Scenery*: Garry Sherman; *Costumes*: Ann Roth; *Lighting*: Thomas Skelton; *Musical Direction*: Charles Austin
Cast: Robert Guillaume (Purlie), Shirley Monroe (Church Soloist), Patti Jo (Lutiebelle), Laura Cooper (Missy), Sherman Hemsley (Gitlow), Every Hayes (Field Hand), Lonnie McNeil (Field Hand), Ted Ross (Field Hand), Douglas Norwick (Charlie), Helen Martin (Idella), Art Wallace (Ol' Cap'n); Dancers: Darlene Blackburn, Deborah Bridges, Raphael Gilbert, Linda Griffin, Every Hayes, Reggie Jackson, Alton Lathrop, Robert Martin, Karen E. McDonald, Lonnie McNeil, Debbie Palmer, Andre Peck, Zelda Pulliam; Singers: Demarest Grey, Barbara Joy, Ursuline Kairson, Shirley Monroe, Alfred Rage, Beverly G. Robnett, Ted Ross, Frances Salisbury, Vanessa Shaw, David Weatherspoon, Joe Williams Jr.
The musical was presented in two acts.
The action takes place "not too long ago" in South Georgia.

Musical Numbers

Act One: "Walk Him Up the Stairs" (Entire Company); "New-Fangled Preacher Man" (Robert Guillaume); "Skinnin' a Cat" (Sherman Hemsley, Every Hayes, Lonnie McNeil, Ted Ross); "Purlie" (Patti Jo); "The Harder They Fall" (aka "Ten Feet Tall") (Robert Guillaume, Patti Jo); "The Barrels of War" (Douglas Norwick); "The Unborn Love" (Douglas Norwick); "Big Fish, Little Fish" (Art Wallace, Douglas Norwick); "I Got Love" (Patti Jo); "Great White Father" (aka "The Great White Father of the Year") (The Cotton Pickers); "Skinnin' a Cat" (reprise) (Sherman Hemsley, Douglas Norwick); "Down Home" (Robert Guillaume, Laura Cooper)
Act Two: "First Thing Monday Mornin'" (The Cotton Pickers); "He Can Do It" (Laura Cooper, Patti Jo); "The Harder They Fall" (reprise) (Sherman Hemsley, Patti Jo, Laura Cooper); "The World Is Comin' to a Start" (Douglas Norwick, Company); "Walk Him Up the Stairs" (reprise) (Entire Company)

The national company of *Purlie* played in New York for a two-week limited engagement as part of its road tour and included original cast members Sherman Hemsley and Helen Martin.

The touring cast was in every respect equal to the original company, and in some ways surpassed it. Robert Guillaume perfectly captured the humorous aspects of the title role, but he also revealed a heretofore unseen poignant and dramatic side to the character. His Purlie was comical, but he also created a memorable portrait of a man brushed with a tragic and noble air in his determination to see his vision fulfilled despite overwhelming odds.

For more information about the musical, see the entry for the original 1970 production.

THE GRAND MUSIC HALL OF ISRAEL

Theatre: Felt Forum
Opening Date: January 4, 1973; *Closing Date*: January 14, 1973
Performances: 14
Direction and *Choreography*: Jonatan (aka Jonathan) Karmon (Gavri Levi, Assistant Director); *Producers*: Madison Square Garden Productions and Hy Einhorn; *Costumes*: Lydia Punkus Ganay *Musical Direction*: Rafi Paz
Cast: Shoshana Damari (Singer), Ron Eliran (Singer), Myron Cohen (Host), Ariela (Xylophone Player), The Marganiot (Zlila and Leah) (Singers), The Tal U'Matar (Drums, Flute, and Vocals: Shlomo; Sitar: Yehezkel); The Karmon Israeli Dancers and Singers: Tami Tomer, Ofira Ofir, Dassy Shahar, Rima Meir, Ora Mor, Brurira Aviv, Varda Amir, Tirza Barir, Ruth Ramati, Tuvia Ofir, Itamar Gur, Arie Baror, Ephraim Zamir, Zvi Granit, Zvika Zohar, Shimon Ashkenzi, Jonathan Nahorai, Avi Zah
The revue was presented in two acts.

Musical Numbers

Act One: "Israeli Rhapsody" (dance) (The Karmon Israeli Dancers); "Israeli Songs" (The Marganiot); "The Fishermen of Kineret" (The Karmon Israeli Dancers); "Rhythm and Sound of the Desert" (The Tal U'Matar); "A Night on the Gilboa Mountains" (The Karmon Israeli Singers); Ron Eliran; "A Panorama of Hassidic Life" (The Karmon Israeli Dancers and Singers)
Act Two: "The Mediterranean Flavor" (The Karmon Israeli Dancers); Ariela; "Fire in the Mountains" (The Karmon Israeli Dancers); Shoshana Damari; "Holiday in the Kibbutz" (The Karmon Israeli Dancers); Finale (Company)

The limited engagement of *The Grand Music Hall of Israel* was another evening of Israeli dances and songs helmed by Jonatan (Jonathan) Karmon. (For a complete list of his revues that played in New York, see ***To Live Another Summer, to Pass Another Winter***.)

Howard Thompson in the *New York Times* found the revue "forthright, fresh and charming" with "ingratiating" performers. He singled out "The Fishermen of Kineret" (which he said was "ever so picturesque"), Shoshana Damari (who sang mostly Hebrew songs as well as a "Jewish-Mexican" number), and Ron Eliran (who performed a "plaintive" shepherd's song and a "rousing" antiwar number). He also noted that the "Panorama of Hassidic Life" ended in a "cheerful" wedding dance that brought on the "heartiest applause" of the evening.

The Felt Forum was later renamed the Paramount Theatre, and today is known as The Theatre at Madison Square Garden.

TRICKS

"A New Musical Comedy"

Theatre: Alvin Theatre
Opening Date: January 8, 1973; *Closing Date*: January 13, 1973
Performances: 8
Book: John Jory
Lyrics: Lonnie Burstein
Music: Jerry Blatt
Based on the 1671 comedy *Les fourberies de Scapin* by Moliere (aka Jean-Baptiste Poquelin).
Direction: John Jory; *Producer*: Herman Levin (Samuel Liff, Associate Producer); *Choreography*: Donald Saddler; *Scenery*: Oliver Smith; *Costumes*: Miles White; *Lighting*: Martin Aronstein; *Musical Direction*: David Frank
Cast: Adale O'Brien (Property Mistress), Walter Bobbie (Octave), Christopher Murney (Sylvestre), Rene Auberjonois (Scapin), Carolyn Mignini (Hyacinthe), Mitchell Jason (Argante), Tom Toner (Geronte), Randy

Herron (Leandre), June Helmers (Zerbinetta), Suzanne Walker (Pantanella), Jo Ann Ogawa (Isabella), Lani Sundsten (Carmella), John Handy (Gondolier); The Commedia: Joe Morton (Arlecchino, Lead Singer), Charlotte Crossley (Charlotta), Ernestine Jackson (Ernestina), Shezwae Powell (Shezwae)

The musical was presented in two acts.

The action takes place in and around Venice.

Musical Numbers

Act One: *Prologue*: "Love or Money" (The Commedia); "Who Was I?" (Walter Bobbie, The Commedia); "Trouble's a Ruler" (Rene Auberjonois, Christopher Murney, Walter Bobbie); "Enter Hyacinthe" (Walter Bobbie, The Commedia); "Believe Me" (Walter Bobbie, Carolyn Mignini, The Commedia); "Tricks" (Rene Auberjonois, Christopher Murney); "A Man of Spirit" (The Commedia); "Where Is Respect?" (Mitchell Jason, Tom Toner); "Somebody's Doin' Somebody All the Time" (Rene Auberjonois, The Commedia); "A Sporting Man" (The Commedia)

Act Two: "Scapin" (Joe Morton); "Anything Is Possible" (Rene Auberjonois, Christopher Murney); "How Sweetly Simple" (Carolyn Mignini, June Helmers); "Gypsy Girl" (June Helmers, The Commedia); Epilogue: "Life Can Be Funny" (Company)

Based on Moliere's comedy *Les fourberies de Scapin*, the commedia dell'arte–styled *Tricks* was an anemic version of the farce that dealt with conniving servant Scapin (Rene Auberjonois) and his wily efforts to ensure that Octave (Walter Bobbie) and Leandre (Randy Herron) marry the girls of their dreams, and not the ones their rich, overbearing fathers have chosen for them. The slight evening wasn't helped by a bland but pleasant-in-a-background-kind-of-way score, or with the musical's attempt to dress up the proceedings with soft rock music and the utilization of a black quartet to comment on the action in song or provide musical support to the leading players.

And why do one's eyes glaze over at the mere mention of commedia dell'arte? It seems that every musical that employs such techniques is doomed to fail (such as *Royal Flush* [1965], ***Comedy***, and *The Green Bird* [2001]) because most writers and directors interpret commedia dell'arte as a license to indulge in overbearingly coy stage business. For example, in *Tricks* we're told two characters are drawing their swords, and then we see them as they proceed to paint swords on a canvas placed upon an easel; various characters entwine a spaghetti of colored ropes, and another one complains that he's lost the plotline; and when the words "simple as can be" are sung, a huge cartoon of a bumble bee makes an appearance.

Douglas Watt in the *New York Daily News* said the "browbeating" production would do "anything for a laugh," but the laughs never came, and he concluded that the "noisy and compulsively energetic" musical was a "sorry trick." Leonard Probst on NBC Radio noted the evening was a "twenty-minute show" stretched over two acts and two hours, and the real trick would have been to hold the audience's attention; and Leonard Harris on WCBSTV2 became weary of the "relentless cuteness" and "sophomoric naughtiness." Clive Barnes in the *New York Times* found the evening "tiring" because its "restless activity" was "insufficiently disciplined by a clearly perceived style." He noted the score was "derivative if quite tuneful" and the lyrics were "mildly apt," but suggested the musical might have been better suited to a more intimate theatre than the Alvin. As for Rene Auberjonois, he "enlivened" and sometimes "electrified" the show with "one of the most engaging and brilliant performances currently to be found in the Broadway theatre."

Kevin Sanders on WABCTV7 felt the musical was too "flimsy and stylized," but he liked the "sometimes excellent" score and noted that Auberjonois gave "the most exhausting single performance on Broadway today." But Harris felt that after his appearances in *Coco* (1969), the 1972 movie *Pete 'n' Tillie*, and now *Tricks*, Auberjonois had "dug himself a deep pit on the old camp grounds."

Martin Gottfried in *Women's Wear Daily* noted that most Broadway musicals now fell into two categories, either the so-called rock musical, which forced the rock beat on stories for which such music was inappropriate, or the economy musical in which décor, cast, and musicians were lost on a large Broadway stage. Unfortunately, *Tricks* was now a merger of both genres, and it was a "dead loss."

The script was published in paperback by Samuel French in an undated edition (probably 1974).

Tricks was first produced by the Actors' Theatre in Louisville, Kentucky, in October 1971, and then was presented at Arena Stage in Washington, D.C., on May 19, 1972. In Louisville, Scapin was played by Eric

Tavaris, and in Washington by Richard Bauer. For Louisville, Washington, and New York, Christopher Murney was Sylvestre. The song "Wonderful!" was dropped prior to New York.

Moliere's Scapin had better luck the following season when Jim Dale scored a personal success (and a Tony nomination for Best Leading Actor in a Play) for the London import *Scapino*, which opened at the Circle in the Square on May 18, 1974, for 121 performances.

Awards

Tony Award Nomination: Best Costume Designer (Miles White)

SHELTER

"A Musical"

Theatre: John Golden Theatre
Opening Date: February 6, 1973; *Closing Date*: March 3, 1973
Performances: 31
Book and *Lyrics*: Gretchen Cryer
Music: Nancy Ford
Direction: Austin Pendleton; *Producers*: Richard Fields and Peter Flood (Julie Hughes, Associate Producer); *Choreography*: Sammy Bayes; *Scenery, Costumes*, and *Projection Design*: Tony Walton; *Lighting* and *Projections Devised* by: Richard Pilbrow; *Musical Direction*: Kirk Nurock
Cast: *Marcia Rodd* (Maud), *Terry Kiser* (Michael), *Susan Browning* (Wednesday November), *Joanna Merlin* (Gloria), Charles Collins (Member of Television Crew), Britt Swanson (Member of Television Crew); Voices: Tony Wells (Voice of Arthur), Philip Kraus (Voice of the Director)
The musical was presented in two acts.
The action takes place during the present time in a television studio.

Musical Numbers

Act One: Overture (Tony Wells); "Changing" (Marcia Rodd, Terry Kiser); "Welcome to a New World" (Terry Kiser, Tony Wells); "It's Hard to Care" (Terry Kiser, Tony Wells, Marcia Rodd); "Woke Up Today" (Marcia Rodd, Tony Wells); "Mary Margaret's House in the Country" (Marcia Rodd, Tony Wells); "Woman on the Run" (Tony Wells); "Don't Tell Me It's Forever" (Marcia Rodd, Terry Kiser, Tony Wells)
Act Two: "Sunrise" (Tony Wells); "I Bring Him Seashells" (Susan Browning); "She's My Girl" (Terry Kiser, Marcia Rodd, Tony Wells); "Welcome to a New World" (reprise) (Marcia Rodd, Terry Kiser, Tony Wells, Susan Browning); "He's a Fool" (Susan Browning, Marcia Rodd); "Goin' Home with My Children" (Marcia Rodd, Tony Wells); "Sleep, Baby, Sleep" (Tony Wells)

For their 1970 Off-Broadway musical *The Last Sweet Days of Isaac*, librettist and lyricist Gretchen Cryer and composer Nancy Ford enjoyed a long-running success that offered a pleasant, easy-listening soft rock score with one really superior number ("I Want to Walk to San Francisco"). The evening was comprised of two short one-act musicals, *The Elevator* and *I Want to Walk to San Francisco*, and the latter was a surreal piece in which Isaac is jailed during a protest, watches televised news reports about the event, and then witnesses his own death on camera. It seems that as Isaac filmed the melee, he accidentally strangled himself with his tape recorder and the instrument recorded his death. (Isaac was performed by Austin Pendleton, who directed *Shelter*.)

Cryer and Ford's *Shelter* marked their Broadway debut and their third New York outing (prior to *The Last Sweet Days of Isaac*, their Off-Broadway musical *Now Is the Time for All Good Men* had opened in 1967). But unlike the year's run of *Isaac*, *Shelter* closed after just one month on Broadway. Like *Isaac*, the new musical utilized electronics to tell its story, which (like ***The Selling of the President***) took place entirely in a television studio. The musical also included a computer character named Arthur (whose voice was that of Tony Wells).

Michael (Terry Kiser) writes television commercials and prefers living in a television studio set that simulates a living room rather than in his suburban home with his wife Gloria (Joanna Merlin) and their seven adopted children, all from different racial backgrounds. Michael's best friend, Arthur, is a computer who's always ready to give advice and counsel; the electronic devices about the studio allow for projections on a cyclorama which depict the bucolic scenery of a farm or the skyscape of a starry night, and thus can transform the sterile environment of the television studio into the semblance of the outside world; a tape recorder provides the comforting sound of crickets chirping away during the evening; and prop plastic flowers are always perfect and never wilt.

Michael soon meets (and sleeps with) Maud (Marcia Rodd), an actress who appears in television commercials and whose husband has walked out on her, and he's also involved with cleaning lady Wednesday November (Susan Browning, who played April in ***Company***). But Gloria sends the two women packing; after all, hers and Michael's marriage may be "no good," but they do have a "working relationship."

Douglas Watt in the *New York Daily News* said the "unnerving bit of musical whimsy" with its "sorry materials" would be "looked down upon as childish by the *Sesame Street* audience," and when Miss November plays a string-less guitar and states she knows "only two chords," he felt the character was speaking directly for the composer. Richard Watts in the *New York Post* found *Shelter* "far inferior" to *Isaac*, but noted that while the evening lacked humor, the songs were "steadily fresh and attractive."

Martin Gottfried in *Women's Wear Daily* said the script was "uncontrolled," the score "unmusical," the leading performances "bland," and the direction "confidently obvious." Edwin Wilson in the *Wall Street Journal* felt the early scenes were promising: during the overture, an electronic image of a red line danced across the curtain, and in Michael's soft-shoe salute to Gloria ("She's My Girl"), his movements were accompanied by an array of flashing electronic pictures of her. But midway through the evening the plot abruptly changed direction, and issues raised in the first act were scuttled in favor of "twenty minutes of pseudo-psychological chatter."

Leonard Probst on NBC Radio liked the "zany, kooky, foolish and essentially improbable" musical, which he felt was a spoof of Broadway sex comedies. Leonard Harris on WCBSTV2 suggested that if the musical had consisted of just the first act, the evening might have been a "smash," but the "disease" of "second-act problems" soon crossed "the line from cute to cutesy." And Kevin Sanders on WABCTV7 said that *Shelter* ranked with ***Dude*** and ***Via Galactica*** as "one of the all-time lousy Broadway musicals"; it was "an utterly pointless, inane, inept waste of time, money and talent."

Clive Barnes in the *New York Post* decided the musical was "very likable" and "most engagingly staged," but whether "this will prove enough remains to be seen." The music was "sweet," the show was "kooky," and while the production wasn't for those who prefer "bold and brassy" musicals, those looking for an "intimate, even cozy" chamber musical would find *Shelter* "a warmly pleasant evening." But he noted the "central situation" about a character living in a television studio set was "unbelievable" and thus the plot detracted from "the wry humor of the writing." In the same newspaper, Walter Kerr indicated the "amusing and possibly pertinent premise for a lightly ironic entertainment" morphed into "routine bedroom farce" and thus replaced "what started out as wryly inverted comment."

Columbia Records recorded the cast album, but due to the musical's short run declined to release it. However, a tape of the album somehow escaped from the company's archives and made the rounds of show music collectors. The script was published in paperback by Samuel French in 1973.

In 1980, Cryer and Ford combined *Isaac*'s *The Elevator* with *Shelter* and the result was *Isaac & Ingrid & Michael*, which was produced at the Center for the Arts in Purchase, New York. A revised version of *Isaac & Ingrid & Michael* was given a limited run at the Off-Off-Broadway York Theatre on April 6, 1997, and was recorded as *Shelter* (Original Cast Records CD # OC-9785). The recording includes most of the songs from *The Elevator*; seven songs from the original *Shelter* ("Woman on the Run," "Changing," "It's Hard to Care," "Mary Margaret's House in the Country," "Sleep, My Baby, Sleep," "I Bring Him Sea Shells," and "She's My Girl"); and two new numbers ("Like a River" and "Goodbye, Plastic Flowers").

Shelter was first presented at the Playhouse in the Park in Cincinnati, Ohio, in June 1972.

A LITTLE NIGHT MUSIC

"A New Musical"

Theatre: Shubert Theatre (during run, the musical transferred to the Majestic Theatre)
Opening Date: February 25, 1973; *Closing Date*: August 3, 1974
Performances: 600
Book: Hugh Wheeler
Lyrics and *Music*: Stephen Sondheim
Based on the 1955 film *Smiles of a Summer Night* (screenplay and direction by Ingmar Bergman).
Direction: Harold Prince; *Producers*: Harold Prince in association with Ruth Mitchell; *Choreography*: Patricia Birch; *Scenery*: Boris Aronson; *Costumes*: Florence Klotz; *Lighting*: Tharon Musser; *Musical Direction*: Harold Hastings
Cast: Benjamin Rayson (Mr. Lindquist), Teri Ralston (Mrs. Nordstrom), Barbara Lang (Mrs. Anderssen), Gene Varrone (Mr. Erlanson), Beth Fowler (Mrs. Segstrom), Judy Kahan (Fredrika Armfeldt), Hermione Gingold (Madame Armfeldt), George Lee Andrews (Frid), Mark Lambert (Henrik Egerman), Victoria Mallory (Anne Egerman), Len Cariou (Fredric Egerman), D. Jamin-Bartlett (Petra), Glynis Johns (Desiree Armfeldt), Despo (Malla), Will Sharpe Marshall (Bertrand), Laurence Guittard (Count Carl-Magnus Malcolm), Patricia Elliott (Countess Charlotte Malcolm), Sherry Mathis (Osa)
The musical was presented in two acts.
The action takes place in Sweden at the turn of the twentieth century.

Musical Numbers

Act One: Overture (Benjamin Rayson, Teri Ralston, Barbara Lang, Gene Varrone, Beth Fowler); "Night Waltz" (aka "Night Waltz I") (Company); "Now" (Len Cariou); "Later" (Mark Lambert); "Soon" (Victoria Mallory, Mark Lambert, Len Cariou); "The Glamorous Life" (Judy Kahan, Glynis Johns, Despo, Hermione Gingold, Teri Ralston, Beth Fowler, Barbara Lang, Benjamin Rayson, Gene Varrone); "Remember?" (Benjamin Rayson, Teri Ralston, Beth Fowler, Gene Varrone, Barbara Lang); "You Must Meet My Wife" (Glynis Johns, Len Cariou); "Liaisons" (Hermione Gingold); "In Praise of Women" (Laurence Guittard); "Every Day a Little Death" (Patricia Elliott, Victoria Mallory); "A Weekend in the Country" (Company)
Act Two: The Sun Won't Set" (Barbara Lang, Beth Fowler, Teri Ralston, Benjamin Rayson, Gene Varrone); "The Sun Sits Low" (aka "Night Waltz II") (Teri Ralston, Gene Varrone); "It Would Have Been Wonderful" (Len Cariou, Laurence Guittard); "Perpetual Anticipation" (Teri Ralston, Beth Fowler, Barbara Lang); "Send in the Clowns" (Glynis Johns); "The Miller's Son" (D. Jamin-Bartlett); Finale (Company)

Despite their praise for Stephen Sondheim's ethereal music and brilliant lyrics, a few critics thought *A Little Night Music* was a letdown after his and Harold Prince's groundbreaking concept musicals ***Company*** and ***Follies***. The new musical was an atmospheric mood piece about the many variations of romantic love, and while there was a story of sorts the work was also somewhat nonlinear in its concept-musical-styled look at romance and how it dominates those who obsess over lost love, present love, and even future love.

Set in turn-of-the-twentieth-century Sweden, the musical centered on Desiree Armfeldt (Glynis Johns), an actress currently on tour with a play that is booked in her home town where her mother Madame Armfeldt (Hermione Gingold) lives on a great estate. Also living in the town is Desiree's old flame, lawyer Fredrik Egerman (Len Cariou), who has no idea he's the father of Desiree's teenage daughter Fredrika (Judy Kahan). Fredrik is married to a young woman just five years older than Fredrika, the lovely Anne (Victoria Mallory), and eleven months after their marriage Anne is still a virgin (but a lyric asks, "What's one small shortcoming?"). Fredrik and Desiree are clearly still interested in one another, just as Henrik (Mark Lambert), Fredrik's young adult son from his first marriage, is clearly attracted to Anne, who alternately taunts and flirts with him. To add to the mix is Desiree's current amour, the pompous and jealous popinjay Count Carl-Magnus Malcolm (Laurence Guittard) who comes upon the scene and is distressed to discover Desiree's involvement with Fredrik, and he's soon followed by his wife Countess Charlotte (Patricia Elliott), who loves her husband and is determined to win him back. On the sidelines are Madame Armfeldt's butler, Frid (George Lee

Andrews), and Anne's maid, Petra (D. Jamin-Bartlett), both of whom view love less cerebrally than the other characters.

Romantic matters come to a head when Madame Armfeldt invites everyone to her country estate for the weekend, and by the end of the weekend the relationships adjust themselves when Henrik runs off with Anne, Fredrik realizes he's always been in love with Desiree, and Charlotte and Carl-Magnus resume their somewhat waspish relationship.

Hugh Wheeler's economical book was generally incisive and direct, and perfectly complemented Sondheim's beautiful waltz-time score (all the songs were in three-quarter time or variations thereof). Sondheim dazzled in number after number. The three-part "Later," "Now," and "Soon" is a brilliant set piece in which Fredrik, Henrik, and Anne address their sexual frustrations and hang-ups; "Liaisons" is Madame Armfeldt's bittersweet look at her past conquests (along the way she acquired position and a "tiny Titian"); Fredrik and Desiree's gorgeous conversational duet "You Must Meet My Wife" is both amusing and rueful; Charlotte and Anne's introspective "Every Day a Little Death" describes how each day's trivialities overtake and diminish one's life, and was thematically related to Wordsworth's comment about the "sad etceteras" of our existence; "The Sun Won't Set" is perhaps the most haunting waltz heard on Broadway in decades; the sweeping "A Weekend in the Country" found the guests anticipating the upcoming weekend; "The Miller's Son" depicts Petra's direct approach to the progress of love and life, where one will "go" dancing in one's youth and "have" dancing in one's home when one is older and richer; and Desiree's wryly beautiful "Send in the Clowns" with its appropriate theatrical imagery became one of the most popular songs of the decade and remains Sondheim's most famous number.

The evening had two annoying flaws, ones that could easily have been corrected during the preproduction and tryout phases of the musical. One was the redundant device of a dumb show that began the musical and in effect played out the plot in shorthand. But its action was oblique, was certainly unclear to most of the audience, and it no doubt was fully grasped only upon a second viewing. The other flaw was equally annoying, but even more distracting because it permeated the entire action of the musical. For some reason, the creators employed a strolling quintet who wandered in and out of the story and commented upon the action in song. They added nothing to the evening, and in fact intruded upon it because they were almost-but-not-quite characters and thus received more attention from the audience than was warranted. At times they seemed to be singing about themselves, and, if so, why? Strangely enough, they were given individual names, and even titles (such as Mrs. Segstrom and Mr. Lindquist), and they came across as too effusive, too smug, and too self-satisfied. Surely Wheeler, Sondheim, and Prince could have eliminated the quintet and found a way to assign most of their music to the main characters.

Martin Gottfried in *Women's Wear Daily* said the "wonderful" and "enchanting" score was "without question" Sondheim's "finest" so far; but the work itself was a "deep disappointment" because the script was bound to the structure of traditional musicals and ignored the "fluid" scripts of Sondheim and Prince's more recent shows. Despite his qualifications about the evening, he noted the work was "still beyond the talent and imagination of most everyone else who does musicals."

Douglas Watt in the *New York Daily News* praised the score, but noted the musical lacked "an actual love song" (but he said "Send in the Clowns" was the show's "most affecting" number). He complained that the overall evening had "little room for the breath of life" and was "too literary and precious a work to stir the emotions." T. E. Kalem in *Time* said he left the theatre with "unbridled admiration and untouched feelings" because the "jeweled music box of a show" was "perhaps too exquisite, fragile and muted ever to be quite humanly affecting." But he said Sondheim's score was a "beauty" and "the best yet in an exceedingly distinguished career." Jack Kroll in *Newsweek* noted that Prince and Sondheim had earned the right "to be measured against the highest standard—their own," and "by any other standards" their new musical was "an emerald in a box of gooseberries." As for Sondheim, his was "one of the most brilliant creative streaks in the history of American musical theatre."

Richard Watts in the *New York Post* found the score "fresh and charming," said the production possessed "style and imagination," and noted the evening's "somewhat unusual quality that combines humor with a strain of sadness." Clive Barnes in the *New York Times* said the musical was "heady, civilized, sophisticated and enchanting," and he praised Sondheim's "breathtaking" lyrics. In the same newspaper, Walter Kerr said the "restlessly inventive" Sondheim had created double soliloquies and trios with "cool crosstalk that snaps like icicles, playing with lyrics as though a keyboard could spell." Here was a score "as friendly as it is musically rich."

During the tryout, Garn Stephens was succeeded by D. Jamin-Bartlett, and the songs "Bang!," "Thoughts on the Terrace," and "Silly People" were cut. George Lee Andrews had introduced the latter, and for the special one-performance-only production *Sondheim: A Musical Tribute* which played at the Shubert Theatre on March 11, 1973, Andrews performed the number, which is included in the *Tribute* cast album (Warner Brothers Records released the two-LP set # 2WS-2705, and RCA issued the two-CD set on # 60515-2).

The script was published in hardback by Dodd, Mead & Company in 1973, and again in hardback by Applause Theatre Book Publishers in 1991. The latter edition includes the lyrics of the unused songs "Two Fairy Tales" and "My Husband the Pig" and the cut songs "Silly People" and "Bang!" "Two Fairy Tales" is also included on the above-referenced *Tribute* album, and is performed by Victoria Mallory and Mark Lambert, whose characters Anne and Fredrik would have sung it had it not been dropped in preproduction. For the 1981 Off-Broadway musical *Marry Me a Little*, the deleted "Two Fairy Tales," "Silly People," and "Bang!" were included (the cast recording was issued by RCA Victor Records LP # ABL1-4159, and the CD by RCA # 7142-2).

The script is also included in the hardback collections *Great Musicals of the American Theatre, Volume Two* (published by the Chilton Book Company in 1976 and edited by Stanley Richards) and *Four by Sondheim* (published by Applause in 2000). The lyrics for the used, unused, cut, and revised songs are in Sondheim's *Finishing the Hat: Collected Lyrics (1954–1981) with Attendant Comments, Principles, Heresies, Grudges, Whines and Anecdotes*, which also includes the unused songs "Numbers" and "Night Waltz III," which seem to have never been recorded.

The original Broadway cast album was recorded by RCA Victor (LP # KS-32265), and later the CD was issued (# CK-32265). Another later CD issue by Sony Classical/Columbia/Legacy (# SK-65284) includes the previously unreleased "Night Waltz II" (aka "The Sun Sits Low"), which had been recorded during the original cast album session but for reasons of length wasn't included on the recording. This CD also includes a bonus track of the rewritten "The Glamorous Life" which was heard in the film version.

The musical has enjoyed four major revivals in New York. The New York City Opera Company presented the work on August 3, 1990, at the New York State Theatre for eleven performances. The cast included Sally Ann Howes (Desiree), Regina Resnik (Madame Armfeldt), Kevin Anderson (Henrik), Michael Maguire (Count Carl-Magnus Malcolm), and Maureen Moore (Countess Charlotte). George Lee Andrews had created the role of Frid for the original Broadway production, and here he performed the role of Fredrik. This revival was shown on public television, but wasn't released on home video. The company brought back the musical a year later with most of the same cast when it opened at the New York State Theatre on July 9, 1991, for seven showings; and on March 7, 2003, the company revived the musical at the New York State Theatre with a cast that included Jeremy Irons (Fredrik), Juliet Stevenson (Desiree), Claire Bloom (Madame Armfeldt), Michele Pawk (Countess Charlotte), and Marc Kudish (Count Carl-Magnus Malcolm).

The fourth revival opened on December 13, 2009, at the Walter Kerr Theatre for 425 performances; the cast included Catherine Zeta-Jones (Desiree) and Angela Lansbury (Madame Armfeldt). Zeta-Jones won the Tony Award for Best Leading Actress in a Musical, and the cast recording was released by Nonesuch/PS Classics (# 523488-2) on a two-CD set.

The first London production opened at the Adelphi Theatre on April 15, 1975, for 406 performances; the cast included Jean Simmons (Desiree), Joss Ackland (Fredrik), Hermione Gingold (Madame Armfeldt), David Kernan (Count Carl-Magnus Malcolm), Diane Langton (Petra), and Liz Robertson (Mrs. Anderssen). The cast album was released by RCA Records (LP # LRL1-5090), and the CD was also issued by RCA (# RCD1-5090).

A second London production opened at the Piccadilly Theatre on October 6, 1989, for 144 performances, and the cast included Dorothy Tutin (Desiree) and Lila Kedrova (Madame Armfeldt). Another London production by the Royal National Theatre opened at the Olivier Theatre on September 26, 1995, with Judi Dench (Desiree), Sian Phillips (Madame Armfeldt), and Lambert Wilson (Count Carl-Magnus Malcolm); for this production, Laurence Guittard (who created the role of the count for the original Broadway production) played Fredric. The revival included a combination of the stage and film versions of "The Glamorous Life" as well as the previously unused "My Husband the Pig."

A 1990 studio cast recording with Sian Phillips (here singing the role of Desiree), Bonaventura Bottone (Henrik), Elisabeth Welch (Madame Armfeldt), and Maria Friedman (Petra) was released by Jay Records (CD # CDTER-1179); a 2000 production seen in Barcelona was released by K Industria Cultural, S.L. (CD # KO26CD); and Terry Trotter's piano recording of songs from the score was released by Varese Sarabande Records (CD # VSD-5819), and includes both the stage and film versions of "The Glamorous Life."

The 1978 film version was produced by New World and Sascha-Wien Films and released by Roger Corman and New World Pictures; directed by Harold Prince, the cast includes Elizabeth Taylor (Desiree), and from the original Broadway production, Len Cariou, Hermione Gingold, and Laurence Guittard. Others in the cast are Diana Rigg (Countess Charlotte) and Lesley-Anne Down (Anne). Sondheim wrote new lyrics for "Night Waltz" (as "Love Takes Time") and "The Glamorous Life," and these are included in the 1991 edition of the script published by Applause as well as in *Finishing the Hat*. Sondheim also revised "Every Day a Little Death" for the film; besides the three revised numbers, the following songs retained for the film are "Now," "Later," "Soon," "You Must Meet My Wife," "A Weekend in the Country," "It Would Have Been Wonderful," and "Send in the Clowns." The soundtrack was released by Columbia Records (LP # JS-35333), and the DVD was issued by Hen's Tooth Video.

Awards

Tony Awards and Nominations: Best Musical (***A Little Night Music***); Best Leading Actor in a Musical (Len Cariou); Best Leading Actress in a Musical (**Glynis Johns**); Best Featured Actor in a Musical (Laurence Guittard); Best Featured Actress in a Musical (**Patricia Elliott**); Best Featured Actress in a Musical (Hermione Gingold); Best Director of a Musical (Harold Prince); Best Book (**Hugh Wheeler**); Best Score (**Stephen Sondheim**); Best Scenic Designer (Boris Aronson); Best Costume Designer (Florence Klotz); Best Lighting Designer (Tharon Musser)

New York Drama Critics Circle Award: Best Musical (1972–1973) (***A Little Night Music***)

IRENE

"A Musical Comedy"

Theatre: Minskoff Theatre
Opening Date: March 13, 1973; *Closing Date*: September 7, 1974
Performances: 604
Book: Hugh Wheeler and Joseph Stein (based on an adaptation by Harry Rigby); original book by James Montgomery
Lyrics: Joseph McCarthy
Music: Harry Tierney
New Lyrics and *Music*: Otis Clements, Charles Gaynor, Wally Harper, and Jack Lloyd
Direction: Gower Champion; *Producers*: Harry Rigby, Albert W. Selden, and Jerome Minskoff (Steven Beckler, Associate Producer); *Choreography*: Peter Gennaro; *Scenery* and *Costumes*: Raoul Pene du Bois; *Costumes* (for Debbie Reynolds): Irene Sharaff; *Lighting*: David F. Segal; *Musical Direction*: Jack Lee
Cast: Patsy Kelly (Mrs. O'Dare), Janie Sell (Jane Burke), Carmen Alvarez (Helen McFudd), Bruce Lea (Jimmy O'Flaherty), *Debbie Reynolds* (Irene O'Dare), Ruth Warrick (Emmeline Marshall), Bob Freschi (Clarkson), Monte Markham (Donald Marshall), Ted Pugh (Ozzie Babson), George S. Irving (Madame Lucy), Kate O'Brady (Arabella Thornsworthy); Debutantes: Arlene Columbo, Meg Bussert, Carrie Fisher, Dorothy Wyn Gehgan, Marybeth Kurdock, Frances Ruth Lea, Jeanne Lehman, Kate O'Brady, Julie Pars, Pamela Peadon, Pat Trott, Sandra Voris, Jeanette Williamson, Penny Worth; Ninth Avenue Fellas: Paul Charles, Dennis Edenfield, David Evans, Bob Freschi, John Hamilton, Bruce Lea, Joe Lorden, Byran Nicholas, Robert Rayow, Dennis Roth, Kenn Scalice, Ron Schwinn, David Steele, Albert Stephenson
The musical was presented in two acts.
The action takes place in New York City and Long Island in 1919.

Musical Numbers

Act One: "The World Must Be Bigger Than an Avenue" (lyric by Jack Lloyd, music by Wally Harper) (Debbie Reynolds); "The Family Tree" (lyric by Joseph McCarthy, music by Harry Tierney) (Ruth Warrick, Debutantes); "Alice Blue Gown" (lyric by Joseph McCarthy, music by Harry Tierney) (Debbie Reynolds);

"They Go Wild, Simply Wild, Over Me" (lyric by Joseph McCarthy, music by Fred Fisher) (George S. Irving, Debutantes); "An Irish Girl" (lyric by Charles Gaynor, music by Otis Clements) (Debbie Reynolds, Company); "Stepping on Butterflies" (programs credit Wally Harper as composer, but at least one credits lyric to Charles Gaynor and music to Otis Clements) (George S. Irving, Debbie Reynolds, Carmen Alvarez, Janie Sell); "Mother, Angel, Darling" (lyric and music by Charles Gaynor) (Debbie Reynolds, Patsy Kelly); "The Riviera Rage" (dance) (music by Wally Harper) (Debbie Reynolds, Company)

Act Two: "The Last Part of Every Party" (lyric by Joseph McCarthy, music by Harry Tierney) (Company); "We're Getting Away with It" (lyric by Joseph McCarthy, music by Harry Tierney) (George S. Irving, Carmen Alvarez, Janie Sell, Ted Pugh); "Irene" (lyric by Joseph McCarthy, music by Harry Tierney) (Debbie Reynolds, Company); "The Great Lover Tango" (lyric by Charles Gaynor, music by Otis Clements) (Monte Markham, Carmen Alvarez, Janie Sell); "You Made Me Love You" (lyric by Joseph McCarthy, music by James V. Monaco) (Debbie Reynolds, Monte Markham); "You Made Me Love You" (reprise) (George S. Irving, Patsy Kelly); Finale (Company)

While ***Seesaw*** was undergoing one of the most agonizing tryouts in Broadway history, the revival of *Irene* was experiencing tryout traumatitis as well. For reasons known only to the gods who hate musical theatre, venerable classical actor John Gielgud was hired to direct the big-budget song-and-dance spectacle, despite his lack of experience in the field. In fact, his first major foray into the genre was a role in the film musical *Lost Horizon*, which at the time of *Irene*'s premiere had been completed but not yet released. Ultimately, the legendarily bad film and the also-ran *Irene* proved to be two unhappy detours in the actor's otherwise distinguished career, and a few years later he won the Oscar for Best Featured Actor in the frothy 1981 comedy *Arthur*. But there wasn't much froth in *Irene*; it was a workmanlike revival with a few pleasant moments, and although it played for eighteen months, it ended up losing a small fortune.

Gielgud was succeeded as director by Gower Champion, but not before one memorable tryout performance in Toronto when star Debbie Reynolds had laryngitis. She mimed the role as Gielgud sat on the sidelines and spoke her lines. The audience was not amused, and Reynolds reportedly croaked that she didn't have to be up there on the stage, she could have been at home with her "seven maids."

During the tryout, the book was credited to Hugh Wheeler and its adaptation to co-producer Harry Rigby, but by New York both Wheeler and Joseph Stein received book credit while Rigby was still listed as adaptor. Veteran Broadway dancer Eddie Phillips left the show when his role was eliminated, and the following new songs were cut: "The Me That I Want to Be" (lyric by Timothy Grey and Hugh Martin, music by Hugh Martin), "Gimme a Shimmy" (lyric by Charles Gaynor, music by Otis Clements), "This Dear Lady" (lyric by Charles Gaynor, music by Otis Clements), "Paint and Plaster" (writers unknown), "The Fight," and "The Fashion Show" (the last two appear to have been choreographed sequences). The Washington, D.C., tryout program also listed "The Riviera Rag" with lyric by Charles Gaynor and music by Otis Clements; for Broadway, the title was altered to "The Riviera Rage" and the music for the dance number was credited to Wally Harper.

The standards "What Do You Want to Make Those Eyes at Me For?" (lyric by Joseph McCarthy and Howard Johnson, music by James V. Monaco) and "I'm Always Chasing Rainbows" (lyric by Joseph McCarthy, music by Harry Carroll; from the 1918 musical *Oh, Look!*) were also dropped during the tryout and weren't listed in the New York opening night program. But the former was apparently added as a first-act number for the chorus soon after the opening, and the latter was reinstated when Jane Powell succeeded Debbie Reynolds during the course of the Broadway run. The choral version of the former can be heard on the cast album, and while it seems Reynolds never performed the latter song on Broadway, she sings it on the cast album. Incidentally, the program indicates the title song is sung by Debbie Reynolds and chorus, but for the album the number is performed by Monte Markham and chorus.

The musical never quite found its tone, and too often seemed to be an assembly-line product from a not-very-inspired musical comedy factory. ***No, No, Nanette*** occasionally winked at the stage conventions of the 1920s, but it didn't play for camp, and the book, songs, direction, choreography, décor, and performances created a birthday cake of a musical. But *Irene* was like a plate of cookies: some were tasty, but others were way past their expiration date.

The performers did their best, and old reliables George S. Irving and Patsy Kelly did what they could with their campy roles. Irving played a non-drag role as dress designer Madame Lucy, and milked every bit of comic juice out of the essentially clichéd and tiresome role (and garnered a Tony Award, to boot), and Kelly portrayed Debbie Reynolds's Irish mother with her welcome shtick of shrugs-with-attitude. As for Reynolds, she was energetic and gave her all, but the evening allowed her just two opportunities to shine: her rousing opening number "The World Must Be Bigger Than an Avenue," which she sang in shivery show business splendor, and a lively second-act dance that found her and the chorus boys carousing all over a piano store, and even on the pianos themselves.

The plot was the old Cinderella story, here set in the New York neighborhoods and Long Island estates of 1919. The plot asked whether the romance between Ninth Avenue piano tuner Irene O'Dare (Reynolds) and society fella Donald Marshall (Monte Markham) could possibly flower, and the answer was a resounding and unsurprising "yes."

Douglas Watt in the *New York Daily News* said Debbie Reynolds made her stage debut "with the aplomb of a veteran" and praised her "charm and easy assurance." *Irene* was the first production to play at the new Minskoff Theatre, and Watt noted the venue was "bare, colorless and unfriendly." He also noted Irving had never been so "downright entertaining" in the "newly fabricated" role of Madame Lucy (but the character wasn't new, and is listed in the program of the original 1919 production). Richard Watts in the *New York Post* liked the "lively and entertaining" musical, and singled out the piano dance in which the piano tops served as a dance floor for Reynolds and the chorus. Kevin Sanders on WABCTV7 said Reynolds was "breathtaking," the choreography "stunningly superb," the music "buoyant and relaxed," and suggested *Irene* was "perfect" for those who considered ***Pippin*** "too sexy."

But T. E. Kalem in *Time* found the show "as playful as a Detroit assembly line." Champion was the "master of mindless mechanics," and Reynolds performed with an aura of "selfless public service that precluded the display of any private pleasure." Martin Gottfried in *Women's Wear Daily* said the theatre was "new, comfortable, acoustically perfect, characterless and very temporary-looking" and mentioned he "wouldn't be surprised" if after each performance the actors were "plugged out, disassembled and put into little boxes for storage" until the next performance. He said the musical had an "industrial heart" with no "style," "purpose," or "human energy." It was "simply manufactured." Edwin Wilson in the *Wall Street Journal* suggested the creators couldn't decide whether *Irene* was "an authentic period piece, a revival, a parody, a potpourri, or just what."

The original production of *Irene* opened at the Vanderbilt Theatre on November 18, 1919, with Edith Day in the title role. When it closed after 670 performances, it was the longest-running musical in Broadway history, "Alice Blue Gown" became one of the biggest song hits of the era, and musicals with Cinderella stories became the rage. Day also appeared in the London production, which opened at the Empire Theatre on April 7, 1920, for 399 performances.

The revival included four songs from the original production ("Alice Blue Gown," "We're Getting Away with It," "The Last Part of Any Party" aka "The Last Part of Every/Ev'ry Party," and the title song) and omitted seven ("Hobbies," "Castle of Dreams," "The Talk of the Town," "To Be Worthy of You," "To Love You," "Sky Rocket," and "There's Something in the Air"). "The Family Tree" (lyric by Joseph McCarthy and music by Harry Tierney) is often cited as part of the 1919 score, but it wasn't listed in the program of the original production (for its inclusion in the 1973 revival, Charles Gaynor revised the lyric).

Except for "There's Something in the Air," the 1920 London cast album includes every song from the original production (the recording was later released by Monmouth-Evergreen Records LP # MES-7057). The 1973 Broadway cast album was released by Columbia Records (LP # KS-32266) and issued on CD by Sony Broadway (# 32266) and includes "What Do You Want to Make Those Eyes at Me For?" and "I'm Always Chasing Rainbows," both of which were added to the revival after its opening. The 1973 Broadway revival was produced in London at the Adelphi Theatre on June 15, 1976, and the cast album was released by EMI Records (LP # EMC-3139/OC-062-06165).

The 1940 film version was released by RKO and the DVD is available on the Warner Brothers Archive Collection. It was directed by Herbert Wilcox, starred Anna Neagle (Mrs. Wilcox), Ray Milland, Alan Marshall, Billie Burke, Roland Young, May Robson, Marsha Hunt, Isabel Jewell, Ethel Griffies, and Arthur Treacher, and includes two new songs by McCarthy and Tierney ("You've Got Me Out on a Limb" and "Sweet Vermosa Brown") and five from the original production ("Alice Blue Gown," "Castle of Dreams," "There's Something in the Air," "To Be Worthy of You," and the title song). The film was photographed in black and white, but changed into Technicolor for a ballroom sequence that included "Alice Blue Gown." A silent version of the musical was released by First National Pictures in 1926 and starred Colleen Moore.

Among the cast members of the revival was Debbie Reynolds's daughter, Carrie Fisher. For her Broadway debut, Jane Powell succeeded Reynolds, but the occasion was one in which she and Champion came to a parting of the ways (they had previously worked together on the 1958 film musical *The Girl Most Likely*, in which she starred and he choreographed). According to John Anthony Gilvey's biography of Champion *Before the Parade Passes By*, Powell called Champion (who was in California), and asked if he would direct her. He refused to return to New York, and furthermore told her he "didn't like" the show, "didn't like" musicals, and was only interested in directing films. He then said that since he was a friend of hers, he could give her "a few minutes." Powell reportedly told him his response showed he wasn't her friend, that she therefore was no longer his friend, and that his ego had "gone too big." As a result, and at Champion's request, his name was removed from the theatre programs.

For one who "didn't like" musicals, Champion was soon back on Broadway and associated with four flops. He directed and choreographed both ***Mack & Mabel*** (1974; despite its winning score by Jerry Herman, the musical was dreary, tiresome, and miscast and played for just sixty-six performances) and ***Rockabye Hamlet*** (1976; seven performances); was an uncredited consultant for ***The Act*** (1977; 233 performances; during Barry Nelson's vacation, Champion spelled for him, and at one memorable matinee Champion was on stage in Nelson's role, and Nelson was in the audience watching him); and he "supervised" ***A Broadway Musical*** (1978; one performance). Of course, there was one more musical in Champion's future, and it was one of the biggest hits in Broadway history. His dance-driven *42nd Street* ran for 3,486 performances, and its premiere on August 25, 1980, was one of a handful of truly legendary Broadway opening nights: at the curtain call when the performers took their bows, producer David Merrick appeared on the stage and informed both the actors and the audience that Champion had died just a few hours earlier. It's seldom that a Broadway opening makes headlines, but this one did.

As for Champion's wish to direct only movies, he did so just twice: *My Six Loves* (which was released in 1963 and starred Debbie Reynolds) and *Bank Shot* (1974).

Seesaw's leading man, Ken Howard, left that show three months after its Broadway opening, and Monte Markham left *Irene* after three months as well (he was succeeded by Ron Husmann). Later in the run of *Irene*, Hans Conried succeeded George S. Irving as Madame Lucy; and at various times Justine Johnston and Mary McCarty were standbys for Patsy Kelly.

Awards

Tony Awards and Nominations: Best Leading Actress in a Musical (Debbie Reynolds); Best Featured Actor in a Musical (**George S. Irving**); Best Featured Actress in a Musical (Patsy Kelly); Best Choreographer (Peter Gennaro)

SEESAW

"A New Musical"

Theatre: Uris Theatre (during run, the musical transferred to the Mark Hellinger Theatre)
Opening Date: March 18, 1973; *Closing Date*: December 8, 1973
Performances: 296
Book: Michael Bennett
Lyrics: Dorothy Fields
Music: Cy Coleman
Based on the 1958 play *Two for the Seesaw* by William Gibson.
Direction: Michael Bennett; *Producers*: Joseph Kipness and Lawrence Kasha, James Nederlander, George M. Steinbrenner III, and Loren E. Price; *Choreography*: Michael Bennett (Grover Dale, Co-Choreographer; Bob Avian and Tommy Tune, Associate Choreographers); *Scenery*: Robin Wagner; *Media Art* and *Photography*: Sheppard Kerman; *Costumes*: Ann Roth; *Lighting*: Jules Fisher; *Musical Direction*: Don Pippin
Cast: *Ken Howard* (Jerry Ryan), *Michele Lee* (Gittel Mosca), Tommy Tune (David), Cecelia Norfleet (Sophie), Giancarlo Esposito (Julio Gonzales), LaMonte Peterson (later changed last name to des Fontaines) (Sparkle), Judy McCauley (Nurse), Cathy Brewer-Moore (Ethel); Citizens of New York: John Almberg, Steve Anthony, Cathy Brewer-Moore, Eileen Casey, Wayne Cilento, Patti D'Beck, Terry Deck, Judy Gibson, Felix Greco, Mitzi Hamilton, Loida Iglesias, Bobby Johnson, Baayork Lee, Amanda McBroom, Judy Mc-

Cauley, Anita Morris, Gerry O'Hara, Michon Peacock, Frank Pietri, Yolanda Raven, Michael Reed, Orrin Reiley, Don Swanson, William Swiggard, Tom Urich, Dona D. Vaughn, Clyde Walker, Thomas J. Walsh, Chris (Crissy) Wilzak

The musical was presented in two acts.

The action takes place during the present time in New York City.

Musical Numbers

Act One: "Seesaw" (Full Company); "My City" (Ken Howard, The Neighborhood Girls); "Nobody Does It Like Me" (Michele Lee); "In Tune" (Michele Lee, Ken Howard); "Spanglish" (Giancarlo Esposito, Michele Lee, Ken Howard, Cecelia Norfleet, Full Company); "Welcome to Holiday Inn!" (Michele Lee); "You're a Lovable Lunatic" (Ken Howard); "He's Good for Me" (Michele Lee); "Ride Out the Storm" (LaMonte Peterson, Cecelia Norfleet, Full Company)

Act Two: "We've Got It" (Ken Howard); "Poor Everybody Else" (Michele Lee); "Chapter 54, Number 1909" (Tommy Tune, Ken Howard, Michele Lee, Dancers); "The Concert" (Michele Lee, Dancers, Tommy Tune, Full Company); "It's Not Where You Start" (Tommy Tune, Full Company); "I'm Way Ahead" (Michele Lee); "Seesaw" (reprise) (Michele Lee)

Seesaw was based on William Gibson's 1958 hit two-character play *Two for the Seesaw*, which starred Anne Bancroft and Henry Fonda and played for 750 performances (it was filmed in 1962 with Shirley MacLaine and Robert Mitchum). The story was about the slightly pathetic and seemingly eternal loser Gittel Mosca (Michele Lee), a Brooklyn Jewish girl, and her affair with visiting WASP lawyer Jerry Ryan (Ken Howard), who is separated from his wife. The two meet and have an affair, but in the end Jerry returns to Omaha and his wife.

Instead of adapting the play in *I Do! I Do!* (1966) fashion as an intimate two-character musical, librettist Michael Stewart (and later Michael Bennett), lyricist Dorothy Fields, and composer Cy Coleman opened up the bittersweet play with incidental characters and time-filler material. As a result, the basic story line was crushed under the weight of a huge production that often forgot to focus on the two leads. In fact, there were really two musical versions of *Seesaw*, one seen during its tryout and the other a revised version that opened on Broadway, and both missed the mark because their traditional Broadway blockbuster mentality didn't trust the small-scale intimacy of the original story.

Seesaw was in many ways reminiscent of Coleman and Fields's 1966 hit *Sweet Charity*. Both shows offered outwardly tough but essentially vulnerable girls in modern-day Manhattan who are always involved with the wrong kind of men and wind up being alone. They even shared the same song: Charity's "Poor Everybody Else" was dropped during the tryout of *Sweet Charity*, but was reinstated for Gittel in *Seesaw*.

Sweet Charity was purposely structured with revue-like episodes peppered with a slightly satiric viewpoint; dance was used to move the story along, and its minor characters were given little in the way of stage time. But *Seesaw* wavered between the doomed love affair of Gittel and Jerry and the out-of-nowhere subplot of Gittel's friend David and his show-business aspirations. The two stories never really merged, and David's scenes and songs were shoehorned into the action; moreover, there was a pointless scene when Puerto Rican characters sang of their "Spanglish" language, and the first act ended with an extraneous nightclub sequence. The musical's big show-stopping number, the effervescent "It's Not Where You Start," was a lavish brew of multicolored lights, balloons, confetti, streamers, a *Hello, Dolly!*–like staircase, white top hats, and a kick line, but it threw the second act off balance because it had nothing to do with the main story. In general, the score was more serviceable than inspired, although the title song had a memorably haunting air about it, and Gittel's establishing number "Nobody Does It Like Me" and at the end her hopeful "I'm Way Ahead," were standouts (and since these two songs reflect the attitude and mood of Charity at the beginning and end of *Sweet Charity*, they could easily be interpolated into a production of that show; in fact, "Nobody Does It Like Me" would be a marked improvement over "Charity's Soliloquy").

When *Seesaw* opened in Detroit, Lainie Kazan starred as Gittel, and others in the cast were Joshie Jo Armstead (Sophie), Bill Starr (Larry), Richard Ryder (Ralph), and Christine (aka Chris and Crissy) Wilzak (Gretchen). There were forty-one players in the company and fifty-six speaking roles, and the book was by Michael Stewart, the direction by Edwin Sherin, and the choreography by Grover Dale. The musical underwent one of the most public and painful of all Broadway tryouts, and between Detroit and New York, Michael Bennett replaced Sherin and Dale (the latter retained credit as co-choreographer, and Bob Avian and Tommy Tune were brought in as associate choreographers). Stewart's book was rewritten by Bennett, and Tommy Tune joined the company along with Baayork Lee, Wayne Cilento, and Anita Morris. But as new cast members were added, some were dropped. Kazan was replaced by Michele Lee, Armstead by Cecelia Norfleet, and the roles of Larry, Ralph, and Gretchen were eliminated (but Wilzak remained with the company as a chorus member and later understudied Cecelia Norfleet and Lucie Arnaz, who starred in the national tour). There were now just eight speaking roles, and the entire company totaled thirty-five players. By the New York opening night, seven songs had been cut: "Pick Up the Pieces," "Big Fat Heart," "Highly Emotional State," "Tutu and Tights," "More People Like You," "Visitors," and "Megatron." (Ken Howard left the musical three months into the New York run, and was temporarily succeeded by Nicholas Coster and then permanently by John Gavin, who later starred in the national tour with Arnaz.)

The musical's grueling birth pains were widely publicized, and the *New York Times* published Patricia Bosworth's in-depth analysis of the tryout's traumas. This article was quickly followed by a lengthy letter to the newspaper by Lainie Kazan, who gave her side of the story. For example, Bosworth reported that three days before the Detroit opening, a representative of Columbia Records had witnessed an "ugly fight" between Sherin and Kazan, and on the following day the company decided not to sign a contract to record the cast album. In her reply, Kazan clearly resented the article's implication that the argument affected Columbia's decision, and she amusingly and waspishly noted in a backhanded slap to Coleman that it is "common knowledge that the decision of a record company to record an original cast album is usually predicated on the quality of the musical score."

The cast album itself (which was eventually recorded by Buddah Records LP # BDS-95006-1-OC/0698) became the subject of another *Times* article, and then a few days after the opening the musical received a torrent of publicity when then-mayor John Lindsay (who bore a striking resemblance to Ken Howard) made a cameo appearance in the early first-act number "My City." But all the attendant publicity didn't help. *Seesaw* ran out the year and played for almost three hundred performances, but reportedly lost an estimated $1.3 million.

Clive Barnes in the *New York Times* said *Seesaw* certainly had its "ups and downs" and there was a "bland and yet efficient slickness" about it. It was "constructed" rather than "inspired," and was "well-crafted" if not "top-drawer." He praised in particular the production's decor, and noted the cityscape projections gave the show a "very good" look. T. E. Kalem in *Time* felt the musical lost the "taste, flavor," and "identity" of Gibson's original play, but the "entertainment hybrid" nonetheless offered lively dances and a pleasant if unmemorable score.

Douglas Watt in the *New York Daily News* complained that the intimate plot and the "big" and "brassy" production "never truly become one." Richard Watts in the *New York Post* said he preferred the original play to the musical, but he praised the "brilliant" performances of Lee and Howard, the "imaginative" dances, and the "steadily agreeable and tuneful score." Jack Kroll in *Newsweek* said the show inspired "more affection" than the season's other musicals, but he felt it somewhat wavered after a promising opening because Bennett was never able to get a perfect "push-pull rhythm" to join both the intimate story and the "expansive" production numbers.

Martin Gottfried in *Women's Wear Daily* liked the "colorful, expansive, cheerful" dances and praised Bennett for giving the evening a "professional look our musical theatre has almost forgotten." These attributes helped assuage the "obvious failure" of the show's intentions, its "patchwork construction," and its "raging inconsistency." The "whole" of *Seesaw* was "less than its individual parts," and while the show wasn't "great" it nonetheless worked.

The script was published in paperback by Samuel French in 1975. The CD of the cast album was released by DRG (# 6108), and the collection *Lost in Boston III* (Varese Sarabande CD # VSD-5563) includes the deleted "Big Fat Heart" and "Pick Up the Pieces."

For the national tour, "Ride Out the Storm" was replaced by "The Party's on Me," and while "Spanglish" was heard during the early months of the tour, it was later cut from the production.

The musical was revived by the Equity Library Theatre on October 29, 1981, for thirty-two performances; the production included "Spanglish" and "The Party's on Me," but not "Ride Out the Storm."

Awards

Tony Awards and Nominations: Best Musical (*Seesaw*); Best Leading Actress in a Musical (Michele Lee); Best Featured Actor in a Musical (**Tommy Tune**); Best Director of a Musical (Michael Bennett); Best Book (Michael Bennett); Best Score (music by Cy Coleman and lyrics by Dorothy Fields); Best Choreographer (**Michael Bennett**)

CYRANO

"A New Musical"

Theatre: Palace Theatre
Opening Date: May 13, 1973; *Closing Date*: June 23, 1973
Performances: 49
Book: Based on an adaptation by Anthony Burgess
Lyrics: Anthony Burgess
Music: Michael J. Lewis
Based on the 1897 play *Cyrano de Bergerac* by Edmond Rostand.
Direction: Michael Kidd; *Producers*: Richard Gregson and APJAC International; *Choreography*: Although uncredited in the program, the dances were staged by Michael Kidd; *Scenery*: John Jensen; *Costumes*: Desmond Heeley; *Lighting*: Gilbert V. Hemsley Jr.; *Musical Direction*: Thomas Pierson
Cast: Paul Berget (Candle Lighter, Cyrano's Page), Anthony Inneo (Candle Lighter, Actor), Bob Heath (Doorman), Tovah Feldshuh (Foodseller), Danny Villa (The Marquis in Yellow), Michael Nolan (Musketeer), Donovan Sylvest (Cavalryman), Geoff Garland (Pickpocket, Capucine Monk), James Richardson (Citizen), Tim Nissen (Citizen's Brother, Boy, Cyrano's Page), Alexander Orfaly (The Marquis in Red), Joel Craig (The Marquis in Beige), Arnold Soboloff (Ragueneau), Mark Lamos (Christian de Neuvillette), Betty Leighton (Madame Aubry, Lise, Sister Marguerite), Janet McCall (Madame de Guemene), Patricia Roos (Barthenoide, Sister Claire), Mimi Wallace (Felixerie), Mary Straten (Urimedonte), James Blendick (Le Bret), Leigh Beery (Roxana), Anita Dangler (Roxana's Duenna, Sister Marthe), Louis Turenne (Count de Guiche), J. Kenneth Campbell (Viscount de Valvert), Richard Schneider (Actor), Vicki Frederick (Actress), Jill Rose (Actress), Michael Goodwin (Jodelet), Patrick Hines (Montfleury), *Christopher Plummer* (Cyrano de Bergerac), Paul Berget (Boy); Bakery Staff: J. Kenneth Campbell, Geoff Garland, Janet McCall, Michael Nolan, James Richardson, Patricia Roos, Mary Straten; Gascon Cadets and Soldiers: J. Kenneth Campbell, Joel Craig, Michael Goodwin, Bob Heath, Anthony Inneo, Gale McNeeley, Michael Nolan, James Richardson, Richard Schneider, Donovan Sylvest, Danny Villa; Georges Spelvinet (Theophraste Renaudot); Nuns: Tovah Feldshuh, Vicki Frederick, Janet McCall, Jill Rose, Mary Straten, Mimi Wallace
The musical was presented in two acts.
The action takes place both in Paris and Arras in 1640 and in 1654.

Musical Numbers

Act One: "Cyrano's Nose" (Christopher Plummer); "La France, La France" (Company); "Tell Her" (James Blendick, Christopher Plummer); "From Now Till Forever" (Christopher Plummer, Company); "Bergerac" (Christopher Plummer, Leigh Beery); "Pocapdedious" (Gascon Cadets); "No, Thank You" (Christopher Plummer); "From Now Till Forever" (reprise) (Christopher Plummer, Mark Lamos)
Act Two: "Roxana" (Mark Lamos, Company); "It's She and It's Me" (Mark Lamos); "You Have Made Me Love" (Leigh Beery); "Thither, Thother, Thide of the" (Christopher Plummer); "Pocapdedious" (reprise) (James Blendick, Gascon Cadets); "Paris Cuisine" (Christopher Plummer, James Blendick, Gascon Cadets); "Love Is Not Love" (Leigh Beery); "Autumn Carol" (Leigh Beery, Nuns); "I Never Loved You" (Christopher Plummer)

Edmond Rostand's play *Cyrano de Bergerac* premiered in Paris at the Theatre de la Porte Saint-Martin on December 28, 1897, with Benoit Constant in the title role; the first Broadway production opened at the

Garden Theatre on October 3, 1898, with Richard Mansfield. The current musical version is one of at least sixteen lyric adaptations of the work (see below), and all of them were jinxed. Not one has found a permanent place in the standard repertoire of opera or musical theatre, and the current version closed after six weeks on Broadway.

The familiar story told of the ugly Cyrano de Bergerac (Christopher Plummer) and his unrequited love for the lovely Roxana (Leigh Beery). The handsome but not particularly bright Christian de Neuvillette (Mark Lamos) also loves Roxana, and so Cyrano helps the young man win her affection by authoring letters that Roxana assumes were written by Christian. Christian dies in battle, and many years later Roxana lives in a convent and is ever true to her love for him. One day the dying Cyrano is brought to the convent, and although he denies having written the letters from Christian that Roxana holds so dear, she comes to realize it was he and not Christian who wrote the letters, and that Cyrano has always loved her.

Edwin Wilson in the *Wall Street Journal* said that Christopher Plummer's "magnificent" performance and the scenes from the play itself were worth seeing; otherwise, the musical side of the evening was redundant, and the score wavered between opera and traditional musical comedy with songs that echoed those in *South Pacific* (1949) and *The Sound of Music* (1959). Douglas Watt in the *New York Daily News* found the evening "awesomely silly" and felt the musical was a "mélange" of *The Vagabond King* (1926), *The Sound of Music* (1959), and *Man of La Mancha* (1965).

Richard Watts in the *New York Post* praised Plummer for making the production an "interesting" one, and said the evening was the performer's "personal triumph." But T. E. Kalem in *Time* said the "dry, businesslike efficiency" of the adaptation affected Plummer's performance. He was too "coolheaded," and while he commanded one's attention, he never captured one's heart. As for the score, it had "the soaring melodic imagination of a computer" and the lyrics were written for "economy" rather than "eloquence."

Martin Gottfried in *Women's Wear Daily* found Plummer "magnificent" but said he had a tendency to "ham"; adding music to the production was "superfluous," and he regretted the story arbitrarily stopped for "unnecessary" songs. For much of the time, the evening was "sluggish," and except for two "beautiful" ballads he found the book "unmusical" and the score reminiscent of "bland movie background music."

While Clive Barnes in the *New York Times* said the production was "altogether very good and partly excellent," he noted the score got in the way of the story. As for Plummer, the actor was giving "one of the best performances in many a season." In the same newspaper, Walter Kerr suggested the songs were a "shade less exhilarating than sheer language might have been" and he felt the musical's creators too often waved the play away "in order to get to production values."

During the tryout, the following songs were cut: "Amorous Morons," "What Does 'I Love You' Mean?," and "Gascon Flute Song."

The cast album was released on a two-LP set by A & M Records (# SP-3702) and includes dialogue sequences; the CD was issued by Broadway Decca (# B0004083-02).

Plummer had previously appeared in the title role of *Cyrano de Bergerac* when a revival of Rostand's play (in a translation by Brian Hooker which was adapted by Michael Langham) was produced by the Stratford Shakespearean Festival in 1962.

The first musical adaptation of Rostand's play opened at the Knickerbocker Theatre on September 18, 1899, for twenty-eight performances with a score by Victor Herbert. Next came Walter Damrosch's operatic adaptation *Cyrano*, which premiered at the Metropolitan Opera House for six performances beginning on February 27, 1913 (Pasquale Amato sang the title role). *Cyrano de Bergerac* (later titled *Roxanne*) closed during its 1932 tryout (book and lyrics by Charles O. Locke, music by Samuel D. Pokrass), but resurfaced during the 1939–1940 season as *The White Plume* (later titled *A Vagabond Hero*) (the book and lyrics were still by Locke, but this time around Pokrass's score was supplemented with new songs by Vernon Duke) and it too closed prior to Broadway.

In between the two Locke versions, Franco Alfano's operatic version premiered in 1936 (and was produced at the Met in 2005). As *Cyrano*, a new musical version opened at Yale University in 1958 with book and lyrics by Richard Maltby Jr., and music by David L. Shire; John Cunningham played the title role, and others in the cast were Richard (Dick) Cavett, Carrie Nye McGeoy, Bill Hinnant, Austin Pendleton, and Roscoe (Lee) Brown. In 1963, a children's version with lyrics and music by Judith Dvorkin opened in North Carolina, and in 1967 and 1973 José Ferrer starred in an adaptation by Robert Wright and George Forrest that played in summer stock as ***A Song for Cyrano***. Ferrer had earlier appeared in a revival of the play at the Alvin (now Neil Simon) Theatre on October 8, 1946, for 195 performances and tied with Fredric March (who starred in

Years Ago) for the Tony Award for Best Leading Actor in a Play; and the 1950 film version brought Ferrer the Academy Award for Best Actor.

On November 21, 1998, a version that had previously been seen in the Netherlands the previous year opened at the Neil Simon Theatre for 137 performances; titled *Cyrano . . . The Musical*, the score was by Ad Van Dijk and the lyrics by Koen Van Dijk (the English lyrics were by Peter Reeves and Sheldon Harnick). In 1992, Reeves had been associated with an Australian version for which he wrote lyrics and music; it seems to have gone unproduced, but in 1994 he was involved with another musical version of the play that was performed in Australia (the book and lyrics were by Hal Shaper, and Reeves composed the music). There have also been three other operatic versions of the play (by Enio Tamberg, Marius Constant, and David DiChiera). The versions by Alfano, Maltby and Shire, Dvorkin, Lewis, Van Dijk, Reeves, Tamberg, and Constant have been recorded, and there are two different recordings of Van Dijk's adaptation, one a Netherlands cast album and the other a symphonic version. With book and lyrics by Leslie Bricusse and music by Frank Wildhorn, the most recent version (as *Cyrano de Bergerac*) was presented in London in 2007, and as of this writing a concept album of the score is scheduled to be released by Global/Vision/Koch. (Counting the Pokrass and later Pokrass/Duke scores as two versions and the 1992 and 1994 productions by Reeves as two versions, there have been at least sixteen musical adaptations of Rostand's play.)

Awards

Tony Awards and Nominations: Best Leading Actor in a Musical (**Christopher Plummer**); Best Featured Actress in a Musical (Leigh Beery)

NASH AT NINE

"A Wordsical"

Theatre: Helen Hayes Theatre
Opening Date: May 17, 1973; *Closing Date*: June 2, 1973
Performances: 21
Verses and *Lyrics*: Ogden Nash
Music: Milton Rosenstock
Direction: Martin Charnin; *Producers*: Les Schecter and Barbara Schwei in association with SRO Enterprises and Arnold Levy; *Scenery*: David Chapman; *Costumes*: Theoni V. Aldredge; *Lighting*: Martin Aronstein; *Musical Direction*: Karen Gustafson
Cast: *E. G. Marshall*, Bill Gerber, Richie Schectman, Virginia Vestoff, Steve Elmore
The revue was presented in one act.

Musical Numbers

Note: The program didn't list individual numbers, but indicated the songs "had been structured from the following works of Ogden Nash."

"Seaside Serenade"; "Fahrenheit Gesundheit"; "The Sniffle"; "Coefficients of Expansion (A Guide to the Infant Season)"; "To a Small Boy Standing on My Shoes While I Am Wearing Them"; "The Madcap Zoologist"; "The Panther"; "The Armadillo"; "The Canary"; "The Shrew"; "Experiment Degustatory"; "The Pig"; "A Bulletin Has Just Come In"; "The Fly"; "The Octopus"; "The Eel"; "The Kipper"; "The Clam"; "The Guppy"; "Barmaids Are Diviner Than Mermaids"; "But I Could Not Love Thee, Ann, So Much, Loved I Not Honore More"; "The Armchair Golfer," or "Whimpers of a Shortchanged Viewer"; "Song of the Open Road"; "From an Antique Land"; "Any Millenniums Today, Lady?"; "Give-Away, Give-Away, Banker Man"; "I Will Arise and Go Now"; "Always Marry an April Girl"; "The Anniversary"; "Love Under the Republicans (or Democrats)"; "A Word to Husbands"; "I'm Sure She Said Six-Thirty"; "To My Valentine"; "Reflections on Ice-Breaking"; "I Do, I Will, I Have"; "The Private Dining Room"; "One Third of a Calendar"; "The Wedding Whistle"; "What's in a Name? Here's What's in a Name, or I Wonder

What Became of John and Mary?"; "No Trouble at All, It's as Easy as Falling Off a Portable Bar"; "Grandpa Is Ashamed"; "A Brief Guide to New York"; "Requiem"; "The Pizza"; "All Quiet Along the Potomac"; "Except the Letter G"; "Shrinking Song"; "Suppose I Darken Your Door"; "You and Me and P.B. Shelley"; "Come, Come, Kerouac! My Generation Is Beater Than Yours"; "The Clean Platter"; "Coffee with the Meal"; "The Middle"; "The Return"; "Peekaboo, I Almost See You"; "Modest Meditations on the Here, the Heretofore, and the Hereafter"; "Birthday on the Beach"; "A Lady Thinks She Is Thirty"; "Crossing the Border"; "For a Good Dog"

The self-described "wordsical" *Nash at Nine* was a modest evening of songs "structured" from the works of poet Ogden Nash. The intimate revue of five performers was a mildly pleasant one, but so wispy it seemed to dissipate as you watched it. The production was far too small for the Helen Hayes Theatre, and probably wouldn't have worked in most Off-Broadway venues, either. Because of the nature of the material, perhaps even a cabaret setting would have been unsuitable. During the 1974–1975 season, the show played Ford's Theatre in Washington, D.C., and even that small house seemed too large for such a small-scale revue.

And just who was the show's target audience? Certainly not tourists, and probably not even regular New York theatergoers. Perhaps the production might have worked best on the college theatre circuit, but even then it might have been too much of Ogden Nash for one sitting. If the concept of the 1955 production *All in One* had taken hold (in which three different theatre pieces shared the same evening), perhaps *Nash at Nine* would have been seen to its best advantage as a short half-hour concert of Nash set to music.

Milton Rosenstock was one of Broadway's major musical directors, and here for the first time he was represented as a composer and not a conductor (he had conducted the original productions of *Gentlemen Prefer Blondes* [1949], *Can-Can* [1953], *Bells Are Ringing* [1956], and *Gypsy* [1959], among others). For *Nash at Nine*, his contributions were pleasant, and one was more than pleasant: the sequence that was based on Nash's "Always Marry an April Girl" was one of the most exquisite theatre ballads of the era. But for the most part Nash's short poems weren't inherently musical and didn't lend themselves to the standard Broadway song treatment.

One particular weakness of the revue was that it lacked a common thread to hold together the dozens of poems. Sometimes the poems were grouped together to suggest a theme (a party or a visit to a zoo), but these devices were somewhat labored. David Chapman's décor helped, because he devised a series of panels upon which were projected definitions of words from a dictionary.

The revue received mixed notices. Douglas Watt in the *New York Daily News* found the evening a "modest, attractive, polished entertainment" and suggested it made the "perfect" after-dinner show (after opening night, all performances were at nine o'clock, as the title indicated). Richard Watts in the *New York Post* liked the "delightful" and "charming" production; Kevin Sanders on WABCTV7 praised the "pleasant," "modest" and sometimes "memorable" evening with its "buoyant" score and "crisp" performances; and Leonard Probst on WNBCTV4 said the show was "mild" but "diverting" and "friendly."

Edwin Wilson in the *Wall Street Journal* had feared an evening of Nash might seem too long, and so he was pleasantly surprised that the revue moved along "like a breeze." But opening the small show in the 1,200-seat Helen Hayes was the "one mistake" that might doom the entire production to "go down the drain." Martin Gottfried in *Women's Wear Daily* said the "white bread" revue "blands you to death," and he noted the material had been written to be read, not performed.

Clive Barnes in the *New York Times* said the revue took Nash's "literate doggerel" and transformed it into "something mongrel." Further, the evening was "unremittingly cute," lacked variety, and thus "*Nash* is no smash" because "a little Nash goes a long way." He noted that while Milton Rosenstock's score was "evanescent" it was also "appropriately gentle"; and the cast was "exceptionally agreeable."

For some of the reviewers, the evening brought to mind television. Gottfried said the cast had been directed "as if for a television screen"; Watt mentioned the revue could very well end up as a television special; and Sanders suggested it was a kind of "relaxed evening-at-home kind of show."

As mentioned, two seasons later the musical was revived for a national tour, which lasted for just six weeks; this time around, the cast was reduced from five to four: Craig Stevens, Harvey Evans, Jane Summerhays, and John Stratton.

SMITH

"A New Musical Comedy"

Theatre: Eden Theatre
Opening Date: May 19, 1973; *Closing Date*: June 3, 1973
Performances: 17
Book: Dean Fuller, Tony Hendra, and Matt Dubey
Lyrics and *Music*: Matt Dubey and Dean Fuller
Direction: Neal Kenyon; *Producers*: Jordan Hott with Robert Anglund, Jack Millstein, Iris Kopelan, and Alexander Bedrosian; *Choreography*: Michael Shawn (Bonnie Walker, Assistant Choreographer); *Scenery*: Fred Voelpel; *Costumes*: Winn Morton; *Lighting*: Martin Aronstein; *Musical Direction*: Richard Parrinello
Cast: Virginia Sandifur (Melody Hazleton), *Don Murray* (Walter Smith), Mort Marshall (Ed Baggett), Carol Morley (Mrs. Smith, Irish Maid), David Horwitz (Pilot, Prompter, Vice President of Slimeroonie), Louis Criscuolo (Ralph), Renee Baughman (Island Beauty), Patricia Garland (Island Beauty, Sydney Jones), Penelope Richards (Island Beauty), Bonnie Walker (Island Beauty, The Dancing Melody), Michael Tartel (Jacques), William James (Policeman, Ernie), David Vosburgh (Policeman, Bruce), Guy Spaull (Chief Punitana), Don Prieur (Servant, Herbie), Ted Thurston (Sinclair Firestone), Nicholas Dante (Hanger-On), Aurelio Padron (Hanger-On), Kenneth Henley (Hanger-On): Singers: Bonnie Hinson, Jacqueline Johnson, Betsy Ann Leadbetter, Shirley Lemmon, David Horwitz, William James, Don Prieur, David Vosburgh; Dancers: Renee Baughman, Patricia Garland, Penelope Richards, Bonnie Walker, John Cashman, Nicholas Dante, Kenneth Henley, Aurelio Padron
The musical was presented in two acts.
The action takes place in the present in New Jersey, New York, and Balinasia.

Musical Numbers

Act One: "Boy Meets Girl" (Ensemble); "There's a Big Job Waiting for You" (Mort Marshall, Ensemble); "There's a Big Job Waiting for You" (reprise) (Carol Morley); "To the Ends of the Earth" (Virginia Sandifur, Passengers); "Balinasia" (Renee Baugham, Patricia Garland, Penelope Richards, Bonnie Walker); "Onh-Honh-Honh!" (Michael Tartel); "Police Song" (William James, David Vosburgh); "You Need a Song" (Louis Criscuolo, Don Murray, Don Prieur, William James, David Vosburgh); "How Beautiful It Was" (Virginia Sandifur, Don Murray, Bonnie Walker); "Island Ritual" (Ensemble); "People Don't Do That" (Don Murray)
Act Two: "You're in New York Now" (Ensemble); "It Must Be Love" (Don Murray, Virginia Sandifur, Ensemble); "Song of the Frog" (Ted Thurston, Don Murray, Mort Marshall); "G'bye" (Virginia Sandifur); "Melody" (Don Murray, Company); "It Must Be Love" (reprise) (Don Murray, Virginia Sandifur)

Smith, the season's final musical, is perhaps one of the decade's cleverest concoctions. It was a major flop, but its amusing conceit is delightful: the nerdy Smith (Don Murray) discovers that his life has turned into a musical comedy and he's the title character. His world goes topsy-turvy and the conventions of musical theatre are the only reality. During the following decades, audiences and critics became used to so-called ironic musicals that kidded the genre, such as *Urinetown* (2002), *The Musical of Musicals* (2003), *Spamalot* (2005), *[title of show]* (2006), *The Drowsy Chaperone* (2006), and *Adrift in Macao* (2007). But prior to *Smith*, only the 1966 Off-Broadway musical *Hooray! It's a Glorious Day . . . and All That* spoofed the genre, and like *Smith* it was generally unappreciated and quickly closed.

But the script of *Smith* reads well, and its catchy songs capture the spirit of the carnival world of 1950s and 1960s musicals. Regional theatres today regurgitate recent musical hits or revive old favorites, and in truth most of their presentations are lazy attempts to bring in box-office cash regardless of whether or not the musicals are appropriate for their small venues. Do major regional theatres really need to produce *Oklahoma!* (1943), *My Fair Lady* (1956), *Les Miserables* (1987), and *Miss Saigon* (1991)? There's a wealth of undiscovered small-scale musicals that would be effective in the regional theatre milieu, but most artistic directors don't have the interest to explore such modest, forgotten gems as *Seventeen* (1951), *Ernest in Love* (1960), *All in Love* (1961), *Riverwind* (1962), and, yes, *Smith*.

Smith is a botanist who works in a dreary laboratory in New Jersey where the lighting is bright fluorescent and the predominant color of the office is gray. Even his secretary Melody (Virginia Sandifur) is plain. One fateful morning he notices a script of a musical on his desk, and realizes it's about him. Suddenly the stage is transformed with music and a dancing chorus, the lab morphs into a room with translucent walls of stained glass the colors of lemon, avocado, and shrimp ("like a salad," Smith notes), and Melody emerges as a beautiful blonde. There's even a stagehand who warns Smith he'd better get used to this new world because he's the star of it.

Suddenly Smith is able to have conversations on prop telephones, and soon he calls his mother to tell her what's happened to him. But his normally understanding and down-to-earth mother instead responds to him with a song and a tap dance. When Smith has to take a business trip to the South Sea Islands (to study a plant that has the properties of both a weight-reducer and an aphrodisiac), he's shocked to discover that a "musical comedy" plane will take him to the island nation of Balinasia where the chief needs a teleprompter in order to say his lines. Meanwhile, Smith has to fight off dressers who appear for his costume changes and who powder his face, and he notes that whenever the lights come up he's "in a perfectly sickening baby pink spot." Balinasia is a true musical comedy island because it has its very own volcano (which eventually erupts with a shower of smoke, dust, papier-mâché lava rock, and orange silly putty).

Smith becomes even more confused when the singing Melody is suddenly replaced by a dancing Melody (Bonnie Walker) who according to the script finishes her number and "acknowledges the audience's applause with a deep reverence and runs off" stage. Smith also has to deal with "finale people" and the fact that despite not liking to rhyme, he's forced to do so when he sings. Another amusing moment occurred early in the second act when a typically Irish musical comedy maid has a one-sided telephone conversation in which she sums up the entire action of the first act and also notes that "it's early afternoon, two weeks later."

Richard Watts in the *New York Post* said the "unheralded" *Smith* was one of the "delights" of the theatre season with an "expertly" handled and "wonderfully fresh and amusing" premise and an "always attractive" score. Leonard Harris on WCBSTV2 got a "kick" out of the "kind of fun" musical, and he found Don Murray "unaffected and charming." And Kevin Sanders on WABCTV7 praised the "bright, funny, ingenious" show with its "double layer of humor," its "wry" characters, and its "pleasantly tuneful" score.

But Martin Gottfried in *Women's Wear Daily* felt the musical's premise was weak and the score "more cliché than mock-cliché." And Douglas Watt in the *New York Daily News* indicated the evening was shapeless and left the "agreeable" cast in search of "something worthwhile to do." But the "catchy" score was in the "cocky, rhythmic and enlivening" mode of Frank Loesser and he singled out the second-act opener "You're in New York Now."

The script was published in paperback by Samuel French in 1972.

Like ***Grease***, *Smith* opened at Off-Broadway's Eden Theatre. *Variety* reported the musical had been slated to open at a traditional Broadway house, but when the musical's projected capitalization of $600,000 wasn't forthcoming the show was re-budgeted for Off Broadway at $375,000. Because the performers had previously signed Broadway contracts, these contracts were in effect for the Off-Broadway run of the musical.

COMEDY

"A Musical Commedia"

The musical opened on November 6, 1972, at the Colonial Theatre in Boston, Massachusetts, and permanently closed there on November 18, 1972.

Book: Lawrence Carra

Lyrics and *Music*: Hugo Peretti, Luigi Creatore, and George David Weiss

Based on the 1622 play *The Great Magician* by Basillo Locatelli.

Direction: Lawrence Carra; *Producers*: Edgar Lansbury, Stuart Duncan, and Joseph Beruh; *Choreography*: Stephen Reinhardt; *Scenery* and *Costumes*: William Pitkin; *Lighting*: Roger Morgan; *Musical Direction*: Joseph Stecko

Cast: Merwin Goldsmith (The Great Magician), George S. Irving (Capitano Cockalorum), Joseph Bova (Coviello), Joseph R. Sicari (Pantalone), Bill McCutcheon (Pulcinella), Jerry Sroka (Doctor Gratiano), Diane J. Findlay (Franceschina, Servant), Frank Vohs (Zanni, Servant), Marty Morris (Melbi, Flavia), George Lee Andrews (Sireno, Silvio), Suellen Estey (Clori, Hortentia), John Witham (Elpino, Lelio), Marc Jordan (Bacchus), Marilyn Saunders (Bacchante), Lana Shaw (Bacchante), Thom Christoph (A Country Fellow), Bobby Lee (Soundman)

The musical was presented in two acts.

The action takes place on the island of Arcadia.

Musical Numbers

Act One: "Comedy" (Troupe); "Open Your Heart" (John Witham, George Lee Andrews, Frank Vohs); "I'm the Cockalorum" (George S. Irving, Joseph Bova, Frank Vohs); "Gotta Hang Out My Wash to Dry" (Diane J. Findlay, John Witham, George Lee Andrews, Frank Vohs, Thom Christoph, Bobby Lee); "Dance Caper" (Diane Findlay, Frank Vohs); "A Friend Is a Friend" (Joseph R. Sicari, Bill McCutcheon, Jerry Sroka); "Where Is My Love" (Suellen Estey, Marty Morris); "God Bless the Fig Tree" (Diane J. Findlay); "Tarantella" (Suellen Estey, Jerry Sroka); "Buttercup" (Joseph Bova, Diane J. Findlay, Troupe); Finale (Troupe)

Act Two: Entr'acte: "Smile, Smile, Smile" (Bobby Lee, Troupe); "Magnetic" (George S. Irving, Marty Morris, Marilyn Saunders, Lana Shaw); "Love Is Such a Fragile Thing" (George Lee Andrews, Suellen Estey, Marty Morris, John Witham); "Breakin' the Spell" (Jerry Sroka, Diane J. Findlay, Frank Vohs, Joseph R. Sicari); "Whirlwind Circle" (Troupe); "Comedy" (reprise) (Troupe)

Comedy billed itself as "A Musical Commedia," and like so many musicals that flirted with a commedia dell'arte framework (see ***Tricks***), it was a fast failure that lasted less than two weeks during its pre-Broadway tryout at Boston's Colonial Theatre. It canceled its scheduled Broadway opening at the Martin Beck (now Al Hirschfeld) Theatre for November 28.

The would-be frolic centered on a group of shipwrecked survivors who come ashore on the strange island of Arcadia, which is ruled by The Great Magician (Merwin Goldsmith) who likes nothing better than to cast spells and cause confusion among everyone. But a happy ending is had by all (except the musical's investors, who reportedly lost $300,000).

Ster in *Variety* complained that the plot was "thin" and was neither "dramatic nor clever enough to sustain interest for long." The score ranged from "rock to country to McGuire Sisters style," and the show incorporated such shticks as fast-talking dialogue routines, vaudeville-type characters, local jokes, and *Hellzapoppin'*-inspired material. *Variety* concluded that the musical had "some potential as a deliberately ridiculous evening, but needs much work before it succeeds on even that level."

During the brief Boston run, choreographer Sammy Bayes was replaced by Stephen Reinhardt.

The cast album was to have been recorded by Bell Records, but was canceled when the musical closed during its tryout.

As *Smile, Smile, Smile* (billed as "A Musical Entertainment"), a revised version of *Comedy* opened Off Broadway at the Eastside Playhouse on April 4, 1973, for seven performances. Clive Barnes's memorably succinct review of *Smile, Smile, Smile* in the *New York Times* stated: "I didn't, I didn't, I didn't." Like *Comedy*, the revised version was scheduled to be recorded by Bell Records, but it too was canceled due to the musical's brief run. The new production included four cast members from *Comedy*, Diane J. Findlay, Bobby Lee, Suellen Estey, and Marilyn Saunders; others in the production were Gary Beach, Rudy Tronto, Donna Liggitt Forbes, and Chip Zien.

Songs in *Smile, Smile, Smile* that were retained from *Comedy* were: "Open Your Heart," "I'm the Cockalorum," "God Bless the Fig Tree," "Buttercup," "Smile, Smile, Smile," "Magnetic," "Love Is Such a Fragile Thing," and "Breakin' the Spell"; songs not used in the revival were: "Comedy," "Gotta Hang My Wash Out to Dry," "Dance Caper," "Where Is My Love," "Tarantella," and "Whirlwind Circle." *Comedy* included the song "A Friend Is a Friend," which may have been rewritten as "Friends" for the new production. New songs included in the revised version were "Haven't I Seen You Somewhere Before?," "Paradise," "To Find True Love," "A Good Old-Fashioned Revolutionary," "Adios," "Garland of Roses," "I'm All for the Good of the People," and "Love Is a Pain."

An earlier production of *Comedy* at the Bucks County Playhouse in New Hope, Pennsylvania, opened during the summer of 1972, and included the song "Sha Na Na Nay" which wasn't heard in the Boston or Off-Broadway versions of the musical.

HALLOWEEN

The musical opened on September 20, 1972, at the Bucks County Playhouse, New Hope, Pennsylvania, and permanently closed there on October 1, 1972.
Book and *Lyrics*: Sidney Michaels
Music: Mitch Leigh
Based on a French play, which was adapted by Sidney Michaels as *Saltpeter in the Rhubarb* (although his musical adaptation of the material was produced as *Halloween*, the straight play version was never staged).
Direction: Albert Marre; *Producers*: Albert Selden and Jerome Minskoff; *Choreography*: Bert Michaels; *Scenery* and *Lighting*: Howard Bay; *Costumes*: Juliellen Weiss; *Musical Direction*: John Lesko
Cast: *David Wayne* (Charley Beddoes), *Dick Shawn* (Lieberwitz), *Margot Moser* (Victoria Bascombe); The Goblins: Billy Barty, Luis de Jesus, Richard Godouse, Tommy Madden, Jerry Maren, Yvonne Moray, Felix Silla, and Emory Souza; John Favorite (Attendant), Dennis M. Fitzpatrick (Attendant), William Simington (Doctor)
The musical was presented in two acts.
The action takes place in Charley's room at a Connecticut mental institution during an evening in autumn.

Musical Numbers

Note: The program didn't list musical numbers; the following is taken from a production presented in early 1972 at Florida State University [for more information, see below]. These titles are given with the names of the performers in the current staging at the Bucks County Playhouse. Some songs may have been cut during or after the Florida production, and thus may not have been heard during the Bucks County tryout.)
Act One: Overture (Ensemble); "Halloween" (David Wayne, Ensemble); "Love in a Barbershop" (Ensemble); "Saltpeter in the Rhubarb" (David Wayne, Ensemble); "This Life Is Fantasy" (David Wayne); "Halloween" (reprise) (David Wayne); "I Want to Be Your Mother" (Dick Shawn); "In the Autumn in the Night" (Margot Moser) ; "It'll Be Green Again" (David Wayne, Ensemble); Dance; Finale
Act Two: Entr'acte (Orchestra); "Organized Sex" (Margot Moser, Dick Shawn); "Would You Marry a Nut Like Me" (Dick Shawn); "Run Away with Me" (Ensemble); "Seduction Is a Holy Thing" (David Wayne); "Where Have I Been?" (Margot Moser); Finale (Margot Moser, David Wayne)

Halloween was first presented at Florida State University (Tallahassee, Florida) in early 1972 with Jose Ferrer, Dick Shawn, Barbara Cook, and Billy Barty. When the musical later opened at the Bucks County Playhouse in New Hope, Pennsylvania, on September 20 of that year, Ferrer and Cook were succeeded by David Wayne and Margot Moser.

Produced by Albert Selden and Jerome Minskoff, the musical had been slated to open in New York on October 24, 1972, and then on October 30 at the Martin Beck (now Al Hirschfeld) Theatre at a capitalization of $450,000, but closed permanently at the Bucks County Playhouse. The season wasn't a good one for the producing team, and all three of their 1972–1973 ventures lost money. Besides *Halloween*, V. J. Longhi's *The Lincoln Mask* (known as *Abraham's Mask* in preproduction) played for eight Broadway performances, and while the revival of ***Irene*** ran for 604 showings it lost most of its investment.

Halloween was a reunion of sorts for many of the creative team from *Man of La Mancha*. Mitch Leigh again composed the score, Howard Bay created the scenery and lighting, and Selden was again the coproducer. Ferrer had played the roles of Cervantes/Don Quixote during the Broadway run of *La Mancha* and on tour.

Like ***Prettybelle***, *Halloween* was set in a mental institution. Prettybelle wrote her memoirs as a form of therapy, and most of the story was comprised of scenes from her past. For *Halloween*, former poetry professor Charley Beddoes (David Wayne) has an active imagination that transports him into all sorts of exotic places, such as haunted mansions and underground caves, and he even conjures up a group of midgets who become supporting players in his dreams. In many ways, Charley is a Don Quixote whose impossible dreams allow him to cope with his personal tragedies, and his haunting "This Life Is Fantasy" summarized his philosophy that illusion is more bearable than reality.

The reason Charley prefers fantasy is because it enables him to deal with the loss of his daughter, who died in an automobile accident. He soon convinces fellow patients Lieberwitz (Dick Shawn) and Victoria Bascombe (Margot Moser) to join him in illusions, and well they might. Lieberwitz is a transvestite, a former actor who is too attached to his Teddy bear, and Victoria drove her husband to suicide. The musical's title derived from Charley's belief that every day should be wrapped in a Halloween state of mind.

Mitch Leigh's richly melodic score included a number of memorable songs, such as "Love in a Barbershop," "Saltpeter in the Rhubarb," "It'll Be Green Again," and the title number. Victoria and Lieberwitz's catchy tango "Organized Sex" had a truly quirky (if innocent) lyric, and most affecting of all was Charley's heartfelt "This Life Is Fantasy," his own version of "The Impossible Dream."

Penny in *Variety* found the musical "insubstantial,' but praised Wayne's "sensitive" and "tender" performance and noted Mitch Leigh's score was "bright at times and relatively tuneful, but lacks excitement."

MARY C. BROWN AND THE HOLLYWOOD SIGN

"A New Musical"

The musical began previews at the Shubert Theatre, Los Angeles, California, on November 12, 1972, and permanently closed there on November 18, 1972.

Book, Lyrics, and *Music*: Dory Previn

Direction: Tom O'Horgan; *Producer*: Zev Bufman; *Scenery*: Robin Wagner; *Costumes*: Randy Barcelo; *Lighting*: Jules Fisher; *Musical Direction*: Gordon Lowry Harrell

Cast: *Elizabeth Ashley* (Mary C. Brown), Philip Thomas (Cully Surroga), Tommy Madden (Reynard), Sorrell Booke (A. Luvian Katzenman), Seth Allen (Priest, B. C. Constantine), Danny Goldman (Masso Pile), Don Chastain (Andrew Roebuck), Delores Hall (Black Nun), Jennifer Ann Lee (Oriental Nun), Walt Wanderman (Man on Malibu Bus), James Sbano (Bus Driver), Penelope Bodry (Waitress, Make-Up Girl), Merria Ross (Script Girl), Ferne Bork (Best Boy)

The musical was presented in two acts.

The action takes place mostly in Hollywood during the present time.

Musical Numbers

Note: The program didn't identify performers of songs.

Act One: "Mary C. Brown and the Hollywood Sign"; "The Holy Man on Malibu Bus Number 3"; "The Midget's Lament"; "Inner Space"; "Cully Surroga, He's Almost Blind"; "Oh, Yes, I Was Afraid"; "Corn"; "The Egbert Souse March"; "The Perfect Lady"; "Don't Put Me Down"; "Left Hand Lost"; "Mary C. Brown and the Hollywood Sign" (reprise); "Starlet, Starlet on the Screen, Who Will Follow Norma Jean?"

Act Two: "Blue"; "Big Mother"; "Play It Again, Sam"; "When a Man Wants a Woman"; "Kong of the Jungle"; "The Perfect Man"; "It's Okay, Babe"; "Four Quarters"; "Jesus Was an Androgyne"; "Morning Star/Evening Star"; "Anima/Animus"

Dory Previn's *Mary C. Brown and the Hollywood Sign* never officially opened. It was scheduled to play for two weeks of previews at the Shubert Theatre in Los Angeles from November 12 through November 25, with an official opening night of November 26. But not only did the musical fail to reach opening night, it didn't even play out its scheduled two-week preview period and instead permanently closed after the first week of performances.

According to the musical's flyer, the story is a "concise musical image of the fantasmagoria that Hollywood represents." Specifically, the musical looked at the brief career of starlet Mary C. Brown (Elizabeth Ashley), who ultimately commits suicide by jumping off the letter "H" of the famous landmark overlooking the Hollywood Hills. (The plot was loosely based on the suicide of actress Peg Entwistle, who jumped to her death from the letter "H" in September 1932.)

The cast album was scheduled to be recorded by United Artists Records, which canceled the recording due to the musical's premature closing. But Dory Previn recorded a number of songs from the show on an album released by United Artists (LP # UAS-5657); the album includes thirteen of the musical's twenty-three numbers, along with their lyrics. Like a few theatre recordings of the era (such as ***Earl of Ruston*** and the Off-Broadway musicals *Exchange* and *House of Leather*), the album gave barely a hint of its theatrical origin.

A note in Elizabeth Ashley's program biography for an early 1973 regional production of Jean Giraudoux's *The Enchanted* stated *Mary C. Brown and the Hollywood Sign* would be seen on Broadway during the 1973–1974 season, but of course the production never materialized.

1973–1974 Season

THE DESERT SONG

Theatre: Uris Theatre
Opening Date: September 5, 1973; *Closing Date*: September 16, 1973
Performances: 15
Book: Otto Harbach, Oscar Hammerstein II, and Frank Mandel
Lyrics: Otto Harbach and Oscar Hammerstein II
Music: Sigmund Romberg
Direction: Henry Butler; *Producers*: Moe Septee in association with Jack L. Wolgin and Victor H. Potamkin (A Lehman Engel Production); *Choreography*: David Nillo; *Scenery* and *Lighting*: Clarke Dunham; *Costumes*: "Supervised" by Sara Brook; *Musical Direction*: Al Cavaliere (for opening night, Lehman Engel was the musical director)
Cast: Nicholas Scarpinati (Mindar), John Ribecchi (Sid El Kar), Dick Ensslen (Hadji), Frederick G. Sampson III (Palace Guard), Mandingo Shaka (Hassi), Ruby Greene Aspinall (Neri), David Cryer (The Red Shadow, Pierre Birabeau), Jerry Dodge (Benjamin Kidd), Stanley Grover (Captain Paul Fontaine), Kent Cottam (Lieutenant Davergne), William Leyerle (Sergeant Boussac), Gloria Rossi (Azuri); Azuri Dancing Girls: Kita Bouroff, Lana Caradimas, Urylee Leonardos, Jane Lucas, Sandra Mannis, Dundi Wright; Osceola Davis (Edith); Britt Swanson (Susan), Shepperd Strudwick (General Birabeau), Chris Callan (Margot Bonvalet), Carol Jeanne Tenny (Margot Bonvalet for Wednesday and Saturday matinees), Gloria Zaglool (Clementina), Michael Kermoyan (Ali Ben Ali); Ensemble: Ruby Greene Aspinall, Marsha Bagwell, Rita Oney Best, Kita Bouroff, Lana Caradimas, Jacqueline Clark, Osceola Davis, Karen Ford, Bonnie Hinson, Urylee Leonardos, Rona Leslie, Jane Lucas, Sandra Mannis, Berdeen E. Pigorsh, Brenda Schaffer, Dundi Wright, Donald Coleman, Bill Collins, Austin Colyer, Kent Cottam, Ronald De Felice, Dennis Dohman, Dick Ensslen, William Leyerle, Frederick G. Sampson III, Nicholas Scarpinati, Peter Schroeder, Arthur Shaffer, Anthony Tamburello, David Vogel, David Weatherspoon
The musical was presented in two acts.
The action takes place during the 1930s in Northern Africa.

Musical Numbers

Act One: "Prelude" and "Feasting Song" (John Ribecchi, Riffs); "The Riff Song" (David Cryer, John Ribecchi, Riffs); "Feasting Song" (reprise) (John Ribecchi, Riffs); "The Riff Song" (reprise) (David Cryer, John Ribecchi); "Margot" (Stanley Grover, Soldiers); "Has Anybody Seen My Bennie?" (new lyric by Edward Smith) (Britt Swanson); "Why Did We Marry Soldiers?" (French Girls); "The French Military Marching Song" (Chris Callan, French Girls, Soldiers); "Romance" (Chris Callan, French Girls); "Then You Will Know" (Chris Callen, David Cryer, Ensemble); "I Want a Kiss" (Chris Callen, David Cryer, Stanley Grover, Ensemble); "It" (new lyric by Edward Smith) (Jerry Dodge, Britt Swanson); "The Desert Song" (aka "Blue

Heaven and You and I") (David Cryer, Chris Callen); "Azuri Dance" (Gloria Rossi, Azuri Girls); "Soft as a Pigeon" (John Rebecchi, Stanley Grover, Ensemble); "The Desert Song" (reprise) (David Cryer, Chris Callen, Ensemble)

Act Two: Entr'acte (Orchestra); "My Little Castagnette" (Gloria Zaglool, Spanish Girls); "Song of the Brass Key" (Gloria Zaglool, Spanish Girls); "One Good Boy Gone Wrong" (new lyric by Edward Smith) (Jerry Dodge, Gloria Zaglool); "Eastern and Western Love": (1) "Let Love Go" (Michael Kermoyan, Male Ensemble), (2) "One Flower Grows Alone in Your Garden" (John Ribecchi, Male Ensemble), and (3) "One Alone" (David Cryer, John Ribecchi, Michael Kermoyan, Male Ensemble); "The Sabre Song" (Chris Callan, David Cryer); "The Desert Song" (reprise) (Chris Callen, David Cryer); "One Alone" (reprise) (David Cryer, Male Ensemble); "The Desert Song" (reprise) (Chris Callan); "It" (reprise) (new lyric by Edward Smith) (Jerry Dodge, Britt Swanson); "Dance of Triumph" (Gloria Rossi); "One Alone" (reprise) (David Cryer, Chris Callan)

During the summer of 1973, the production team of Moe Septee, Jack L. Wolgin, Victor H. Potamkin, and Lehman Engel presented two hit Sigmund Romberg operettas from the mid-1920s, *The Desert Song* and ***The Student Prince***. The former played on Broadway for two weeks, and the latter played out its scheduled summer and early fall run but didn't risk New York. Both productions were reasonably lavish, had large casts, and avoided the trap of retaining only the musical highlights of the operettas. These weren't "greatest hit" revivals and both (but especially *The Desert Song*) retained most of the original scores (for *The Desert Song*, Edward Smith wrote new lyrics for three of the numbers).

The Desert Song was played straight by the leads David Cryer (as Pierre Birabeau and his alter ego The Red Shadow) and Chris Callan (Margot), while Jerry Dodge (Bennie), Britt Swanson (Susan), Gloria Rossi (Azuri), and Gloria Zaglool (Clemintina) kidded their campy roles and sometimes over-the-top songs. The result was a genial revival that in earlier decades would probably have enjoyed tolerant reviews and a reasonably long run. But the critics saw "summer stock" written all over the production, and were merciless. As a result, some fine singing and performances and some grand Romberg melodies were gone within two weeks.

When the operetta premiered in 1926, it was actually a contemporary piece that was very loosely based on then-current political events in North Africa. The plot centered on the mysterious Red Shadow, described as a "Riff Robin Hood" who leads the rebellious Riff tribes against the Europeans in Morocco. The Red Shadow is actually Pierre Birabeau, the son of Governor-General Birabeau, and Pierre poses as a meek and mild-mannered introvert in order to protect his identity as the Red Shadow. As Pierre, his attempts to court the beautiful Margot Bonvalet are doomed because she wants to escape from her "humdrum world" and find a "rough and ready" man who will "master" her, not some nerdy bookworm like Pierre. So as the Red Shadow, Pierre abducts her and thus fulfills her fantasies of romantic adventure. But when his father wants to duel the Red Shadow, Pierre of course can't agree to it and thus disappears, much to the chagrin of Margot, who now believes her hero has turned coward. Later, Pierre "kills" the Red Shadow, and when he brings the Red Shadow's clothes to the French headquarters he's considered a hero. But Pierre's father realizes his son is the Red Shadow and comes to understand that with Pierre's help the Moroccans and the Europeans can peaceably coexist. And when Pierre is alone with Margot he dons the Red Shadow's mask and cape, and she realizes that the seemingly wimpy Pierre is actually the "rough and ready" man of her dreams.

During the 1926 tryout, the musical was known as *Lady Fair* and the stars were Robert Halliday and Vivienne Segal. The production opened at the Casino Theatre on November 30, 1926, for 471 performances and became one of the era's most popular operettas. The score offered lushly romantic melodies ("Romance"; the title song, which is also known as "Blue Heaven and You and I"; and a fascinating three-part sequence with the overall title "Eastern and Western Love," which includes "Let Love Go," "One Flower Grows Alone in Your Garden," and "One Alone"); stirring choral numbers ("The Riff Song," "The French Military Marching Song"); and some surprisingly sly ones (a salute to Elinor Glyn and that "indefinable thing" known as "It," "One Good Boy Gone Wrong," and "Then You Will Know").

Richard Watts in the *New York Post* had reviewed the original 1926 production, and now he noted that the show was "silly stuff" that had "the virtue of knowing that it is." The score was still "charming," David Cryer was "dashing," and as the comic newspaper reporter Jerry Dodge was "no braver than he should be." Douglas Watt in the *New York Daily News* noted the revival was a "respectable mounting," and while the story was "enthrallingly stupid," both "first-rate" singer David Cryer and the fetching Chris Callan treated it with "splendid aplomb." Edwin Wilson in the *Wall Street Journal* said the production "rediscovered the voice," and thus the singers could "carry a tune and hit the back wall of the theatre with the high notes." He said *The Desert Song* was a "carefree" way to open the new theatre season, and one reason the revival worked so well was that the cast played their roles seriously and not for laughs; instead, they let the audience laugh at the operetta's conventions.

But Martin Gottfried in *Women's Wear Daily* disliked the "cut-rate revival" (although he praised Romberg's "wonderful" score), and Jack Kroll in *Newsweek* found the production a "barren waxworks" that demonstrated "Broadway's adeptness at burying its head in the sand."

The musical was filmed three times (in 1929 with John Boles and Carlotta King; in 1943 with Dennis King and Irene Manning and an updated story that included Nazis in North Africa; and in 1953 with Gordon MacRae and Kathryn Grayson). The 1943 and 1953 versions are available on DVD by the Warner Brothers Archive Collection. In his review of the 1943 version, Bosley Crowther in the *New York Times* described the operetta as a "sheik-and-shimmy romance." And for the 1953 version, in what was perhaps a nod to the political climate of the era, Pierre's alter ego was named El Khobar instead of The Red Shadow. An NBC television adaptation by William Friedberg, Neil Simon, and Will Glickman was aired on May 7, 1955, with Nelson Eddy and Gail Sherwood.

Besides the current production, the musical had been previously revived on Broadway at City Center on January 8, 1946, for forty-five performances with Walter Cassel and Dorothy Sandlin. There were also two revivals by the New York City Opera Company, both at the New York State Theatre; the first opened on August 25, 1987, for sixteen performances, and the second on August 29, 1989, for seven showings.

The original London production opened at the Drury Lane on April 7, 1927, for 432 performances and starred Harry Welchman and Edith Day.

The script was published in paperback by Samuel French in 1954, and the lyrics are included in *The Collected Lyrics of Oscar Hammerstein II*. There are numerous recordings of the score, including a studio cast by RCA Victor Records (released on CD by ArkivMusic/RCA Masterworks Broadway # 88725-42771-2) with Giorgio Tozzi, Kathy Barr, and Peter Palmer. A delightful recording with Mario Lanza and Judith Raskin was also released by RCA (LP # LM-2440).

RAISIN

"The New Musical"

Theatre: 46th Street Theatre (during run, the musical transferred to the Lunt-Fontanne Theatre)
Opening Date: October 18, 1973; *Closing Date*: December 7, 1975
Performances: 847
Book: Robert Nemiroff and Charlotte Zaltzberg
Lyrics: Robert Brittan
Music: Judd Woldin
Based on the 1959 play *A Raisin in the Sun* by Lorraine Hansberry.
Direction and *Choreography*: Donald McKayle; *Producers*: Robert Nemiroff (Sydney Lewis and Jack Friel, Associate Producers); *Scenery*: Robert U. Taylor; *Costumes*: Bernard Johnson; *Lighting*: William Mintzer; *Musical Direction*: Howard A. Roberts
Cast: Al Perryman (Pusher), Loretta Abbott (Victim), Ernestine Jackson (Ruth Younger), Ralph Carter (Travis Younger), Helen Martin (Mrs. Johnson), Joe Morton (Walter Lee Younger), Deborah Allen (Beneatha Younger), Virginia Capers (Lena Younger aka Mama), Elaine Beener (Bar Girl), Ted Ross (Bobo Jones), Walter P. Brown (Willie Harris), Robert Jackson (Joseph Asagai), Chief Bey (African Drummer), Herb Downer (Pastor), Marenda Perry (Pastor's Wife), Richard Sanders (Karl Lindner); People of the Southside: Chuck Thorpes, Eugene Little, Karen Burke, Zelda Pulliam, Elaine Beener, Renee Rose, Paul Carrington, Marenda Perry, Gloria Turner, Don Jay, Glenn Brooks, Marilyn Hamilton
The musical was presented in two acts.
The action takes place in Chicago during the 1950s.

Musical Numbers

Act One: Prologue (Company); "Man Say" (Joe Morton); "Whose Little Angry Man" (Ernestine Jackson); "Runnin' to Meet the Man" (Joe Morton, Company); "A Whole Lotta Sunlight" (Virginia Capers); "Booze" (Elaine Beener, Ted Ross, Joe Morton, Walter P. Brown, Company); "Alaiyo" (Robert Jackson, Deborah Allen); "African Dance" (Deborah Allen, Joe Morton, Company); "Sweet Time" (Ernestine Jackson, Joe Morton); "You Done Right" (Joe Morton)

Act Two: "He Come Down This Morning" (Herb Downer, Marenda Perry, Virginia Capers, Helen Martin, Ernestine Jackson, Ralph Carter, Company); "It's a Deal" (Joe Morton); "Sweet Time" (reprise) (Ernestine Jackson, Joe Morton); "Sidewalk Tree" (Ralph Carter); "Not Anymore" (Joe Morton, Ernestine Jackson, Deborah Allen); "Alaiyo" (reprise) (Robert Jackson); "It's a Deal" (reprise) (Joe Morton); "Measure the Valleys" (Virginia Capers); "He Come Down This Morning" (reprise) (Company)

Lorraine Hansberry's 1959 drama *A Raisin in the Sun* was a groundbreaking work, for here was a first: a hit Broadway play by a female black playwright about black family life. It ran for 530 performances, won the New York Drama Critics' Circle Award for Best Play, was filmed in 1961, has enjoyed television versions in 1989 and 2008, and was revived on Broadway in 2004 and 2014.

The catalyst for the story turns on a $10,000 insurance policy left to Mama Younger (Virginia Capers) by her late husband. She and her family live together in an apartment in a Chicago ghetto; besides Mama, there's her daughter Beneatha (Deborah Allen), her son Walter Lee (Joe Morton), his wife Ruth (Ernestine Jackson), and their young son Travis (Ralph Carter). Mama plans to use the insurance money to buy a house in the suburbs, but others in the family have different ideas about how to invest the inheritance. Beneatha wants the legacy to fund her medical studies, and Walter Lee plans to buy a share in a local liquor business. The latter loses his portion when his business associates abscond with it, but there's enough money left to help Beneatha and to put a down payment on a house. Soon a representative from their prospective neighborhood arrives with the news that he and his neighbors will pay the Youngers for not moving there. But the Youngers are determined to leave the ghetto for a better life and despite the unpromising future of a potentially hostile new neighborhood they decide to move anyway.

When the musical opened up Hansberry's intimate story, it too often fell into clichéd Broadway territory. The most effective moments occurred when in chamber-musical style it centered on the intimate and touching details of the characters' lives. Thanks to Judd Woldin's music and Robert Brittan's lyrics, there were many such affecting moments, including Mama's hopes for her family, herself, and even for her scraggly houseplant, in "A Whole Lotta Sunlight"; Mama's admonition that the sum of a man's life must be measured by the whole and not just the parts in "Measure the Valley"; Walter Lee's bitter diatribe against Mama's values in "You Done Right"; and Travis's "Sidewalk Tree." The latter was one of the finest musical moments of the decade as it depicted the little boy's farewell to an old neighborhood tree that was as important to him as his games and his playmates.

Otherwise, the musical often lost itself in extraneous numbers. The opening prologue was a dance sequence, described in the script as a "jazz ballet," that depicts the Youngers' squalid neighborhood during the early morning hours when drunks and drug pushers own the streets. Early-morning numbers had been the rage in the mid-1940s when *On the Town* (1944) began with "I Feel Like I'm Not out of Bed Yet," *Are You with It?* (1945) asked for "Five Minutes More in Bed," *The Duchess Misbehaves* (1946) looked at "Morning in Madrid," and *The Girl from Nantucket* (1945) lost "Morning in Manhattan" during its pre-Broadway tryout. And certainly a close cousin to *Raisin*'s "jazz ballet" is the "Five A.M. Ballet" from *Watch Out, Angel!* (1945; closed prior to New York), which the program describes as a peek at "the sounds common to the dawn of a great city" and includes such types as a sailor and a street girl.

In later seasons, early-morning numbers morphed into specific depictions of the morning and evening rush hours, and *Raisin*'s commuter song "Runnin' to Meet the Man" was a reminder of the Broadway of the early 1960s in which the rush-hour was a de rigueur musical moment: *Let It Ride!* (1961) offered "Run, Run, Run"; *How to Succeed in Business without Really Trying* (1961) wearily noted that "It's Been a Long Day"; and "Subway Rush" in *Subways Are for Sleeping* (1961) looked at dancing commuters in Grand Central Station.

Other extraneous songs in *Raisin* were ""Booze" (one of the Broadway musical's many salutes to drinking) and "He Come Down This Morning" (yet another in an almost endless series of the era's gospel numbers).

Moreover, the African-oriented "Alaiyo," its second-act reprise, and "African Dance" seemed out of place and held up the action.

Douglas Watt in the *New York Daily News* said the musical "always seems on the verge of striking home but never does," and he felt the poignancy and urgency of the original play never quite emerged; as a result, the evening was "efficient, likeable and rather bland." T. E. Kalem in *Time* noted that the black dream of moving into a white neighborhood was now "hopelessly dated" considering the rise of black separatism; instead of updating the play, *Raisin* was simply "soap operetta."

Martin Gottfried in *Women's Wear Daily* said the adaptation was "skimpy" and unless one knew the original play the story was "barely followable." The evening was in the nature of an "outline," and the work wasn't truly musicalized. There were "noisy, trite, spiritless, indistinguishable" dances, and the décor consisted of what looked like scaffolding and "shabby abstract sticks of furniture," which gave the musical a "bare-boned look ironically consistent with its bare-boned nature."

Richard Watts in the *New York Post* said the musical was a "superior work," but found the songs "pleasant" instead of "exciting"; he praised Virginia Capers's "heroic quality," and said the "delightful" Ralph Carter matched her in "brilliance" and "justified" the idea of child performers. Clive Barnes in the *New York Times* praised the musical, which had "a heartbeat very much its own" as it "warms the heart and touches the soul." As for "that mighty little atom" Ralph Carter, Barnes suggested that even W. C. Fields could grow to love him.

Geoffrey Holder on WNBC4TV said he hadn't cared for the original play, which he termed "a black soap opera," but now the "marvelous" musical version "got rid of the soap opera and made [the play] into an opera." Leonard Harris on WCBSTV2 praised the "winner" with its "good" songs, "honest-to-goodness" dances, and "fine performances," and Leonard Probst on NBC Radio felt the musical improved upon the original drama and had "heart, honesty, and terrific dancing."

During the tryout, Shezwae Powell was succeeded by Deborah Allen, and the numbers "Just Tell Me," "Moving Day Dance," and "Later, Gator" were cut.

The script was published in paperback by Samuel French in 1978, and the cast album was released by Columbia Records (LP # KS-32754). The CD was issued by Sony Broadway (also # SK-32754) and includes the previously unreleased "Booze."

On May 14, 1981, the musical was revived by the Equity Library Theatre for thirty-six performances.

Awards

Tony Awards and Nominations: Best Musical (***Raisin***); Best Leading Actor in a Musical (Joe Morton); Best Leading Actress in a Musical (**Virginia Capers**); Best Featured Actor in a Musical (Ralph Carter); Best Featured Actress in a Musical (Ernestine Jackson); Best Director of a Musical (Donald McKayle); Best Book (Robert Nemiroff and Charlotte Zaltzberg); Best Score (lyrics by Robert Brittan, music by Judd Woldin); Best Choreographer (Donald McKayle)

MOLLY

"The New Broadway Musical" / "The New Musical"

Theatre: Alvin Theatre
Opening Date: November 1, 1973; *Closing Date*: December 29, 1973
Performances: 68
Book: Louis Garfinkle and Leonard Adelson
Lyrics: Leonard Adelson and Mack David
Music: Jerry Livingston
Based on the characters created by Gertrude Berg for the radio series *The Goldbergs*.
Direction: Alan Arkin; *Producers*: Don Saxon, Don Kaufman, and George Daley in association with Complex IV (Larry Falon and Richard Vonella, Associate Producers); *Choreography*: Grover Dale; *Scenery*: Marsha L. Eck; *Costumes*: Carrie F. Robbins; *Lighting*: Jules Fisher; *Musical Direction*: Jerry Goldberg

Cast: Suzanne Walker (Angelina Frazini), Camila Ashland (Mrs. Sullivan), Eddie Phillips (Mr. Sullivan), Justine Johnston (Mrs. Frazini), *Kay* (Kaye) *Ballard* (Molly), Molly Stark (Mrs. Kramer), Ruth Manning (Belle Seidenschneer), Hazel Weber Steck (Mrs. Bloom), Toni Darnay (Mrs. Dutton), Lisa Rochelle (Rosalie), Lee Wallace (Jake), Eli Mintz (Uncle David), Daniel Fortus (Sammy), Connie Day (Stella Hazelcorn), Swen Swenson (Michael Stone), Mitchell Jason (Cousin Simon), Martin Garner (Max); Ensemble: Don Bonnell (Skeeter), Rodney Griffin (Ralph), Bob Heath (Reggie), Don Percassi (Harold), Sal Pernice (Vinnie), Linda Rose (Sheala), Leland Schwantes (George), Gerald Teijelo (Waiter), Mimi Wallace (Ellen), Miriam Welch (Sarah)

The musical was presented in two acts.

The action takes place during the spring of 1933 in the Bronx.

Musical Numbers

Note: * = lyric by Leonard Adelson; ** = lyric by Mack David.

Act One: "There's a New Deal on the Way" (**) (Suzanne Walker, Company); "If Everyone Got What They Wanted" (**) (Kay Ballard, Company); "A Piece of the Rainbow" (**) (Kay Ballard); "Cahoots" (**) (Swen Swenson, Kay Ballard); "Sullivan's Got a Job" (*) (Company); "In Your Eyes" (**) (Daniel Fortus); "Cahoots" (**) (reprise) (Ruth Manning, Kay Ballard); "High Class Ladies and Elegant Gentlemen" (**) (Swen Swenson, Connie Day, Kay Ballard, Lee Wallace, Daniel Fortus, Lisa Rochelle); "So I'll Tell Him" (**) (Kay Ballard); "Appointments" (*) (Eli Mintz); "There's Gold on the Trees" (**) (Lee Wallace, Kay Ballard, Company)

Act Two: "The Mandarin Palace on the Grand Concourse" (**) (Company); "I Want to Share It with You" (**) (Swen Swenson, Connie Day, Company); "In Your Eyes" (**) (reprise) (Daniel Fortus); "I Was There" (**) (Kay Ballard, Lee Wallace); "Oak Leaf Memorial Park" (*) (Kay Ballard); "If Everyone Got What They Wanted" (**) (reprise) (Eli Mintz, Lisa Rochelle); "I See a Man" (lyric and music by Norman L. Martin) (Kay Ballard); "The Tremont Avenue Cruisewear Fashion Show" (*) (Company); "I've Got a Molly" (*) (Lee Wallace); "Go in the Best of Health" (*) (Kay Ballard)

Gertrude Berg wrote and starred in the highly successful radio series *The Goldbergs* about a Jewish family in the Bronx that consisted of Molly Goldberg and her husband, Jake; their son, Sammy and daughter, Rosalie; and Uncle David (Eli Mintz, who re-created his role for the current musical). The series ran from 1929 to 1946, and then in 1948 was adapted for the stage by Berg as *Molly and Me*; she reprised her role of Molly, and also starred in a 1950 film version titled *The Goldbergs*, which was later retitled *Molly*. The stories were also adapted into Berg's popular television series *The Goldbergs*, which ran on various networks from 1949 to 1956. Gertrude Berg made Molly her own indelible character, and so the musical adaptation in 1973 had to contend with her strong and memorable characterization of the friendly soul in the Old Bronx who innocently meddles in the lives of her family and neighbors. The musical came across as an adaptation of an old episode of the show, and centered on Molly's efforts to help Jake make a go of it in the garment business (he does so by inventing two-piece bathing suits for women).

For the musical, Kay Ballard looked the part, but a few critics felt she didn't bring the necessary qualities to the role. Jack Kroll in *Newsweek* suggested Ballard exuded "more minestrone than chicken soup"; Leonard Probst on NBC Radio felt she didn't "mix well" with the "real Bronx Jewish folk-humor" of Eli Mintz and Daniel Fortus; and T. E. Kalem in *Time* said she spun through her numbers like a "treadless tank" and lacked "the remotest trace of that sweetly enveloping maternal musk with which Gertrude Berg so winningly invested her creation." Douglas Watt in the *New York Daily News* noted that Ballard was a "resourceful" comedienne and a "talented" singer, and while she was "valiant" and tried "her level best to carry" off the characterization, she "simply" could not. Leonard Harris on WCBSTV2 said the "talented" Ballard managed a "tentative grip" on the title role when she spoke her lines but when she sang she "lost it totally" because she was "too big and nightclubby a singer for Molly Goldberg." But Geoffrey Holder on WNBC4TV was glad to see the "brilliant" Ballard back on Broadway and Richard Watts in the *New York Post* said she played the title role with her "characteristic skill."

As for the musical itself, Kroll found it "pallid," Kalem pronounced it "the latest nostalgia dud," and Martin Gottfried in *Women's Wear Daily* said the "shabbily professional" and "unamusing, untouching, uninteresting, and unnecessary" musical was a "mess" and "utterly without imagination or originality."

Gottfried described the score as "all-purpose, nondescript, dated but period-less Broadway" but praised the "lovely" "In Your Eyes," which was sung by Daniel Fortus. Watt noted "I See a Man" was Ballard's "finest moment" and the song was "the only pointed number in the whole silly score"; he also enjoyed the "fast-stepping" sequence "The Mandarin Palace on the Grand Concourse," which was "a welcome change of scene from the claustrophobic Goldberg household."

In preproduction, the musical was titled *The Goldbergs*. During the tryout and preview period, director Paul Aaron and choreographer Bert Michaels were respectively succeeded by Alan Arkin and Grover Dale. The following songs were dropped either in preproduction or during the tryout: "Cancelling" (*), "The Kinder" (*), "I Had a Night" (*), "In the Afternoon of Our Years," (*), "My Chosen Man" (*), "Now That You Mention It" (*), "I've Got to Change" (*), "We've Got a Lot in Common" (*), "California" (*), "In the Lobby of the Roxy" (*), "Yoohoo" (*), "You Remember" (*) (best guess title), "Simon" (*) (best guess title), and "The Neighbors' Song" (**).

Leonard Adelson had begun the adaptation and lyrics, and after his death Louis Garfinkle completed the book and Mack David wrote the remaining lyrics.

Recordings of Ballard singing "Go in the Best of Health" and "I See a Man" and the unused "In the Afternoon of Our Years" are included in the collection *Forgotten Broadway* (unnamed company; LP # T-101).

During the period of the production of *Molly*, Ballard changed her first name from Kaye to Kay, reportedly from the advice of an astrologer. But the name change didn't bring her luck with *Molly* and so she soon reverted to the original spelling.

GIGI

"A New Musical for Broadway"

Theatre: Uris Theatre
Opening Date: November 13, 1973; *Closing Date*: February 10, 1974
Performances: 103
Book and *Lyrics*: Alan Jay Lerner
Music: Frederick Loewe
Based on the 1944 novella *Gigi* by Colette, and the 1958 film *Gigi* (screenplay by Alan Jay Lerner and direction by Vincente Minnelli).
Direction: Joseph Hardy; *Producers*: A Saint-Subber Production of the Los Angeles and San Francisco Civic Light Opera Production (produced by Edwin Lester and Saint-Subber); *Choreography*: Onna White; *Scenery*: Oliver Smith; *Costumes*: Oliver Messel; *Lighting*: Thomas Skelton; *Musical Direction*: Ross Reimueller
Cast: *Alfred Drake* (Honore Lachailles), *Daniel Massey* (Gaston Lachailles), Sandahl Bergman (Liane d'Exelmans), *Maria Karnilova* (Inez Alvarez aka Mamita), Karin Wolfe (Gigi), *Agnes Moorehead* (Aunt Alicia), Gordon De Vol (Charles), Joe Ross (Head Waiter, Receptionist, Telephone Installer, Maitre d'Hotel), Leonard John Crofoot (Waiter, Law Clerk), Thomas Stanton (Waiter, Law Clerk), Thomas Anthony (Liane's Dance Partner), Patrick Spohn (Artist), Joel Pressman (Count), Randy Di Grazio (Sandomir), Gregory Drotar (Dancing Teacher), Truman Gaige (Manuel), George Gaynes (Maitre Du Fresne), Howard Chitjian (Maitre Duclos); Ensemble: Thomas Anthony, Alvin Beam, Russ Beasley, Robyn Blair, Leonard John Crofoot, Gordon De Vol, Randy Di Grazio, John Dorrin, Gregory Drotar, Janis Eckhart, Margit Haut, Andy Keyser, Beverly Kopels, Diane Lauridsen, Merilee Magnuson, Kelley Maxwell, Vickie Patik, Joel Pressman, Patrick Spohn, Thomas Stanton, Cherie Suzanne, Marie Tillmanns, Sallie True; Little Girls: Patricia Daly, Jill Turnbull
The musical was presented in two acts.
The action takes place mostly in Paris at the turn of the twentieth century.

Musical Numbers

Act One: "Thank Heaven for Little Girls" (Alfred Drake); "It's a Bore" (Alfred Drake, Daniel Massey); "The Earth and Other Minor Things" (Karin Wolfe); "Paris Is Paris Again" (Alfred Drake, Ensemble); "She Is Not Thinking of Me" (Daniel Massey); "It's a Bore" (reprise) (Alfred Drake, Daniel Massey, Truman Gaige, Agnes Moorehead); "The Night They Invented Champagne" (Karin Wolfe, Daniel Massey, Maria Karnilova); "I Remember It Well" (Alfred Drake, Maria Karnilova); "I Never Want to Go Home Again" (Karin Wolfe, Ensemble)

Act Two: "Gigi" (Daniel Massey); "The Contract" (Agnes Moorehead, Maria Karnilova, Howard Chitjian, George Gaynes); "I'm Glad I'm Not Young Anymore" (Alfred Drake); "In This Wide, Wide World" (Karin Wolfe); "Thank Heaven for Little Girls" (reprise) (Alfred Drake)

Gigi was one of many failed attempts to transform a classic MGM film musical into an equally classic stage production. The adaptation lasted just three months and reportedly lost some $400,000 of its initial investment, and over the years *Seven Brides for Seven Brothers* (1982, five performances), *Singin' in the Rain* (1985, 367 performances), and *Meet Me in St. Louis* (1989, 253 performances) also stumbled because they couldn't measure up to the originals. See below for information regarding new stage versions of *Gigi* as well as two other classic MGM musicals, *The Band Wagon* and *An American in Paris*.

In his review of *Gigi*, Martin Gottfried in *Women's Wear Daily* complained that the production was "indicative of the current depressing attitude toward the musical theatre as a marketplace for packaged versions of established properties." His prescient comment describes what has happened to Broadway with its unending stream of predigested musicals, most of which are little more than commercial and manufactured products devised by committees who sell brand-name musicals to audiences already familiar with their sources, such as movies, cartoons, television shows, and song catalogs. And so as soon as it premiered, the stage version of *Gigi* already seemed like a tired revival whose shelf life was quickly expiring.

The 1958 film version was a gorgeous adult fairy tale, a bon-bon of a musical about the title character (Leslie Caron for the film, Karin Wolfe for the current stage version) who lives with her grandmother, Mamita (Hermione Gingold/Maria Karnilova), and (in a running joke throughout the film) her unseen mother, and who is tutored by her elegant Aunt Alicia (Isabel Jeans/Agnes Moorehead) in the ways of the world so that she can become a great courtesan in the family tradition. Among Mamita and Gigi's circle of friends is the rich and handsome playboy Gaston (Louis Jourdan/Daniel Massey) who has known Gigi since she was an awkward little girl and now realizes she's a poised and graceful young woman. But Gigi isn't content to be his mistress; love and marriage are on her mind, and when Gaston realizes he's fallen in love for the first time in his life, he proposes to her. The film's characters also include Honore (Maurice Chevalier/Alfred Drake), Gaston's uncle and a former lover of Mamita, who hovers on the sidelines and acts as occasional host to the audience.

The film was perfectly cast, and boasted lovely songs by Alan Jay Lerner and Frederick Loewe, a witty screenplay by Lerner, clever direction by Vincente Minnelli, and a sumptuous production designed by Cecil Beaton that captured the luxurious world of fin de siècle Paris. A few sequences were filmed in Paris, including the color-drenched interiors of Maxim's, and so the film's atmosphere was authentic with on-location shooting. *Gigi* won nine Academy Awards (plus a special honorary Oscar for Chevalier), including Best Picture, Best Song (the title number), Best Direction (Minnelli), Best Adapted Screenplay (Lerner), Best Costume Design, Best Cinematography, Best Art Direction, Best Editing, and Best Score.

The film was Lerner and Loewe's first musical since the premiere of *My Fair Lady* on Broadway two years earlier (and its advertisement as "The *My Fair Lady* of the Screen" confused some, who thought it was the official film adaptation of *My Fair Lady*). The film was indeed an Event, and it played a road show engagement for one year in a regular Broadway house (the Royale, now the Bernard B. Jacobs Theatre); programs were distributed to the audience, souvenir programs were sold in the lobby, and the film had its own window card. Incidentally, the title and basic lyric of "I Remember It Well" had been used by Lerner in the 1948 Broadway musical *Love Life* (music by Kurt Weill), and the title number is technically in two parts, "Gaston's Soliloquy" and "Gigi," but most recordings and programs refer to the overall sequence as "Gigi."

Both *My Fair Lady* and *Gigi* employed similar stories of awkward young women who are transformed into lovely and elegant ones, and both musicals also shared one song. During the tryout of *My Fair Lady*, Julie Andrews sang "Say a Prayer for Me Tonight" in anticipation of attending the embassy ball. The song was dropped prior to the Broadway opening, but was heard in *Gigi* when duckling-turned-swan Gigi looks forward to her evening at Maxim's with Gaston. Incidentally, the basic plots of *My Fair Lady* and *Gigi* resonate in two other Lerner musicals, *On a Clear Day You Can See Forever* (1965) and ***Lolita, My Love***.

The current adaptation cut three songs from the film ("The Parisians," "Gossip," and "Say a Prayer for Me Tonight") and added five ("The Earth and Other Minor Things," "Paris Is Paris Again," "I Never Want to Go Home Again," "The Contract," and "In This Wide, Wide World"). "The Contract" was a much revised version of "À toujours," which was written for but never used in the film, but can be heard on *Gigi*, RCA Victor's contemporary album of the film's score (LP # LPM-1716) where it is sung by Gogi Grant.

During the pre-Broadway tryout, "The Parisians" was used but eventually dropped for Broadway, and "Da Da Da Da" may have been a new title for "Gossip"; like "The Parisians," it too was cut prior to New York. During the tryout a new song titled "Everything French Is Better" was deleted. Teresa Stevens played the title role for much of the tryout, but was succeeded by Karin Wolfe. George Gaynes and Marijane Maricle played the roles of Honore's brother and sister-in-law, but when the characters were eliminated Maricle left the company; Gaynes had played the roles of both Honore's brother and the attorney Du Fresne, and so he remained with the production in the latter role. During the Broadway run, Arlene Francis succeeded Agnes Moorehead due to the latter's illness.

The musical toured for a few months during the 1984–1985 season, but never risked Broadway. The cast included Louis Jourdan (this time around in the role of Honore), Betsy Palmer (Aunt Alicia), Taina Elg (Mamita), Tom Hewitt (Gaston), and Lisa Howard (Gigi). Except for "Gossip," all the songs from the film were included, and only one number from the 1973 production was retained ("The Contract").

A London production opened in September 1985 at the Lyric Theatre with a cast that included Beryl Reid (Mamita), Jean-Pierre Aumont (Honore), Sian Phillips (Aunt Alicia), Geoffrey Burridge (Gaston), and Amanda Waring (Gigi). The film songs "Gossip" and "Say a Prayer for Me Tonight" weren't retained, but four of the five numbers written for the 1973 version were kept: "The Earth and Other Minor Things" (here, "I Know about the Earth"), "Paris Is Paris Again," "The Contract," and "In This Wide, Wide World."

The Broadway cast album was released by RCA Victor (LP # ABL1-0404 and CD # 09026-68070-2), and the cast album of the London production was recorded by Safari Records (LP # 1). The best recording of the score is the expanded soundtrack which was issued by Rhino Movie Music (CD # R271962) and includes extended versions of the "Waltz at Maxim's" (a variation of "She Is Not Thinking of Me") and "Gossip" (and its reprise version). As a bonus, the CD includes tracks of Leslie Caron singing "The Parisians" and "Say a Prayer for Me Tonight" as well as a version of "The Night They Invented Champagne" with Caron, Jourdan, and Gingold (for the completed film, Caron's vocals were dubbed by Betty Wand).

Almost all the leads in the current production were criticized in one way or another. Douglas Watt in the *New York Daily News* found Karin Wolfe and Daniel Massey charmless; T. E. Kalem in *Time* said Massey was "miscast" and that Wolfe was a "Barbie doll" with "a chilling absence of presence"; and Gottfried felt Drake was miscast, Maria Karnilova was "mildly distracting" with her "leftover Yiddish dialect from *Fiddler on the Roof*," Massey was "too boyishly exuberant" for the worldly Gaston, and Wolfe was a "perfectly ordinary ingénue."

Watt said the evening was "pleasant" but the movie's "magic" had disappeared; Richard Watts in the *New York Post* found the adaptation "entertaining" and "agreeable" if not "sensational"; and the headlines for the weeklies were succinctly to the point: "For the Geritol Set" (*Time*) and "Frozen Food" (*Newsweek*). Clive Barnes in the *New York Times* gave the musical a positive if somewhat ambivalent nod. He asked if it were possible to "re-invent" champagne, decided you could because "champagne is champagne," but cautioned that "it may come out tasting just a little more like New York State than *Veuve Clicquot* the second time around."

In a devastating statement about the quality of the current state of the Broadway musical circa 1973 and 1974, *Gigi* was awarded the Tony for Best Score despite the fact that nine of its fourteen musical numbers were from the 1958 film.

Gigi was adapted from Colette's 1944 novella, and in 1949 the French (nonmusical) film version was released (Daniele Delorme played the title role). Anita Loos's nonmusical stage adaptation premiered on Broadway at the Fulton Theatre for 219 showings on November 24, 1951, with Audrey Hepburn as Gigi, and the London production of the play opened on May 23, 1956, at the New Theatre for 317 performances with Leslie Caron in the title role. The two-DVD set of the 1958 film musical is paired with the 1949 film version (Warner Brothers # 3000017734).

Gottfried's remark about "musical theatre as a marketplace for packaged versions of established properties" is again appropriate. In 2015, a new production of *Gigi* with a "re-envisioned" book by Heidi Thomas opened at the Neil Simon Theatre on April 8. All the songs from the film version were retained (including "The Parisians," "Gossip," "Say a Prayer for Me Tonight," and the unused film song "À toujours") and all but one ("The Earth and Other Minor Things") of the songs written for the 1973 production were included in the new package. Gigi's "Say a Prayer for Me Tonight" was assigned to Mamita as "Say a Prayer"; Honore's solo "I'm Glad I'm Not Young Anymore" became a duet for him and Mamita; and, in order not to offend the delicate sensibilities of the politically correct, Honore's "Thank Heaven for Little Girls" was assigned to Mamita and Aunt Alicia. In his review of the musical for the *Washington Post*, Peter Marks stated that *Gigi* was not "great" and was "nothing really special," and a sub-headline in the review noted that *Gigi* "affirms its undistinguished status." The production closed on Broadway after eighty-six performances.

Further, a perhaps Broadway-bound *The Band Wagon* was presented by Encores! on November 6, 2014, with a book by Douglas Carter Beane (Ben Brantley in the *New York Times* said the "big, bright balloon of a show" wouldn't "inflate" and added that "even hot air would be welcome"). *An American in Paris* opened on Broadway at the Palace Theatre on April 12, 2015, in an adaptation by Craig Lucas, and seems poised to become a long-running crowd-pleaser.

Awards

Tony Awards and Nominations: Best Leading Actor in a Musical (Alfred Drake); Best Score (**Frederick Loewe** and **Alan Jay Lerner**); Best Scenic Designer (Oliver Smith); Best Costume Designer (Oliver Messel)

GOOD EVENING

"Comedy with Music"

Theatre: Plymouth Theatre
Opening Date: November 14, 1973; *Closing Date*: November 30, 1974
Performances: 438
Sketches: Peter Cook and Dudley Moore
Direction: Jerry Adler; *Producers*: Alexander H. Cohen and Bernard Delfont; *Scenery*: Robert Randolph
Cast: *Peter Cook, Dudley Moore*
The revue was presented in two acts.

Sketches and Musical Numbers

Note: All sketches and musical numbers were performed by Peter Cook and Dudley Moore.

Act One: "Hello"; "On Location"; "Madrigal"; "Six of the Best"; "Die Flabbergast"; "Down the Mine"; "One Leg Too Few"; "Chanson"; "Soap Opera"

Act Two: "Gospel Truth"; "Mini-Drama"; "The Kwai Sonata" ("Colonel Bogey March," music by K. J. Alford); "The Frog and Peach"; "On Appeal"; "Tea for Two"

Along with Alan Bennett and Jonathan Miller, Peter Cook and Dudley Moore first appeared on Broadway in 1962's London import *Beyond the Fringe*, one of the theatrical highlights of that era. The foursome wrote their own material, and the evening's rapier wit skewered politics, trends, and the arts. The production opened in London in 1961 and ran for 1,189 performances, and the New York edition played for 667 showings.

In 1971, Cook and Moore's revue *Behind the Fridge* opened in Australia and New Zealand for a five-month run; two performances were taped, and the highlights (which were later released on DVD) were shown on Australian television. The revue was later produced in London where it opened at the Cambridge Theatre on November 21, 1972, for a nine-month run. For Broadway, the title was changed to *Good Evening*, where it played over a year and then enjoyed a national tour.

Even though *Good Evening* was less biting than *Beyond the Fringe*, a few sequences caused a bit of controversy. "Gospel Truth" found Cook and Moore in biblical times, with Cook as a reporter named Matthew for the *Bethlehem Star* who has an in-depth interview with one of the three shepherds who witnessed the birth of Christ. The latter seems unimpressed with the event, and notes he had been abiding in the fields, and he just never could abide the fields. "One Leg Too Few" looked at an awkward interview between a director and a one-legged actor who auditions for the title role in an upcoming Tarzan movie; the director must tell him he's not quite right for the part, but assures the actor that his other leg is quite nice.

Good examples of the duo's quirky humor were the opening sequence "Hello" and the second-act "The Frog and Peach." In the former, two men who are supposedly old friends run into one another and enthusiastically gush over how good it is to see the other again, but it turns out the two have never met before. In the latter, a television reporter interviews the owner of a restaurant called The Frog and Peach, which after thirty-five years is still unpopular with the public. Perhaps its location (in the boggy moors) and its extremely limited menu (see title of restaurant) have something to do with the public's disinterest. In another sketch, a mother gives her son a ring, and he says he'll wear it "everywhere." The mother replies, "Just your finger will do."

Martin Gottfried in *Women's Wear Daily* liked the production's "high spirits and brightness" which were "refreshing and contagious." The evening wasn't "side-splittingly funny" but it was nonetheless enjoyable "in an adult, breezy way." Douglas Watt in the *New York Daily News* said Moore and Cook were "certifiably insane" and he found the former a "cheerful rodent" and a "dazzling runt of a jester" while the latter's "quizzical stare" hovered "over a body whose parts seem wired together." T. E. Kalem in *Time* said the twosome were "stark-raving bonkers," with Moore a "libidinous opossum" and Cook a man with "the imperturbable aplomb of a tightly furled umbrella." Richard Watts in the *New York Post* said they were "two of the funniest and most inventive men in the world," and Kevin Sanders on WABCTV7 seconded that with the comment they were "arguably the funniest comedy team in the world today."

But Geoffrey Holder on NBC4TV said the "boring" evening lacked "taste, rhyme or reason" and some of the sketches would offend Christians, feminists, and gays. Regarding the latter, for the sketch "Soap Opera" Moore portrayed a "flaming flit" (per Watt) of a gay actor and part-time maid who yearns to play Othello.

A holdover from *Beyond the Fringe* was Moore's classic piano rendition of the "Colonel Bogey March" (played in the styles of Bach, Chopin, and Mozart) in which he can't seem to finish the piece as it exasperatingly goes on and on with a life of its own. Three other sequences had also been seen in the earlier revue: "Sitting on the Bench" (here titled "Down the Mine") about a coal miner who always wanted to be a judge or a writer; "Deutscher Chansons" (here "Die Flabbergast"), a spoof of French and German music; and the above-mentioned "One Leg Too Few" (the latter was added to *Beyond the Fringe* when its revised edition opened in New York on January 8, 1964).

The cast album of *Beyond the Fringe* (Parlophone Records LP # PMC-1145, Capitol Records LP # S/W-1792, and Broadway Angel CD # ZMD-0777-7-64771-2-1) includes "Deutscher Chansons" ("Die Flabbergast") and "Sitting on the Bench" ("Down the Mine"); and the DVD of *Fringe* (Acorn Media # AMP-7990) includes "Deutscher Chansons," "One Leg Too Few," and "Sitting on the Bench."

Awards

Tony Award: Special Award to the "co-stars and authors of *Good Evening*" (**Peter Cook** and **Dudley Moore**)

BETTE MIDLER

Theatre: Palace Theatre
Opening Date: December 3, 1973; *Closing Date*: December 23, 1973
Performances: 19
Technical Direction: Don Stern; *Producers*: Aaron Russo in association with Ron Delsener; *Choreography*: Andre DeShields, Michael Bennett; *Scenery*: Richard Mason; *Costumes*: Bob DeMora; *Lighting*: John Te desco; *Musical Direction*: Barry Manilow
Special Material: Bill Hennessey, Bruch Vilanch

Cast: *Bette Midler*, The Harlettes (Charlotte Crossley, Robin Grean, Sharon Redd), Nick Brown's Hawaii '73 (Singers: Jimmy Kaina, Marvin Stein, Betty Kawamura, Cindy Curtin, and Helen Estol; Musicians: Luther Rix, Frank Vento, Will Lee, and Don Grolnick)

The revue was presented in two acts.

Bette Midler's concert-cum-revue was an evening devoted to many of the favorites in her repertoire, including "Friends" (lyric and music by Mark Klingman and Buzzy Linhart); "Do You Wanna Dance?" (lyric and music by Bobby Freeman); and "Da Doo Ron Ron" (lyric and music by Jeff Barry, Ellie Greenwich, and Phil Spector). And since she happily appropriated many songs from the 1930s and 1940s into her concerts and recordings, the evening also offered "Am I Blue?" (1929 film *On with the Show*; lyric by Grant Clarke, music by Harry Akst); "Lullaby of Broadway" (1935 film *Gold Diggers of 1935*; lyric by Al Dubin, music by Harry Warren); "Optimistic Voices" (1939 film *The Wizard of Oz*; lyric by E. Y. Harburg, music by Harold Arlen and Herbert Stothart); "The Boogie Woogie Bugle Boy from Company 'B'" (1941 film *Buck Privates*; lyric and music by Don Raye and Hughie Prince); and the Glenn Miller standard "In the Mood" (lyric by Andy Razaf, music by Joe Garland).

Otis L. Guernsey Jr., in *Best Plays* didn't include the production in his seasonal annual because he considered it a concert (but ***Liza*** was part of the series' annual summary, tucked right in there between the drama *Find Your Way Home* and ***Lorelei***). However, *Theatre World* decided Midler's revue was a part of the Broadway season (as did the Tony Award committee, who presented both Midler and Minnelli with special Tony Awards "for adding lustre to the Broadway season"). Besides Midler and Minnelli, the season also saw visits from Josephine Baker (***An Evening with Josephine Baker***) and Sammy Davis Jr. (***Sammy***).

Ian Dove in the *New York Times* noted that Midler had been a chorus replacement during the original Broadway run of *Fiddler on the Roof*, and with her current show she just "may have emerged a star." With "ferocious pizzazz" she sang a "'real' Warner Bros. Presents'" version of "Lullaby of Broadway," and her "energy" was "a cross between Sadie Thompson and Martha Raye." And the evening was different from her earlier New York club appearances because she now emphasized "some classy put downs and invective." Dove also commented that the revue's musical director, Barry Manilow, was the show's pianist, and at one point he performed three songs that proved he was a "talent in his own right."

Bette Midler returned in 1975 with ***Bette Midler's Clams on the Half-Shell Revue*** and in 1979 with ***Bette! Divine Madness***.

Awards

Tony Award: Special Tony Award "for adding lustre to the Broadway season" (**Bette Midler**)

THE PAJAMA GAME

"The New Musical Production"

Theatre: Lunt-Fontanne Theatre
Opening Date: December 9, 1973; *Closing Date*: February 3, 1974
Performances: 65
Book: George Abbott and Richard Bissell
Lyrics and Music: Richard Adler and Jerry Ross
Based on the 1953 novel *7½ Cents* by Richard Bissell.
Direction: George Abbott; *Producers*: Richard Adler and Bert Wood in association with Nelson Peltz; *Choreography*: Bob Fosse; *Scenery* and *Costumes*: David Guthrie; *Lighting*: John Gleason; *Musical Direction*: Joyce Brown
Cast: *Cab Calloway* (Hines), Marc Jordan (Prez), Gerrit de Beer (Joe), Willard Waterman (Hasler), Sharron Miller (Gladys), *Hal Linden* (Sid Sorokin), Mary Jo Catlett (Mabel), David Brummel (First Helper), Jon Engstrom (Second Helper), Tiger Haynes (Charlie), *Barbara McNair* (Babe Williams), Margret Coleman (Mae), Chris Calloway (Brenda), Wyetta Turner (Poopsie), Hal Norman (Salesman), Baron Wilson (Pop); Dancers: Dru Alexandrine, Eileen Casey, Vicki Frederick, Mickey Gunnersen, Sally Neal, Jo Ann Ogawa,

P. J. Benjamin, Hank Brunjes, Jon Engstrom, Ben Harney, Randal Harris, Dallas Johann, David Kressler Jr., Cameron Mason, Chester Walker; Singers: Chalyce Brown, Susan Dyas, Rebecca Hoodwin, Patricia Moline, Marie Santell, Cynthia White, Gerrit de Beer, David Brummel, Doug Carfrae, Stan Page, Ward Smith, Teddy Williams

The musical was presented in two acts.

The action takes place in a small town in the Middle West.

Musical Numbers

Act One: "The Pajama Game" (Cab Calloway); "Racing with the Clock" (Girls and Boys); "A New Town Is a Blue Town" (Hal Linden); "I'm Not at All in Love" (Barbara McNair, Girls); "I'll Never Be Jealous Again" (Cab Calloway, Mary Jo Catlett); "Hey, There" (Hal Linden); "Her Is" (Marc Jordan, Sharron Miller); "Sleep-Tite" (Barbara McNair, Boys and Girls); "Once-a-Year Day" (Hal Linden, Barbara McNair, Company; danced by Sharron Miller, Dallas Johann, and Hank Brunjes); "Her Is" (reprise) (Marc Jordan, Margret Coleman); "Small Talk" (Hal Linden, Barbara McNair); "There Once Was a Man" (Hal Linden, Barbara McNair); "Hey, There" (reprise) (Hal Linden)

Act Two: "Steam Heat" (Sharron Miller, David Kressler Jr., P. J. Benjamin); "Watch Your Heart" (Barbara McNair); "Think of the Time I Save" (Cab Calloway, Girls); "Hernando's Hideaway" (Hal Linden, Sharron Miller, Company); "7½ Cents" (Barbara McNair, Marc Jordan, Girls and Boys); "There Once Was a Man" (reprise) (Hal Linden, Barbara McNair); "The Pajama Game" (reprise) (Company)

Except for a limited-engagement City Center revival in 1957, the current production of *The Pajama Game* was the first major Broadway mounting of the lively 1954 musical. The revival was well cast with Hal Linden (Sid), Barbara McNair (Babe), and Cab Calloway (Hines) in the leads, offered the fresh perspective of a pajama factory in the Midwest populated by both blacks and whites, and included a "new" song by Richard Adler for McNair. The number "Watch Your Heart" (aka "If You Win, You Lose") was a revised version of Adler's haunting ballad "What's Wrong with Me?" from his 1961 musical *Kwamina*, where it had been introduced by Sally Ann Howes.

As for the interracial romance between Sid and Babe, the script didn't play coy and ignore the racial differences between the two, but it didn't emphasize matters, either. In some ways, the jolly integration of blacks and whites in a small Midwestern town and its pajama factory was a stretch. This was the 1950s, after all, where women are named Babe and Poopsie and where factory workers get head-over-heels excited about an office picnic. Since this was an old-fashioned musical comedy, it was wise of the revival's creators to avoid turning it into a Brechtian tirade about racial issues and the capitalist system. But for all its picnic gaiety goings-on, the smooth, easy-going production never gave off the steam-heat blast of musical comedy nirvana and it lacked the pizzazz of the brilliantly re-imagined 1994 revival of Adler and Jerry Ross's *Damn Yankees*.

The story took on management-versus-labor issues at a pajama factory in a small Midwestern town and centered on the somewhat rocky romance between new factory superintendant Sid Sorokin (Linden) and factory worker and union representative Babe Williams (McNair). Comic shenanigans were provided by the secondary leads, the factory's time-study-obsessed executive Hines (Calloway) who is insanely jealous of his secretary Gladys (Sharron Williams). The lighthearted book was beautifully complemented by the delightful score, which yielded such standards as "Hey, There," "Hernando's Hideaway," and "Steam Heat."

Richard Watts in the *New York Post* said the original production was "pleasant" and "tuneful," but the revival seemed "even better" and was in fact "brilliant" and sure to be a "resounding success"; Douglas Watt in the *New York Daily News* felt the original novelty of the musical's factory setting had worn off, but the show was still "rousing"; Leonard Harris on WCBSTV2 praised the "lovely" revival of the "marvelous" musical with its "formidable" score and "splendid" cast; and Geoffrey Holder on WNBC4TV said "welcome back" to the "wonderful" musical with its "brilliant" songs and its "light, charming" story. Martin Gottfried in *Women's Wear Daily* found the musical "miraculously as fresh as a daisy and just as welcome." The evening was "invariably cheerful" and he liked the score ("remarkably consistent for melody and charm") and the book (it "may be silly but is at least adult and well-made").

But Clive Barnes in the *New York Times* wasn't enthusiastic. He enjoyed the "great and charming" songs, but felt the book had "worn very badly" and he suggested the production could "have been better" and "more imaginatively done." He was also cool to the leads, whom he felt were mostly miscast, but praised Sharron Miller, who was "a tightly packaged bundle of charm."

During the revival's tryout, the "Jealousy Ballet" (performed by Cab Calloway, Sharron Miller, Mary Jo Catlett, and Boys) was dropped.

The original production opened at the St. James Theatre on May 13, 1954, for a long run of 1,063 performances and won six Tony Awards, including Best Musical, Best Score, and Best Choreography. Immediately after the 1954 Broadway opening, the second-act ballad "The World around Us" was cut and a reprise of "Hey, There" was substituted.

The script was published in hardback by Random House in 1954, and an undated paperback edition was published in Great Britain by Williamson Music. The libretto is also included in the 2014 Library of Congress hardback collection *American Musicals*, which includes the scripts of fifteen other musicals. The original cast album of the 1954 production was released by Columbia Records (LP # OL-4840) and the CD by Sony Classical/Columbia/Legacy (# SK-89253) and includes a number of bonus tracks such as "The World around Us" and "Sleep-Tite." The 1997 studio cast recording by Jay Records (# CDJAY2-1250) includes the complete "Jealousy Ballet" (here titled "I'll Never Be Jealous Again Ballet") as well as the factory slowdown music, the entr'acte, and the finale, curtain, and exit music (but the recording ignores "The World around Us").

The London production opened at the Coliseum on October 13, 1955, for 588 performances, and the cast members included Elizabeth Seal (as Gladys). The cast album was released by Axis/EMI Records (CD # 7017902) and by Sepia Records (CD # 1072).

The faithful 1957 film version released by Warner Brothers was directed by George Abbott and Stanley Donen and choreographed by Bob Fosse. With the exception of Janis Paige (who was replaced by Doris Day), virtually all the stage principals reprised their roles for the film. A new song for Day by Adler called "The Man Who Invented Love" was filmed but cut prior to the film's release; its outtake is included as a bonus on the DVD issued by Warner Brothers (# 70599).

As mentioned, the musical was first revived in New York at City Center by the New York City Center Light Opera Company on May 15, 1957, for twenty-three performances. After the current revival, the work was produced by the New York City Opera Company at the New York State Theatre on March 3, 1989, for fifty-one performances; and the most recent revival was offered by the Roundabout Theatre Company at the American Airlines Theatre on February 23, 2006, for 129 performances. The latter production included "The World around Us"; "If You Win, You Lose" (aka "Watch Your Heart"); and "The Three of Us," a new song by Adler. The cast album was released on a two-CD set by Columbia (# CK-99036). One CD is devoted to selections from Harry Connick Jr.'s 2001 musical *Thou Shalt Not*, and the second CD to *The Pajama Game* (and includes "The World around Us," "If You Win, You Lose," "The Three of Us," "Sleep-Tite," and the factory slowdown music).

Co-librettist Richard Bissell had seen his novel *7½ Cents* adapted into *The Pajama Game*, and was later inspired to write the novel *Say, Darling* (1957), about a writer's observations when his novel is adapted into a hit musical. This slightly Pirandelloesque approach resulted in the adaptation of *Say, Darling* into the 1958 play-with-music, also called *Say, Darling* (and subtitled "a comedy about a musical").

THE BEGGAR'S OPERA

Theatre: Billy Rose Theatre
Opening Date: December 22, 1973; *Closing Date*: December 31, 1973
Performances: 6
Book and *Lyrics*: John Gay
Music: Music arranged by Roland Gagnon (probably from the music adapted by Johann Christoph Pepusch for the original 1728 production)
Direction: Gene Lesser; *Producer*: City Center Acting Company (John Houseman, Artistic Director; Margot Harley, Producing Director; Porter Van Zandt, Executive Director); *Choreography*: Elizabeth Keen; *Scenery*: Robert Yodice; *Costumes*: Carrie F. Robbins; *Lighting*: Martin Aronstein; *Musical Direction*: Roland Gagnon

Cast: Norman Snow (Filch), Benjamin Hendrickson (Beggar), David Ogden Stiers (Peachum), Mary Lou Rosato (Mrs. Peachum, Betty Coaxer), Cynthia Herman (Polly Peachum), Kevin Kline (Macheath), Richard Ooms (Matt of the Mint), Peter Dvorsky (Jemmy Twitcher), Joel Colodner (Harry Paddington), David Schramm (Wat Dreary), Jared Sakren (Crook-Finger'd Jack), Gerald Shaw (Nimming Ned), Nita Angeletti (Mrs. Trapes), Leah Chandler (Dolly Trull), Mary-Joan Negro (Jenny Diver), Gisela Caldwell (Suky Tawdry), Sam Tsoutsouvas (Lockit), Patti LuPone (Lucy Lockit)

The musical was presented in two acts.

The action takes place in eighteenth-century London in and around Newgate Prison.

Musical Numbers

Note: The program didn't list individual musical numbers.

The short-lived City Center Acting Company presented a season of five works, all of which were limited engagements. Besides *The Beggar's Opera*, the company offered revivals of Anton Chekhov's *The Three Sisters*, William Shakespeare's *Measure for Measure*, James Saunders's *Next Time I'll Sing to You*, and a special performance for children of Moliere's *Scapin*. The cast of *The Beggar's Opera* was impressive, with early New York performances by Patti LuPone, Kevin Kline, and David Ogden Stiers. Roland Gagnon conducted an offstage orchestra of three musicians (who played organ, guitar, reed, and percussion).

Richard Watts in the *New York Post* praised the "likeable romp" and singled out Patti LuPone ("just right"), Kevin Kline ("properly debonair"), and David Ogden Stiers ("amusingly outrageous"). He also noted the production was "at its best" when "the riffraff and strumpets go in for lively and exultant dances." Douglas Watt in the *New York Daily News* felt the evening was "good-natured, workmanlike, but rather dull," and things only picked up when Patti LuPone's Lucy Lockit appeared in the second act. The role called for "a spirited actress," and LuPone met the role "head on in a salty, admirably alert comedy performance."

The Beggar's Opera premiered in London at the Drury Lane in 1728 with book and lyrics by John Gay and music adapted by Johann Christoph Pepusch. The work spoofed the mores and manners of the middle class as well as the conventions of opera itself. The cynical mood piece dealt with London lowlifes, including Macheath (Kline in the current revival), his criminal gang of pickpockets and thieves, and a group of prostitutes. Macheath is romantically involved with the pure Polly Peachum (Cynthia Hermam) and the amoral Lucy Lockit (LuPone), but his crimes catch up with him and he's sentenced to death. But the lovable scoundrel is also the hero of the opera, and a hero can't possibly go to the gallows. So Macheath is pardoned and he and Polly head for the altar.

The work was first seen in the United States during the 1855–1856 theatre season, and of course was the inspiration for Bertolt Brecht and Kurt Weill's *The Threepenny Opera*, which premiered in Berlin in 1928 and New York in 1933.

The New York City Center Light Opera Company revived *The Beggar's Opera* on March 13, 1957, for 15 performances in an adaptation by Richard Baldridge (Daniel Pinkham adapted the music); the production starred two husband-and-wife teams, Jack Cassidy and Shirley Jones, and George S. Irving and Maria Karnilova. On March 21, 1972, the musical was revived by the Chelsea Theatre Center of Brooklyn at the Brooklyn Academy of Music for 29 performances, and then on May 30, 1972, transferred to Off-Broadway's McAlpin Rooftop Theatre for 224 performances (the score was "newly realized" by Ryan Edwards).

In 1981, a complete rendering of the score was released on a two-LP set by London Records (# LDR-72008) with a cast that included Kiri Te Kanawa, Joan Sutherland, James Morris, Angela Lansbury, Alfred Marks, Regina Resnik, and Michael Hordern. A 1953 film version of *The Beggar's Opera* was directed by Peter Brook, and the cast included Laurence Olivier, Stanley Holloway, Dorothy Tutin, Hugh Griffith, and Laurence Naismith. There have been three film adaptations of *The Threepenny Opera* (in 1931, 1964, and 1989).

A number of musicals have been inspired by *The Beggar's Opera*, including the 1946 Broadway musical *Beggar's Holiday* (book and lyrics by John LaTouche and music by Duke Ellington); the 1961 Chicago *Big Deal* (book by Paul Sills, lyrics by David Shepherd, and music by William Mathieu); and the 1979 Off-Off-Broadway *The Beggar's Soap Opera* (book and lyrics by Dolores Prida and music by Paul Radelat), which managed to spoof the original work as well as Spanish television soap operas.

AN EVENING WITH JOSEPHINE BAKER

Theatre: Palace Theatre
Opening Date: December 31, 1973; *Closing Date*: January 6, 1974
Performances: 7
Direction: Patrick Horrigan ("Stage Director"); *Producers*: The Palace Theatre (under the direction of the Messrs. Nederlander); *Lighting*: Don Stern ("Lighting Consultant"); *Musical Direction*: Not credited
Cast: *Josephine Baker*, G. Keith Alexander (Master of Ceremonies), Roberto Lorco and Company (Paco Juanas, Guitarist; Domingo Alverado, Singer); Baby Laurence ("The World's Greatest Tap Percussionist"); The Michael Powell Ensemble: Michael Powell, Joey Coleman, Leeroy Cooks, Vinson Cunningham, Bernadette Doctor, Dorthea Doctor, Norman Hawkins, Ricardo Portlette, Charlene Ricks, Barbara Rolle, Calvin Van Meter, Esther Westbrook, Peggy Williams, and Shirley Williams
The revue was presented in two acts.

Musical Numbers

Note: Most numbers were sung by Josephine Baker.
Act One: "People" (*Funny Girl*, 1964; lyric by Bob Merrill, music by Jule Styne); "Sourire"; "(It's) Impossible" (English lyric by Sid Wayne, music by Armando Manzareno); "Avec" (from the revue *Paris mes amours*; lyric and music by Henri Betti, Bruno Coquatrix, and Andre Hornez); "Love Story" ("Where Do I Begin?") (1968 film *Love Story*; lyric by Carl Sigman, music by Francis Lai); "Hello, Young Lovers" (*The King and I*, 1951; lyric by Oscar Hammerstein II, music by Richard Rodgers); Medley
Act Two: "Lend Your Ear"; "Si me faltas tu" (lyric and music by Armando Manzareno); Medley from *My Fair Lady* (1956; lyrics by Alan Jay Lerner, music by Frederick Loewe); "Demain" (lyric and music by Donaggio, Pallavicini, Annoux, and Vallade); "La vie en rose"(lyric by Edith Piaf, music by Marguerite Monnot and Louis Guglielmi aka Louiguy); "Yesterday" (lyric and music by Paul McCartney); "J'ai deux amours" (lyric and music by Georges Koger, Henri Varna, and Vincent Baptiste Scotto); "My Sweet Lord" (lyric and music by George Harrison)

Singer Josephine Baker (1906–1975) made her Broadway debut in *The Chocolate Dandies* at the Colonial Theatre on September 1, 1924. Most of her life and career were centered in Paris, where she became a superstar, a French citizen, and, as they say, the toast of the continent. Irving Berlin's 1933 revue *As Thousands Cheer* paid homage to her in the sequence "Josephine Baker Still the Rage of Paris" in which Ethel Waters portrayed the wealthy international headliner who confesses that she still has "Harlem on My Mind."

Baker later appeared on Broadway in the 1936 edition of the *Ziegfeld Follies*, which premiered at the Winter Garden Theatre on January 30 for two engagements that totaled 227 performances, but her Broadway-bound revue *Paris Sings Again* closed during its tryout in 1948. Her next New York appearance was *Josephine Baker and Her Company*, which opened at the Brooks Atkinson Theatre on February 4, 1964, for a limited engagement of sixteen performances but reopened at Henry Miller's Theatre on March 31 for an additional twenty-four showings. She then appeared at Carnegie Hall for a special celebration (billed as "50 Years in Show Business/Golden Jubilee") on June 5 through June 8, 1973, and the current limited engagement on December 31 of that year marked her final New York appearances.

The June 1973 concert was recorded live and released on the two-LP set *Josephine Baker Live at Carnegie Hall* (unnamed label # JB-001). The recording includes most of the songs that were heard in the December 1973 engagement and is representative of her repertoire during the era. Songs on the album that were in the December production are: "People," "Sourire," "Impossible," "Avec," "Hello, Young Lovers," "Se me faltas tu," a medley of two songs from *My Fair Lady* ("On the Street Where You Live" and "I Could Have Danced All Night"), "Demain," "La vie en rose," "J'ai deux amours," and "My Sweet Lord." Although she didn't perform "Island in the West Indies" in the 1936 *Ziegfeld Follies*, she included the song in the Carnegie Hall celebration and it can be heard on the recording.

In reviewing the current program, Howard Thompson in the *New York Times* stated Baker was "a real singer" with "luscious, honeyed tones in the middle register and hearty top ones belted out when she chooses." In one sequence the glamorous personality appeared in denims next to a motorcycle, and then later she emerged "dripping ermine and feathers" as she led two Russian wolfhounds (both of which "balked" and thus displayed "the evening's only flash of temperament"). Thompson noted that, besides Baker, the "sight" of the show was the audience's response to her invitation to join her on the stage for a dance contest. The first-nighters "eagerly" filled the aisles, many of them "in exotic garb" that rivaled what Baker wore, and one tall man ("prancing rhapsodically and adorned like a Christmas tree") "drew a wary glance from the star."

The number "Mira Bra" (which was apparently performed by the Roberto Lorco Company) was choreographed by Maria Rosa Merced.

The biographical film *The Josephine Baker Story* was shown on the Home Box Office channel in 1991 (Lynn Whitfield played the title role), and there have been at least five musicals written about Baker's life and career, four of them produced. *Josephine* was presented as a showcase production in London in the 1980s at the Fortune Theatre with Heather Gillespie in the title role and a score by Michael Wild; *Looking for Josephine* was produced in regional theatre; Wally Harper and Sherman Yellen's *Josephine Tonight*, which focused on Baker's early life, was also seen in regional theatre; and *The Sensational Josephine Baker*, which was written and performed by Cheryl Howard, opened Off Broadway at the Beckett Theatre on June 26, 2012, for a scheduled run of twelve weeks. The one as yet unproduced show is untitled but was once mentioned for a Broadway production. The London *Josephine* was recorded, and the *Josephine Tonight* score was praised by the *Washington Post*, which noted "the ragtime-and-blues-inspired songs often sparkle with wit, melodiousness and infectious rhythm."

LIZA

Theatre: Winter Garden Theatre
Opening Date: January 6, 1974; *Closing Date*: January 26, 1974
Performances: 23
Continuity: Written by Fred Ebb
Original Musical Material: Lyrics by Fred Ebb and music by John Kander
Direction: Bob Fosse; *Producers*: The Shubert Organization in association with Ron Delsener; *Choreography*: Bob Fosse, Ron Lewis; *Lighting*: Jules Fisher; *Musical Direction*: Jack French
Cast: *Liza Minnelli*; Dancers: Pam Barlow, Spencer Henderson, Jimmy Roddy, Sharon Wylie
The concert was presented in two acts.

Musical Numbers

All songs were performed by Liza Minnelli; division of acts unknown.
Overture (Orchestra) (overture included "Liza with a 'Z'" [1972 television special of the same name; lyric by Fred Ebb, music by John Kander], "Ring Them Bells" [1972 television special *Liza with a "Z"*; lyric by Fred Ebb, music by John Kander], "I Can See Clearly Now" [lyric and music by Johnny Nash], "Maybe This Time" [independent song interpolated into 1972 film version of *Cabaret*; lyric by Fred Ebb, music by John Kander], and "Cabaret" [title song of 1966 Broadway musical; lyric by Fred Ebb, music by John Kander]); "If You Could Read My Mind" (lyric and music by Gordon Lightfoot); "Come Back to Me" (*On a Clear Day You Can See Forever*, 1965; lyric by Alan Jay Lerner, music by Burton Lane); "Shine on, Harvest Moon" (*Ziegfeld Follies of 1908*; lyric and music by Nora Bayes and Jack Norworth); "Exactly Like Me" (lyric by Fred Ebb, music by John Kander); "The Circle" (English lyric by Fred Ebb, music by Edith Piaf); "More Than You Know" (*Great Day!*, 1929; lyric by Billy Rose and Edward Eliscu, music by Vincent Youmans); "I'm One of the Smart Ones" (lyric by Fred Ebb, music by John Kander); "Natural Man" (lyric and music by Bobby Hebb and Sandy Baron); "I Can See Clearly Now" (lyric and music by Johnny Nash); "And I in My Chair" ("Et moi dans mon coin") (lyric and music by Jeff Davis, Charles Aznavour, and Fred Ebb); "There Is a Time" ("Les temps") (lyric and music Jeff Davis, Charles Aznavour, and Gene Lees); "A Quiet Thing" (*Flora, The Red Menace*, 1965; lyric by Fred Ebb, music by John Kander); "Anywhere You Are" (lyric by Fred Ebb, music by John Kander); "I Believe You" (lyric by Fred Ebb, music by John Kander); "Cabaret" (*Cabaret*, 1966; lyric by Fred Ebb, music by John Kander) ; "Ring Them Bells" (1972 television special *Liza with a "Z"*; lyric by Fred Ebb, music by John Kander); "I Gotcha" (1972 television special *Liza*

with a "Z"; lyric and music by Joe Tex); "Bye Bye Blackbird" (1972 television special *Liza with a "Z"*; lyric by Mort Dixon, music by Ray Henderson); *Note*: Other songs performed by Minnelli in the concert were: "You and I" (lyric and music by Stevie Wonder); "It Had to Be You" (lyric by Gus Kahn, music by Isham Jones); "My Shining Hour" (1943 film *The Sky's the Limit*; lyric by Johnny Mercer and music by Harold Arlen); and "Yes" (*70, Girls, 70*, 1971; lyric by Fred Ebb, music by John Kander); "My Mammy" (lyric by Joe Young and Sam M. Lewis, music by Walter Donaldson); and "It Was a Good Time" (1970 film *Ryan's Daughter*; lyric by Mack David and Mike Curb, music by Maurice Jarre).

Liza Minnelli's concert was titled *Liza* on the program cover, and *Liza Minnelli* on the program's title page, but this detail didn't matter to her fans, who turned the limited engagement into a complete sell-out that broke all records at the Winter Garden Theatre. The production was virtually a one-woman show; Minnelli sang every number, and was occasionally backed by four dancers.

Clive Barnes in the *New York Times* said Minnelli's appeal was due to "some exciting internal tension" in which she was always "on" but alternated between "coming on strong doing a Jolson number as Miss Show Business of 1932" and then as "a little girl lost in a Lord Fauntleroy velvet suit." The evening was a "winner" and the "exciting" Minnelli made the Winter Garden seem like summer.

For the first three numbers performed in Minnelli's successful 1972 television special *Liza with a "Z"* ("Ring Them Bells," "I Gotcha," and "Bye Bye Blackbird"), Bob Fosse recreated his original choreography. Ron Lewis choreographed "Natural Man" and "I Can See Clearly Now."

The concert was recorded on LP by Columbia Records as *Liza Minnelli Live at the Winter Garden*, and released on CD by Sony/Masterworks Broadway (the latter includes three numbers not included on the original release, "I Gotcha," "It Had to Be You," and "My Shining Hour," all of which had been performed and recorded at the concert).

Awards

Tony Award: Special Tony Award "for adding lustre to the Broadway season" (**Liza Minnelli**)

LORELEI, or GENTLEMEN STILL PREFER BLONDES

"A MUSICAL COMEDY"

Theatre: Palace Theatre
Opening Date: January 27, 1974; *Closing Date*: November 3, 1974
Performances: 321
Book: Anita Loos and Joseph Fields; *New Book*: Kenny Solms and Gail Parent
Lyrics: Leo Robin; *New Lyrics*: Betty Comden and Adolph Green
Music: Jule Styne

Based on the 1925 novel *Gentlemen Prefer Blondes: The Intimate Diary of a Professional Lady* by Anita Loos (the book had been previously serialized in *Harper's Bazaar*); in 1926, a nonmusical stage adaptation by Loos and her husband John Emerson opened on Broadway.

Direction: Robert Moore; *Producers*: Lee Guber and Shelly Gross; *Choreography*: Ernest G. Flatt; *Scenery*: John Conklin; *Costumes*: Alvin Colt; *Carol Channing's Costumes*: Ray Aghayan and Bob Mackie; *Lighting*: John Gleason; *Musical Direction*: Milton Rosenstock

Cast: *Carol Channing* (Lorelei Lee, Dessert), Lee Roy Reams (Henry Spofford), Dody Goodman (Mrs. Ella Spofford), Jack Fletcher (Lord Francis Beekman), Jean Bruno (Lady Phyllis Beekman), Brandon Maggart (Josephus Gage), Tamara Long (Dorothy Shaw), Peter Palmer (Gus Esmond), Ray Cox (Bartender, Pierre, Announcer), Steve Short (Frank, Gendarme), Bob Daley (George, Engineer), Robert Riker (Charles, Master of Ceremonies), Bob Fitch (Robert Lemanteur), Ian Tucker (Louis Lemanteur), Brenda Holmes (Lobster), Linda McClure (Caviar, Bridesmaid), Aniko Farrell (Pheasant, Bridesmaid), Marie Halton (Salade, Bridesmaid), Willard Beckham (Maitre D'), Joela Flood (Zizi), Gina Ramsel (Fifi), Sherrill Harper (Simone Duval, Bridesmaid), David Neuman (Mr. Esmond); Ship's Personnel, Passengers, Olympic Team Members, Waiters, Wedding Guests: Aniko Farrell, Joela Flood, Marie Halton, Marian Haraldson, Sherrill Harper, Brenda

Holmes, Linda Lee MacArthur, Linda McClure, Susan Ohman, Gina Ramsel, Roxanna White, Willard Beckham, Ray Cox, Bob Daley, Bob Fitch, Gregg Harlan, Wayne Mattson, Jonathan Miele, Jeff Richards, Robert Riker, Rich Schneider, Steve Short, Don Swanson, Ian Tucker

The musical was presented in two acts.

The action takes place in 1944 and in the mid-1920s in Paris, at sea, and in New York

Musical Numbers

Note: * = lyrics by Leo Robin; and ** = lyrics by Betty Comden and Adolph Green.

Act One: "Looking Back" (**) (Carol Channing); "Bye, Bye, Baby" (*) (Peter Palmer, Carol Channing, Passengers, Tourists); "A Little Girl from Little Rock" (*) (Carol Channing); "I Love What I'm Doing" (*) (Tamara Long); "It's Delightful Down in Chile" (*) (Carol Channing, Jack Fletcher, Stewards); "I Won't Let You Get Away" (**) (Lee Roy Reams, Tamara Long); "Keeping Cool with Coolidge" (*) (Lee Roy Reams, Tamara Long, Dody Goodman, Guests); "Men" (**) (Carol Channing)

Act Two: "Coquette" (*) (Tamara Long, Carol Channing, Show Girls); "Mamie Is Mimi" (*) (Carol Channing, Bob Fitch, Ian Tucker); "Diamonds Are a Girl's Best Friend" (*) (Carol Channing); "Homesick" (aka "Homesick Blues") (*) (Carol Channing, Peter Palmer, Lee Roy Reams, Tamara Long, Brandon Maggart, Dody Goodman); "Miss Lorelei Lee" (**) (Lee Roy Reams, Tamara Long, Dody Goodman, Brandon Maggart, Bob Fitch, Ian Tucker, Wedding Guests); "Button Up with Esmond" (*) (Carol Channing, Bridesmaids); "Diamonds Are a Girl's Best Friend" (reprise) (*) (Carol Channing)

Carol Channing became an instant legend with her performance as Lorelei Lee in *Gentlemen Prefer Blondes*. As the dizzy but not dumb blonde diamond hunter (of the tiara variety), she created one of the most memorable roles in the history of the Broadway musical. In their reviews of the original 1949 production, Brooks Atkinson in the *New York Times* wrote that in regard to Channing there had "never been anything like this before in human society" and Ward Morehouse in the *New York Sun* noted that with her "vacuous stare" and "mincing steps" she was about as "helpless as a fretful boa constrictor."

Lorelei was a revised version of the earlier musical, with a new book by Kenny Solms and Gail Parent and some new songs by Jule Styne, Betty Comden, and Adolph Green. For the revision, the prologue began in 1944 when the widowed Lorelei sails off to Paris and reminisces about her adventures back in the 1920s. And from there on in, the musical was a flashback set in Paris with Lorelei's crony Dorothy (Tamara Long), her boyfriend and future husband Gus Edmond (Peter Palmer), and assorted colorful types from her flapper days.

The production retained ten numbers from the original ("Bye, Bye, Baby," "A Little Girl from Little Rock," "I Love What I'm Doing," "It's Delightful Down in Chile," "Keeping Cool with Coolidge," "Coquette," "Mamie Is Mimi," "Diamonds Are a Girl's Best Friend," "Homesick Blues," and "Button Up with Esmond") and added four ("Looking Back," "I Won't Let You Get Away," "Men," and "Miss Lorelei Lee"). During the year-long pre-Broadway national tour, four numbers from the original production were heard at one time or another, but were dropped before the New York opening ("It's High Time," "I'm A'Tingle, I'm A'Glow," "We're Just a Kiss Apart," and "Sunshine," which was rewritten as "Paris" [aka "Paris, Paris"]). Three numbers from the original production ("You Say You Care," "A House on Rittenhouse Square," and the title song) didn't seem to make the cut at all, and apparently were never performed during the tryout of the revised production. The tryout also included two new songs ("A Girl Like I" and "Lorelei") which were dropped by the time the show reached New York.

The production was bright and summery, and Channing was a delight. She knocked out audiences all over again with her definitive interpretations of "A Little Girl from Little Rock" and "Diamonds Are a Girl's Best Friend," and made a great comic impression with the new song "Men" which literally brought down the curtain on both her and the first act.

During the tryout, John Mineo was succeeded by Ian Tucker and Brooks Morton by Jack Fletcher. Joe Layton was the director and choreographer and Ernie (aka Ernest G.) Flatt was credited with additional choreography; at one point during the tryout, Betty Comden and Adolph Green were given directorial credit; and by New York, Robert Moore was the director of record and Flatt was the choreographer.

There were two cast albums of *Lorelei*. The pre-Broadway tour was recorded by MGM/Verve (LP # MV-5097-OC) and includes "I'm A'Tingle, I'm A'Glow," "Just a Kiss Apart," "Paris, Paris," and Peter Palmer's smooth version of the lovely title song, which was eventually dropped. The Broadway cast album (MGM LP # M3G-55) includes numbers added after the touring production had been recorded ("It's Delightful Down in Chile, "Men," and "Miss Lorelei Lee"). The CD (released by Decca Broadway # B0001407-02) includes all the songs from the two LPs as well as both overtures (the first overture included "A Girl Like I," which was dropped during the pre-Broadway tour).

Richard Watts in the *New York Post* felt the new book let Channing down, but because she kept the evening going with her limitless vitality and enthusiasm there would never be an energy crisis. Douglas Watt in the *New York Daily News* said the book was "creaky" and "something of a nuisance," but Channing looked great and still spoke "with that measured baby voice that can suddenly plummet to the bottom of the scale." Clive Barnes in the *New York Times* said "her timing is such that if she were a railroad system, even Mussolini would have eaten his heart out"; and in the same newspaper Walter Kerr noted she was the only performer "who can live up to a Hirschfeld" and "the only entertainer left who can carry a whole show by herself, portal to portal."

Martin Gottfried in *Women's Wear Daily* said the production was "the first genuinely professional musical of the season"; it had "million dollar looks" and "energy, polish, and style." As for Channing, "every one of today's manufactured superstars should be dragged to the Palace to take a look at her and see what work, talent, showmanship, clout and class really are."

Gentlemen Prefer Blondes opened at the Ziegfeld Theatre on December 8, 1949, for 740 performances (Milton Rosenstock was conductor for the original production as well as for *Lorelei*); the original cast album was released by Columbia Records (LP # ML-4290), and issued on CD by Sony Broadway (# SK-48013). A slightly revised version opened on Broadway at the Lyceum Theatre on April 10, 1995, for twenty-four performances; K. T. Sullivan was Lorelei, and the production was recorded by DRG Records (CD # 94762). A concert version by Encores! with Megan Hilty as Lorelei played at City Center for a limited engagement of seven performances beginning on May 9, 2012, and was recorded by Masterworks Broadway (CD # 88725-44451-2).

The London production opened at the Princes Theatre on August 20, 1962, for 223 performances with Dora Bryan in the leading role; the cast album was released by HMV Records (LP # 1464) and later by That's Entertainment Records (LP # TER-1059).

The splashy 1953 film version released by Twentieth Century-Fox starred Marilyn Monroe (Lorelei) and Jane Russell (Dorothy), and in her own way Monroe's Lorelei is as iconic as Channing's. The film retained three songs from the Broadway production ("Bye, Bye, Baby," "Diamonds Are a Girl's Best Friend," and "A Little Girl from Little Rock") and added two new ones ("When Love Goes Wrong" and "Ain't There Anyone Here for Love?") with lyrics by Harold Adamson and music by Hoagy Carmichael.

Awards

Tony Award Nomination: Best Leading Actress in a Musical (Carol Channing)

RAINBOW JONES

"A Musical Fable" / "A New Musical"

Theatre: Music Box Theatre
Opening Date: February 13, 1974; *Closing Date*: February 13, 1974
Performances: 1
Book, Lyrics, and *Music*: Jill Williams
Direction: Gene Persson; *Producers*: Rubykate, Incorporated in association with Phil Gillin and Gene Bambic; *Choreography*: Sammy Bayes; *Scenery*: Richard Ferrer; *Costumes*: James Berton Harris; *Lighting*: Spencer Mosse; *Musical Direction*: Danny Holgate
Cast: Ruby Persson (Rainbow Jones), Peggy Hagen Lamprey (Leona), Andy Rohrer (Bones), Gil Robbins (C. A. Fox), Stephanie Silver (Cardigan), Peter Kastner (Joey Miller), Kay St. Germain (Aunt Felicity), Daniel Keyes (Uncle Ithaca)
The musical was presented in two acts.
The action takes place during the present in New York City and in Ohio.

Musical Numbers

Act One: "A Little Bit of Me in You" (Peggy Hagen Lamprey, Andy Rohrer, Gil Robbins, Stephanie Silver); "Free and Easy" (Ruby Persson); "Do unto Others" (Ruby Persson, Peggy Hagen Lamprey, Andy Rohrer, Gil Robbins, Stephanie Silver); "I'd Like to Know You Better" (Peter Kastner); "Bad Breath" (Peggy Hagen Lamprey, Andy Rohrer, Gil Robbins, Stephanie Silver); "I'd Like to Know You Better" (reprise) (Peter Kastner, Ruby Persson, Peggy Hagen Lamprey, Andy Rohrer, Gil Robbins, Stephanie Silver); "Alone, at Last, Alone" (Kay St. Germain); "Free and Easy" (reprise) (Ruby Persson); "Her Name Is Leona" (Ruby Persson, Andy Rohrer, Stephanie Silver, Gil Robbins, Peggy Hagen Lamprey); "We All Need Love" (Stephanie Silver, Andy Rohrer, Gil Robbins, Peggy Hagen Lamprey)

Act Two: "We All Need Love" (reprise) (Stephanie Silver, Gil Robbins, Andy Rohrer); "The Only Man for the Job" (Andy Rohrer); "It's So Nice" (Kay St. Germain, Daniel Keyes); "Wait a Little While" (Peggy Hagen Lamprey); "It's So Nice" (reprise) (Ruby Persson, Kay St. Germain, Daniel Keyes, Peter Kastner); "One Big Happy Family" (Peter Kastner, Gil Robbins, Andy Rohrer, Stephanie Silver, Peggy Hagen Lamprey); "Who Needs the Love of a Woman" (Peter Kastner, Ruby Persson); "We All Need Love" (reprise) and "A Little Bit of Me in You" (reprise) (Peter Kastner, Ruby Persson, Stephanie Silver, Andy Rohrer, Gil Robbins, Peggy Hagen Lamprey)

With one performance and out, *Rainbow Jones* was the season's shortest-running musical and certainly one of the most insufferable ones of the decade. The overly coy and precious plot dealt with Beatrice Jones (Ruby Persson), who likes to be called Rainbow Jones. She can't seem to hold down a job, never stays very long in any of the schools she attends, and likes to spend her time in Central Park reading *Aesop's Fables* and visiting with friends. In this case, her friends are a quartet of animals that only she (and later jogger-in-the-park and soon-to-be-boyfriend Joey [Peter Kastner]) can see, lion Leona (Peggy Hagen Lamprey), dog Bones (Andy Rohrer), fox C. A. Fox (Gil Robbins), and sheep Cardigan (Stephanie Silver). The animals chat with her, they give her advice, they sometimes squabble among themselves . . . and within minutes of watching this foolishness one realized that being petrified with boredom was perhaps not just an expression.

The nonsensical plot and dialogue, the generally vapid songs, the unimaginative décor, and the bland performances did the show in, and nothing could salvage it. Well, almost nothing. For a brief few minutes midway into the first act, Rainbow's Aunt Felicity (Kay St. Germain) ripped into the rather jaunty, Charleston-inflected "Alone, at Last, Alone" and fantasized about a life without Rainbow. The moment was a spontaneous and jubilant one, and the audience could easily relate to Aunt Felicity's joy at the prospect of being rid of Rainbow.

Martin Gottfried in *Women's Wear Daily* noted that coyness was bad enough in a small Off-Broadway venue and was even worse on Broadway, where it became as "embarrassing" as "an aunt in pigtails." He felt it appropriate that Rainbow Jones's only reading matter was *Aesop's Fables* because she didn't seem literate enough "for anything more difficult." He also mentioned that the music was as "invisible" as the animals and the show itself, and so at intermission he too became invisible.

Leonard Harris on WCBSTV2 found the musical "a drowsy bit of whimsy," and Clive Barnes in the *New York Times* said the "coy and simpering" evening had book, lyrics, and music that were "very even in quality" because "the book is as bad as the music, the music as bad as the lyrics, and the lyrics are as bad as either."

Douglas Watt in the *New York Daily News* said musicals with "moony speculations" came along at least once every season, and mentioned *Celebration* (1969), ***Park***, and ***Shelter***. As for most of the performers, he wouldn't mention their names because "I don't really ever want to see any of them again," and for the "common good" librettist-lyricist-composer Jill Williams should "be denied access either to a typewriter or a musical instrument of any kind." The book was "extremely silly" and "it would be dignifying her songs to call them commonplace." He felt sorry for the venerable Music Box Theatre. It was a desirable house and producers once fought to book their shows there, and now it had to "suffer fools."

But Richard Watts in the *New York Post* liked the musical's "delightful idea" and its "wonderful conception," and regretted Williams didn't employ the "proper inventiveness" to carry it off. The musical was "always pleasant" and "far from being a disaster," but it was "nevertheless disappointing" and the score wasn't "very interesting."

During its tryout, the musical was titled *R.J.*, and the songs "Listen to Me," "One Just Portion," and "Ju, Ju, Jupiter" were cut. For Broadway, Richard Kuller (Bones), Jay Bonnell (C. A. Fox), and Peter Johl (Uncle

Ithaca) were respectively succeeded by Andy Rohrer, Gil Robbins, and Daniel Keyes. When the tryout was first advertised, Barbara Baxley was named as one of the production's leads (apparently in the role of Aunt Felicity).

The script was published in paperback by Pioneer Drama Service in 1979.

SEXTET

"A New Musical"

Theatre: Bijou Theatre
Opening Date: March 3, 1974; *Closing Date*: March 10, 1974
Performances: 9
Book: Harvey Kerr and Lee Goldsmith
Lyrics: Lee Goldsmith
Music: Lawrence Hurwit
Direction and *Choreography*: Jered Barclay (Mary Jane Houdina, Assistant Choreographer); *Producers*: Balemar Productions and Lawrence E. Sokol; *Scenery*: Peter Harvey; *Costumes*: Zoe Brown; *Lighting*: Marc B. Weiss; *Musical Direction*: David Frank
Cast: Robert Spencer (David), John Newton (Paul), Mary Small (Fay), Harvey Evans (Kenneth), Dixie Carter (Ann), Jerry Lanning (Leonard)
The musical was presented in one act.
The action takes place in New York City during the present time.

Musical Numbers

"Nervous" (Company); "What the Hell Am I Doing Here?" (John Newton); "Keep on Dancing" (Robert Spencer, Harvey Evans, Mary Small, John Newton); "Spunk" (Mary Small, Robert Spencer, Harvey Evans); "Visiting Rights" (Dixie Carter); "Going-Staying" (Company); "I Wonder" (Dixie Carter, Mary Small); "Women and Men" (Jerry Lanning, Robert Spencer, Harvey Evans); "I Love You All the Time" (Jerry Lanning); "Keep on Dancing" (reprise) (Company); "Hi" (Harvey Evans); "Roseland" (Company); "How Does It Start?" (Robert Spencer); "Roseland" (reprise) (Company)

After ***Company***, any musical set in contemporary Manhattan that focused on singles and married couples was bound to be measured against Stephen Sondheim's iconic work. And so naturally *Sextet* was compared to the earlier musical, and the title of its song "Going-Staying" certainly brought to mind Sondheim's "Sorry-Grateful." Other musicals during the decade that also dealt with ***Company***-like themes were such Off-Broadway items as *Wonderful Lives* (1977) and *Piano Bar* (1978).

Sextet took place at a small dinner party given by gay couple David (Robert Spencer) and Kenneth (Harvey Evans), and among the guests are David's widowed mother Fay (Mary Small) and her boyfriend Paul (John Newton). Back in his college days, David had an unreciprocated crush on his straight roommate Leonard (Jerry Lanning), and now Leonard's in town from Seattle and has arrived at the party with his wife Ann (Dixie Carter). (For a while, it seemed *Sextet* had cross-pollinated ***Company*** with *The Boys in the Band*.)

Nothing much really happens at the party. David wonders what it would be like to be straight and seems somewhat attracted to Ann (or is this just a bit of transference, since Ann is Leonard's wife?). Meanwhile, Ann discovers Leonard has women on the side, Fay discovers that Paul has no interest in marriage, and Kenneth decides to spend the remainder of the night at the baths. That was it, and Douglas Watt in the *New York Daily News* said at the show's conclusion everyone just accepted his or her lot in life.

Watt described the musical as "a poor man's *Company*" which had "no genuinely amusing nor interesting comments" to make on its subject; John Beaufort in the *Christian Science Monitor* found the evening "drab," the characters "dreary," and the proceedings "mercifully short" (the intermission-less musical was seventy-five minutes in length); and Clive Barnes in the *New York Times* said the score was "faintly familiar" and "not at all unpleasant," but the work lacked "intellectual assurance and emotional worldliness" and thus its "gloss is glassy, its diamonds are paste, and the dry martinis are wet and warm."

Richard Watts in the *New York Post* said *Sextet* was "an amiable and quite agreeable little show" but he was doubtful if its "pleasant qualities" would "set Broadway on fire." He "especially" liked Dixie Carter's performance, and of all the songs in the "tuneful" score, "Roseland" was the highlight. He also noted that the relationship between David and Kenneth was so vaguely delineated that some in the audience might assume they were just friends, but then he decided that in "this suspicious age" it was unlikely anyone would miss the point.

Kevin Sanders on WABCTV7 found the musical "occasionally entrancing." The score was "lively," the lyrics "intelligent" and "contemporary," and the cast "excellent" (he singled out Dixie Carter). He mentioned he was a bit tired of "splashy nostalgic Broadway sideshows" of the ***Irene*** and ***Gigi*** variety, and felt a modern-day musical such as *Sextet* was "infinitely more enjoyable."

Martin Gottfried in *Women's Wear Daily* said the "mostly terrific" *Sextet* (a sort of "Son of *Company*") was "ambitious" in its "non-linear way" and he liked the "layered and mingling" dialogue in which "one character talks to a second, who responds to a third who reacts to a fourth." The score was a "marvelous mix of satire and original material," and one number ("Roseland") was certainly an homage to ***Follies***. Like Watt, he noted that the evening concluded with the characters' realization that they are "stuck with who they are."

OVER HERE!

"AMERICA'S BIG BAND MUSICAL" / "THE NEW BIG BAND MUSICAL"

Theatre: Shubert Theatre
Opening Date: March 6, 1974; *Closing Date*: January 4, 1975
Performances: 348
Book: Will Holt
Lyrics and *Music*: Richard M. Sherman and Robert B. Sherman; special dance music by Louis St. Louis
Direction: Tom Moore; *Producers*: Kenneth Waissman and Maxine Fox (Lou Kramer, Associate Producer); *Choreography*: Patricia Birch; *Scenery*: Douglas W. Schmidt; *Media Design*: Stan J. Goldberg and Jeanne H. Livingston; *Costumes*: Carrie F. Robbins; *Lighting*: John Gleason; *Musical Direction*: Joseph Klein
Cast: Jim Weston (Make-Out), Douglass Watson (Norwin Spokesman), MacIntyre Dixon (Father), Bette Henritze (Mother), William Griffis (Rankin), Marilu Henner (Donna), Phyllis Somerville (Wilma), Ann Reinking (Maggie), Janie Sell (Mitzi), John Travolta (Misfit), Treat Williams (Utah), John Mineo (Lucky), William Newman (Sarge), Samuel E. Wright (Sam), April Shawhan (June), John Driver (Bill), *The Andrews Sisters—Maxene Andrews* (Pauline de Paul) and *Patty Andrews* (Paulette de Paul)
The musical was presented in two acts.
The action takes place in the United States of America during the War Forties on a cross-country train trip.

Musical Numbers

Act One: "The Beat Begins" (Overture) (The Big Band, Company); "Since You're Not Around" (Jim Weston, Company); "Over Here" (Patty Andrews, Maxene Andrews, Company); "Buy a Victory Bond" (Company); "My Dream for Tomorrow" (April Shawhan, Soldiers); "Charlie's Place" (Maxene Andrews, Ann Reinking, John Mineo, The Big Band, Company); ""Hey, Yvette" ("The Grass Grows Green") (Douglass Watson, William Griffis, MacIntyre Dixon); "My Dream for Tomorrow" (reprise) (April Shawhan, John Driver); "The Good-Time Girl" (aka "The V.D. Polka") (Patty Andrews, Company); "Wait for Me, Marlena" (Janie Sell, Company); "We Got It" (Patty Andrews, Maxene Andrews, Janie Sell, Company)
Act Two: "The Beat Continues" (Entr'Acte) (The Big Band, Company); "Wartime Wedding" (Patty Andrews, Maxene Andrews, Company); "Don't Shoot the Hooey to Me, Louie" (Samuel E. Wright); "Where Did the Good Times Go?" (Patty Andrews); "Dream Drummin'" and "Soft Music" (John Travolta, Phyllis Somerville, The Big Band, Company); "The Big Beat" (Patty Andrews, Maxene Andrews, Janie Sell); "No Goodbyes" (Patty Andrews, Maxene Andrews, Company)

Over Here! was one of the delights of the decade, a nostalgia-laden musical of the War Forties that starred two legends of the big-band years, Patty and Maxene Andrews (LaVerne, the third Andrews Sister, died in

1967). Here was an unpretentious old-fashioned lark that gently kidded the conventions of the era with an array of soldiers, spies, and ingénues all taking a cross-country train trip to the big-band beat of jitterbugs and lindy hops, boogie-woogie and beat-me-daddy-eight-to-the-bar blasts, and creamy Glenn Miller-styled ballads. *Over Here!* was one of the funniest and sunniest musicals of its time, one that deserves reconsideration: Will Holt's pitch-perfect book and the Sherman Brothers' tuneful score are in drape shape with a reet pleat, and with inspired choices for its two leading roles, the musical might well become the blockbuster hit it deserved to be in 1974.

The passengers on the cross-country train ride are mostly soldiers heading for New York and embarkation to Europe, including Misfit (John Travolta), Utah (Treat Williams), Lucky (John Mineo), and Bill (John Driver) as well as the latter's girlfriend June (April Shawhan), who has secretly hopped aboard. Also along for the ride are genial older couple Mother (Bette Henritze) and Father (MacIntyre Dixon) as well as Pauline de Paul (Maxene Andrews) and Paulette de Paul (Patty Andrews), the hostesses of the train's canteen and a singing sister duo who know all too well that to make the Hit Parade you need a three-girl group. Another passenger on the train is the mysterious Mitzi (Janie Sell, in a Tony Award-winning performance for Best Featured Actress in a Musical) whom the script describes as a German cabaret singer who learned English in the 1930s and whose slang is now way behind the times.

Mitzi is in fact a Nazi spy who hopes to pick up military secrets from the soldiers. Her compact is really a camera, and with the help of her handy dandy tube of lipstick (which includes a secret transmitter) she can send messages directly to Germany (no wonder Mitzi the Nazi is always touching up her lips, and sometimes when it appears a soldier is on the verge of revealing vital information, she practically shoves the lipstick tube in his face). When Pauline and Paulette discover that Mitzi can sing, they commandeer her for their act, which is going to be broadcast live on radio from the train. Mitzi is delighted to join them because she plans to include a Morse code message to Germany as they sing the scat part of the song "The Big Beat." Meanwhile, Bill puts pressure on June to "go all the way," but she resolutely refuses because "My Dream for Tomorrow" ("is to keep what I have today"). But when she finally offers herself to him, he nobly tells her that they must wait until after marriage.

Douglas W. Schmidt's stunning set was drenched in Twentieth Century-Fox Technicolor and was backed by the orchestra, which first emerged from beneath the stage and in big band style was seen throughout the performance upstage. The proscenium itself was dominated by three huge rainbow arcs, each one offering a collage of photos and advertisements from the era, including bond campaign slogans and photos of Frank Sinatra, Betty Grable, Kate Smith, Dorothy Lamour, and Benny Goodman; and towering above center stage on the highest arc was a photo of FDR himself (Schmidt used this visual design on a smaller scale in ***Grease***, and for that musical a photo of James Dean looked down upon the proceedings).

Despite the potentially confining space of a train setting, Schmidt's décor utilized the entire Shubert stage to depict the various cars of the train, and he gave plenty of room for spectacular jitterbugging by Ann Reinking and John Mineo, who burned the floor in "Charlie's Place." One of the most elaborate production numbers of the era was the fantasy "America Dreams of Tomorrow" in which the characters look to a rosy postwar future. A treadmill transports them across the stage, and, this being an American fantasy, their dreams are immersed in an MGM and Twentieth Century-Fox carnival of show business glory. Utah envisions himself as a successful drummer a la Gene Krupa ("Dream Drummin'"); Wilma (Phyllis Somerville) sees herself as an ingénue songster in the June Allyson tradition ("Sweet Music"); in the style of Esther Williams, Maggie (Ann Reinking) and other girls "swim" across the stage on the moving treadmill; the black porter Sam (Samuel E. Wright) becomes a Joe Louis dancing champ; June and Bill morph into Sonja Henie and Tyrone Power in a skating sequence; Lucky turns into a tap-dancing singer (and gangster) à la James Cagney; Donna (Marilu Henner) is crowned Miss America and strikes the iconic Betty Grable pin-up girl pose; and even Mother and Father get in the mood with a Jeanette MacDonald and Nelson Eddy operetta-styled spoof.

As for Mitzi the Nazi, you'll be glad to know she's captured before she can do any damage to national security. It seems when she sings the national anthem she knows all the words of the second stanza, and as Lucky says, "no *real* American knows the second verse to the 'Star-Spangled Banner.'" Mitzi tries in vain to prove her mom-and-apple-pie credentials but becomes flustered: "I prove to you Mitzi's no Mitzi, Mister. I mean, Matzoh. Mister, no Mitzi naster. No nasty Mitzi." But she gives up, defeated by our "verstunkene language."

If all this 1940s fantasy wasn't enough, after the curtain calls Maxene and Patty Andrews performed a "third" act in which they sang many of their old hits. The audience went wild, and nostalgia never got any better than this.

John Beaufort in the *Christian Science Monitor* hailed "the big, brassy bonanza" that offered "some of the liveliest show tunes" since the end of the big band era, and he liked Holt's book, an affectionate lampoon with "occasional moments of sentiment" that were "affectingly genuine." Richard Watts in the *New York Post* said the "delightful and exhilarating" *Over Here!* was a "vivid and tuneful victory" for the Andrews Sisters. And although Douglas Watt in the *New York Daily News* was a bit cool to the show, he admitted it was "reasonably diverting" despite its need for "more dash" and "a more irreverent spirit." He singled out the "stunning" Ann Reinking whose "chiseled bad-girl good looks alone should take her far."

Clive Barnes in the *New York Times* said that despite his "better judgment" he "warmed to the show enormously." It was "preposterously bad" but also "preposterously engaging and, in its way, devilish clever." But Martin Gottfried in *Women's Wear Daily* felt the musical condescended to the past and wasn't a "true, loving memory of it." But he liked the "smash" opening with the introduction of the big-band orchestra, Patricia Birch's "wonderful" choreography, and the "superb" Ann Reinking. Lance Morrow in *Time* didn't care for the musical but noted "the sheer energy expended here could power every pacemaker in the country for the next 75 years."

Leonard Harris on WCBSTV2 liked the "fun musical" with its "charmingly corny" book and "fun" songs; Kevin Sanders on WABCTV7 said *Over Here!* was "the most exuberant new musical" in years and its "effervescent display" of "dazzling" dances and "lush and vivacious" songs made it an "exhilarating big, brassy breeze." Jack Kroll in *Newsweek* said the musical was conceived as "an explosion of 1940s archetypes, like a theme show taking place at some Radio City Music Hall in the skies," and he praised the "spine-chilling" big band; "brilliant" direction; the "joyous, sly and touching" choreography; the "knockout" dancers Ann Reinking and John Mineo; and the "pleasing and intelligent" score that was a "pastiche of every '40s genre as well as an affectionate commentary on their mixture of hope and self-deception."

During the tryout, the "America Dreams of Tomorrow" sequence included the cut numbers "Cottage Small," "Blue-Chip Portfolio," "Aren't-Cha Itch-In?," "Brand-New Automobile," and "Penthouse."

The script was published in paperback by Samuel French in 1979, and Columbia Records recorded the cast album (LP and CD # KS-32961).

Besides the appearances of legends Patty and Maxene Andrews, the cast included an astonishing number of young performers who would soon enjoy successful careers on Broadway, television, and film, including John Travolta, Treat Williams, Marilu Henner, and Ann Reinking.

A special note in the program from Richard M. Sherman, Robert B. Sherman, and Louis St. Louis thanked Walter Weschler's "creative contribution" for the numbers "Over Here," "We Got It," and "The Big Beat."

Three years earlier, the Sherman Brothers had written another World War II musical with a canteen setting, and it too starred an Andrews Sister (in this case, Patty). *Victory Canteen* opened at the Ivar Theatre in Hollywood on January 27, 1971, but none of its songs were recycled for *Over Here!* However, like *Over Here!*'s "Hey, Yvette" ("The Grass Grows Green"), *Victory Canteen* also included a musical salute to World War One, in this case "Lafayette, We're Here." For the record, the other songs in the score were: "The Victory Canteen," "Doughnuts," "L-O-V-E," "The South American Number," "Ax the Axis Polka," "Hawks," "Loose Lips," "Va-Va-Va-Vee," "My Window Full of Stars," "Let's Go Native," "South Sea Island Rhapsody," "We Two," and "Smoke 'Em Up, Smoke 'Em Up, Smoke 'Em Up."

Awards

Tony Awards and Nominations: Best Musical (*Over Here!*); Best Featured Actress in a Musical (**Janie Sell**); Best Director of a Musical (Tom Moore); Best Costume Designer (Carrie F. Robbins); Best Choreographer (Patricia Birch)

CANDIDE

Theatre: Broadway Theatre
Opening Date: March 10, 1974; *Closing Date*: January 4, 1976
Performances: 740
Book: Hugh Wheeler

Lyrics: Richard Wilbur; additional lyrics by Stephen Sondheim, John LaTouche, and Leonard Bernstein
Music: Leonard Bernstein
Based on the 1759 novel *Candide, or Optimism* by Voltaire (Francois-Marie Arouet).
Direction: Harold Prince; *Producers*: The Chelsea Theatre Center of Brooklyn (Robert Kalfin, Artistic Director; Michael David, Executive Director; Burl Hash, Productions' Director) in conjunction with Harold Prince and Ruth Mitchell; *Choreography*: Patricia Birch; *Scenery* and *Costumes*: Eugene Lee and Franne Lee; *Lighting*: Tharon Musser; *Musical Direction*: Paul Gemignani
Cast: Lewis J. Stadlen (Doctor Voltaire, Doctor Pangloss, Governor, Host, Sage), Jim Corti (Chinese Coolie, Westphalian Soldier, Priest, Spanish Don, Rosary Vendor, Sailor, Lion, Guest), Mark Baker (Candide), David Horwitz (Huntsman, First Recruiting Officer, Agent, Spanish Don, Cartagenian, Priest, Sailor, Eunuch), Deborah St. Darr (Paquette), Mary-Pat Green (Baroness, Harpsichordist, Penitente, Steel Drummer, Houri), Joe Palmieri (Baron, Grand Inquisitor, Slave Driver, Captain, Guest), Maureen Brennan (Cunegonde), Sam Freed (Maximillian), Robert Hendersen (Servant, Agent of the Inquisition, Spanish Don, Cartagenian, Sailor), Peter Vogt (Second Recruiting Officer, Aristocrat, Cartagenian), Gail Boggs (Penitente, Whore, Houri), Lynne Gannaway (Penitente, Cartagenian, Houri), Carolann Page (Aristocrat, Cartagenian, Second Sheep), Carlos Gorbea (Bulgarian Soldier, Aristocrat, Fruit Vendor, Pygmy, Cow), Kelly Walters (Bulgarian Soldier, Penitente, Cartagenian, Sailor, Cow), Chip Garnett (Westphalian Soldier, Agent, Governor's Aide, Pirate, Guest), Jeff Keller (Rich Jew, Judge, Man in Black, Cartagenian, Pirate, German, Botanist, Guest), Becky McSpadden (Aristocrat, Cartagenian, Houri), Kathryn Ritter (Aristocrat, Whore, Houri, alternate for Cunegonde for matinees), Renee Semes (Lady with Knitting, Cartagenian, First Sheep), June Gable (Old Lady); Swing Girl: Rhoda Butler
The musical was presented in one act.
The action occurs in Westphalia, Paris, Buenos Aires, Venice, and sundry places throughout the world.

Musical Numbers

"Life Is Happiness Indeed" (lyric by Stephen Sondheim) (Mark Baker, Maureen Brennan, Sam Freed, Deborah St. Darr); "The Best of All Possible Worlds" (new lyric by Stephen Sondheim) (Lewis J. Stadlen, Mark Baker, Maureen Brennan, Sam Freed, Deborah St. Darr); "Oh, Happy We" (lyric by Richard Wilbur) (Mark Baker, Maureen Brennan); "It Must Be So" (lyric by Richard Wilbur) (Mark Baker); "O Miserere" (lyricist not identified) (Carolann Page, Lynne Gannaway, Gail Boggs, Robert Hendersen); "Oh, Happy We" (reprise) (Mark Baker, Maureen Brennan); "Glitter and Be Gay" (lyric by Richard Wilbur) (Maureen Brennan); "Auto Da Fe" ("What a Day") (lyric by John LaTouche and Stephen Sondheim) (Company); "This World" (aka "Candide's Lament") (lyric by Stephen Sondheim) (Mark Baker); "You Were Dead, You Know" (lyric by John LaTouche) (Mark Baker, Maureen Brennan); "I Am Easily Assimilated" (lyric by Leonard Bernstein) (June Gable, Jim Corti, Robert Hendersen, David Horwitz); "I Am Easily Assimilated" (reprise) (June Gable, Mark Baker, Maureen Brennan); "My Love" (lyric by John LaTouche and Richard Wilbur) (Lewis J. Stadlen, Sam Freed); "Alleluia" (lyricist not identified) (Company); "Sheep's Song" (lyric by Stephen Sondheim) (Renee Semes, Carolann Page, Jim Corti, Deborah St. Darr, Mark Baker); "Bon Voyage" (lyric by Richard Wilbur) (Lewis J. Stadlen, Company); "The Best of All Possible Worlds" (reprise) (June Gable, Mark Baker, Deborah St. Darr, Renee Semes, Carolann Page); "You Were Dead, You Know" (reprise) (Mark Baker, Maureen Brennan); "Make Our Garden Grow" (lyric by Richard Wilbur) (Company)

The 1971 revival of the 1956 musical ***Candide*** closed prior to its Broadway premiere, but was a generally faithful version of the original. The current production was a radically different but unfortunately disappointing interpretation from previous *Candide* revivals and unaccountably received raves from most of the critics and won a slew of awards. The misguided production began life at the Brooklyn Academy of Music, where it opened on December 11, 1973, and played for forty-eight performances.

In March 1974, the musical moved to the luckless Broadway Theatre, which had recently undergone the indignity of the so-called environmental staging of ***Dude***, or ***The Highway Life*** in which the theatre underwent a drastic physical overhaul to accommodate the demands of the script and the staging of that rock musical. So much work, so much *carpentry*, and it all went down after sixteen performances.

With *Candide*, the theatre was saddled with yet another musical that required an environmental staging. And so the house was again turned upside down, and the normally seventeen hundred–seat theatre was reduced to some eight-hundred-and-fifty bleacher-styled seats that were scattered all over the venue in various nooks and crannies. Further, there were now ten multileveled playing areas of small stages throughout what remained of the house as well as four separate sections where the orchestra members were deposited. The script noted that all these areas were connected by ramps, drawbridges, trap doors, and "hidden passageways." What all this had to do with *Candide* was moot. But if the mise-en-scène made one cringe, the production itself was jaw-droppingly obvious. The script, the performances, and the staging were done cute with unbearably coy dumbed-down shtick. The brittle wit of Bernstein's brilliant score was subjugated to *Laugh-In*-styled antics, and Lillian Hellman's sardonic and acerbic book was replaced by the kindergarten-styled humor of Hugh Wheeler's new adaptation.

And so of course most of the critics adored it: "I love *Candide*" (Richard Watts in the *New York Post*); "This is a doll of a show" (Clive Barnes in the *New York Times*); "If there is a lovelier *Candide* than this, it is difficult to imagine" (Lance Morrow in *Time*); "*Candide* is unquestionably the season's most brilliant musical to date" (John Beaufort in the *Christian Science Monitor*); and *Candide* is "a splendid new musical on Broadway" (Leonard Harris on WCBSTV2).

Douglas Watt in the *New York Daily News* rightly praised "the century's wittiest operetta score," but noted Wheeler's book was "something of a drag and even confusing at times" and didn't "really hold up" for the two-hour intermission-less performance. Martin Gottfried in *Women's Wear Daily* said the evening was a "salvage job rather than something begun afresh." Despite Wheeler's elimination of an abundance of scenes and settings, he caused a new problem by creating a narrator to tell the story rather than letting the performers act it out. Further, the actor (Lewis J. Stadlen) who played the narrator also played four other roles and so the conception of the narrator caused more problems than it solved.

Although the production played for 740 performances, it lost money. The positive side of the revival is that it brought the work into the mainstream and introduced it to a wider public, and so *Candide* was no longer a cult musical primarily known to just the cognoscenti. But the downside was that most new productions of the work now draw upon the carnival mood and atmosphere of the revival. So what was a sardonic and bitter musical for adults in 1956 is now a feel-good bit of circus-like fun. The satiric lyrics and music are blunted, and the bitter story is softened by silliness. Surely there must be a compromise where *Candide* can be both slyly humorous and darkly satiric.

The script was published in a lavish hardback edition by Schirmer Books/MacMillan Performing Arts Series in 1976. The cast album was recorded by Columbia Records on a two-LP set (# S2X-32923), and the two-CD set was issued by Sony/Masterworks Broadway Records (# 82876-88391-2).

For more information about the musical, see entry for the 1971 revival.

Awards

Tony Awards and Nominations: Best Leading Actor in a Musical (Lewis J. Stadlen); Best Featured Actor in a Musical (Mark Baker); Best Featured Actress in a Musical (Maureen Brennan); Best Featured Actress in a Musical (June Gable); Best Director of a Musical (**Harold Prince**); Best Book (**Hugh Wheeler**); Best Scenic Designer (**Eugene Lee** and **Franne Lee**); Best Costume Designer (**Franne Lee**); Special Tony Award to the production of *Candide* as "an outstanding contribution to the artistic development of the musical theatre"; *Note*: The program credited Eugene Lee and Franne Lee for both scenery and costumes, but the Tony Award for Best Costume Designer was given only to Franne Lee (but both were awarded the Tony for Best Scenic Design).

New York Drama Critics' Circle Award: Best Musical (1973–1974) (***Candide***)

THE CONSUL

Theatre: New York State Theatre
Opening Date: March 27, 1974; *Closing Date*: April 28, 1974
Performances: 4 (in repertory)

Libretto and *Music*: Gian-Carlo Menotti

Direction: Gian-Carlo Menotti; *Producer*: The New York City Opera Company; *Scenery*: Horace Armistead; *Costumes*: Not credited; *Lighting*: Not credited; *Musical Direction*: Christopher Keene

Cast: John Darrenkamp (John Sorel), Olivia Stapp (Magda Sorel), Muriel Costa-Greenspon (The Mother), Edward Pierson (Secret Police Agent), Jack Sims (First Plainclothesman), Ray Van Orden (Second Plainclothesman), Sandra Walker (The Secretary), Don Yule (Mr. Kofner), Judith De Rosa (Foreign Woman), Barbara Hocher (Anna Gomez), Nico Castel (Nika Magadoff [The Magician]), Virginia Brobyn (Vera Boronel), William Ledbetter (Assan), Mabel Mercer (Voice on the Record)

The opera was presented in three acts.

The action takes place somewhere in Europe during the recent past.

The current revival of Gian-Carlo Menotti's Cold War opera *The Consul* by the New York City Opera Company was its seventh of eight productions of the work.

The opera premiered on Broadway at the Ethel Barrymore Theatre on March 15, 1950, for 269 performances, with Patricia Neway in the leading role of Magda Sorel. The work was named Best Musical by the New York Drama Critics' Circle and received the 1950 Pulitzer Prize for music. The powerful self-described "musical drama" depicted an unnamed totalitarian country whose citizens are persecuted by secret police and a Kafkaesque bureaucracy. Underground protestor John Sorel has escaped from the country and has sent word to his wife Magda to get the necessary visa papers so that she, their baby, and his ailing mother can join him. But Magda is shadowed by the police and becomes entangled in the spider's web of the bureaucratic maze of the consul's office, which is run by his coldly efficient secretary who informs Magda that "your name is a number, your story is a case, your need a request, your hopes will be filed." (The consul himself is never seen.) But the visa papers are elusive, as there's always one more necessary document which must be executed in the unending morass of papers and questionnaires. Ultimately, John returns to help his family, but it's too late: he's arrested, his mother has succumbed to illness, his baby has died of starvation, and Magda has committed suicide.

Allen Hughes in the *New York Times* praised the "polished" revival and said Olivia Stapp was a "stirring" Magda and Muriel Costa-Greenspon a "sympathetic" and "touching" mother. He also noted that Christopher Keene "conducted the work authoritatively," but complained that the music itself was only "serviceable." While it was not a score "to arouse admiration for inspiration or refined workmanship," it nonetheless "makes its points, and it works."

The original cast album was released by Decca Records (LP # DX-101), and two other recordings of the score have been issued, one from the Spoleto Festival (Chandos CD # CHAN-9706-2) and one of a production by the Berkshire Opera Company (Newport Classics CD # NPD-85645/2). The libretto was published in paperback by G. Schirmer in 1950.

The first City Opera revival was produced on October 8, 1952, for three performances, and was followed by revivals on April 16, 1953 (three performances [estimated]), February 14, 1960 (two performances), March 28, 1962 (four performances), March 17, 1966 (three performances), October 6, 1966 (two performances; see entry), the current production on March 27, 1974 (four performances), and March 22, 1975 (two performances). The first four revivals were seen at City Center, and the last four at the New York State Theatre. Neway reprised her original role of Magda for the first six revivals.

The 1960 production was shown on pay-per-view television (the DVD version was released by Video Artists International # 4266), and is one of eight U.S. and international television versions of the opera.

MUSIC! MUSIC!

"A Cavalcade of American Music with Footnotes by Alan Jay Lerner"

Theatre: City Center 55th Street Theatre

Opening Date: April 11, 1974; *Closing Date*: May 12, 1974

Performances: 37

Text: Alan Jay Lerner

Lyrics and *Music*: (See list of musical numbers for individual credits.)

Direction: Martin Charnin; *Producers*: The City Center of Music and Drama, Inc. (Norman Singer, Executive Director) and Alvin Bojar (Robert P. Brannigan and Chuck Eisler, Producers for City Center) (Howard P.

Effron, Associate Producer); *Choreography*: Tony Stevens; *Scenery*: David Chapman; *Costumes*: Theoni V. Aldredge; *Lighting*: Martin Aronstein; *Musical Direction*: John Lesko

Cast: *Gene Nelson, Larry Kert, Karen Morrow, Donna McKechnie, Robert Guillaume,* Will MacKenzie, Gail Nelson, Ted Pritchard, Arnold Soboloff, Russ Thacker; Singing and Dancing Ensemble: Renee Baughman, Trish Garland, Denise Mauthe, Michon Peacock, Tom Offt, Michael Radigan, Yolanda R. Raven, Freda Soiffer, Thomas J. Walsh

The revue was presented in two acts.

Musical Numbers

Note: Singing assignments unknown.

Act One: 1895–1941: "Basin Street Blues" (lyric and music by Spencer Williams); "When the Saints Go Marching In" (traditional); "The Merry Widow Waltz" (*The Merry Widow*, 1905; original German lyric by Victor Leon and Leo Stein, English lyricist for this version unknown, music by Franz Lehar); "Yankee Doodle Dandy" (*Little Johnny Jones*, 1906; lyric and music by George M. Cohan); "Over There" (independent song, 1918; lyric and music by George M. Cohan); "I Didn't Raise My Boy to Be a Soldier" (lyric and music by Alfred Bryan and Al Piantadosi); "How Ya Gonna Keep 'Em Down on the Farm?" (lyric by Sam Lewis and Joe Young, music by Walter Donaldson); "Hinky Dinky Parlay Voo" (lyric and music by Al Dubin, Irving Mills, Jimmy McHugh, and Julian Dash); "Look for the Silver Lining" (*Sally*, 1921; lyric by B. G. "Buddy" DeSylva, music by Jerome Kern); "Bill" (*Show Boat*, 1927; lyric by P. G. Wodehouse, music by Jerome Kern); "Yes, Sir, That's My Baby" (lyric by Gus Kahn, music by Walter Donaldson); George Gershwin Medley: "Fascinating Rhythm" (*Lady, Be Good!*, 1924; lyric by Ira Gershwin); "Somebody Loves Me" (*George White's Scandals of 1924*; lyric by B. G. "Buddy" DeSylva and Ballard MacDonald); "The Babbitt and the Bromide" (*Funny Face*, 1927; lyric by Ira Gershwin); "Funny Face" (*Funny Face*, 1927; lyric by Ira Gershwin); "(I'll Build a) Stairway to Paradise" (*George White's Scandals of 1922*; lyric by Ira Gershwin and B. G. "Buddy" DeSylva); "The Man I Love" (lyric by Ira Gershwin; the song was dropped during the 1924 tryout of *Lady, Be Good!*; was used in the 1927 version of *Strike Up the Band*, which closed during its pre-Broadway tryout; and was considered for but not used in *Rosalie*, 1928); "Oh, Lady Be Good" (*Lady, Be Good!*, 1924; lyric by Ira Gershwin); and "Someone to Watch Over Me" (*Oh, Kay!*, 1927; lyric by Ira Gershwin); "Manhattan" (*The Garrick Gaieties of 1925*; lyric by Lorenz Hart, music by Richard Rodgers); "The Girl Friend" (*The Girl Friend*, 1925; lyric by Lorenz Hart, music by Richard Rodgers); "Stouthearted Men" (*The New Moon*, 1928; lyric by Oscar Hammerstein II, music by Sigmund Romberg); "Lucky Lindy" (lyric and music by Abel Bauer and L. Wolfe Gilbert); "Brother, Can You Spare a Dime?" (*Americana*, 1932; lyric by E. Y. Harburg, music by Jay Gorney); "I'll See You Again" (*Bitter Sweet*, 1929; lyric and music by Noel Coward); "Great Day" (*Great Day!*, 1928; lyric by Edward Eliscu and Billy Rose, music by Vincent Youmans); "Stormy Weather" (*Cotton Club Revue of 1933*; lyric by Ted Koehler, music by Harold Arlen); "Bess, You Is My Woman Now" (*Porgy and Bess*, 1935; lyric by Ira Gershwin and Dubose Heyward, music by George Gershwin); "I Loves You, Porgy" (*Porgy and Bess*, 1935; lyric by Ira Gershwin and DuBose Heyward, music by George Gershwin); "Hooray for Hollywood" (1937 film *Hollywood Hotel*; lyric by Johnny Mercer, music by Richard A. Whiting); "Lullaby of Broadway" (film *Gold Diggers of 1935*; lyric by Al Dubin, music by Harry Warren)

Act Two: 1941–1974: "In the Mood" (lyric by Andy Razaf, music by Joe Garland); "There Are Such Things" (lyric and music by George W. Meyer, Abel Baer, and Stanley Adams); "The White Cliffs of Dover" (lyric and music by Walter Kent and Nat Burton); Medley of songs from *Oklahoma!* (1943; lyrics by Oscar Hammerstein II, music by Richard Rodgers); "Call Me Mister" (*Call Me Mister*, 1946; lyric and music by Harold Rome); "The Composers' Song" (recitation written by Alan Jay Lerner); Rock and Roll Recitation; "Whiffenpoof Song" (parody); Medley of songs from *My Fair Lady* (1956; lyrics by Alan Jay Lerner, music by Frederick Loewe); Medley of songs from *West Side Story* (1957; lyrics by Stephen Sondheim, music by Leonard Bernstein); Dance sequences from *The Music Man* (1957; music by Meredith Willson), *Camelot* (1960; music by Frederick Loewe); *Bye Bye Birdie* (1960; music by Charles Strouse); and *Gypsy* (1959; music by Jule Styne); Medley of songs from *Hello, Dolly!* (1964; lyrics and music by Jerry Herman); Medley of songs from *Fiddler on the Roof* (1964; lyrics by Sheldon Harnick, music by Jerry Bock); "Abraham, Martin and John" (lyric and music by Dick Holler); "Maman" (*Mata Hari*, 1967; closed during its pre-Broadway tryout; lyric by Martin Charnin, music by Edward Thomas); "I Believe in Music" (lyric and music by Mac Davis)

The revue *Music! Music!* was a self-described cavalcade of American music, and was one of a few similar revues that popped up during the period of the country's bicentennial. ***A Musical Jubilee*** opened a year later (with *Music! Music!* alum Larry Kert in its cast), as did ***Sing America Sing***, which was produced in Washington, D.C., but never risked New York (like *Music! Music!*, its choreographer was Tony Stevens).

The revue purported to be a salute to American music, and for the most part it was (and it emphasized songs from Broadway and film musicals). But why did it include "The Merry Widow Waltz?" from Franz Lehar's 1905 Viennese operetta *The Merry Widow* and Noel Coward's "I'll See You Again" from *Bitter Sweet*, an operetta that premiered in London in 1929?

Clive Barnes in the *New York Times* noted that "tedium was continually threatening to run riot" throughout the evening, and said the production was "just like a record album, or a television special done on the cheap"; Martin Gottfried in *Women's Wear Daily* found the revue "as smooth and cold as a television program taped without an audience"; and while Douglas Watt in the *New York Daily News* liked the "reasonably engaging" production, he said it was "overlong" and had the "glossy look and sound" that suggested it could "hardly wait—with editing, of course—to make it to the TV screen."

But Lance Morrow in *Time* praised the "delightful musical blowout" and found it "as much fun and entertainment as anything on Broadway," and Richard Watts in the *New York Post* hailed the "splendid imagination" behind the "simply and tastefully done" revue.

WORDS AND MUSIC

Theatre: John Golden Theatre
Opening Date: April 16, 1974; *Closing Date*: August 3, 1974
Performances: 127
Lyrics: Sammy Cahn
Music: Various composers (see below)
Direction: Jerry Adler; *Producers*: Alexander H. Cohen in association with Harvey Granat; *Scenery*: Robert Randolph; *Lighting*: Marc B. Weiss; *Musical Direction*: Richard Leonard
Cast: Sammy Cahn, Kelly Garrett, Jon Peck, Shirley Lemmon
The revue was presented in one act.

Musical Numbers

Note: The program didn't include a list of songs; the following alphabetical list is based on newspaper reviews and other sources; song assignments unknown.

"All the Way" (1957 film *The Joker Is Wild*; music by Jimmy Van Heusen); "Bei mir bist du schon" (independent song; Yiddish lyric by Jacob Jacobs, English lyric by Sammy Cahn and Saul Chaplin, music by Sholom Secunda); "Be My Love" (1950 film *The Toast of New Orleans*; music by Nicholas Brodszky); "Call Me Irresponsible" (1963 film *Papa's Delicate Condition*; music by Jimmy Van Heusen); "Come Fly with Me" (independent song; music by Jimmy Van Heusen); "Day by Day" (independent song; music by Axel Stordahl and Paul Weston); "Give Me Five Minutes More" (independent song; music by Jule Styne); "High Hopes" (1959 film *A Hole in the Head*; music by Jimmy Van Heusen); "I Fall in Love Too Easily" (1945 film *Anchors Aweigh*; music by Jule Styne); "I Guess I'll Hang My Tears Out to Dry" (*Glad to See You*, 1944 musical which closed prior to Broadway opening; music by Jule Styne); "I Should Care" (independent song; music by Axel Stordahl and Paul Weston); "I'll Walk Alone" (1944 film *Follow the Boys*; music by Jule Styne); "It's Been a Long, Long Time" (independent song; music by Jule Styne); "It's Magic" (1948 film *Romance on the High Seas*; music by Jule Styne); "I've Heard That Song Before" (1944 film *Youth on Parade*; music by Jule Styne); "Let It Snow! Let It Snow! Let It Snow!" (independent song; music by Jule Styne); "Love and Marriage" (1955 television musical *Our Town*; music by Jimmy Van Heusen); "My Kind of Town (Chicago Is)" (1964 film *Robin and the Seven Hoods*; music by Jimmy Van Heusen); "Papa, Won't You Dance with Me?" (*High Button Shoes*, 1947; music by Jule Styne); "Rhythm Is Our Business" (independent song; music by Saul Chaplin); "The Second Time Around" (1960 film *High Time*; music by Jimmy Van Heusen); "Teach Me Tonight" (independent song; music by Gene de Paul); "(Love Is) The Tender Trap" (1955 film *The Tender Trap*; music by Jimmy Van Heusen); "The Things We Did Last Summer" (independent song; music by Jule Styne); "Thoroughly Modern Millie" (1967 film *Thoroughly Modern Millie*; music by Jimmy Van Heusen); "Until the Real Thing Comes Along" (independent song; various sources credit the lyric and music to Sammy Cahn, Saul Chaplin, L. E. Freeman, Mann Holiner, and Alberta Nichols); "Walking Happy" (*Walking Happy*, 1966; music by Jimmy Van Heusen); in the revue, Cahn also performed songs by other lyricists and composers, such as "White Christmas" (1942 film *Holiday Inn*; lyric and music by Irving Berlin) and "You'll Never Know" (1943 film *Hello, Frisco, Hello*; lyric by Mack Gordon, music by Harry Warren).

Words and Music was an intimate and amiable evening that starred veteran lyricist Sammy Cahn, who sang and discussed many of the hit songs from his career, most of which had been introduced in films and musicals. He was accompanied by Richard Leonard at the piano and was joined by singers Jon Peck, Shirley Lemmon, and Kelly Garrett (during the run, the latter was succeeded by Kay Cole).

Cahn's Broadway musicals were *Glad to See You* (1944; music by Jule Styne; closed prior to Broadway, and included the classic torch song "Guess I'll Hang My Tears Out to Dry"); *High Button Shoes* (1947; music by Jule Styne); *Skyscraper* (1965; music by Jimmy Van Heusen); *Walking Happy* (1966; music by Jimmy Van Heusen); and ***Look to the Lilies*** (1970; music by Jule Styne).

Four of Cahn's songs won the Academy Award for Best Song: "Three Coins in the Fountain" (film of same title, 1954; music by Jule Styne); "All the Way" (1957 film *The Joker Is Wild*; music by Jimmy Van Heusen); "High Hopes" (1959 film *A Hole in the Head*; music by Jimmy Van Heusen); and "Call Me Irresponsible" (1963 film *Papa's Delicate Condition*; music by Jimmy Van Heusen). Moreover, twenty-three others were nominated for Best Song. He also wrote the holiday classics "Let It Snow! Let It Snow! Let It Snow!" and "The Christmas Waltz" ("frosted window panes"), both with music by Jule Styne.

The singular interpreter of Sammy Cahn was Frank Sinatra, who introduced and popularized an astonishing number of Cahn's songs over a period of three decades, including "I Fall in Love Too Easily" (1945 film *Anchors Aweigh*; music by Jule Styne); "Time After Time" (1946 film *It Happened in Brooklyn*; music by Jule Styne); "Three Coins in the Fountain" (1954 film title song; music by Jule Styne); "Love and Marriage" (1955 television musical *Our Town*; music by Jimmy Van Heusen); "All the Way" (1957 film *The Joker Is Wild*; music by Jimmy Van Heusen); "High Hopes" (1959 film *A Hole in the Head*; music by Jimmy Van Heusen); and "My Kind of Town (Chicago Is)" (1964 film *Robin and the Seven Hoods*; music by Jimmy Van Heusen). Sinatra also introduced such Cahn classics as the independent songs "Saturday Night Is the Loneliest Night of the Week" (music by Jule Styne), "Come Fly with Me" (music by Jimmy Van Heusen), and "Come Dance with Me" (music by Jimmy Van Heusen).

The critics enjoyed the affable, often self-effacing Cahn, who not only sang his famous songs but also provided gossip-like chatter about Doris Day's first screen test and how it came about that he and Jule Styne wrote the title song for the film *Three Coins in the Fountain*.

Clive Barnes in the *New York Times* "adored" the evening and praised Cahn as "the best bad singer in the world," whose lyrics possessed the qualities of genius and love, which were the very ingredients of the thing that "makes Sammy run." Martin Gottfried in *Women's Wear Daily* liked the "warm, funny, utterly congenial evening" and said Cahn maintained a "disarming amateurism" that was "thoroughly professional." And Richard Watts in the *New York Post* praised the "wonderful show" and noted it was "a great pleasure to meet Sammy Cahn in person."

Douglas Watt in the *New York Daily News* reported that for "My Kind of Town (Chicago Is)," Cahn offered a second version with a "Manhattan Is" chorus. The critic also noted that Cahn "could sell you the Brooklyn Bridge if it had a tune to go with it" (in fact, for the 1946 film musical *It Happened in Brooklyn* Cahn had actually written the lyric, set to Jule Styne's music, of a song titled "The Brooklyn Bridge" for Frank Sinatra).

SAMMY

Theatre: Uris Theatre
Opening Date: April 23, 1974; *Closing Date*: May 4, 1974
Performances: 14
Direction: Darrell Giddens; *Producers*: Nederlander in association with Sy Marsh; *Musical Direction*: George Rhodes
Cast: *Sammy Davis Jr.*, Freda Payne, The Nicholas Brothers

The concert was presented in two acts.

Sammy was in the nature of an extended version of Sammy Davis Jr.'s nightclub act. He sang many songs with which he was associated, and the evening included dances by the legendary Nicholas Brothers and vocals by Freda Payne.

The program for the limited engagement didn't include a list of musical numbers, but Davis performed a number of songs including "I've Got to Be Me" (*Golden Rainbow*, 1968; lyric and music by Walter Marks); "Mr. Bojangles" (lyric and music by Jerry Jeff Walker); and "(I Did It) My Way" (English lyric by Paul Anka, music and original lyric by Jacques Revaux and Claude Francois). He also sang a medley of songs by Leslie Bricusse and Anthony Newley, including three from the team's *Stop the World—I Want to Get Off* (London, 1961; Broadway, 1962) ("What Kind of Fool Am I?," "Once in a Lifetime," and "Gonna Build a Mountain"); one from the team's *The Roar of the Greasepaint—The Smell of the Crowd* (closed prior to London opening in 1964; Broadway, 1965) ("Who Can I Turn To?"); one from the team's 1971 film *Willy Wonka and the Chocolate Factory* ("The Candy Man"); and the title song from the 1964 film *Goldfinger* (lyric by Bricusse and Newley, music by John Barry). Later in the decade, Davis starred on Broadway in a revival of ***Stop the World—I Want to Get Off***.

Mel Gussow in the *New York Times* said Davis was a "powerhouse" performer in what was "essentially a nightclub show" with the star "as the featured act." After an overture of show tunes (played by an onstage orchestra conducted by George Rhodes), Davis chatted with the audience and then sang a medley of songs by Bricusse and Newley; he was followed by the Nicholas Brothers and Freda Payne; and it wasn't until 10:00 PM when Davis returned to the stage with a forty-five minute session of songs, including "Mr. Bojangles," the evening's "high point."

RIDE THE WINDS

"A New Musical"

Theatre: Bijou Theatre
Opening Date: May 16, 1974; *Closing Date*: May 18, 1974
Performances: 3
Book, *Lyrics*, and *Music*: John Driver
Direction: Lee D. Sankowich; *Producers*: Bertra Walker and Bill Tchakirides; *Choreography*: Jay Norman; *Scenery* and *Costumes*: Samuel C. Ball; *Lighting*: Jeff Davis; *Musical Direction*: Robert Brandzel
Cast: Irving Lee (Musashi), Sab Shimono (Yamada), Ernesto Gonzalez (Sensei Takuan), Nate Barnett (Joshu), Chip Zien (Inari), Tom Maysusaka (Banzo), Fanny Cerito Assoluta (Ya Ta), Elaine Petricoff (Lan), Marion Jim (Toki), Alexander Orfaly (Oda); Tellers: Laura May Lewis, John Gorrin; Priests, Kendo Students, Soldiers: Kenneth Frett, John Gorrin, Richard Loreto, Ken Mitchell
The musical was presented in two acts.
The action takes place during feudal times in a country in the Far East.

Musical Numbers

Act One: "Run, Musashi, Run" (Company); "The Emperor Me" (Irving Lee); "The Gentle Buffoon" (Nate Barnett, Chip Zien); "Those Who Speak" (Irving Lee, Nate Barnett, Chip Zien); "Flower Song" (Ernesto Gonzalez, Elaine Petricoff, Nate Barnett, Ensemble); "You're Loving Me" (Irving Lee); "Breathing the Air" (Marion Jim); "Remember That Day" (Ernesto Gonzalez, Sab Shimono); "Tengu" (Ensemble)

Act Two: "Ride the Winds" (Company); "Are You a Man?" (Elaine Petricoff); "Ride the Winds" (reprise) (Company); "Every Days" (Elaine Petricoff, Marion Jim, Inari Priests); "Loving You" (Elaine Petricoff, Irving Lee); "Pleasures" (Alexander Orfaly); "Someday I'll Walk" (Irving Lee); "That Touch" (Elaine Petricoff); Finale (Company)

During the 1972–1973 season, ***Dude***, ***Hurry, Harry***, and ***Pippin*** focused on young men in search of themselves, and the current season offered *Ride the Winds*, in which yet another hero is out there with symbolic binoculars. Set in feudal times in the Far East, the hero Musashi (Irving Lee) wants an extraordinary life, decides being a Samurai is his destiny, finds that war is morally objectionable, and so settles down to a quiet life with his nice girlfriend. If all this sounds familiar, it's because New York had already been there and done that with ***Pippin***, in which a young man in feudal times seeks his destiny, finds war reprehensible, and ultimately settles down with a nice young widow and her young son. As a result, *Ride the Winds* blew away after three performances. It was written by John Driver (currently in the cast of *Over Here!*).

And there were more medieval sagas to come. The 1975 Off-Broadway musical *The Glorious Age* veered into ***Pippin*** territory, and advertised itself as "A Light Look at the Dark Ages." But in his review for the *New York Times*, Clive Barnes noted the "light" look was "heavy, heavy, heavy." And Off-Broadway's *Bodo* (1983) closed at the last minute (literally, because the programs were already printed and delivered to the theatre) and never gave a single performance; it took place in 1125 and dealt with the titular hero, whom librettist Hugh Wheeler described as "the first modern man."

Mel Gussow in the *New York Times* found *Ride the Winds* a "mild" musical "so wispy that one fears it might blow right off the stage," and noted the music was "rockish without being raucous," the lyrics "bland," and the choreography "crowded." Leonard Harris on WCBSTV2 said his review of the "kung fu"-styled musical was "about to deliver an unkind karate chop right to the box-office."

Richard Watts in the *New York Post* found the evening "lively and colorful" with "pleasant" songs and "vigorous and effective" dances, and while he "enjoyed quite a lot of it," he nonetheless felt the overall evening "just misses out in being more than moderately enlivening as a whole." The headline of Ernest Leogrande's review in the *New York Daily News* stated that "Ill *Winds*' Has Weak Plot," and while he noted the musical had "the velocity of a spring breeze" it was nonetheless "pleasant."

The critics couldn't help quoting some of the musical's inadvertently awkward and smirk-inducing dialogue. At one point, the hero Musashi goes to a Buddhist monk to seek spiritual guidance, and is helpfully told that "To know one's self, one must know the world, but to know the world one must know oneself." And Musashi later states, "I do not know if I can walk the road of which you speak, but I will try."

The most dramatic aspects of the evening took place offstage. The critics reported that the musical was picketed by the Oriental Actors of America (some of whom said they preferred the term "Asian American") who protested that of the musical's fifteen performers, only three were of Asian descent. Further, they were upset because the leading role of Musashi had been given to Irving Lee, a black actor. The picketers reported that the musical's producers said "it would be discriminatory to hire only Asians," and so they wondered why the same rule didn't apply to ***Raisin***, which had an all-black cast. Further, the producers stated that for an open Equity call, a total of 475 performers showed up and were auditioned, and of this number only 25 were Asian American. (Gussow noted that Irving Lee was "not a convincing Oriental," and Leogrande said that native Puerto Rican Ernesto Gonzalez, who played the role of the Buddhist priest, "still carries the accent of that island.")

THE MAGIC SHOW

Theatre: Cort Theatre
Opening Date: May 28, 1974; *Closing Date*: December 31, 1978
Performances: 1,920
Book: Bob Randall
Lyrics and *Music*: Stephen Schwartz
Magic: Doug Henning
Direction and *Choreography*: Grover Dale; *Producers*: Edgar Lansbury, Joseph Beruh, and Ivan Reitman (Nan Pearlman, Associate Producer); *Scenery*: David Chapman; *Costumes*: Randy Barcelo; *Lighting*: Richard Nelson; *Musical Direction*: Stephen Reinhardt

Cast: Robert LuPone (Manny), David Ogden Stiers (Feldman), Annie McGreevey (Donna), Cheryl Barnes (Dina), Dale Soules (Cal), Doug Henning (Doug), Ronald Stafford (Mike), Loyd Sannes (Steve), Anita Morris (Charmin), Sam Schacht (Goldfarb)

The musical was presented in one act.

The action takes place at the Passaic Top Hat, a "nite club" in New Jersey.

Musical Numbers

"Up to His Old Tricks" (Company); "Solid Silver Platform Shoes" (Cheryl Barnes, Annie McGreevey); "Lion Tamer" (Dale Soules); "Style" (David Ogden Stiers, Company); "Charmin's Lament" (Anita Morris); "Two's Company" (Cheryl Barnes, Annie McGreevey); "The Goldfarb Variations" (Cheryl Barnes, David Ogden Stiers, Annie McGreevey, Robert LuPone, Anita Morris); "Doug's Act" (Doug Henning); "A Bit of Villany" (David Ogden Stiers, Cheryl Barnes, Annie McGreevey); "West End Avenue" (Dale Soules); "Sweet, Sweet, Sweet" (Anita Morris, Robert LuPone, Ronald Stafford, Loyd Sannes); "Before Your Very Eyes" (Cheryl Barnes, Annie McGreevey, David Ogden Stiers)

The Magic Show was not only the season's final musical, it was also its longest-running, with a marathon showing of 1,920 performances.

The small-scale, one-set musical with a cast of ten and a seven-piece orchestra took place in a tacky nightclub in Passaic, New Jersey, and its negligible plot and serviceable score provided the framework for jaw-dropping magic tricks by Doug Henning, who amazed both critics and audiences with his sleight of hand.

The flimsy story centered on the owner and entertainers of the Passaic Top Hat night club. The club's owner Manny (Robert LuPone) employs a black-and-white singing duo in the Bette Midler tradition (Cheryl Barnes and Annie McGreevey), two tap dancers (Ronald Stafford and Loyd Sannes), an over-the-hill and almost always drunk magician named Feldman (David Ogden Stiers), and his sexy assistant Charmin (Anita Morris). When Manny replaces Feldman with the young magician Doug (Doug Henning) and his assistant Cal (Dale Soules), the fortunes of the club look bright, and everyone becomes excited when they discover that the well-known casting agent Goldfarb (Sam Schacht) will be dropping in to scout the club for new talent. In the meantime, Charmin joins Cal as one of Doug's assistants, and Feldman hopes to sabotage Doug's success.

Henning wasn't content to pull rabbits out of a hat, and so in one amazing I-don't-believe-I-actually-saw-that sequence, he turns Charmin into a lion. Martin Gottfried in *Women's Wear Daily* "couldn't believe his eyes" as he watched Henning perform acts of levitation, sawing women in half, and even rearranging their bodies in various boxes so that heads were where torsos should be and knees were below feet. Henning also handcuffed a girl and tied her in a sack, and placed the sack in a padlocked chest. In an instant, Henning is somehow handcuffed and locked in the chest and the girl is triumphantly standing atop it. (Clive Barnes in the *New York Times* noted that this "sure beats Bingo!") Henning further incinerates a girl into a skeletal crisp, skewers a man's body with a sword, transforms a dove into a rabbit, and shreds a copy of the *New York Times* and then proceeds to make it whole. And along the way he was also impaled by a block of spikes which dropped from the ceiling.

Barnes said Henning was "the greatest illusionist" he'd ever seen; Gottfried said he was "the most terrific magician" he'd ever seen; Richard Watts in the *New York Post* said he was "a brilliant master of his art"; Jack Kroll in *Newsweek* hailed him as "one of the great illusionists"; and T. E. Kalem in *Time* found him a "master illusionist."

As for the story and score, Edwin Wilson in the *Wall Street Journal* suggested Henning should have "made them disappear forever," Barnes said "they should keep the magic and abandon the show," and Douglas Watt in the *New York Daily News* noted that the lion pulled off "the best trick of the evening" because its magical appearance "took everybody's mind off the story."

The cast album was issued by Bell Records (LP # 9003) and then later was released on CD by January Records (# 7001). A revised version of the musical (which didn't include the entire score) was filmed on stage in Canada, and while it was apparently intended for theatrical release it seems to have taken the direct-to-video route and was issued on DVD by Image Entertainment (# ID0697CODVD). Directed by Norman Campbell and scripted by Jerry Ross, the film stars Henning and Anita Morris, and others in the cast are Didi Conn and Jon Finlayson.

Henning returned to Broadway in the title role of the lavish musical *Merlin*, which opened at the Mark Hellinger Theatre on February 13, 1983, and played for 199 performances. Henning's magical feats were again the highlight of the evening, although Chita Rivera and Nathan Lane gave amusingly campy performances and Elmer Bernstein's score offered one memorable song, the opening number "It's About Magic." Henning also appeared in *Doug Henning and His World of Magic*, which opened at the Lunt-Fontanne Theatre on December 11, 1984, for a limited engagement of fifty-six performances.

Awards

Tony Award Nominations: Best Featured Actor in a Musical (Doug Henning); Best Director of a Musical (Grover Dale)

BRAINCHILD

"A Musical in the Mind"

The musical opened at the Forrest Theatre, Philadelphia, Pennsylvania, on March 25, 1974, and permanently closed there on April 6, 1974.
Book: Maxine Klein
Lyrics: Hal David
Music: Michel Legrand
Direction: Maxine Klein; *Producer*: Adela Holzer; *Choreography*: Leigh Abdallah (billed as "choreographic assistant to the director"); *Scenery*: Kert Lundell; *Costumes*: Joseph G. Aulisi; *Lighting*: Thomas Skelton; *Musical Direction*: Thomas Pierson
Cast: Adrian—Tovah Feldshuh (Adrian's Self Image), Marilyn Pasekoff (Adrian's Emotional Self), Barbara Niles (Adrian's Mental Self); Adrian's Memories—Dorian Harewood (Raymond), Barbara Niles (Adrian's mother), Gene Lindsey (Jim), Nancy Ann Denning (Bonnie, Nun), Mark Siegel (Irving), Louise Hoven (Teacher, Telephone Operator), Signa Joy (Sally Ensalada); Adrian's Fantasies—Louise Hoven (Hag, New York Lady), Dorian Harewood (Rock Singer), Nancy Ann Denning (Weatherball Mermaid), Signa Joy (Low Bottom Woman); Adrian's Nerve Cells—Francesca Bartoccini, Nancy Dalton, Ben Harney, Scott Johnston, Tony Padron, Justin Ross, Harriet Scalici
The musical was presented in one act.
The action takes place in Adrian's mind in both the present and the past.

Musical Numbers

"Everything That Happens to You" ("unfinished" song, performed in the present time) (Tovah Feldshuh); "I'm Tired of Me" (present time) (Tovah Feldshuh, Marilyn Pasekoff, Barbara Niles); "No Faceless People" (fantasy) (Nancy Dalton, Nancy Ann Denning, Signa Joy, Harriet Scalici); "The First Time I Heard a Bluebird" (memory) (Marilyn Pasekoff); "I Know You Are There" (memory) (Dorian Harewood, Ben Harney, Scott Johnston, Tony Padron, Justin Ross); "Don't Talk, Don't Think" (fantasy) (Nancy Ann Denning, Gene Lindsey); "Low Bottom Woman" (fantasy) (Signa Joy); "I've Been Starting Tomorrow" (fantasy) (Dorian Harewood, Ben Harney, Signa Joy); "I've Been Starting Tomorrow" (reprise) (fantasy) (Tovah Feldshuh, Dorian Harewood, Ben Harney, Signa Joy); "Everything That Happens to You" (reprise) (present) (unfinished) (Tovah Feldshuh, Marilyn Pasekoff, Barbara Niles); "Let Me Think for You" (present) (Marilyn Pasekoff, Barbara Niles); "I Never Met a Russian I Didn't Like" (fantasy) (Ben Harney, Scott Johnston, Tony Padron, Justin Ross); "Sally Ensalada" (memory) (Signa Joy, Ben Harney, Tony Padron, Dorian Harewood, Scott Johnston, Justin Ross); "Let Me Be Your Mirror" (memory) (Dorian Harewood); "Just a Little Space Can Be a Growing Place" (memory) (Barbara Niles); "What Is It?" (present) (Tovah Feldshuh, Marilyn Pasekoff, Barbara Niles); "Don't Pull Up the Flowers" (fantasy) (Tovah Feldshuh, Company); "Everything That Happens to You" (reprise) (fantasy) (Tovah Feldshuh, Company)

Brainchild was a pretentious exercise that never braved Broadway and quickly folded during its Philadelphia tryout. The program notes explained that the action took place in Adrian's mind, and, yes, like Arthur Laurents's drama *A Clearing in the Woods* (1957) and Dan Goggins's 1992 Off-Broadway musical *Balancing Act*, *Brainchild* was one of those tiresome shows that found it necessary to utilize different performers to represent various aspects of a single character. In Laurents's play, Virginia (Kim Stanley) is also performed by three other actresses who portray Virginia as a child, a young girl, and a younger woman, and Goggins's musical found five performers acting out the ambitious, sensitive, optimistic, skeptical, and humorous sides of the same person.

In Adrian's case, there is Adrian's self-image (Tovah Feldshuh), Adrian's "emotional self" (Marilyn Pasekoff), and Adrian's "mental self" (Barbara Niles). But wait. There are also Adrian's nerve cells, and these were performed by Francesca Bartoccini, Nancy Dalton, Ben Harney, Scott Johnston, Tony Padron, Justin Ross, and Harriet Scalici. Besides characters and scenes that took place in the present, there were also excursions into Adrian's memories and fantasies (and the program placed each song number in one or the other of these categories).

Adrian is a songwriter who, according to the program notes, is "like most composers" and thus "is always somewhere in between procrastinating and writing a song." She's also waiting for her lover, and he is late "as usual." Swin in *Variety* indicated the evening might appeal to "committed feminists" because the plot dealt with Adrian's "self-debate over ravages she has endured at the hands of a sexist society." The review mentioned that the performers never rose above the level of an "agreeably amateur presence" and that the book was "utterly joyless," the lyrics "neither clever nor provocative," the music "ordinary," and the costumes "overbearingly ugly." Further, there were "desperate attempts" at "vulgarity for its own sake."

Ernest Schier in the *Philadelphia Evening Bulletin* noted "*Brainchild* celebrates an almost empty mind" and Jay Samuels in the *Courier-Post* called the musical "a soggy psycho-saga."

With the exception of "Let Me Think for You," a demo album of the entire score was released by RFO (Rescued from Oblivion) Records (LP # RFO-104) with unidentified singers. Michel Legrand and Lena Horne's recording *Lena & Michel* (originally released on LP by RCA Victor Records and later issued on CD by BMG and RCA) includes three songs from the score, "Everything That Happens to You Happens to Me," "I've Been Starting Tomorrow All My Life," and "Let Me Be Your Mirror."

GONE WITH THE WIND

The production opened on August 28, 1973, at the Dorothy Chandler Pavilion in Los Angeles, and closed there on October 20; it then opened at the Curran Theatre in San Francisco on October 23, and permanently closed there on November 24, 1973.

Book: Horton Foote

Lyrics and *Music*: Harold Rome

Based on the 1936 novel *Gone with the Wind* by Margaret Mitchell.

Direction and *Choreography*: Joe Layton; *Producers*: Harold Fielding (A Joe Layton Production); *Scenery*: David Hays (Tim Goodchild and Romain Johnston, Associate Scenic Designers); *Costumes*: Patton Campbell; *Lighting*: H. R. Poindexter; *Musical Direction*: Jay Blackton

Cast: At Tara, the O'Hara Plantation—*Lesley Ann Warren* (Scarlett O'Hara); Cheryl Robinson (Prissy), Pamela Johnson (Suellen O'Hara), Jennifer Williams (Careen O'Hara), Anne Turner (Ellen O'Hara), James Cutlip (Gerald O'Hara), Malaika Ahraam (Cookie), Dolores Davis (Dilcey), E. B. Smith (Big Sam), Elimu Goss Jr. (Pork), Lawrence Hyman (Brent Tarleton), Gene Castle (Stuart Tarleton), Melinda Sherwood (Randa Tarleton), Ginny Gagnon (Mrs. Tarleton), Norman Fontaine (Mr. Tarleton), Robert Nichols (Frank Kennedy), Nadine Moody (Karen Elsing), Shari White (Maybelle Merriwether), Al Jessup (Mr. Elsing), Maryalice Jessup (Mrs. Elsing), Polly Wood (Mrs. Taylor), Peter Kevoian (Rene Picard), Philip Sweatman (Hugh Elsing), Paddy McIntyre (Alex Fontaine), Lou Manor (Cade Calvert), Tucker Smith (Hugh Munroe), Bob Bakanic (Phil Meade), Tom Westerman (Darcy Meade), Geraldine Decker (Mrs. Meade), Ellen Cadwallader (Cathleen Calvert), Eileen MacMillan (Sally Munroe), William Sisson (Doctor Meade), Lynda Sue Marks (Mrs. Merriwether), Lloyd Bunnell (Mr. Merriwether), Russell Chambers (Tommy Wellburn), Greg Macosko (Charles Hamilton), Jordan Bowers (Mr. Wilkes), Debbie Henry (Honey Wilkes), Nancy Robinson (India Wilkes), Udana Power (Melanie Hamilton), Terence Monk (Ashley Wilkes), *Pernell Roberts* (Rhett Butler); At the Bazaar in the Atlanta Armory—William Sisson (Doctor Meade), Evelyn Bell (Aunt Pittypat), Tom Westerman (Soldier); In Atlanta during the Siege—Ann Hodges (Belle Watling); Belle's Girls: Debbie Henry, Shari White, and Ellen Cadwallader; Confederate Soldiers: Joshua Aaron, Les Cockayne, William Cullen, Anthony De Fonte, Michael Greer, Charles Luxemberg, Dale MacKenzie, Anthony Orr; On the Road to Tara—Paddy McIntyre (Yankee Deserter); Atlanta and Tara After the Civil War—Tucker Smith (Yankee Guard); Carpetbaggers: Gene Castle, Nadine Moody, Elimu Goss Jr., Malaika Ahraam; Peter Kevoian (Tom), Al Jessup (Mr. Parker), Polly Wood (Mrs. Taylor), Ginny Gagnon (Mrs. Tarleton), Tucker Smith (Contractor); The Mansion Home of Rhett and Scarlett—Heather O'Connell (Bonnie [age two]), Eileen McDonough (Bonnie [age five])

The musical was presented in two acts.

The action takes place in Tara and Atlanta during the time of the Civil War and the years immediately following.

Musical Numbers

Act One: "Today's the Day" (Leslie Ann Warren); "Cakewalk" (Orchestra); "We Belong to You" (Udana Power); "Scarlett" (Terrence Monk); "We Belong to You" (reprise) (Terrence Monk, Greg Macosko, Udana Power, Leslie Ann Warren); "Bonnie Blue Flag" (Soldiers); "Bazaar Hymn" (People of Atlanta); "Virginia Reel" (Orchestra); "Quadrille" (Orchestra); "Two of a Kind" (Pernell Roberts); "Two of a Kind" (reprise) (Lesley Ann Warren); "Blissful Christmas" (Cheryl Robinson, Theresa Merritt, Evelyn Bell, Udana Power, Leslie Ann Roberts); "My Soldier" (Udana Power, Lesley Ann Warren); "Tomorrow Is Another Day" (Lesley Ann Warren); "Ashley's Departure" (People of Atlanta, Soldiers); "Where Is My Soldier Boy?" (People of Atlanta, Soldiers); "Why Did They Die?" (People of Atlanta, Soldiers); "Johnny Is My Darling" (People of Atlanta, Soldiers); "Bonnie Blue Flag" (reprise) (People of Atlanta, Soldiers); "Lonely Stranger" (Ann Hodges, Soldiers); "Lonely Stranger" (reprise) (Ann Hodges, Pernell Roberts); "Atlanta Burning" (People of Atlanta, Soldiers); "Tomorrow Is Another Day" (reprise) (Leslie Ann Warren)

Act Two: "If Only" (The Old South); "How Often" (Pernell Roberts); "Gone with the Wind" (Terrence Monk); "How Lucky" (Robert Nichols); "A Southern Lady" (Pernell Roberts, Ladies of the Old South); "A Southern Lady" (reprise) (Atlanta Workers); "Marrying for Fun" (Pernell Roberts); "Brand New Friends" (Lesley Ann Warren, Pernell Roberts, The New South); "Miss Fiddle-Dee-Dee" (Pernell Roberts); "Blueberry Eyes" (Theresa Merritt, Pernell Roberts, Udana Power); "Bonnie Gone" (Theresa Merritt, Pernell Roberts, Mourners); "Two of a Kind" (reprise) (Lesley Ann Warren); "It Doesn't Matter Now" (Pernell Roberts)

Can you make a classic musical out of Margaret Mitchell's 1936 best-selling novel *Gone with the Wind* and its definitive 1939 film version? Apparently not, although the formidable undertaking didn't stop Harold Rome, and for a six-year period four major productions of his adaptation were produced and three albums of his score were recorded.

In November 1966, a straight-play, two-part version of the novel was presented by Kazuo Kikuta in Tokyo (the first part lasted five hours, the second three). From there, he commissioned a musical version for which he wrote the book and Harold Rome the lyrics and music (the Japanese adaptation of the lyrics was by Tokiko Iwatani and Ryo Fukui). As *Scarlett*, the musical opened at Tokyo's Imperial Theatre on January 2, 1970, with direction and choreography by Joe Layton, décor by David Hays, costumes by Patton Campbell, and musical direction by Lehman Engel. The cast album was released on a lavish two-LP set by (RCA) Victor/World Group Records (# SJET-9210-11), and the two-CD set was later issued by DRG Records (# 13105).

As *Gone with the Wind*, the musical was then produced in London at the Drury Lane on May 3, 1972, for a run of 397 performances; with a revised book by Horton Foote, the musical was again directed and choreographed by Layton, the scenery was designed by Hays and by Tim Goodchild, and the costumes were by Campbell. The cast included June Ritchie (Scarlett O'Hara), Harve Presnell (Rhett Butler), Patricia Michael (Melanie Wilkes), Robert Swann (Ashley Wilkes), Brian Davies (Frank Kennedy), Bessie Love (Aunt Pittypat), and Marion Ramsey (Prissy). The cast album was recorded by EMI/Columbia Records (LP # SCXA-9252) and the CD was issued by Kritzerland Records (# KR-20018-2); of the thirty-seven individual numbers (including reprises), nineteen were heard on the album. During the time of the production, Harold Rome recorded an album of songs from the musical that was released by Chappell Records (LP # CHP-101).

Songs heard in the Tokyo production (but not in London) were: "He Loves Me," "Scarlett," "Goodbye, My Honey," "What Is Love?," "Gambling Man," "O'Hara," and "The Newlyweds' Song." Added for London, were: "Cakewalk," "Tara," "Bazaar Hymn," "Virginia Reel," "Quadrille," "Ashley's Departure," "Tomorrow Is Another Day," "Why Did They Die?," "Johnny Is My Darling," "Atlanta Burning," "A Soldier's Goodbye," "If Only," "How Often, How Often," "The Wedding," "A Southern Lady," "Marrying for Fun," and "It Doesn't Matter Now." Rome's recording of the score includes two songs not heard in either the Tokyo or London productions, "Because There's You" and a title song. The number "Bonnie Gone" was a recycled version of Rome's "Like the Breeze Blows" from his 1965 play-with-music *The Zulu and the Zayda*.

In reviewing the London production, Pit in *Variety* said the musical was "too fragmentary and overlong, musically too busy and lacking in sock production numbers." The score "wasn't memorable," but "as spectacle" the musical was "at its best."

The current American production was headed for Broadway but never made it. The cast included Lesley Ann Warren (Scarlett), Pernell Roberts (Rhett Butler), Udana Power (Melanie), Terence Monk (Ashley), Theresa Merritt (Mammy), and Cheryl Robinson (Prissy). Edwa in *Variety* said the long evening resulted in "boredom," Rome's score was "unmemorable" and "forgettable" and his lyrics "even worse," and because of Monk and Power's "excellent" performances the show might well have been titled *Ashley and Melanie*; otherwise, Warren was a "disappointing" Scarlett and the "dashing" Roberts wasn't up to the demands of the score. The production added "Miss Fiddle-Dee-Dee," "How Lucky," "Brand New Friends," and a title song; and reinstated "Scarlett" from the Tokyo production.

On June 14, 1976, the musical was revived for a cross-country tour, where it played in such cities as Dallas, Kansas City, and Atlanta. Directed by Lucia Victor, the cast included Sherry Mathis (Scarlett), David Canary (Rhett), Leigh Berry (Melanie), and Laurence Guittard (Ashley). *Variety* said that while the production was "no smash," it was nonetheless an "entertaining evening on the basis of the story." As for the score, *Variety* found it undistinguished and felt it sometimes got in the way of the plot.

A different musical adaptation of the novel opened in London on April 22, 2008, at the New London Theatre for seventy-nine performances. The book and lyrics were by Margaret Martin, and her book was adapted by Trevor Nunn.

RACHAEL LILY ROSENBLOOM AND DON'T YOU *EVER* FORGET IT!

"A New Musical"

The musical played preview performances at the Broadhurst Theatre from November 26 to December 1, 1973, before permanently closing prior to its scheduled opening night of December 5.

Book: Paul Jabara and Tom Eyen

Lyrics and Music: Paul Jabara

Direction: Tom Eyen; *Producers*: Robert Stigwood and Ahmet Ertegun (R. Tyler Gatchell Jr., and Peter Neufeld, Associate Producers); *Choreography*: Tony Stevens ("Choreography Supervision" by Grover Dale); *Scenery*: Robin Wagner; *Costumes*: Joseph G. Aulisi; *Lighting*: Jules Fisher; *Musical Direction*: Gordon Lowry Harrell

Cast: Ellen Greene (Barbara's Voice, Rachael Lily Rosenbloom), Paul Jabara (Joey, Raymond de la Troya, Doctor), Marion Ramsey (Academy Awards Guest, Glinda, Rachael's Echo, One-Man Girl, Jeanette), Anita Morris (Academy Awards Guest, Stella Starfuckoff, Rachael's Ocho Rios Twin, One-Man Girl, Doris O'Laski), Richard Cooper Bayne (Academy Awards Guest, Brooklynite, Delivery Boy, Huck, Troy Denning, Hollywood Boy, Party Guest, Starving Actor, Quartet, Go-Go Boy, Sun Worshipper, Calypso Chorus, Arab, Sailor), Carole (Kelly) Bishop (Academy Awards Guest, Brooklynite, Dream Girl, Ice Cream Cone, Flapper, Jogger, Mona, Party Guest, Sun Worshipper, Calypso Chorus, Arab Girl, One-Man Girl), Kenneth Carr (Academy Awards Announcer, Brooklynite, Delivery Boy, Mr. Walton, Trick Donning, Hollywood Boy, Party Guest, Party Announcer, Quartet, Go-Go Boy, Sun Worshipper, Calypso Chorus, Arab, Bartender), Andre de Shields (Academy Awards Announcer, Brooklynite, Delivery Boy, Glinda's Angel, List Reciter, Pimp, Hollywood Boy, Borneo, Party Guest, Party Doctor, Quartet, Go-Go Boy, Beach Boy, Arab, Black), Judy Gibson (Academy Awards Guest, Brooklynite, Fish Stand Owner's Friend, Can of Tab, Flapper, Jogger, Party Guest, Dykette, Starving Actor, Sun Worshipper, Calypso Chorus, Arab Girl, One-Man Girl, Black), Michon Peacock (Academy Awards Guest, Brooklynite, Dream Girl, Hot Dog, Flapper, Jogger, Party Guest, Starving Actor, Go-Go Girl, Sexy Announcer, Sun Worshipper, Calypso Chorus, Arab Girl, One-Man Girl), Jozella Reed (Academy Awards Guest, Brooklynite, Fish Stand Owner, Hooker, Flapper, Jogger, Party Guest, Dykette, Starving Actor, Sun Worshipper, Calypso Chorus, Arab Girl, One-Man Girl, Black), Jane Robertson (Barbara, Brooklynite, Fish Stand Owner's Friend, Dancing Partner, Flapper, Jogger, Rona, Party Guest, Gloria, Sun Worshipper, Calypso Chorus, Arab Girl, One-Man Girl), Thomas Walsh (Academy Awards Guest, Brooklynite, Delivery Boy, Dancing Partner, Waiter, Hollywood Boy, Rachael's Stud, Go-Go Boy, Sun Worshipper, Doctor Osho Rios Twin, Arab, Sailor), Anthony White (Academy Awards Guest, Brooklynite, Delivery Boy, Glinda's Angel, Dancing Partner, Hollywood Boy, Rachael's Stud, Barbara's House Control Voice, Quartet, Go-Go Boy, Sun Worshipper, Calypso Chorus, Arab, Jamaican Announcer, Sailor, Black)

The musical was presented in two acts.

The action takes place mostly in New York City and Los Angeles during the present time.

Musical Numbers

Act One: "Academy Awards Theme" (Company); "Dear Miss Streisand" (Ellen Greene); "Delivery Boys' Lament" (Richard Cooper Bayne, Kenneth Carr, Andre de Shields, Thomas Walsh, Anthony White); "Me and My Perch" (lyric by Paul Jabara and David Debin) (Ellen Greene, Richard Cooper Bayne, Kenneth Carr, Andre de Shields, Thomas Walsh, Anthony White); "Gorgeous Lily" (Ellen Greene, Paul Jabara, Michon Peacock, Carole Bishop); "Get Your Show Rolling" (Marion Ramsey, Ellen Greene, Andre de Shields, Anthony White, Company); "Hollywood, Hollywood!" (Marion Ramsey, Ellen Greene, Paul Jabara, Andre de Shields, Anthony White); "East Brooklyn Blues" (Kenneth Carr, Richard Cooper Bayne, Ellen Greene, Judy Gibson, Michon Peacock, Carole Bishop, Andre de Shields, Jozella Reed, Company); "Broadway Rhythm" (Anita Morris, Girls); "Hollywood Is Dying" (Boys); "Broadway, I Love You" (Anita Morris); "Ramond's Song" (Paul Jabara, Ellen Greene); "Seduction Samba" (Marion Ramsey, Andre de Shields, Anthony White, Company); "Rona, Mona and Me" (Paul Jabara, Carole Bishop, Jane Robertson); "Working for Stella" (Anita Morris, Ellen Greene); "Silver Diamond Rhinestone Glasses" (Ellen Greene); "Party Sickness" (Company); "Take Me Savage" (Anita Morris, Judy Gibson, Jozella Reed); "Overdose" (Company); "Get Your Show Rolling" (reprise) (Marion Ramsey, Ellen Greene, Company)

Act Two: "Academy Awards Theme" (reprise) (Company); "Change in Raquel" (Ellen Greene, Paul Jabara, Richard Cooper Bayne, Kenneth Carr, Anthony White, Andre de Shields); "Raquel Gives the Dish" (Ellen Greene, Anthony White, Michon Peacock, Kenneth Carr, Thomas Walsh, Andre de Shields, Richard Cooper Bayne); "Gorgeous Lily" (reprise) (Ellen Greene, Paul Jabara, Michon Peacock, Carole Bishop); "Ochos Rios" (lyric by Paul Jabara and Paul Issa) (Ellen Greene, Andre de Shields, Anita Morris, Paul Jabara, Thomas Walsh, Company); "Cobra Woman" (Ellen Greene, Company); "Things" (lyric by Paul Jabara and Paul Issa) (Ellen Greene, Kenneth Carr, Thomas Walsh, Richard Cooper Bayne, Anthony White); "One Man" (Ellen Greene, Anita Morris, Marion Ramsey, Girls); "We'll Be There" (lyric by Paul Jabara and Paul Issa) (Marion Ramsey, Andre de Shields, Anthony White, Jozella Reed, Judy Gibson); "One Man" (reprise) (Anita Morris, Marion Ramsey); "Broadway Rhythm" (reprise) (Company); "We'll Be There" (reprise) (Company)

Rachael Lily Rosenbloom and Don't You Ever *Forget It!* may have died of terminal camp. *New York* summarized the plot as about "a lady from Brooklyn with a weight problem who goes off to Hollywood." And the title character (Ellen Greene) is indeed a slavey from Brooklyn whose origins include a job in a fish market. Because Miss Streisand dropped the "a" from her first name, Rachael acquires it and adds it to hers, and soon she's on the road to success and reaches the heights of fame and glory as a Hollywood gossip columnist—but not before she undergoes a nervous breakdown. In the meantime, her world is knee-deep in Hollywood boys, go-go boys, sun worshippers, party guests, pimps, studs, and other assorted tinsel town hangers-on, and the song titles seemed to say it all ("Dear Miss Streisand," "Me and My Perch," "Hollywood! Hollywood!," "Rona, Mona and Me," "Silver Diamond Rhinestone Glasses," "Overdose," "Raquel Gives the Dish," and "Cobra Woman").

Variety first reported that the musical was budgeted at $500,000, and that after an out-of-town tryout would open on Broadway in mid-October 1973, probably at the Shubert Theatre. Ellen Greene, Paul Jabara,

Melba Moore, and Gretchen Wyler were scheduled to star, and Ron Link was to direct. But instead of a traditional tryout (Jabara told the *New York Times* "it was not possible to take [the musical] out of town" because it was "specifically designed for New York audiences"), the show opted for a series of Broadway previews at the Broadhurst Theatre, which was just around the corner from the Shubert. The roles mentioned for Moore and Wyler were played by Marion Ramsey and Anita Morris, and Ron Link was succeeded by Tom Eyen.

RSO Records had planned to record the cast album, which was canceled due to the musical's premature closing.

A SONG FOR CYRANO

"A New Musical Romance"

The musical played the summer stock circuit in 1973, including engagements at the Tappan Zee Playhouse in Nyack, New York, for the week of July 18–21 and at the Falmouth Playhouse, Falmouth, Massachusetts, for the week of July 23–July 28.

Book: J. Vincent Smith

Lyrics and *Music*: Robert Craig Wright and George Forrest

Based on the 1897 play *Cyrano de Bergerac* by Edmond Rostand.

Direction: Jose Ferrer; *Producer*: Sidney Gordon (A Producing Managers Company Project); *Choreography*: Rich Rahn; *Dueling Sequences*: Directed by Edward Easton; *Scenery*: Gary R. Langley ("Design Concept" by James Riley); *Costumes*: "Supervised" by Neal Cooper; *Lighting*: Bob Sessions; *Musical Direction*: Dobbs Frank

Cast: Adam Petroski (Montfleury), Keith Kaldenberg (Theophraste Renaudot), Genette Lane (Barmaid), Stephen Fenning (Porter), Al DeSio (Shepherd, Bertrandou the Piper), Joy Chutz (Shepherdess), Marie King (Shepherdess), Louise Reichlin (Shepherdess), *Jose Ferrer* (Cyrano de Bergerac), Marshall Borden (Comte Antoine de Guiche), Richard Miller (Bellrose), Edward Easton (Baron Pierre de Valvert), Willi Burke (Roxane), Helon Blount (Duenna. Mother Marguerite), Edmund Lyndeck (Captain Henri Le Bret); Cadets: James Anthony, Samuel Bruce, Al DeSio, Edward Easton, Stephen Fenning, Robert Hendersen, Richard Miller, Curt Ralston, Burt Rodriguez, Hank Schob, and Clyde P. Walker; Don McKay (Baron Christian de Neuvillette), James Anthony (Monk, Cyrano de Bergerac in "The Ambush" sequence); Nuns: Joy Chutz, Marie King, Genette Lane, Melanie Lerner, Louise Reichlin, and Susan Von Suhrke

The musical was presented in two acts.

The action takes place in Paris and environs during 1640 and 1654.

Musical Numbers

Act One: "All Paris!" (Keith Kaldenberg); "Sleep, Sheep, Sleep" (Al DeSio, Joy Chutz, Marie King, Louise Reichlin); "Phoebus Apollo" (Adam Petroski); "My Nose, My Plume, My Life" (Jose Ferrer, Crowd); "A Bit of a Ballad" (Jose Ferrer, Edward Easton, Keith Kaldenberg, Crowd); "My Love Does Not Know" (Jose Ferrer); "The Ambush" (James Anthony, Ruffians); "Morning Song" (Joy Chutz, Marie King, Genette Lane, Melanie Lerner, Louise Reichlin, Susan Von Suhrke); "My Love Does Not Know" (reprise) (Willi Burke); "Take Care of Him" (Willi Burke); "Second to None" (Cadets); "Now and Always Yours" (Don McKay, Jose Ferrer, Willi Burke, Helon Blount)

Act Two: "The Kiss" (Jose Ferrer, Willi Burke, Don McKay); "Moment in the Dark"/"Roxane"/"Definition of a Kiss"/"On the Moon" (Jose Ferrer, Marshall Borden); "To the Battle!" (Willi Burke, Cadets); "Take Care of Him" (reprise) and "Second to None" (reprise) (performers unidentified in programs; probably Willie Burke and Cadets); "A Melancholy Melody" (Don McKay, Al DeSio, Cadets); "The Other You" (Willi Burke, Don McKay); "The Battle" (Cadets, Spanish Army); "Evening Song" (Joy Chutz, Marie King, Genette Lane, Melanie Lerner, Louise Reichlin, Susan Von Suhrke); "One Friend" (Willi Burke); "The Gazette" (Jose Ferrer); "His Last Letter" (Jose Ferrer, Willi Burke); "Now and Always Yours" (performers unidentified in programs; probably Jose Ferrer and Willie Burke); "A Song for Cyrano" (Helon Blount, Willi Burke, Don McKay, Cadets, Nuns)

A Song for Cyrano had toured in stock with Jose Ferrer during the summer of 1967, and then during the summer of 1973 Ferrer again hit the tent circuit with the musical. Perhaps the 1972 Broadway production of ***Cyrano*** sparked the interest of Ferrer, Robert Wright, and George Forrest to revive the musical, or maybe Ferrer just enjoyed the role because of his great successes in the 1946 Broadway revival of *Cyrano de Bergerac* (for which he won the Tony Award for Best Leading Actor in a Play) and its 1950 film version (for which he won the Academy Award for Best Actor). But after the musical's current tour, *A Song for Cyrano* seems to have completely disappeared.

During the summer run, the intermission was changed and came directly before "A Melancholy Melody."

There have been at least sixteen lyric adaptations of Edmund Rostand's play; for more information, see ***Cyrano***.

THE STUDENT PRINCE

The musical opened on June 5, 1973, at the Academy of Music, Philadelphia, Pennsylvania, and permanently closed on October 21, 1973, at the Dallas State Fair.

Book and *Lyrics*: Dorothy Donnelly

Music: Sigmund Romberg

Based on the 1901 play *Alt-Heidelberg* by Wilhelm Meyer-Forster (which in turn had been adapted from Meyer-Forster's 1898 novel *Karl Heinrich*).

Direction: George Schaefer; *Producers*: Moe Septee in association with Jack L. Wolgin and Victor H. Potamkin (A Lehman Engel Production); *Choreography*: David Nillo; *Scenery* and *Lighting*: Clarke Dunham; *Costumes*: Supervised by Winn Morton and Sara Brook; *Musical Direction*: John Lesko (for the Philadelphia premiere, Lehman Engel conducted)

Cast: Lackeys—Eric Ellenberg, Homer Foil, Wayne Scherzer, and Michael Merrill; Robert Symonds (Prime Minister Von Mark), Richard Torigi (Doctor Engel), Harry Danner (Prince Karl Franz), Jon Garrison (Prince Karl Franz for matinee performances), John Mintun (Ruder), Patti Allison (Gretchen), Warren Galjour (Toni), George Rose (Lutz), Theodore Tenley (Hubert), Brad Tyrrell (Von Asterberg), Don Estes (Lucas), Ed Dixon (Count Hugo Detlef), Bonnie Hamilton (Kathie), Fran Stevens (Grand Duchess), Sandra Thornton (Princess Margaret), William Covington (Captain Tarnitz), Peter Atherton (Baron Arnheim), Mary Roche (Countess); Students, Waitresses, Patrons of the Inn, and Ladies and Gentlemen of the Court: Neal Antin, Peter L. Atherton, Marta Brennan, Michael Carrier, Peter Damon, Doreen DeFeis, Eric Ellenberg, Tricia Ellis, Patti Farmer, John Franz, Homer Foil, James Fredericks, George Holland, Mark Jacoby, Howard Johnson, Robert Kunar, Valerie Lemon, George Maguire, Jason McAuliffe, Michael Merrill, Sal Mistretta, Mary Roche, Anthony Santelmo, Wayne Scherzer, Dana Talley, David Varnum, Richard Walker, John West, Peter Whitehead, Parker Willson

The musical was presented in two acts.

The action takes place during the years 1830–1832 in Karlsburg and Heidelberg, Germany.

Musical Numbers

Act One: "By Our Bearing So Sedate" (Eric Ellenberg, Homer Foil, Wayne Scherzer, Michael Merrill); "Golden Days" (Richard Torigi, Harry Danner); "To the Inn We're Marching" (Ed Dixon, Brad Tyrrell, Don Estes, Students); "Drinking Song" (aka "Drink, Drink, Drink") (Ed Dixon, Brad Tyrrell, Don Estes, Students); "I'm Coming at Your Call" (Bonnie Hamilton, Students); "Come, Boys" (Bonnie Hamilton, Students); "Entrance of the Prince and Engel" (Harry Danner, Richard Torigi, Bonnie Hamilton, John Mintun, Patti Allison, Girls); "Gaudeamus Igitur" (traditional) (Students); "Golden Days" (reprise) (Richard Torigi); "Deep in My Heart, Dear" (Bonnie Hamilton, Harry Danner); "Serenade" (aka "Overhead the Moon Is Beaming") (Harry Danner, Ed Dixon, Brad Tyrrell, Don Estes, Students); Finale (Harry Danner, Bonnie Hamilton, Richard Torigi, Ed Dixon, Brad Tyrrell, Don Estes, Patti Allison, Students, Waitresses)

Act Two: "Student Life" (Harry Danner, Richard Torigi, Ed Dixon, Brad Tyrrell, Don Estes, Bonnie Hamilton, Patti Allison, Students); Finale (Bonnie Hamilton, Harry Danner, Richard Torigi); "Just We Two" (Sandra Thornton, William Covington, Officers); "The Flag That Flies" (Ensemble); Finale (Harry Danner, Richard

Torigi); "To the Inn We're Marching" (reprise) (Ed Dixon, Brad Tyrrell, Don Estes, Students); "Serenade" (reprise) (Harry Danner, Ed Dixon, Brad Tyrrell, Don Estes, Students); "Come, Boys" (reprise) (Ed Dixon, Brad Tyrrell, Don Estes, Students); Finale Ultimo (Harry Danner, Bonnie Hamilton)

During the summer months of 1973, producers Moe Septee, Jack L. Wolgin, and Victor H. Potamkin presented Lehman Engel's revivals of Sigmund Romberg's popular 1920s operettas *The Student Prince* (originally titled *The Student Prince in Heidelberg*) and ***The Desert Song***. Both productions provided a welcome opportunity to hear Romberg's sentimental ballads and stirring marches in a theatrical setting with strong voices and a large orchestra. But the era wasn't much interested in operettas, and thus chances to see and hear fully staged revivals of Romberg, Rudolf Friml, and Victor Herbert's works became increasingly rare. The public and the critics weren't overwhelmed with the Romberg revivals, and so while ***The Desert Song*** braved Broadway, it lasted for just two weeks, and *The Student Prince* played out its bookings for the summer and early fall and finally closed at the Dallas State Fair in early October without chancing Broadway.

The operetta had premiered on Broadway at Jolson's Theatre on December 2, 1924, for 608 performances, and Romberg's gorgeously romantic score included the glorious ballads "Deep in My Heart, Dear" and "Serenade" (aka "Overhead the Moon Is Beaming"), the lilting waltz "Just We Two," the stirring march "To the Inn We're Marching," the impish backhanded salute to "Student Life," and perhaps the ultimate Broadway toast to spirits, the irresistible "Drinking Song" (aka "Drink, Drink, Drink") with its full-blooded male chorus. And serving as a theme song throughout the evening was the bittersweet "Golden Days."

The simple story was told in a straightforward manner and without a touch of camp. Prince Karl (Harry Danner) attends college at Heidelberg University for a few months and falls in love with the barmaid Kathie (Bonnie Hamilton), a waitress from the nearby Three Golden Apples Inn. But when the prince's father dies, royal duty calls. He becomes king and must enter into an arranged marriage with Princess Margaret (Sandra Thornton).

The operetta was first revived on Broadway at the Majestic Theatre on January 29, 1931, for forty-five performances, and then played at the Broadway Theatre on June 8, 1943, for 153 showings. The work was revived five times by the New York City Opera Company at the New York State Theatre: on August 29, 1980 (thirteen performances); August 27, 1981 (six performances); July 5, 1985 (nine); July 7, 1987 (fourteen); and August 14, 1993 (fifteen). For the 1985 revival, Jerry Hadley sang the role of Prince Karl.

The original London production opened at His Majesty's Theatre on February 3, 1926, for ninety-six performances, and there have been two film versions released by MGM. The 1928 silent adaptation was directed by Ernst Lubitsch and starred Ramon Novarro (Prince Karl) and Norma Shearer (Kathie). The second version released in 1954 was a colorful and melodic look at the familiar story and had a rather quaint and ingratiating charm about it. Directed by Richard Thorpe, the film was to have starred Mario Lanza in the title role, but weight and other problems caused him to be replaced by Edmund Purdom (whose singing voice was dubbed by Lanza). Ann Blyth was Kathie, and others in the cast were Louis Calhern, S. Z. "Cuddles" Sakall, Edmund Gwenn, John Williams, Betta St. John, and Evelyn Varden. The film included three pleasant new songs (all with lyrics by Paul Francis Webster and music by Nicholas Brodszky), "Summertime in Heidelberg," "I'll Walk with God," and "Beloved." Lanza recorded the score for RCA Victor (LP # LM-2339), which included the three new songs; later, the set was released with other vocals by Lanza on Sepia CD # 1200.

The most complete recording of the score is a two-CD studio cast album by That's Entertainment Records (# CDTER2-1172).

Alt-Heidelberg was first produced on Broadway at the Princess Theatre on December 15, 1902, as *Heidelberg, or When All the World Was Young*; as *Old Heidelberg*, another version of the story was seen at the Lyric Theatre on October 12, 1903.

Romberg's musical adaptation of *Alt-Heidelberg* wasn't the first lyric version of the work. The opera *Eidelberga mia* premiered in Genoa, Italy, in 1908 (music by Ubaldo Pacchierotti and libretto by Alberto Colantuoni).

1974–1975 Season

THE MERRY WIDOW

Theatre: City Center 55th Street Theatre
Opening Date: June 4, 1974; *Closing Date*: June 9, 1974
Performances: 7
Book and *Lyrics*: Victor M. Leon and Leo Stein; Spanish adaptation by Miguel Padilla
Music: Franz Lehar
Direction: Miguel de Grandy; *Producers*: VICMAN Productions (Victor del Corral, Manolo Alonso); *Choreography*: Armando Suez; *Scenery*: Sormani di Milano; *Costumes*: Stivanello; *Lighting*: Lawrence Metzler; *Musical Direction*: Alfredo Munar
Cast: Hernando Chaviano (Viscount Zancada), Miguel de Grandy (Baron Mirko Zeta), Rosendo Gali Menendez (Kromow), Carlos de Leon (Raul de Saint Brioche), Nydia del Rivero (Olga Kromow), Ruddi Fanetti (Bogdanovitch), Jesus Zubizaretta (Pritzy), Puli Toro (Valencienne), Rafael Le Bron (Camilo de Rosillon), Lolina Gutierrez (Prascovia), Manolo Alvan (Niegus), Georgina Granados (Ana de Glavari), Tomas Alvarez (Count Danilo), Lisette Palacio (Silviana Bogdanovitch); Waiters: Pablo Alamo, Eddie Gonzales, Mario Santisteban, and Pedro Trujillo; Chorus: German Acosta, Frank Acosta, Jose Calazan, Nina Cruz, Frank Cruz, Isis Fergueroa, Lourdes Galaya, Luis Gotay, Orika Gutierrez, Ernesto Gutierrez, Hector Lomba, Maria Mainegra, Rafael Morales, Amparo Navarro, Josefa Navarro, Soledad Navarro, Luis Pena, Juan Sabache, Flora Santana, Antonio Tarazona, Amparo Viccini, Elda Zubizarreta; Dancers: Kate Antrobus, Joan Baker, Marissa Benetsky, Sandy Italiano, Barbara Klein, Henry Boyer, Marcos Dinnerstein, Daryl Gray, Gerald Moreno, Stephen Rockford
The musical was presented in three acts.
The action takes place in and around Paris during the early 1900s.

The revival of Franz Lehar's operetta *The Merry Widow* (here, *La viuda alegre*) was a short-lived but ambitious attempt by producers Victor del Corral and Manolo Alonso to introduce full-scale musical productions performed in Spanish for New York audiences. But the limited engagement of seven performances seems to have been the first and last of such offerings by the team.

Allen Hughes in the *New York Times* liked the "colorful and energetic" evening and Lehar's "lovely" music, and suggested the mounting should be "commended more for good intentions than for musical and theatrical achievement." The book showed signs of age, and he wondered if the old jokes and wheezes might have sounded better in Spanish than in English. Tomas Alvarez was not always ideal in the role of Danilo, but he possessed "theatrical know-how" and was the "most experienced and authoritative personality" in the musical. Georgina Granados as the widow was "good-looking" with an "attractive and assertive" voice in the upper reaches which faded in the middle register.

As *Die lustige witwe*, the operetta premiered in Vienna at the Theatre an der Wien on December 30, 1905, with Mizzi Gunther and Louis Treumann in the leading roles. The story centers on the impoverished Ruritanian kingdom of Marsovia and the attempts of its politicians to see that the fortune of its wealthiest citizen

Sonia (here, Ana) will remain in the country. To this end, Danilo is sent to Paris to woo her into marriage and thus keep her fortune in Marsovia. Of course, the two fall in love to the accompaniment of Lehar's gorgeous score and their romantic happy ending is also a financially happy one for the coffers of the government.

The operetta has enjoyed some twenty-one productions in New York; the first starred Ethel Jackson and Donald Brian at the New Amsterdam Theatre on October 27, 1907, for 416 performances.

There have been various film versions, the most memorable one directed by Ernst Lubitsch for MGM in 1934 with Jeanette MacDonald and Maurice Chevalier (most of the lyrics were by Lorenz Hart, and additional music was by Richard Rodgers and Herbert Stothart).

There are many recordings of the score, including the cast album of the 1964 Music Theatre of Lincoln Center production which starred Patrice Munsel and Bob Wright (RCA Victor Records LP # LOC/LSO-1094; the CD was released by Sony Masterworks Broadway # 88697-88567-2). A two-CD set (with libretto) performed in German was released by Deutsche Grammophon (# 439-911-2) by the Wiener Philharmoniker and the Monteverdi Choir (orchestra conducted by John Eliot Gardiner, and with Cheryl Studer and Boje Skovhus in the leading roles).

For information about the Australian Ballet version of the operetta, see entry for the 1976 production, and for the New York City Opera Company's adaptation see entries for April 1978, September 1978, and September 1979.

DIE FLEDERMAUS

Theatre: New York State Theatre
Opening Date: September 18, 1974; *Closing Date*: November 7, 1974
Performances: 9 (in repertory)
Libretto: Carl Haffner and Richard Genee (English adaptation by Ruth and Thomas Martin)
Music: Johann Strauss
Based on the play *Le reveillon* by Henri Meilhac and Ludovic Halevy.
Direction: Gerald Freedman; *Producer*: The New York City Opera Company; *Choreography*: Joyce Trisler; *Scenery*: Lloyd Evans; *Costumes*: Theoni V. Aldredge; *Lighting*: Hans Sondheimer; *Musical Direction*: Mario Bernardi
Cast: Gary Glaze (Alfred), Ruth Welting (Adele), Johanna Meier (Rosalinda von Eisenstein), Alan Titus (Gabriel von Eisenstein), Howard Fried (Doctor Blind), Dominic Cossa (Doctor Falke), Spiro Malas (Frank), Diana Kehrig (Sally), Jack Sims (Ivan), David Rae Smith (Prince Orlofsky), Coley Worth (Frosch); Solo Dancers: Esperanza Galan, Juliu Horvath; Ensemble: The New York City Opera Chorus and Dancers
The operetta was presented in three acts.
The action takes place in a summer resort near Vienna during the latter part of the nineteenth century.

The New York City Opera Company's revival of Johann Strauss's *Die Fledermaus* (*The Bat*) marked the operetta's one-hundredth birthday, and Harold C. Schonberg in the *New York Times* noted that the "masterpiece" was "the most insouciant of operettas and always welcome." The revival was presented in "good taste" (although it found a way to allude to "W-t-r-gate"), and while there "were really no outstanding voices" the "handsome" cast was "competent." Because the work was given in English, he noted some of the Viennese flavor was lost, but there was "a gain in intelligibility." During the run, Donald Henahan in the same newspaper reviewed the replacement cast, and noted the translation was replete with "aged jests" and that Gerald Freedman's direction was "equally tired." He suggested that if one didn't mind "domestic champagne" then the production was "palatably fizzy stuff" because the cast worked hard to keep Strauss "from going flat." Later in the season, the production returned for an additional four performances in repertory beginning on March 18, 1975.

The operetta premiered on April 5, 1874, at the Theatre an der Wien in Vienna, and became an instant favorite because of Strauss's enchanting music and the light-as-air plot of amorous misbehavior, marital deceptions, and mistaken identities.

The New York premiere was given in German at Brooklyn's Thalia Theatre on October 18, 1879, for seven performances in repertory, and the first English adaptation (by Sydney Rosenfeld) opened at the Casino Theatre on March 16, 1885, for forty-two performances. The operetta has been revived in New York numerous times in both German and English. Among the adaptations: *The Merry Countess* (Casino Theatre, August

20, 1912, for 135 performances; adaptation by Gladys Unger, lyrics by Arthur Anderson); *A Wonderful Night* (Majestic Theatre, October 31, 1929, for 125 performances with Archie Leach, who later changed his name to Cary Grant; adaptation by Fanny Todd Mitchell); *Champagne, Sec* (Morosco Theatre, October 30, 1933, for 113 performances; adaptation by Alan Child [aka Lawrence Langner], lyrics by Robert A. Simon); and the most successful of all, *Rosalinda* (44th Street Theatre, October 28, 1942, for 521 performances; adaptation by Gottfried Reinhardt and John Meehan Jr., which was based on an earlier adaptation by Max Reinhardt). In 1943, *The Rose Masque* was another adaptation of the operetta; in this instance, the production was seen in Los Angeles and San Francisco but never risked Broadway.

There are innumerable recordings of Strauss's score, but there doesn't seem to be one of the Reinhardt and Meehan adaptation, which has proven to be the most popular of all the English versions.

GYPSY

"A Musical Fable"

Theatre: Winter Garden Theatre
Opening Date: September 23, 1974; *Closing Date*: January 4, 1975
Performances: 120
Book: Arthur Laurents
Lyrics: Stephen Sondheim
Music: Jule Styne
Based on the 1957 *Gypsy*: *A Memoir* by Gypsy Rose Lee.
Direction: Arthur Laurents; *Producers*: Barry M. Brown, Fritz Holt, Edgar Lansbury, and Joseph Beruh; *Choreography*: Jerome Robbins (choreography reproduced by Robert Tucker); *Scenery* and *Lighting*: Robert Randolph; *Costumes*: Raoul Pene du Bois (Angela Lansbury's costumes by Robert Mackintosh); *Musical Direction*: Milton Rosenstock
Cast: John C. Becher (Uncle Jocko, Kringelein, Cigar), Don Potter (George, Mr. Goldstone), Craig Brown (Clarence), Donna Elio (Balloon Girl), Lisa Peluso (Baby Louise), Bonnie Langford (Baby June), *Angela Lansbury* (Rose), Peewee (Chowsie), Ed Riley (Pop, Phil); Newsboys: Craig Brown, Anthony Marciona, Sean Rule, and Mark Santoro; Charles Rule (Weber), Rex Robbins (Herbie), Zan Charisse (Louise), Maureen Moore (June), John Sheridan (Tulsa), Steven Gelfer (Yonkers), David Lawson (L.A.), Jay Smith (Little Rock), Dennis Karr (San Diego), Serhij Bohsdan (Boston, Bourgeron-Couchon), Edith Ann (Gigolo), Patricia Richardson (Waitress), Gloria Rossi (Miss Cratchitt, Mazeppa); Hollywood Blondes: Pat Cody, Jinny Kordek, Jan Neuberger, Marilyn Olson, and Patricia Richardson; Denny Dillon (Agnes), Richard J. Sabellico (Pastey), Mary Louise Wilson (Tessie Tura), Sally Cooke (Electra), Bonnie Walker (Maid)
The musical was presented in two acts.
The action takes place during the period from the early 1920s to the early 1930s in various cities throughout the country.

Musical Numbers

Act One: "Let Me Entertain You" (Bonnie Langford, Lisa Peluso); "Some People" (Angela Lansbury); "Small World" (Angela Lansbury, Rex Robbins); "Baby June and Her Newsboys" (Bonnie Langford, Lisa Peluso, Newsboys); "Mr. Goldstone, I Love You" (Angela Lansbury, Company); "Little Lamb" (Zan Charisse); "You'll Never Get Away from Me" (Angela Lansbury, Rex Robbins); "Dainty June and Her Farmboys" (Maureen Moore, Zan Charisse, Farmboys); "If Momma Was Married" (Zan Charisse, Maureen Moore); "All I Need Is the Girl" (John Sheridan); "Everything's Coming Up Roses" (Angela Lansbury)
Act Two: "Toreadorables" (Maureen Moore, Hollywood Blondes); "Together" (Angela Lansbury, Rex Robbins, Zan Charisse); "You Gotta Get a Gimmick" (Gloria Rossi, Sally Cooke, Mary Louise Wilson); "The Strip" (Zan Charisse); "Rose's Turn" (Angela Lansbury)

The current limited-engagement revival of *Gypsy* marked the musical's first production on Broadway since the original had opened at the Broadway Theatre on May 21, 1959, for 702 performances with Ethel

Merman as Rose in what was not only the most brilliant performance of her career but one of the greatest of all Broadway turns. It took courage for Angela Lansbury to take on such an iconic role that was so closely associated with Merman, but the challenge paid off. While her voice was no match for Merman's (of course, no one's was a match for Merman's), she sang well enough and had the acting chops to make the role her own.

Lansbury's blistering bare stage aria "Rose's Turn" was jaw-dropping and included an incredible touch that said volumes about Rose and her failed ambitions. As Lansbury finished the number, the audience applauded her. But Lansbury made no acknowledgment of the applause, even as she gracefully bowed toward the house. She bowed, and she bowed, a great lady taking in the adulation due her. But it wasn't Lansbury on the stage anymore. She had completely submerged herself into the character of Rose, and it was Rose and Rose alone on an empty stage in an empty theatre who bowed and bowed to a spectral audience that would never see or hear her. The clapping in the Winter Garden finally stopped, but Rose kept bowing. This was her tragedy. At the end of *The Music Man*, the almost defeated Harold Hill says, "There's always a band, kid." For Rose there is always the burning ambition to be the star performer, but the only cheers she'll ever know is the imaginary applause in her head.

The revival was initially produced in London at the Piccadilly Theatre on May 29, 1973, for three hundred performances and marked the musical's West End premiere. The cast included Lansbury, Zan Charisse (Louise), and Bonnie Langford (Baby June), all of whom reprised their roles for the Broadway production, and the London cast album was released on CD by RCA/BMG (# 60571-2-RG).

Martin Gottfried in the *New York Post* said the "powerful" production was to experience theatre "at full tilt," and Jule Styne and Stephen Sondheim's "magnificent" score was "probably the most consistent one in all of musical theatre, and as a whole may well be the best." Lansbury "spearheads the show's brutality and then overcomes it with devastating compassion," and her "Rose's Turn" was "unparalleled." Edwin Wilson in the *Wall Street Journal* praised Lansbury's "Rose's Turn" as a "rare moment" in which everything the actress had ever done in film or on stage had come together in an instant. Louis Snyder in the *Christian Science Monitor* said Lansbury had carved out "a resplendent new niche for herself in Broadway history." While she seemed to top herself in each succeeding number, "nothing" compared to her "grand finale" in "Rose's Turn," which "is to *Gypsy* what the Immolation Scene is to *Goetterdaemmerung*."

In comparing Lansbury to Merman, Howard Kissel in *Women's Wear Daily* found Lansbury's Rose "more vulnerable, and in her moments of crisis, more affecting"; Merman's Rose was created with her "incredible voice," and Lansbury's through "a more encompassing physical performance." Clive Barnes in the *New York Times* said Lansbury was "enchanting, tragic, bewildering and bewildered"; Jack Kroll in *Newsweek* felt that her overall performance had "honesty, velocity and strength"; Pat Collins on WCBSTV2 said she was "wonderful"; and Leonard Probst on NBC Radio said she was "so good that right now a Tony should be set aside for the best performance of an actress in a musical" (which is what indeed happened).

But T. E. Kalem in *Time* had a terrible evening. *Gypsy* was "gaudy-awful" with "implausibilities" and it was "blighted" by "thoroughly unappealing characters"; the choreography had more "spoof than snap"; the score was "innocuously springy and clever"; and Lansbury injected "self-kidding, campy humor" into her role and couldn't "sound the classic Merman brass." He concluded that *Gypsy* was "not a show that will stay with you after the curtain drops."

As of this writing, *Gypsy* has been revived in New York five more times: on November 16, 1989, at the St. James Theatre for 476 performances (Tyne Daly was Rose and won the Tony Award for Best Leading Actress in a Musical; the cast album was released by Elektra Nonesuch CD # 9-79239-2, the production won the Tony Award for Best Revival, and Daly appeared in a return engagement at the Marquis Theatre on April 28, 1991, for 105 showings); on May 1, 2003, at the Shubert Theatre for 451 performances (Bernadette Peters; the CD was released by Angel Records # 7243-5-83858-2-3); on July 14, 2007, by Encores! at City Center for fifteen performances (Patti LuPone); and on March 27, 2008, at the St. James Theatre for 332 performances (LuPone won the Tony Award for Best Actress in a Musical, and Laura Benanti as Louise won for Best Featured Actress in a Musical; the CD was issued by Time Life # 80020-D and includes a number of bonus tracks of cut and unused songs).

The surprisingly faithful 1962 Warner Brothers film starred Rosalind Russell (and original cast member Faith Dane reprised her unforgettable Mazeppa) and retained the entire score except for "Together" (which was filmed but cut before the final release); the DVD by Warner Brothers (# 16755) includes "Together" as well as the duet version of "You'll Never Get Away from Me." The soundtrack was issued by Rhino (CD #

R2-73873) and has various extras, including outtake versions of five songs, a previously unreleased full version of "Dainty June and Her Farmboys," and both "album" and "film" versions of "Rose's Turn."

A television adaptation was presented by CBS on December 12, 1993, with Bette Midler. Hallmark Entertainment released an unnumbered DVD, and the CD was issued by Atlantic Records (# 82551-2).

Other recordings of the score include six selections from a late 1990s German revival produced by the Theatre des Westens (Pallas Group CD # LC-6377); a jazz version by Annie Ross and the Buddy Bregman Band (Pacific Jazz CD # CDP-7243-8-33574-2-0); the 2015 London cast (First Night CD # 117) with Imelda Staunten; and perhaps the rarest of all *Gypsy* recordings, the South African production (circa 1976) with Libby Morris (Rose) and Bonnie Langford (Baby June), which was released by Philips Records (LP # STO-774). Of all the *Gypsy* recordings, only one is truly essential, and of course that is the 1959 original cast recording (Columbia Records LP # OL-5240), which was reissued by Masterworks Broadway (CD # 88697-49406-2) and includes deleted and unused songs. And floating around the fringes in the world of theatre collectors is a private and unauthorized two-CD recording of the complete closing-night performance of the original Broadway production on March 25, 1961.

The script was published in hardback by Random House in 1960, and in paperback by the Theatre Communications Group in 1994. The libretto is also included in the 2014 Library of Congress hardback collection *American Musicals*, which includes the scripts of fifteen other musicals. The lyrics are included in Sondheim's *Finishing the Hat: Collected Lyrics (1954–1981) with Attendant Comments, Principles, Heresies, Grudges, Whines and Anecdotes*. Keith Garebian's *The Making of "Gypsy"* was published by ECW Press in an undated edition.

It's common knowledge that Sondheim's voice is heard on the original Broadway cast album as Rose's father (he tells Rose she ain't gettin' eighty-eight cents from him), but it's generally forgotten that while the 1959 production was nominated for eight Tony Awards (including Best Musical, Best Actress, and Best Direction), it walked away without a single award!

Awards

Tony Awards and Nominations: Best Leading Actress in a Musical (**Angela Lansbury**); Best Featured Actress in a Musical (Zan Charisse); Best Director of a Musical (Arthur Laurents)

MACK & MABEL

"The Musical Romance of Mack Sennett's Funny and Fabulous Hollywood" / "A Musical Love Story"

Theatre: Majestic Theatre
Opening Date: October 6, 1974; *Closing Date*: November 30, 1974
Performances: 65
Book: Michael Stewart
Lyrics and *Music*: Jerry Herman; incidental and dance music by John Morris
Direction and *Choreography*: Gower Champion (Buddy Schwab, Associate Choreographer); *Producer*: David Merrick in association with Edwin H. Morris (Jack Schlissel, Associate Producer); *Scenery*: Robin Wagner; *Costumes*: Patricia Zipprodt; *Lighting*: Tharon Musser; *Musical Direction*: Donald Pippin
Cast: Stanley Simmonds (Eddie), *Robert Preston* (Mack Sennett), Lisa Kirk (Lottie Ames), Nancy Evers (Ella), Roger Bigelow (Freddie), Christopher Murney (Charlie Muldoon), Robert Fitch (Wally), Jerry Dodge (Frank Wyman), *Bernadette Peters* (Mabel Normand), Tom Batten (Mr. Kleinman), Bert Michaels (Mr. Fox), Marie Santell (Iris), James Mitchell (William Desmond Taylor), Cheryl Armstrong (Phyllis Foster), Frank Root (Sege); The Grips: John Almberg, Roger Bigelow, George Blackwell, Frank Bouley, Gerald Brentte, Lonnie Burr, Chet D'Elia, Igors Gavon, Jonathan Miele, Don Percassi, Frank Root; The Mack Sennett Bathing Beauties: Cheryl Armstrong, Claudia Asbury, Sandahl Bergman, Chrystal Chambers, Nancy Dafgek, Prudence Darby, Elaine Handel, Paula Lynn, Patricia Michaels, Carol Perea, L. J. Rose, Rita Rudner, Marianne Selbert, Jo Speros, Pat Trott, Geordie Withee
The musical was presented in two acts.
The action takes place during the years 1938, 1911, 1912, 1919, 1923, and 1929 in Brooklyn, Los Angeles, and Manhattan.

Musical Numbers

Act One: "Movies Were Movies" (Robert Preston); "Look What Happened to Mabel" (Bernadette Peters, Robert Fitch, Christopher Murney, Jerry Dodge, Grips); "Big Time" (Lisa Kirk, Family); "I Won't Send Roses" (Robert Preston); "I Won't Send Roses" (reprise) (Bernadette Peters); "I Wanna Make the World Laugh" (Robert Preston, Company); "I Wanna Make the World Laugh" (reprise) (Robert Preston, Company); "Wherever He Ain't" (Bernadette Peters, Waiters); "Hundreds of Girls" (Robert Preston, Bathing Beauties)
Act Two: "When Mabel Comes in the Room" (Stanley Simmonds, Company); "My Heart Leaps Up" (Robert Preston); "Time Heals Everything" (Bernadette Peters); "Tap Your Troubles Away" (Lisa Kirk, Girls); "I Promise You a Happy Ending" (Robert Preston)

Michael Stewart's book for *Mack & Mabel* was perhaps his weakest and certainly the strangest of his career. He used a flashback device that began in 1938 when legendary silent film director Mack Sennett (Robert Preston) looks back on his heyday in the pre-Talkie era when his two-reeler brand of custard-pies-in-face, Keystone Kops, bathing beauties, and leading lady Mabel Normand (Bernadette Peters) were the rage. But the sketchy book never delineated the characters and didn't develop the story, and far too much happened off stage than on. Mabel leaves Sennett and the studio toward the end of the first act, returns early in the second, and is greeted by a welcome mat of a song ("When Mabel Comes in the Room") as if she'd been away for decades, just like Norma Desmond. In context, the song made no sense because we'd never really experienced Mabel's departure and how it affected the studio and its employees, and in stage time it seemed she'd just left the room a few minutes ago. But practically the entire company comes out to pay homage to Mabel as she glides above the audience on a huge camera dolly. But why all the hoopla? Well, Dolly was greeted by the waiters after all those years, and she and they promenaded on a catwalk that brought them around the orchestra pit and into the house itself, and so apparently Mabel needed the same treatment.

Later, we're suddenly informed that Mabel is addicted to cocaine, and then just as suddenly Sennett tells us she's dead. Again, there was little to prepare the audience for these lurching twists and turns of the plot, and their potentially dramatic punch was lost because they seemed to have occurred in scenes left on the long and winding tryout road.

In another bit of folly, Lisa Kirk's role as the fictitious silent-film star Lottie Ames was virtually a non-starter because she was given no character to play. Although she was third-billed, Kirk had only eighteen lines of dialogue in the first act and five in the second. She participated in a production number ("Big Time"), and was the lead singer for the ingratiating "Tap Your Troubles Away," but the ironic song was poorly staged as it depicted both the filming of the number on a sound stage and a parallel sequence at a Hollywood party where Mabel is seen taking cocaine just minutes before her companion William Desmond Taylor (James Mitchell) is murdered.

As for the flashback device, it never worked because it forced Sennett into the roles of narrator and bystander and never quite allowed him to be the leading man. And the final sequence was truly dreadful. Mack had always promised Mabel a ring and a happy ending, but she died at the age of thirty-seven, and there was nothing happy about her death. But Sennett devises a happy ending for the two of them, and as the curtain falls Mabel has returned to life (or to Sennett's memory) and the two are wed (according to the script, the two "start down the long sunlit road that stretches far away to the horizon"). But Mabel's dead, there's no happy ending, and so what was the point? The awkward and almost laughable scene was there only to end the musical on an upbeat note.

Besides its major book troubles, the musical was painful to watch. Robin Wagner's décor consisted of what seemed to be endless acres of polished wood, supposedly the interior of a movie studio. But the plainness only added to the sour tone of the evening. Moreover, neither Preston nor Peters seemed at ease in their roles. He looked uncomfortable, and while she got by with her usual kewpie-doll shtick in the early scenes, she never conveyed the innate tragedy of her character. But on the cast album they both sparkled. For here was one of Jerry Herman's most melodic scores, one which cried out for an old-fashioned musical comedy book. His Victrola overflowed with the bouncy rhythms of "Look What Happened to Mabel," "Wherever He Ain't," and "Hundreds of Girls," the somewhat bittersweet splendor of the cakewalk "When Mabel Comes in the Room," the gorgeous ballad "I Won't Send Roses," and the splendid torch song "Time Heals Everything." Even the overture was wonderful, an irresistible collection of melody overflowing with the brass and gusto of Old Broadway.

Clive Barnes in the *New York Times* suggested the musical had "book trouble so bad that it is practically library trouble"; Howard Kissel in *Women's Wear Daily* said the evening offered "a rather thin gloomy, morose" story; and Pat Collins on WCBSTV2 found the score "undistinguished" but said Champion used "first-rate" techniques of "razzle-dazzle" (and reported that Michael Kidd had lent him a hand). Although Leonard Probst on NBC Radio complained that the characters were "wooden" and the "boring" story line deadened the production, he noted that the score had a "solid beat," the dances were "terrific," and the two leads were wonderful . . . but these positive attributes required "another story" than the one on stage.

"Reel Sad" was the headline of T. E. Kalem's review in *Time*. The book had a "static narrative line," Preston and Peters didn't "seem to take any real pleasure in each other," and the entire evening resulted in "a case of 'Give my regrets to Broadway.'" Douglas Watt in the *New York Daily News* said he "spent the evening feeling sorry" for the "amiable fool of a musical," which clearly tried hard to please, and Jack Kroll in *Newsweek* found the musical a "sad waste" and noted that unlike Glynis Johns, Peters "hasn't learned how to express an entire personality through the 'cuteness' which is her leading trait."

Martin Gottfried in the *New York Post* felt the huge permanent set gave the impression that "everything seems to be happening in the same place." He also noted that the end of the second act stopped in order for Preston to "tell the audience in minutes an end to the story that should have taken scenes." He also noted that Lisa Kirk's role was "a meaningless part impossible to describe." In all, *Mack & Mabel* was "professionalism without identity."

The script was published in paperback by Samuel French in 1976. The original cast album was released by ABC Records (LP # ABCH-830), and the CD was issued by Broadway Gold/MCA Classics (# MCAD-10523).

"Today I'm Gonna Think about Me" was cut in preproduction, and "Hit 'Em on the Head" was deleted during the tryout (and replaced with "My Heart Leaps Up"); for the published script, "Hit 'Em on the Head" was reinstated.

The one-performance-only *Mack & Mabel in Concert* was presented in London at the Drury Lane on February 21, 1988, and was recorded by First Night Records; the cast includes George Hearn, Tommy Tune, Denis Quilley, Stubby Kaye, Debbie Shapiro, and Georgia Brown. A West End production opened at the Piccadilly Theatre on November 7, 1995, for 270 performances; Howard McGillin and Caroline O'Connor were the leads, and a note in the program thanked Michael Stewart's sister Francine Pascal for her assistance on the musical's book. The cast recording was released by EMI Records (CD # 7243-8-36771-2-2). A later London production was presented at the Criterion Theatre on April 10, 2006, with David Soul and Janie Dee, and *Variety* voiced the old complaints which still made the show so unworkable: the flashback device (here with voice-overs) was "dramatically desperate" and the book should have allowed the audience "to see and feel what the characters are going through, not hear about it."

The musical's overture was featured in the 1982 World Figure Skating Championship when skaters Torvill and Dean used the Broadway cast album's overture to accompany their skating routine.

A 1998 German production mounted in Karlsruhe was recorded by Bella Musica (CD # LC-0562); there were two casts, and the performers alternate on the recording.

Mack and Mabel (but not *Mack & Mabel*) returned to the musical stage in *Keystone*, which opened at the GeVa Theatre in Rochester, New York, on March 10, 1981; the book was by John McKellar, lyrics by Dion McGregor and McKellar, music by Lance Mulcahy, and the cast included Scott Bakula (Mack) and Ann Morrison (Mabel). Doug in *Variety* found the book "interesting" and the score "tuneful and lingering," and Clive Barnes in the *New York Post* said the work was "no match" for the "genuine thump, thunder and throb of Broadway magnificence" offered by Herman's version, but *Keystone* was nonetheless a "very enjoyable show" and Mulcahy's score offered "piano-rag flavor and hearts-and-flowers sentiment." The work was later presented at Princeton University's McCarter Theatre on January 13, 1982, with John Sloman and Randy Graff in the leads; the production was shown on cable television, and in 1983 a version of the musical was released on videocassette by Sony Video Software with Wayne Bryan and Ann (Leslie) Morrison in the main roles.

Awards

Tony Award Nominations: Best Musical (*Mack & Mabel*); Best Leading Actor in a Musical (Robert Preston); Best Leading Actress in a Musical (Bernadette Peters); Best Director of a Musical (Gower Champion); Best Book (Michael Stewart); Best Costume Designer (Patricia Zipprodt); Best Choreographer (Gower Champion)

CHARLES AZNAVOUR ON BROADWAY

Theatre: Minskoff Theatre
Opening Date: October 15, 1974; *Closing Date*: October 27, 1974
Performances: 16
Lyrics and *Music*: Unless otherwise noted, all lyrics and music by Charles Aznavour
Technical Direction: Michael Cadieux; *Producers*: Lee Guber, Shelly Gross, and Joseph Harris (A Music Fair-Enterprises, Inc., Production); *Lighting*: Marc B. Weiss; *Musical Direction*: Aldo Frank
Cast: *Charles Aznavour*
The concert was presented in two acts.

Musical Numbers

All songs performed by Charles Aznavour
Act One: "Le temps" (English lyric by Herbert Kretzmer, music by J. Davis); "Happy Anniversary" (English lyric by Herbert Kretzmer); "I Live for You" (English lyric by Herbert Kretzmer); "Un par un"; "Our Love, My Love" (lyric by Erich Segal); "The Ham" (English lyric by B. Morrisson, music by Georges Garvarentz); "La mamma" (lyric by Robert Gall); "To Die of Love" (English lyric by Howard Liebling); "No, I Could Never Forget" (English lyric by Al Kasha and Joel Hirschhorn, music by Georges Garvarentz); "I Have Lived" (English lyric by Al Kasha and Joel Hirschhorn); "La boheme" (lyric by Jacques Plante); "What Makes a Man" (English lyric by R. Craig); "Emmenez-moi"
Act Two: "La Baraka" (English lyric by Herbert Kretzmer); "Reste" (lyric by Bachelor); "We Can Never Know" (English lyric by Al Kasha and Joel Hirschhorn); "You've Let Yourself Go" (English lyric by Marcel Stellman); "Trousse chemise" (lyric by J. Mareuil); "The 'I Love You' Song" (lyric by G. Bontempelli, English lyric by Herbert Kretzmer); "She" (English lyric by Herbert Kretzmer); "Que c'est triste Venise" (lyric by F. Dorin); "And I in My Chair" (English lyric by D. Newburg); "Yesterday When I Was Young" (English lyric by Herbert Kretzmer); "Isabelle"; "(Dance in) The Old-Fashioned Way" (English lyric by Al Kasha and Joel Hirschhorn, music by Georges Garvarentz); "Les comediens" (music by Jacques Plante); "You've Got to Learn" (English lyric by Marcel Stellman)

Charles Aznavour returned for another evening of songs (see ***Charles Aznavour*** for more information about his Broadway appearances), and with his concert the season began a series of visits from popular singers and musicians, all of which were limited runs and were booked mostly into the cavernous Minskoff or Uris Theatres (***In Concert: Andy Williams with Michel Legrand***, ***Tony Bennett & Lena Horne Sing***, ***Anthony Newley & Henry Mancini***, ***Johnny Mathis***, ***The 5th Dimension***, ***Raphael in Concert***, and ***Bette Midler's Clams on the Half-Shell Revue***).

Ian Dove in the *New York Times* noted that Aznavour was a "master" of lyric interpretation, and most of the numbers were love songs "for people still wearing suits and ties." He mentioned that "What Makes a Man" was a "gay liberation blues" performed in a "realistic and sympathetic manner."

IN CONCERT: ANDY WILLIAMS WITH MICHEL LEGRAND

Theatre: Uris Theatre
Opening Date: October 16, 1974; *Closing Date*: October 27, 1974
Performances: 15
Direction: "Stage direction" by Jerry Grollnek; *Producer*: Nederlander; *Scenery*: Neil Peter Jampolis; *Lighting*: Jane Riesman; *Musical Direction*: Jack Feierman
Cast: *Andy Williams*, Michel Legrand, Eileen Duffy
The concert was presented in two acts.

Musical Numbers

Act One: For the first act, composer Michel Legrand performed a number of his film songs, including a cantata-like presentation of music from his 1964 film *The Umbrellas of Cherbourg*; he was assisted by singer Eileen Duffy.
Act Two: Andy Williams performed various songs, and for the finale was joined by Michel Legrand.

On the program's title page, the name of the concert was *Andy Williams*, but for the program cover it was called *In Concert: Andy Williams with Michel Legrand*. The popular singer and the film composer teamed up for an evening of what John Rockwell in the *New York Times* described as "middle-of-the-road" entertainment, which was "slick" and "smoothly flowing."

For the first act, Legrand performed his film songs, and the centerpiece was an extended sequence from the score of his 1964 film *The Umbrellas of Cherbourg*, which featured singer Eileen Duffy. Rockwell felt the *Cherbourg* sequence was too "bathetic," and noted the trouble with middle-of-the-road entertainment was that it quickly degenerated from "the honestly simple-minded" to the "self-important" where it became "kitsch of the silliest kind."

As for the "appealing" Andy Williams, he tamped down the television-styled slickness of the evening with his "self-deprecating" and "shy" humor. His baritone voice was "workable" but not "very special," and his phrasing didn't get much beyond "a subdued relaxedness." The critic noted the concert marked Williams's first New York booking since his appearance at the Copacabana in 1959.

THE BIG WINNER

Theatre: Eden Theatre
Opening Date: October 20, 1974; *Closing Date*: February 2, 1975
Performances: 119
Book: David Opatoshu
Lyrics: Wolf Younin
Music: Sol Kaplan
Based on an unidentified play by Sholem Aleichem.
Direction: David Opatoshu (Bryna Wasserman, Assistant to the Director); *Producers*: Harry Rothpearl and Jewish Nostalgic Production, Inc.; *Choreography*: Sophie Maslow; *Scenery* and *Costumes*: Jeffrey B. Moss; *Lighting*: Tom Meleck; *Musical Direction*: Jack Easton
Cast: Bruce Adler (Old Man, Kopel), Stan Porter (Motel), Diane Cypkin (Bailke), Miriam Kressyn (Ety-Meny), *David Opatoshu* (Shimele Soroker), David Carey (Solomon Fine), Herschel Rosen (Osher Fine), Shifra Lerer (Perel, Madame Flaum), Jack Rechtzeit (Solovaitchik), William Gary (Goldentaller), Elia Patron (Mendel), Shmulik Goldstein (Rubinchik), Jaime Lewin (Vigdorchik, Sexton), Reizl Bozyk (Madame Fine); Townspeople, Guests: Richard Ammon, Winifred Berg, Susan Fox, Joseph Goode, Cheryl Hartley, Marcus Williamson
The musical was presented in two acts.
The action takes place during 1910 in a Jewish town in Russia.

Musical Numbers

Act One: "How Can I Tell Him She Loves Me?" (Stan Porter, Bruce Adler); "We're the People" (David Opatoshu, Miriam Kressyn, Stan Porter, Bruce Adler, Diane Cypkin); "Lottery Celebration" (Company); "Money, Wealth, Gold" (Stan Porter, Bruce Adler); "It's Delicious" (David Opatoshu, Miriam Kressyn); "Move Montage" (David Opatoshu, Miriam Kressyn, Shmulik Goldstein, Jaime Lewin); "I Am a Tailor's Daughter" (Diane Cypkin); "Tango Rehearsal" (David Opatoshu, Miriam Kressyn)
Act Two: "The Tango" (Company); "In-Laws" (Miriam Kressyn, Reizl Bozyk); "Love Song" (Stan Porter, Diane Cypkin); "Winners, Losers" (Bruce Adler); "Wedding Dance" (David Opatoshu, Miriam Kressyn, Stan Porter, Diane Cypkin, Bruce Adler)

The Big Winner was performed in Yiddish but was accompanied by an English narration. The musical played at the Eden Theatre, an Off-Broadway house where productions were sometimes presented under a Middle or Limited Broadway contract. It's unclear if *The Big Winner* was under such a contract, but to be as inclusive as possible the musical is included in this book (but with the caveat that contractually it may not have been a full-fledged Broadway production).

The story took place in a small Jewish village in Russia in 1910, and dealt with the town's poor tailor Shimele (David Opatoshu, who also adapted and directed the production) who wins a lottery of 200,000 rubles. His daughter Bailke (Diane Cypkin) has been courted by two of Shimele's humble apprentices Motel (Stan Porter) and Kopel (Bruce Adler), but with his new-found wealth Shimele in conjunction with the town's matchmaker hopes to marry her off into a wealthy family. When Shimele is swindled of his fortune by two con artists, he realizes he had lost his values and forgotten his roots. Bailke chooses Motel for her husband, and all ends well with a happy wedding celebration. Shimele may have lost his fortune, but he's a big winner when it comes to understanding life's true values.

Richard F. Shepard in the *New York Times* praised the "lively, creative and contemporary" songs, which included an amusing tango number, and he noted that the scenery and costumes were beautifully designed, that the choreography was "decorative," and that the cast included a "happy mixture" of Yiddish theatre veterans and young performers.

The musical was revived at the Folksbiene Theatre in 1989 where it was taped from a live performance and was released on video cassette by the Jewish Video Library (# 1333).

Composer Sol Kaplan had written the score for *Shootin' Star*, a musical about Billy the Kid which closed in 1946 during its pre-Broadway tryout. His next major musical was the 1962 Off-Broadway production *The Banker's Daughter*.

TONY BENNETT & LENA HORNE SING

Theatre: Minskoff Theatre
Opening Date: October 30, 1974; *Closing Date*: November 24, 1974
Performances: 37
Direction: Technical direction by Serge Descheneaux; *Producers*: Lee Guber, Shelly Gross, and Joseph Harris (A Music Fair-Enterprises, Inc., Production); *Costumes*: Lena Horne's costumes designed by Georgio Sant'Angelo; *Musical Direction*: Torrie Zito (for Tony Bennett) and Robert Freedman (for Lena Horne)
The concert was presented in two acts.

Musical Numbers

Act One: Lena Horne performed songs by Harold Arlen, Bloom, John Denver, Freedman, Kris Kristofferson, Cole Porter, Andy Razaf, Joseph Raposo, and Stevie Wonder.
Act Two: Tony Bennett performed songs by Harold Arlen and Ted Koehler, Burt Bacharach, Sammy Cahn and Barrie, Cross and Cory, Fred Ebb, Duke Ellington, George Gershwin, George Harrison, Paul McCartney, Jimmy McHugh, Miller, Anthony Newley and Leslie Bricusse, Richard Rodgers and Lorenz Hart, and Jule Styne. At the end of the second act, Horne joined Bennett and the two sang a number of songs by Arlen.

John S. Wilson in the *New York Times* noted that for the concert Tony Bennett found himself in an "impossible situation" because he had to follow the "electrifying" first act in which Lena Horne had stunned the audience with her "intense and dramatic" singing. She was in "complete command" of her material and at intermission she left the audience "with a high from which there was no place to go but down."

Bennett was an "earthbound" singer with "limited vocal and emotional range" who performed his songs with "a genial, puppy-dog smile" and a "thin" and "uncertain" voice that sometimes faltered into "raggedness." As for the lengthy late second-act tribute to Harold Arlen, the medley was fragmented into "bits and pieces" and didn't allow Horne or Bennett "to get deeply" into the songs.

If Lena Horne wowed them in 1974, she would knock them out in 1981 when she returned to Broadway in her one-woman show *Lena Horne: The Lady and Her Music*, which devastated both audiences and critics and played for 333 performances.

ANTHONY NEWLEY/HENRY MANCINI

Theatre: Uris Theatre
Opening Date: October 31, 1974; *Closing Date*: November 10, 1974
Performances: 15
Producer: Nederlander; *Scenery*: Neil Peter Jampolis; *Lighting*: Jerry Grollnek and Pat Barson (Jane Reisman, Lighting Design for the Uris Theatre); *Musical Direction*: Ian Fraser (for Anthony Newley)
Cast: *Anthony Newley, Henry Mancini*

Musical Numbers

Act One: All songs played by Henry Mancini and His Orchestra: Overture from *Tommy* (music by Pete Townshend); Medley—Baby Elephant Walk" (1962 film *Hatari!*; music by Henry Mancini) and "Mr. Lucky" (1959 television series *Mr. Lucky*; music by Henry Mancini); "Love Theme"(1968 film *Romeo and Juliet*; music by Nino Rota); Overture from 1974 film *That's Entertainment*: "The Trolley Song" (1944 film *Meet Me in St. Louis*; lyric and music by Hugh Martin and Ralph Blane); "Over the Rainbow" (1939 film *The Wizard of Oz*; lyric by E. Y. Harburg, music by Harold Arlen); "Hi-Lili, Hi-Lo" (1953 film *Lili*; lyric by Helen Deutsch, music by Bronislau Kaper); "It's a Most Unusual Day" (1948 film *A Date with Judy*; lyric by Harold Adamson, music by Jimmy McHugh); "Singin' in the Rain" (film *Hollywood Revue of* 1929; lyric by Arthur Freed, music by Nacio Herb Brown); "San Francisco" (title song of 1936 film; lyric by Gus Kahn, music by Bronislau Kaper and Walter Jurmann); "Love" (1946 film *Ziegfeld Follies*; lyric and music by Hugh Martin and Ralph Blane); and "That's Entertainment" (1953 film *The Band Wagon*; lyric by Howard Dietz, music by Arthur Schwartz); Theme from *The Pink Panther* (1964 film; music by Henry Mancini); Medley: "Love's Theme" (music by White) and "T.S.O.P." (lyric and music by Gamble and Huff); The Big Band Montage: "I'm Getting Sentimental over You" (lyric by Ned Washington, music by George Bassman); "Blue Flame"; "Let's Dance" (lyric and music by Fanny Baldridge, Gregory Stone, and Joseph Bonine); "Ciribiribin" (lyric and music by A. Pestalozza and Rudolf Thaler); "Artistry in Rhythm"; "Nightmare"; "Leapfrog"; and "Take the 'A' Train" (lyric by Joya Sherrill, music by Billy Strayhorn); Theme from *Peter Gunn* (1958 television series) (music by Henry Mancini); Ballads by Henry Mancini (all lyrics by Johnny Mercer): "Dear Heart" (title song from 1964 film); "The Sweetheart Tree" (1965 film *The Great Race*); "Days of Wine and Roses" (title song from 1962 film); and "Moon River" (1961 film *Breakfast at Tiffany's*)

Act Two: All songs performed by Anthony Newley: "It's a Musical World" Medley (unless otherwise credited, all lyrics and music are by Anthony Newley and Leslie Bricusse)—"It's a Musical World" (1971 British musical *The Good Old Bad Old Days*); "The Good Old Bad Old Days" (title song of 1971 British musical); "Gonna Build a Mountain" (1961 British musical *Stop the World—I Want to Get Off*); "On a Wonderful Day Like Today" (1964 British musical *The Roar of the Greasepaint—The Smell of the Crowd*, which closed during pre-London tryout and its 1965 Broadway production); "Goldfinger" (title song of 1964 film; lyric by Anthony Newley and Leslie Bricusse, music by John Barry); "The Good Things in Life" (1971 British musical *The Good Old Bad Old Days*); "The Candy Man" (1971 film *Willy Wonka and the Chocolate Factory*); "Once in a Lifetime" (1961 British musical *Stop the World—I Want to Get Off*); "Talk to the Animals" (1967 film *Doctor Dolittle*; lyric and music by Leslie Bricusse); "Love Has the Longest Memory of All" (1968 film *Mr. Quilp* aka *The Old Curiosity Shop*; lyric and music by Anthony Newley); "Middle Age Rock & Roll Star" (lyric and music by Anthony Newley); "No Such Thing as Love" (lyric and music by Anthony Newley and Ian Fraser); "Who Can I Turn To?" (1965 Broadway musical *The Roar of the Greasepaint—The Smell of the Crowd*); "Feeling Good" (1965 Broadway musical *The Roar of the Greasepaint—The Smell of the Crowd*); A Broadway Melody—"Everything's Coming Up Roses" (*Gypsy*, 1959; lyric by Stephen Sondheim, music by Jule Styne); "Tonight" (*West Side Story*, 1957; lyric by Stephen Sondheim, music by Leonard Bernstein); "Get Me to the Church on Time" (*My Fair Lady*, 1956; lyric by Alan Jay Lerner, music by Frederick Loewe); "If I Were a Rich Man" (*Fiddler on the Roof*, 1964; lyric by Sheldon Harnick, music by Jerry Bock); "People" (*Funny Girl*, 1964; lyric by Bob Merrill, music by Jule Styne); "I'll Never Fall in Love Again" (*Promises, Promises*, 1968; lyric by Hal David, music by Burt Bacharach); "Hello, Dolly!" (*Hello, Dolly!*, 1964; lyric and music by Jerry Herman); and "What Kind of Fool Am I?" (1961 British musical *Stop the World—I Want to Get Off*; lyric and music by Anthony Newley and Leslie Bricusse)

For the first act of the limited-engagement concert, Henry Mancini and his orchestra performed selections of his film music as well as tributes to MGM musicals and the big band era, and then for the second Anthony Newley performed both stage and film songs that he and Leslie Bricusse had written as well as a selection of Broadway numbers.

Ian Dove in the *New York Times* noted the unadventurous concert was "safe," "familiar," and "firmly middle of the road." But what else could it have been? Mancini offered up Boston Pops-styled selections, and an emphasis on his movie and television work was certainly what his audience wanted to hear. Similarly, fans of Newley expected to hear him performing the songs most identified with him, of which there were many. Dove found Mancini's orchestra "dutifully efficient in all respects" and said Newley's decision to perform many of his own songs showed "a certain amount of self-confidence"; moreover, his voice also showed self-confidence. Newley and Bricusse's songs ranged from "the best" (the numbers from *Stop the World* and *Greasepaint*) to the "silliest" (the theme from *Goldfinger* was "a prime example of the high art of nonsense film-title songs").

MOURNING PICTURES

Theatre: Lyceum Theatre
Opening Date: November 10, 1974; *Closing Date*: November 10, 1974
Performances: 1
Play and *Lyrics*: Honor Moore
Music: Susan Ain
Direction: Kay Carney; *Producers*: Samuel H. Schwartz (A Lenox Arts Center/Music-Theatre Performing Group Production; Lyn Austin and Mary Silverman, Producers); *Scenery*: John Jacobsen; *Costumes*: Whitney Blausen; *Lighting*: Spencer Mosse
Cast: Kathryn Walker (Margaret), Leora Dana (Maggie), Donald Symington (Philip), Leslie Ackerman (Abigail), Daniel Landon (David), Philip Carlson (Doctors Rumbach, Cassidy, Berryman, and Potter), Dorothea Joyce (Singer); Musicians: Amy Rubin (Electric and Acoustic Piano), John Carbonne (Acoustic and Fender Base), Sue Ann Kahn (Soprano and Alto Flute), Joe Passaro (Percussion)
The play with music was presented in two acts.
The action takes place in Connecticut, New York, and Washington, D.C., from March to May and from June to September.

Musical Numbers

Note: All songs were performed by Dorothea Joyce.
Act One: "What Will She Leave Me?"; "It's Such a Beautiful Day"; "What Are You Saying About Me Now?"; "Sweet Clear Sun"
Act Two: "The Garden"; "Wait Until the Sun"; "I Want to Go Home"; "Paul Arrives"; "There Is a Birthday"

Like ***The Sign in Sidney Brustein's Window***, *Mourning Pictures* was a play throughout which incidental songs were performed by a singer who wasn't part of the stage action, but whose songs commented upon the plot or enhanced its mood. A program note stated that "grief was given visible form in the mourning picture, popular in the early nineteenth century, especially in New England. Mourning pictures were stitched or painted by young women as gifts for the bereaved family."

Mourning Pictures was an autobiographical play in which the author and poet Honor Moore described the final illness and death of her mother. It was clearly a personal work and one that was heartfelt in its depiction of a loving parent's final days. But the critics found fault with the evening, and it became the season's shortest-running lyric work with just one performance.

Clive Barnes in the *New York Times* suggested Moore had written the play as a "personal memorial for herself and her family" and he wasn't convinced that "this very personal memorial should have been opened to the public." He hoped the play had been "essential therapy" for Moore and perhaps her family, and suggested that only those who could identify with the situation would get much out of the evening. As for the songs, they were "plaintive but irrelevant, even a trifle arty." Barbara Ettorre in *Women's Wear Daily* said the songs often sank into "whining bathos" and as musical counterpoint to the action were "too jarring"; as for the play, it was "too shrill" and lacked delicacy, but she noted there were "glimmers of truth" in the evening, "mostly due to Leora Dana," who brought the mother "gloriously to life."

Martin Gottfried in the *New York Post* noted the play contained some "lovely writing" but wasn't memorable as poetry or as theatre. The actors often spoke directly to the audience, and the songs, while "not without musical sophistication" and which ran the gamut of styles from Joni Mitchell to Samuel Barber, were "uninvolved and uninvolving." Douglas Watt in the *New York Daily News* felt the play "deliberately avoids the pulse of drama" and so instead of real characters there were "simply figures in a mourning landscape" who under Kay Carney's direction moved about "like so many lifeless objects." But he found the music "lovely" and said the lyrics contained some of Moore's "most effective writing."

JOHNNY MATHIS

Theatre: Uris Theatre
Opening Date: November 13, 1974; *Closing Date*: November 24, 1974
Performances: 15
Producers: Ron Delsener and Nederlander (Jonathan Scharer, Associate Producer for Ron Delsener); *Scenery*: Neil Peter Jampolis; *Lighting*: Jane Reisman; *Musical Direction*: Jim Barnett
Cast: *Johnny Mathis*, the Miracles
The limited engagement concert starred popular singer Johnny Mathis and featured the five-member soul-singing group the Miracles. Ian Dove in the *New York Times* reported that Mathis sang a number of his hit songs from the 1950s (such as "Wonderful, Wonderful" and "Chances Are") but also added contemporary flavor to his repertoire with songs by Paul Williams and Michel Legrand and even reached back decades earlier to Ivor Novello. As a result, Mathis proved he had "survived all the fads and fantasies of popular music during the last decade by not endlessly recycling his golden oldies."

SGT. PEPPER'S LONELY HEARTS CLUB BAND ON THE ROAD

"A Rock Spectacle"

Theatre: Beacon Theatre
Opening Date: November 17, 1974; *Closing Date*: January 5, 1975
Performances: 66
Adaptation: Robin Wagner and Tom O'Horgan
Lyrics and *Music*: John Lennon and Paul McCartney
Based on the 1967 record album *Sgt. Pepper's Lonely Hearts Club Band.*
Direction: Tom O'Horgan; *Producers*: Robert Stigwood in association with Brian Avnet and Scarab Productions, Inc. (Gatchell and Neufeld, Associate Producers; "presented" at the Beacon Theatre by Steven Singer and Steve Metz; Howard Dando, "Presenter"); *Scenery*: Robin Wagner; *Costumes*: Randy Barcelo; *Lighting*: Jules Fisher; *Musical Direction*: Gordon Lowry Harrell
Cast: Maxwell's Silver Hammermen: Allan Nicholls (Jack), William Parry (Sledge), and B. G. Gibson (Claw); Ted Neeley (Billy Shears), Alaina Reed (Lucy), Walter Rivera (Flattop), David Patrick Kelly (Sun Queen, Lovely Rita, Polythene Pam, Sgt. Pepper), Kay Cole (Strawberry Fields); Hammeroids: Blake Anderson, Edward O. Bhartonn, Arlana Blue, Ron Capozzoli, Michael Meadows, Stoney Reece, and Jason Roberts
The musical was presented in two acts.

Musical Numbers

Note: * = song from the *Sgt. Pepper*'s album.

Act One: Opening (Orchestra); "Sgt. Pepper's Lonely Hearts Club Band" (*) (Hammermen); "With a Little Help from My Friends" (*) (Ted Neeley, Hammermen); "Nowhere Man" (Hammermen); "With a Little Help from My Friends" (reprise) (Ted Neeley, Hammermen); "Lucy in the Sky with Diamonds" (*) (Alaina Reed, Ted Neeley, Hammermen); "I Want You" (Ted Neeley, Alaina Reed, Hammermen); "Come Together" (Alaina Reed, Walter Rivera, Friends); "Nowhere Man II" (Hammermen); "Sun Queen" (All); "Lovely Rita" (David Patrick Kelly, Ted Neeley, Hammermen, Alaina Reed); "Polythene Pam" (David Patrick Kelly, Ted Neeley, Hammermen, Alaina Reed); "She Came In Through the Bathroom Window" (Hammermen, featuring Allan Nicholls); "You Never Give Me Your Money" (Ted Neeley, David Patrick Kelly, Hammermen, Alaina Reed); "Lovely Rita" (*) (reprise) (Ted Neeley, David Patrick Kelly, Hammermen, Alaina Reed); "Her Majesty" (Ted Neeley); "A Day in the Life" (*) (Ted Neeley); "She's Leaving Home" (*) (Hammermen, featuring B. G. Gibson); "Strawberry Fields Forever" (Kay Cole, Ted Neeley); "Getting Better" (*) (Ted Neeley, Kay Cole, Hammermen)

Act Two: Opening (Orchestra); "Because" (Ted Neeley, Kay Cole); "When I'm Sixty-Four" (*) (Ted Neeley, Kay Cole); "Because" (reprise) (Ted Neeley, Kay Cole); "Good Morning, Good Morning" (*) (Hammermen); "Being for the Benefit of Mr. Kite" (*) (Hammermen, Alaina Reed); "Oh Darling" (Kay Cole); "Fixing a Hole" (*) (Ted Neeley); "Oh Darling" (reprise) (Kay Cole); "Being for the Benefit of Mr. Kite II" (Hammermen): "Mean Mr. Mustard" (Alaina Reed); "Maxwell's Silver Hammer" (Hammermen); "Being for the Benefit of Mr. Kite III" (Hammermen); "Carry That Weight" (Hammermen); "Golden Slumbers" (Ted Neeley); "Carry That Weight" (reprise) (Hammermen); "The Long and Winding Road" (Ted Neeley); "Get Back" (David Patrick Kelly, Ted Neeley, Alaina Reed, Hammermen); "Sgt. Pepper's Lonely Hearts Club Band" (reprise) (All); "The End" (All)

The Beatles' 1967 album *Sgt. Pepper's Lonely Hearts Club Band* was a song cycle of serious and humorous numbers that didn't tell a story but offered a moody and surreal atmosphere permeated with hallucinatory drug-related references (some listeners were surprised to realize that "Lucy in the Sky with Diamonds" might be a reference to LSD).

Robin Wagner and Tom O'Horgan's misguided stage version was a failed attempt to impose a storyline on the album, and to that end they added seventeen songs from John Lennon and Paul McCartney's catalog. But the nebulous plot with no dialogue was weak, and so the evening was more in the nature of a rock concert with over-the-top scenic effects, including giant balloons, huge puppets, a monstrous walking hand, a huge jar of French's mustard (for "Mean Mr. Mustard"), and gimmicks such as the cast hurtling colorful sponge Frisbees at the audience and a snowfall of confetti falling from the rafters. As for the plot, it looked at poor little innocent rock star Billy Shears (Ted Neeley) who loses his artistic soul to the commercial music business. It was Clifford Odets's 1951 play *The Big Knife* all over again, it was a later ***Soon***, and in a few weeks ***Black Picture Show*** covered much of the same territory albeit from a racial angle.

The critical consensus was that *Sgt. Pepper* wasn't worth its salt, and with *Hair*, ***Jesus Christ Superstar***, ***Dude***, and now the Beatles' musical behind him, O'Horgan needed to get over his obsession for overproduced rock musicals and concentrate on fresh subject matter.

Martin Gottfried in the *New York Post* said the "clumsy concert with dance movement and Thanksgiving parade props" was "leaden and cheap." James Spina in *Women's Wear Daily* pounced on Neeley's "terrible singing" and O'Horgan's "dated" staging techniques and noted there were "so many idiotic things going on that you never know where to look." T. E. Kalem in *Time* said the "germy display" had a "faggy odor," and he regretted that the Beatles' songs "were trampled under the dreck" of O'Horgan's "grimagination."

Leonard Propst on NBC Radio said the work was "a revival of old rock spectacles, without a focus or central idea" and suggested the music worked much better if one simply listened to the original Beatles' recordings. And Patricia O'Haire in the *New York Daily News* felt that the "spectacular" and "overwhelming staging" devices "all but obscures the music."

Clive Barnes in the *New York Times* noted that the "inflated" show tried for a "psychedelic fantasy" but the trip was "mostly through Mr. O'Horgan's attic," and thus the "terrific" music was "submerged" by constant visual and aural sound effects.

The production was scheduled to play in New York for a limited engagement and then tour nationally. But after the indifferent reviews, the show closed for good.

The only song on the original *Sgt. Pepper*'s album that wasn't included in the musical was "Within You Without You."

The Beatles' music was more successful in the long-running 1977 ***Beatlemania***, which played for over one thousand performances, and a few months before the Broadway premiere of *Sgt. Pepper* the 1974 British musical *John, Paul, George, Ringo . . . and Bert* opened for an eventual run of 418 showings. There were three shows about John Lennon, two were titled *Lennon*, and both flopped, one Off Broadway in 1982 and one on Broadway in 2005, and another Off-Broadway Lennon tribute was the concert-styled revue *Lennon: Through a Glass Onion* which opened in 2014. There was also the 1987 German production *Elvis & John*, two one-act musicals.

EDDY ARNOLD

Theatre: Palace Theatre
Opening Date: November 25, 1973; *Closing Date*: November 30, 1973
Performances: 8
Producer: Nederlander
Cast: *Eddy Arnold*, George Gobel, The Establishment

The popular country-and-western singer Eddy Arnold appeared at the Palace for a one-week limited engagement.

Ian Dove in the *New York Times* praised the "very palatable piece of entertainment" and said Arnold was "deceptively simple, melodic and soothing" and his program had "low-keyed polish." George Gobel (who had last appeared on Broadway as the lead in the 1961 musical *Let It Ride!*) was a "superior" comic, and a young singing group called The Establishment provided Arnold with vocal backup.

THE 5TH DIMENSION

Theatre: Uris Theatre
Opening Date: November 27, 1974; *Closing Date*: December 8, 1974
Performances: 15
Producers: Marc Gordon in association with Nederlander; *Choreography* (for the 5th Dimension): Bert Woods; *Choreography* (for Jo Jo's Dance Factory): Jo Jo Smith; *Scenery*: Robin Wagner; *Costumes*: Michael Travis; *Lighting*: Jane Reisman; *Musical Direction* (for the 5th Dimension): John Myles; *Musical Direction* (for Jo Jo's Dance Factory): William Daniel
Cast: *The 5th Dimension*, Jo Jo's Dance Factory

The popular singing group the 5th Dimension appeared in this limited-engagement concert. Also on the bill were dances by Jo Jo's Dance Factory. John Rockwell in the *New York Times* said the five-member 5th Dimension "sang well" and "the way they knit several songs into a cohesive medley is unusual." But their "on-stage demeanor" looked "simply stiff" and overall the show "lacked shape and pacing." And "worst of all" was Jo Jo's Dance Factory, "an inept and out-of-shape collection of vulgarized jazz dancers."

RAPHAEL IN CONCERT

Theatre: Uris Theatre
Opening Date: December 19, 1974; *Closing Date*: December 22, 1974
Performances: 6
Producer: Nederlander; *Scenery*: Neil Peter Jampolis; *Lighting*: Jane Reisman
Cast: *Raphael*, the Voices of New York

The popular Spanish singer and actor Raphael (aka Miguel Rafael [Raphael] Martos Sanchez) appeared in this limited-engagement concert, and was backed by the singing group the Voices of New York.

Ian Dove in the *New York Times* reported that the concert was performed almost entirely in Spanish, and Raphael "more than justifies his reputation as one of the biggest pop singers in the Latin field." He moved "quickly, smoothly and efficiently through his large song bag," and, in keeping with the season, performed an *a capella* version of "The Little Drummer Boy." Otherwise, he sometimes indulged in the "somewhat overblown gesture," such as when against a backdrop his shadow was seen "in crucifixion pose."

WHERE'S CHARLEY?

Theatre: Circle in the Square Theatre
Opening Date: December 20, 1974; *Closing Date*: February 23, 1975
Performances: 76
Book: George Abbott
Lyrics and *Music*: Frank Loesser
Based on the 1892 play *Charley's Aunt* by Brandon Thomas.
Direction: Theodore Mann; *Producer*: Circle in the Square, Inc. (Theodore Mann, Artistic Director; Paul Libin, Managing Director); *Choreography*: Margo Sappington; *Scenery*: Marjorie Kellogg; *Costumes*: Arthur Boccia; *Lighting*: Thomas Skelton; *Musical Direction*: Tom Pierson
Cast: Louis Beachner (Brassett), Jerry Lanning (Jack Chesney), *Raul Julia* (Charley Wykeham), Carol Jo Lugenbeal (Kitty Verdun), Marcia McClain (Amy Spettigue), Peter Walker (Sir Francis Chesney), Tom Aldredge (Mr. Spettigue), Taina Elg (Donna Lucia D'Alvadorez), Dennis Cooley (Reggie); Students and Young Ladies: Pamela Burrell, Jacqueline Clark, Dennis Cooley, Karen Jablons, Jack Neubeck, Craig Sandquist, Leland Schwantes, Miriam Welch
The musical was presented in two acts.
The action takes place at Oxford University in 1892.

Musical Numbers

Act One: "Where's Charley?" (Students and Young Ladies); "Better Get Out of Here" (Marcia McClain, Carol Jo Lugenbeal, Raul Julia, Jerry Lanning); "The New Ashmolean Marching Society and Students Conservatory Band" (Ensemble); "My Darling, My Darling" (Carol Jo Lugenbeal, Jerry Lanning); "Make a Miracle" (Raul Julia, Marcia McClain); "Serenade with Asides" (Tom Aldredge); "Lovelier Than Ever" (Taina Elg, Peter Walker, Students, Young Ladies); "The Woman in His Room" (Marcia McClain); "Pernambuco" (Raul Julia, Company)
Act Two: "Where's Charley?" (Marcia McClain); "Once in Love with Amy" (Raul Julia, Students); "The Gossips" (Pamela Burrell, Jacqueline Clark, Karen Jablons, Miriam Welch); "At the Red Rose Cotillion" (Jerry Lanning, Carol Jo Lugenbeal, Ensemble); Finale (Ensemble)

Circle in the Square brought back Frank Loesser's *Where's Charley?*, but it was a scaled-down, bare-bones revival with sixteen performers and an orchestra of six (the original production featured a cast of forty-four, and an orchestra of approximately twenty-six musicians). The sets were basically drops and movable skeletal pieces, and the small orchestra was perched atop a gazebo at the back of the stage. No one made the case that *Where's Charley?* was a masterpiece of musical theatre, but the critics generally enjoyed the production and praised Frank Loesser's melodic score (which unfortunately lost some of its effectiveness due to the small orchestra, and so the brass-band antics of "The New Ashmolean Marching Society and Students Conservatory Band" were more placid with harpsichord and piano effects).

Based on Brandon Thomas's 1892 farce *Charley's Aunt*, the proceedings revolved around the shenanigans at Oxford University when students Charley Wykeham (Raul Julia) and Jack Chesney (Jerry Lanning) devise a scheme for Charley to impersonate his rich aunt Donna Lucia D'Alvadorez (Taina Elg) so that "she" can chaperone Amy Spettigue (Marcia McClain) and Kitty Verdun (Carol Jo Lugenbeal) when they visit Charley and Jack in their rooms for lunch. Soon Charley is darting in and out of the room in Aunt Lucia drag, and is later pursued by both Amy's uncle Mr. Spettigue (Tom Aldredge) and Jack's father Sir Francis (Peter Walker). And just when the confusion couldn't get any more confused, in walks the real Aunt Lucia from Brazil ("where the nuts come from").

The revival generated some controversy over the casting of Raul Julia as a British Oxford student of the early 1890s; he apparently made no attempt to alter his Puerto Rican accent, and so a few critics felt this was jarring for the musical's time period and locale. Martin Gottfried in the *New York Post* complained of the "absurdity" of Julia's casting, the "obvious and spiritless" production, and the "uneven" company. He said there was "no excuse" for Julia's retaining his accent, which sounded "positively ridiculous" for the musical's time and place, but noted that Jerry Lanning was "very funny" and turned "My, Darling, My Darling" into a "show-stopper." Although the revival was "mediocre" and Julia's casting "disastrous," Gottfried emphasized that the musical itself had "class" and Loesser's score offered "melody, lilt, theatricality, simplicity and instinctive musical sophistication."

Douglas Watt in the *New York Daily News* felt that Julia wasn't "entirely comfortable" as Charley; John Beaufort in the *Christian Science Monitor* suggested his casting was "something less than inspired"; and Edwin Wilson in the *Wall Street Journal* noted that Julia couldn't seem to make up his mind as to whether he believed in the "foolishness" of the plot or not, and so sometimes he seemed to be "in" the musical and other times "outside it." But Clive Barnes in the *New York Times* indicated Julia was the "raison d'etre" of the revival and "proves himself a star," and Keitha McLean in *Women's Wear Daily* said he "walks away with the show."

McLean noted that the musical was an "absolutely smashing" family entertainment for the holiday season, but Wilson felt the production lacked style and Leonard Probst on NBC Radio noted the evening suffered from "chaotic" direction.

The original production opened at the St. James Theatre on October 11, 1948, for 792 performances. Ray Bolger won the Tony Award for Best Leading Actor in a Musical, and the show enjoyed two hit songs, "Once in Love with Amy" and "My Darling, My Darling." Because of the ASCAP musicians' strike, there was no cast album, but Bolger recorded "Once in Love with Amy." The script was published in paperback by Samuel French (London) in an undated edition circa 1958, and the lyrics for all the used and unused songs are included in the collection *The Complete Lyrics of Frank Loesser*.

The production was revived in New York for a limited-run return engagement with Bolger which opened at the Broadway Theatre on January 29, 1951, for forty-eight performances; it was next seen at City Center on May 25, 1966, for fifteen performances by the New York City Center Light Opera Company as part of its Frank Loesser tribute (Darryl Hickman was Charley); and after the current revival it was presented at City Center by Encores! on March 17, 2011, for five performances (Rob McClure was Charley).

The faithful film version was made in Great Britain by Warner Brothers with original cast members Bolger, Allyn Ann McLerie (Amy), and Horace Cooper (Mr. Spettigue); Robert Shackleton had played the part of Jack during the original national tour, and reprised the role for the film version, which also featured Jean Marsh as a dancer. Directed by David Butler and choreographed by Michael Kidd, the adaptation is surprisingly faithful to its source and is an excellent visual record of the show and its performance style (because of rights issues, the film has unfortunately not been seen in public for decades).

The London production opened at the Palace Theatre on February 20, 1958, for 404 performances; Norman Wisdom was Charley, and this time around the choreography was created by Hanya Holm. Happily, the London version was recorded by Columbia (LP # 33SX1085), and the CD was issued by EMI/West End Angel (# 0777-7-89058-2-0). The CD was later released on a pairing with the 1959 London cast album of *Chrysanthemum* on Must Close Saturday Records (# MCSR-3044). A college production at the University of Vermont was recorded and privately issued during the early 1960s.

The current revival dropped one song from the original production ("The Years before Us").

Awards

Tony Award Nominations: Best Leading Actor in a Musical (Raul Julia); Best Featured Actor in a Musical (Tom Aldredge); Best Featured Actress in a Musical (Taina Elg); Best Costume Designer (Arthur Boccia); Best Choreographer (Margo Sappington)

GOOD NEWS

"The 30's Musical Comedy"

Theatre: St. James Theatre
Opening Date: December 23, 1974; *Closing Date*: January 4, 1975

Performances: 16
Book: Laurence Schwab, B. G. (Buddy) De Sylva, and Frank Mandel; book adapted by Garry Marshall
Lyrics: B. G. (Buddy) De Sylva and Lew Brown
Music: Ray Henderson; dance and incidental music by Luther Henderson
Direction: Michael Kidd; *Producers*: Harry Rigby and Terry Allen Kramer (Robert Anglund, Stan Hurwitz, and Frank Montalvo, Associate Producers); *Choreography*: Not credited, but apparently by Michael Kidd (Gary Menteer, Associate Choreographer); *Scenery*: Donald Oenslager; *Costumes*: Donald Brooks; *Lighting*: Tharon Musser; *Musical Direction*: Liza Redfield
Cast: *Gene Nelson* (Bill Johnson), Scott Stevensen (Tom Marlowe), Joseph Burke (Beef Saunders), Wayne Bryan (Bobby Randall), Stubby Kaye (Pooch Kearney), Rebecca Urich (Flo), Paula Cinko (Millie), Jana Robbins (Pat), Barbara Lail (Babe O'Day), Terry Eno (Windy), Jimmy Brennan (Slats), Tommy Breslin (Sylvester), *Alice Faye* (Professor Kenyon), Marti Rolph (Connie Lane), Margaret (Muffin), Ernie Pysher (Colton Player); Happy Days Quartet: Tim Cassidy, Randall Robbins, Scott Stevensen, and David Thome; Acrobats: Lisa Guignard, Mary Ann Lipson, Ernie Pysher, and Jeff Spielman; Baton Twirlers: Tim Cassidy, Lynda Goodfriend, and Lisa Guignard; Tap Dancers: Terry Eno and Jimmy Brennan; Coeds: Paula Cinko, Robin Gerson, Lynda Goodfriend, Lisa Guignard, Anne Kaye, Mary Ann Lipson, Sally O'Donnell, Rebbeca Urich, and Marcia Lynn Watkins; The Boys: Michael Austin, Jimmy Brennan, Tim Cassidy, Ernie Pysher, Randall Robbins, Jeff Spielman, and David Thome
The musical was presented in two acts.
The action takes place during the mid-1930s on and around the campus of Tait College.

Musical Numbers

Note: * = song was from the original 1927 production.
Act One: Overture (Orchestra and Company); "He's a Ladies' Man" (*) (Jana Robbins, Paula Cinko, Rebecca Urich, Students); "The Best Things in Life Are Free" (*) (Alice Faye, Students); "Just Imagine" (*) (Marti Rolph with Jana Robbins, Paula Cinko, and Rebecca Urich); "Happy Days" (*) (Scott Stevensen, Jana Robbins, Paula Cinko, Rebecca Urich, Tommy Breslin, Boys); "Button Up Your Overcoat" (from *Follow Thru*, 1929) (Wayne Bryan, Barbara Lail); "Lucky in Love" (*) (Marti Rolph, Scott Stevensen, Students); "You're the Cream in My Coffee" (from *Hold Everything*, 1928) (Alice Faye, Gene Nelson); "The Varsity Drag" (*) (Barbara Lail, Students); "Together" (independent song) (Alice Faye); "Tait Song" (*) (Gene Nelson, Stubby Kaye, Students); "Lucky in Love" (reprise) (Company)
Act Two: "Today's the Day" (*) (Girls); "The Girl of the Pi Beta Phi" (*) (Jana Robbins, Girls); "Good News"(*) (Alice Faye, Marti Rolph, Students); "Keep Your Sunny Side Up" (from 1929 film *Sunny Side Up*) (Stubby Kaye, Boys); "The Best Things in Life Are Free" (reprise) (Marti Rolph, Scott Stevensen); "Life Is Just a Bowl of Cherries" (from *George White's Scandals*, 1931; lyric by Lew Brown, music by Ray Henderson) (Alice Faye, Marti Rolph, Barbara Lail); "The Professor and the Students" (origin unknown) (Alice Faye, Stubby Kaye, Company); Finale (Company)

The current production of *Good News* was its first and (as of this writing) only Broadway revival. The smash hit originally opened at the 46th Street Theatre on September 6, 1927, and ran for 551 performances, and the delightful score included four songs that became standards ("The Best Things in Life Are Free," "Lucky in Love," "Just Imagine," and "The Varsity Drag"). The show was the epitome of the carefree flapper era with its lighthearted look at life on a college campus where dates and football are clearly more important than math and astronomy. As for the plot, two words sum it up: campus capers.

Even the titles of the show's songs are reflective of the evening's insouciance and easy-going nature: "Flaming Youth," "Happy Days," "He's a Ladies' Man," "The Girls of the Pi Beta Phi," "On the Campus," "Lucky in Love," "Baby! What?," "The Best Things in Life Are Free," the rousing title song, and perhaps most of all, the show's irresistible dance routine "The Varsity Drag." Despite its hit status, the musical wasn't revived on Broadway for decades, maybe because college musicals were something of a staple and came along every few years and thus satisfied the college-musical market (the visits to colleges, prep schools, and girls' boarding schools included *You Said It*, 1931; *Too Many Girls*, 1939; *Best Foot Forward*, 1941; *What's Up*, 1943; *Barefoot Boy with Cheek*, 1947; *Hold It!*, 1948; and *All American*, 1962).

Clearly the nostalgia craze of the early 1970s paved the way for the revival of *Good News*. It was a familiar title (thanks mostly to the popular 1947 film version, which made regular appearances on the late show), and it seemed to have everything going for it: the reunion of Twentieth Century-Fox's Alice Faye and John Payne, a bright supporting cast, a sheaf of melodic songs, lively choreography, and a lavish production with knockout costumes (Donald Oenslager, who had designed the 1927 production, also designed the décor for the revival). The revival changed the time of the musical from the 1920s to the 1930s, perhaps because ***No, No, Nanette*** had taken full theatrical ownership of the earlier decade.

The revival toured for a year, and when it opened and abruptly closed after two weeks on Broadway, those who had seen the tour during its early months were astounded. How could the critics have pounced on such a wonderfully entertaining show? But Edwin Wilson in the *Wall Street Journal* perhaps had the answer. He'd seen the musical during the early part of its tryout almost a year earlier when director and adaptor Abe Burrows "with tremendous love and warmth" had created an "affectionate Valentine" to the never-land world of college days; but when Burrows was replaced by director Michael Kidd and book adaptor Garry Marshall, the work became a "slick glossy, fast-paced" musical that the material wasn't able to support and thus the show proceeded to lose its heart. As a result, the "bright-faced" performers were now "calculating pros" who aimed for laughs, and some of the sincere songs were "hoked up beyond recognition."

Douglas Watt in the *New York Daily News* said that after a year-long tour the Broadway opening was less a "triumphant revival" than "the end of the road"; Martin Gottfried in the *New York Post* noted that at a critics' preview two different programs were in circulation and because both credited different creative personnel (see below) the show lacked a consistent style, but he praised the "dazzling harmonizations and stylings" by vocal arranger Hugh Martin; and Jack Kroll in *Newsweek* was generally unenthusiastic about the "silly but friendly" musical, felt Alice Faye sang "too sedately," and quoted Wilson Mizner's old comment: "Don't miss it if you can."

But Howard Kissel in *Women's Wear Daily* said the production was a "perfect example of the Broadway musical showmanship we too seldom see," found the score "fresh as ever," and noted that Alice Faye had a "star's aura" and a "still splendid voice"; and Leonard Probst on NBC Radio said Faye was "just right" and the show itself was "fast-paced, high spirited, simple, silly, and well done."

During the tryout and almost to opening night, Abe Burrows was the director and adaptor of record, Donald Saddler the choreographer, and Arthur Faria the assistant director. Burrows was succeeded by Michael Kidd as director, and presumably Kidd took over the choreography (the program didn't list a choreographer, and Gary Menteer was billed as associate choreographer), and Garry Marshall was officially credited as the book's adaptor. John Payne was with the company for a year, and appeared in early New York previews; when he left the musical, he was replaced by Gene Nelson. During the tryout, Harry Rigby was the producer of record, but for New York was joined by Terry Allen Kramer.

A number of songs were cut during the year-long national tour and New York preview period, including "On the Campus," "Tait Song," "After Commencement," "Football Drill," "I Want to Be Bad," and "Never Swat a Fly." The first two numbers were from the original production; "After Commencement" seems to have been newly composed by Hugh Martin (but there was a song in the original production titled "After Commencement, What?" and so perhaps Martin wrote new music for the original lyric); "Football Drill" was a dance number that utilized music from the score; "I Want to Be Bad" was from *Follow Thru* (1929); and the irresistible "Never Swat a Fly" was from the 1930 film *Just Imagine* (the latter was a science-fiction musical comedy that borrowed its title from the song in *Good News* [but the song itself was not part of the film's score]).

The script was published in paperback by Samuel French in 1959, and while there wasn't an official cast album of the revival, a lavish two-LP recording was privately issued (unnamed company and unnumbered LP) that included songs from the Broadway production, numbers cut during the tour, and such esoterica as rehearsal tracks, Alice Faye's entrance at the first tryout performance, and the Broadway finale, which includes Gene Nelson in the cast.

A cast album of a 1993 revival by the Music Theatre of Wichita was released by That's Entertainment Records (CD # CDTER-1230) and includes eleven songs from the original production and seven interpolations by De Sylva, Brown, and Henderson, most of which were from their stage and screen musicals. The recordings of the 1974 and 1993 revivals provide an almost complete rendering of the original 1927 score except for "Flaming Youth," Baby! What?," "In the Meantime," and "After Commencement" (aka "After Commencement, What?").

MGM filmed the musical twice, in 1930 and 1947. The first version is delightful, as far as it goes; unfortunately, the final reel is lost (or, at least, hasn't turned up). But what remains is an entertaining bit of high-jinks, including a rousing "Varsity Drag" in which even the amoebas under the science-class microscope are seen dancing away. The film's players include original cast member Mary Lawlor as well as Cliff Edwards, Bessie Love, and Lola Lane. And if Shirley MacLaine wants to know what she was doing in 1930, all she has to do is watch Dorothy McNulty's performance: Dorothy *is* Shirley, or maybe Shirley *is* Dorothy (McNulty later changed her name to Penny Singleton and of course achieved her greatest success in a series of twenty-eight *Blondie* movies released between 1938 and 1950).

The second version is a Technicolor delight with June Allyson, Peter Lawford, Mel Tormé, Joan McCracken Patricia Marshall, and Ray McDonald. Eight songs were retained from the stage version, and there were two new ones, "Pass That Peace Pipe" (lyric and music by Roger Edens, Hugh Martin, and Ralph Blane) and "The French Lesson" (lyric by Betty Comden and Adolph Green, music by Roger Edens). An expanded soundtrack album issued by Rhino (CD # RHM2-7763) includes various outtakes (such as the deleted song "An Easier Way," lyric by Comden and Green and music by Edens) and two numbers from the soundtrack of the 1930 version ("The Varsity Drag" and the title song, both sung by McNulty). The DVD of the 1947 film was issued by Artiflix (unnumbered DVD).

THE WIZ

"The New Musical Version of *The Wonderful Wizard of Oz*"

Theatre: Majestic Theatre (during run, the musical transferred to the Broadway Theatre)
Opening Date: January 5, 1975; *Closing Date*: January 28, 1979
Performances: 1,672
Book: William F. Brown
Lyrics and *Music*: Charlie Smalls
Based on the 1900 novel *The Wonderful Wizard of Oz* by L. Frank Baum (who also wrote thirteen other *Oz* novels).
Direction: Geoffrey Holder; *Producer*: Ken Harper; *Choreography*: George Faison; *Scenery*: Tom H. John; *Costumes*: Geoffrey Holder; *Lighting*: Tharon Muser; *Musical Direction*: Charles H. Coleman
Cast: Tasha Thomas (Aunt Em), Nancy (Toto), Stephanie Mills (Dorothy), Ralph Wilcox (Uncle Henry), Evelyn Thomas (Tornado); Munchkins: Phylicia Ayers-Allen, Pi Douglass, Joni Palmer, Andy Torres, and Carl Weaver; Clarice Taylor (Addaperle); Yellow Brick Road: Ronald Dunham, Eugene Little, John Parks, and Kenneth Scott; Hinton Battle (Scarecrow); Crows: Wendy Edmead, Frances Morgan, and Ralph Wilcox; Tiger Haynes (Tinman), Ted Ross (Lion); Kalidahs: Phillip Bond, Pi Douglass, Rodney Green, Evelyn Thomas, and Andy Torres; Poppies: Lettie Battle, Leslie Butler, Eleanor McCoy, Frances Morgan, and Joni Palmer; Field Mice: Phylicia Ayers-Allen, Pi Douglass, Carl Weaver, and Ralph Wilcox; Danny Beard (Gatekeeper); Emerald City Citizens: Lettie Battle, Leslie Butler, Wendy Edmead, Eleanor McCoy, Frances Morgan, Joni Palmer, Evelyn Thomas, Philip Bond, Ronald Dunham, Rodney Green, Eugene Little, John Parks, Kenneth Scott, and Andy Torres; Andre De Shields (The Wiz), Mabel King (Evillene), Ralph Wilcox (Lord High Underling), Carl Weaver (Soldier Messenger), Andy Torres (Winged Monkey), Dee Dee Bridgewater (Glinda); Pit Singers: Frank Floyd, Sam Harkness, Jozella Reed, and Tasha Thomas
The musical was presented in two acts.
The action takes place in Kansas, Munchkin Land, and Oz.

Musical Numbers

Act One: "The Feeling We Once Had" (Tasha Thomas); "Tornado Ballet" (Company); "He's the Wizard" (Clarice Taylor, Munchkins); "Soon as I Get Home" (Stephanie Mills); "I Was Born on the Day Before Yesterday" (Hinton Battle, Crows); "Ease on Down the Road" (Stephanie Mills, Hinton Battle, Yellow Brick Road); "Slide Some Oil to Me" (Tiger Haynes, Stephanie Mills, Hinton Battle); "Mean Ole Lion" (Ted Ross); "Kalidah Battle" (Friends, Kalidahs, Yellow Brick Road); "Be a Lion" (Stephanie Mills, Ted Ross); "Lion's Dream" (Ted Ross, Poppies); "Emerald City Ballet" ("Pssst") (lyric by Timothy Graphenreed, music by George Faison) (Friends, Company); "So You Wanted to Meet the Wizard" (Andre De Shields); "To Be Able to Feel" (Tiger Haynes)

Act Two: "No Bad News" (Mabel King); "Funky Monkeys" (Monkeys); "Everybody Rejoice" (lyric and music by Luther Vandross) (Friends, Winkies); "Who Do You Think You Are?" (Friends); "Believe in Yourself" (Andre De Shields); "Y'all Got It!" (Andre De Shields); "A Rested Body Is a Rested Mind" (Dee Dee Bridgewater); "Believe in Yourself" (reprise) (Dee Dee Bridgewater); "Home" (Stephanie Mills)

The Wiz was an updated and urbanized black version of L. Frank Baum's *The Wonderful Wizard of Oz*, and if it was never able to match the charm of the 1939 MGM film adaptation and its classic score by E. Y. Harburg and Harold Arlen, it nonetheless was a crowd-pleaser that played for 1,672 performances and became the season's longest-running musical. It won a number of Tony Awards, including Best Musical, and "Ease on Down the Road" became one of the era's popular songs.

William F. Brown's book followed the basic plot of the original story, and for his score Charlie Smalls came up with musical numbers that often mirrored the same moods of the songs from the 1939 film ("Home" was a yearning ballad in what was essentially the "Over the Rainbow" number; "Ease on Down the Road" was a riff on "Follow the Yellow Brick Road"; and "Everybody Rejoice" was in spirit like "Optimistic Voices"). Brown's book had some nice touches, such as transforming the yellow brick road into a quartet of dancers with blonde Afros and oversized yellow shoes, and the ingenious conceit of a tornado character (Evelyn Thomas) resulted in one of the most thrilling stage effects of the era. Thomas whirled across the stage while a strip of black cloth emerged from her headdress, and soon the cloth morphed into a huge winding one which enveloped the entire stage. While Dorothy and her porch were spinning in limbo, Thomas continued dancing while a chorus dressed in black appeared with inverted umbrellas and swirling streamers on poles. And when the storm and the tornado characters had played themselves out, suddenly Dorothy was in Oz, surrounded by Munchkins.

But the evening quickly became a one-joke musical with its constant street-smart vernacular and outlook, and the score was generally a disappointment. However, the rich Technicolor look of the production and the lively dances kept things moving, and the show was seldom dull. One of the most delightful aspects of the evening was Mabel King's very, very evil Evillene, the Wicked Witch of the West. She made her entrance telling everyone to shut up because "I'm evil with everyone today!" and in her show-stopping number warned her toadies not to bring her "No Bad News."

Clive Barnes in the *New York Times* noted that while there was much to enjoy in *The Wiz*, he never really enjoyed it. The "somewhat charmless" book gave the story a treatment that he found "tiresome" and without magic; the score was "too insistent and oddly familiar" with "blaring, relentless rhythms"; and while the décor was handsome and the costumes "wackily imaginative," the overall "scenic spectacle" was "a little cold." Douglas Watt in the *New York Daily News* found the evening "enormously good-natured" and "hard to resist," but said the score was "mostly dull" with "commonplace" lyrics and "uninspired" music. While Martin Gottfried in the *New York Post* found the first act "fabulous," he noted that things "fell apart" in the second, and as a result the musical was "half of something when it might have been something and a half." Edwin Wilson in the *Wall Street Journal* said the book was undistinguished, and suggested the musical was "performed by blacks for blacks"; he praised Andre De Shields as the Wiz ("the coolest, meanest dude in town"), Tiger Haynes's Tinman (who danced like Bill Robinson), and Mabel King's Evillene ("the last of the Red Hot Mamas").

John Beaufort in the *Christian Science Monitor* noted the score was "workmanlike," but otherwise the "gorgeous prismatic extravaganza" was an "all-exuberant retelling" of the well-known story. Howard Kissel in *Women's Wear Daily* praised the "entertaining" production with its "dazzling" décor, "excellent" choreography, and Brown's book, which was full of "sassy archness" (when toward the end of the musical someone tells Glinda she could have saved everyone a lot of time by telling Dorothy the secret about clicking her heels, Glinda looks around at the cast members and says, "Well, of course I could have! But look at all the people I'd of put out of work"). T. E. Kalem in *Time* said the musical displayed "a breathtaking flamboyance of design and color" and flaunted "the gaudy hues of an exploding rainbow." And Jack Kroll in *Newsweek* felt the evening's parade of characters provided most of the fun, including De Shields's Wiz who was "the apotheosis of all ghetto con artists, a shyster preacher, pimp and politician."

During the tryout, director Gilbert Moses III was replaced by Geoffrey Holder; Stu Gilliam (Scarecrow) was succeeded by Hinton Battle, who had been in the chorus of the musical; Butterfly McQueen was the Queen of the Mice, but once the role was eliminated she no longer appeared in the musical (but remained as standby for Clarice Taylor); the canine performer Meg was succeeded by Nancy; and the following songs were cut: "Which Where, Which What, Witch Why?," "You Can't Win," "Don't Cry, Girl," and "Who Do

You Think You Are?" During the Broadway run, "To Be Able to Feel" was retitled "What Would I Do If I Could Feel."

The script was published in paperback by Samuel French, in 1979, and was included in the hardback collection *Great Rock Musicals* (edited by Stanley Richards and published by Stein and Day in 1979). The original cast album was released by Atlantic Records (LP # SD-18137), and later issued the CD (# 18137).

The Wiz was revived on May 24, 1984, at the Lunt-Fontanne Theatre for thirteen performances (Mills was again Dorothy); the era wasn't particularly receptive to visits from recently produced musicals, and other short-running revivals were ***Hair, Jesus Christ Superstar***, *Shenandoah, Ain't Misbehavin'*, and *Dreamgirls*. *The Wiz* was later seen in New York on March 16, 1993, at the Beacon Theatre for sixteen showings (Mills and De Shields revisited their original roles) and in a special concert presentation by Encores! at City Center on June 18, 2009, for twenty-one performances. As of this writing, *The Wiz* is scheduled to be telecast live by NBC on December 3, 2015 (with Mills in the role of Aunt Em).

The dreary and overblown 1978 film version by Universal Pictures was directed by Sidney Lumet and designed and costumed by Tony Walton; the adaptation included a miscast Diana Ross as a misconceived adult Dorothy (who is now a school teacher), and others in the film were Michael Jackson (Scarecrow), Nipsey Russell (Tinman), Richard Pryor (The Wiz), Lena Horne (Glinda), Thelma Carpenter (Miss One), Theresa Merritt (Aunt Em), and, reprising their original stage roles, Ted Ross (Lion) and Mabel King (Evillene). The film added some new songs and background music, including "Can I Go On?" and "Is This What Feeling Gets?" (both with lyrics and music by Quincy Jones, Nick Ashford, and Valerie Simpson), and "Emerald City Sequence" ("Green" and "Red") (lyric by Charlie Smalls, music by Quincy Jones). The soundtrack was issued on a two-LP set by MCA Records (# MCA2-14000), and the DVD was released by Universal.

Awards

Tony Awards and Nominations: Best Musical (***The Wiz***); Best Featured Actor in a Musical (**Ted Ross**); Best Featured Actress in a Musical (**Dee Dee Bridgewater**); Best Director of a Musical (**Geoffrey Holder**); Best Book (William F. Brown); Best Score (**Charlie Smalls**); Best Costume Designer (**Geoffrey Holder**); Best Choreographer (**George Faison**)

BLACK PICTURE SHOW

Theatre: Vivian Beaumont Theatre
Opening Date: January 6, 1975; *Closing Date*: February 9, 1975
Performances: 41
Play: Bill Gunn
Lyrics and *Music*: Sam Waymon
Direction: Bill Gunn; *Producer*: The New York Shakespeare Festival Lincoln Center (Joseph Papp, Producer); *Scenery*: Peter Harvey; *Costumes*: Judy Dearing; *Lighting*: Roger Morgan; *Musical Direction*: Sam Waymon
Cast: Sam Waymon (Vocalist), Albert Hall (J.D.), Derek Anthony Williams (Alexander), Graham Brown (Norman), Carol Cole (Rita), Paul-David Richards (Phillipe), Linda Miller (Jane)
The play with music was presented in one act.
The action takes place during the present in New York City.

Musical Numbers

"I'm So Glad" (Overture); "Mose Art" (Second Movement); "Bird of Paradise"; Variation on "Chopin in E Minor"; "Memory"; "Black Picture Show" (lyric by Bill Gunn); "Mose Art" (First Movement); "Bitch in Heat"; "Digits"; "Science Fiction"; "I Feel So Good" (lyric by Bill Gunn); "Vintage '51"; "Afghanistan"; "Terminate"

Like ***The Sign in Sidney Brustein's Window*** and ***Mourning Pictures***, Bill Gunn's *Black Picture Show* was a drama with incidental songs. The numbers were performed by the play's lyricist and composer Sam Waymon (who doubled on the keyboard), and he was backed by five musicians. The six characters weren't part of the musical sequences, but they nonetheless acknowledged and reacted to the music.

The plot dealt with Alexander (Derek Anthony Williams), a dying poet and playwright confined to a mental institution who is visited by his son J.D. (Albert Hall), a successful film director who seems to have made peace with his career choices even if he isn't proud of them. The play skips around in the past as Alexander obsesses over his choices and his sell-out to Hollywood. He's presented as the victim of the white Hollywood establishment who exploited him, and now on his deathbed he regrets his actions. But it's difficult to sympathize with a writer who willingly goes along with the Hollywood establishment in order to enjoy a lavish lifestyle and a hefty bank account. This was the same problem, and weakness, of Clifford Odets's variation of the same theme in 1951's *The Big Knife*. The story rang as hollow then as it does now.

Douglas Watt in the *New York Daily News* said the "self-indulgent and arty" play was "more pretentious nonsense" from the New York Shakespeare Festival. The mostly "slovenly" writing was replete with "four-letter words and toilet talk," and the evening was a "flapdoodle" that combined "muddled thinking, confused playwriting and old-fashioned theatre." T. E. Kalem in *Time* said the basic premise was "twaddle" because an artist corrupts himself in the marketplace only if he's a "willing accomplice." Further, Kalem noted the play reeked of reverse racism because Gunn persisted in the notion that "some whitey somewhere is prostituting the black brothers for gain"; further, all the white characters were depicted as disgusting human beings. Jack Kroll in *Newsweek* felt the unfocused play was "thrown out of whack by racial overlay" and outdated "racial polemics."

But Martin Gottfried in *Women's Wear Daily* and Clive Barnes in the *New York Times* seem to have witnessed an entirely different play. For Gottfried, the "emotionally overwhelming" evening was "a tremendous work of theatre" with "gorgeous writing," and it was "hard to think of its match among recent work for sustained power" and "literary skill." Barnes felt that Gunn was a "splendid dramatic writer" and the play was "worth seeing just as it was very much worth producing."

Barnes mentioned that the "pleasant" score provided musical commentary on the action, and Gottfried said the "ingenious" score was a "mix of mockery and intensity ranging from silken jazz to Chopin." But Kroll felt the use of music didn't work.

The script was published in paperback by Reed Cannon & Johnson in 1975.

Awards

Tony Award Nomination: Best Featured Actor in a Play (Dick Anthony Williams)

SHENANDOAH

Theatre: Alvin Theatre (during run, the musical transferred to the Mark Hellinger Theatre)
Opening Date: January 5, 1975; *Closing Date*: August 7, 1977
Performances: 1,050
Book: James Lee Barrett, Peter Udell, and Philip Rose
Lyrics: Peter Udell
Music: Gary Geld
Based on the 1965 film *Shenandoah* (screenplay by James Lee Barrett and direction by Andrew V. McLaglen).
Direction: Philip Rose; *Producers*: Philip Rose and Gloria and Louis K. Sher; *Choreography*: Robert Tucker; *Scenery*: C. Murawski; *Costumes*: Pearl Somner and Winn Morton; *Lighting*: Thomas Skelton; *Musical Direction*: Lynn Crigler
Cast: John Cullum (Charlie Anderson), Ted Agress (Jacob), Joel Higgins (James), Jordan Suffin (Nathan), David Russell (John), Penelope Milford (Jenny), Robert Rosen (Henry), Joseph Shapiro (Robert [The Boy]), Donna Theodore (Anne), Chip Ford (Gabriel), Charles Welch (Reverend Byrd, Tinkham), Gordon Halliday (Sam), Edward Penn (Sergeant Johnson), Marshall Thomas (Lieutenant), Casper Roos (Carol), Gary Harger (Corporal), Gene Masoner (Marauder), Ed Preble (Engineer), Craig Lucas (Confederate Sniper); Ensemble: Tedd Carrere, Stephen Dubov, Gary Harger, Brian James, Robert Johanson, Sherry Lambert, Craig Lucas, Gene

Masoner, Paul Myrvold, Dan Ormond, Casper Roos, J. Kevin Scannell, Jack Starkey, E. Allan Stevens, Marshall Thomas, Matt Gavin
The musical was presented in two acts.
The action takes place in the Shenandoah Valley of Virginia during the period of the Civil War.

Musical Numbers

Act One: "Raise the Flag of Dixie" (Confederate and Union Soldiers); "I've Heard It All Before" (John Cullum); "Pass the Cross to Me" (Congregation); "Why Am I Me" (Joseph Shapiro, Chip Ford); "Next to Lovin' (I Like Fightin')" (Ted Agress, Joel Higgins, Jordan Suffin, David Russell, Robert Rosen); "Over the Hill" (Penelope Milford); "The Pickers Are Comin'" (John Cullum); "Next to Lovin'" (reprise) (Ted Agress, Joel Higgins, Jordan Suffin, David Russell, Robert Rosen, Penelope Milford); "Meditation I" (John Cullum); "We Make a Beautiful Pair" (Donna Theodore, Penelope Milford); "Violets and Silverbells" (Penelope Milford, Gordon Halliday, Family); "It's a Boy" (John Cullum)
Act Two: "Freedom" (Donna Theodore, Chip Ford); "Violets and Silverbells" (reprise) (Joel Higgins, Donna Theodore); "Papa's Gonna Make It Alright" (John Cullum); "The Only Home I Know" (Gary Harger, Soldiers); "Papa's Gonna Make It Alright" (reprise) (Penelope Milford); "Meditation II" (John Cullum); "Pass the Cross to Me" (reprise) (Congregation)

Most of the critics noted that *Shenandoah* was in the Rodgers and Hammerstein tradition, and despite the musical's defects it offered a straightforward linear story, foursquare characters, and a pleasant if not particularly memorable score. For audiences turned off by rock musicals, *Shenandoah* was just the ticket, and it played for 1,050 performances, enjoyed a long tour, and managed to turn a profit. It was nominated for six Tony Awards, and John Cullum's stalwart performance won him the Tony for Best Leading Actor in a Musical and the librettists won for Best Book.

Based on the 1965 film of the same name that starred James Stewart, the musical was coscripted by James Lee Barrett, who had written the screenplay. The story centered on widower Charlie Anderson (Cullum), who lives in Virginia's Shenandoah Valley and runs his farm with the help of his sons, five of whom are adults and one still a little boy. The country is enmeshed in the Civil War, but Charlie, with his pacifist if not isolationist beliefs, wants no part of it. Nevertheless, the war soon comes to Charlie and his family: his boy Robert (Joseph Shapiro) is kidnapped by Union soldiers, his son James (Joel Higgins) and James's wife Anne (Donna Theodore) are killed by marauders, and Nathan (Jordan Suffin) is killed by a Yankee sniper. In retaliation for the latter, Charlie kills the sniper, shooting him over and over again.

The musical was clearly on the era's antiwar bandwagon, but the final scenes seemed to turn the show's message upside down: Charlie says that only undertakers win wars, but then spouts some cracker-barrel wisdom about how some dreams are worth dying for, and if some men have to die, then others have to do the killing. Or something like that. It was rather confusing, as if the musical's antiwar message also acknowledged that war and killing are sometimes necessary.

The somewhat episodic plot moved along rather briskly, and if the production values were minimal and the dances very occasional, the score was pleasant if sometimes bombastic. The songs included a soldiers' chorus ("Raise the Flag of Dixie"), a lullaby ("Papa's Gonna Make It Alright"), a hymn ("Pass the Cross to Me"), and a dainty wedding ballad ("Violets and Silverbells"). And while its country-and-western flavor may have been slightly pronounced, "We Make a Beautiful Pair" was one of the score's most ingratiating moments. The musical threw in a nod to racial equality ("Freedom"), but the number was a bit obvious, as were Charlie's heartfelt if somewhat overwrought "I've Heard It All Before" and his two "Meditation" sequences. The evening's crowd-pleaser was the brothers' roughhouse song-and-dance "Next to Lovin' (I Like Fightin')"; one or two critics said it could have been part of the score for the 1954 film *Seven Brides for Seven Brothers*, but everyone liked it and the number eventually found its way into the repertoire of Lee Theodore's ***The American Dance Machine*** (and was included on the video cassette collection *The American Dance Machine: A Celebration of Broadway Dance* released by CBS Video # CV-400056).

The book offered some lump-in-the-throat moments, and the most effective one took place in the final scene at a church service. Robert had been kidnapped by the Yankees, and Charlie and the family presume he's dead. But as the service is in progress, Robert enters the church, hobbling and a bit shaky, but all in one piece. As he sees Charlie, the boy speaks the musical's final line of dialogue: "I'm home, sir." Believe me, there wasn't a dry eye in the house. (The national tour ended with the church service but the character of Robert never made an appearance, and those who'd seen the musical on Broadway were astounded that such a sure-fire emotional ending had been scuttled.)

Douglas Watt in the *New York Daily News* said the "dumb" story had a leading character who refuses to take sides in the war but "winds up making a mess of things, anyway" and despite being an "enlightened pacifist" he turns into a "sort of desperado" who is "dangerously demented." He also noted that the first act was "static" and the score "insipid." Jack Kroll in *Newsweek* admired what the musical tried to do, but suggested that "emotional and moral simplicities" were "the hardest of tasks on stage" and thus *Shenandoah* "just misses" the "intellectual toughness" required to tell its story.

Clive Barnes in the *New York Times* found the evening "very likable" and said the musical's "aspirations are brave" and would most please those who prefer musicals both "a little serious and a trifle old-fashioned." John Beaufort in the *Christian Science Monitor* found the score bland and the choreography "derivative" but nonetheless felt audiences would find the "wholesome and attractive sampler thoroughly enjoyable." And Leonard Probst on NBC Radio praised the "first-rate" musical and said he hoped it would enjoy a long run (he found the acting and dancing "good," the music "spirited," and the lyrics "weak").

T. E. Kalem in *Time* said Cullum held together the "rambling" show with his "strong stage presence" and "robust" baritone, but felt his "general manner" was a "trifle too Broadway-slick" for the widower farmer. Martin Gottfried in the *New York Post* noted the musical's "homespun wisdom and sentimental Americana should be sold at Disneyland souvenir shops." As for Cullum, he played the role of the "sexless stud" who is "altogether manly but somehow uninterested in women" and is "so liberal" he calls all the young men "boy" except for the character of the young black slave. But Gottfried praised Cullum's voice as "one of the most beautiful in the theatre."

The script was published in paperback by Samuel French in 1975 (the script includes stanzas from "Raise the Flag of Dixie" with the notation that they "have been removed from the original Broadway production" and that the copyright owners recommend the stanzas "also be cut from regional productions"). The cast album was released by RCA Victor Records (LP # ARL11019), which later issued the CD (# 3763).

The musical was revived on Broadway with John Cullum on August 8, 1989, at the Virginia Theatre for thirty-one performances.

Awards

Tony Awards and Nominations: Best Musical (*Shenandoah*); Best Leading Actor in a Musical (**John Cullum**); Best Featured Actress in a Musical (Donna Theodore); Best Book (**James Lee Barrett, Peter Udell**, and **Philip Rose**); Best Score (lyrics by Peter Udell, music by Gary Geld); Best Choreographer (Robert Tucker)

MAN ON THE MOON

"A New Musical"

Theatre: Little Theatre
Opening Date: January 29, 1975; *Closing Date*: February 1, 1975
Performances: 5
Book, Lyrics, and *Music*: John Phillips
Direction: Paul Morrissey; *Producers*: Andy Warhol in association with Richard Turley; *Choreography*: Joy Javits, Assistant to Paul Morrissey for Musical Numbers; *Scenery*: John J. Moore; *Costumes*: Marsia Trinder (Michael Yeargan, Costume Design Supervision); *Lighting*: Jules Fisher; *Musical Direction*: Karen Gustafson
Cast: Harlan S. Foss (Dr. Bomb), Eric Lang (Ernie Hardy), Mark Lawhead (Leroy), *Dennis Doherty* (President, King Can), Genevieve Waite (Angel), Monique Van Vooren (Venus); Celestial Choir: Brenda Bergman (Mercury, Miss America), John Patrick Sundine (Mars), Jennifer Elder (Neptune), E. Lynn Nickerson (Pluto), Jeanette Chastonay (Saturn)
The musical was presented in one act.
The action takes place in the future on Earth, Moon, and Canis Minor.

Musical Numbers

Prologue (Harlan S. Foss); "Boys from the South" (Eric Lang); "Midnight Deadline Blastoff" (Eric Lang); "Mission Control" (Harlan S. Foss, Eric Lang, Mark Lawhead, Dennis Doherty, Brenda Bergman); "Speed of Light"(Eric Lang, Mark Lawhead); "Though I'm a Little Angel" (Genevieve Waite); "Girls" (Dennis Doherty, Monique Van Vooren, Genevieve Waite); "Canis Minor Bolero Waltz" (Genevieve Waite); "Starburst" (Genevieve Waite); "Penthouse of Your Mind" (Dennis Doherty); "Champagne and Kisses" (Monique Van Vooren); "Star-Stepping Stranger"/"Convent" (Eric Lang, Genevieve Waite); "My Name Is Can" (Dennis Doherty); "American Man on the Moon" (Genevieve Waite); "Welcome to the Moon" (Company); "Sunny, Sunny Moon" (Monique Van Vooren, Harlan S. Foss); "Love Is Coming Back" (Genevieve Waite, Eric Lang); "Truth Cannot Be Treason" (Mark Lawhead); "Place in Space" (Eric Lang, Genevieve Waite); "Family of Man" (Harlan S. Foss); "Yesterday I Left the Earth" (Company); "Stepping to the Stars" (Company)

Man on the Moon dealt with evil scientist Dr. Bomb (Harlan S. Foss), who plans to blow up the moon, and along for the ride is a dwarf named Leroy (Mark Lawhead), part man and part big red box, who is a human bomb. *Man on the Moon* clearly tempted theatrical fate by bringing up the subject of bombs, and fate couldn't resist the temptation. As a result, the musical bombed after five performances. "Bring back ***Via Galactica***!" demanded Clive Barnes in the *New York Times*, and Douglas Watt in the *New York Daily News* said the "low-budget ***Via Galactica***" contained such precious lines of dialogue as "I have created the biggest bomb of my career" and "I had the most awful dream last night—I dreamed I laid an egg."

Dr. Bomb is the head of the U.S. space program, and he once sent his brother, King Can (Dennis Doherty), and sister-in-law, Venus (Monique Van Vooren), to Canis Minor, where they and their daughter, Angel (Genevieve Waite), now run a hotel without customers. The doctor's ambition is to send a rocket to the moon, bomb the orb, and thus keep Canis Minor in eternal darkness. But instead of landing on the moon, the rocket and its astronaut Ernie (Eric Lang) somehow end up on Canis Minor where he and Angel immediately fall in love. In the meantime, there's that dwarf robot and walking time bomb Leroy to worry about. (After trying to explain the plot, Martin Gottfried in the *New York Post* wrote, "I'd rather not go on with this.")

Originally titled *S-P-A-C-E*, the musical was written by John Phillips, the songwriter and one of the members of the singing group the Mamas and the Papas, and one of the musical's stars was his wife, Genevieve Waite. During previews, Phillips played the roles of King Can and the U.S. President, and Dennis Doherty, the lead singer of the Mamas and the Papas, was Dr. Bomb. When Phillips dropped out of the performing side of the show, Doherty assumed his roles and Dr. Bomb was performed by Harlan S. Foss.

Gottfried said Van Vooren was "made to look and behave in the grotesque style peculiar to the worst kind of camp," Genevieve Waite's "squeaky voice" was "cute at first and then less cute. And less cute," and Eric Lang "muscles around like a male hustler." Keitha McLean in *Women's Wear Daily* said Lang looked "like a reject from a Marlboro ad" and played his role "with all the voice and vigor of a palace eunuch," and Barnes said he sang "with a strong microphone." McLean mentioned that Waite warbled "slightly off-key" and tripped around the stage "with a vapid inanity surpassed only by her lack of voice and stage presence." Watt reported that the performers "often appeared to be mouthing their lyrics to recordings."

Andy Warhol produced the musical, and one or two critics noted that the minutes preceding the first act curtain (which was delayed by a half-hour) provided the best entertainment of the evening because the opening night audience included Warhol and all the beautiful "in" people (Barnes wistfully noted that he wished he'd brought his camera). Kevin Sanders on WABCTV7 said the audience was replete with "the renowned and obscure," including Pat Ast, Peggy Cass, Kurt Vonnegut Jr., and Peter Boyle, and thus "the throng of the beautiful, the bizarre, and the glamorous" was a haven for autograph hunters (others in the audience were Warren Beatty, Geraldo Rivera, Rex Harrison, Yoko Ono, Jules Feiffer, and Diana Vreeland).

Phillips's score didn't overwhelm the critics, but they found it pleasant. McLean said many of the songs were "fresh, interesting and full of good rock potential" and for her the "standouts" were "Penthouse of Your Mind," "Yesterday I Left the Earth," "Love Is Coming Back," and "Star-Stepping Stranger." McLean suggested that Phillips should put together an album of the score's songs. He never did, but thirty-four years later a CD of the score was released by Varese Sarabande Records (CD # 302-066-965-2), which included twenty-two studio recordings by Phillips; six songs recorded live from the Broadway production; six recordings by Waite; two studio recording out-takes; and three video sequences of rehearsal footage from the production (not all the numbers on the CD were used in the final Broadway version). A year before the musical was produced on Broadway, Genevieve Waite's solo album *Romance Is on the Rise* (Paramour Records LP # PR5088SD; issued on CD by Chrome Records # CDCD-5006) included three songs later heard in the show ("Girls," "American Man on the Moon," and "Love Is Coming Back").

The Mamas and the Papas were the subject of *Dream a Little Dream*, an Off-Broadway tribute revue that opened at the Village Theatre on April 23, 2003, for approximately 119 performances.

DANCE WITH ME

"A Comedy with Music"

Theatre: Mayfair Theatre
Opening Date: January 23, 1975; *Closing Date*: January 4, 1976
Performances: 396
Play: Greg Antonacci
Lyrics and *Music*: The score consisted of popular rock-and-roll songs.
Direction and *Choreography*: Joel Zwick; *Producers*: Ted Ravinett and Steve Rubenstein; *Scenery* and *Lighting*: Scott Johnson; *Costumes*: Susan Hum Buck
Cast: Anne Abbott (Tommie Sincere), Greg Antonacci (Honey Boy), John Bottoms (Jimmy Dick II), Peter Frumkin (Thumbs Bumpin), Patricia Gaul (Judy Jeanine), Scott Robert Redman (Wendell Crunchall), Deborah Rush (Goldie Pot), Stuart Silver (Smitner Tuskey), Skip Zipf (Don Tomm), Joel Zwick (Bulldog Allen)
The play with music was presented in two acts.
The action takes place during the present in a subway station and in the memories of Honey Boy.

Musical Numbers

The program didn't list musical numbers. The following alphabetical list is taken from songs mentioned in various reviews of the production: "Chantilly Lace" (lyric and music by Jerry Foster, Bill Rice, and Jiles Perry Richardson); "He's So Fine" (lyric and music by Ronald Mack); "In the Still of the Night" (lyric and music by Fred Parris); "Let's Go to the Hop" (aka "At the Hop") (lyric and music by Artie Singer, John Medora, and David White); "(This) Little Girl of Mine" (lyric and music by Ray Charles); "The Loco-Motion" (lyric and music by Gerry Goffin and Carole King); and "Will You Still Love Me Tomorrow?" (lyric and music by Gerry Goffin and Carole King)

As *Dance wi' Me*, Greg Antonacci's play *Dance with Me* had first been produced at La Mama Experimental Theatre Club (ETC), and from there was mounted at the Anspacher Theatre at the Public on June 10, 1971, for fifty-three performances. Antonacci and director, choreographer, and cast member Joel Zwick had appeared in this production, as they did in the current one (which had been presented in New Orleans prior to the Broadway opening).

The action takes place in a subway station where stock boy Honey Boy (Antonacci) is late on his way to somewhere; both his personal and professional lives are falling apart, and as he waits for his train, he discovers that subways are for daydreaming as a rush of memories envelop him and he reenacts his high school days of the 1950s with its dating rituals, record hops, and basketball games. Although the locale of the subway station remained throughout the evening, the subway commuters morphed into the people from Honey Boy's past. The play utilized rock-and-roll songs of the 1950s to enhance the mood of the era, and Zwick staged an occasional dance sequence.

Martin Gottfried in the *New York Post* liked the play's use of theatrical devices to tell the story: actors froze in place when necessary, at other times performed in slow motion, and they quickly transitioned from dialogue to song because the directorial effects utilized quick dissolves to depict the changes from the real to the surreal. But the main problem with the semi-autobiographical evening was that Honey Boy just wasn't all that interesting a character and the story never quite held together.

The headline of Douglas Watt's notice in the *New York Daily News* proclaimed that the musical won the booby prize; he found it "disreputable" and "defenseless" and after showings at La Mama and the Public, he predicted the Mayfair Theatre would be the "last stop" for the show (but the show attracted audiences, and managed to play for a year). Barbara Ettorre in *Women's Wear Daily* noted that the play might superficially remind one of ***Grease***, but the script had more on its mind with its "charmingly befuddled and confused" Honey Boy who looks upon the 1950s as a safe haven from the present-day world. She also noted that "the shifts and changes in action are crisp and wholly diverting." But Leonard Probst on NBC Radio suggested there would be "few takers" for the "derivative, dumb, dull" evening, and while Honey Boy dreamed of the 1950s, the critic said he dreamed he "was someplace else than at this play."

Clive Barnes in the *New York Times* had enjoyed the show in an earlier production, but now found it "out of all recognition to the original." Everything was "overblown" and the previous charm had "evaporated." He said 1975 didn't seem to be "the time" for the show, and the Mayfair Theatre wasn't "the place."

As for "the place," the Mayfair Theatre was a traditional Off-Broadway theatre that for the current production was considered a Broadway house. The musical was reviewed as a Broadway production by the critics and was eligible for Tony Award consideration (and was in fact nominated for three). Gottfried noted the show opened "on Broadway" but "none too easily" because the Mayfair was an "Off-Broadway kind of house," Kevin Sanders on WABCTV7 mentioned that the Mayfair was "more or less on Broadway," and Watt noted the venue was "buried in a midtown basement."

Perhaps the most striking aspect of the production was Scott Johnson's realistic subway setting (which garnered him a Tony nomination). Gottfried found it "fabulous," with perspectives that gave the illusion of "an astonishingly realistic subway station," and Ettorre said it was "perfectly delightful." Barnes noted it was "well and carefully designed," and Watts said the "remarkable" design overpowered the show and the theatre with its "strikingly realistic representation" of the 34th Street subway station, right down to its columns, tiled walls, platform, and tracks, which disappeared into the distance on either side of the stage.

Awards

Tony Award Nominations: Best Featured Actor in a Musical (John Bottoms); Best Scenic Designer (Scott Johnson); Best Choreographer (Joel Zwick)

THE NIGHT THAT MADE AMERICA FAMOUS

Theatre: Ethel Barrymore Theatre
Opening Date: February 26, 1975; *Closing Date*: April 6, 1975
Performances: 47
Lyrics and *Music*: Harry Chapin
Direction: Gene Frankel; *Producers*: Edgar Lansbury and Joseph Beruh in association with The Shubert Organization (Nan Pearlman, Associate Producer); *Choreography*: Doug Rogers; *Scenery*: Kert Lundell; *Multi-Media Design*: Imero Fiorentino Associates (Multi-Media Development Consultants), Jim Sant'Andrea (Multi-Media Execution), and Multi-Media under the direction of Joshua White; *Costumes*: Randy Barcelo; *Lighting*: Imero Fiorentino (lighting supervised by Fred Allison); *Musical Direction*: Stephen Chapin
Cast: *Harry Chapin*, Kelly Garrett, Delores Hall, Gilbert Price, Bill Starr, Alexander Borrie, Mercedes Ellington, Sid Marshall, Ernie Pysher, Lynne Thigpen
The revue was presented in two acts.
The action takes place "during the last fifteen years."

Musical Numbers

Act One: 1960's: Prologue (Company); "Six-String Orchestra" (Harry Chapin, Company); "Give Me a Road" (Company); "Sunday Morning Sunshine" (Harry Chapin, Company); "It's My Day" (Kelly Garrett); "Give Me a Cause" (Company); "Welfare Rag" (Delores Hall, Bill Starr, Gilbert Price, Company); "Better Place to Be" (Harry Chapin, Company); "Give Me a Wall" (Company); "Peace Teachers" (Kelly Garrett); "Pigeon Run" (Gilbert Price); "Changing of the Guard" (Gilbert Price); "When I Look Up" (Delores Hall); "Sniper" (Harry Chapin, Company)

Act Two: 1970's: "Great Divide" (Harry Chapin); "Taxi" (Harry Chapin, Kelly Garrett); "Cockeyed John" (Company); "Mr. Tanner" (Harry Chapin, Gilbert Price); "Maxie" (Kelly Garrett); Fugue: "Love Can't" (Bill Starr), "When Maudy Wants a Man" (Delores Hall), and "It's a Wonderfully Wicked Woman" (Kelly Garrett); "Battleground Bummer" (Gilbert Price); "Stoopid" (Gilbert Price); "Cat's in the Cradle" (Harry Chapin, Company); "Cockeyed John, Give Me My Dream" (Company); "Too Much World" (Kelly Garrett, Delores Hall, Bill Starr, Gilbert Price, Harry Chapin, Company); "As I Grow Older" (Kelly Garrett); "Beginning of the End" (Company); Epilogue: "The Night That Made America Famous" (Harry Chapin, Company)

Singer and songwriter Harry Chapin, who specialized in story songs and protest numbers, starred in *The Night That Made America Famous*, an evening of his material that included his hits "Taxi" and "Cat's in the Cradle." He was backed by a group of singers, among them Gilbert Price, Delores Hall, and Kelly Garrett, and the production utilized various multimedia effects, some of which were quickly becoming somewhat old-hat, including the use of technicians who carried handheld television cameras that transmitted live images of the performers via closed-circuit TV to a huge circular screen (the Off-Broadway revival of *Rise and Fall of the City of Mahagonny* had experimented with this concept five years earlier).

Clive Barnes in the *New York Times* noted that Chapin was less a protest singer than one of "ironic dissatisfaction," and his subjects included the generation gap, women's liberation, welfare, and the Vietnam War. Barnes found his work "platitudinous" and the production pretentious, and noted the singer had once been called "the Jacques Brel of Brooklyn Heights." Douglas Watt in the *New York Daily News* said "Jacques Brel he ain't," and the critic stated the material was "pretty flat."

Edwin Wilson in the *Wall Street Journal* said "monotony" set in because of the "constant hammering" away of the protest songs, and John Beaufort in the *Christian Science Monitor* also mentioned that "monotony" prevailed because of the "banality" of the "sentimental" lyrics, the "heavy irony," and the "earnest propaganda." James Spina in *Women's Wear Daily* said Chapin had taken his "cringing-couplets" and "shucked the mess to Broadway." And so he gave Harry some advice: "Jump into your proverbial 'Taxi' and go home. Your family needs you. Broadway doesn't."

But Martin Gottfried in *Women's Wear Daily* rather enjoyed the evening. Despite Chapin's "limited" voice and "unexceptional presence" he nonetheless had a "contagious amiability which survives the ardor of his liberalism." Although the evening was more in the nature of a concert than a Broadway show, it was "magnificently performed," "handsomely staged," and was "as musical a musical as you're going to see."

Incidentally, Barnes explained that the title derived from Chapin's belief that Americans have the wrong American dream, and when they realize this mistake it will be "The Night That Made America Famous."

Chapin died in an automobile accident a few months before his song cycle *Cotton Patch Gospel* opened Off Broadway at the Lamb's Theatre on October 21, 1981, for 193 performances (the work had previously played in Boston as *Somethin's Brewin' in Gainesville*). It was revived Off Off Broadway on November 14, 1997, by the Melting Pot Theatre Company for twenty-six performances. The tribute revue *Chapin* played in Chicago in 1977, and in 1985 another retrospective revue *Lies & Legends: The Musical Stories of Harry Chapin* opened at the Village Gate on April 24, 1985, for seventy-nine performances. The 1981 cast album of *Cotton Patch Gospel* was released by Chapin Productions Records (LP # CP-101), and a Chicago production of *Lies & Legends* was released on a two-LP cast album by Titanic Productions Records (# T-0184).

Awards

Tony Award Nominations: Best Featured Actor in a Musical (Gilbert Price); Best Featured Actress in a Musical (Kelly Garrett)

GOODTIME CHARLEY

"A New Musical"

Theatre: Palace Theatre
Opening Date: March 3, 1975; *Closing Date*: May 31, 1975
Performances: 104

Book: Sidney Michaels
Lyrics: Hal Hackady
Music: Larry Grossman; incidental music by Arthur B. Rubinstein; dance music by Danny Troob
Direction: Peter H. Hunt; *Producers*: Max Brown and Byron Goldman in association with Robert Victor and Stone Widney; *Choreography*: Onna White; *Scenery*: Rouben Ter-Arutunian; *Costumes*: Willa Kim; *Lighting*: (Abe) Feder; *Musical Direction*: Arthur B. Rubinstein
Cast: Brad Tyrrell (Henry V, Second Soldier), Hal Norman (Charles VI, Second English Captain, Herald, Third Soldier), Grace Keagy (Isabella of Bavaria), Rhoda Butler (Queen Kate), Charles Rule (Phillip of Burgundy, First English Captain, Chef, Guard), Peggy Cooper (Yolande), Nancy Killmer (Marie), Ed Becker (Pope), *Joel Grey* (Charley), Jay Garner (Archbishop Regnault de Chartres), Louis Zorich (General George de la Tremouille), George Ramos (Servant), Ross Miles (Servant), Pat (Patrick) Swayze (Servant), Cam Lorendo (Servant), Susan Browning (Agnes Sorel), Andy Hostettler (Jester), Gordon Weiss (Jester), Ann Reinking (Joan of Arc), Richard B. Shull (Minguet), Kenneth Bridges (Third English Captain, First Soldier); Citizen Trio, Soldier Trio, Peasant Trio, and Hostile Trio: Kenneth Bridges, Brad Tyrrell, and Ed Becker; Dan Joel (Louis), Kathe Dezina (Estelle); Singers: Rhoda Butler, Peggy Cooper, Kathe Dezina, Nancy Killmer, Jane Ann Sargia, Ed Becker, Kenneth Bridges, Hal Norman, Charles Rule, Brad Tyrrell; Dancers: Andy Hostettler, Cam Lorendo, Dan Joel, Glen McClaskey, Ross Miles, Tod Miller, Sal Pernice, George Ramos, Pat Swayze, Gordon Weiss, Jerry Yoder, Julie Pars, Kathleen Robey
The musical was presented in two acts.
The action takes place in France during the years 1429, 1431, and 1461.

Musical Numbers

Act One: "History" (Brad Tyrrell, Hal Norman, Grace Keagy, Rhoda Butler, Charles Rule, Peggy Cooper, Nancy Killmer, Ed Becker, Ensemble); "Goodtime Charley" (Joel Grey, Ensemble); "Visions and Voices" (Ann Reinking); "Merlin the Magician" (Courtiers); "Bits and Pieces" (Joel Grey, Ann Reinking); "To Make the Boy a Man" (Ann Reinking); "Why Can't We All Be Nice?" (Joel Grey, Susan Browning); "Born Lover" (Joel Grey); "I Am Going to Love (the Man You're Going to Be)" (Ann Reinking); "Castles of the Loire" (dance) (music by Arthur B. Rubinstein) (Ann Reinking, Soldiers); "Coronation" (Joel Grey, Ann Reinking, Ensemble)
Act Two: "You Still Have a Long Way to Go" (Ann Reinking, Joel Grey); "Merci, bon Dieu" (Richard B. Shull, Susan Browning); "Confessional" (Louis Zorich, Jay Garner); "One Little Year" (Ann Reinking); "I Leave the World" (Joel Grey)

Goodtime Charley was probably the most schizoid musical of the decade. The title of Sidney Michael's book logically led one to assume the story focused on first-billed Joel Grey as Charley, the Dauphin and eventual King Charles VII of France. But Joan of Arc was the show's second major character, and since history remembers her more than the Dauphin, it seemed possible the musical might really be about her. The evening of course dealt with both of them, and centered on Joan's vision to save France from England and to ensure that Charley ascends the throne. But the musical was always off-kilter because the story wavered between the musical comedy world of Charley and the musical play where Joan lived. Her three solos were from the school of serious musical drama ("To Make the Boy a Man," "I Am Going to Love the Man You're Going to Be," and "One Little Year"), while his were old-fashioned Broadway whoop-dee-do (the title song, and, especially, "Born Lover," which would have been a natural for Eddie Cantor). Only in the musical's epilogue, which took place three decades later, did the older and dying Charley have a serious and introspective moment ("I Leave the World").

Larry Grossman and Hal Hackady's unappreciated songs underscored the duality inherent in the book. As noted, Joan's songs were generally serious and Charley's mostly old-time Broadway; and numbers by the minor characters were tongue-in-cheek, including the ironic "Merci, Bon Dieu" and "Confessional," and the brilliant opening "History," which summed up the plot's backstory.

"History" took place against the musical's spectacular permanent set, which was designed by Rouben Ter-Arutunian. It depicted a huge white semicircular colonnade with a cascade of marble-like steps topped off by eight towering columns. Scattered about the colonnade and between the columns are ten statues representing among others King Charles VI of France, King Henry V of England, Queen Isabella of Bavaria, Pope Eugene, Queen Yolande of Sicily, Marie of France, and Phillip of Burgundy. Like the figures of Seurat's painting in *Sunday in the Park with George* (1984), the statues come to life and complain about their lot (Charles has had a cramp in his foot since 1421, he and Henry lament that "we're not even good art," and they wryly note that their signatures will eventually fade and become unreadable). With their squabbling and their smug notion that they'll make "damn sure history repeats," the living statues provide the background leading up to the musical's first scene, in which the terrified Charley wakes up. It turns out "History" is the depiction of his nightmare, and, worst of all, upon his awakening the nightmare doesn't go away because it's all true.

For the lyrical pyrotechnics of "Visions and Voices," Joan was serious but could laugh at herself, and Joan and Charley's "Bits and Pieces" was a charming duet in which he discussed the details of a suit of armor, including the most important piece of all, the jock strap.

The work was a serious musical trying to be a musical comedy, and, conversely, a musical comedy trying to be a musical play, and despite the wonderful score (which is more effective as a recording than it was in the theatre), the show never quite worked and could muster only three months on Broadway. It's a failed musical that no one seems to talk about anymore, and it never attained the status of a cult show. But it was fascinating to watch and to observe how the two-shows-in-one never quite merged into a unified whole, and the cast recording is a memorable souvenir of a score that is all over the place in style and tone but nonetheless is melodic and listenable.

Douglas Watt in the *New York Daily News* said the "bloodless" musical had a "dreadful air of solemnity and lifelessness," and while the music was "often provocative," the lyrics were "of considerably less interest." But Martin Gottfried in the *New York Post* praised the "superb" lyrics which developed character and were "technically ingenious." However, he found the music "strictly in the Broadway vernacular under the subdivision labeled Frederick Loewe-Burton Lane." The evening was "gloriously good looking" and the "gorgeous" décor underwent "spectacular" changes, including the sudden appearances of a "tremendous" autumn tree as well as "giant" stained glass windows. But unfortunately there was a "basic confusion" about which story to focus on.

T. E. Kalem in *Time* complained that "cutesie Broadway vulgarity" had met the "bones of history"; further, Grey played Charley as less a womanizer than a tot who'd "be happier in a sandbox than a boudoir" and he never became "quite the man that [Joan] is." But he praised the "majestic" décor and said Reinking danced "across the stage like a thoroughbred in the stretch."

Edwin Wilson in the *Wall Street Journal* proclaimed the musical as "one of the most elegant and elaborate shows of the season" and noted that when the autumnal tree descended from above it was one of the "largest" and "loveliest" ever designed for the theatre, and its red leaves and huge roots dominated the stage. John Beaufort in the *Christian Science Monitor* praised the "spectacular" Maxfield Parrish–like décor, but cautioned that the musical itself sounded like an Al Capp comic strip. The "odd' evening was "more galling than Gallic," and despite the "pleasant" score, the musical belittled a "tremendous historic drama."

Clive Barnes in the *New York Times* felt the book's tone was "uncertain" and said we never found out if the story was about Charley or Joan; the music was "agreeably lyrical without being memorably tuneful" and the lyrics "efficient but unsurprising" (he singled out Joan and Charley's argument-duet "You Still Have a Long Way to Go" in which each one accuses the other of not being saintly or regal). And like the other reviewers he was impressed with Ter-Arutunian's "most stylish" décor and Willa Kim's "elegant" costumes.

During the tryout, choreographer Dennis Nahat was succeeded by Onna White, and the following songs were cut: "Charge," "All She Can Do Is Say No," "I Thank You," "There Goes the Country," and "Tomorrow's Good Old Days."

The script was published in paperback by Samuel French in 1985, and includes a verse from "Why Can't We All Be Nice?" which wasn't performed in the Broadway production. The cast album was released by RCA Victor (LP # ARL1-1011; later issued on CD # 09026-68935-2).

Joan of Arc (but not Charley) has been the subject of a number of lyric works, including the Off-Broadway musicals *The Survival of St. Joan* (1971) and Al Carmines's *Joan* (1972), and Norman Dello Joio's opera *The Triumph of St. Joan*, produced by the New York City Opera Company in 1959 (the work had first premiered at Sarah Lawrence College in 1950 and then in a revised version was seen on NBC in 1956 as *The Trial at Rouen*).

Awards

Tony Award Nominations: Best Leading Actor in a Musical (Joel Grey); Best Leading Actress in a Musical (Ann Reinking); Best Featured Actor in a Musical (Richard B. Shull); Best Featured Actress in a Musical (Susan Browning); Best Scenic Designer (Rouben Ter-Arutunian); Best Costume Designer (Willa Kim); Best Lighting (Abe Feder)

THE LIEUTENANT

"A New Rock Opera"

Theatre: Lyceum Theatre
Opening Date: March 9, 1975; *Closing Date*: March 16, 1975
Performances: 9
Book, *Lyrics*, and *Music*: Gene Curty, Nitra Scharfman, and Chuck Strand
Direction: William Martin; *Producers*: Joseph S. Kutrzeba and Spofford J. Beadle; *Choreography*: Dennis Dennehy; *Scenery* and *Costumes*: Frank J. Boros; *Lighting*: Ian Calderon; *Musical Direction*: Chuck Strand
Cast: Eddie Mekka (Lieutenant), Gene Curty (Judge, OCS Sergeant), Joel Powers (Recruiting Sergeant, Senator), Chet D'Elia (First General), Eugene Moose (Second General), Danny Taylor (Third General), Don McGrath (Chaplain, First Congressman), Walt Hunter (Captain); "C" Company: Jim Litten (Sergeant), Steven Boockvor, Clark James, Jim-Patrick McMahon, Joseph Pugliese, Burt Rodriguez, and Tom Tofel; Tom Tofel (G.I., Second Reporter), Jim Litten (Clergyman, First Reporter), Burt Rodriguez (Second Congressman, Prosecutor), Jo Speros (Third Reporter), Gordon Grody (Defense Attorney), Alan K. Siegel (New Recruit)
The musical was presented in two acts.
The action takes place in Vietnam and the United States over a three-year period.

Musical Numbers

Act One: "The Indictment" (Eddie Mekka, Gene Curty); "Join the Army" (Eddie Mekka, Joel Powers, Recruits); "Look for the Men with Potential" (Chet D'Elia, Eugene Moose, Danny Taylor); "Kill" (Gene Curty); "I Don't Want to Go Over to Vietnam" (Eddie Mekka, "C" Company); "Eulogy" (Don McGrath); "At 0700 Tomorrow" (Walt Hunter, "C" Company); "Massacre" (Walt Hunter, Eddie Mekka, "C" Company, Vietnamese); "Something's Gone Wrong" (Walt Hunter, Eddie Mekka); "Twenty-Eight" (Chet D'Elia, Eugene Moose, Danny Taylor, Walt Hunter, Eddie Mekka); "Let's Believe in the Captain" (Chet D'Elia, Eugene Moose, Danny Taylor); "Final Report" (Chet D'Elia); "I Will Make Things Happen" (Tom Tofel)
Act Two: "He Wants to Put the Army in Jail" (Joel Powers, Don McGrath, Jim Litten, Burt Rodriguez); "There's No Other Solution" (Chet D'Elia, Eugene Moose, Danny Taylor); "I'm Going Home" (Eddie Mekka, "C" Company); "We've Chosen You, Lieutenant" (Chet D'Elia, Eugene Moose, Danny Taylor); "The Star of This War" (Jim Litten, Tom Tofel, Jo Speros, Eddie Mekka); "(Here I Am) On Trial for My Life" (Eddie Mekka); "The Conscience of a Nation" (Burt Rodriguez); "Damned No Matter How He Turned" (Gordon Grody); "On Trial for My Life" (reprise) (Eddie Mekka); "The Verdict" (Gene Curty, Jurors); Finale (Alan K. Siegel, Joel Powers, Company)

The Lieutenant was a short-running, self-described rock musical based on the My Lai massacre, which occurred on March 16, 1968. The virtually sung-through musical centered on the events leading up to the incident, the massacre itself, and then the aftermath, including the court martial of the Army lieutenant who was part of the company involved in the episode and who, according to Douglas Watt in the *New York Daily News*, is depicted as a victim of the Vietnam war machine. Watt noted the musical was thematically related to ***Johnny Johnson***, but the score lacked distinction and despite the production's "right tone" the evening had "no real substance." But he said Eddie Mekka was "excellent" in the title role, and the dance sequence accompanying "I'm Going Home" was "one of the most exultant" he'd seen on Broadway for a long time.

Barbara Ettorre in *Women's Wear Daily* also found Mekka "excellent," and she praised the "exhilarating" and "smashing" choreography created by Dennis Dennehy. But rock music didn't suit the material (the genre was "dead, dead, dead"). She asked that "somebody please make the boredom go away" because the rock musical was "time-worn and about five years behind the pace . . . we need a new form for the mid-70s." Kevin Sanders on WABCTV7 said Mekka was "raw but vital" and the rock score itself was "one of the most dynamic and soaring since *Jesus Christ Superstar*." He also made the interesting but unelaborated comment that the show was not so much "anti-war" as it was "anti-military."

Clive Barnes in the *New York Times* liked the "passion and vitality" of the musical, and said its viewpoint was that "American militarism" was the "real villain." He noted that Dennehy's choreography used the motif of Army calisthenics, but he felt the dances relied too much "on the relentless show-biz pressure of a TV dance routine or an industrial show."

Martin Gottfried in *Women's Wear Daily* said the musical was as much a "disaster" as the Vietnam War itself. It was written "on a summer camp level without the vaguest notion of professional standards," the music was "embarrassingly derivative" of ***Tommy***, and "the lyrics are what the score deserves." As for the choreography, it seemed Dennehy "was apparently under the impression that he was auditioning for industrial shows."

The musical had first been presented Off Off Broadway at the Queens Playhouse on September 18, 1974; the showcase was presented for one week, and Eddie Mekka played the title role.

A private two-LP recording (unnumbered and by an unnamed company) seems to have been recorded at the time of the Off-Off-Broadway production. Between the numbers "At 0700 Tomorrow" and "Massacre," the album includes three musical sequences not heard on Broadway ("Quiet Village," "The Attack," and "The Orders"), and between "Damned No Matter How He Turned" and "The Verdict," there was another number not part of the Broadway production ("I Won't Beg"). As a bonus track, the album also offers a variant version of "The Star of This War."

There are opening night programs for the musical that are dated March 11, 1975, and so *The Lieutenant* reversed the usual trend of postponing opening night and instead moved it forward a notch (to March 9).

Awards

Tony Award Nominations: Best Musical (*The Lieutenant*); Best Leading Actor in a Musical (Eddie Mekka); Best Book (Gene Curty, Nitra Scharfman, and Chuck Strand); Best Score (Gene Curty, Nitra Scharfman, and Chuck Strand)

THE ROCKY HORROR SHOW

Theatre: Belasco Theatre
Opening Date: March 10, 1975; *Closing Date*: April 6, 1975
Performances: 32
Book, Lyrics, and Music: Richard O'Brien
Direction: Jim Sharman (Nina Faso, Assistant Director); *Producers*: Lou Adler (The Michael White Production) (John Beug, Associate Producer); *Choreography*: Not credited; *Scenery*: Brian Thomson (Peter Harvey, Set Supervisor); *Costumes*: Sue Blane (Pearl Somner, Costume Supervisor) (Costumes executed by Larry Lefler); *Lighting*: Chipmonck; *Musical Direction*: D'Vaughn Pershing
Cast: Jamie Donnelly (The Belasco Popcorn Girl [Trixie], Magenta); Abigale Haness (Janet), Bill Miller (Brad), William Newman (Narrator), Ritz (Richard) O'Brien (Riff-Raff), Boni Enten (Columbia), *Tim Curry* (Frank N. Furter), Kim Milford (Rocky), Meat Loaf (Eddie, Doctor Scott)
The musical was presented in one act.
The action takes place mostly in Frank N. Furter's castle.

Musical Numbers

"Science Fiction" (aka "Double Feature") (Jamie Donnelly); "Wedding Song" (aka "Damn It, Janet") (Bill Miller, Abigale Haness); "Over at the Frankenstein Place" (Bill Miller, Abigale Haness); "Sweet Transvestite" (Tim Curry); "Time Warp" (Jamie Donnelly, Boni Enten, Ritz O'Brien, William Newman); "The

Sword of Damocles" (Kim Milford); "Charles Atlas Song" (aka "Hot Patootie" and "Bless My Soul") (Tim Curry); "What Ever Happened to Saturday Night" (Meat Loaf); "Charles Atlas Song" (reprise) (Tim Curry); "Eddie's Teddy" (Meat Loaf, Boni Enten, Company); "Once in a While" (Bill Miller); "Planet Schmanet Janet" (aka "Wise Up, Janet Weiss") (Tim Curry); "It Was Great When It All Began" (aka "Rose Tint My World") (Company); "Super Heroes" (Company); "Science Fiction" (reprise) (Jamie Donnelly); "Sweet Transvestite" (reprise) (Company); "Time Warp" (reprise) (Company)

A gender-bending spoof of 1950s mores and science fiction movies, *The Rocky Horror Show* premiered in London at the Royal Court Theatre/Up Stairs on June 19, 1973, for a marathon run of 2,960 performances; Tim Curry was the lead, and the cast album was recorded by UK Records (LP # UKAL-1006); the CD was issued by First Night Records (# CD-17). Curry also starred in the U.S. premiere at the Roxy Theatre in Los Angeles on March 24, 1974; this production, which ran for nine months and spawned its own cast album on Ode Records (LP # SP-77026; and Rhino Records CD # 70090), led to the Broadway production with Curry, which bombed after four weeks.

Perhaps New York wasn't quite ready for an ironic blend of horror movie spoofs and transvestite musicals. *Little Shop of Horrors* (Off Broadway, 1982; Broadway, 2003) would come along later, but despite its success horror spoofs and even straight horror musicals (such as those of the vampire variety) never quite found their niche in musical theatre. On the other hand, it seemed that soon every theatre season featured at least one drag musical or drama, such as *La Cage Aux Folles* (1983, 2004, and 2010), *Pageant* (Off Broadway, 1991), *Kiss of the Spider Woman* (1993), *Whoop-Dee-Doo!* aka *Howard Crabtree's Whoop-Dee-Doo!* (Off Broadway, 1993), *Splendora* (Off Broadway, 1995), *When Pigs Fly* aka *Howard Crabtree's When Pigs Fly* (1996), *Hedwig and the Angry Inch* (Off Broadway, 1998; Broadway, 2014), *The Producers* (2001), *Hairspray* (2002), *I Am My Own Wife* (2003), *Priscilla Queen of the Desert* (2011), *Kinky Boots* (2013), and others. But the timing for the current production of *Rocky Horror* wasn't quite right, at least for Broadway; perhaps the musical would have been more at home in the casual and laidback atmosphere of an Off-Broadway theatre.

The tongue-in-cheek story of *The Rocky Horror Show* began with an ode to science fiction films, which cited such celluloid icons as Michael Rennie and *The Day the Earth Stood Still*, Anne Francis and *Forbidden Planet*, Leo G. Carroll and *Tarantula*, and Janette Scott and *The Day of the Triffids*. Soon we're introduced to the foursquare All-American Brad (Bill Miller) and Janet (Abigale Haness), who have just attended a wedding (we're informed that an hour ago the bride was just "plain Betty Munroe" and now she's Mrs. Ralf Hapshatt) and unfortunately take a wrong turn (a *very wrong* turn) and end up at the castle of the demented, dangerous, and *strictly out-for-unmentionable-kicks* Frank N. Furter (Tim Curry), a sight to behold in black lipstick, garter belts, black corsets, high heels, and fishnet stockings. His bizarre establishment includes a creature he's made for his *very own* pleasure; first seen wrapped in bandages, the creature makes quite an impression when the bandages are stripped away to reveal the handsome, muscular, and scantily clad Rocky (Kim Milford), who, according to T. E. Kalem in *Time*, wears briefs much smaller than swimming trunks but a bit bigger than a jock strap (Janet notes that she doesn't care for overly muscular men, and Frank quickly replies, "I didn't make him for *you*"). Eventually, Rocky separately seduces Janet *and* Brad (both morning-after seduction scenes are staged and performed in exactly the same manner and with the same dialogue), and soon all hell breaks loose with abandoned sex and unadulterated cross-dressing that celebrate the hedonistic philosophy of "don't dream it—be it." All this, and there's even time for the latest dance craze, "The Time Warp." And throughout the evening a portentous narrator commented on the plot with grave affectation in the manner of solemn movie voice-overs (as Brad and Janet approach the castle, the narrator tells us "It's true there were dark storm clouds . . . it was a night out they were to remember for a very—long—time").

For the Broadway production, the orchestra section was gutted and in cabaret fashion sets of tables and chairs replaced the rows of orchestra seats. One or two critics didn't think the new seating arrangements added much to the evening, although Kalem mentioned that with drinks served throughout the performance the audience had the chance "to get as bombed as the show."

Clive Barnes in the *New York Times* said the plot had enough for everyone to "like" or "dislike," and he complained that unlike the London production which was "tacky, tacky, tacky," the musical was now "too flashy, expensive and overstaged" and had lost its modest charms. Indeed, Martin Gottfried in the *New York Post* reported that the staging included a bulb-lit runway, steaming dry ice, neon bolts of lightning, and rear-screen projections but, curiously enough, a "surprisingly bad" sound system that made the lyrics "largely unintelligible" (though he quickly added this was perhaps a "blessing"); Douglas Watt in the *New York Daily News* said the "noisy and spirited farrago" was a "leering *Hellzapoppin*" whose style seemed "a bit dated" and so he "quickly grew bored" with the evening; James Spina in *Women's Wear Daily* disliked the "overexposed spoof" and found Tim Curry "mildly irritating in his sweaty drive to blend the mannerisms of Mick Jagger, Alice Cooper, and Fay Wray"; and, like Gottfried, Kalem noted the "deafening" sound system made the lyrics "unintelligible" and said the new seating system of café tables and chairs had been arranged "without regard for comfort or pleasure."

Edwin Wilson in the *Wall Street Journal* cautioned that the work wasn't a typical camp production that emphasized "style and aesthetics"; instead, it was a "subverted" means of "exploitation" that delivered a message from "the homosexual or bisexual point of view"; in this case, the innocent Brad and Janet "must be ridiculed and seduced until they are won over" and thus they must acknowledge that "their captors are right." Leonard Probst on NBC Radio found the show "so completely silly" that it was "fun" and "happily sick." He noted it was "delightfully decadent, a step beyond tiresome, straight old-fashioned homosexuality" and answered his question "What next?" with "Maybe incest."

As noted above, there were cast albums of the London and Los Angeles productions; and Ode Records also released *Songs from the Vaults: A Collection of Rocky Horror Rarities*. The script was published in paperback by Samuel French in 1983. In 1995, Jay Records/That's Entertainment Records (CD # TER-1221) released a studio cast album of the score, which included Christopher Lee (Narrator), Tim Flavin (Brad), Kim Criswell (Janet), and Howard Samuels (Frank N. Furter).

The musical was revived on Broadway on November 15, 2000, at the Circle in the Square for 436 performances; the cast included Tom Hewitt (Frank N. Furter), Jarrod Emick (Brad), Alice Ripley (Janet), Daphne Rubin-Vega (Usherette and Magenta), Raul Esparza (Riff Raff), Sebastian LaCause (Rocky), Joan Jett (Usherette and Columbia), Lea DeLaria (Dr. Scott), and Dick Cavett (Narrator). The cast album was released by RCA Victor (CD # 09026-63801-2).

The Twentieth Century-Fox film version (as *The Rocky Horror Picture Show*) was released in 1975, and quickly became a cult favorite with popular midnight showings in which legions of fans ritualistically interacted with the proceedings on screen. Sharman wrote the screenplay and again directed; Curry, Meat Loaf, and O'Brien reprised their stage roles; and other cast members included Barry Bostwick (Brad), Susan Sarandon (Janet), and Peter Hinwood (Rocky). The soundtrack album was issued by Ode Records (LP # 9009), the CD by Castle Records (# CHRCD-296), and Twentieth Century-Fox released the DVD.

A sequel of sorts emerged in 1981 with the release of the film *Shock Treatment*, in which Janet (Jessica Harper) and Brad (Cliff De Young) find themselves trapped in a television game show. Directed by Jim Sharman and with a cast that included Richard O'Brien, the film is scheduled to be adapted for a London stage production in 2015.

Awards

Tony Award Nomination: Best Lighting Designer: (Chipmonck)

SEALS AND CROFTS

Theatre: Uris Theatre
Opening Date: March 11, 1975; *Closing Date*: March 16, 1975
Performances: 6
Stage Direction: Tim McCarthy and Randall Woods; *Production Direction*: Bud Becker and Rich Cohen; *Producers*: Marcia Day and Marc Lamkin (the latter was also Executive Producer); *Lighting*: Jay Baker and Ron Cohen, Lighting Consultants
Cast: *James (Jim) Seals*, *Darrell (Dash) Crofts*, Walter Heath

The soft rock duo of Seals and Crofts (James "Jim" Seals and Darrell "Dash" Crofts) appeared in concert at the Uris Theatre for a limited engagement of six performances. Singer and songwriter Walter Heath was also on the bill as their special guest star.

DOCTOR JAZZ

"A New Musical"

Theatre: Winter Garden Theatre
Opening Date: March 19, 1975; *Closing Date*: March 22, 1975
Performances: 5
Book, Lyrics, and *Music*: "Mostly by" Buster Davis
Direction and *Choreography*: Donald McKayle ("Entire Production Supervised" by John Berry); *Producer*: Cyma Rubin (A Pyxidium Ltd. Production); *Scenery* and *Costumes*: Raoul Pene du Bois (Mason Arvold, "Scenic Coordinator"; and David Toser, "Costume Coordinator"); *Lighting*: Feder; *Musical Direction*: Joyce Brown
Cast: *Bobby Van* (Steve Anderson); Spasm Band: Quitman D. Fludd III, Bruce Heath, Hector Jaime Mercado, and Jeff Veazey; Jack Landron (Jonathan Jackson Jr.), Paul Eichel (Henry, Rudy, Harry), Peggy Pope (Harriet Lee), *Lillian Hayman* (Georgia Sheridan), *Lola Falana* (Edna Mae Sheridan); Georgia's Girls: Bonita Jackson, Michele Simmons, and Annie Joe Edwards; Harriet's Girls: Gail Benedict, Sarah Coleman, Maggy Gorrill, Kitty Jones, Diana Mirras, Sally Neal, Yolanda R. Raven, and Catherine Rice; Hector Jaime Mercado (Lead Dancer); The Group: Bruce Heath, Bonita Jackson, Sally Neal, Yolanda R. Raven, and Michele Simmons; Eron Tabor (Pete); Dancers: Gail Benedict, Quitman D. Fludd III, Maggy Gorrill, Bob Heath, Bruce Heath, David Hodo, Bonita Jackson, Michael Lichtefeld, Hector Jaime Mercado, Diana Mirras, Sally Neal, Yolanda R. Raven, Catherine Rice, Michele Simmons, Dan Strayhorn, and Jeff Veazey; Singers: James Braet, Annie Joe Edwards, Paul Eichel, Marian Haraldson, Evelyn McCauley, and Eron Tabor; Showgirls: Sarah Coleman, Kitty Jones; Onstage Musicians: George Davis Jr., Dennis Drury, John Gill, Vince Giordano, Haywood Henry, Danny Moore, Sam Pilafian, Candy Ross, Bob Stewart, Allan Vache, Warren Vache Jr., Earl Williams, and Francis Williams
The musical was presented in two acts.
The action takes place between 1917 and the mid-1920s in New Orleans, Chicago, and New York City.

Musical Numbers

Note: Unless otherwise specified, all songs by Buster Davis.
Act One: "Doctor Jazz" (lyric and music by King Oliver and Howard Melrose) (Bobby Van, Musicians, Spasm Band); "We've Got Connections" (Bobby Van, Lillian Hayman, Peggy Pope); "Georgia Shows 'Em How" (Lillian Hayman, Georgia's Girls); "Cleopatra Had a Jazz Band" (lyric by Jack Coogan, music by J. L. Morgan) (Bobby Van, Ballyhoo Band); "Juba Dance" (Lola Falana, Spasm Band); "Charleston Rag" (music by Eubie Blake) (Jonathan's Band, Harriet's Girls); "I've Got Elgin Watch Movements in My Hips" (Lola Falana); "Blues My Naughty Sweetie Gave to Me" (lyric and music by Swanstone, McCarren, and Morgan) (Ballyhoo Band); "Good-Time Flat Blues" (lyric and music by A. J. Piron) (Lillian Hayman); "Evolution Papa" (Lola Falana, Hector Jaime Mercado, Troupe); "Rehearsal Tap" (The Group); "Blues My Naughty Sweetie Gave to Me" (reprise) (Bobby Van); "I Love It" (Lola Falana) (lyric and music by E. Ray Goetz and Harry von Tilzer); "Anywhere the Wind Blows" (Bobby Van)
Act Two: "Those 'Sheik-of-Araby' Blues" (Singers and Dancers); "Look Out for Lil" (Lola Falana, Dancers); "Swanee Strut" (Bobby Van); "All I Want Is My Black Baby Back" (Lola Falana); "Everybody Leaves You" (Bobby Van); "Free and Easy" (Lola Falana, Company); "I Love It" (reprise) (Bobby Van, Lola Falana)

Forty-two New York previews couldn't prevent *Doctor Jazz* from being one of the biggest theatrical train wrecks of the decade. The chaotic five weeks included rewriting, recasting, and the elimination of almost a dozen songs, but nothing helped and the musical mustered just five official performances before calling it quits.

During previews, Buster Davis and Paul Carter Harrison received book credit, but by opening night Harrison's name had been removed from the program and Davis received a "mostly by" credit for book, lyrics, and music (an uncredited Joseph Stein also worked on the script). Donald McKayle was director and choreographer, but the opening night program added a "production supervised by" credit for John Berry.

Joan Copeland was succeeded by Peggy Pope, and Frank Owens by Jack Landron; and when her role of Gale Bennett was eliminated, Marcia Watkins left the show. The musical had been presented in one act, but there were two by opening night, and at least eleven songs (a mixture of new numbers as well as older ones) were cut during previews: "Storyville Theme," "Miss Harriet Lee," "He's Always Ticklin' the Ivories" (sung in drag by Michael Lichtefeld and Jeff Veazey), "Just a Closer Walk with Thee," "I Wish I Was in Peoria" (lyric by Billy Rose and Mort Dixon, music by Harry Woods), "I Want a Little Lovin', Sometimes" (lyric and music by Chris Smith), "Chicago Montage," "It's Getting Very Dark on Old Broadway" (lyric and music by Louis A. Hirsch, Gene Buck, and Dave Stamper), "Our Medicine Man" (aka "Our Medicine Man's a Music Maker Now"), "Welcome to Edna Mae," and "Sorry, I've Made Other Arrangements."

The slim plot followed the rags-to-riches saga of naive singer Edna Mae (Lola Falana), who catapults to stardom from gigs in a New Orleans brothel to Broadway glory. While singing at the brothel, she meets Steve (that is, Doctor Jazz) (Bobby Van), a would-be trumpeter who works there hustling up customers for the girls, and together Edna Mae and Steve try to make their mark in show business as they travel to Chicago and New York. Edna Mae makes it big on Broadway, but Steve apparently realizes he has no future there or with her, and so returns to New Orleans. She finds It's Lonely at the Top, but soon happiness comes her way when she's reunited with a piano player she had met in Chicago.

The skeletal story was essentially told between numerous and lavish songs and dances, all of which were performance numbers taking place in the theatrical venues where the characters appeared, such as brothels, theatres, and clubs (there were hardly any book songs). Clive Barnes in the *New York Times* said "nothing happened" in *Doctor Jazz* because it was "a nonevent, an unhappening" and its "story line" was "more of a dash than a line." Here was "unlimited tedium" in which Van, Falana, and the other performers tried their best but to no avail. Douglas Watt in the *New York Daily News* said the "noisy, sluggish and senseless" musical seemed left over from the World's Fair (and quickly added, "the 1939 one"), and the "numbingly dull" evening had a "flaccid" book that "even the performers can't seem to take seriously." Christopher Sharp in *Women's Wear Daily* said the highlight of the musical was the "stunning" choreography devised by McKayle, dances that were "hedonistic joy rides." Leonard Probst on NBC Radio noted the "dull" musical had a score that was "derivative and dull, loud but limp," and the only funny moments were provided by Peggy Pope as a brothel madam (but Watt complained there was too much "maddening baby talk" in her portrayal).

Martin Gottfried in the *New York Post* regretted the musical that never was, as he seemed to see in *Doctor Jazz* a completely different musical that had been suppressed by the exigencies of Broadway commercialism. He felt the "might have been" musical could have depicted what he termed the "corruption" of black jazz to its "homogenization by the white swing bands of the Forties" and the saga of a black singer under the influence of a white man's guidance. But instead the production provided a "hackneyed" backstage story. The décor was "gorgeous," the costumes "fabulous," and the choreography "wonderful" (the show was the season's most "dancingest"), but ultimately the evening was "shallow" and "senseless."

Six songs from the production were included in the collection *18 Interesting Songs from Unfortunate Shows* (Take Home Tunes Records LP # THT-777): "Everybody Leaves You," "Elgin Watch Number" (aka "I've Got Elgin Watch Movements in My Hips"), "Anywhere the Wind Blows," "Sorry, I've Made Other Arrangements," "Our Medicine Man's a Music Maker Now," and the deleted "He's Always Ticklin' the Ivories." Original cast member Bobby Van reprised his songs "Everybody Leaves You" and "Anywhere the Wind Blows," and lyricist and composer Buster Davis sang the other four numbers.

Awards

Tony Award Nominations: Best Costume Designer (Raoul Pene du Bois); Best Choreographer (Donald McKayle)

A LETTER FOR QUEEN VICTORIA

"An Opera in Four Acts"

Theatre: ANTA Theatre
Opening Date: March 22, 1975; *Closing Date*: April 6, 1975
Performances: 16
Text: Robert Wilson
Music: Alan Lloyd in collaboration with Michael Galasso

Direction: Robert Wilson; *Producer*: The Byrd Hoffman Foundation, Inc.; *Choreography*: Andrew deGroat; *Scenery* and *Costumes*: Supervised by Peter Harvey; *Lighting*: Supervised by Beverly Emmons assisted by Carol Mullins; *Musical Direction*: Michael Galasso; Additional Credits: Christopher Knowles (Verbal Tape Constructions, The Sundance Kid Speech), Stefan Brecht (Introductory Letter), Cynthia (Cindy) Lubar (Act III Dialogue), James Neu (First Speech of Chinaman), Francis Brooks (Slides)

Cast: Sheryl Sutton (1, Civil War Soldier, 2C, 3, 1), Cynthia (Cindy) Lubar (2, 2, 2E, 4, 2), George Ashley (1A, 1, 2B, George), Stefan Brecht (2, Pilot, 2A, 4, 1A, 2A, Pilot), Kathryn Cation (1, Billy, 3, 2D), Alma Hamilton (Queen Victoria), Christopher Knowles (3, Pilot, Chris, 1C), James Neu (24, Pilot, 4, 1D, 1), Scotty Snyder (Warden, 2A, 2), Robert Wilson (4), Andrew deGroat (Dancer, 1E), Julia Busto (Dancer, 2B); Musicians: Michael Galasso (First Violin), Susan Krongold (Second Violin), Kevin Byrnes (Violin), Laura Epstein (Cello), Kathryn Cation (Flute)

The opera was performed in four acts.

Robert Wilson's experimental pieces were usually of the silent variety, in which motion, dance, and visual effects were the primary form of communication with the audience. And his works were lengthy: *KA MOUNTAIN AND GUARDenia TERRACE* was performed on a mountainside in Iran and the performance took a full week for a total of 168 hours, and *The Life and Times of Joseph Stalin*, which played at the Brooklyn Academy of Music in 1973, ran for twelve hours. *A Letter for Queen Victoria* was unusual for Wilson: it ran just under three hours and it employed dialogue (as well as primal screams and dog-barking) to tell its non-story.

And a "non-story" it was. It wasn't really about Queen Victoria (although the character, played by Wilson's eighty-eight-year-old grandmother Alma Hamilton, appeared in two scenes), and four characters do indeed read a letter to her, but since all speak simultaneously with overlapping dialogue the content of the letter is purposely unclear because for Wilson the sound of the words, and not their meaning is what is important; the "characters" included ones with such names as 1, 2, 2C, and 4; and throughout the evening Andrew deGroat and Julia Busto danced on the sidelines in whirling dervish fashion. The evening was mostly a display of dadaesque verbal pyrotechnics with dialogue so convoluted that according to T. E. Kalem in *Time* it made Gertrude Stein "at her murkiest sound like a paragon of pellucid clarity." (Some of the dialogue ran to: "Ok Ok Ok Ok Okay/Okayk Ok Ok O" and "Pirup Birup Pirup Birup.")

Two sequences in particular were singled out by the critics. One took place in a fashionable café where five couples in turn-of-the-century finery are chatting away in gibberish (behind them, a backdrop with the phrase "chitter chatter" was endlessly repeated). Occasionally, a café patron is shot to death, but he quickly revives and starts chatting again. Another sequence (described in detail by Edwin Wilson in the *Wall Street Journal*) revealed a black woman (Sheryl Sutton) dressed in black and a white woman (Cynthia Lubar) dressed in white; they speak in non sequiturs about washing dishes and the Civil War, repeat their dialogue three times with different actions and gestures. Then they remove their outer garments, and the black woman is now dressed in white and the white woman in black.

A few critics cautioned that one had to attend *A Letter for Queen Victoria* without the preconceptions of traditional theatre, but Martin Gottfried in the *New York Post* felt the venue of a commercial Broadway house was all wrong for the piece, which rightly belonged in the repertory of a ballet company. He noted the limited four-week run was "doubtless doomed," and indeed the work played for just half that time.

Otherwise, Gottfried felt the evening's word fragmentations didn't succeed and became "mere irritants, separated by boredom, connected with no structural arc" and thus were "conclusively unsatisfying"; Clive Barnes in the *New York Times* "loved" the work and said what he expected to happen didn't, and what he didn't expect to happen did; and Edwin Wilson felt that Robert Wilson had "fused the arts of painting, theatre, dance, and music in a way no one else has," and while some in the audience "will be bored out of their minds" the work offered "intriguing possibilities" for the theatre and Wilson's conception might possibly be "on the brink of important discoveries."

Douglas Watt in the *New York Daily News* said that despite Wilson's "striking images" the work was "fantastic but bloodless" and he complained about the "lack of communicativeness or expressiveness even in abstract terms." And John Beaufort in the *Christian Science Monitor* said the "phantasmagoric enigma" offered "sometimes striking and beautiful images" that should be interpreted in the words of the old standard "Life Is Just a Bowl of Cherries" (from the 1931 *George White's Scandals*, lyric by Lew Brown, music by Ray Henderson): "Don't take it serious / It's too mysterious."

Kevin Sanders on WABCTV7 said the "undeniably impressive" work was "vapid and sterile and intellectually arid." He reported that for one sequence Wilson stood on the stage and barked like a dog "for a very, very long time" and the barking was so amplified that many in the audience who were seated near the speakers had to leave their seats. He also noted many left the theatre, and that Andy Warhol (who "usually seems to thrive on this kind of stuff") didn't return after intermission.

As for Alan Lloyd's score, Gottfried said it was "the only fine work in this production"; Barnes said it sounded "white-wigged and baroque"; Wilson praised the "melodic chamber music"; and Watt liked the "salon-music accompaniment a great deal."'

The opera had originally been produced in Paris at the Theatre des Varieties from December 5, 1974, through January 5, 1975. The script was published in France in a paperback edition (in both English and French) in an undated edition by an unnamed publisher.

Awards

Tony Award Nomination: Best Score (Alan Lloyd)

THE CONSUL

Theatre: The New York State Theatre
Opening Date: March 22, 1975; *Closing Date*: April 6, 1975
Performances: 2 (in repertory)
Libretto and *Music*: Gian-Carlo Menotti
Director: Francis Rizzo; *Producer*: The New York City Opera Company; *Scenery*: Horace Armstead; *Costumes*: Not credited; *Lighting*: Not credited; *Musical Direction*: Christopher Keene
Cast: John Darrenkamp (John Sorel), Olivia Stapp (Magda Sorel), Muriel Costa-Greenspon (The Mother), Edward Pierson (Secret Police Agent), Jack Sims (First Plainclothesman), Tom Barrett (Second Plainclothesman), Sandra Walker (The Secretary), Don Yule (Mr. Kofner), Judith De Rosa (Foreign Woman), Barbara Hocher (Anna Gomez), John Lankston (Nika Magadoff aka The Magician), Sophia Steffan (Vera Boronel), William Ledbetter (Assan), Mabel Mercer (Voice on the Record)
The opera was presented in three acts.
The action takes place somewhere in Europe during the recent past.

The New York City Opera Company's revival of Gian-Carlo Menotti's *The Consul* was its eighth and final production of the Cold War opera. The previous revival had been seen a year earlier, and except for Nico Castel (Nika Magadoff, the magician) and Virginia Brobyn (Vera Boronel) who were succeeded by John Lankston and Sophia Steffan, all the members from the previous production returned, and Christopher Keene was again the conductor.

For more information about the opera, see entry for the 1974 revival.

BETTE MIDLER'S CLAMS ON THE HALF-SHELL REVUE

Theatre: Minskoff Theatre
Opening Date: April 17, 1975; *Closing Date*: June 21, 1975
Performances: 67
Special Material: Bruce Vilanch, Jerry Blatt, and Bill Hennessy
Direction and *Choreography*: Joe Layton (Andre De Shields, Associate Choreographer); *Producers*: Aaron Russo in association with Ron Delsener; *Scenery* and *Costumes*: Tony Walton; *Lighting*: Beverly Emmons; *Musical Direction*: Don York
Cast: *Bette Midler*, Lionel Hampton, the Michael Powell Ensemble (Michael Powell, Joey Coleman, Lee Roy Cooks, Vinson Cunningham, Dorothea Doctor, Norman P. Hawkins, Clifford Jamerson, Jeannie Page, Ricardo Portlette, Charlene Ricks, Shirley Underwood, and Peggy Williams), the Harlettes (Charlotte Crossley, Robin Grean, and Sharon Redd)
The revue was presented in two acts.

Musical Numbers

Act One: *Oklahoma!* Overture (1943 musical; music by Richard Rodgers) (Orchestra); "Nobody Knows the Trouble I've Seen"; "The Moon of Manakoora" (1937 film *The Hurricane*; lyric by Frank Loesser, music by Alfred Newman); "Ol' Man River" (*Show Boat*, 1927; lyric by Oscar Hammerstein II, music by Jerome Kern); Medley of Bette Midler's Greatest Hits; "The Bitch Is Back" (lyric and music by Elton John and Bernie Taupin); "Delta Dawn" (lyric and music by Alex Harvey and Larry Collins); The Toilet Medley (A 1950s Rock-and-Roll Medley); "Sentimental Journey" (lyric by Bud Green, music by Les Brown and Ben Horner); "Ain't No Love" (lyric and music by John Gary Williams); Saloon Sequence: (1) "Back in the Bars Again" (lyric and music by Susan Taylor); (2) "Drinking Again" (lyric by Johnny Mercer, music by Doris Tauber); (3) "Fiesta in Rio" (lyric and music by Bette Midler and Jerry Blatt); (4) "Strangers in the Night" (instrumental theme from 1966 film *A Man Could Get Killed*; music by Bert Kaempfert, later English lyrics by Eddie Snyder and Charles Singleton): and (5) "Do You Wanna Dance?" (lyric and music by Bobby Freeman); "If Love Were All" (*Bitter Sweet*, 1929; lyric and music by Noel Coward); "Friends" (lyric and music by Mark Klingman and Buzzy Linhart); "I'm Wishing" (1938 film *Snow White and the Seven Dwarfs*; lyric by Larry Morey, music by Frank Churchill); "A Dream Is a Wish Your Heart Makes" (1950 film *Cinderella*; lyric and music by Mack David, Al Hoffman, and Jerry Livingston); "Lullaby of Broadway" (1935 film *Gold Diggers of 1935*; lyric by Al Dubin, music by Harry Warren)

Act Two: "In the Mood" (lyric by Andy Razaf, music by Joe Garland; additional lyric by Bette Midler and Barry Manilow); "Hey Ba-Ba-Re-Bop"; "Flying Home" (lyric and music by Lionel Hampton, Benny Goodman, and Sid Ramin); Lionel Hampton; "We'll Be Together Again" (lyric and music by Carl Fischer and Frankie Laine); "Shiver Me Timbers" (lyric and music by Tom Waits); "I Don't Want the Night to End" (lyric and music by Phoebe Snow); Sophie Tucker Jokes; "Hello in There" (lyric and music by John Prine); "Higher and Higher" (lyric and music by Gary Lee Jackson, Carl W. Smith, and Raynard Miner); "The Boogie-Woogie Bugle Boy from Company 'B'" (1941 film *Buck Privates*; lyric and music by Don Raye and Hughie Prince); "Chapel of Love" (lyric and music by Jeff Barry, Ellie Greenwich, and Phil Spector)

Bette Midler's Clams on the Half-Shell Revue was another visit from The Divine Miss M, and unlike her previous appearance ***Bette Midler***, which was pretty much in the nature of a straightforward concert, the current production was a dolled-up revue with direction and choreography by Joe Layton, scenery and costumes by Tony Walton, a guest appearance by Lionel Hampton and his seventeen-member orchestra, the twelve-member gospel troupe the Michael Powell Ensemble, and, of course, Bette's trio the Harlettes.

In typically Midleresque and skewed fashion, the evening began with the overture to *Oklahoma!* and was soon followed by the Michael Powell Ensemble singing "Ol' Man River." But fear not. Her Divinity soon appeared: a huge clam shell opened, and there she was in all her spangled magnificence in a homage to Dorothy Lamour and "The Moon of Manakoora." According to Douglas Watt in the *New York Daily News*, she told a couple of truly "filthy" Sophie Tucker jokes (but somehow managed to create an aura of "wholesomeness") and she chatted up the customers (Jack Kroll in *Newsweek* reported that she told a drag queen in the audience that "It's very 1971 of you to come in that dress"). Kroll also reported that for the first-act finale "Lullaby of Broadway" she was seen in the grip of a King Kong atop the Empire State Building; but instead of screaming, she squealed "Nicky Arnstein, Nicky Arnstein, Nicky Arnstein!" (no doubt an homage to Barbra Streisand, which perhaps only the inner-most circle of the cognoscenti would understand).

Clive Barnes in the *New York Times* said Midler was the "tackiest girl in town" who was playing at the "tackiest theatre on Broadway"; she was "the low priestess of her own juke-box subculture, an explosion of energy and minutely calculated bad taste." And so of course New York was her town and she "is still its best Bette." Leonard Probst on NBC Radio hailed the "new type of Broadway bombshell" who is "part brilliant, part bagel."

Other songs performed during the run were: "Bad Sex" (lyric and music by Bill Hennessey and Bruce Vilanch); "A Day in the Life" (lyric and music by Paul McCartney and John Lennon); "Deep Purple" (lyric by Mitchell Parish, music by Peter DeRose); "How High the Moon" (*Two for the Show*, 1940; lyric by Nancy Hamilton, music by Morgan Lewis); "I've Never Been to Flushing"; "When a Man Loves a Woman" (lyric and music by Calvin Lewis and Andrew Wright); and "You Will Never Be Lonely" (lyric and music by Tom Pacheco).

Later in the decade, the star returned to Broadway in the concert ***Bette! Divine Madness***.

RODGERS & HART

Theatre: Helen Hayes Theatre
Opening Date: May 13, 1975; *Closing Date*: August 16, 1975
Performances: 111
Lyrics: Lorenz Hart
Music: Richard Rodgers
Direction: Burt Shevelove; *Producers*: Lester Osterman Productions (Lester Osterman and Richard Horner) in association with Worldvision Enterprises, Inc.; *Choreography*: Donald Saddler (Arthur Faria, Associate Choreographer); *Scenery*: Gordon Jenkins; *Costumes*: Stanley Simmons; *Lighting*: Ken Billington; *Musical Direction*: Buster Davis
Cast: Barbara Andres, Jimmy Brennan, Wayne Bryan, David-James Carroll, Jamie Donnelly, Tovah Feldshuh, Mary Sue Finnerty, Laurence Guittard, Stephen Lehew, Jim Litten, Virginia Sandifur, Rebecca York
The revue was presented in two acts.

Musical Numbers

Note: The program listed musical numbers alphabetically without indicating names of performers. At the end of this entry is an alphabetical list of the songs, followed by source information.

The season's final offering was a tribute to Richard Rodgers and Lorenz Hart. The evening was a collection of almost one hundred songs that were listed in the program in alphabetical order and without song assignments (but not all the numbers were actually performed in the revue). The first act emphasized ballads, the second satiric and topical numbers. The revue was pleasant but somewhat bland, and as one or two critics noted it would have been better served as the basis for a television special. Further, far too many numbers were shortened into medley sequences, and so just snatches of songs were performed.

Martin Gottfried in the *New York Post* noted the revue had "more aplomb than flair," emphasized the evening was more in the nature of a staged concert or television special, and said the production lacked an overriding concept or pattern; he also complained that the emphasis was on the team's more obscure songs. Kevin Sanders on WABCTV7 felt the show suffered from an often "sterile, anti-septic look," the costumes looked "like something left over from the Johnny Mann Singers," and the evening almost seemed like an episode of *The Lawrence Welk Show* or "a staged version of Muzak."

Clive Barnes in the *New York Times* praised the "champagne-fizz of an evening," and suggested the team of Rodgers and Hart was successful because of the inspired mating of the "cynical realism" of Hart's lyrics and Rodgers' "dry-martini" music. Like many of the reviewers, he singled out *Pal Joey*'s "Zip," which in this instance was sung by a leather-clad male hustler type. But Barnes complained that the "cheap" and awkward set "looked a little like a forgotten foyer in the Radio City Music Hall." Ernest Leogrande in the *New York Daily News* said the cast offered "so much gee-gosh puppy-dog energy" he thought he'd "die of the cutes," but was soon won over by the production's "party feeling," and Keitha McLean in *Women's Wear Daily* hoped there would be a cast album (there wasn't) and singled out the "splendid" Laurence Guittard.

The following songs were listed in the program: "At the Roxy Music Hall" (*I Married an Angel*, 1938); "Babes in Arms" (*Babes in Arms*, 1937); "Bewitched, Bothered and Bewildered" (*Pal Joey*, 1940); "Blue Moon" (with a different lyric, the song was written as "Prayer" and was intended for the 1934 film *Hollywood Party*; it was later revised but unused as "Manhattan Melodrama"/"It's Just That Kind of Play" for the 1934 film *Manhattan Melodrama*, and was heard in that film as "The Bad in Every Man"; as an independent song not presented in a musical or film, the song became popular as "Blue Moon"); "Blue Room" (*The Girl Friend*, 1926); "Bye and Bye" (*Dearest Enemy*, 1925); "Can't You Do a Friend a Favor?" (1943 revival of *A Connecticut Yankee*); "Careless Rhapsody" (*By Jupiter*, 1942); "Cause We Got Cake" (*Too Many Girls*, 1939); "Come with Me" (*The Boys from Syracuse*, 1938); "Dancing on the Ceiling" (1930 London musical *Ever Green*; as "He Dances on My Ceiling," the song was cut from *Simple Simon* [1930] during its tryout); "Dear Old Syracuse" (*The Boys from Syracuse*, 1938); "Did You Ever Get Stung?" (*I Married an Angel*, 1938); "Disgustingly Rich" (*Higher and Higher*, 1940); "Do I Hear You Saying 'I Love You?'" (*Present Arms*, 1928); "Down by the River" (1935 film *Mississippi*); "Easy to Remember" (1935 film *Mississippi*); "Everybody Loves You" (cut from the tryout of *I'd Rather Be Right*, 1937); "Ev'rything I've Got" (*By Jupiter*, 1942); "Falling in Love with Love" (*The Boys from Syracuse*, 1938); "From Another World" (*Higher and Higher*, 1940); "The Gateway of the Temple of Minerva" (*By Jupiter*, 1942); "The Girl Friend" (*The Girl Friend*, 1926); "Give It Back to the Indians" (*Too Many Girls*, 1939); "Glad to Be Unhappy" (*On Your Toes*, 1936); "Great Big Town" (aka "Chicago") (*Pal Joey*, 1940); "Happy Hunting Horn" (*Pal Joey*, 1940); "Have You Met Miss Jones?" (*I'd Rather Be Right*, 1937); "He and She" (*The Boys from Syracuse*, 1938); "He Was Too Good to Me" (cut from the tryout of *Simple Simon*, 1930); "The Heart Is Quicker Than the Eye" (*On Your Toes*, 1936); "Here in My Arms" (*Dearest Enemy*, 1925); "How About It?" (*America's Sweetheart*, 1931); "How Was I to Know?" (cut from tryout of *She's My Baby*, 1928; and rewritten as "Why Do You Suppose?" for *Heads Up!*, 1929); "I Could Write a Book" (*Pal Joey*, 1940); "I Didn't Know What Time It Was" (*Too Many Girls*, 1939); "I Like to Recognize the Tune" (*Too Many Girls*, 1939); "I Married an Angel" (*I Married an Angel*, 1938); "I Wish I Were in Love Again" (*Babes in Arms*, 1937); "I'll Tell the Man in the Street" (*I Married an Angel*, 1937); "Imagine" (*Babes in Arms*, 1937); "Isn't It Romantic?" (1932 film *Love Me Tonight*); "It Never Entered My Mind" (*Higher and Higher*, 1940); "It's Got to Be Love" (*On Your Toes*, 1936); "I've Got Five Dollars" (*America's Sweetheart*, 1931); "Johnny One Note" (*Babes in Arms*, 1937); "Jupiter Forbid" (*By Jupiter*, 1942); "The Lady Is a Tramp" (*Babes in Arms*, 1937); "Love Me Tonight" (1932 film *Love Me Tonight*); "Love Never Went to College" (*Too Many Girls*, 1939); "A Lovely Day for a Murder" (*Higher and Higher*, 1940); "Lover" (1932 film *Love Me Tonight*); "Manhattan" (first edition of *The Garrick Gaieties*, 1925); "Me for You" (*Heads Up!*, 1929); "Mimi" (1932 film *Love Me Tonight*); "Morning Is Midnight" (1926 London production of *Lido Lady*; later cut from tryout of *She's My Baby*, 1928); "Mountain Greenery" (second edition of *The Garrick Gaieties*, 1926); "My Funny Valentine" (*Babes in Arms*, 1937); "My Heart Stood Still" (*A Connecticut Yankee*, 1927); "My Prince" (*Too Many Girls*, 1939); "My Romance" (*Jumbo*, 1935); "Nobody's Heart" (*By Jupiter*, 1942); "Nothing but You" (*Higher and Higher*, 1940); "Oh, Diogenes" (*The Boys from Syracuse*, 1938); "On Your Toes" (*On Your Toes*, 1936); "Quiet Night" (*On Your Toes*, 1936); "Sentimental Me" (added to the 1925 edition of *The Garrick Gaieties* during its Broadway run); "She Could Shake the Maracas" (*Too Many Girls*, 1939); "A Ship without a Sail" (*Heads Up!*, 1929); "The Shortest Day of the Year" (*The Boys from Syracuse*, 1938); "Sing for Your Supper" (*The Boys from Syracuse*, 1938); "Slaughter on Tenth Avenue" (*On Your Toes*, 1936); "Soon" (1935 film *Mississippi*); "Spring Is Here" (probably the song "Spring Is Here" ["why doesn't my heart go dancing?"] from *I Married an Angel* [1938], and not the title song "Spring Is Here" ["in person"] from *Spring Is Here* [1929]); "Take Him" (*Pal Joey*, 1940); "Ten Cents a Dance" (*Simple Simon*, 1930); "That Terrific Rainbow" (*Pal Joey*, 1940); "There's a Small Hotel" (*On Your Toes*, 1936); "This Can't Be Love" (*The Boys from Syracuse*, 1938); "This Funny World" (*Betsy*, 1926); "This Is My Night to Howl" (1943 revival of *A Connecticut Yankee*); "Thou Swell" (*A Connecticut Yankee*, 1927); "The Three B's" (*On Your Toes*, 1936); "To Keep My Love Alive" (1943 revival of *A Connecticut Yankee*); "Too Good for the Average Man" (*On Your Toes*, 1936); "A Tree in the Park" (*Peggy-Ann*, 1927); "Wait Till You See Her" (*By Jupiter*, 1942); "Way Out West" (*Babes in Arms*, 1937); "What's the Use of Talking?" (second edition of *The Garrick Gaieties*, 1926); "Where or When" (*Babes in Arms*, 1937); "Where's That Rainbow?" (*America's Sweetheart*, 1931); "Why Can't I?" (*Spring Is Here*, 1929); "With a Song in My Heart" (*Spring Is Here*, 1929); "You Always Love the Same Girl" (1943 revival of *A Connecticut Yankee*); "You Are Too Beautiful" (1933 film *Hallelujah, I'm a Bum*); "You Have Cast Your Shadow on the Sea" (*The Boys from Syracuse*, 1938); "You Mustn't Kick It Around" (*Pal Joey*, 1940); "You Took Advantage of Me" (*Present Arms*, 1928); "You're Nearer" (1940 film version of *Too Many Girls*); "Zip" (*Pal Joey*, 1940)

I GOT A SONG

"A View of the Life and Times Through the Lyrics of E. Y. Harburg"

The revue opened on September 26, 1974, at the Studio Arena Theatre, Buffalo, New York, and permanently closed there on October 20.

Text: "Dramatized" by E. Y. Harburg and Fred Saidy

Lyrics: E. Y. Harburg

Music: See list of musical numbers for names of composers

Direction: Harold Stone; *Producers*: A Joel Schenker and Claire Nichtern Production (Paul Repetowski, Associate Producer) presented by Studio Arena Theatre (Neal Du Brock, Executive Director); *Choreography*:

Geoffrey Holder; *Scenery*: R. J. Graziano; *Costumes*: Theoni V. Aldredge; *Lighting*: Tom Skelton; *Musical Direction*: Marty Henne

Cast: D'Jamin Bartlett, Alan Brasington, Norma Donaldson, Bonnie Franklin, Miguel Godreau, Gilbert Price

The revue was presented in two acts.

Musical Numbers

Note: The program didn't list performers of specific songs.

Act One: "Look to the Rainbow" (*Finian's Rainbow*, 1947; music by Burton Lane); "I Got a Song" (*Bloomer Girl*, 1944; music by Harold Arlen); "There's a Great Day Coming Manana" (*Hold on to Your Hats*, 1940; music by Burton Lane); "Brother, Can You Spare a Dime?" (*New Americana*, 1932; music by Jay Gorney); "April in Paris" (*Walk a Little Faster*, 1932; music by Vernon Duke); "Let's Take a Walk around the Block" (*Life Begins at 8:40*, 1934; lyric by Ira Gershwin and E. Y. Harburg, music by Harold Arlen); "Necessity" (*Finian's Rainbow*); "The Money Cat" (1962 film *Gay Purr-ee*; music by Harold Arlen); "When the Idle Poor Become the Idle Rich" (*Finian's Rainbow*); "Happiness Is Just a Thing Called Joe" (1943 film version of *Cabin in the Sky*; music by Harold Arlen); "Silent Spring" (independent song, 1963; music by Harold Arlen); "The Eagle and Me" (*Bloomer Girl*); "Monkey in the Mango Tree" (*Jamaica*, 1957; music by Harold Arlen); "Jump, Children, Jump" (aka "Jump, Little Chillun!") (*Flahooley*, 1951; music by Sammy Fain); "Noah" (dropped from *Jamaica*); "We're Off to See the Wizard" (1939 film *The Wizard of Oz*; music by Harold Arlen)

Act Two: "We're Off to See the Wizard" (reprise) (*The Wizard of Oz*); "Napoleon" (*Hooray for What!* and *Jamaica*; see below); "Ain't It the Truth" (1943 film *Cabin in the Sky* and *Jamaica*; see below); "Leave the Atom Alone" (*Jamaica*); "(We're in) The Same Boat, Brother" (1945 radio program *Unity Fair*; music by Earl Robinson); Love Medley: "If This Isn't Love" (*Finian's Rainbow*), "The World Is Your Balloon" (*Flahooley*), "Old Devil Moon" (*Finian's Rainbow*), and "Right as the Rain" (*Bloomer Girl*); "Over the Rainbow" (*The Wizard of Oz*); "Eagle Dance" (medley of unspecified songs); "That Great Come-and-Get-It Day" (*Finian's Rainbow*); "It's Only a Paper Moon" (aka "If You Believed in Me") (1932 play *The Great Magoo*; lyric by Billy Rose and E. Y. Harburg, music by Harold Arlen)

The tribute revue *I Got a Song* featured lyrics by E. Y. Harburg, almost all of which had first been performed in Broadway and film musicals.

The production was scheduled for Broadway, but closed after its engagement in Buffalo. *Variety* noted the evening lacked a point of view (surprising, considering Harburg's social and political outlooks were clearly reflected in many of the songs chosen for the revue) and required revision and tightening.

Harburg and Harold Arlen's "Napoleon" was heard in *Jamaica*, and is a different song from their "Napoleon's a Pastry" from *Hooray for What!* (1937). "Ain't It the Truth" was written for the 1943 film version of *Cabin in the Sky* where it was sung by Lena Horne, but was cut prior to the film's release; it was later added to *Jamaica*, where it was again performed by Horne.

MISS MOFFAT

"A New Musical"

The musical opened on October 7, 1974, at the Shubert Theatre, Philadelphia, Pennsylvania, and permanently closed there on October 16.

Book: Emlyn Williams and Joshua Logan

Lyrics: Emlyn Williams

Music: Albert Hague

Based on the 1938 play *The Corn Is Green* by Emlyn Williams.

Direction: Joshua Logan; *Producers*: Eugene V. Wolsk, Joshua Logan, and Slade Brown (Jim Milford, Associate Producer); *Choreography*: Donald Saddler; *Scenery* and *Lighting*: Jo Mielziner; *Costumes*: Robert Macintosh; *Musical Direction*: Jay Blackton

Cast: Rudolf Lowe (Champ), Jason Walker (Ty), Nat Jones (Absie), Gian Carlo Esposito (Zeke), Dorian Harewood (Morgan Evans), Kevin Dearinger (Jim), Randy Martin (Jerry), Michael Calkins (Larry), Lee Goodman (Mr. Jones), Anne Francine (Mrs. Sprode), Dody Goodman (Miss Ronberry), David Sabin (The Senator), Marion Ramsey (Bessie Watty), Nell Carter (Mrs. Watty), *Bette Davis* (Miss Moffat), Avon Long (Ole Mr. Pete), Gil Robbins (Marse Jeff); Schoolchildren, Parents, and Others: Wendell Brown, Vicki Geyer, Yolande Graves, Helen Jennings, Betty Lynd, Pamela Palluzzi, Lacy Darryll Phillips, Sandra Phillips, Janet Powell, Christine Tordenti

The musical was presented in two acts.

The action takes place during three years early in the twentieth century on and around a small plantation in the South.

Musical Numbers

Act One: "A Wonderful Game" (Bette Davis); "A Wonderful Game" (reprise) (Bette Davis, Lee Goodman, Dody Goodman, Children); "Pray for the Snow" (Dorian Harewood); "Here in the South" (David Sabin, Bette Davis, Ensemble); "Tomorrow" (Bette Davis); "Tomorrow" (reprise) (Bette Davis, Ensemble); "There's More to a Man Than His Head" (Marion Ramsey, Avon Long, Boys); "Time's A-Flyin'" (Company); "Here in the South" (reprise) (Bette Davis, David Sabin); "You Don't Need a Nailfile in a Cornfield" (Dorian Harewood); "There's More to a Man Than His Head" (reprise) (Marion Ramsey); "The Words Unspoken" (Bette Davis)

Act Two: "Peekaboo, Jehovah!" (Nell Carter, Ensemble); "The Words Unspoken" (reprise) (Bette Davis); "Go Go Morgan" (Ensemble); "I Can Talk Now" (Dorian Harewood, Bette Davis, Ensemble); "If It Weren't Me" (Bette Davis, David Sabin); "What Could Be Fairer Than That?" (Marion Ramsey); "The Debt I Owe" (Dorian Harewood); "I Shall Experience It Again" (Bette Davis)

Miss Moffat was one of the biggest disasters of the era. The first tryout stop of a proposed almost year-long tour was set for Baltimore's Mechanic Theatre, but because of Bette Davis's illness the Baltimore booking was canceled. The musical was then scheduled to premiere at Philadelphia's Shubert Theatre, but its opening there was postponed for two weeks. When it finally opened, it met with scathing reviews and played for little more than one week before permanently closing; future bookings in such venues as the Shubert Theatre in Boston on October 28 and the O'Keefe Center in Toronto on November 18 were scuttled.

The musical was based on Emlyn Williams's semiautobiographical 1938 London play *The Corn Is Green*, which starred Sybil Thorndike as Miss Moffat and Williams as Morgan Evans; the Broadway production opened at the National Theatre on November 26, 1940, and ran for 477 performances with Ethel Barrymore and Richard Waring in the leading roles. Set in a Welsh mining village, the story centered on dedicated spinster school teacher Miss Moffat, who believes that young student Morgan has the potential for greater things than a life in the mines. Because of Miss Moffat's mentoring, Morgan becomes a successful writer. When the play was filmed in 1945, Bette Davis played Miss Moffat (John Dall was Morgan). The play was revived on Broadway in 1943, 1950, and 1983; and there have been five television versions (1946, two in 1956, 1968, and 1979).

With director Joshua Logan, Williams cowrote the book of the musical, and he penned all the lyrics. The adaptation took place in the American South, and here Miss Moffat (Bette Davis) encourages young black student Morgan Evans (Dorian Harewood) to believe in himself and his abilities.

Ernest Scheir in the *Philadelphia Evening Bulletin* found the musical "uncertain and frequently boring," and Jonathan Takiff in the *Philadelphia Daily News* found the score "dismal," the book and lyrics "cornball," and the direction "surprisingly stilted." As for Bette Davis, Takiff noted there was a "thrill" in seeing the screen legend on the stage, and Swin in *Variety* said her singing voice revealed "a metrical mastery within a very narrow talk-song range."

Variety found the musical an "honest mistake" and noted "much work" was needed to salvage the show, and it seemed "dubious" that the musical's "inherent deficiencies" could be overcome. The score was "doggedly undistinguished," the book seemed like a straight play in which songs were "ushered in out of a feeling of obligation," and Jo Mielziner's sets suggested an "economy line." The critic singled out "Peekaboo, Jehovah!" as "delightful," and although the song wasn't "organic to the drama" it provided "lift" to the proceedings.

The song "There's a Stranger on My Doorstep" was apparently intended for the production, but was never performed due to the musical's premature closing.

The cast album was scheduled to be recorded by RCA Victor Records, but was canceled due to the show's abrupt closing. On May 2, 1975, the Friends of the Theatre and Music Collection of the Museum of the City of New York presented a tribute to Joshua Logan at the Imperial Theatre. Titled *A Gala Tribute to Joshua Logan*, the production included songs and dialogue sequences from musicals and plays directed by Logan, and the cast included Henry Fonda, James Stewart, Ethel Merman, José Ferrer, Dolores Gray, James Michener, Ray Walston, Diosa Costello, Sheila Bond, and Patricia Marand. The evening included two songs from *Miss Moffat* with original cast members: "Peekaboo, Jehovah!" (sung by Nell Carter, Avon Long, and the *Miss Moffat* company [excluding Bette Davis]) and "The Debt I Owe" (Dorian Harewood). The tribute was privately recorded on a two-LP set (unnamed company and unnumbered album) and was made available to the public for a limited period.

1975–1976 Season

CHICAGO

"A Musical Vaudeville"

Theatre: 46th Street Theatre
Opening Date: June 3, 1975; *Closing Date*: August 27, 1977
Performances: 898
Book: Fred Ebb and Bob Fosse
Lyrics: Fred Ebb
Music: John Kander
Based on the 1926 play *Chicago* by Maurine Dallas Watkins.
Direction and *Choreography*: Bob Fosse; *Producers*: Robert Fryer and James Cresson in association with Martin Richards, Joseph Harris, and Ira Bernstein; *Scenery*: Tony Walton; *Costumes*: Patricia Zipprodt; *Lighting*: Jules Fisher; *Musical Direction*: Stanley Lebowsky
Cast: *Chita Rivera* (Velma Kelly), *Gwen Verdon* (Roxie Hart), Christopher Chadman (Fred Cassidy), Richard Korthaze (Sergeant Fogarty), Barney Martin (Amos Hart), Cheryl Clark (Liz), Michon Peacock (Annie), Candy Brown (June), Graciela Daniele (Hunyak), Pamela Sousa (Mona), Michael Vita (Martin Harrison), Mary McCarty (Matron), *Jerry Orbach* (Billy Flynn), M. O'Haughey (Mary Sunshine), Charlene Ryan (Go-to-Hell Kitty), Paul Solen (Harry), Gene Foote (Aaron), Ron Schwinn (The Judge), Gary Gendell (Court Clerk); The Band: Sy Berger, Harry DeVito, Hank Freedman, Karen Gustafson, John Monaco, Anthony Pagano, Waymon Reed, James Sedlar, Charles Spies, William Stanley, Art Wagner, Frank Weiss, Tony Posk
The musical was presented in two acts.
The action takes place in Chicago, Illinois, during the late 1920s.

Musical Numbers

Act One: "All That Jazz" (Chita Rivera, Company); "Funny Honey" (Gwen Verdon); "Cell Block Tango" (Chita Rivera, Cheryl Clark, Michon Peacock, Candy Brown, Graciela Daniele, Pamela Sousa); "When You're Good to Mama" (Mary McCarty); "Tap Dance" (Gwen Verdon, Barney Martin, Boys); "All I Care About" (Jerry Orbach, Girls); "A Little Bit of Good" (M. O'Haughey); "We Both Reached for the Gun" (aka "The Press Conference Rag") (Jerry Orbach, Gwen Verdon, M. O'Haughey, Company); "Roxie" (Gwen Verdon, Boys); "I Can't Do It Alone" (Chita Rivera); "Chicago after Midnight" (The Band); "My Own Best Friend" (Gwen Verdon, Chita Rivera)
Act Two: "I Know a Girl" (Chita Rivera); "Me and My Baby" (Gwen Verdon, Christopher Chadman, Gene Foote); "Mister Cellophane" (Barney Martin); "When Velma Takes the Stand" (Chita Rivera, Boys); "Razzle Dazzle" (Jerry Orbach, Company); "Class" (Chita Rivera, Mary McCarty); "Nowadays" (Gwen Verdon); "Nowadays" (reprise) (Gwen Verdon, Chita Rivera); "R.S.V.P." (Gwen Verdon, Chita Rivera); "Keep It Hot" (Gwen Verdon, Chita Rivera)

Chicago was a sardonic and cynical look at everything it touched: marriage, show business, the media, and the justice system. Its attitudes may have been obvious and sophomoric, but the book was genuinely amusing in its saga of murderesses and show-biz wannabes Roxie Hart (Gwen Verdon) and Velma Kelly (Chita Rivera), their shyster lawyer Billy Flynn (Jerry Orbach), and the on-the-take prison-matron-with-vaudeville-connections (Mary McCarty). The musical's moral is the more the immorality, the greater the reward, and the show's only decent character is the hapless Hunyak, who is executed for a murder she didn't commit. But Roxie and Velma hit it big on the vaudeville circuit and prove that vice is its own reward.

John Kander and Fred Ebb's score was a series of knockout songs choreographed and staged to blockbuster perfection by Bob Fosse, whose seamless direction kept the musical moving at top speed. The production was presented as a series of vaudeville turns accompanied by occasional Brechtian-like announcements from various cast members who introduced and commented upon the numbers (we're told that Roxy and Velma's "My Own Best Friend" is "a song of unrelenting determination and unmitigated ego"). When a piano glides on stage with Roxie atop, she sings in Helen Morgan style the insincere "Funny Honey" about her husband Amos (Barney Martin); Billy's press conference for reporters to meet and interview Roxy is staged as a puppet-and-ventriloquist act with Roxie the puppet on Billy's lap as he sings the words, which she mouths; and the virtually invisible Amos sings "Mister Cellophane" in the manner of Ted Lewis. (And the score even turned on itself. The music of "Funny Honey" was ingratiatingly tender and delicate and the first part of the lyric was in the manner of classic torch songs of the "My Man" variety; but soon the number morphed into an excoriating damnation of Amos by Roxie.)

Tony Walton's stunning décor framed the proscenium with swirling translucent pillars decorated with photos of the era's figures, and high above center stage the orchestra was placed on a circular art deco platform of neon lights and tubing. Patricia Zipprodt's imaginative costumes were often shaggy with sagging stockings and a go-to-hell look reminiscent of a George Grosz nightmare.

If ***A Chorus Line*** hadn't opened during the same period, *Chicago* would clearly have been the season's biggest hit. But the musical was completely shut out of the Tony Awards, and while it received favorable reviews and had a profitable run of almost 1,000 performances, it was lost in the shadow of the Michael Bennett musical. But fate sometimes rights old wrongs, and as of this writing the 1996 Broadway revival of *Chicago* is still playing on Broadway and is the longest-running American musical in Broadway history (some 7,700 performances, and counting). Only the British import *The Phantom of the Opera* has played longer.

The critics admired Fosse's brilliant staging, the score, the performances, and the stylish decadence that permeated every aspect of the musical. But some were turned off by the cold and selfish characters. The dancers in ***A Chorus Line*** had heart and vulnerability, but the denizens of *Chicago* were icy and bloodless and could have quite comfortably fit into the world of ***The Threepenny Opera***. But twenty years after *Chicago*'s premiere, the country had become more cynical and had witnessed show-business-styled media trials on television, and so the 1996 revival of *Chicago* became the hottest ticket on Broadway.

In reviewing the original production, Martin Gottfried in the *New York Post* said *Chicago* was the most "dazzling demonstration of the craft of musical theatre as you're ever going to see on a Broadway stage." He cautioned however that while the "tremendous accomplishment" was "a sight to see," its "ingenuity of stylization" kept the characters "unreal and remote." Overall, the show was a "great accomplishment" that presented a "simply incredible unity of work" from its creators. The score was Kander's best and was a "superb series of period pieces" that were nonetheless "surreal and still musical and heart-catching" and Ebb's lyrics were "masterful." Clive Barnes in the *New York Times* found the evening a disappointment, but said it was "easily one of the best musicals of the season." He noted that everywhere there was style which dripped "like a dowager with opals." But for all its technical savvy, he felt the production didn't seem to go anywhere.

Douglas Watt in the *New York Daily News* said the "cynical and stylish" and "luridly effective spectacle" nonetheless "misses the mark" but was still a "corrosive cabaret show." There was an "overall brilliance" to Fosse's choreography, and he created "the sexiest dance routines imaginable." Watt's main complaint was that the underlying comparison of *Cabaret*'s Berlin to Chicago wasn't valid and "the two corrupt cultures" were "dissimilar." Jack Kroll in *Newsweek* said the musical was Fosse's "best work" but its "astringency" and "clinched tightness" would alienate some of its audience; he also noted the show lacked the "humane texture" of ***A Chorus Line***. The word "Fossephorescence" was the headline of T. E. Kalem's review in *Time*, and he predicted the musical was a "cinch to take a bite out of the Big Apple"; Fosse was "the most paganly sexual of choreographers" and Shubert Alley was his "mother earth."

Edwin Wilson in the *Wall Street Journal* said the "hard-edged, angular movement" of Fosse's cakewalks, Charlestons, and soft-shoe dances were "executed with verve and precision"; if the musical was sometimes uneven, it nonetheless followed "its own dictum and absolutely bedazzles the eyes." John Beaufort in the *Christian Science Monitor* noted the musical was "a piece of masterfully crafted showmanship" but seemed "hollow, melancholy, and abrasively alienating." But perhaps all this was "what Mr. Fosse intended."

Perhaps the strangest comment came from Kevin Sanders on WABCTV7, who said there was "nothing really wrong" with the "big, bright, generally better than average Broadway musical," but it had "no unifying theme," had no "center," and was "searching for an idea."

During the tryout, David Rounds played the role of Henry Glassman, a sleazy publicity agent who helps Roxie and Velma in their mania for publicity and stardom. When his role and song "Ten Percent" were written out of the show, part of his character morphed into the prison matron, who then became both warden and agent. Besides "Ten Percent," other songs cut in preproduction or during the tryout were "No," "It," "Curtain," "Rose-Colored Glasses," "Pansy Eyes," and "Loopin' the Loop" (the latter was heard as the musical's overture and as part of "Chicago after Midnight").

The script was published in paperback by Samuel French in 1976, and the original cast album was released by Arista Records (LP # 9005; later issued on CD # 07822-18952-2). The CD was also issued by Bay Cities Records (# BCD-3003). There were two orchestral versions of the score. Lee Konitz's *Chicago 'n All That Jazz* (Groove Merchant Records LP # GM-3306) was a big-band jazz interpretation of the score that included the cut songs "Ten Percent" and "Loopin' the Loop"; and *Chicago . . . and All That Jazz* (Varese Sarabande CD # VSD-5798) by the Brad Ellis Little Big Band included "Loopin' the Loop." *Forgotten Broadway* (unnamed company; LP # T-101) includes a live tryout performance of "It" by Verdon and Rivera. *Lost in Boston* (Varese Sarabande CD # VSD-5475) includes "Ten Percent" (sung by Harry Groener), and *Contemporary Broadway Revisited* (Painted Smiles Records CD # PSCD-131) includes "Ten Percent" and "Loopin' the Loop."

The first London production opened in 1979 for six hundred performances, and the second, which was based on the 1996 Broadway revival (see below), opened at the Adelphi Theatre on November 18, 1997, and played for approximately five thousand performances. As of this writing, the second revival holds the record as the longest-running American musical in West End history; it starred Ruthie Henshall, Ute Lemper, and Henry Goodman, and the cast album was released by RCA Victor/BMG Records (CD # 09026-63155-2). Two European productions based on the 1996 revival (both of which were recorded live) are the 1997 Austrian company (Reverso/BMG Records CD # 74321-583552) and the 1999 Dutch company (Endemol Records two-CD set # ENCD-99143).

The 1996 Broadway revival was first seen in a concert production by Encores! at City Center, where it opened on May 2, 1996, and played for a limited engagement of four performances with Ann Reinking (Roxie), Bebe Neuwirth (Velma), James Naughton (Billy Flynn), and Joel Grey (Amos). With all the leading players, this version opened on Broadway later in the year on November 14 at the Richard Rodgers (formerly 46th Street) Theatre, where of course the original production had opened twenty-one years earlier. It was fitting that the revival played at Fosse and Verdon's old stomping ground, for the 46th Street was not only the original home of *Chicago* but also of three other Fosse and Verdon collaborations: *Damn Yankees* (1955), *New Girl in Town* (1957), and *Redhead* (1959).

The Broadway revival's chic bare-bones look of stylishly black Victoria's Secret–like costumes, essentially skeletal platform-styled scenery, and an orchestra placed onstage emphasized the sardonic book, score, and dances. The choreography ("in the style of Bob Fosse") was by Reinking, and every vaudeville turn was developed into a show-stopping sequence. The revival opened to unanimously rave reviews, and almost twenty years later it is still playing on Broadway. This version omitted the orchestral sequence "Chicago after Midnight" as well as two dance numbers, "R.S.V.P." and "Keep It Hot." These last two were replaced by "Hot Honey Rag" (with choreography credited to Fosse), and it may be that "Hot Honey Rag" was a new overall title for "R.S.V.P." and "Keep It Hot."

The new production won six Tony Awards, including Best Revival of a Musical; Best Leading Actress in a Musical (Bebe Neuwirth); Best Leading Actor in a Musical (James Naughton); Best Director of a Musical (Walter Bobbie); Best Choreography (Ann Reinking); and Best Lighting Designer (Ken Billington).

The 1996 cast album was released by RCA Victor/BMG Records (CD # 09026-68727-2) and includes the first recording of "I Know a Girl," which wasn't recorded for the 1975 cast album.

The dazzling 2002 film version directed and choreographed by Rob Marshall was a clever cinematic adaptation that used stage-bound techniques in imaginative and exciting ways. Rather than presenting the songs as vaudeville-styled numbers introduced by various cast members, the musical sequences were staged as visions by the star-struck Roxie, who blows up everything in her life into colorful show-business turns. The film was a huge critical and financial success, was nominated for thirteen Academy Awards, and won six, including Oscars for Best Picture and Best Supporting Actress (Catherine Zeta-Jones, who played Velma). Others in the cast were Renee Zellweger (Roxie), Richard Gere (Billy Flynn), Queen Latifah (Matron), and John C. Reilly (Amos); there was even a classy nod to Chita Rivera, who was seen in a brief cameo appearance.

The film retained most of the songs from the two Broadway productions: "All That Jazz," "Funny Honey," "When You're Good to Mama," "Cell Block Tango," "All I Care About," "We Both Reached for the Gun," "Roxie," "I Can't Do It Alone," "Mister Cellophane," "Razzle Dazzle," "Nowadays," and "Hot Honey Rag." Omitted were "A Little Bit of Good," "My Own Best Friend," "I Know a Girl," "Me and My Baby," "R.S.V.P.," "Keep It Hot," and "Class." The latter was filmed but cut prior to the film's release, but was included on the soundtrack album and its outtake is an extra on the DVD release. The film included one new song, the vampy "I Move On," which was sung over the end credits by Roxie and Velma. There have been numerous releases of the CD and DVD, including a "special limited edition" CD (Epic/Sony Music Soundtrax # EK-89059) and a special two-DVD set ("The Razzle-Dazzle Edition") by Miramax (# 35001). A soundtrack was also issued in Russian (by Epic/Sony Music Soundtrax CD # 511952-2). The screenplay was published in a lavish hardback edition by Newmarket Press in 2003.

Awards

Tony Award Nominations: Best Musical (*Chicago*); Best Leading Actor in a Musical (Jerry Orbach); Best Leading Actress in a Musical (Chita Rivera); Best Leading Actress in a Musical (Gwen Verdon); Best Director of a Musical (Bob Fosse); Best Score (lyrics by Fred Ebb, music by John Kander); Best Scenic Designer (Tony Walton); Best Costume Designer (Patricia Zipprodt); Best Lighting Designer (Jules Fisher); Best Choreographer (Bob Fosse)

A CHORUS LINE

Theatre: Shubert Theatre
Opening Date: July 25, 1975; *Closing Date*: April 28, 1990
Performances: 6,137
Book: James Kirkwood and Nicholas Dante
Lyrics: Edward Kleban
Music: Marvin Hamlisch
Direction and *Choreography*: Michael Bennett (Bob Avian, Co-Choreographer); *Producers*: A New York Shakespeare Festival Production (Joseph Papp, Producer; Bernard Gersten, Associate Producer) in association with Plum Productions; *Scenery*: Robin Wagner; *Costumes*: Theoni V. Aldredge; *Lighting*: Tharon Musser; *Musical Direction*: Don Pippin
Cast: Scott Allen (Boy), Renee Baughman (Kristine), Carole (Kelly) Bishop (Sheila), Pamela Blair (Val), Wayne Cilento (Mike), Chuck Cissel (Butch), Clive Clerk (Larry), Kay Cole (Maggie), Ronald Dennis (Richie), Donna Drake (Tricia), Brandt Edwards (Tom), Patricia Garland (Judy), Carolyn Kirsch (Lois), Ron Kuhlman (Don), Nancy Lane (Bebe), Baayork Lee (Connie), Priscilla Lopez (Diana), Robert LuPone (Zach), Cameron Mason (Mark), Donna McKechnie (Cassie), Don Percassi (Al), Michael Serrecchia (Frank), Michel Stuart (Greg), Thomas J. (Thommie) Walsh (Bobby), Sammy Williams (Paul), Crissy Wilzak (Vicki); John Mineo and Carole Schweid were general understudies.
The musical was presented in one act.
The action takes place "now" (in 1975) and "here" (in a Broadway theatre).

Musical Numbers

"I Hope I Get It" (Company); "I Can Do That" (Wayne Cilento); "'And' . . ." (Thomas J. Walsh, Ronald Dennis, Pamela Blair, Patricia Garland); "At the Ballet" (Carole Bishop, Nancy Lane, Kay Cole); "Sing!" (Renee

Baughman, Don Percassi); "Hello Twelve, Hello Thirteen, Hello Love" (Company); "Nothing" (Priscilla Lopez); "Dance: Ten; Looks: Three" (Pamela Blair); "The Music and the Mirror" (Donna McKechnie); "One" (Company); "The Tap Combination" (Company); "What I Did for Love" (Priscilla Lopez, Company); "One" (reprise) (Company)

A Chorus Line was a concept musical about a group of some two-dozen dancers who audition for a new Broadway show. They line up across the stage, and the director Zach (Robert LuPone) asks each one to step forward and talk about him- or herself. Throughout the evening, he eliminates the dancers until finally eight are chosen for the new musical. For the finale of *A Chorus Line*, the entire cast appears in a fantasy extravaganza of glitter and gold as they sing the new musical's big number ("One"), which is designed to showcase the "singular sensation" of the unseen female star of the upcoming production. But instead of featuring the star, the finale celebrates the dancing chorus who are momentarily stars, each one a "singular sensation."

All the elements of the production supported the thin, revue-like story and while some were less successful than others the musical nonetheless struck a note with audiences who made the work one of the most successful in the history of Broadway.

Director and choreographer Michael Bennett made the evening spectacular because he fused every facet of the production into a continuous flow of musical movement. The book, lyrics, music, décor, and performances all supported his vision, and so the evening was one of the most fluid stagings ever seen in New York. His brilliant stage groupings were like images from a sharply edited film as the dancers weaved in and out of the action on wings of movement.

Marvin Hamlisch's score worked in perfect tandem with Bennett's concept, and the music permeated the mood of the production with a dance-oriented score that infused the action and provided a musical background for such expansive sequences as "At the Ballet," Hello Twelve, Hello Thirteen, Hello Love," "The Music and the Mirror," "The Tap Combination," and "One."

Only once did Bennett's choreography miss the mark. "The Music and the Mirror" was overwrought and brought to mind the worst excesses of interpretive dancing.

Although James Kirkwood and Nicholas Dante's book was spare and supported the staging techniques and the choreography, it was often excessively maudlin with its naval-gazing characters who overanalyzed themselves to the point of parody. The musical was a product of the so-called Me Decade, and so the constant babbling by some of the characters was right in step with the zeitgeist (if these people were around today, they'd be screaming into their cell phones and texting themselves into oblivion).

The story's basic premise was also weak. It was simply not believable that a director would require prospective cast members to submit to such probing questions in a public forum; and why would the dancers themselves go along with him? Didn't any of them have a notion of what personal matters are, of what privacy is? One might go along with a serious one-on-one interview between a director and a performer, but the group therapy confessional approach was hard to accept. It was also somewhat distasteful to witness the dancers all but grovel while they swallowed their pride in order to get a spot in the new show. But perhaps all of them were exhibitionists and enjoyed baring their souls.

The characters also complained so much about their chosen profession that one suspected some weren't suited for a life in the theatre. No vocation is perfect, and why should theirs be any different? Hopefully they all attended ***Working*** a few years later and picked up some tips about non–show business jobs.

Edward Kleban's lyrics were generally ordinary and were in no way a match for Hamlisch's score. And like the librettists, he emphasized the self-pitying and self-obsessed aspects of many of the characters.

The constant self-pity and overanalyzing were burdens that threatened to constantly bog down the evening, but the music, direction, and choreography came through to salvage the smug, self-satisfied atmosphere of sharing one's most personal issues with a group of strangers.

The musical was first seen Off Broadway, where it opened at the Public's Newman Theatre on April 15, 1975, for 101 performances. Its top-ticket price was $8.00, and the cheapest seats were $3.50, and Mike's song "Joanne" was replaced by "I Can Do That." With rave reviews and instant sell-out status, it was a given that the show would transfer to Broadway, and so the first performance at the Shubert Theatre occurred on July 25; due to a musicians' strike, there was a later "official" opening on October 19.

The musical became an instant sensation and played at the Shubert for 6,137 performances; it was the season's longest-running musical, and when it closed was the longest-running show in Broadway history (as of this writing it's in sixth place). There were numerous touring companies, and a London production opened on July 22, 1976, at the Drury Lane for an approximate three-year run.

Martin Gottfried in the *New York Post* found the musical "purely and simply magnificent" and "a major event in the development of the American musical theatre." Hamlisch provided that "rare animal," a "theatre *score*" that wasn't "just a series of songs but an evening's worth of music designed to function as part of the stage work." But the "quasi-group therapy" aspect of the musical was "weak" and Zach came across as "God the psychotherapist." Clive Barnes in the *New York Times* said the "tremendous" and "terrific" musical would take its place in the history of musical theatre, and even the "hokum" of the dancer who once worked in drag shows and the backstory of Cassie and Zach's romance and her brief movie career worked because they were "undisguised and unapologetic."

Douglas Watt in the *New York Daily News* praised the "splendid achievement" as "the most exciting Broadway musical in several seasons"; Edwin Wilson in the *Wall Street Journal* said the "most exciting musical of the season" offered a finale "so sensational that it's bound to go down in show business annals as one of the most exciting finishes in modern musicals"; Christopher Sharp in *Women's Wear Daily* exclaimed that Bennett had created a musical "to make the heart pound"; and John Beaufort in the *Christian Science Monitor* said the musical would be "superior entertainment in any season" because it was "original, full of style and flair, at times quite breathtaking, and essentially very touching."

The script was belatedly published in hardback by Applause Books in 1995. The original cast album was released by Columbia Records (LP # PS-33581); the CD was issued by Sony Classical/Columbia/Legacy Records (# SK-65282) and includes an expanded version of "Hello Twelve, Hello Thirteen, Hello Love." Other recordings of the score include the 1983 Oslo cast (NorDisc Records LP # NORLP-422); the 1988 German cast (LP # 835-485-1 and CD # 835-485-2; company unknown); and the 1990 Italian cast (Carisch Records CD # CL-36). Columbia Records also released the LP collection *Andre Kostelanetz Plays "A Chorus Line," "Treemonisha" and "Chicago."*

There have been numerous books written about *A Chorus Line*, including: *What They Did for Love: The Untold Story Behind the Making of "A Chorus Line"* by Denny Martin Flinn (Bantam Books, 1989; paperback); *On the Line: The Creation of "A Chorus Line"* by Robert Viagas, Baayork Lee, and Thommie Walsh (William Morrow & Company, 1990, hardback; reprinted in paperback by Limelight Editions in 2006); and *The Longest Line: Broadway's Most Singular Sensation: "A Chorus Line"* by Gary Stevens and Alan George (Applause Theatre & Cinema Books, 1995; hardback).

The disappointing and lackluster 1985 film version by Polygram Pictures was indifferently directed by Richard Attenborough and included two new songs ("Surprise, Surprise" and "Let Me Dance for You"); the soundtrack was released by Casablanca and Filmworks Records (LP # 826-306-1M-1) and MGM issued the DVD.

The musical was revived at the Gerald Schoenfeld Theatre on October 5, 2006, for 759 performances, and the cast recording was released by Sony Masterworks Broadway Records (CD # 82876-89785-2). *Every Little Step: The Journey of "A Chorus Line"* is a documentary about the 2006 revival and the dancers who auditioned for it; the DVD was released by Sony Pictures Home Entertainment.

The musical's title was first used for an unproduced play by George Furth, who had of course written the book for ***Company***, which had been choreographed by Michael Bennett; the play was announced for production in 1970 and had been optioned by David Merrick.

Awards

Tony Awards and *Nominations*: Best Musical (***A Chorus Line***); Best Leading Actress in a Musical (**Donna McKechnie**); Best Featured Actor in a Musical (Robert LuPone); Best Featured Actor in a Musical (**Sammy Williams**); Best Featured Actress in a Musical (**Carole Bishop**); Best Featured Actress in a Musical (Priscilla Lopez); Best Director of a Musical (**Michael Bennett**); Best Book (**James Kirkwood** and **Nicholas Dante**); Best Score (music by **Marvin Hamlisch** and lyrics by **Edward Kleban**); Best Costume Designer (Theoni V. Aldredge); Best Lighting Designer (**Tharon Musser**); Best Choreographer (**Michael Bennett**)

New York Drama Critics' Circle Award: Best Musical (1974–1975): ***A Chorus Line***

Pulitzer Prize (1975–1976): ***A Chorus Line***

DIE FLEDERMAUS

Theatre: The New York State Theatre
Opening Date: August 29, 1975; *Closing Date*: November 1, 1975
Performances: 5 (in repertory)
Libretto: Carl Haffner and Richard Genee (English adaptation by Ruth and Thomas Martin)
Music: Johann Strauss
Direction: Gerald Freedman (Richard Getke, Stage Direction); *Producer*: The New York City Opera Company; *Choreography*: Thomas Andrew; *Scenery*: Lloyd Evans; *Costumes*: Theoni V. Aldredge; *Lighting*: Hans Sondheimer; *Musical Direction*: Alexis Hauser
Cast: Gary Glaze (Alfred), Arlene Randazzo (Adele), Johanna Meier (Rosalinda von Eisenstein), Alan Titus (Gabriel von Eisenstein), Joaquin Romaguerra (Doctor Blind), David Holloway (Doctor Falke), Spiro Malas (Frank), Puli Toro (Sally), Jack Sims (Ivan), David Rae Smith (Prince Orlofsky), Coley Worth (Frosch); Solo Dancers: Sandra Balestracci, Esperanza Galan, Juliu Horvath; Ensemble: The New York City Opera Chorus and Dancers
The operetta was presented in three acts.

Johann Strauss's 1874 operetta *Die Fledermaus* had been revived twice by the New York City Opera Company during the previous season, when it opened on September 18, 1974, and then on March 18, 1975, for a total of thirteen performances in repertory. For the current revival, most of the principal from the previous year's production returned, including Johanna Meier, Alan Titus, Spiro Malas, and David Rae Smith.

Raymond Ericson in the *New York Times* noted that for the operetta's current engagement, Gerald Freedman's direction was still "lively and neat" and the ballroom scene had been choreographed by Thomas Andrew to make "effective use" of the limited stage space. The orchestra played "crisply" under Alexis Hauser's baton, Johanna Meier "dominated the singing" with her "warmth, power and elan," Gary Glaze had "the right light comic touch" for Alfred, and Coley Worth provided a "lovely comedy routine" as Frosch. Ericson concluded his review by praising the "good show," which "lifted the audience's spirits."

The production returned later in the season when it opened on February 29, 1976, for an additional five performances in repertory.

For more information about the operetta, see entry for the 1974 production.

THE ROBBER BRIDEGROOM

Theatre: Harkness Theatre
Opening Date: October 7, 1975; *Closing Date*: October 18, 1975
Performances: 15
Book and *Lyrics*: Alfred Uhry
Music: Robert Waldman
Based on the 1942 novella *The Robber Bridegroom* by Eudora Welty.
Direction: Gerald Freedman; *Producer*: The Acting Company (John Houseman, Artistic Director; Margot Harley, Producing Director); *Choreography*: Donald Saddler; *Scenery*: Douglas Schmidt; *Costumes*: Jeanne Button; *Lighting*: David F. Segal; *Musical Direction*: Not credited
Cast: Kevin Kline (Jamie Lockhart), Norman Snow (Mike Fink), David Schramm (Clemment Musgrove), Robert Bacigalupi (Goat), J. W. Harper (Little Harp), Anderson Matthews (Big Harp), Brooks Baldwin (Kyle Nunnery), Richard Ooms (Tom Plymale), Nicolas Surovy (Billy Brenner), Roy K. Stevens (John Oglesby), Peter Dvorsky (Ernie Summers), Michael Tolaydo (Herman McLaughlin), Mary Lou Rosato (Salome), Patti LuPone (Rosamund), Glynis Bell (Goat's Mother), Sandra Halperin (Airie), Elaine Hausman (Raven), Cynthia Dickason (Queenie Sue Stevens), Alan Kaufman (The Fiddler); Orchestra—The Wretched Refuse: Bob Jones (Guitar), Alan Kaufman (Fiddle, Mandolin), David Markowitz (Bass), Richard Shulberg (Fiddle), and Steve Tannenbaum (Banjo)
The musical was presented in one act.
The action takes place "in legendary Mississippi."

Musical Numbers

"With Style" (Kevin Kline, Company); "The Real Mike Fink" (Kevin Kline, David Schramm, Norman Snow); "The Pricklepear Bloom" (Mary Lou Rosato); "Nothin' Up" (Patti LuPone); "Deeper in the Woods" (Company); "Riches" (David Schramm, Kevin Kline, Mary Lou Rosato, Patti LuPone); "Love Stolen" (Kevin Kline); "Poor Tied Up Darlin'" (J. W. Harper, Robert Bacigalupi); "Goodbye Salome" (Company); "Sleepy Man" (Patti LuPone)

The Robber Bridegroom was performed in repertory with three nonmusicals produced by The Acting Company, Christopher Marlowe's *Edward II*, William Saroyan's *The Time of Your Life*, and Anton Chekhov's *The Three Sisters*. Prior to the New York engagement, The Acting Company had first presented the musical at the Saratoga Performing Arts Center, Saratoga Springs, New York, on July 28, 1975.

Set in "legendary Mississippi," the quirky if slight fable-like story centered on charming Robin Hood–like robber Jamie Lockhart (Kevin Kline), who becomes romantically involved with Rosamund (Patti LuPone) when he saves her father, Clemment Musgrove (David Schramm), from a gang of robbers. But Rosamund's stepmother Salome (Mary Lou Rosato) has designs on Jamie and so she plans to murder Rosamund. Her scheme fatally boomerangs, and along the way there are misunderstandings, disguises, and mistaken identities to contend with before the requisite happy ending for everyone (except Salome).

Martin Gottfried in the *New York Post* said the "delightful" blend of Southern folklore and Grimm fairy tales had a "whimsical and fresh" book, a "melodic" and "theatrical" score, and a "grand" company, and Clive Barnes in the *New York Times* found the evening "as lively as a fiddle at a wedding" and was "much taken" with Patti LuPone and Kevin Kline. Douglas Watt in the *New York Daily News* said the "screwy" musical was a "humdinger" that resembled a "lewd comic strip set to attractive and rather sophisticated country music." The lyrics were "salty," the production was "superbly" directed, Patti LuPone gave "a thoroughly engaging and smart comedy performance," and her ballad "Sleepy Man" was "lovely."

Christopher Sharp in *Women's Wear Daily* liked the "cornball evening of nonsense," which was "light and alternately funny and childish," and mentioned some of the evening's off-the-wall touches: when the simpleminded Goat (Robert Bacigalupi) quotes his mother, he speaks in a woman's voice (thanks to ventriloquism); when a character hears Goat approaching from offstage, he comments that "something stupid" is coming; and a pet raven owned by one of the gang members is played by an actress (Elaine Hausman). Edwin Wilson in the *Wall Street Journal* suggested the musical was a bit too long, but otherwise was "delightful," and he praised the score, which had "the flavor of a Southern hoedown or square dance."

John Beaufort in the *Christian Science Monitor* thought the "fiddle-faddle foolery" went a long way, but he liked the "fetching" score and "boisterous" dances; and Leonard Probst on NBC Radio praised the "strange, lusty, light-hearted laugh show" which was a "barnyard country folk-opera."

At the time of the musical's opening, Broadway was in the midst of a musicians' union strike, but in his review Barnes noted that because the Harkness Theatre was operating under a special contract with the union until 1977, the musical was unaffected.

Prior to the musical's production by The Acting Company, the work had first been seen Off Off Broadway at St. Clement's Church on November 4, 1974, for six performances where it was produced by St. Clement's and The Stuart Ostrow Foundation. As he did for the subsequent 1975 and 1976 Broadway productions, Gerald Freedman directed, and the 1974 cast included Raul Julia (Jamie Lockhart), Rhonda Coullet (Rosamund), and Susan Berger (Salome). (For information about the expanded 1976 production, see entry.)

The script was published in hardback by Drama Books Specialists in 1978, and the 1976 Broadway production was recorded by CBS Records as part of their "Collectors' Series" (LP # P-14589). The CD was issued by Original Cast Records. Patti LuPone performs "Sleepy Man" on the two-CD *Patti LuPone Live* (RCA Victor # 09026-61797-2) which was recorded live from her concert performances at the Westwood Playhouse in Los Angeles, California, in January 1993.

With the present booking by The Acting Company, the Harkness Theatre became a legitimate Broadway theatre again after spending many decades as a movie house and television studio. The venue first opened its doors in 1905 as the Colonial, and perhaps its most famous tenant was the 1923 musical *Runnin' Wild*, which introduced the most iconic Roaring Twenties song of them all, "Charleston." In 1974, the house was renamed the Harkness and was intended as the home base for the Harkness Ballet Company, which briefly performed there. But the theatre had poor luck in its bookings (such as ***So Long, 174th Street***, which opened later in the season) and in 1977 was demolished.

Awards

Tony Award Nominations: Best Featured Actress in a Musical (Patti LuPone); Best Book of a Musical (Alfred Uhry)

THE 5TH SEASON

Theatre: Eden Theatre
Opening Date: October 12, 1975; *Closing Date*: January 25, 1976
Performances: 122
Book: Luba Kadison
Lyrics and *Music*: Dick Manning; Yiddish adaptation of lyrics by Isaac Dogim
Based on the 1953 play *The Fifth Season* by Sylvia Regan.
Direction: Joseph Buloff; *Producers*: Harry Rothpearl and Jewish Nostalgic Productions, Inc.; *Choreography*: Sophie Maslow; *Scenery* and *Costumes*: Jeffrey B. Moss; *Lighting*: Bob McCarthy; *Musical Direction*: Renee Solomon
Cast: Elias Patron (Mr. Katz), Gerri-Ann Frank (Shelly), Raquel Yossiffon (Laurie), David Carey (Perl), *Joseph Buloff* (Max Pincus), Stan Porter (Benny Goodwin), Evelyn Kingsley (Frances Goodwin), Gene Barrett (Marty Goodwin), Miriam Kressyn (Miriam Oppenheim), Jack Rechtzeit (Mr. Lewis); Models: Franceska Fischler, Cathy Carnevale, Barbara Joan Frank
The musical was presented in two acts.
The action takes place during the present time in a Seventh Avenue fashion showroom.

Musical Numbers

Act One: "Believe in Yourself" (Stan Porter, Raquel Yossiffon); "My Son, The Doctor" (Stan Porter, Evelyn Kingsley, Gene Barrett); "Goodbye" (Stan Porter, Raquel Yossiffon); "The Fifth Season" (Ensemble)
Act Two: "Friday Night" (lyric by Lisa Kadison) (Joseph Buloff, Miriam Kressyn); "Mom! You Don't Understand!" (Gene Barrett, Evelyn Kingsley); "How Did This Happen to Me?" (Stan Porter); "From Seventh Avenue to Seventh Heaven" (Stan Porter, Ensemble)

The 5th Season was a Yiddish and English musical adaptation of Sylvia Regan's hit 1953 comedy *The Fifth Season*, which despite dismissive reviews from the critics played on Broadway for 645 performances. The play's star Menasha Skulnik received rave notices, and he no doubt was the major reason for the show's long run.

The wispy plot dealt with Max Pincus (Joseph Buloff) and Benny Goodwin (Stan Porter), who are partners in a Seventh Avenue dress firm that always seems to have creditors at the door. And there were a few romantic entanglements: the married Benny becomes briefly involved with a model, while Max is pursued by Miriam Oppenheim (Miriam Kressyn).

The play's title referred to the five seasons of the garment industry, Spring, Summer, Fall, Winter, and Slack (and "slack" didn't refer to leisure apparel).

In reviewing the original play, Walter Kerr in the *New York Herald Tribune* noted that Sylvia Regan had forgotten about another season—the theatrical one, in which "work done on Broadway is expected to be professional" (he provided a sample of the dialogue: "I feel like Hamlet"; "A partner of yours?"); but Robert Sylvester in the *New York Daily News* said Menasha Skulnik was "one of the funniest men who ever lived" and he didn't care if *The Fifth Season* was a good play or not as long as "my Menasha" was in it.

As for the musical version, Thomas Lask in the *New York Times* said it was "an ebullient and engaging evening" with a "fistful" of "romantic" and "nostalgic" songs, none of them "strictly necessary." But Joseph

Buloff (who had created the role of Ali Hakim in the original production of *Oklahoma!*) was "never less than perfect" and his "consummate skills" made the show worth seeing.

TREEMONISHA

Theatre: Uris Theatre (during run, the opera transferred to the Palace Theatre)
Opening Date: October 21, 1975; *Closing Date*: December 14, 1975
Performances: 64
Libretto and *Music*: Scott Joplin
Direction: Frank Corsaro; *Producers*: Adela Holzer, James Nederlander, and Victor Lurie; A Houston Grand Opera Association Production; *Choreography*: Louis Johnson; *Scenery* and *Costumes*: Franco Colavecchia; *Lighting*: Nananne Porcher; *Musical Direction*: Gunther Schuller
Cast: Ben Harney (Zodzetrick), Willard White (Ned), Betty Allen (Monisha), Carmen Balthrop (Treemonisha), Curtis Rayam (Remus), Kenneth Hicks (Andy), Cora Johnson (Lucy), Edward Pierson (Parson Alltalk), Raymond Bazemore (Simon), Dwight Ransom (Cephus), Dorceal Duckens (Luddud); Dancers (The Louis Johnson Dance Theatre): Clyde-Jacques Barrett, Thea Barnes, Dwight Baxter, Renee Brailsford, Karen Burke, Veda Jackson, Reggie Jackson, Julia Lema, Anita Littleman, Rick Odums, Dwayne Phelps, Ivson Polk, Mabel Robinson, Martial Roumain, Katherine Singleton, James Thurston, Bobby Walker, Pamela Wilson; Singers: Earl L. Baker, Kenneth Bates, Barbara Christopher, Steven Cole, Ella Eure, Gregory Gardner, Melvin Jordan, Patricia McDermott, Janette Moody, Marion Moore, Vera Moore, Lorna Myers, Glover Parham, Patricia Pates, William Penn, Dwight Ransom, Cornel Richie, Patricia Rogers, Christine Spencer, Walter Turnbull, Gloria Turner, Peter Whitehead, Arthur Williams, Barbara Young; *Note*: For Saturday matinee performances, Lorna Myers sang the role of Monisha, and for Wednesday and Saturday matinees, Kathleen Battle sang the role of Treemonisha.
The opera was presented in two acts.
The action takes place during one day in 1884 on a plantation settlement in Arkansas.

Musical Numbers

Act One: Overture (Orchestra, with Ben Harney and Dancers); "The Bag of Luck" (Carmen Balthrop, Betty Allen, Curtis Rayam, Willard White, Ben Harney); "The Corn-Huskers" (Carmen Balthrop, Chorus); "We're Goin' Around" (Carmen Balthrop, Betty Allen, Cora Johnson, Curtis Rayam, Willard White, Chorus, Dancers); "The Wreath" (Carmen Balthrop, Betty Allen, Cora Johnson); "The Sacred Tree" (Betty Allen); "Surprise" (Carmen Balthrop); "Treemonisha's Bringing Up" (Carmen Balthrop, Betty Allen); "Good Advice" (Edward Pierson, Chorus); "Confusion" (Betty Allen, Cora Johnson, Curtis Rayam, Willard White); "Superstition" (Raymond Sizemore, Dwight Ransom); "Treemonisha in Peril" (Ben Harney, Raymond Sizemore, Dorceal Duckens, Dwight Ransom); "The Frolic of the Bears" (Dancers); "The Wasp Nest" (Raymond Sizemore, Dwight Ransom); "The Rescue" (Carmen Balthrop, Curtis Rayam); "We Will Rest Awhile" (Quartet); "Going Home" (Carmen Balthrop, Curtis Rayam, Foreman [unidentified performer]); "Aunt Dinah Has Blowed de Horn" (Chorus, Dancers)
Act Two: Prelude (Orchestra); "I Want to See My Child" (Betty Allen, Willard White); "Treemonisha's Return" (Carmen Balthrop, Betty Allen, Curtis Rayam, Willard White, Kenneth Hicks); "Wrong Is Never Right" (Curtis Rayam, Chorus); "Abuse" (Carmen Balthrop, Kenneth Hicks); "When Villains Ramble Far and Near" (Willard White); "Conjurors Forgiven" (Carmen Balthrop, Kenneth Hicks); "We Will Trust You as Our Leader" (Carmen Balthrop, Betty Allen, Cora Johnson, Willard White, Curtis Rayam, Kenneth Hicks, Chorus); "A Real Slow Drag" (Company); "Aunt Dinah Has Blowed de Horn" (reprise) (Company)

The successful 1973 film *The Sting* introduced Scott Joplin's ragtime music to a new generation, and the enormous popularity of the music resulted in an interest in Joplin's all-but-lost opera *Treemonisha,* which was assumed by many to be a "ragtime opera." Joplin completed the work in 1910, the piano score was published in 1911, and in 1915 a disastrous concert version was presented by Joplin in Harlem where the opera was reputedly scorned by the audience of blacks and whites. Decades later the score was reconstructed and staged in Atlanta, and in 1976 the Houston Grand Opera presented the work, which eventually opened on Broadway. The production had originally been intended as a limited three-week engagement at the Uris, and reportedly was an immediate sell-out. So even before opening night, an extended but limited run was booked for the Palace Theatre. (The Broadway production had been postponed for a few weeks due to the musicians' strike, and once the strike was settled Joplin's long-aborning opera finally saw its first full-length New York performance.)

Walter Kerr in the *New York Times* noted that if the opera wasn't "everything" Joplin had hoped for, it nonetheless wasn't "fake" and was as "strangely soothing, simple and sweet as a cradlesong." He correctly predicted that *Treemonisha* wouldn't find a place in the permanent operatic repertory and thus "we shan't see it often." So the current production was a rare opportunity to see a lavish and fully staged version of the work.

Treemonisha was definitely not the "ragtime opera" everyone hoped it would be, and perhaps that's where its fault lies. Joplin basically wrote in the European tradition, and the opera might have been more forceful had he followed his natural musical instincts and composed a completely "American" opera in a vernacular musical style. In this way, his opera would have been thoroughly American in music and story. Unfortunately, the score offered only a few "American" and recognizably Joplinesque moments, and these were truly memorable: the gentle barbershop-styled quartet "We Will Rest Awhile," the rousing "Aunt Dinah Has Blowed de Horn," and the undulating contours of the mesmerizing "A Real Slow Drag." Joplin truly found his voice in these sequences, and if the remainder of the score had reached this level *Treemonisha* would surely have found its place in American opera along with *Porgy and Bess*, *The Tender Land*, *Susannah*, and *The Ballad of Baby Doe*.

Besides Joplin's emphasis on European operatic conventions, his libretto was paper-thin and offered little in the way of drama, conflict, and character. The action takes place within a twenty-four-hour period in 1884 in a small plantation settlement in Arkansas where Treemonisha (Carmen Balthrop) is the only educated black in an area rife with conjurors and superstitious practices. Because the conjurors view Treemonisha as a threat to their power, they kidnap and prepare to kill her, but she's saved by her friend Remus (Curtis Rayam). Through the force of her beliefs and her vision, the entire community decides to make her their leader and to follow her mantra that education is the only way to become enlightened and truly free.

Martin Gottfried in the *New York Post* felt that *Treemonisha* wasn't "very good opera, very good theatre, or very good Joplin" because of its "boring" libretto and the "sheer slumber" of most of the first act (and the second act seemed to forget about the story and for all purposes turned into a concert). But he praised "Aunt Dinah Has Blowed de Horn" and especially "A Real Slow Drag" which was "so beautiful and so fresh" it practically justified the entire evening. Leonard Probst on NBC Radio said the work didn't offer "especially good music" and the libretto was "simple beyond belief," and so the "reverential but uninspired" evening was at best "historical curiosity."

Clive Barnes in the *New York Times* praised the production but noted the first act didn't generate much in the way of excitement; however, he liked the score and singled out five songs. Douglas Watt in the *New York Daily News* found a "disarming sweetness and simplicity about the score" and said the opera was "a very special evening of delight"; and Edwin Wilson in the *Wall Street Journal* liked the "lyrical and surprisingly varied" score but felt the work "faltered" when Joplin tried "to graft a home-spun story onto a strictly European form."

John Beaufort in the *Christian Science Monitor* noted that Joplin's opera was "visionary" in its attitudes toward feminism and black enlightenment, and Howard Kissel in *Women's Wear Daily* said that the Houston Grand Opera made a "powerful case for this beautiful work" which was "an event no one who cares about American musical theatre can miss."

During the tryout, Edward Pierson succeeded Clark Morgan as Parson Alltalk.

The cast album was released on a two-LP set with the complete libretto by Deutsche Grammophon Records (LP # 2702-083), which later issued a CD set, and New World Records released a two-CD version of the opera with Anita Johnson and the Paragon Ragtime Orchestra. A piano interpretation of the score by Richard Zimmerman was released on LP by Olympic Records, and *Andre Kostelanetz Plays "A Chorus Line," "Treemonisha," and "Chicago"* was issued on LP by Columbia Records.

A 1985 Houston Grand Opera revival with Carmen Balthrop and Obba Babatunde was shown on public television in 1986 and was released on video cassette.

Awards

Tony Award Nomination: Best Score (Scott Joplin)

ME AND BESSIE

"A Musical Evening"

Theatre: Ambassador Theatre (during run, the revue transferred to the Edison Theatre)
Opening Date: October 22, 1975; *Closing Date*: December 5, 1976
Performances: 453
Text: Will Holt and Linda Hopkins
Lyrics and *Music*: For credits, see song list below.
Direction: Robert Greenwald; *Producers*: Lee Apostoleris (A Center Theatre Group/Mark Taper Forum and Lee Apostoleris Production); *Choreography*: Special Dance Sequences by Lester Wilson; *Scenery*: Donald Harris; *Costumes*: Pete Menefee; *Lighting*: Tharon Musser; *Musical Direction*: Howlett Smith
Cast: *Linda Hopkins* (Bessie Smith), Lester Wilson (Man), Gerri Dean (Woman); The Band: Howlett Smith (Leader, Piano), Bob Bushnell (Bass), Ray Mosca (Drums), Dick Griffin (Trombone), and Lenny Hambro (Clarinet, Saxophone)
The revue was presented in two acts.

Musical Numbers

Note: Virtually all the songs were performed by Linda Hopkins, who was backed by Lester Wilson and Gerri Dean.

Act One: "I Feel Good" (lyricist and composer unknown); "God Shall Wipe All Tears Away" (lyricist and composer unknown); "Moan You Mourners" (lyricist and composer unknown); "New Orleans Hot Scop Blues" (lyricist and composer unknown); "Romance in the Dark" (lyric and music by Lil Green); "Preach Them Blues" (lyric and music by Bessie Smith); "A Good Man Is Hard to Find" (lyric and music by Eddie Green); "T'Ain't Nobody's Bizness If I Do" (lyric and music attributed to Porter Grainger, Everett Robbins, Clarence Williams, and Graham Prince); "Gimme a Pigfoot (and a Bottle of Beer)" (lyric and music by Wesley Wilson); "Put It Right Here" (lyric and music by Porter Grainger); "You've Been a Good Old Wagon" (lyric and music by J. Henry); "Trombone Cholly" (lyricist and composer unknown); "Jazzbo Brown" (lyricist and composer unknown); "After You've Gone" (lyric by Henry Creamer, music by Turner Layton)

Act Two: "(There'll Be a) Hot Time in the Old Town Tonight" (lyric by Joe Hayden, music by Theodore August Metz); "Empty Bed Blues" (lyric and music by J. C. Johnson); "Kitchen Man" (lyric by Andy Razaf, music by Alex Belledna); "Mama Don't 'Low" (lyricist and composer unknown); "Do Your Duty" (lyric and music by Wesley Wilson); "Fare Thee Well" (lyricist and composer unknown); "Nobody Knows You When You're Down and Out" (lyric and music by Jimmy Cox); "Trouble" (lyric and music by D. Akers); "The Man's All Right" (lyricist and composer unknown)

Me and Bessie was a tribute revue to blues singer Bessie Smith (1894–1937), known as the Empress of the Blues. Although Linda Hopkins was identified in the program as playing the role of Bessie Smith, she didn't necessarily impersonate her. She said, "I ain't Bessie. But, you know, there's a whole lot of Bessie in me." And so she morphed between Smith and her own persona (and her specialty of gospel songs) throughout the evening, and was backed by dancers and singers Lester Wilson and Gerri Dean and a five-piece band. As the evening progressed, Hopkins provided occasional background information about Smith's life and career (the text was written by both Hopkins and Will Holt).

Clive Barnes in the *New York Times* noted that the "tremendous" Hopkins was more a gospel than a blues singer, but she nonetheless could be "funny" in "(There'll Be a) Hot Time in the Old Town Tonight" and "cheerfully bawdy" in "Kitchen Man." He suggested that not only was there some Bessie Smith in her, there was also a touch of Pearl Bailey. Martin Gottfried in the *New York Post* said Hopkins's voice was "stunning"; Edwin Wilson in the *Wall Street Journal* noted it was doubtful if anyone but Smith herself could have provided a more authentic presentation of the blues singer and her repertoire; T. E. Kalem in *Time* noted that Smith sang from "pain" and Hopkins from "joy," and if the latter never quite became Smith she was nonetheless a "champ"; Barbara Ettorre in *Women's Wear Daily* said Hopkins's "happily innocent sophistication warms" the theatre and she "more than balances some of the lightweight aspects of the show"; and John Beaufort in the *Christian Science Monitor* praised the "virtuosic voice range and resources" of Hopkins's voice but cautioned that the evening was "by no means entertainment for all tastes."

Douglas Watt in the *New York Daily News* said the "pleasant" revue never moved him, and suggested Hopkins "lacks that final thrust as a singer to make you cheer." He also noted that when she received a standing ovation after "Trouble," the "moment seemed cued" (and for her appearance in ***Inner City***, there was a similar moment which seemed "plotted").

Prior to the New York production, the revue had been produced in other cities such as Los Angeles and Washington, D.C.; dropped prior to Broadway was the song "Careless Love." When the revue transferred from the Ambassador to the Edison Theatre, Norman Kean became coproducer and during part of the revue's run at the Edison the production alternated with performances of ***Oh! Calcutta!***

The cast album was recorded by Columbia Records (LP # PC-34032).

At least two critics noted that the revue made no mention of the circumstances of Bessie Smith's death, and both referred to her being turned away from a white hospital after a traffic accident. But this story seems to have been discredited, and so perhaps that's why Holt and Hopkins didn't refer to it. It appears that after the accident, an ambulance took Smith directly to a black hospital (the hospital, located in Clarksdale, Tennessee, was then known as the G.T. Thomas Afro-American Hospital and today is called the Riverside Hospital).

HELLO, DOLLY!

Theatre: Minskoff Theatre
Opening Date: November 6, 1975; *Closing Date*: December 21, 1975
Performances: 51
Book: Michael Stewart
Lyrics and *Music*: Jerry Herman
Based on the 1955 play *The Matchmaker* by Thornton Wilder, which was a revised version of his 1938 play *The Merchant of Yonkers* (which in turn was based on the 1842 Austrian play *Einen jux will er sich machen* by Johann Nestroy, which had been based on the 1835 British play *A Day Well Spent* by John Oxenford).
Direction: Lucia Victor; *Producers*: Robert Cherin in association with Theatre Now, Inc.; *Choreography*: Gower Champion (choreography re-created by Jack Craig); *Scenery*: Oliver Smith; *Costumes*: "supervised by" Robert Pusilo; *Lighting*: John Gleason; *Musical Direction*: Al Cavaliere
Cast: *Pearl Bailey* (Mrs. Dolly Gallagher Levi), Bessye Ruth Scott (Ernestina), Howard Porter (Ambrose Kemper), Kathy Jennings (Horse), Karen Hubbard (Horse, Ermengarde), Billy Daniels (Horace Vandergelder), Terrence Emanuel (Cornelius Hackl), Grenoldo Frazier (Barnaby Tucker), Mary Louise (Irene Malloy), Chip Fields (Minnie Fay), Birdie M. Hale (Mrs. Rose), Jonathan Wynne (Rudolph), Ted Goodridge (Judge), Ray Gilbert (Court Clerk); Townspeople, Waiters, Others: Sally Benoit, Terry Gene, Pat Gideon, Ann Given, Birdie M. Hale, Karen Hubbard, Gwen Humble, Eulaula Jennings, Francie Mendenhall, Bessye Ruth Scott, Sachi Shimizu, Guy Allen, Don Coleman, Richard Dodd, Ray Gilbert, Charles Goeddertz, Ted Goodridge, Clark James, James Kennon-Wilson, Richard Maxon, Charles Neal, Howard Porter, Jimmy Rivers, Ken Rogers, David Staller, Teddy Williams, Jonathan Wynne
The musical was presented in two acts.
The action takes place in New York City and in Yonkers in the 1890s.

Musical Numbers

Act One: "I Put My Hand In" (Pearl Bailey, Company); "It Takes a Woman" (Billy Daniels, The Glee Club); "Put on Your Sunday Clothes" (Terrence Emanuel, Grenoldo Frazier, Pearl Bailey, Howard Porter, Karen

Hubbard); "Put on Your Sunday Clothes" (reprise) (Passengers); "Ribbons Down My Back" (Mary Louise); "Motherhood" (Pearl Bailey, Billy Daniels, Mary Louise, Chip Fields, Terrence Emanuel, Grenoldo Frazier); "Dancing" (Pearl Bailey, Terrence Emanuel, Grenoldo Frazier, Chip Fields, Mary Louise, Dancers); "Before the Parade Passes By" (Pearl Bailey, Billy Daniels, Company)

Act Two: "Elegance" (Mary Louise, Terrence Emanuel, Chip Fields, Grenoldo Frazier); "The Waiters' Gallop" (Jonathan Wynne, Waiters); "Hello, Dolly!" (Pearl Bailey, Jonathan Wynne, Waiters, Cooks); "The Polka Contest" (Howard Porter, Karen Hubbard, Mary Louise, Terrence Emanuel, Chip Fields, Grenoldo Frazier, Contestants); "It Only Takes a Moment" (Terrence Emanuel, Mary Louise, Prisoners, Policemen); "So Long, Dearie" (Pearl Bailey, Billy Daniels); "Hello, Dolly!" (reprise) (Pearl Bailey, Billy Daniels); Finale (Company)

Pearl Bailey's visit in *Hello, Dolly!* might well have been called *The Pearl Bailey Show* because the irrepressible entertainer took over the proceedings with her usual steam-roller aplomb. You either loved her chutzpah or you shook your head and sighed in bemused annoyance. The revival was a limited six-week engagement as part of the musical's national tour, and after the next stop in Washington, D.C., the tour ended and with it Bailey's final appearance in a book musical. She had delighted theatre audiences since her 1946 debut in *St. Louis Woman*, but hers was a unique talent that was never quite comfortable within the strictures of a book musical and the night club was her true forte.

Martin Gottfried in the *New York Post* was appalled by the proceedings. Here was a "wonderful" musical that had been "masterfully controlled" by director and choreographer Gower Champion in its original 1964 production, but the current revival lacked respect for the show and the audience. He'd "never seen stage behavior so unprofessional." This kind of "vulgar" production was "the reason they invented Chicago" and its limited run was the only good thing about it. He reported that Bailey broke out of character and chatted up the audience because she apparently thought she was playing Vegas, and her "compulsion" was "to be her night club self whatever the cost to the show." Further, Billy Daniels, "dapper" and with pinkie rings, was "far too supper club" in his performance and he missed the "wonderfully cranky" aspects of Horace Vandergelder's character.

Howard Kissel in *Women's Wear Daily* said the evening showed few signs of life, and the cast didn't seem to understand the book's purposely "arch tone" with intentionally clichéd dialogue. He suspected the cast knew this was a "humdrum" production, and hence the performance ended with a third act in which Bailey and Daniels sang a few standards (she performed "Manhattan," he sang "That Old Black Magic," and they joined together for "Easy to Love").

Clive Barnes in the *New York Times* praised Bailey, who was "exultant," "triumphant," and "as relaxed as if she were on a swing in her own backyard," and John Beaufort in the *Christian Science Monitor* said "the Bailey joie de vivre" bubbled over and there would "never be another Dolly quite like her." But Leonard Probst on NBC Radio complained that Bailey "never got out of neutral" and that Daniels "seemed so uninterested that at one point he was physically off-stage even before he had finished his song."

The original production of *Hello, Dolly!* opened at the St. James Theatre on January 16, 1964, for 2,844 performances with Carol Channing in her Tony Award–winning role (the show won a total of ten Tony Awards, including Best Musical), and she was succeeded by Ginger Rogers, Martha Raye, Betty Grable, Bibi Osterwald, Phyllis Diller, and Ethel Merman; Channing reprised her role on tour, and others who performed in national touring companies were Eve Arden and Dorothy Lamour; and Mary Martin created the role for the 1965 London production.

About midway through the original Broadway run, producer David Merrick pulled a casting stunt which brought new life to the show when an all-black *Hello, Dolly!* with Bailey and Cab Calloway opened in 1967, played for two years, and even enjoyed its own cast album.

The charmless film version, directed by Gene Kelly and released by Twentieth Century-Fox in 1969, was a bloated production which starred a miscast Barbra Streisand.

The current production was the first of three New York revivals; the second opened on March 5, 1978, at the Lunt-Fontanne Theatre for 147 performances with Channing and Eddie Bracken (see entry), and the third on October 19, 1995, at the Lunt-Fontanne Theatre for 118 performances with Channing and Jay Garner. Incidentally, while Bailey's first appearance during the original Broadway run was with an all-black cast, the current revival was a mixture of both black and white performers.

The script was published in hardback by DBS Publications in 1968 with a memorable misprint on both its dust jacket and title page that credits the musical's source to "Thorton" Wilder. There are numerous recordings of Jerry Herman's melodic, old-fashioned score, but the definitive version is the original Broadway cast album by RCA Victor Records (LP # LOC/LSO-1087; issued on CD by RCA # 82876-514321-2). Besides the Bailey cast album, Merman recorded a 45 RPM single of two new songs ("World, Take Me Back" and "Love, Look in My Window") she introduced when she assumed the role in 1970. There are also a number of foreign cast albums (Great Britain, Brazil, Germany, Israel, France, Mexico, Czechoslovakia, and Italy).

A MUSICAL JUBILEE

Theatre: St. James Theatre
Opening Date: November 13, 1975; *Closing Date*: February 1, 1976
Performances: 92
Text: Max Wilk
Lyrics and *Music*: For credits, see list of musical numbers.
Direction: Morton Da Costa; *Producers*: The Theatre Guild and Jonathan Conrow (Merle D. King, Associate Producer); *Choreography*: Robert Tucker; *Scenery*: Herbert Senn; *Costumes*: Donald Brooks; *Lighting*: Thomas Skelton; *Musical Direction*: John Lesko
Cast: *Patrice Munsel, John Raitt, Tammy Grimes, Cyril Ritchard, Dick Shawn, Larry Kert, Lillian Gish*; Ensemble: Steven Boockvor, Eric Brotherson, Marcia Brushingham, Igors Gavon, Nana, David King, Jeanne Lehman, Bettye Malone, Estella Munson, Julie Pars, Dennis Perren, Leland Schwantes, Craig Yates
The revue was presented in two acts.

Musical Numbers

Act One: *Opening*: "Happy Days" (lyric by Howard Dietz, music by Johann Strauss II) (Company); *American Frontier*: "Whoa-Haw" (traditional folk song) (Larry Kert); "Lorena" (lyric by Reverend H. D. L. Webster, music by J. P. Webster) (John Raitt); "Sweet Betsy from Pike" (traditional folk song) (Tammy Grimes); "Skip to My Lou" (traditional folk song) (Patrice Munsel, Larry Kert); "Whoa-Haw" (reprise) (Company); *American Military*: "Hold On Abraham" (lyric and music by William L. Bradbury) (Ensemble); "Bonnie Blue Flag" (lyric by H. Macarthy, music by Valentine Vousden) (Larry Kert, Steven Boockvor, Igors Gavon, David King, Dennis Perren, Leland Schwantes, Craig Yates); "It's a Long Way to Tipperary" (lyric and music by Jack Judge and Henry Williams) (Tammy Grimes, Male Ensemble); "I Didn't Raise My Boy to Be a Soldier" (lyric and music by Alfred Bryan and Al Piantadosi) (Lillian Gish); "Mademoiselle from Armentieres" (lyric and music attributed to Harry Carlton and Joe Tunbridge) (Cyril Ritchard, Dick Shawn); "Over There" (independent song, 1918; lyric and music by George M. Cohan) (Patrice Munsel, Male Ensemble); "Battle Hymn of the Republic" (lyric by Julia Ward Howe, music by William Steffe) (John Raitt, Company); *Old Vienna*: "Wien, Wien, You're Calling Me" (lyric and music by Rudolf Sieczynski and King) and "I'm in Love with Vienna" (1938 film *The Great Waltz*; lyric by Oscar Hammerstein II, music by Johann Strauss II) (Patrice Munsel, John Raitt, Ensemble); "Der Shimmy" (lyric by King, music by Emmerich Kalman) (Tammy Grimes); "I've Got Something" (lyric by Harry B. Smith and Robert B. Smith, music by Franz Lehar) (Cyril Ritchard, Marcia Brushingham, Nana, Jeanne Lehman, Bettye Malone, Julie Pars, Estella Munson); "Oh, the Women" (lyricist unknown, music by Franz Lehar) (Larry Kert, Igors Gavin, Dennis Perrin); "Gypsy Love" (*Ziegeunerliebe*, 1909; produced in New York as *Gypsy Love* in 1911; lyric by Harry B. Smith and Robert B. Smith, music by Franz Lehar) (Patrice Munsel, Ensemble); *Britain*: "And Her Mother Came Too" (London revue *A to Z*, 1921; lyric by Dion Titheradge, music by Ivor Novello) (Cyril Ritchard); *Early Broadway*: "Song of the Vagabonds" (*The Vagabond King*, 1925; lyric by Brian Hooker, music by Rudolf Friml) (John Raitt, Male Ensemble); "Totem Tom Tom" (*Rose-Marie*, 1924; lyric by Oscar Hammerstein II and Otto Harbach, music by Rudolf Friml) (Tammy Grimes, Female Ensemble); "Serenade" (aka "Overhead the Moon Is Beaming") (*The Student Prince*, 1924; lyric by Dorothy Donnelly, music by Sigmund Romberg) (Larry Kert); "Violetta" (lyricist and composer unknown)

(Cyril Ritchard, Tammy Grimes, Larry Kert, Eric Brotherson); "Moonstruck" (*Our Miss Gibbs*, London [1909] and New York [1910]; lyric by James T. Tanner, music by Ivan Caryll and Lionel Monckton; some sources credit both lyric and music to Monckton only) (Lillian Gish, Male Ensemble); "You Are Love" (*Show Boat*, 1927; lyric by Oscar Hammerstein II, music by Jerome Kern) (Patrice Munsel, John Raitt); "I've Told Ev'ry Little Star" (*Music in the Air*, 1932; lyric by Oscar Hammerstein II, music by Jerome Kern) (Dick Shawn, Female Ensemble); "Why Was I Born?" (*Sweet Adeline*, 1929; lyric by Oscar Hammerstein II, music by Jerome Kern) (Patrice Munsel); "The Best Things in Life Are Free" (*Good News*, 1927; lyric by B. G. Buddy DeSylva and Lew Brown, music by Ray Henderson) (Larry Kert, Ensemble); "They Didn't Believe Me" (*The Girl from Utah*, 1914; lyric by Herbert Reynolds, music by Jerome Kern) (Tammy Grimes); "The Song Is You" (*Music in the Air*, 1932; lyric by Oscar Hammerstein II, music by Jerome Kern) (John Raitt); "Something Seems Tingle Ingleing" (added to *High Jinks* [1913] during Broadway run; lyric by Otto Harbach, music by Rudolf Friml) (Cyril Ritchard, Female Ensemble); "I Want to Hear a Yankee Doodle Tune" (*Mother Goose*, 1903; lyric and music by George M. Cohan)

Act Two: *The Smart Set*: "We're Blasé" (1932 London revue *Bow Belles*; lyric by Bruce Sievier, music by Ord Hamilton; some sources credit lyric to Desmond Carter and music to Henry Sullivan) (Patrice Munsel, John Raitt, Tammy Grimes, Cyril Ritchard, Dick Shawn); "Poor Little Rich Girl" (London revue *On with the Dance*, 1925; lyric and music by Noel Coward) (Tammy Grimes); "You Go to My Head" (lyric by Haven Gillespie, music by J. Fred Coots) (John Raitt); "Find Me a Primitive Man" (*Fifty Million Frenchmen*, 1929; lyric and music by Cole Porter) (Patrice Munsel, Tammy Grimes); "I Guess I'll Have to Change My Plan" (*The Little Show*, 1929; lyric by Howard Dietz, music by Arthur Schwartz) (Dick Shawn); "Sophisticated Lady" (lyric by Mitchell Parish and Irving Mills, music by Duke Ellington) (Larry Kert); "Love Me or Leave Me" (*Whoopee!*, 1928; lyric by Gus Kahn, music by Walter Donaldson) (Patrice Munsel); "Gilbert the Filbert" (*The Girl from Utah*, 1914; lyric by Arthur Wimperis, music by Herman Finck [song may also have been performed in *The Passing Show of 1914*) (Cyril Ritchard); "We're Blasé" (reprise) (Patrice Munsel, John Raitt, Cyril Ritchard, Tammy Grimes, Dick Shawn, Larry Kert); *Vaudeville*: "At the Moving Picture Ball" (lyric by Howard Johnson, music by Joseph H. Santly) (Ensemble); "Miss Annabelle Lee" (lyric by Sidney Clare and Harry Richman, music by Lew Pollack) (Dick Shawn); "I Wanna Be Loved by You" (*Good Boy*, 1928; lyric and music by Herbert Stothart, Bert Kalmer, and Harry Ruby) (Patrice Munsel, Tammy Grimes, Lillian Gish); "The Green Eye of the Little Yellow God" (lyric and music by Reginald Purdell; lyric based on the poem by Milton Hayes) (Cyril Ritchard, Dick Shawn, Eric Brotherson); *Jazz*: "How Jazz Was Born" (lyric by Andy Razaf and Henry Creamer, music by Fats Waller) (Larry Kert, Ensemble); "Ain't Misbehavin'" (*Hot Chocolates*, 1929; lyric by Andy Razaf, music by Fats Waller and Harry Brooks) (Larry Kert); "I'm Just Wild About Harry" (*Shuffle Along*, 1921; lyric by Noble Sissle, music by Eubie Blake) (Tammy Grimes); "Me and My Shadow" (lyric by Billy Rose, music by Dave Dreyer; Al Jolson may have contributed to the lyric) (Dick Shawn); "Sometimes I'm Happy" (*Hit the Deck*, 1927; lyric by Irving Caesar, music by Vincent Youmans) (Patrice Munsel); "Great Day!" (*Great Day!*, 1929; lyric by Billy Rose and Edward Eliscu, music by Vincent Youmans) (John Raitt); "How Jazz Was Born" (reprise) (Patrice Munsel, John Raitt, Tammy Grimes, Dick Shawn, Larry Kert, Ensemble); *Later Broadway*: "Lullaby of Broadway" (film *Gold Diggers of 1935*; lyric by Al Dubin, music by Harry Warren) (Ensemble); "Lucky Day" (*George White's Scandals of 1926*; lyric by B. G. Buddy DeSylva and Lew Brown, music by Ray Henderson) (Dick Shawn); "If You Knew Susie (Like I Know Susie)" (interpolated into the score of *Big Boy*, 1925; lyric by B. G. Buddy DeSylva, music by Joseph Meyer) (Cyril Ritchard); "'S Wonderful" (*Funny Face*, 1927; lyric by Ira Gershwin, music by George Gershwin) (Lillian Gish); "Fascinating Rhythm" (*Lady, Be Good!*, 1924; lyric by Ira Gershwin, music by George Gershwin) (Larry Kert); "Liza" (*Show Girl*, 1929; lyric by Ira Gershwin and Gus Kahn, music by George Gershwin) (Tammy Grimes); "Where or When" (*Babes in Arms*, 1937; lyric by Lorenz Hart, music by Richard Rodgers) (Patrice Munsel); "Hallelujah!" (*Hit the Deck*, 1927; lyric by Leo Robin and Clifford Grey, music by Vincent Youmans) (John Raitt, Company)

A Musical Jubilee first saw life as an entertainment package presented on a passenger ship. One can't resist asking: Was it the *Titanic*? Perhaps the misbegotten revue was produced for the poor souls who missed Lillian Gish in her first appearance in a musical (*Anya* in 1965), and thus gave them a final chance to see and hear her in another Broadway musical. Or perhaps the revue was for camp followers, because how often is one given the opportunity of hearing Tammy Grimes sing "Totem Tom-Tom" from *Rose-Marie*? Otherwise, this dreary offering (like ***Music! Music!*** and ***Sing America Sing***) was just another Bicentennial smorgasbord of song that purported to celebrate American music. If so, it had a strange way of doing so, as the evening was peppered with numbers from Viennese operettas and British revues.

Moreover, the production was divided into such arbitrary categories as "Early Broadway," "Later Broadway," and "The Smart Set." Songs from the 1930s (such as "I've Told Ev'ry Little Star" and "The Song Is You," both from the 1932 musical *Music in the Air*) were included as "early" show tunes and yet "Later Broadway" offered selections from a decade earlier. Couldn't the producers afford a calendar? Further, "The Smart Set" sequence made no sense: such categories as "American Frontier" and "American Military" at least pulled together folk songs for the former and military and war-related ones for the latter. But "The Smart Set"? Was it a subgenre of music that somehow escaped the notice of music historians? It turns out the numbers were mostly pickings from the songbooks of Cole Porter, Duke Ellington, and Noel Coward, and since many had been introduced in musicals, their being lumped together in a "Smart Set" category made no sense. Neither did the "Vaudeville" sequence, which included a song from a book musical ("I Wanna Be Loved by You") that had nothing to do with vaudeville.

The evening was sloppily conceived by people who should have known better, and with its relatively small cast and modest scenery it was clearly pulled together in order to make a quick buck and capitalize on the Bicentennial. It lost its investment, but somehow managed to hang on for about ten weeks.

The critics didn't quite know what to make of it, although one or two commented that late in the second act the revue announced its intention: to present Broadway music as well as songs that influenced the Broadway musical. But wait. "Sweet Betsy from Pike" influenced the Broadway sound? And "The Battle Hymn of the Republic"? By this definition, every song ever written could be considered influential. Clearly, Monteverdi's 1643 opera *The Coronation of Poppea* could have been included in the revue because it offered a drinking song, and drinking songs have always been a staple on Broadway (there could easily be a three-CD set devoted just to Broadway Drinking Songs).

It was all very bewildering, and the reader is encouraged to seek out Martin Gottfried's complete review of *A Musical Jubilee* in the *New York Post*. Along with Brooks Atkinson and Walter Kerr, Gottfried was both an insightful and entertaining reviewer, and his hilarious comments about the revue are more entertaining than anything actually seen in the show itself. Gottfried wondered if "the producer knew what the director was doing, whether the director knew what his company were doing, and whether the performers knew what each other was doing." The show, "if that is what it was," must have been "some kind of award show," but "God knows what the whole thing was supposed to be." The performers were caught in a "giddy nightmare," and instead of "being embarrassed" or "walking through it," they had "the class of the theatre" and "showed why they were performers" and "what had made them stars."

Christopher Sharp in *Women's Wear Daily* said the "small-minded" evening offered little more than routine sequences "in a daytime variety TV show"; Kevin Sanders on WABCTV7 found the revue "fairly standard" and "run-of-the-mill"; Leonard Probst on NBC Radio said *A Musical Jubilee* was a "musical jumble"; and John Beaufort in the *Christian Science Monitor* noted that the production was "more mishmash than melody, more jumble than jubilee."

But Edwin Wilson in the *Wall Street Journal* praised the "bona fide Bicentennial musical"; Clive Barnes in the *New York Times* said the company performed "with consummate skill and grace" and director Morton Da Costa ensured that the evening avoided "the frozen spirit of the TV spectacular"; and Douglas Watt in the *New York Daily News* singled out Patrice Munsel's "rich lyric soprano, an uncommon sound on the musical-comedy stage."

Numbers deleted during the pre-Broadway tryout were: "Love Is a Rider" (*American Frontier* sequence); "Three Wonderful Letters from Home" (*American Military*); "Yours Is My Heart Alone" (*Old Vienna*); and "Bidin' My Time" (*Girl Crazy*, 1930; lyric by Ira Gershwin, music by George Gershwin) (*The Smart Set*).

Well, at least *A Musical Jubilee* served its purpose and gave audiences a chance to see Lillian Gish in her second and final musical and to hear her sing "boop-boop-a-doop" when she accompanied Patrice Munsel and Tammy Grimes in "I Wanna Be Loved by You."

BOCCACCIO

"A Musical"

Theatre: Edison Theatre
Opening Date: November 24, 1975; *Closing Date*: November 30, 1975
Performances: 7
Book and *Lyrics*: Kenneth Cavender
Music: Richard Peaslee
Based on Giovanni Boccaccio's stories from *The Decameron* (approximately one hundred stories written circa 1348–1353). For the musical adaptation, six stories were used: *Devil in Hell*, Day II, Story 10; *Masetto*, Day III, Story 1; *Ferondo*, Day III, Story 8; *The Doctor's Daughter*, Day III, Story 9; *Madonna Isabella*, Day VII, Story 6; and *Anichino*, Day VII, Story 7.
Direction: Warren Enters; *Producers*: Rita Fredericks, Theatre Now, Inc., and Norman Kean; *Choreography*: "Musical staging" by Julie Arenal; *Scenery*: Robert U. Taylor; *Costumes*: Linda Fisher; *Lighting*: Patrika Brown; *Musical Direction*: Ken Bichel
Cast: Michael Zaslow (Beltramo, Egano), Virginia Vestoff (Giletta, Abbess), Armand Assante (Masetto, Ferondo), Caroline McWilliams (Beatrice, Sister Teresa, Ferondo's Wife), D'Jamin Bartlett (Madonna Isabella, Sister Angelica), Jill Choder (Alibech, Sister Makaria), Munson Hicks (Rustico, Leonetto, Brother Perdurabo), Richard Bauer (Anichino, Nuto, Abbot)
The musical was presented in two acts.
The action takes place at a villa outside Florence, Italy, in 1348.

Musical Numbers

Act One: *Introduction* (Company); *Masetto*: "Masetto's Song" (Armand Assante, Richard Bauer); "Nun's Song" (Virginia Vestoff, Nuns); "God Is Good" (Armand Assante, Nuns); and "Now My Season's Here" (Company); *Anichino*: "Only in My Song" (Richard Bauer); "Egano D'Galluzzi" (Richard Bauer, Michael Zaslow); "The Men Who Have Loved Me" (Caroline McWilliams); "In the Garden" (Richard Bauer, Michael Zaslow); and "Lucky Anichino" (Company); "Pretend You're Living" (D'Jamin Bartlett); "(Put the) Devil in Hell" (Jill Choder, Munson Hicks, Company)
Act Two: *The She Doctor* (aka *The Doctor's Daughter*): "She Doctor" (Virginia Vestoff, Michael Zaslow); "Lover Like a Blind Man" (Virginia Vestoff); "If You Had Seen" (Virginia Vestoff); and "Love Was Just a Game" (Michael Zaslow); "Madonna Isabella" (D'Jamin Bartlett, Company); *Ferondo*: "My Holy Prayer" (Richard Bauer, Monks) and "Hold Me Gently" (Caroline McWilliams); Finale (Company)

Boccaccio was based on Giovanni Boccaccio's *The Decameron*, a collection of approximately one hundred stories he wrote during the middle of the fourteenth century. The musical adapted six of the stories, and centered on a group of refugees who seek safety in a villa near Florence from the scourge of the Black Death, the plague that killed upwards of half of Europe's population during the fourteenth century. In order to pass the time, they entertain one another with stories, mostly earthy in nature because death could strike at any moment and take away the pleasures of the flesh.

Clive Barnes in the *New York Times* suggested that the "plague" was the musical itself because the book and lyrics had little in the way of grace, cleverness, tone, and style, and the score was "somewhat worse" with its "musical chatter"; Martin Gottfried in the *New York Post* said the musical was "overdirected" with an "excess of performance," the music was "self-conscious" with a *Godspell*-like sound of "art music with a rock beat," and the lyrics were unmusical and "too crammed with information"; Douglas Watt in the *New York Daily News* felt the musical "never once makes a strong impression of any kind" and only induces "a polite yawn"; and Howard Kissel in *Women's Wear Daily* said the adaptation oversimplified Boccaccio's "intriguing" stories and the "amiable" music didn't "seem consistent enough in style or rich enough for the original material." Leonard Probst on NBC Radio said the evening had an "unpretentious" and "almost collegiate" air about it, and he praised Armand Assante, who was "like an Al Pacino with a very good singing voice."

During previews, Warren Enters succeeded Gene Lesser as director, Julie Arenal was credited with musical staging (in previews, Elizabeth Keen was credited with "movement"), and lighting designer Patrika Brown followed William Mintzer. The songs "The Best of Times," "Let Your Body Have Its Way," "Apples in the Garden," and "My Holy Prayer" were dropped, and the title of "A Game I've Lost" was changed to "Love Was Just a Game." Two sequences, both titled "Recitativo" and "Aria," may have been reworked as "Egano D'Galluzzi" and "In the Garden." In previews, "Time to Go" was included as part of the introductory sequence, but wasn't listed in the official opening night program; it may have been included as part of the overall opening number.

The musical had first been seen in a showcase production at the Williamstown Playhouse in Williamstown, Massachusetts, in 1972, was followed by a presentation at the Manhattan Theatre Club in 1973, and was produced at Arena Stage in Washington, D.C., where it opened on November 15, 1974 (from the latter production, only Jill Choder was in the cast of the New York version; others in the Arena presentation were Robert LuPone).

Another adaptation of Boccaccio's stories was the Off-Broadway musical *The Decameron*, which opened at the East 74th Street Theatre on April 12, 1961, for thirty-nine performances (Howard Taubman in the *New York Times* said the evening offered more entertainment "than some of the higher-priced musicals in town").

VERY GOOD EDDIE

Theatre: Booth Theatre
Opening Date: December 21, 1975; *Closing Date*: September 5, 1976
Performances: 304
Book: Guy Bolton
Lyrics: Various lyricists (see credits below)
Music: Jerome Kern
Based on the 1911 play *Over Night* by Phillip Bartholomae.
Direction: Bill Gile; *Producers*: David Merrick, Max Brown, and Byron Goldman (A Goodspeed Opera House Production; produced for the Goodspeed Opera House by Michael P. Price); *Choreography*: Dan Siretta; *Scenery* and *Lighting*: Fred Voelpel; *Costumes*: David Toser; *Musical Direction*: Russell Warner
Cast: James Harder (Steward, Al Cleveland), David Christmas (Mr. Dick Rivers), Travis Hudson (Mme. Matroppo), Cynthia Wells (Miss Elsie Lilly), Joel Craig (M. de Rougemont); Spring Fairbank (Mrs. Georgina Kettle), Charles Repole (Mr. Eddie Kettle), Nicholas Wyman (Mr. Percy Darling), Virginia Seidel (Mrs. Elsie Darling), Wendy Young (Miss Lily Pond), Karen Crossley (Miss Chrystal Poole), Gillian Scalici (Miss Carrie Closewell), Robin Herbert (Miss Alwys Innit), Russ Beasley (Mr. Tayleurs Dumme), Jon Engstrom (Mr. Dayr Thurst), Larry McMillian (Mr. Dustin Stacks), Hal Shane (Mr. Rollo Munn)
The musical was presented in two acts.
The action takes place during June 1913 on a Hudson River dayliner and in the lobby of Honeymoon Inn in the Catskills.

Musical Numbers

Act One: "We're on Our Way" (lyric by Schuyler Greene) (Ensemble); "Some Sort of Somebody" (although the song is from the 1915 musical *Miss Information*, it was included in the original production of *Very Good Eddie*; lyric by Elsie Janis) (Cynthia Wells, David Christmas); "Thirteen Collar" (lyric by Schuyler Greene) (Charles Repole); "Bungalow in Quogue" (*The Riviera Girl*, 1917; lyric by P. G. Wodehouse) (Virginia Seidel, Nicholas Wyman); "Isn't It Great to Be Married?" (lyric by Schuyler Greene); (Virginia Seidel, Spring Fairbank, Charles Repole, Nicholas Wyman); "Good-Night Boat" (*The Night Boat*, 1920; lyric by Anne Caldwell and Frank Craven) (Ensemble); "Left All Alone Again Blues" (*The Night Boat*, 1920; lyric by Anne Caldwell) (Virginia Seidel); "Hot Dog!" (dropped from *The Bunch and Judy*, 1922; lyric by Anne Caldwell) (Ensemble); "If You're a Friend of Mine" (London musical *Lady Mary*, 1928; lyric by Harry Graham) (Virginia Seidel, Charles Repole); "Wedding Bells Are Calling Me" (although the song is from the 1915 musical *Nobody Home,* it was included in the original production of *Very Good Eddie;* lyric by Harry B. Smith) (Ensemble)

Act Two: "Honeymoon Inn" (*Have a Heart,* 1917; lyric by P. G. Wodehouse) (Cynthia Wells, Ensemble); "I've Got to Dance" (lyric by Schuyler Greene; written for, but not used in, the original production of *Very Good Eddie*) (Joel Craig, Ensemble); "Moon of Love" (*Hitchy-Koo 1920* [fourth edition]; lyric by Anne Caldwell) (Travis Hudson, Ensemble); "Old Boy Neutral" (lyric by Schuyler Greene) (Cynthia Wells, David Christmas); "Babes in the Wood" (lyric by Jerome Kern and Schuyler Green) (Virginia Seidel, Charles Repole); "Katy-did" (*Oh, I Say!,* 1913; lyric by Harry B. Smith) (Travis Hudson); "Nodding Roses" (lyric by Schuyler Greene and Herbert Reynolds) (Cynthia Wells, David Christmas); Finale (lyric by John E. Hazzard and Herbert Reynolds)

The revival of Jerome Kern's 1915 musical *Very Good, Eddie* was a surprise hit that enjoyed a nine-month run and managed to turn a profit. The production had originated at Goodspeed Opera House in East Haddam, Connecticut, where it had opened on July 6, 1975, and the transfer from that small house to the reasonably intimate Booth Theatre worked well. Intimate musicals often got lost in Broadway theatres, but the Booth and *Very Good Eddie* were a perfect fit. A program note mentioned that the musical's producers hoped the Booth would become the permanent home for a series of intimate musicals, but unfortunately nothing ever came of their proposal.

The lighter-than-air plot of *Very Good Eddie* dealt with two mismatched just-married couples, the tall Georgina Kettle (Spring Fairbank) and the short Eddie Kettle (Charles Repole), and the short Elsie Darling (Virginia Seidel) and the tall Percy Darling (Nicholas Wyman). Both couples plan a day trip up the Hudson River to the Honeymoon Inn in the Catskills, but in ways known only to musical comedies Georgina and Percy are inadvertently left at the dock. Romance blossoms between Eddie and Elsie, and when Georgina and Percy eventually arrive at the inn, there's much comic ado in the way of mistaken identities, similar names which cause confusion (two characters are named Elsie and a third is known as "L.C."), and a Marx Brothers–like sequence that involved hotel-room doors that are repeatedly opened and slammed. There were also characters who sported such names as Lily Pond, Chrystal Poole, Alwys Innit, and Dayr Thurst. And of course all ends well, when Eddie matches up with Elsie and Georgina with Percy.

The revival opened almost sixty years to the day of the original production, and since it was Christmas week, T. E. Kalem in *Time* mentioned that while producer David Merrick usually sent out macabre holiday greeting cards, for the revival of *Very Good Eddie* he was "obviously wishing all of us a happy '76." Clive Barnes in the *New York Times* said the revival was "Merrick's Christmas present to New York" because the evening was "absolutely enchanting" and Kern's score a "pure delight." Douglas Watt in the *New York Daily News* said Bolton's book was "cheerfully unassuming and unabashedly corny"; and Martin Gottfried in the *New York Post* praised the "charming and disarming entertainment," which was a "beautifully wrapped present" with "an excellent basic plot" and "lovely period music."

But Howard Kissel in *Women's Wear Daily* warned that "tedium" set in because of the "deadly coyness of the material"; and Leonard Probst on NBC Radio said the musical was "not very good" with its "feeble" jokes, "bland" dialogue, "insipid" lyrics, and unmemorable music. And while John Beaufort in the *Christian Science Monitor* found the "fresh, agile and amiable" evening "rather engaging," he felt it was "perhaps better suited to a summer outing than to Broadway's winter winds and prices."

Charles Repole played the title role (which had been created by Ernest Truex in the original production), and in 1979 he played another "Eddie" when he appeared in the 1979 revival of ***Whoopee!*** and re-created the leading role originated by Eddie Cantor in 1928. In his review of *Very Good Eddie,* Gottfried mentioned Repole's "remarkable" resemblance to Cantor, and Watt too noticed the likeness. Barnes said he "enjoyed very much" Repole's "kind of Eddie Cantor imitation," and Kissel found Repole "extremely engaging." No doubt the comments about Repole's Cantor-like looks and performance led Goodspeed to produce *Whoopee!* for the comic, who gave one of the most amusing performances of the decade in that production.

Very Good Eddie wasn't a completely faithful rendering of the original; five songs from the 1915 production were dropped ("The Same Old Song," "On the Shore at Le Lei Wi," "If I Find the Girl," "The Fashion Show," and "I Wish I Had a Million"), and as noted in the song list above, eight songs from the original score were retained (including two interpolations that had been heard in the original production); eight songs were borrowed from other Kern musicals; and one number cut from the original score was reinstated.

The cast album of the revival was released by DRG Records (LP # DRG-6100; issued on CD # CDRG-6100).

Very Good Eddie was one of a series of Kern's musicals that were known as the Princess shows because they played at the intimate venue located at Sixth Avenue and 39th Street. These were small-scale "smart" musicals in the mode of musical comedy instead of operetta, and employed one set per act. The original production of *Very Good Eddie* opened on December 23, 1915, and while the score didn't yield any Kern standards the show managed a ten-month run that totaled 341 performances.

The musical's first London production opened in 1918 and ran for a disappointing 43 performances, and the London revival of the Goodspeed version took place on March 23, 1976, at the Piccadilly Theatre where it played for 411 showings.

Awards

Tony Award Nominations: Best Featured Actor in a Musical (Charles Repole); Best Featured Actress in a Musical (Virginia Seidel); Best Director of a Musical (Bill Gile)

HOME SWEET HOMER

"A Musical Romantic Comedy" / "A New Musical Comedy"

Theatre: Palace Theatre
Opening Date: January 4, 1976; *Closing Date*: January 4, 1976
Performances: 1
Book: Roland Kibbee and Albert Marre
Lyrics: Charles Burr and Forman Brown
Music: Mitch Leigh
Based on Homer's epic poem *The Odyssey* (written between the eighth and sixth centuries B.C.).
Direction: Albert Marre; *Producer*: Kennedy Center Productions, Inc.; *Choreography*: Musical Staging by Albert Marre (Michael Mann, Choreographic Assistant); *Scenery* and *Lighting*: Howard Bay; *Costumes*: Howard Bay and Ray Diffen; *Musical Direction*: Ross Reimueller
Cast: *Yul Brynner* (Odysseus), Joan Diener (Penelope), Russ Thacker (Telemachus); Penelope's Suitors: Martin Vidnovic (Antinous), Ian Sullivan (Pilokrates), Bill Mackey (Ktesippos), Daniel Brown (Eurymachus), Brian Destazio (Leokritos), John Aristedes (Primteus), Bill Nabel (Melios), and Les Freed (Polybos); Shev Rodgers (King Alkinoos), Diana Davila (Nausikaa); Handmaidens: Suzanne Sponsler (Therapina), Cecile Santos (Melantho), and Christine Uchida (Hippodameia); Darel Glaser (Kerux), P. J. Mann (Dekati Evdomi)
The musical was presented in one act.
The action takes place nine years after the Trojan War, in and around the palace at Ithaka as well as on various islands on Odysseus's travels.

Musical Numbers

Note: There were at least two different opening night programs; the list below reflects the songs listed in one program, and incorporated into the list, in performance order and in brackets, are the songs listed in a second program.

["The Tales" (Joan Diener, Suitors)]; ["The Future" (Joan Diener)]; "The Sorceress" (Joan Diener, Suitors); "The Departure" (Yul Brynner, P. J. Mann); "Home Sweet Homer" (Yul Brynner); "The Ball" (Diana Davila, Handmaidens); "How Could I Dare to Dream" (Yul Brynner, Russ Thacker); "I Never Imagined Goodbye" (Joan Diener); "Love Is the Prize" (Yul Brynner); "Penelope's Hand" (Martin Vidnovic); "He Will Come Home Again" (Russ Thacker); "Did He Really Think" (Joan Diener); "I Was Wrong" (Yul Brynner); "The Rose" (Joan Diener); "Tomorrow" (Martin Vidnovic, Suitors); "The Contest" (Yul Brynner, Russ Thacker, Martin Vidnovic, Suitors); ["He Sang Songs" (Joan Diener, Yul Brynner)]

Like ***Lorelei***, ***Good News***, and other musicals of the era, *Home Sweet Homer* undertook a year-long *Odyssey* (its title for most of the tryout) before reaching Broadway. But it collapsed after its first performance, and perhaps the show's only distinction is its status as the season's shortest-running musical.

A year before the New York opening, two viewings provided clear evidence that the production was hopelessly inept. Bereft of production values and with a small cast, the musical seemed lost on a large stage, and the weak, episodic script offered vague, ill-defined characters, a negligible score, and scant choreography. All these factors would normally have doomed the show to a quick out-of-town closing, but star Yul Brynner was the musical's one and only attraction, and his name sold tickets and enabled the show to run for over a year on the long odyssey to Broadway. The show did good business, but the costs of running the tour and the extensive rewrites added up, and the musical was reportedly $1 million in the red after it closed. Once the musical faced the New York critics, it was indeed all over for *Home Sweet Homer*, and Brynner's only subsequent Broadway visits were in revivals of *The King and I.*

Brynner brought his personal charisma to the role of Odysseus, and clearly did all he could to generate life into the characterless character; Diana Davila, Russ Thacker, and Martin Vidnovic tried as well, but their material defeated them and gave them little to work with. As a result, the evening was often an unintentionally pompous pageant-like re-telling of the familiar story of the aftermath of the Trojan War with its focus on the final year of Odysseus's ten-year journey to Ithaca and his homecoming with his wife Penelope (Joan Diener), his son Telemachus (Russ Thacker), and the suitors who pursue Penelope because they assume Odysseus is dead. There was also some tiresome business with Brynner in various disguises so that he can secretly observe the intrigues and goings-on in hometown Ithaca.

Musically, the show had little to offer (only the flowing rhythms of "Tomorrow" were attractive and had musical muscle), and, speaking of muscles, the show definitely had its camp moments, especially those scenes that centered on Penelope's scantily clad, exhibitionist suitors who performed as though they'd rather be spending an evening with one another at the baths.

Martin Gottfried in *Women's Wear Daily* said the musical was "in the hands of the ill-equipped in the pursuit of the misconceived" and it all seemed to take place "in the lounge of a Las Vegas hotel." As for Penelope's muscle men, he noted they looked and acted "like competitors in a moron's beefcake contest." And Joan Diener was the "silliest" of all the performers; she was "obnoxious" in the "snide, supercilious and sophisticated style of an arid, idle suburban housewife." "Suburbs" seems to be the key word here, because Douglas Watt in the *New York Daily News* commented that besides her "shaky, semi-legit" singing voice, she was "something else again" in her speech and carriage, and she managed to create the impression of "an imperious hostess in a suburban restaurant." He said he wouldn't have been surprised to see her "walk on at some point carting an armload of menus."

Clive Barnes in the *New York Times* also mentioned Penelope's suitors, and said their "boorish" attempts at martial arts and "loutish pranks" led him to think they were performing a parody called *Kung Fu Comes to Athens*. Howard Kissel in *Women's Wear Daily* said one of the numbers in the "appallingly banal" production reminded him of "some Israeli song" he used to sing at summer camp, that Brynner's role was so "campily written" it would have been a natural for Dom De Luise, and the dialogue zigged and zagged between would-be grandiloquence and arch humor.

The headline of John Beaufort's review in the *Christian Science Monitor* proclaimed that "Homer Fizzles," and he noted the evening vacillated between "technique and tedium." Kevin Sanders on WABCTV7 said the musical was "a bit like a Disneyland version of Homer's *Odyssey*," while Leonard Probst on NBC Radio said he was "stunned" by the musical's "uniform inferiority" and said it was so bad "you have to see it to believe it."

Besides the title change from *Odyssey* to *Home Sweet Homer* (in preproduction the musical had been known as *A Hero's Song*), the show underwent major rewrites and the two acts were compressed into one. At the beginning of the tryout, Erich Segal was credited with book and lyrics, but as the tour continued he requested that his name and material be removed. And so a new book by Roland Kibbee (and director Albert Marre) and new lyrics by Charles Burr and Forman Brown were added. Billy Wilson was the original choreographer of record, but soon Marre took over the musical staging and Michael Mann was credited as the choreographic assistant. Catherine Lee Smith left the show when her role of Kalypso was eliminated.

For reasons perhaps known only to Mitch Leigh, many of his musicals (*Man of La Mancha* during its early months on Broadway and the tryouts of *Chu Chem*, **Halloween**, and *An April Song*) dispensed with song lists in their programs, and *Odyssey* was no exception. But for the New York programs, song titles were added, and there were in fact two opening night programs (actually matinee programs because the musical opened and closed at a Sunday afternoon performance), both with slightly different song lists.

There was no cast recording, but *Forgotten Broadway Volume II* (LP # T-102, unnamed company) includes Brynner and Russ Thacker's performance of "How Could I Dare to Dream," which was apparently taken from a television talk-show broadcast.

PACIFIC OVERTURES

Theatre: Winter Garden Theatre
Opening Date: January 11, 1976; *Closing Date*: June 27, 1976
Performances: 193
Book: John Weidman; additional material by Hugh Wheeler
Lyrics and *Music*: Stephen Sondheim; dance music by Danny Troob
Direction: Harold Prince; *Kabuki Consultant*: Haruki Fijimoto; *Producers*: Harold Prince in association with Ruth Mitchell; *Choreography*: Patricia Birch; *Scenery*: Boris Aronson; *Costumes*: Florence Klotz; *Masks* and *Dolls*: E. J. Taylor; *Lighting*: Tharon Musser; *Musical Direction*: Paul Gemignani
Cast: Mako (Reciter, Shogun, Jonathan Goble), Yuki Shimoda (Abe [First Councilor]), Sab Shimono (Manjiro), James Dybas (Second Councilor, Old Man, French Admiral), Alvin Ing (Shogun's Mother, Observer, Merchant, American Admiral), Freddy Mao (Third Councilor, Samurai's Daughter), Isao Sato (Kayama), Soon-Teck Oh (Tamate, Samurai, Storyteller, Swordsman), Ernest Abuba (Samurai, Adams, Noble), Richard Tobia (Samurai), Haruiki Fijimoto (Servant, Commodore Matthew Calbraith Perry), Ricardo Tobia (Observer), Jae Woo Lee (Fisherman, Sumo Wrestler, Lord of the South), Timm Fujii (Son, Priest, Girl, Noble, British Sailor), Conrad Yama (Grandmother, Sumo Wrestler, Japanese Merchant), Mark Hsu Syers (Thief, Soothsayer, Warrior, Russian Admiral, British Sailor), Larry Hama (Williams, Lord of the South), Freda Foh Shen (Shogun's Wife), Ernest Harada (Physician, Madam, British Admiral), Gedde Watanabe (Priest, Girl, Boy), Patrick Kinser-Lau (Shogun's Companion, Girl, Dutch Admiral, British Sailor), Leslie Watanabe (Girl), Tom Matsusaka (Imperial Priest), Joey Ginza (Musician); Proscenium Servants, Sailors, Townspeople: Susan Kikuchi, Diane Lam, Kim Miyori, Freda Foh Shen, Kenneth S. Eiland, Timm Fujii, Joey Ginza, Patrick Kinser-Lau, Tony Marinyo, Kevin Maung, Dingo Secretario, Mark Hsu Syers, Ricardo Tobia, Gedde Watanabe, Leslie Watanabe; Musicians: Fusako Yoshida (Shamisen), Genji Ito (Percussion)
The musical was presented in two acts.
The action takes place in Japan during July 1853 and "from then on."

Musical Numbers

Act One: "The Advantages of Floating in the Middle of the Sea" (Mako, Company); "There Is No Other Way" (Soon-Teck Oh, Alvin Ing, Ricardo Tobia); "Four Black Dragons" (Jae Woo Lee, Mark Hsu Syers, Mako, Townspeople); "Chrysanthemum Tea" (Mako, Alvin Ing, Freda Foh Shen, Mark Hsu Syers, Tim Fujii, Gedde Watanabe, Patrick Kinser-Lau, Ernest Harada, Conrad Yama, Jae Woo Lee); "Poems" (Isao Sato, Sab Shimono); "Welcome to Kanagawa" (Ernest Harada, Timm Fujii, Patrick Kinser-Lau, Gedde Watanabe, Leslie Watanabe); "Someone in a Tree" (James Dybas, Mako, Gedde Watanabe, Mark Hsu Syers); "Lion Dance" (Haruki Fujimoto)
Act Two: "Please Hello" (Yuki Shimoda, Mako, Alvin Ing, Ernest Harada, Patrick Kinser-Lau, Mark Hsu Syers, James Dybas); "A Bowler Hat" (Isao Sato, Sab Shimono); "Pretty Lady" (Timm Fujii, Patrick Kinser-Lau, Mark Hsu Syers); "Next" (Mako, Company)

Pacific Overtures was a magnificent concept musical that, like ***Follies***, looked at change and the passing of time. But in this case, the change was about a country. For some two hundred fifty years, Japan lived in self-imposed isolation from the world, but when Commodore Matthew Calbraith Perry (Haruki Fujimoto) visited the nation in 1853 there was no going back. The West wanted to open up the nation for trade, and soon emissaries from the major Western nations arrived to hammer out the diplomatic and business details for the export and import of goods. The "floating" world of delicate sliding screens, chrysanthemum tea, and haiku vanished, and the nation would eventually boast that in 1976 it exported sixteen million kilograms of monosodium glutamate and four hundred thousand tons of polyvinyl chloride resin. The country's transformation was personified by Kayama (Isato Sato) and his song "A Bowler Hat," one of the most memorable numbers in Stephen Sondheim's brilliant score and one of the greatest songs in his catalog. At first, Kayama is impressed by the bowler hats worn by the Europeans; soon he's actually sporting one himself; and eventually he dismisses the hat as old-hat and is contemptuous of anyone who would wear one.

All the performers were Asian-Americans, and the musical was conceived as if practitioners in the art of Kabuki theatre had written a Kabuki-like production in the style of an American musical. And so in Kabuki fashion, many of the actors wore outlandish wigs and make-up in order to immediately reflect the nature of their characters; stagehands who changed scenery were dressed completely in black and were thus "invisible" to the audience; and only male actors were seen during most of the evening, including those who portrayed females. Women appeared only in the musical's explosive final scene, which catapulted the action from Japan's past into the garish world of mid-1970s Tokyo, where Japanese wear pantsuits, T-shirts, leather jackets, and sunglasses and where the weather bureau proudly proclaims that during calendar year 1975 Tokyo had "acceptable" air quality for 162 days. Here the remnants of Kabuki theatre *and* musical comedy were tossed aside and *Pacific Overtures* became an industrial show that sold the products of Japan, such as Toyotas and Seiko watches. And there was the somewhat ominous comment that 57 percent of the bicentennial souvenirs hawked in Washington, D.C., during 1975 were . . . made in Japan.

Besides "A Bowler Hat," Sondheim's dazzling score included some of the most impressive songs heard on Broadway in decades. "Chrysanthemum Tea" was for all purposes a story of murder. The Western ships are in the harbor with a letter to convey to the Shogun (Mako), who procrastinates and tries to pretend they aren't there; as the days pass, his mother (Alvin Ing) continually serves him tea ("an herb that's superb / For disturbances at sea") and finally tells him she decided if there's no Shogun to receive the letter, maybe the ships will go away. Hence, as he dies she explains that "*in the tea*, my lord" she has added "an informal variation / On the normal recipe."

"Please Hello" was an out-and-out Broadway blast of a show-stopper in which the American, British, Dutch, Russian, and French admirals present their countries' respective positions concerning trade agreements, and each admiral's song reflects his national music: for the American admiral, a Sousa-like march; for the British, a Gilbert and Sullivan tongue-twisting patter song; for the Dutch, a waltz-clog ice-skating song; for the Russian, something akin to "The Song of the Volga Boatmen"; and for the French an Offenbach-styled can-can.

And supreme in Sondheim's endless cornucopia of masterful songs was "Someone in a Tree," possibly the masterpiece of his entire canon. History shows that while the United States cataloged its negotiations with Japan, no official record was kept by the Japanese and so nothing is known about Japan's accounts and observations concerning their side of the treaty. "Someone in a Tree" reflects what a young boy and a warrior observe during the negotiations, but because nothing is known about the event from the Japanese perspective the song is actually about . . . nothing. Only Sondheim would have had the audacity, the daring, and the genius to write a such a number: these characters are absolutely clueless about the momentous events they have tangentially witnessed. An old man (James Dybas) recalls the negotiations when as a young boy (Gedde Watanabe) he hid in a tree near the treaty house (Boris Aronson created an impossibly beautiful tree that bloomed in the nature of an ornate Japanese fan). The boy reports that as "a fragment of the day" he saw men with gold on their coats and he witnessed notes being passed back and forth. In the meantime, a warrior who hid beneath the floor of the treaty house reports that he heard creaks, thumps, clinks, shouts, growls, droning, and knocks as well as the banging of a fist and the swish of handheld fans. The boy and the warrior understand absolutely nothing of what is going on, but nonetheless are witnesses to "cups of tea / And history."

The memorable tree was only one aspect of Boris Aronson's sumptuous production designs, which included almost choreographed movements of delicately painted Japanese screens. And the appearance of Perry's ship, the USS *Powhatan*, was, along with Aronson's Fragonard-like designs for the Loveland sequence in ***Follies***, one of the two most memorable scenic effects of the decade. As the terrified villagers watch and then run away in horror, the monstrous ship seems to come out of nowhere as it takes shape and moves from stage right toward the edge of the stage; the lights in its portholes are like the flashing orange eyes of a nightmarish dragon and the navy personnel stand on the decks and prow with their rifles raised in salute, or possibly in threat.

Martin Gottfried in the *New York Post* praised the "exquisite, enchanting, touching, intelligent and altogether remarkable work of theatre art." The musical brought its story "into the same dimension as music and dance and musical staging" and was thus the first musical he'd ever seen that didn't "stop being musical when involved with plot." He noted that Aronson's "gorgeous" physical production included gliding screens and that director Harold Prince staged the work to reflect a "scheme of gliding, appearing and disappearing visions."

Clive Barnes in the *New York Times* said the musical was "very serious" and "almost inordinately ambitious." Sondheim's lyrics were "devilish, wittily and delightfully clever" and he was "the most remarkable man in the Broadway musical today." Barnes felt that John Weidman's book didn't "always rest happily within the conceptual format" of the production and the "narrative balance" of the two acts lost continuity and tone. But *Pacific Overtures* was "so bold" in its attempt and "so fascinating" in its achievement that its "obvious faults demand to be overlooked."

Howard Kissel in *Women's Wear Daily* found the musical "the most original, the most profound, the most theatrically ambitious of the Prince-Sondheim collaborations." It was "a triumph of sophistication, taste and craft" and the physical production conveyed "the brightness and eloquence of the overall conception." John Beaufort in the *Christian Science Monitor* said the "stunning and unique stage spectacle is not to be missed," but noted the work's "trendy liberal yen for national recrimination" presented Perry as a "barbarian" and he wondered if Prince and Weidman really preferred the old Japan of "feudalism and the samurai code." Like Beaufort, Jack Kroll in *Newsweek* noted that the book became slightly didactic with a "fuzzy seriousness" that blamed America for bringing evil upon "poor little Nippon." But otherwise *Pacific Overtures* presented "as brilliant a first act as you'll see in any musical" and the production "voluptuates with invention and sheer beauty."

T. E. Kalem in *Time* found the musical "as arid and airless as the moon" and said it was "audaciously ambitious and flagrantly pretentious." He also stated the work belonged to the "flagellant school of contemporary American self-criticism," which believes that the opening of Japan caused "the whirlwind of Pearl Harbor and global commercial competition." If so, no amount of beautiful scenery could "conceal the simple-mindedness of that line of thought."

Douglas Watt in the *New York Daily News* said the "prevailingly dull, semi-documentary" dealt with "the corrupting influence of Western civilization on Asian culture" and thus the work was "as thin and insubstantial as the painted screens used for scenery."

During the tryout, the somewhat harsh music of "Chrysanthemum Tea" was restructured into a lighter, flowing melody and the lyric was rewritten; "Prayers" was partially dropped (Tamate's prayer was completely cut, but the Councilor's prayer was incorporated into the lyric of "Chrysanthemum Tea"); a processional through the auditorium was eliminated; and the title of "The Advantages of Being Set in the Middle of the Sea" was altered to "The Advantages of Floating in the Middle of the Sea" ("We Float" was an earlier opening number that according to Sondheim was heard during the Boston tryout performances; *Variety*'s Boston review indicates "The Advantages of Being Set in the Middle of the Sea" was heard at the Boston opening). The musical played on Broadway for over five months, and was followed by a brief national tour in which one of the performances was taped and later shown on Japanese television.

"Someone in a Tree" was the subject of the March 28, 1976, telecast of the CBS series *Camera Three* (the episode was titled "Anatomy of a Song").

The script was published in hardback by Dodd, Mead & Company in 1976, and in both hardback and paperback editions by the Theatre Communications Group in 1991. All the lyrics written for the musical are included in Sondheim's collection *Finishing the Hat: Collected Lyrics (1954–1981) with Attendant Comments, Principles, Heresies, Grudges, Whines and Anecdotes*. The original Broadway cast album was released by RCA Victor Records (LP # AR1-1-1367 and CD # RCD1-4407), and the 1987 production by the English National Opera was released on a two-LP set by That's Entertainment Records (LP # TER2-1151) which was later issued on a two-CD set (# TER2-1152).

The musical was revived Off Off Broadway by the York Theatre Company at the Church of the Heavenly Rest on March 27, 1984, for twenty performances, and the same production was seen Off Broadway at the Promenade Theatre on October 25 of that year for 109 showings. The Lincoln Center Festival 2002 presented a Japanese production of the musical by the New National Theatre (Tokyo) at Avery Fisher Hall for five performances beginning on July 9, 2003; and a Broadway revival by the Roundabout Theatre at Studio 54 opened on December 2, 2004, for sixty-nine performances and was recorded by PS Classics (CD # PS-528).

Awards

Tony Award Nominations and Awards: Best Musical (*Pacific Overtures*); Best Leading Actor in a Musical (Mako); Best Featured Actor in a Musical (Isao Sato); Best Director of a Musical (Harold Prince); Best Book (John Weidman); Best Score (lyrics and music by Stephen Sondheim); Best Scenic Designer (**Boris Aronson**); Best Costume Designer (**Florence Klotz**); Best Lighting Designer (Tharon Musser); Best Choreographer (Patricia Birch)
New York Drama Critics' Circle Award: Best Musical (1975–1976) (***Pacific Overtures***)

ROCKABYE HAMLET

"A Musical"

Theatre: Minskoff Theatre
Opening Date: February 17, 1976; *Closing Date*: February 21, 1976
Performances: 7
Book, *Lyrics*, and *Music*: Cliff Jones
Based on the play *Hamlet* by William Shakespeare (written circa 1599–1602).
Direction and *Choreography*: Gower Champion (Tony Stevens, Co-Choreographer); *Producers*: Lester Osterman Productions (Lester Osterman and Richard Horner) and Joseph Kipness in association with Martin Richards and Victor D'Arc and Marilyn Strauss by arrangement with Champlain Productions, Limited; *Scenery*: Kert F. Lundell; *Costumes*: Joseph G. Aulisi; *Lighting*: Jules Fisher; *Musical Direction*: Gordon Lowry Harrell
Cast: Rory Dodd (Horatio), Larry Marshall (Hamlet), Alan Weeks (Claudius), Leata Galloway (Gertrude), Meat Loaf (Priest), Randal Wilson (Polonius), Beverly D'Angelo (Ophelia), Kim Milford (Laertes), Christopher Chadman (Rosencrantz), Winston DeWitt Hemsley (Guildenstern), Irving Lee (Player), Judy Gibson (Playeress, Honeybelle Huckster); Acolytes, Swordsmen, Nobles, Courtesans: Tommy Aguilar, Steve Anthony, Terry Calloway, Prudence Darby, George Giraldo, Larry Hyman, Kurt Johnson, Clinton Keen, Paula Lynn, Joann Ogawa, Sandi Orcutt, Merel Poloway, Joseph Pugliese, Yolanda Raven, Michelle Stubbs, Dennis Williams; Singers: James Braet, Judy DeAngelis, B. G. Gibson, Judy Gibson, Pat Gorman, Suzanne Lukather, Bruce Paine, William Parry; Roadies: David Fredericks, David Lawson, Jeff Spielman; *Rockabye Hamlet* Band: Gordon Lowry Harrell, Allen Herman, Michael Levinson, Peter Phillips, Phil Davis, Billy Schwartz, Richie Resnicoff, Erik Frandsen, Ron McClure, Lowell Hershey, Peter Yellin, Bruce Shaffel, Bill Schneider, Gene Lowinger, Marc Horowitz
The musical was presented in two acts.
The entire action takes place at a rock concert.

Musical Numbers

Act One: "Why Did He Have to Die?" (Rory Dodd, Chorus); "The Wedding" (Larry Marshall, Alan Weeks, Leata Galloway, Meat Loaf, Chorus); "That It Should Come to This" (Larry Marshall); "Set It Right" (Alan Weeks, Larry Marshall, Leata Galloway, Chorus); "Hello-Hello" (Beverly D'Angelo, Larry Marshall); "Don't Unmask Your Beauty to the Moon" (Larry Marshall, Kim Milford); "If Not to You" (Beverly D'Angelo, Chorus); "Have I Got a Girl for You" (Christopher Chadman, Winston DeWitt Hemsley, Larry Marshall, Chorus); "Tis Pity, Tis True" (Randal Wilson, Alan Weeks, Leata Galloway); "Shall We Dance" (Larry Marshall, Leata Galloway); "All My Life" (Leata Galloway); "Something's Rotten in Denmark" (Larry Marshall, Irving Lee, Judy Gibson, Chorus); "Denmark Is Still" (Larry Marshall, Beverly D'Angelo, Chorus); "Twist Her Mind" (Rory Dodd, Larry Marshall, Beverly D'Angelo, Chorus); "Gentle Lover" (Beverly D'Angelo); "Where Is the Reason" (Larry Marshall); "The Wart Song" (Irving Lee, Judy Gibson, Chorus); "He Got It in the Ear" (Judy Gibson); "It Is Done" (Larry Marshall, Rory Dodd)
Act Two: "Midnight—Hot Blood" (Larry Marshall); "Midnight Mass" (Larry Marshall, Leata Galloway, Alan Weeks, Meat Loaf, Choir); "Hey . . . !" (Christopher Chadman, Winston DeWitt Hemsley, Alan Weeks); "Sing Alone" (Larry Marshall); "Your Daddy's Gone Away" (Rory Dodd); "Rockabye Hamlet" (Beverly

D'Angelo); "All by Yourself" (Kim Milford); "The Rosencrantz and Guildenstern Boogie" (Alan Weeks, Chorus Girls); "Laertes' Coercion" (Alan Weeks, Kim Milford, Leata Galloway, Chorus Girls); "The Last Blues" (Leata Galloway); "Didn't She Do It for Love" (Meat Loaf, Alan Weeks, Larry Marshall, Kim Milford, Chorus); "If My Morning Begins" (Larry Marshall); "Swordfight" (Alan Weeks, Larry Marshall, Kim Milford, Leata Galloway, Rory Dodd)

Advertisements for *Rockabye Hamlet* proclaimed it was "An Experience as Limitless as Your Imagination!" But critics and audiences were able to contain themselves, and the show went down in flames after seven performances. A glance at the program might have misled the unwary: the song titles "Shall We Dance" and "Have I Got a Girl for You" certainly had a familiar ring to them. But other titles were a foreboding of things to come: "The Rosencrantz and Guildenstern Boogie" and "The Wart Song" (but this version omitted such road kill as "Pass Them Biscuits, Mama" and "Trojan Boogie").

The program indicated the action took place at a rock concert, and there was much in the way of microphones passing back and forth between performers, not to mention mikes rising from beneath the floor of the stage or moving overhead on a boom above the actors. In this spirit, Ophelia (Beverly D'Angelo) conveniently commits suicide not by drowning but by strangling herself on the cord of her microphone. The scenic design played up the concert motif, and so there were steps and platforms on both sides of the stage for the musicians, and the stage was flanked by rows and rows of neon lights, sound equipment, and other such paraphernalia endemic to rock concerts. There was also a huge ramp in the middle of the stage that was frequently raised and lowered like a seesaw, and the production seemed to grasp at each and every effect in order to make some kind of impression (for example, when the players perform for Claudius, they wear electric blue cowboy outfits, and the leading player is a black actor in white face).

Martin Gottfried in *Women's Wear Daily* said it all was "perfectly and impeccably awful" and there was no way to truly convey "the foolishness and waste" of the show. The ramp seemed to "obsess" director and choreographer Gower Champion, and it kept going up and down throughout the evening "like a drawbridge to disaster"; his dances were variations on the frug and the monkey, and thus were outdated by about ten years; and Larry Marshall (Hamlet) was "so withdrawn" he could have been portraying Fortinbras. Leata Galloway (Gertrude) was a "slinky sexpot" who made up the trio of the black royal family that included Hamlet and Claudius (Alan Weeks), and Gottfried suggested only Champion knew what Galloway was supposed "to be up to." He ruefully concluded his notice by saying that perhaps ***Home Sweet Homer*** wasn't so bad after all.

Clive Barnes in the *New York Times* found the production "quite disturbingly banal—empty, vacuous and a little conceited," said librettist-lyricist-composer Cliff Jones was "a second-rate musician with a third-rate mind" whose lyrics were "deplorable" (and when a country-western tune started up, Barnes wondered "which country?"). Edwin Wilson in the *Wall Street Journal* said the musical was "guilty of overkill, both in the elaborate spectacle and in the underlying cynicism." And Douglas Watt in the *New York Daily News* said the "bloated" and "misguided" musical "flopped about the stage like a dying swordfish," the score was "utterly without distinction, with lyrics to match," and the scenery looked "like an electrical appliances warehouse" and was one of the "ugliest stage settings I have ever seen."

Howard Kissel in *Women's Wear Daily* suggested the musical's title should have been *Hamlet Goes to Las Vegas*, said the material lacked "honesty" and "genuineness," and noted that the scenery gave the production the "tawdry tone" required by the "Vegas-styled evening." Kevin Sanders on WABCTV7 said the musical was "crassly and crudely" adapted from *Hamlet*, and the costumes looked as if they'd been "ransacked from Sonny and Cher's wardrobe." Hobe in *Variety* said the performers were "incomprehensibly costumed" and the musical had "little relation to human drama"; and Leonard Probst on NBC Radio complained that the production was "tacky and tasteless" with "rock Muzak" and thus was "the most painful show" he'd seen all year.

A recording of songs from the musical by Rising Records (LP # RILP-103) includes vocals by Cliff Jones, Cal Dodd, and Rory Dodd; the ten numbers on the album are: "With a Pick and a Shovel," "If My Morning Begins," "That It Should Come to This," "Hello-Hello," "All by Yourself," "The Last Blues (I'll Ever Sing)," "Sing Alone," "All My Life," "Denmark Is Still," and "Somebody Wrote the Wrong Words to My Song." The liner notes stated that five critics "killed" *Rockabye Hamlet*, and the album provided quotes from various celebrities who praised the show: Bob Fosse said it was "a landmark in musical theatre history"; "with tears in her eyes" Chita Rivera said it was "the most wonderful experience I've ever had in the theatre"; and not to be outdone, Carol Channing saw *Rockabye Hamlet* twice and said the musical gave her the "greatest thrill of my life." Two songs from the musical ("If My Morning Begins" and "The Last Blues") are included in the collection *Shakespeare on Broadway* (Varese Sarabande Records CD # VSD-5622)

As *Kronberg: 1582*, *Rockabye Hamlet* had originally been commissioned by the Canadian Broadcasting Company's Radio Variety Department for a two-hour presentation in December 1, 1973, with Cal Dodd (Hamlet) and Nancy White (Ophelia). Again as *Kronberg: 1582*, the musical was presented at the Charlottetown Festival, Prince Edward Island, at the Confederation Center on July 1, 1974, and returned to the festival during the following summer (of the Charlottetown cast members, Rory Dodd, as Horatio, also appeared in the Broadway version). In reviewing the 1974 production, Add in *Variety* found it a "likeable, rollicking, striking" show that was "something special," and said at first hearing several songs had a "commercial sound and could stand on their own." (The review also helpfully explained that *Hamlet* is "often considered by scholars of the theatre the greatest play ever written.")

The musical subsequently toured Canada with Brent Carver (Hamlet) and Beverly D'Angelo (Ophelia), and of course the latter appeared in the Broadway production.

Songs heard in *Kronberg: 1582* that weren't retained for the Broadway production were: "To Thine Own Self Be True," "Trojan Boogie," "Get Thee to a Nunnery," "To Have Seen What I Have Seen," "Pass Them Biscuits, Mama," "I Cannot Turn to Love," "Somebody Wrote the Wrong Words to My Song," "Song of the Flowers," "Willy Nilly," and "Words."

A few years after the *Rockabye Hamlet* debacle, Cliff Jones revised the musical as *Something's Rockin' in Denmark!*, and the work was presented at the Odyssey Theatre in Los Angeles in 1981. The production contained forty-nine separate musical sequences, and the following numbers seem to have been written just for this version: "The First Watch," "I Cannot Believe It," "The Ceremony," "Hello, Hello" (extended version), "Good-bye," "Father-Daughter," "It Is My Belief," "The Second Watch," "Set It Right" (blues version), "The Boogie," "Something's Rockin' in Denmark," "Chat," "It Is Better to Live," "Hamlet's Request," "If I Could," "Hamlet's Explanation," "A Hurtin' Song," "It Is Better," "Midnight Ritual," "Hey!" (ballet version), "Set It Right" (chant version), "Street Cries," "With a Pick and a Shovel," "Funeral Procession," "Her Death Was Doubtful," "The Trap," "The Letter," "No Use Pretending," "The Set-Up," and "Epilogue." Some of the numbers were probably the same ones from the Charlottetown or Broadway versions with title variations (e.g., "Something's Rockin' in Denmark" and "Something's Rotten in Denmark" and "Midnight Ritual" and "Midnight Mass").

BUBBLING BROWN SUGAR

"A New Musical Revue"

Theatre: ANTA Theatre
Opening Date: March 2, 1976; *Closing Date*: December 31, 1977
Performances: 766
Book: Loften Mitchell
Lyrics and *Music*: See song listing for specific credits.
Direction: Robert M. Cooper; *Producers*: J. Lloyd Grant, Richard Bell, Robert M. Cooper, and Ashton Springer in association with Moe Septee, Inc. (A Media House Production); *Choreography*: Billy Wilson; *Scenery*: Clarke Dunham; *Projections*: Lucie D. Grosvenor and Clarke Dunham; *Costumes*: Bernard Johnson; *Lighting*: Barry Arnold; *Musical Direction*: Danny Holgate
Cast: Lonnie McNeil (Skip, Young Checkers), Vernon Washington (Bill, Time Man, Bumpy, Emcee), Newton Winters (Ray, Young Sage), Carolyn Byrd (Carolyn, Gospel Lady, Female Nightclub Singer), Karen Grannum (Norma), Alton Lathrop (Gene, Gospel Lady's Son); Dyann Robinson (Helen), Charlise Harris (Laura), Vivian Reed (Marsha, Young Irene), Anthony Whitehouse (Tony, Waiter, Dutch), Josephine Premice (Irene Paige), Avon Long (John Sage, Rusty), Joseph Attles (Checkers, Dusty), Chip Garnett (Jim, Male Nightclub Singer), Ethel Beatty (Ella), Barbara Rubenstein (Judy, Dutch's Girl), Barry Preston (Charlie, Count); The Solitunes: Alton Lathrop, Lonnie McNeil, Newton Winters; Chorus: Murphy Cross, Nedra Dixon, Emme Kemp, Stanley Ramsey
The revue was presented in two acts.
The action takes place in Harlem at the present time and in the period from 1920 to 1940.

Musical Numbers

Act One: "Harlem '70" (music by Danny Holgate) (Company); "Bubbling Brown Sugar" (lyric and music by Danny Holgate, Emme Kemp, and Lillian Lopez) (Company); "That's What Harlem Is to Me" (lyric and music by Andy Razaf) (Josephine Premice); "Bill Robinson Specialty" (Vernon Washington); "Harlem, Sweet Harlem" (lyric by Emme Kemp, music by Danny Holgate) (Company); "(I Ain't Never Done Nothing to) Nobody" (*Ziegfeld Follies of 1910*; lyric by Axel Rogers, music by Bert Williams) (Avon Long); "Goin' Back in Time" (music by Danny Holgate) (Vernon Washington) "Some of These Days" (lyric and music by Shelton Brooks) (Barbara Rubenstein); "Moving Uptown" (lyric by Loften Mitchell and Emme Kemp, music by Danny Holgate) (Vernon Washington); "Strolling" (music by Danny Holgate) (Alton Lathrop, Charlise Harris, Lonnie McNeil, Karen Grannum, Newton Winters, Dyann Robinson); "I'm Gonna Tell God All My Troubles" (traditional) (Alton Lathrop); Medley: "His Eye Is on the Sparrow" (traditional) and "Swing Low, Sweet Chariot" (traditional) (Carolyn Byrd, Company); "Sweet Georgia Brown" (lyric and music by Kenneth Casey, Ben Bernie, and Maceo Pinkard) (Vivian Reed, Lonnie McNeil, Newton Winters); "Honeysuckle Rose" (nightclub revue *Load of Coal*, 1929; lyric by Andy Razaf, music by Thomas "Fats" Waller) (Josephine Premice, Avon Long); "Stormy Monday Blues" (lyric and music by Earl "Fatha" Hines, Billy Eckstein, and Bob Crowder) (Carolyn Bird); "Rosetta" (lyric and music by Earl "Fatha" Hines) (Alton Lathrop, Lonnie McNeil, Newton Winters); "Sophisticated Lady" (lyric by Irving Mills and Mitchell Parish, music by Duke Ellington) (Chip Garnett; danced by Vernon Washington and Dyann Robinson); "In Honeysuckle Time (When Emmaline Said She'd Be Mine)" (*Shuffle Along*, 1921; lyric by Noble Sissle, music by Eubie Blake) (Avon Long, Joseph Attles); "In My Solitude" (lyric by Eddie DeLange and Irving Mills, music by Duke Ellington) (Vivian Reed, Alton Lathrop, Lonnie McNeil, Newton Winters); "C'mon Up to Jive Time" (music by Danny Holgate) (Vernon Washington); Medley: "Stompin' at the Savoy" (lyric by Andy Razaf, music by Edgar Sampson) and "Take the 'A' Train" (lyric by Joya Sherrill, music by Billy Strayhorn) (Company)

Act Two: "Harlem-Time" (music by Danny Holgate) (Vernon Washington); "Love Will Find a Way" (*Shuffle Along*, 1921; lyric by Noble Sissle, music by Eubie Blake) (Chip Garnett, Ethel Beatty); "Dutch's Song" (lyric and music by Emme Kemp) (Anthony Whitehouse); "Brown Gal" (lyric and music by Avon Long and Lil Armstrong) (Avon Long); "Pray for the Lights to Go Out" (lyric and music by Renton Tunnan and William E. Skidmore) (Joseph Attles); "I Got It Bad (and That Ain't Good)" (from 1941 musical *Jump for Joy* which closed during its pre-Broadway tryout; lyric by Paul Francis Webster, music by Duke Ellington) (Ethel Beatty); "Harlem Makes Me Feel!" (lyric and music by Emme Kemp) (Barry Preston); "Jim, Jam, Jumpin' Jive" (lyric and music by Cab Calloway) (Vernon Washington, Lonnie McNeil, Newton Winters); "There'll Be Some Changes Made" (lyric and music by W. Benton Overstreet, Billy Higgins, and William Blackston) (Josephine Premice, Vivian Reed); "God Bless the Child" (lyric and music by Arthur Herzog Jr., and Billie Holiday) (Vivian Reed); "It Don't Mean a Thing" (lyric by Irving Mills, music by Duke Ellington) (Chip Garnett, Anthony Whitehouse, Vivian Reed, Josephine Premice, Company)

The musical *Bubbling Brown Sugar* credited Loften Mitchell with its book, but the evening was for all purposes a glorified revue, and what a revue it was! The thin storyline, which was a happy excuse for a series of show-stopping musical numbers, starts in the present when a trio of former black entertainers look back on their glory days as part of Harlem's night life and entertainment spots. They proceed to take some young people, including a tourist or two, on a time trip into the past where they all see (and often participate in) songs and dances from the 1920s, 1930s, and 1940s.

The old-timers were Avon Long, Joseph Attles, and Josephine Premice, and in ***Follies*** fashion they meet up with their youthful selves (Newton Winters, Lonnie McNeil, and Vivian Reed). But unlike ***Follies*** this is a happy occasion for laughs, songs, and dances; no regrets and recriminations here. The 1970s offered a number of musical tributes to both black composers and to Harlem's past, and *Bubbling Brown Sugar* was the best of them all. ***Ain't Misbehavin'*** was entertaining but modest and lacked a certain variety in its presentation, and *Sophisticated Ladies* seemed far too calculated for its own good. But *Bubbling Brown Sugar* was the real thing, an old-fashioned slam-bang entertainment that offered show-stopper after show-stopper. Its pleasures were genuine, and it was one of the most delightful productions of the decade. Although the critics showered the show with rave reviews, they nonetheless groaned about the early book scenes that established the evening's premise. But once the evening traveled to Harlem's past, all was well and the evening was a cornucopia of sizzling song and dance. And Vivian Reed received some of the most rapturous notices of the decade for her knockout performance; with her clarion voice and electric dancing, she was the personification of Old-Time Broadway.

Avon Long and Joseph Attles cavorted impishly throughout the proceedings. Long made musical magic with Josephine Premice in "Honeysuckle Rose" and as Attles cavorted through the naughty "Pray for the Lights to Go Out" he seemed to shock himself by the lyric's implications. Vivian Reed razzle-dazzled with her brassy voice and heavenly high kicks in "Sweet Georgia Brown" (hers may well be the definitive version of the song) and she later shook the rafters with her spiritual-like interpretation of "God Bless the Child." In the meantime, Vernon Washington, Lonnie McNeil, and Newton Winters never touched the floor in "Jim, Jam, Jumpin' Jive" because their smooth and undulating dancing proved they were made of air and weren't bound by the laws of gravity. And for the evening's grand finale, all the leads appeared in a snowstorm of white gowns and tuxedos and proceeded to knock the daylights out of "It Don't Mean a Thing."

Martin Gottfried in the *New York Post* said there might be much that was "technically wrong" with *Bubbling Brown Sugar* but there was one thing that was "technically perfect" because the show was "terrific." The going-back-in-time premise may have been awkward, but the show was "gorgeous entertainment" with "regularly wonderful" choreography. Here was an evening of "contagious effervescence" and "simply exhilarating" numbers, and the finale could have gone on "forever." As for Vivian Reed, she was a "show stealer" and a "show topper."

Douglas Watt in the *New York Daily News* loved the "ebullient, tonic entertainment" and "joyous occasion," and Barry Preston was "the most dazzling eccentric and pure show dancer to turn up on Broadway since Ray Bolger was a colt." Clive Barnes in the *New York Times* said after a slow start the revue picked up speed and "came to the boil." Here was an "unexpectedly endearing" entertainment and Billy Wilson's dances were "some of the best to be seen currently on Broadway." As for Vivian Reed, she was a "knockout" in "Sweet Georgia Brown."

Edwin Wilson in the *Wall Street Journal* praised the "effervescent, explosive musical loaded with fresh talent and marvelous music." The choreography was "impressive" and Vivian Reed "knocks the audience dead with 'Sweet Georgia Brown.'" Howard Kissel in *Women's Wear Daily* said the revue was "enormous fun"; as for Vivian Reed, she was "the most impressive talent on the stage" and looked and sounded "spectacular." Her "Sweet Georgia Brown" was "elegant" and "witty," and it "met with a thundering ovation and cries of 'One More Time.'"

Kevin Sanders on WABCTV said the nonstop songs and dances were performed by a "superlative" cast; Billy Wilson's choreography was "stunning"; and Vivian Reed's "Sweet Georgia Brown" was "the sexiest single song on Broadway today." Like all the critics, T. E. Kalem in *Time* wasn't happy with the book (it's "for the wastebasket"), but the show itself came from the "torrid zone" with its expert performers. Vivian Reed had "the fresh, flaming force of a new comet entering the earth's orbit"; she was "sinuous" and "magnetic" and "torchy" and "sans Con Edison, she could light up a Broadway marquee."

The revue was based on a concept by Rosetta LeNoire and was first produced Off Off Broadway by her AMAS Repertory Theatre, Inc., at the Church of St. Paul and St. Andrew for twelve performances beginning on February 14, 1975. A national tour began during that summer, and the musical opened on Broadway late the following winter and played for 766 performances. During the pre-Broadway tour, Thelma Carpenter was succeeded by Josephine Premice and Danny Beard by Chip Garnett. Songs cut from the Off-Off-Broadway run were: "Through the Years," "S'posin'," and "It's All Your Fault." For the post-Broadway tour, "Dutch's Song" was dropped and "Ain't Misbehavin'" was added (lyric by Andy Razaf, music by Thomas "Fats" Waller and Harry Brooks), and a later national tour with Cab Calloway included "Minnie the Moocher" (lyric by Cab Calloway, Clarence Gaskill, and Irving Mills, music by Cab Calloway) and "Them There Eyes" (lyric and music by Maceo Pinkard, Doris Tauber, and William Tracey).

The script (but not the lyrics) was published in paperback by Broadway Play Publishing in 1985, and the original cast album was released by H & L Records (LP # 69011-698). The London production opened at the Royalty Theatre on September 28, 1977, and a two-LP cast album was released by Pye Records (# NSPD-504).

Awards

Tony Award Nominations: Best Musical (*Bubbling Brown Sugar*); Best Leading Actress in a Musical (Vivian Reed); Best Choreographer (Billy Wilson)

MY FAIR LADY

Theatre: St. James Theatre
Opening Date: March 25, 1976; *Closing Date*: February 20, 1977
Performances: 377
Book and *Lyrics*: Alan Jay Lerner
Music: Frederick Loewe
Based on the 1912 play *Pygmalion* by George Bernard Shaw and the 1938 film *Pygmalion* (among others, Shaw was one of the film's writers, and he won an Oscar for the screenplay).
Direction: Jerry Adler (based on the original direction by Moss Hart); *Producer*: Herman Levin; *Choreography*: Crandall Diehl (based on the original choreography by Hanya Holm); *Scenery*: Oliver Smith; *Costumes*: Cecil Beaton (W. Robert Lavine, Special Costume Assistant); *Lighting*: John Gleason; *Musical Direction*: Theodore Saidenberg
Cast: Debra Lyman (Busker), Stan Picus (Busker), Ernie Pysher (Busker), Eleanor Phelps (Mrs. Eynsford-Hill), Jerry Lanning (Freddy Eynsford-Hill), *Christine Andreas* (Eliza Doolittle), Robert Coote (Colonel Pickering), *Ian Richardson* (Henry Higgins), Kevin Marcum (First Cockney), Jack Starkey (Second Cockney), William James (Third Cockney, Flunkey), Stan Page (Fourth Cockney, Footman), Kevin Lane Dearinger (Bartender, Servant, Footman), John Clarkson (Harry, Lord Boxington, Zoltan Karpathy), Richard Neilson (Jamie, Ambassador), *George Rose* (Alfred P. Doolittle), Sylvia O'Brien (Mrs. Pearce), Margaretta Warwick (Mrs. Hopkins, Lady Boxington), Clifford Fearl (Butler, Bartender), Sonja Anderson (Servant), Lynn Fitzpatrick (Servant), Karen Gibson (Servant, Queen of Transylvania), Vicki Patik (Servant), Brenda Forbes (Mrs. Higgins), Jack Karcher (Chauffer), Timothy Smith (Constable), Dru Alexandrine (Flower Girl), Sonja Stuart (Mrs. Higgins' Maid); Singing Ensemble: Sonja Anderson, Alyson Bristol, Lynn Fitzpatrick, Karen Gibson, Cynthia Meryl, Vickie Patik, Kevin Lane Dearinger, Clifford Fearl, William James, Kevin Marcum, Stan Page, Jack Starkey); Dancing Ensemble: Dru Alexandrine, Sally Benoit, Marie Berry, Debra Lyman, Mari McMinn, Gina Ramsel, Catherine Rice, Sonja Stuart, Bonnie Walker, Richard Ammon, Jeremy Blanton, David Evans, Jack Karcher, Richard Maxon, Stan Picus, Ernie Pysher, Rick Schneider, Timothy Smith
The musical was presented in two acts.
The action takes place in London in 1912.

Musical Numbers

Act One: "Street Entertainers" (Debra Lyman, Stan Picus, Ernie Pysher); "Why Can't the English?" (Ian Richardson); "Wouldn't It Be Loverly?" (Christine Andreas, Kevin Marcum, Jack Starkey, William James, Stan Page); "With a Little Bit of Luck" (George Rose, John Clarkson, Richard Neilson); "I'm an Ordinary Man" (Ian Richardson); "With a Little Bit of Luck" (reprise) (George Rose, Ensemble); "Just You Wait" (Christine Andreas); "The Rain in Spain" (Ian Richardson, Christine Andreas, Robert Coote); "I Could Have Danced All Night" (Christine Andreas, Sylvia O'Brien, Maids); "Ascot Gavotte" (Ensemble); "On the Street Where You Live" (Jerry Lanning); "The Embassy Waltz" (Ian Richardson, Robert Coote, Christine Andreas, John Clarkson, Ensemble)
Act Two: "You Did It" (Ian Richardson, Robert Coote, Sylvia O'Brien, Servants); "Just You Wait" (reprise) (Christine Andreas); "On the Street Where You Live" (reprise) (Jerry Lanning); "Show Me" (Christine Andreas, Jerry Lanning); "Wouldn't It Be Loverly?" (reprise) (Christine Andreas, Kevin Marcum, Jack Starkey, William James, Stan Page); "Get Me to the Church on Time" (George Rose, John Clarkson, Richard Neilson, Ensemble); "A Hymn to Him" (Ian Richardson); "Without You" (Christine Andreas, Ian Richardson); "I've Grown Accustomed to Her Face" (Ian Richardson)

The critics generally liked the twentieth-anniversary revival of Alan Jay Lerner and Frederick Loewe's *My Fair Lady*, which opened almost exactly twenty years after the Broadway premiere of the original 1956 production. Despite a run of almost one year, the musical closed in the red. The critics offered wildly divergent views on the performances of Ian Richardson (Henry Higgins) and Christine Andreas (Eliza Doolittle), and the cast also included George Rose (as Doolittle, a role he had first performed in New York at City Center in 1968), Robert Coote (who reprised his role of Colonel Pickering from the original production), and Jerry Lanning (Freddy Eynsford-Hill).

John Beaufort in the *Christian Science Monitor* found Richardson "stagey instead of stylish," and T. E. Kalem in *Time* said the actor approached the English language as "the lineal descendant of Shakespeare" and the text couldn't "bear the weight of that sort of gravity and eloquence." Leonard Probst on NBC Radio felt Richardson lacked "magnetism" and was "always the actor, not the man he is playing"; Jack Kroll in *Newsweek* said Richardson was "miscast" and didn't convey Higgins's "warmth and eccentricity"; and Martin Gottfried in the *New York Post* found him a "disappointment" because he wasn't cruel and intense enough and thus missed the quality of Higgins's strength. But Clive Barnes in the *New York Times* said Richardson "took command" of the revival and his Higgins was more in keeping with Shaw's vision; and Douglas Watt in the *New York Daily News* noted that the actor performed his numbers "with style" and that his "graceful and intelligent" interpretation of the role brought to mind Leslie Howard's Higgins in the 1938 film version of *Pygmalion*.

Beauford found Andreas "miscast"; Gottfried said she was "disappointing" and "not up to acting the role"; Barnes suggested her "transformation from cabbage leaf to daffodil was not quite convincing"; and Kroll noted that despite her being a "real singer" she lacked "the star quality of Julie Andrews and even the semi-star quality of Sally Ann Howes" (who succeeded Andrews in the original Broadway production). But Watt praised the "gorgeous" actress whose "supple" voice did justice to her songs; Edwin Wilson in the *Wall Street Journal* liked her "fresh interpretation" of Eliza and noted she possessed "a remarkably beautiful singing voice"; and Howard Kissel in *Women's Wear Daily* praised her "rich voice" and suggested she brought "greater human vulnerability to the role" than did Andrews.

George Rose's acting style was mannered and smug, and a little bit of him went a long way. For his performance in *My Fair Lady*, the critics as usual adored him and his Alfred P. Doolittle brought him a Tony Award for Best Leading Actor in a Musical for a role that was clearly a supporting one (imagine a revival of *Carousel* in which the performer playing Carrie Pipperidge wins the Tony Award for Best Leading Actress in a Musical). As mentioned, Rose had previously played Doolittle in a revival produced by the New York City Center Light Opera Company in 1968. Gottfried found Jerry Lanning's performance as Freddy Eynsford-Hill "remarkable"; the role was usually a thankless one, but somehow Lanning "found a hook" to make the character interesting and thus he was "delightful."

As for the musical itself, Kroll said it was "a masterwork of the American musical stage," and while Gottfried found it "among the very best of the Broadway book musicals," he made a strange comment that the work "is not a musical that will prove classic because its construction as theatre is too often awkward."

The revival was recorded by Columbia Records (LP # PS-34197).

The original Broadway production opened on March 15, 1956, at the Mark Hellinger Theatre for a then record-breaking 2,717 performances. Besides the current revival, there have been four others of the musical. The New York City Center Light Opera Company revived the work at City Center on June 28, 1964, for forty-seven performances with Myles Eason and Marni Nixon, and then on June 13, 1968, for twenty-two performances (Fritz Weaver and Inga Swenson; and George Rose was Doolittle); on August 18, 1981, at the Uris (now Gershwin) Theatre for 119 performances (Rex Harrison reprised his original role, and Nancy Ringham was Eliza); and on May 1, 1994, for 165 performances at the Virginia Theatre (Richard Chamberlain and Melissa Errico).

The first London production opened on April 30, 1958, at the Drury Lane for 2,281 performances with Harrison, Andrews, Stanley Holloway, and Robert Coote all reprising their original roles.

For the Warner Brothers' 1964 film version, Harrison and Holloway re-created their stage roles, and Audrey Hepburn was Eliza (her singing voice was dubbed by Marni Nixon). The film won eight Academy Awards, including Best Picture.

The musical's script was published in hardback by Coward-McCann in 1956, and is also one of sixteen scripts included in the 2014 Library of Congress hardcopy collection *American Musicals*. There are numerous recordings of the score, but the definitive one is the original 1956 cast album (Columbia Records LP # OL-5090), which has been twice issued on CD (the most recent by Sony Classical/Columbia/Legacy # SK-89997 includes interviews with Harrison, Andrews, and Lerner and Loewe). Beware of the London cast recording; it's far too studied and lacks spontaneity. One particularly interesting cast album is the 1959 Mexico City production *Mi Bella Dama*, which includes a young Placido Domingo as one of the quartet that accompanies Eliza in "Wouldn't It Be Loverly?"

For more information about *My Fair Lady*, Keith Garebian's *The Making of "My Fair Lady"* (published by ECW Press in 1993) is recommended, and another solid resource is Dominic McHugh's *Loverly: The Life and Times of "My Fair Lady"* (Oxford University Press, 2012).

Awards

Tony Awards and Nominations: Best Leading Actor in a Musical (Ian Richardson); Best Leading Actor in a Musical (**George Rose**)

MONTY PYTHON LIVE!

Theatre: City Center 55th Street Theatre
Opening Date: April 14, 1976; *Closing Date*: May 2, 1976
Performances: 23
Sketches and *Direction*: By the Monty Python performers
Producer: Artist Consultants; *Scenery*: Karl Eigsti ("American Scenic Supervision"); *Lighting*: John Gleason
Cast: The Monty Python performers—Terry Gilliam (Chunky Neanderthal Painter), Terry Jones (Dusky Welchman), John Cleese (Lofty Gagster), Eric Idle (Winsome Seventh Day Adventist), Graham Chapman (Svelte Non-Mexican), Michael Palin (Languid Empiricist); Neil Innes, Carol Cleveland
The revue was presented in two acts.

Sketches and Musical Numbers

Note: The program didn't list individual sketches and musical sequences.

Monty Python Live! was an evening of comic sketches (and a few musical sequences) by the British team Monty Python, whose television series *Monty Python's Flying Circus* was popular on British and U.S. television. But "live" may not be quite accurate, as the evening seems to have consisted of a combination of film sequences from the series as well as cartoons; besides appearances by the troupe, there were also two guest performers. A few critics reported that the team's familiar routines were rapturously greeted by their fans, and the evening took on the trappings of a rock concert where the audience turns out in droves to hear their favorite songs. Benjamin Stein in the *Wall Street Journal* noted that as soon as the very first words of a sketch were spoken, and "before anything funny has happened," the audience went "crazy with laughter."

The program included a sampling of critical quotes about the revue, including: "Terrific, Fantastic, Wonderful, Great" (Roget's *Thesaurus*); "A must for all the family" (Al Capone); and "Good entertainment for all ages—particularly the Paleolythic and Mezzozoic" (*Archeological Review*). (For the latter, were the misspellings part of the joke?)

Among the routines were Graham Chapman's one-man wrestling match; a TV quiz show called *Blackmail* in which Karl Marx, Che Guevara, Mao Tse-tung, and Vladimir Ilyich Ulanov (the latter "popularly known as Lenin") compete for prizes; a sequence in which stately judges remove their wigs and robes to reveal they're wearing silky black undergarments; a cast member who hawks a dead albatross to audience members; a movie about dancing dentures; a song about the swimming habits of llamas; impersonations of Elton John, Bob Dylan, and Paul McCartney; and a musical interlude by an inept guitarist (who tells the audience, "I suffered for my music, and now it's your turn").

Martin Gottfried in the *New York Post* said the evening was "the maddest and brightest comedy revue" since *Beyond the Fringe*, but Douglas Watt in the *New York Daily News* thought it "a kind of poor man's *Beyond the Fringe*," and one sequence reminded him of a shtick performed by Dudley Moore in ***Good Evening***. Clive Barnes in the *New York Times* said the revue was one of "pure, adulterated madness" which combined the "wry savagery of Tom Lehrer and the poetic anarchy of *Hellzapoppin'*." Stein felt the one-joke sketches went on too long, but he noted that for "Python addicts desperate for a fix," the City Center was the place to be.

David Sterritt in the *Christian Science Monitor* noted the sketches ranged "from sublimely funny to oafishly crude," and he liked the sequence in which one of the cast members "sings pop music astride platform shoes higher than most platforms." Howard Kissel in *Women's Wear Daily* said many sketches had a "giddy brilliance"; and T. E. Kalem in *Time* noted that "no matter how high the brow or how low" the revue "creases it with jet-propelled mirth."

Watt mentioned that the evening sometimes consisted of "explicit material," and he noticed that a father in his row left early with his young child; Watt suggested that if one brought a child to the show, it was best to leave at intermission by telling the youngster the show was over (a "trick" he learned when he used to take his children to the circus).

SHIRLEY MACLAINE

Theatre: Palace Theatre
Opening Date: April 19, 1976; *Closing Date*: May 1, 1976
Performances: 14
Dialogue: Fred Ebb; additional material by Bob Wells
Direction and *Choreography*: Tony Charmoli (*Special Choreography*: Alan Johnson); *Producer*: HMT Associates; *Lighting*: Richard Winkler (Graham Large, Lighting Consultant); *Musical Direction*: Donn Trenner
Cast: *Shirley MacLaine*; Shirley's Gypsies: Adam Grammis, Candy Brown, Gary Flannery, Jo Ann Lehmann, Larry Vickers; Drummer: Tom Duckworth
The revue was presented in one act.

Musical Numbers

Overture (Orchestra); "If My Friends Could See Me Now" (*Sweet Charity*, 1966; lyric by Dorothy Fields, music by Cy Coleman); (Shirley MacLaine, Adam Grammis, Gary Flannery); "My Personal Property" (1969 film version of *Sweet Charity*; lyric by Dorothy Fields, music by Cy Coleman); "Remember Me?" (1937 film *Mr. Dodd Takes the Air*; lyric by Al Dubin, music by Harry Warren; new lyric may have been written by Bob Wells) (Shirley MacLaine); "Hey, Big Spender" (*Sweet Charity*, 1966; lyric by Dorothy Fields, music by Cy Coleman) (Candy Brown, Jo Ann Lehmann, Shirley MacLaine); "I'm a Person, Too" (lyric by Bob Wells; composer unknown, but probably Cy Coleman; sequence included a monologue from 1959 film *Some Came Running*) (Shirley MacLaine); "Irma La Douce" (Shirley MacLaine) (the sequence may have used music by Marguerite Monnot from the 1960 Broadway production or from the 1963 film version with music mostly by Andre Previn); "The Gypsy in My Soul" (from 1937 University of Pennsylvania Mask and Wig Show; lyric by Moe Jaffe, music by Clay Boland) (Shirley MacLaine, Gypsies); "It's Not Where You Start" (*Seesaw*, 1973; lyric by Dorothy Fields, music by Cy Coleman) (Shirley MacLaine, Gypsies); "Every Little Movement (Has a Meaning All Its Own)" (*Madame Sherry*, 1910; lyric by Otto Harbach, music by Karl Hoschna) (Shirley MacLaine, Gypsies); "The Hustle" (Shirley MacLaine, Gypsies) (the discotheque-styled dance was based on "The Donkey Serenade" from the 1937 film *The Firefly*; lyric by Robert Wright and George Forrest, music by Rudolf Friml and Herbert Stothart); "(She's a) Star" (lyric and music by Serge Lama, A. Dona, and Fred Ebb) (Shirley MacLaine); "I'm a Brass Band" (*Sweet Charity*, 1966; lyric by Dorothy Fields, music by Cy Coleman)

The limited-engagement revue marked Shirley MacLaine's first Broadway appearance in over two decades. She had made her debut in the dancing chorus of Richard Rodgers and Oscar Hammerstein II's 1953 musical *Me and Juliet*, and the following year appeared as a member of the chorus and as Carol Haney's understudy in Richard Adler and Jerry Ross's *The Pajama Game*. And the rest was the stuff of Broadway legend: Haney injured her foot, MacLaine went on in the role, a Hollywood talent scout was in the audience, and the next year MacLaine starred in her first film, Alfred Hitchcock's *The Trouble with Harry*. During her lengthy Hollywood career, she appeared in three films that won the Academy Award for Best Picture (*Around the World in Eighty Days*, *The Apartment*, and *Terms of Endearment*) and picked up five Best Actress nominations, including her win for *Terms of Endearment*. But MacLaine hadn't forgotten her Broadway roots, and so her engagement included a quintet of Broadway gypsies who backed her in a series of musical numbers, many of which were from Broadway musical film adaptations in which she had starred.

Kevin Sanders on WABCTV7 found the revue "one of the liveliest one-person shows in a long time," and John Beaufort in the *Christian Science Monitor* said the entertainment was "worthy of the Palace tradition," including the twenty-seven-member "first-rate" onstage band. But Richard Eder in the *New York Times* felt the evening was "strained and disappointing" and that MacLaine "withheld" her personality, and Martin Gottfried in the *New York Post* said the evening was "simply a slick act" with "the polished blandness of big-time night clubs." However, he noted MacLaine was "one hell of a dancer" and could be a "tremendous" performer in a traditional Broadway musical.

Unfortunately, one of MacLaine's comments dominated many of the reviews and caused a major controversy. In the first half of the 1970s, New York City was at its nadir, and in an ad-lib moment MacLaine noted that New York was "the Karen Quinlan of American cities." The Quinlan case had dominated the news during this period, as the young woman had been in a coma for a year and her plight was at the center of a right-to-life court battle. The critics pounced on MacLaine's comment, and according to *Time* the audience "sat in silence." But MacLaine had the class to quickly apologize, and she explained that her allusion was to the federal government, which had the power of life or death over cities such as New York; further, two days later she called Quinlan's parents to apologize and later wrote them a letter.

Two months after the revue closed, the production made a return engagement that opened at the Palace on July 9 for a limited run of twenty performances. For this visit, Candy Brown was succeeded by Barbara Alston, and two numbers were dropped ("My Personal Property" and "Irma La Douce"). MacLaine visited Broadway again in *Shirley MacLaine on Broadway*, which opened at the Gershwin Theatre on April 19, 1984, for forty-seven performances.

REX

Theatre: Lunt-Fontanne Theatre
Opening Date: April 25, 1976; *Closing Date*: June 5, 1976
Performances: 49
Book: Sherman Yellen
Lyrics: Sheldon Harnick
Music: Richard Rodgers
Direction: Edwin Sherin; *Producers*: Richard Adler in association with Roger Berlind and Edward R. Downe Jr.; *Choreography*: Dania Krupska; *Scenery* and *Costumes*: John Conklin; *Lighting*: Jennifer Tipton; *Musical Direction*: Jay Blackton
Cast: Charles Rule (Norfolk), William Griffis (Cardinal Wolsey), Tom Aldredge (Will Somers), *Nicol Williamson* (Henry VIII), Ed Evanko (Mark Smeaton), Barbara Andres (Queen Catherine), Glenn Close (Princess Mary), April Shawhan (Lady Jane Seymour), Stephen D. Newman (Francis), Danny Ruvolo (English Herald, "Te Deum" Herald), Jeff Phillips (French Herald), Martha Danielle (Queen Claude of France, Lady Margaret, Queen Katherine Parr), Penny Fuller (Anne Boleyn, Princess Elizabeth), Keith Koppmeier (Dauphin), Merwin Goldsmith (Comus), Melanie Vaughan (Nursemaid), Michael John (Prince Edward); Ladies and Gentlemen of the Courts: Dennis Daniels, Harry Fawcett, Paul Forrest, Pat Gideon, Ken Henley, Dawn Herbert, Robin Hoff, Don Johanson, Jim Litten, Craig Lucas, Carol Jo Lugenbeal, Valerie Mahaffey, Eugene Moose, Jeff Phillips, Charles Rule, Danny Ruvolo, Lillian Shelby, Jo Speros, Gerald R. Teijelo Jr., Candice Tovar, John Urlrickson, Melanie Vaughan; Sword Dancers: Dennis Daniels, Ken Henley, Don Johanson, Jim Litten, Jeff Phillips, Danny Ruvolo
The musical was presented in two acts.
The action takes place in England during the period 1520–1547.

Musical Numbers

Note: Almost every reference source disagrees about which songs were performed on opening night. Based on a number of sources, including opening night reviews, the following seems to reflect what the first-nighters heard.

Act One: "Te Deum" (Company); "No Song More Pleasing" (Ed Evanko); "At the Field of Cloth of Gold" (Company); "Where Is My Son?" (Nicol Williamson); "Basse Dance" (Company); "The Chase" (Merwin Goldsmith, Tom Aldredge, Ed Evanko, Gentlemen of the Court); "Away from You" (Nicol Williamson); "As Once I Loved You" (Barbara Andres); "Away from You" (reprise) (Penny Fuller, Nicol Williamson);

"Elizabeth" (Ed Evanko, Martha Danielle, Melanie Vaughan); "What Now?" (Nicol Williamson); "No Song More Pleasing" (reprise) (April Shawhan, Nicol Williamson); "Te Deum" (Company)

Act Two: "Christmas at Hampton Court" (Penny Fuller, Michael John, Glenn Close); "The Wee Golden Warrior" and "The Masque" (Tom Aldredge, Michael John, Penny Fuller, Glenn Close, Ladies and Gentlemen of the Court); "Sword Dance" (Sword Dancers); "From Afar" (Nicol Williamson); "In Time" (Penny Fuller, Tom Aldredge); "In Time" (reprise) (Penny Fuller, Michael John); "Te Deum" (reprise) (Company)

Rex was one of the season's three "historical" musicals, and while ***Pacific Overtures*** and ***1600 Pennsylvania Avenue*** were concept musicals that treated their subjects in an imaginative and somewhat abstract manner, *Rex* was deplorably literal and tedious in its depiction of Henry VIII (Nicol Williamson) and his obsession to produce a male heir to the throne. It was all very ponderous and dull, but there were a few memorable songs by Richard Rodgers, including the lovely and indeed pleasing "No Song More Pleasing" and "Away from You." The finest song of all was "So Much You Loved Me," which was apparently dropped late in New York previews but was happily included on the cast album.

As for the book, Henry and his problems soon became tiresome. The historical figures on stage were sketchy, and the book skimmed along too quickly and didn't always develop story and character. Most disappointing was Williamson's generally indifferent portrayal of Henry. Most of the critics went overboard in praise of his performance, but in truth he came across as puny and weak and he lacked the gravitas that the role demanded. He was never convincing as a king, and seemed out of place in a musical. The most incisive performance was given by Penny Fuller, who played the dual roles of Anne Boleyn and Elizabeth. Considering the raves over Williamson's performance and some favorable comments about the score, the six-week run was surprising and it marked the shortest run of any Rodgers musical since 1928's *Chee-Chee*, which played for thirty-one performances (*Chee-Chee* is best remembered as Broadway's first eunuch musical).

Martin Gottfried in the *New York Post* said *Rex* wasn't a "disaster" but was nonetheless "a bad idea with half a salvage job" (incidentally, during part of the tryout, the uncredited Harold Prince assisted with the direction). Gottfried indicated the first act was "more than bearable" but the second was performed "as if it couldn't wait to get itself over with," and he noted that while Williamson had a "splendid" singing voice, "he ambles through the role as if it were beneath him." Clive Barnes in the *New York Times* mentioned that *Rex* had "almost everything not going for it" and thus the show seemed "more of an abdication ceremony than a musical celebration." He also wondered what kind of score should be composed about a musical dealing with Henry VIII: "Airy-fairy madrigals, lute-songs jazzed up for a Broadway orchestra, a short mixture of Benjamin Britten and Irving Berlin?" He decided this was what Rodgers had done, and as a result the score seemed to be "an anthology of songs from *Camelot* that were ditched on the road."

Douglas Watt in the *New York Daily News* found the musical "dull" and "solemn," and noted Williamson wasn't "essentially a romantic actor" and this worked against the character's succession of courtship scenes. And while T. E. Kalem in *Time* said Williamson was "one of the acting comets of the age," he noted that Rodgers's score often seemed "more suited to rocking a cradle than stirring a realm" and Sheldon Harnick's lyrics confused "spareness with childishness." John Beaufort in the *Christian Science Monitor* judged the whole of the evening as "not so much a sum of its parts as it is a miscellany of fragments" and "more like a patchwork quilt than a seamless tapestry."

Howard Kissel in *Women's Wear Daily* praised Rodgers's "beautiful" songs, but noted the book was "basically conventional" and "rarely probed very deeply" into the "complex characters"; and Kevin Sanders on WABCTV7 said the "glorious" evening had "lush" music, "magnificent" costumes, and "majestic" sets.

During the run, Henry's "What Now?" was dropped and "Why?" substituted (the latter is included on the cast album). As noted above, it seems that Anne's "So Much You Loved Me" was cut during New York previews (but was included on the cast album). The "Basse Dance" had originally been part of a longer choreographed sequence given the overall title "Court Dances," which included "Basse," "Pavanne," "Galliard," and "Volta." Among the songs dropped during the tryout were "I'll Miss You," "Tell Me, Daisy" "I Brought You a Gift," "Dear Jane," "Feast Dance," "The Pears of Anjou," "Long Live the King," and the title song (one wag commented that when Williamson sang "Rex" he appeared to be calling for his dog).

The original cast album was released by RCA Victor Records (LP # ABL1-1683; issued on CD # 09026-68933-2). *Shelly Manne Plays Richard Rodgers' "Rex"* (Discovery Records LP # DS-783) includes "What Now?" The demo album (# ARS-2476A/B) includes "Tell Me" (aka "Tell Me, Daisy") and "I Brought You a Gift."

Rex is now best remembered for one of its New York curtain calls. As the performers took their bows, one member of the company whispered something to another. Williamson overheard the apparently innocuous comment but misinterpreted it, and then Williamson proceeded to slap the actor in full view of the cast and audience.

SO LONG, 174TH STREET

Theatre: Harkness Theatre
Opening Date: April 27, 1976; *Closing Date*: May 9, 1976
Performances: 16
Book: Joseph Stein
Lyrics and *Music*: Stan Daniels
Based on the 1958 novel *Enter Laughing* by Carl Reiner and its 1963 stage adaptation of the same name by Joseph Stein.
Direction: Burt Shevelove; *Producers*: Frederick Brisson in association with The Harkness Association and Wyatt Dickerson; *Choreography*: Alan Johnson; *Scenery*: James Riley; *Costumes*: Stanley Simmons; *Lighting*: Richard Nelson; *Musical Direction*: John Lesko
Cast: *Robert Morse* (David), Joe Howard (Stage Manager), Freda Soiffer (Girl), Gene Varrone (Barrymore, Waiter, Pike, Ziegfeld), Robert Barry (Pope, Harry Hamburger), Richard Marr (King, Peabody), David Berk (Roosevelt), Nancy Killmer (Eleanor Roosevelt), Mitchell Jason (Mr. Foreman), Loni Ackerman (Wanda), Lawrence John Moss (Marvin), Sydney Blake (Miss B), Chuck Beard (Don Baxter), Michael Blue Aiken (Don Darwin), Barbara Lang (Angela), George S. Irving (Marlowe, Butler, Judge), Lee Goodman (Papa), James Brennan (Soda Jerk, Man); Ensemble: Jill Cook, Nancy Killmer, Meribeth Kisner, Denise Mauthe, Rita Rudner, Freda Soiffer, Michael Blue Aiken, Chuck Beard, David Berk, Joe Howard, Richard Marr, William Swiggard
The musical was presented in one act.
The action takes place during the present time and in the late 1930s in New York City.

Musical Numbers

"David Kolowitz, the Actor" (Robert Morse, Ensemble); "It's Like" (Robert Morse, Loni Ackerman); "Undressing Girls with My Eyes" (Robert Morse, Lawrence John Moss, Girls); "Bolero on Rye" (Robert Morse, Sydney Blake, Gene Varrone); "Whoever You Are" (Robert Morse); "Say the Words" (Barbara Lang); "My Son the Druggist" (Lee Goodman); "You Touched Her" (Robert Morse, Lawrence John Moss, Men); "Men" (Loni Ackerman, James Brennan, Girls); "Boy, Oh Boy" (Robert Morse, Company); "The Butler's Song" (George S. Irving); "Being with You" (Loni Ackerman, Robert Morse); "If You Want to Break Your Father's Heart" (Robert Morse, Lee Goodman, George S. Irving, Jury); "So Long, 174th Street" (Robert Morse, Family, Friends, Neighbors); "David Kolowitz, the Actor" (reprise) (Company); Finale (Company)

Carl Reiner's semi-autobiographical 1958 novel *Enter Laughing* and its 1963 stage adaptation by Joseph Stein told the story of David (Alan Arkin in the play, Robert Morse in the musical), a nice Jewish boy from the Bronx who wants to be an actor despite the objections of his parents who insist he become a druggist (further, there's no evidence that he has any real acting talent). The play opened at Henry Miller's Theatre on March 13, 1963, for 419 performances and included a title song by Sheldon Harnick and Jerry Bock; a 1967 film version directed by Reiner starred Reni Santoni in the leading role.

Stein adapted his play into the musical, which followed the basic story of David's ambition to be an actor and emphasized his fantasies of being a Broadway star and sexual stud. Unfortunately, the talented Robert Morse was all wrong for the role: David is a Jewish New Yorker in his late teens, and Morse didn't convey any of this, especially since he was twice the age of the character he portrayed.

Martin Gottfried in the *New York Times* felt Stein's play hadn't been "anything special," and now his book for the musical adaptation was "the shell of what was once mediocre"; Stan Daniels's score consisted of "one bland, stereotyped number after another"; James Riley's décor was all in tan colors "for reasons best known to him"; the choreography was strictly on the level of an industrial show; Robert Morse was a "non-Jewish middle-aged adolescent" who "managed to even outmug himself"; and Lawrence John Moss won "the year's award for the most invisible performance in the most invisible role."

Howard Kissel in *Women's Wear Daily* said there was "no honest feeling" in the plot and the evening was "totally synthetic" and "absolutely without character." Clive Barnes in the *New York Times* couldn't resist the temptation to say "So Long!" to the musical, a "formula show" that "thudded" into town. Edwin Wilson in the *Wall Street Journal* found the evening "too coy and cute," and to expect the "appealing" Morse to play a seventeen-year-old was "too much to ask." Jack Kroll in *Newsweek* said the "manic schlock" of a musical was "dated, dopey and vulgar," and he pounced on the controversial "Butler's Song" (he found it tasteless, while Kissel had thought it "clever"). And Kevin Sanders on WABCTV7 was disappointed with the "thin" score, "belabored" comedy, and the lack of "style or imagination."

Douglas Watt in the *New York Daily News* liked the "irresistible" musical, and although there wasn't "much" in the way of a book or a score, the evening "bubbled" along because it was "a plain, honest-to-goodness musical comedy." Morse was "deft and utterly charming," the dances were "lively," and "The Butler's Song" was "hilarious." John Beaufort in the *Christian Science Monitor* generally liked the show's "catchy" songs and "lively" dances, and said he couldn't imagine "a more brilliant musical comedy performer" than Morse.

During the tryout, the musical was presented in two acts; songs cut during the tryout and New York previews were: "You," "Hot Cha Cha," and "Do What You Want to Do."

In 1981, a combination original and studio cast recording was released by Original Cast Records (LP # OC-8131; later issued on CD # OC-9341) with original cast members Robert Morse, George S. Irving, Barbara Lang, and Loni Ackerman; Patti Karr sang the role of Miss B, and the role of David's father was changed to the role of his mother, which was sung by Kaye Ballard. The deleted songs "You" and "Hot Cha Cha" were included on the recording, the latter sung by Stan Daniels.

On September 10, 2008, the York Theatre Company presented a revised version of the musical as *Enter Laughing* at the Theatre at St. Peter's Church for forty-one performances (a return engagement on January 29, 2009, played for fifty-one showings); the production was directed and choreographed by Stuart Ross (who wrote additional lyrics for "Undressing Girls with My Eyes" and "Hot Cha Cha"), and the cast included Josh Grisetti as David and George S. Irving in his original roles from the 1976 production (others in the company were Jill Eikenberry and Paul Binotto). The revival omitted "Bolero on Rye," added "The Man I Can Love," and also included "You" and "Hot Cha Cha." The cast album was released by Jay Records (CD # CDJAY-1417).

THREEPENNY OPERA

Theatre: Vivian Beaumont Theatre
Opening Date: May 1, 1976; *Closing Date*: January 23, 1977
Performances: 307
Book and *Lyrics*: Bertolt Brecht (adaptation by Ralph Manheim and John Willett)
Music: Kurt Weill
Based on the 1728 opera *The Beggar's Opera* (libretto by John Gay, music by Johann Pepusch); Brecht based his adaptation on Elisabeth Hauptmann's German translation of the opera.
Direction: Richard Foreman; *Producer*: Joseph Papp (Bernard Gersten, Associate Producer; A New York Shakespeare Festival Production); *Scenery*: Douglas W. Schmidt; *Costumes*: Theoni V. Aldredge; *Lighting*: Pat Collins; *Musical Direction*: Stanley Silverman
Cast: Roy Brocksmith (The Ballad Singer), Raul Julia (Mack the Knife), Ellen Greene (Jenny Towler), C. K. Alexander (Jonathan Peachum), Tony Azito (Samuel), Ed Zang (Charles Filch), Elizabeth Wilson (Mrs. Peachum), Ralph Drischell (Matt), Caroline Kava (Polly Peachum), William Duell (Jake), K. C. Wilson (Bob), Rik Colitti (Ned), Robert Schlee (Jimmy), Max Gulack (Walt), David Sabin (Tiger Brown), Glen Kezer (Smith), Blair Brown (Lucy Brown); Beggars and Policemen: Pendleton Brown, M. Patrick Hughes, George McGrath, Rick Petrucelli, John Ridge, Craig Rupp, Armin Shimerman, Jack Eric Williams, Ray Xifo; Whores: Penelope Bodry, Nancy Campbell, Gretel Cummings, Brenda Currin, Mimi Turque; *Note*: The program identifies Raul Julia's character as Mack the Knife, but the song list and liner notes of the cast album refer to the character as Mac the Knife and Macheath, respectively.

The musical was presented in three acts.
The action takes place in London in 1837 at the time of Queen Victoria's coronation.

Musical Numbers

Note: The program didn't list musical numbers; the following list is taken from the LP and CD releases of the revival's cast album.

Act One: "Ballad of Mack the Knife" (Roy Brocksmith, Tony Azito, Robert Schlee, Jack Eric Williams); "Peachum's Morning Hymn" (C. K. Alexander); "'No They Can't' Song" (C. K. Alexander, Elizabeth Wilson); "Wedding Song for the Less Well-Off" (Gang and Beggars); "For That's My Way" (Caroline Kava); "Cannon Song" (Raul Julia, David Sabin, Gang); "Liebeslied" (Caroline Kava, Raul Julia); "Barbara Song" (Caroline Kava); "First Threepenny Finale" ("Concerning the Insecurity of the Human State") (Caroline Kava, C. K. Alexander, Elizabeth Wilson)

Act Two: "Polly's Lied" (Caroline Kava, Raul Julia); "Ballad of Sexual Obsession" (Elizabeth Wilson); "Pirate Jenny" (Ellen Greene); "Ballad of Immoral Earnings" (Ellen Greene, Raul Julia); "Ballad of Gracious Living" (Raul Julia); "Jealousy Duet" (Blair Brown, Caroline Kava); "Second Threepenny Finale" ("What Keeps Mankind Alive?") (Raul Julia, Ellen Greene, Chorus)

Act Three: "Song of the Insufficiency of Human Endeavor" (C. K. Alexander); "Solomon Song" (Ellen Greene); "Call from the Grave" (Raul Julia); "Ballad in Which Macheath Begs All Men for Forgiveness" (Raul Julia); "Third Threepenny Finale" (David Sabin, Glenn Kezer, Roy Brocksmith, Jack Eric Williams, Elizabeth Wilson, C. K. Alexander, Raul Julia, Caroline Kava, Blair Brown, Ellen Greene, Chorus); "Ballad of Mack the Knife" (reprise) (Roy Brocksmith)

Much ado was made of Ralph Manheim and John Willett's new adaptation of Bertolt Brecht's book and lyrics of *The Threepenny Opera* (for this revival, the musical was titled *Threepenny Opera*), which boasted it was more faithful to the original German text than Marc Blitzstein's popular translation. Blitzstein's version had brought Kurt Weill and Brecht's musical back from obscurity because the April 13, 1933, New York premiere (in an adaptation by Gifford Cochran and Jerrold Krimsky) closed after just twelve performances at the Empire Theatre, and the work virtually disappeared in the United States. Blitzstein's version (which premiered on June 14, 1952, at the Festival of the Creative Arts at Brandeis University) was briefly performed Off Broadway in 1954 and then returned in 1955 for a marathon run. Blitzstein's adaptation of the fable-like satire of London riffraff that includes the amoral gang leader Macheath (played in the current revival by Raul Julia) and his assorted underground cronies such as the prostitute Jenny (Ellen Greene) was a smash and played for a total of 2,707 performances. "Mack the Knife," Blitzstein's version of the musical's opening song "Moritat," became one of the most popular of all theatre songs (especially in versions by Louis Armstrong and Bobby Darin) and topped the Hit Parade.

A special insert in the current revival's program by producer Joseph Papp complained that Blitzstein had "excised much" of the original's "political and sexual thrust" and his adaptation was "clearly at odds with [Brecht's] purpose and dramatic sensibilities." All this may be true (although it's debatable that Blitzstein was "clearly at odds" with Brecht's intentions), but Blitzstein's adaptation was much more enjoyable than the current one, and his omission of Brecht's four-letter words in no way softened the original: it simply omitted expletives that weren't spoken in musicals during the 1950s. Papp apparently believed the new production would show the "true power" of the original, as if Blitzstein's version wasn't powerful. The critics liked the new translation, although Jack Kroll in *Newsweek* said that Manheim and Willett "can't compete with Blitzstein as theatrical lyricists."

The critics were more focused on avant-garde director Richard Foreman's staging techniques, which were unique variations of Brecht's celebrated alienation devices that strived to create for the audience a sense of emotional detachment from the stage action, as though to remind the audience it was watching an artificial theatre performance. The device has always seemed a bit suspect and a trifle pretentious because unless a member of the audience is completely clueless, or perhaps asleep, one suspects that most viewers are well aware they are in a theatre watching a theatrical performance that isn't real life. In a musical, the very presence of music with singers and an orchestra is technically an alienation device that reminds the audience it's witnessing a theatrical event.

But alienation devices can enhance a production with theatrical effects, and in the current revival Foreman's performers moved like slow-motion marionettes. (Was this a nod to the 1966 Broadway production, which used actors, marionettes, and life-size cut-outs to represent the characters?) Tony Azito's Samuel (a newly created character for the musical) was singled out for his erratic, eccentric, and almost surreal movements. Throughout the evening, background characters froze in place when a performer sang, the actors were dressed in costumes of blacks, grays, and browns, and stark smudgy lighting picked up stage action in cold and merciless light. To add to the alienation effect, Howard Kissel in *Women's Wear Daily* noted that Jenny's exultant, bitter, and triumphant "Pirate Jenny" wasn't performed in this usual manner and instead was sung by Ellen Greene with dead, glazed-over eyes.

Douglas Watt in the *New York Post* said Brecht and Weill's "blazing masterpiece" with Weill's "brilliantly poisonous score" was a "gigantic robot show whose dehumanized characters perform with mechanical predictability the inhuman acts of man." Clive Barnes in the *New York Times* also called the work a "blazing masterpiece"; and Martin Gottfried in the *New York Post* said if the 1954 production reflected Blitzstein's and not Brecht's vision, then the current one reflected Foreman's instead of Brecht's. Further, Foreman's staging didn't capture the spirit of the Berliner Ensemble's production any more than Blitzstein's did, and in fact was "considerably less effective" than Blitzstein's.

Edwin Wilson in the *Wall Street Journal* said Weill had "forged a unique musical signature which still sounds fresh fifty years after it was written," and he noted the movements of the performers were "highly stylized and artificial" and that Azito gave the impression of a "walking cadaver" with "double-joined arms and legs flying akimbo." Jack Kroll in *Newsweek* liked the "complex dance of death going on in the gutters, jails and brothels of Victorian London" and said the work was "the greatest musical of all time." And T. E. Kalem in *Time* praised the "satanic brilliance" of the production.

John Beaufort in the *Christian Science Monitor* noted the irony behind the revival. The musical was contemptuous of the middle class and of capitalism itself, but here it was at Lincoln Center, "that citadel of bourgeois culture," which is "lavishly subsidized by millionaires and the foundations they have formed." Further, there was the "double irony" that in his politics Brecht allied himself with "totalitarian tyranny." Incidentally, for their help in funding the revival, the program thanked the U.S. federal government and the New York State government as well as nine specific entities, including foundations (such as the Andrew W. Mellon Foundation), individuals (John D. Rockefeller III), and other groups (including the Lincoln Center Consolidated Corporate Fund Drive).

Kalem noted that Raul Julia moved "like a Fred Astaire of gangsterdom" and Barnes said he was the "ideal" Mack the Knife, but Gottfried echoed his complaint about the actor's performance in ***Where's Charley?*** ("he simply must get rid of" his Puerto-Rican accent). Watt said Ellen Greene gave the evening's "most electrifying performance," and Kroll found her "chillingly seductive" with her "absinthe voice," but Gottfried said she was "lost" as Jenny (but he blamed Foreman for his "lack of guidance").

The revival was recorded by Columbia Records (LP # PS-34325), and the CD release was issued by Arkiv/Sony Records (# 51520) and includes a previously unreleased track ("For That's My Way"). The script was published in hardback in 1977 by Random House in *Collected Plays, Vol. 2* by Brecht, and was also published in a single volume in 1977 by Vintage Books/Random House in a special hardback edition for the now defunct Fireside Theatre book club.

As *Die Dreigroschenoper*, the original production of *The Threepenny Opera* premiered in Berlin on August 31, 1928, at the Theatre am Schiffbuerdamm with Harold Paulson (Macheath), Lotte Lenya (Jenny), and Ernest Busch (The Street Singer).

The 1954 revival opened at the Theatre de Lys on March 10, and reopened there on September 20, 1955. Lenya appeared as Jenny in both productions as did Scott Merrill (Macheath), Jo Sullivan (Polly), and Beatrice Arthur (Lucy Brown); for the 1954 version, Gerald Price was the Street Singer, and for 1955 Tige Andrews. The cast album of the 1954 production was released by MGM Records (LP # E/SE-3121), and the CD was issued by Decca Broadway Records (# 012-159-463-2) and includes a bonus track of "Mack the Knife" sung by Lenya, who is accompanied by Blitzstein at the piano.

There have been a number of other New York revivals of the musical. On March 11, 1965, *Die Dreigroschenoper* opened at City Center by the New York City Opera Company with Kurt Kasznar (Macheath), George S. Irving (The Street Singer), Lilia Skala (Mrs. Peachum), and Martha Schlamme (Jenny) in a production that marked the work's first U.S. performance in German (the above-cited 1933 Broadway premiere was performed in English). On October 27, 1966, the Stockholm Marionette Theatre of Fantasy presented the musical for thirteen performances at the Billy Rose (now Nederlander) Theatre (the production used prerecorded music taken from the original Off-Broadway cast album, and it marks the only time Blitzstein's version was heard on Broadway); on November 5, 1989, an adaptation by Michael Feingold opened at the Lunt-Fontanne Theatre for sixty-five performances with Sting (Macheath), Suzzanne Douglas (Jenny), Maureen McGovern (Polly), and Georgia Brown (Mrs. Peachum); and on April 20, 2006, an adaptation by Wallace Shawn opened at Studio 54 for seventy-seven performances with Alan Cumming (Macheath), Cyndi Lauper (Jenny), and Jim Dale (Mr. Peachum).

On October 26, 1995, an Off-Broadway revival by the National Youth Music Theatre opened at City Center for a limited run of three performances (it's unclear which translation was used), and the current 1976 production was revived Off Broadway for a limited engagement of twenty-seven performances at the Delacorte Theatre on June 28, 1977, with Philip Bosco (who had succeeded Raul Julia during the Lincoln Center run) and Ellen Greene.

There have been three film versions of the musical. The first was produced in Germany in 1931, was directed by G. W. Pabst, and starred Rudolph Forster (Macheath) and Lotte Lenya (Jenny). A 1962 version used Blitzstein's lyrics and starred Curt Jurgens, Hildegarde Neff, Gert Frobe, and June Ritchie (Sammy Davis Jr., was the Street Singer), and the score was conducted by Samuel Matlowsky (aka Matlovsky), who had been the musical director for the 1954 Off-Broadway production. Jo Wilder, who had succeeded Jo Sullivan during the 1955 engagement, was the singing voice of Polly (the soundtrack was issued by RCA Victor Records LP # LOC/LSO-1086). The most recent film version was released in 1989 as *Mack the Knife* and starred Raul Julia and Julia Migenes; some of Blitzstein's lyrics were used (the soundtrack was released by CBS Records, Inc., LP # SM-45630).

Awards

Tony Awards and Nominations: Best Revival (*Threepenny Opera*); Best Leading Actor in a Musical (Raul Julia); Best Featured Actress in a Musical (Ellen Greene); Best Costume Designer (Theoni V. Aldredge); Best Lighting Designer (Pat Collins)

1600 PENNSYLVANIA AVENUE

"A Musical about the Problems of Housekeeping"

Theatre: Mark Hellinger Theatre
Opening Date: May 4, 1976; *Closing Date*: May 8, 1976
Performances: 7
Book and *Lyrics*: Alan Jay Lerner
Music: Leonard Bernstein
Direction and *Choreography*: "Entire Production Co-Directed and Staged and Choreographed by" Gilbert Moses and George Faison; *Producers*: Roger L. Stevens and Robert Whitehead (produced by arrangement with Saint Subber); *Scenery*: "Supervised by" Kert Lundell; *Costumes*: "Supervised by" Whitney Blausen and Dona Granata; *Lighting*: Tharon Musser; *Musical Direction*: Roland Gagnon
Cast: *Ken Howard* (The President), *Patricia Routledge* (The President's Wife), *Gilbert Price* (Lud), Emily Yancy (Seena), Guy Costley (Little Lud), David E. Thomas (The Stage Manager); The Thirteen Delegates—Howard Ross (Massachusetts), Reid Shelton (New York), Ralph Farnsworth (Pennsylvania), J. T. Cromwell (New Hampshire), Lee Winston (Rhode Island), Richard Chappell (Connecticut), Walter Charles (New Jersey), Edwin Steffe (Virginia), John Witham (North Carolina), Richard Muenz (South Carolina), Alexander Orfaly (Delaware), Raymond Cox (Maryland), and Randolph Riscol (Georgia); The Staff—Raymond Bazemore (Henry), Urylee Leonardos (Rachel), Carl Hall (Coley), Janette Moody (Joby), Howard Ross (Broom), Cornel J. Richie (Jim), and Louise Heath (Sally); The British—Walter Charles (Ordway), John Witham (Pimms), Lee Winston (Barker), Raymond Cox (Glieg), Alexander Orfaly (Maitland), Edwin Steffe (Ross), Richard Chappell (Pratt), J. T. Cromwell (Scott), Richard Muenz (Budgen), and Reid Shelton (Cockburn); Bruce A. Hubbard (Reverend Bushrod), Lee Winston (Auctioneer, Mr. Henry, Babcock), Edwin Steffe (James Hoban, Judge), Randolph Riscol (Royal Visitor), Howard Ross (Secretary of the Senate), Reid

Shelton (Senator Roscoe Conkling); Singers: Raymond Bazemore, Elaine Bunse, Nancy Callman, Richard Chappell, Walter Charles, Raymond Cox, J. T. Cromwell, Beth Fowler, Carl Hall, Louise Heath, Bruce A. Hubbard, Kris Karlowski, Urylee Leonardos, Joyce MacDonald, Janette Moody, Richard Muenz, Sharon Powers, Cornel J. Ritchie, Randolph Riscol, Martha Thigpen, Lee Winston; Dancers: Jo-Ann Baldo, Clyde-Jacques Barrett, Joella Breedlove, Allyne DeChalus, Linda Griffin, Bob Heath, Michael Lichtefeld, Diana Mirras, Hector Jaime Mercado, Cleveland Pennington, Al Perryman, Renee Rose, Juliet Seignious, Thomas J. Stanton, Clayton Strange, Mimi Wallace; Swings: Leah Randolph, Martial Roumain

The musical was presented in two acts.

The action occurs in Washington, D.C., during the approximate period of 1789–1909.

Musical Numbers

Act One: "Rehearse!" (Ken Howard, Patricia Routledge, Gilbert Price, Emily Yancy, Guy Costley, Company); "If I Was a Dove" (Guy Costley); "On Ten Square Miles by the Potomac River" (Ken Howard, Delegates); "Welcome Home, Miz Adams" (Raymond Bazemore, Urylee Leonardos, Staff); "Take Care of This House" (Ken Howard, Patricia Routledge, Guy Costley, Staff); "The President Jefferson Sunday Luncheon Party March" (Ken Howard, Guy Costley, Guests); "Seena" (Gilbert Price); "Sonatina" ("The British"): (1) "Allegro con Brio"; (2) "Tempo di Menuetto" (Program Note: This sequence includes "an authentic harmonization of "To Anacreon in Heav'n" [1740], later known as "The Star-Spangled Banner."); and (3) "Rondo" (Reid Shelton, Officers, Citizens); "Lud's Wedding" (Gilbert Price, Emily Yancy, Chorus); "I Love My Wife" (Gilbert Price, Emily Yancy, Staff); "Auctions" (Lee Winston, Buyers); "The Little White Lie" (Ken Howard, Patricia Routledge); "We Must Have a Ball" (Ken Howard); "The Ball" (Company)

Act Two: "Forty Acres and a Mule" (Staff); "Bright and Black" (Emily Yancy, Staff); "Duet for One" ("The First Lady of the Land") (Patricia Routledge *and* Patricia Routledge, Company); "The Robber-Baron Minstrel Parade" (Minstrels); "Pity the Poor" (Minstrels); "The Red White and Blues" (Minstrels); "I Love This Land" (Ken Howard); "Rehearse!" (reprise) (Company)

Alan Jay Lerner and Leonard Bernstein's *1600 Pennsylvania Avenue* was one of the most ambitious concept musicals ever produced, but was so out of control it stumbled all over its message. The creators tried too hard, and, conversely, they didn't try hard enough. Much of the musical was undeveloped and sketchy, and other aspects of the show seem to have been remnants of staging ideas that had been mostly discarded during preproduction or in rehearsals. As a result, tornadic confusion reigned throughout the evening.

The work called itself "a musical about the problems of housekeeping" and used the White House itself as an emblem of the nation's ideals that must always be safeguarded. In *Love Life* (1948), Lerner had used the same actor and actress (Ray Middleton and Nanette Fabray) to portray a married couple who symbolize the status of marriage throughout the history of the United States, and for *1600* two performers (Ken Howard and Patricia Routledge) played all the presidents and first ladies. But perhaps the word *all* is misleading. As the musical began, it appeared that the evening's revue-like structure would look at all the presidents and first ladies throughout American history and examine how they directly or indirectly dealt with the protection of our constitutional freedoms. But the book didn't follow up on this approach, and so the cavalcade of presidents began with George Washington and abruptly ended with Teddy Roosevelt (along the way, we're told that James Buchanan may have been the only gay president).

Moreover, the musical tried for an *Upstairs, Downstairs* effect by contrasting upstairs life with the black servants who work below. To this end, the same black couple Lud (Gilbert Price) and Seena (Emily Yancy) were played by the same performers as they covered the "downstairs" territory (but someone forgot to tell Lerner that white servants also worked in the White House). It was in its depiction of racial issues that the musical really lost its way, because Lerner seemed obsessed over these matters, as if race was the *only* issue in American life. The musical quickly became a soapbox, and the first ladies were Lerner's mouthpieces regarding racial awareness; as a result, they came across as intellectual scolds who never stopped nagging their somewhat doltish presidential husbands (in some ways, this approach mirrored sexist television advertisements and sitcoms of the period, which always seemed to portray wives as wise, all-knowing figures and husbands as spaced-out fools).

Further, the musical touched upon the concept of using a theatrical rehearsal to make its political points (the opening number was in fact titled "Rehearse!," and the program listed one of the characters as "Stage Manager"), the idea being that the official business of the country is never finished and thus the nation must continue to rehearse in order to get it right. This concept was carried over into the décor and costumes, which had a half-unfinished look as if the musical were giving a Sunday afternoon gypsy run-through before going out of town for the tryout (particularly unfortunate were the ridiculous-looking and unattractive costumes foisted off on the female chorus, who were clad in a combination of casual rehearsal clothing and traditional Yankee-Doodle-styled Revolutionary War garb). But the rehearsal motif was never developed and got in the way of the already top-heavy if underdeveloped main plot.

The work also had leftover remnants of what appeared to be another early concept, one of a minstrel show. This might have led to a fascinating approach for a musical focused on racial matters, but like the rehearsal concept the minstrel show device was never really developed and was used only in the later scenes of the second act.

So with *1600 Pennsylvania Avenue*, Broadway saw one of the most ambitious but confusing musicals to ever open. The hopeless book was a shambles, and despite a two-month tryout in Philadelphia and Washington, D.C., the musical was never clear and direct about the important matters it wanted to discuss. The reviews were devastatingly harsh, and the show never got beyond its first week in New York.

If the score had been on the level of the book, *1600* would have become a forgotten Broadway Bicentennial moment. But Bernstein's brilliant contributions and Lerner's mostly clever lyrics were among the best of the era, and so the demise of *1600* was heartbreaking. One returned to *1600* over and over again, just to hear Bernstein's glorious music.

Only a two-LP set could have captured all of Bernstein's bountiful score, but the proposed cast album by Capitol Records was canceled due to the musical's quick closing. Over the years a few songs from the score were included in various Broadway collections, and later a studio cast album was released on CD (for more information about recordings of the score, see below).

The evening's highlight was the hilarious "Duet for One" sung by Patricia Routledge in the roles of Julia Grant and Lucy Hayes. It's one of the most brilliant songs ever written for a Broadway musical and was given a classic performance by Routledge, who was surrounded by a forest of gorgeously tinted red, white, and blue parasols as she literally flipped her wig in order to morph into either Julia or Lucy. The sequence takes place in two different time levels during the reading of the oath of office at Hayes's inauguration. While the oath is read (which in real time takes about thirty seconds to administer), a musical time zone the length of ten minutes took place between the words and phrases of the oath as Julia morosely groans about leaving Washington while the gushingly jubilant Lucy delights in the prospect of "counting my sheep at night / Where Van Buren and Polk used to sleep at night." Routledge's performance of the song was breathtakingly funny and is one of the greatest moments in all musical theatre.

Other memorable songs were the gorgeous anthem "Take Care of This House"; the rollicking and irresistible "The President Jefferson Sunday Luncheon Party March"; a mini "Sonatina" when the British burn the White House; and the scorching "The Red, White and Blues" for part of the minstrel show sequence. Here was glorious theatre music on a grand scale, and if the book had matched its genius the musical would have run for seven years instead of seven performances.

Variety's review (by Hari) of the Philadelphia opening was an ominous preview of what was to come when the critics in Washington and New York saw the musical. The work was a "black polemic" that quickly became a "Bicentennial bore" of "three hours of mea-culpating" as it "relentlessly chastises whites in the audience for their forebears' unarguable mistreatment of blacks."

In his review for the *New York Times*, Clive Barnes pleaded "Bring back *Rex*!" and suggested if this was a Bicentennial offering then we should all wait for the "Tricentennial." The work was "done in the most tedious and simplistic way imaginable" and was "bleak and patronizing," but Patricia Routledge was "often deliciously funny" and he praised "Duet for One" (and hailed the "elegant vivacity" of "The President Jefferson Sunday Luncheon Party March"). The headline of Douglas Watt's review in the *New York Daily News* read "Sorry, Wrong Number" and the critic suggested the evening was "more suitable to a school pageant than a Broadway musical." The work was an "impossible enterprise, just one more Bicentennial burden." But he noted that Routledge's "Duet for One" was the score's "liveliest sally." Hobe in *Variety* said there was more "schoolbook history than entertainment" in the new musical but said "Duet for One" was a "good comedy number" in which Routledge depicted the "infuriated" Mrs. Grant and the "smugly exultant" Mrs. Hayes. The critic also noted that the musical cost $1,300,000 to open.

Alan Rich in *New York* said Bernstein's music was "awful," and wondered "was this the Lenny we had known and loved? Or was it all some ghastly joke?" But he praised Patricia Routledge's "delicious" moment in her simultaneous portrayal of the two first ladies. Howard Kissel in *Women's Wear Daily* said the musical was a "colossal embarrassment" presented in the nature of "a series of collegiate skits." The intent may have been "allegorical" but the "impression is of amateurism." He also mentioned that the United States presidents were the object of "sophomoric ridicule," but all the black characters were treated with "condescending affection." J. K. (Jack Kroll) in *Newsweek* said the musical was a victim of "myasthenia gravis conceptualis," or "crummy idea." He noted "Duet for One" was the score's best song, and Routledge "would have stopped the show, if there had been one to stop."

Martin Gottfried in the *New York Post* found the evening an "embarrassment," and "of all the patched-up musicals that have limped into New York, this is the most pitifully pieced together one I have ever seen." But he praised the score; the "superb" overture was "destined" to join the *Candide* overture as a "concert staple"; "The President Jefferson Sunday Luncheon Party March" was "irresistibly catchy"; and "Take Care of This House" was "stirring." Here was "melodic, ambitious" music set to "surprising rhythms" and "expansive lengths."

During the chaotic tryout, director Frank Corsaro and choreographer Donald McKayle were replaced by Gilbert Moses and George Faison, and while Tony Walton was credited with the scenery and costumes, his name wasn't in the Broadway opening night program (New York preview programs credited Kurt Lundell with the scenery, and Whitney Blausen and Dona Granata received "costumes supervised by" credit; by opening night, Lundell was no longer given a "scenery designed by" credit, and instead received a "scenery supervised by" credit).

During the Philadelphia tryout, the musical's official producers were Roger L. Stevens and Robert Whitehead by arrangement with Saint Subber and in association with The Coca-Cola Company. But after the Philadelphia reviews, Coca-Cola withdrew its name from the advertising and a lavish party planned by the company for the Washington run was abruptly canceled (but Coca-Cola's portion of the investment, a reputed $900,000, remained). As musical theatre historian Steven Suskin has noted, the Philadelphia program has a hilarious credit: the Ginger Ale used in the production is by the courtesy of the Canada Dry Corporation. (*Note*: The credit was blacked out of the program, but by slanting the blacked-out lines toward the light one can read the words of this outrage!)

During the tryout and preview period, the following songs were deleted: "The Nation That Wasn't There," "The Mark of a Man," "The Grand Old Party," "American Dreaming," "Middle C," "To Make Us Proud" (aka "Proud"), and "This Time."

The musical was originally announced as *Opus 1*; a September 6, 1974, article in the *Washington Post* reported that at a gathering of the Foreign Correspondents Club, Lerner said the new musical would tell the "terribly important story of the little white lie that our country has been living with since its inception—to which I mean the big black lie." The *Post* later reported the musical would have its world premiere on December 31, 1975, at the Kennedy Center's Opera House for a month-long engagement followed by tryout stops in Philadelphia and Detroit and with a Broadway opening in March 1976. Instead, the musical's first tryout stop was at Philadelphia's Forrest Theatre; it was followed by a month of performances at the National Theatre in Washington, D.C., and then opened on Broadway in May 1976.

As *A White House Cantata* ("Scenes from *1600 Pennsylvania Avenue*"), the musical was recorded by Deutsche Grammophon (CD # 289-463-448-2) by the London Symphony Orchestra conducted by Kent Nagano (the leading singers are Thomas Hampson and June Anderson). The recording features an opening prelude followed by "On Ten Square Miles by the Potomac River," "If I Was a Dove," "Welcome Home, Miz Adams," "Take Care of This House," "The President Jefferson Sunday Luncheon Party March," "Seena," "Sonatina," "Lud's Wedding," "The Monroviad" (a combination of "The Little White Lie" and the deleted "The Mark of a Man"), "This Time," "We Must Have a Ball," "Bright and Black," "Duet for One," three sequences from the minstrel show ("Minstrel Parade," "Pity the Poor," and "The Grand Old Party"), and "To Make Us Proud." While the recording is a welcome one, it unfortunately is not as theatrical as it should be, and June Anderson completely misses the delirious madness of "Duet for One."

The collection *Leonard Bernstein Revisited* (Painted Smiles CD # PSCD-107) includes three numbers from the score ("Bright and Black," "The President Jefferson Sunday Luncheon Party March," and "Take Care of This House").

The best way to sample the score of *1600 Pennsylvania Avenue* is the magnificent collection *Broadway Showstoppers* (Broadway Angel CD # 0777-7-54586-2-6) conducted by John McGlinn. The recording offers two songs from the score, both electric interpretations: "The President Jefferson Sunday Luncheon Party March" (Davis Gaines) and "Duet for One" (Judy Kaye).

In 1992, the University of Indiana Opera Theatre revived the musical with a restored score that included both deleted ("The Nation That Wasn't There," "American Dreaming") and unused ("Me," "Philadelphia," "What Happened?") songs. The revival was presented for a limited run of three performances at the Kennedy Center's Eisenhower Theatre beginning on August 11, 1992. Daniel Selznick in *Variety* praised the "charm" of Lerner's lyrics and the "undeniable quality" of Bernstein's score, and noted that the musical's premise that racism is America's original sin "seems, in hindsight, both naïve and unnecessary" and suggested future productions of the musical concentrate on the "thankless roles assigned to blacks through the years" and how over the years changing attitudes have evolved. Octavio Roca in the *Washington Times* said the new production was "fabulous" and the "overall result is more successful than the original Broadway production." Here was a musical which "deserves another chance."

SOMETHING'S AFOOT

"A New Murder Mystery Musical"

Theatre: Lyceum Theatre
Opening Date: May 27, 1976; *Closing Date*: July 18, 1976
Performances: 61
Book, Lyrics, and *Music*: James McDonald, David Vos, and Robert Gerlach; additional music by Ed Linderman
Direction and *Choreography*: Tony Tanner; *Producers*: Emanuel Azenberg, Dasha Epstein, and John Mason Kirby; *Scenery*: Richard Seger; *Costumes*: Walter Watson and Clifford Capone; *Lighting*: Richard Winkler; *Musical Direction*: Buster Davis
Cast: Neva Small (Lettie), Marc Jordan (Flint), Sel Vitella (Clive), Barbara Heuman (Hope Langdon), Jack Schmidt (Doctor Grayburn), Gary Beach (Nigel Rancour), Liz Sheridan (Lady Grace Manley-Prowe), Gary Gage (Colonel Gillweather), Tessie O'Shea (Miss Tweed), Willard Beckham (Geoffrey)
The musical was presented in two acts.
The action takes place on an English country estate in 1935.

Musical Numbers

Act One: "A Marvelous Weekend" (Company); "Something's Afoot" (Tessie O'Shea, Company); "Carry On" (Tessie O'Shea, Liz Sheridan, Neva Small, Barbara Heuman); "I Don't Know Why I Trust You (but I Do)" (Barbara Heuman, William Beckham); "The Man with the Ginger Moustache" (Liz Sheridan, Gary Gage); "Suspicious" (Company)
Act Two: "The Legal Heir" (Gary Beach); "You Fell Out of the Sky" (Barbara Heuman); "Dinghy" (Marc Jordan, Neva Small); "I Owe It All" (Tessie O'Shea, Barbara Heuman, Willard Beckham); "New Day" (Barbara Heuman, Willard Beckham)

Something's Afoot was one of the guilty pleasures of the decade, a delightful little musical that spoofed murder mysteries of the Agatha Christie–*And Then There Were None* genre. But the audience-pleasing show never found its audience, and the critics were in a grumpy mood and failed to enjoy the show's retro charms. A later London production managed a run of seven months, but the lack of a Broadway or a London cast album seems to have relegated the show to theatrical limbo. Had a cast album been recorded, the musical might have become better known and enjoyed many productions, perhaps even an Off-Broadway revival (which is probably where the musical should have opened in the first place).

Prior to the Broadway production, the musical was occasionally seen in regional theatre over a three-year period beginning in 1972, and among the actresses who played the role of Miss Tweed were Mary Jo Catlett, Lu Leonard, and Pat Carroll.

The musical takes place in 1935 on a lonely English estate located on a small island in the middle of a lake (appropriately in the Lake District) where weekenders have been invited to enjoy a "celebrating, rusticating" weekend. The party is composed of a group of stock (and suspicious) figures: two Cockneys, Lettie the maid (Neva Small) and Flint the handyman (Marc Jordan); the supercilious butler Clive (Sel Vitella); the lovely ingénue Hope Langdon (Barbara Heuman); the handsome juvenile Geoffrey (Willard Beckham); the family doctor Grayburn (Jack Schmidt); an oily and dissolute nephew (Gary Beach); a possibly would-be grande-dame Lady Grace Manley-Prowe (Liz Sheridan); the clichéd old Army bore Colonel Gillweather (Gary Gage); and amateur detective and spinster Miss Tweed (Tessie O'Shea). Almost as soon as the weekend in the country begins, Clive is blown to bits, an event that leads the others to assume something suspicious is afoot (but they must admit that in this case "the butler didn't do it").

As the weekend progresses, guests are bumped off one by one, and soon the survivors become increasingly suspicious of one another. No spoiler here, but rest assured the authors worked out the plot to the nth degree: every character is in one way or another involved in the mystery.

The plot was delightful, the set was picture-perfect in its depiction of an old stately manor, and the score was catchy and captured the spirit of the evening: "A Marvelous Weekend" was a sweeping opening number that introduced all the characters; the title song was a nice piece of nonsense; "I Don't Know Why I Trust You (but I Do)" a cautionary but carefree ballad for Hope and Geoffrey; the first-act finale "Suspicious" found the survivors pushing the panic button as they're swept up in a maelstrom of "malice, mayhem, mystery, murder"; the cheesy but amusing duet "Dinghy" (Flint informs Lettie he's got "a teeny little dinghy" to share with her, and of course he's alluding to a small craft which will take them away from the island); and Hope's rapturous ballad to Geoffrey "You Fell Out of the Sky" was climaxed by a chandelier which crashes to the floor and just barely misses her. And best of all was Miss Tweed's eleven o'clock number, "I Owe It All," a delirious soft-shoe salute to her favorite fictional detectives and their authors who have inspired her, and, yes, most especially she owes it all to Agatha Christie.

But Clive Barnes in the *New York Times* felt the musical was "terrible," the lyrics "clumsy," and the direction was "camp taken to lengths that are almost as distasteful as they are ridiculous." He said the murders were "innocuous," the performances "frantic," and "the music should have been left somewhere else." In the same newspaper, Walter Kerr noted that "something's amiss" with *Something's Afoot* but admitted that the evening began "hale and hearty," having a "fairly rousing, houseful of baritones and wild sopranos, then steadily reduces its octets to quartets, its quartets to duets, its duets to—well, that would be telling too much."

The script was published in paperback by Samuel French circa 1977.

The London production opened at the Ambassadors Theatre in 1977 for 232 performances. A television version was presented on Showtime on December 9, 1982, with Jean Stapleton (Miss Tweed) and Andy Gibb (Geoffrey).

THE BAKER'S WIFE

The musical opened on May 11, 1976, at the Dorothy Chandler Pavilion in Los Angeles, California; played at the Curran Theatre, San Francisco; at the MUNY in St. Louis, Missouri; at the Shubert Theatre in Boston, Massachusetts; and permanently closed at the Opera House at the Kennedy Center in Washington, D.C., on November 13, 1976.

Book: Joseph Stein

Lyrics and *Music*: Stephen Schwartz

Based on the 1938 film *La Femme du Boulanger* (screenplay by Marcel Pagnol and Jean Giono and direction by Pagnol).

Direction: Joe Hardy; *Producer*: David Merrick; *Choreography*: Dan Siretta; *Scenery*: Jo Mielziner; *Costumes*: Theoni V. Aldredge; *Lighting*: Jennifer Tipton; *Musical Direction*: Don Jennings

Cast: Timothy Jerome (Teacher), Gordon Connell (Antoine), Pierre Epstein (Barnaby), Portia Nelson (Therese), Darlene Conley (Henriette), Benjamin Rayson (Claude), Keene Curtis (Marquis), Tara Leigh (Colette), Cynthia Parva (Melissa), Jean McLaughlin (Denise), David Rounds (Priest), (*Chaim*) *Topol* (Aimable), Carole Demas (Genevieve), Kurt Peterson (Dominique), Tony Schultz (Raoul)

The musical was presented in two acts.

The action takes place during the recent past in Concorde, a small village in Provence, France.

Musical Numbers

Act One: "Welcome to Concorde" (Keene Curtis, Timothy Jerome, David Rounds, Villagers); "A Little Taste of Heaven" (Topol, Carole Demas); "Gifts of Love" (Topol, Carole Demas); "Bread" ("A Paene to le Pain") (Villagers); "Proud Lady" (Kurt Peterson); "Serenade" (Kurt Peterson, Tony Schultz, Topol, Carole Demas); "Meadowlark" (Carole Demas); "Any-Day-Now Day" (Topol, Villagers)

Act Two: "Something's Got to Be Done" (Men of the Village); "Romance" (Portia Nelson, Darlene Conley, Jean McLaughlin, Nieces); "Endless Delights" (Kurt Peterson, Carole Demas); "The Luckiest Man in the World" (Benjamin Rayson, Gordon Connell, Pierre Epstein, Keene Curtis, Nieces, Villagers); "If I Have to Live Alone" (Topol); "Where Is the Warmth?" (Carole Demas); Finale (Carole Demas, Topol)

Based on the 1938 French film *Le Femme du Boulanger*, *The Baker's Wife* underwent a tumultuous six-month tryout, but despite major casting changes (both leads were replaced), the replacements of the original director and choreographer, the constant rewrites of the book, and the numerous songs that were added and dropped throughout the pre-Broadway tour, producer David Merrick decided not to risk New York and thus canceled the planned Broadway opening at the Martin Beck (now Al Hirschfeld) Theatre on November 21, 1976, where previews were scheduled to begin on November 17.

The show was an intimate, low-key musical full of modest charms as its villagers went about their daily routines and sang of the heavenly delight of the fresh-baked bread by the town's baker Aimable (Topol, who was succeeded by Paul Sorvino late in the run). When his young wife Genevieve (Carole Demas, who was replaced by Patti LuPone early in the run) runs off with handsome young chauffeur Dominique (Kurt Peterson), the village faces a crisis of monumental proportions because Aimable is so distraught over his wife's desertion that he won't bake the bread they all die for. So it's up to the villagers to devise a scheme to bring Genevieve back to him.

The older-man-young-woman-and-young-man triangle was a familiar one and brought to mind two earlier musicals also set in France: Merrick's very own *Fanny* (1954), which was based on a play by Marcel Pagnol, who had directed and also cowritten the screenplay of *La Femme de Boulanger*, and the 1964 film *The Umbrellas of Cherbourg* (which was produced Off Broadway in 1979). The plot was also reminiscent of Frank Loesser's 1956 musical *The Most Happy Fella* and the nonmusical film *Wild Is the Wind* (1957).

Stephen Schwartz's score for *The Baker's Wife* is his best, a richly melodic one that includes a bouquet of beautiful songs that delineate the love story: "Merci, Madame," "Gifts of Love," "Serenade," "If I Have to Live Alone," "Where Is the Warmth?," and, especially, Genevieve's towering and elegiac "Meadowlark," a stunning art song in which she describes her favorite childhood fairy tale about a meadowlark torn between her love for the "old king" and her attraction to a "beautiful young god." The shimmering "Meadowlark" is not only the score's finest moment, it's also one of the towering achievements of American musical theatre, a dramatic, incisive character song in which the storybook elements of Genevieve's childhood fairy tale mirror the emotional war going on within her. Along with Ethel Merman's "Rose's Turn," Patti LuPone's memorable interpretation of "Meadowlark" belongs in the pantheon of great musical theatre performances.

In reviewing the opening of the Los Angeles production, Edwa in *Variety* said that "somewhere" there was a musical in the material, but it hadn't yet been found. The script was "mediocre," the choreography "disappointing," and the score "should be better." Demas's role was "undefined" and thus her performance was limited, as was Kurt Peterson's, who had "very little dialogue." But he praised Jo Mielziner's "beautifully designed" stage settings (sadly, these were the last ones created by the legendary designer who had died two months before the Los Angeles premiere).

For the tryout's final stop, the headline of Richard L. Coe's review in the *Washington Post* proclaimed that the musical was "Only Half a Loaf." The evening was "listless," the director seemed to be "loafing on his job," and the characters were "cardboard figures." As for Topol, he often seemed "unrelated" to his fellow performers. Later in the Washington run, Coe re-reviewed the production and stated that Sorvino was an improvement over Topol. The latter hadn't much bothered with the "amiability" of his character, but Sorvino was indeed amiable and was thus "far more credible and touching" than Topol. David Richards in the *Washington Star* noted that Sorvino's "strong lyric voice" was an asset to the score (Topol had tended to "croak"), and he brought a "quiet sincerity" to the role which was "an improvement over Topol's petulance."

Besides the replacements of Topol and Carole Demas, Benjamin Rayson was succeeded by Charles Rule; the role of Denise (Claude's wife) was added, and played by Teri Ralston (Jean McLaughlin had played a role named Denise, and her character's name was now changed to Simone); and another character (Jean-Paul) was added and played by Bill Mullikin.

Craig Zadan in *New York* reported that Topol said "he hated the show" and that in the presence of the entire company Merrick told him, "You won't perform to the best of your ability and you say you're unhappy in the show. . . . So why don't you leave?" Topol then reportedly told Merrick he would "give the production his cooperation, but not his enthusiasm." When Topol was eventually replaced by Sorvino, the critics noted the improvement, for Sorvino brought a heart-breaking intensity to the role, a warm brio of emotional depth that had completely eluded Topol.

During the tryout, director John Berry replaced Joe Hardy, choreographer Robert Tucker replaced Dan Siretta, and musical director Robert Billig succeeded Don Jennings.

During the course of the run, the following songs were heard either during the Los Angeles run or in other tryout stops, and were eventually cut from the score and not heard in the final Washington performances: "Welcome to Concorde," "A Little Taste of Heaven," "Proud Lady," "Look for the Woman," "When She Comes Home Tomorrow," "Something's Got to Be Done," and "Romance." The following numbers were added after the Los Angeles opening night and during the course of the tour were still in the production by the end of the Washington run: "Chanson," "Merci, Madame," "The Baking," "Not in the Market," "Perfect Every Time," and "What's a Man to Do?"

The original cast album was to have been recorded by Motown Records, but was canceled due to the show's pre-Broadway closing. But Sorvino, LuPone, and Peterson later participated in a delightful recording of the score that was released by Original Cast Records (LP # THT-772; CD # THT-CD-891). "Meadowlark" is included on the two-CD *Patti LuPone Live* (RCA Victor # 09026-61797-2), which was recorded from one of her concert performances at the Westwood Playhouse in Los Angeles, California, in January 1993.

Various sources couldn't agree on how much money the musical lost. *The New York Times* estimated the loss at $572,300, but *Variety* reported the show closed in the red by "about" $1 million.

During the years following the pre-Broadway closing, various regional productions of the musical were mounted, and on March 24, 1985, the York Theatre Company presented a revival at the Church of the Heavenly Rest for a limited engagement of twenty performances (Jack Weston was Aimable).

A major London production opened at the Phoenix Theatre on November 27, 1989, but ran for a disappointing fifty-six performances; happily, it was recorded on a two-LP set by That's Entertainment Records (LP # TER2-175; CD # CDTER-1175).

A number of songs were written by Schwarz for various post-1976 productions seen regionally, at the York Theatre, or in London, and these include: "Voila," "New Musketeers," "I Could Never Get Enough of You," "Feminine Companionship," "If It Wasn't for You," "Plain and Simple," and "Buzz-a-Buzz."

SING AMERICA SING

"A Bicentennial Musical Celebration of America"

The revue opened on September 8, 1975, at the Concert Hall at the John F. Kennedy Center for the Performing Arts and closed there on September 21.

Text: Oscar Brand

Lyrics and *Music*: See list of musical numbers, below.

Direction: Oscar Brand; *Producers*: The Kennedy Center (Roger L. Stevens, Producer) and The Prudential Insurance Company of America; *Choreography*: Tony Stevens (Yolanda R. Raven, Assistant to Choreography); *Scenery*: Special Visual Effects by George Pickow; *Musical Direction*: Ron Frangipane

Cast: *John Raitt*, Jean Ritchie, Gil Robbins, Glory Van Scott, Oscar Brand, Lyn Hardy, Jay Ungar, Jonathan Pickow, Peter Pickow; Ensemble: Tommy Aguilar, Steve Anthony, Phyllis Bash, Jill Cook, David Dusing, Iony, Gina Paglia, Yolanda R, Raven, Catherine Rice, Rick Schneider, Timm Stetzner, and Cliff Townsend

The revue was presented in two acts.

Musical Numbers

Act One: "Sing America Sing" (lyric and music by Oscar Brand) (John Raitt, Chorus); "Amazing Grace" (traditional) (Jean Ritchie, Chorus); "Deer Dance Chant" (traditional) (Oscar Brand); "Las Mananitas"

(traditional) (Jay Unger); "Alouette" (traditional) (Oscar Brand); "Wonderful Country" (lyric and music by Oscar Brand) (John Raitt, Gil Robbins); "Wondrous Free" (lyric and music by F. Hopkinson and T. Parnell) (Jean Ritchie); "Free Americay" (lyric by Dr. Joseph Warren, music traditional) (Chorus); "Follow Washington" (new music by Oscar Brand) (Chorus); "Farewell to America" (new music by Oscar Brand) (Glory Van Scott, Cliff Townsend); "Jefferson and Liberty" (traditional) (Oscar Brand); "The Alamo" (traditional) (John Raitt); "Square Dance" (traditional; music arranged by Jay Ungar) (Jay Ungar, Band); "Blow the Man Down" (traditional) (Cliff Townsend); "A Is for Axe" (traditional) (David Dusing); "I Got a Mule" (traditional) (Gil Robbins); "Anti-Lincoln Song" (traditional) (Lyn Hardy, Jay Ungar); "Motherless Child" (traditional) (Phyllis Bash); "Bonny Blue Flag" (lyric by H. Macarthy, music by Valentine Vousden) (Chorus); "The Union Forever" (traditional) (Chorus); "We Are the Negro Soldiers" (lyric by Sojourner Truth, music traditional) (Cliff Townsend); "Tenting Tonight" (lyric and music by W. Kittredge) (Unidentified trio); "Slavery Chain" (traditional) (Glory Van Scott, Chorus); "John Wilkes Booth" (new music by Jean Ritchie) (Jean Ritchie); "I Ride an Old Paint" (traditional) (John Raitt); "Chisholm Trail" (traditional) (Jonathan Pickow); "Lullaby" (traditional) (Oscar Brand); "Bury Me Not" (traditional) (Peter Pickow); "Blood on the Saddle" (traditional) (Oscar Brand); "Laredo" (traditional) (Peter and Jonathan Pickow); "Home on the Range" (lyric and music by D. E. Kelley) (John Raitt); "Filleemeeooree Ooreeay" (traditional) (Gil Robbins); "John Henry" (traditional) (Cliff Townsend); "Hanged Be the Bureaucrats" (lyric and music by Oscar Brand) (John Raitt); "Sing America Sing" (John Raitt, Chorus)

Act Two: Entr'acte (music by Ron Frangipane) (Orchestra); "Hail to the Chief" (lyric by Sir Walter Scott, music by J. S. Sanderson) (Chorus); "(There'll Be a) Hot Time in the Old Town Tonight" (lyric by Joe Hayden, music by Theodore August Metz) (Glory Van Scott); "Sousa March" (music by John Phillip Sousa, music arranged by Ron Frangipane) (Orchestra); "Solidarity Forever" (lyric by R. Chapin, music traditional) (Jean Ritchie, Lyn Hardy, Glory Van Scott); "St. Louis Blues" (lyric and music by W. C. Handy) (Iony); "The Long, Long Trail" (lyric and music by S. King and A. Elliott) (John Raitt); "It's a Long Way to Tipperary" (lyric and music by Jack Judge and Henry Williams) and "The Long, Long Trail" (reprise) (John Raitt and Gil Robbins); "Mademoiselle from Armentieres" (lyric and music attributed to Harry Carlton and Joe Tunbridge) (Chorus); "How Ya Gonna Keep 'Em Down on the Farm" (lyric by Joe Young and Sam M. Lewis, music by Walter Donaldson) (Peter and Jonathan Pickow); "Russian Lullaby" (independent song; lyric and music by Irving Berlin) (Oscar Brand); "This Land Is Your Land" (lyric and music by Woody Guthrie) (Gil Robbins, Jean Ritchie, Lyn Hardy); "Happy Days Are Here Again" (1930 film *Chasing Rainbows*; lyric by Jack Yellen, music by Milton Ager) (John Raitt); "Remember Pearl Harbor" (lyric by Don Reid, music by Don Reid and Sammy Kaye) (Jean Ritchie); "I'm Just Wild about Harry" (*Shuffle Along*, 1921; lyric by Noble Sissle, music by Eubie Blake) (John Raitt); "You'll Never Walk Alone" (*Carousel*, 1945; lyric by Oscar Hammerstein II, music by Richard Rodgers) (John Raitt); "The Leaves Turn to Paper" (lyric and music by Oscar Brand) (Oscar Brand); "Aquarius" (*Hair*, 1968; lyric by James Rado and Gerome Ragni, music by Galt MacDermot) (Glory Van Scott, Chorus); "Okie from Muskogee" (lyric and music by Merle Haggard) (Lyn Hardy, Jay Ungar); "Roar, Lion, Roar" (traditional) (John Raitt, Chorus); "The Trojan Fight Song" (lyric and music by G. Grant and M. Sweet) (John Raitt, Chorus); "Rambling Wreck from Georgia Tech" (lyric and music by F. Roman) (John Raitt, Chorus); "Hail to the Victors" (lyric and music by L. Elbel) (John Raitt, Chorus); "On, Wisconsin" (lyric and music by W. T. Purdy and C. Beck) (John Raitt, Chorus); "Boola, Boola" (traditional) (John Raitt, Chorus); "Now Is the Cool of the Day" (lyric and music by Jean Ritchie) (Jean Ritchie); "One Step Farther Than the Moon" (lyric and music by Oscar Brand) (John Raitt, Chorus); "Sing America Sing" (reprise) (John Raitt, Chorus)

During the period of the nation's Bicentennial, a handful of revues surfaced that celebrated the American song book. ***Music! Music!*** and ***A Musical Jubilee*** were briefly seen on Broadway, and *Sing America Sing* seems to have been produced only at the Kennedy Center in Washington, D.C. (it's unclear if the revue had been intended for other cities besides Washington, and whether a New York booking had been considered).

The concert-styled evening was put together by Oscar Brand, who directed and was among the cast members; he also wrote the narration as well as a few new songs. The production starred John Raitt, who had appeared in Brand's short-lived 1966 Broadway musical *A Joyful Noise*. Raitt had also appeared in ***A Musical Jubilee***.

For the souvenir program of *Sing America Sing*, Brand noted that the evening was a "one-nighter" musical profile of America, and suggested there should be a series of *Sing America Sing* concerts to do full justice to the nation's songbook. He mentioned that trying to pull together songs for "the definitive Bicentennial Song Sampler" was "like trying to collect the best fifty waves in the Indian Ocean."

Sing America Sing was pleasant but bland, and went on far too long. The concert would probably have been more effective as a one-hour, one-act retrospective of American music or as a television special.

TRUCKLOAD

The musical played at the Lyceum Theatre for six previews from September 6 through September 11, 1975, before permanently closing.

Book: Hugh Wheeler

Lyrics: Wes Harris

Music: Louis St. Louis

Direction and *Choreography*: Patricia Birch; *Producers*: Adela Holzer, The Shubert Organization, and Dick Clark; *Scenery*: Douglas W. Schmidt; *Costumes*: Carrie F. Robbins; *Lighting*: John Gleason; *Musical Direction*: Louis St. Louis

Cast: Louis St. Louis (Driver), Kelly Ward (Heustis), Ilene Graff (Bonnie), Donny Burks (Horace), Laurie Prange (Amelia), Cheryl Barnes (Glory), Sherry Mathis (Darleen), Doug McKeon (Leon), Kenneth S. Eiland (Lee Wu), Ralph Strait (Whitfield), Deborah (Debbie) Allen (Rosa), Jose Fernandez (Ricardo), Rene Enriquez (Carlos); Louis St. Louis and His All Nite Drivers: Louis St. Louis (Musical Director, Piano), Richard Weinstock (Keyboards), Jimmy Young (Drums), Steve Mack (Bass), Dickie Frank (Guitar), Jack Cavari (Guitar), and Luther Rix (Latin Percussion)

The musical was presented in one act.

The time is "last night" and the action takes place on "any open road."

Musical Numbers

The Highway—"Truckload" (Louis St. Louis, Company); "Find My Way Home" (Cheryl Barnes, Louis St. Louis, Company); *The Come On Inn*—"Cumbia"/"Wedding Party" (Deborah Allen, Rene Enriquez, Jose Fernandez, Company); "Step-Mama" (Sherry Mathis, Kelly Ward, Company); "Look at Us" (Deborah Allen, Jose Fernandez); "Standing in This Phone Booth" (Ralph Strait); *All-Night Driving*—"Amelia's Theme" (Laurie Prange); "I Guess Everything Will Turn Out All Right" (Kelly Ward, Ralph Strait, Company); "Rest Stop" (Sherry Mathis, Louis St. Louis); *Plaza Truck Stop*—"Boogie Woogie Man" (Donny Burks with Kenneth S. Eiland, Ilene Graff, Sherry Mathis, Kelly Ward); "Ricardo's Lament" ("Man in the Middle") (Jose Fernandez with Deborah Allen and Rene Enriquez); "Hash House Habit" (Kenneth S. Eiland); "Dragon Strikes Back" (Kenneth S. Eiland, Company); "Bonnie's Song" ("Sometimes I Get to Stay All Nite") (Ilene Graff); "Pour Out Your Soul" (Cheryl Barnes, Company); "Jesus Is My Main Man" (Cheryl Barnes, Company); "There's Nothing Like Music" (Louis St. Louis); "Hello, Sunshine" (Louis St. Louis, Company); "Truckload" (reprise) (Company)

Truckload didn't go on the road, and instead chose to give a series of New York previews beginning on September 6, 1975, with a scheduled opening night of September 23. But after just six previews, the musical permanently closed.

Although it didn't have a subtitle, the musical might well have borrowed the one from producer Adela Holzer's earlier musical ***Dude***, or ***The Highway Life***. The plot dealt with an itinerant group of travelers who hitch-hike across the country in a huge musical-comedy bus which includes a giant piano played by composer Louis St. Louis as the Driver. Some of the passengers' stories seemed a trifle obvious and tantamount to soap opera, and the musical's quick closing indicates the proceedings left much to be desired. In its seasonal preview, *New York* suggested the show "could be a wow or a ***Dude***," and asked if the plot was "real" or "fantasy." "Or do we care?"

With a $15 top, the first preview took in an estimated $500, and the next five showings brought in ticket sales of $5,823 (at sell-out, the show could take in $85,000). When the musical closed, it was $500,000 in the red.

1976–1977 Season

AN EVENING WITH DIANA ROSS

Theatre: Palace Theatre
Opening Date: June 14, 1976; *Closing Date*: July 3, 1976
Performances: 24
Special Material: Bill Goldenberg and Bill Dyer
Additional Material: Bruce Vilanch
Direction: Joe Layton; *Producer*: Danny O'Donovan (A Danny O'Donovan/Sagittarius Entertainment Presentation); *Lighting*: John Gleason; *Musical Direction*: Gil Askey
Cast: *Diana Ross*; Mimes: Howard Coleman, Don McLeod, and Stewart Fischer; The Jones Sisters: Shirley, Brenda, and Valorie
The concert was presented in two acts.

Musical Numbers

Note: All songs were performed by Diana Ross, who was occasionally accompanied by the Jones Sisters.

Act One: Overture (Orchestra); "Here I Am" (lyric by Hal David, music by Burt Bacharach); "I Wouldn't Change a Thing" (lyric by Hal David, music by Burt Bacharach); "The Lady Is a Tramp" (*Babes in Arms*, 1937; lyric by Lorenz Hart, music by Richard Rodgers); "Touch Me in the Morning" (lyric by Ron Miller, music by Michael Masser); "One Love in My Lifetime" (lyric and music by Larry Brown, Theresa McFaddin, and Leonard Perry); "Smile" (1936 film *Modern Times*; music by Charlie Chaplin; lyric for the song was later written by John Turner and Geoffrey Parsons);"Love Hangover" (lyric and music by Pamela Sawyer and Marilyn McLeod); "Girls" (lyric and music by John Phillips); Medley of songs from *The Point*: "Everybody's Got 'Em," "Me and My Arrow," and "Lifeline" (concept album and later film and stage production with lyrics and music by Harry Nilsson); "Lady Sings the Blues" (lyric and music by Billie Holiday and Herbie Nichols); "'Tain't Nobody's Biz-ness If I Do" (lyric and music by Porter Grainger and Everett Robbins); "Hawaii" (lyric and music by Pascal Bastia and Jean Bastia); "Stormy Weather" (*Cotton Club Parade*, 1933 [twenty-second edition]; lyric by Ted Koehler, music by Harold Arlen); "(I Need a Little) Sugar in My Bowl" (lyric and music by C. Williams, D. Small, and T. Brymn); "My Man" (first performed in various Parisian and New York revues in 1920 and 1921, most notably in the 1921 edition of the *Ziegfeld Follies* where it was sung by Fannie Brice; original French lyric by Albert Willemetz and Jacques-Charles, English lyric by Channing Pollock, music by Maurice Yvain)

Act Two: "Motown History"; "The Supremes"; Medley from *A Chorus Line* (1975; lyrics by Edward Kleban, music by Marvin Hamlisch): "Play Me the Music," "What I Did for Love," and "T & A" (aka "Dance: Ten, Looks: Three"); "Theme from *Mahagony*" (aka "Do You Know Where You're Going To?") (1975 film *Mahagony*; lyric by Gerald Goffin, music by Michael Masser); "Ain't No Mountain High Enough" (lyric and music by Nickolas Ashford and Valerie Simpson); "Reach Out and Touch (Somebody's Hand)" (lyric and music by Nickolas Ashford and Valerie Simpson)

Diana Ross's limited-engagement concert-like revue at the Palace included talk about, and songs from, her Motown and Supreme days (the three Jones Sisters provided backup vocals); she discussed and sang numbers from her films *Lady Sings the Blues* (1972) and *Mahagony* (1975); dedicated a sequence (from Harry Nilsson's *The Point*) to her three daughters who were in the audience; and included a medley of songs from ***A Chorus Line***. She also left the stage and appeared in the auditorium itself where she mingled with the audience, sang "Reach Out and Touch (Somebody's Hand)," and asked the customers to do just that with one another.

Joe Layton directed the concert, and the critics singled out two clever staging touches. Ross first appeared in a gown of flowing white, and three male performers (who appeared throughout the evening and were identified in the program as the Mimes) held the train of her gown, which was suddenly and magically transformed into a huge movie screen that showed films and stills of the star. Another talked-about sequence occurred when Ross stopped singing "Love Hangover" and prepared to leave the stage. But the song continued as a prerecording, and suddenly a life-sized cardboard cut-out of the star materialized. Ross jokingly told the audience that they didn't *really* think she'd been singing live all evening, did they?

Clive Barnes in the *New York Times* said Ross had "style and class," her voice had a "velvet vibrancy," and her "stage command had a nervy security to it"; Martin Gottfried in the *New York Post* said she ranged from a "baby panther to the most teasing of tigers" and might well be the "only glamorous" entertainer to emerge from the 1960s; and Don Nelsen in the *New York Daily News* noted she "commanded all eyes and ears of the theatre" with the "mastery of her performance."

John Beaufort in the *Christian Science Monitor* said Ross had "the indispensible knack of taking an audience into her confidence" and then "putting it into her pocket"; and Leonard Probst on NBC Radio said the "triumphant entertainer" had a "marvelous" voice that was "vibrant and velvet."

But James Spina in *Women's Wear Daily* suggested Ross had "disappeared under a veneer of Vegas-fungus" and that director Layton had spent too much time watching reruns of the Sonny and Cher show. And Maureen Orth in *Time* found the evening "cloying and cute" and "as much a fashion show as a performance."

Awards

Tony Award: A special Tony was awarded to Diana Ross for her concert performance.

GODSPELL

Theatre: Broadhurst Theatre (during run, the musical transferred to the Plymouth and the Ambassador Theatres)
Opening Date: June 22, 1976; *Closing Date*: September 4, 1977
Performances: 527
Based on the Gospel According to St. Matthew.
Book: John-Michael Tebelak
Lyrics and *Music*: Stephen Schwartz
Direction: John-Michael Tebelak; *Producers*: Edgar Lansbury, Stuart Duncan, and Joseph Beruh and The Shubert Organization, Inc. (Charles Haid, Associate Producer); *Scenery*: Not credited; *Costumes*: Susan Tsu; *Lighting*: Spencer Mosse; *Musical Direction*: Paul Shaffer
Cast: Lamar Alford, Laurie Faso, Lois Foraker, Robin Lamont, Elizabeth Lathram, Bobby Lee, Tom Rolfing, Don Scardino, Marley Sims, Valerie Williams; Band: Paul Shaffer (Conductor, Keyboard), Mark Zeray (Guitar), Chris Warwin (Bass), and Michael Redding (Percussion)
The musical was presented in two acts.

Musical Numbers

Act One: "Tower of Babble" (Company); "Prepare Ye the Way of the Lord" (Tom Rolfing, Company); "Save the People" (Don Scardino, Company); "Day by Day" (Robin Lamont, Company); "Learn Your Lessons

Well" (Marley Sims); "Bless the Lord" (Valerie Williams, Company); "All for the Best" (Don Scardino, Tom Rolfing); "All Good Gifts" (Lamar Alford, Company); "Light of the World" (Laurie Faso)

Act Two: "Learn Your Lessons Well" (reprise) (Lamar Alford, Company); "Turn Back, O Man" (Lois Foraker, Company); "Alas for You" (Don Scardino); "By My Side" (lyric by Jay Hamburger, music by Peggy Gordon) (Elizabeth Lathram, Company); "We Beseech Thee" (Bobby Lee, Company); "On the Willows" (Band); Finale (Company)

An early version of *Godspell* was first presented Off Off Broadway at Café La Mama as part of John-Michael Tebelak's graduate project at Carnegie-Mellon University, and a revised production opened Off Broadway at the Cherry Lane Theatre on May 17, 1971, for a marathon run of 2,124 performances. The informal evening presented a ragtag, fast-and-loose interpretation of the Gospel according to St. Matthew in what amounted to a Gospel for Dummies, but the lighthearted nature of the musical along with Stephen Schwartz's catchy score (which included "Day by Day," one of the era's few popular theatre songs; "All for the Best," a sardonic vaudeville-styled number; and "Turn Back, O Man," a lowdown honky-tonk shuffle) propelled the musical into one of the decade's major theatre events, the kind of show attended by people who didn't usually go to shows. During the lengthy Off-Broadway run, a number of touring companies played throughout the country, many of which settled into long runs in various cities.

A week after the Off-Broadway production closed, it transferred to Broadway for a healthy run of 527 showings and the cast included Robin Lamont and Lamar Alford, both from the original Off-Broadway cast.

The revue-like retelling of the Gospel according to St. Matthew found the cast members coyly cavorting about in Superman, Raggedy Ann, and Disney-styled costumes and performing in a slightly improvisational manner with occasional mime-like clownish affectations against a setting that resembled an abandoned school's playground.

Douglas Watt in the *New York Daily News* suggested the musical required "a touch of the old nasty" because it was far "too cute." Further, its old-hat 1960s staging techniques (such as having the performers mix with the audience, offer them paper cups of wine, and invite them on stage during intermission) were tiresome. He also noted that the evening had been updated to include references to ***A Chorus Line*** and the Concorde. Edwin Wilson in the *Wall Street Journal* noted that the cast continuously impersonated past and current entertainers (such as Ed Wynn, Jack Benny, George Burns, Jimmy Durante, Groucho Marx, Paul Lynde, and Joanne Worley) because the musical's creators perhaps felt the audience couldn't take its religion "straight."

John Beaufort in the *Christian Science Monitor* suggested the musical had lost some of its "spontaneous exuberance" and now had an "excessive busyness" about it with performers who were "allowed to overindulge in crowd-pleasing specialties." Leonard Probst on NBC Radio doubted if *Godspell* would "cast a spell" on Broadway because it was "now too young to be nostalgic and too old to be fresh."

Martin Gottfried in the *New York Post* said the "*Hair* with a haircut" musical was "amateurish" and "accusably calculated to be inoffensive." When he had seen it at Café La Mama, he left at intermission because the work was "so obnoxiously precocious." The "love child" costumes were "whimsical enough for a hippie window at Macy's" and the performers were "so terribly cute" as they "spread so much love" that he yearned "for hatred." As for the musical's structure, he noted the performers were called by their real names, and there was no explanation of who they were supposed to be and why they were acting out the gospel in a schoolyard.

The musical's second Broadway engagement opened on November 7, 2011, at the Circle in the Square Theatre for 264 performances. The original London company opened on November 17, 1971, at Wyndham's Theatre for 1,128 performances with Jeremy Irons (in the Judas role). The 1973 film version by Columbia Pictures included Victor Garber (as Jesus) along with original Off-Broadway cast members Robin Lamont, Victor Haskell, and Gilmer McCormack and included a new song, "Beautiful City." An Off-Broadway revival was produced at the Lamb's Theatre on June 12, 1988, for 225 performances.

The original Off-Broadway cast album was released by Bell Records (LP # BELL-1102), and the same company also issued the London cast album (LP # BELLS-203) and the film's soundtrack (LP # BELL-1118). Other recordings of the score include the Australian cast album (Lewis Young Productions Records LP # SFL-934486); a 1993 studio cast recording by That's Entertainment Records (CD # CDTER-1204); a 1994 "UK Cast Recording for the 90's" by Playback Records (CD # GSCD-01); and a studio cast album performed by The Last Galaxie (General American Records LP # GAR-11312).

Awards

Tony Award Nomination: Best Score (lyrics and music by Stephen Schwartz)

THE MERRY WIDOW

Theatre: Uris Theatre
Opening Date: June 22, 1976; *Closing Date*: July 3, 1976
Performances: 15
Libretto and *Lyrics*: Victor M. Leon and Leo Stein (English scenario by Robert Helpmann and English lyrics by Christopher Hassall)
Music: Franz Lehar (musical adaptation by John Lanchbery)
Direction: Robert Helpmann; *Producers*: S. Hurok by arrangement with The Australian Ballet Foundation (Robert Helpmann, Director); *Choreography*: Ronald Hynd; *Scenery* and *Costumes*: Desmond Heeley; *Lighting*: "supervised" by John Gleason; *Musical Direction*: John Lanchbery
Cast: (*Note*: The dancers alternated roles during the run; the first-named are the ones who appeared in the opening night performance.) Robert Olup/Colin Peasley (Baron Mirko Zeta), Lucette Aldous/Maria Lang/Ai-Gul Gaisina (Valencienne), John Meehan/Jonathan Kelly (Count Danilo), Kelvin Coe/Walter Bourke/Dale Baker (Camille de Rosillon), Ray Powell/Alan Alder (Njegus), Dale Baker/Rex McNeill (Kromow), Mark Brinkley/Paul de Masson (Pritschitsch), Margot Fonteyn/Marilyn Rowe (Hanna Glawari), Paul Saliba/Danilo Radojevic (Pontevedrian Dancer), Paul Siliba (Maitre d' at Chez Maxime); Guests at the Embassy, Pontevedrians, Can-Can Ladies, Others: Members of the Australian Ballet
The ballet was presented in three acts.
The action takes place in Paris during the year 1905.

Clive Barnes in the *New York Times* said the Australian Ballet's version of Franz Lehar's 1905 operetta *The Merry Widow* played like a musical comedy. The production was "good, lighthearted summer entertainment for the family," the "sumptuous" costumes and décor were "a strange mixture of fin de siècle and art nouveau," and there was even some vocalizing to Lehar's famous score. The production was clearly a vehicle for ballet legend Margot Fonteyn, and while she may have been less limber than before, her "sense of authority" and her "wit and charm" couldn't be matched. Further, she was offering "now" and perhaps "forever" one of "the most emotional experiences in dance."

For more information about *The Merry Widow*, see entry for the June 1974 production.

PAL JOEY

Theatre: Circle in the Square Theatre
Opening Date: June 26, 1976; *Closing Date*: August 29, 1976
Performances: 73
Book: John O'Hara
Lyrics: Lorenz Hart
Music: Richard Rodgers
Based on a series of short stories by John O'Hara that were published in the *New Yorker* (the first story appeared in the October 22, 1938, issue); the collected short stories were published in book format in 1939.
Direction: Theodore Mann; *Producer*: Circle in the Square Theatre (Theodore Mann, Artistic Director, and Paul Libin, Managing Director); *Choreography*: Margo Sappington; *Scenery*: John J. Moore; *Costumes*: Arthur Boccia; *Lighting*: Ron Wallace; *Musical Direction*: Scott Oakley
Cast: Harold Gary (Mike), *Christopher Chadman* (Joey), Terri Treas (Kid), *Janie Sell* (Gladys), Gail Benedict (Gail), Murphy Cross (Murphy), Rosamond Lynn (Rosamond), Marilu Henner (Marilu), Deborah Geffner (Debbie), Boni Enten (Linda), *Joan Copeland* (Vera), David Hodo (Gent), Austin Colyer (Ernest), Denny Martin Flinn (Waldo), Michael Leeds (Victor), Kenn Scalice (Delivery Boy), Adam Petroski (Louis [The Tenor]), *Dixie Carter* (Melba), *Joe Sirola* (Ludlow Lowell), Ralph Farnworth (O'Brien); Boys and Girls: Gail

Benedict, Murphy Cross, Deborah Geffner, Marilu Henner, Rosamond Lynn, Terri Treas, Denny Martin Flinn, David Hodo, Michael Leeds, Kenn Scalice

The musical was presented in two acts.

The action takes place in Chicago during the late 1930s.

Musical Numbers

Act One: "You Mustn't Kick It Around" (Christopher Chadman, Janie Sell, Girls); "I Could Write a Book" (Christopher Chadman, Boni Enten); "Chicago" (Girls); "That Terrific Rainbow" (Janie Sell, Girls); "What Is a Man?" (Joan Copeland); "Happy Hunting Horn" (Christopher Chadman, Boys and Girls); "Bewitched, Bothered and Bewildered" (Joan Copeland); "Pal Joey" (Christopher Chadman); "Joey Looks into the Future" (Christopher Chadman, Gail Benedict, Company)

Act Two: "The Flower Garden of My Heart" (Adam Petroski, Janie Sell, Boys and Girls; Show Girls—Heather: Rosamond Lynn; Violet: Deborah Geffner; Sunflower: Murphy Cross; Lilac: Gail Benedict; Lily: Marilu Henner; American Beauty: Terri Treas); "Zip" (Dixie Carter); "Plant You Now, Dig You Later" (Janie Sell, Joe Sirola, Boys and Girls); "In Our Little Den (of Iniquity)" (Joan Copeland, Christopher Chadman); "Do It the Hard Way" (Joe Sirola, Janie Sell); "Take Him" (Boni Enten, Joan Copeland); "Bewitched, Bothered and Bewildered" (reprise) (Joan Copeland)

The revival of *Pal Joey* was one of the most troubled of the era. During previews, leading man Edward Villella (Joey) resigned, as did leading lady Eleanor Parker (Vera), both of whom were succeeded by their understudies Christopher Chadman and Joan Copeland. Even musical director Gene Palumbo left and was replaced by Scott Oakley. The *New York Times* reported that Parker complained of the "total lack of communication" and the "climate of hate" within the production, and as the first preview performance drew near, there was grumbling that director Theodore Mann had yet to block all the show. (One anonymous source said the revival should be called the musical version of *Jaws*.) The major source of friction centered around Margo Sappington's choreography for Villella. The *Times* said he was "uncomfortable" with her "angular, exuberant movements" and asked that his friends George Balanchine and Jerome Robbins unofficially create new choreography for him. Sappington "strenuously" objected to Balanchine's contributions because the new balletic choreography was at odds with the kind of dancing that small-time hoofer Joey would know. And so when Villella left the production, that old villain "artistic differences" was blamed for the parting of the ways. Opening night had been scheduled for June 17, but instead took place on June 26.

Considering the blood bath, the critics were somewhat generous in their assessments of the show, but poor Christopher Chadman was given little leniency (although one or two reviewers admitted he had inherited the role at practically the last minute). Clive Barnes in the *Times* said the "ill-fated" revival opened "after many birth pangs and much heartburn." Mann's direction was "heavy-handed," Sappington's choreography was "rather weak-legged," and the "charmless" Chadman danced "indifferently," sang "gratingly," and acted "as if he had had one disastrous acting lesson and decided not to go back." But Barnes said Joan Copeland's Vera was a "knock-out" and he also praised Dixie Carter, Janie Sell, Joe Sirola, and Harold Gary.

Martin Gottfried in the *New York Post* said Chadman "plays Joey like the understudy he was" and "goes through the show like a chorus boy at an audition for the lead," and Theodore Mann's staging alternated between "no choices and mistakes." Gottfried particularly complained about the placements of the band on both a specially constructed stage (which represented the night club stage) as well as in a pit next to the back of the stage. Book scenes were performed on the night club stage and some of the club numbers were presented on the regular stage itself, and so the separate worlds of the story and of the night club were never clearly defined.

Howard Kissel in *Women's Wear Daily* said the revival rarely went beyond the "conventional," and complained that the staging emphasized the proscenium part of the stage at the far end of the theatre (the Circle's thrust stage is designed so that the audience surrounds three sides of it) and underutilized the other areas of the proscenium. As for Chadman, he sang and danced well but didn't fully convey Joey's "sleazy charm." Edwin Wilson in the *Wall Street Journal* said Chadman lacked "personal magnetism," but he liked Dixie Carter, Janie Sell, and the "just right" performance of Joan Copeland. T. E. Kalem in *Time* said Chadman was "pallid" and "rather like a gypsy dropped from the audition of *A Chorus Line*."

But Douglas Watt in the *New York Daily News* said Chadman was a "just right" Joey with a "ratty charm," and he was also a "fine" dancer whose dream dance with Gail Benedict was "a nifty Astaire-Rogers take-off."

The musical was a tough portrait of conceited, small-time hoofer Joey and his cheap world of seedy show business, and its first few lines of dialogue signaled it wasn't going to mince words. When a nightclub manager meets Joey, he offers him a drink, drugs, women, or, if he prefers, a young man. Joey's ambition is to own a nightclub, and so he sleeps with society matron Vera Simpson, who agrees to bankroll him, and he also becomes involved with the innocent Linda English. By evening's end both the worldly and amoral Vera and nice-girl Linda dump him.

The original production opened on December 25, 1940, at the Ethel Barrymore Theatre for 374 performances, and theatrical legend has it that the musical was a failure that no one appreciated until it was revived on Broadway in 1952. But in truth *Pal Joey* was a hit, and when it closed was the second-longest-running of all the musicals by Richard Rodgers and Lorenz Hart (only the team's 1927 *A Connecticut Yankee* had played longer with 418 showings, and in 1942 *By Jupiter* topped out as their longest-running show with 427 performances).

The original production was also well received by most of the critics. Richard Watts in the *New York Herald-Tribune* found the show "a hard-boiled delight" and "an outstanding triumph"; Sidney B. Whipple in the *New York World-Telegram* said it was "bright, novel, gay and tuneful"; and Burns Mantle in the *New York Daily News* gave the musical three out of four stars and said the show heralded "signs of new life" for the American musical. John Mason Brown in the *New York Post* felt the story was "unimportant" but nonetheless noted the creators had attempted to discard the "old conventions" of musical comedy in their depiction of a leading man who is a "bum." And Richard Lockridge in the *New York Sun* said the musical's "amusedly ruthless examination" of Joey created one of the "most substantial" characters to ever "stand among the shadows of musical comedy."

Brooks Atkinson in the *New York Times* described the story as "odious" and Joey as a "heel," a "punk," and a "rat infested with termites," and then asked the most famous question in the annals of theatre-reviewing, "Can you draw sweet water from a foul well?" But even his question is misleading because he said the musical was "expertly done" with "inventive" choreography and a score of "wit and skill."

The first Broadway revival opened at the Broadhurst Theatre on January 3, 1952, for 540 performances and won three Tony Awards as well as the New York Drama Critics' Circle Award for Best Musical. Two revivals were produced at City Center by the New York City Center Light Opera Company, both with Bob Fosse in the title role; the first opened on May 31, 1961, for thirty-one performances, and the second on May 29, 1963, for fifteen showings. A concert version presented by Encores! played at City Center for a limited run of four performances beginning on May 4, 1995, and on December 18, 2008, the musical was revived at Studio 54 for eighty-four performances.

The first London production opened on March 11, 1954, at the Prince's Theatre for 245 performances, and the considerably revised and softened 1957 film version by Columbia nonetheless offered one of Frank Sinatra's best performances (here, Joey was a singer, not a hoofer).

There have been numerous recordings of the score, but the best is the 1950 studio cast album by Columbia Records (LP # 4364; issued on CD by Sony Classical/Columbia/Legacy # SK-86856) with Vivienne Segal reprising her Vera from the original 1940 production and Harold Lang as Joey. This recording sparked new interest in the musical and it led to the 1952 Broadway revival which starred Segal and Lang.

The script was published in hardback by Random House in 1952, and the lyrics are included in the collection *The Complete Lyrics of Lorenz Hart*. The script is also one of sixteen published by the Library of Congress in the 2014 hardcopy collection *American Musicals*.

LET MY PEOPLE COME

"A SEXUAL MUSICAL"

Theatre: Morosco Theatre
Opening Date: July 7, 1976; *Closing Date*: October 2, 1976
Performances: 108
Lyrics and *Music*: Earl Wilson Jr.

Direction: Phil Oesterman; *Producer*: Phil Oesterman; *Choreography*: Charles Augins; *Scenery* and *Lighting*: Duane F. Mazey ("Set and costumes supervised" by Douglas W. Schmidt; Clarence Sims, "Wardrobe Supervisor"; and lighting "supervised" by John Gleason); *Musical Direction*: Glen Roven

Cast: Brandy Alexander, Joanne Baron, Dwight Baxter, Pat Cleveland, Lorraine Davidson, Joelle Erasme, Yvette Freeman, Paul Gillespie, Gloria Goldman, Tulane Howard II, Bob Jockers, Empress Kilpatrick, Dianne Legro, Allan Lozito, Bryan Miller, Rod R. Neves, Rozaa, Don Scotti, Sterling Saint-Jacques, Bryan Spencer, Dean Tait, Lori Wagner, Charles Whiteside

The revue was presented in two acts.

Musical Direction

Act One: Opening (aka "Screw") (Company); "Mirror" (Bryan Spencer, Gloria Goldman, Paul Gillespie, Empress Kilpatrick, Rod R. Neves, Lori Wagner, Tulane Howard II, Joelle Erasme, Dean Tait, Pat Cleveland, Sterling Saint-Jacques); "Whatever Turns You On" (Company); "Give It to Me" (Lorraine Davidson, Lori Wagner); "Giving Life" (Empress Kilpatrick, Bryan Miller, Paul Gillespie, Rod R. Neves, Lori Wagner, Joelle Erasme, Dean Tait, Pat Cleveland, Sterling Saint-Jacques); "The Ad" (Charles Whiteside); "Fellatio 101" (Allan Lozito, Students); "I'm Gay" (Bob Jockers, Bryan Miller, Rod R. Neves, Paul Gillespie); "Linda, Georgina, Marilyn and Me" (Joanne Baron); "Dirty Words" (Company); "I Believe My Body" (Company)

Act Two: "The Show Business Nobody Knows" (Company); "Take Me Home with You" (Bryan Miller); "Choir Practice" (Allan Lozito, Company); "And She Loved Me" (Rozaa, Empress Kilpatrick, Lori Wagner, Joelle Erasme); "Poontang" (Company); "Come in My Mouth" (Empress Kilpatrick); "The Cunnilingus Champion of Company C" (Bryan Miller, Pat Cleveland, Joanne Baron, Charles Whiteside); "Doesn't Anybody Love Anymore" (Rozaa); "Let My People Come" (Company)

The self-described "sexual musical" *Let My People Come* began Broadway performances on July 7, 1976, never held an official opening night, and closed after three months. Prior to the opening, the lyricist and composer Earl Wilson Jr., told the *New York Times* that the Broadway cast would consist "of some of our country's brightest attractive young talent." Once performances got underway, there were various cast changes as well as a major reordering of the musical numbers, and Wilson requested that his name be omitted from the program because according to the *Times* Wilson felt his once "innocent and joyous" show had lost its "innocence" and the "subtlety" of his lyrics was no longer present. But producer Phil Oesterman countered that Wilson hadn't waived his royalties, and regarding the lyrics (the titles of the numbers ranged from "Fellatio 101" to "Come in My Mouth" to "The Cunnilingus Champion of Company C") the producer asked, "What subtlety?"

The revue had originally been seen Off Broadway, where it began performances at the Village Gate on January 8, 1974, and played for 1,167 showings. Like the Broadway edition, the revue embraced sexual liberation but wasn't liberated enough to hold an official opening night performance and face the critics, who eventually reviewed the production anyway. The Off Broadway edition was recorded by Libra Records (LP # LR-1069), and on August 19, 1974, the revue opened in London at the Oxford Circus Theatre for a long run. For Off Broadway, Peachena was one of the cast members, and while she didn't return for the Broadway run, all was not lost because Rozaa joined the production.

In reviewing the Off-Broadway edition, Mel Gussow in the *New York Times* stated the skits "lack the wit and sophistication of *Oh! Calcutta!* (and that's a claim I never expected to make for any show)."

Let My People Come was the season's first of two sexual-oriented revues; it was followed by ***Oh! Calcutta!*** which had also been first produced Off Broadway.

GUYS AND DOLLS

"A Musical Fable of Broadway"

Theatre: Broadway Theatre
Opening Date: July 21, 1976; *Closing Date*: February 13, 1977
Performances: 239

Book: Jo Swerling and Abe Burrows
Lyrics and *Music*: Frank Loesser
Based on various characters in short stories by Damon Runyon, including "Blood Pressure" (1930) and "The Idyll of Miss Sarah Brown" (1933).
Direction: Billy Wilson ("entire production under the supervision" of Abe Burrows); *Producers*: Moe Septee in association with Victor H. Potamkin (Ashton Springer and Carmen F. Zollo, Associate Producers); *Choreography*: Billy Wilson; *Scenery*: Tom H. John; *Costumes*: Bernard Johnson; *Lighting*: Thomas Skelton; *Musical Direction*: Howard Roberts
Cast: Ken Page (Nicely-Nicely Johnson), Christophe Pierre (Benny Southstreet), Sterling McQueen (Rusty Charlie), Ernestine Jackson (Sister Sarah Brown), John Russell (Harry the Horse), Clark Morgan (Lieutenant Brannigan), Robert Guillaume (Nathan Detroit), Jymie Charles (Angie the Ox), Norma Donaldson (Miss Adelaide), James Randolph (Sky Masterson), Emett "Babe" Wallace (Arvid Abernathy), Irene Datcher (Agatha), Alvin Davis (Calvin), Marion Moore (Martha), Derrick Bell (Joey Biltmore, Waiter), Andy Torres (Master of Ceremonies, Drunk), Prudence Darby (Mimi), Edye Byrde (General Cartwright), Walter White (Big Jule); The Guys: Derrick Bell, Toney Brealond, Jymie Charles, Alvin Davis, Nathan Jennings Jr., Bill Mackey, Sterling McQueen, Andy Torres, Eddie Wright Jr.; The Dolls: Prudence Darby, Jacquelyn DuBois, Anna Maria Fowlkes, Helen Gelzer, Julia Lema, Jacqueline Smith-Lee
The musical was presented in two acts.
The action takes place in New York City.

Musical Numbers

Act One: "Runyonland" (Company); "Fugue for Tinhorns" (Ken Page, Christophe Pierre, Sterling McQueen); "The Oldest Established" (Ken Page, Christophe Pierre, Robert Guillaume, The Guys); "I'll Know" (Ernestine Jackson, James Randolph); "A Bushel and a Peck" (Norma Donaldson, The Hot Box Girls); "Adelaide's Lament" (Norma Donaldson); "Guys and Dolls" (Ken Page, Christophe Pierre); "El Café Felicidad" (Company); "If I Were a Bell" (Ernestine Jackson); "My Time of Day" (James Randolph); "I've Never Been in Love Before" (James Randolph, Ernestine Jackson)
Act Two: "Take Back Your Mink" (Norma Donaldson, The Hot Box Girls); "Adelaide's Lament" (reprise) (Norma Donaldson); "More I Cannot Wish You" (Emett "Babe" Wallace); "Crapshooters' Dance" (The Guys); "Luck, Be a Lady Tonight" (James Randolph, The Guys); "Sue Me" (Norma Donaldson, Robert Guillaume); "Sit Down, You're Rockin' the Boat" (Ken Page, Company); "Marry the Man Today" (Ernestine Jackson, Norma Donaldson); "Guys and Dolls" (reprise) (Company)

The all-black revival of *Guys and Dolls* was a mixed blessing. As Martin Gottfried in the *New York Post* pointed out, the work had been written "very white and very Jewish" and the transposition to black was sometimes uneasy and awkward. Perhaps if the revival had been completely reconceived, it might have worked. But instead its overall concept faithfully adhered to the original production and thus it lacked both Jewish and black flavor and might well have been set in an anonymous city.

The production also had a summer-stock ambience about it, as if the designers hadn't been allotted enough money to lavish the show with the décor needed to create the fairy-tale look of a never-never-land New York City. As for the principals, Robert Guillaume (Nathan Detroit), Norma Donaldson (Miss Adelaide), and especially Ernestine Jackson (Sarah Brown) were delightful, and the latter's joyous "If I Were a Bell" made the song seem newly minted with her fresh interpretation. But James Randolph (Sky Masterson) seemed subdued and somewhat uncomfortable as the dashing gambler.

Gottfried had serious reservations about the decision to use an all-black cast, but most of the critics lavished praise on the production (and all agreed that the spiritual-like "Sit Down, You're Rockin' the Boat" was the one number that clearly worked in the all-black production). Despite mostly favorable reviews, the musical managed just seven months on Broadway and didn't return its investment. After the current revival, there were occasional all-black versions of earlier Broadway musicals (***Timbuktu!***, which was based on *Kismet*, and the 1991 version of *Oh, Kay!*), but both were financial failures and soon producers gave up on all-black revivals and instead looked toward casting revivals with a mixture of black and white performers. Sometimes this worked (the 1999 revival of *Kiss Me, Kate* and the 2002 revival of *Man of La Mancha*), but other times did not (Lincoln Center's 1994 production of *Carousel* and the 1995 *How to Succeed in Business without Really Trying*).

Gottfried was one of the era's finest theatre critics, but sometimes seemed a bit ornery. Like the recent revival of ***My Fair Lady***, he said *Guys and Dolls* wasn't a classic musical. But if these two aren't classic, then apparently there are no Broadway musical classics. He was more on target with his criticisms of the all-black casting gimmick, which he found "condescending" to blacks and made no theatrical sense in light of the specific material.

Clive Barnes in the *New York Times* suggested the evening was "a completely new look at an old work" and said the musical was "as wry and as funny, as enchanting and as entrancing as ever." Kevin Sanders on WABCTV7 suggested the musical was now "very innocent, brash and dated" and thus depended on the "novelty" of its black cast. And John Beaufort in the *Christian Science Monitor* praised the "brilliant" cast and said the musical was "in the best Broadway tradition."

The headline of T. E. Kalem's review in *Time* was "Almost-Nicely," and he complained that the revival's "most troubling interference is the blackface." Except for the character of Nathan Detroit, who was "completely himself" in Robert Guillaume's performance, the other leads were "a darker shade of make-up uneasily applied over white characters." He noted the evening's highlights were Jackson's "If I Were a Bell" and Ken Page's "Sit Down, You're Rockin' the Boat," both of which were performed in a "soul-stirring manner that is genuinely all-black."

Howard Kissel in *Women's Wear Daily* said the revival was one of "uneasy compromise" and felt Norma Donaldson's Miss Adelaide and Ernestine Jackson's Sarah Brown were "a little uneasy" because Adelaide was conceived as "very Brooklyn Jewish" and Sarah as "very, very WASP goyish." John S. Cooper in the *Wall Street Journal* complained that the revival made "almost no concessions to the black idiom" and thus there was at times "a faintly distasteful Amos 'n' Andy flavor to the performance." He noted that the performers probably had better singing voices than the original cast members, but said he was reluctant to be "too praiseful" because "the next thing you know they'll all be consigned to something like an all-black *My Fair Lady*."

During the revival's tryout, Norman Matlock (Lieutenant Brannigan) and Bill Mackey (Rusty Charlie) were succeeded by Clark Morgan and Sterling McQueen, respectively (but Mackey remained with the production as a chorus member).

The original Broadway production opened at the 46th Street (now Richard Rodgers) Theatre on November 24, 1950, for 1,200 performances, and besides the current edition the show has been revived in New York five times. Three productions were produced at City Center by the New York City Center Light Opera Company (April 20, 1955, 31 performances; April 28, 1965, 15 performances; and June 8, 1966, 23 performances). The somewhat overrated 1992 revival opened at the Martin Beck (now Al Hirschfeld) Theatre on April 14 for 1,143 performances, and the most recent one opened on March 1, 2009, at the Nederlander Theatre for 121 showings.

The original London production opened at the Coliseum on May 28, 1953, for 555 performances, and the somewhat enjoyable if overly long and talky film version was released by Samuel Goldwyn in 1955 with Marlon Brando (Sky Masterson), Jean Simmons (Sarah Brown), Frank Sinatra (Nathan Detroit), and Vivian Blaine (Miss Adelaide), who reprised her original Broadway role (Blaine also appeared in the 1966 New York revival and in the London production). The film included three new songs by Frank Loesser, "Adelaide," "(Your Eyes Are the Eyes of) A Woman in Love," and "Pet Me, Poppa."

Incidentally, in a bow to then-current politics, the 1965, 1966, and 1976 revivals found Sky taking Sarah to Puerto Rico (not Cuba) for the weekend. But for the 1992 and 2009 revivals they flew to Havana.

There are numerous recordings of the score, but the definitive one is the original Broadway cast album released by Decca Records (# DL-8036) and later on CD by Decca Broadway (# 012-159-112-2). The script was published in paperback by Doubleday Anchor in the 1956 collection *From the American Drama*: *The Modern Theatre Series, Volume Four* (edited by Eric Bentley). The script is also included in *The "Guys and Dolls" Book*, published by Methuen in 1982 (the volume also contains Runyon's short story "The Idyll of Miss Sarah Brown" and articles about Loesser and the 1982 British National Theatre production). The script is also one of sixteen included in the 2014 hardcover collection *American Musicals*, published by the Library of Congress. The lyrics for all the used and unused songs written for the musical are included in *The Complete Lyrics of Frank Loesser*.

The original production of *Guys and Dolls* won seven Tony Awards, including Best Musical, Best Direction, Best Choreography, Best Book, and Best Score. It also won the New York Drama Critics' Circle Award for Best Musical.

Awards

Tony Award Nominations: Best Revival (*Guys and Dolls*); Best Leading Actor in a Musical (Robert Guillaume); Best Leading Actress in a Musical (Ernestine Jackson)

DIE FLEDERMAUS

Theatre: New York State Theatre
Opening Date: September 11, 1976; *Closing Date*: November 7, 1976
Performances: 4 (in repertory)
Libretto: Carl Haffner and Richard Genee (English adaptation by Ruth and Thomas Martin)
Music: Johann Strauss
Direction: Gerald Freedman; *Producer*: The New York City Opera Company; *Choreography*: Thomas Andrew; *Scenery*: Lloyd Evans; *Costumes*: Theoni V. Aldredge; *Lighting*: Hans Sondheimer; *Musical Direction*: Imre Pallo
Cast: Gary Glaze (Alfred), Gianna Rolandi (Adele), Johanna Meier (Rosalinda von Eisenstein), Charles Roe (Gabriel von Eisenstein), Jerold Siena (Doctor Blind), Thomas Jamerson (Doctor Falke), Spiro Malas (Frank), Diana Kehrig (Sally), Jack Sims (Ivan), David Rae Smith (Prince Orlofsky), James Billings (Frosch); Solo Dancers: Sandra Balestracci, Esperanza Galan, and Jiliu Horvath; Ensemble: The New York City Opera Chorus and Dancers
The operetta was presented in three acts.
The action takes place in a summer resort near Vienna during the latter part of the nineteenth century.

Peter G. Davis in the *New York Times* found the current revival of Johann Strauss's *Die Fledermaus* (*The Bat*) a "perplexing affair." Gerald Freedman's direction was "smooth" and "ungimmicked," the cast was "energetic," and the décor was "handsome." Nonetheless, the evening lacked flavor and was "little more than humdrum" and he suspected the English translation by Ruth and Thomas Martin was the culprit because it conveyed "as much wit as a prime-time TV situation comedy script."

Davis noted that Johanna Meier stood out with her "subtle humor" and "vocal refinement" but felt the male singers, such as Charles Roe and Gary Glaze, were "adequate" but "nondescript."

The production returned the following winter, opening on February 26, 1977, and closing on April 30, 1977, for six performances in repertory for a total of ten showings during the season.

For more information about the operetta, see the entry for the September 1974 production.

DEBBIE

Theatre: Minskoff Theatre
Opening Date: September 16, 1976; *Closing Date*: September 26, 1976
Performances: 14
Direction and *Choreography*: Ron Lewis; *Producers*: Raymax Productions (Robert Fallon, Producer); *Scenery*: Billy Morris; *Costumes* and *Gowns*: Bob Mackie; *Lighting*: Jerry Grollnek; *Musical Direction*: Tom Nygaard
Cast: *Debbie Reynolds*, Bruce Lea, Albert Stevenson, Ray Chabeau, Joel Blum, Louis McKay, Gene Myers, George Eiferman, Penny Worth, Dani MiCormick, Steven Lardas
The revue was presented in two acts.

Musical Numbers

Act One: Overture (Tom Nygaard and Orchestra); "(Gee, but) It's Great (Good) to Be Here" (*Happy Hunting*, 1956; lyric by Matt Dubey, music by Harold Karr) (Debbie Reynolds, Company); Medley: "Reach Out and Touch (Somebody's Hand)" (lyric and music by Nickolas Ashford and Valerie Simpson); "He's Got the Whole World in His Hands" (traditional); "Touch a Hand" and "Higher and Higher" (lyric and music by Gary Lee Jackson, Carl W. Smith, and Raynard Miner) (Debbie Reynolds, Company); Singers' Medley (unidentified songs) (Steven Lardas, Penny Worth, Dani McCormick); Film Sequence and Medley (Debbie Reynolds); " I Ain't Down Yet" (*The Unsinkable Molly Brown*, 1960 [film, 1964]; lyric and music by Meredith Willson); "Debbie's Salute to Show Business" (Company)

Act Two: Entr'acte (Tom Nygaard and Orchestra); Medley from *Irene* (1919; revival, 1973): "Irene" (lyric by Joseph McCarthy, music by Harry Tierney), "I'm Always Chasing Rainbows" (lyric by Joseph McCarthy, music by Harry Carroll [song originally introduced in the 1918 musical *Oh, Look!* and wasn't performed in the original 1919 production of *Irene*]), "Alice Blue Gown" (lyric by Joseph McCarthy, music by Harry Tierney), and "You Made Me Love You" (independent song not performed in the original 1919 production of *Irene*; lyric by Joseph McCarthy, music by James V. Monaco) (Debbie Reynolds, Boys); "Premier Night . . . Impressions" (Debbie Reynolds); "Bicentennial Salute to America" (sequence includes "God Bless America" [lyric and music by Irving Berlin] and "Strike Up the Band"[*Strike Up the Band*, 1930; lyric by Ira Gershwin, music by George Gershwin]) (Company)

Debbie Reynolds's Las Vegas-styled revue *Debbie* played a limited engagement at the Minskoff Theatre, where a few seasons earlier she had appeared in ***Irene***. The critics were able to contain themselves, and weren't overly enthusiastic about Reynolds or her revue. The star was backed by three singers (Steven Lardas, Penny Worth, and Dani McCormick) and six dancers (Bruce Lea, Albert Stevenson, Ray Chabeau, Joel Blum, Louis McKay, and Gene Myers).

Reynolds made her entrance on a display of marquee lights that spelled out her first name as it descended from the ceiling to the stage. And as Diana Ross did earlier in the season, Reynolds stepped out into the auditorium and chatted with the audience, and, like Ross, she sang "Reach Out and Touch (Somebody's Hand)." She also narrated a memory-lane-styled sequence in which she showed film clips from her movies; she performed "I Ain't Down Yet" (from her 1964 film version of *The Unsinkable Molly Brown*) and a medley of songs from ***Irene***; she did impressions (of Marlene Dietrich, Zsa Zsa Gabor, Mae West, and Barbra Streisand); and concluded the evening with a "bicentennial salute to America."

Jan Hodenfield in the *New York Post* said Reynolds was "a gorgeously tough tiny terrier" who deserved a better show. Her imitations were cringe-inducing ("Barbra Streisand" complains that she hates her initials but at least takes comfort that her name isn't Vic Damone), and the patriotic salute looked like "a Radio City Music Hall production number propelled by LSD." The headline of Douglas Watt's review in the *New York Daily News* read "Debbie in Schlockland," and he noted the "garish evening" lacked "a genuine showman stage center." He mentioned that he'd never seen Reynolds in a movie and "maybe that's the trouble." Mel Gussow in the *New York Times* said the star had a "certain amount" of talent but needed "a show to stop instead of this loosely strung necklace of nightclub numbers" (but he noted the "devastating" Streisand parody was a "showstopper" which proved Reynolds could be funny).

Christopher Sharp in *Women's Wear Daily* said Reynolds's "talent" was the ability "to combine her lesser talents into a palatable form," and her revue revealed "no single quality" that could "earn her a star standing." He criticized her parodies of the styles of other performers because the sequence showed she had "no style of her own" and the Bicentennial salute was "magnificently stupid."

Leonard Probst on NBC Radio said Reynolds was at her best advantage when the clips from her films were shown; otherwise, when the lights came up she looked "smaller, slighter and somewhat lost." He also thought her chats with the customers were "tasteless." Kevin Sanders on WABCTV7 found Reynolds "bright and cute and bland and coy," said her impersonations were "unexpectedly funny," and the "best impression of all" was "that of the well-known 1950's character called Debbie Reynolds."

GOING UP

"An Uplifting Musical Comedy"

Theatre: John Golden Theatre
Opening Date: September 19, 1976; *Closing Date*: October 31, 1976
Performances: 49
Book and *Lyrics*: Otto Harbach
Music: Louis A. Hirsch
Based on the 1910 play *The Aviator* by James Montgomery.
Direction: Bill Gile; *Producers*: Ashton Springer, William Callahan, Stephens-Weitzenhoffer Productions in association with Stephen R. Friedman and Irwin Meyer (James L. D. Roser, Associate Producer) (A Goodspeed Opera House Production; Michael P. Price, Producer); *Choreography*: Dan Siretta; *Scenery*: Edward Haynes; *Costumes*: David Toser; *Lighting*: Peter M. Ehrhardt (Lighting Supervision by Edward Haynes); *Musical Direction*: Lynn Crigler
Cast: Pat Lysinger (Miss Zonne), Calvin McRae (Alex), Larry Hyman (Gus, Louis), Stephen Bray (John Gordon), Kimberly Farr (Grace Douglas), Lee H. Doyle (F. H. Douglas), Michael Tartel (Jules Gaillard), Walter Bobbie (Hopkinson Brown), Maureen Brennan (Madeline Manners), Noel Craig (James Brooks), Brad Blaisdell (Robert Street), Ronn Robinson (Sam Robinson), James Bontempo (Dwayne), Deborah Crowe (Faye), Michael Gallagher (Howell), Terri Gill (Ennis), Barbara McKinley (Mollie)
The musical was presented in two acts.
The action takes place in Lenox, Massachusetts, in 1919.

Musical Numbers

Act One: "Paging Mr. Street" (Pat Lysinger, Stephen Bray, Bellboys, Ensemble); "I Want a Determined Boy" (Maureen Brennan, Walter Bobbie, Four Aviators); "If You Look in Her Eyes" (Kimberly Farr, Brad Blaisdell, Maureen Brennan); "Going Up" (Brad Blaisdell, Company); "Hello, Frisco" (*Ziegfeld Follies of 1915*; lyric by Gene Buck) (Pat Lysinger, Four Aviators); "Down, Up, Left, Right" (Brad Blaisdell, Walter Bobbie, Noel Craig, Ronn Robinson); "Kiss Me" (Kimberly Farr, Michael Tartel); "The Tickle Toe" (Kimberly Farr, Ensemble)
Act Two: "Brand New Hero" (Ensemble); "I'll Think of You" (*The Rainbow Girl*, 1918; lyric by Renold Wolf) (Kimberly Farr, Brad Blaisdell); "I'll Think of You" (reprise) (Kimberly Farr, Brad Blaisdell); "Do It for Me" (Maureen Brennan, Walter Bobbie); "My Sumurun Girl" (*The Whirl of Society*, 1912; lyric by Al Jolson); "Going Up" (reprise)/"Down, Up, Left, Right" (reprise)/"The Tickle Toe" (reprise) (Company)

The program didn't indicate *Going Up* was a revival, but the musical was based on the hit that opened on December 25, 1917, at the Liberty Theatre where it played for 351 performances. The revival had originated at the Goodspeed Opera House, East Haddam, Connecticut, where it opened on June 22, 1976, and the Broadway production came between the company's New York revivals of ***Very Good, Eddie*** and ***Whoopee!*** These two revivals played on Broadway for almost a year apiece, but *Going Up* crashed after six weeks.

The lighter-than-air plot dealt with Robert Street (Brad Blaisdell), the author of *Going Up*, a best-selling book about aviation. But there's one major problem: Robert knows nothing about flying, and so while his friends expect him to take to the air and entertain them with aerial stunts, Robert must find numerous ways to keep both feet on the ground.

Mel Gussow in the *New York Times* said the plot occasionally dawdled but otherwise he noted the evening's "pleasure" was in the musical's "smallness" and "unpretentiousness" and that "The Tickle Toe" was a "knee-twisting, foot-kicking miniature frolic." While Martin Gottfried in the *New York Post* liked the "pleasant, innocuous" songs and "ingratiating" dances, he suggested the book took up more time "than it has any right to" and he felt the show might have been "more fun" at Goodspeed than on Broadway.

Douglas Watt in the *New York Daily News* said *Going Up* was "earthbound" and that Hirsch was a "workmanlike" composer whose score was a "lifeless" collection of songs. The direction was "excessively campy," but the décor's highlight was a mock-up biplane that "seemed just right" and the "bright and cheerful" costumes were more so than the show itself. And Jack Kroll in *Newsweek* suggested Goodspeed's "recycled cuteness" of "antediluvian romps is beginning to be oppressive."

But T. E. Kalem in *Time* found the musical "sappy but ingratiating" and said "The Tickle Toe" was "marvelously agile." Howard Kissel in *Women's Wear Daily* said the show was "thoroughly disarming" with "good-natured humor" and "lively, exciting" dances. And John Beaufort in the *Christian Science Monitor* liked the "beguilingly fresh" show with its "catchy" songs, "uncampy" direction, and fetching costumes; here was a musical that "skims over improbabilities and soars with delights."

The revival interpolated three songs from other scores by Hirsch ("Hello, Frisco," "I'll Think of You," and "My Sumurun Girl" [see details in above song list]), and eliminated four from the original production ("I'll Bet You," "The Touch of a Woman's Hand," "Here's to the Two of You," and "When the Curtain Falls," the latter by Irving Berlin, which was added to the score during the Broadway run). The original production was performed in three acts, the revival in two, and while the original took place in 1917, the revival moved the action to 1919.

A silent film adaptation directed by Lloyd Ingraham was released in 1923 by Douglas MacLean Productions (MacLean played the role of Robert Street).

A recording of the score was released by Operetta Archives Records (CD # OA-1033).

LA BELLE HELENE

Theatre: The New York State Theatre
Opening Date: September 21, 1976; *Closing Date*: October 29, 1976
Performances: 5 (in repertory)
Libretto: Henri Meilhac and Ludovic Halevy (adaptation by Geoffrey Dunn with revisions by Julius Rudel)
Music: Jacques Offenbach
Direction: Jack Eddleman; *Producers*: The New York City Opera Company and Gert von Gontard; *Choreography*: Thomas Andrew; *Scenery*: Lloyd Evans; *Costumes*: Patton Campbell; *Lighting*: Hans Sondheimer; *Musical Direction*: Julius Rudel
Cast: Richard McKee (Calchas), Joaquin Romaguera (Philocomos), Joan Campbell (First Young Lady), Myrna Reynolds (Second Young Lady), Don Yule (Euthycles), Karan Armstrong (Helen), Puli Toro (Daphne), David Griffith (Orestes), Vicki Grof (Jocanthis), Valeria Orlando (Anthea), Madeline Mines (Phantis), Joyce Tomanec (Chloe), Henry Price (Paris), Jerold Siena (Ajax I), Melvin Lowery (Ajax II), John Lankston (Achilles), James Billings (Menelaus), David Holloway (Agamemnon), Richard McKee (Calchas); Dancers: Sandra Balestracci and Mikhail Korogodsky; Ensemble: The New York City Opera Company Chorus and Dancers
The operetta was presented in three acts.
The action takes place in ancient Greece.

The operetta *La belle Helene* premiered in Paris at the Theatre des Varietes on December 17, 1864, and was first seen in New York at the French Theatre on March 26, 1868, for thirty-seven performances, where it was sung in French. The first English adaptation (by Louis Harrison) was presented at the Casino Theatre on January 12, 1899, for fifty-two showings.

In the early 1930s, the operetta enjoyed renewed popularity in Europe with a new production by Max Reinhardt. In 1941, an all-black Broadway-bound version (with Avon Long and Joseph Attles, who teamed up thirty-four years later in the hit ***Bubbling Brown Sugar***) shuttered in summer stock, and other adaptations also failed: *Helen Goes to Troy* (1944; musical adaptation by Wolfgang Korngold, lyrics by Herbert Baker, and book by Gottfried Reinhardt and John Meehan Jr.) played ninety-seven performances on Broadway and *La Belle* (1962; musical adaptation by William Roy, lyrics by Marshall Barer, and book by Brendan Gill) closed during its pre-Broadway tryout. Another new version was presented Off Broadway in 1986 by Rosetta LeNoire's AMAS Repertory Theatre for sixteen performances (LeNoire herself had played Bacchis in the 1941 production) with lyrics by David Baker and book by John Fearnley.

Other musicals about Helen of Troy include John LaTouche and Jerome Moross's glorious *The Golden Apple* which opened Off Broadway in 1954 and soon transferred to Broadway for a total run of 173 performances; the irreverent and merry 1961 Off-Broadway musical *Sing Muse!* which played for thirty-nine performances (book and lyrics by Erich Segal and music by Joe Raposo); and 1978's *Helen*, another version which played at the AMAS for twelve showings (book by Lucia Victor and lyrics and music by Johnny Brandon).

Harold C. Schonberg in the *New York Times* said City Opera's English version was a "good show" more in keeping with Broadway than Paris. Offenbach's score was "brilliant," and as Helen the "beauteous" Karan Armstrong "invested the role with just the right amount of burlesque." Schonberg also praised James Billings's Menelaus and his "Victor Moore routine." For the same newspaper, Robert Sherman later reviewed the production when Carole Farley assumed the title role; he found her vocally "uneven" but physically she was "the Helen of anybody's dreams" and she showed a "delectable" comic flair. Allen Hughes in the *Times* noted that later in the run John Miner conducted and that Joseph Evans made his City Opera debut in the role of Paris.

The production returned during the company's spring season when it opened on February 27, 1977, for four showings (for a total run of nine performances during the season). John Rockwell in the *Times* said the New York State Theatre was "too big" for the production and English seemed "slightly incongruous" for the goings-on. But the "flaccid charade" offered a few compensations, including the "affection and buoyancy" of conductor David Effron and the charming score. As for Billings, he could easily transfer into a production of *A Funny Thing Happened on the Way to the Forum*, and Sharon Daniels's Helen was sung "decently enough." And when Patricia Brooks assumed the role of Helen, Donal Henahan in the *Times* noted she portrayed the character "as a kind of burlesque queen who had made good." But overall the "broad" English adaptation and the "flat" humor "did little to redeem a dreary evening."

OH! CALCUTTA!

"THE WORLD'S LONGEST-RUNNING EROTIC STAGE MUSICAL"

Theatre: Edison Theatre
Opening Date: September 26, 1976; *Closing Date*: August 6, 1989
Performances: 5,959
Sketches: Jules Feiffer, Dan Greenburg, Lenore Kandel, John Lennon, Jacques Levy, Leonard Melfi, David Newman and Robert Benton, Sam Shepard, Clovis Trouille, Kenneth Tynan, and Sherman Yellen
Lyrics and *Music*: Robert Dennis, Peter Schickele, and Stanley Walden; additional music and lyrics by Stanley Walden and Jacques Levy
Direction: Production "conceived" and directed by Jacques Levy (production "devised" by Kenneth Tynan); *Producers*: Hillard Elkins, Norman Kean, and Robert S. Fishko; *Choreography*: Margo Sappington; *Scenery*: James Tilton; *Projected Media Design*: Gardner Compton; *Costumes*: Kenneth M. Yount ("supervised" by James Tilton); *Lighting*: Harry Silverglat; *Musical Direction*: Michael Tschudin
Cast: Haru Aki, Jean Andalman, Bill Bass, Dorothy Chansky, Cress Darwin, John Hammil, William Knight, Cy Moore, Pamela Pilkington, Peggy Jean Walker; The Band: Michael Tschudin (Keyboards, Vocals), Dan Carter (Guitar, Vocals). Robin Gould III (Drums), Jeff Gerson (Percussion), and Harvey Swartz (Bass)
The revue was presented in two acts.

Musical Numbers

Act One: "Taking Off the Robe" (Company); "Will Answer All Sincere Replies" (Sue Ellen: Dorothy Chansky; Dale: John Hammil; Monte: William Knight; Cherie: Jean Andalman); "Rock Garden" (Man: William Knight; Boy: Cress Darwin); "One on One" (Haru Aki, Bill Bass; during this sequence, "Clarence" sung by Jean Andalman); "Suite for Five Letters" (John Hammil, William Knight, Dorothy Chansky, Jean Andalman, Pamela Pilkenton); "The Paintings of Clovis Trouille": (1) "Much Too Soon" (Cress Darwin) and (2) "Dance for George" (Pamela Pilkenton)
Act Two: "Jack and Jill" (Pamela Pilkenton, John Hammil); "Spread Your Love Around" (Jean Andalman; during sequence, "Love Lust Poem" performed by Pamela Pilkenton and Haru Aki); "Delicious Indignities" (Helen: Dorothy Chansky; Alfred: William Knight); "Playin'" (John Hammil); "Was It Good for You, Too?" (Perlmutter: Cress Darwin; Interviewer: Haru Aki; Doctor Bronson: Jean Andalman; Doctor Jaspers: William Knight; Nurse: Pamela Pilkenton; Attendant: Bill Bass; Woman: Dorothy Chansky; Gypsies: John Hammil and Haru Aki; Gypsy Dog: G. Grover Lightstone); "Coming Together, Going Together" (Company)

The revue *Oh! Calcutta!* originally opened Off Broadway at the Eden Theatre on June 17, 1969, for 704 performances and then transferred to Broadway on February 26, 1971, for 610 showings; the current revival played at the Edison Theatre for 5,959 performances. This production was presented under a Middle or Limited Broadway contract and occasionally gave ten weekly performances instead of the standard eight showings. For the first part of the run, the revue alternated with ***Me and Bessie*** and then after early December 1976 was presented solo. For more information about the revue, see entry for the February 1971 production.

The current version was based on one that opened at the Coconut Grove Playhouse in Miami, Florida, on April 6, 1976, and closed there on September 5, 1976 ("a record-breaking 23 weeks," according to the program).

In reviewing the current revival, Clive Barnes in the *New York Times* noted the revue had been "feeble" when it first opened and was still feeble. Further, it was "so silly" he felt more like musing upon the show than reviewing it because it was "still the most humorless exploration of human sexuality the theatre has so far experienced." When he first reviewed the production seven years earlier, he had written that *Oh! Calcutta!* could "give pornography a bad name." For the current revival, he noted that a nearby audience member viewed the proceedings through opera glasses, and this "could give opera a bad name."

The revised production omitted four numbers heard in the two earlier New York presentations ("Dick & Jane," "Green Pants," "I Like the Look," and "Four in Hand") and added four ("Clarence," "Dance for George," "Spread Your Love Around," and "Love Lust Poem").

PORGY AND BESS

Theatre: Uris Theatre
Opening Date: September 25, 1976; *Closing Date*: January 9, 1977
Performances: 122
Libretto: DuBose Heyward
Lyrics: DuBose Heyward and Ira Gershwin
Music: George Gershwin
Based on the 1927 play *Porgy* by Dorothy and DuBose Heyward (which in turn had been adapted from DuBose Heyward's 1925 novel *Porgy*).
Direction: Jack O'Brien (Mabel Robinson and Helaine Head, Assistant Directors); *Producers*: Sherwin M. Goldman and The Houston Grand Opera; *Choreography*: Mabel Robinson; *Scenery*: Robert Randolph (additional "scenic elements" for the Kittiwah Island scene designed by John Rothgeb); *Costumes*: Nancy Potts; *Lighting*: Gilbert V. Hemsley Jr.; *Musical Direction*: Ross Reimueller
Cast: Clay Fullum (Jasbo Brown), Betty Lane (Clara; alternates: Elizabeth Graham, Alma Johnson, Myra Merritt), Bernard Thacker (Mingo), Alexander B. Smalls (Jake; alternate: Bruce A. Hubbard), Larry Marshall (Sportin' Life), Glover Parham (Robbins), Delores Ivory-Davis (Serena; alternates: Wilma Shakesnider, Shirley Baines); Hartwell Mace (Jim), Mervin Wallace (Peter), Myra Merritt (Lily), Barbara Ann Webb (Maria; alternate: Queen Yahna), Alex Carrington (Scipio), Donnie Ray Albert (Porgy; alternates: Abraham Lind-Quendo, Robert Mosley), George Robert Merritt (Crown; alternate: John D. Anthony), Clamma Dale (Bess; alternates: Esther Hinds, Phyllis Bash), Hansford Rowe (Detective), William Gammon (Policeman), Cornel Richie (Undertaker), Shirley Baines (Annie), Earl Grandison (Frazier), Kenneth Barry (Mr. Archdale), Phyllis Bash (Strawberry Woman; alternate: Barbara Buck), Steven Alex-Cole (Crab Man), John B. Ross (Coroner); Ensemble: John D. Anthony, Shirley Baines, Earl Baker, Phyllis Bash, Kenneth Bates, Barbara Buck, Steven Alex-Cole, Ella Eure, Wilhelmenia Fernandez, Elizabeth Graham, Earl Grandison, Loretta Holkmann, Bruce A. Hubbard, Alma Johnson, Christal Lockley, Roberta Long, Hartwell Mace, Patricia McDermott, Myra Merritt, Naomi Moody, Glover Parham, William Penn, Dwight Ransom, Cornel Richie, Rodrick Ross, Bernard Thacker, Mervin Wallace, Wardell Woodard, Denice Woods, Barbara L. Young
The opera was presented in two acts.
The action takes place in Catfish Row, Charleston, South Carolina, and on nearby Kittiwah Island in 1935 (the original Broadway production's program indicated the time was in "the recent past").

Musical Numbers

Act One: Introduction (Piano); "Brown Blues" (Piano); "Summer Time" (lyric by DuBose Heyward) (Betty Lane); "A Woman Is a Sometime Thing" (lyric by DuBose Heyward) (Alexander B. Smalls, Men); "Here Come De Honey Man" (lyric probably by DuBose Heyward) (Mervin Wallace); "They Pass By Singin'" (lyric by DuBose Heyward) (Donnie Ray Albert); "Oh Little Stars" (lyric probably by DuBose Heyward) (Donnie Ray Albert); "Gone, Gone, Gone" (lyric by DuBose Heyward) (Ensemble); "Overflow" (lyric by DuBose Heyward) (Ensemble); "My Man's Gone Now" (lyric by DuBose Heyward) (Delores Ivory-Davis); "Leavin' for the Promise' Lan'" (lyric probably by DuBose Heyward) (Clamma Dale, Ensemble); "It Take a Long Pull to Get There" (lyric by DuBose Heyward) (Alexander B. Smalls, Men); "I Got Plenty o' Nuthin'" (lyric by Ira Gershwin and DuBose Heyward) (Donnie Ray Albert, Ensemble); "Buzzard Song" (lyric probably by DuBose Heyward) (Donnie Ray Albert, Ensemble); "Bess, You Is My Woman Now" (lyric by DuBose Heyward and Ira Gershwin) (Donnie Rae Albert, Clamma Dale); "Oh, I Can't Sit Down!" (lyric by Ira Gershwin) (Ensemble); "I Ain't Got No Shame" (lyric by DuBose Heyward) (Ensemble); "It Ain't Necessarily So" (lyric by Ira Gershwin) (Larry Marshall, Ensemble); "What You Want wid Bess?" (lyric by DuBose Heyward) (Clamma Dale, George Robert Merritt)

Act Two: "Oh, Doctor Jesus" (lyric by DuBose Heyward) (Delores Ivory-Davis, Barbara Ann Webb, Mervin Wallace, Myra Merritt, Donnie Rae Albert); "I Loves You, Porgy" (lyric by Ira Gershwin and DuBose Heyward) (Donnie Rae Albert, Clamma Dale); "Oh, Heav'nly Father" (lyric by Ira Gershwin and DuBose Heyward) (Ensemble); "Oh, de Lawd Shake de Heavens" (lyric by DuBose Heyward) (Ensemble); "Oh, Dere's Somebody Knockin' at de Do'" (lyric probably by DuBose Heyward) (Ensemble); "A Redheaded Woman" (lyric by Ira Gershwin) (George Robert Merritt, Ensemble); "Clara, Clara" (lyric by DuBose Heyward) (Ensemble); "There's a Boat Dat's Leavin' Soon for New York" (lyric by Ira Gershwin) (Larry Marshall, Clamma Dale); "Good Mornin', Sistuh!" (lyric probably by DuBose Heyward) (Donnie Rae Albert); "Oh, Bess, Oh Where's My Bess" (lyric by Ira Gershwin) (Donnie Rae Albert, Delores Ivory-Davis, Barbara Ann Webb); "Oh, Lawd, I'm on My Way" (lyric by DuBose Heyward) (Donnie Rae Albert, Ensemble)

As revivals of George Gershwin's *Porgy and Bess* were produced over the years, it became something of a cliché for many of them to proclaim how different they were from other productions of the opera. One revival announced it had cleared away the recitative and would present the songs in traditional musical comedy fashion; another restored the recitative and other discarded music to make the work more operatic; and yet another declared how it would "explain" the characters and provide more backstory. In truth, ever since its world premiere performance at the Colonial Theatre in Boston on September 30, 1935, the work has been almost always revised in one respect or another. During the tryout itself, the work was considerably shortened and the "Buzzard Song" was cut from the score.

The current production by the Houston Grand Opera had the right to proclaim it was unique, for here was a true operatic version with the cuts (including the "Buzzard Song" and the recitative portions) fully restored. As to whether the work was an opera or a musical, this was an old debate that probably will never end; but this being the 1970s, a new debate arose among some critics concerning the issue of white writers and a white composer creating a work about blacks that was intended to be performed by them. If this is objectionable, then will every work be subject to politically correct scrutiny? Is it "proper" for a Jewish composer to write a musical about Christians? If not, then banish *The Sound of Music* and ***Mass*** and "White Christmas"! And what about black composer Thomas "Fats" Waller's basically all-white musical *Early to Bed*? The list could go on and on, and the debates seem pointless.

Porgy and Bess takes place in the environs of Charleston's Catfish Row and nearby Kittiwah Island, and its folk-like story has taken on a mythic quality with its tale of the crippled Porgy who against all odds and reason loves the selfish and sluttish Bess. When the demonic Sportin' Life seduces her with drugs and the promise of the "high life" in New York, she abandons Porgy without a qualm. With only a cart pulled by a goat, Porgy sets off from Charleston to New York to find her, and despite the soaring hopefulness of "Oh, Lawd, I'm on My Way," one suspects Porgy is off on a futile quest that will only lead him to more unhappiness and frustration.

Clive Barnes in the *New York Times* said the "best musical on Broadway tonight is not a musical" but an "opera," for this *Porgy and Bess* was a "revelation" in its "finally authentic version" and for him it was a "masterpiece." Douglas Watt in the *New York Daily News* proclaimed the "masterpiece" was now "revealed grander than ever" and was "being given its full due in an enthralling production." Edwin Wilson in the *Wall Street Journal* said the Houston company came "as close to the heavenly land of American musical theatre as anyone is likely to get." Howard Kissel in *Women's Wear Daily* noted that the production "could not be improved" upon and with its "breathtaking" singing was "the best show in town." David Sterritt in the *Christian Science Monitor* found the work "wholly operatic, yet urgent and direct enough to satisfy any entertainment-craving Broadway audience." And Jack Kroll in *Newsweek* said the production "fills a crucial gap in the history of the American musical theatre" and was the result of the Houston Opera's "labor of loving professionalism," which "took guts as well as talent and money to bring it off."

Martin Gottfried in the *New York Post* noted that Gershwin's score was "the most prodigious ever written by a composer of the American musical theatre." He mentioned that the opera was "sung to the hilt" and even the Uris Theatre's "troublesome acoustics" were "shamed into cooperation." And while the music was "more like Gershwin" than "like black music" and the dialogue was "often a weird, white idea of rural, Southern black speech patterns," he noted that "after all, everything black doesn't have to have the urban soul sound."

After its world premiere in Boston at the Colonial Theatre on September 30, 1935, the original production opened at the Alvin (now Neil Simon) Theatre on October 10, 1935, for 124 performances. Since then, the work has been revived in New York sixteen times and has enjoyed a total of 1,376 performances, a New York record for an American opera. The first revival in 1942 dropped the recitative, more than doubled the run of the original with 286 performances, and for a time held the record as the longest-running New York revival of a musical. During the next two years the opera returned three times, for a total of 88 showings, and the 1953 revival ran for 350 performances and holds the record for the opera's longest Broadway run (this revival restored earlier cuts and added about twenty minutes of music that reportedly had never been heard in any previous production).

The opera was then produced at City Center four times, in 1961, 1962, 1964, and 1965; the first three revivals were sponsored by the New York City Center Light Opera Company and the latter by the New York City Opera Company. After the current 1976 revival, the opera was presented at Radio City Music Hall in 1983, and then by the Metropolitan Opera during the 1984–1985, 1989–1990, and 1990–1991 seasons for a total of fifty-four showings. In 2000 and 2002, the opera was presented by the New York City Opera Company at the New York State Theatre, and in 2012 the work was revived on Broadway where it played for 293 performances and won the Tony Award for Best Revival of a Musical (as did the current 1976 revival).

The lavish 1959 film version released by Columbia Pictures was personally produced by Samuel Goldwyn and directed by Otto Preminger; it has all but disappeared during the past few decades, reportedly because of the Gershwin estate's displeasure with the film (it has never been shown on cable television or released on any home video format). However, the March 20, 2002, performance by the New York City Opera Company was shown live on public television.

Beginning in 1958, the libretto has been published in paperback editions by the Chappell Music Company. There are numerous recordings of the score, including one with many members of the original 1935 and 1942 casts, including Todd Duncan and Anne Brown, both of whom created the original title roles (Decca LP # DL-7-9024), and one of the most complete recordings is EMI's 1985 three-CD set (# CDS-7-49568-2). Joseph Horowitz's *On My Way: The Untold Story of Rouben Mamoulian, George Gershwin, and "Porgy and Bess"* was published in 2013 by W.W. Norton.

Awards

Tony Awards and Nominations: Best Revival (***Porgy and Bess***); Best Leading Actress in a Musical (Clamma Dale); Best Featured Actor in a Musical (Larry Marshall); Best Director of a Musical (Jack O'Brien); Best Scenic Designer (Robert Randolph); Best Costume Designer (Nancy Potts)

SIAMSA

"A Folk Entertainment"

Theatre: Palace Theatre
Opening Date: September 27, 1976; *Closing Date*: October 2, 1976
Performances: 8

Direction: Pat Ahern; *Producer*: Brannigan-Eisler Performing Arts International, Inc.; *Choreography*: Patricia Hanafin; *Costumes*: Phyllis O'Donoghue, Wardrobe Supervisor

Cast: Sean O'Mahony (The Merrymaker), Liam Heaslip (The Gardener), Sean Ahern (The Shoemaker); Solo Dancers: Patricia Hanafin, Jimmy Smith, Jerry Nolan, and John McCarthy; Solo Singers: Mary Deady, Sean Ahern, Liam Heaslip, and Sean O'Mahony; Folk Dancers: Philomena Daly, Susan Rohan, Catherine Hurley, Michael O'Shea, and Aidan O'Carroll; Children: Mary Lyons, Marie O'Donoghue, Sandra O'Reilly, Catherine Spangler, Sean Heaslip, Oliver Hurley, and John Fitzgerald; Musicians: Pat Kennington, Gerald Buckley, Nicholas McAuliffe, Timmy O'Shea, Pierce Heaslip, and Audrey O'Carroll

The revue was presented in two acts.

Musical Numbers

Note: All musical sequences were performed by the entire company.
Act One: "Samhra"
Act Two: "Cois Teallaigh"; "Casadh An tSugain"; "Siamsa an Fomhair"

Siamsa, the National Folk Theatre of Ireland, presented a limited engagement of *Siamsa*, which the program described as "a folk entertainment which recaptures the spirit of the age in Ireland which Irish was the spoken language, the age from which Ireland inherited her great treasure of folk music and song. It aims to show something of the simple way of life of the people who gave her that heritage." The word *siamsa* roughly translates as "an evening of merriment."

The entertainment in the first act was titled "Samhra" (summertime) and depicted the members of a typical Irish homestead going about their daily chores, and by evening they and their neighbors sing love songs and celebrate "traditional bonfire revelry" and worship. The second act included love songs, country dances, and concluded with a traditional harvest festival dance.

Clive Barnes in the *New York Times* found the evening "as beguiling as a troupe of emerald-green leprechauns emerging unexpectedly out of a Celtic mist" and after watching "the absolutely delightful show" he wanted to catch the next plane to Dublin.

A recording taken from a live performance in Kerry, Ireland, was released by Rex Records (LP # SPR-1016). The sequences include dances such as "A Kerry Set" (a polka-like number) and "Biodh Ril Againn" (a set of reels) as well as a ballad about unrequited love ("An Ciarraioch Mallaithe"), a work song ("Amhran na Cuiginne"), and a milking song ("Aililliu na nGamhna"). Another number describes a bird's search for a place to build a nest safe from children ("Gogai O Gaog") and another dealt with a farmer protecting his apple tree from children ("An Crann Ull").

THE ROBBER BRIDEGROOM

Theatre: Biltmore Theatre
Opening Date: October 9, 1976; *Closing Date*: February 13, 1977
Performances: 145
Book and *Lyrics*: Alfred Uhry
Music: Robert Waldman
Based on the 1942 novella *The Robber Bridegroom* by Eudora Welty.

Direction: Gerald Freedman; *Producers*: John Houseman, Margot Harley, and Michael B. Kapon by arrangement with The Acting Company (Porter Van Zandt, Associate Producer); *Choreography*: Donald Saddler; *Scenery*: Douglas W. Schmidt; *Costumes*: Jeanne Button; *Lighting*: David F. Segal; *Musical Direction*: Not credited

Cast: Barry Bostwick (Jamie Lockhart), Stephen Vinovich (Clemment Musgrove), Rhonda Coullet (Rosamund), Barbara Lang (Salome), Lawrence John Moss (Little Harp), Ernie Sabella (Big Harp), Trip Plymale (Goat), Susan Berger (Goat's Mother), Jana Schneider (Airie), Carolyn McCurry (Raven); The Residents of Rodney: George DeLoy (Kyle Nunnery), Gary Epp (Harmon Harper), B. J. Hardin (Norman Ogelsby), Mary

Murray (Queenie Brenner), Melinda Tanner (Rose Otto), Dennis Warning (Gerry G. Summers), Tom Westerman (K. K. Pone); Orchestra: The McVoutie River Volunteers
The musical was presented in one act.
The action takes place in and around Rodney, Mississippi.

Musical Numbers

"Once Upon the Natchez Trace" (Company); "Two Heads" (Ernie Sabella, Lawrence John Moss); "Steal with Style" (Barry Bostwick); "Rosamund's Dream" (Rhonda Coullet); "The Pricklepear Bloom" (Barbara Lang); "Nothin' Up" (Rhonda Coullet); "Deeper in the Woods" (Company); "Riches" (Stephen Vinovich, Barry Bostwick, Barbara Lang, Rhonda Coullet); "Love Stolen" (Barry Bostwick); "Poor Tied Up Darlin'" (Lawrence John Moss, Trip Plymale); "Goodbye, Salome" (Company); "Sleepy Man" (Rhonda Coullet); "Where Oh Where" (Barry Bostwick, Stephen Vinovich, Rhonda Coullet)

The Robber Bridegroom had been presented for a limited engagement at the Harkness Theatre during the previous season (see entry, which also includes more information about the musical).

This time around the production was open-ended, and while it managed only four months on Broadway (and according to *Variety* closed in the red by $363,000), it garnered a Tony Award for Barry Bostwick as Best Leading Actor in a Musical. From the earlier production, Barbara Lang reprised her role of the evil stepmother Salome, and Rhonda Coullet, who had created the role of Rosamund when the musical had first been produced Off Off Broadway in 1975, reprised her original role (for the 1975 production, Patti LuPone portrayed Rosamund).

The current mounting was an expanded version of the previous year's presentation and included four new songs ("Once Upon the Natchez Trace," "Two Heads," "Rosamund's Dream," and "Where Oh Where") and omitted one ("The Real Mike Fink").

Martin Gottfried in the *New York Post* said the musical was as "refreshing" as the previous year's production, and he praised Robert Waldman's "ingenious" score, which was "country and theatrical, melodic and interesting, catchy but not obvious." But the concept of performers in the present day at a square dance reenacting the story of the nineteenth-century gentleman bandit was awkward; the production made almost no use of the square-dance motif and instead the script should have told the story without the confusing concept. Gottfried praised the "wonderful" Barry Bostwick, but reported that the performer had suffered a broken elbow (which had occurred during rehearsals when he had taken a twelve-foot fall onto the stage) and had to perform with his arm in a sling. Presumably many in the audience thought the sling was part of the plot, and Gottfried suggested that a line or two of dialogue should have been added to the script in order to explain the sling.

Clive Barnes in the *New York Times* found the musical "astonishingly deft and smooth" and felt the score "more varied and interesting" than it had been the year before; and T. E. Kalem in *Time* said Gerald Freedman directed at "cannonball pace without sacrificing the illusion that the show is taking place in an enchanted glade." But Christopher Sharp in *Women's Wear Daily* missed the "improvisational" effect of the previous year's production and felt the current one was "too slick and professional."

Douglas Watt in the *New York Daily News* liked the "humdinger" of an evening and singled out "Sleepy Man" as one of the score's best songs. He also noted that the title role was now more "sharply focused," but felt the production stretched out its "thin" story.

A later production played at Ford's Theatre in Washington, D.C., with a cast that included Tom Wopat (Jamie), Rhonda Coullet (Rosamund), and John Goodman (Little Harp). The musical was revived Off Broadway by The Equity Library Theatre on January 6, 1983, for thirty performances and was presented in two acts.

Awards

Tony Award: Best Leading Actor in a Musical (**Barry Bostwick**)

DON'T STEP ON MY OLIVE BRANCH

"A NEW MUSICAL"

Theatre: Playhouse Theatre
Opening Date: November 1, 1976; *Closing Date*: November 14, 1976
Performances: 16
Book: Harvey Jacobs
Lyrics and *Music*: Ron Eliran
Direction and *Choreography*: Jonatan (aka Jonathan) Karmon; *Producers*: The Yael Company and Norman Kean; *Scenery*: James Tilton; *Costumes*: Pierre D'Alby; *Lighting*: William H. Bachelder; *Musical Direction*: David Krivoshei
Cast: Rivka Raz, Ron Eliran, Ruthi Nixon, Riki Gal, Hanan Goldblatt, Gail Benedict, Darleen Boudreaux, Donald Ronci, Karen DiBianco, Carla Farnsworth, David Kottke, Joel Robertson, Lisa Gould Rubin, Daniel Stewart, John Windsor
The revue was presented in one act.

Musical Numbers

Note: The program didn't identify individual singers and dancers for the musical numbers.
"Moonlight"; "The World's Greatest Magical Act"; "I Believe"; "Only Love"; "My Land"; "We Love a Conference"; "Come with Me"; "Tired Heroes"; "Have a Little Fun"; "I Hear a Song"; "I Live My Life in Color"; "Young Days"; "Somebody's Stepping on My Olive Branch"; "It Was Worth It"; "Jerusalem"

Jonatan (Jonathan) Karmon's *Don't Step on My Olive Branch* was a revue that included songs, dance, and commentary about the precarious state of being Jewish and living in the Middle East. Despite the underlying seriousness of the material, the evening was generally satiric in its outlook on politics. An early version of the revue was produced in Israel; the current production was presented in English with five Israeli and ten Broadway cast members.

Clive Barnes in the *New York Times* said the combined cast of Israeli and New York performers blended well and the songs of love, patriotism, and nostalgia were "more pleasing than memorable." The evening was "unabashedly ethnic and partisan" in its attempts at political satire, and the choreography (which he described as a blend of *West Side Story* and *Fiddler on the Roof*) wasn't "unduly subtle." But the production was often "genuinely touching" and he predicted many would enjoy it.

Martin Gottfried in the *New York Post* suggested the "amateurish" revue played "like the floor show at the world's most expensive bar mitzvah" and "if Israel can survive [Karmon's revues], it can survive anything." The score was "watered-down rock songs," the dances were "in the television special vernacular," and the company was "undirected when not misdirected entirely." Douglas Watt in the *New York Daily News* said the evening of "almost suffocating ordinariness" pandered to ethnic theatergoers "with the grinning insincerity of a beggar in a marketplace" and had the "quality of a Las Vegas floor show than of Israeli theatre." Christopher Sharp in *Women's Wear Daily* noted the revue had "the strength and the weakness of a high school pep rally." The strength was "the pluckiness of Israel" in the face of political threats, and the weakness was Karmon's belief that the theme didn't require "theatrical embellishment" and so he "spreads it on a medley of forgettable songs and jokes as if he were spreading peanut butter."

During previews, the revue was presented in two acts (with an intermission between "Jerusalem" and "Tired Heroes"); when the production was condensed into one act, "Jerusalem" was presented as the evening's final number. "Nothing Like Home" was deleted and "I Live My Life in Color" was added. Ron Eliran's 1977 Off-Broadway revue *Nightsong* included seven of his songs from *Don't Step on My Olive Branch* ("I Believe," "My Land," "Come with Me," "Have a Little Fun," "I Hear a Song," "Young Days," and "It Was Worth It").

Don't Step on My Olive Branch was Karmon's sixth and final musical production about Jewish life in the Middle East. The others were the 1962 dance revue *Karmon Israeli Dancers*; *The Grand Music Hall of Israel* (1968); *The New Grand Music Hall of Israel* (1969); ***To Live Another Summer, to Pass Another Winter*** (1971); and a new version of ***The Grand Music Hall of Israel*** (1973).

THE SAINT OF BLEECKER STREET

Theatre: The New York State Theatre
Opening Date: November 5, 1976; *Closing Date*: November 10, 1976
Performances: 3 (in repertory)
Libretto and *Music*: Gian-Carlo Menotti
Direction: Francis Rizzo; *Producer*: The New York City Opera Company; *Scenery*: Beeb Salzer; *Costumes*: Carol Luiken; *Lighting*: Hans Sondheimer; *Musical Direction*: Cal Stewart Kellogg
Cast: Jane Shaulis (Assunta), Howard Hensel (A Young Man), Judith De Rosa (Maria Corona), Ron Boucher (Corona's Son), Diana Soviero (Carmela), Diana Kehrig (A Young Woman), Irwin Densen (Don Marco), Catherine Malfitano (Annina), Enrico DiGiuseppe (Michele), Danielle Brisebois (Concettina), Jeanne Piland (Desideria), Jerold Siena (First Guest), Alan Baker (Second Guest), William Ledbetter (Salvatore), Don Henderson (Bartender), Charlott Thyssen (A Nun), Ronald Kelley (A Young Priest), Kenn Dovel (Neighbor), James Sergi (Neighbor); Neighbors, Friends, Policemen, Others: The New York City Opera Chorus
The opera was presented in three acts.
The action takes place in the Little Italy neighborhood of New York City during the present time.
(The program didn't list musical numbers.)

The New York City Opera Company's production of Gian-Carlo Menotti's *The Saint of Bleecker Street* was the opera's first major New York revival since the company had presented it in 1965. The powerful work was in the *verismo* (or realistic) tradition of Italian opera and centered on the sickly Annina (Catherine Malfitano), whose religious visions, healing powers, and mark of the stigmata are derided by her atheist brother Michele (Enrico DiGiuseppe), who views religion and Anna's desire to become a nun as emblematic of an Old-World culture alien to modern-day America. These differing views erupt in the opera's most vivid sequence, which takes place during Little Italy's San Gennaro festival. The ghetto's devout Catholics revere Annina and claim her as part of their Good Friday procession, but Michele forbids Annina to join them. The participants in the festival then proceed to beat him, handcuff him to a chain-link fence in crucifix fashion, and carry Annina off to the festival.

Later, at a neighborhood wedding, Michele's sluttish girl friend Desideria (Jeanne Piland) accuses him of having incestuous desires for his sister and he stabs her to death. On the run from the law, Michele visits the dying Annina for the last time. The Church has given her special dispensation to join a religious order and so in her last moments she becomes a nun and the Bride of Christ.

The libretto wedded religious mysticism, murder, jealousy, and a semi-incestuous relationship into a powerful and lyrical score that captured the passions of the characters and the milieu of New York's Little Italy with its San Gennaro street festival, an Italian wedding, deserted street corners, and garbage-strewn subway stations (Menotti's insinuating "subway" music for the beginning of the third act was particularly atmospheric).

In reviewing the revival, Allen Hughes in the *New York Times* said Menotti was "so faithful" to the style of Italian operatic realism that the opera had "not dated at all, and it seems unlikely that it ever will. As a matter of fact, the older it gets, the less anachronistic it will seem."

The original production's world premiere took place at the Broadway Theatre on December 27, 1954, for ninety-two performances (the work was billed as "A Musical Drama") and won the New York Drama Critics' Circle Award for Best Musical and the Pulitzer Prize for Best Music.

The opera was first revived by the New York City Opera Company at City Center on March 18, 1965, and on September 29, 1965, for two performances apiece, and after the current production it was revived on April 13, 1978, for three performances (see entry).

The libretto was published in paperback by G. Schirmer, and the original cast album was recorded by RCA Victor Records on a three-LP set (# LM-6032; later reissued on LP # CBM-2714) and later issued on a two-CD set by Arkiv Music/Masterworks Broadway/RCA (# 88697-91220-2). A 2001 production by the Spoleto Festival was recorded on a two-CD set by Chandos Records (# CHAN-9971-2). Ken Wlaschin in *Gian-Carlo Menotti on Screen: Opera, Dance and Choral Works on Film, Television and Video* reports that the opera has been televised in four different adaptations, including one on May 15, 1955, by *NBC Opera Theatre* just six weeks after the opera closed on Broadway and with many of the original cast members. The April 19, 1978, performance by the New York City Opera Company was telecast live on public television.

BING CROSBY ON BROADWAY

Theatre: Uris Theatre
Opening Date: December 7, 1976; *Closing Date*: December 19, 1976
Performances: 12
Direction: Robert Sidney; *Producers*: William Loeb and Robert Paterson; *Lighting*: Martin Aronstein
Cast: *Bing Crosby*, Rosemary Clooney, Joe Bushkin, The Joe Bushkin Quartet, Kathryn Crosby, Harry Crosby III, Mary-Frances Crosby, Nathaniel Crosby, Ted Rogers, The Billy Byers Orchestra
The concert was presented in two acts.

Bing Crosby on Broadway marked the legendary singer and actor's first appearance on the New York stage since he had headlined a stage show at the Paramount in 1931. This time around, he was flanked by two musical groups (the Billy Byers Orchestra and the Joe Bushkin Quartet), his *White Christmas* costar Rosemary Clooney, his wife Kathryn, and their children Harry, Mary-Frances, and Nathaniel, and British comedian Ted Rogers. The concert was presented for a limited engagement of twelve performances, and its net proceeds were earmarked for the Association for the Help of Retarded Children and the Mannes College of Music.

Clive Barnes in the *New York Times* "loved" Crosby's "sweet, accomplished," and "gorgeous" voice. He was still a "great singer" who performed with "astonishing and enchanting skill" and was one of few men who "carry through their voices, and perhaps even more their styles, the remembrances, fantasies and aspirations of a generation."

John Beaufort in the *Christian Science Monitor* found the evening "sentimental and nostalgic," said old troupers didn't fade away, they simply mellowed, and noted Crosby performed with an "effortless ease that is the hallmark of precise and totally mastered technique"; Jan Hodenfield in the *New York Post* said Crosby sounded "terrific" and his "mastery of phrasing and command of every syllable, as he glides through the lower registers, provokes lulled astonishment"; Leonard Probst on NBC Radio praised the "incredibly good" and "remarkable" performer who was "the greatest crooner of them all"; an unsigned review in *Time* said Crosby's baritone "seemed as full as ever"; and Douglas Watt in the *New York Daily News* noted that Crosby's "charm, glibness and deft, easygoing way with a song are still very much in evidence" (but Watt mentioned his surprise that the theatre "was only partially filled, with the rear section practically empty despite reportedly last-minute attempts to 'paper' the house").

With the Joe Bushkin Quartet, Crosby sang an extended medley of his most famous hits, but throughout the evening he performed many other songs, including such recent show and film numbers as "My Cup Runneth Over" (*I Do! I Do!*, 1966; lyric by Tom Jones, music by Harvey Schmidt), "Send in the Clowns" (***A Little Night Music***, 1973; lyric and music by Stephen Sondheim), and "The Way We Were" (1974 film *The Way We Were*; lyric by Marilyn and Alan Bergman, music by Marvin Hamlisch) and two songs from London productions, "The Pleasure of Your Company" (*The Good Companions*, 1974; lyric by Johnny Mercer, music by Andre Previn) and "At My Time of Life" (*Great Expectations*, 1975; lyric by Hal Shaper, music by Cyril Ornadel). With Rosemary Clooney, Crosby sang "On a Slow Boat to China" (lyric and music by Frank Loesser), and Clooney performed her hit "Tenderly" (which had been featured in the campy 1953 Joan Crawford vehicle *Torch Song*; lyric and music by Jack Lawrence and Walter Gross) as well as "By Myself" (*Between the Devil*, 1937; lyric by Howard Dietz, music by Arthur Schwartz). As noted, Crosby sang a generous medley of songs he had popularized over the decades, including, of course, "White Christmas" (1942 film *Holiday Inn*; lyric and music by Irving Berlin).

MUSIC IS

Theatre: St. James Theatre
Opening Date: December 20, 1976; *Closing Date*: December 26, 1976
Performances: 8
Book: George Abbott
Lyrics: Will Holt
Music: Richard Adler
Based on the play *Twelfth Night* by William Shakespeare (written circa 1600 or 1601).

Direction: George Abbott (Judith Abbott, Assistant Director); *Producers*: Richard Adler, Roger Berlind, and Edward R. Downe Jr.; *Choreography*: Patricia Birch; *Scenery*: Eldon Elder; *Costumes*: Lewis D. Rampino; *Lighting*: H. R. Poindexter; *Musical Direction*: Paul Gemignani

Cast: Daniel Ben-Zali (William Shakespeare, Feste [Clown]), William McClary (Valentine), David Holliday (Duke Orsino), David Brummel (Curio, First Officer), Catherine Cox (Viola), Paul Michael (Captain), Laura Waterbury (Maria), David Sabin (Sir Toby Belch), Christopher Hewett (Malvolio), Sherry Mathis (Olivia), Marc Jordan (Antonio), Joel Higgins (Sebastian), Joe Ponazecki (Sir Andrew Aguecheek), Doug Carfrae (Second Officer), Helena Andreyko (Cupid), Ann Crowley (Cupid); Court Musicians: Donald Hettinger (Reeds), Steve Uscher (Guitar); Members of the Court: Helena Andreyko, Doug Carfrae, Jim Corti, Ann Crowley, Dennis Daniels, Dawn Herbert, Dana Kyle, Wayne Mattson, Jason McAuliffe, Carolann Page, Susan Elizabeth Scott, Denny Shearer, Melanie Vaughan, Mimi B. Wallace

The musical was presented in two acts.

The action takes place during the Elizabethan era.

Musical Numbers

Act One: "Music Is" (Daniel Ben-Zali, Company); "When First I Saw My Lady's Face" (David Holliday); "Lady's Choice" (Catherine Cox, Paul Michael); "The Time Is Ripe for Loving" (Company); "Should I Speak of Loving You" (Catherine Cox); "Dance for Six" (Helena Andreyko, Ann Crowley, Mimi B. Wallace, Denny Shearer, Dennis Daniels, Jim Corti); "Hate to Say Good-Bye to You" (Marc Jordan, Joel Higgins); "Big Bottom Betty" (Daniel Ben-Zali); "Twenty-One Chateaux" (Catherine Cox, Sherry Mathis, Company); "Sudden Lilac" (Sherry Mathis); "Sing Hi" (David Sabin, Joe Ponazecki, Daniel Ben-Zali, Laura Waterbury); "Blindman's Bluff" (dance) (Catherine Cox, David Holliday, Company)

Act Two: "The Tennis Song" (David Holliday, William McClary, Company); "I Am It" (Christopher Hewett); "No Matter Where" (Sherry Mathis, Catherine Cox); "The Duel" (David Sabin, Catherine Cox, Joe Ponazecki, Daniel Ben-Zali); "Please Be Human" (Sherry Mathis, Joel Higgins); "What You Will" (Daniel Ben-Zali, Company)

Music Is was a fast-moving, charmingly performed, and melodically impressive version of Shakespeare's *Twelfth Night*. A few critics praised the show and score, but most were in bad humor and failed to appreciate the evening's special qualities. The intimate musical wasn't served well in a large theatre, and one suspects the critical reception would have been more positive had the show opened Off Broadway in a smaller venue such as the Promenade Theatre.

Music Is was George Abbott's second musical inspired by a Shakespearean comedy. In 1938, he directed and wrote the book for Richard Rodgers and Lorenz Hart's *The Boys from Syracuse*, which was based on *The Comedy of Errors*. *Syracuse* was one of the era's biggest hits, but this time around Abbott's book and direction didn't impress most of the critics and the new musical lasted just one week on Broadway (*Variety* reported the musical lost its entire capitalization of $757,300).

The familiar story centered on disguises and mistaken identities when the shipwrecked Viola (Catherine Cox) pretends to be her twin brother Sebastian (Joel Higgins) and soon falls in love with Duke Orsino (David Holliday) who in turn loves Olivia (Sherry Mathis) who in turn falls in love with Viola because she assumes Viola is a man. Meanwhile, Sebastian soon comes upon the scene with his servant Antonio (Marc Jordan) and promptly falls in love with Olivia. The lighthearted plot, the ingratiating performances, the lively choreography by Patricia Birch, the modest yet colorful décor, and Will Holt and Richard Adler's clever and melodic songs provided a delightfully civilized evening. Among the score's highlights were Viola's haunting "Should I Speak of Loving You," one of the most shimmering ballads of the era; "Please Be Human" and "Sudden Lilac" were likewise impressive; the title song was bouncy; and "Hate to Say Good-Bye to You," a comic duet for Sebastian and Antonio, had a flippant lyric and a wound-up hurdy-gurdy melody that could have come from a Marx Brothers' movie.

Martin Gottfried in the *New York Post* said Abbott's dialogue was the "characterless English familiar to students of old musical scripts" and his "inserted jokes" were jokes only "in the technical sense." Richard Adler's "melodic," "pleasant" and "innocuous" score was "odd" with its mixture of traditional show tunes, rock, and Elizabethan-styled numbers, and Will Holt's lyrics were "sappy."

Clive Barnes in the *New York Times* said the evening lacked "tone" and was "like elaborate window dressing without goods." Adler's romantic music was "pleasant," the songs were "appropriately catchy," and the composer had "an ear for lyricism." But overall the score seemed "caught between a lute and an electric guitar" and Holt's lyrics lacked brightness and cleverness. But Barnes singled out "I Am It," which had "the zip of expertise and the zap of conviction." Douglas Watt in the *New York Daily News* suggested there was no reason why another musical version of *Twelfth Night* wasn't welcome, especially since the songs from *Your Own Thing* (a 1968 Off-Broadway version of Shakespeare's comedy) hadn't endured. *Music Is* was "gorgeous" to look at, but required more lift and imagination; however, "Should I Speak of Loving You" and "Please Be Human" had "grace and expressiveness," "Hate to Say Good-bye to You" had spirit, and the dance "Blindman's Bluff" was "lively."

Howard Kissel in *Women's Wear Daily* noted that the musical began in a breezy and droll manner with the cast singing the title song and parading across the stage carrying banners with the names of the show and its creators, a look reminiscent of Tom Morrow's artwork for the original 1956 production of *Candide*. But the "carefree, bouncy," and "engagingly performed" musical was "short on substance." As for the score, "Should I Speak of Loving You" was a "beautiful" ballad and "Please Be Human" a "lovely" duet.

Edwin Wilson in the *Wall Street Journal* admired how Abbott had trimmed Shakespeare's plot "down to musical comedy size" and he even suggested Abbott's ending was "more felicitous than the original." He also liked Adler's "versatile and lively" music, including "two lovely ballads, a rousing quartet number, and several strong comedy songs."

During the tryout, the following songs were cut: "Masquerade," "Paeans of Paradise," "Needing No One," "Time Gone By," and "Isn't It Better to Be a Man."

Soon after the closing, Adler was reportedly approached by a record company that wanted to record the score, but he wasn't open to the idea (perhaps he was still smarting from the musical's dismissively short run). It's a shame, because the album would have introduced the score to a wide audience and once small theatre companies discovered the musical it might have had a busy afterlife in college, community, and regional theatre. Happily, "Shall I Speak of Loving You" was later included in the collection *Shakespeare on Broadway* (Varese Sarabande Records CD # VSD-5622), which also offers two incidental songs composed by Rupert Holmes for a nonmusical version of *Twelfth Night* which was produced by the New York Shakespeare Festival at the Delacorte Theatre in 1986.

Music Is is the third of five musicals that played in New York and were based on *Twelfth Night*. Two opened Off Broadway a few days apart in January 1968: *Love and Let Love* (lyrics by John Lollos and Don Christopher, music by Stanley Jay Gelber) played for 14 performances and *Your Own Thing* (lyrics and music by Hal Hester and Danny Apolinar) played for 933 showings and unaccountably won the New York Drama Critics' Award for Best Musical. Both productions were recorded, but neither can match Adler's score for *Music Is*. A fourth adaptation was a black version titled *Play On!* that opened on Broadway in 1997 for 61 showings; instead of new music, the score consisted by standards by Duke Ellington. A fifth musical titled *What You Will* played Off Off Broadway in 2001 for 17 performances (with an adaptation by Andrew Sherman and Rusty Magee).

BARRY MANILOW ON BROADWAY

Theatre: Uris Theatre
Opening Date: December 21, 1976; *Closing Date*: January 2, 1977
Performances: 12
Special Material: Bruce Sussman
Direction: Jack Hofsiss, "Staging Consultant"; *Producers*: Lee Guber, Shelly Gross, and Miles Lourie; *Choreography*: Barry Manilow and Lady Flash; *Costumes*: Barry Manilow's clothes by Patrick Elliott and Lady Flash's clothes by Arthur Boccia; *Lighting*: Lighting designed by Michael Newton-Brown and lighting supervised by Spencer Mosse; *Musical Direction*: Not credited
Cast: *Barry Manilow*, Lady Flash, Debra Byrd, Reparata, Monica Burruss; the City Rhythm Band: Lee Gurst, Alan Axelrod, Keith Loving, Steven Donaghey, Harold "Ricardo" Alexander
The concert was presented in two acts.

Singer and songwriter Barry Manilow performed a number of popular songs and ballads, and was backed by a few singers and the City Rhythm Band. There weren't any Broadway numbers in his repertoire, but he performed his hits, such as "Mandy" (lyric and music by Scott English and Richard Kerr). Other songs heard during the evening were "This One's for You" (lyric and music by Marty Panzer and Manilow), "Could It Be Magic" (lyric and music by Manilow, Frederic Chopin, and Adrienne Anderson), and "I Write the Songs" (lyric and music by Bruce Johnson).

John Rockwell in the *New York Times* noted Manilow sang with a "pleasantly malleable baritone" and played piano with "great fluency." But too often he came across with "the costuming and stage accoutrements of a Las Vegas middle-of-the-road schlock entertainer" who veered between references to "New York–camp 'trash'" and "the awkward nice guy" image. As a result, it was hard to know what was real and what was calculated; further, Manilow built the "genuinely affecting" sentiments of songs like "Why Don't We Live Together" (lyric and music by Peter Thom and Phil Galston) into "raucous, grandiose production numbers."

Manilow returned to Broadway in his concert *Barry Manilow at the Gershwin*, which opened at the Gershwin Theatre on April 18, 1989, for forty-four performances and in *Barry Manilow's Showstoppers*, which opened at the Paramount Theatre on September 25, 1991, for four performances.

Awards

Tony Award: A special Tony was awarded to Barry Manilow for his concert performance.

YOUR ARMS TOO SHORT TO BOX WITH GOD

"The Songplay for the Seventies!"

Theatre: Lyceum Theatre
Opening Date: December 22, 1976; *Closing Date*: January 1, 1978
Performances: 429
Text: Vinnette Carroll
Lyrics and *Music*: Alex Bradford; additional lyrics and music by Micki Grant; dance music by H. B. Barnum
Based on the *Book of Matthew*.
Direction: Vinnette Carroll; *Producers*: Frankie Hewitt and The Shubert Organization in association with Theatre Now, Inc. (A Ford's Theatre Production); *Choreography*: Talley Beatty; *Scenery* and *Costumes*: William Schroder (Michael Hotopp, "Set Supervisor"); *Lighting*: Gilbert V. Hemsley Jr.; *Choral Direction*: Chapman Roberts
Cast: Featured Soloists—Salome Bey, Clinton Derricks-Carroll, David St. Charles, Sheila Ellis, Delores Hall, William Hardy Jr., Hector Jaime Mercado, Mabel Robinson, and William Thomas Jr.; Deborah Lynn Bridges, Sharon Brooks, Thomas Jefferson Fouse Jr., Michael Gray, Cardell Hall, Bobby Hill, Lidell Jackson, Edna Krider, Leon Washington, Marilyn Winbush
The concert-styled revue was presented in one act.

Musical Numbers

Note: * = Music by Micki Grant; ** = Music by Alex Bradford; *** = Music by H. B. Barnum; **** = Composer unknown.
"Beatitudes" (*) (Company); "We're Gonna Have a Good Time" (*) (Clinton Derricks-Carroll, Company); "There's a Stranger in Town" (**) (Clinton Derricks-Carroll, Bobby Hill, Company); "Do You Know Jesus?" (**) and "He's a Wonder" (**) (Thomas Jefferson Fouse Jr., Company); "Just a Little Bit of Jesus Goes a Long Way" (**) (Delores Hall, Company); "We Are the Priests and Elders" (*) (William Hardy Jr., Clinton Derricks-Carroll, Bobby Hill, Michael Gray); "Something Is Wrong in Jerusalem" (*) (Salome Bey, Mabel Robinson, Company); "It Was Alone" (**) (William Thomas Jr., David St. Charles); "I Ain't Had My Fill" (****) (Clinton Derricks-Carroll, David St. Charles); "Be Careful Whom You Kiss" (**) (Salome Bey,

Company); "I Know I Have to Leave Here" (**) (William Hardy Jr., Company); "It's Too Late" (*) (Company); "Judas Dance" (***) (Hector Jamie Mercado); "Your Arms Too Short to Box with God" (**) (Delores Hall, Company); "Give Us Barabas" (**) (Company); "See How They Done My Lord" (**) (Salome Bey, Company); "Come On Down" (**) (Sheila Ellis, Clinton Derricks-Carroll, Michael Gray); "That's What the Bible Say" (****) (Michael Gray, Company); "Were You There When They Crucified My Lord?" (****) (Salome Bey); "Can't No Grave Hold My Body Down" (**) (Bobby Hill, Company); "Beatitudes" (reprise) (*) (Bobby Hill, Company); "Didn't I Tell You" (**) (William Hardy Jr., Company); "When the Power Comes" (**) (William Hardy Jr., Company); "As Long as I Live" (**) (Salome Bey); "Everybody Has His Own Way" (**) (Clinton Derricks-Carroll, Michael Gray, Thomas Jefferson Fouse Jr.); "I Love You So Much Jesus" (**) (Delores Hall, Company); "I Left My Sins Behind Me" (****) (Delores Hall, Company); "On That Day" (**) (Clinton Derricks-Carroll, Thomas Jefferson Fouse Jr., Bobby Hill, Michael Gray); "The Band" (**) (William Hardy Jr., Company)

The apostrophe-challenged *Your Arms Too Short to Box with God* was a gospel song cycle loosely adapted from the *Book of Matthew.* It seemed to aspire to be a black version of ***Jesus Christ Superstar*** and ***Godspell***, the latter of which had transferred from Off Broadway to Broadway earlier in the season. Although the former had been overproduced and the latter had major structural problems, their scores were at least varied, ***Superstar*** with rock-styled music which veered occasionally into operatic-like moments and traditional Broadway numbers and ***Godspell*** with light gospel and traditional theatre music.

But *Your Arms Too Short to Box with God* was a full evening of gospel-styled singing, foot-stomping, and hand-clapping, all of which soon became monotonous; it would have helped if Alex Bradford and Micki Grant's score had been stronger and more inventive, but the evening was too one-note and quickly became tiresome. With a few exceptions, the critics gushed over the evening and treated it as the Second Coming.

The production took place in a church in which the parishioners reenact the story of Christ's Passion. The character of Jesus never spoke or sang, and the major solo dance was by Judas. At the conclusion of the revue and once Matthew's story had been reenacted, the evening for some reason morphed into a tribute to singers such as Mahalia Jackson and Louis Armstrong.

Martin Gottfried in the *New York Post* complained that the production lacked theatricality and its high spirits became "monotonous"; further, the music wasn't "all that good" and the choreography was sometimes "embarrassing examples of what used to be called interpretive dance." Despite the "fine" singing, the show "was not enough to be theatre." Edwin Wilson in the *Wall Street Journal* said the production "overreaches" with its "incessant roll of kettle drums and a clashing of cymbals" whenever "something important is to happen" and the evening's coda, which saluted Louis Armstrong and other gospel-styled singers seemed unnecessary. Christopher Sharp in *Women's Wear Daily* suggested that if ***Jesus Christ Superstar*** wasn't your idea of "fun," then *Your Arms Too Short,* which owed the earlier rock musical a "huge debt," would "seem even more tedious." Because ***Superstar*** wasn't "solid enough" to "warrant imitations," the new musical's "attempt to emulate [***Superstar***] is like grafting jelly onto Jello."

But the remaining critics wrote valentines. Clive Barnes in the *New York Times* praised the "festive occasion" and "infectious happiness" of the "enchanted" evening. John Beaufort in the *Christian Science Monitor* said the work's "impact is irresistible" and was "something special to celebrate." Jack Kroll in *Newsweek* hailed the "irresistible" show and said "no one knows how to energize a stage better than" Vinnette Carroll, whose "combination of religious fervor with joyous and intelligent sensuality is a delightful characteristic of her shows." T. E. Kalem in *Time* found the production "luminous," while Bob Lape on WABCTV7 liked the production's "totally infectious" and "irresistible momentum and heart," and Leonard Probst on NBC Radio said the musical was "sizzling" (and made the strange comment that it was "sort of like a black *Fiddler on the Roof*").

Prior to the New York production, the musical had premiered at the Festival of Two Worlds, Spoleto, Italy, in Summer 1975 and then was produced at Ford's Theatre in Washington, D.C.

Songs dropped prior to the Broadway opening (all of which had lyrics and music by Alex Bradford) were: "Hail the Saviour Prince of Peace," "There Are Days I'd Like to Be," "See How They Done My Lord," "Somebody Here Don't Believe in Jesus," "What Have I Done to Thee," "Following Jesus," "I Know He'll Look Out for Me," "How Can I Make It," and "The Hour of Darkness" (dance).

The cast album was recorded by ABC Records (LP # AB-1004).

The musical was revived on Broadway twice. The first opened at the Ambassador Theatre on June 2, 1980, for 149 performances; and the second at the Alvin Theatre on September 9, 1982, for 70 performances with a cast that included Patti LaBelle and Al Green.

In later productions, the following songs were added: "Trial" (*), "Me and Jesus" (*), "I Know I Have to Leave Here" (**), "Running for Jesus" (**), "Couldn't Keep It to Myself," (**) "Veil of the Temple" (****), and "Down by the Riverside" (traditional). Later productions were restructured into two acts.

Awards

Tony Awards and Nominations: Best Featured Actress in a Musical (**Delores Hall**); Best Director of a Musical (Vinnette Carroll); Best Choreographer (Talley Beatty)

FIDDLER ON THE ROOF

"A MUSICAL"

Theatre: Winter Garden Theatre
Opening Date: December 28, 1976; *Closing Date*: May 21, 1977
Performances: 167
Book: Joseph Stein
Lyrics: Sheldon Harnick
Music: Jerry Bock
Based on various short stories by Sholem Aleichem.
Direction: Ruth Mitchell (reproduced from the original direction by Jerome Robbins); *Producers*: The Shubert Organization & Nederlander Producing Company of America, Inc., and The John F. Kennedy Center for the Performing Arts in association with Theatre Now, Inc.; *Choreography*: Tom Abbott (who reproduced the original choreography by Jerome Robbins); *Scenery*: Boris Aronson; *Costumes*: Patricia Zipprodt; *Lighting*: Ken Billington; *Musical Direction*: Milton Rosenstock
Cast: *Zero Mostel* (Tevye), Thelma Lee (Golde), Elizabeth Hale (Tzeitel), Christopher Callan (Hodel), Nancy Tompkins (Chava), Davia Sacks (Shprintze), Tiffany Bogart (Bielke), Ruth Jaroslow (Yente), Irwin Pearl (Motel), Jeff Keller (Perchik), Leon Spelman (Mordcha), Paul Lipson (Lazar Wolf), Charles Meyer (Rabbi), Paul A. Corman (Mendel), Merrill Plaskow II (Avram), David Masters (Nachum), Duane Bodin (Grandma Tzeitel, Yussel), Joyce Martin (Fruma Sarah, Rivka), Alexander Orfaly (Constable), Rick Friesen (Fyedka), Jeanne Grant (Shandel), Sammy Bayes (The Fiddler), Matthew Inge (Shloime), Don Tull (Yitzuk), Glen McClaskey (Chaim), Wallace Munro (Duvidel, Sasha), Lynn Archer (Surcha, Sima), Tog Richards (Label), David Horwitz (Schmeril), Patrick Quinn (Yakov), Myron Curtis (Hershel), Hope Katcher (Fredel), Debra Timmons (Bluma), Maureen Sadusk (Mirala), Robert L. Hultman (Vladimer), Shelley Wolf (Bascha), Neal Thompson (Pinchas), Lorenzo Bianco (Igor), Annette Pirrone (Lifsha), John Kirshy (Baruch); Bottle Dancers: Tog Richards, Myron Curtis, Matthew Inge, Wallace Munro
The musical was presented in two acts.
The action takes place in the Russian village of Anatevka during 1905, on the eve of the revolutionary period.

Musical Numbers

Act One: "Tradition" (Zero Mostel, Villagers); "Matchmaker, Matchmaker" (Elizabeth Hale, Christopher Callan, Nancy Tompkins); "If I Were a Rich Man" (Zero Mostel); "Sabbath Prayer" (Zero Mostel, Thelma Lee, Villagers); "To Life" (Zero Mostel, Paul Lipson, Villagers); "Miracle of Miracles" (Irwin Pearl); "The Tailor, Motel Kamzoil" (Zero Mostel, Thelma Lee, Duane Bodin, Joyce Martin, Villagers); "Sunrise, Sunset" (Zero Mostel, Thelma Lee, Villagers); "Bottle Dance" (Tog Richards, Myron Curtis, Matthew Inge, Wallace Munro); "Wedding Dance" (Villagers)
Act Two: "Now I Have Everything" (Jeff Keller, Christopher Callan); "Do You Love Me?" (Zero Mostel, Thelma Lee); "Far From the Home I Love" (Christopher Callan); "Chava" (Zero Mostel); "Anatevka"

(Zero Mostel, Thelma Lee, Ruth Jaroslow, Paul Lipson, Paul A. Corman, Merrill Plaskow II); "Epilogue" (Company)

The revival of *Fiddler on the Roof* was a first-class production that could have been a brand-new musical receiving its first Broadway showing. There was nothing tired or slipshod here: Boris Aronson's original scenic designs in the style of Marc Chagall, Patricia Zipprodt's evocative and colorful costumes, a huge company, and an authentic reproduction of Jerome Robbins's original direction and choreography made this the most definitive *Fiddler* revival Broadway will ever see. And the crowning glory of the production was Zero Mostel, the original Tevye, re-creating one of the greatest of all Broadway musical roles. Mostel was as fresh and funny and touching as he had been in 1964, and the revival gave audiences one final opportunity to see the master clown in one of his legendary performances. The production had been touring for a few months, and now the show's final booking was the current five-month engagement at the Winter Garden.

The musical's concept was that of change, and its brilliant opening number "Tradition" dealt with that theme. The plot looked at the personal changes in Tevye's well-ordered, Jewish Orthodox life: one daughter moves away to be with her husband, and another marries a gentile. And there are the frightening political changes: Tevye and the villagers of Anatevka must first endure pogroms and then are forced to leave their homeland. Some plan to immigrate to the United States while others head for middle Europe, and a special poignancy resulted when one realized that by escaping the ravages of the Russian pogroms, many of the villagers were walking right into the Holocaust that would soon envelop Europe.

Douglas Watt in the *New York Daily News* praised Mostel's "masterful" performance, but commented that *Fiddler* itself wasn't a "masterpiece" because Joseph Stein's book was "crowded with incident" and was sometimes too "gaggy," and thus was "unable to contain all the events comfortably, to do them justice"; Jack Kroll in *Newsweek* said *Fiddler* was "a terrific piece of work" and Mostel's was "one of the gigantic performances of our time"; and Martin Gottfried in the *New York Post* noted that Mostel "owns the role of Tevye" and his "stagemanship is tremendous."

The original production opened on September 22, 1964, at the Imperial Theatre for 3,242 performances and has been revived on Broadway four times. Besides the current revival, the others opened on July 9, 1981, at the New York State Theatre for 53 performances (Herschel Bernardi was Tevye); on November 18, 1990, at the Gershwin Theatre for 240 performances (Topol aka Chaim Topol); and on February 26, 2004, at the Minskoff Theatre for 781 performances (Alfred Molina); the latter included "Topsy-Turvy," a new and minor song by Jerry Bock and Sheldon Harnick. The original production won nine Tony Awards, including Best Musical, and also won the New York Drama Critics' Circle Award for Best Musical.

The first London production opened at Her Majesty's Theatre on February 16, 1967, for 2,030 performances with Topol, and the bloated and dreary film version, which was released by United Artists in 1971, was directed by Norman Jewison and starred Topol.

The script was first published in hardback in 1965 by Crown, and is also one of sixteen scripts included in the 2014 Library of Congress collection *American Musicals*. A fascinating account of the musical is *The Making of a Musical: "Fiddler on the Roof"* by Richard Altman and Mervyn Kaufman (Crown, 1971), and two other books about the production are Alisa Solomon's *Wonder of Wonders: A Cultural History of "Fiddler on the Roof"* (Henry Holt, 2013) and Barbara Isenberg's *Tradition!: The Highly Improbable, Ultimately Triumphant Broadway-to-Hollywood Story of "'Fiddler on the Roof," The World's Most Beloved Musical* (St. Martin's, 2014).

The original Broadway cast album was released by RCA Victor Records (LP # LSO/LOC-1093), and RCA's CD (# 51430) includes "I Just Heard," which had been recorded for the 1964 cast album session but hadn't been included on the LP release because of space limitations (the song was also omitted from the current Broadway revival). There are numerous recordings of the score, many of which offer cut songs (such as "If I Were a Woman," "When Messiah Comes," "Dear Sweet Sewing Machine," and "A Little Bit of This") as well as music not recorded for the original cast album ("Wedding Dance" and the Chava sequence).

In his review of the revival, Watt noted Mostel had to leave the production in late May in order to begin preparing for a role in a new play. This was Arnold Wesker's *The Merchant*, which opened on Broadway at the Plymouth Theatre on November 16, 1977, for five performances. Sadly, Mostel died during the drama's Philadelphia tryout (he was succeeded by Joseph Leon), and so the *Fiddler* revival was his last New York appearance in a Broadway career that spanned thirty-five years.

IPI-TOMBI

Theatre: Harkness Theatre
Opening Date: January 12, 1977; *Closing Date*: February 13, 1977
Performances: 39
Lyrics: Gail Lakier
Music: Bertha Egnos
Direction: Not credited (probably Bertha Egnos); *Producers*: A. Deshe (Pashanel) and (Chaim) Topol by arrangement with Ray Cooney Productions, Ltd., and Academy and Brooke Theatre, Johannesburg (A Bertha Egnos Production); *Choreography*: Sheila Wartski (additional choreography by Neil McKay and cast members); *Scenery*: Elizabeth MacLeish (American scenic supervision by Robert Mitchell); *Costumes*: Costume Supervision by David Toser; *Lighting*: Timothy Heale and John Wain (American lighting supervision by Jeremy Johnson); *Musical Direction*: Not credited
Cast: Count Wellington Judge, Daniel Pule, Jabu Mbalo, Matthew Bodibe, Gideon Bendile, Elliot Ngubane, Andrew Kau, Sam Hlatschwayo, Philip Gama, David Mthethwa, Shadrack Moyo, Martha Molefe, Dorcas Faku, Lydia Monamodi, Busi Dlamini, Zelda Funani, Thembi Mtshali, Linda Tshabalala, Betty-Boo Hlela, Dudu Nzimande, Coreen Pike, Nellie Khumalo; Junior Tshanalala (Chief Drummer), Simon Nkosi (Drummer), Ali Lerefolo (Drummer)
The revue was presented in two acts.

Musical Numbers

Note: The program didn't identify names of the performers for the musical sequences.
Act One: Overture: "Ipi-tombi" ("Where Are the Girls?"); "Sesiyahamba" ("We Are Going About Our Labors"); "Hamba bhekile" ("Let the Drinks Be Served"); "Uthando luphelile" ("Love Is Lost, Love Is Gone"); "Madiwa-madiwa" ("Calling for Rain"); "Qhobosha" ("The Unfaithful One Will Die"); "Mokhibo" ("The Sotho Girls' Dance"); "Ntaba zenyuka" ("The Mountains Are High"); "Orgy, The Temptress"; "Moriva"; "Shamanile"; "Shangaan" ("A Dance of Happiness"); "Nadia" ("Song of Hope"); "Emdudeni" ("Street Sweepers"); "Oo-le-le"; "A Xhosa Proposition"; "The Refuse Collectors"; "Arieni" ("Let's Dance"); "Gum Boot Dance"; "Ipi-Tombi" (reprise)
Act Two: "Bayakhala" ("The Child"); "Mama Tembu's Wedding"; "Baby Baby"; "Phata phata" ("Touch Touch"); "Wishing"; "Zimbaba"; "Baby Baby" (reprise); "Shosholoza" ("A Work Song"); "Going Home"; "The Warriors" (dance)

The South African revue *Ipi-tombi* had originally premiered in Johannesburg at the Brooke Theatre in March 1974, and a later production was still playing in London when the short-lived Broadway version opened. The virtually plotless evening, which compared life in a small African village to that of a large city like Johannesburg, consisted of dances, songs, and rituals associated with village life and included work songs, gum boot dances, warrior dances, baptism rituals, weddings, and pleas for rain. There was even a "click" number in which members of the cast spoke in the clicking sounds of the Xhosa tongue, and there was a sequence that contrasted the ancient practices of witch doctors with modern-day Christianity.

The evening was an attempt to capture the folk culture of the Zulu population much in the same manner that ***Siamsa*** had looked at Ireland's musical heritage and the way that many Israeli and New York revues viewed the shtetl life of European Jews before the Holocaust swept away much of that culture.

The program twice noted that the revue's title translated as "Where Are the Girls?," but in an early example of political correctness one critic apparently couldn't bear the horror of such a title and so referred to the evening as "Where Are the Women?"

In general, the reviewers felt the production was too monotonous in its presentation and theme. Martin Gottfried in the *New York Post* said the material was "superficial" and "perfectly harmless," but the company's voices were "rich and fine" and the dancing was "often exciting" and "culturally interesting." Clive Barnes in the *New York Times* said the dancing was "moderately good" but "everything else" was "tedious." Douglas Watt in the *New York Daily News* felt the show offered "surprisingly little over-all excitement" and noted the dancing was "lively enough," but otherwise much of the material "meant little to most members of the audience." T. E. Kalem in *Time* found the cast "breathtaking" in their "agility, grace and energy" and said the "Dionysian frenzy" of the warrior dance was the "best" part of the evening. Bob Lape on WABCTV7 also praised the warrior dance and felt it was "as exciting a piece of stagecraft as you'll see." And while Leonard Probst on NBC Radio liked the "energetic" dances and "colorful" costumes, he found the revue "tiresome" and "disappointing" with an "endless, pointless, and sometimes joyless quality."

The offstage drama surrounding *Ipi-tombi* was perhaps more exciting than anything onstage. Controversy swirled around the production, and the performances were picketed by the Patrice Lumumba Coalition and the Socialist Workers Party, both of which alleged that the revue served as a propaganda piece for South Africa's apartheid policies. The pickets tried to discourage audiences from seeing the show, and they hoped to close it down. For whatever reasons, the show closed after five weeks and according to *Variety* lost its investment of $327,300.

But John Beaufort in the *Christian Science Monitor* felt it was unfair that visiting black South African performers should be victimized by "the crossfire of a propaganda campaign by black American activists against the racist policies of the South African government." Barnes wryly noted that in the past artistic groups from many oppressive regimes had heretofore played in New York without protests. Indeed, the Moiseyev dance troupe and the Bolshoi Ballet had performed in Broadway theatres and at the old Met, and political activists were noticeably silent that the companies came from a country that embraced oppressive and totalitarian Stalinist policies.

The producers of *Ipi-tombi* distributed literature explaining that the revue was privately produced and was not sponsored or supported by the South African government, and that in fact the South African government "would not be disturbed at all if *Ipi-tombi* were closed and left Broadway and returned home" (the reviewers noted that the current production *included* three numbers that had been censored by the South African government because of their political content). The producers stated that the revue's intention was to preserve African music and dance, and that the cast members were under full American Actors' Equity Association contracts.

Edwin Wilson in the *Wall Street Journal* said a musical should be judged on its content, not on the political policies of its native country. He noted that audiences attend *Oklahoma!* without focusing on the U.S. government's treatment of American Indians and that *My Fair Lady* is enjoyed without worrying about Great Britain's "colonial wars." Wilson also noted that the black South African performers in *Ipi-tombi* were at a loss to understand "their strange welcome to the U.S." and he criticized the "hysterical demeanor" of the protestors, whose views "preclude any enjoyment of art or thought that isn't pointed against the injustice of the hour."

The South African cast recording was released on a two-LP set by Ashtree Records (# ASH-26000).

A PARTY WITH BETTY COMDEN AND ADOLPH GREEN

Theatre: Morosco Theatre (during run, the concert transferred to the Little Theatre)
Opening Date: February 10, 1977; *Closing Date*: April 30, 1977
Performances: 92
Lyrics: Betty Comden and Adolph Green
Music: See song list for names of composers.
Technical Direction: Mitch Miller; *Producers*: Arthur Cantor and Leonard Friedman; *Costumes*: Betty Comden's gowns by Donald Brooks; *Lighting*: Andrea Wilson
Cast: *Betty Comden, Adolph Green*; Paul Trueblood (Piano)

Musical Numbers

Note: All numbers were performed by Betty Comden and Adolph Green, who were accompanied by Paul Trueblood at the piano; all the lyrics were by Comden and Green and all the Revuers' sketches by the Revuers [Comden, Green, John Frank, Alvin Hammer, and Judy Tuvim, who later changed her last name to Holiday]. The list below of the material presented during the performance is given chronologically.

Sketches from the Revuers (nightclub act, early 1940s): "The Reader's Digest," "The Screen Writers" (aka "Beautiful Girls"), "The Banshee Sisters," and "The Baroness Bazooka" (The latter was a spoof of operettas and had been performed by the Revuers during the 1942 pre-Broadway tryout of *My Dear Public*, which closed prior to Broadway. A revised edition opened in New York the following year, but without the Revuers and "The Baroness Bazooka.");

On the Town (1944; music by Leonard Bernstein; book by Comden and Green): "New York, New York," "Lonely Town," "Lucky to Be Me," "Some Other Time," and "Carried Away";

Bonanza Bound (1947; music by Saul Chaplin; book by Comden and Green): "Inspiration" (The musical closed during its pre-Broadway tryout, and Adolph Green, who was in the cast, sang the number with his then-wife Allyn Ann McLerie.);

Good News (1947 film; screenplay by Comden and Green): "The French Lesson" (music by Roger Edens);

Two on the Aisle (1951; music by Jule Styne; sketches by Comden and Green): "If" (aka "If You Hadn't, But You Did") and "Catch Our Act at the Met";

Wonderful Town (1953; music by Leonard Bernstein): "A Hundred Easy Ways to Lose a Man," "Ohio," and "Wrong Note Rag";

Peter Pan (1954; music by Jule Styne): "Captain Hook's Waltz," "Never Never Land," and "Mysterious Lady";

It's Always Fair Weather (1955 film; screenplay by Comden and Green; music by Andre Previn): "I Said Good Morning" (The song was written for, but not used in, the film.);

Bells Are Ringing (1956; music by Jule Styne; book by Comden and Green): "Just in Time" and "The Party's Over";

Do Re Mi (1960; music by Jule Styne): "Make Someone Happy";

Subways Are for Sleeping (1961; music by Jule Styne; book by Comden and Green): "Capital Gains" (aka "Swing Your Projects"); and

Straws in the Wind (1975; music by Cy Coleman): "The Lost Word" and "Simplified Language" (The revue played Off Broadway at the American Place Theatre for thirty-four subscription performances, but never held an official opening night for the critics.)

Lyricists and performers (as well as writers of sketches, books of musicals, and screenplays) Betty Comden and Adolph Green brought their welcome party to Broadway almost twenty years after their first one. The wait was too long. The two were extraordinarily ingratiating, and they chatted about their stage and film musicals and presented a generous sampling of their material on a stage devoid of scenery except for two bar stools. There was no orchestra, and they were accompanied only by Paul Trueblood on the piano.

Comden and Green were natural performers, and had first appeared in nightclubs as part of the Revuers, and from there wrote the book and lyrics for their first Broadway musical *On the Town* (1944) in which they also created the comic roles of Claire de Loone and Ozzie. As the years went by, they wrote the lyrics and sometimes books for a number of Broadway musicals as well as occasional screenplays, including two classic 1950s MGM musicals, *Singin' in the Rain* (1952) and *The Band Wagon* (1953). For *Singin' in the Rain*, they also wrote the lyric for "Moses" (music by Roger Edens). Their longest-running Broadway musical *The Will Rogers Follies* opened in 1991 and played for 983 performances.

Clive Barnes in the *New York Times* said Comden and Green were "fantastic performers" with "dazzling charm," and were the kind of entertainers "you would really like to invite into your home" because they were "clearly having such a good time"; Douglas Watt in the *New York Daily News* praised the twosome, who blended together well with her "ineffable calm" and his "craziness" and "manic charm"; Charles Michener in *Newsweek* said the "smashing bash" filled the theatre with "a spectacle that puts most recent million-dollar musicals to shame," and he noted that Comden and Green brought fresh meaning to the word "class"; Gerald Clarke in *Time* felt that "rarely has so much wit and fun been packed into two hours"; John Beaufort in the *Christian Science Monitor* said it was "hard to imagine a more enjoyable evening," and he singled out the tongue-twisting madness of "If" ("an effusion of daffily spiffy iffiness"); and Howard Kissel in *Women's Wear Daily* said the two "superb" performers were the best interpreters of the "sparkle" and "giddy charms" of their material.

Martin Gottfried in the *New York Post* praised the "easygoing and delightful" retrospective and noted that few recent lyricists could "match their wit and honest intelligence." But he wondered if some of their more recent (and disappointing) shows were the result of "mismatings with composers." Jule Styne was their most frequent collaborator, but their best work was with Leonard Bernstein (*On the Town* and *Wonderful*

Town), and Styne's best scores (*Gypsy* and *Funny Girl*) were with other lyricists. He too liked the yin and yang of the two performers, and he noted that Comden had a "certain formal distance" about her which complemented Green's "exuberance."

The team had first performed an evening of their songs and sketches Off Broadway at the Cherry Lane Theatre in *Betty Comden and Adolph Green in a Program of Their Own Material*, which opened on November 10, 1958, and played for approximately five consecutive Monday night performances. From there, the revue opened at the John Golden Theatre on December 23, 1958, for thirty-eight performances and then reopened at the same theatre on April 16, 1959, for forty-four more showings for a total run of eighty-two performances.

The original cast recording was released by Capitol Records (LP # SWAO-1197; CD by Broadway Angel Records # 764773) and was taken from a live performance. The 1977 revival was issued by Stet Records on a two-LP set (# S2L-5177) which was recorded live at Arena Stage, Washington, D.C., on May 1, 1977 (the two-CD set was released by DRG Records # 5177).

PIAF . . . A REMEMBRANCE

Theatre: The Playhouse
Opening Date: February 14, 1977; *Closing Date*: March 5, 1977
Performances: 21
Play: David Cohen
Lyrics and *Music*: See song list below for specific credits.
Direction: Lee Rachman; *Producers*: Michael Ross and Eddie Vallone; *Scenery* and *Lighting*: Ralph Alswang; *Costumes*: Robert Troie; *Musical Direction*: John Marino
Cast: Gregory Salata (Theo Sarapo), Edmund Lyndeck (Louis Leplee), Lou Bedford (Marcel Cerdan), Juliette Koka (Edith Piaf), Douglas Andros (Loulou Barrier), Donald Hampton (Henri, Doctor)
The play with music was presented in two acts.

Musical Numbers

Note: All songs were performed by Juliette Koka.

Act One: "Padam" (lyric and music by Norbert Glanzberg and Henri Contet); "Bal dans ma rue" (lyric and music by Michel Emer); "L'etranger" (lyric by Robert Malleron, music by Marguerite Monnot); "Bravo pour le clown" (lyric and music by Henri Contet and Louiguy); "Mon Dieu" (lyric and music by Charles Dumont and Michel Vaucaire); "L'accordioniste" (lyric and music by Michel Emer); "Mon ménage à moi" (lyric by Jean Constantin, music by Norbert Glanzberg); "Milord" (lyric by G. Moustaki, music by Marguerite Monnot)

Act Two: "La vie en rose" (lyric by Edith Piaf, music by Louiguy); Medley: "Les trios cloches" (lyric and music by J. Villard and B. Reisfeld); "Under Paris Skies" ("Sous le ciel de Paris") (lyric and music by Jean Drejac and Hubert Giraud); "La goulante de pauvre Jean" (lyric by P. de Lange and possibly cowritten with R. Roulaud, music by Marguerite Monnot); "Hymne a l'amour" (lyric by Edith Piaf, music by Marguerite Monnot); "La foule" ("Carnival") (lyric and music by Michel Rivgauche, Charles Dumont, and possibly A. Cabral); "Les blouses blanches" ("The Ones in White") (lyric by Michel Rivgauche, music by Marguerite Monnot); "Non, je ne regrette rien" (lyric and music by Charles Dumont and Michel Vaucaire)

Piaf . . . A Remembrance was an evening that depicted the life and songs of Edith Piaf (1915–1963), who was otherwise known as the "Little Sparrow." The chanteuse divided her critics: some thought she was the eminent interpreter of melancholy song, but others found her pretentious and overly dramatic. Juliette Koka had put together an evening of Piaf's songs and had performed them in a New Jersey nightclub, and when the current production was in the offing, she was chosen to play the title role.

The evening was essentially a recital by Koka which was punctuated by comments from three men who played major roles in her life, Louis Leplee (Edmund Lyndeck), who discovered her; Marcel Cerdan (Lou Bedford), a prizefighter with whom she had an affair; and Theo Sarapo (Gregory Salata), a singer and hairdresser with whom she apparently had a conflicted relationship. As they spoke, all the men stood behind a scrim on platforms high above both the stage and the on-stage band; they also seem to have occasionally intoned the word "Piaf" over and over ("pure off-off Broadway," complained Martin Gottfried in the *New York Post*).

Mel Gussow in the *New York Times* noted Koka was "a reasonably good singer" but he wasn't "convinced" by her acting; as for the play itself, it was "a maudlin B-movie biography" and author David Cohen should have eliminated the gimmick of the three men and "got himself a new typewriter." Douglas Watt in the *New York Daily News* said the evening was a "foolhardy enterprise" and a "gigantic mistake," and while Piaf was "a presence and incomparable," Koka was "scarcely even a shadow." Howard Kissel in *Women's Wear Daily* said the "travesty" had a "cliché-ridden" and "amateurish" script and "leaden" direction.

But Bob Lape on WABCTV7 found the evening "pure magic" and an "absolute delight" and said Koka was "the belle of Broadway" with her "memorable" performance. Gottfried commented that Koka was an "utter discovery" and a "rather remarkable singer" who sent "electricity through the house almost every time she sings." As for the "unimaginatively constructed" book, "it could pass for educational television."

Koka returned as Piaf in *Piaf . . . Remembered*, which opened at the Theatre Arielle on June 16, 1993, for 175 performances. Piaf has in fact become something of a cottage industry, and some two-dozen plays, films, and ballets are about her. Besides the two separate evenings that featured Koka, there were the Off-Off-Broadway *Dear Piaf* (The Theatre at Mama Gail's, December 29, 1975, for 74 performances); the London import *Piaf* by Pam Gems, which opened on Broadway (Plymouth Theatre, February 5, 1981, for 165 performances and won Jane Lapotaire a Tony Award for Best Leading Actress in a Play); the 2007 film *La vie en rose* (for which Marion Cotillard won the Academy Award for Best Actress); and the 2007 Off-Broadway self-described "musical drama" *Piaf: Love Conquers All* by Roger Peace (Soho Playhouse, December 8, 2007, for a two-month limited engagement). After all this, one can only paraphrase the title of a 1962 Off-Broadway musical and say *Fly, Sparrow*.

I LOVE MY WIFE

"A NEW MUSICAL"

Theatre: Ethel Barrymore Theatre
Opening Date: April 17, 1977; *Closing Date*: May 20, 1979
Performances: 872
Book and *Lyrics*: Michael Stewart
Music: Cy Coleman
Based on the 1975 play *Viens chez moi, J'habite chez une copine* by Luis Rego.
Direction: Gene Saks; *Producers*: Joseph Kipness, Terry Allen Kramer, and Harry Rigby (Frank Montalvo, Associate Producer); *Choreography*: Onna White; *Scenery*: David Mitchell; *Costumes*: Ron Talsky; *Lighting*: Gilbert V. Hemsley Jr.; *Musical Direction*: John Miller
Cast: Ilene Graff (Cleo), Joanna Gleason (Monica), James Naughton (Wally), Michael Mark (Stanley), Joe Saulter (Quentin), John Miller (Harvey), Ken Bichel (Norman), Lenny Baker (Alvin)
The musical was presented in two acts.
The action takes place during the present time in Trenton, New Jersey.

Musical Numbers

Act One: "We're Still Friends" (Company); "Monica" (Lenny Baker, Joanna Gleason, The Four Guys); "By Threes" (James Naughton, Lenny Baker, John Miller); "A Mover's Life" (Lenny Baker, The Four Guys); "Love Revolution" (Ilene Graff); "Someone Wonderful I Missed" (Joanna Gleason, Ilene Graff); "Sexually Free" (Lenny Baker, Ilene Graff, James Naughton)

Act Two: "Hey There, Good Times" (John Miller, Michael Mark, Joe Saulter, Ken Bichel); "Lovers on Christmas Eve" (Joanna Gleason, James Naughton, Ken Bichel); "Scream" (John Miller, Michael Mark, Joe Saulter, Ken Bichel); "Everybody Today Is Turning On" (Lenny Baker, James Naughton); "Married Couple Seeks Married Couple" (Lenny Baker, Ilene Graff, James Naughton, Joanna Gleason); "I Love My Wife" (Lenny Baker, James Naughton)

A small-scale musical about wife-swapping in New Jersey didn't sound all that promising, but Cy Coleman and Michael Stewart's *I Love My Wife* fooled everyone and became a surprise hit that ran over two years and was one of Coleman's longest-running Broadway musicals. The show was the first in a trio of hit musicals to open in April, and was followed within a few days by ***Side by Side by Sondheim*** and ***Annie***. But *I Love My Wife* now seems to have fallen off the theatrical radar and has become something of a forgotten hit.

Based on a French farce, the story was reset in Trenton and focused on would-be swinger Wally (James Naughton), who suggests to his inhibited buddy Alvin (Lenny Baker) that they and their respective wives Monica (Joanna Gleason) and Cleo (Ilene Graff) form a sexual foursome. But despite such songs as "By Threes," "Love Revolution," "Sexually Free," "Married Couple Seeks Married Couple," and "Everybody Today Is Turning On," the couples remained properly and suburbanly chaste and the evening ended with Wally and Alvin's singing the title song to their wives.

With just four characters and no real production numbers, the small musical might have fared even better in an Off-Broadway house, but with good reviews and its offbeat subject matter the musical caught on and chalked up a total of 872 performances. The score didn't yield a hit song but contained one gem, the country-and-western flavored "Someone Wonderful I Missed" in which Monica and Cleo are "almost sure" they don't regret their choice of husbands. "Hey There, Good Times" was a bouncy feel-good Broadway number; the old-time melodic ambience of "Everybody Today Is Turning On" had a decidedly modern lyric that notes that Amyl Nitrate used to be "some guy's name"; and "Lovers on Christmas Eve" was an ingratiating ballad.

Lenny Baker stole the show as the somewhat reluctant swinger who does all he can do to postpone the "action." At one point, he strips to his shorts, all the while taking his sweet time by slowly and meticulously folding his clothes, and then later insisting on a snack before a possible sexual showdown.

Besides the four characters, the script utilized four musicians who weaved in and out of the action, and while some reviewers thought this quite innovative, one (Howard Kissel in *Women's Wear Daily*) recalled that *No Strings* had employed the same device in 1962. And like *Subways Are for Sleeping*, another musical from the 1961–1962 season, the musician-chorus donned Santa Claus outfits while performing one number.

Martin Gottfried in the *New York Post* noted that the evening took a while to get going, but once it did the musical proved to be "friendly and charming" because it was all innocence and wasn't about "to challenge our morals." He praised Coleman's "singable" music but mentioned that Stewart's lyrics were "not always professional in technique," and he noted that Lenny Baker had the "plum" role of the evening. Clive Barnes in the *New York Times* found the show "bright, inventive, amusing and breezy" with a "cigarette-paper thin" plot that was presented in a "lighthearted, light-fingered and original" manner. As for the score, it was "tuneful, infectious and slightly impish," the cast was "gorgeous," and Baker's "heroic idiocy" and "baffled mind" were a "total joy."

T. E. Kalem in *Time* enjoyed the innocent saga of the would-be liberated couples who "only manage to get their toes wet," and he found the score "thoroughly beguiling" and the lyrics "saucily intelligent." Jack Kroll in *Newsweek* liked the "impudent" musical, and Bob Lape on WABCTV7 found *I Love My Wife* "lovable." John Beaufort in the *Christian Science Monitor* cautioned that the show might prove "too frank" for some, but "its basic outlook is healthy and its heart is in the right place."

Douglas Watt in the *New York Daily News* liked the "brisk, bouncy and gently melodic" score, the "engaging" lyrics, the "trim" book, and Baker's "resourceful comic performance." But Kissel was a bit cool to the show, although he praised Baker's "standout" performance and said David Mitchell's backdrop ("a splendid evocation of one of the world's most satisfying vistas—the lights of industrial New Jersey") was the evening's "high point."

In preproduction, the musical was titled *Fourscore*, and early press reports stated the musical would star Lenny Baker, Priscilla Lopez, Jim Norton, and Joanna Hall. Baker and Hall appeared in the Broadway production, the latter as Joanna Gleason (she is the daughter of television personality Monty Hall).

The script was published in paperback by Samuel French in 1980. The original cast album was released by Atlantic Records (LP # SD-19107) and later issued on CD by DRG Records (# 6109). The Australian cast album was released by Festival Records (LP # L-37934), and the 1978 South African cast album by EMI/Brigadiers Records (LP # EMCJL-11552). During the course of the Broadway run, the two male leads were succeeded by Dick Smothers and Tom Smothers, and then by black principals which included Lawrence-Hilton Jacobs and Hattie Winston.

MGM bought the film rights to the musical, and *Variety* reported that Allan Carr and Neil Machlis would produce and executive produce the screen version (which of course was never made).

The London production opened on October 6, 1977, at the Prince of Wales Theatre for 401 performances with a cast which included Ben Cross and Liz Robertson.

Awards

Tony Awards and Nominations: Best Musical (*I Love My Wife*); Best Featured Actor in a Musical (**Lenny Baker**); Best Director of a Musical (**Gene Saks**); Best Book (Michael Stewart); Best Score (lyrics by Michael Stewart, music by Cy Coleman); Best Choreography (Onna White)

SIDE BY SIDE BY SONDHEIM

"A Musical Entertainment"

Theatre: Music Box Theatre (during run, the revue transferred to the Morosco Theatre)
Opening Date: April 18, 1977; *Closing Date*: March 19, 1978
Performances: 384
Text (*"Continuity"*): Ned Sherrin
Lyrics: Stephen Sondheim
Music: Unless otherwise noted, all music by Stephen Sondheim
Direction: Ned Sherrin; *Producers*: Harold Prince in association with Ruth Mitchell and by arrangement with The Incomes Company Ltd.; *Musical Staging*: Bob Howe; *Scenery*: Peter Docherty (Jay Moore, Scenery Supervision); *Costumes*: Florence Klotz; *Lighting*: Ken Billington; *Musical Direction*: Ray Cook
Cast: Millicent Martin, Julie N. McKenzie, David Kernan, Ned Sherrin; Pianists: Danny Troob and Albin Konopka
The revue was presented in two acts.

Musical Numbers

Act One: "Comedy Tonight" (*A Funny Thing Happened on the Way to the Forum*, 1962) and "Love Is in the Air" (cut from *A Funny Thing Happened on the Way to the Forum*, 1962) (Millicent Martin, Julia N. McKenzie, David Kernan); "If Momma Was Married" (*Gypsy*, 1959; music by Jule Styne) (Millicent Martin, Julia N. McKenzie); "You Must Meet My Wife" (*A Little Night Music*, 1973) (Millicent Martin, David Kernan); "The Little Things You Do Together" (*Company*, 1970) (Julia N. McKenzie, David Kernan); "Getting Married Today" (*Company*, 1970) (Millicent Martin, Julia N. McKenzie, David Kernan); "I Remember" (1966 television musical *Evening Primrose*) (David Kernan); "Can That Boy Foxtrot" (cut from *Follies*, 1971) (Millicent Martin, Julia N. McKenzie); "Company" (*Company*, 1970) (Millicent Martin, Julia N. McKenzie, David Kernan); "Another Hundred People" (*Company*, 1970) (Julia N. McKenzie); "Barcelona" (*Company*, 1970) (Julia N. McKenzie, David Kernan); "Marry Me a Little" (cut from *Company*, 1970) (performer unknown; probably David Kernan); "I Never Do Anything Twice" (1976 film *The Seven-Per-Cent Solution*) (Millicent Martin); "Bring on the Girls" (dropped during preproduction of *Follies*, 1971) (David Kernan); "Ah, Paree!" (*Follies*, 1971) (Millicent Martin); "Buddy's Blues" (aka "The God-Why-Don't-You-Love-Me Blues") (*Follies*, 1971) (David Kernan, Millicent Martin, Julia N. McKenzie); "Broadway Baby" (*Follies*, 1971) (Julia N. McKenzie); "You Could Drive a Person Crazy" (*Company*, 1970) (Millicent Martin, David Kernan, Julia N. McKenzie)

Act Two: "Everybody Says Don't" (*Anyone Can Whistle*, 1964) (Millicent Martin, David Kernan, Julia N. McKenzie); "Anyone Can Whistle" (*Anyone Can Whistle*, 1964) (David Kernan); "Send in the Clowns" (*A Little Night Music*, 1973) (Millicent Martin); "We're Gonna Be All Right" (*Do I Hear a Waltz?*, 1965; music by Richard Rodgers) (Millicent Martin, David Kernan); "A Boy Like That" and "I Have a Love" (*West Side Story*, 1957; music by Leonard Bernstein) (Millicent Martin, Julia N. McKenzie); "The Boy From . . ." (*The Mad Show*, Off Broadway,1966; music by Mary Rodgers) (Millicent Martin); "Pretty Lady" (*Pacific Overtures*, 1976) (Millicent Martin, Julia N. McKenzie, David Kernan); "You Gotta Have a Gimmick" (*Gypsy*, 1959; music by Jule Styne) (Millicent Martin, Julia N. McKenzie, David Kernan); "Losing My

Mind" (*Follies*, 1971) (Julia N. McKenzie); "Could I Leave You?" (*Follies*, 1971) (David Kernan); "I'm Still Here" (*Follies*, 1971) (Millicent Martin); "Conversation Piece" (medley of songs from various Sondheim musicals); "Side by Side by Side" (*Company*, 1970) (Millicent Martin, Julia N. McKenzie, David Kernan)

The tribute revue *Side by Side by Sondheim* originated in London at the Mermaid Theatre on May 4, 1976, and then later transferred to Wyndham's Theatre on July 7, 1976; both productions featured Millicent Martin, Julia N. McKenzie, David Kernan, and Ned Sherrin, all of whom appeared in the Broadway edition. The evening offered some two-dozen songs by Sondheim, most of which were thoroughly familiar to Sondheim devotees, and along with 1973's special one-night *Sondheim: A Musical Tribute*, there began a decades-long parade of Sondheim evenings, tributes, salutes, galas, celebrations, and retrospectives.

Besides offering familiar material, the revue was laboriously peppered with Ned Sherrin's sometimes arch and overly precious "continuity" material. But at least the production offered the songs in a generally straight, concert-styled evening and avoided the mistakenly conceived *Marry Me a Little* (Off Broadway, 1981) and *Putting It Together* (Off Broadway, 1993; Broadway, 1999) which forced songs written for specific Sondheim productions into newly created plot situations.

Clive Barnes in the *New York Times* said the production was "a dream of a show" which proved Sondheim was "the master lyricist of American popular music, and one of the two or three most interesting theatre composers around"; Howard Kissel in *Women's Wear Daily* praised the "enormously entertaining" revue with its "expert" cast; Douglas Watt in the *New York Daily News* hailed the "ravishing musical retrospective"; the headline of T. E. Kalem's review in *Time* said the evening was a "String of Pearls" and that Sondheim was "the master jewel cutter of the modern U.S. musical theatre"; Jack Kroll in *Newsweek* proclaimed that Sondheim was the theatre's "poet laureate of urban regret, pain and irony"; and Edwin Wilson in the *Wall Street Journal* said the production found the "right sensibility" and the "right key" to present the songs.

But Martin Gottfried in the *New York Post* thought the evening was "presumptuous" because Sondheim had written only six musicals as a composer-lyricist, and this was "not enough" to crown him as a "legendary figure." Further, unlike the work of George Gershwin, Irving Berlin, Cole Porter, and Richard Rodgers, Sondheim had yet to win "the heart of the American people." The production had no imagination and concept, and the numbers were sung in an "imitation" of earlier cast-album performances. As for Ned Sherrin, he played "to the boys in the balcony" and colored the evening in "lavender blue." His "supercilious manner" and "campy attitude" were "smarmy and topical in an undergraduate way" and he was "simply sycophantic" with his "trivial, familiar and obsequious" stories.

"Being Alive" (*Company*, 1970) and "There Is No Other Way" (*Pacific Overtures*, 1976) were heard in the London production but were dropped for New York and replaced by "Marry Me a Little" and "Pretty Lady." The Broadway version included "Could I Leave You?," which was dropped during the course of the run, and both the London and New York productions included "Conversation Piece," which was a medley of songs from various Sondheim shows. During the London and New York engagements, various songs were dropped, and others added; among the latter were "There Won't Be Trumpets" (*Anyone Can Whistle*, 1964) for London (which was included on the cast recording) and for New York "The Two of You" (which Sondheim had written in 1952 as a proposed number for the *Kukla, Fran and Ollie* television show).

The London cast album was issued on a two-LP set by RCA Victor Records (# CBL2-1851) and was later released on a two-CD set (# 1851-2-RG). The Dublin production opened at the Gaiety Theatre on May 31, 1977, with a cast that included Gemma Craven, and the cast album of highlights from the revue was recorded as *Songs of Sondheim* (Ram Records LP # RMLP-1026). The Australian production opened at the Theatre Royal in Sydney on September 27, 1977, and its two-LP cast recording was released by RCA Victor Records (LP # VRL2-0156) and includes the "Conversation Piece" sequence. The Brazilian production (in Portuguese) opened on August 31, 2005, at the Centro Cultural Banco do Brasil's Theatre in Rio de Janeiro and highlights were recorded as *Lado a Lado com Sondheim* (Axion Records unnumbered CD).

The revue was revived by The Equity Theatre on January 7, 1988, for thirty-two performances; it reinstated "Could I Leave You?" and added "Beautiful Girls" (*Follies*, 1971).

Awards

Tony Award Nominations: Best Musical (*Side by Side by Sondheim*); Best Featured Actor in a Musical (David Kernan); Best Featured Actor in a Musical (Ned Sherrin); Best Featured Actress in a Musical (Millicent Martin); Best Featured Actress in a Musical (Julia N. McKenzie)

ANNIE

"A New Musical"

Theatre: Alvin Theatre (during run, the musical transferred to the ANTA, Eugene O'Neill, and Uris Theatres)
Opening Date: April 21, 1977; *Closing Date*: January 2, 1983
Performances: 2,377
Book: Thomas Meehan
Lyrics: Martin Charnin
Music: Charles Strouse
Based on the comic strip *Little Orphan Annie* by Harold Gray, which first appeared in the *New York Daily News* in 1924.
Direction: Martin Charnin; *Producers*: Mike Nichols; produced by Irwin Meyer, Stephen R. Friedman, and Lewis Allen; produced by Alvin Nederlander Associates, Inc., and Icarus Productions; and produced in association with Peter Crane; *Choreography*: Peter Gennaro; *Scenery*: David Mitchell; *Costumes*: Theoni V. Aldredge; *Lighting*: Judy Rasmuson; *Musical Direction*: Peter Howard
Cast: Danielle Brisebois (Molly), Robyn Finn (Pepper), Donna Graham (Duffy), Janine Ruane (July), Diana Barrows (Tessie), Shelley Bruce (Kate), Andrea McArdle (Annie), Dorothy Loudon (Miss Hannigan), James Hosbein (Bundles McCloskey, Sound Effects Man, Ickes), Steven Boockvor (Dog Catcher, Jimmy Johnson, Honor Guard), Donald Craig (Dog Catcher, Bert Healy, Kaltenborn's Voice, Hull), Sandy (Himself), Richard Ensslen (Lieutenant Ward, Morgenthau, Justice Brandeis), Raymond Thorne (Harry, FDR), Laurie Beechman (Sophie, Cecille, A Star to Be, Bonnie Boylan, Perkins), Sandy Faison (Grace Farrell), Edwin Bordo (Drake), Edie Cowan (Mrs. Pugh, Connie Boylan), Penny Worth (Annette, Ronnie Boylan), Reid Shelton (Oliver Warbucks), Robert Fitch (Rooster Hannigan), Barbara Erwin (Lily St. Regis), Bob Freschi (Fred McCracken, Howe), Mari McMinn (NBC Page); Hooverville-ites, Policemen, Warbuck's Servants, New Yorkers: Laurie Beechman, Steven Boockvor, Edwin Bordo, Edie Cowan, Donald Craig, Richard Ensslen, Barbara Erwin, Bob Freschi, James Hosbein, Mari McMinn, Penny Worth
The musical was presented in two acts.
The action takes place in New York City and Washington, D.C., from December 11 to December 25, 1933.

Musical Numbers

Act One: "Maybe" (Andrea McArdle); "It's the Hard-Knock Life" (Andrea McArdle, Orphans); "It's the Hard-Knock Life" (reprise) (Orphans); "Tomorrow" (Andrea McArdle); "We'd Like to Thank You" (The Hooverville-ites); "Little Girls" (Dorothy Loudon); "I Think I'm Gonna Like It Here" (Sandy Faison, Andrea McArdle, Edwin Bordo, Laurie Beechman, Penny Worth, Edie Cowan, Other Servants); "N.Y.C." (Reid Shelton, Sandy Faison, Andrea McArdle, Laurie Beechman, New Yorkers); "Easy Street" (Dorothy Loudon, Robert Fitch, Barbara Erwin); "You Won't Be an Orphan for Long" (Sandy Faison, Edwin Bordo, Edie Cowan, Laurie Beechman, Penny Worth, Servants, Reid Shelton)
Act Two: "You're Never Fully Dressed without a Smile" (Donald Craig, Laurie Beechman, Edie Cowan, Penny Worth, "The Hour of Smiles" Family); "You're Never Fully Dressed without a Smile" (reprise) (Orphans); "Easy Street" (reprise) (Dorothy Loudon, Robert Fitch, Barbara Erwin); "Tomorrow' (reprise) (Andrea McArdle, Raymond Thorne, Reid Shelton, Cabinet); "Something Was Missing" (Reid Shelton); "I Don't Need Anything but You" (Reid Shelton, Andrea McArdle); "Annie" (Sandy Faison, Edwin Bordo, Staff); "Maybe" (reprise) (Andrea McArdle); "A New Deal for Christmas" (Andrea McArdle, Reid Shelton, Sandy Faison, Raymond Thorne, Staff)

Based on the cartoon character of *Little Orphan Annie*, *Annie* was set during the Depression and focused on the title character (Andrea McArdle) who lives in an orphanage under the domination of Miss Hannigan (Dorothy Loudon), whose only reason for living is to hate little girls. Annie hopes to someday find her parents, but in the meantime is chosen by Grace Farrell (Sandy Faison), the private secretary to multibillionaire Oliver Warbucks (Reid Shelton), to spend Christmas at his luxurious Fifth Avenue mansion. Although Warbucks hopes to adopt Annie, he realizes it's his duty to help in her search for her parents, and when he offers a reward for information, Miss Hannigan, her brother Rooster (Robert Fitch), and his girlfriend Lily St. Regis (Barbara Erwin) devise a scheme to pawn off Rooster and Lily as the parents so they all can live on easy street (upon meeting Miss Hannigan, Lily says her last name is like that of the hotel—to which Miss Hannigan replies, "Which floor?"). And when Annie's "parents" say they can't wait for her to come live with them in their home in New Jersey, Annie ruefully and resignedly says to herself, "New Jersey." But all ends well: Annie will be able to live in New York! The villains are captured, Warbucks adopts Annie, and it seems certain that Warbucks and Grace are headed for the altar.

Annie's score offered one of the last hit songs to emerge from a Broadway musical when "Tomorrow" became as ubiquitous as "Send in the Clowns" and "What I Did for Love," and later "It's the Hard-Knock Life" became a popular rap number. "Maybe" (Annie's "wanting" song for her mother and father), was a haunting ballad, but the score's most theatrical numbers were Miss Hannigan's hateful ode to "Little Girls" and her, Rooster, and Lily's wickedly gleeful vaudeville-like salute to "Easy Street" when they hope to cash in on their scheme. Another highlight was the orphans' reprise of "You're Never Fully Dressed without a Smile" in which the little girls went into a chorus-line salute to the keep-your-chin-up-styled song.

Clive Barnes in the *New York Times* noted that in recent years the Broadway musical had become "somewhat tarnished," but *Annie* worked "on all levels" and was "that now rare animal—the properly built, handsomely groomed Broadway musical." He singled out Dorothy Loudon's "deliciously and deliriously horrid" Miss Hannigan, liked the "tuneful" if neither "unduly inventive nor memorable" music, and said the lyrics were the "worst aspect" of the show.

Martin Gottfried in the *New York Post* said the musical was "thoroughly, even brazenly conventional," but "the damned thing works" and "working" was "the theatre's absolute excuse." He praised Charles Strouse's score as his best since *Bye Bye Birdie* (1960), but wished there had been fewer reprises (the second act had no less than four) and more musical "fidelity" to the 1930s. Howard Kissel in *Women's Wear Daily* reported that "the house came down" when Loudon sang "Little Girls," a song that "would have delighted W. C. Fields"; Edwin Wilson in the *Wall Street Journal* noted that the musical lacked "a sharp edge and a consistent point of view" and its "political ideology" showed a "confusion of values" that vilified conservative President Hoover but glorified the "arch-conservative" Warbucks. And Douglas Watt in the *New York Daily News* said the plot of the "big, splashy, sentimental, old-fashioned" musical soon turned "pure marshmallow." There was "thin musical material" (the lyrics were "usually commonplace" and the music was "dismayingly commonplace"), and Andrea McArdle was only "adequately cast" in the title role (in truth, McArdle sang in a clarion voice, but otherwise she came across as somewhat sullen and remote).

Jack Kroll in *Newsweek* praised McArdle as a "mini-Merman" and said the "maniacally baroque performance" of Loudon "raises mugging to a high art." John Beaufort in the *Christian Science Monitor* said the score was "dandy" with its "wistful to rousing" songs, and Bob Lape on WABCTV7 said the show "might run forever." But Leonard Probst on NBC Radio suggested it was impossible to "dislike" the score because you couldn't "remember" it, the lyrics were "banal," there was "little" in the way of dancing, and the show "belabors the obvious."

T. E. Kalem in *Time* said Andrea McArdle brought an "aridity of mood" that pervaded the evening; she kept "any warmth or vulnerability on a very tight leash." Loudon's performance would "surely appall any admirer of acting restraint," the music "would scarcely inspire an organ-grinder's monkey to rattle his cup," and the lyrics were "for beginning lip readers." But even without Alpo, Sandy proved himself an "artful trouper even if he doesn't say "Arf.'"

For some reason, a few critics objected to FDR's portrayal. Watt said it was a "tasteless caricature," and Kalem complained that FDR was "tastelessly trundled on in a wheelchair" and was "smarmily caricatured."

The original cast album was released by Columbia Records (LP # PS-34712), and the CD issue (Sony Classical/Columbia/Legacy # SK-60723) includes bonus tracks of the cut songs "Apples," "We Got Annie," "Just Wait," "That's the Way It Goes," "Parents," and "I've Never Been So Happy" as well as the first recorded performance of "Tomorrow." There have been numerous foreign cast recordings of the score, including the Madrid production, which premiered at the Teatro Principe on September 25, 1981, and was recorded by Bocaccio Records (LP # BS-32137); it includes "Mañana," "Nueva York," "Huerfanas," and "Felices Navidades, por fin." Time-Life released a thirtieth-anniversary recording of the score on a two-CD set, and in 2008 Lifetime Channel aired the documentary *Life after Tomorrow*, which focused on interviews with many of the now grown-up little girls who had played the orphans in various productions.

The musical premiered at Goodspeed Opera House, East Haddam, Connecticut, on August 10, 1976; Kristen Vigard was the original Annie, and Andrea McArdle played an orphan known as "The Toughest" (the orphans in the chorus line for the Goodspeed production were nameless and were instead identified by their characteristics, e.g., The Toughest, The Littlest, etc.). Vigard was soon replaced by McArdle, but Vigard remained with the production as McArdle's standby. For Goodspeed, Maggie Task was Miss Hannigan. Songs cut during this phase of the tryout (which reopened the following March at the Kennedy Center's Eisenhower Theatre in Washington, D.C.) include "Apples," "We Got Annie," "Just Wait," "That's the Way It Goes," "He Doesn't Know," "That's Our Annie," and "I've Never Been So Happy." With the same music, the lovely ballad "Something Was Missing" had earlier been heard as the lowdown Charleston "You Rat, You" (lyric by Lee Adams) in the 1968 film *The Night They Raided Minsky's* where it was sung in a speakeasy by Lillian Hayman. Thomas Meehan's *Annie*: *An Old-Fashioned Story* was published in hardback by Macmillan in 1980.

The musical has been revived twice on Broadway. The first opened at the Martin Beck (now Al Hirschfeld) Theatre on March 26, 1997, with Nell Carter (Miss Hannigan), Conrad John Schuck (Warbucks), Brittny Kissinger (Annie), and Sutton Foster (in various roles). From the original production, Raymond Thorne reprised his FDR, and the score included the new song "You Make Me Happy." The second opened at the Palace Theatre on November 8, 2012, for 487 performances with Kate Finneran (Miss Hannigan) and Lilla Crawford (Annie); it included "You Make Me Happy" and introduced a new song, "Why Should I Change a Thing?"

The first London production opened at the Victoria Palace Theatre on May 3, 1978, for 1,485 performances, and during the first few weeks of the run Andrea McArdle reprised the title role. The cast album was released by CBS Records (LP # 70160). A later London revival opened on September 30, 1998.

Columbia Pictures' charm-free film version was released in 1982; directed by John Huston and choreographed by Arlene Phillips, the unmemorable adaptation starred Aileen Quinn (Annie), Albert Finney (Warbucks), Carol Burnett (Miss Hannigan), Bernadette Peters (Lily), Ann Reinking (Grace), Tim Curry (Rooster), Edward Herrmann (FDR), and, in two roles that were part of the comic strip but not the Broadway musical, Geoffrey Holder (Punjab) and Roger Minami (Asp). The film omitted six songs ("We'd Like to Thank You," "N.Y.C.," "You Won't Be an Orphan for Long," "Something Was Missing," "Annie," and "A New Deal for Christmas"), added four ("Dumb Dog," "Sandy," "Let's Go to the Movies," and "Sign"), and reinstated "We Got Annie" from the tryout. The soundtrack album was released by Columbia Records (LP # JS-38000).

A Walt Disney television production was shown on ABC on November 7, 1999, and was livelier than the desultory 1982 film. Directed by Rob Marshall, the cast included Alicia Morton (Annie), Kathy Bates (Miss Hannigan), Victor Garber (Warbucks), Alan Cumming (Rooster), Kristin Chenoweth (Lily), Audra McDonald (Grace), and Andrea McArdle as the Star to Be (the latter is surely destined to one day play Miss Hannigan in a revival). The soundtrack album was released by Sony Records (CD # SK-89008).

A radically revised second theatrical film version was released in 2014 by Sony Pictures Entertainment. The story now took place in present-day New York, eliminated the character of Warbucks, and offered a racially diverse cast that included Quvenzhane Wallis (Annie), Cameron Diaz (Miss Hannigan), Rose Byrne (Grace), Jamie Foxx, and Bobby Cannnavale. The lyrics and music for some of the songs were altered for a few of the stage version's numbers ("Maybe," "It's a Hard Knock Life," "Tomorrow," "I Think I'm Going to Like It Here," "You're Never Fully Dressed without a Smile," "Little Girls," "Easy Street," and "I Don't Need Anything but You" were retained), and there were a few new songs ("Moonquake Lake," "The City's Yours," "Opportunity," and "Who Am I?") by Sia, Greg Kurstin, and Will Gluck. The *Hollywood Reporter* called the film a "toxic mess" and noted that most of the stage score had been "shredded" and thus retained "just a signature line or two" with "desperately hip polyrhythmic sounds, aurally assaultive arrangements and inane new lyrics." A. O. Scott in the *New York Times* said the "hacky, borderline-incompetent production" was a "chaotic shambles."

In his liner notes for the cast album's release, book writer Thomas Meehan stated that *Annie* had been written "as a reaction to the Nixonian America of 1972," but with "James Earl Carter in the White House, the message of hope in *Annie* is no longer antithetical to the mood of the country." Who knew that the bubbly musical carried so much political weight? And since Meehan is the one who brought up the subject of politics . . . maybe he was too quick to put on his rose-colored glasses. For it was Carter who soon told the nation it had a "crisis of confidence" (otherwise known as Carter's "malaise speech"), and when inflation rates soared to 14.8% and interest rates hit 18%, perhaps the nation was not all that immersed in hope. Further, the song "We'd Like to Thank You" accused Herbert Hoover of being the sole cause of the Wall Street Crash of 1929 and the Depression. Who knew Hoover had such power? It's surprising Hoover wasn't blamed for the divorce of Joan Crawford and Douglas Fairbanks Jr.

Sequels in the theatre almost always fail, and the one for *Annie* was no exception. In 1989, *Annie 2: Miss Hannigan's Revenge* seemed poised to become a blockbuster and hopes were high because the original creators (librettist Meehan, lyricist Charnin, composer Strouse, scenic designer Mitchell, costume designer Aldredge, and musical director Howard) were back on hand and Dorothy Loudon was set to reprise her memorable Miss Hannigan (as FDR, Raymond Thorne was another holdover from the original production). But those hopes were completely dashed almost as soon as the curtain went up on the first preview performance at the Kennedy Center's Opera House on December 22. The sequel was jaw-droppingly sour, unfunny, and confusing, and despite an occasionally amusing (if politically incorrect) joke and sometimes atmospheric décor, the evening was a complete bust. The show closed in Washington without risking Broadway, but the creators didn't give up, and the following summer *Annie Warbucks* opened at the Goodspeed Opera House's Norma Terris Theatre. In 1992, the production toured and finally opened Off Broadway at the Variety Arts Theatre on August 9, 1993, for two hundred performances; the new version retained four songs from the 1989 debacle ("A Younger Man," "When You Smile," "Tenement Lullaby," and "Changes") and perhaps a fifth (the current version included "I Got Me," which may have been a reworking of "All I've Got Is Me" from the 1989 sequel). The cast album was released on a two-CD set by Broadway Angel Records (# CDQ-7243-5-55040-29).

Awards

Tony Awards and Nominations: Best Musical (***Annie***); Best Leading Actor in a Musical (Reid Shelton); Best Leading Actress in a Musical (**Dorothy Loudon**); Best Leading Actress in a Musical (Andrea McArdle); Best Director of a Musical (Martin Charnin); Best Book (**Thomas Meehan**); Best Score (**Charles Strouse**, music; **Martin Charnin**, lyrics); Best Scenic Designer (**David Mitchell**); Best Costume Designer (**Theoni V. Aldredge** in a tie with Santo Loquasto for *The Cherry Orchard*); Best Choreography (**Peter Gennaro**)
New York Drama Critics' Circle Award: Best Musical (1976–1977): ***Annie***

THE KING AND I

Theatre: Uris Theatre
Opening Date: May 2, 1977; *Closing Date*: December 30, 1978
Performances: 696
Book and *Lyrics*: Oscar Hammerstein II
Music: Richard Rodgers
Based on the 1944 novel *Anna and the King of Siam* by Margaret Landon.
Direction: Yuriko; *Producers*: Lee Guber and Shelly Gross (Fred Walker, Associate Producer); *Choreography*: Jerome Robbins (re-created for this production by Yuriko); *Scenery*: Peter Wolf; *Costumes*: Stanley Simmons (costumes based on the original costume designs by Irene Sharaff); *Lighting*: Thomas Skelton; *Musical Direction*: John Lesko
Cast: Larry Swansen (Captain Orton), Alan Amick (Louis Leonowens), Constance Towers (Anna Leonowens), Jae Woo Lee (The Interpreter), Michael Kermoyan (The Kralahome), *Yul Brynner* (The King), June Angela (Tuptim), Hye-Young Choi (Lady Thiang), Gene Profanato (Prince Chulalongkorn), Julie Woo (Princess Ying Yaowalak), Martin Vidnovic (Lun Tha), John Michael King (Sir Edward Ramsay); The Royal Dancers and Wives: Su Applegate, Jessica Chao, Lei-Lynne Doo, Dale Harimoto, Pamela Kalt, Susan Kikuchi, Faye Fujisaki Mar, Sumiko Murashima, Libby Rhodes, Cecile Santos, Hope Sogawa, Mary Ann Teng, Patricia K. Thomas; Princesses and Princes: Ivan Ho, Clark Huang, Annie Lam, Connie Lam, Jennifer Lam, Paul Siu, Tim Waldrip, Kevan Weber, Kym Weber, Julie Woo, Mary Woo; Nurses and Amazons: Sydney Smith, Marianne Tatum, Patricia K. Thomas, Patricia Weber, Rebecca West; Priests and Slaves: Kaipo Daniels, Barrett Hong, Jae Woo Lee, Ric Ornellas, Simeon Den, Chandra Tanna, Robert Vega
The musical was presented in two acts.
The action takes place in and around the King's Palace in Bangkok, Siam, during the early 1860s.

Musical Numbers

Act One: "I Whistle a Happy Tune" (Constance Towers, Alan Amick); "My Lord and Master" (June Angela); "Hello, Young Lovers" (Constance Towers); "March of the Siamese Children" (Constance Towers, Yul Brynner, The King's Wives and Children); "A Puzzlement" (Yul Brynner); "The Royal Bangkok Academy" (Constance Towers, Pupils); "Getting to Know You" (Constance Towers, Wives, Children, Patricia Weber); "We Kiss in a Shadow" (June Angela, Martin Vidnovic); "A Puzzlement" (reprise) (Gene Profanato, Alan Amick); "Shall I Tell You What I Think of You?" (Constance Towers); "Something Wonderful" (Hye-Young Choi); Finale (Company)

Act Two: "Western People Funny" (Hye-Young Choi, Wives); "I Have Dreamed" (June Angela, Martin Vidnovic); "Hello, Young Lovers" (reprise) (Constance Towers); "The Small House of Uncle Thomas" (ballet) (Narrator: June Angela; Uncle Thomas: Jessica Chao; Topsy: Lei-Lynne Doo; Little Eva: Dale Harimoto; Eliza: Susan Kikuchi; King Simon: Rebecca West; Angel: Patricia Weber; Royal Dancers: Barrett Hong, Faye Fujisaki Mar, Ric Ornellas, Libby Rhodes, Simeon Den, Cecile Santos, Sydney Smith, Hope Sogawa, Chandra Tanna, Patricia K. Thomas; Propmen: Kaipo Daniels, Jae Woo Lee, Thomas J. Rees, Robert Vega); "Shall We Dance?" (Constance Towers, Yul Brynner); Finale (Company)

The revival of Richard Rodgers and Oscar Hammerstein II's *The King and I* gave New York an opportunity to see Yul Brynner re-create on stage his role of the King for the first time since the original Broadway production opened some twenty-six years earlier. Audiences took advantage of the occasion, for here was the original actor reprising his legendary performance in one of the most famous roles in all musical theatre. The revival played for 696 showings (some sources cite 719), and even when Brynner (and his Anna, Constance Towers) took a vacation, the production was an occasion because Angela Lansbury played the role of Anna for three weeks (during this time, Michael Kermoyan stepped up from the role of The Kralahome to play the King, which he had performed in a 1968 New York revival with Constance Towers).

Douglas Watt in the *New York Daily News* said the revival of *The King and I* was "the most beautiful show in town, musically and in all other respects" and that Brynner now seemed "even better" because he had aged into the role of the mature monarch. Clive Barnes in the *New York Times* praised the charming and yet dominating Brynner, said Constance Towers was "piquantly ladylike and sweet without being dangerously saccharine," and Rodgers's score was "a happy swirl of melody." An unsigned review in *Time* said Brynner was "the first and only true King" and that the production itself "dwarfs recent musicals in opulence." Edwin Wilson in the *Wall Street Journal* found the production "a feast for the eyes as well as the ears" and "was amazed all over again" by the "many unforgettable" songs that Rodgers and Hammerstein wrote for the musical. And Charles Michener in *Newsweek* found "new depth" in Brynner's performance and said his death scene struck "the fleeting but unmistakable note of genuine tragedy."

But Howard Kissel in *Women's Wear Daily* found the revival "for the most part a good summer stock production" and noted Hammerstein's book hadn't "aged well" with a "quaintness" and "operettaishness" about it. But it was "wonderful" to see Brynner "performing the part again so powerfully." And as he had noted with the recent revivals of ***My Fair Lady*** and ***Guys and Dolls***, Martin Gottfried in the *New York Post* said *The King and I* wasn't a classic musical. But the score was "flawless" and "magnificent," and Jerome Robbins's choreography was "masterful." As for the book, it had "many flaws of stagecraft" that were "irritating" and couldn't be overlooked; and while Brynner hadn't "quite the intensity and power of the past" he was nonetheless "one hell of a King of Siam and had every right to own the role."

The original production opened on Broadway at the St. James Theatre on March 29, 1951, for 1,246 performances with Gertrude Lawrence and Brynner in the leading roles. It won five Tony Awards, including Best Musical, Best Leading Actress in a Musical (Lawrence), and Best Featured Actor in a Musical for Brynner (at the time, the rules of the Tony Award committee considered any performer whose name was billed below the title to be a featured player).

As of this writing, the musical has been revived in New York nine times for over three thousand performances. The first five were limited-engagement institutional revivals, four produced by the New York City Center Light Opera Company at City Center (April 18, 1956, for twenty-three performances with Jan Clayton and Zachary Scott; May 11, 1960, for twenty-four performances with Barbara Cook and Farley Granger; June 12, 1963, for fifteen performances with Eileen Brennan and Manolo Fabregas; and May 28, 1968, for twenty-two performances with Constance Towers and Michael Kermoyan) and one produced by the Music Theatre of Lincoln Center at the New York State Theatre on July 6, 1964, for forty performances with Rise Stevens and Darren McGavin.

After the current revival, the musical returned on January 7, 1985, at the Martin Beck (now Hirschfeld) Theatre for 191 performances with Brynner and Mary Beth Peil, and on April 11, 1996, at the Neil Simon Theatre for 781 performances with Donna Murphy and Lou Diamond Phillips. A ninth revival opened at the Vivian Beaumont Theatre on April 16, 2015, with Kelli O'Hara and Ken Watanabe.

The first London production opened at the Drury Lane on October 9, 1953, for 926 performances with Valerie Hobson and Herbert Lom, and other West End revivals in 1973 and 1999 starred Sally Ann Howes and Elaine Paige, respectively.

The 1956 film version was released by Twentieth Century-Fox with Brynner (who won the Academy Award for Best Actor) and Deborah Kerr, and an animated version was released by Warner Brothers Family Entertainment in 1999.

The script of the musical was published in hardback by Random House in 1951, and all the used and unused lyrics are included in the collection *The Complete Lyrics of Oscar Hammerstein II*. There are numerous recordings of the classic score, including later ones that are more complete than the original cast album (Decca Records LP # DL-7-9008 and MCA CD # MCAD-10049), but the original is the essential one to own.

Perhaps the strangest review of *The King and I* was Henry Hewes's appraisal Lincoln Center's 1964 revival. Writing in *Saturday Review*, he said Anna is a "smug representative of Western colonialism" and her purported "'goodness' now emerges as a hypocritical disguise for intolerance of another country's traditions and for her ruthless drive to emasculate a man." He further stated that Anna "succeeds in destroying" the King. Talk about a puzzlement!

HAPPY END

Theatre: Martin Beck Theatre
Opening Date: May 7, 1977; *Closing Date*: July 10, 1977
Performances: 75
Book: Dorothy Lane or Elisabeth Hauptmann (but probably by Bertolt Brecht; see below); book adapted by Michael Feingold
Lyrics: Bertolt Brecht; lyrics adapted by Michael Feingold
Music: Kurt Weill
Direction: Direction and Staging by Robert Kalfin and Patricia Birch; *Producers*: Michael Harvey and The Chelsea Theatre Center (Robert Kalfin, Artistic Director, and Michael David, Executive Director) (Wilder Luke Burnap, Associate Producer); *Scenery*: Robert U. Taylor; *Costumes*: Carrie F. Robbins; *Lighting*: Jennifer Tipton; *Musical Direction*: Roland Gagnon
Cast: The Gang—*Christopher Lloyd* (Bill Cracker), Benjamin Rayson (Sam "Mammy" Wurlitzer), Tony Azito (Doctor Nakamura aka The Governor), John A. Coe (Jimmy Dexter aka The Reverend), Robert Weil (Bob Marker aka The Professor), Raymond J. Barry (Johnny Flint aka Baby Face), *Grayson Hall* (Lady in Gray aka The Fly), Donna Emmanuel (Miriam); The Army—*Meryl Streep* (Lieutenant Lillian Holiday aka Hallelujah Lil), Liz Sheridan (Major Stone), Joe Grifasi (Captain Hannibal Jackson), Prudence Wright Holmes (Sister Mary), Alexandra Borrie (Sister Jane), Christopher Cara (Brother Ben Owens); The Fold—Kristin Jolliff, Frank Kopyc, Tom Mardirosian, Martha Miller, Victor Pappas; David Pursley (Cop)
The musical was presented in three acts.
The action takes place in Chicago during December 1915.

Musical Numbers

Act One: Prologue (Company); "The Bilbao Song" (Christopher Lloyd, The Gang); "Lieutenants of the Lord" (Meryl Streep, The Army); "March Ahead" (The Army); "The Sailors' Tango" (Meryl Streep)
Act Two: "Brother, Give Yourself a Shove" (The Army, The Fold); "Song of the Big Shot" (Tony Azito); "Don't Be Afraid" (Alexandra Borrie, The Army, The Fold); "In Our Childhood's Bright Endeavor" (Joe Grifasi); "The Liquor Dealer's Dream" (Joe Grifasi, Tony Azito, Alexandra Borrie, The Army, The Fold)

Act Three: "The Mandalay Song" (Benjamin Rayson, The Gang); "Surabaya Johnny" (Meryl Streep); "Song of the Big Shot" (reprise) (Christopher Lloyd); "Ballad of the Lily of Hell" (Grayson Hall); "The Happy End" (Company)

Bertolt Brecht and Kurt Weill's *Happy End* was here receiving its first Broadway production some fifty years after the musical's world premiere in Berlin at the Theatre am Schiffbauerdamm on September 2, 1929 (Michael Feingold's adaptation had first been produced at the Yale Repertory Theatre, New Haven, Connecticut, on April 6, 1972).

The title of the original German production was in English, and besides opening almost a year to the day after Brecht and Weill's *The Threepenny Opera*, which had premiered at the same theatre, the original productions of both musicals shared the same director (Erich Engel), scenic designer (Caspar Neher), and conductor (Theo Mackeben). The cast members were Carola Neher (Lillian), Oskar (Oscar) Homolka (Bill), Helene Weigel (A Lady in Gray), and Peter Lorre (Doctor Nakamura).

Like Brecht and Weill's later *Rise and Fall of the City of Mahagonny* (1930), the world premiere of *Happy End* caused a riot in the theatre because of its cynical ending, and police were summoned. And like *Mahagonny*, the work took place in the United States (specifically the Chicago of 1915), where a local branch of the Salvation Army tries to reform a group of gangsters. But the plot upends itself when the gangsters and the preachers join forces to fleece the city's wealthy citizens because they believe it's more ethical to rob a bank than to own one.

The basic plot was vaguely similar to the later ***Guys and Dolls***, which had been revived on Broadway earlier in the 1976–1977 season. (Damon Runyon's short story "The Idyll of Miss Sarah Brown" had first been published in 1933 and was one of the sources for the 1950 musical.) Incidentally, Off-Off-Broadway's Drama Committee Repertory Theatre had presented a revival of George Bernard Shaw's *Major Barbara* (1905) earlier in the season, and so New York theatergoers had the opportunity to see three "Salvation Army" plays and musicals during a single season (Shaw's play dealt with a Salvation Army worker who becomes unnerved when she discovers that manufacturers of war matériel and alcohol contribute to the Christian cause).

As for the musical's book, it was originally attributed to Dorothy Lane (who apparently never existed) and then to Brecht's secretary Elisabeth Hauptmann. But it was probably written by Brecht himself. (Douglas Watt in the *New York Daily News* commented that "whoever" wrote it had created a "throwaway" story.)

The current production of *Happy End* was first seen Off Broadway at the Brooklyn Academy of Music's Chelsea Theatre Center (BAM) on March 8, 1977, with Shirley Knight as Lillian. Because of casting and directorial issues, the work temporarily closed on April 3 after thirty-two showings, and when performances resumed on April 12 Meryl Streep had succeeded Knight. The revival played at BAM through April 30 for an additional twenty-four showings, and then on May 7 opened on Broadway for seventy-five more performances (the Off-Broadway and Broadway runs totaled 131 performances). Streep continued with the musical for part of the Broadway run, and was succeeded by Janie Sell.

The world premiere in Berlin had opened in chaos (due to the riot in the theatre and the controversy about the musical's cynical ending), and BAM's production underwent a grueling birth as well. When Knight left the production, Streep took over her role at the last minute; then leading man Christopher Lloyd injured his leg during rehearsals and was temporarily replaced by his understudy Bob Gunton (some of the reviewers saw the production when Gunton was the lead); a bout of measles affected some of the cast members; and the original director Michael Posnick was replaced by BAM's artistic director Robert Kalfin. (By the time the musical opened on Broadway, Kalfin and Patricia Birch were together credited for direction and staging.) Ironically, the 1970 New York premiere of *Rise and Fall of the City of Mahagonny* also underwent a chaotic preview period that stretched into nine weeks and saw no less than three performers in the leading role of Jimmy Mahoney.

Watt praised Feingold's "top-notch" adaptation and the "beauty" of Weill's score (which included such cabaret favorites as "Surabaya Johnny," "The Sailors' Tango," and "The Bilbao Song"), and noted that while the musical was still set in 1915, the flavor of the evening captured the gangland Chicago of the 1920s. Clive Barnes in the *New York Times* liked Feingold's "excellent" translation and said the story was "constantly entertaining" and the score "sheer genius." But Martin Gottfried in the *New York Post* found the musical "painfully uninteresting" and complained that Feingold's adaptation played "fast and loose" with the material and thus wasn't Brechtian, German, or American.

John Beaufort in the *Christian Science Monitor* found the evening "fluffy stuff" with "fabulous" music, and if the reader didn't mind "nonintellectual fare" the evening was enjoyable. T. E. Kalem in *Time* said

Weill's score was the "marvel" of the production and noted the show had "no redeeming social value save delight." Howard Kissel in *Women's Wear Daily* said that the book lacked "bite" and seemed "a somewhat silly, enervating context for the great score."

The first recording of the musical was sung in German and was released by Columbia Records (LP # OL-5630 and OS-2032) with Lotte Lenya as Lillian. Michael Feingold's current adaptation was later heard in a 2006 production by the American Conservatory Theatre in San Francisco, which was recorded by Ghostlight Records (CD # 7915584418-2). The script was published in soft back by Samuel French, Inc., in 1982.

Because the current production was the musical's first on Broadway, it was considered eligible for Best Musical Tony Award, and was so nominated.

Awards

Tony Award Nominations: Best Musical (*Happy End*); Best Book (Elisabeth Hauptmann, adaptation by Michael Feingold); Best Score (music by Kurt Weill, lyrics by Bertolt Brecht with adaptation by Michael Feingold)

TOLLER CRANSTON'S THE ICE SHOW

Theatre: Palace Theatre
Opening Date: May 19, 1977; *Closing Date*: July 10, 1977
Performances: 61
Original Music: Al Kasha and Joel Hirschhorn
Direction: Myrl A. Schreibman; *Producers*: Dennis Bass and Robin Cranston (Executive Producers), and Myrl A. Schreibman; *Choreography*: Choreography and Staging by Brian Foley (Ellen Burka, Additional Choreography); *Scenery*: Anthony Sabatino and William H. Harris; *Costumes*: Miles White; *Lighting*: D. Scott Linder; *Musical Direction*: probably Bill Courtney
Cast: *Toller Cranston*, Jim Millns and Colleen O'Connor, Gordon McKellen Jr., Ken Shelley, Wendy Burge, Candy Jones and Don Fraser, Kath Malmberg, Barbara Berezowski and David Porter, Elizabeth Freeman, Jack Courtney and Emily Benenson, Janet and Mark Hominuke
The ice revue was presented in two acts.

Skating and Musical Numbers

Act One: Overture and Introduction (music by Al Kasha and Joel Hirschhorn) (Full Company); *Trilogy*—"Thus Spoke Zarathustra" (Don Fraser and Candy Jones); "Candide" (Elizabeth Freeman); "Somewhere" (*West Side Story*, 1957; lyric by Stephen Sondheim, music by Leonard Bernstein) (David Porter and Barbara Berezowski); "Captain from Castile" (Don Fraser, Candy Jones, Elizabeth Freeman, David Porter, Barbara Berezowski); "Son of a Gun" (Ken Shelley and Colleen O'Connor); "Let's Hear It for Me" (Wendy Burge); "Free Again" (Kath Malmberg); "On the Waterfront" (Jack Courtney and Emily Benenson); and "Nicholas and Alexandra" (Toller Cranston); *Dance Medley*—"(We're Gonna) Rock around the Clock" (lyric and music by Max C. Freedman and James E. Myers aka Jimmy De Knight) (Candy Jones and Don Fraser); "Charleston" (*Runnin' Wild*, 1923; lyric by Cecil Mack, music by James P. Johnson) (Jack Courtney and Emily Benenson); "Tango" (Jack Courtney and Emily Benenson); "Nola" (Candy Jones and Don Fraser); "Sugar Blues" (Candy Jones and Don Fraser); and "Fascination" (French lyric by Maurice de Feraudy, English lyric by Dick Manning, music by Fermo Dante Marchetti), "The Varsity Drag" (*Good News*, 1927; lyric by Buddy B. G. "Buddy" DeSylva and Lew Brown, music by Ray Henderson), and "The Darktown Strutters' Ball" (lyric and music by Shelton Brooks) (All the Couples); *Russian Ode*—"The Young and the Restless" (Jim Millns and Colleen O'Connor); "Innocence" (Janet and Mark Hominuke); "Love Duet" (Toller Cranston and Emily Benenson); "The Warlords" (Gordon McKellen Jr., and Jack Courtney); "Loneliness of War" (Toller Cranston); "Vision" (David Porter, Barbara Berezowski); "Dream of Love" (Toller Cranston and Emily Benenson); and "Emptiness and Longing" (Toller Cranston)

Act Two: *Toller's Ball*—"Le prophete" (Full Company); "Graduation Ball I" (Toller Cranston); "Corsaire I" (Don Fraser and Candy Jones); "Graduation Ball II" (Toller Cranston); "Corsaire II" (Jim Millns and Colleen O'Connor); "Graduation Ball III" (Toller Cranston); and "La prophete" (reprise) (Full Company); "Gaiete parisienne" (Elizabeth Freeman); "Raymonda" (Wendy Burge); "Pas de deux" (Janet and Mark Hominuke); "Black Orpheus" (Kath Malmberg); "MacArthur Park" (lyric and music by Jimmy Webb) (Don Fraser and Candy Jones); "Tick-Tock" (Don Fraser and Candy Jones); *Latino*—"Rodrigo" (Jack Courtney and Emily Benenson); "Habanera" (Jim Millns and Colleen O'Connor); "La Carioca" (David Porter and Barbara Berezowski); "Scheherazade" (Ken Shelley); "A Fifth of Beethoven" (Jim Millns and Colleen O'Connor); "I Pagliacci" (Toller Cranston); Finale (Full Company)

Canadian Olympic medalist Toller Cranston made his professional debut in his ice-skating revue *The Ice Show* with a company that included a number of solo performers as well as a few professional ice-skating and ice-dancing couples.

Anna Kisselgoff in the *New York Times* said Cranston was "terrific" and her headline proclaimed he was "A Nureyev on Skates." He possessed "the same flamboyance and daring of the Soviet ballet stars at their most entertaining" and was truly "a wayward spirit in his own art" with "strong discipline" and "virtuoso tricks." The others in the company also delighted, including Gordon McKellen Jr., "whose razor-sharp virtuosity nearly catapults him off the thrust stage" (she noted that the close proximity of the skaters to the audience was "one of the show's breathtaking aspects").

The program didn't credit individual musical sources, although some were obvious, such as "Somewhere" and "The Varsity Drag." Otherwise, it appears that most of the music was drawn from classical and popular music. Perhaps the sequences titled "Captain from Castile," "On the Waterfront," and "Nicholas and Alexandra" used music from the films of those titles (by the respective composers Alfred Newman, Leonard Bernstein, and Richard Rodney Bennett) and probably the "Candide" selection was from Bernstein's musical. The program credited the song-writing team Al Kasha and Joel Hirschhorn for the music of the overture and the introduction, but otherwise didn't cite their material.

HELLZAPOPPIN

"A Musical Circus"

The revue opened on November 22, 1976, at the Mechanic Theatre in Baltimore, Maryland, played at the National Theatre, Washington, D.C., and then at the Colonial Theatre, Boston, Massachusetts, where it permanently closed on January 22, 1977.

Sketches: Abe Burrows, Bill Heyer, and Hank Beebe

Lyrics: Bill Heyer and Carolyn Leigh

Music: Hank Beebe and Jule Styne; additional music by Cy Coleman; dance music by Gordon Lowey Harrell

Direction: Jerry Adler; *Producers*: Alexander H. Cohen; coproduced by Hildy Parks and Roy A. Somlyo; *Choreography*: Donald Saddler; *Scenery* and *Lighting*: Robert Randolph; *Costumes*: Alvin Colt; *Musical Direction*: John Lesko

Cast: *Jerry Lewis*, Lynn Redgrave, Herb Edelman, Joey Faye, Brandon Maggart, Robert Fitch, Tom Batten, Mace Barrett, Justine Johnston, Bob Harvey, The Volantes, Bob Williams and Louie, Leonardo, Jill Choder; Ensemble: Marie Berry, Terry Calloway, Susan Danielle, Mercedes Ellington, Trudie Green, Lisa Guignard, Lisa Haapaniemi, Peter Heuchling, Gwen Hillier, Holly Jones, Michael Mann, P. J. Mann, Dana Jo Moore, Rick Pessagno, Rodney Reinber, Terry Rieser, Catherine Rice, Jeff Richards, Tudy Roach, Jane Robertson, Karen St. George, Fred Siretta, Robin Stone, Melanie Winter

The revue was presented in two acts.

Sketches and Musical Numbers

Act One: "Hellzapoppin" (lyric by Carolyn Leigh, music by Jule Styne) (Company); The Volantes; "Dare to Do" (lyric by Bill Heyer, music by Hank Beebe) (Jerry Lewis, Herb Edelman, Company); "Bouncing Back for More" (lyric by Carolyn Leigh, music by Cy Coleman) (Jerry Lewis); "A Husband, a Lover, a Wife" (lyric by Bill Heyer, music by Hank Beebe) (Lynn Redgrave, Brandon Maggart, Robert Fitch, Joey Faye, Mace Barrett); "Let's Put a Man on the Sun" (lyric by Bill Heyer, music by Hank Beebe) (Jerry Lewis, Senators); Bob Williams and Louie; "Hello, Mom" (lyric by Bill Heyer, music by Hank Beebe) (Company)

Act Two: "Once I've Got My Cane" (lyric by Bill Heyer, music by Hank Beebe) (Jerry Lewis, Ladies); "A Miracle Happened" (lyric by Bill Heyer, music by Hank Beebe) (Jill Choder); Leonardo; "Eighth Avenue" (lyric by Carolyn Leigh, music by Jule Styne) (Lynn Redgrave, Ladies); "The Four Faces of Arthur" (Jerry Lewis, Herb Edelman, Ladies); "A Hymn to Her" (Lynn Redgrave, The Hellzapoppin Glee Club); "One to a Customer" (lyric by Carolyn Leigh, music by Jule Styne) (Jerry Lewis); Finale (Company)

Hellzapoppin (without the apostrophe) was based on Ole Olsen and Chic Johnson's 1938 free-wheeling revue *Hellzapoppin'* (with apostrophe). When the latter closed, it was the longest-running musical in Broadway history, but the new incarnation was one of the most publicized bombs of the 1970s. After playing in Baltimore and Washington, D.C., the revue permanently closed in Boston and according to *Variety* lost $1,250,000.

In reviewing the opening night of the Baltimore tryout, Cedr in *Variety* said the revue was "only half the fun it could be" and needed "tons" of work as well as "pruning." Lewis was "quite funny" and Lynn Redgrave made "valuable" contributions to the evening, but both stars deserved better material. *Variety* noted that the old *Hellzapoppin'* shticks had been incorporated into the new production, including the woman who wanders through the audience shouting out for "Oscar"; the man who hopes to deliver a plant (and each time he appears the plant is larger and larger); the usherette who hopes to become a star (and announces that "a Jerry Lewis show is not a laughing matter"); and assorted hecklers who were placed throughout the auditorium.

Richard Coe in the *Washington Post* praised the first act, which began with a "boom-bang-blare" of an overture and then proceeded to demolish ***A Chorus Line***, but the second act required "considerable sharpening." David Richards in the *Washington Star* apologized to the lady in the row in front of him because he was "instinctively reaching out for the knob to change the channel." The revue was a "run-of-the-mill TV special" and never managed "to rise above the level of tired mediocrity."

Elliot Norton in the *Boston Herald American* said the revue "wasn't poppin' brightly enough," and Kevin Kelly's headline in the *Boston Globe* read "Hellzasplutterin'" because the critic said the revue had "embarrassingly inept material" and an "eminently miscast" star who was no "more than a fifth-rate movie madman."

But the revue had its moments, and Jerry Lewis shined throughout. The spoof of ***A Chorus Line*** found the cast members strung across the stage in the familiar manner of that show's logo, and when an unseen director commands one of the cast members to step forward and tell his story, Jerry Lewis stepped out of line, knock-kneed his way forward toward the apron of the stage, and proceeded to fall *splat!* into the orchestra pit. Another amusing skit focused on two television anchors who hate one another and do all they can to upstage the other, and Lewis performed in a savvy old-time show-biz manner the nostalgic "Once I've Got My Cane" and "One to a Customer." And Bob Williams and Louie impressed everyone, for the terrier Louie was completely unimpressed with being on the stage and thus refused to do tricks for his imploring master.

Once the debacle permanently closed, *New York* ran a cover story of the revue with the headline "Hellzafloppin!" and *People*'s title was "The Final Curtain Falls on *Hellzapoppin* but Nobody Is Applauding." The feuds between Lynn Redgrave and Lewis, and between producer Alexander Cohen and Lewis, were widely reported in the press, but in an interview with the *New York Times* two months after the Broadway closing Redgrave "swiftly cut short discussions of the rumored tensions between herself and Jerry Lewis." Almost a year after the revue shuttered, *Variety* reported there were two legal actions surrounding the production, including one by Cohen against Lewis that alleged that the star had "caused the musical's failure" or "at least" had prevented "effective doctoring" of the show, due to the claim that Lewis refused to appear with Redgrave and declined to rehearse with her. The trade paper later reported that the suit was settled out of court when Lewis reportedly agreed to pay an undisclosed settlement to Cohen (which *Variety* reported was "understood to be somewhere between $75,000 and $100,000").

During the course of the tryout, "Dare to Do," "Let's Put a Man on the Sun," and "The Four Faces of Arthur" were dropped, and The Villams (a juggling and acrobatic act) were added to the cast. "Bouncing Back for More" had originally been written for (but never used in) Cy Coleman and Carolyn Leigh's 1960 musical *Wildcat*, and the song is included in Sara Zahn's collection *Witchcraft: The Songs of Carolyn Leigh* (Harbinger Records CD # HCD-1702).

The revue had been scheduled to play previews at the Minskoff Theatre for the period January 25–February 12, 1977, prior to the official opening on February 13. NBC's *Big Event* had planned to televise live the first thirty minutes of the opening night performance, but with the revue's collapse the network quickly substituted a rerun of the 1968 film *2001: A Space Odyssey*.

As noted, Ole Olsen and Chic Johnson's 1938 revue *Hellzapoppin'* ("The Screamlined Revue") was an enormous hit; it played for 1,404 performances and excelled in zany, off-the-wall humor and cast interaction with the audience; it was followed by the team's *Sons o' Fun* which opened in 1941 and played for 742 performances; then by *Laffing Room Only* (1944; 233 showings); *Funzapoppin'* (1949; thirty-seven performances); *Pardon Our French* (1950; 100 performances); a one-month appearance at the Palace in 1952; and the 1954 revue *Pardon Our Antenna*, which closed during its pre-Broadway tryout.

Prior to the current 1976–1977 *Hellzapoppin*, Alexander Cohen had presented *Hellzapoppin' '67* ("The World's Funniest Musical") at Montreal's Expo '67 where it opened on July 1, 1967. The cast included Soupy Sales, Luba Lisa, Ted Thurston, Will B. Able, and Brandon Maggart (the latter also appeared in the 1976–1977 production), and the score was by Marian Grudeff and Raymond Jessel, who had written the songs for Cohen's 1965 Broadway musical *Baker Street*. The revue was set to open on Broadway in December 1967 as *Hellzapoppin' '68*, but it never got out of Montreal.

On March 1, 1972, Cohen then presented a *Hellzapoppin'* television special on the *ABC Comedy Hour* with Lynn Redgrave, Bob Williams and Louie, and The Volantes, all of whom were seen in the 1976–1977 production; others in the television version were Jack Cassidy, Rex Reed, Lyle Waggoner, The Jackson Five, and, from the 1967 production, Will B. Able. *Variety* said the *Laugh-In*-styled show proved "there's still life left in the *Hellzapoppin'* concept" and thought the show "was promising enough to warrant consideration as a summer replacement series" and might eventually find itself on ABC's regular prime-time schedule. But a series never materialized and the March 1 episode was the revue's first and only television showing.

1977–1978 Season

BEATLEMANIA

Theatre: Winter Garden Theatre
Opening Date: May 31, 1977; *Closing Date*: October 17, 1979
Performances: 920
"Editorial Content": Robert Rabinowitz, Bob Gill, and Lynda Obst
Lyrics and *Music*: Unless otherwise noted, all songs by John Lennon and Paul McCartney (some numbers were primarily written by one or the other, some in collaboration, and all were officially credited to both).
Direction: "Production supervised" by Jules Fisher and "Visuals" Direction by Charles E. Hoefler; *Producers*: David Krebs and Steven Leber; *Scenery*: Robert D. Mitchell; *Multi-Media Images*: Robert Rabinowitz, Bob Gill, Shep Kerman, and Kathleen Rabinowitz; *Costumes*: Not credited; *Lighting*: Jules Fisher; *Musical Direction*: Not credited (Sandy Yaguda was cited for "Musical Supervision")
Cast: The Group: Joe Pecorino (Rhythm Guitar), Mitch Weissman (Bass Guitar), Leslie Fradkin (Lead Guitar), Justin McNeill (Drums)
The concert was presented in two acts.

Musical Numbers

Note: All songs were performed by the four-member cast; see "The Group," above.
Act One: Camelot and Pre-Beatles: "Let's Twist Again" (lyric and music by Kal Mann and Dave Appell); "Roll Over Beethoven" (lyric and music by Chuck Berry); "Bye Bye Love" (lyric and music by Felice and Boudleaux Bryant); "Hound Dog" (lyric and music by Jerry Lieber and Mike Stoller); and "Roll Over Beethoven" (reprise); The Coming: "I Want to Hold Your Hand" and "She Loves You"; Making It: "Help!"; "If I Fell"; "Can't Buy Me Love"; "Day Tripper"; Listening: "Yesterday"; "Eleanor Rigby"; "We Can Work It Out"; and "Nowhere Man"; Tripping: "A Day in the Life"; "Strawberry Fields Forever"; "Penny Lane"; "Magical Mystery Tour"; and "Lucy in the Sky with Diamonds"
Act Two: Dropping Out: "Lady Madonna"; "The Fool on the Hill"; "Got to Get You Into My Life"; "Michelle"; and "Get Back"; Flower Power: "Come Together"; "With a Little Help from My Friends"; and "All You Need Is Love"; Bottoming Out: "Revolution"; "Helter Skelter"; and "Hey Jude"; Moving On: "I Am the Walrus"; "The Long and Winding Road"; and "Let It Be"

Best Plays reported that *Beatlemania* began performances on May 26, 1977, but never scheduled an official opening night. Newspaper critics eventually began to attend performances and reviewed the show, and, in conjunction with the League of New York Theatres and Producers, the producers of *Beatlemania* agreed that May 31 was the formal opening date. *Best Plays* also reported that during the final weeks of the run the production gave additional performances "on an irregular and unrecorded schedule" and that the final number of showings totaled 920.

The evening was a four-man concert of songs by Beatle lookalikes and was divided into segments in which songs were performed to reflect the 1960s and the Beatles' career. The clichéd and somewhat pretentious program notes thus titled the segments as "The Coming," "Tripping," "Dropping Out," and "Flower Power," among others. For "Moving On," the concert's final sequence, the program stated the Beatles had moved "beyond their audiences."

John Rockwell in the *New York Times* said the evening was "unobjectionable" and "ingratiating enough" if you didn't take it too seriously; the songs "plowed along chronologically" and slides provided "simple-minded news headlines" to evoke the era. He noted that the four performers did "a pretty fine job" of imitating the Beatles, and Mitch Weissman (in the Paul McCartney role) was "downright creepy in his accuracy."

DIE FLEDERMAUS

Theatre: The New York State Theatre
Opening Date: September 2, 1977; *Closing Date*: November 1, 1977
Performances: 7 (in repertory)
Libretto: Carl Haffner and Richard Genee (English adaptation by Ruth and Thomas Martin)
Music: Johann Strauss
Direction: Gerald Freedman (Richard Getke, Stage Director); *Producer*: The New York City Opera Company; *Choreography*: Thomas Andrew; *Scenery*: Lloyd Evans; *Costumes*: Theoni V. Aldredge; *Lighting*: Hans Sondheimer; *Choral Master*: Lloyd Walser; *Musical Direction*: Julius Rudel
Cast: Henry Price (Alfred), Beverly Sills (Adele), Johanna Meier (Rosalinda von Eisenstein), Charles Roe (Gabriel von Eisenstein), Melvin Lowery (Doctor Blind), David Holloway (Doctor Falke), Richard McKee (Frank), Puli Toro (Sally), Jack Sims (Ivan), David Rae Smith (Prince Orlofsky), Coley Worth (Frosh); Solo Dancers: Sandra Balestracci, Esperanza Galan, Juliu Horvath; Ensemble: The New York City Opera Company Chorus and Dancers

Johann Strauss's *Die Fledermaus* had been revived twice by the New York City Opera Company during the 1975–1976 season. For the current production, Johanna Meier and David Rae Smith reprised their respective roles of Rosalinda and Prince Orlofsky, and, in a surprise bit of casting, Beverly Sills sang the role of Adele. Richard Traubner in the *New York Times* reported that in October 1955 Sills had made her City Opera debut as Rosalinda and had reprised the role numerous times throughout her career. When Julius Rudel, the artistic director of City Opera and frequent conductor for the company, asked Sills to sing Rosalinda for the current production she said she had become "bored" with the role and suggested she would prefer to sing Adele instead.

John Rockwell in the *New York Times* felt that Johanna Meier was "well-suited" to the role of Rosalinda "but both musically and dramatically" she lacked the "confidence" which the part demanded. He found Sills "an amusingly wry, endearing duckling of an Adele," and noted her voice was in "good shape" with only occasional "slight edginess."

The production returned for the City Opera's spring season when it opened on March 8, 1978, and closed on April 11, 1978, for three performances, for a seasonal total of ten showings. One of the spring performances included Noelle Rogers as Rosalinda, whom Joseph Horowitz in the *New York Times* found "tall, willowy and enticing" with a "substantial and colorful" lyric soprano that had "style and enthusiasm to spare." The spring revival also included the addition of a second-act dance sequence for New York City Ballet principal Patricia McBride. Horowitz also noted that Stefan Minde made his City Opera debut as conductor, and "without the benefit of orchestral rehearsals" he "made a fine impression."

For more information about the operetta, see entry for the 1974 production as well as for the August 1975 revival.

MAN OF LA MANCHA

Theatre: Palace Theatre
Opening Date: September 15, 1977; *Closing Date*: December 31, 1977
Performances: 124

Book: Dale Wasserman
Lyrics: Joe Darion
Music: Mitch Leigh
Based on the novel *Don Quixote* by Miguel de Cervantes (Volume One of the novel was published in 1605, and Volume Two in 1615); also based on the 1959 telefilm *I, Don Quixote* by Dale Wasserman.
Direction: Albert Marre (Greg Hirsch, Assistant to Director); *Producer*: Eugene V. Wolsk; *Choreography*: Not Credited; *Scenery* and *Lighting*: Howard Bay; *Costumes*: Howard Bay and Patton Campbell; *Musical Direction*: Robert Brandzel
Cast: *Richard Kiley* (Don Quixote, Cervantes), Tony Martinez (Sancho), Ben Vargas (The Horse, Tenorio), Hector (Jaime) Mercado (The Mule, Jose), Bob Wright (The Innkeeper), Marceline Decker (Maria), Chev Rodgers (Pedro), Ted Forlow (Anselmo, The Barber), Mark Holliday (Juan), Anthony DeVecchi (Paco), Emily Yancy (Aldonza), Joan Susswein (Fermina, Moorish Dancer), Robin Polseno (Guitarist), Edmond Varrato (Jorge), David Wasson (Fernando, Guard), Harriett Conrad (Antonia), Margaret Coleman (The Housekeeper), Taylor Reed (The Padre), Ian Sullivan (Doctor Carrasco, The Knight), Renato Cibelli (The Captain), Michael St. Paul (Guard)
The musical was presented in one act.
The action takes place at the end of the sixteenth century in a dungeon in Seville and in the imagination of Cervantes.

Musical Numbers

"Man of La Mancha" ("I, Don Quixote") (Richard Kiley, Tony Martinez, Ben Vargas, Hector Mercado); "It's All the Same" (Emily Yancy, Muleteers); "Dulcinea" (Richard Kiley; later, Muleteers); "I'm Only Thinking of Him" (Taylor Reed, Harriett Conrad, Margaret Coleman; later, Ian Sullivan); "I Really Like Him" (Tony Martinez); "What Does He Want of Me?" (Emily Yancy); "Little Bird, Little Bird" (Ted Forlow, Muleteers); "Barber's Song" (Ted Forlow); "Golden Helmet of Mambrino" (Richard Kiley, Tony Martinez, Ted Forlow, Muleteers); "To Each His Dulcinea" (Taylor Reed); "The Quest" ("The Impossible Dream") (Richard Kiley); "The Combat" (Richard Kiley, Emily Yancy, Tony Martinez, Muleteers); "The Dubbing" (Bob Wright, Emily Yancy, Tony Martinez); "The Abduction" (Emily Yancy, Muleteers); "Moorish Dance" (Ensemble); "Aldonza" (Emily Yancy); "The Knight of the Mirrors" (Richard Kiley, Ian Sullivan, The Knight's Attendants); "A Little Gossip" (Tony Martinez); "Dulcinea" (reprise) (Emily Yancy); "Man of La Mancha" (reprise) (Richard Kiley, Emily Yancy, Tony Martinez); "The Psalm" (Taylor Reed); "The Quest" (reprise) (Company)

The current limited-engagement revival of *Man of La Mancha* was part of a national tour in which Richard Kiley re-created his original role of Cervantes/Don Quixote. The performer had first appeared in the musical's world premiere at the Goodspeed Opera House, East Haddam, Connecticut, in the summer of 1965, and then on Broadway the following fall where he won the Tony Award for Best Leading Actor in a Musical. He also appeared in a limited-engagement revival at Lincoln Center in 1972, and the current production marked his last New York performances in the role (later New York revivals starred Raul Julia and Brian Stokes Mitchell). (The current production was yet another dubious opportunity to experience what is perhaps the most annoying and cringe-inducing character in all musical theatre, Sancho, who seems to come not from La Mancha but from La Borscht Belt.)

Richard Eder in the *New York Times* said Sancho was the "best character" in the musical, but noted that Aldonza was a "pretty unworkable" and "stock character." Eder stated that the production was "big and generally first-rate" and it would have been "hard to improve upon Mr. Kiley's performance." Douglas Watt in the *New York Daily News* noted that Kiley "cut a superb figure" in his dual roles, but the musical itself was starting to show its "holes" with its "serviceable enough" book and a score that didn't equal "the profundities" of the original novel.

Martin Gottfried in the *New York Post* said Kiley was giving "the performance of his career," and while he was "excellent" in 1965, he was now "superior" and brought "depth and compassion perhaps greater than exists in the script." Gottfried noted the book was "awkward" and the lyrics "weak," and while Mitch Leigh's music was "less of Spain than of movie Westerns set in Spanish California," it was nonetheless "musicianly" (Leigh incidentally conducted the overture for the opening night performance).

Although Jack Cole had created and heretofore had always been credited for the musical's choreography, the current production omitted his name from the program and in fact didn't even list a choreographer. Gottfried said the late Cole "deserves credit for his work" because his dances had been "reconstructed" for the revival.

For more information about the musical, see entry for the 1972 revival.

ESTRADA

"The 1977 Music and Dance Festival from the Soviet Union"

Theatre: Majestic Theatre
Opening Date: September 20, 1977; *Closing Date*: September 26, 1977
Performances: 7
Producer: United Euram (Nikolai Laktionov, Artistic Director; and Nadezhda Kazantzeva, Administrative Director); *Choreography*: Tamara Golovanova
Cast: Nani Bregvadze (Singer), Grigori Davidenko and Vladimir Kononovich (Ukrainian Comic Dance Team), Natalia and Oleg Kiriushkin (Mimes), Larisa Kudeyarova (Acrobat), Yefim Levinson and Galina Korzina (Puppet Masters), Orera (Georgian Vocal Instrumental Group), Pesnyary (Pop-Rock Group), Vladimir Serov (Cyclist and Aerialist), Souvenir Ensemble (Dance Ensemble), Alla, Vyacheslav, and Vyacheslav Jr., Rasshivkin (Acrobats)
The revue was presented in two acts.

Musical Numbers

Act One: "Moscow Nights" (lyric and music by V. Soloviev-Sedoy) (Company); "Korobeiniki" (Russian Dance) (Souvenir Ensemble); Four Contemporary Byelorussian Folk Songs (Pesnyary); "Dva kuma" (Comic Dance) (Vladimir Kononovich and Grigori Davidenko); "Northern Festive Dance" (Souvenir Ensemble); "A Friendship That Never Came to Be" (Souvenir Ensemble); Puppet Sketches (Yefim Levinson and Galina Korzina); "Barynya" (Russian Dance) (Souvenir Ensemble)

Act Two: "Sabre Dance" (Souvenir Ensemble); Medley including "Give My Regards to Broadway" (*Little Johnny Jones*, 1904; lyric and music by George M. Cohan) and "The Sidewalks of New York" ("East Side, West Side, All Around the Town") (lyric by James W. Blake, music by Charles B. Lawlor) (Orera); Bicycle on the Wire (Vladimir Serov); "Serdtse" (lyric and music by I. Dunaevsky) (Orera); "Svetlyachok" (Georgian Folk Song) (Orera); "Tbiliso" (lyric by Peter Gruzinsky, music by Revaz Lagidze) (Nani Bregvadze); "Dorogoy Dlinoyu" (Old Song) (Nani Bregvadze); Acrobatic Sketch with a Hoop (Larisa Kudeyarova); "Gypsy Fantasy" (Souvenir Ensemble); Acrobatic Sketch (Alla, Vyacheslav, and Vyacheslav Jr., Rasshivkin); Specialty (Natalia and Olga Kiriushkin); "Potekha" (Comic Dance) (Souvenir Ensemble); Finale (Company)

The Russian revue *Estrada* (which roughly translates as "variety") was an evening of dance, song, mime, and puppet, acrobatic, cyclist, and aerialist acts from the Soviet Union, but unlike ***Ipi-Tombi*** the revue wasn't picketed by groups protesting abuse of human rights in the native country of the performers.

Richard Eder in the *New York Times* found occasional "charm" and "mild excitement" in the entertainment but felt the proceedings sometimes had the depressing air of "the displays at airport souvenir stands" and few seemed "authentic." But the Orera singers offered "exuberant, roaring" voices with a touch of yodeling and scat-singing that soon morphed into "soft, crooning" melody, and the overall "surrealistic" effect gave the impression "of lions doing gazelle impersonations." The Souvenir dance ensemble was "agreeable" in several folk routines, but a gypsy dance (with taped music) was "limp and painfully banal."

When the Orera singers offered a brief medley of such American songs as "Give My Regards to Broadway" and "East Side, West Side," Eder felt they were out of their element (but this nice-sounding touch seems to have been a friendly gesture from the Russians to Broadway and New York).

The Broadway engagement was booked for three weeks, but closed after just seven performances. The company then began a U.S. national tour.

COMEDY WITH MUSIC

"A Musical Entertainment by Victor Borge"

Theatre: Imperial Theater
Opening Date: October 3, 1977; *Closing Date*: November 27, 1977
Performances: 66
Producers: The Edgewood Organization, Inc. (Lewis Friedman and John W. Ballard, Executive Directors) (Dean Lenz and Allison McLeod, Associate Producers); *Scenery* and *Lighting*: Neil Peter Jampolis; *Costumes*: Marylyn Mulvey's gown by Donald Brook
Cast: *Victor Borge*, Marylyn Mulvey

Musical Numbers

Act One: In order of appearance—Victor Borge
Act Two: In order of disappearance—The Concert; Marylyn Mulvey; Victor Borge; The Audience

Comedy with Music was another evening of Victor Borge's whimsical evenings of word and music play where he excelled in comical confrontations with his piano: sometimes the piano lost, sometimes Borge lost, but the audience always won.

He had first appeared on Broadway in the revised edition of the revue *Crazy with the Heat*, which opened on January 14, 1941, at the 44th Street Theatre for ninety-nine performances. His one-man revue *Comedy in Music* premiered on October 2, 1953, for 849 performances and *Comedy in Music*: *Opus 2* opened on November 9, 1964, at the John Golden Theatre for 192 showings. After the current production, Borge appeared in New York one more time on December 5, 1989, with *Victor Borge on Broadway* at the Brooks Atkinson Theatre for eight performances.

The current limited engagement was part of a national tour. Borge revisited a few of his old routines and offered new ones, and in the second act was briefly joined by soprano Marylyn Mulvey for a demolition of Russian opera.

T. E. Kalem in *Time* was happy that "one of the master funnymen of the age is back," and noted one could never be sure if Borge regarded the piano, the piano bench, and the microphone as "allies or enemies." Douglas Watt in the *New York Daily News* praised the "incomparable" performer who was a "boulevardier continually wandering up the wrong boulevard." Howard Kissel in *Women's Wear Daily* noted that Borge was a specialist at "genial silliness" but was also a pianist of "great delicacy and power" and thus no one would object "if he played some piece straight through." And Martin Gottfried in the *New York Post* found Borge "one of the legitimate international stars and the rare comic one" and said the performer defined the term "class act."

Although Richard Eder in the *New York Times* admitted Borge was a comic of "grace and civility," he found his stage patter "tired" and noted that some of the routines lacked "energy." In the past, Borge had been a "mixture of charm and perilousness" but now the latter was gone and the performance seemed "long and fumbling"; although some of the charm remained, Borge was now "limping badly."

The cast album of the 1953 production of *Comedy in Music* was recorded live by Columbia Records (LP # CL-554), and in 1956 Borge brought his evening to television in two representative specials titled *Comedy in Music: The Victor Borge Show*.

CLEO ON BROADWAY

Theatre: Minskoff Theatre
Opening Date: October 5, 1977; *Closing Date*: October 9, 1977
Performances: 6
Producer: Ron Delsener; *Lighting*: Andrea Wilson; *Musical Direction*: John Dankworth
Cast: *Cleo Laine*, Bill Conti, John Dankworth and His Orchestra
The concert was presented in one act.

Singer Cleo Laine appeared in a limited engagement concert of six performances with her husband, the conductor and composer John Dankworth and his orchestra. Also on the bill was conductor and film composer Bill Conti.

Robert Palmer in the *New York Times* said Laine's voice was "perhaps a more remarkable instrument than any other jazz vocalist." But he complained that she was "cool, cool" and he couldn't tell "whether the songs mean something personal to her or not." But if you didn't expect "a great deal of emotional involvement" from her, then you would "love" her. He noted that Dankworth was a "canny" musical director whose saxophone and clarinet were "an effective foil for his wife's spectacular voice." For a segment of movie music, Conti conducted the orchestra "with such hammy over-emphasis that one suspects he might be parodying Leonard Bernstein."

HAIR

"The American Tribal Love Rock Musical"

Theatre: Biltmore Theatre
Opening Date: October 5, 1977; *Closing Date*: November 6, 1977
Performances: 43
Book and *Lyrics*: Gerome Ragni and James Rado
Music: Galt MacDermot
Direction: Tom O'Horgan; *Producers*: Michael Butler (George Milman, Associate Producer); *Choreography*: Julie Arenal (Wesley Fata, Assistant Choreographer); *Scenery*: Robin Wagner; *Costumes*: Nancy Potts; *Lighting*: Jules Fisher; *Musical Direction*: Kirk Nurock
Cast: Randall Easterbrook (Claude), Michael Hoit (Berger), Scott Thornton (Woof), Cleavant Derricks (Hud), Ellen Foley (Sheila), Iris Rosenkrantz (Jeanie), Alaina Reed (Dionne), Kristen Vigard (Crissy), Michael Leslie (Shopping Cart Lady); Mothers: Annie Golden, Louis Mattioli, and Perry Arthur; Fathers: James Rich, Eva Charney, and Martha Wingate; Principals: Carl Woerner, Michael Leslie, and Linda Myers; Perry Arthur (Tourist), Carl Woerner (Tourist, General Grant), Linda Myers (Abraham Lincoln), Byron Utley (Sergeant), Lori Wagner (Parent), James Rich (Parent); Tribe: Perry Arthur, Emily Bindiger, Paul Binotto, Eva Charney, Loretta Devine, Doug Katsaros, Michael Leslie, Louis Mattioli, Linda Myers, Raymond Patterson, James Rich, James Sbano, Deborah Van Valkenburgh, Lori Wagner, Doug Wall, Martha Wingate, Carl Woerner, Charlaine Woodard
The musical was presented in two acts.
The action takes place in the 1960s in the East Village.

Musical Numbers

Act One: "Aquarius" (Raymond Patterson, Company); "Donna" (Michael Hoit, Company); "Hashish" (Company); "Sodomy" (Scott Thornton, Company); "Colored Spade" (Cleavant Derricks); "Manchester" (Randall Easterbrook); "Ain't Got No" (Scott Thornton, Cleavant Derricks, Alaina Reed, Company); "Dead End" (Charlaine Woodard, Loretta Devine, Byron Utley, Raymond Patterson, Michael Leslie); "I Believe in Love" (Ellen Foley); "Air" (Annie Golden, Kristen Vigard, Alaina Reed); "Initials" (Company); "I Got Life" (Randall Easterbrook, Company); "Going Down" (Michael Hoit, Company); "Hair" (Randall Easterbrook, Michael Hoit, Company); "My Conviction" (Perry Arthur or Carl Woerner); "Easy to Be Hard" (Ellen Foley); "Don't Put It Down" (Michael Hoit, Scott Thornton, Cleavant Derricks, Doug Wall); "Frank Mills" (Kristen Vigard); "Be-In" (Company); "Where Do I Go" (Randall Easterbook, Company)
Act Two: "Electric Blues" (Peter Gallagher, Lori Wagner, Eva Charney, Louis Mattioli, James Sbano); "Black Boys" (Ellen Foley, Lori Wagner, Deborah Van Valkenberg); "White Boys" (Loretta Devine, Alaina Reed, Charlaine Woodard); "Walking in Space" (Company); "Abie Baby" (Cleavant Derricks, Byron Utley, Raymond Patterson, Linda Myers); "Three-Five-Zero-Zero" (Company); "What a Piece of Work Is Man" (Raymond Patterson, James Rich); "Good Morning Starshine" (Ellen Foley, Company); "The Bed" (Company); "The Flesh Failures" ("Let the Sun Shine In") (Randall Easterbook, Ellen Foley, Alaina Reed, Company)

The revival of *Hair* came along five years after the original closed, and for most of the critics and audiences the bloom was off the rose. The musical was perhaps too old to be fresh and timely and too young to be a period piece (but a 2009 revival did well, and so perhaps later audiences viewed the show as a time capsule of the mid- and late 1960s).

The revival opened at the Biltmore Theatre, the home of the original Broadway production, and virtually the entire original creative team was involved in the new mounting. After a two-month preview period of seventy-nine performances, the musical opened to poor reviews and lasted just five weeks. During previews, the show underwent an inordinate number of major casting changes. For the role of Claude, David Patrick Kelly was succeeded by Randall Easterbrook (incidentally, Peter Gallagher was the understudy for the role); for Berger, Doug Katsaros, then James Sband, and then finally Michael Hoit played the role; Soni Moreno was Crissy, and was succeeded by Kristen Vigard; and Trudy Perkins was succeeded by Alaina Reed for the role of Dionne.

Hair first opened at the Public Theatre's Anspacher Theatre on October 20, 1967, for forty-nine performances; transferred to the Cheetah Theatre on December 22, 1967, for forty-five showings; and then to Broadway at the Biltmore on April 29, 1968, for a marathon run of 1,750 performances. The musical was an atmospheric mood piece that emphasized a particular point of view rather than plot and character, and hence was the first successful concept musical (for more information about this genre, see ***Company***).

The hippies and drops-outs of *Hair* railed against the establishment and celebrated their counterculture life style of illegal drugs, casual sex, and protest (specifically against the draft and the Vietnam War). Like the later *Rent* (1996) and its sentimental glorification of Village-type misfits, *Hair*'s message and its more-sensitive-than-thou hippies were passé even before the musical opened. But the combination of Galt MacDermot's lively score (which included a number of songs that enjoyed Hit Parade status, including "Aquarius," "Good Morning Starshine," and "Let the Sun Shine In"), the edginess of its clearly non-mainstream attitude, and its rather innocent and sometimes tongue-in-cheek vulgarity (including its celebrated, gratuitous, and pretentious nude scene) made *Hair* the era's zeitgeist.

The headlines of the critics' reviews for the revival seemed to say it all: "Revived *Hair* Shows Its Gray" (Richard Eder, *New York Times*), "Defoliated" (T. E. Kalem, *Time*), and "Bald" (Jack Kroll, *Newsweek*). Eder said "nothing ages worse than graffiti," and thus *Hair* was too old to be "timely" and too young for "nostalgia." And when a cast member dropped his pants, Eder could only reflect that "pants are in fact an older and sturdier human tradition than pantlessness." As for the character of Claude, the role was now the "least sufferable" with its "saintly attitudes," and Eder suggested that someone should "drop a guitar" on him. Kalem noted the musical was "lavish in dispraise of things American" and gave vent to a generation that was "overprivileged, overindulged, and woefully underdisciplined"; and Kroll stated "the Revelation According to St. Hippie is both too close chronologically and too distant emotionally to work now."

Howard Kissel in *Women's Wear Daily* said the original production of *Hair* brought an "era of amateurism" to Broadway and was the "progenitor" of the three "most horrendous" musicals he had ever seen (***Two Gentlemen of Verona***, ***Via Galactica***, and ***Inner City***). The revival revealed that the hippies of the 1960s were as passé as 1940s bobbysoxers and 1950s greasers; further, the show was constructed in four-minute "segments" that were "strung together no more tightly than *The Johnny Carson Show*" (and "only the commercials are missing").

Martin Gottfried in the *New York Post* said the musical was always "adolescent, disorganized and unprofessional" and now was "terribly dated" because it was difficult to be interested or involved in a musical that had no "connecting thread." But like all the critics, he felt MacDermot's score was the "best part" of the evening.

Douglas Watt in the *New York Daily News* said the days of the 1960s were "gone, kids, gone, lost in a marijuana cloud." But he rightly predicted future success for the musical because "a whole new audience of thirty-ish oldsters" might see the show as representing a "gritty, lusty, aching Nirvana whose true name is Youth."

RCA Victor Records released both the 1967 Off-Broadway (LP # LSO-1143) and the 1968 Broadway (LP # LSO-1150) cast albums, and a later LP reissue (# 1150-1-RC) included previously unreleased material that was recorded at the time of the Broadway cast album session ("Going Down" and "Electric Blues"). A 1988 CD release of the Broadway cast album included five previously unissued songs ("I Believe in Love," "The Bed," and reprise versions of "Ain't Got No," "Manchester, England," and "Walking in Space"). In 2003, RCA released a "deluxe" two-CD edition (# 82876-56085-2) of both the Off-Broadway and Broadway cast albums, including previously unreleased tracks from the 1967 production (an "Opening" sequence; "Red Blue and White" [which became "Don't Put It Down" for the Broadway version]; and "Sentimental Ending" [a finale that wasn't listed in the Off-Broadway program but was included in the published script]).

Besides the above, RCA released *DisinHAIRited* (LP # LSO-1163), later issued on CD by RCA/Arkiv Music (# 05095), a collection of songs written for but not used in the musical as well as ones especially written for the recording, including "One-Thousand-Year-Old Man," "So Sing the Children on the Avenue," "Manhattan Beggar," "Mr. Berger," "I'm Hung," and "Mess o' Dirt" (among the performers are James Rado, Gerome Ragni, Galt MacDermot, Melba Moore, Susanna Nordstrom, Donnie Burks, and Leata Galloway). Other recordings include: a British studio cast album (Polydor Records LP # 583-043), a Paris cast album (Philips Records LP # 844-987-BY), the Tokyo cast album (RCA LP # LSO-1170), a 2004 concert version that was a benefit for the Actors' Fund of America (Ghostlight Records CD # 1968-2), and *Hair Styles*, a selection of songs from the musical by the Terminal Barbershop (Atco Records LP # SD-33-301).

The script was published in paperback by Pocket Books in 1969, and was also included in the hardback collection *Great Rock Musicals*, edited by Stanley Richards and published by Stein and Day in 1979. In 2003, *Let the Sun Shine In*: *The Genius of "Hair"* by Scott Miller was published in paperback by Heinemann, and in 2010 *"HAIR"*: *The Story of the Show That Defined a Generation* by Eric Grode (with a forward by James Rado) was published in hardback by Running Press.

Besides the current revival, the musical was performed in concert by Encores! at City Center on May 3, 2001 ("Dead End" and "Oh Great God of Power" were added to the score), and in 2004 there was a special Actors' Fund concert performance (referenced above).

On September 22, 2007, the musical was presented for three concert showings at Central Park's Delacorte Theatre; directed by Diane Paulus, the concert was the genesis for the later 2009 revival, which she also directed. The production opened at the Al Hirschfeld (formerly Martin Beck) Theatre on March 31, 2009, and was more successful than the current mounting. It chalked up 519 performances, won the Tony Award for Best Musical Revival, was recorded by Ghostlight Records (CD # 8-44-67), and was the subject of the 2009 documentary film *"Hair"*: *Let the Sun Shine In*. The two Paulus productions added a number of songs not in the original: "Ain't Got No Grass," "Hello, There," "Oh Great God of Power," "Minuet," "Yes, I's Finished on Y'alls Farmlands," "Give Up All Desires," "How Dare They Try," "Eyes Look Your Last," "The Stone Age," and "Sheila Franklin"; "Colored Spade" was included, but was retitled "I'm Black."

A weak and disappointing film version was released by United Artists in 1979, and a two-LP soundtrack was issued by RCA (# CBL2-3274). During this era, many film adaptations of Broadway musicals were helmed by directors who seemed clueless about the genre (Richard Attenborough's *Oh! What a Lovely War* and *A Chorus Line*; Sidney Lumet's *The Wiz*; and John Houston's *Annie*), but when Milos Forman was announced as the film's director he at least seemed like an inspired choice because his style and sensibility appeared to be a natural match for the iconoclastic material. However, his film version of *Hair* proved as uninteresting as *Annie* and most other film adaptations of the era.

The original London production of *Hair* opened on September 27, 1968, at the Shaftesbury Theatre for 1,998 performances, which surpassed the lengthy run of the original Broadway mounting.

There was a sequel of sorts to *Hair*. James Rado wrote the lyrics and music and cowrote the book with Ted Rado for *Rainbow*, which opened Off Broadway at the Orpheum Theatre on December 18, 1972, for forty-eight performances. In 1973, a revised version briefly (*very* briefly) toured with James Rado as *The Rainbow Rainbeam Radio Show*, and was subtitled *Heavenszapopin'*. The confusing concert-like musical (which included some pleasant songs) focused on the spirit of a young man who was killed in the Vietnam War and who now travels throughout the universe in search of peace. Perhaps he was *Hair*'s Claude, who was drafted and sent to Vietnam.

THE ACT

"The New Musical Drama" / "A New Musical"

Theatre: Majestic Theatre
Opening Date: October 29, 1977; *Closing Date*: July 1, 1978
Performances: 240
Book: George Furth

Lyrics: Fred Ebb
Music: John Kander
Direction: Martin Scorsese; *Producers*: The Shubert Organization (A Feuer and Martin Production); *Choreography*: Ron Lewis; *Scenery*: Tony Walton; *Costumes*: Halston; *Lighting*: Tharon Musser; *Musical Direction*: Stanley Lebowsky
Cast: Christopher Barrett (Lenny Kanter), *Liza Minnelli* (Michele Craig), Arnold Soboloff (Nat Schreiber), Barry Nelson (Dan Connors), Roger Minami (Arthur), Mark Goddard (Charley Price), Gayle Crofoot (Molly Connors); The Boys: Wayne Cilento, Michael Leeds, Roger Minami, Albert Stephenson; The Girls: Carol Estey, Laurie Dawn Skinner
The musical was presented in two acts.
The action takes place during Michelle Craig's Las Vegas nightclub act as well as in her memories.

Musical Numbers

Act One: "Shine It On" (Liza Minnelli, Ensemble); "It's the Strangest Thing" (Liza Minnelli); "Bobo's" (Liza Minnelli, Ensemble); "Turning" ("Shaker Hymn") (Ensemble); "Little Do They Know" (Ensemble); "Arthur in the Afternoon" (Liza Minnelli, Roger Minami); "Hollywood, California" (Liza Minnelli, Ensemble); "The Money Tree" (Liza Minnelli)
Act Two: "City Lights" (Liza Minnelli, Ensemble); "There When I Need Him" (Liza Minnelli); "Hot Enough for You?" (Liza Minnelli, Dancers); "Little Do They Know" (reprise) (Ensemble); "Finale" (Liza Minnelli); "My Own Space" (Liza Minnelli)

The Act offered an interesting concept: as famous entertainer Michelle Craig (Liza Minnelli) performs her act in a Las Vegas nightclub, she weaves back and forth in time and recalls the events and the people of her past. The problem was that her story wasn't very interesting and compelling, George Furth's book was paper thin, and John Kander and Fred Ebb's score was one of their mildest. The show-stopper "City Lights" was a happy exception with its genuine old-time razz-ma-tazz (and it neatly complemented their title song from the previous year's film *New York, New York*, which Minnelli had memorably introduced), "Arthur in the Afternoon" was amusing (although it wasn't composed for *The Act* and was in fact a reworked version of "Mamie in the Afternoon," a song cut from Kander's 1962 flop *A Family Affair*), and a third superior song, "Please, Sir," was dropped during the tryout. If the story had given Michelle's life a complexity and a sense of urgency and had the nightclub songs reflected a double reality as performance numbers that also mirrored the flashbacks in Michelle's memory, the work might have been a fascinating stream-of-consciousness musical. But the book never matched its ambitions, and for the most part came across as an extended Liza Minnelli concert.

Soon after the opening, the finale sequence (a number that was unspecified in the program) was replaced by "Walking Papers," which had been heard during the tryout. During the course of the New York run, "Hollywood, California" was dropped.

During the tryout, the musical (which in preproduction was known as *In Person*) was titled *Shine It On*, and the following songs were cut: "Good Thing Going," "The Princess," "Love Songs," "Please, Sir," "Walking Papers," and "The Only Game in Town." Costume designer Thea Van Runkle was replaced by Halston, and the unnamed character of the musician (played by Christopher Barrett) was called Lenny Kanter for New York. Leonard Gaines played the role of Ted Kincaid, but by New York he was longer in the show; he was first replaced by Lorry Goldman and then by Arnold Soboloff (and the character's name was changed to Nat Schreiber).

Gower Champion unofficially took over as director and apparently retooled the musical staging (but Martin Scorsese remained the director of record, and Ron Lewis continued to receive credit for the choreography). Late in the run, Champion spelled Barry Nelson when the latter was on vacation. Pirandello would certainly have enjoyed one matinee when Champion played Nelson's role while Nelson himself was in the audience watching Champion perform the role he had created (this provided an amusing conceit far more entertaining than anything in Furth's book).

The musical made news because it was the first to charge $25 for its top ticket price, but the tumultuous and expensive tryout increased the show's production costs and so despite a small cast, good ticket sales, and the highest-priced tickets in Broadway history, the production had a long way to go before it could possibly hope to turn a profit. When Liza Minnelli missed a number of performances (which totaled almost one full month of the show's eight-month run) and when eventually the musical's weekly performance schedule was reduced from eight to seven and then finally to six showings in order to accommodate her, the situation was hopeless and the show closed in the red. Despite rumors that part of Minnelli's singing was lip-synched and despite the reduction of her weekly performances, she won a Tony Award for Best Leading Actress in a Musical.

Martin Gottfried in the *New York Post* said the "striking and intense" evening had a "solid" concept with a "well-constructed cinematic style" that used a nightclub act for "metaphoric value." But Furth's book was "soggy, skimpy and unaffecting" and the score didn't take the nightclub songs to a "mythic level," and so if the evening was "too uncertainly focused" it was still an "ambitious and big time musical with terrific entertainment values and stage excitement."

Douglas Watt in the *New York Daily News* said Minnelli was a performer "out to kill an audience" and that "on her own terms she emerges triumphant." But the evening was put together with "cold perfection," its love story was "glacial," and Minnelli was incapable of radiating "warmth." The musical was "all technique and expertise." John Beaufort in the *Christian Science Monitor* noted that *The Act* "ratified Minnelli's position in the glittery pantheon of show-business superstars," but the musical itself lacked a "heartbeat" and only the performers could bring "the throb of humanity" to the evening.

Richard Eder in the *New York Times* praised Minnelli's "breathtaking presence" but noted the "thin" book made *The Act* "a first-rate cabaret show expanded for theatre, rather than theatre itself." Howard Kissel in *Women's Wear Daily* noted the book was more of an "outline" and the score was "devoid of content, musical or otherwise," and so the evening offered "the hollowest material for Broadway in memory." And while Bob Lape on WABCTV7 found the book "skimpy" and the songs "unmemorable," he said Minnelli was an "irresistible" and "wonderful mix of vulnerability and energy."

Edwin Wilson in the *Wall Street Journal* said the evening was "quite possibly the most schizoid musical ever written" because of "the confusion of identities" in which the character Michelle Craig and the performer Liza Minnelli merged into one and then proceeded to morph into Judy Garland (especially in "City Lights," a "blockbuster" that nonetheless brought a sense of *déjà vu* because of its staging, costuming, and performance style).

As for Minnelli, Jack Kroll in *Newsweek* said "you've never seen anyone work so hard on a stage before" and "she fights [Furth's book] with ferocious good nature until at last it slinks away with its banality between its legs, leaving her onstage in exhausted triumph." T. E. Kalem in *Time* didn't think the star was "extraordinary or unique" in the fields of singing, dancing, and acting, but she was the center of a "cult" and he admitted she was "a tornado of energy" with "hypnotic appeal."

The script was published in paperback by Samuel French in 1987, and includes "Hollywood, California" and "Walking Papers." The cast album was released by DRG Records (LP # DRG-6101 and CD # CDRG-6101) and includes "Walking Papers." A live performance of "Hollywood, California" by Minnelli is included in the collection *Forgotten Broadway Volume II* (unnamed company, LP # T102); the collection *Lost in Boston II* (Varese Sarabande CD # VSD-5485) includes "The Only Game in Town"; and the collection *Contemporary Broadway Revisited* (Painted Smiles CD # PSCD-1311) offers "Please, Sir" and "The Only Game in Town." The collection *Celebrating New York, New York! Chicago! Cabaret! A Tribute to Kander and Ebb* (BBC Records CD # WMEU-0017-2) includes "City Lights," "Arthur in the Afternoon," and "My Own Space" (the latter sung by Claire Moore with John Kander at the piano).

Awards

Tony Awards and Nominations: Best Leading Actor in a Musical (Barry Nelson); Best Leading Actress in a Musical (**Liza Minnelli**); Best Score (lyrics by Fred Ebb, music by John Kander); Best Costume Designer (Halston); Best Lighting Designer (Tharon Musser); Best Choreographer (Ron Lewis)

JESUS CHRIST SUPERSTAR

Theatre: Longacre Theatre
Opening Date: November 23, 1977; *Closing Date*: February 12, 1978
Performances: 96

Lyrics: Tim Rice
Music: Andrew Lloyd Webber
Direction: William Daniel Grey; *Producer*: Hal Zeiger; *Choreography*: Kelly Carrol; *Costumes*: Joan Lucas ("Wardrobe Supervisor"); *Musical Direction*: Peter Phillips (*Note*: The program didn't provide any other production credits.)
Cast: Patrick Jude (Judas Iscariot), William Daniel Grey (Jesus of Nazareth), Barbara Niles (Mary Magdalene), Doug Lucas (First Priest, Apostle), Richard Tolin (Second Priest, Apostle), Christopher Cable (Caiaphas), Steve Schochet (Annas), Bobby London (Simon Zealotes), Randy Martin (Peter), Randy Wilson (Pontius Pilate), D. Bradley Jones (Soldier, Tormentor), George Bernhard (Soldier, Tormentor), Freida Ann Williams (Soul Girl), Pauletta Pearson (Soul Girl), Claudette Washington (Soul Girl), Celeste Hogan (Maid by the Fire), David Cahn (Apostle), Ken Samuels (Apostle), Lennie Del Duca (Apostle), Mark Syers (King Herod)
The musical was presented in two acts.
The action takes place during a seven-day period in 33 AD in Bethany, Jersusalem, The Garden of Gethsemane, and on Golgotha.

Musical Numbers

Act One: Overture (Company); "Heaven on Their Minds" (Patrick Jude); "What's the Buzz" (William Daniel Grey, Barbara Niles, The Apostles and Their Women); "Strange Thing Mystifying" (Patrick Jude, William Daniel Grey, The Apostles and Their Women): "Everything's All Right" (Barbara Niles, Patrick Jude, William Daniel Grey, The Apostles and Their Women); "This Jesus Must Die" (Christopher Cable, Steve Schochet, The Priests, Company); "Hosanna" (Christopher Cable, William Daniel Grey, Company); "Simon Zealotes" (Bobby London, Freida Ann Williams, Pauletta Pearson, Claudette Washington); "Poor Jerusalem" (William Daniel Grey); "Pilate's Dream" (Randy Wilson); "The Temple" (William Daniel Grey, Company); "I Don't Know How to Love Him" (Barbara Niles, William Daniel Grey); "Damned for All Time" (Patrick Jude, Steve Schochet, Christopher Cable, The Priests)
Act Two: "The Last Supper" (William Daniel Grey, Patrick Jude, The Apostles); "Gethsemane" (William Daniel Grey); "The Arrest" (Randy Martin, William Daniel Grey, The Apostles, The Reporters, Christopher Cable, Steve Schochet); "Peter's Denial" (Celeste Hogan, Randy Martin, Soldier, Old Man, Barbara Niles); "Pilate and Christ" (Randy Wilson, Soldier, William Daniel Grey, Company); "King Herod's Song" (Mark Syers); "Could We Start Again, Please" (Barbara Niles, Randy Wilson); "Judas' Death" (Patrick Jude, Steve Schochet, Christopher Cable); "Trial Before Pilate" (Randy Wilson, Christopher Cable, William Daniel Grey, The Mob); "Superstar" (Patrick Jude, Freida Ann Williams, Pauletta Pearson, Claudette Washington); "John 19:41" (Orchestra)

The current revival of *Jesus Christ Superstar* was a New York booking of a concert-styled production that toured the country. Virtually ignored by the critics, the musical managed to hang on for almost three months. For more information about the work, see entry for the 1971 production.

LOU RAWLS ON BROADWAY

Theatre: Mark Hellinger Theatre
Opening Date: November 23, 1977; *Closing Date*: December 4, 1977
Performances: 15
Producers: Larry Tarnofsky (Glenn Lipnick, Associate Producer); *Scenery*: Production Design by Salvatore Tagliarino and Multi-Media Design by Stig Edgren; *Lighting*: Lighting by Stig Edgren and Lighting Supervision by Fred Allison; *Musical Direction*: Denny Gore
Cast: *Lou Rawls*, The MFSB Orchestra; Vocalists: Althea Rogers, Debbie Morris, and Cindy Jordan
The concert was presented in two acts.

The popular singer Lou Rawls offered a limited engagement of fifteen concert performances in which he was backed by the MFSB Orchestra and three female vocalists.

John S. Wilson in the *New York Times* noted that during his career Rawls had been described as a jazz, pop, blues, folk, rock, and soul singer, and with his current appearance he could now add "Broadway singer" to the list (and, in fact, Rawls sang one Broadway number, "Send in the Clowns" from ***A Little Night Music***). Because Rawls performed his hit songs, a medley of big-band numbers, a touch of disco, and salutes to Louis Armstrong, Duke Ellington and Nat King Cole (the latter tribute included "Mona Lisa" and "Impossible"), Wilson said Rawls emerged as "a prototypical middle-of-the-road singer" who was an "unruffled performer" in "whatever musical area he is in." He possessed a "friendly, engaging manner" which reached "easily across the footlights" with "an inner sense of sincerity."

ELVIS THE LEGEND LIVES

Theatre: Palace Theatre
Opening Date: January 31, 1978; *Closing Date*: April 30, 1978
Performances: 101
Production Concept: John Finocchio, Larry Marshak, and David Zaan
Music: Title music by Doc Pomus and Bruce Foster
Direction: Jim Sotos and Henry Scarpelli; *Producer*: DL Theatrical Productions, Inc.; *Visual Concepts* and *Design*: Productions II; *Lighting*: Barry Arnold; *Musical Direction*: Peter Dino
Cast: Rick Saucedo (Elvis Presley), the Jordanaires (Vocal Quartet: Gordon Stoker, Neal Matthews, Hoyt Hawkins, and Ray Walker), D. J. Fontana (Drummer), Will Jordan (Ed Sullivan), Kharisma (Vocal Trio: Bernice Frazier, Judith O'Dell, and April Epps); The Elvis Presley Tribute Orchestra
The revue was presented in two acts.

Musical Numbers

Note: Most songs were performed by Rick Saucedo, who was backed by the male vocal quartet the Jordanaires and the female vocal trio Kharisma. The program didn't credit performers for individual songs and didn't list the names of the lyricists and composers of the musical numbers.
Act One: "Mood Indigo"; "Anytime"; "When the Saints Go Marching In"; "In the Mood"; "Johnny Be Good"; "C.C. Rider"; "Blue Moon of Kentucky"; "When My Blue Moon Turns to Gold Again"; "Heartbreak Hotel"; "How Great Thou Art"; Medley: "Reddy Teddy" and "Tutti Fruiti"; "Don't Be Cruel"; "One Night with You"; "Lawdy, Miss Clawdy"; "A Fool Such as I"; "Hound Dog"
Act Two: "Theme from 2001"; "Burning Love"; "Are You Lonesome Tonight?"; "I Just Can't Help Believing"; "You've Lost That Lovin' Feeling"; "Polk Salad Annie"; "The Wonder of You"; "My Way"; "Moody Blue"; "Little Darlin'"; "In the Ghetto"; Medley: "Whole Lot of Shakin' Goin' On" and "Hound Dog"; "Sweet Caroline"; "Suspicious Minds"; "The Legend Lives On"; "American Trilogy"

The revue *Elvis The Legend Lives* (sometimes given as *Elvis: The Legend Lives!*) was a revue-and-concert-styled evening that paid tribute to Elvis Presley. The first act looked at the singer's early years and his first recording sessions and radio and television appearances, including his famous debut on Ed Sullivan's *Toast of the Town* television variety show. The second act was a re-creation of Presley's appearance in Las Vegas at the International Hotel.

Rick Saucedo portrayed Presley, and was supported by the male vocal quartet the Jordanaires (who had backed Presley on his recordings and concerts over a fourteen-year period) and by D. J. Fontana (who was Presley's drummer for sixteen years). Will Jordan impersonated Ed Sullivan, and the female vocal trio Kharisma also provided backing for some of the musical numbers.

John Rockwell in the *New York Times* said the "lame" production was "an inept and witless mess" that was presented "amateurishly and simplistically." Saucedo was "kind of cute" but "only intermittently convincing" as Elvis, and Jordan "grotesquely exaggerated" Ed Sullivan. He noted the evening included out-of-focus slides as well as what he assumed were plants in the audience who screamed and offered pink and yellow flowers to Saucedo. As for the Jordanaires and D. J. Fontana, he said they should be "ashamed" of their participation in the production.

ON THE TWENTIETH CENTURY

"A New Musical Comedy"

Theatre: St. James Theatre
Opening Date: February 19, 1978; *Closing Date*: March 18, 1979
Performances: 453
Book and *Lyrics*: Betty Comden and Adolph Green
Music: Cy Coleman
Based on the 1932 play *Twentieth Century* by Ben Hecht and Charles MacArthur (which was based on an earlier and unproduced play by Bruce Millholland).
Direction: Harold Prince; *Producers*: The Producers Circle 2, Inc. (Robert Fryer, Mary Lea Johnson, James Cresson, and Martin Richards) in association with Joseph Harris and Ira Bernstein (Sam Crothers and Andre Pastoria, Associate Producers); *Choreography*: Larry Fuller; *Scenery*: Robin Wagner; *Costumes*: Florence Klotz; *Lighting*: Ken Billington; *Musical Direction*: Paul Gemignani
Cast: Ken Hilliard (Priest), Charles Rule (Bishop), Ray Gill (Stage Manager), Maris Clement (Joan), Carol Lurie (Wardrobe Mistress, Hospital Attendant), Hal Norman (Actor), George Coe (Owen O'Malley), Dean Dittman (Oliver Webb), Keith Davis (Porter), Quitman Fludd III (Porter), Ray Stephens (Porter), Joseph Wise (Porter), Rufus Smith (Congressman Lockwood), Tom Batten (Conductor Flanagan), Stanley Simmonds (Train Secretary Rogers), *Imogene Coca* (Letitia Primrose), Mel Johnson Jr. (Redcap), Carol Lugenbeal (Anita), *John Cullum* (Oscar Jaffee), George Lee Andrews (Max Jacobs), Willi Burke (Imelda, Doctor Johnson), David Horwitz (Maxwell Finch), *Madeline Kahn* (Mildred Plotka aka Lily Garland), Sal Mistretta (Otto Von Bismark, Hospital Attendant), Kevin Kline (Bruce Granit), Judy Kaye (Agnes); Female Singers: Susan Cella, Maris Clement, Peggy Cooper, Karen Gibson, Carol Lugenbeal, Carol Lurie, Melanie Vaughan; Male Singers: Ray Gill, Ken Hilliard, David Horwitz, Craig Lucas, Sal Mistretta, Hal Norman, Charles Rule, David Vogel
The musical was presented in two acts.
The action takes place in the early 1930s, mainly on the Twentieth Century Limited from Chicago to New York City.

Musical Numbers

Act One: Overture; "Stranded Again" (Charles Rule, Hal Norman, Singers); "On the Twentieth Century" (Porters, Imogene Coca, Tom Batten, Stanley Simmonds, Passengers); "I Rise Again" (John Cullum, George Coe, Dean Dittman); "Indian Maiden's Lament" (Willi Burke, Madeline Kahn); "Veronique" (Madeline Kahn, Male Singers); "I Have Written a Play" (Tom Batten); "Together" (Porters, Passengers, John Cullum); "Never" (Madeline Kahn, George Coe, Dean Dittman); "Our Private World" (Madeline Kahn, John Cullum); "Repent" (Imogene Coca); "Mine" (John Cullum, Kevin Kline); "I've Got It All" (Madeline Kahn, John Cullum); "On the Twentieth Century" (reprise) (Company)
Act Two: Entr'acte (Porters); "Five Zeros" (George Coe, Dean Dittman, Imogene Coca, John Cullum); "Sextet" (George Coe, Dean Dittman, John Cullum, Imogene Coca, Madeline Kahn, Kevin Kline); "She's a Nut" (Company); "Max Jacobs" (George Lee Andrews); "Babette" (Madeline Kahn); "The Legacy" (John Cullum); "Lily, Oscar" (Madeline Kahn, John Cullum)

Betty Comden, Adolph Green, and Cy Coleman's *On the Twentieth Century* was one of the wittiest and most elegant musicals of the era, an art deco operetta with a farcical plot, purposely over-the-top hammy performances, and a richly melodic score, arguably Coleman's best (and certainly most atypical). Further, Robin Wagner and Florence Klotz designed a stupendously gorgeous production. Wagner's train was a fantasy of scalloped silvers and creams that depicted drawing rooms, observation cars, corridors, and platforms. Other striking visuals included a lit miniature train that crossed the stage and depicted the train's route, a head-on view of the huge engine with flashing lights that (like Commodore Perry's ship in ***Pacific Overtures***) headed straight toward the audience, and periodically steam rose from the orchestra pit to simulate the speeding train.

Egotistical director Oscar Jaffee (John Cullum) is trying to resuscitate his career, and when he discovers his old flame and former leading lady Mildred Plotka aka Lily Garland (Madeline Kahn) is on the Twentieth

Century Limited bound for New York from Chicago, he hops aboard in order to woo her into signing for his next play. Lily is now a famous (but unfortunately very temperamental) movie star, and her presence in his new production will ensure box office platinum. There are numerous romantic, financial, and contractual mix-ups, not to mention such quirky characters as Bruce Granit (Kevin Kline), an egotistical boy-toy being kept by Lily, and Letitia Primrose (Imogene Coca), a crazed and, yes, nutty kook who tries to save the world from sin (but is grateful she "did it all" before she repented and got religion).

The merry plot machinations never let up, and the rich score was a cornucopia of delight. For Barrymore-like Oscar's establishing number "I Rise Again" ("full size again"), he showed his determination to again hit the top of his profession, and his later kiss-off "The Legacy" was a wonderful "Jack Cassidy" number that was cousin to Cassidy's show-stopping "Grand Knowing You" in the 1963 musical *She Loves Me*. Lily's flashback "Veronique" was a glimpse at the show that made her a star, and its second-act counterpart, "Babette," looked at her dilemma in choosing her next role—a comedy in which she'll play the shallow Babette, a tony Mayfair society type, or a biblical epic where she'll portray Mary Magdalene (the programs, cast album, and published script couldn't agree if the song's title was "Babette" or "Babbette"). Lily and Oscar shared two amusing duets, "I've Got It All" (in which Lily brandishes her Academy Award, which decorates her drawing room) and the succinct and spoofy "Lily, Oscar." There were also staggeringly impressive, extended tongue-in-cheek solo and choral numbers: "Together," "Never," "Five Zeros," "Sextet," the title song, and the rabid "She's a Nut." This was a score written in purely comic terms, and virtually every number exuded sardonic magic in various musical salutes to insincerity and selfishness, and the flippant lyrics were cleverly contrasted with often lush and romantic music. Even Lily and Oscar's (almost) conventional ballad "Our Private World" wasn't "straight" and employed theatrical imagery throughout to describe their relationship.

Richard Eder in the *New York Times* praised the "funny, elegant and totally cheerful" evening, which had "exuberance" and a "bubbly confidence in its own life." The book offered "civilized wit and wild humor," the score was "strong," and the show "brought back what seemed dead or at least endangered: the comedy in musical comedy." Howard Kissel in *Women's Wear Daily* commented that the "marvelously stylish show" had "visual sumptuousness" and "several marvelously theatrical numbers," and the score offered "lovely ballads" and "wonderful spoofs." Clive Barnes in the *New York Post* said the "lovely" score ran the "gorgeous gamut" from Jacques Brel to Gian-Carlo Menotti, that director Harold Prince had done a "tremendous job," and "if ever there was a musical that could even appeal to people with tin ears but stylish eyesight, this would be it." And John Beaufort in the *Christian Science Monitor* noted that the evening was a "stunning example of Broadway craftsmanship and technology" with a "railroad glamour wondrous to behold" and a score that combined the "satirical sketch" with "borrowings from opera bouffe."

But the headline in Edwin Wilson's review in the *Wall Street Journal* read, "A Lavish Musical Loses Track of Itself," and the headline in T. E. Kalem's review in *Time* was "Monorail." Wilson wondered how screwball farce could be presented in the 1970s, and suggested the musical's creators didn't know the answer. The result was therefore a "mélange that is part musical comedy, part operetta, part parody and part pure bombast." Kalem said the musical lacked "inspired lunacy" and thus Prince opted for "camp and stylistic cartoonery," while Coleman's score went "clickety-clack in its monotony." Jack Kroll in *Newsweek* said Coleman's "strong theatricality" offered "effective pastiche" with "deft echoes" of Offenbach, Jerome Kern, and Gilbert and Sullivan.

During the tryout, the song "This Is the Day" was deleted. After the Broadway opening, Madeline Kahn began missing performances and permanently left the production; on April 24, 1978, Kahn's understudy Judy Kaye (who had also played the role of Agnes) officially assumed the role for the remaining ten months of the Broadway run.

The script was published in hardback by Drama Book Specialists in 1981. The cast album was released by Columbia Records (LP # JS-35330) and the CD by Sony Broadway (# SK-35330), which included three short previously unreleased tracks ("I Have Written a Play" and both the first act and curtain call reprises of the title song).

The London production opened at Her Majesty's Theatre on March 19, 1980, for 165 performances; the cast included Keith Mitchell, Julia McKenzie, Mark Wynter, and Ann Beach.

The York Theatre Company's revival opened on October 25, 1985, for twenty showings, and another revival opened on March 12, 2015, at the American Airlines Theatre, with Kristin Chenoweth and Peter Gallagher ("The Legacy" was revised as "Because of Him" by Green's daughter Amanda); the two-CD cast album was issued by PS Classics # PS-1532.

Awards

Tony Awards and Nominations: Best Musical (*On the Twentieth Century*); Best Leading Actor in a Musical (**John Cullum**); Best Leading Actress in a Musical (Madeline Kahn); Best Featured Actor in a Musical (**Kevin Kline**); Best Featured Actress in a Musical (Imogene Coca); Best Director of a Musical (Hal Prince); Best Book (**Betty Comden** and **Adolph Green**); Best Score (lyrics by **Betty Comden** and **Adolph Green**, music by **Cy Coleman**); Best Scenic Designer (**Robin Wagner**)

TIMBUKTU!

"A MUSICAL FABLE BASED ON *KISMET*"

Theatre: Mark Hellinger Theatre
Opening Date: March 1, 1978; *Closing Date*: September 10, 1978
Performances: 221
Book: Luther Davis
Lyrics and *Music*: Robert Wright and George Forrest; music based on themes by Alexander Borodin and African folk music; incidental music by Charles H. Coleman
Based on the 1953 musical *Kismet* (book by Charles Lederer and Luther Davis; lyrics and music by Robert Wright and George Forrest [music based on themes by Alexander Borodin]) and the 1911 play *Kismet* by Edward Knoblock.
Direction and *Choreography*: Geoffrey Holder; *Producers*: Luther Davis in association with Sarnoff International Enterprises, William D. Cunningham, and the John F. Kennedy Center for the Performing Arts; *Scenery*: Tony Straiges; *Costumes*: Geoffrey Holder; *Lighting*: Ian Calderon; *Musical Direction*: Charles H. Coleman
Cast: Obba Babatunde (The Chakaba [The Stiltwalker], Orange Merchant, Antelope), Harold Pierson (Beggar, Witchdoctor), Shezwae Powell (Beggar, Woman in the Garden), Louis Tucker (Beggar), Ira Hawkins (Hadji), *Melba Moore* (Marsinah), Deborah Waller (Child), Daniel Barton (M'Ballah), Eleanor McCoy (Najua), George Bell (The Wazir), Bruce A. Hubbard (Chief Policeman), *Eartha Kitt* (Sahleem-La-Lume); The Three Princesses of Baguezne: Deborah K. Brown, Sharon Cuff, and Patricia Lumpkin; Miguel Godreau (Munshi), *Gilbert Price* (The Mansa of Mali); Birds in Paradise: Miguel Godreau and Eleanor McCoy; Luther Fontaine (Antelope), Vanessa Shaw (Zubbediya); The Citizens of Timbuktu: Obba Babatunde, Gregg Baker, Daniel Barton, Joella Breedlove, Deborah K. Brown, Tony Carroll, Sharon Cuff, Cheryl Cummings, Luther Fontaine, Michael F. Harrison, Dyane Harvey, Marzetta Jones, Jimmy Justice, Eugene Little, Patricia Lumpkin, Joe Lynn, Tony Ndogo, Harold Pierson, Ray Pollard, Shezwae Powell, Ronald Richardson, Vanessa Shaw, Louis Tucker, Deborah Waller, Renee Warren
The musical was presented in two acts.
The action takes place during a period of twenty-four hours in 1361 in Timbuktu in the Ancient Empire of Mali in West Africa.

Musical Numbers

Act One: "Rhymes Have I" (Ira Hawkins, Melba Moore, Harold Pierson, Shezwae Powell, Louis Tucker); "Fate" (Ira Hawkins); "In the Beginning, Woman" (Eartha Kitt); "Baubles, Bangles and Beads" (Melba Moore, Merchants); "Birds in Paradise Garden" (dance) (Miguel Godreau, Eleanor McCoy); "Stranger in Paradise" (Gilbert Price, Melba Moore); "Gesticulate" (Ira Hawkins, Council); "Night of My Nights" (Gilbert Price, Courtiers)
Act Two: "Nuptial Celebration" (dance) (People of Mali); "My Magic Lamp" (Melba Moore); "Stranger in Paradise" (reprise) (Melba Moore); "Rahadlakum" (Eartha Kitt, Ladies of the Harem); "And This Is My Beloved" (Ira Hawkins, Melba Moore, Gilbert Price, George Bell); "Golden Land, Golden Life" (Bruce A. Hubbard, Nobles of the Court); "Zubbediya" and "Dances" (Vanessa Shaw, Princesses, Other Marriage Candidates, Court Acrobat); "Night of My Nights" (reprise) (Gilbert Price, Melba Moore, Ira Hawkins, Nobles of the Court); "Sands of Time" (Ira Hawkins, Eartha Kitt)

There seems to be no middle ground on *Kismet*. Either you love its lavish, melodic, and old-time musical comedy shtick or you recoil in horror at its peacocks-and-monkeys-in-purple-adornings ornamentation and its our-beggars-more-distinctly-aromatic-here salute to civic pride. The musical's dissenters just don't seem to get it: *Kismet* has a cleverly written book and lyrics that are tongue-in-cheek with dreamily over-the-top purple prose, and its score is one of the most lush and romantic imaginable. And so it was with the musical's new incarnation *Timbuktu!*, which had its adherents and scoffers. The latter won the day, and the musical closed at a loss after little more than six months on Broadway. But it was a thoroughly enjoyable old-fashioned show, now with an all-black cast who live in the fabled African city rather than in Old Baghdad.

The revival lacked a striking Hadji (Ira Hawkins replaced William Marshall during the tryout, but in fact both were rather bland and lacked the panache required for the role), but Eartha Kitt was a smashing Lalume (here Sahleem-La-Lume), a predatory voluptuary bored with her older husband the Wazir (George Bell) and on the prowl for virile and younger flesh. She made one of the most spectacular entrances of the era. Amid a bevy of gorgeously draped citizens in downtown Timbuktu, many of whom held aloft colorful birthday cake-like parasols which reached for the sky, Kitt was regally carried on stage in a canopied couch hoisted by four nearly naked men. As her entourage reached stage center, she looked at the audience in her inimitable dead-pan style and in her gravelly lowdown voice announced, "I'm here."

The story takes place during a twenty-four-hour period and centers on the beggar-poet Hadji and his lovely daughter Marsinah (Melba Moore) who make their living selling rhymes to passersby. She catches the eye of the Mansa of Mali (Gilbert Price), and they immediately fall in love. Meanwhile, Hadji becomes involved in court intrigues and soon becomes the willing lover of the luscious Sahleem-La-Lume.

Robert Wright and George Forrest adapted the music from themes of Alexander Borodin, and reshaped his music into one of the theatre's most ingratiating scores, including the glorious ballads "Stranger in Paradise," "And This Is My Beloved," and "Baubles, Bangles and Beads." Except for "Not Since Nineveh," "Bazaar of the Caravans," "He's in Love!," and "The Olive Tree," *Timbuktu!* retained most of the original *Kismet* score (as noted below, the latter two songs were heard during the tryout of *Timbuktu!*), and included three new ones ("In the Beginning, Woman," "My Magic Lamp," and "Golden Land, Golden Life") and two new dances ("Birds in Paradise Garden" and "Nuptial Celebration").

John Beaufort in the *Christian Science Monitor* said the "opulent operetta" was a "costume ball" (thanks to designer Geoffrey Holder, who also directed and choreographed) and Eartha Kitt gave "a show-stopping comic performance." Clive Barnes in the *New York Post* had serious reservations about the musical, but praised Holder's "brilliant" and "dazzling conception" of "a musical as a masque" in which the choreography "prances through the landscape of an impossible fairy-tale." Here was a "great visual production," and he noted that Eartha Kitt lit up the stage "like a perversely silver sun."

Howard Kissel in *Women's Wear Daily* said the "lively" book and "beautiful" score of *Kismet* had been reduced to "rubble," the evening was "disastrous," and Melba Moore did "some of the ugliest singing I have ever heard." Douglas Watt in the *New York Daily News* found Moore "sweet and saucy" but said *Timbuktu!* was a "gaudy bore with a pearl named Melba bobbing about in it." As for the costumes, T. E. Kalem in *Time* said "the undress is almost more spectacular than the dress" and the "virile, muscular" men of the chorus might "restore to fashion the jeweled codpiece"; and Edwin Wilson in the *Wall Street Journal* noted that when the dancing and pageantry stopped "so did the play," but "literally and figuratively" Eartha Kitt stood "above the rest of the proceedings" and leveled "everything in sight."

Richard Eder in the *New York Times* thought the dances "agreeably energetic," the music "dull," and the lyrics "soggy," but noted the book was "cheerful and perfectly workable." As for Eartha Kitt, in the very same moment she was able to combine "vast sultriness" and "gleeful mockery." She moved "unexpectedly," was "motionless unexpectedly," kept the audience "off balance," and with "Rahadlakum" she stopped the show.

Jack Kroll in *Newsweek* was disappointed with Melba Moore and Gilbert Price. He said the former "hardly sings" and instead "caterwauls, ululates and even yodels," and the latter resorted "to some of the same soul-shattering affectations." But Eartha Kitt was a "stunning, stealthy-stepping, chop-licking panther" who "cruises the stage with imperial raunch" and "mewed" her songs with "catnip relish." The critic said he'd love to see her and Yul Brynner "fight it out sumo style for the champion stage presence of the world."

The critics pounced on the theatre's sound system. Kissel said it "constantly crackles"; Eder reported the performers were "solidly 'miked up,' and something was badly wrong with the sound system." Wilson complained that with "three banks of ten-foot speakers" the system "sometimes distorts the voices so completely that the human dimension disappears." Beaufort said the musical was "abominably amplified"; and

Watt noted that the "heavily miked" evening sounded "like a recording, and a faulty one, at that," with an overhead speaker that was "spitting and scratching from time to time."

During the tryout, William Marshall was succeeded by Ira Hawkins, and the new song "Power!" (for George Bell and the Policemen) was deleted. Also briefly heard during part of the tryout were two songs from the original *Kismet*, "He's in Love!" (for Eartha Kitt, Eleanor McCoy, and Company) and "The Olive Tree" (for William Marshall).

The original production of *Kismet* opened at the Ziegfeld Theatre on December 3, 1953, for 583 performances and won five Tony Awards, including Best Musical, Best Book, and Best Leading Actor in a Musical (Alfred Drake). It was revived at the New York State Theatre three times, first by the Music Theatre of Lincoln Center on June 25, 1965, for forty-eight performances (with Drake reprising his original Broadway role) and twice by the New York City Opera Company, on October 3, 1985, and on July 13, 1986, for thirteen and eight respective performances.

Besides the 1955 film version released by MGM and directed by Vincente Minnelli, there was also an ABC television adaptation that was aired on October 24, 1967. The London premiere opened at the Stoll Theatre on April 20, 1955, for 648 performances and included three members from the original Broadway cast, Drake, Joan Diener (Lalume), and Doretta Morrow (Marsinah).

There are numerous recordings of *Kismet*, but the best is the sparkling original cast album by Columbia (LP # OL-4850); the CD was issued by Sony Classical/Columbia/Legacy (# SK-89252). It is one of the most vivid and electric of all cast recordings, so spectacularly produced that it seems the singers and orchestra are performing in your living room. Two other notable versions are the two-CD studio cast album by That's Entertainment Records (# CDTER2-1170), which includes "Bored" (written for the 1955 film version and which is sometimes interpolated into stage revivals of the musical), as well as the new songs for *Timbuktu!* ("In the Beginning, Woman," "My Magic Lamp," "Golden Land, Golden Life," and "Power!," the last performed during the tryout of *Timbuktu!* but dropped prior to New York) and the lush Sony Broadway studio cast album (CD # SK-46438), which includes Samuel Ramey (Haji [for *Timbuktu!*, Hadji]) and Jerry Hadley (The Caliph [for *Timbuktu!*, The Mansa]).

A demo recording of *Timbuktu!* (LP # SS-33782-01A/02B; unnamed company) includes two numbers performed by Eartha Kitt ("In the Beginning, Woman" and "Rahadlakum") as well as songs by Johnny Mathis ("Sands of Time"), Sarah Vaughan ("And This Is My Beloved"), Lena Horne ("Baubles, Bangles and Beads"), and two versions of "Stranger in Paradise" (a ballad version by Della Reese and a disco version by Isaac Hayes).

The script of *Kismet* was published in hardback by Random House in 1954, and a paperback was published in an undated edition by Frank Music Co. in Great Britain.

Awards

Tony Award Nominations: Best Leading Actor in a Musical (Gilbert Price); Best Leading Actress in a Musical (Eartha Kitt); Best Costume Designer (Geoffrey Holder)

HELLO, DOLLY!

Theatre: Lunt-Fontanne Theatre
Opening Date: March 5, 1978; *Closing Date*: July 9, 1978
Performances: 145
Book: Michael Stewart
Lyrics and *Music*: Jerry Herman
Based on the 1955 play *The Matchmaker* by Thornton Wilder, which was a revised version of his 1938 play *The Merchant of Yonkers* (which in turn was based on the 1842 Austrian play *Einen jux will er sich machen* by Johann Nestroy, which had been based on the 1835 British play *A Day Well Spent* by John Oxenford).
Direction: Lucia Victor (based on the original direction by Gower Champion) (production "supervised" by Jerry Herman); *Producers*: James M. Nederlander and The Houston Grand Opera (Robert Buckley, Associate Producer); *Choreography*: Jack Craig (based on the original choreography by Gower Champion); *Scenery*: Oliver Smith; *Costumes*: Freddy Wittop; *Lighting*: Martin Aronstein; *Musical Direction*: Jack Everly

Cast: *Carol Channing* (Mrs. Dolly Gallagher Levi), P. J. Nelson (Ernestina), Michael C. Booker (Ambrose Kemper), Carole Banninger and Debra Pigliavento (Horse), Eddie Bracken (Horace Vandergelder), K. T. Baumann (Ermengarde), Lee Roy Reams (Cornelius Hackl), Robert Lydiard (Barnaby Tucker), Alexandra Korey (Minnie Fay), Florence Lacey (Irene Molloy), Marilyn Hudgins (Mrs. Rose), John Anania (Rudolph), Bill Bateman (Judge), Randolph Riscol (Court Clerk); Townspeople, Waiters, Others: Diane Abrams, Carole Banninger, JoEla Flood, Marilyn Hudgins, Deborah Moldow, Janyce Nyman, Jacqueline Payne, Debra Pigliavento, Theresa Rakov, Barbara Ann Thompson, Richard Ammon, Bill Bateman, Kyle Cittadin, Ron Crofoot, Don Edward Detrick, Richard Dodd, Rob Draper, David Evans, Tom Garrett, Charlie Goeddertz, James Homan, Alex MacKay, Richard Maxon, Randy Morgan, Randolph Riscol, Mark Waldrop
The musical was presented in two acts.
The action takes place in New York City and Yonkers in the 1890s.

Musical Numbers

Act One: "I Put My Hand In" (Carol Channing, Company); "It Takes a Woman" (Eddie Bracken, The Instant Glee Club); "Put on Your Sunday Clothes" (Lee Roy Reams, Robert Lydiard, Carol Channing, Michael C. Booker, K. T. Baumann); "Put on Your Sunday Clothes" (reprise) (The People of Yonkers); "Ribbons Down My Back" (Florence Lacey); "Motherhood" (Carol Channing, Eddie Bracken, Florence Lacey, Alexandra Korey, Lee Roy Reams, Robert Lydiard); "Dancing" (Carol Channing, Lee Roy Reams, Robert Lydiard, Alexandra Korey, Florence Lacey, Dancers); "Before the Parade Passes By" (Carol Channing, Eddie Bracken, Company)
Act Two: "Elegance" (Florence Lacey, Lee Roy Reams, Alexandra Korey, Robert Lydiard); "The Waiters' Gallop" (John Anania, Waiters); "Hello, Dolly!" (Carol Channing, John Anania, Waiters, Cooks); "The Polka Contest" (Michael C. Booker, K. T. Baumann, Florence Lacey, Lee Roy Reams, Alexandra Korey, Robert Lydiard, Contestants); "It Only Takes a Moment" (Lee Roy Reams, Florence Lacey, Prisoners, Policemen); "So Long, Dearie" (Carol Channing); "Hello, Dolly!" (reprise) (Carol Channing, Eddie Bracken); Finale (Company)

The current *Hello, Dolly!* came along just two seasons after Pearl Bailey's visit, but this production was special because it starred Carol Channing, the original Dolly, in her first of two New York revivals of the lighthearted and melodic old-fashioned musical (she reprised the role on Broadway one more time, in 1995). The four-month engagement was part of two national tours in which Channing (and costar Eddie Bracken) had appeared during the latter part of the decade.

Douglas Watt in the *New York Daily News* said Channing was "at the top of her form in what now amounts to an immaculate musical comedy performance." Bracken made a "well-nigh perfect" Horace Vandergelder, and the production itself went like "a house afire" and was "as fresh as the paint on the star's animated face." Clive Barnes in the *New York Post* reported "nobody knows the Dollies I've seen," but Channing's was "the first, the last, and in some ways the only Dolly." He noted that her "movements are mannered beyond the point of mannerism" and she had "that gift of performing for every individual, individually. She emerges one to one with the audience." (In her curtain call speech at a tryout performance of ***Lorelei*** at the National Theatre in Washington, D.C., she noted the number of times she'd played the National over the years [in *Gentlemen Prefer Blondes*, *Wonderful Town*, *The Vamp*, *Show Girl*, the original *Dolly!*, and *Four on a Garden*], and when members of the audience began to clap after the names of certain productions, Channing suddenly stopped speaking, looked astounded, aghast, and excited, proceeded to point toward where the applause had come from, and said something along the lines of: "Why, I *remember* you at *The Vamp*! But then you were sitting in the eighth row, and not the sixth!"

For more information about the musical, see entry for the 1975 production which starred Pearl Bailey.

DANCIN'

"A New Musical Entertainment"

Theatre: Broadhurst Theatre (during run, the dance revue transferred to the Ambassador Theatre)
Opening Date: March 27, 1978; *Closing Date*: June 27, 1982

Performances: 1,774
Lyrics and *Music*: See list of musical numbers for names of lyricists and composers
Direction and *Choreography*: Bob Fosse; *Producers*: Jules Fisher, The Shubert Organization, and Columbia Pictures (Patty Grubman, Associate Producer); *Scenery*: Peter Larkin; *Costumes*: Willa Kim; *Lighting*: Jules Fisher; *Musical Direction*: Gordon Lowry Harrell
Cast: Gail Benedict, Sandahl Bergman, Karen G. Burke, Rene Ceballos, Christopher Chadman, Wayne Cilento, Jill Cook, Gregory B. Drotar, Vicki Frederick, Linda Haberman, Richard Korthaze, Edward Love, John Mineo, Ann Reinking, Blane Savage, Charles Ward
The dance revue was presented in three acts.

Musical Numbers

Act One: *Opening*: Prologue—"Hot August Night" (lyric and music by Neil Diamond) and "Crunchy Granola Suite" (lyric and music by Neil Diamond) (Company; Singers: Wayne Cilento and John Mineo); *Recollections of an Old Dancer*—"Mr. Bojangles" (lyric and music by Jerry Jeff Walker) (Mr. Bojangles: Christopher Chadman; Mr. Bojangles' Spirit: Gregory B. Drotar; Singer: Wayne Cilento); *The Dream Barre*—"Chaconne" (a transcription from Johann Sebastian Bach's Sonata for Violin Solo No. 4) (A Boy: Charles Ward; A Girl: Ann Reinking; Ballet Master: Richard Korthaze; Company); *Percussion*—Part I (Rene Ceballos, Vicki Frederick, Linda Haberman); Part II (Christopher Chadman, Wayne Cilento, John Mineo); Part III (Sandahl Bergman, Gail Benedict, Karen G. Burke, Jill Cook, Gregory B. Drotar, Edward Love, Ann Reinking, Blane Savage); Part IV *"Ionisation"* (music by Edward Varese) (Charles Ward)
Act Two: *Dancin' Man*—"I Wanna Be a Dancin' Man" (1952 film *The Belle of New York*; lyric by Johnny Mercer, music by Harry Warren) (Company); *Three in One*—"Big Noise from Winettka" (lyric and music by Bob Haggart, Ray Bauduc, Gil Rodin, and Bob Crosby) (Karen G. Burke, Wayne Cilento, Jill Cook); *Joint Endeavor*—"If It Feels Good, Let It Ride" (lyric and music by Carole Bayer Sager and Melissa Manchester) and "Easy" (lyric and music by Carole Bayer Sager and Melissa Manchester) (Pas de Deux: Vicki Frederick and Charles Ward, Rene Ceballos and Gregory B. Drotar, Sandhal Bergman and Blane Savage; "Easy": Ann Reinking; Singers: Christopher Chadman, Wayne Cilento, Edward Love, John Mineo); *A Manic Depressive's Lament*—"I've Got Them Feelin' Too Good Today Blues" (lyric and music by Jerry Leiber and Mike Stoller) (Edward Love); *Fourteen Feet*—"Was Dog a Doughnut" (lyric and music by Cat Stevens) (Sandahl Bergman, Christopher Chadman, Wayne Cilento, Gregory B. Drotar, Vicki Frederick, Ann Reinking, Blane Savage)
Act Three: *Benny's Number*—"Sing, Sing, Sing" (lyric and music by Louis Prima) Part I (Company); Part II (Trombone Solo: Vicki Frederick, Blane Savage, Charles Ward; Trumpet Solo: Ann Reinking; Clarinet Solo: Company; Piano Solo: Wayne Cilento, John Mineo); *The Female Star Spot*—"Here You Come Again" (lyric and music by Barry Mann and Cynthia Weil) (Sandahl Bergman, Karen G. Burke, Rene Ceballos, Vicki Frederick); *America*—"(I'm a) Yankee Doodle Dandy" (aka "The Yankee Doodle Boy") (*Little Johnny Jones*, 1904; lyric and music by George M. Cohan) (Company); "Gary Owen" (Gail Benedict, Linda Haberman, Gregory B. Drotar); "Stout-Hearted Men" (*The New Moon*, 1928; lyric by Oscar Hammerstein II, music by Sigmund Romberg) (Sandahl Bergman, Vicki Frederick, Ann Reinking); "Under Double Eagle" (Wayne Cilento, John Mineo, Blane Savage); "Dixie" (Karen G. Burke, Edward Love); "When Johnny Comes Marching Home" (Ann Reinking); "Rally Round the Flag" (Rene Ceballos); "Pack Up Your Troubles in Your Old Kit Bag and Smile, Smile, Smile" (lyric by George Asaf, music by Felix Powell) (Vicki Frederick, Gail Benedict, John Mineo); "The Stars and Stripes Forever" (music by John Philip Sousa) (Charles Ward); "Yankee Doodle Disco" (choreographed by Christopher Chadman); *Improvisation*—"Dancin'" (music by Ralph Burns) (Company)

Bob Fosse's *Dancin'* was a dance revue, and so finally Fosse didn't have to bother with lyricists, composers, and book writers, and with plots and characters. Instead he was completely in his element, a program in three acts of non-stop dancin', as opposed to dancing. According to Jack Kroll in *Newsweek*, "dancing" is a "great art form," but for Fosse "dancin'" was his "giant claim for popular dance as something worth looking at and admiring in its own right." The show was the longest running of the season, played for over four years, and Fosse won the Tony Award for Best Choreographer.

Some complained that *Dancin'* wasn't a *musical*. Would they have groused that the *Ziegfeld Follies* were revues and not book musicals? It seems the notion of a Broadway evening of dances was a revolutionary horror to some, and for others there was the angst that the show lacked original music. But when ***Ain't Misbehavin'*** came along a few weeks later and didn't include a note of original music, no one seemed to be bothered. Susan Stroman's brilliant *Contact* (2000) met with similar criticism: she created mini-dance musicals set to preexisting music, and despite the fact that her choreography was some of the most explosive and exciting seen on Broadway since the heyday of Fosse, Michael Bennett, and Gower Champion, some criticized the show for not being a "real" musical.

But *Dancin'* (and *Contact*) found receptive audiences who were happy to see an evening of original choreography by one of Broadway's masters. There were a few sequences that weren't up to the level of the evening's best, but by and large *Dancin'* was a memorable series of show-stoppers. Among the highlights were "I Wanna Be a Dancin' Man," a fabulous soft-shoe tribute to Fred Astaire in which the entire cast appeared in vanilla-ice-cream-colored summer suits with gloves and sherbet-hued straw boaters, and "Swing, Swing, Swing," a jaw-dropping tribute to 1940s swing music. There was also a lively patriotic finale, not to mention the amusing if gimmicky "Was Dog a Doughnut" in which seven dancers cavorted through the number while remaining in shoes nailed to the floor. Other highlights were the snazzy trio "Big Noise from Winettka" and the pulsating "Percussion" for the entire company.

Perhaps the weakest number was the "Dream Barre"/"Chaconne" sequence, which was a bit too balletic as well as tiresomely pretentious in its desperate need to be sexually with it (another flaccid number was the would-be hip "Joint Endeavor"). For some, "Recollections of an Old Dancer"/"Mr. Bojangles" was memorably effective, but it was perhaps too weepy and sentimental for its own good.

Richard Eder in the *New York Times* said the dances needed the weight of a plot ("even a silly plot") to give them the "intensity" and "seriousness" to stand alone without the trappings of traditional musical comedy. Dance without musical comedy structure was like "frosting declaring its independence from the cake," and *Dancin'* was more of a "spectacular recital" than an "integrated musical show." T. E. Kalem in *Time* complained that the evening lacked a cohesive theme, and John Beaufort in the *Christian Science Monitor* found *Dancin'* "entrancin'" but felt there was so much "razzle dazzle" that the evening lacked "humanity" and was "more overwhelming than stirring."

Douglas Watt in the *New York Daily News* said Fosse had pulled together his "enormous vocabulary of seductive and humorous body language" from his years on Broadway and in Hollywood and was thus at his "lustrous and unstinting best" in "the most stylish musical you'll ever witness." Clive Barnes in the *New York Post* felt that *Dancin'* "should run for as near forever as forever can be," and suggested that Fosse had created "a new theatrical form" that was "glorious" and a "knockout." Howard Kissel in *Women's Wear Daily* noted that Fosse didn't care about developing dance to create a character or advance a plot. He was more concerned with dance that "stops the show" rather than "merely" moving it along. As a result, his work was "as full of light, energy and excitement as Times Square" and while it might contain some "vulgarity" it was also "exhilarating entertainment."

All the dancers were praised, but Ann Reinking was singled out. Kalem said dance was "her manifest and incandescent destiny" for she was "terpsiglorious"; Kroll said she was a "meteor," and her solo dance in "Sing, Sing, Sing" was "a breath-taking explosion of beauty, grace and power"; Eder said she was "clearly" the star of the evening; and Barnes found her "something special."

There was, perhaps understandably, no cast album, but sadly there was no film version of the material. Once the revue closed, it would have seemed an obvious candidate for a public television special, but unfortunately a film version never materialized.

During the tryout, the "Welcome to the Big City" sequence (which used the music of Erik Satie's "Trois Gymnopedies") was dropped and the "America" tribute was substituted.

Awards

Tony Awards and Nominations: Best Musical (*Dancin'*); Best Featured Actor in a Musical (Wayne Cilento); Best Featured Actress in a Musical (Ann Reinking); Best Director of a Musical (Bob Fosse); Best Costume Designer (Willa Kim); Best Lighting Designer (**Jules Fisher**); Best Choreographer (**Bob Fosse**)

A HISTORY OF THE AMERICAN FILM

Theatre: ANTA Theatre
Opening Date: March 30, 1978; *Closing Date*: April 16, 1978
Performances: 21
Play and *Lyrics*: Christopher Durang
Music: Mel Marvin
Direction: David Chambers; *Producers*: Judith Gordon and Richard S. Bright (Marc Howard, Associate Producer); *Choreography*: Graciela Daniele; *Scenery*: Tony Straiges; *Costumes*: Marjorie Slaiman; *Lighting*: William Mintzer; *Musical Direction*: Clay Fullum
Cast: Maureen Anderman (Contract Player # 1: Blessed Virgin Mother, Speakeasy Patron, Nurse, Voice of Anna Karenina, Ma Joad, Cucumber Girl, Dolores, Voice of Sonja Henie), Gary Bayer (Jimmy), Walter Bobbie (Contract Player # 2: Michael, Salad Chef), Jeff Brooks (Contract Player # 3: Ticket Man, Newsboy, Young Speakeasy Patron, Young Reporter, Grandma Joad, Mickey), Bryan Clark (Contract Player # 4: Cop, Bartender, Judge, Edward Mortimer, Voice of Vronsky, Von Leffing, Navy Officer, Victor Henreid, Voice of John, Wally Marvin, Voice of Academy Award Announcer, Voice of FBI Narrator, Voice of God, Theatre Manager), David Cromwell (Contract Player # 5: Jesus, Ferruchi, Ernie the Reporter, Abdhul, Pa Joad, Make-Up Man, Harkness, Uncle Sam, Marine Officer, Robot, Windsor Phelps), David Garrison (Contract Player # 6: Minstrel, Clarinet Man, "Big" Hit Man, David, Fife), Ben Halley Jr. (Contract Player # 7: Piano Man, Viola, Indian, Ito, Sailor, Stuart), Swoosie Kurtz (Bette), Kate McGregor-Stewart (Contract Player # 8: Orphanage Lady, Ma O'Reilly, Allison Mortimer, Prison Warden, Lettuce Girl, Gold Star Mother, WAC, Elizabeth Purtidge), Joan Pape (Eve), April Shawhan (Loretta), Brent Spiner (Hank), Eric Weitz (Contract Player # 9: God, "Little" Hit Man, Eric, Santa, Snare, Voice of Robot), Mary Catherine Wright (Contract Player # 10: "Silent" Mother, Bartender's Girl, Clara Mortimer, Carrot Girl); Rob Fisher (On Stage Pianist)
The musical was presented in two acts.

Musical Numbers

Act One: "The Silent Years" (Company); "Minstrel Song" (David Garrison); "Shanty Town Romance" (Gary Bayer, April Shawhan); "They Can't Prohibit Love" (Swoosie Kurtz); "We're in a Salad" (Brent Spiner; Salad Girls: Bean—April Shawhan, Tomato—Swoosie Kurtz, Celery—Joan Pape, Cucumber—Maureen Anderman, Lettuce—Kate McGregor-Stewart, Carrot—Mary Catherine Wright; David Garrison, Eric Weitz, Walter Bobbie); "Euphemism" (April Shawhan); "Ostende Nobis Tosca" (Swoosie Kurtz, Brent Spiner, David Garrison, Eric Weitz); "The Red, the White and the Blue" (Joan Pape, Company)
Act Two: "Pretty Pin-Up" (Joan Pape, April Shawhan, Swoosie Kurtz, Mary Catherine Wright); "Apple Blossom Victory" (Swoosie Kurtz, Joan Pape, Kate McGregor Stewart); "Isn't It Fun to Be in the Movies" (David Garrison, Erick Weitz); "Search for Wisdom" (Gary Bayer, April Shawhan, Company)

A History of the American Film was a look at America's obsession with the movies and its stars, and how the clichés of the screen have permeated our culture. The setting was the auditorium of an old-time movie palace, replete with rows of seats that faced the actual theatre where *A History of the American Film* was presented; there were also balcony seats, and high above was a film projector. The cast members sat and watched the movies, and, of course, they were actually watching the audience. The seats were easily movable, and so throughout the evening some of the cast members left their seats and took part in a phantasmagoric film that encapsulated most of the screen genres and its stars, from the silent era to the present day. Those cast members who weren't involved in a particular scene returned to their seats and watched the ongoing movie.

The leading roles were movie stars known as Bette (Swoosie Kurtz), the tough leading lady of the Bette Davis and Barbara Stanwyck variety; Loretta (April Shawhan), the angelic leading lady a la Loretta Young and Norma Shearer; Hank (Brent Spiner), the "aw-shucks" hero in the Henry Fonda and James Stewart tradition; Jimmy (Gary Bayer), the hard-boiled hero in the style of James Cagney and Humphrey Bogart; and Eve (Joan Pape), the dead-pan sidekick in the mode of Eve Arden. From the silent era and through the 1930s, everything seen on stage was in black and white (including gray orange juice as well as a gray grapefruit shoved in Loretta's face by Jimmy), but from the 1940s onward the décor and costumes were splashed in Technicolored hues.

After each movie segment, Loretta hopes it really is "the end" of the movie so that she and Jimmy can get on with their lives back in shanty town, but the end never comes because the movies go on forever. The evening kidded all film genres, including gangster films, backstage musicals (with the big production number "We're in a Salad"), detective movies, war stories, prison movies (up the river and to the slammer at the Big House for Women, the governor pardons Esther Blodgett, Norma Desmond, Mildred Pierce, Tootie Smith, and Florence Ziegfeld), romances, biblical epics, and sci-fi and disaster flicks. In one of the most amusing sequences, Jimmy goes through the complicated mechanics of lighting two cigarettes at the same time, and when he proffers one to Bette she informs him she doesn't smoke. Among other delightful moments was a glimpse at an Oscar ceremony where we discover that Loretta is nominated for her role as an alcoholic ex-ingenue with polio in *I'll Cry with a Song in My Heart Tomorrow*. And no matter how serious the situation, Eve can't control her obsessive wise-cracking. We also hear about all sorts of movies, including *Seven Brides for Twelve Angry Men* and *Love Me or Leave Me in the Snake Pit*.

Despite the evening's drolleries and generally favorable reviews, the show lasted less than three weeks. It was another in a long string of essentially small-scale musicals that probably should have opened in an intimate Off-Broadway theatre rather than in a large Broadway house.

Richard Eder in the *New York Times* liked the "mostly very funny carnival," and while it sometimes "stalls or bogs down" it "always gets going again." He felt the evening was "too long" and "too much," but it nonetheless was an "authentic, inspired and possessed comedy." Clive Barnes in the *New York Post* said the show was "rather more of a dangerously clever joke than a play" but Durang's book was "sharp and funny" and Mel Marvin's score was "cheerfully accurate pastiche." And John Beaufort in the *Christian Science Monitor* praised Durang's "mischievous guided tour through cinema non-verite," said Swoosie Kurtz "proves again that she is simply one of our deftest young comediennes," and singled out "Isn't It Fun to Be in the Movies" as the score's best song.

But Howard Kissel in *Women's Wear Daily* said the musical was "no less banal than the clichés it intends to mock," and Douglas Watt in the *New York Daily News* indicated the evening was like a "gussied-up varsity show" in which "inanity becomes an end in itself." Jack Kroll in *Newsweek* noted that an early regional production had "satiric bite and a certain rueful affection for a fantasy-fed nation," but somewhere "along the regional theatre trail" the work "developed a bad case of elephantiasis" and was now a "puffed-up travesty."

The musical had first been presented in a showcase production at the Eugene O'Neill Memorial Theatre Foundation in Waterford, Connecticut, and then in three separate and fully staged productions at the Hartford Stage Company, Hartford, Connecticut, the Mark Taper Forum in Los Angeles, and at the Kreeger Theatre at the Arena Stage in Washington, D.C.

The script was published in paperback by Avon Books in 1978.

Awards

Tony Award Nomination: Best Book (Christopher Durang)

THE MERRY WIDOW

Theatre: New York State Theatre
Opening Date: April 2, 1978; *Closing Date*: April 27, 1978
Performances: 8 (in repertory)
Libretto and *Lyrics*: Victor M. Leon and Leo Stein; English adaptation and dialogue by Ursula Eggers and Joseph De Rugeris and English lyrics by Sheldon Harnick
Music: Franz Lehar
Direction: Tito Capobianco (Gigi Denda, Stage Director); *Producer*: The New York City Opera (Julius Rudel, Director; John S. White, Managing Director); *Choreography*: Gigi Denda; *Scenery* and *Costumes*: Carl Toms; *Lighting*: Ken Billington; *Chorus Master*: Lloyd Walser; *Musical Direction*: Julius Rudel
Cast: David Rae Smith (Baron Mirko Zeta), Glenys Fowles (Valencienne), Alan Titus (Count Danilo Danilovitch), Beverly Sills (Anna Glawari), Bruce Reed (Camille de Rosillon), Harlan Foss (Vicomte Cascada), Howard Hensel (Raoul St. Brioche), John Lankston (Bogdanovitch), Jane Shaulis (Sylviane), William Ledbetter (Kromov), Sandra Walker (Olga), Jonathan Green (Pritchitch), Puli Toro (Praskovia), James Billings

(Njegus); Grisettes: Candace Itow (Lolo), Jane Shaulis (Dodo), Sandra Walker (Jou-Jou), Toni-Ann Gardella (Frou-Frou), Puli Toro (Clo-Clo), Emilietta Ettlin (Margot); Members of Petrovenian and Parisian Society, Dancers, Servants, Waiters: The New York City Opera Company Chorus and Dancers
The operetta was presented in three acts.
The action takes place in Paris during the early 1900s.

The current revival of Franz Lehar's operetta *The Merry Widow* was a new version that had first been produced by the San Diego Opera in 1977 and directed by Tito Capobianco. The original German text was adapted by Ursula Eggers and Joseph De Rugeriis, and new English lyrics were by Sheldon Harnick. The production starred Beverly Sills and Alan Titus, and was recorded by Angel Records (LP # S-37500). For the new production, an aria from Lehar's *Giuditta* (1934) was interpolated for Beverly Sills in the third act.

Harold C. Schonberg in the *New York Times* said the revival was "cheap-looking" and the unit set and the "paucity" of props weren't "particularly imaginative" and were "serviceable" at best. The "handsome" and "romantic" Titus sang "suavely" but was "occasionally next to inaudible" ("perhaps he had a cold"), and although Sills made a "gallant try" her "vocal resources" were now "sadly diminished" (but she still exuded "glamour").

For more information about *The Merry Widow* see entry for the June 1974 production (also see entry for the ballet version, which opened in June 1976).

THE SAINT OF BLEECKER STREET

Theatre: New York State Theatre
Opening Date: April 13, 1978; *Closing Date*: April 23, 1978
Performances: 3 (in repertory)
Libretto and *Music*: Gian-Carlo Menotti
Direction: Francis Rizzo; *Producer*: The New York City Opera Company; *Scenery*: Beeb Salzer; *Costumes*: Carol Luiken; *Lighting*: Hans Sondheimer; *Chorus Master*: Lloyd Walser; *Musical Direction*: Cal Stewart Kellogg
Cast: Jane Shaulis (Assunta), Alan Kays (A Young Man, First Guest), Judith De Rosa (Maria Corona), Bobby Scalese (Corona's Son), Diana Soviero (Carmela), Martha Thigpen (A Young Woman), Irwin Densen (Don Marco), Catherine Malfitano (Annina), Enrico DiGiuseppe (Michele), Lila Herbert (Concettina), Sandra Walker (Desideria), Alan Baker (Second Guest), William Ledbetter (Salvatore), Kenn Dovel (Bartender), Charlott Thyssen (A Nun), Ron Boucher (A Young Priest), Don Henderson (Neighbor), Harris Davis (Neighbor); Neighbors, Friends, Policemen, Others: The New York City Opera Company Chorus
The opera was presented in three acts.
The action takes place in the Little Italy neighborhood of New York City during the present time.
(The program didn't list musical numbers.)

Like the previous season's revival of Gian-Carlo Menotti's opera *The Saint of Bleecker Street*, The New York City Opera Company's production included Catherine Malfitano (Annina) and Enrico DiGiuseppe (Michele) in the leading roles. Donal Henahan in the *New York Times* noted that "with her pure and sweet soprano voice and her darkly fragile beauty," Malfitano was "as fine an Annina as could be imagined" and that DiGiuseppe created an "interesting mixture" of "angered befuddlement and intelligence." He noted the production made a "good stab" at capturing "the lurid, verismo mood" of the story and that Cal Stewart Kellogg was a "precise" and "tasteful" conductor.

The April 19 performance was telecast live on public television.

For more information about the opera, see entry for the November 1976 revival.

AIN'T MISBEHAVIN'

"The New FATS WALLER Musical Show"

Theatre: Longacre Theatre (during run, the musical transferred to the Plymouth and Belasco Theatres)
Opening Date: May 9, 1978; *Closing Date*: February 21, 1982

Performances: 1,604
Lyrics and *Music*: See list of musical numbers for specific credits
Direction: Richard Maltby Jr. (Murray Horwitz, Associate Director); *Producers*: Emanuel Azenberg, Dasha Epstein, The Shubert Organization, Jane Gaynor, and Ron Dante; *Choreography*: Arthur Faria; *Scenery*: John Lee Beatty; *Costumes*: Randy Barcelo; *Lighting*: Pat Collins; *Musical Direction*: Hank Jones
Cast: Nell Carter, Andre De Shields, Armelia McQueen, Ken Page, Charlaine Woodard; Luther Henderson (Piano)
The revue was presented in two acts.

Musical Numbers

Act One: "Ain't Misbehavin'" (*Hot Chocolates*, 1929; lyric by Andy Razaf, music by Thomas "Fats" Waller and Harry Brooks) (Company); "Lookin' Good but Feelin' Bad" (lyric by Lester A. Santly, music by Thomas "Fats" Waller) (Company); "'T Ain't Nobody's Biz-ness If I Do" (lyric and music by Porter Grainger and Everett Robbins; additional lyric by Richard Maltby Jr. and Murray Horwitz) (Andre De Shields, Company); "Honeysuckle Rose" (lyric by Andy Razaf, music by Thomas "Fats" Waller) (Ken Page, Nell Carter); "Squeeze Me" (lyric by Clarence Williams, music by Thomas "Fats" Waller) (Armelia McQueen); "Handful of Keys" (lyric by Richard Maltby Jr. and Murray Horwitz, and based on an idea by Marty Grosz) (Company); "I've Got a Feeling I'm Falling" (lyric by Billy Rose, music by Thomas "Fats" Waller and Harry Link) (Nell Carter, Company); "How Ya Baby" (lyric by J. C. Johnson, music by Thomas "Fats" Waller) (Andre De Shields, Charlaine Woodard, Company); "The Jitterbug Waltz" (lyric by Richard Maltby Jr., music by Thomas "Fats" Waller) (Company); "The Ladies Who Sing with a Band" (*Early to Bed*, 1943; lyric by George Marion, music by Thomas "Fats" Waller) (Andre De Shields, Ken Page); "Yacht Club Swing" (lyric by J. C. Johnson, music by Thomas "Fats" Waller and Herman Autry) (Charlaine Woodard); "When the Nylons Bloom Again" (*Early to Bed*, 1943; lyric by George Marion, music by Thomas "Fats" Waller) (Armelia McQueen, Charlaine Woodard, Nell Carter); "Cash for Your Trash" (lyric by Ed Kirkeby, music by Thomas "Fats" Waller) (Nell Carter); "Off-Time" (lyric by Andy Razaf, music by Thomas "Fats" Waller and Harry Brooks) (Company); "This Joint Is Jumpin'" (lyric by Andy Razaf and J. C. Johnson, music by Thomas "Fats" Waller) (Company)
Act Two: Entr'acte (Company); "Spreadin' Rhythm Around" (lyric by Ted Koehler, additional lyric by Richard Maltby Jr., music by Jimmy McHugh) (Company); "Lounging at the Waldorf" (lyric by Richard Maltby Jr., music by Thomas "Fats" Waller) (Armelia McQueen, Charlaine Woodard, Ken Page, Nell Carter); "The Viper's Drag" (music by Thomas "Fats" Waller) and "The Reefer Song" (traditional) (Andre De Shields, Company); "Mean to Me" (lyric and music by Roy Turk and Fred E. Ahlert) (Nell Carter); "Your Feet's Too Big" (lyric and music by Ada Benson and Fred Fisher) (Ken Page); "That Ain't Right" (lyric and music by Nat "King" Cole, additional lyric by Richard Maltby Jr. and Murray Horwitz) (Andre De Shields, Armelia McQueen, Company); "Keepin' Out of Mischief Now" (lyric by Andy Razaf, music by Thomas "Fats" Waller) (Charlaine Woodard); "Find Out What They Like" (lyric by Andy Razaf, music by Thomas "Fats" Waller) (Armelia McQueen, Nell Carter); "Fat and Greasy" (lyric and music by Porter Grainger and Charlie Johnson) (Andre De Shields, Ken Page); "Black and Blue" (*Hot Chocolates*, 1929; lyric by Andy Razaf, music by Thomas "Fats" Waller and Harry Brooks) (Company); Finale: "I'm Gonna Sit Right Down and Write Myself a Letter" (lyric by Joe Young, music by Fred E. Ahlert) (Ken Page); "Two Sleepy People" (1938 film *Thanks for the Memory*; lyric by Frank Loesser, music by Hoagy Carmichael) (Armelia McQueen, Ken Page); "I've Got My Fingers Crossed" (1936 film *King of Burlesque*; lyric by Ted Koehler, music by Jimmy McHugh) (Armelia McQueen, Charlaine Woodard, Ken Page); "I Can't Give You Anything but Love" (*Blackbirds of 1928*; lyric by Dorothy Fields, music by Jimmy McHugh) (Andre De Shields, Charlaine Woodard); "It's a Sin to Tell a Lie" (lyric and music by Billy Mayhew) (Nell Carter, Company); and "Honeysuckle Rose" (reprise) (Company)

After *Dancin'*, the "Fats" Waller (Thomas "Fats" Waller) (1904–1943) tribute revue *Ain't Misbehavin'* was the second-longest-running musical of the season with 1,604 performances. It was one of the most popular hits of the era, and won Tony Awards for Best Musical, Best Director of a Musical (Richard Maltby Jr.), and

Best Featured Actress in a Musical (Nell Carter). Later there was a television special; a Broadway revival; various recordings and national tours; and London productions.

The evening received rapturous reviews from the critics, and audiences loved it. But this viewer found it somewhat disappointing. The tribute began life at the intimate Manhattan Theatre Club, a perfect venue for a pocket-sized show with five cast members, but looked somewhat forlorn when it transferred to the Longacre Theatre on Broadway. The Longacre is a relatively small house, but was too large for the show, which seemed lost and undernourished on its stage. During the era, there were a number of revues that paid tribute to black music. The Duke Ellington tribute *Sophisticated Ladies* (1981) was bloated and overblown, and *Ain't Misbehavin'* looked underproduced. As the evening progressed, it became slightly monotonous and it clearly needed more textured musical flavoring with a chorus of supporting singers and dancers. The revues ***Bubbling Brown Sugar*** and ***Eubie!*** (the Eubie Blake tribute) were far more satisfying because each one found an inspired middle ground that was intimate and yet offered a variation in its presentational style that included singing and dancing choruses.

The songs fell into four categories: songs composed solely by Waller (with lyrics by various writers); songs co-composed by Waller and other composers (with lyrics by various writers); songs composed by Waller without lyrics, but were here presented with lyrics especially written by Maltby and Murray Horwitz; and songs by other composers that Waller had popularized via his recordings.

Richard Eder in the *New York Times* said the revue was "a cluster of marvels," not the least of which was Nell Carter, who in "I've Got a Feeling I'm Falling" could "blare like a trumpet" and in "Mean to Me" could sing "quietly, but with a silvery, delicate pungency that could lead an army." The "heart" of the "heart-stopping show" was "Black and Blue" (aka "What Did I Do to Get So Black and Blue"), which was a spiritual, madrigal, "or any other musical work that operates on pure spirit." The evening's "one real failure" was "The Viper's Drag."

Clive Barnes in the *New York Post* praised the "joyous celebration" and said it was "quite simply a Broadway show that you will never forget." Howard Kissel in *Women's Wear Daily* said the evening was "two hours of sheer, solid pleasure" and noted that with Off-Broadway's *Starting Here, Starting Now* (a 1977 retrospective revue of songs by David Shire and Maltby) and *Ain't Misbehavin'*, director Maltby "may single-handedly make revues respectable again."

Douglas Watt in the *New York Daily News* noted that Nell Carter was a "black Mae West with a voice that could sound reveille for an entire regiment or croon it to sleep" with her raucous "Cash for Your Trash" and her delicate "Mean to Me." Jack Kroll in *Newsweek* found the revue "blazingly entertaining"; he said the evening's one misstep was "Honeysuckle Rose," which was sung "with startling crassness and vulgarity," and the "most moving moment" was "Black and Blue," a song with a "splendid, sorrowing pun" that transformed "an immensely appealing show" into "a deeply poignant one."

The revue premiered at the Manhattan Theatre Club's Cabaret on February 8, 1978, for twenty-eight performances and except for Irene Cara (who was succeeded by Charlaine Woodard), the others in the cast transferred to Broadway. The cast album was released by RCA Victor Records on a two-LP set (# CBL2-2965; CD # 2965-2-RC). A televised version was produced by NBC on June 21, 1985, with the original Broadway cast, who also appeared in a Broadway revival that opened on August 15, 1988, at the Ambassador Theatre for 176 performances.

A 1995 national tour with the Pointer Sisters apparently had Broadway in mind, and while it didn't play in New York, a recording of highlights from the production was released by RCA (CD # 68415). There have been two London productions, at Her Majesty's Theatre on March 22, 1979, and one that opened at the Tricycle Theatre in 1995 and was recorded by First Night Records.

The revue included two songs from Waller's 1943 Broadway musical *Early to Bed* ("The Ladies Who Sing with a Band" and "When the Nylons Bloom Again"). The 1988 Broadway revival of *Ain't Misbehavin'* added a third song from the 1943 musical, "This Is So Nice" (for Nell Carter).

Awards

Tony Awards and Nominations: Best Musical (***Ain't Misbehavin'***); Best Featured Actress in a Musical (**Nell Carter**); Best Featured Actress in a Musical (Charlaine Woodard); Best Director of a Musical (**Richard Maltby Jr.**); Best Choreographer (Arthur Faria)

ANGEL

"A New Musical"

Theatre: Minskoff Theatre
Opening Date: May 10; 1978; *Closing Date*: May 13, 1978
Performances: 5
Book: Ketti Frings and Peter Udell
Lyrics: Peter Udell
Music: Gary Geld
Based on the 1929 novel *Look Homeward, Angel* by Thomas Wolfe and its 1957 stage adaptation of the same name by Ketti Frings.
Direction: Philip Rose; *Producers*: Philip Rose and Ellen Madison (Karen Wald and Norman Main, Associate Producers); *Choreography*: Robert Tucker; *Scenery*: Ming Cho Lee; *Costumes*: Pearl Somner; *Lighting*: John Gleason; *Musical Direction*: William Cox
Cast: Donna Davis (Helen Gant), Joel Higgins (Ben Gant), Patti Allison (Mrs. Fatty Pert), Grace Carney (Mrs. Snowden), Don Scardino (Eugene Gant), *Frances Sternhagen* (Eliza Gant), Elek Hartman (Will Pentland), Rebecca Seay (Florry Mangle), Justine Johnston (Mrs. Clatt), Gene Masoner (Jake Clatt), Billy Beckham (Mr. Farrell), Jayne Barnett (Miss Brown), Leslie Ann Ray (Laura James), *Fred Gwynne* (W. O. Gant), Daniel Keyes (Doctor Maguire), Rex David Hays (Joe Tarkington), Carl Nicholas (Reed McKinney), Norman Stotz (Tim Laughran), Patricia Englund (Madame Victoria)
The musical was presented in two acts.
The action takes place in Altamount, North Carolina, during Autumn 1916.

Musical Numbers

Act One: "Angel Theme" (Orchestra); "All the Comforts of Home" (Boarders); "Like the Eagles Fly" (Joel Higgins); "Make a Little Sunshine" (Frances Sternhagen, Don Scardino, Joe Higgins); "Fingers and Toes" (Fred Gwynne, Norman Stotz, Carl Nicholas, Rex David Hays); "Fatty" (Joel Higgins); "Astoria Gloria" (Patti Allison, Boarders); "Railbird" (Don Scardino); "If I Ever Loved Him" (Leslie Ann Ray); "A Dime Ain't Worth a Nickel" (Joel Higgins, Patti Allison); "I Got a Dream to Sleep On" (Don Scardino); "Drifting" (Frances Sternhagen)
Act Two: "I Can't Believe It's You" (Fred Gwynne, Patricia Englund); "Feelin' Loved" (Don Scardino, Leslie Ann Ray); "A Medley" (Joe Higgins, Patti Allison, Frances Sternhagen, Leslie Ann Ray); "Tomorrow I'm Gonna Be Old" (Fred Gwynne); "Feelin' Loved" (reprise) (Don Scardino, Leslie Ann Ray); "How Do You Say Goodbye" (Leslie Ann Ray); "Gant's Waltz" (Fred Gwynne, Frances Sternhagen); "Like the Eagles Fly" (reprise) (Don Scardino)

Angel, which in preproduction was known as *All the Comforts of Home* and during its tryout as *Look Homeward, Angel*, was based on Thomas Wolfe's 1929 novel *Look Homeward, Angel* and its 1957 stage adaptation of the same name by Ketti Frings. The drama won the Pulitzer Prize and the New York Drama Critics' Circle Award for Best Play, and ran for 564 performances. The musical version was co-authored by Frings, and ran for just five performances.

Wolfe's semiautobiographical novel and its stage adaptations looked at the sad lives of the Gant family who live in Altamount (Asheville), North Carolina, and centered on Eugene (the Thomas Wolfe role), who was played by Don Scardino. The family's home is also a boarding house (called "Dixieland") run by Eugene's cold and domineering mother Eliza (Frances Sternhagen), and other family members are his ineffectual stonecutter father W. O. (Fred Gwynne), who never seems able to finish the sculpture of an angel, and his older brother Ben (Joel Higgins), who is dying of consumption. On the periphery of the story were the few boarders who made up the remainder of the depressing household. At the end of the story, Ben has died and left Eugene some money, and so the young man breaks free of Altamount, Dixieland, and his mother and goes off to make his own life.

Richard Eder in the *New York Times* suggested that *Angel* was less a "disaster" than a "desert." The musical was "a damp and oppressive amalgam of bathos" that lacked "feeling." Instead, "slickness" prevailed and the oddities of Wolfe's hometown were "flattened out into marshmallows" and were "hooked together in awkward and absurd transitions." Douglas Watt in the *New York Daily News* said the evening was "prevailingly nice" but "bland"; John Beaufort in the *Christian Science Monitor* found the musical "oddly constructed and not very happily pieced together"; and Clive Barnes in the *New York Times* said the musical was "far from a disaster" but just "didn't work."

Eder noted the lyrics had "the consistency of cornbread soaked in milk" and the banal score was sufficient enough "to furnish a number or two for the piped music on airplanes waiting to take off"; Christopher Sharp in *Women's Wear Daily* said the music opted "for a sound that is as unimposing as Muzak"; and Barnes mentioned that the score "sounds faintly like agreeably tuneful music in someone else's elevator." The evening offered one outstanding rhythmic song ("Astoria Gloria") which had nothing to do with the plot (someone says "they just loved this down at the saloon," and then proceeds to sing it).

Scenic designer Ming Cho Lee created a huge Victorian home and boarding house that revolved at will to reveal exteriors and interiors. Watt felt that the "expansive two-story" design was "exactly right" and Barnes said the set was a "knockout." Holly Hill in the *Wall Street Journal* praised the "attractive" house of gray-green hues set against a "leafy" cyclorama, and said Pearl Somner's "graceful" costumes were in "autumnal shades" that reflected the evening's "subdued mood." She also mentioned that Robert Tucker's choreography was in keeping with the era's soft-shoe and Castle Walk–styled dances.

During the tryout, the musical was presented in three acts, the lighting was designed by David Kissel, and Madame Victoria was played by Peg Lamprey.

A recording of the entire score (including "Dixieland Rag," which wasn't listed in the program, as well as a "playoff" version of "Astoria Gloria" and a second act reprise of the "Angel Theme") with some of the cast members was privately released (Geld/Udell/Abrams LP # GUA-001) and was briefly available for sale to the public. The script was published in paperback by Samuel French in 1979.

Awards

Tony Award Nomination: Best Leading Actress in a Musical (Frances Sternhagen)

RUNAWAYS

Theatre: Plymouth Theatre
Opening Date: May 13, 1978; *Closing Date*: December 31, 1978
Performances: 199
Text, Lyrics, and *Music*: Elizabeth Swados
Direction: Elizabeth Swados; *Producers*: Joseph Papp (Bernard Gersten, Associate Producer); *Choreography*: Elizabeth Swados (and members of the cast); *Scenery*: Douglas W. Schmidt and Woods MacKintosh; *Costumes*: Hilary Rosenfeld; *Lighting*: Jennifer Tipton; *Musical Direction*: Not Credited
Cast: Bruce Hlibok (Hubbell), Lorie Robinson (Interpreter for Hubbell), Carlo Imperato (A.J.), Rachael Kelly (Jackie), Ray Contreras (Luis), Nan-Lynn Nelson (Nikki Kay Kane), Jossie De Guzman (Lidia), Randy Ruiz (Manny), Jon Matthews (Eddie), Bernie Allison (Sundar), Venustra K. Robinson (Roby), David Schechter (Lazar), Evan H. Miranda (Eric), Jonathan Feig (Iggy), Kate Schellenbach (Jane), Leonard Brown (EZ), Mark Anthony Butler (Mex-Mongo), Trini Alvarado (Melinda), Karen Evans (Deidre), Sheila Gibbs (Mocha); Chorus: Paula Anderson, Kenya Brome, Jerome Dekie, Karin Dekie, Lisa Dekie, John Gallogly, Timothy Michaels, Toby Parker; Musicians: Judith Fleisher (Piano, Toy Piano), John Schimmel (String Bass), Leopoldo F. Fleming (Congas, Timbales, Bongos, Bells, Siren, Others), David Sawyer (Trap Set, Triangle, Glass, Ratchet), Patience Higgins (Saxophones, Flutes), Elizabeth Swados (Guitar)
The musical was presented in two acts.
The action takes place during the present time in a playground in New York City.

Musical Numbers and Speeches

Act One: "You Don't Understand" (Bruce Hlibok; improvisation by Hlibok); "I Had to Go" (Carlo Imperato, John Schimmel); "Parent/Kid Dance" (Company) "Appendectomy" (Rachael Kelly); "Where Do People Go" (Company); "Footsteps" (Nan-Lynn Nelson, John Schimmel, Jossie De Guzman, Randy Ruiz; "Spanish Argument" in this sequence by Guzman and Ruiz); "Once Upon a Time" (Jossie De Guzman, Company); "Current Events" (Jon Matthews); "Every Now and Then" (Carlo Imperato, Bernie Allison, Company); "Out on the Street" (Bruce Hlibok, Lorie Robinson; improvisation by Hlibok); "Minnesota Strip" (Venustra K. Robinson); "Song of a Child Prostitute" (Rachael Kelly, Jossie De Guzman, Randy Ruiz, Ray Contreras); "Christmas Puppies" (Nan-Lynn Nelson); "Lazar's Heroes" (David Schechter; improvisation by Schechter); "Find Me a Hero" (David Schechter, Company); "Scrynatchkielooaw" (Nan-Lynn Nelson); "The Undiscovered Son" (Evan H. Miranda, Judith Fleisher, John Schimmel); "I Went Back Home" (Jonathan Feig, Kate Schellenbach); "This Is What I Do When I'm Angry" (Carlo Imperato, Nan-Lynn Nelson); "The Basketball Song" (Leonard Brown, Company; dance by Ray Contreras and Mark Anthony Butler); "Spoons" (Randy Ruiz); "Lullaby for Luis" (Jossie de Guzman, Ray Contreras, Patience Higgins, Company); "We Are Not Strangers" (Evan H. Miranda, Company)

Act Two: "In the Sleeping Line" (Company; A.J.'s Dream: Carlo Imperato; Roby's Dream: Venustra K. Robinson; Jackie's Dream: Rachael Kelly; Eddie's Dream: Jon Matthews; Nightmares in Spanish: Jossie De Guzman, Randy Ruiz, Ray Contreras); "Lullaby from Baby to Baby" (Trini Alvarado, Bruce Hlibok, Karen Evans); "Tra Gog Vo in Den Whole" ("I Will Not Tell a Soul") (David Schechter, Bruce Hlibok); "Revenge Song" (Company); "Enterprise" (Karen Evans, Nan-Lynn Nelson, Mark Anthony Butler, Company); "Sometimes" (Venustra K. Robinson, David Schechter, Company); "Clothes" (Jonathan Feig); "We Are Not Strangers" (reprise) (Sheila Gibbs, Leonard Brown, Company); "Mr. Graffiti" (Mark Anthony Butler); "The Untrue Pigeon" (Nan-Lynn Nelson); "Senoras de la Noche" (Jossie De Guzman, Randy Ruiz, Nan-Lynn Nelson); "We Have to Die?" (Karen Evans); "Where Are Those People Who Did *Hair*?" (David Schechter, Karen Evans, Company); "Appendectomy II" (Rachael Kelly, Trini Alvarado); "Let Me Be a Kid" (Company); "To the Dead of Family Wars" (Karen Evans); "Problem after Problem" (Bruce Hlibok, Lorie Robinson); "Lonesome of the Road" (Ray Contreras, Bernie Allison, Company)

Runaways was first presented Off Broadway at the Public Theatre's Martinson Hall on February 21, 1978, for seventy-six performances. It transferred to Broadway in late spring and managed to run for the remainder of the year, but despite many favorable reviews and a batch of Tony Award nominations, the dreary work has all but disappeared and its only major recent production was a special single performance at Joe's Pub on March 25, 2007, in a revised version by Rodney Hicks.

The revue-like evening was a bleeding-heart look at runaway teenagers, and through the work's prism it seems runaways exist because of the failures of society and parents. Elizabeth Swados wrote most of the material, directed and choreographed the production, and played the guitar in the small six-piece orchestra. Like the earlier ***The Me Nobody Knows***, *Runaways* sentimentalized its subject, and its characters were perhaps too self-aware. Swados stated the work was based on interviews and sessions with runaways, but it seems most of the lyrics and dialogue was written by her. Perhaps the piece would have been more authentic and more touching if the subjects themselves had written the entire piece (with a few minor exceptions, the entire text, lyrics, and music were by Swados).

In her program notes, Swados made the curious comment that she had an "intuition about the potential of adolescents and how they have been grossly underestimated." She then noted that the runaway children are from broken and "solid" homes; as for the latter, it was unclear if they were *with* their families or if they just decided to take off on their own. (Were they simply unmotivated and directionless?) Further, Swados mentioned that some of the cast members were runaways. If so, these runaways had impressive show business credentials because the majority of them had been on national television (*The Mike Douglas Show* as well as commercials for Pepsi-Cola, Bell Telephone, and Life Savers), Off Broadway (in recent productions of *The Landscape of the Body*, *The Cherry Orchard*, and *Agamemnon*), and had theatre exposure with the Lee Strasberg Institute, the Boston Repertory Theatre, and Arena Stage in Washington, D.C. Swados's intention was to present a "collage" that dealt with "the profound effects of our deteriorating families," but reading the script and listening to the cast album reveals a well-meaning show that wasn't particularly affecting and gripping.

The musical was also another in the mode of ***A Chorus Line*** in which a group of people gather together to talk about themselves. After its success with Michael Bennett's groundbreaking musical, the Public Theatre was particularly taken with this happily short-lived genre (which T. E. Kalem in *Time* once termed the "confessional musical"). The Public also offered the monotonous (nonmusical) *For Colored Girls Who Have Considered Suicide When the Rainbow Is Enuf* (1976) (perhaps it should have been titled *A Colored Girls' Line*?) and the musical *On-the Lock-In* (1977), a bleeding-heart look at prisoners (*A Prisoners' Line*?) who smugly tell the audience members that they too are in a prison. And during the same month *Runaways* opened on Broadway, another confessional-style revue, ***Working***, opened.

In reviewing the Broadway production of the musical, Douglas Watt in the *New York Daily News* said *Runaways* was like "an overlong graduate production by the sociology department of a well-endowed university," and despite the "spirited" cast the evening had "not been transformed into art." The show struck "the same note repeatedly" with "growing monotony."

Although Richard Eder in the *New York Times* found the work "remarkable," he felt the move to Broadway "weakened" the show's spirit and now the cast was "performing its discoveries rather than making them." Clive Barnes in the *New York Post* said the evening was "strange and brilliant" and "a theatrical experience that should not be missed" (but the song "Where Are Those People Who Did *Hair*?" offered a "sour note" when Swados "quite insultingly" tried to deny that show's influence and thus was "the one moment of bad taste and insecurity in her show").

In reviewing the production when it played Off Broadway, the critics were mixed in their assessments. Christopher Sharp in *Women's Wear Daily* noted the production wasn't "particularly dynamic" and there was "little attempt to form all the raw material beyond setting it to some lively music." But sometimes the linking together of musical "fragments" made him feel he'd missed "several tunes by a few inches" and this in some ways was appropriate for Swados's "unresolved" book, which "doesn't wind down as much as it whines down."

Edwin Wilson in the *Wall Street Journal* said the evening's "overall achievement" was "considerable," but the material was too "one-note"; further, its assumption that all young people's problems "should be laid exclusively on the doorstep of their parents" was simplistic. T. E. Kalem in *Time* felt Swados's score was "eclectic" but lacked "her own signature," and she "sadly indulges in a punitive blame game charging parents with a shortfall of love."

But John Beaufort in the *Christian Science Monitor* found the evening "an extraordinary theatrical experience," and Jack Kroll in *Newsweek* said the work was an "extraordinary urban pop cantata" and "to call it far and away the best musical of the season is to insult it."

The script was published in paperback by Bantam Books in 1979 and then by Samuel French in 1980. The Broadway cast album was released by Columbia Records (LP # JS-35410), and the CD was later issued by DRG.

Carol Lawson in the *New York Times* reported that a film version of *Runaways* was on Twentieth Century-Fox's production schedule, but of course the film was never made.

In his review of Swados's 1982 Off-Broadway musical *Lullabye and Goodnight*, Frank Rich in the *New York Times* said the new work was in essence an expanded version of two songs from *Runaways* ("Minnesota Strip" and "Song of a Child Prostitute").

Awards

Tony Award Nominations: Best Musical (*Runaways*); Best Director of a Musical (Elizabeth Swados); Best Book (Elizabeth Swados); Best Score (lyrics and music by Elizabeth Swados); Best Choreographer (Elizabeth Swados)

WORKING

"A New Musical"

Theatre: 46th Street Theatre
Opening Date: May 14, 1978; *Closing Date*: June 4, 1978
Performances: 25

Text: Stephen Schwartz

Lyrics and *Music*: Craig Carnelia, Micki Grant, Mary Rodgers and Susan Birkenhead, Stephen Schwartz, James Taylor; incidental music by Michele Brourman

Based on the 1974 book *Working: People Talk about What They Do All Day and How They Feel about What They Do* by Studs Terkel.

Direction: Stephen Schwartz (Nina Faso, Associate Director); *Producers*: Stephen R. Friedman and Irwin Meye; *Choreography*: Onna White; *Scenery*: David Mitchell; *Costumes*: Marjorie Slaiman; *Lighting*: Ken Billington; *Musical Direction*: Stephen Reinhardt

Cast: Susan Bigelow (Kate Rushton, Housewife), Steven Boockvor (John Fortune, Advertising Copy Chief; Marco Camerone, Hockey Player), Rex Everhart (Herb Rosen, Corporate Executive; Booker Page, Seaman), Arny Freeman (Anthony Palazzo, Stonemason; Joe Zutty, Retired Shipping Clerk), Bob Gunton (Bud Jonas, Football Coach; Frank Decker, Interstate Trucker), David Patrick Kelly (Brett Meyer, Boxboy; Benny Blue, Bar Pianist; Charlie Blossom, Copy Boy), Robin Lamont (Barbara Herrick, Agency Vice President; Sharon Atkins, Receptionist; Cathleen Moran, Hospital Aide), Matt Landers (Conrad Swibel, Gas Meter Reader; Tom Patrick, Fireman; Tim Devlin, Salesman; Ralph Werner, Tie Salesman), Bobo Lewis (Rose Hoffman, Teacher; Grace Clements, Millworker; Lucille Page, Seaman's Wife), Patti LuPone (Nora Watson, Editor; Roberta Victor, Call Girl), Joe Mantegna (Emilio Hernandez, Migrant Worker; Dave McCormick, Interstate Trucker), Matthew McGrath (John Rushton, Newsboy), Lenora Nemetz (Babe Secoli, Supermarket Checker; Terry Mason, Stewardess; Delores Dante, Waitress), David Langston Smyrl (Al Calinda, Parking Lot Attendant; Will Robinson, Bus Driver), Brad Sullivan (Mike LeFevre, Steel Worker), Lynne Thigpen (Diane Wilson, Secretary; Heather Lamb, Telephone Operator; JoAnn Robinson, Bus Driver's Wife; Maggie Holmes, Cleaning Woman), Terri Treas (Jill Torrance, Model; Carla Devlin, Salesman's Wife)

The revue was presented in two acts.

Musical Numbers

Act One: "All the Livelong Day" (based on poem "I Hear America Singing" by Walt Whitman) (words by Walt Whitman, additional lyric by Stephen Schwartz, music by Stephen Schwartz) (Company); "Lovin' Al" (lyric and music by Micki Grant) (David Langston Smyrl, Ensemble); "The Mason" (lyric and music by Craig Carnelia) (David Patrick Kelly); "Neat to Be a Newsboy" (lyric and music by Stephen Schwartz) (Matthew McGrath, Newsboys); "Nobody Tells Me How" (lyric by Susan Birkenhead, music by Mary Rodgers) (Bobo Lewis); "Treasure Island Trio" (music by Michele Brourman) (danced by Terri Treas, Lenora Nemetz, Lynne Thigpen); "Un Mejor Dia Vendra" (Spanish lyric by Graciela Daniele and Matt Landers, music by James Taylor) (Joe Mantegna, Matt Landers, Migrants); "Just a Housewife" (lyric and music by Craig Carnelia) (Susan Bigelow, Housewives); "Millwork" (music by Michele Brourman and Stephen Schwartz) (Robin Lamont, David Patrick Kelly, Matt Landers; danced by Terri Treas); "Nightskate" (music by Michele Brourman and Stephen Schwartz) (danced by Steven Boockvor); "Joe" (lyric and music by Craig Carnelia) (Arny Freeman); "If I Could've Been" (lyric and music by Micki Grant) (Company)

Act Two: "It's an Art" (lyric and music by Stephen Schwartz) (Lenora Nemetz, Customers); "Brother Trucker" (lyric and music by James Taylor) (Joe Mantegna, Bob Gunton, David Patrick Kelly, Matt Landers); "Husbands and Wives" (music by Michele Brourman) (Rex Everhart and Bobo Lewis, David Langston Smyrl and Lynne Thigpen, Matt Landers and Terri Treas); "Fathers and Sons" (lyric and music by Stephen Schwartz) (Bob Gunton); "Cleanin' Women" (lyric and music by Micki Grant) (Lynne Thigpen); "Something to Point To" (lyric and music by Craig Carnelia) (Company)

Stephen Schwartz's well-meaning and earnest revue *Working* was a series of songs and vignettes based on Studs Terkel's oral history of ordinary people doing their ordinary jobs. There were no glamorous types here, no one in the arts or in politics, no models and fashion designers, and instead the evening looked at waitresses, tie salesmen, truck drivers, supermarket checkers, and the like. But for the most part the evening lacked theatrical excitement and was unfocused. Perhaps there were too many creators (seven lyricists and composers in all), and had the score been written just by Schwartz it might have had a more cohesive point of view.

Richard Eder in the *New York Times* said the adaptation lacked "a workable form and combines elements that don't agree." He felt that on paper Terkel captured the "drama of real people" while the musical offered "dramatic fictions" that were "frail" and "overburdened." And while James Taylor's contributions (including the "stunning" song "Millwork") were "interesting and effective," many of the other songs were "musically uninteresting" with "trite and sentimental" and "inflated and banal" lyrics. Clive Barnes in the *New York Post* pointed out that "lengthy" conversations set to "the bland sound of muzak" could never result in a "truly stimulating evening of theatre," and unfortunately *Working* was "fundamentally an attempt to make statistics into musical drama."

Howard Kissel in *Women's Wear Daily* said the evening's best moments were when the cast delivered segments from Terkel's book as if they were "dramatic monologs"; otherwise, the show had "no shape." He noted that if ***A Chorus Line*** lacked a plot it at least had a "direction" in which the director Zach chooses the gypsies for his new musical. But *Working*, like ***Runaways***, lacked a "sense of momentum." Douglas Watt in the *New York Daily News* liked the "exceptionally talented" cast and noted the evening began "marvelously" with the workers seen on a large sign of lighted letters that spelled out the show's title while they sang "I Hear America Singing." He regretted that the show "hadn't been edited more carefully and given a few more strong songs."

T. E. Kalem in *Time* said the adaptation faltered because instead of the characters "doing" their jobs they were always "talking" about their work; further, the dances were "tangential" because only dancers "dance out" their "work life." As for the score, it "was written by too many hands to possess a distinctive signature."

But John Beaufort in the *Christian Science Monitor* said *Working* was "a labor of love" and that Schwartz and his collaborators had "expended talent generously and bestowed laudable devotion" to create the musical equivalent of Terkel's oral history. And Bob Lape on WABCTV7 said Schwartz had "worked a miracle" to ensure that the characters were "both real and robustly entertaining."

During the Chicago tryout, Graciela Daniele was the choreographer (for New York, she was succeeded by Onna White). Performers who were seen in both Chicago and New York were: Robin Lamont, Lynne Thigpen, Steven Boockvor, Rex Everhart, Bobo Lewis, Joe Mantegna, Matt Landers, David Patrick Kelly, Terri Treas, and Brad Sullivan. Performers in Chicago who weren't in the New York production were: Joe Ponazecki, Jay Flash Riley, Anne DeSalvo, Stephen Reinhardt, Jay Footlik, and Jo Henderson. Henderson played Kate (the housewife), and for New York was succeeded by D'Jamin Bartlett, who played the role in previews and was herself succeeded by Marilyn Cooper and then by Susan Bigelow (Cooper was the general standby for the female performers in the company).

Dropped during the Chicago tryout were: "American Dreaming" (lyric and music by James Taylor), "Nobody Goes Out Anymore" (lyric and music by Craig Carnelia), and the dance "The Working Girl's Apache."

The cast album was released by Columbia Records (LP # 35411), and issued on CD by Fynsworth Alley (# 302-062-114-2). The latter includes additional tracks: three demo recordings performed by Stephen Schwartz ("The Mason," "Joe," and "Lovin' Al"); a recording of "Fathers and Sons" performed by Schwartz; "Hots Michael at the Piano" (an unused song for the production written, composed, and performed by Craig Carnelia); and a new song ("I'm Just Movin'," performed by Kenna Ramsey) which was written by Schwartz for a 1999 Los Angeles production. The collection *Lost in Boston IV* (Varese Sarabande CD # VSD-5768) includes "Hots Michael at the Piano."

The revue was presented on the public television series *American Playhouse* in 1982, and was produced Off Off Broadway at St. Bart's Playhouse during the 1984–1985 season.

Awards

Tony Award Nominations: Best Featured Actor in a Musical (Steven Boockvor); Best Featured Actor in a Musical (Rex Everhart); Best Book (Stephen Schwartz); Best Score (lyrics and music by Stephen Schwartz; lyrics and music by Craig Carnelia; lyrics and music by James Taylor; lyrics and music by Micki Grant; lyric by Susan Birkenhead, music by Mary Rodgers); Best Scenic Designer (David Mitchell); Best Lighting Designer (Ken Billington)

ALICE

"A New Musical"

The musical opened at the Forrest Theatre, Philadelphia, Pennsylvania, on May 31, 1978, for a scheduled ten-week run, but permanently closed there on June 11, 1978, and canceled its anticipated late summer Broadway opening.

Book: Vinnette Carroll

Lyrics and *Music*: Micki Grant

Based on the novels *Alice's Adventures in Wonderland* (1865) and *Through the Looking Glass* (1872) by Lewis B. Carroll (Carroll was a pseudonym for Charles Lutwidge Dodgson).

Direction: Vinnette Carroll; *Producers*: Mike Nichols and Lewis Allen, and presented in association with Urban Arts Corporation and Anita MacShane; *Choreography*: Talley Beatty; *Scenery*: Douglas W. Schmidt; *Costumes*: Nancy Potts; *Lighting*: Jennifer Tipton; *Musical Direction*: Joyce Brown

Cast: Charlene Harris (Charlie), Clinton Derricks-Carroll (Caterpillar [The Dee-Jay], [the other] Caterpillar, Tweedledum, The Black Knight's Horse, Fish), Alberta Bradford (Bartender, Mushroom), Thomas Pinnock (Gryph [The Bouncer], Gryphon), Marilynn Winbush (Waitress), Cleavant Derricks (Carpenter, Tweedledee, The White Knight's Horse, Fish), Douglas Houston (Chauffeur, The Black Knight), Jane White (Duchess, The Duchess), Alice Ghostley (Lily White, White Queen), Hamilton Camp (Ted White, White King, The White Knight), Roumel Reaux (Prima), Clif De Raita (Secunda), Christopher Deane (Tertia), Paula Kelly (Regina, Black Queen), Debbie Allen (Alice), Jeffrey Anderson-Gunter (Eric, Cheshire Cat, Mock Turtle), Ronald Dunham (Ronnie); Cooks: Alberta Bradford, Cleavant Derricks, Clinton Derricks-Carroll, Charlene Harris, Douglas Houston, Thomas Pinnock, and Roumel Reaux; The Cheshire Cat's Girls: Brenda Braxton, Linda James, Juanita Grace Tyler, and Kiki Shepard; Disco Dancers, Mushroom People, Chess Pieces, Croquet Game Guests, Lobsters: Adrian Bailey, Brenda Braxton, Roslyn Burrough, Nora M. Cole, Christopher Deane, Clif De Raita, Ronald Dunham, Ralph Farrington, Maggy Gorrill, Charlene Harris, Linda James, Dwayne Phelps, Roumel Reaux, Kiki Shepard, Juanita Grace Tyler, Marilynn Winbush, Charles Wynn

The musical was presented in two acts.

The action takes place during the present time in New York City and in Wonderland.

Musical Numbers

Act One: "Disco" (Company); "Hall of Mirrors Ballet" (Debbie Allen); "Father William" (Alberta Bradford, Debbie Allen, The Mushroom People, Clinton Derricks-Carroll); "Chess" (Paula Kelly, The Chess Pieces); "Workin' for the Man" (Clinton Derricks-Carroll, Cleavant Derricks); "I Am Real" (Debbie Allen, Hamilton Camp, Clinton Derricks-Carroll, Cleavant Derricks); "Children Are" (Jane White, The Cooks); "Everybody's Mad" (Jeffrey Anderson-Gunter, The Cheshire Cat's Girls); "Alice" (Hamilton Camp)

Act Two: "Workin' for the Man" (reprise) (Clinton Derricks-Carroll, Cleavant Derricks); "Fun and Games" (Company); "It's Lonely" (Debbie Allen); "Lobster Rock" (Cleavant Derricks, Clinton Derricks-Carroll, Lobsters); "I Am Real" (reprise) (Debbie Allen); "Consider" (Paula Kelly); "Disco" (reprise) (Company)

Vinnette Carroll's adaptation of Lewis B. Carroll's *Alice's Adventures in Wonderland* and *Through the Looking Glass* made for an unhappy collision between the two Carrolls. The updated version began in a Manhattan disco called The Rabbit Hole in which teenager Alice (Debbie Allen) gets high on cocktails and soon becomes part of a wonderland dream world. Unfortunately, the musical lacked a point of view, the atmosphere of the Victorian and disco worlds clashed, and the surreal episodes in Alice's hallucination didn't resonate and were remote and uninteresting.

The cast was a mixture of black and white performers, and for a while it seemed as if the new adaptation might cleverly comment on racial relationships. But if so the idea was never developed. For example, Alice Ghostley played the White Queen as a faded Southern belle adorned in a ragged Confederate flag; the conceit seemed to indicate an implicit racial statement, but nothing came of it. Later, there was a duel between the White Knight (Hamilton Camp) and the Black Knight (Douglas Houston), but both were portrayed by white actors and so any racial tension between the two symbolic characters was lost. Further, Tweedledee (Cleavant Derricks) and Tweedledum (Clinton Derricks-Carroll) sang an inconclusive would-be protest work song ("Workin' for the Man") which went nowhere.

Besides Carroll's scattershot approach to the *Alice* stories, Micki Grant's score was generally disappointing and so the book, lyrics, and music were major let-downs. But the musical had many redeeming qualities. Debbie Allen proved that besides her acting, singing, and dancing talents, she also possessed a striking stage presence. Further, Douglas W. Schmidt's décor was dazzlingly inventive and used the patterns of a chess board as the set's unifying visual concept. If the yellow brick road in ***The Wiz*** paved the way for Dorothy's eventual return to Kansas, the chess board served as the means for Alice to play a chess game in order to win her way out of Wonderland and back to reality, and to find her way from childhood to adulthood. Schmidt's designs and his use of a surreal series of seemingly endless mirrors were handsomely complemented by Jennifer Tipton's lighting design, and Talley Beatty's choreography lent excitement to the evening. The "Disco," "Hall of Mirrors Ballet," and "Lobster Rock" had energy and imagination, but otherwise the musical sequences failed to impress.

William B. Collins in the *Philadelphia Inquirer* suggested Carroll was too timid in her approach to the material and thus she never completely reimagined the Victorian *Alice* stories for contemporary black interpretation. The musical had "staggering" book problems, the songs were "flavorless," and the merging of the traditional *Alice* stories and characters with the newly created modern-day disco setting was "puzzlingly pointless." Hari in *Variety* said Alice's champagne cocktails at the disco produced more "fizzle than fizz" and noted the revue-like episodes had little "momentum" with their "arbitrarily jumbled" sequences where Wonderland too often seemed like "blunderland." But he noted that Debbie Allen was "charismatic" and that Alice Ghosley made the most of her "few comic opportunities."

Variety reported that the musical lost $1,050,000, and that during its brief run played to less than 20 percent capacity.

There have been numerous musical adaptations of Carroll's *Alice* stories. Eva Le Gallienne and Florida Friebus's version (with music by Richard Addinsell) was first produced on Broadway at the Civic Repertory on December 12, 1932, for 127 performances; it was revived on April 5, 1947, at the International Theatre for 100 performances and on December 23, 1982, at the Virginia Theatre for 21 performances (for all three productions, Le Gallienne played the role of the White Queen). There were also a number of Off-Broadway and Off-Off-Broadway adaptations, including *Alice with Kisses* (which closed in previews in 1964); *Alice in Wonderland* (Bil Baird's 1975 marionette version); *For the Snark Was a Boojum, You See* (1977); *The Passion of Alice* (1977); *Alice in Concert* (a 1980 adaptation by Elizabeth Swados); and *Alice* (1995; adapted by Robert Wilson and music cowritten by Tom Waits).

Vinnette Carroll followed up her *Alice* adaptation with another version titled *But Never Jam Today*, which opened Off Off Broadway in a workshop production at the Urban Arts Corps Theatre in August 1978 for twelve performances, just two months after *Alice* closed in Philadelphia. Carroll's first version of *But Never Jam Today* had been developed with Anita MacShane in 1962 at the Actors' Studio, and then on April 23, 1969, it was presented for one performance at City Center with music by Gershon Kingsley (Marie Thomas was Alice and Sherman Hemsley was the Mad Hatter). The final version of ***But Never Jam Today*** opened on Broadway in 1979 and played for just one week (see entry for more information).

There was even an Off-Off-Broadway "adult" musical version called *Alice in Wonderland* that opened in 2007; set in a trailer park in Weehawken, New Jersey, the musical's flyer proclaimed that Alice finds herself in an "erotic Wonderland." The most recent Broadway adaptation of the material was *Wonderland*, which opened in 2011 (lyrics by Jack Murphy and music by Frank Wildhorn).

In 1951, Disney's cartoon film version offered a somewhat chilly Alice, which was softened by gorgeous visuals and a charming score by Bob Hilliard and Sammy Fain that included "I'm Late," "All in a Golden Afternoon," and "Painting the Roses Red."

BARBARY COAST

Theatre and *Performance Dates*: The musical opened on February 28, 1978, at the Orpheum Theatre in San Francisco, California, and permanently closed there on March 11.
Book, *Lyrics*, and *Music*: William Penzner

Direction: Jack Bunch; *Producer*: Barbary Coast Productions, Inc. (William Penzner); *Choreography*: Ed Nolfi; *Scenery*: William Morris; *Costumes*: Madeline Graneto; *Lighting*: Martin Aronstein; *Musical Direction*: Joseph Stecko

Cast: Jerry Lanning (Gentleman Jim Corbett), Marcia Rodd (Cynthia Carter), Ben Wrigley (Biff Mahoney), Lette Rehnolds (Princess Zara), Gillian Scalici (Rita Lorraine), Philip Kenneally (Officer Miority, Trainer), Dan Ferrone (Rod Van de Vere), Sab Shimono (Captain Chung), Michael Byers (Lee Matson), Lola Fisher (Mrs. Mary R. Carter), Chao-Li Chi (Bing Lu Lee), Timm Fujii (Kim), Jack Driscoll (Joe "Killer" Choynski), Marnie Mosiman (Lillian Russell), Michael Magnusen (Dispatcher), Charles Spoerri (Referee); Cabaret Girls: Helena Andreyko, Cynthia DeVore, Mary Ann Dunroe, Spence Ford, Alyson Reed, and Lynne Savage; Roxann Pyle (Carrie Nation), M. G. Hawkins (C. Barrington Fairchild); Reporters: M. G. Hawkins, Michael Magnusen, Jeffrey Reynolds, and James Whitson; Ensemble Singers: James D. Armstrong, Eileen Duffy, Catherine Fiasca, M. G. Hawkins, Terry Iten, Michael Magnusen, Carla Manning, Brad Maule, Marnie Mosiman, Roxann Pyle, Jeffrey Reynolds, Charles Spoerri, Brian Taylor, Leslie Tinnaro, Kathy Vestuto, James Whitson; Ensemble Dancers: John Addis, Helena Andreyko, Ron Cisneros, Cynthia DeVore, Mary Ann Dunroe, Denny Martin Flinn, Spence Ford, Shuan Soo Lee, Lynne Savage, Ricky Schussel, Wilfredo Suarez; Richard Laster (Organ-Grinder), Charlie (Monkey)

The musical was presented in two acts.

The action takes place in San Francisco, California, from mid-August 1897 to 1906.

Musical Numbers

Act One: Overture (Orchestra); "You're on the Barbary Coast" (Ben Wrigley, Ensemble); "The Fight" (Jerry Lanning, Jack Driscoll, The Fight Fans); "Everybody Loves a Winner" (The Fight Fans); "They Struck Her Name from the Blue Book Set 'Cause She Made Headlines in the Pink Police Gazette" (Marcia Rodd, Ensemble); "Love, Love, Love" (Gillian Scalici, Cabaret Girls); "The Pink Police Gazette" (Marcia Rodd, Marnie Mosiman, Gillian Scalici, Ensemble); "The Count of Ten" (Jerry Lanning); "Love Is Everything" (Ben Wrigley, Lette Rehnolds, Michael Byers, Gillian Scalici, Ensemble); "There's Nothing Stranger Than Love" (Jerry Lanning, Marcia Rodd); "Love Is Everything" (reprise) (Jerry Lanning, Marcia Rodd, Ensemble); "Monkey Dance" Ben Wrigley, Charlie); "Happy Time Rag" (Dancers, Ensemble); "Is It Love or Fascination" (Lette Rehnolds, Jerry Lanning, Marcia Rodd, Ensemble); "Without You There Is No Me" (Marcia Rodd); "The Count of Ten" (reprise) (Jerry Lanning, Reporters, Philip Kenneally); "When Miss Park Avenue Does the Bumps" (Marcia Rodd, Chao-Li Chi, Two Dancers)

Act Two: Entr'acte (Orchestra); "The Tong War" (Marcia Rodd, Jerry Lanning, Ben Wrigley, Timm Fujii, Philip Kenneally, Sab Shimono, Chinese Tongs); "There's Nothing Stranger Than Love" (reprise) (Jerry Lanning, Marcia Rodd); "I Can See It All" (Lette Rehnolds, Dan Ferrone, Ben Wrigley); "Gentlemen Jim" (Ben Wrigley, Philip Kenneally, Chao-Li Chi, Lette Rehnolds, Cabaret Girls, Ensemble); "When You Dance with the One You Love" (Jerry Lanning, Marcia Rodd, Ensemble); "How Long Can a Heart Go On Loving" (Marcia Rodd); "Barbary Coast" (Ben Wrigley, Roxann Pyle); "Searching" (Jerry Lanning); "Ride, Ride, Ride" (The Cabaret Girls); "Go, Don't Want to Love You No More" (Gillian Scalici, Chao-Li Chi, Cabaret Girls); "You're on the Barbary Coast" (reprise) (Gillian Scalici, Cabaret Girls); "Searching" (reprise) (Jerry Lanning, Marcia Rodd); "Love Is Everything" (reprise) (Company)

Barbary Coast had all the markings of a vanity production. The book, lyrics, and music were by William Penzner who bankrolled the musical (under the name of Barbary Coast Productions, Inc.) for the reported amount of $700,000–$1 million, and after devastatingly bad reviews the show gave up on a Broadway transfer and permanently closed.

The musical dealt with opposite-sides-of-the-tracks Barbary Coast boxer and saloon owner Gentleman Jim Corbett (Jerry Lanning) and Nob Hill society girl Cynthia Carter (Marcia Rodd), and their romance was set against a tourist's-eye view of Old San Francisco. There were Nob Hill mansions and low-life saloons, visits to boxing matches and luxurious yachts, Chinatown with its exotic opium dens, a ballet depicting the Tong Wars, scenes on the city's waterfront and atop Telegraph Hill, a movable cable car, and even the 1906 earthquake. And in a bow to the clichés of old-hat operettas from the 1940s, the musical utilized celebrity walk-ons (here, Lillian Russell and Carrie Nation).

William Hogan in the *San Francisco Chronicle* found the musical "tiresomely old-fashioned" and noted that the "expensive nonsense" went "on and on" to the point where you didn't care if the star-crossed lovers ever got together (but the earthquake was good for something, because it broke down "social barriers" and provided a romantic ending for the pair). Stanley Eichelbaum in the *San Francisco Examiner* said the "spectacularly bad" musical was a "dud" and a "fiasco" which brought "triteness to a new low" with its "derivative, perfectly awful songs" and lyrics "worse than the music." Both critics provided examples of the show's idea of humor ("Shall we join the girls?" "Why, are they coming apart?"; and, in response to the comment "She's a peach!," a character replies, "She's not a peach, she's a whole bloody orchard!").

Herb in *Variety* found the book "frantic but listless" and the score "derivative" (as for the lyrics, "well, they rhyme"). The "failure" lacked "substance" and all was "for naught" in an evening that "desperately hungers for song and story."

However, the critics agreed that William Morris's décor and Madeline Graneto's costumes were "fetching" and "well-crafted." Herb said the "artistry and inventiveness" of Morris's scenery could have outfitted three or four more musicals; Hogan praised the interior of a Nob Hill mansion, a promenade atop Telegraph Hill, and the poop deck of a luxurious yacht; and Eichelbaum said the production was "gorgeous" with "handsome" and "overwhelming" effects, including a stained-glass gazebo and a revolving cable car. Hogan noted that forty-two stagehands were needed to move the scenery and twenty-three dressers were employed to help the forty-one cast members in and out of Graneto's "elegant, quite stunning costumes."

During the run there was some reordering of the songs in the second act, and the "Monkey Dance," "When You Dance with the One You Love," and "Go, Don't Want to Love You No More" were deleted and "Without You Waltz" was added.

THE LAST MINSTREL SHOW

The musical opened at the Playhouse Theatre, Wilmington, Delaware, on March 30, 1978, and closed at the New Locust Theatre, Philadelphia, Pennsylvania, on April 30, 1978.

Book: Joe Taylor Ford

Lyrics and *Music*: See song list for credits

Direction and *Choreography*: Donald McKayle; *Producers*: Ken Marsolais in association with Martin Markinson and Donald Tick; *Scenery*: Edward Burbridge; *Costumes*: Robert Mackintosh; *Lighting*: Ian Calderon; *Musical Direction*: Howard Roberts

Cast: Roger Alan Brown (Forbes), *Della Reese* (Black Sally), Gregory Hines (J. J. Jones [Mr. Shine]), Ned Wright (George Cole [Mr. Tambo]), Eugene Jackson (Uncle Tom Taylor [Mr. Salt]), Dick Vance (Brother Bo Taylor [Mr. Pepper]), Jeffrey V. Thompson (Sam Parks Jr. [Mr. Pompey), Howard Roberts (Preacher Simmons [Mr. Moses]), Tucker Smallwood (Jimmie "Tuskegee" White [Rastus]), Ralston Hill (Al Perletter [Mr. Interlocutor]), Clebert Ford (Bert Pine [Mr. Bones]), Rene Levant (Patton Bridges)

The musical was presented in two acts.

The action takes place at the Variety Theatre in Cincinnati, Ohio, on the night of March 15, 1926.

Musical Numbers

Act One: Overture (Minstrels); "Down Where the Watermelon Grows" (lyric and music by George Evans and Shields) (Clebert Ford, Ned Wright, Minstrels); "Shine! Shine! Shine!" (lyricist and composer unknown) (Dick Vance, Minstrels); "At the Garbage Gentleman's Ball" (lyric and music by Joseph M. Daly and Thomas S. Allen) (Gregory Hines, Tucker Smallwood, Jeffrey V. Thompson, Minstrels); "'Tain't No Sin to (Take Off Your Skin and) Dance Around in Your Bones" (lyric by Edgar Leslie, music by Walter Donaldson) (Eugene Jackson, Dick Vance, Howard Roberts, Minstrels); "Turkey in the Straw" (lyric and music by Otto Bonnell) (Gregory Hines, Jeffrey V. Thompson, Tucker Smallwood, Minstrels); "I'll Lend You Anything" (lyric and music by Jean Havez and Harry von Tilzer) (Ned Wright with Clebert Ford, Howard Roberts, Minstrels); "When the Bell in the Lighthouse Rings Ding Dong" (lyric and music by Lamb and Solman) (Ralston Hill); "Stack Dat Cotton" (lyricist and composer unknown) (Clebert Ford, Ned Wright); "Hello, Baby" (lyric and music by Magidson, Washington, and Cleary) (Clebert Ford, Ned Wright, Gregory

Hines); "Darktown Is Out Tonight" (lyric and music by Will Marion) (Ralston Hill, Minstrels); "Waiting for the Robert E. Lee" (lyric by L. Wolfe Gilbert, music by Lewis F. Muir) (Minstrels)

Act Two: "Oh, Dem Golden Slippers" (lyric and music by James A. Bland) (Clebert Ford, Ned Wright); "Good News" (lyricist and composer unknown) (Della Reese, Minstrels); "Sister Low Down" (lyricist and composer unknown) (Della Reese, Minstrels); "Happy Days in Dixieland" (lyric and music by Kerry Mills) (Della Reese, Minstrels); "She's Getting' More Like the White Folk Every Day" (lyric by Bert Williams, music by Bert Williams and George Walker) (Della Reese, Minstrels); "I Don't Mind Walkin' in the Rain" (lyric and music by Max Rich and Al Hoffman) (Della Reese with Howard Roberts, Clebert Ford, Minstrels); "Keep On Goin'" (lyric and music by Al Bernard and Paul Crane) (Della Reese, Eugene Jackson); "The Pickaninny's Paradise" (lyric and music by Sam Ehrlich and Nat Osborne) (Della Reese, Minstrels); "Strut Miss Lizzie" (*Strut Miss Lizzie*, 1922; lyric by John Turner Layton, music by Henry Creamer) (Della Reese, Minstrels); "Do Lord, Remember Me" (lyricist and composer unknown) (Della Reese); "Gee, I'm Glad I'm from Dixie" (lyric by Noble Sissle, music by Eubie Blake) (Della Reese); "Rufus Rastus Johnson Brown" (lyric and music by Sterling and von Tilzer) (Della Reese); "Can't You Hear Me Callin' Caroline" (lyric and music by Gardner and Roma) (Minstrels); "Always Left Them Laughing" (lyric and music by Howard Roberts and Maureen Meloy) (Della Reese)

The Last Minstrel Show was an ambitious concept musical that closed during its pre-Broadway tryout. The work looked at the last performance of an all-black minstrel show (with black performers in blackface), which is closed down due to protests that it's racist and demeaning to blacks. Ironically, there were some who found *The Last Minstrel Show* itself racially offensive.

Joe Taylor Ford's script was ambitious, and the use of actual songs from the minstrel show era added to the atmosphere. Della Reese gave a memorable performance as Black Sally, the owner of the minstrel show, and her powerful stage presence and singing were impressive. The minstrel sequences were superbly sung and danced, and Gregory Hines was a particular standout.

Ernest Schier in the *Philadelphia Evening Bulletin* felt that the evening's "potential" was "barely touched" upon by Ford's "clumsy treatment," but said the minstrel sequences made for "a rousing evening" and was a "personal triumph" for Reese. William B. Collins in the *Philadelphia Inquirer* felt a "certain discomfiture" in watching black performers in blackface presenting songs and dances "with infectious skill," and *Variety* noted the production was "lively and entertaining" and the musical numbers didn't get in the way of the evening's message.

During the tryout, the following numbers were added: "A High Old Time in Dixie" (lyric and music by Lowen and Schleifforth); "Wait Till the Sun Shines, Nellie" (lyric by Andrew B. Sterling, music by Harry von Tilzer); "What He's Done for Me" (lyricist and composer unknown); and "Dixie" (lyric and music by Dan Emmett). In a credits' section of the program, the following songs were listed and may have been intended for, or perhaps at some point were heard in, the production: "A Hot Time in the Old Town Tonight" (lyric by Joe Hayden, music by Theodore H. Metz); "Remus Takes the Cake" (lyric and music by Jacob Henry Ellis and Wallace H. Becker); "At a Georgia Camp Meeting" (lyric and music by Kerry Mills); and "Brother Low Down" (lyric and music by Al Bernard and Larry Briers).

The musical had been scheduled to begin previews at the Helen Hayes Theatre on May 4, 1978, with an opening night of May 8. A few seasons later the musical was revived by the Rutgers Theatre Company at the Levin Theatre at Rutgers University in New Brunswick, New Jersey. Linda Hopkins portrayed Black Sally, and Tiger Haynes was George Cole/Mr. Tambo; from the original 1978 cast were Roger Allen Brown, Clebert Ford, Ralston Hill, and Jeffrey V. Thompson, and Howard Roberts was again the musical's conductor.

NEFERTITI

"A Musical Romance"

The musical opened on September 20, 1977, at the Blackstone Theatre, Chicago, Illinois, and permanently closed there on October 22, 1977.

Book and *Lyrics*: Christopher Gore

Music: David Spangler

Direction: Jack O'Brien; *Producer*: Sherwin M. Goldman; *Choreography*: Daniel Lewis; *Scenery, Costumes,* and *Visuals*: Sam Kirkpatrick; *Lighting*: Gilbert V. Hemsley Jr.; *Musical Direction*: Robert Billig

Cast: Patrick Kinser-Lau (Messenger from Egypt), Marilyn Cooper (Penmut), Benjamin Rayson (Tushratta, General Ramose), Andrea Marcovicci (Tadukhipa, later named Nefertiti), Michael Nouri (Hap), Michael V. Smartt (Ipy), Jane White (Tiy), Robert LuPone (Akhenaton), C. Eugene Moose (Mitanni Scribe), Francisco La Gueruela (Tutmose), George Connor (Sennet); Citizens of Mitanni, Citizens of Thebes, and Citizens of Everything Else in the Ancient World: Georgia Connor, Ann Crumb, Florie Freshman, Sylvia Miranda, Anthony Balcena, Ramon Colon, Michael Corbett, Simeon Den, Patrick Kinser-Lau, Francisco La Gueruela, G. Eugene Moose, Ernest Pagnano

The musical was presented in two acts.

The action takes place in Egypt circa 1350 BC.

Musical Numbers

Act One: "The Diary of a Dying Princess" (Andrea Marcovicci, Marilyn Cooper, Benjamin Rayson, Citizens of Mitanni); "Lama Su Apapi" (Marilyn Cooper); "Penmut's Apology" (Marilyn Cooper); "Everything Is Possible" (Andrea Marcovicci); "The Diary of a Dying Princess" (reprise) (Andrea Marcovicci, Michael Nouri, Marilyn Cooper); "Breakfast at Thebes" (Jane White, Household Staff); "Father" (Robert LuPone); "Pardon Me a Minute" (Andrea Marcovicci); "Beautiful Has Come" (Robert LuPone, Attendants); "Whatever Happened to Me?" (Michael Nouri); "Whatever Happened to Me?" (reprise) (Michael Nouri); "It Happens Very Softly" (Andrea Marcovicci, Handmaidens); "Legions of the Night" (Michael V. Smartt, Priests); "Light Will Shine" (Robert LuPone, Citizens of Thebes); "Everything Is Possible" (reprise) (Andrea Marcovicci, Robert Lupone)

Act Two: "Under the Sun" (Robert LuPone, Andrea Marcovicci, Their Followers); "The New World" (Robert LuPone); "A Free Translation" (Michael Nouri, Benjamin Rayson, Mitannites); "Someone Was Here" (Andrea Marcovicci, Artists); "Another Free Translation" (Michael Nouri, Benjamin Rayson); "Dinner at Thebes" (Jane White, Michael V. Smartt, Michael Nouri); "Take Off the Sandal" (Andrea Marcovicci)

In response to the title character's statement, "I'm Nefertiti," someone replied, "Never Who?"

And at the same time there was the stately and earnest love triangle of the princess Nefertiti (Andrea Marcovicci), the pharaoh Akhenaton (Robert LuPone), and the Egyptian soldier Hap (Michael Nouri).

And there was also the story of Akhenaton's desire to introduce the idea of monotheism to his people.

The musical *Nefertiti* was at war with itself, and never found its voice and tone. It ranged from the lighthearted to the serious, and by the time the musical began its Chicago tryout it was probably too late to radically revise the book and focus on a unifying concept. The musical closed in Chicago after playing there for five of its scheduled six-week engagement and canceled its November 10 New York opening.

Glenna Syse in the *Chicago Sun-Times* told the musical's creators to "get out the papyrus and start writing." The show was sometimes an "artsy-craftsy historical portrait," sometimes a "martyred love story," at other times was pure "Molly Goldberg," and seemed to be at war with itself in trying to decide if it was *Hair* or *Porgy and Bess*. The critic also regretfully noted that some of Robert LuPone's unfortunate costumes looked distressingly like diapers or tutus. (Later, Aaron Gold in the *Chicago Tribune* reported the musical would be shortened by about twenty minutes and would undergo new opening sequences for both acts; he also noted there would be replacements for "some costumes that didn't work," and so presumably they changed the diapers.)

Linda Winer in the *Chicago Tribune* said the evening was a combination of "well-intentioned but leaden intellectual vision" and "all-out musical comedy burlesque." Too often the show seemed to be about "three nice, talented kids in funny costumes trying to change the world." Sydney J. Harris in the *Chicago Daily News* said *Nefertiti* met "the mark of competence" but lacked that something special that would transform it "from the merely pleasant to the genuinely memorable"; and Mor in *Variety* said the "muddled musical" had an "aimless" book and "pleasant, unexciting songs."

Harris said Marcovicci was "most fetching, in face, voice, and manner"; Gold reported that a "New York theatre expert" found Nouri the "handsomest and most masculine musical star to hit the stage in 20 years"; and while Winer noted LuPone had the chance to show his "booming dance talent," he was "nearly crushed by playing straight man in an impossibly written, goody-goody role."

Beloved Broadway Baby Marilyn Cooper played Nefertiti's nurse (that is, maid), and the critics pounced on her interpretation. *Variety* said she needed "lessons in restraint and a curb on her inappropriate Yiddish accent"; Winer noted she employed "an inexplicable Jewish-Puerto Rican accent as the burlesque nurse"; and Harris said Cooper seemed to have "arrived in Egypt by way of Minsk, Pinsk, and Tomsk."

The critics mentioned that the décor was somewhat spartan, but Harris noted the designs were "simple, tasteful, imaginative and dramatic" and said that while the musical might have been "economically tailored" it was not "cheap and sleazy" looking. In fact, the November-December 1977 issue of *Theatre Crafts* devoted a cover story to the musical. Patricia MacKay discussed the show's design scheme in an in-depth eight-page article that included nine photographs from the production. She described Sam Kilpatrick's "elegant, monochromatic environment" which utilized a hydraulically controlled "broad open space [that] is limited and defined by a trapezoidal 'sail' of silk and rayon flown from a downstage pipe." MacKay reported the sail could be raised and lowered "like a curtain or float freely as if puffed up by the wind." The musical also employed a huge mechanical camel that was part puppet and part man (Winer said the fantasy camel was "wonderful").

The musical's original cast album was released by Take Home Tunes! Records (LP # THT-7810) with Andrea Marcovicci, Robert LuPone, Michael Nouri, Jane White, Michael V. Smartt, and chorus (the album includes a special insert with song lyrics). The recording offers twelve songs from the Chicago production ("Everything Is Possible," "Father," "Pardon Me a Minute," "Beautiful Has Come," "Whatever Happened to Me?," "It Happens Very Softly," "Legions" aka "Legions of the Night," "Under the Sun," "The New World," "Someone Was (Is) Here," "Take Off the Sandal," and "Dinner at Thebes"); omitted seven ("The Diary of a Dying Princess," "Lama Su Apapi," "Penmut's Apology," "Breakfast at Thebes," "Light Will Shine," "A Free Translation," and "Another Free Translation"); and added two ("Egypt Is Egypt Again" and "Where Did the Day Go?").

Akhenaton returned to the musical stage in Philip Glass's opera *Akhnaten* (libretto by Glass, Shalom Goldman, Robert Israel, and Richard Riddell), which premiered at the Stuttgart State Opera on March 3, 1984. Later that year, the opera was produced by the New York City Opera Company and the Houston Grand Opera Company at the New York State Theatre on November 4. The two-CD set recording by the Stuttgart State Opera, Orchestra, and Chorus was released by Sony Classical Records (# SM2K-91141).

THE PRINCE OF GRAND STREET

The musical opened on March 7, 1978, at the Forrest Theatre, Philadelphia, Pennsylvania, and permanently closed on April 15, 1978, at the Shubert Theatre, Boston, Massachusetts.

Book, Lyrics, and *Music*: Bob Merrill

Direction: Gene Saks; *Producers*: Robert Whitehead and Roger L. Stevens and The Shubert Organization; *Choreography*: Lee Theodore; *Scenery*: David Mitchell; *Costumes*: Jane Greenwood; *Lighting*: Tom Skelton; *Musical Direction*: Colin Romoff

Cast: *Robert Preston* (Nathan Rashumsky), Darlene Anders (Jenny Abromowitz), Steven Gelfer (Moishe Zweigman), Bernice Massi (Yetta Feinstein), Derek Wolshonak (Martin Malovsky), Duane Bodin (Sam Teitelbaum, A Sexton), Annette C. Winter (Mrs. Schumacher), Molly Stark (Mrs. Schwartz), Alexander Orfaly (Mr. Ginsburg, Foreman, Stephen Douglas), Bob Carroll (Mr. Gittleson), Alan Manson (Goldman), Sammy Smith (Krantz), David Margulies (Harry Metzger); Mourners: Dean Badolato, Duane Bodin, Bob Carroll, Walter Charles, Steven Gelfer, Clyde Laurents, Richard Muenz, Alexander Orfaly, Derek Wolshonak; Neva Small (Leah); Criers: Shellie Chancellor, Susan Edwards, Patricia Gadonnieux, Molly Stark, Annette C. Winter; Werner Klemperer (Julius Pritkin), Sam Levene (Itzak Goldfarb); Workers: Darlene Anders, Shellie Chancellor, Susan Edwards, Patricia Gadonnieux, Patti Mariano, Nana, Molly Stark, Annette C. Winter; Susan Edwards (Sarah), Nana (Young Mother), Dean Badolato (Yashka), Walter Charles (Stage Manager), Addison Powell (Mark Twain), Clyde Laurents (Jim), Richard Muenz (Hamlet); Swing Dancers and Singers: Eleanor Treiber and Duane Bodin

The musical was presented in two acts.

The action takes place in 1908 in New York City and Atlantic City.

Musical Numbers

Act One: "A Grand Street Tivoli Presentation" (Company); "Fifty Cents" (Mourners); "I'm a Girl with Too Much Heart" (Neva Small); "I Know What It Means to Be Alone" (Neva Small, Robert Preston); "I'm a Star" (Robert Preston); "Sew a Button" (Neva Small, Factory Workers); "Do I Make You Happy?" (Neva Small, Robert Preston); "A Grand Street Tivoli Presentation" (Company)
Act Two: "A Grand Street Tivoli Presentation" (Ensemble); "A Place in the World" (Neva Small); "My Potential" (Bernice Massi, Alan Manson, Sammy Smith); "The Youngest Person I Know" (Neva Small, Robert Preston, Ensemble); "A Grand Street Tivoli Presentation" (Ensemble); "What Do I Do Now?" (Neva Small); "What Do I Do Now?" (reprise) (Neva Small)

The Prince of Grand Street centered on the early years of Yiddish theater in New York City at the turn of the twentieth century. Robert Preston was Nathan Rashumsky, a character based on a composite of Jacob Adler and Boris Tomashefsky, both of whom were stars of Yiddish theatre. Like his real-life counterparts, Rashumsky specialized in playing characters much younger than himself, and he presented classics in which even the tragedies sported happy endings.

The musical was a dreary and tiresome show that never found its voice. The spoofs of *Romeo and Juliet* (with Preston playing the young hero with a rewritten ending that allowed Romeo and Juliet to live happily ever after and depicted a lavish wedding celebration in which the Capulets and the Montagues all join hands in joy) and *The Adventures of Huckleberry Finn* (with Preston an unlikely Huck) should have been devastatingly funny, but instead fell flat. And Preston was all wrong for the role: Rashumsky is a Jewish New Yorker, and Preston came across like a WASP from the mid-West. If Zero Mostel had been alive, he might have been the perfect Rashumsky, but with Mostel dead, Sam Levene far too old (although he played a minor role in the musical), and perhaps Sid Caesar unavailable, the show lacked a leading man with the fire, the chutzpah, and the madness required for the theatrical spoofs.

Bob Merrill's book lacked humor, the theatrical take-offs were unfunny, the romance between Rashumsky and Leah (Neva Small) wasn't interesting and lacked chemistry, the dances were negligible, and Merrill's score was bland and seldom offered much in the way of ingratiating lyrics and music. David Mitchell's décor occasionally had inventive ideas, but even it was disappointing.

The musical had been scheduled to open at the Palace Theatre on May 11, 1978, after tryouts in Philadelphia and Boston; but the production canceled its final two weeks in Boston and reportedly lost around $1 million.

Bill Wine in the *Camden* (New Jersey) *Courier-Post* said the "uneven tribute" to old-time Yiddish theatre needed to be "pruned, shaped, restructured, revamped, fleshed out, slimmed down and spruced up. In a word, overhauled." Ernest Schier in the *Philadelphia Bulletin* stated the book had "as much continuity as a map of Chinatown," there were only two or three songs "worth hearing," and the dances "seem to have been borrowed from the annual high school musical." He found the show "remarkably tuneless," said Preston came across as "desperate," and remarked that the evening of "boring nonsense" needed "one good kosher idea."

Elliot Norton in the *Boston Herald American* said the musical offered "a surprising amount of warmth and tenderness" as well as "a good deal of muddle and confusion"; further, the humor was sometimes "crude and embarrassing." The headline of Kevin Kelly's review in the *Boston Globe* read "Merrill's '*Fiddler in the Basement*'" and the critic noted that the "shloomp" of a musical was a "perfect, unfortunate example of oy-oy-oy!!!" He noted that "poor Sam Levene" had virtually "nothing to do" and said Preston's Rashumsky was a "stock embarrassment" and his Huck Finn was "painful" to watch. Hari in *Variety* said there were "deficiencies" in both book and songs and that *The Prince of Grand Street* had a long way to go if it was to "qualify as Broadway royalty."

During the course of the tryout, four songs were added ("Stay with Me," "Where Does Love Go?," "Look at Me," and a title number) and two were deleted ("I'm a Star" and "My Potential"). In Philadelphia, the action took place in 1908, but in Boston the year was given as 1907.

Neva Small's *Not Quite an Ingenue* (Small Penny Enterprises Records, unnumbered CD) includes one song from the musical, "I'm a Girl with Too Much Heart" (her collection of mostly theatre songs is one of the finest in recent years). In 1990, Merrill's Off-Broadway musical *Hannah . . . 1939* (which included Neva Small in its cast) lasted just forty-six performances but its cast album was recorded by That's Entertainment

Records (CD # CDTER-1192) and includes one song from *The Prince of Grand Street*, "Sew a Button," which apparently had been interpolated into *Hannah*'s score during previews but dropped prior to opening night.

We're Home, the Off-Broadway 1984 retrospective of Merrill's work, included two songs from *The Prince of Grand Street*, "A Place in the World" and "I'm a Girl with Too Much Heart."

In preproduction, the musical was titled *A Place in the World!* and included a few songs that were dropped prior to the tryout, including "Who Can Comprehend?," "Why Is the Bride So Young?," "Ev'ry Nighttime of Life," "What Does a Londoner Do in New York?," and "A Little While" (all are best-guess titles).

SPOTLIGHT

Theatre and *Performance Dates*: The musical gave one preview performance on January 10, 1978, at the National Theatre and officially opened there on January 11 before permanently closing on January 15 after six regular performances.
Book: Richard Seff
Lyrics: Lyn Duddy
Music: Jerry Bresler
Based on a story by Leonard Starr.
Direction: David Black; *Producer*: Sheldon R. Lubliner; *Choreography*: Tony Stevens; *Scenery*: Robert Randolph; *Costumes*: Robert Mackintosh; *Lighting*: Roger Morgan; *Musical Direction*: Jack Lee
Cast: *Gene Barry* (Jack Beaumont), Marc Jordan (Siggy Zimmer), D'Jamin Bartlett (Holly Beaumont), David-James Carroll (Chip Beaumont), William McClary (Mr. Kleinsinger), John Leslie Wolfe (Carey), Garon Douglass (Cosmo), James Braet (Charlie, Waiter), Clare Culhane (Myrna), Lenora Nemetz (Marie), Debbie Shapiro (Louisa May), Gary Daniel (Brawn), Cynthia Stewart (Mona), Freda Soiffer (First Contender), Michelle Stubbs (Second Contender, Young Woman), Eileen Casey (Third Contender), Terry Calloway (Lu Ellen), Michon Peacock (Janet, Night Woman), Loyd Sannes (Passerby), Wayne Mattson (Leaflet Man), Jeffrey Spielman (Young Man), Polly Rowles (Louise Pembley)
The musical was presented in two acts.
The action takes place during the present time and in 1955, mostly in Hollywood and New York.

Musical Numbers

Act One: "No Regrets" (Gene Barry); "What Am I Bid" (Gene Barry, D'Jamin Bartlett, David-James Carroll, Marc Jordan, William McClary, Ensemble); "Spotlight" (Gene Barry, Ensemble, Lenora Nemetz); "You Need Someone" (Gene Barry, Lenora Nemetz); "Round and Round" (Gene Barry, Lenora Nemetz, Michon Peacock, Freda Soiffer, Michelle Stubbs, Eileen Casey, Ensemble); "Tricks of the Trade" (Gene Barry, D'Jamin Bartlett); "Notice Me" (David James-Carroll); "Everything" (D'Jamin Bartlett)
Act Two: "Didn't You Used to Be Him?" (Gene Barry, Ensemble); "Such a Business" (Marc Jordan); "The Stranger in the Glass" (David James-Carroll); "You Are You" (Gene Barry, D'Jamin Bartlett); "Where Is Everybody?" (Gene Barry, Ensemble); "Spotlight" (reprise) (Gene Barry, D'Jamin Bartlett)

Spotlight was one of the decade's biggest disasters. It was set for a four-week tryout at the National Theatre in Washington, D.C., beginning on January 10, 1978, but after one preview and six regular performances it canceled the remainder of its scheduled run through February 4 as well as its announced opening in New York on February 12 at the Palace Theatre. *Variety* reported the potential take for the show's seven performances was $180,633, but the musical took in only $23,420, and Richard L. Coe in the *Washington Post* reported that *Spotlight* was the National Theatre's shortest-ever tryout.

Capitalized at $850,000, the musical was first announced as a vehicle for Dan Dailey and was scheduled for tryout stops at the National on November 7, 1977, and at the Colonial Theatre in Boston on December 7, with a Broadway opening at the Palace on January 10, 1978, after a week of New York previews. Once Dailey became ill, the production was postponed and eventually Gene Barry assumed the leading role.

The plot dealt with now down-and-out Broadway entertainer Jack Beaumont (Barry) who became a popular film star and is now reduced to seeing the memorabilia from his career go on the auction block. When his top hat and cane are up for bidding, he recalls his unhappy life and unfulfilling career, including three failed marriages (his wives were played by Lenora Nemetz, Michon Peacock, and Terry Calloway) and two unhappy and alienated children (D'Jamin Bartlett and David-James Carroll). But all ends sort of well: in the final moments of the musical he meets a fan (Polly Rowles) who tells him how much inspiration his films gave her.

The plot creaked and groaned, and the score was almost as bad as legend has it, but the title song was a good solid second-tier show-business salute, and the auction number "What Am I Bid" had a nice sweep to it. More interesting were some of scenic designer Robert Randolph's conceits and one particularly ingenious bit of musical staging by choreographer Tony Stevens. Randolph created a series of mesmerizing blackout effects that were the stage equivalent of the dissolves used in movies. As the audience watched, a projection of a city street was suddenly enveloped by an almost cartoon-like effect of black swirls, spirals, and optical effects that magically wiped away the scene in preparation for the next one. And for the strange "Round and Round" sequence, which looked at Jack and his succession of wives and girlfriends, Stevens staged the surreal number as a roundelay that transformed a realistic setting into a fantasy which seemed to come out of nowhere and just as quickly faded into limbo.

In his review, Coe said *Spotlight* lacked focus and never glowed, the story was "dreary" and "familiar," and the score was conducted at a "drearily slow pace." He "charitably assumed" that Barry sang with "the heaviest cold known to living man." David Richards in the *Washington Star* said the story was "overbaked cliché, stuffed with drivel and platitudes" with its "hoary backstage drama" and its "hoary generation gap drama." And he couldn't resist quoting some of the dialogue: "I know you love her, but you've got to love her enough to let her go" and "We're not into good and bad, we're into what is" and "I did it the only way I knew how." As for the music, it was "vaguely derivative" and the lyrics had "Jack and Jill rhymes" with the "vapidness of sentiment." He assumed the producers of *Spotlight* were less concerned with repairing the musical than deciding when to pull the plug.

Paul in *Variety* said *Spotlight* had "so many maladies it defies attempts at first aid." The performances were "dismal," Barry was "wooden from start to finish," the music was "awful," and the lyrics were "correspondingly inane." And in the typical fashion of so many flops, the producer announced the show would close for revisions and then reopen. But, again in typical fashion, this never happened.

But Gene Barry got to the Palace after all, and in one of the biggest hits of the 1980s. He costarred with George Hearn in Jerry Herman's *La Cage aux Folles*, which ran for 1,761 performances. He received a Tony Award nomination for Best Leading Actor in a Musical, and he introduced two of the loveliest numbers in Herman's song book, "Look Over There" and "Song on the Sand."

1978–1979 Season

THE AMERICAN DANCE MACHINE

"A Living Archive of Broadway Theatre Dance"

Theatre: Century Theatre
Opening Date: June 14, 1978; *Closing Date*: December 3, 1978
Performances: 199
Direction: Lee Theodore; *Producers*: Lee Theodore and Louis K. and Gloria Sher; *Choreography*: See list of musical numbers for specific credits; *Costumes*: John David Ridge; *Lighting*: Jeremy Johnson; *Musical Direction*: David Krane
Cast: Guest Artists—Harold Cromer, Patti Mariano, and Don Swanson; Soloists—Nancy Chismar, Louise Hickey, Don Johanson; Ensemble—Helena Andreyko, Amy Lester, Greg Minahan, Christine Oren, Candice Prior, Kevin Ryan, Alexandra Visitor, Derek Wolshonak, Donald Young; *Note*: *Best Plays* also listed the following performers who appeared during the run (some for the opening night performance)—Janet Eilber, Denny Shearer, Steven Gelfer, Joseph Pugliese, Liza Gennaro, Kristina Koebel, Gina Martin, Morgan Richardson, John Jones, Brian Kelly, David Kottke, Zan Charisse.
The dance revue was presented in two acts.

Musical Numbers

Act One: "Mamie Is Mimi" (*Gentlemen Prefer Blondes*, 1949; lyric by Leo Robin, music by Jule Styne) (choreography by Agnes de Mille; dance reconstructed by Evelyn Taylor) (Janet Eilber); "Popularity" (*George M!*, 1968; music by George M. Cohan) (choreography by Joe Layton; reconstructed by Karin Baker and Patti Mariano) (Patti Mariano, Company); "June Is Bustin' Out All Over" (*Carousel*, 1945; lyric by Oscar Hammerstein II, music by Richard Rodgers) (choreography by Agnes de Mille, reconstructed by Gemze de Lappe) (Janet Eilber, Female Ensemble); "Whip Dance" (*Destry Rides Again*, 1959; music by Harold Rome) (choreography by Michael Kidd; reconstructed by Swen Swenson) (Morgan Richardson, Greg Minahan, and Donald Young); "All Aboard for Broadway" (*George M!*, 1968; lyric and music by George M. Cohan) (choreography by Joe Layton; reconstructed by Karin Baker and Patti Mariano) (Denny Shearer, Steven Gelfer, Helena Andreyko, Liza Gennaro); "Won't You Charleston with Me?" (*The Boy Friend*, 1970 revival; music by Sandy Wilson) (choreography by Buddy Schwab; reconstructed by Eleanor Treiber) (Don Johanson, Company); "The Telephone Dance" (*Cabaret*, 1966; lyric by Fred Ebb, music by John Kander) (choreography by Ron Field; reconstructed by Marianne Selbert) (Company); "Next to Lovin' (I Like Fightin')" (***Shenandoah***, 1975; lyric by Peter Udell, music by Gary Geld) (choreography and reconstruction by Bob Tucker) (Don Swanson, Don Johanson, David Kottke, Greg Minahan, Derek Wolshonak); "Rich Kids' Rag" (*Little Me*, 1962; music by Cy Coleman) (choreography by Bob Fosse, reconstructed by Gene Gavin) (Patti Mariano, Don Johanson, Company)

Act Two: *Note*: Intermission dances were performed by Harold Cromer, including "Mr. Bojangles" (lyric and music by Jerry Jeff Walker). "If the Rain's Got to Fall" (*Half a Sixpence*, 1965; lyric and music by David Heneker) (choreography by Onna White; reconstructed by Tom Panko, Ron Bostick, and Eric Paynter) (Denny Shearer, Company); "Satin Doll" (from a 1962 television episode of *The Ed Sullivan Show*; lyric by Johnny Mercer, music by Duke Ellington and Billy Strayhorn) (choreography by Carole Haney; reconstructed by Buzz Miller) (Joe Pugliese, Liza Gennaro, Patti Mariano); "Monte Carlo Crossover" and "Up Where the People Are" (*The Unsinkable Molly Brown*, 1960; music by Meredith Willson) (choreography by Peter Gennaro; reconstructed by Vito Durante) (Company); "Come to Me, Bend to Me" and "Funeral Dance" (*Brigadoon*, 1947; lyric by Alan Jay Lerner, music by Frederick Loewe) (choreography by Agnes de Mille; reconstructed by Gemze de Lappe and Jamie Jamieson) (Janet Eilber, Female Ensemble); "Quadrille" (*Can-Can*, 1953; music by Cole Porter) (choreography by Michael Kidd; reconstructed by Eleanor Treiber and Ken Urmstrum) (Louise Hickey, Don Johanson, Company); "You Can Dance with Any Girl at All" (***No, No, Nanette***, 1971 revival; lyric by Irving Caesar, music by Vincent Youmans) (choreography by Donald Saddler; reconstructed by Helen Gallagher, Donald Saddler, and Swen Swenson) (Janet Eilber, Denny Shearer); "Clog Dance" (*Walking Happy*, 1966; music by Jimmy Van Heusen) (choreography by Danny Daniels; reconstructed by Dick Korthaze) (Denny Shearer, Male Ensemble)

Thanks to Lee (Becker) Theodore, the visionary founder of The American Dance Machine, a number of lost Broadway dances were authentically reconstructed for posterity. Although scripts and cast albums of musicals are generally available, the choreography often disappears after the final curtain falls. But the "living archive" of Broadway dances will hopefully ensure that many memorable theatre dances will survive for future audiences to enjoy.

Theodore was a Broadway dancer who appeared as Anybodys (the tomboy) in the original production of *West Side Story* (1957), and was later a Broadway choreographer for such musicals as *Baker Street* (1965), *Flora, the Red Menace* (1965), and *The Apple Tree* (1966).

Frances Herridge in the *New York Post* said the company's name was "somewhat forbidding" (in truth, the name doesn't indicate that the repertoire consists of Broadway dances, and it's a shame Theodore didn't come up with a better descriptive title for her troupe), but noted the evening provided "diversion and nostalgia." Howard Kissel in *Women's Wear Daily* praised the "excellent" dancers, said the company performed a "valuable" service, and he hoped the troupe would be around "for a long time." He singled out a number of dances, including the "Clog Dance" ("wonderfully giddy") and the "Whip Dance" ("a bizarre, but riveting conception"). T. E. Kalem in *Time* saluted the "handsome retrospective"; and Douglas Watt in the *New York Daily News* said the dances were "deserving," but felt some were under a "strain" because they were presented out of context (he also mentioned that the company was "dully named").

Jack Anderson in the *New York Times* suggested that by their very nature Broadway dances were "climaxes," and so the evening was somewhat one-note in its "jollity" (and he was glad the "Funeral Dance" from *Brigadoon* offered some "striking contrast"). But the company hinted at what could be done to preserve Broadway's choreographic history, and he hoped the works of Helen Tamiris, Hanya Holm, George Balanchine, and Jerome Robbins would soon be reconstructed. (Of course, Robbins took things in hand with his own dance tribute and retrospective *Jerome Robbins' Broadway*, which opened in 1989 and won the Tony Award for the season's Best Musical.) John Beaufort in the *Christian Science Monitor* said *The American Dance Machine* was "the greatest invention since the cartwheel" and suggested that "a livelier, more stylish, more personable archive would be hard to imagine."

Clearly, the performer of the evening was the strikingly beautiful and talented dancer Janet Eilber. Kalem said "some celestial potter who fashions divinity from clay must be responsible" for her "absolute skill and mesmeric dramatic presence." Herridge said she was "gorgeous to look at and even more so when she moves," and Kissel noted she danced "with a commanding blend of grace and sensuality."

Later dances reconstructed for the company were: "Hornpipe" (*Carousel*, 1945; music by Richard Rodgers) (choreography by Agnes de Mille; reconstructed by Gemze de Lappe); "Dance o' the Golden Crock" (*Finian's Rainbow*, 1947; music by Burton Lane) (choreography by Michael Kidd; reconstructed by Anita Alvarez); "That Terrific Rainbow" (*Pal Joey*, 1952 revival; lyric by Lorenz Hart, music by Richard Rodgers) (choreography by Robert Alton; reconstructed by Helen Gallagher); "Shriners' Ballet" (*Bye Bye Birdie*, 1960; music by Charles Strouse) (choreography by Gower Champion; reconstructed by Edmond Kresley); "Little Old New

York" (*Tenderloin*, 1960; lyric by Sheldon Harnick, music by Jerry Bock) (choreography by Joe Layton; reconstructed by Joe Layton and Lee Theodore); "I've Got Your Number" (*Little Me*, 1962; lyric by Carolyn Leigh, music by Cy Coleman) (choreography by Bob Fosse; reconstructed by Swen Swenson); "Rat-Tat-Tat-Tat" (*Funny Girl*, 1964; lyric by Bob Merrill, music by Jule Styne) (choreography by Carol Haney; reconstructed by Edie Cowan); "The Fight Sequence" (*Golden Boy*, 1964; music by Charles Strouse) (choreography by Donald McKayle; reconstructed by Buck Heller); "Hair" (*Hair*, 1968; lyric by Gerome Ragni and James Rado, music by Galt MacDermot) (choreography and reconstruction by Julie Arenal); "Charlie's Place" (***Over Here!***, 1974; lyric and music by Richard M. Sherman and Robert B. Sherman) (choreography and reconstruction by Patricia Birch); "Cane Dance" (***The Magic Show***, 1974; music by Stephen Schwartz) (choreography and reconstruction by Grover Dale); "Harlem Makes Me Feel!" (***Bubbling Brown Sugar***, 1975; lyric and music by Emme Kemp) (choreography by Billy Wilson; reconstructed by Barry Preston); "The Aggie Song" (***The Best Little Whorehouse in Texas***, 1978; lyric and music by Carol Hall) (choreography by Tommy Tune; reconstructed by Jerry Yoder); "They're Playing My Song" (***They're Playing Our Song***, 1979; lyric by Carole Bayer Sager, music by Marvin Hamlisch) (choreography and reconstruction by Patricia Birch); and "Once in Love with Amy" (from 1980 revue *Perfectly Frank*; the song and dance was originally from *Where's Charley?*, 1948; lyric and music by Frank Loesser) (choreography by Tony Stevens; reconstructed by Wayne Cilento).

In 1981, a few of the company's dances were released on video cassette (# CV-400056) by MGM/CBS Home Video. Gwen Verdon was the host, and the dancers included Janet Eilber, Lee Roy Reams, Wayne Cilento, and John Jones.

In 1982, *Steps in Time* was a sequel of sorts to *The American Dance Machine* and it too was helmed by Lee Theodore. The production played in at least one venue, Ford's Theatre in Washington, D.C., and the evening included such dance numbers as: "Moon-Faced, Starry-Eyed" (*Street Scene*, 1947; lyric by Langston Hughes, music by Kurt Weill) (the choreography was created and danced by Sondra Lee and Richard Tone for the 1959 New York City Opera revival, and was reconstructed by them for *Steps in Time*); "Another Autumn" (*Paint Your Wagon*, 1951; lyric by Alan Jay Lerner, music by Frederick Loewe) (choreography by Agnes de Mille; reconstructed by Gemze de Lappe and David Evans); "I Guess I'll Have to Change My Plan" (1953 film *The Band Wagon*; lyric by Howard Dietz, music by Arthur Schwartz) (choreography by Michael Kidd, who apparently reconstructed the dance for *Steps in Time*); and "Express Yourself" (*Flora, the Red Menace*, 1965; lyric by Fred Ebb, music by John Kander) (choreography and reconstruction by Lee Theodore).

The American Dance Machine was briefly revived at City Center for a limited engagement for the period February 4–February 16, 1986.

One of the happiest surprises of the 2014–2015 theatrical season was the resurrection of the dance company as The American Dance Machine for the 21st Century (aka ADM21), which is now helmed by Nikki Feirt Atkins (Artistic Producer) and Margo Sappington (Artistic Director). The company presented evenings of three different dance programs at the Joyce Theatre for a total of eight performances November 11–November 16, 2014. Among the musicals represented were: *Promises, Promises* (1968), *Oh! Calcutta!* (1969), ***A Chorus Line***, ***The Act***, *A Day in Hollywood/A Night in the Ukraine* (1980), *42nd Street* (1980), *Big Deal* (1986), *Black and Blue* (1989), *Billion Dollar Baby* (1945, as reproduced in *Jerome Robbins' Broadway* [1989]), and *Contact* (2000).

The Century Theatre was located on West 46th Street in the Paramount Hotel, and from 1938 to 1951 was the original home of the legendary nightclub Billy Rose's Diamond Horseshoe. The venue was later the Mayfair Theatre, and then later was renamed the Century Theatre.

THE BEST LITTLE WHOREHOUSE IN TEXAS

Theatre: 46th Street Theatre
Opening Date: June 19, 1978; *Closing Date*: March 27, 1982
Performances: 1,576
Book: Larry L. King and Peter Masterson
Lyrics and *Music*: Carol Hall
Based on the magazine article "The Best Little Whorehouse in Texas," which was published in the April 1974 issue of *Playboy*.

Direction: Peter Masterson and Tommy Tune; *Producer*: Universal Pictures; *Choreography*: Tommy Tune (Thommie Walsh, Associate Choreographer); *Scenery*: Marjorie Kellogg; *Costumes*: Ann Roth; *Lighting*: Dennis Parichy; *Musical Direction*: Robert Billig

Cast: Craig Chambers (Rio Grande Band Leader), Clint Allmon (Farmer, Melvin P. Thorpe), Gerry Burkhardt (Shy Kid, Aggie # 7), Edna Milton (Miss Wulla Jean), Jay Garner (Traveling Salesman, C. J. Scruggs, Chip Brenster, Governor), K. C. Kelly (Slick Dude, Soundman, Ukranian Placekicker Aggie # 1), Pamela Blair (Amber), Joan Ellis (Shy), Delores Hall (Jewel), Carlin Glynn (Miss Mona Stangley); Girls at Miss Mona's: Donna King (Linda Lou), Lisa Brown (Dawn), Louise Quick-Brown (Ginger), Jan Merchant (Beatrice), Carol Chambers (Taddy Jo), Becky Gelke (Ruby Rae), Marta Sanders (Eloise), Debra Zalkind (Durla); Bradley Clayton King (Leroy Sliney, Aggie # 77), Tom Cashin (Stage Manager, Cameraman, Aggie # 12, Specialty Dancer), Henderson Forsythe (Sheriff Ed Earl Dodd), J. Frank Lucas (Mayor Rufus Poindexter, Senator Wingwoah), Don Crabtree (Edsel Mackey), Susan Mansur (Doatsey Mae, Reporter # 1), Larry L. King (Voice of TV Announcer), Lisa Brown (Angelette, Imogene Charlene), Paul Ukena Jr. (Aggie # 21, Reporter # 2), Michael Scott (Aggie # 71, Reporter # 3), Jay Bursky (Aggie # 11, Governor's Aide), James Rich (Aggie # 17); Girls: Lisa Brown, Carol Chambers, Donna King, Susan Mansur, Louise Quick-Brown, Debra Zalkind; Cowboys: Jay Bursky, Bradley Clayton King, Michael Scott, Paul Ukena Jr.; Choir: Jay Bursky, Becky Gelke, Edwina Lewis, Jan Merchant, James Rich, Marta Sanders; The Dogettes: Gerry Burkhardt, Jay Bursky, Michael Scott, Paul Ukena Jr.; Melvin Thorpe Singers: Becky Gelke, Bradley Clayton King, Susan Mansur, Jan Merchant, James Rich, Marta Sanders; Townspeople: Carol Chambers, Bradley Clayton King, Edna Milton, James Rich, Marta Sanders; Angelettes: Becky Gelke, Carol Chambers, Donna King, Debra Zalkind, Jan Merchant; Photographers: Michael Scott, Paul Ukena Jr., James Rich, Jay Bursky

The musical was presented in two acts.

The action takes place during the present time in Texas.

Musical Numbers

Act One: "Prologue" (Craig Chambers, The Rio Grande Band); "20 Fans" (Craig Chambers, The Girls, The Cowboys, Clint Allmon, Gerry Burkhardt, Edna Milton, Jay Garner, K. C. Kelly, The Choir); "A Lil Ole Bitty Pissant Country Place" (Carlin Glynn, The Girls); "Girl, You're a Woman" (Carlin Glynn, Joan Ellis, Delores Hall, The Girls); "Watch Dog Theme" (The Dogettes); "Texas Has a Whorehouse in It" (Clint Allmon, The Melvin P. Thorpe Singers, The Dogettes); "Twenty-Four Hours of Lovin'" (Delores Hall, The Girls); "Watch Dog Theme" (reprise) (The Dogettes); "Texas Has a Whorehouse in It" (reprise) (Clint Allmon, The Dogettes); "Doatsey Mae" (Susan Mansur); "Angelette March" (Lisa Brown, The Angelettes); "The Aggie Song" (The Aggies); "Bus from Amarillo" (Carlin Glynn)

Act Two: "The Sidestep" (Jay Garner, Jay Bursky, J. Frank Lucas, The Reporters, Clint Allmon, The Dogettes, The Melvin P. Thorpe Singers); "No Lies" (Carlin Glynn, Delores Hall, The Girls); "Good Old Girl" (Henderson Forsythe, The Aggies); "Hard Candy Christmas" (Pamela Blair, Donna King, Louise Quick-Brown, Lisa Brown, Becky Gelke, Jan Merchant); "Hard Candy Christmas" (reprise) (The Girls); Finale (Company)

And with that title, how could it miss? And so *The Best Little Whorehouse* was the season's biggest hit and longest-running show. The musical was about the legendary century-old Texas whorehouse now run by heart-of-gold madam Miss Mona (Carlin Glynn), her flock of happy "girls," and the even happier businessmen and high school football players who patronize the old-fashioned institution. The fable-like story took on an almost mythic quality as it described the long-ago rise and fall of the quaint establishment that existed in a kind of never land of sex and sweetness. But the bluenoses win the day, and the house closes its door forever. There was a certain bittersweet aura about the story, and while there was cheerful vulgarity in the proceedings, the show was never offensive. Tommy Tune's ingenious ideas were full of surprises (for the drill tap routine "Angelette March," a cheerleader chorus girl appears with cut-out life-sized cheerleader dolls attached to each shoulder; soon five more girls join her in similar costumes, and the six-member chorus line is suddenly transformed into eighteen girls) and Carol Hall's tuneful score included the show-stopping "The Sidestep" for Jay Garner's slippery and noncommittal governor, and the girls' yearning and nostalgic "Hard Candy Christmas" was one of the finest theatre songs of the era.

Most of the critics reviewed the Off-Broadway production, which had opened two months prior to the Broadway premiere. Richard Eder in the *New York Times* said the book wasn't "really strong enough" and suggested the evening had been assembled "too loosely and blandly." Some of the dialogue was "sharply written" with "fine lines" that were "unprintable" for his review, and he liked the "agreeable" songs, such as "Texas Has a Whorehouse in It" ("forthright") and "No Lies" ("a fine ironic duet"). The evening's "brilliant" number was "Angelette March" with its "hilarious" chorus line of cheerleaders and dolls (the latter bounce "even more idiotically than the dancers"). Clive Barnes in the *New York Post* said the sometimes "predictable" story was "a strange old-fashioned, new-fashioned musical, full of simple sentiments" and "dirty words." The score had the "rustic air of a country fair" and the "Angelette March" was a "riot." Douglas Watt in the *New York Daily News* found the evening "sunny enough and funny enough," and he liked the "Angelette March" ("funny") and "Hard Candy Christmas" ("a musical nod to Stephen Sondheim").

Jack Kroll in *Newsweek* felt Hall's score was "fresh, but saucy rather than meaty" and Tune's musical staging "makes your eyes smile without making your heart dance"; T. E. Kalem in *Time* found the evening "a font of fun and friendliness" and said the "Angelette March" would "induce laughsphyxia"; and Christopher Sharp in *Women's Wear Daily* said the musical was "a delightful evening that is respectably profane" and he praised Tune's "heel-kicking" dances.

In reviewing the Broadway opening, Alfred L. Malabre Jr. in the *Wall Street Journal* said the musical's transition from Off Broadway to Broadway was "highly successful." The music was in the nature of "Western swing," the "Angelette March" had "fresh originality," and in paraphrasing W. C. Fields, he noted that "any musical that doesn't cater to little children can't be all bad" and in fact "can be very good." But he noted there was "nothing at all amusing" about prostitution and the musical's theme might "prove off-putting" to some.

The musical had originally been produced in a workshop engagement at the Actors' Studio in November 1977 (with choreography by Christopher "Spider" Duncan) and then Off Broadway at the Entermedia Theatre on April 17, 1978, for 64 performances. Four songs were cut after the workshop production ("A Little Bit of Fixin'", "Memory Song," "Two Blocks from the Capitol Building," and "Goddam Everything"), and for the Off-Broadway version Tommy Tune joined the musical as choreographer and codirector. A week after the Off-Broadway closing, the musical opened on Broadway on June 19, 1978, and closed on March 27, 1982, after 1,576 performances (due to a dispute with the musicians' union, the musical closed on March 27, 1982, played an engagement in Boston, and then reopened in New York at the Eugene O'Neill Theatre on May 31, 1982, in what was termed a return engagement for a run of 63 additional performances; this volume considers the second run as an extension of the first and not as a separate production).

The script was published in paperback by Samuel French in 1983, and the Broadway cast album was released by MCA Records (LP # MCA-3049 and CD # MCAD-11683). The national tour (which starred Alexis Smith as Miss Mona) included a new song ("Lonely at the Top" for Melvin P. Thorpe). The London production opened at the Drury Lane on February 26, 1981, for 204 performances with Glynn and Forsythe reprising their original roles. In 2001, a national tour with Ann-Margret included a new song ("A Friend to Me") and the cast recording was issued by Fynsworth Alley (CD # 302-062-1172). The collection *Lost in Boston IV* (Varese Sarabande CD # VSD-5768) includes the unused song "Have a Memory on Me."

A disappointing film version was released by Universal in 1982 with Dolly Parton, Burt Reynolds, Dom DeLuise, Jim Nabors, Theresa Merritt, and Lois Nettleton; a handful of songs was retained ("20 Fans," "A Lil Ole Bitty Pissant Country Place," "The Aggie Song," "Watch Dog Theme," "Texas Has a Whorehouse in It," "Hard Candy Christmas," and the film's best musical sequence, "The Sidestep," which was memorably performed by Charles Durning); Hall contributed a new number called "Courtyard Shag," and two numbers written by Parton were interpolated into the score, a new one called "Sneakin' Around" and her earlier hit "I Will Always Love You." The soundtrack was released by MCA (CD # MCAD-31007), and the DVD was issued by Universal Studios.

Musical sequels almost never work (*Of Thee I Sing* [1931]/*Let 'Em Eat Cake* [1933], *Bye Bye Birdie* [1960]/*Bring Back Birdie* [1981], and *Annie* [1977]/*Annie 2: Miss Hannigan's Revenge* [1989]), and so it was with *The Best Little Whorehouse Goes Public*. King and Masterson again wrote the book and Hall the lyrics and music, and Tommy Tune returned (here as codirector and co-choreographer). The musical opened at the Lunt-Fontanne Theatre on May 10, 1994, and lasted for just fifteen performances. The splashy production was lost in a preposterous plot in which Miss Mona becomes president of the United States. But Hall's score had many attractive numbers ("It's Been a While" and "Change in Me") and one jaw-droppingly tasteless sequence ("Call Me") in which boxer-shorts-clad men enjoy phone sex with Miss Mona's girls. The cast album was released by Varese Sarabande Records (CD # VSD-5542), and the script was published in paperback by Samuel French in 1999.

As of this writing, *The Best Little Whorehouse in Texas* is scheduled to be revived on Broadway in 2015 with direction and choreography by Rob Ashford.

Awards

Tony Awards and Nominations: Best Musical (*The Best Little Whorehouse in Texas*); Best Featured Actor in a Musical (**Henderson Forsythe**); Best Featured Actress in a Musical (Joan Ellis); Best Featured Actress in a Musical (**Carlin Glynn**); Best Director of a Musical (Peter Masterson and Tommy Tune); Best Book (Larry L. King and Peter Masterson); Best Choreographer (Tommy Tune)

STOP THE WORLD I WANT TO GET OFF

Theatre: New York State Theatre
Opening Date: August 3, 1978; *Closing Date*: August 27, 1978
Performances: 30
Book, Lyrics, and *Music*: Leslie Bricusse and Anthony Newley
Direction: Mel Shapiro; *Producers*: James and Joseph Nederlander in association with City Center of Music and Drama, Inc. (The Hillard Elkins Production) (Barbara Platoff, Associate Producer); *Choreography*: Billy Wilson; *Scenery* and *Costumes*: Santo Loquasto; *Lighting*: Pat Collins; *Musical Direction*: George Rhodes
Cast: *Sammy Davis Jr.* (Littlechap), Dennis Daniels (Baton Twirler, Death, MC at Snobbs Country Club), Donna Lowe (Schoolgirl, Election Newscaster), Marian Mercer (Evie, Anya, Ilse, Lorene), Debora Masterson (First Girl in Crow's Nest), Joyce Nolen (Second Girl in Crow's Nest, MC of Hadassah, Solo Singer in Sunvale), Wendy Edmead (Susan), Patrick Kinser-Lau (Guitar Player, MC of Spanish Group), Shelly Burch (Jane), Charles Willis Jr. (The Boy), Edwetta Little (MC of Black Organization, Speaker of the House); Ensemble: Marcus B. F. Brown, Dennis Daniels, Karen Giombetti, Linda Griffin, Patrick Kinser-Lau, Edwetta Little, Donna Lowe, Debora Masterson, Billy Newton-Davis, Joyce Nolen, Robert Yori-Tanna
The musical was presented in two acts.

Musical Numbers

Act One: "I Wanna Be Rich" (Sammy Davis Jr.); "Typically English" (Marian Mercer); "Lumbered" (Sammy Davis Jr.); "Welcome to Sludgeville" (Chorus); "Gonna Build a Mountain" (Sammy Davis Jr.); "Glorious Russian" (Marian Mercer); "Meilinki Meilchick" (Sammy Davis Jr., Marian Mercer); "Family Fugue" (Sammy Davis Jr., Marian Mercer, Wendy Edmead, Shelly Burch); "Typische Deutsche" (Marian Mercer); "Life Is a Woman" (Sammy Davis Jr.)
Act Two: "All-American" (Marian Mercer); "Once in a Lifetime" (Sammy Davis Jr.); "Mumbo Jumbo" (Sammy Davis Jr.); "Welcome to Sunvale" (Chorus); "Someone Nice Like You" (Sammy Davis Jr., Marian Mercer); "What Kind of Fool Am I?" (Sammy Davis Jr.)

The revised revival of Leslie Bricusse and Anthony Newley's 1961 London musical *Stop the World—I Want to Get Off* (in a bold move, the current version removed the dash) was clearly a vehicle for Sammy Davis Jr., and the production toured for a few months, including a four-week engagement at the New York State Theatre. Except for its three hit songs ("What Kind of Fool Am I?," "Once in a Lifetime," and "Gonna Build a Mountain"), the musical never had much going for it, and this time around the critics were particularly dismissive.

The self-described "New-Style Musical" opened in London on July 20, 1961, at the Queen's Theatre for 485 performances with Newley and Anna Quayle in the leading roles, which they reprised for the Broadway production that opened at the Shubert Theatre on October 3, 1962, for 556 showings. The action took place in a circus tent–like setting, the performers wore clownish Marcel Marceau–like makeup and togs, and occasionally mime was used to tell the story. The inflated, predictable, and pretentious evening followed the revue-like exploits of Littlechap, who marries the boss's daughter, Evie, but has numerous affairs with Russian, German, and American women, and occasionally announces, "Stop the world, I want to get off!" (in light of his sexual adventures, the title took on a double meaning). Littlechap succeeds in both business and politics, but at the end of his life wonders What Was It All For. All for naught, apparently, because he was a fool who never realized Evie was his only real love. (Some audience members could be forgiven for briefly thinking they were seeing a musical version of Archibald MacLeisch's 1958 Pulitzer Prize-winning drama *J.B.*, which had also looked at the world from the perspective of the circus tent and dwelt upon the life of a very much put-upon businessman.)

The tiresome allegorical nonsense was somewhat redeemed by the musical's obvious but ingratiating power ballads and its mildly amusing comedy songs, and both the London and New York productions played for over a year and Quayle won the Tony Award for Best Featured Actress in a Musical. The London cast album was released by Decca Records (LP # LK-4408 and # SKL-4142) and was later released on CD by Must Close Saturday Records (# MCSR-3028), and the Broadway production was recorded by RCA Victor Records (LP # CSO/COP-106); the CD was issued by Polydor (# 820261).

A 1966 film version by Warner Brothers was released for what seems like five minutes, and was essentially a filmed stage production. Directed by Philip Saville, the film starred Tony Tanner (who had played the role in London when he succeeded Newley) and Millicent Martin. The movie began in black and white, then switched to color, and included two new songs by Al Ham ("The New York Scene" and "I Believed It All"). Littlechap's affairs include one with a Japanese girl, and so "Typically Japanese" replaced "Typische Deutsche." The soundtrack album was released by Warner Brothers Records (LP # B-1643) and the film was later issued on videocassette and laser disk. The work was revived in London in 1989 at the Lyric Theatre; Newley reprised his original role, and also directed the production. This version omitted "A Special Announcement" and "Typische Deutsche," added "Welcome to Wedlock," and "What Kind of Fool Am I?" both began and ended the show. In 1995, Jay Records released a studio cast album (CD # CDJAY-1236), which included previously unrecorded material such as the entr'acte and exit music as well as "Welcome to Sludgepool" and "Welcome to Sunvale."

The current revival cut "The A.B.C. Song," "A Special Announcement," and "Nag! Nag! Nag!," added the new number "Life Is a Woman," changed the title of "Welcome to Sludgepool" to "Welcome to Sludgeville," included updated references (such as jogging), and found Littlechap elected as the first black president of the United States. The cast recording was released by Warner Brothers Records (LP # HS-3214), and a 1978 film version titled *Sammy Stops the World* was produced by SEE Theatre Network and was directed by Mel Shapiro; like the 1966 film version, the new one was essentially a filmed stage production and it too had a limited theatrical release.

Mel Gussow in the *New York Times* said Sammy Davis Jr., "can light up any stage," but his vehicle was "a pretentious, sentimental act of self-piety" with "heavy-handed" political and social satire. Davis's Littlechap begins his career as a self-described "coffee-colored coffee vendor" and ends up as president of the country and wins "the Ignoble Prize for political doubletalk." "Mumbo Jumbo" depicted his presidential campaign in which he swaggers around in sunglasses in order to capture the black vote; and per T. E. Kalem in *Time*, goes into "hip-swiveling tangomania" for the Hispanic vote and then wears a Tevye-styled hat and dons a Yiddish accent to charm the Hadassah (which, come to think of it, is pretty much what the title character of *Fiorello!* [1959] did when he ran for office in the expansive production number "The Name's LaGuardia").

Douglas Watt in the *New York Daily News* said the evening was a "sappy" allegory in which Davis seemed "lost," and suggested Davis and the audience would have been better off had the entertainer performed non-Newley and Bricusse songs in concert. Clive Barnes in the *New York Post* found the revival a "vulgar" production and a "disaster on wheels that overplays everything that was bad in the original." Like Watt, he suggested Davis belonged on the concert stage or in "a new musical."

Kalem said Davis, like Liza Minnelli, projected "the image of an overage child parched for affection" who "aggressively" demands "approval." These "personality pushers" market "their mannerisms like commodities" and their fan base attends their shows in order "to bathe in the effulgence of celebrityhood." Howard Kissel in *Women's Wear Daily* said Davis's opening night audience "lapped it up" and the critic quoted Wright Morris in his 1957 novel *Love among the Cannibals* in which he described the "new show business" as one in which "You tell [the audience] what they're going to like, they like it, then they all stand and applaud themselves."

Incidentally, Littlechap wasn't the first musical comedy character to cry out, "Stop the world, I want to get off!" In 1951, the B. G. Bigelow character in *Flahooley* (who was played by Ernest Truex) also shouted out such a wish.

NAUGHTY MARIETTA

Theatre: New York State Theatre
Opening Date: August 31, 1978; *Closing Date*: September 10, 1978
Performances: 14
Book: New book adapted by Frederick S. Roffman from the original book by Rida Johnson Young
Lyrics: Rida Johnson Young; additional lyrics by Frederick S. Roffman
Music: Victor Herbert
Direction: Gerald Freedman; *Producer*: The New York City Opera Company (Julius Rudel, Director; John S. White, Managing Director); *Choreography*: Graciela Daniele; *Scenery*: Oliver Smith; *Costumes*: Patricia Zipprodt; *Lighting*: Ken Billington; *Choral Direction*: Lloyd Walser; *Musical Direction*: John Mauceri
Cast: Gianna Rolandi (Marietta d'Altena), Jacque Trussel (Captain Richard Warrington of Kentucky aka Captain Dick), Alan Titus (Etienne Grandet), Joanna Simon (Adah Le Clercq), Russ Thacker (Private Silas Slick), James Billings (Acting Governor Grandet), Brooks Morton (Florenze), Don Yule (Sergeant Harry Blake), Harlan Foss (Rudolfo), Richard McKee (Pierre La Farge), Dan Kingman (Pirate), James Sergei (Pirate), Rita Metzger (Sister Domenique); Casquette Girls: Patricia Price, Sally Lambert, and Lee Bellaver; Herbert Hunsberger (Ranger), Edward Vaughan (Town Crier), Susan Delery-Whedon (Flower Girl), Sally Lambert (Flower Girl), George Bohachevsky (Flower Vendor), Louis Perry (Bird Vendor, Durand), Robert Brubaker (Fruit Vendor, Another Vendor), Harris Davis (Sugar Cane Vendor, Beaurivage); Citizens: Leslie Luxemburg, Lila Herbert, and Marie Young; Men: James Brewer, Louis Perry, Herbert Hunsberger, and Edward Vaughan; Jose Bourbon (Giovanni), Don Carlo (Gambler), Kenn Dovel (Pierre), Herbert Hunsberger (Robillard), James Brewer (Plauche), Glenn Rowen (Major-Domo), Esperanza Galan (Spanish Dancer); Quadroons: Sharon Claveau, Rosalie Tisch, Rita Metzger, Marie Young, Madeleine Soyka, and Lila Herbert; French Girls: Susan Delery-Whedon, Sally Lambert, Jean Rawn, and Myrna Reynolds; James Sergi (Bordenave), Dan Kingman (La Fourche); San Domingo Ladies: Toni-Ann Gardella, Candace Itow, and Rebeka Pradera
The operetta was presented in two acts.
The action takes place in Louisiana in 1803, on the island of Barataria at the mouth of the Mississippi River and in New Orleans.

Musical Numbers

Act One: Prologue (Gianna Rolandi), "It Never, Never Can Be Love" (Gianna Rolandi, Jacque Trussel); "Opening Chorus" (Ensemble); "This Brave New Land" (Joanna Simon, Alan Titus); "Tramp, Tramp, Tramp" (Jacque Trussel, Rangers); "Taisez-vous" (Ensemble); "All I Crave Is More of Life" (Gianna Rolandi); "Italian Street Song" (Gianna Rolandi, Ensemble); "Intermezzo" (Orchestra); "Opening Music" (Gianna Rolandi, Harlan Foss); "Naughty Marietta" (Gianna Rolandi); "If It Were Anybody Else but Me" (Russ Thacker, Gianna Rolandi); Dance (Orchestra); Finale (Principals, Ensemble)
Act Two: "New Orleans Jeunesse Doree" (Male Ensemble); "You Marry a Marionette" (Alan Titus, Men); "'Neath the Southern Moon" (Joanna Simon); "Loves of New Orleans" (Ensemble); "It's Pretty Soft for Silas" (Russ Thacker); "Live for Today" (Gianna Rolandi, Joanna Simon, Jacque Trussel, Alan Titus, Ensemble); "The Sweet By and By" (James Billings); "I'm Falling in Love with Someone" (Jacque Trussel); "Ah, Sweet Mystery of Life" (Gianna Rolandi, Jacque Trussel, Company)

The New York City Opera Company's revival of Victor Herbert's *Naughty Marietta* was the operetta's first New York production in forty-eight years. The original had opened at the New York Theatre on November 7, 1910, for 136 performances, and told the story of Marietta d'Altena (Gianni Rolandi in the current production) who flees Italy for New Orleans in order to escape an arranged marriage with a man she doesn't love.

In New Orleans, she's courted by both Etienne Grandet (Alan Titus) and military officer Captain Warrington (Jacque Trussel) and so is faced with the age-old operetta dilemma of whom to choose. Herbert's score was a music box of delightful melody: the stirring march "Tramp, Tramp, Tramp"; the merry "Italian Street Song"; the sweeping waltz "I'm Falling in Love with Someone"; and one of the ultimate examples of operetta music (which is perhaps rivaled only by Rudolf Friml's "Indian Love Call" from 1924's *Rose-Marie*), the haunting ballad "Ah, Sweet Mystery of Life." The latter (like *Lady in the Dark*'s "My Ship") is a dream melody that haunts Marietta: she can never remember the entire song, but when the Captain completes it, she knows he's her man. Other memorable musical interludes in the score were the lighthearted "It Never, Never Can Be Love" and the pleasant if somewhat lugubrious "'Neath the Southern Moon."

The operetta was revived for a limited engagement of sixteen performances at Jolson's Theatre on October 21, 1929, and then in two slightly separated engagements was produced for limited runs at Erlanger's Theatre on November 16, 1931, for a total of twenty-four showings. After the current City Opera production, the company revived the work two more times, on August 30, 1979, for six performances (see entry) and on August 30, 1988, for fourteen showings.

The work is best remembered today as the film that first teamed Jeanette MacDonald and Nelson Eddy. Directed by W. S. Van Dyke II, the 1935 MGM film was a huge success and catapulted MacDonald and Eddy into cinematic immortality with a series of eight films in the operetta vein. Five numbers were retained for the adaptation: "Tramp, Tramp, Tramp," "'Neath the Southern Moon," "Italian Street Song," "I'm Falling in Love with Someone," and "Ah, Sweet Mystery of Life."

According to Raymond Erickson in the *New York Times*, the current City Opera revival had undergone a tumultuous birth. Two directors and one choreographer were replaced, and the original libretto was altered to the point where the "already tricky" plot was made even more nonsensical. But after the current run, Beverly Sills, who had now become the company's new general director and who had faith in the work, asked Jack Eddleman to "start over from scratch and give me a hit!" And so the following year a revised production opened.

The current revival included one interpolation, "This Brave New Land," which had originally been written for (but perhaps not performed in) Herbert's *The Prince Ananais* (1894); the lyric was by Francis Neilson.

The most complete recording of the score was released as part of the Smithsonian American Musical Theatre Series in a two-LP boxed set (Smithsonian Collection # N-026).

THE MERRY WIDOW

Theatre: New York State Theatre
Opening Date: September 17, 1978; *Closing Date*: November 11, 1978
Performances: 6 (in repertory)
Libretto and *Lyrics*: Victor M. Leon and Leo Stein; English adaptation and dialogue by Ursula Eggers and Joseph D. Rugeris and English lyrics by Sheldon Harnick
Music: Franz Lehar
Direction: Tito Capobianco; *Producer*: The New York City Opera Company (Julius Rudel, Director; John S. White, Managing Director); *Choreography*: Jessica Redel; *Scenery* and *Costumes*: Carl Toms; *Lighting*: Ken Billington; *Musical Direction*: Imre Pallo
Cast: David Rae Smith (Baron Mirko Zeta), Diana Soviero (Valencienne), Howard Hensel (Count Danilo Danilovitch), Johanna Meier (Anna Glawari), Bruce Reed (Camille de Rosillon), Harlan Foss (Vicomte Cascada), Alan Kays (Raoul St. Brioche), Herbert Hunsberger (Bogdanovitch), Kathleen Murphy (Sylviane, Dodo), William Ledbetter (Kromov), Myrna Reynolds (Olga, Jou-Jou), Louis Perry (Pritchitch), Susan Delery-Whedon (Praskovia, Clo-Clo), James Billings (Njegus), Candace Itow (Lolo), Toni-Ann Gardella (Frou-Frou), Raven Wilkinson (Margot); Members of Petrovenian and Parisian Society, Dancers, Servants, and Waiters: The New York City Opera Company Chorus
The operetta was presented in three acts.
The action takes place in Paris during the early 1900s.

The New York City Opera Company had presented the new production of Franz Lehar's 1905 operetta *The Merry Widow* five months earlier with Beverly Sills and Alan Titus in the leading roles of Anna and Danilo. This time around, Johanna Meier and Howard Hensel were the leads. The production had originally been produced by the San Diego Opera in 1977.

For more information about the operetta and its recent New York presentations, see entries for the April 1978 productions and the 1974 and 1976 revivals.

EUBIE!

Theatre: Ambassador Theatre
Opening Date: September 20, 1978; *Closing Date*: October 7, 1979
Performance: 439
Lyrics: See song list for individual credits.
Music: Eubie Blake
Direction: Julianne Boyd (Ron Abbott, Production Supervisor); *Producers*: Ashton Springer in association with Frank C. Pierson and Jay J. Cohen (John N. Hart Jr., Associate Producer); *Co-Choreography* and *Tap Choreography*: Henry LeTang; *Co-Choreography* and *Musical Staging*: Billy Wilson; *Scenery*: Karl Eigsti; *Costumes*: Bernard Johnson; *Lighting*: William Mintzer; *Musical Direction*: Vicki Carter
Cast: Ethel Beatty, Terry Burrell, Leslie Dockery, Lynnie Godfrey, Gregory Hines, Maurice Hines, Mel Johnson Jr., Lonnie McNeil, Janet Powell, Marion Ramsey, Alaina Reed, Jeffery V. Thompson
The revue was presented in two acts.

Musical Numbers

Act One: Prologue: "Good Night, Angeline" (*Shuffle Along*, 1921) and "Charleston Rag" (Company); "Shuffle Along" (*Shuffle Along*, 1921) (lyric by Noble Sissle) (Company); "In Honeysuckle Time (When Emmaline Said She'd Be Mine)" (*Shuffle Along*, 1921) (lyric by Noble Sissle) (Lonnie McNeil, Janet Powell, Company); "I'm Just Wild about Harry" (*Shuffle Along*, 1921) (lyric by Noble Sissle) (Maurice Hines, Janet Powell, Lynnie Godfrey, Marion Ramsey, Ethel Beatty); "Baltimore Buzz" (*Shuffle Along*, 1921) (lyric by Noble Sissle) (mime staged by Dana Manno) (Lonnie McNeil, Jeffery V. Thompson, Mel Johnson Jr., Janet Powell, Gregory Hines, Leslie Dockery); "Daddy (Won't You Please Come Home)" (*Shuffle Along*, 1921) (lyric by Noble Sissle) (Lynnie Godfrey); "There's a Million Little Cupids in the Sky" (written for, but not used in, *Chocolate Dandies*, 1924) (lyric by Noble Sissle) (Maurice Hines, Lonnie McNeil, Gregory Hines, Ethel Beatty, Mel Johnson Jr., Jeffery V. Thompson, Marion Ramsey, Janet Powell, Leslie Dockery, Alaina Reed); "I'm a Great Big Baby" (*Tan Manhattan*, 1940) (lyric by Andy Razaf) (Jeffery V. Thompson); "My Handy Man Ain't Handy Anymore" (possibly written for, but not used in, *Blackbirds of 1930*) (lyric by Andy Razaf) (Alaina Reed, Mel Johnson Jr.); "Low Down Blues" (*Shuffle Along*, 1921) (lyric by Noble Sissle) (Gregory Hines); "Gee, I Wish I Had Someone to Rock Me in the Cradle of Love" (lyric by Noble Sissle) (Ethel Beatty); "I'm Just Simply Full of Jazz" (*Shuffle Along*, 1921) (lyric by Noble Sissle) (Company)
Act Two: "High Steppin' Days" (lyric by Johnny Brandon) (Company); "Dixie Moon" (*Chocolate Dandies*, 1924) (lyric by Noble Sissle) (Mel Johnson Jr., Gregory Hines, Maurice Hines, Company); "Weary" (*Tan Manhattan*, 1940) (lyric by Andy Razaf) (Terry Burrell, Company); "Roll, Jordan" (*Blackbirds of 1930*) (lyric by Andy Razaf) (Alaina Reed, Terry Burrell, Janet Powell, Company); "Memories of You" (*Blackbirds of 1930*) (lyric by Andy Razaf) (Ethel Beatty); "If You've Never Been Vamped by a Brownskin, You've Never Been Vamped at All" (*Shuffle Along*, 1921) (lyric by Noble Sissle) (Marion Ramsey, Mel Johnson Jr., Lynnie Godfrey, Gregory Hines, Jeffery V. Thompson, Leslie Dockery, Janet Powell, Maurice Hines, Lonnie McNeil); "You Got to Git the Gittin While the Gittin's Good" (lyric by F. E. Miller) (Maurice Hines); "Oriental Blues" (*Shuffle Along*, 1921) (lyric by Noble Sissle) (Jeffery V. Thompson, Ethel Beatty, Lynnie Godfrey, Janet Powell, Marion Ramsey); "I'm Craving for That Kind of Love" (*Shuffle Along*, 1921) (lyric by Noble Sissle) (Lynnie Godfrey); "Hot Feet" (lyric by Noble Sissle) (Gregory Hines); "Goodnight, Angeline" (lyric by Noble Sissle and Jim Europe) (Ethel Beatty, Mel Johnson Jr., Lonnie McNeil, Janet Powell); Finale (Company)

Eubie! was a delightful tribute to composer Eubie Blake (1897–1983); the evening was one of a number of the era's revues that saluted black music, and while the earlier ***Ain't Misbehavin'*** was somewhat monotonous with a lack of dancing and choral flavoring in its song presentation and the later *Sophisticated Ladies* was overproduced, *Eubie!* (along with ***Bubbling Brown Sugar***) was just right in its mix of dance and song and in its varied presentation of musical numbers.

T. E. Kalem in *Time* reported that at the end of the evening, Blake appeared on the stage, accepted a rose, engaged in "amiable banter," and soon the cast and audience sang "I'm Just Wild about Eubie." Kalem noted that the revue was "thoroughly entertaining and unerringly professional, but it bubbles more often than it blazes." He said Gregory Hines and Maurice Hines were the "magnetic high spots" of the show, and that overall he preferred ***Ain't Misbehavin'***. Jack Kroll in *Newsweek* said the revue was a "handsome homage to a man who is himself a living century of music." Blake wrote true "theatre music," and Kroll noted that Lynnie Godfrey had a "voice that could crush diamonds" and the Hines brothers danced like "men possessed." The costumes were "eye-drenching" and the choreography created "velvety, snapping patterns." Christopher Sharp in *Women's Wear Daily* felt the evening didn't have the sophistication of the "Fats" Waller revue, but the songs had "the impact of a magical tapestry set into sound" and he praised the "exciting" tap dancing; and Edwin Wilson in the *Wall Street Journal* noted that Blake defined the term "living legend," and his songs ranged from "ragtime, blues and spirituals to sophisticated melodies like 'Memories of You.'"

Walter Kerr in the *New York Times* said the "eminently suitable" tribute displayed Blake's "tinkly, raggy, eagerly syncopated rhythms" and said "no one taps faster" than the Hines brothers. He further praised Lynnie Godfrey, Alaina Reed, and Ethel Beatty, who "belted, cooed, and growled most effectively." Clive Barnes in the *New York Post* noted that the stylish revue contained "some of the best tap-dancing ever seen" and said the show was "full of nostalgia and rockets."

During the tryout, the dance number "Slewfoot Nelson" was dropped.

The cast album was released by Warner Brothers Records (LP # 0898). For the national tour, the song "Baltimo' Joe" (composed by Blake in 1935 and with newly revised lyrics by Cheryl Hardwick) was added.

Eubie! included eleven songs from Blake and Noble Sissle's hit 1921 revue *Shuffle Along*, which opened on May 23, 1921, at the 63rd Street Music Hall for 504 performances; the numbers were: "Shuffle Along," "In Honeysuckle Time (When Emmaline Said She'd Be Mine)," "I'm Just Wild about Harry," "Baltimore Buzz," "Daddy (Won't You Please Come Home)," "Low Down Blues," "I'm Just Simply Full of Jazz," "If You've Never Been Vamped by a Brownskin, You've Never Been Vamped at All," "Oriental Blues," "I'm Craving for That Kind of Love," and "Goodnight, Angeline"). An archival recording of *Shuffle Along* released by New World Records (LP # NW-260) includes "Bandana Days," "Love Will Find a Way," "Gypsy Blues," and "Gee, I'm Glad I'm from Dixie," all of which weren't included in *Eubie!*

Awards

Tony Award Nominations: Best Featured Actor in a Musical (Gregory Hines); Best Score (music by Eubie Blake, lyrics by Noble Sissle, Andy Razaf, F. E. Miller, Johnny Brandon, and Jim Europe); Best Choreographer (Henry Le Tang and Billy Wilson)

KING OF HEARTS

"A New Musical"

Theatre: Minskoff Theatre
Opening Date: October 22, 1978; *Closing Date*: December 3, 1978
Performances: 48
Book: Joseph Stein
Lyrics: Jacob Brackman
Music: Peter Link
Based on the 1966 film *King of Hearts* (screenplay by Philippe de Broca, Maurice Bessy, and Daniel Boulange and direction by Philippe de Broca).
Direction and *Choreography*: Ron Field (John Calvert, Assistant to the Director; and Marianne Selbert, Assistant to the Choreographer); *Producers*: Joseph Kipness and Patty Grubman in association with Jerome Minskoff (Lee Minskoff and Charlotte Dicker, Associate Producers; Nan Pearlman, Production Associate); *Scenery*: Santo Loquasto; *Costumes*: Patricia Zipprodt; *Lighting*: Pat Collins; *Musical Direction*: Karen Gustafson

Cast: The Inmates—Gary Morgan (Demosthenes), Millicent Martin (Madeleine), Mitzi Hamilton (Genevieve), Marilyn D'Honau (Simone), Isabelle Farrell (Dahlia), Bob Gunton (Raoul), Pamela Blair (Jeunefille), Neva Rae Powers (Valerie), Rex David Hays (Jacques), Michael McCarty (DuBac), Maria Guida (Therese), Gerrianne Raphael (Isolde), Gordon J. Weiss (Claude), Timothy Scott (Guy-Louis), David Thomas (M. Clichy), Bryan Nicholas (Philippe), Julia Shelley (Marie-Claire), Will Roy (Henri), Wilbur (Le Porc); American Soldiers—Donald Scardino (Private Johnny Perkins), Jay Devlin (Lieutenant McNeill), Robert Brubach (Frank), Harry Fawcett (Steve), John Scoullar (Joe), Jamie Haskins (Tom), Richard Christopher (Phillip); German Soldiers—Scott Allen (Hans), Alexander Orfaly (Kapitan Kost), Scott Barnes (Siegfried), Robert Berdahl (Fritz), Timothy Wallace (Karl), Karl Heist (Willie)

The musical was presented in two acts.

The action takes place during one day in September 1918 toward the end of World War I in the French town of DuTemps and the trenches that surround it.

Musical Numbers

Act One: "A Stain on the Name" (Inmates); "Déjà vu" (Millicent Martin); "Promenade" ("The Transformation") (Inmates); "Turn Around" (Millicent Martin, Inmates); "Nothing, Only Love" (Pamela Blair, Donald Scardino, Millicent Martin); "King of Hearts" (Gary Morgan, Pamela Blair, Bob Gunton, Millicent Martin, Inmates); "Close Upon the Hour" (Donald Scardino); "A Brand New Day" ("The Coronation") (Michael McCarty, Donald Scardino, Inmates)

Act Two: "Le Grand Cirque de Provence" (Bob Gunton, Inmates); "Hey, Look at Me, Mrs. Draba" (Donald Scardino); "Going Home Tomorrow" (Soldiers); "Somewhere Is Here" (Millicent Martin); "Nothing, Only Love" (reprise) (Bob Gunton, Millicent Martin, Pamela Blair, Donald Scardino); "March, March, March" (Donald Scardino, Inmates); "The Battle" (Soldiers)

King of Hearts was based on the 1966 cult film of the same name, which took place in a small village in France toward the end of World War I. The townspeople have fled because the Germans have hidden bombs in the village that are intended to kill the advancing American soldiers. Only the placid and peaceful inmates of the local asylum remain in the town, and they soon resume the lives they led before their incarceration, and so one (Millicent Martin) become's the town's madam, another a hairdresser, another a bishop, and so on. When Private Johnny Perkins (Donald Scardino) and his regiment arrive to dismantle the bombs, at first they don't realize the villagers are actually the inhabitants of the sanitarium, but eventually they catch on, especially when the inmates crown Johnny as their king. Ultimately, the inmates return to the asylum, and when Johnny decides they are saner than the world outside, he joins them.

The fey notion that the world is mad and the insane are sane was a popular one in the 1960s and 1970s (Stephen Sondheim and Arthur Laurents's 1964 musical *Anyone Can Whistle* and Ken Kesey's *One Flew Over the Cuckoo's Nest*, which was first a book, a Broadway play, then a long-running Off-Broadway play, and finally an Oscar-winning film, explored this notion). Perhaps if the book of *King of Hearts* had retained the charm and simplicity of its source material and if the score had been stronger, the musical might have had a chance. But the unenthusiastic reviews and the lack of a star name relegated the show to a six-week run, and *Variety* reported the musical lost the staggering amount of $1,764,805.

Clive Barnes in the *New York Post* felt Peter Link's "serviceable" score lacked the "magic kiss" to transform the fantasy into satisfying musical theatre because the songs were "characterless" and alternated "vapid lyricism" with "ooh-la-la gusto"; Jack Kroll in *Newsweek* noted that the creators never found "the alchemic mix that turns professionalism into pure gold" (but he singled out the score's best song, the soldiers' *a cappella* "Going Home Tomorrow"); John Beaufort in the *Christian Science Monitor* mentioned that with all the evening's set pieces (the transformation scene when the inmates take over the town; a cathedral rooftop for Johnny's coronation; and a lavish circus sequence) the libretto's "simple message" got "lost" in "a lurching and overladen delivery vehicle."

Howard Kissel in *Women's Wear Daily* suggested the musical's "brash theatricality" worked against its "innocent high-mindedness" and so a can-can should have reflected something of the skewed attitudes of the inmates rather than a predictable and conventional version of the dance. But Link's score was "best" when it aimed "highest," and so "Going Home Tomorrow," the coronation sequence, and "Close upon the Hour" were impressive; otherwise, the music was too "close to conventional Broadway material" and wound up "colorless." Walter Kerr in the *New York Times* said the book "wanders about loosely" and "forgets which narrative it ought to attend to next"; an unsigned review in the *New York Daily News* noted that "story and music" were "almost nonexistent"; and Daniel Henninger in the *Wall Street Journal* said that the musical "lacked narrative coherence, memorable music or wit" and thus was in "antic free fall."

Hobe in *Variety* stated that "practically nothing" worked in a production "in which virtually everything is bloated beyond reason." The "box office dud" had a "painfully overwritten" book, "mostly tuneless and instantly forgettable" songs, and "energetic, pointless and endless" dances. Martin Gottfried in *Cue* said the musical found its voice in the coronation scene and in the "compactly European, unthreateningly surreal" circus sequence, and having captured the perfect tone for the evening in these two numbers director Ron Field should have "gone back" and "chucked" all the first-act plot exposition and reinvented the material. As for Link's score, it was "musicianly, theatrical, and melodic."

Virtually all the critics agreed that the star of the evening was Santo Loquasto's imaginative décor. When his turntable set revolved, it depicted different perspectives of the town and its interiors. Barnes noted it was a true "toy-town of the spirit" which was "a mixture of gothic, French provincial and pure wit"; Kissel mentioned that the striking interior of the asylum offered the inmates' beds arranged in topsy-turvy fashion "in an almost Chagallian defiance of gravity"; and Kerr praised the "sheer spectacle" and "eye-popping scenery" of Loquasto's décor.

Fourteen months before the Broadway premiere, an early version of the musical opened at the Westport Country Playhouse, Westport, Connecticut, with an almost completely different creative team: the book was by Steve Tesich, direction by A. J. Antoon, choreography by Miguel Godreau, scenery by Ernest Allen Smith, costumes by Bosha Johnson, lighting by Ian Calderon, and musical direction by Paul Gemignani. The cast included Robby Benson (Johnny), and others in the production were Abigale Haness (Jeunefille), Judith Anna Roberts (Madeliene), Elliott Savage, Kurt Knudson, and Laura Waterbury. Songs heard in Westport that were dropped for Broadway were: "Ready or Not," "Down at Madeliene's," "The Only Time Is Now," "Say Mama," "With My Friends," "The World Is a Jungle," "Now We Need to Cry," "Any Old Girl," and "A Day in Our Life."

During the Boston tryout of the revised version, "Femme Fatale" and "The Truce" were cut.

The cast album was released in 1980 by Original Cast Records (LP # OC-8028; CD # THT-9225), and offers music not heard in the Broadway production, including a prologue, "Here Come Mine," "A Day in Our Life," and "With My Friends." A revival by the Los Angeles Harbor College's Music and Theatre Departments used the original book by Steven Tesich, and the cast album was released in a two-LP boxed set (Audio Engineering Associates # AEA-1375). In 2002, Goodspeed Opera House, East Haddam, Connecticut, also revived the musical with Tesich's book.

Awards

Tony Award Nomination: Best Featured Actress in a Musical (Millicent Martin)

STREET SCENE

Theatre: New York State Theatre
Opening Date: October 28, 1978; *Closing Date*: November 12, 1978
Performances: 4 (in repertory)
Book: Elmer Rice
Lyrics: Langston Hughes and Elmer Rice
Music: Kurt Weill
Based on the 1929 play *Street Scene* by Elmer Rice.
Direction: Jack O'Brien (Antoni Jaworski, Assistant Director); *Producer*: The New York City Opera Company (Julius Rudel, Director, and John S. White, Managing Director); *Choreography*: Patricia Birch; *Scenery*: Paul Sylbert; *Costumes*: Nancy Potts; *Lighting*: Gilbert V. Hemsley Jr.; *Choral Direction*: Leann Hillmer; *Musical Direction*: John Mauceri

Cast: Martha Thigpen (Greta Fiorentino), Diane Curry (Emma Jones), Rosemarie Freni (Olga Olsen), Ralph Bassett (Carl Olsen), Marie Young (Neighborhood Woman, Nursemaid), Lynn Cohen (Shirley Kaplan), Nico Castel (Abraham Kaplan), Myrna Reynolds (Salvation Army Girl), Kay Schoenfeld (Salvation Army Girl), Andrew Smith (Henry Davis), Robert Sapolsky (Willie Maurrant), Eileen Schauler (Anna Maurrant), Alan Kays (Sam Kaplan), James Clark (Daniel Buchanan), Lila Herbert (Mrs. Buchanan), William Chapman (Frank Maurrant), Robert Paul (George Jones), William Ledbetter (Steve Sankey), Jonathan Green (Lippo Fiorentino), Sally Lambert (Mrs. Hildebrand), Kathleen Hegierski (Jenny Hildebrand), Denise Adoff (Graduate), Vanessa Williams (Graduate), Timothy Eaton (Charlie Hildebrand), Dela Bartolini (Mary Hildebrand), Kimara Love (Grace Davis), Catherine Malfitano (Rose Maurrant), Alan Titus (Harry Easter), Bronwyn Thomas (Mae Jones), Daniel Levans (Dick McGann), Bill Herndon (Vincent Jones), Don Carlo (Doctor Wilson), Kenn Dovel (Officer Murphy), Robert Brubaker (Milkman), Ann Cawlo (Joan), Alexandra Sabin (Myrtle), Harris Davis (Workman), John Henry Thomas (Eddie), Brigitte Stocker (Sally), Billy Ross (Joe), Richard Nelson (Strawberry Seller, Policeman), Susan Delery-Whedon (Corn Seller), Don Yule (James Henry), Alan Baker (Fred Cullen), Dan Kingman (Old Clothes Man), Frank Tippie (Man, Furniture Mover), James Brewer (Man), Herbert Hunsberger (Man), Ken Rubenfeld (Grocery Boy), Edward Vaughan (Ambulance Driver), Patricia Charbonneau (Music Student), James Sergi (Intern), Rita Metzger (Nursemaid), Don Henderson (Policeman), Dan Kingman and Harriet Greene (Middle-Aged Couple); Off-Stage Voices: Vanessa Williams, Timothy Eaton, Lila Herbert

The opera was presented in two acts.

The action takes place on the stoop and front sidewalk of a New York City tenement during a period of twenty-four hours in June.

Musical Numbers

Unless otherwise noted, all lyrics are by Langston Hughes.

Act One: "Ain't It Awful, the Heat?" (lyric by Langston Hughes and Elmer Rice) (Martha Thigpen, Diane Curry, Rosemarie Freni, Nico Castel, Ralph Bassett); "I Got a Marble and a Star" (Andrew Smith); "Get a Load of That" (lyric by Langston Hughes and Elmer Rice) (Diane Curry, Martha Thigpen, Rosemarie Freni); "When a Woman Has a Baby" (lyric by Langston Hughes and Elmer Rice) (James Clark, Martha Thigpen, Diane Curry, Eileen Schauler); "Somehow I Never Could Believe" (Eileen Schauler); "Get a Load of That" (reprise) (Diane Curry, Martha Thigpen, Robert Paul, Rosemarie Freni); "Ice Cream" (lyric by Langston Hughes and Elmer Rice) (Jonathan Green, Diane Curry, Martha Thigpen, Andrew Smith, Robert Paul, Ralph Bassett, Rosemarie Freni); "Let Things Be Like They Always Was" (William Chapman); "Wrapped in a Ribbon and Tied in a Bow" (lyric by Langston Hughes and Elmer Rice) (Kathleen Hegierski, Neighbors); "Lonely House" (Alan Kays); "Wouldn't You Like to Be on Broadway?" (lyric by Langston Hughes and Elmer Rice) (Alan Titus); "What Good Would the Moon Be?" (Catherine Malfitano); "Moon-Faced, Starry-Eyed" (Daniel Levans, Bronwyn Thomas); "Remember That I Care" (Alan Kays, Catherine Malfitano)

Act Two: "Catch Me If You Can" (aka "Children's Game") (lyric by Langston Hughes and Elmer Rice) (Children); "There'll Be Trouble" (lyric by Langston Hughes and Elmer Rice) (William Chapman, Eileen Schauler, Catherine Malfitano); "A Boy Like You" (Eileen Schauler); "We'll Go Away Together" (Alan Kays, Catherine Malfitano); "The Woman Who Lived Up There" (Ensemble); "Lullaby" (lyric by Elmer Rice) (Marie Young, Rita Metzger); "I Loved Her, Too" (lyric by Langston Hughes and Elmer Rice) (William Chapman, Catherine Malfitano, Ensemble); "Don't Forget the Lilac Bush" (lyric by Langston Hughes and Elmer Rice) (Alan Kays, Catherine Malfitano); "Ain't It Awful, the Heat?" (reprise) (Martha Thigpen, Diane Curry, Rosemarie Freni, Nico Castel)

The New York City Opera Company's new production of Kurt Weill's *Street Scene* was their sixth of eight revivals of the self-described "dramatic musical." Elmer Rice's Pulitzer Prize-winning play of the same name premiered at the Playhouse Theatre on January 10, 1929, and ran for 601 performances, and the musical version opened at the Adelphi Theatre on January 9, 1947, for 148 showings. The story takes place on the stoop and front sidewalk of a New York City tenement during the twenty-four-hour period of a miserably hot and steaming day and night in June, and depicted both the trivialities and tragedies of the people who live there, including the Maurrant family. The doomed Anna (Eileen Schauler) is unhappily married to the insanely jealous Frank (William Chapman), and their daughter Rose (Catherine Malfitano) seems prey to the bitterness and futility of the hardscrabble underside of Manhattan life.

The score perfectly captured both the tragic and mundane worlds of the tenement dwellers. Anna's aria "Somehow I Never Could Believe" is one of the crown jewels of lyric theatre in its powerful introspective character study, and Frank's "I Loved Her, Too" is a gripping musical self-analysis in which he explains but doesn't justify himself after he has murdered Anna. But there were lighter numbers, too, including the gossips and their "Ain't It Awful, the Heat?" and "Get a Load of That"; the joyous ode to "Ice Cream" on a hot summer's day; and the scorching jitterbug "Moon-Faced, Starry-Eyed" for two of the neighborhood's hep cats.

The cast album of the 1947 production was recorded by Columbia Records (LP # OL-4139) and later issued on CD by CBS Masterworks (# MK-44668); for the album, the role of Frank is sung by Randolph Symonette, who was Norman Cordon's understudy and who eventually assumed the role. A 1949 radio broadcast from the Hollywood Bowl was released by Naxos Records (CD # 8-120885) with Polyna Stoska and Brian Sullivan from the original cast. Both the 1947 and 1949 recordings are abridged, but there are two complete versions that were released on two-CD sets. The English National Opera recording (That's Entertainment Records # CDTER-2-1185) is based on a production that opened on October 13, 1989, and the second one on Decca Records (# 433-371-2) was conducted by John Mauceri, who also conducted the current revival. During the tryout of the original production, the song "Italy in Technicolor" was cut, but is included in two collections, *Kurt Weill Revisited* (Painted Smiles Records CD # PSCD-108) and *Lost in Boston II* (Varese Sarabande CD # VSD-5485).

Besides the current revival, the opera was produced by City Opera on April 2, 1959 (two performances); September 17, 1959 (two performances); February 13, 1960 (three performances); and April 26, 1963 (three performances), all at City Center; the February 24, 1966, production (six performances), the current revival, and the ones produced on October 13, 1979 (five performances; see entries) and September 7, 1990 (six performances) were presented at the New York State Theatre.

The 1979 revival was shown on public television on October 27, 1979, and a joint production by the Houston Grand Opera, the Theatre im Pfalabau Ludwigshafen, and the Theatre des Westens was released on DVD by Image Entertainment (# ID924-ORADVD).

All lyrics, spoken dialogue, and music were included in an undated paperback edition published by Chappell & Co.

In reviewing the current production, John Rockwell in the *New York Times* said *Street Scene* was "a landmark in the evolution of American musical theatre" and urged his readers to see it. For the performance he reviewed, Sharon Daniels was Anna, and he noted that she "sang attractively and projected a most moving and convincing portrayal"; he said Daniel Levans and Bronwyn Thomas did "lovely justice" to Patricia Birch's "snazzy yet never vulgar choreography" for "Moon-Faced, Starry-Eyed."

GOREY STORIES

"An Entertainment with Music"

Theatre: Booth Theatre
Opening Date: October 30, 1978; *Closing Date*: October 30, 1978
Performances: 1
Text: Written by Edward Gorey and adapted by Stephen Currens
Music: David Aldrich
Based on Edward Gorey's short story collections *Amphigorey* (1972) and *Amphigorey Too* (1975).
Direction: Tony Tanner; *Producers*: Terry Allen Kramer, Harry Rigby, Hale Matthews, John Wulp; *Scenery and Costumes*: Edward Gorey (scenery supervised by Lynn Pecktal and costumes supervised by David Murin); *Furs*: Ben Kahn; *Lighting*: Roger Morgan; *Musical Direction*: Martin Silvestri
Cast: Gemze de Lappe (Mona), Sel Vitella (Harold), Julie Kurnitz (Lady Celia), June Squibb (Mary Rosemarsh), Susan Marchand (Ortenzia Caviglia), Tobias Haller (Little Henry), Dennis McGovern (Jasper Ankle), Leon Shaw (C. F. Earbrass), John Michalski (Hamish)
The revue was presented in two acts.
The action takes place in Lady Celia's drawing room and in the summer house.

Sketches and Musical Numbers

Note: During previews, the musical underwent a reordering of some of the sketches and songs; the following list is taken from a special "corrected running order" insert in the program.

Act One: "Assembly" (Company); "The Hapless Child" (Gemze de Lappe, Sel Vitella, June Squibb, Leon Shaw, Dennis McGovern, John Michalski, Julie Kurnitz, Susan Marchand); "The Wuggly Ump" (song) (Company); "The Curious Sofa" (Company); "The Sinking Spell" (Company); "The Gilded Bat" (Company); "The Insect God" (song) (Company); "The Willowdale Handcar" (Company); "The Doubtful Guest" (Company); "The Blue Aspect" (song) (lyrics by Stephen Currens) (Company)

Act Two: "The Unstrung Harp, or Mr. Earbrass Writes a Novel" (Julie Kurnitz, Leon Shaw); "The Pious Infant" (Company); "The Osbick Bird" (song) (Sel Vitella, Tobias Haller); "The Deranged Cousins" (Leon Shaw, Dennis McGovern, Susan Marchand, June Squibb); Limericks from "The Listing Attic" (Company); "The Lost Lions" (John Michalski, Leon Shaw, Julie Kurnitz); "The Loathsome Couple" (Company); "The Gashlycrumb Tinies" (song) (Company)

Gorey Stories was an evening of sketches and songs that were adapted from Edward Gorey's peculiar and quirky brand of arch and fiendish stories. It was conceived and adapted for the stage by Stephen Currens and was first produced by the University of Kentucky's Department of Theatre Arts and premiered in New York in an Off-Off-Broadway production at the WPA Theatre on December 8, 1977, for twelve performances. A later production at George Mason University, in Fairfax, Virginia, worked rather well in a casual campus environment, but for Broadway the work was clearly too wispy, and so along with ***A Broadway Musical*** and ***The Utter Glory of Morrissey Hall*** the Gorey evening was one of the 1978–1979 season's three one-performance flop musicals.

Clive Barnes in the *New York Post* said the work was "unique, odd, perverse and engagingly entertaining" and one which you'd not "easily forget." But, paradoxically, it was "theatrical" without being "theatre" because Gorey's writings didn't easily translate into a dramatic context. Howard Kissel in *Women's Wear Daily* felt the first act was too coy and fey, and commented that the essence of Gorey was too "sporadic" to be effective; but the second act was more structured and possessed a "sense of style." He noted that Tony Tanner's direction was "generally inventive" but "frequently too cute."

John Beaufort in the *Christian Science Monitor* said Gorey's "weird characters and horrid happenings" arrived just in time for Halloween, but unfortunately the evening wasn't "particularly theatrical" and the unending comic horror eventually became "tedious." Dennis Cunningham on WCBSTV2 noted that while Gorey's stories "read well, they sure don't play well." The "thin" evening sometimes seemed like a *Sophomore Spring Follies* and it had "no business being anywhere in the vicinity of Broadway."

Martin Gottfried in *Cue* found the "sophisticated" evening appropriate for those "bored with virtue and children and normalcy." The company was "gifted and well-drilled," and the show was "what is nowadays called 'special taste' entertainment," which was "code language for the urbane and clever" and "was getting rarer every day."

In regard to the horrors depicted throughout the evening, one segment ("The Gashlycrumb Tinies") provided an alphabetical list of twenty-six people who come to ghastly ends (one was "assaulted by bears," one was "devoured by mice," and another "died of ennui"). Another ("The Hapless Child") told the tale of a little girl's short and miserably tragic life. She eventually goes blind and is killed when her long-lost father accidentally runs over her. And a limerick noted that the Almighty was offended by a mother's behavior and so punished her by making her newborn a "cripple."

During previews, the song "The Eleventh Episode" was cut.

The script was published in paperback by Samuel French in 1983.

Other works based on Gorey's writings (some of which used material that had been adapted for *Gorey Stories*) include *Amphigorey* (Off Broadway; Perry Street Theatre, April 7, 1994; fifty performances; an early version was titled *Tinned Lettuce*) and *The Gorey Details* (Off Broadway; The Century Theatre for the Performing Arts, October 16, 2000; sixty-five performances). Gorey's most successful theatrical venture was the revival of *Dracula*, which opened on October 20, 1977, at the Martin Beck (now Al Hirschfeld) Theatre for 925 performances. Gorey designed a black-and-white (with occasional reds) fantasy of sets and costumes and won the Tony Award for Best Costume Design.

PLATINUM

"THE MUSICAL WITH A FLIP-SIDE"

Theatre: Mark Hellinger Theatre
Opening Date: November 12, 1978; *Closing Date*: December 10, 1978
Performances: 33
Book: Will Holt and Bruce Vilanch
Lyrics: Will Holt
Music: Gary William Friedman
Direction and *Choreography*: Joe Layton (Damita Jo Freeman, Assistant Choreographer); *Producers*: Gladys Rackmil, Fritz Holt, and Barry M. Brown (A Joe Layton Production); *Scenery*: David Hays; *Multi-Media Design*: Sheppard Kerman; *Costumes*: Bob Mackie; *Lighting*: John Gleason; *Musical Direction*: Fred Thaler
Cast: Tony Shultz (Shultz), *Alexis Smith* (Lila Halliday), Ronnie B. Baker (Snake), Jonathan Freeman (Minky, Alan Fairmont), John Hammil (Boris), Damita Jo Freeman (Damita), Robin Grean (Robin), Avery Sommers (Avery), Stanley Kamel (Jeff Leff), Lisa Mordente (Crystal Mason), Richard Cox (Dan Danger), Christine Faith (Christine), Wenndy Leigh MacKenzie (Wenndy); The Sidemen—Fred: Fred Thaler (Conductor, Piano), Greg: Gregory Bloch (Violin), Dick: Dick Frank (Guitar), Steve: Steve Mack (Bass), Roy: Roy Markowitz (Drums); *Wings of Destiny* (film sequence conceived and directed by Joe Layton): War Bride: Alexis Smith (as Lila Halliday), Mack: Jonathan Freeman (as Alan Fairmont)
The musical was presented in two acts.
The action takes place during the present time "in the newest environmental recording studio" in Hollywood.

Musical Numbers

Act One: "Back with a Beat"/"Nothing But" (Alexis Smith); "Sunset" (Lisa Mordente, Avery Sommers, Damita Jo Freeman, Robin Grean); "Ride Baby Ride" (Richard Cox, Damita Jo Freeman, Robin Grean, Avery Sommers); "Destiny" (Alexis Smith); "Disco Destiny" (Lisa Mordente, Avery Sommers, Damita Jo Freeman, Robin Grean); "I Am the Light" (Richard Cox); "Move Star Mansion" (Richard Cox, Alexis Smith)
Act Two: "Platinum Dreams" (Avery Sommers, Damita Jo Freeman, Robin Grean); "Trials and Tribulations"/"I Like You" (Lisa Mordente, Alexis Smith); "1945" (Richard Cox, Alexis Smith); "Too Many Mirrors" (Alexis Smith); "Old Times, Good Times" (Alexis Smith, Company)

Platinum wasn't a musical about 1930s platinum blonde Jean Harlow, but instead focused on a fictitious movie star from the 1940s named Lila Halliday (Alexis Smith), who hopes to make a comeback by recording disco songs. In this instance, platinum is the Holy Grail of the music industry because it denotes that a record has sold a million copies. The action takes place in the "newest environmental studio in Hollywood," and the gargantuan single set was a maze of recording equipment, speakers, consoles, microphones, intercoms, closed-circuit television monitors, lighting grids, transparent mirrors, a movie screen, and even a pinball machine and a hot tub (the latter allowed for a glimpse of a nude Richard Cox emerging from the tub, which Howard Kissel in *Women's Wear Daily* noted would please one segment of "the traditional Broadway audience").

Lila arrives at the studio to record a demo record, and while there she meets various singers, including the up-and-coming hot singer Crystal Mason (Lisa Mordente, who, incidentally, is the daughter of Chita Rivera and Tony Mordente) and rock singer Dan Danger (Cox), who at thirty-one is afraid he's already on the verge of becoming a has-been. And "has-been" is something Lila knows all too well as she now spends most of her time on the road touring in second-rate productions of hit musicals (she drily notes, "I *am* the road") and comments that one time during a performance of *Hello, Dolly!* in Columbus, Ohio, she started singing the title song from *Mame*. But it was OK, because she was performing the show in a dinner theatre and the audience was so nauseated it didn't notice her flub. Lila and Dan are briefly attracted to one another, but by the musical's end go their separate ways. Unfortunately, the musical's denouement was inconclusive and the evening's generation-gap theme seemed to indicate that swing and disco can merge into a new form called disco tap, and so the glittery, almost out-of-nowhere finale came across as cousin to "One" from ***A Chorus Line***.

There were clearly major holes in the story. It seemed unlikely that a film actress from the 1940s would suddenly find a second career as a disco singer, and the romance between the chic and stylish Lila and the grungy and shaggy Dan was never credible. But the musical offered a number of amusing lines and Alexis Smith's witty and brittle performance was saturated with star quality. Moreover, the lyrics by Will Holt and the music by Gary William Friedman offered an array of clever and melodic songs, and their *Platinum* score is one of the most underrated of the era. Lila's opening number, a two-part sequence titled "Back with a Beat" and "Nothing But," was an impressive character analysis; the former was dazzling with a confident lyric that was undermined by tentative, uneasy, and abrupt beats in the music, and for "Nothing But" Lila describes her War Forties array of film roles in which she played "war brides, WACs, and waifs on the run."

Lila and Dan shared two moments that reflected their glory days. In the big-band stomp of "1945," Lila recalled the era when "every gate would gain a rep for being hip when hip was hep," and in "Movie Star Mansion" Dan looked back on the heady summer of love in 1968 when he and his rocker friends shared a Hollywood estate. There was also an amusing contrast between 1940s and modern-day music in "Destiny," a song in Lila's old movie *Wings of Destiny* from which a black-and-white film sequence was shown (with Smith as a war bride and Jonathan Freeman as a guy named Mack). For the 1940s, "Destiny" was a sultry bolero that was soon transformed into the 1970s blast "Disco Destiny" for Crystal and the girl-singing trio. Crystal and Lila also shared an ingratiating two-part duet, "Trials and Tribulations" and "I Like You." "Sunset" was a tribute to "the life they call LA," and was strikingly orchestrated and sung, and "Old Times, Good Times" was an old-fashioned show tune in the Jerry Herman tradition.

Martin Gottfried in *Cue* praised Alexis Smith's "intelligent presence, adult and classy beauty, gorgeous legs" and "delightful dance talent." The show itself was "not-too-bright," but Friedman's music was "excellent—melodic, ambitious, ingenious, and decidedly theatrical" and Holt's lyrics were "clean and crafty." John Simon in *New York* was unimpressed with the evening, but noted Smith acted "with great poise and style, and exudes in equal measure grace and sexiness." Brendan Gill in the *New Yorker* said Smith performed "with grace and valor and a simulation of zest that under the circumstances" was "downright uncanny." Hobe in *Variety* found Smith a "magnetic" performer who was "not merely a stunning woman who can sing and dance, but also a skillful, resourceful actress who can command an audience and at times carry along inept fellow-players." And Clive Barnes in the *New York Post* said Smith had a "special quality of gentle steel, of unstressed chutzpah, of opalescent glitter."

David Ansen in *Newsweek* said *Platinum* was "all premise" that hoped to capitalize "on three of the hottest musical modes of the moment—rock, disco and the '40s revival." Although the show "miscalculated" its ability "to capture an audience of all generations," the "playfully seductive" "Movie Star Mansion" was the "one sustained moment" when the heart of *Platinum* seemed "made of something more than metal." Richard Eder in the *New York Times* pounced on the weak ending ("all is synthesis, harmony and mush") but praised Smith as a "graceful star" whose "Nothing But" was "the show's one good song," which benefited from "a strongly accented, astringent musical line." Kissel noted that throughout the "dreary" musical Smith managed "to move through" the "mess with class and dignity" and the show's one good song was "1945," which had "a simple, bouncy Forties feeling."

Douglas Watt in the *New York Daily News* said the musical was "full of electricity and sends you into the night charged-up." *Platinum* was "the first big fat hit" of the Broadway season, and Smith was "vibrant and smashing-looking." He singled out the songs "Destiny" and "Movie Star Mansion." In all, the show was "a triumphant piece of musical staging" that achieved "pure excitement." John Beaufort in the *Christian Science Monitor* noted the evening had its faults but was nonetheless "a big, comically boisterous, light-and-sound spectacular" with a "stunning" and "Soignée with a capital 'S'" performance by Smith and such outstanding songs as "Movie Star Mansion" and "Too Many Mirrors."

The musical had first been produced as *Sunset* a year prior to the Broadway production when it opened on September 30, 1977, at the Studio Area Theatre in Buffalo, New York, with Alexis Smith and Lisa Mordente and a book by Louis LaRusso II and direction by Tommy Tune. Songs heard in this version that were cut for Broadway were: "Sunset City," "Rock Is My Way of Life," "Waltz," "Retreat," "Moments," "Montage," "If," and "True Music." During the tryout of *Platinum* a year later, "Retreat" and "Moments" were included in the score but were dropped prior to the New York production (as was "Gonna Get Hot").

A limited-edition private cast recording taken from a live performance of the Broadway production was briefly on sale during the months following the New York closing.

A revised production of *Platinum* (which now reverted to *Sunset*, the show's original title) opened Off Broadway on November 7, 1983, at the Village Gate Downstairs and promptly closed after one performance. The new version centered on three fading entertainers and an up-and-coming one who happen to meet one night. The program didn't credit a book writer, and the new production included a cast of four, Tammy Grimes (Lila Halliday), Kim Milford (Dan Danger, now named Danger Dan Hardin), and two new characters played by Ronee Blakley (Marta Gibson) and Walt Hunter (Jamie). The production's choreography was by Buzz Miller. (Ellen Hanley was Grimes's standby, and Jessica Molaskey was the standby for Blakley.) The production was recorded by That's Entertainment Records (CD # CDTER-1180).

Songs in the Off-Broadway production that had been heard in the Buffalo version of *Sunset* or in the tryout of *Platinum* but which weren't used for Broadway were: "Sunset City," "Rock Is My Way of Life," "Retreat," and "Moments"; numbers that had been heard in *Platinum* were: "Nothing But," "Destiny," "Back with a Beat," "Sunset Dreams," "1945," "I Am the Light," "Old Times, Good Times"; and various unused songs that hadn't been included in the original *Sunset* production or in *Platinum* (some of which had been written for these earlier productions) were: "La Bamba," "Funky," "Standing in Need," "Rap," "Cheap Chablis," "Stuck on the Windshield of Life," and "This One's for Me."

Platinum was heavily backed by Paramount Pictures as a silent investor. According to *Variety*, the film company believed "the project will ultimately prove to have strong cinematic values," and *New York* reported that if Paramount went ahead with a film version "look for" Shirley MacLaine and Rod Stewart as the leads. Of course, a film never materialized, and *Variety* later said the musical lost $1,743,153.

Awards

Tony Award Nominations: Best Leading Actress in a Musical (Alexis Smith); Best Featured Actor in a Musical (Richard Cox)

ICEDANCING

Theatre: Minskoff Theatre
Opening Date: December 19, 1978; *Closing Date*: December 31, 1978
Performances: 16
Production Supervisor: Ruth Mitchell; *Producers*: Charlotte Kirk, David Singer, and Cubby Downe in association with Peter Wiese; *Choreography*: Jean-Pierre Bonnefous, Robert Cohan, John Curry, Norman Maen, Kenneth MacMillan, Peter Martins, Douglas Norwick, Donald Saddler, Twyla Tharp; *Scenery*: Tony Straiges; *Costumes*: Supervised by Florence Klotz and Designed by Nadine Baylis, Sara Brook, Norberto Chiesa, Joe Eula, Florence Klotz, Harry Lines, Santo Loquasto, D. D. Ryan; *Lighting*: Marilyn Rennagel
Cast: John Curry, JoJo Starbuck, Angela Adney, Ron Alexander, Yvonne Brink, Lorna Brown, Jack Courtney, Patricia Dodd, Cathy Foulkes, Brian Grant, Deborah Page, Paul Toomey
The ice revue was presented in two acts.

Skating Numbers

Act One: "Palais de glace" (music by Giacomo Meyerbeer; choreography by Donald Saddler; costumes by Florence Klotz) (Major Domo: Ron Alexander; Lovers: Cathy Foulkes and Jack Courtney; Famous Poet: Paul Toomey; Famous Dancer: Patricia Dodd; A Darling of Paris: Deborah Page; Young Count: Brian Grant; American: Lorna Brown; Another Darling of Paris: JoJo Starbuck; Prince: John Curry); "Scoop" (music composed and played by Donald Ashwander; choreography by Douglas Norwick; costumes by Sara Brook) (Paul Toomey, Deborah Page, Yvonne Brink, Jack Courtney); "After All" (music by Tomasso Albinoni; choreography by Twyla Tharp; costumes by Santo Loquasto) (John Curry); "Moon Dances" (music by Camille Saint-Saëns; choreography by John Curry) (Cathy Foulkes, Lorna Brown, Patricia Dodd, Ron Alexander, Brian Grant, Paul Toomey); "Tango-Tango" ("Tango" by Igor Stravinsky and "Jalousie" by Jakob Gade; choreography by Peter Martins; costumes by D. D. Ryan) (John Curry, JoJo Starbuck)
Act Two: "Afternoon of a Faun" (music by Claude Debussy; choreography by Norman Maen; costumes by Nadine Baylis) (John Curry, Cathy Foulkes); "Anything Goes" (music by Leonard Bernstein; choreography by John Curry) (JoJo Starbuck, Jack Courtney, Deborah Page); "Feux follets" (music by Franz Liszt;

choreography by Kenneth MacMillan; costume by Harry Lines) (John Curry); "Night and Day" (pas de deux from *Myth*) ("Masque of Separation" composed by Burt Alcantara; choreography by Robert Cohan; costumes designed by Norberto Chiesa and executed by Suzanne Joelson) (JoJo Starbuck, Jack Courtney); "IceMoves" (music by Hector Berlioz; choreography by Jean-Pierre Bonnefous; costumes by Joe Eula) (John Curry, Cathy Foulkes, Patricia Dodd, Yvonne Brink, Lorna Brown, Deborah Page, Ron Alexander, Jack Courtney)

John Curry's *IceDancing* had previously been produced at Felt Forum from November 21 through December 3, 1978, for twenty-one performances. In mid-December, the ice revue transferred to Broadway at the Minskoff Theatre for an additional sixteen performances.

In reviewing the production at Felt Forum, Anna Kisselgoff in the *New York Times* said Curry was "elegance personified" and the choreographers "allowed the skaters movements that only skaters can do, but have given them the form and structured context of theatrical dance." Choreographer Kenneth MacMillan was "fantastically successful" with "Feux follets." Here was the "dragonfly image" of Curry "darting around in a whirlwind series of turns, many of them low slung." The images were "astounding," and then "without warning" Curry "shot off" the stage through an opening in the scenery and it was "literally as if he had flown out the window."

In 1980, Curry returned to Broadway in the memorable but sadly short-running revival of *Brigadoon* in which he danced the role of Harry Beaton to James Jamieson's re-creation of Agnes de Mille's original choreography.

BALLROOM

Theatre: Majestic Theatre
Opening Date: December 14, 1978; *Closing Date*: March 24, 1979
Performances: 116
Book: Jerome Kass
Lyrics: Alan and Marilyn Bergman
Music: Billy Goldenberg
Based on the 1975 television film *Queen of the Stardust Ballroom* (teleplay by Jerome Kass, lyrics by Alan and Marilyn Bergman, and music by Billy Goldenberg).
Direction and *Choreography*: Michael Bennett (Bob Avian, Co-Choreographer); *Producers*: Michael Bennett (Bob Avian, Bernard Gersten, and Susan MacNair, Co-Producers); *Scenery*: Robin Wagner; *Costumes*: Theoni V. Aldredge; *Lighting*: Tharon Musser; *Musical Direction*: Don Jennings
Cast: The Family—*Dorothy Loudon* (Bea Asher), Sally-Jane Heit (Helen), John Hallow (Jack), Dorothy Danner (Diane), Peter Alzado (David); At the Stardust Ballroom—*Vincent Gardenia* (Alfred Rossi), Lynn Roberts (Marlene), Bernie Knee (Nathan Bricker), Patricia Drylie (Angie), Howard Parker (Johnny "Lightfeet"), Barbara Erwin (Martha), Gene Kelton (Petey), Liz Sheridan (Shirley), Michael Vita (Paul), Danny Carroll ("Scooter"), Jayne Turner (Eleanor), Janet Stewart White (Pauline Krim), Roberta Haze (Faye), Victor Griffin (Harry "the Noodle"), Adriana Keathley (Marie), Mary Ann Niles (Emily), Terry Violino (Mario), Svetlana McLee Grody (Anitra), David Evans (Carl), Mavis Ray (Margaret), Peter Gladke (Thomas), Rudy Tronto (Bill); And—Marilyn Cooper, Dick Corrigan, Bud Fleming, Carol Flemming, Mickey Gunnersen, Alfred Karl, Dorothy D. Lister, John J. Martin, Joe Milan, Frank Pietri; Customers at Bea's Store—Marilyn Cooper (Natalie), Roberta Haze (Estelle), Carol Flemming (Kathy)
The musical was presented in one act.
The action takes place during the present time in the Bronx.

Musical Numbers

"A Terrific Band and a Real Nice Crowd" (Dorothy Loudon); "A Song for Dancing" (Foxtrot) (The Ballroom Regulars; Lynn Roberts and Bernie Knee); "One by One" (The Lindy) (Patricia Drylie, Howard Parker, The Ballroom Regulars; Lynn Roberts and Bernie Knee); "The Dance Montage" (The Ballroom Regulars);

"Dreams" (Lynn Roberts); "Somebody Did Alright for Herself" (Dorothy Loudon); "The Tango Contest" (Mary Ann Niles and Terry Violino, Dorothy Loudon and Vincent Gardenia, Barbara Erwin and Gene Kelton, Svetlana McLee Grody and David Evans, Liz Sheridan and Michael Vita, Mavis Ray and Peter Gladke, Adriana Keathley and Victor Griffin); "Goodnight Is Not Goodbye" (The Ballroom Regulars; Lynn Roberts and Bernie Knee); "I've Been Waiting All My Life" (Rhumba) (The Ballroom Regulars; Bernie Knee); "I Love to Dance" (Dorothy Loudon, Vincent Gardenia); "More of the Same" (Hustle) (The Ballroom Regulars; Lynn Roberts and Bernie Knee); "Fifty Percent" (Dorothy Loudon); "The Stardust Waltz" (The Ballroom Regulars); "I Wish You a Waltz" (Dorothy Loudon)

Michael Bennett's *Ballroom* was the dance musical of the era. Bennett's work for *Promises, Promises* (1968), *Coco* (1969), ***Company***, ***Follies***, ***Seesaw***, and ***A Chorus Line*** offered thrilling and memorable moments, but nothing topped *Ballroom*, his choreographic masterpiece. While ***A Chorus Line*** depicted young Broadway gypsies who live for their art, *Ballroom* focused on mostly sad and lonely middle-aged souls who come alive only at the Stardust Ballroom, which is their portal to a fantasy world where reality never intrudes and where dance is an escape into enchantment. These average people may be waitresses or mailmen by day, but on the Stardust's floor they are neighborhood Nijinskys.

The Stardust is a never-land dominated by a swirling mirror ball that spreads flames of silver across the room and reflects the sparkling lights of the dance hall with its red plush walls and glittering mirrors. While a big band plays upstage with two singers on the bandstand, the Stardust regulars foxtrot, lindy, tango, rhumba, hustle, and waltz. Bennett's six breathtaking dances flowed throughout the evening, and the audience was treated to one show-stopper after another. Here was a dazzling example of old-time Broadway grandeur, and possibly never before or since have there been such masterful variations of ensemble dancing on the musical stage. For "More of the Same," the stage brimmed with couples hustling in unison, and even the costumes seemed choreographed: when the female dancers moved to the same step, each one's dress flared up at the same moment and in the same direction as the others. And in the foxtrot "A Song for Dancing," each couple had their own moment on the dance floor and their steps provided glimpses of their physical and personality quirks as well as their dancing styles. These were flesh-and-blood characters, not amorphous chorus dancers. Bennett's direction and choreography as well as his perfect casting choices of almost two-dozen seasoned Broadway veterans created finely etched mini-characterizations: for example, the moment Harry the "Noodle" (Victor Griffin) is introduced, we feel we know exactly who he is and what he's like as a person and a dancer, and, like the others, he always stood out on the ballroom floor.

The story focused on widowed Bea Asher (Dorothy Loudon) who has resigned herself to an endless stream of empty days working in her thrift shop. Her friend, waitress Angie (Patricia Drylie) urges her to go to the Stardust, and eventually the reluctant Bea gives in, much to the consternation of her family, who feel she should live a quiet life of widowhood ("perpetual purdah," according to T. E. Kalem in *Time*). At the ballroom, Bea meets Al Rossi (Vincent Gardenia) and the lonely twosome find a new life with one another. When Alfred reveals he's in a loveless marriage but can never consider divorce, Bea decides that 50 percent is 100 percent more of what she had before she met him.

Unfortunately, Jerome Kass's book got in the way of the evening, and Bennett didn't find a successful means of reducing the book to a skeletal framework that emphasized the ballroom scenes and played down the non-ballroom ones. Bea's family was a collection of clichéd joy-killing bores and they were allotted far too much stage time (one wanted to tell the show's creators, we get it, we get it, we *understand* that the family members are selfish and self-centered). In the memorable 1956 film *All That Heaven Allows*, the main character shared Bea's suffocating widowhood and loneliness, and director Douglas Sirk came upon an ingenious image to quickly telegraph her plight: her children give her a television for Christmas and she sits alone in her semi-darkened living room, stares at the unplugged set, and sees her reflection imprisoned on the blank screen. More and more musicals such as ***Company***, ***Follies***, ***A Chorus Line***, ***Chicago***, and ***Pacific Overtures*** had minimal books that formed the glue to hold together their concepts, songs, dances, and staging techniques. Books supplied the functional framework to pull the plot together, but the shows themselves no longer required lengthy expository book scenes, which slowed down the action.

Unfortunately, the dreary non-ballroom scenes were made even worse because of a few equally doleful and tiresome book songs. Numbers like Bea's "Somebody Did All Right for Herself" and "Fifty Percent" were the kind of rambling, groan-inducing songs one expected to hear in the most ordinary kind of musical, and *Ballroom* was too good for this kind of triteness. As the musical traveled to Broadway, Bennett eliminated more and more of the book songs, but unfortunately didn't go all the way by relegating the musical numbers to only those in the ballroom scenes. The daily lives of the characters in *Ballroom* were devoid of song and dance, and only at night in the ballroom did they become alive, and the song placement should have reflected this. Lyricists Alan and Marilyn Bergman and composer Billy Goldenberg created perfect pastiche for the ballroom sequences, songs that sometimes lightly commented on the action but didn't dwell on it ("Dreams," "I've Been Waiting All My Life," and "I Wish You a Waltz"). The team was criticized for what some felt was a lackluster score, but Goldenberg's music was indeed made for dancing, and the Bergmans' ballroom lyrics had just the right touch of glossiness and occasional poignancy.

If Loudon and the dancers were perfectly cast, one pivotal role was not. Unfortunately, the interesting character actor Vincent Gardenia (who later shined in the 1987 film *Moonstruck*) didn't quite have the required charm that the role required and seemed out of his element in a musical. Because the evening included book songs, it's telling that he was given little to sing; his character had at least two solos during the tryout and New York previews, but they were cut before opening night.

Martin Gottfried in *Cue* said that despite its faults *Ballroom* was "one of the most beautiful and sizable and skillfully made musicals in recent years" and the musical numbers were "simply stunning" in "size and accomplishment" and were "the most beautiful stage images." John Simon in *New York* couldn't recall a Broadway show in which "every part" was "so perfectly cast" and "devastatingly right" and he said the "flawless cast is worthy of the Nobel Prize for chemistry." Bennett's dances were "delightful" and "perfectly poised on the razor's edge between what the Stardust's clients could manage and only what a shrewd, skillful choreographer could create."

Kalem said the dances were the evening's "glory" and Bennett was a "choreographic Picasso" who created a "stage canvas for a riot of disciplined motion." The musical was "rejuvenating enchantment" and may have been "what Ponce de Leon was looking for." But Kalem disliked the score, and suggested the production should have used standard songs rather than new ones. In *Time*'s annual survey of the theatre year's best productions, *Ballroom* was hailed as "an entrancing musical with a rare grace note of affection." Jack Kroll in *Newsweek* said Bennett had "no peer" and his dances were "engaging and rousing, and he establishes the whirling rhythm as a kind of human dynamo, continually spinning voltage into the lives of the characters."

Howard Kissel in *Women's Wear Daily* stated that *Ballroom* was "a major achievement in widening our understanding of the potential of musical theatre," and he noted that Bennett's "masterful" dances offered "marvelous, imaginative patterns" of "genuine theatre choreography" that created "characters and drama." John Beaufort in the *Christian Science Monitor* said Bennett filled the stage with "montages of graceful movement" in which his "marvelously responsive" dancers spun and glided across the stage. Clive Barnes in the *New York Post* noted that the "trivial" story was hardly worth an answer by "Dear Abby," but he liked the Bergmans' "agreeably literate" lyrics and the "agreeably unmemorable" but "cheerful pastiche" of Goldenberg's score. He praised Bennett, who could "adroitly place dances in their dramatic context," and concluded that "from start to finish" the musical had the "ephemeral but great grace of style" that brought "class" to Broadway.

Edwin Wilson in the *Wall Street Journal* noted that "no such ballroom actually exists—in the Bronx or anywhere else" and was thus a ballroom of the imagination. And so Bennett "magically created" a "fantasy world" where couples "swirl" to "lively" and "enchanting" dances. Dennis Cunningham on WCBSTV2 suggested the story was too light to support the production, but the evening offered "lovely theatrical magic" and for the "vibrant" and "exciting" hustle "More of the Same" the audience "absolutely went berserk."

However, Richard Eder in the *New York Times* found the musical "weak" and suggested the work was "condescending" to its characters. But he singled out "One by One" and "A Song for Dancing," and noted that the latter gave "individuality" to the dancers and created "an autobiography in movement." Douglas Watt in the *New York Daily News* said the production lacked "bite and excitement" and suggested the "spectral figures" danced to "past sounds into a silent future" that "seems to evaporate before our eyes."

Ballroom couldn't overcome the mixed reviews, and closed after three months at a loss of almost \$2.5 million (even its last week did poor business; *Variety* reported that at capacity the musical could have taken in \$268,486, but instead brought in just \$118,791 or 66.4 percent of its gross potential).

During the tryout and New York preview period, the following songs were cut: "Who Gave You Permission?," "The Job Application," and "If Anyone Had Told Me" (all for Bea), and "Like Her" and "How Can I Tell Her?" (for Alfred). For some New York preview performances, the musical was presented with an intermission.

The script was published in paperback by Samuel French in 1981, and the cast recording was released by Columbia Records (LP # 35762) and later issued on CD by Sony Broadway (# SK-35762). The collection *Lost in Boston IV* (Varese Sarabande CD # VSD-5768) includes the cut songs "Who Gave You Permission?" and "The Job Application" and one number that seems to have been dropped in preproduction ("Suddenly There's You"), all sung by Karen Morrow. The collection *Forgotten Broadway Volume II* (unnamed company, LP # T-102) includes "The Job Application" (sung by Georgia Brown).

During summer 1979, the musical was revived for a five-city tour that starred Janis Paige and Forrest Tucker as well as a few cast members from the Broadway production (Patricia Drylie, Howard Parker, Gene Kelton, Liz Sheridan, Victor Griffin, and Mavis Ray); Parker and Drusilla Davis reproduced the direction and choreography originally created by Bennett and Bob Avian. The revival was presented in two acts, with an intermission between "I Love to Dance" and "More of the Same." A later California production with Tyne Daly and Charles Durning (who had created the role of Al in the 1975 telefilm [see below] included "Who Gave You Permission?" As *Queen of the Stardust Ballroom*, a revised Chicago revival reinstated the musical's original television title and its downbeat ending (of Bea's sudden death). The production starred Louisa Flaningam and Joel Hatch, and included five new songs ("The Stardust Ballroom," "Family Counsel," "A Big Mistake," "Call Me a Fool," and "The Stardust Waltz"), three reinstated songs ("Who Gave You Permission?," "The Job Application," and "Suddenly There's You"), and nine from the original production ("A Terrific Band and a Real Nice Crowd," "A Song for Dancing," "Dreams," "Somebody Did Alright for Herself," "I Wish You a Waltz," "Goodnight Is Not Goodbye," "I've Been Waiting All My Life," "I Love to Dance," and "Fifty Percent").

The musical was based on the CBS made-for-television movie *Queen of the Stardust Ballroom*, which was telecast on February 13, 1975, with Maureen Stapleton and Charles Durning in the leading roles; others in the cast were big-band singer Martha Tilton and character actors Gil Lamb and Charlotte Rae. The production was directed by Sam O'Steen and choreographed by Marge Champion. As they did for the later Broadway production, Jerome Kass wrote the script, Alan and Marilyn Bergman the lyrics, and Billy Goldenberg the music. The songs heard in this version were: "Who Gave You Permission?," "Call Me a Fool," "Pennies and Dreams," "Suddenly There's You," and "I Love to Dance." For Broadway, "Who Gave You Permission?" had been deleted during the tryout and "Suddenly There's You" seems to have been considered for the original stage version but dropped during preproduction (but as noted above, it was heard in the Chicago revival). The film of the television version was released on videocassette (Prism Entertainment # 1204) and DVD (VCI Video).

Awards

Tony Awards and Nominations: Best Musical (*Ballroom*); Best Leading Actor in a Musical (Vincent Gardenia); Best Leading Actress in a Musical (Dorothy Loudon); Best Director (Michael Bennett); Best Book (Jerome Kass); Best Costume Designer (Theoni V. Aldredge); Best Lighting Designer (Tharon Musser); Best Choreographer (**Michael Bennett** and **Bob Avian**)

A BROADWAY MUSICAL

"A Musical about a Broadway Musical"

Theatre: Lunt-Fontanne Theatre
Opening Date: December 21, 1978; *Closing Date*: December 21, 1978
Performances: 1
Book: William F. Brown
Lyrics: Lee Adams
Music: Charles Strouse
Direction and *Choreography*: Not credited, but the program cited that the production was "supervised" by Gower Champion and that the co-choreographer was George Bunt; *Producers*: Norman Kean and Garth H. Drabinsky; *Scenery*: Peter Wexler; *Costumes*: Randy Barcelo; *Lighting*: John De Santis; *Musical Direction*: Kevin Farrell
Cast: Nate Barnett (Policeman, Nathaniel), Irving Allen Lee (James Lincoln), Warren Berlinger (Eddie Bell), Larry Riley (Lonnie Paul), Jackee Harry (Melinda Bernard), Alan Weeks (Stan Howard), Patti Karr (Maggie

Simpson), Gwyda Donhowe (Stephanie Bell), Christina Kumi Kimball (Kumi-Kumi); "Smoke and Fire" Back-Up Singers: Maris Clement, Loretta Devine, and Jackee Harry; Richie Taylor's Lawyers: Sydney Anderson and Michael Gallagher; Jo Ann Ogawa (Auditionee One, Richie's Secretary), Prudence Darby (Auditionee Two), Maggy Gorrill (Auditionee Three), Sharon Ferrol (Auditionee Four), Gwen Arment (Rehearsal Pianist), Larry Marshall (Richie Taylor), Anne Francine (Shirley Wolfe); Theatre Party Associates: Sydney Anderson, Maris Clement, and Loretta Devine; Albert Stephenson (Male Dancer One, Big Jake), Robert Melvin (Male Dancer Two, Junior), Martin Rabbett (Male Dancer Three, Jake), Tiger Haynes (Sylvester Lee), Marilynn Winbush (Flower Delivery Girl), Reggie Jackson (Western Union Delivery Man, Louis); Ensemble: Sydney Anderson, Gwen Arment, Nate Barnett, Maris Clement, Prudence Darby, Don Edward Detrick, Loretta Devine, Sharon Ferrol, Michael Gallagher, Scott Geralds, Maggy Gorrill, Jackee Harry, Leon Jackson, Reggie Jackson, Carleton Jones, Christina Kumi-Kimball, Michael Kubala, Robert Melvin, Jo Ann Ogawa, Karen Paskow, Martin Rabbett, Albert Stephenson, Marilynn Winbush, Brad Witsger

The musical was presented in two acts.

The action takes place during the past year in New York City and Washington, D.C.

Musical Numbers

Act One: "Broadway, Broadway" (New Kids in Town, Nate Barnett, Irving Allen Lee); "A Broadway Musical" (Warren Berlinger, Irving Allen Lee, Larry Riley, Gwyda Donhowe, Alan Weeks, Patti Karr, Ensemble); "I Hurry Home to You" (Warren Berlinger, Gwyda Donhowe); "Smoke and Fire" (Alan Weeks, Christina Kumi Kimball, Irving Allen Lee, Ensemble); "Lawyers" (Warren Berlinger, Gwyda Donhowe, Sydney Anderson, Michael Gallagher); "Yenta Power" (Anne Francine, Sydney Anderson, Maris Clement, Loretta Devine); "Let Me Sing My Song" (Larry Marshall); "A Broadway Musical" (Warren Berlinger, Gwyda Donhowe, Irving Allen Lee, Anne Francine, Patti Karr, Larry Riley, Alan Weeks, Ensemble)

Act Two: "The 1934 Hot Chocolate Jazz Babies Revue" (Tiger Haynes, Irving Allen Lee, Members of the Ensemble); "Let Me Sing My Song" (reprise) (Larry Marshall, Friends); "It's Time for a Cheer-Up Song" (Alan Weeks, Patti Karr, Larry Riley, Irving Allen Lee); "You Gotta Have Dancing" (Patti Karr, Irving Allen Lee, Ensemble); "What You Go Through" (Gwyda Donhowe, Warren Berlinger); "Don't Tell Me" (Warren Berlinger); "Together" (Irving Allen Lee, Warren Berlinger, Staff); "Together" (reprise) (Company); "A Broadway Musical" (reprise) (Company)

A Broadway Musical was a failed attempt to spoof Broadway musicals created by whites that are about blacks. When the musical began its unusual tryout (for more information, see below), it employed a black director-choreographer (George Faison), but ironically he was soon replaced by Gower Champion. The show was clearly in trouble during its tryout, and despite major creative and cast changes, book rewriting, and the tossing of ten songs, the musical was a huge failure and along with ***Gorey Stories*** and ***The Utter Glory of Morrissey Hall*** was one of the season's three single-performance flops.

The plot centered on director Eddie Bell (Warren Berlinger) who acquires the rights to produce a musical based on *The Final Point*, a serious book about how basketball exploits blacks by earnest young black writer James Lincoln (Irving Allen Lee). As *Sneakers*, the musical is produced as a frothy old-fashioned lark with snazzy Las Vegas performer Richie Taylor (Larry Marshall) as its star, but it bombs in Washington during its out-of-town tryout and Taylor quickly returns to Vegas. Lincoln has heretofore been appalled by the destruction of his book, but suddenly volunteers to take over as the star of the mindless musical adaptation (it turns out he has singing and dancing talents we didn't know about) and so the show is a big hit.

There was probably some incisive satire to be found in the nooks and crannies of the plot, but the production failed to capitalize on the inherent strengths of the potential humor. Further, the musical attempted to laugh at various aspects of show business, including theatre party ladies (the song "Yenta Power"); show business lawyers ("Lawyers"); egotistical rock stars; and pushy, steamroller producers.

Douglas Watt in the *New York Daily News* said the book was "impossible" and that the season was still looking for a big hit musical. He noted that the opening night program listed one song that wasn't performed (probably "I Hurry Home to You"), and another ("a love song made up of show-review quotations" [clearly "'Smashing'—*New York Times*," a number cut from ***Applause***]) which was performed but not listed. Like most of the critics, he singled out two numbers: Tiger Haynes's tribute to old-time musicals ("The 1934 Hot Chocolate Jazz Babies Revue") and Patti Karr's salute to show business-styled dances ("You Gotta Have Dancing").

Mel Gussow in the *New York Times* said the musical was less directed and written than "glued together from spare parts" with a "slack" score and "show business wisecracks." The cast performed "with eagerness even as the show sinks" and Champion clearly had tried to "streamline this tired vehicle." But he concluded his review by quoting one of the show's lyrics, which he felt summed up the show: "nada, nothing, zero, zip." Clive Barnes in the *New York Times* suggested the evening was less concerned with the creation of a Broadway musical than about "the making of a Broadway disaster." The "grotesquely wrong-headed venture" had a "major stumbling block" of a book and a "less than inspired" score, and although Champion had done a "skilful job" in trying to pull the show together, he was defeated by the "conceptual banality." Dennis Cunningham on WCBSTV2 found *A Broadway Musical* an "unholy mess" and wryly noted that the show was undoubtedly the first to end by "*celebrating*" a young man who compromises his integrity.

Howard Kissel in *Women's Wear Daily* said the musical lacked a "unifying form" and had been "polished almost to the point of sterility." But "Jazz Babies" was "outstanding" with its "wistful beauty" and was "beautifully realized" by Tiger Haynes, and "You Gotta Have Dancing" had a "delicious sound." John Beaufort in the *Christian Science Monitor* found the book "haphazard" and the score "rather uneven" (but he too praised "Jazz Babies" and "You Gotta Have Dancing"), and noted that while Champion couldn't have been "expected to do the impossible" he nonetheless brought "pizzazz" to the show.

Instead of a traditional out-of-town tryout, the musical opened Off Broadway on October 10, 1978, at the Theatre of the Riverside Church for twenty-six performances (the flyer touted the work as an "exciting" and "brilliant new work"). This production was directed and choreographed by George Faison, and the cast included Julius La Rosa, Helen Gallagher, and Ron Ferrell, who were respectively succeeded by Warren Berlinger, Patti Karr, and Irving Allen Lee for Broadway. Songs heard in this version that were cut for Broadway included: "Here in the *Playbill*," "You Only Get One Chance," "A Wrong Song," "Who Says You Always Have to Be Happy?," "Who Am I," "Out-A-Town," "Jokes," "Goin' to Broadway," "I've Been in Those Shoes," and "Be Like a Basketball and Bounce Right Back."

The Broadway preview programs didn't cite a director or choreographer (but listed George Bunt as co-choreographer); for the opening night program, Champion was credited as the production's supervisor. As mentioned, "'Smashing'—*New York Times*" was almost certainly performed (by Warren Berlinger and Gwyda Donhowe in the second act), but in his collection *Charles Sings Strouse* (PS Classics Records CD # PS-646), the composer notes that the song "never found a show" because it was cut from *Applause* and was only "considered" for *A Broadway Musical*. The collection *Unsung Musicals II* (Varese Sarabande CD # VSD-5564) includes "'Smashing'—*New York Times*" and "Lawyers," and the liner notes indicate "'Smashing'" was heard in *A Broadway Musical*.

Norman Kean was the musical's coproducer, and his wife, Gwyda Donhowe, was one of the leads. In 1988, they came to tragic ends when he stabbed her to death and then jumped from the roof of their apartment building. The show's other coproducer, Garth Drabinsky, was later convicted and sentenced to prison for fraud and forgery and was the subject of the 2012 documentary *Show Stopper*: *The Theatrical Life of Garth Drabinsky*.

A Chorus Line began a mini-trend of musicals that looked at shows from behind the scenes. Besides *A Broadway Musical*, Champion's final show, *42nd Street* (1980) as well as *Musical Chairs* and *A Backers' Audition* (both 1982) explored such territory, and of course Richard Rodgers and Oscar Hammerstein II's *Me and Juliet* had earlier dealt with the subject.

MONTEITH AND RAND

Theatre: Booth Theatre
Opening Date: January 2, 1979; *Closing Date*: March 10, 1979
Performances: 79
Material: John Monteith and Suzanne Rand
Producer: James Lipton Productions; *Costumes*: Donald Brooks; *Lighting*: Gilbert V. Hemsley Jr.
Cast: John Monteith, Suzanne Rand, Bill-Boy Russell

The revue was presented in two acts.

The improvisational comedy team of John Monteith and Suzanne Rand (with an assist from Bill-Boy Russell) presented their brand of topical and improvisational humor, some of it prepared in advance and some created on the spot. The team had previously performed Off Off Broadway the previous summer at Theatre East on July 25, 1978, for thirty-one performances.

Edwin Wilson in the *Wall Street Journal* said you'd have to go back to Mike Nichols and Elaine May to find a comic duo with whom Monteith and Rand could be compared; Gerald Clarke in *Time* found the team "the funniest" and "most inventive to come along in years, recalling the days of Nichols and May"; and Clive Barnes in the *New York Post* said he'd like a journalism award "for having written this entire [review] without mentioning" Nichols and May.

The critics reported that about two-thirds of the evening consisted of written sketches, and about a third were improvisations based on suggestions from the audience. As for the latter, the team asked the audience to supply the title of a book, from which they would then invent a folk song whose last line would incorporate the book's title. Wilson reported that a member of the audience suggested *The World According to Garp*, and to this end Monteith created a song about a man who owned a guitar as well as an accordion which was shaped like the globe; when the man died, he left his "world accordion to Garp."

In one of the written skits, Rand in Doris Day mode played a stewardess who must land a jet liner (the pilot has died, the copilot has parachuted out, and a bland voice from the control tower [provided by Monteith] gives her helpful flying and landing suggestions despite the fact that she's completely unmechanical and in fact flunked her car-driving exam four times). In another, Monteith tries to pick up a girl (Rand) at a bar by pretending he's gay and wants to go to bed with a woman for the first time (but his ploy backfires, and the girl tells him he's convinced her . . . that she should try a woman, too).

Howard Kissel in *Women's Wear Daily* liked the team's "perverse wit" and "the cogent, dramatic ways they reach weirdly logical conclusions." He suggested that for future performances they plan more time for improvisations because "that seems when they and their audience are in closest rapport."

Richard Eder in the *New York Times* noted that some of Monteith and Rand's material was "fairly slight or obvious," and suggested the Booth Theatre was perhaps too large a venue for their brand of humor. But they made the evening "almost always agreeable, frequently delightful and once in a while brilliant."

THE GRAND TOUR

"THE MUSICAL"

Theatre: Palace Theatre
Opening Date: January 11, 1979; *Closing Date*: March 4, 1979
Performances: 61
Book: Michael Stewart and Mark Bramble
Lyrics and *Music*: Jerry Herman
Based on Franz Werfel's 1944 play *Jacobowsky und der Oberst*, which opened on Broadway during the same year in an adaptation by S. N. Behrman as *Jacobowsky and the Colonel.*
Direction: Gerald Freedman; *Producers*: James M. Nederlander, Diana Shumlin, and Jack Schlissel in association with Carole J. Shorenstein and Stewart F. Lane; *Choreography*: Donald Saddler (Mercedes Ellington, Assistant Choreographer); *Scenery*: Ming Cho Lee; *Costumes*: Theoni V. Aldredge; *Lighting*: Martin Aronstein; *Musical Direction*: Wally Harper
Cast: *Joel Grey* (S. L. Jacobowsky), Grace Keagy (Mme. Bouffier, Peasant Woman, Bride's Mother, Sister Roland), Jack Karcher (Cziesno), Mark Waldrop (Jeannot, Groom), Ron Holgate (Colonel Tadeusz Boleslav Stjerbinsky), Stephen Vinovich (Szabuniewicz), Stan Page (Chauffeur, Peddler), George Reinholt (Captain Mueller), Chevi Colton (Mme. Vauclain, Mme. Manzoni, Bride's Aunt), Florence Lacey (Marianne), Gene Varrone (Conductor, Bride's Father), Travis Hudson (Mme. Marville, Mother Madeleine), Jay Pierce (Stiltwalker, Papa Clairon), Kenneth Kantor (Hugo), Jay Stuart (Man with Flower in His Lapel), Jo Speros (Claudine), Michelle Marshall (Bride), Bob Morrisey (Commissaire of Police); Refugees, Parisians, Train Travelers, Carnival Performers, German Soldiers, Wedding Guests, Sisters of Charity: Bjarne Buchtrup, Carol Dorian, Kenneth Kantor, Jack Karcher, Debra Lyman, Michelle Marshall, Bob Morrisey, Stan Page,

Tina Paul, Jay Pierce, Linda Poser, Theresa Rakov, Paul Solen, Jo Speros, Mark Waldrop, Jeff Veazey, Bonnie Young

The musical was presented in two acts.

The action takes place from June 13 to June 18, 1940, between Paris and the Atlantic Coast of France.

Musical Numbers

Act One: "I'll Be Here Tomorrow" (Joel Grey); "For Poland" (Ron Holgate, Grace Keagy, Parisians); "I Belong Here" (Florence Lacey); "Marianne" (Ron Holgate); "We're Almost There" (Florence Lacey, Stephen Vinovich, Joel Grey, Ron Holgate, Travis Hudson, Gene Varrone, Passengers); "Marianne" (reprise) (Joel Grey); "More and More"/"Less and Less" (Florence Lacey, Ron Holgate); "One Extraordinary Thing" (Joel Grey, Florence Lacey, Ron Holgate, Stephen Vinovich, The Carnival Manzoni); "One Extraordinary Thing" (reprise) (Joel Grey)

Act Two: "Mrs. S. L. Jacobowsky" (Joel Grey); "Wedding Conversation" (Joel Grey, Gene Varrone); "Mazeltov" (Gene Varrone, Wedding Guests); "I Think, I Think" (Ron Holgate); "Domine, Domine" (Sisters of Charity); "For Poland" (reprise) (Florence Lacey, Travis Hudson, Sisters of Charity); "You I Like" (Ron Holgate, Joel Grey); "I Belong Here" (reprise) (Florence Lacey); "I'll Be Here Tomorrow" (reprise) (Joel Grey)

Jerry Herman's *The Grand Tour* was based on the popular 1944 play *Jacobowsky and the Colonel*. Set in occupied France during World War II, the musical dealt with Jacobowsky (Joel Grey), a Jewish refugee who hopes to escape to Britain, and the pompous Polish aristocrat Colonel Stjerbinsky (Ron Holgate) who must deliver important political "papers" to exiled Polish government officials in Britain. Along with the colonel's lady, Marianne (Florence Lacey), the odd couple join forces in a plan to escape from Paris and travel from there to the Atlantic Coast. The "papers" are sewn into Marianne's hat for hiding, but in a fracas with the Germans the hat is lost and Jacobowsky is separated from Stjerbinsky and Marianne. But he miraculously recovers the "papers," is ultimately able to deliver them to the colonel, and the small group finally reaches the wharf where a small boat will take them to Britain and freedom. The vessel, however, has room for just two more passengers, and so Jacobowsky relinquishes his place to Marianne. She and Stjerbinksy head for Britain, and Jacobowsky, truly a Wandering Jew all alone in Nazi-occupied France, is nonetheless certain that somehow he'll be around for "tomorrow."

The musical had definite possibilities because the basic story had substance, the time and setting were colorful and dramatic, and the yin and yang of the two major characters promised conflict, albeit of the sitcom kind. Unfortunately, the libretto offered a grand tour of highlights from other musicals, and so the evening overflowed with filler material of the déjà vu variety. There was a carnival/circus sequence (which always seems to pop up in musicals set in France, such as *Fanny* [1954], *Carnival!* [1961], and the current season's ***King of Hearts***); in another vignette, Jacobowsky becomes involved in a Jewish wedding, and naturally the wedding and the song "Mazeltov" were reminiscent of *Fiddler on the Roof*; and finally there was a scene in a convent where nuns sang "Domine, Domine," and this of course brought to mind *The Sound of Music*. Even the all-important "papers" seemed something out of old-hat melodrama.

The book was obvious and overly familiar, and unfortunately Herman's pleasant but generally ordinary score was by-the-numbers and only once soared into musical theatre nirvana. Jacobowsky's "I'll Be Here Tomorrow" was a typical anthem of hope and defiance against overpowering odds; Stjerbinsky's "Marianne" offered a lovely melody that was unfortunately marred by a flowery lyric of purple prose; and, in general, the songs never rose above the functional. But toward the end of the evening, Jacobowsky and the colonel realize that despite their differences they have much in common and thus reach an understanding of, and an admiration for, the other and extol their unlikely friendship in the sweeping and thrilling "You I Like," which exploded into a joyful and jaunty polka. If the entire score had matched this inspired moment, *The Grand Tour* might have had a chance. As it was, the musical received mixed reviews and with some forcing managed to struggle along for six weeks before closing at an enormous loss.

Richard Eder in the *New York Times* said the "patchwork" evening gave the effect of "first-rate talents working at their occasional second-best, and having occasional third thoughts about it." The "central weakness" of the production was its "lack of conviction, the sense of tinkering, of putting in a bit of this and a bit of that because some of it is bound to work." And like a few other critics, Eder found fault with the cast. Grey's performance was sometimes "self-indulgent" and he had "things his own way just a bit too often," and at one point Lacey didn't manage to hold her own in a duet with Holgate. Clive Barnes in the *New York Post* said Lacey's character was "little more than an ingénue," and Howard Kissel in *Women's Wear Daily* found her voice "odd" because it wasn't "rich enough" for "old-fashioned legit" and "not brassy enough for contemporary musicals," and Grey spent too much time "being winsome and pathetic." Even the always enjoyable and reliable Ron Holgate annoyed at least one reviewer: Jack Kroll in *Newsweek* said he was allowed "to pulverize the brave but bombastic colonel into the noisiest of Polish jokes" and his strong bass-baritone was sometimes "almost apoplectic with machismo."

Although Kroll praised Grey's "total professionalism," he nonetheless felt his Jacobowsky was "too brittle and cuddly," and Dennis Cunningham on WCBSTV2 stated Grey was "not a star," had little "stage presence," and "if he were not center stage in a spotlight I'm sure you'd have a hard time finding him." Cunningham found his "boyish cuteness" both "annoying" and "embarrassing" and said Grey's true métier was as a character actor, not as a leading man.

Douglas Watt in the *New York Daily News* suggested there was nothing to really "dislike" about *The Grand Tour*. But the musical had an "insistent mediocrity that seems to make it such an awful waste of everybody's time." Barnes said the show was "a grand mess" but "an oddly successful mess," and he praised Herman's "tuneful and effective" score and said Grey was "brilliant." Kissel said Herman "trivialized" the original source material and reduced it "to a varsity show kind of cuteness," but Edwin Wilson in the *Wall Street Journal* liked the "rousing" songs and said Grey was "perfect" and "the complete musical comedy man." T. E. Kalem in *Time* said Herman's score was "romantic as candlelight," Lacey "appealingly played" Marianne, and Grey had "never done finer work." Kalem mentioned that Grey's "balletic grace" made him (in a good way) "a *Fiddler* on the run"; but the headline of Kroll's review was "*Fiddler* on the Run," and it wasn't a compliment. The critic complained that the would-be spirit of the musical was "fogged with a drabness of concept and tone," and he noted that Grey sang of dreaded knocks on the door at night "with all the terror of someone expecting the Fuller Brush man."

During the tryout and New York preview period, the songs "Two Possibilities," "Having Someone There," "What I Am with You," and "I Want to Live Each Night" were cut. "You I Like" is not the song of the same title from Herman's 1961 Off-Broadway musical *Madame Aphrodite*.

The script was published in paperback by Samuel French in 1980, and the cast album was recorded by RCA Victor Records (LP # JS-35761) and first issued on CD by Fynsworth Alley (# FA-2139/A-53955) and then by Sony/Masterworks Broadway/Arkiv (# 60001). Along with the Fynsworth Alley release, the company also issued a free sampler, not-for-sale CD that included rehearsal versions of the deleted songs "What I Am with You" and "I Want to Live Each Night" and a live performance of the reprise version of "You I Like" (which was performed during the curtain calls). The demo recording (# MPA-921-A) of the score also includes "What I Am with You" and "I Want to Live Each Night."

The musical was later revived by the Jewish Repertory Theatre on June 14, 1988, for a limited engagement.

As *Jacobowsky and the Colonel*, S. N. Behrman's adaptation of Franz Werfel's *Jacobowsky und der Oberst* opened on Broadway in 1944 and played for 417 performances at the Martin Beck (now Al Hirschfeld) Theatre (Oscar Karlweis and Louis Calhern played the two leads), and a 1958 film version was released by Columbia as *Me and the Colonel* with Danny Kaye and Curt (aka Curd) Jurgens (the background music was by George Duning). Herman's musical was the second lyric adaptation of the material. In 1965, the German opera *Jacobowsky und der Oberst* premiered with a score and libretto by Giselher Wolfgang Klebe.

The Grand Tour was also the name of a 1951 drama by Elmer Rice, and it too played at the Martin Beck. The title also served for Richard Maltby Jr., and David Shire's college musical that was produced at Yale University in 1959. Coincidentally, both works dealt with school teachers and their trips to Europe.

Awards

Tony Award Nominations: Best Leading Actor in a Musical (Joel Grey); Best Featured Actor in a Musical (Ron Holgate); Best Score (lyrics and music by Jerry Herman)

SARAVA

Theatre: Mark Hellinger Theatre (during run, the musical transferred to the Broadway Theatre)
Opening Date: January 11, 1979; *Closing Date*: June 17, 1979
Performances: 177
Book and *Lyrics*: N. Richard Nash
Music: Mitch Leigh
Based on the 1966 novel *Dona Flor and Her Two Husbands* by Jorge Amado (which was filmed under the same title in 1978).
Direction and *Choreography*: Rick Atwell; *Producers*: Eugene V. Wolsk (A Mitch Leigh Production); *Scenery* and *Costumes*: Santo Loquasto; *Lighting*: David F. Segal; *Musical Direction*: David Friedman
Cast: P. J. Benjamin (Vahinho), *Tovah Feldshuh* (Flor), Roderick Spencer Sibert (Arigof), Doncharles Manning (Costas), Wilfredo Suarez (Manuel), Jack Neubeck (Dealer, Senhor Baldez), Carol Jean Lewis (Dionisia), Loyd Sannes (Policeman), Gaean Young (Policeman), Betty Walker (Dona Paiva), Randy Graff (Rosalia), Alan Abrams (Antonio), Ken Waller (Priest), Michael Ingram (Teo), David Kottke (Pinho); The People of Bahia: Steve J. Ace, Frank Cruz, Donna Cyrus, Marlene Danielle, Adrienne Frimet, Brenda Garratt, Trudie Green, Jane Judge, David Kottke, Daniel Lorenzo, Doncharles Manning, Jack Neubeck, Thelma Anne Nevitt, Ivson Polk, Wynonna Smith, Michelle Stubbs, Wilfredo Suarez, Ken Waller, Freida Ann Williams, John Leslie Wolfe, Gaetan Young
The musical was presented in two acts.
The action takes place in Bahia, Brazil, "from Carnival to Carnival."

Musical Numbers

Act One: "Sarava" (P. J. Benjamin, Tovah Feldshuh, Others); "Makulele" (Wilfredo Suarez, Doncharles Manning, P. J. Benjamin, Roderick Spencer Sibert); "Vadinho Is Gone" (Tovah Feldshuh); "Hosanna" (Tovah Feldshuh, Others); "Nothing's Missing" (Michael Ingram, Tovah Feldshuh); "Nothing's Missing" (reprise) (Tovah Feldshuh); "I'm Looking for a Man" (Carol Jean Lewis, Others); "A Simple Man" (Michael Ingram); "Viva a Vida" (All)
Act Two: "Muito Bom" (Tovah Feldshuh, Michael Ingram, Others); "Nothing's Missing" (reprise) (Tovah Feldshuh, Michael Ingram); "Play the Queen" (Tovah Feldshuh, P. J. Benjamin, Roderick Spencer Sibert, Others); "Which Way Do I Go?" (Tovah Feldshuh); "Remember" (P. J. Benjamin); "A Simple Man" (reprise) (Michael Ingram); "You Do" (Carol Jean Lewis); "A Single Life" (P. J. Benjamin); "Vadinho Is Gone" (reprise) (Tovah Feldshuh); "Sarava" (reprise) (All)

Sarava cut short its Boston tryout at the Colonial Theatre, and on January 11, 1979, began a long series of Broadway preview performances at the Mark Hellinger Theatre. The production announced at least two official opening dates, but each time cancelled them, continued with the ongoing series of previews, and never officially opened. In the meantime, tickets were sold at full price and the New York City area was flooded with television ads for the musical. At one point, a few of the newspaper critics decided to buy tickets for the show and review it in mid-February, and most of the other critics followed suit about a week later.

Best Plays reported its decision to assign the official opening date as January 11, the day of the first preview, and noted that a spokesman for the musical said the producers had "no objection" if the annual chose January 11 as the "opening date of record." But hardly anyone else agreed as to when (if ever) the musical officially opened, and there was also a disagreement as to the number of the show's "official" performances. Using *Best Plays* as the arbiter in the matter, January 11 seems as good a date as any for the official opening, and the annual's performance total of 177 showings is based on a count of every single New York performance of the show. But if there was disagreement about the show's official opening date and the number of its performances, at least everyone was in happy agreement that the musical permanently closed on June 17, 1979.

The title wasn't the name of the heroine, but instead, like "Shalom" from *Milk and Honey* (1961), the word translated as "hello," "goodbye," or any such pleasantry. The musical was based on Jorge Amado's 1966 novel *Dona Flor and Her Two Husbands* (which was later filmed in 1978). It some respects the story was a variation of Noel Coward's *Blithe Spirit* in its marital mix-ups when Dona Flor (Tovah Feldshuh) must contend with her staid and sexually uninteresting new husband, the pharmacist Teo (Michael Ingram), and the ghost of her sexually charged deceased spouse, Vadinho (P. J. Benjamin). Not all that much happened during the evening, and while the book, lyrics, and score were decidedly average, the musical was pleasant enough with lush and flowery summer garden décor and lively choreography.

Clive Barnes in the *New York Times* suggested the producers should have used machine guns ("or at least employed program ladies well-versed in karate") to keep the critics from reviewing the "vulgar" and "tacky" musical with a book as "obvious as a TV sit-com" and a score "slightly to the West of Xavier Cugat." As for Tovah Feldshuh, she was "beautiful" and had a "lovely" singing voice, but she was perhaps "just a little smug." Douglas Watt in the *New York Daily News* said the "commonplace" book, lyrics, and score were "hackwork" and lacked "inner energy." But Santo Loquasto's décor was "visually stunning," David F. Segal's lighting was romantic, and Rick Atwell did a "credible" job of direction and his choreography was "brisk." But the musical's few strengths were unfortunately "like a shine on an ill-made pair of boots."

John Beaufort in the *Christian Science Monitor* said the "florid extravaganza" and "overblown entertainment" offered some "charming" songs and he noted Loquasto had "festooned the stage with crepe blossoms, woven abstracts, and a huge, delicately tinted petal" which screened the onstage orchestra. But the evening was nonetheless "ponderous and rather trashy." Edwin Wilson in the *Wall Street Journal* praised the "lavish" production and said the score offered many "tuneful" songs; but the lyrics were "predictable," the show wavered between "the serious and the comic," and sometimes the numbers were staged "with the self-conscious seriousness of grand opera."

Dennis Cunningham on WCBSTV2 was unimpressed with the leads. For all his "bumping and grinding and leering," P. J. Benjamin didn't come across as "rambunctiously sexy," and Feldshuh had "minimal talent" and "would do well to start all over again in summer stock and try to master basic acting." But Joel Siegel on WABCTV7 found Benjamin "slinky and sexy" and said Feldshuh was "stunningly beautiful" and had "a strong singing voice" (and noted that while she looked like a young Lauren Bacall, she danced like Humphrey Bogart).

Richard Eder in the *New York Times* said the first two-thirds of the musical offered "specific delights" and "held together with intelligence and integrity." Its story may have been purposely far-fetched, but the plot was handled with comedy and poignancy. And then suddenly "everything" went "wrong" and the evening "inflated to tragedy": there was a "dreadful, hyped-up" song ("Which Way Do I Go?"), the characters sang with "the desperation of grand opera," and the music "surged pompously" with "swollen aria."

During the tryout, Fran Stevens was succeeded by Betty Walker and the following songs were cut: "Take Love," "Condomble," and "We're Alive."

Roadshow Records had originally been scheduled to record the cast album, but the production went unrecorded. However, Roadshow released an LP single with two songs from the score in disco versions, the title number and "You Do" (LP # YD-11455).

Awards

Tony Award Nomination: Best Leading Actress in a Musical (Tovah Feldshuh)

THEY'RE PLAYING OUR SONG

Theatre: Imperial Theatre
Opening Date: February 11, 1979; *Closing Date*: September 6, 1981
Performances: 1,082
Book: Neil Simon
Lyrics: Carole Bayer Sager
Music: Marvin Hamlisch
Direction: Robert Moore; *Producer*: Emanuel Azenberg; *Choreography*: Patricia Birch; *Scenery and Projections*: Douglas W. Schmidt; *Costumes*: Ann Roth; *Lighting*: Tharon Musser; *Musical Direction*: Larry Blank

Cast: Robert Klein (Vernon Gersch), Lucie Arnaz (Sonia Walsk); The Voices of Vernon Gersch: Wayne Mattson, Andy Roth, Greg Zadkov; The Voices of Sonia Walsk: Helen Castillo, Celia Celnik Matthau, Debbie Shapiro; Philip Cusack (The Voice of Phil the Engineer)
The musical was presented in two acts.
The action takes place during the present time in New York City, Long Island, and Los Angeles.

Musical Numbers

Act One: "Fallin'" (Robert Klein); "God, He's Such a Genius" (Lucie Arnaz); "Workin' It Out" (Robert Klein, Lucie Arnaz, The Voices of Sonia Walsk, The Voices of Vernon Gersch); "If He (She) Really Knew Me" (Lucie Arnaz, Robert Klein); "They're Playing Our Song" (Robert Klein, Lucie Arnaz); "If She (He) Really Knew Me" (reprise) (Robert Klein, Lucie Arnaz); "Right" (Lucie Arnaz, The Voices of Sonia Walsk, Robert Klein); "Just for Tonight" (Lucie Arnaz)
Act Two: "When You're in My Arms" (Robert Klein, Lucie Arnaz, The Voices of Sonia Walsk, The Voices of Vernon Gersch); "I Still Believe in Love" (Lucie Arnaz); "I Still Believe in Love" (reprise) (Voice of Johnny Mathis); "Fill in the Words" (Robert Klein, The Voices of Vernon Gersch)

They're Playing Our Song was a low-key, minor effort by book writer Neil Simon, lyricist Carole Bayer Sager, and composer Marvin Hamlisch. It was essentially a two-character play with incidental songs that purportedly drew upon the personal and professional relationship of Sager and Hamlisch. For the musical, lyricist Sonia Walsk (Lucie Arnaz) is a rather dizzy kook and composer Vernon Gersch (Robert Klein) is a serious, no-nonsense type. But as numerous show business sagas have taught us, including some by Simon, odd couple types sometimes make the best couples. And so it was with the musical, which occasionally seemed like an expanded sitcom episode that ends on a high cute note before the fade-out, or, in this case, before the final curtain. Each character is given an "endearing" trait (she wears outfits from plays and musicals that have closed, and he incessantly talks into his tape recorder), and there was even the popular sitcom device of an unseen character (in this case, Sonia's former boyfriend Leon).

Although everyone seemed to be working at half-speed, their contributions were nonetheless amiably pleasant. Simon's book moved along at a decent clip, and if the score was from the second drawer, it was almost always soothing in a middle-of-the-road kind of way. Further, while their roles weren't in the least challenging, Klein and Arnaz were always lively and charming. In order to bolster the thin evening, Simon came up with the conceit of using three back-up girl singers and three back-up boy singers to represent the alter egos of Sonia and Vernon. Although Clive Barnes in the *New York Post* thought the device "somewhat tiresome," it ensured that all the songs weren't relegated to solos and duets for the two leading characters, and thus the choral flavorings added some variety to the score. In a hospital scene, there was also some amusing business for Vernon and his "boys" with a toy piano, a gift from Sonia when Vernon has broken his leg.

Although some critics had qualifications about the evening, they were in a generous mood and so the show got by with better reviews than it deserved. T. E. Kalem in *Time* gushed that "great joy has come to Shubert Alley"; Jack Kroll in *Newsweek* hailed the "stylish piece of work" which "exemplifies that sometimes ambiguous thing known as Broadway professionalism"; John Beaufort in the *Christian Science Monitor* crowned the show as "Broadway musical a la mode"; and Edwin Wilson in the *Wall Street Journal* said the evening was "expertly put together." Wilson even felt compelled to explicate how the songs "operate on two levels" as numbers that the characters write together and songs "as they would appear in a regular musical" (this analysis certainly seemed a stretch for the slight and wispy score).

Richard Eder in the *New York Times* felt the evening's occasional "buoyancies" weren't enough "to keep the show afloat"; the work was one of Simon's "weakest" and its "leaden seriousness" in regard to self and mutual analysis was "conducted in clichés that sound like a magazine counseling column." He also noted that the two leading characters "meet cute," "love cute," "work cute," "quarrel cute," "separate cute," and "make up cute."

During the tryout, "If We Give It Time" was deleted.

The script was published in hardback by Random House in 1980, and the original cast album was released by Casablanca Records (LP # NBLP-7141) and later issued on CD (# 826240). There have been at least nine foreign cast albums, including one from the first London production (see below) which was issued by Chopper

Records (LP # CHOP-E-6) and later on CD by That's Entertainment Records (# TER-1035); a 1979 Australian production issued by Festival Records (LP # 37356); and an Italian version (*Stanno Suonando la Nostra Canzone*) released by Polydor Records (LP # 2448-129).

The original London production opened on October 1, 1980, at the Shaftesbury Theatre for a nineteen-month run and starred Tom Conti and Gemma Craven.

Perhaps it was fated that Lucie Arnaz's Broadway debut would take place at the Imperial Theatre. It was at the Imperial where Lucy, Ricky, Fred, and Ethel saw *The Most Happy Fella* in a memorable episode of *I Love Lucy*, and Desi Arnaz's Broadway debut also took place at the Imperial when he appeared in Richard Rodgers and Lorenz Hart's 1939 hit musical *Too Many Girls* (it was during the making of the film version the following year that Desi Arnaz and Lucille Ball first met). Further, William Frawley appeared at the Imperial in the hit 1929 musical *Sons o' Guns* and Vivian Vance was also there in Cole Porter's long-running 1941 musical *Let's Face It!*

Awards

Tony Award Nominations: Best Musical (*They're Playing Our Song*); Best Leading Actor in a Musical (Robert Klein); Best Director of a Musical (Robert Moore); Best Book (Neil Simon)

WHOOPEE!

Theatre: ANTA Theatre
Opening Date: February 14, 1979; *Closing Date*: August 12, 1979
Performances: 204
Book: William Anthony McGuire
Lyrics: Gus Kahn
Music: Walter Donaldson
Based on the short story "The Wreck" by E. J. Rath, Robert Hobart Davis, and possibly G. Howard Watt and the 1923 play *The Nervous Wreck* by Owen Davis.
Direction: Frank Corsaro; *Producers*: Ashton Springer, Frank C. Pierson, and Michael P. Price (Martin Markinson, Joseph Harris, and Donald Tick, Associate Producers); *Choreography*: Dan Siretta (Larry McMillan, Assistant Choreographer); *Scenery*: John Lee Beatty; *Costumes*: David Toser; *Lighting*: Peter M. Ehrhardt; *Musical Direction*: Lynn Crigler
Cast: J. Kevin Scannell (Sheriff Bob), Carol Swarbrick (Mary Custer), Bob Allen (Judson Morgan), Beth Austin (Sally Morgan), Charles Repole (Henry Williams), Franc Luz (Wanenis), Leonard Drum (Black Eagle), Garrett M. Brown (Chester Underwood), Catherine Cox (Harriet Underwood), Peter Boyden (Jerome Underwood), Vic Polizos (Mort), Bill Rowley (Andy McNab), Al Micacchion (Jim), Steven Gelfer (Slim), Rick Pessagno (Jack), Paul M. Elkin (Pete), Brent Saunders (Red Buffalo), Candy Darling (Metape), Susan Stroman (Leslie), Robin Black (Becky), Diane Epstein (Tilly), Teri Corcoran (Olive)
The musical was presented in two acts.
The action takes place in Arizona during the 1920s.

Musical Numbers

Act One: "Let's All Make Whoopee Tonight" (Ensemble); "Makin' Whoopee" (Charles Repole, Bridesmaids); "Go Get 'Im" (J. Kevin Scannell, Ensemble); "Until You Get Somebody Else" (Charles Repole, Beth Austin); "Go Get 'Im" (reprise) (J. Kevin Scannell, Ensemble); "Love Me or Leave Me" (Carol Swarbrick, Charles Repole); "I'm Bringing a Red, Red Rose" (Franc Luz, Beth Austin); "My Baby Just Cares for Me" (Charles Repole, Ensemble); Finaletto: "Go Get 'Im" (reprise) (J. Kevin Scannell, Ensemble)
Act Two: "Out of the Dawn" (Franc Luz, Beth Austin); "The Tapahoe Tap" (Indian Ensemble); "Reaching for Someone" (J. Kevin Scannell); "You" (lyric by Harold Adamson) (Catherine Cox); "Yes, Sir, That's My Baby" (Charles Repole, Ensemble); "Makin' Whoopee" (reprise) (Charles Repole, Company)

Whoopee! was a delightful revival of the 1928 musical, and it deserved a much longer run than its six months on Broadway. Charles Repole was a joy in the Eddie Cantor role, and the merry evening rolled along briskly with its corny but amusing plot, amiable supporting cast, lively dances, and Gus Kahn and Walter Donaldson's tuneful score (among the dancers in the production was future choreographer Susan Stroman).

Set in Arizona (the original production took place in California), the lighthearted plot dealt with hypochondriac Henry Williams (Repole) who is out west for a rest and a cure at a dude ranch with his love-smitten and somewhat battle-ax nurse Mary Custer (Carol Swarbrick). Local Sally Morgan (Beth Austin) is pursued by two men, Sheriff Bob (J. Kevin Scannell) and the Indian Wanenis (Franz Luc), and while she's betrothed to Bob she really loves Wanenis (who is a recent Dartmouth graduate). She gives Henry the impression she wants to meet Bob in a nearby town and persuades him to drive her there, and when Bob discovers the two have disappeared, he assumes they're an item and goes off in hot pursuit. But all ends well, except for Sheriff Bob, who loses the girl; otherwise Sally and Wanenis pair up, as do Henry and Mary.

The musical was given a lavish production by Florenz Ziegfeld when it opened on December 4, 1928, at the New Amsterdam Theatre and played for 379 performances. Besides Cantor, the cast included Ethel Shutta (Mary Custer), Frances Upton (Sally Morgan), Ruth Etting (Leslie Daw), Tamara Geva (Yolandi), Paul Gregory (Wanenis), John Rutherford (Sheriff Bob), and George Olsen and His Band (the latter were succeeded by Paul Whiteman and His Band); and later the Ritz Quartet joined the production. The score included such hit songs as the sly and naughty almost-title-song "Makin' Whoopee," the ballad "I'm Bringing a Red, Red Rose," and the now-classic torch song "Love Me or Leave Me" (in the original, the number was performed by Ruth Etting; her character Leslie Daw was eliminated for the revival and the song was assigned to Mary Custer).

The entertaining Technicolor film version was released in 1930 by Samuel Goldwyn and United Artists, and is a rare opportunity to see a reasonably faithful film version of a hit Broadway musical of the era, and a chance to see Cantor reprise his classic stage role. Other cast members who appeared in the film are Ethel Shutta, Paul Gregory, and John Rutherford (and in the film's chorus is a young Betty Grable); Sally was played by Eleanor Hunt, who had been in the dancing chorus of the stage production. Kahn and Donaldson wrote four new songs for the film ("Cowboys," "A Girl Friend of a Boy Friend of Mine," "Today's the Day," and "My Baby Just Cares for Me"); the latter became the fourth hit song from the classic score. A fifth new song ("I'll Still Belong to You") was written by lyricist Edward Eliscu and composer Nacio Herb Brown. Three songs from the stage version were retained ("Makin' Whoopee," "Stetson," and "The Song of the Setting Sun"). The film is available on DVD by the Warner Brothers Archives Collection.

The Broadway revival was presented at Goodspeed Opera House, East Haddam, Connecticut, for the period June 20–August 26, 1978, with Charles Repole, Catherine Cox, and J. Kevin Scannell. Virginia Seidel was Sally and Bonnie Leaders was Mary, but for the pre-Broadway tryouts in Wilmington and Washington, D.C., and for New York they were succeeded by Beth Austin and Carol Swarbrick. The song "Out of the Dawn" was dropped after the Goodspeed mounting, and "Indian War Dance" became "The Tapahoe Tap."

The program for the Kennedy Center tryout included the article "The American Musical" by Martin Gottfried, and if you happen to have the program and notice that a page is missing, it's not the publisher's error. The missing page included a photograph of Charles Repole as well as one from the original 1928 production with Cantor (in blackface) and Charles Rutherford, and one of the revival's producers insisted that the page be torn out of the programs because he considered Cantor's photograph offensive. (So much for theatre history, and chalk one up for political correctness.)

The revival retained seven songs from the original production ("Makin' Whoopee," "I'm Bringing a Red, Red Rose," "Go Get 'Im," "Until You Get Somebody Else," "Love Me or Leave Me," "Out of the Dawn," and "Reaching for Someone"); one from the film ("My Baby Just Cares for Me"); and two interpolations, "You" (lyric by Harold Adamson and music by Donaldson) and "Yes, Sir, That's My Baby" (by Kahn and Donaldson). "Let's All Make Whoopee Tonight" was probably a new lyric based on a song from the original production, and "The Tapahoe Tap" was a newly created dance number for the revival.

Numbers in the 1928 production that weren't retained for the revival were: "It's a Beautiful Day Today," "Here's to the Girl of My Heart," "Gypsy Joe," "Taps," "Come West, Little Girl, Come West," "The Movietone of the Gypsy Song," "Where the Sunset Meets the Sea," "Gypsy Dance," "Stetson," "The Song of the Setting Sun," "Love Is the Mountain" (a variation of "The Song of the Setting Sun"), "Red Mama," "We'll Keep on Caring," "Mohave War Dance," "Invocation to the Mountain God" (which included three sequences, "The Prayer," "The Dance," and "The Offering of Beauty"), "Hallowe'en Tonight," "Modernistic Ballet in Black," and "Hallowe'en Whoopee Ball."

There was no cast album of the revival, but an archival recording was released as part of the Smithsonian American Musical Theatre Series (RCA Special Products LP # DPM1-0349/R-012). It includes original cast members (Cantor performs "Makin' Whoopee" and Ruth Etting "Love Me or Leave Me") as well as Etting's "I'm Bringing a Red, Red Rose," a number she didn't sing in the production. The album also includes three other songs from the score, "Until You Get Somebody Else," "Come West, Little Girl, Come West," and "Gypsy Song" (aka "Where the Sunset Meets the Sea") as well as various vocal and instrumental versions of these numbers. During the original production, Cantor appeared in a "Singing Waiter" sequence, and sang a number of popular songs not written by Kahn and Donaldson, and three of his recordings are included on the album, "Hungry Women" (lyric by Jack Yellen, music by Milton Ager), "Automobile Horn Song" (lyric and music by Gaskill, Tobias, Bennett, and Carlton), and "I Faw Down an' Go Boom!" (lyric and music by James Brockman, Leonard Stevens, and B. B. Berman). As the "Singing Waiter," Cantor also performed "My Blackbirds Are Bluebirds Now" (lyric by Irving Caesar, music by Cliff Friend), and for the recording Etting sings the number. Both George Olsen and Paul Whiteman's bands are represented on the album, as well as the Ritz Quartet.

In reviewing the revival, Richard Eder in the *New York Times* said the production was "a frequent delight but not an unmitigated one." Although he complained that the evening occasionally dragged and the jokes were wheezy, he praised Repole, who was the "dynamic improbability that keeps the whole creaky plot going." Repole's diminutive frame was a perfect match for the stalwart Swarbrick, and when she did a bump and grind he was "blown off the stage altogether." Further, his "enlivening" dances found him in "desperate glee" as he darted among the chorus dancers, and when he performed a soft-shoe tap he glowed with "a kind of delighted surprise" that he could do it.

Clive Barnes in the *New York Post* proclaimed that "nostalgia got a giant-sized shot in the arm" with *Whoopee!* because it was one of the "happiest" events on Broadway with "marvelous" staging and a "fantastic" performance by Repole. T. E. Kalem in *Time* said the show was "transparently mindless and totally exhilarating" with dances that "blaze across the stage like prairie fire." The "endearingly cuddlesome" Repole moved with "the erratic precision of a broken watch spring" and he danced in "the style that Walter Mitty's dreams are made of."

But Howard Kissel in *Women's Wear Daily* stated that of all the musicals he'd seen at Goodspeed, *Whoopee!* was the only one he "genuinely disliked." The book was "silly," the performances "sillier," and Repole was devoid of "charisma" (he also noted that what must have been "cloying" with Cantor was "unbearable" with Repole). Douglas Watt in the *New York Daily News* said the production and performances were of "stock-company quality" and so *Whoopee!* was "nothing to shout about." He commented that Repole's role was now stripped of the old blackface gags, Jewish gags, and probably most of the Indian gags, and Repole was "simply not a strong enough performer to carry" the show. But Dan Siretta's dances provided the evening's "livelier moments." (Watt referred to a song titled "That Certain Party," which wasn't listed in the program.)

A revised post-Broadway production of the revival briefly toured as *Makin' Whoopee!* It added one song from the original 1928 version ("Come West, Little Girl, Come West") and one ("My Heart Is Just a Gypsy") of unknown origin. The tour's cast included Ted Pritchard, Mamie Van Doren, Imogene Coca, and King Donovan.

Awards

Tony Award Nomination: Best Choreography (Dan Siretta)

COQUELICO

Theatre: 22 Steps Theatre
Opening Date: February 22, 1979; *Closing Date*: April 1, 1979
Performances: 45
Text: Josef Svoboda
Music: O. F. Korte

Direction: Josef Svoboda; *Producers*: Olivier Coquelin in cooperation with Michael Butler, Gene Kelly, and Alan Jay Lerner (A National Theatre of Prague Production); *Choreography*: Karel Vrtiska; *Scenery* and *Costumes*: Josef Svoboda; *Musical Direction*: O. F. Korte; Film written and directed by Evald Schorm
Cast: Members of the National Theatre of Prague (*Note*: There was no official program except a souvenir program, which didn't list the individual names of cast members.)
The evening was presented in two acts.

Coquelico was a ninety-minute multimedia theatre piece imported from the National Theatre of Prague, Czechoslovakia, for a limited run of six weeks. The work used a mixture of filmed and live performers who enacted a charade that featured two clowns and their adventures, including their pursuit of the goddess Venus while they in turn are pursued by a devil figure. What made the evening unusual was that upstage were three large movie screens a total of forty-four feet in width that resembled the cyclorama-like screens of the Cinerama and CinemaScope movies of the 1950s. The audience watched performers in the film, and, in sync with the movie, the live actors who portrayed the characters on screen emerged from between slits in the panels and gave the effect that the movie had come to life. For example, the screen showed two large eggs floating down a river, from which burst two clowns, and then suddenly the two clowns emerged from a slit in the screen and tumbled onto the stage. The effect was startling and eminently theatrical, and although a critic or two hoped that traditional opera and ballet companies might appropriate some of these techniques to enhance their presentations, nothing seems to have ever come from the experiment.

The work was also known as *The Enchanted Circus*, and John Rockwell in the *New York Times* explained that the word *coquelicot* meant *poppy* in French and that the plot did indeed include a poppy in its narrative. However, the New York producer of *Coquelico* was named Olivier Coquelin, and so Rockwell noted that "suspicions do arise" about that title. But a spokesman for the production "flatly denied" any connection between the title of the show and the producer's last name. Rockwell said composer O. F. Korte's "sound collage" was "adept," and Clive Barnes in the *New York Post* found the background music pleasant. Barnes said the production was "brilliant, fascinating and theatrically unbridled" and commented that the notion of a live performer who is "almost inside a cinematic image is a dizzying concept."

Howard Kissel in *Women's Wear Daily* liked the "delightful" and surreal images of the "loosely plotted" evening, and suggested the work would have been stronger had it employed "a more unifying, compelling narrative structure." But even with its faults, *Coquelico* was a "visual treat." Douglas Watt in the *New York Daily News* felt the "in-and-out affair" had "a vagrant charm that keeps wearing thin," and suggested the work would have been more effective at half its length. But he praised a "grotesque doll dance" and noted the dance's "pennywhistle waltz tune" by Korte was heard throughout the evening along with "musical chestnuts" that also accompanied the action.

The National Theatre of Prague had earlier visited New York on August 3, 1964, when *Laterna Magika* opened at Carnegie Hall for twenty-three performances. Directed by Milos Forman, the production consisted of two pieces, *Tales of Hoffman* and *Variations*, and both combined live and movie action to tell their stories.

Like the Century Theatre on West 46th Street, which had been the site of the fabled nightclub Billy Rose's Diamond Horseshoe, the 450-seat 22 Steps Theatre (so named because one ascended twenty-two steps to reach the theatre, which was on the second floor of a building) had once been a popular nightclub, the Latin Quarter. The venue was located at Broadway and West 47th Street, and after its glory years as a popular night spot, it eventually deteriorated into an X-rated movie house before it was briefly resurrected as a traditional theatre. The venue was generally considered both an Off-Broadway and Broadway house, although it appears that most if not all its productions were under a Middle or Limited Broadway contract (during the era these terms weren't used as formally as they had been in the earlier years of the decade). *Best Plays* considered *Coquelico* a Broadway production, as did the *New York Theatre Critics' Reviews* annual, but *Theatre World* designated it as an Off-Broadway offering.

Coquelico was the first show to open at the 22 Steps, and was followed by ***My Old Friends***. During the following year, the theatre's name was changed to the Princess, and by 1984 it reverted to its original name, the Latin Quarter. The final show to play there was Charles Strouse's *Mayor*, which transferred from Off Broadway in 1985. In 1989, the building that housed the theatre was demolished and today a hotel stands on the site.

SWEENEY TODD, THE DEMON BARBER OF FLEET STREET

"A Musical Thriller"

Theatre: Uris Theatre
Opening Date: March 1, 1979; *Closing Date*: June 29, 1980
Performances: 557
Book: Hugh Wheeler
Lyrics and *Music*: Stephen Sondheim
Based on the 1970 play *Sweeney Todd, the Demon Barber of Fleet Street* by Christopher Bond.
Direction: Harold Prince; *Producers*: Richard Barr, Charles Woodward, Robert Fryer, Mary Lea Johnson, and Martin Richards in association with Dean and Judy Manos (Marc Howard, Associate Producer); *Dance* and *Movement*: Larry Fuller; *Scenery*: Eugene Lee; *Costumes*: Franne Lee; *Lighting*: Ken Billington; *Musical Direction*: Paul Gemignani
Cast: Victor Garber (Anthony Hope), *Len Cariou* (Sweeney Todd), Merle Louise (Beggar Woman), *Angela Lansbury* (Mrs. Lovett), Edmund Lyndeck (Judge Turpin), Jack Eric Williams (The Beadle), Sarah Rice (Johanna), Ken Jennings (Tobias Ragg), Joaquin Romaguera (Pirelli), Robert Ousley (Jonas Fogg); The Company: Duane Bodin, Walter Charles, Carole Doscher, Nancy Eaton, Mary-Pat Green, Cris Groenendaal, Skip Harris, Marthe Ihde, Betsy Joslyn, Nancy Killmer, Frank Kopyc, Spain Logue, Craig Lucas, Pamela McLernon, Duane Morris, Robert Ousley, Richard Warren Pugh, Maggie Task
The musical was presented in two acts.
The action takes place in London during the nineteenth century in London.

Musical Numbers

Act One: "The Ballad of Sweeney Todd" ("Attend the tale of Sweeney Todd") (Company); "No Place Like London" (Victor Garber, Len Cariou, Merle Louise); "The Barber and His Wife" (Len Cariou); "The Worst Pies in London" (Angela Lansbury); "Poor Thing" (Angela Lansbury); "My Friends" (Len Cariou, Angela Lansbury); "The Ballad of Sweeney Todd" ("Lift your razor high, Sweeney!") (Company); "Green Finch and Linnet Bird" (Sarah Rice); "Ah, Miss" (Victor Garber, Merle Louise); "Johanna" ("I'll steal you, Johanna") (Victor Garber); "Pirelli's Miracle Elixir" (Ken Jennings, Len Cariou, Angela Lansbury, Company); "The Contest" (Joaquin Romaguera); "The Ballad of Sweeney Todd" ("Sweeney pondered and Sweeney planned") (Beggar Woman, Company); "Wait" (Angela Lansbury); "The Ballad of Sweeney Todd" ("His hands were quick, his fingers strong") (Three Tenors); "Kiss Me" (Sarah Rice, Victor Garber); "Ladies in Their Sensitivities" (Jack Eric Williams); "Quartet" (Sarah Rice, Victor Garber, Jack Eric Williams, Edmund Lyndeck); "Pretty Women" (Len Cariou, Edmund Lyndeck); "Epiphany" (Len Cariou); "A Little Priest" (Len Cariou, Angela Lansbury)

Act Two: "God, That's Good!" (Ken Jennings, Angela Lansbury, Len Cariou, Merle Louise, Customers); "Johanna" ("I feel you, Johanna") (Victor Garber, Len Cariou, Sarah Rice, Merle Louise); "By the Sea" (Angela Lansbury); "The Ballad of Sweeney Todd" ("Sweeney'd waited too long before—" (Quintet); "Wigmaker" and "Letter Sequence" (Len Cariou, Victor Garber, Quintet); "Not While I'm Around" (Ken Jennings, Angela Lansbury); "Parlor Songs" ("Sweet Polly Plunkett" and "Ding Dong") (Jack Eric Williams, Angela Lansbury); "City on Fire!" (Lunatics, Sarah Rice, Victor Garber); "Final Sequence" (Victor Garber, Merle Louise, Len Cariou, Edmund Lyndeck, Angela Lansbury, Sarah Rice, Ken Jennings); "The Ballad of Sweeney Todd" ("Lift your razor high, Sweeney!") (Company); "The Ballad of Sweeney Todd" ("Attend the tale of Sweeney Todd") (Entire Company)

With *Sweeney Todd, the Demon Barber of Fleet Street*, Stephen Sondheim rounded out the 1970s with his fifth brilliant musical; like ***Company***, ***Follies***, ***A Little Night Music***, and ***Pacific Overtures*** before it, *Sweeney Todd* was exciting and compelling musical theatre, and if ***Follies*** is his masterwork, *Sweeney Todd* is clearly his second-most-important creation. It was virtually sung through, and dealt with revenge, murder, and cannibalism, and of its ten major speaking roles, seven characters are murdered (one is burned alive, one is shot, and five have their throats slit) and an eighth goes insane. Yet despite the horrific story, Sondheim's music was, after ***A Little Night Music***, his most lushly romantic and lyrical score and contained some of the most gorgeous theatre music of the era.

The story of Sweeney Todd has undergone several variations from its earliest beginnings in the nineteenth century, and Sondheim and Hugh Wheeler's adaptation was directly inspired by and used the title of Christopher Bond's 1970 play. The barber Benjamin Barker (Len Cariou), who has taken the alias of Sweeney Todd, returns to London after fifteen years to seek his wife, Lucy, and their daughter, Johanna (Sarah Rice). He was falsely imprisoned on trumped-up charges by the corrupt Judge Turpin (Edmund Lyndeck) and once Todd was incarcerated and transported to Australia, Turpin raped Lucy and raised the beautiful Johanna as his ward and virtual prisoner with the plan of eventually marrying her.

Todd rents a room from Mrs. Lovett (Angela Lansbury), who runs a dilapidated and unprofitable pie shop. She recognizes Todd as the former Benjamin Barker and is clearly attracted to him, and the two form an unholy alliance in which he slices the throats of his enemies while they're in the barber chair and she bakes them into meat pies. Soon Todd's compulsive need for revenge compels him to kill indiscriminately, and so Mrs. Lovett's business booms with her endless supply of fresh and tasty meat. Her assistant is the simple boy Tobias Ragg (Ken Jennings), who is unaware of the ingredients that go into the pies, and while he trusts Mrs. Lovett, he's instinctively leery of Todd. Meanwhile, Mrs. Lovett revels in her newfound success and hopes to buy a seaside cottage where she and Todd can take the sea air in style, but Todd is dead inside and is consumed with killing Turpin and freeing his daughter, who has become enamored of the young sailor Anthony Hope (Victor Garber).

Events come to a head with frightening speed when Todd finally slices the judge's throat but is recognized by one of the local neighborhood characters known as the Beggar Woman (Merle Louise), and so he murders her as well. Tragically, he realizes that the Beggar Woman is Lucy and that Mrs. Lovett knew it all along, and so he dispatches Mrs. Lovett by waltzing her toward the door of one of her huge ovens, pushes her inside, and slams the door. In the meantime, the judge had placed Johanna in an asylum, but with the help of Anthony she escapes when she shoots and kills one of the asylum's officials. Anthony disguises her as a sailor and dispatches her to Mrs. Lovett's shop, where he thinks she'll be safe. When Todd comes upon her and realizes that the "sailor" has witnessed one of his murders, he plans to kill the sailor, too. But the girl escapes and neither she nor Todd ever know they are father and daughter. Overcome by the horror of what has happened, Toby goes mad, and as he sees the grief-stricken Todd kneeling and keening over Lucy's body, the young boy slits Todd's throat.

Broadway had never seen a musical like this, and at the time the unrelenting gore was considered shocking and over the top. And perhaps it was all the more vivid and upsetting to audiences because Sondheim drenched the bloody story in ravishing melody with shimmering ballads and riotous comedy songs. "My Friends" was Todd's nostalgic reunion with his old razors, and his salute to them was as delicate and soothing as a lullaby; Mrs. Lovett's admonishment for him to "Wait" until the right time to kill was a lovely ballad; and her and Tobias's "Not While I'm Around" was another caressing lullaby-like number. Anthony's "Johanna" was an explosion of musical grandeur, one of the most soaring ballads ever heard in lyric theatre, and Johanna's "Green Finch and Linnet Bird" was pure art song. The frisson of the staging of Todd and Turpin's haunting ode to "Pretty Women" was almost unbearable. Turpin sits in the barber chair while Todd shaves him ("the closest I ever gave," he promises), and their haunting duet was an uneasy moment for the audience because it appeared that at any second Todd was going to slit the judge's throat.

The musical also had its lighthearted comedy songs, of which the highlight was "A Little Priest" when Todd and Mrs. Lovett observe that the flavor of the pies reflects the professions of the men who provide the filling (the chimney sweep has dark meat, a piccolo player is piping hot, a politician is oily, and an actor is always overdone); Mrs. Lovett's irresistible fantasy "By the Sea" was pure English music hall; and her description of "The Worst Pies in London" was a whirligig of intricate lyrics and eccentric stage business as she went about her kitchen tasks with a filthy rag to protect her pies from dust, dirt, and the occasional bug.

Sondheim also wrote sweeping choral interludes, including the ominous "The Ballad of Sweeney Todd," which bookended the evening and in snippets was sung throughout the production in different variations (seven times in all); the thundering "City on Fire"; the almost operatic intensity of the "Quartet" and "Final Sequence" interludes; and the expansive opera comique qualities of "Pirelli's Miracle Elixir" and "The Contest"; and "God, That's Good!," the choral salute to Mrs. Lovett's culinary creations.

"Epiphany" was a striking solo in which Todd goes completely mad; he's no longer a man who seeks revenge on those who falsely sentenced him and stole his wife and daughter. Now he wants to obliterate everyone, including the innocent. Len Cariou's chilling and knowing interpretation was staged so that at one point his character seemed to leap out and accuse the audience for its complicity in the wrongs society has inflicted upon him.

Eugene Lee's impressive scenic design represented an industrialized nightmare of the interior of a gargantuan foundry, projections that showed drawings of Victorian London, and a huge backdrop depicting the caste system of "The British Bee Hive." The foundry was like a robotic monster with its clattering machinery, iron beams, stairways, catwalks, cloudy and dirty glass panes, and a cyclorama of corrugated metal that dominated the upstage wall, and for once in the few years of its existence the barn-like Uris (now Gershwin) Theatre had an enormous physical production which matched the vastness of the playhouse's interior.

If the musical had a flaw, it was the special pleading that somehow everyone is responsible for all the evil in the world. There was a bit too much of an accusatory air to the proceedings, and it seemed as though Prince, Wheeler, and Sondheim were trying to surround the musical with the techniques and temperament of living newspaper and agitprop theatre. The somewhat Brechtian outlook occasionally succeeded and sometimes the musical was reminiscent of the tone and style found in Brecht and Kurt Weill's *The Threepenny Opera* (but Sweeney Todd makes Mack the Knife look like the new kid on the block). There was also too much finger-pointing (literally, for during the final chorus of "The Ballad of Sweeney Todd," the company members pointed their fingers at the audience and warned that there were Sweeneys throughout the auditorium).

Richard Eder in the *New York Times* had reservations about the musical, but said it was "necessary to give the dimensions of the event" because the work was "a musical and dramatic achievement" with an "endlessly inventive" and "extraordinary" score and "brilliant and abrasive" lyrics. But he noted the effort to achieve "sardonic social commentary" didn't work, and while this "defect" was a "vital" one, the work was nonetheless "an extraordinary, fascinating, and often ravishingly lovely effort."

Clive Barnes in the *New York Post* said the "sensationally entertaining" musical was "simply great" and Sondheim's score was "the most distinguished to grace Broadway in years." The work was not simply "next month's cocktail party conversation" because "it will be talked about for years." Douglas Watt in the *New York Daily News* stated the musical was a "triumphant occasion" in which Cariou was a "magnificently obsessed" Todd and Lansbury "the grandest, funniest, most bewitching witch of a fairy-tale fright you're ever likely to encounter."

Howard Kissel in *Women's Wear Daily* noted that Sondheim's score was his "most melodic, richest work" and suggested *Sweeney Todd* was "not just a musical—it is total theatre, a brilliant conception and a shattering experience." Edwin Wilson in the *Wall Street Journal* said the score was "probably" Sondheim's "best so far" and the evening's emotions "flooded" the audience with "sights and sounds so powerful that the effect is one usually achieved only in opera." John Beaufort in the *Christian Science Monitor* praised Sondheim's "dazzling achievement of variety and invention" and noted that "by any Broadway standard, this is a triumph of audacious theatricalism."

T. E. Kalem in *Time* was somewhat cool to the production, but noted "most of Stephen Sondheim's score matches the best competition—Stephen Sondheim." He also praised Lee's "broodingly ominous iron-clad set," said Cariou was "like a scion of the House of Usher summoned forth by Poe," and felt Lansbury was "quite wonderful" as "a blowsy pragmatist as wickedly succulent as one of her pies." Jack Kroll in *Newsweek* suggested the musical "slashes the jugular instead of touching the heart." But "in sheer ambition and size" there had never been "a bigger musical on Broadway." He praised Sondheim's "eloquent" score and said that with the array of "sheer theatrical talent" the musical "must be seen by anyone who cares about the gifts and risks of Broadway at its best."

Martin Gottfried in *Saturday Review* said *Sweeney Todd* was a "musical accomplishment of the first order" with a "huge score" of "melodic, even soaring" music and "faultlessly" honed lyrics. But the evening had "no basic theatrical motivation" and "no reason for its existence." It was a "brilliant exercise" that despite its score had nothing "theatrical to accomplish." John Simon in *New York* faulted the score for its contrast of "serious" songs and lighthearted ones that were a "jejune retreat to tried-and-true show-biz razzmatazz." Although the work was "more spectacular and provocative than finished and satisfying," it "has to be seen" because it was a "historic event on Broadway."

During previews, Judge Turpin's version of "Johanna" was cut, but the controversial scene (in which he fantasizes about Johanna and flagellates himself until he ejaculates) has been reinstated for most subsequent productions. The tooth-pulling part of "The Contest" was also cut.

The script was published in hardback and paperback editions by Dodd, Mead & Company in 1979, and includes the cut "Johanna" and tooth-pulling sequences. A later edition that contains background material about the musical was published in hardback and paperback by the Applause Musical Library in 1991. The script is also included in the hardback collection *Four by Sondheim* (published by Applause in 2000). All the lyrics for *Sweeney Todd* are included in Sondheim's hardback collection *Finishing the Hat: Collected Lyrics (1954–1981) with Attendant Comments, Principles, Heresies, Grudges, Whines and Anecdotes*, published in 2010 by Alfred A. Knopf.

The original Broadway cast album was released on a two-LP set and two-CD set by RCA Victor Records (LP # CBL2-3379 and CD # 3379-2-RC), and includes the Judge's version of "Johanna."

During the musical's national tour with Angela Lansbury and George Hearn, a performance at the Dorothy Chandler Pavilion in Los Angeles was taped and shown on the Entertainment Channel on September 12, 1982. This version was released on DVD by Warner Home Video, Inc. (# T-6750).

The musical has been revived eight times in New York. The first of two Broadway revivals was presented at the Circle in the Square Theatre on September 14, 1989, for 189 performances (Bob Gunton and Beth Fowler), and was based on an Off-Broadway production by the York Theatre Company at the Church of the Heavenly Rest on March 31, 1989, which played for a limited engagement of twenty-four performances; and the second Broadway revival opened at the Eugene O'Neill Theatre on November 3, 2005, for 384 showings (Michael Cerveris and Patti LuPone) in a controversial staging by John Doyle, which, like his Broadway revival of ***Company***, eliminated the traditional orchestra and instead used the gimmick in which the performers themselves play the musical instruments (and this time around the musical was set in a mental institution). The cast album of the 2005 production was released on a two-CD set by Nonesuch Records (# 79946-2).

The musical was revived three times by the New York City Opera Company at the New York State Theatre: on October 11, 1984, for thirteen performances (Timothy Nolen/Stanley Wexler and Rosalind Elias/Joyce Castle); on July 29, 1987, for eleven performances (Nolen/Wexler and Marcia Mitzman/Castle); and on March 1, 2004, for twenty-eight performances (Timothy Nolen/Mark Delavan and Elaine Paige/Myrna Paris). The work was also twice presented in concert at Lincoln Center's Avery Fisher Hall with the New York City Philharmonic: on May 4, 2000, for three performances (George Hearn and Patti LuPone) and on March 5, 2014, for five performances (Bryn Terfel and Emma Thompson). The 2000 concert was released on a two-CD set by Philharmonic Special Editions (# NYP-2001/2002), and a later production of the concert was presented with Hearn and LuPone at Davies Symphony Hall in San Francisco and was released on DVD by Image Entertainment (# ID1529EMDVD). The 2014 concert was shown on public television on September 26, 2014.

There have been three major London stagings (in 1980, 1994, and 2012, and the last two won the Olivier Award for Best Musical Revival). The 1980 production opened at the Drury Lane on July 2 and ran for 157 performances, starred Denis Quilley and Sheila Hancock, and included a new second-act musical sequence ("Beggar Woman's Lullaby") for the Beggar Woman (played by Dilys Watling, who had been Broadway's ***Georgy*** a decade earlier). A recording of highlights from the 2012 production was released by First Night Records (CD # CASTCD-113) with Michael Ball and Imelda Staunton.

The 2007 film version was released by Dreamworks Pictures and Warner Brothers Pictures; directed by Tim Burton and with a screenplay by John Logan, the film starred Johnny Depp and Helena Bonham Carter. Although the adaptation didn't include all the musical numbers, it nonetheless captured the mood of the original stage production and Depp made an arresting Todd. Two sequences stood out: "Epiphany" began in Todd's tonsorial parlor and then surreally catapulted him into the streets of London while he glowered at and sang to unseeing passersby; and the film's atmospherically dark look exploded into a Technicolor MGM musical moment when Mrs. Lovett envisions her life "By the Sea" where she and Todd promenade on the boardwalk against the blue sky and sparkling water. The two-CD set was released by Nonesuch Records (# 368572-2), the DVD was issued on a special two-disk edition by Dreamworks Home Entertainment (# 13215), and a lavish hardback published by Titan Books in 2007 includes articles about the musical and the making of the film and offered a generous sampling of photographs from the movie.

Other recordings of the score include a two-CD set of the 1995 Barcelona production *Sweeney Todd, el barber diabolic del carrer Fleet* (Horus Records # CD-25002); a 2012 two-CD German recording which was sung in English (BR Classics # 900316); a two-CD "accompaniment" recording with tracks without vocals and complete tracks with guide vocals (Stage Stars Records # RPT-516); and The Trotter Trio's *Sweeney Todd . . . In Jazz* (Varese Sarabande CD # VSD-5603), an instrumental album with a vocal by Lorraine Feather for one selection ("Not While I'm Around"). There was also a disco version of "The Ballad of Sweeney Todd" released by RCA Records/Red Seals Disco (# PD-11687) and performed by His Master's Fish and featuring Gordon Grody.

Awards

Tony Awards and Nominations: Best Musical (***Sweeney Todd***); Best Leading Actor in a Musical (**Len Cariou**); Best Leading Actress in a Musical (**Angela Lansbury**); Best Director of a Musical (**Harold Prince**); Best Book (**Hugh Wheeler**); Best Score (lyrics and music by **Stephen Sondheim**); Best Scenic Designer (**Eugene Lee**); Best Costume Designer (**Franne Lee**); Best Lighting Designer (Ken Billington)
New York Critics' Circle Award: Best Musical 1978–1979 (***Sweeney Todd***)

SPOKESONG, OR THE COMMON WHEEL

"A New Play with Music and Bicycles"

Theatre: Circle in the Square Theatre
Opening Date: March 15, 1979; *Closing Date*: May 20, 1979
Performances: 77
Play and *Lyrics*: Stewart Parker
Music: Jimmy Kennedy
Direction: Kenneth Frankel; *Producers*: Circle in the Square (Theodore Mann, Director; Paul Libin, Managing Director) and The Long Wharf Theatre (Arvin Brown, Artistic Director; M. Edgar Rosenblum, Executive Director); *Scenery*: Marjorie Kellogg; *Costumes*: Bill Walker; *Lighting*: John McLain; *Musical Direction*: Thomas Fay (Piano)
Cast: *Joseph Maher* (The Trick Cyclist), *John Lithgow* (Frank), *Virginia Vestoff* (Daisy), *Josef Sommer* (Francis), *Maria Tucci* (Kitty), *John Horton* (Julian)
The play with music was presented in two acts.
The action takes place in a bicycle shop in Belfast, Northern Ireland, during the 1970s "and the eighty years preceding."

Musical Numbers

Note: The program didn't identify musical numbers, and the list below is taken from the published text.
Act One: "On a Bicycle Built for Two" (aka "Daisy Belle (Bicycle Built for Two)" (lyric and music by Harry Dacre) (Joseph Maher, Company); "On a Bicycle Built for Two" (reprise) (John Lithgow); "The Parlour Song" (Josef Sommer); "The Cocktail Song" (Joseph Maher); "The Cowboy Song" (Joseph Maher); "On a Bicycle Built for Two" (reprise) (Joseph Maher, Company)
Act Two: "The Music Hall Song" (Joseph Maher, John Lithgow); "The Parlour Song" (reprise) (Joseph Maher); "The Army Song" (Joseph Maher); "The Spinning Song" (lyric by Madelyne Bridges) (John Lithgow); "The Army Song" (reprise) (Joseph Maher); "The Anthem" (Maria Tucci, Josef Sommer); "On a Bicycle Built for Two" (reprise) (Joseph Maher, John Horton)

Stewart Parker's play with music *Spokesong*, or *The Common Wheel* was one of a series of four limited engagements that were produced by the Circle in the Square Company at the Circle in the Square Theatre during its 1978–1979 season (although the fourth actually opened at the beginning of the 1979–1980 season). It was preceded by Nikolai Gogol's *The Inspector General* and George Bernard Shaw's *Man and Superman*, and was followed by Michael Weller's *Loose Ends*. *Spokesong* was coproduced with the Long Wharf Theatre Company, New Haven, Connecticut, where the work had received its American premiere a year earlier on February 2, 1978, with the same cast that later played in the Broadway production. The play's world premiere occurred in 1975 at the Dublin Theatre Festival, and the following year was produced in London.

Part of the play took place in contemporary Ireland and focused on Frank (John Lithgow), who runs a bicycle shop that was founded by his long-dead grandparents Francis (Josef Sommer) and Kitty (Maria Tucci). For Frank, the bicycle is a symbol of a safer and saner world, one that was calmer before the invention of the automobile. The story contrasted the old and new worlds, and throughout the evening there is always the simmering hostility between Ireland and Great Britain. A more personal conflict arises when Frank's leftist half-brother Julian (John Horton) makes a rare visit and comes between Frank and his girlfriend Daisy (Virginia Vestoff).

Part of the play took place eighty years prior to the present, and depicted the lives of Frank's grandparents. Along with the play's two time levels as well as the political and personal conflicts, there was also the added layer of the ambiguous character of The Trick Cyclist (Joseph Maher) who appeared throughout the evening as a kind of master of ceremonies. He performed skits and sang original songs (and was sometimes joined by the other characters), and the use of music added a certain Brechtian flavor to the atmosphere.

Needless to say, the work was not the typically easy and lighthearted Broadway entertainment, and its complicated subject matter and equally challenging presentation probably scared off potential ticket-buyers. If the play had received uniformly rave reviews, perhaps it would have been successful and warranted a transfer for a commercial run. But instead it played out its limited engagement and now seems to have disappeared from the repertory of New York and regional theatre companies.

Clive Barnes in the *New York Post* had seen *Spokesong* a year earlier at Long Wharf, and he noted it was the kind of play that had a life of its own outside the theatre because its ideas became "embedded" in one's mind and its many layers resonated with rich images and metaphors. The cast was "splendid" and Parker's ideas threw off "dramatic tricks with the showy naivety of a guileless conjuror." Barnes's only complaint was that the "essentially oblong" playing space of the Circle in the Square was not the best venue for the drama.

John Beaufort in the *Christian Science Monitor* said the play "touches the heart, stirs the mind, and delights the imagination." Here was a "folk comedy" which dealt with civil strife as well as fond memories of things past, and Parker dealt with these disparate elements "with exceptional skill." Richard Eder in the *New York Times* commented that many plays had been written about the strife between Britain and Ireland, but none of them had "approached so closely an artistic vision of the subject as" *Spokesong*, which was a "small, undoubtedly flawed and cheerfully instructive play." Parker's "vision and wit" were "fresh" and his and Jimmy Kennedy's songs were "delightful."

Edwin Wilson in the *Wall Street Journal* praised the play as "one of the most delightful and thoughtful" of the season, and Christopher Sharp in *Women's Wear Daily* said the work was "more good-natured than good" and was "pleasant without being particularly impressive." As for Douglas Watt in the *New York Daily News*, his headline proclaimed, "*Spokesong* Lets the Air Out of Its Tires," and he apologized that on the morning of March 16 he had "to give the back of one's hand to an Irish play" that was "downright tiring."

Composer Jimmy Kennedy had enjoyed a number of popular song hits over the years, including "Red Sails in the Sunset," "Harbor Lights," "My Prayer," "Isle of Capri," and "South of the Border." All of his and Parker's contributions to the play were original numbers, and only one was interpolated, the 1892 hit song "On a Bicycle Built for Two," aka "Daisy Belle (Bicycle Built for Two)," lyric and music by Harry Dacre.

The play was published in paperback by Samuel French in 1980, and was later included in the paperback collection *Parker Plays*, which was published by Methuen in 2000.

Awards

Tony Award Nomination: Best Featured Actor in a Play (Joseph Maher)

ZOOT SUIT

"A New American Play"

Theatre: Winter Garden Theatre
Opening Date: March 25, 1979; *Closing Date*: April 29, 1979
Performances: 41
Play: Luis Valdez
Direction: Luis Valdez (Jack Bender, Assistant Director); *Musical Sequences* and *Production*: Daniel Valdez; *Producers*: The Shubert Organization, Center Theatre Group of Los Angeles, and Gordon Davidson (A Mark Taper Forum Production); presented in association with Lou Adler; *Choreography*: Patricia Birch; *Scenery*: Thomas A. Walsh (based on a concept by Roberto Morales and Thomas A. Walsh); *Costumes*: Peter J. Hall; *Lighting*: Dawn Chiang; *Musical Direction*: Not Credited

Cast: Edward James Olmos (El Pachuco), Daniel Valdez (Henry Reyna); His Family—Abel Franco (Enrique Reyna), Lupe Ontiveros (Dolores Reyna), Roberta Delgado Esparza (Lupe Reyna), and Tony Plana (Rudy Reyna); His Friends—Charles Aidman (George Shearer) and Karen Hensel (Alice Bloomfield); His Gang—Rose Portillo (Della Barrios), Geno Silva (Smiley Torres), Mike Gomez (Joey Castro), Paul Mace (Tommy Roberts), Julie Carmen (Elena Torres), and Angela Moya (Bertha Villareal); Los Angelinos—Dennis Stewart (Swabbie), Kim Miyori (Manchuka), Lewis Whitlock (Zooter), and Darlene Bryan (Little Blue); The Downey Gang—Miguel Delgado (Rafas), Lee Mathis (Ragman), Richard Jay-Alexander (Hobo), Luis Manuel (Cholo), Gela Jacobson (Guera), Helen Andreyko (Blondie), and Michele Mais (Hoba); The Law—Vincent Duke Milana (Lieutenant Edwards) and Raymond Barry (Sergeant Smith); The Press—Arthur Hammer (Press), Dennis Stewart (Cub Reporter), and Lee Mathis (Newsboy); The Court—Vincent Duke Milana (Judge F. W. Charles) and Raymond Barry (Bailiff); The Prison—Vincent Duke Milana (Guard); The Military—Dennis Stewart (Sailor), Lee Mathis (Sailor), Raymond Barry (Sailor), and Richard Jay-Alexander (Marine)

The play with music was presented in two acts.

The action takes place in Los Angeles, San Quentin Prison, and in the mind of Henry Reyna between the fall of 1942 and the fall of 1944.

The program notes for Luis Valdez's *Zoot Suit* stated that while the play (with incidental songs and dances) was "loosely based" on two generally unrelated news stories of the early 1940s, the 1942 Sleepy Lagoon murder case and the zoot suit riots of 1944, some events in the play occurred while others did not. The characters were "merely representatives or composites" and the play was "a dramatization of the imagination" and "not a documentary." Despite enthusiastic word-of-mouth during its Los Angeles engagement (where it had opened at the Mark Taper Forum on April 20, 1978, and was still running at the time of the play's Broadway premiere) and the story's attempt to create an epic look at its subject matter, the work received a combination of mostly mild and negative notices in New York and couldn't muster a run of more than five weeks.

The murder took place on August 2, 1942, when a young Mexican American man was found dying near a popular swimming reservoir called the Sleepy Lagoon, and it was believed his death resulted from a skirmish among warring Chicano gang members. Seventeen Mexican American men were arrested for the murder and nine were sentenced to San Quentin, but in 1944 their convictions were overturned and they were freed. The zoot suit riots took place in 1944 and were the result of clashes between young male civilian Mexican Americans (who sported zoot suits as a symbol of their defiant attitudes and beliefs) and white American servicemen who believed the Mexican Americans were unpatriotic and should have joined the armed forces.

The play created the fictional character of El Pachuco (Edward James Olmos) who in iconic zoot suit garb served as the evening's narrator as well as the alter ego of Henry Reyna (Daniel Valdez), the leader of a zoot suit gang implicated in the Sleepy Lagoon murder. Two people believe in Reyna's innocence—a lawyer (Charles Aidman) and a Jewish female reporter of a left-wing newspaper (Karen Hensel). Otherwise, it seems the public, the police, the politicians, and the press are guilty of the indictments and subsequent sentencings—in other words, We All Are Guilty. Newspapers served as the visual motif for the evening, and as the production began a huge blow-up of the front page of a newspaper served as a curtain. Then suddenly a knife ripped through the newspaper and El Pachuco stepped through and made his entrance. Further, stacks of newspapers served as props, such as furniture, and even a clothes line was hung with newspapers.

The play included lindy and jitterbug dances created by Patricia Birch, and these were accompanied by recordings of Glenn Miller's and Harry James's bands. There was also some original music, including "Los Chucos Suaves," "Vamos a Bailar," and "Chicas Patas Boogie" (lyrics and music by Lalo Guerrero) and "*Zoot Suit* Theme" (aka "Put On a Zoot Suit") (lyric and music by Daniel Valdez).

Edwin Wilson in the *Wall Street Journal* noted that virtually every white in the play was "brutal, insensitive and sadistic" and "so unremittingly evil that they border on caricatures." And he found it telling that when the (white) appeals court reversed the convictions, the event was not staged and was merely announced by a newspaper headline. The headline of T. E. Kalem's review in *Time* read "Threads Bare," and the critic said the play reduced the stage to a "soapbox and the meaningless ritual of preaching to the already converted." While Valdez tried for a mix of "myth, documentation and fantasy," he never got "past the ABCs in any category." Clive Barnes in the *New York Post* said that while the Los Angeles production was "street theatre of very effective force," Broadway was "not the street where it lives." The play's tone was "simplistic" in its "sterile investigation into past social injustice" and the critic felt that "television does it better."

Christopher Sharp in *Women's Wear Daily* suggested the evening was "better" as a fashion show than a play, and noted that the work "grinds its axe so monotonously that it can cause an Excedrin headache by the second act." He felt Valdez was "condescending" and that he "insulted" the audience, and as an example mentioned a flashback scene of the murder when the narrator shouts "Stop the play," and, referring to the audience out front, states "That's exactly what they pay to see, one Mexican killing another one." Douglas Watt in the *New York Daily News* said *Zoot Suit* was "poorly written and atrociously directed" and diminished its subject. He found the play "Brechtian in its didactic approach, but in the worst sense," and the evening was "flat and boring." But Birch's choreography ("similar" to what she created for ***Over Here!***) was "lively and enjoyable."

John Beaufort in the *Christian Science Monitor* noted that the play borrowed elements from the living newspaper, semi-documentary, and agitprop styles of theatre, and while the characters were "one-dimensional" with an "awkward, overwritten script," the play dealt with "an actual, emotion-packed subject." Jack Kroll in *Newsweek* praised the "theatrical whirligig," which wasn't "a masterpiece of form" but nonetheless presented "the image and energy of a culture that's never been seen on a Broadway stage before." He said the evening's "magnetic field" was "reinforced" by Patricia Birch's "rousing" jitterbug dances set to the era's big-band music.

Richard Eder in the *New York Times* found *Zoot Suit* "overblown and undernourished" in its "bewildering" mix of styles, and said the play's political points were "presented in stilted and paper-thin terms." He noted that the play had been revised for New York, and while the mythical El Pachuco had been played by Olmos in a dominating manner with "comic ferocity" in Los Angeles, he was now "less effective" and his persona became a "stage mannerism." Further, Arthur Hammer's reporter was "nicely played" in Los Angeles but was now "merely affected."

The script was published in paperback by Arte Publico in the collection *"Zoot Suit" and Other Plays*. The movie version, which was filmed on stage before a live audience, was released by Universal Pictures in 1981; the screenplay and direction were by Luis Valdez, and the performers included original cast members Edward James Olmos, Daniel Valdez, and Charles Aidman (John Anderson and Tyne Daly were also in the cast). The soundtrack album was issued by MCA Records (LP # MCA-5267), and the DVD was released by Universal.

Awards

Tony Award Nomination: Best Featured Actor in a Play (Edward James Olmos)

CARMELINA

"A New Musical"

Theatre: St. James Theatre
Opening Date: April 8, 1979; *Closing Date*: April 21, 1979
Performances: 17
Book: Alan Jay Lerner and Joseph Stein
Lyrics: Alan Jay Lerner
Music: Burton Lane
Direction: José Ferrer; *Producers*: Roger L. Stevens, J. W. Fisher, Joan Cullman, and Jujamcyn Productions; *Choreography*: Peter Gennaro; *Scenery*: Oliver Smith; *Costumes*: Donald Brooks; *Lighting*: Feder; *Musical Direction*: Don Jennings
Cast: Marc Jordan (Bellini), Gonzalo Madurga (Mayor Nunzio Manzoni), *Cesare Siepi* (Vittorio Bruno), Grace Keagy (Rosa), Ian Michael Towers (Salvatore), *Georgia Brown* (Signora Carmelina Campbell), Judy Sabo (Signora Bernardi), Joseph d'Angerio (Roberto Bonafaccio), Frank Bouley (Father Tommaso), Jossie de Guzman (Gia Campbell), Gordon Ramsey (Walter Braddock), Howard Ross (Steve Karzinski), John Michael King (Carlton Smith), Virginia Martin (Flo Braddock), Kita Bouroff (Mildred Karzinski), Caryl Tenney (Katherine Smith), David E. Thomas (Father Federico); Ensemble: Frank Bouley, Kita Bouroff, Kathryn Carter, Karen DiBianco, Spence Ford, Ramon Galindo, Liza Gennaro, Laura Klein, Michael Lane, Morgan Richardson, Judy Sabo, Charles Spoerri, Caryl Tenney, David E. Thomas, Ian Michael Towers, Kevin Wilson, Lee Winston

The musical was presented in two acts.
The action takes place somewhere in Italy during 1961.

Musical Numbers

Act One: "It's Time for a Love Song" (Cesare Siepi); "Why Him?" (Georgia Brown, Cesare Siepi); "I Must Have Her" (Cesare Siepi); "Someone in April" (Georgia Brown); "Signora Campbell" (Grace Keagy, Georgia Brown, Frank Bouley, Gonzalo Madurga, Townspeople); "Love before Breakfast" (Georgia Brown, Cesare Siepi); "Yankee Doodles Are Coming to Town" (Townspeople); "One More Walk around the Garden" (Gordon Ramsey, Howard Ross, John Michael King); "All That He'd Want Me to Be" (Jossie de Guzman, Friends); "It's Time for a Love Song" (reprise) (Cesare Siepi)
Act Two: "Carmelina" (Cesare Siepi); "The Image of Me" (Gordon Ramsey, Howard Ross, John Michael King); "I'm a Woman" (Georgia Brown); "The Image of You" (Virginia Martin, Gordon Ramsey); "It's Time for a Love Song" (reprise) (Georgia Brown)

Despite an often lush and melodic score by Burton Lane and sometimes alternately clever and touching lyrics by Alan Jay Lerner, *Carmelina* disappeared after two weeks on Broadway. Lerner and Joseph Stein's mostly dreary book and José Ferrer's lackluster direction all but did the show in; the by-the-numbers evening offered little in the way of stage magic and theatrical surprise, and the result was a long evening's journey to the curtain calls. Although the program didn't credit a source for the musical, it was clearly inspired by the 1968 film *Buona Sera, Mrs. Campbell.* Unwed Italian mother Carmelina Campbell (Georgia Brown) receives child support from three different American men (played by Gordon Ramsey, Howard Ross, and John Michael King), each one of whom served in Italy during the war and assumes he's the father of Carmelina's child Gia (Jossie de Guzman). Because Carmelina slept with all three, she doesn't know who the father is, but she borrowed her last name from a soup can, has told Gia and the villagers that she's the widow of an American soldier and is now supported by his family, and thus she collects three checks a month from the former GIs.

Matters come to a head when the American regiment that liberated the village returns for a reunion, and of course among the group are Carmelina's former lovers (as well as their wives). Each man is unaware that the other two were also involved with Carmelina, and so each assumes he's Carmelina's one and only and is the father of Gia. In the meantime, café owner Vittorio Bruno (Cesare Siepi) is in love with Carmelina, who secretly loves him but spurns his advances because of her assumed role of the ever-faithful Widow Campbell. (In reading the summary of the plot, the reader may well exclaim, "*Mamma Mia!*")

Parts of the score were distressingly ordinary ("Yankee Doodles Are Coming to Town," "All That He'd Want Me to Be," and the title song), but Lerner and Lane also came up with the beautiful "One More Walk around the Garden," in which the three former soldiers hope to recapture the past before it's too late. Another impressive song was "The Image of Me," which the trio sings about Gia. Siepi's "It's Time for a Love Song" was perhaps a bit obvious, but was nonetheless a pleasant ballad, and his "Love before Breakfast" had a lovely, sweeping melodic arc. And while "Why Him?" and "I'm a Woman" were a bit frantic, Georgia Brown brought a vivid intensity to them. Further, "Someone in April" offered a gorgeous melody and incisive lyric, and with "One More Walk around the Garden" was among the finest theatre songs of the era. ("Someone in April" was reportedly written by Lerner and Lane for their 1965 Broadway musical *On a Clear Day You Can See Forever*.)

Richard Eder in the *New York Times* found the evening "at best an exercise in harmlessness"; the show was "frail," the direction and choreography were "equally tired," the décor was "routine," and some of the lyrics seemed "like something inspired by a 3 AM vigil in a hotel room." But he noted that the "fervent" and "well-constructed" "One More Walk around the Garden" was the score's "best" song. Clive Barnes in the *New York Post* liked the show, and said the score was "as Neapolitan as a rich spaghetti sauce." But the evening was "just too old-fashioned" and should have been produced ten years earlier. As a result, its "romantic" music and "honest" sentiment resulted in a "friendly" musical that "is not going anywhere it hasn't been."

Douglas Watt in the *New York Daily News* enjoyed much of the show, but felt it was strongest when the characters looked back on the past and was weakest when it dealt with the present. The first act picked up with "Someone in April," and the three former soldiers stole the show with "The Image of Me" and "One More Walk around the Garden" (the latter "a beautifully conceived piece"). He also liked "I'm a Woman," but noted "a flamenco rhythm strangely" appeared in the music. Edwin Wilson in the *Wall Street Journal* mentioned that the production didn't utilize modern staging techniques and thus during scene changes there were full blackouts while scenery "ponderously" rolled on and off; further, the book was "equally ponderous," the music tried too hard "for an Italian leitmotif," and the lyrics too often reached for "easy rhymes." But "One More Walk around the Garden" was an "excellent" song and an "exception" to the general trend of the score.

Howard Kissel in *Women's Wear Daily* said the musical "played at slow speed" and "whatever life" it might have had was "strained out" by the "slow pace" assigned to the evening by director José Ferrer. But "One More Walk around the Garden" was the evening's "crowd-pleasing" number, a "sentimental song with a sweet, timeless tune." T. E. Kalem in *Time* said the musical was like "going on an archaeological dig" that yielded "dusty relics" instead of "King Tut treasures." He noted the choreography looked like a "jogger's nightmare," but he suggested some of the songs (such as "It's Time for a Love Song," "One More Walk around the Garden," and "I'm a Woman") would "bear rehearing in some other musical."

However, John Beaufort in the *Christian Science Monitor* said the "expertly crafted" and "winningly performed" musical offered "beguiling" songs and the evening resulted in "a handsome, old-fashioned comic extravaganza." He singled out "One More Walk around the Garden" as the evening's show-stopper, but also praised "It's Time for a Love Song," "Someone in April," "Yankee Doodles Are Coming to Town," and "The Image of Me" (the latter was "tenderly expressed" by the former soldiers).

The recording was released with a mixture of original cast members and studio cast performers by Original Cast Records (LP # OC-8019; later on CD # THT-CD-9224). Siepi refused to participate in the recording, and so Paul Sorvino sang the role for the album. "One More Walk around the Garden" is included in the collection *Julie Andrews' Broadway: Here I'll Stay, The Words of Alan Jay Lerner* (Philips Records CD # 446-219-2) and Barbara Brussell's collection *Lerner in Love* (LML Music Records [unnumbered CD]) includes "It's Time for a Love Song" and "One More Walk around the Garden."

Awards

Tony Award Nomination: Best Score (lyrics by Alan Jay Lerner, music by Burton Lane)

MY OLD FRIENDS

"A New Musical"

Theatre: 22 Steps Theatre
Opening Date: April 12, 1979; *Closing Date*: May 27, 1979
Performances: 53
Book, Lyrics, and *Music*: Mel Mandel and Norman Sachs
Direction: Philip Rose; *Producers*: Larry Abrams in association with Belwin/Mills Publishing Corp.; *Choreography*: Bob (Robert) Tucker; *Scenery*: Leon Munier; *Costumes*: George Drew; *Lighting*: Barry Arnold; *Musical Direction*: Larry Hochman
Cast: Allen Swift (Catlan), Leslie Barrett (Fineberg), Robert Weil (Slocum), Norberto Kerner (Arias), Grace Carney (Mrs. Polianoffsky), Maxine Sullivan (Mrs. Cooper), Sylvia Davis (Heloise Michaud), Peter Walker (Peter Schermann), Brenda Gardner (Mrs. Stone), Fred Morsell (A Carpenter, Gettlinger); Norman Sachs (Piano), Larry Hochman (Piano), Thom Janusz (Bass)
The musical was presented in one act.
The action takes place during the present time at the Golden Days Retirement Hotel.

Musical Numbers

"I'm Not Old" (Residents); "My Old Friends" (Peter Walker); "For Two Minutes" (Robert Weil, Norberto Kerner, Allen Swift, Leslie Barrett); "What We Need around Here" (Peter Walker, Sylvia Davis); "Oh, My Rose" (Peter Walker); "I Bought a Bicycle" (Leslie Barrett, Residents); "The Battle at Eagle Rock" (Sylvia Davis, Residents); "Dear Jane" (Residents); "The Only Place for Me" (Residents); "I Work with Wood" (Peter Walker, Robert Weil); "Mambo '52" (Noberto Kerner, Maxine Sullivan); "A Little Starch Left" (Maxine Sullivan); "Our Time Together" (Sylvia Davis); "You've Got to Keep Building" (Peter Walker)

Before transferring to Broadway, *My Old Friends* had first been produced Off Off Broadway at La Mama Experimental Theatre Club (ETC) on November 24, 1978, and then Off Broadway at the Orpheum Theatre on January 12, 1979, for one hundred performances.

The musical was one of a number during the era that looked at the lives of the middle-aged and the elderly, among them John Kander and Fred Ebb's ***70, Girls, 70***; the 1973 Off-Broadway *Antiques*; the current season's ***Ballroom***; and the 1982 Off-Broadway *Taking My Turn*. *My Old Friends* marked a comeback for veteran Maxine Sullivan, whose song "Loch Lomond" was a popular hit in the 1930s and who in the 1939 Broadway musical *Swingin' the Dream* introduced one of the most ethereal of all Broadway ballads, "Darn That Dream."

Walter Kerr in the *New York Times* suggested that the subject matter of *My Old Friends* was "limited" in its somewhat obvious look at the geriatric set (the characters wear sweaters because they're cold all the time, they have trouble hearing, etc.), but he liked the "moderately pleasant switch" of the title song, which wasn't a look at one's fellow retirement-home residents but was instead about one's stash of pills and medicines. And he praised Maxine Sullivan's "A Little Starch Left" and noted she was "lovely, the nearest thing to spring I've come upon this year." He also enjoyed one choice bit of dialogue in which a character mentions that we definitely live in a democracy because one's neglectful children will one day be old, too.

The script was published in paperback by Samuel French in 1980.

The musical was revived Off Off Broadway by the American Jewish Theatre at the 92nd Street Y on May 1, 1985, for thirty-six performances; Maxine Sullivan was again in the cast, and was joined by Imogene Coca and King Donovan. Richard F. Shepard in the *New York Times* praised the "sparkling" and "charming" revival, which didn't once "wheeze" during its two-hour playing time. He noted that Sullivan stopped the show with "A Little Starch Left," and that she and Coca together performed the "fine" duet "Before My Time."

Two songs in *My Old Friends* ("I Bought a Bicycle" and "Our Time Together") had first been introduced in Mel Mandel and Norman Sachs's *After You, Mr. Hyde*, an adaptation of Robert Louis Stevenson's *The Strange Case of Dr. Jekyll and Mr. Hyde*, which played in regional theatre in 1968. The two songs were later heard in *Dr. Jekyll and Mr. Hyde*, a 1973 television adaptation of *After You, Mr. Hyde*; this version starred Kirk Douglas and included songs by Lionel Bart. In 1990, a revised version opened at the George Street Playhouse, New Brunswick, New Jersey, as *Jekyll & Hyde*.

Awards

Tony Award Nomination: Best Featured Actress in a Musical (Maxine Sullivan)

THE UTTER GLORY OF MORRISSEY HALL

"A New Musical"

Theatre: Mark Hellinger Theatre
Opening Date: May 13, 1979; *Closing Date*: May 13, 1979
Performances: 1
Book: Clark Gesner and Nagle Jackson
Lyrics and *Music*: Clark Gesner
Direction: Nagle Jackson; *Producers*: Arthur Whitelaw, Albert W. Selden, and W. Ridgely Bullock in association with Marc Howard (Sandy Stern, Associate Producer); *Choreography*: Buddy Schwab; *Scenery* and *Lighting*: Howard Bay; *Costumes*: David Graden; *Musical Direction*: John Lesko
Cast: Administration—*Celeste Holm* (Julia Faysle), Marilyn Caskey (Elizabeth Wilkins); Staff—Patricia Falkenhain (Foresta Studley), Laurie Franks (Teresa Winkle), Taina Elg (Mrs. Delmonde), Karen Gibson (Miss Newton), John Wardwell (Mr. Weyburn); Sixth Form Students—Mary Saunders (Carswell), Gina Franz (Vickers), Adrienne Alexander (Boody), Jill P. Rose (Dale), Kate Kelly (Dickerson), Polly Pen (Haverfield); Fifth Form Students—Cynthia Parva (Alice), Becky McSpadden (Helen), Dawn Jeffory (Frances), Bonnie Hellman (Angela), Anne Kaye (Marjorie), Lauren Shub (Mary); Visitors—Willard Beckham (Richard Tidewell), John Gallogly (Charles Hill), Robert Lanchester (Mr. Osgood)
The musical was presented in two acts.
The action takes place during the present time at the Morrissey School for Girls in England.

Musical Numbers

Act One: Overture (Orchestra) (*Note*: The overture was composed by Clark Gesner, but as a musical joke to match the arch proceedings of the musical, the music was attributed to a fictional composer named Desmond Gorss [1885–1958] from the "At the Fair" sequence from his *County Fair*; the overture is arranged and conducted for the Morrissey Hall Concert Orchestra by Evelyn Potts, Director of Music [who is actually the musical's conductor John Lesko in temporary drag]); "Promenade" (Company); "Proud, Erstwhile, Upright, Fair" (Celeste Holm, Patricia Falkenhain, Marilyn Caskey); "Elizabeth's Song" (Marilyn Caskey); "Way Back When" (Celeste Holm, Patricia Falkenhain); "Lost" (The Sixth Form Girls); "Morning" (Taina Elg, Dancing Class); "The Letter" (Becky McSpadden, John Gallogly, Company); "Oh, Sun" (Anne Kaye, Bonnie Hellman, Becky McSpadden, Dawn Jeffory, Lauren Shub, Taina Elg); "Give Me That Key" (Celeste Holm, Becky McSpadden, Marilyn Caskey); "Duet" (Marilyn Caskey, Willard Beckham, Company)

Act Two: "Interlude" and "Gallop" (Orchestra, Students); "You Will Know When the Time Has Arrived" (Laurie Franks, Mary Saunders, The Fifth and Sixth Form Students); "You Would Say" (Becky McSpadden, John Gallogly, The Fifth Form Girls); "See the Blue" (Celeste Holm, Flowers); "Dance of Resignation" (Taina Elg); "Reflection" (Celeste Holm); "The War" (the sequence includes "Les Preludes" by Franz Liszt) (Company); "Oh, Sun" (reprise) and "The Ending" (Company)

Clark Gesner's *The Utter Glory of Morrissey Hall* was an arch and quirky musical that didn't seem to have a target audience. It's hard to imagine Broadway theatergoers embracing a twee and intimate look at the arcane goings-on at an exclusive British girls' school. Perhaps the work might have found a small niche in college or community theatre, but it certainly didn't belong in the concrete world of Broadway and the cavernous Mark Hellinger Theatre. The evening met with mostly disdainful reviews and along with ***Gorey Stories*** and ***A Broadway Musical*** was the season's shortest-running musical.

The work was certainly inspired by (if not credited to) the British film *The Belles of St. Trinian's* (the first in the *Trinian's* series of comic escapades at a British girls' school was released in 1954), and it focused on the dotty and sometimes surreal goings-on at Morrissey Hall, which is run by headmistress Julia Faysle (Celeste Holm). There's an eternal war going on between the girls in the Fifth and Sixth forms which includes torture when a girl in the Fifth Form is suspended and chained spread-eagled and upside down inside a closet and threatened with "painful" and "horrible" death. Eventually the animosities between the two forms erupt into full-fledged battle with bombs, cannons, crossbows, and armored infantry garb. Equally strange, but not as dangerous, are the bizarre staff members, such as the headmistress's secretary Elizabeth Wilkins (Marilyn Caskey) and her would-be suitor and traveling salesman Richard Tidewell (Willard Beckham) who sing a repressed love song ("Duet") and dance teacher Mrs. Delmonde (Taina Elg), who often dances out her dialogue. When the latter turns in her resignation, the headmistress admonishes her that she hasn't followed the school's book of rules in regard to tendering her notice, and so Delmonde goes into her "Dance of Resignation." According to the script, she proceeds to shred and destroy the rule book while she performs "a dance of classic grandeur and grace, in the style of Isadora Duncan." And along the way a schoolboy hides out in a steamer trunk, and later when the girls are shown a movie, a pornographic one is shown by mistake.

Howard Kissel in *Women's Wear Daily* noted that some of the season's musicals had been "aggressively, offensively bad," but *Morrissey Hall* was simply "innocuous" with "unimaginative" direction and choreography that "constantly" veered toward "The Cute"; Joel Siegel on WABCTV7 said the evening tried for a *Laugh-In*-styled "theatrical insanity" but there was "no story and no characters" and thus the show wasn't "very interesting"; Douglas Watt in the *New York Daily News* said the "leaden affair" and "empty work" had "insipid" and "lifeless" music and "witless" dialogue; and Clive Barnes in the *New York Post* found the musical "particularly tedious" and noted that what was "bad" during the evening could be "summed up in eight words—book, lyrics, music, direction, choreography, setting and costumes."

Richard Eder in the *New York Times* said the evening was "untidy, uneven and often a mess," but it nonetheless had a certain "charm and sprightliness that are never quite extinguished." He noted that Gesner's score varied between the "agreeable" and the "undistinguished" and suggested the highlight was "You Will Know When the Time Has Arrived," a "rousing number with a suggestion of Gilbert and Sullivan to it." Celeste Holm was "graceful" and "sometimes amusing," but instead of "lighting up with the growing chaos, she wilts" and she tended to be a "bystander" when what the musical demanded was a "true mistress of the revels."

The script was published in paperback by Samuel French in 1982, and the original cast album was released by Original Cast Records (LP # OC-7918, later CD # OC-8738).

The musical had premiered in 1976 at the Pacific Conservatory of the Performing Arts in Santa Maria, California (this production was recorded by an unnamed company [LP # 44037]). In 1977, the work was presented in a one-act version at the McCarter Theatre Company at Princeton University in a production that credited the book to Gesner. Patricia Falkenhain and Jane Rose played the respective roles of Julia Faysle and Emily Stokes (for New York, the former played the character of Foresta Studley and the role of Emily Stokes was eliminated). Others in the cast were Gary Beach and Jeffrey Jones. Songs heard in the Princeton production but cut for New York were "Whose Little Bird Are You" and "Triumphal Re-entry of the Gladiators." Eileen Heckart had been scheduled to play the role of Julia for the Princeton mounting, but left just prior to the opening of the production. From Princeton, the musical then played at the Annenberg Center at the University of Pennsylvania, where it opened on November 25, 1977; it included the song "Like a Rock," which hadn't been heard at Princeton and was later cut prior to the 1979 Broadway production.

Morrissey Hall was a disappointing end to Gesner's once promising career. As a Princeton undergraduate, he contributed songs to such Triangle Club musicals as *After a Fashion!* (1957) and *Breakfast in Bedlam* (1959), both of which were recorded; he then wrote songs for the occasional Off-Broadway revue (*Bits and Pieces XIV* [1964]); and in 1967 his smash hit *You're a Good Man, Charlie Brown* opened Off Broadway and played for 1,597 performances (for more information, see entry for the 1971 Broadway production). After *Charlie Brown*, he was one of the contributors to *New Faces of 1968*, and his only full-length Broadway musical was *Morrissey Hall*. In 1998, he appeared in his Off-Broadway revue *The Jello Is Always Red*, which was a retrospective of his old and new songs (it was recorded by Harbinger Records CD # HCD-1502). He died in 2002.

UP IN ONE

Theatre: Biltmore Theatre
Opening Date: May 23, 1979; *Closing Date*: June 30, 1979
Performances: 46
Lyrics and *Music*: See song list for credits
Additional Written Material: Bruce Vilanch
Direction: Craig Zadan (Neil Meron, Assistant Director); *Producers*: Ron Delsener (A Dee Anthony Production) (Vince Mauro, Executive Producer); *Choreography*: Betsy Haug; *Scenery*: Douglas W. Schmidt; *Projections*: Douglas W. Schmidt and Wendall K. Harrington; *Costumes*: Charles Suppon; *Lighting*: Marilyn Rennagel; *Musical Direction*: Marc Shaiman
Cast: *Peter Allen*, Lenora Nemetz; Background Vocals: Janis Cercone, Louis Cortelezzi, Corky Hale, and Al Scotti; The PA System: Marc Shaiman (Musical Director, Keyboards), Louis Cortelezzi (Reeds), Corky Hale (Harp, Flute, Electric Piano), Doane Perry (Drums), Jose Rossi (Percussion), Larry Saltzman (Guitar), Al Scotti (Bass)
The concert was presented in one act.

Musical Numbers

Note: The program stated the songs for the evening would be taken from the following alphabetical list. (* = songs introduced in the concert.)
"Dixie" (lyric and music by Peter Allen); "Don't Cry Out Loud" (lyric and music by Peter Allen and Carole Bayer Sager); "Don't Wish Too Hard" (lyric and music by Peter Allen and Carole Bayer Sager); "Everything Old Is New Again" (lyric and music by Peter Allen and Carole Bayer Sager); "Fly Away" (*) (lyric and music by Peter Allen and Carole Bayer Sager); "Harlem on My Mind" (*As Thousands Cheer*, 1933; lyric and music by Irving Berlin); "I Could Have Been a Sailor" (lyric and music by Peter Allen); "I Could Really Show You Around" (*) (lyric and music by Peter Allen and Dean Pitchford); "I'd Rather Leave While I'm in Love" (lyric and music by Peter Allen and Carole Bayer Sager); "If You Were Wondering" (lyric and music by Peter Allen); "I Go to Rio" (lyric and music by Peter Allen and Adrienne Anderson); "I Honestly Love You" (lyric and music by Peter Allen and Jeff Barry); "Impatient Heart" (*) (lyric and music by Peter Allen

and Marsha Malamet); "I Never Thought I'd Break" (*) (lyric and music by Peter Allen and Dean Pitchford); "Just a Gigolo" (lyric and music by Leonello Casucci and Irving Caesar); "Love Crazy" (lyric and music by Peter Allen and Adrienne Anderson); ""Make 'Em Pay" (*) (lyric and music by Peter Allen and Dean Pitchford); "More Than I Like You" (lyric and music by Peter Allen and Carole Bayer Sager); "Only Wounded" (*) (lyric and music by Peter Allen and Carole Bayer Sager); "Paris at 21" (lyric and music by Peter Allen); "Planes" (lyric and music by Peter Allen and Carole Bayer Sager); "Puttin' Out Roots Again" (lyric and music by Peter Allen); "6:30 Sunday Morning" (lyric and music by Peter Allen); "Tenterfield Saddler" (lyric and music by Peter Allen); "Two Boys" (lyric and music by Marvin Hamlisch, Carole Bayer Sager, and Peter Allen); "We've Come to an Understanding" (lyric and music by Peter Allen); "What Am I Doing Here?" (*) (lyric and music by Peter Allen and Dean Pitchford); "You Oughta Hear Me Sing" (*) (lyric and music by Peter Allen and Dean Pitchford)

Australian singer and songwriter Peter Allen (1944–1992) charmed many but was quite resistible to others. He had appeared in the flop ***Soon***, and would later star in the flop *Legs Diamond* (1988), for which he also wrote the lyrics and music (the latter was the last booking for the legendary Mark Hellinger Theatre before it was sold and converted into a church). Allen is perhaps best remembered as one of Liza Minnelli's husbands; as a Best Song Oscar winner for "Arthur's Theme" ("Best That You Can Do") from the 1981 film *Arthur* (the song was cowritten by Burt Bacharach, Carole Bayer Sager, Christopher Cross, and Allen); and as the subject of the musical *The Boy from Oz* (which premiered in Sydney in 1998 and on Broadway in 2003 where Allen was portrayed by Hugh Jackman, who won the Tony Award for Best Actor in a Musical).

The small cast of *Up in One* included singer and dancer Lenora Nemitz, a group of background vocalists (some of whom doubled as band members), and the band itself was called the PA System and was conducted by Marc Shaiman, who later composed the music and cowrote the lyrics for the hit *Hairspray* (2002). The concert's overture was arranged by Marvin Hamlisch.

In reviewing the evening, John Rockwell in the *New York Times* said "it would be wrong to say [Allen] scored a raving, hysterical triumph," but the evening could "be warmly recommended to almost anybody." The show wasn't "perfect," Allen was perhaps "too guarded," and his baritone wasn't "the most commanding instrument imaginable." But the concert was nevertheless "an honest, amusing and sometimes moving affair."

I REMEMBER MAMA

Theatre: Majestic Theatre
Opening Date: May 31, 1979; *Closing Date*: September 2, 1979
Performances: 108
Book: Thomas Meehan
Lyrics: Martin Charnin; additional lyrics by Raymond Jessel
Music: Richard Rodgers
Based on the Kathryn Forbes 1943 short story "Mama's Bank Account" (which first appeared in the *Reader's Digest*) and other *Mama* stories by Forbes; and on the 1944 stage adaptation *I Remember Mama* by John Van Druten.
Direction: Cy Feuer; *Producers*: Alexander H. Cohen and Hildy Parks (Roy A. Somlyo, Coproducer); *Choreography*: Musical numbers "staged by" Danny Daniels; *Scenery*: David Mitchell; *Costumes*: Theoni V. Aldredge; *Lighting*: Roger Morgan; *Musical Direction*: Jay Blackton
Cast: Maureen Silliman (Katrine), Carrie Horner (Christine), Tara Kennedy (Dagmar), Kristen Vigard (Johanne), Ian Ziering (Nils), George Hearn (Papa), *Liv Ullmann* (Mama), Dick Ensslen (Mr. McGuire), Elizabeth Hubbard (Aunt Trina), Dolores Wilson (Aunt Jenny), Betty Ann Grove (Aunt Sigrid), Armin Shimerman (Mr. Thorkelson), George S. Irving (Uncle Chris), Janet McCall (Lucie), Sigrid Heath (Nurse), Stan Page (Doctor Anderson), Myvanwy Jenn (Dame Sybil Fitzgibbons); Steiner Street Neighbors: Austin Colyer, John Dorrin, Mickey Gunnersen, Daniel Harnett, Danny Joel, Jan Kasni, Kevin Marcum, Richard Maxon, Marisa Morell, Frank Pietri, Elissa Wolfe
The musical was presented in two acts.
The action takes place in San Francisco during the summer and fall of 1910 and the spring of 1911.

Musical Numbers

Note: * = lyric by Raymond Jessel.

Act One: "I Remember Mama" (Maureen Silliman); "A Little Bit More" (*) (Liv Ullmann, George Hearn, Children); "A Writer Writes at Night" (Maureen Silliman, Liv Ullmann); "Ev'ry Day (Comes Something Beautiful)" (Liv Ullmann, Company); "The Hardangerford" (dance) (Company); "You Could Not Please Me More" (choreography by Graciela Daniele) (George Hearn, Liv Ullmann); "Uncle Chris" (*) (Elizabeth Hubbard, Dolores Wilson, Betty Ann Grove); "Easy Come, Easy Go" (*) (George S. Irving, Friends); "It's Not the End of the World" (Family)

Act Two: "Mama Always Makes It Better" (Children); "Lars, Lars" (*) (Liv Ullmann); "Fair Trade" (Myvanwy Jenn, Liv Ullmann); "It's Going to Be Good to Be Gone" (George S. Irving); "Time" (Liv Ullmann); "I Remember Mama" (reprise) (Maureen Silliman)

In 1944, Richard Rodgers and Oscar Hammerstein II produced *I Remember Mama*, John Van Druten's stage adaptation of Kathryn Forbes's warm and touching short stories about a woman's memories of growing up in San Francisco in a family of Norwegian immigrants in the early years of the twentieth century. The play opened at the Music Box Theatre on October 19, 1944, and was one of the era's biggest hits with 714 performances; the cast included Mady Christians (Mama), Joan Tetzel (Katrin), Oscar Homolka (Uncle Chris), and Marlon Brando (Nels). The memorable film version was released in 1948 and was directed by George Stevens; Homolka reprised his role of Uncle Chris, and the cast included Irene Dunne (Mama) and Barbara Bel Geddes (Katrin). As *Mama*, the popular CBS television series starred Peggy Wood and played from 1949 to 1957. But for his lyric version Rodgers received some of his worst notices, and the musical closed at an enormous loss after just three months of performances. *I Remember Mama* was Rodgers's final work (he died four months after the production closed), and his long and distinguished career ended on a sour note.

The musical is now better remembered for its chaotic tryout than its score. Lyricist Martin Charnin (who had written the lyrics for Rodgers's ***Two by Two***) was the original director, but by New York had been succeeded by producer and sometime director Cy Feuer; and during the course of the tryout Raymond Jessel was brought in to supply new lyrics (by the time of the Broadway opening, the lyrics of four of the thirteen songs were credited to him). Graciela Daniele was the musical's original choreographer, but by New York she had been replaced by Danny Daniels, who was given a "musical numbers staged by" credit (Daniele received program credit for the choreography of "You Could Not Please Me More"). Kate Dezina played the role of Katrin (name later changed to Katrine) and Kristen Vigard the role of Young Katrin. When the role of Young Katrin was eliminated, Dezina left the production and was succeeded by Maureen Silliman, and Vigard was given the newly created role of Johanne. Justine Johnston was Florence Dana Moorhead, but was succeeded by Myvanwy Jenn (and the character's name became Dame Sybil Fitzgibbons); and during the tryout the role of Mr. Hyde was created by Truman Gaige and then in New York previews was played by Francis Bethencourt, who left the production when the character was written out of the show.

During the tryout, seven songs were cut: "Maybe, Maybe, Maybe," "Midsummer Night," "(He's) A Most Disagreeable Man," "When?," "An Old City Boy at Heart," "Such Good Fun," and "A Fam'ly (Family) We Will Be." During New York previews, two songs (with lyrics by Jessel) were added and then cut, "Where We Came From" and "I Don't Know How."

The music for "Mama Always Makes It Better" was originally heard as "Getting Married to a Person" during the tryout of ***Two by Two***. During the New York run, the second-act reprise of the title song was cut, and, according to *The Rodgers and Hammerstein Fact Book*, a song called "Lullaby" was performed in the first act by Liv Ullmann.

Richard Eder in the *New York Times* noted that the musical's "choppy" road to Broadway resulted in "a mass of clichés and a pervading, forced cuteness." Most of the score was "fairly bland" (but he singled out "Fair Trade" as the evening's "best" song) and Thomas Meehan's book and most of the lyrics were "flat" when "not painful." As for Ullmann, she was "unsuited" to the musical and while she brought "force and subtlety" to her screen performances she was here "hopelessly lost" in a production of "sugary simplicity."

Douglas Watt in the *New York Daily News* said the evening was like a "faded" picture postcard in which the outlines remained but the color was missing. He generally liked Rodgers's score (and felt it was better than his work for ***Two by Two*** and ***Rex***), but found the lyrics "pedestrian," the direction "routine," and the book, while "literate and direct," was also "too gentle and sketchy to sustain" interest. Although Ullmann was an "enchanting" actress, she was here "shortchanged" and was given "only scattered acting opportunities." Howard Kissel in *Women's Wear Daily* said the "dimly conceived" musical was "one of those big, soulless, commercial vehicles." Rodgers's music was one of "unimaginable thinness" (he noted the best song was "Time"), Charnin's lyrics were "too pat," and Jessel's were "the worst lyrics I think I've ever heard." As for Ullmann, she had no "real material" to work with and he praised her for being a "good sport."

T. E. Kalem in *Time* noted that looking over the names of the musical's cast and creators was like reading a "casualty list." Rodgers's music wouldn't be "pressed in anyone's memory book" and the lyrics were "weary, stale, flat and unprofitable." Charles Michener in *Newsweek* said the musical was a "mess" of "confusions" and Meehan's "scrambled re-writing of Van Druten" resulted in "some of the least-developed cartoon characters ever to populate a musical."

But Clive Barnes in the *New York Post* said the show was "a warm-souled, family musical with a good and proper Rodgers score" and with a performance of "glorious luminosity" by Ullmann; and John Beaufort in the *Christian Science Monitor* noted the work had a "warmly endearing quality" with "several choice musical numbers," and he said the "jolly" and "fleet-footed" dance "The Hardangerford" was Daniels's "most ebullient contribution."

There was no cast recording at the time of the production, but six years later Polydor Records released a combination Broadway and studio cast album (LP # 827-336-1-Y-1); the CD was issued by That's Entertainment Records (# CDTER-1102). George Hearn and George S. Irving reprised their original roles, and other singers on the recording are Sally Ann Howes (Mama), Ann Morrison (Katrin), Patricia Routledge (Aunt Jenny), Elizabeth Seal (Aunt Sigrid), Gay Soper (Aunt Trina), and Sian Phillips (Dame Sybil Fitzgibbons). The recording retains all the songs heard in the Broadway production (including the second act reprise of the title song), but not the dance number "The Hardangerford." The album also includes two cut songs, "A Most Disagreeable Man" and "When?," as well as "Lullaby," which, as noted, seems to have been performed at some point during the Broadway production.

Rodgers's adaptation of *I Remember Mama* was actually the second lyric version of the material. On January 6, 1972, *Mama* opened at Buffalo's Studio Arena Theatre with Celeste Holm (Mama), Jill O'Hara (Katrin), Michael Kermoyan (Uncle Chris), and Wesley Addy (Papa). The lyrics and music were by John Clifton and the book was by Neal Du Brock.

BACK COUNTRY

The musical opened on September 8, 1978, at the Wilbur Theatre in Boston, Massachusetts, and permanently closed there on September 23, 1978.
Book and *Lyrics*: Jacques Levy
Music: Stanley Walden
Based on the 1907 play *The Playboy of the Western World* by John Millington Synge.
Direction: Jacques Levy; *Producers*: Eugene V. Wolsk in association with Harvey Granat; *Choreography*: Margo Sappington; *Scenery*: Peter Larkin; *Costumes*: Pearl Somner; *Lighting*: Neil Peter Jampolis; *Musical Direction*: Susan Romann
Cast: Stuart Germain (Philly Cullen), Rex Everhart (Michael James), Suzanne Lederer (Pegeen Mike), Harry Groener (Floyd Beavis), Ken Marshall (Christy Mahon), Terri Treas (Evalina), Pamela Pilkenton (Bitsy), Nancy Holcombe (Sister), Barbara Andres (Lucy Jane DuRambeau Finletter), John G. Kellogg (Passerby), Malita Barron (Angel Voice)
The musical was presented in two acts.
The action takes place in the early spring of 1894 in a rustic tavern located in an out-of-the-way rural area in West Kansas.

Musical Numbers

Act One: "Mother of Spring" (Stuart Germain, Rex Everhart); "Little Girl Again" (Suzanne Lederer); "Child of the Devil" (Ken Marshall); "Mr. Moon and Lady Fire" (Suzanne Lederer, Ken Marshall); "Heaven on My Mind" (Harry Groener, Ken Marshall); "Hay Pitchin'" (Ken Marshall, Harry Groener, Terri Treas, Pamela

Pilkenton, Nancy Holcombe); "The Western Slope" (Ken Marshall, Suzanne Lederer); "All the Men in My Life" (Barbara Andres); "Diamond Jim Brady" (Ken Marshall, Harry Groener); "Mother of Spring" (reprise) (Rex Everhart, Stuart Germain)

Act Two: "The Fiddler's Tune" (Ken Marshall, Harry Groener, Terri Treas, Pamela Pilkenton, Nancy Holcombe, Rex Everhart, Stuart Germain, Barbara Andres); "As a Boy" (Rex Everhart); "Too Much Pain" (Suzanne Lederer); "As a Girl" (Rex Everhart); "Old Man" (Ken Marshall); "If You Will Spend Your Life with Me" (Ken Marshall, Suzanne Lederer)

Back Country was one of at least three failed lyric versions of John Millington Synge's classic 1907 play *The Playboy of the Western World*. For the current retelling, the story's setting was moved from Ireland to Kansas and centered on braggart Christy Mahon (Ken Marshall) who arrives in town with his tall tale of having murdered his own father. He impresses everyone in the small community, and when it's eventually revealed he never harmed his father it makes no matter to local lass Pegeen Mike (Suzanne Lederer), who has fallen in love with him.

Variety felt the story lost its charm with its relocation to the American Midwest. Further, the evening offered "musical loquaciousness" and "overloud music" and thus its "very noise" worked against its success. The musical reportedly lost $430,000.

Prior to the Boston engagement, the musical had premiered at the Cohoes Music Hall in Cohoes, New York, on August 15, 1978. Songs deleted prior to the Boston production were: "Champeen of the World," "Talk," "Through the Shadows," and "Till She Comes out the Door."

Other musical versions of Synge's play are *The Heart's a Wonder* and *Christy*. The former opened in London at the Westminster Theatre on September 18, 1958, for a brief run (the score was based on traditional Irish airs), and on October 14, 1975, the latter opened Off Broadway at the Bert Wheeler Theatre for a run of forty performances (the book and lyrics were by Bernie Spiro, the music by Lawrence J. Blank with additional music by Robert Billig), and the cast recording was issued by Original Cast Records (LP # OR-7913).

HOME AGAIN, HOME AGAIN

"An All-American Musical Extravaganza" / "A New Musical Comedy"

The musical opened at the American Shakespeare Theatre, Stratford, Connecticut, on March 10, 1979, and closed there on March 17; it then opened on March 19 at the Royal Alexandra Theatre, Toronto, Ontario, Canada, and permanently closed there on April 14.

Book: Russell Baker

Lyrics: Barbara Fried

Music: Cy Coleman

Direction: Gene Saks; *Producers*: Irwin Meyer and Stephen R. Friedman in association with Kenneth D. Laub and Warner Plays, Inc. (Joseph Harris, Associate Producer); *Choreography*: Onna White (Martin Allen, Associate Choreographer); *Scenery*: Peter Larkin; *Costumes*: Jane Greenwood; *Lighting*: Neil Peter Jampolis; *Musical Direction*: Stanley Lebowsky

Cast: James Lockhart (Voice, Winckelmann, Watchman), *Ronny Cox* (TJ), *Dick Shawn* (Hamilton Witherspoon, The Editor, The Judge, The Reverend, The Governor, The Banker, The Maitre'D, The Sergeant, The Boss), Lisa Ann Cunningham (Grandmother), *Mike Kellin* (Hugo), Rex Everhart (Riley), William Morrison (Young TJ), Dale Christopher (Copy Boy, Lieutenant), Bob Freschi (Chicken, Harris), David Horwitz (Cop, Edmund), Teri Ralston (Helen), Anita Morris (Lila), *Lisa Kirk* (Andrea), Robert Polenz (Robert), Jeannine Taylor (Linda), Tim Waldrip (Kenneth), Mordecai Lawner (Corveen), Susan Cella (Unborn Woman); Singers: Susan Cella, Dale Christopher, Ned Coulter, Lisa Ann Cunningham, Bob Freschi, D. Michael Heath, David Horwitz, Terry Iten, Deborah Moldow; Dancers: Lisa Guignard, Ken Henley, Dirk Lumbard, Bill Nabel, Caroline Nova, Philomena Nowlin, Don Swanson, Karen Tamburrelli

The musical was presented in two acts.

The action takes place in the United States from 1925 to the present.

Musical Numbers

Act One: "America Is Bathed in Sunlight" (Dick Shawn, Mike Kellin, Rex Everhart, Chorus); "Thomas Jefferson Witherspoon" (Chorus); "When the Going Gets Tough" (Dick Shawn, Ronny Cox); "I'm Your Guy" (Ronny Cox, Dick Shawn, Reporters); "All for Love" (Teri Ralston, Ronny Cox, Anita Morris); "When It Comes to Loving" (Lisa Kirk, Chorus); "Wedding Song" (Dick Shawn, Teri Ralston, Ronny Cox, Wedding Guests); "That Happy American Dream" (Chorus); "Home Again" (Ronny Cox, Teri Ralston, Robert Polenz, Jeannine Taylor, Tim Waldrip); "Superland" (Chorus); "What'll It Take" (Robert Polenz); "Big People" (Ronny Cox, Teri Ralston)
Act Two: "I Gotta" (Male Chorus); "French" (Dick Shawn); "Thomas Jefferson Witherspoon" (reprise) (Chorus); "Tell It to Me, Dad" (Robert Polenz, Draftees); "Traveling Together" (Lisa Kirk, Tim Waldrip); "Winter Rain" (Ronny Cox); "America Don't Know How Anymore" (Mike Kellin, Rex Everhart, Mordecai Lawner); "The Way I See It" (Ronny Cox); "Home Again" (reprise) (Company)

Cy Coleman's *Home Again, Home Again* never made it to New York, where it had been scheduled to open at the Mark Hellinger Theatre on April 26, 1979. Instead, the musical closed during its tryout at a loss of $1,250,000. An early full-page advertisement in the *New York Times* stated the new musical would be "an all American Musical Extravaganza," and an article in the same newspaper described the musical as a look at three generations of an American family and their reactions to the changes in American life from the 1930s to the 1970s as the nation moves from the country to the city to the suburbs.

According to Ed in *Variety* (who reviewed the musical during its first tryout stop in Stratford, Connecticut), to say the "mediocre" musical needed work was "the understatement of the year." Further, there was "nothing wrong with the show that a new book, score, cast, direction, choreography, sets and costumes wouldn't help." He stated that any musical which began "with a heavenly voice in conversation with an unborn child" was immediately in trouble.

Variety noted that the fifty-year survey of the American Dream suggested "an impoverished rerun" of Richard Rodgers and Oscar Hammerstein II's *Allegro*, and, indeed, besides *Allegro* the musical also seems somewhat reminiscent of other concept musicals that looked at a broad span of American life, such as *Love Life* (1948), *Hallelujah, Baby!* (1967), ***Different Times*** (1972), and ***1600 Pennsylvania Avenue*** (1976). Incidentally, Lisa Kirk had appeared in *Allegro* as well as *Home Again, Home Again*, but by the end of the first leg of the tryout her part had been written out of the show.

Variety felt the evening lacked a coherent point of view, and the book seemed to say that nice guys don't get ahead. To add to the evening's confusion, the second act began with a "bewildering" pre-French Revolution dance number that turned out to be part of a floor show taking place in a Las Vegas restaurant, and it was followed by a "pointless" fashion show that needed to be cut. Although the well-regarded *Times* columnist Russell Baker had written the book, *Variety* said his journalistic comic style didn't transfer well to the musical stage. As for Coleman's songs, only "French" was impressive with a "certain, minimal flair." After the Stratford engagement, the musical stumbled on to Toronto, where it permanently closed at the end of its scheduled four-week run.

It's a shame Coleman's score never had a wider hearing because some of his songs were highly melodic ("America Is Bathed in Sunlight") and others had a pleasantly quirky and jittery quality ("Thomas Jefferson Witherspoon" and the title song).

OH, KAY!

"A Musical Comedy"

After three previews, the revival opened on July 20, 1978, at the Royal Alexandra Theatre in Toronto, Ontario, Canada, and closed on August 12, 1978, for a total of thirty-one performances, and then opened on August 22 at the John F. Kennedy Center's Opera House in Washington, D.C., for forty-seven performances (including preview performances from August 16 to 21) before permanently closing there on September 23.
Book: Guy Bolton and P. G. Wodehouse; new book adaptation by Thomas Meehan
Lyrics: Ira Gershwin
Music: George Gershwin

Direction and *Choreography*: Donald Saddler (Mercedes Ellington, Associate Choreographer); *Producer*: Cyma Rubin (A Cyma Rubin Production produced in association with the Kennedy Center for the Performing Arts) (Raoul Pene du Bois, Nathan J. Miller, and Keith Davies, Associate Producers); *Scenery* and *Costumes*: Raoul Pene du Bois; *Lighting*: Beverly Emmons; *Musical Direction*: Wally Harper

Cast: Jack Weston (Shorty McGee), Jane Summerhays (Lady Kay Wellington), David-James Carroll (Jimmy Winter), Gene Castle (Tommy Potter), Marie Cheatham (Constance Washburn), David Cromwell (Agent Baldwin), Reno Roop (Oliver Wellington [The Duke of Argylle]), Alexandra Korey (Velma Delmar), Thomas Ruisinger (Senator Albert G. Washbrook), Janet and Louise Arters (Polly and Molly), Joe Palmieri (Minister, Master of Ceremonies); The *Oh, Kay!* Ladies: Barbara Hanks, Holly Jones, Jean McLaughlin, Annette Michelle, Diana Lee Mirras, Dana J. Moore, Terry Reiser, Yveline Semeria, Dorothy Stanley, Roxanna White; The *Oh, Kay!* Gentlemen: Stephen Bray, Jameson Foss, Tom Garrett, Peter Heuchling, Timothy R. Kratoville, Michael Lichtefeld, Dirk Lumbard, Bob Morrisey, Richard Parrott, Danny Robins, J. Thomas Smith, Thomas J. Stanton

The musical was presented in three acts.

The action takes place in and around Southampton, Long Island, during the summer of 1933.

Musical Numbers

Act One: Overture (Orchestra); "I've (We've) Got to Be There" (Gene Castle, Couples); "Bootleggers' Lament" (Jack Weston, Rum Runners); "Heaven on Earth" (lyric by Ira Gershwin and Howard Dietz) (The *Oh, Kay!* Ladies); "Maybe" (Jane Summerhays, David-James Carroll); "Blah, Blah, Blah" (Jack Weston); "Do, Do, Do" (Jane Summerhays, David-James Carroll); "Clap Yo' Hands" (Alexandra Korey, Ensemble); Finaletto (Company)

Act Two: "Stiff Upper Lip" (The *Oh, Kay!* Ladies, Rum Runners, and an uncredited performer); "Someone to Watch Over Me" (Jane Summerhays); "Oh, So Nice" (David-James Carroll); "Oh, Kay!" (lyric by Ira Gershwin and Howard Dietz) (Jack Weston, Jane Summerhays, The *Oh, Kay!* Gentlemen); "Bride and Groom" (Company); Finaletto (Company)

Act Three: Medley (unidentified songs) (Couples); "Fidgety Feet" (Gene Castle, Ensemble); "Don't Ask!" (Jack Weston, Alexandra Korey); Finale (Company)

The team who put together the popular and profitable revival of ***No, No, Nanette*** hoped to mine another nostalgic mother lode with the revival of George and Ira Gershwin's 1926 Broadway hit *Oh, Kay!* Cyma Rubin was back as producer, Donald Saddler was again the choreographer (and now also the director), and Raoul Pene du Bois returned to design the scenery and costumes. As the tryout progressed, *Nanette*'s director Burt Shevelove unofficially stepped in for a time to help with the direction.

But the revival of *Oh, Kay!* was in trouble from the very beginning of its short and arduous life. The *New York Times* reported that John Guare had begun a revision of the original book by Guy Bolton and P. G. Wodehouse which Muriel Resnik (who had scored with the hit comedy *Any Wednesday* in 1964) had completed. By the time the musical began its tryout, Guare and Resnik were gone and the adaptation was credited to Thomas Meehan, who had recently written the book for the hit ***Annie***. The Toronto program was so confused it identified a character named Skeets in the song list (as participating in the number "Stiff Upper Lip"), but there was no Skeets listed in the cast of characters and none of the performers' biographies indicated an actor was playing such a role. This in itself may seem a small matter, but in retrospect is indicative of what was to become a chaotic tryout. The opening night in Toronto ran for three hours and twenty minutes, and a unicycle number (perhaps a wannabe reprise in the style of ***No, No, Nanette***'s beach ball sequence?) was almost immediately dropped.

By the time the musical reached Washington, D.C., a month later, its three acts had been compressed into two; its leading man David-James Carroll had been replaced by Jim Weston; and David Cromwell (who played a secondary character, the comical Agent Baldwin) was succeeded by Eddie Lawrence, who was perhaps best known as the librettist and lyricist of the legendary 1965 flop musical *Kelly*. In Toronto, Gene Castle played the role of Tommy Potter, but for the Washington programs his character was identified as both Freddy LaRue and Fidgety Feet Man. In Toronto, Reno Roop portrayed Oliver Wellington (the Duke of Argylle), but the role was written out of the musical and so for Washington Roop played a new character named Righty. Further,

Joe Palmieri was the minister and the master of ceremonies in Toronto, but in Washington was given a third role, a new character named Luigi Spagnoli (and heretofore chorus member Annette Michelle was now listed among the principals as a newly added character, Lucia Spagnoli).

The addition of new characters and the deletion of others reflect the amount of rewriting that went on during the tryout. Further, by Washington two numbers had been deleted ("Bootleggers' Lament" and an unidentified medley sequence) and three added ("I've Got a Crush on You," "Dear Little Girl," and "How Long Has This Been Going On?").

David Richards in the *Washington Star* reported that Shevelove unofficially joined the company to assist Saddler, and that by the end of the Washington run the musical appeared "to be in the hands of" Barbara Cook, who had been working with Jane Summerhays as her vocal coach. Cook was then asked by Rubin to stay on and "rework the show and stage some of the new numbers." But it was all for naught, and *Oh, Kay!* permanently closed at the Opera House at a loss of $1 million. The musical cancelled its scheduled New York opening night of October 5 at the Lunt-Fontanne Theatre (where previews had been set to begin on September 26).

But for all the firings, rewriting, restaging, and song shifting, the show was surprisingly entertaining. The musical numbers were the thing, and they were joyfully performed by the game cast of singers and dancers. And Saddler's dances were lively and inventive. In particular, "Fidgety Feet" was a show-stopper of the first order. Breathtakingly danced by Gene Castle and the chorus, the number was one of the quirkiest dances seen in a musical in years, and while some hated its jiggly and nervous style, others were enchanted.

The action occurred during the Prohibition era, and while the original production took place in the mid-1920s, the revival was set in 1933 (instead of another look at the 1920s, the ***No, No, Nanette*** team clearly wanted a different atmosphere and thus opted for a 1930s look and tone [which was perhaps best reflected in the musical's striking poster artwork, which combined cubism with art deco touches]).

The feathery plot dealt with the shenanigans surrounding on-her-uppers Lady Kay (Jane Summerhays) and bootlegger Shorty McGee (Jack Weston), who join forces to supply illegal hooch to a nightclub owner. They store the booze in the basement of a huge Long Island mansion owned by absentee playboy Jimmy Winter (David James Carroll, later succeeded by Jim Weston), but when Jimmy suddenly shows up, musical comedy complications ensue, including romantic ones because Jimmy has just brought his latest bride home with him, and Kay is determined that she and she alone should be the bride for Jimmy.

In reviewing the Toronto production, Adil in *Variety* said the musical was "far from ready for even a break-in showing" and noted there were "many intermission walkouts" during the "mishmash." The book was "disorganized," the direction "bewildering," the sets "ill-fitting," the tempos of the orchestra were part of "the potted stew," and some of the performers were miscast. For the Kennedy Center run, Judith Martin (aka Miss Manners) in the *Washington Post* noted that the jokes were on the level of "If it's the wrong number, how come you answered the phone?," and she commented that Summerhays was "better at being Lady Kay pretending to be the maid than she is at pretending to be a lady" and that Jack Weston tried for two approaches to his role ("the naïve and the Don Rickles modern") and the two styles didn't "mesh."

Richard L. Coe in the *Washington Post* felt the musical hadn't found its tone, and what should have been "light" was instead a "yarn" that "plods, plods and plods." But the "fine, attractive" dancers turned "Do, Do, Do" and "Clap Yo' Hands" into "major production numbers." Richards noted that the revival lacked a "single galvanizing performance" and that the cast was "so short of charisma that you have to look to the mirrors in the second act casino set for any suggestion of sparkle." Like Martin, he groaned over the show's idea of humor ("If I'm not back in five minutes, I'll be back in ten"); and he found the "Fidgety Feet" dance more "spastic" than "fidgety." As for the score's "lilting melodies, witty lyrics and jazzy syncopations," he asked what were "such nice songs doing in a show like this?"

The original production of *Oh, Kay!* opened at the Imperial Theatre on November 8, 1926, for 256 performances with Gertrude Lawrence (Kay), Victor Moore (Shorty McGee), and Oscar Shaw (Jimmy). The Gershwin score included eleven songs, and at one point or another during the revival's tryout ten were heard (only "The Woman's Touch" wasn't used). The songs interpolated into the revival (all with lyrics by Ira Gershwin) were: "How Long Has This Been Going On?" (cut from *Funny Face*, 1927, and later used in *Rosalie*, 1928); "I've Got a Crush on You" (*Treasure Girl*, 1928, and later used in *Strike Up the Band*, 1930); "Oh, So Nice" (*Treasure Girl*, 1928); "Blah, Blah, Blah" (1931 film *Delicious*); "I've Got to Be There" (*Pardon My English*, 1933); and "Stiff Upper Lip" (1937 film *A Damsel in Distress*). The source of "Bootleggers' Lament" (which was heard during the Toronto portion of the tryout) is unclear.

A silent film version was released by First National Pictures in 1928; directed by Mervyn LeRoy, the cast included Colleen Moore (Kay), Lawrence Gray (Jimmy), Ford Sterling (Shorty), and Alan Hale (Jansen).

A few months after the original Broadway production closed, a return engagement opened at the Century Theatre on January 2, 1928, for sixteen performances; the cast included Julia Sanderson, Frank Crumit, and John E. Young. The work was later revived Off Broadway on April 16, 1960, at the East 74th Street Theatre for eighty-nine performances (Marti Stevens was Kay, and others in the cast were David Daniels, Bernie West, Penny Fuller, Linda Lavin, and Eddie Phillips). The cast recording was released by 20th Fox MasterArts (LP # FOX-4003) and was later reissued by Stet Records (LP # DS-15017). On November 1, 1990, David Merrick's Broadway revival opened at the Richard Rodgers Theatre for seventy-seven performances. The book was adapted by James Racheff, and the story took place in Harlem with a cast that included Angela Teek, Brian (Stokes) Mitchell, and Gregg Burge. Later in the season, Merrick brought back a revamped production that played for sixteen preview performances at the Lunt-Fontanne Theatre beginning on April 2, 1991, before permanently closing; the leading cast members were Rae Dawn Chong, Ron Richardson, and Gregg Burge.

A charming studio cast album of the score was released by Columbia Records in the 1950s (LP # OS-2550 and OL-7050); issued on CD by Sony Classical/Columbia/Legacy Records (# SK-60703) with Barbara Ruick, Jack Cassidy, and Alan Case. In 1978, a recording issued by the Smithsonian American Musical Theatre Series (released by RCA Special Products Records LP # DPL1-0310) included original cast performances by Gertrude Lawrence and duo pianists Victor Arden and Phil Ohman as well as solo piano recordings by Gershwin himself. In 1995, Nonesuch Records (CD # 79361-2) released the most complete recording of the score with a cast that included Dawn Upshaw, Kurt Ollmann, and Patrick Cassidy.

1979 Season

THE MADWOMAN OF CENTRAL PARK WEST

"An Original Musical Comedy"

Theatre: 22 Steps Theatre
Opening Date: June 13, 1979; *Closing Date*: August 25, 1979
Performances: 85
Book: Phyllis Newman and Arthur Laurents
Lyrics and *Music*: See song list for specific credits
Direction: Arthur Laurents; *Producers*: Gladys Rackmil, Fritz Holt, and Barry M. Brown; *Scenery*: Phillipp Jung; *Costumes*: Theoni V. Aldredge; *Lighting*: Ken Billington; *Musical Direction*: Herbert Kaplan
Cast: *Phyllis Newman*
The revue-like musical was presented in two acts.

Musical Numbers

Note: All songs were performed by Phyllis Newman.
Act One: "Up, Up, Up" (from unproduced musical *The Skin of Our Teeth*; lyric by Betty Comden and Adolph Green, music by Leonard Bernstein); "My Mother Was a Fortune-Teller" (lyric by Phyllis Newman, music by John Clifton); "Cheerleader" (lyric by Fred Ebb, music by John Kander); "What Makes Me Love Him" (*The Apple Tree*, 1966; lyric by Sheldon Harnick, music by Jerry Bock); "Don't Laugh" (*Hot Spot*, 1963; lyric by Martin Charnin and Stephen Sondheim, music by Mary Rodgers); "No One's Toy" (lyric and music by Joe Raposo); *Note*: "No One's Toy" included a "Woman's Medley" of the following fifteen songs: "I Enjoy Being a Girl" (*Flower Drum Song*, 1958; lyric by Oscar Hammerstein II, music by Richard Rodgers); "The Girl That I Marry" (*Annie Get Your Gun*, 1946; lyric and music by Irving Berlin); "Thank Heaven for Little Girls" (1958 film *Gigi*; lyric by Alan Jay Lerner, music by Frederick Loewe); "I Say a Little Prayer" (lyric by Hal David, music by Burt Bacharach); "Homework" (*Miss Liberty*, 1949; lyric and music by Irving Berlin); "Try a Little Tenderness" (lyric by Harry Woods, Jimmy Campbell, and Reginald Connelly, music by Harry Woods); "Happy to Keep His Dinner Warm" (*How to Succeed in Business without Really Trying*, 1961; lyric and music by Frank Loesser); "I'm Having His Baby" (lyricist and composer unknown) (possibly a parody of "[You're] Having My Baby," lyric and music by Paul Anka); "Everybody Ought to Have a Maid" (*A Funny Thing Happened on the Way to the Forum*, 1962; lyric and music by Stephen Sondheim); "Pretty Women" (*Sweeney Todd, The Demon Barber of Fleet Street*, 1979; lyric and music by Stephen Sondheim); "There Is Nothin' Like a Dame" (*South Pacific*, 1949; lyric by Oscar Hammerstein II, music by Richard Rodgers); "A Hymn to Him" (*My Fair Lady*, 1956; lyric by Alan Jay Lerner, music by Frederick Loewe); "My Lord and Master" (*The King and I*, 1951; lyric by Oscar Hammerstein II, music by Richard Rodgers); "You Are Woman" (*Funny Girl*, 1964; lyric by Bob Merrill, music by Jule Styne); and "A Woman Is a Sometime Thing" (*Porgy and Bess*, 1935; lyric by DuBose Heyward, music by George Gershwin).

Act Two: "Up, Up, Up" (reprise); "Better" (lyric and music by Ed Kleban); "Don't Wish" (lyric by Carole Bayer Sager, music by Peter Allen); "Copacabana" (lyric and music by Bruce Sussman, Jack Feldman, and Barry Manilow); "My New Friends" (lyric and music by Leonard Bernstein); "List Song" (aka "A Song of Lists") (lyric by Phyllis Newman, music by John Clifton); "My Mother Was a Fortune-Teller" (reprise)

Phyllis Newman's one-woman show *The Madwoman of Central Park West* was a semi-autographical look at three stages of her life, first as a performer, and then as a wife and mother. She now decides it's time to balance her private life and get back into show business.

Newman was married to lyricist Adolph Green, and appeared in plays, musicals, and television shows. For her delicious performance in *Subways Are for Sleeping* (1961), she won the Tony Award for Best Featured Actress in a Musical, and during the run of *The Apple Tree* (1966) she often spelled Barbara Harris in the musical's three leading female roles.

Richard Eder in the *New York Times* said Newman's performance in *Madwoman* was "mostly good and sometimes winning" but occasionally lacked a "specific flavor." Her character's "rueful kookiness" became "very tiresome" after the first thirty minutes, but when she dropped her "tepid personage" and began a "marvelous" medley of songs about women she was full of "verve and humor." Douglas Watt in the *New York Daily News* found Newman "bright, amusing and in full command of her material" but asked that "somebody please find Phyllis Newman a job in a full-fledged musical show." Howard Kissel in *Women's Wear Daily* noted Newman performed the "women's medley" with "wonderfully ironic bite" and said she was "versatile and sympathetic"; and Joel Siegel on WABCTV7 felt the evening would have been better served in a cabaret setting, and noted that while the audience was asked to sympathize with her "autobiographical setbacks," it was "impossible to sympathize with someone who is A, beautiful; B, talented; C, rich; D, all of the above."

Clive Barnes in the *New York Post* found the show "utterly delightful," and the result of Newman's decision to "take her psyche off in public and give it a wash and a whirl" resulted in a "crazy, brilliant and rather touching" evening. Newman was "all Broadway" and her show was "an idiotic charmer full of vitality, fun, fantasy and guts." He noted he had occasionally met her at cocktail parties and restaurants, and she seemed "terrifyingly bright" and made him feel like a "klutz." But in *Madwoman* she was "totally vulnerable" and "under that tough Manhattan carapace of art-deco stone there beats a heart of pure heart."

As *My Mother Was a Fortune-Teller*, the musical had first opened at the Hudson Guild Theatre on May 5, 1978, for twenty-four performances, and was directed by Arthur Laurents, who performed the same duty for the revised version which was now titled *The Madwoman of Central Park West* (and with Newman he collaborated on the script of the new version). Numbers heard in *Fortune-Teller* which weren't used in *Madwoman* are: "South American Medley" (arranged by John Clifton); "Woman in the Moon" (lyric by Barbra Streisand, music by Kenny Asher); "Some People" (*Gypsy*, 1959; lyric by Stephen Sondheim, music by Jule Styne); "Wait Till You See Her" (*By Jupiter*, 1942; lyric by Lorenz Hart, music by Richard Rodgers [the song was performed during the tryout of *By Jupiter*, and though it was listed in the New York programs, it appears the song was never performed during the Broadway run]); "Come in from the Rain" (lyric and music by Carole Bayer Sager, Melissa Manchester, and Robert Turner); and "Not Easy Being Green" (lyric and music by Joe Raposo). Between the Hudson Guild and 22 Steps productions, *The Madwoman of Central Park West* was produced at the Studio Arena Theatre in Buffalo, New York.

The "Women's Medley" was a sequence of fifteen songs that were allegedly sexist and offensive to women (for most of these, Newman was hopefully kidding). Ed Kleban's "Better" later turned up in the dreary tribute revue *A Class Act* (Off Broadway, 2000; Broadway, 2001) and was recorded for that show's cast album as well as for *The Madwoman of Central Park West* (the CD was released by DRG Records # CDSL-5212).

BRUCE FORSYTH ON BROADWAY!

"A One Man Show"

Theatre: Winter Garden Theatre
Opening Date: June 12, 1979; *Closing Date*: June 16, 1979
Performances: 5
Producers: Lee Guber and Shelly Gross (A Music Fair Concerts Presentation); *Lighting*: Richard Nelson; *Musical Direction*: Don Hunt

Cast: *Bruce Forsyth*
The revue was presented in two acts.

Musical Numbers

Note: All numbers performed by Bruce Forsyth.
Act One: Overture (medley of songs from *Little Me*, 1962 [London, 1964], music by Cy Coleman) (Orchestra); "Just in Time" (*Bells Are Ringing*, 1956; lyric by Betty Comden and Adolph Green, music by Jule Styne); Monologue; "It's Never Too Late" (lyric and music by Carmen Lombardo and John Jacob Loeb); "Claire de Lune" (piano solo) (music by Claude Debussy); "Stardust" (lyric by Mitchell Parish, music by Hoagy Carmichael); "Nola" (lyric by Sammy Skylar, music by Felix Arndt); "Singin' in the Rain" (*Hollywood Revue of 1929*; lyric by Arthur Freed, music by Nacio Herb Brown); "The Old Soft Shoe" (*Three to Make Ready*, 1946; lyric by Nancy Hamilton, music by Morgan Lewis); "New York, New York" (1976 film *New York, New York*; lyric by Fred Ebb, music by John Kander); "The Laughing Policeman" (lyric and music by Billie Grey) and "Dance Competition" (based on sequences from television show *The Generation Game*)
Act Two: Entr'acte (Orchestra); "My Shining Hour" (1943 film *The Sky's the Limit*; lyric by Johnny Mercer, music by Harold Arlen); Impression (of Noel Coward); "La vie en rose" (skit); "Valencia" (skit); "It's the Ending of My Day"; "Savoire Faire" (skit); Impressions (of Tom Jones, Dean Martin, Frank Sinatra, Sammy Davis Jr., and Anthony Newley)

Successful British stage and television personality Bruce Forsyth here made his Broadway debut in his limited engagement one-man revue. For followers of American musical theatre, the singer-comedian was best known for his performance in the 1964 London version of the 1962 Broadway musical *Little Me*, in which he played seven roles which had been performed by Sid Caesar in the New York production..

In reviewing the evening, Mel Gussow in the *New York Times* was able to contain himself. He noted Forsyth was backed by a "brassy band" and an "enormous ego," and his act was "casually vulgar and very broad." The performer "might be amusing" in a nightclub or as the opening act at a Friars' Roast, but otherwise two hours at the Winter Garden Theatre was "a bit much by anyone's standards." At the end of the second act Forsyth impersonated various celebrities (such as Tom Jones, Dean Martin, Frank Sinatra, Sammy Davis Jr., and Anthony Newley), and Gussow reported that on opening night Forsyth was joined on stage by Newley and then by Davis. It was then that the evening "came to life," and Gussow could only surmise what would happen when Newley and Davis weren't around to liven up matters.

The concert-like evening tied with *Censored Scenes from King Kong* and *Heartaches of a Pussycat* (both of which opened later in the season) as the shortest-running musical of the season (all three shows played for five performances apiece).

GOT TU GO DISCO

Theatre: Minskoff Theatre
Opening Date: June 25, 1979; *Closing Date*: June 30, 1979
Performances: 8
Book: John Zodrow
Lyrics and *Music*: Kenny Lehman, John Davis, Ray Chew, Nat Adderly Jr., Thomas Jones, Wayne Morrison, Steve Boston, Eugene Narmore, Betty Rowland, Jerry Powell, Marc Benecke, and Mitch Kerper
Based very loosely on the 1697 fairy tale *Cinderella* by Charles Perrault.
Direction: Larry Forde; *Film Sequences*: Robert Rabinowitz; *Producers*: Jerry Brandt and Gotta Dance, Inc., in association with Roy Rifkind, Julie Rifkind, Bill Spitalsky, and WKTU-Radio 92; *Choreography*: Jo Jo Smith and Troy Garza, with additional choreography by George Faison; *Scenery*: James Hamilton; *Costumes*: Joe Eula; *Lighting*: S. A. Cohen; *Musical Direction*: Kenny Lehman
Cast: Joe Masiell (Narration, Vitus), Irene Cara (Cassette), Patrick Jude (Billy), Lisa Raggio (Minnie), Laurie Dawn Skinner (Contact), Patti Karr (Antwerp), Jane Holzer (Lila), Charlie Serrano (Cubby), Rhetta Hughes (Snap-Flash), Justin Ross (Pete), Marc Benecke (Marc), Bob Pettie (Spinner); Singers: Robin Lynn Beck,

Gloria Covington, Gerri Griffin, Jack Magradey, Billy Newton-Davis; Dancers: Conni Marie Brazleton, Prudence Darby, Ronald Dunham, Miguel Gonz, Christine Jacobsen, Peter Kapetan, Patrick Kinser-Lau, Julia Lema, Bronna Lipton, Mark Manley, Jodi Moccia, Jamie Patterson, Dee Ranzweiler, Adrian Rosario, Willie Rosario, Sue Samuels

The musical was presented in two acts.

The action takes place during the present time in New York City.

Musical Numbers

Note: * = choreography by George Faison.

Act One: "Puttin' It On" (lyric and music by Kenny Lehman and Steve Boston) (Ensemble; Lead Vocalist: Robin Lynn Beck); "Disco Shuffle" (lyric and music by Ray Chew with assistance from Nat Adderly Jr.) (*) (Patrick Jude, Irene Cara); "All I Need" (lyric and music by Thomas Jones and Wayne Morrison) (Irene Cara); "It Won't Work" (lyric and music by John Davis) (Joe Masiell); "Trust Me" (lyric and music by Kenny Lehman and Steve Boston) (Charlie Serrano, Laurie Dawn Skinner); "In and Out" (lyric and music by Kenny Lehman and Steve Boston, with additional lyrics by Marc Benecke) (Marc Benecke, Company); "Got Tu Go Disco" (lyric and music by John Davis) (Ensemble; Lead Vocalist: Billy Newton-Davis); "Pleasure Pusher" (lyric and music by Eugene Narmore) (Justin Ross); "If That Didn't Do It, It Can't Be Done" (lyric and music by Ray Chew with assistance from Nat Adderly Jr.) (*) (Company)

Act Two: "Inter-Mish-Un" (lyric and music by Kenny Lehman, Thomas Jones, and Wayne Morrison) (Billy Newton-Davis); "Hanging Over and Out" (lyric and music by Kenny Lehman and Steve Boston) (Joe Masiell); "Chic to Cheap" (lyric and music by Jerry Powell) (Rhetta Hughes); "Bad, Glad, Good and Had" (lyric and music by John Davis) (Irene Cara); "Cassie" (lyric and music by Ray Chew with assistance from Nat Adderly Jr.) (Patrick Jude); "Takin' the Light" (lyric and music by Kenny Lehman, Thomas Jones, and Wayne Morrison) (Irene Cara, Patrick Jude, Ensemble with Lead Vocalist: Gerri Griffin); "Gettin' to the Top" (lyric and music by John Davis) (*) (Patti Karr)

The new Broadway season stumbled badly with its first two book musicals, *Got Tu Go Disco* and ***But Never Jam Today***. Both were hip versions of children's stories (*Cinderella* and *Alice in Wonderland*), and both played for just eight performances. For its time, *Got Tu Go Disco* was the most expensive flop in Broadway history, and according to Steven Suskin in *More Opening Nights on Broadway* the musical's $3 million capitalization "went down the disco drain."

Perhaps the title of *Got Tu Go Disco* said it all, and if it didn't, then maybe the heroine's name Cassette told you enough. The musical was set in a disco-obsessed New York City and included songs with such titles as "Disco Shuffle," "Inter-Mish-Un," "Bad, Glad, Good and Had," and the title song. There were also characters who sported such names as Snap-Flash, Vitus, and Spinner. Cassette works in a boutique (the Disco Rag Store) which sells disco clothes, but she cares naught for disco dancing, even though her mother Antwerp (Patti Karr) and sister Lila ([Baby] Jane Holzer, of Andy Warhol fame) are dedicated to the God of Disco. Cassette's boyfriend Billy (Patrick Jude) urges her to go to the very in and chic discotheque The Dream Palace. Cassette's shoppe provides her with an appropriate disco outfit, she dazzles the nightclub with her disco dancing and wins the evening's dance contest, and then quickly disappears into the night. The disco's proprietor Vitus (Joe Masiell) searches for her, happily finds her, takes her back to the Dream Palace, and there she's crowned Queen of the Disco. It just doesn't get any better than that.

Richard Eder in the *New York Times* noted that the "sheer mediocrity" of the evening barely suggested "theatre of any kind." The songs lacked "noticeable character," and the performances were strangely conceived. Irene Cara was "droopy" in her pre-disco scenes and was "still droopy" in her queen-of-the-disco moments; Patrick Jude was "bland" (and as the "lover," he shouldn't have wiped his mouth after a kiss); and Masiell was "agreeable" but not "compelling." But Rhetta Hughes (as Snap-Flash, the queen of the disco who is dethroned by Cassette) was "the live one among the zombies" and provided a "slinky and gleefully poisonous performance." Eder and other critics noted how important microphones were to the performers, and mentioned that Cara and Jude clutched their mikes "as if they were ice-cream cones they were unwilling to put down."

Clive Barnes in the *New York Post* said the book was "obviously an exercise in camp-trash of the sub-Bette Midler variety" and noted that twelve lyricists and composers had created the "memorably unmemorable" score and suggested their labors "must have been like being called up for jury duty." Douglas Watt in the *New York Daily News* said the "amateurish" and "leaden and humorless" musical was "pure trash" and "as meaningless as its title." The choreography was "elementary," the songs were "exceedingly monotonous," and while the costumes and décor were "striking in a cheap way" the evening was little more than "a combination fashion show and disco concert."

Christopher Sharp in *Women's Wear Daily* said that at best the musical was "harmless and inoffensive," and noted that one "fine" sequence showed that clothes were the "passport into the disco" and that the performers themselves took on "the appearance of accessories to their fashions." Dennis Cunningham on WCBSTV2 said the show was "so dreary, inept and amateurish" that it made *Bowling for Dollars* look "inspired." The dialogue was "unspeakable," the performances "shockingly bad," and the score "monotonously unmemorable."

During previews, the team of Ashford and Simpson was credited as contributors to the score, and Robby Monk, the lighting designer, was succeeded by S. A. Cohen. The songs "Dance Forever" and "Higher Places" were cut, and while the title page of the program included Betty Rowland as one of the contributors of the lyrics and music, the specific music credits didn't list her name. The original director was John Zadrow, who was succeeded by costume designer Joe Eula, who himself was followed by Larry Forde, and in the role of Billy, Scott Holmes was succeeded by Patrick Jude.

The cast album was to have been recorded by Casablanca Records, but was cancelled due to the musical's short run.

BROADWAY OPRY '79

"A Little Country in the Big City"

Theatre: St. James Theatre
Opening Date: July 27, 1979; *Closing Date*: August 2, 1979
Performances: 6
Creative Director: Jonas McCord; *Producer*: Family Affair Enterprises, Inc. (David S. Fitzpatrick and Edward J. Lynch Jr., Executive Producers; Spyros Venduras and Joseph D'Alesandro, Associate Producers); *Scenery* and *Lighting*: Michael J. Hotopp and Paul de Pass
Cast: Program One—*Tanya Tucker*, Floyd Cramer, Don Gibson, Mickey Newbury; Program Two—*Waylon Jennings*, the Crickets, the Waylors
The revue was presented in two acts. (*Note*: The program didn't list individual musical numbers.)

Broadway Opry '79 was an ambitious series that intended to offer fifteen programs of country-and-western music over a two-month period on Broadway. Due to indifferent attendance for the first two programs, the remaining thirteen were cancelled. The plan was for the programs to change every Tuesday and Friday, with each program giving a total of four performances during a three-day period. But some performances for the first two programs were cancelled and ticket prices were suddenly cut from $16, $13, and $9 to $12, $10, and $8.

Cheaper ticket prices and two positive reviews from the *New York Times* didn't help, and the series shut down after its first week (among the performers who had been scheduled to appear during the course of the series were: Conway Twitty, Larry Gatlin, Earl Scruggs, George Jones, Brenda Lee, Johnny Paycheck, and Roger Miller). The program's notes optimistically reported that the *Broadway Opry* series would visit Broadway on an annual basis, and the next season of performances would begin the following spring at the Broadway Opry House, "a permanent oasis" in the "concrete jungle" that would "be fashioned after Mickey Gilley's legendary bar in Texas and . . . feature mechanical bronco busting rodeos, macho strength testers . . . and the biggest bar east of the Pecos." (Presumably, a currently existing legitimate Broadway or movie house was to have been refurbished for the projected venue.)

Robert Palmer in the *New York Times* found the first program "one of the most appealing country music shows imaginable." Don Gibson was the evening's "most rousing" performer, and the popular Tanya Tucker gave "indication of a talent that should last longer than her present notoriety as a country music sex symbol." In the same newspaper, John Rockwell reviewed the second program and said it was "a deeply enjoyable show." He praised Waylon Jennings's "down-to-earth sophistication" and "artistic imagination," and noted that the repertoire of the Crickets, who performed with "unpretentious charm," mostly consisted of numbers associated with their Buddy Holly heyday.

The program with Earl Scruggs was of course scrubbed, and it marked the performer's second luckless Broadway venture. But at least his first show, the 1954 revue *Hayride* (a self-described "hillbilly, folk musical") made it to Broadway and lasted for twenty-four performances.

EVERY GOOD BOY DESERVES FAVOUR

"A PLAY FOR ACTORS AND ORCHESTRA"

Theatre: Metropolitan Opera House
Opening Date: July 30, 1979; *Closing Date*: August 4, 1979
Performances: 8
Play: Tom Stoppard
Music: Andre Previn
Direction: Tom Stoppard; *Producers*: The Kennedy Center and The Metropolitan Opera (Roger L. Stevens, Producer); *Scenery* and *Costumes*: Eldon Elder; *Lighting*: Thomas Skelton; *Musical Direction*: David Gilbert
Cast: *Rene Auberjonois* (Ivanov), *Eli Wallach* (Alexander), Carol Teitel (Teacher), Bobby Scott (Sacha), *Remak Ramsay* (Doctor), Carl Low (Colonel Rozinsky)
The play with music was presented in one act.
The action takes place in a totalitarian country during the present time.

Tom Stoppard's play *Every Good Boy Deserves Favour* was a London import that opened in New York at the Metropolitan Opera House for a limited engagement of eight performances. The play, which lasted about seventy minutes and included music by Andre Previn, was written and staged to include a full-piece symphony orchestra (the work has also been produced with a chamber orchestra).

The story was set in a totalitarian country during the present time, and focused on two inmates who share a cell in a mental institution. Ivanov (Rene Auberjonois) is mad, and truly believes that a symphony orchestra hovers about and that in an instant he can command it to play (which of course it does). His cellmate is political dissident Alexander (Eli Wallach), who is incarcerated because of his political views. According to the logic of the government, Alexander must be insane because only an insane person would believe the government would institutionalize a sane person.

Stoppard's verbal wit, coupled with the musical interludes by the orchestra, made for an unusual if somewhat precious and gimmicky evening. Like some of Stoppard's other plays, *Every Good Boy Deserves Favour* was perhaps too clever for its own good, and thus was occasionally tiresome and pretentious.

Mel Gussow in the *New York Times* said the work was "an unusual theatrical and musical event" and one of the "oddest" productions seen at the Met since Phillip Glass and Robert Wilson's opera *Einstein on the Beach* (1976). He also noted that the full orchestra gave the play "a richness and even an opulence that embellishes the author's comic point of view." Douglas Watt in the *New York Daily News* found the play "a mid-summer blessing" and noted the music was an "entertaining pastiche" that was "grounded in Stalinist musical ethic" with occasional touches of Prokofiev. Clive Barnes in the *New York Post* praised the "brilliant and desperately funny" evening but was disappointed with the "solidly upbeat" ending (both Ivanov and Alexander are released because of a bureaucratic error).

John Beaufort in the *Christian Science Monitor* said he'd "never encountered a comparable experiment," and the play was more than just "an audacious novelty." While there were musical references to Tchaikovsky, Shostakovich, and Prokofiev, Previn's score was "no mere pastiche" because it enhanced "the mood, emotion, and tension of the drama." Edwin Wilson in the *Wall Street Journal* mentioned that Previn's contributions were "deliberately derivative" of Russian composers, and the "first-rate" evening melded into "a witty, moving and absolutely unique theatre experience."

But Jack Kroll in *Newsweek* had reservations about the play. It was "one of the most unwieldy curiosities of our time" and its inherent ironies were "suddenly dissipated by pathos" and "the buzz of agitprop." The evening had "brilliance" but was "finally the work of a new boy scout who had let his matches get wet." As for Previn's score, it was "a puncturing pastiche" of Tchaikovsky, Shostakovich, and Prokofiev, but at times was also "straight-faced movie music."

The play's world premiere took place at London's Royal Festival Hall on July 1, 1977, as the opening work of the John Player Centenary Festival. Directed by Trevor Nunn, the cast included Ian Richardson (Ivanov), Ian McKellen (Alexander), and Patrick Stewart (Doctor), and Andre Previn conducted the London Symphony Orchestra.

One year prior to the New York production, the work had opened at the Kennedy Center's Concert Hall on August 29, 1978; Andre Previn conducted the Pittsburgh Symphony Orchestra, and except for John Wood (who played Ivanov), all the cast members in the production reprised their roles for the later New York run. For the Kennedy Center production, Wood was also the director.

The script was published in hardback and paperback by Faber and Faber in 1978 (in an edition that also included Stoppard's play *Professional Foul*). The original London cast album was released by RCA Victor/Red Seal Records (LP # ABL1-2855) and includes dialogue and musical interludes. A film version was produced for BBC in 1978 with a cast that included Ian McKellen (Alexander) and Ben Kingsley (Ivanov).

BUT NEVER JAM TODAY

Theatre: Longacre Theatre
Opening Date: July 31, 1979; *Closing Date*: August 5, 1979
Performances: 8
Book: Vinnette Carroll and Bob Larimer
Lyrics: Bob Larimer
Music: Bert Keyes and Bob Larimer; dance music by H. B. Barnum; incidental music by Donald Johnston
Based on Lewis B. Carroll's novels *Alice's Adventures in Wonderland* (1865) and *Through the Looking Glass* (1872).
Direction: Vinnette Carroll (Robert L. Borod, Production Supervisor); *Producers*: Arch Nadler, Anita MacShane, and The Urban Arts Theatre; *Choreography*: Talley Beatty; *Scenery* and *Costumes*: William Schroder; *Lighting*: Ken Billington; *Musical Direction*: Donald Johnston
Cast: Marilynn Winbush (Alice), Cleavant Derricks (Caterpillar, Tweedledee, The Seven of Spades), Lynne Thigpen (Persona Non Grata); Mushrooms: Brenda Braxton, Clayton Strange, Sharon K. Brooks, Garry Q. Lewis, Celestine DeSaussure, and Jeffrey Anderson-Gunter; Lynne Clifton-Allen (The Black Queen), Jeffrey Anderson-Gunter (The White Rabbit, The Cheshire Cat, The Mock Turtle), Reginald Vel Johnson (The Duchess, Humpty-Dumpty, The King of Hearts); Cooks: Cleavant Derricks, Sheila Ellis, and Celestine DeSaussure; Jai Oscar St. John (The Mad Hatter, Tweedledum, The Two of Spades), Sheila Ellis (The March Hare, The Five of Spades), Celestine DeSaussure (The Dormouse), Charlene Harris (The White Queen, The Queen of Hearts); Guards: Clayton Strange and Garry Q. Lewis
The musical was presented in two acts.
The action takes place in Wonderland.

Musical Numbers

Act One: "Curiouser and Curiouser" (Marilynn Winbush); "Twinkle, Twinkle, Little Star" (Cleavant Derricks, Lynne Thigpen, Company); "Long Live the Queen" (Lynne Clifton-Allen, Marilynn Winbush); "A Real Life Lullabye" (Reginald Vel Johnson, Cooks); "The More I See People" (Jeffrey Anderson-Gunter); "My Little Room" (Marilynn Winbush); "But Never Jam Today" (Charlene Harris, Marilynn Winbush); "Riding for a Fall" (Lynne Thigpen, Reginald Vel Johnson, Marilynn Winbush); "All the Same to Me" (Jai Oscar St. John, Cleavant Derricks); "I've Got My Orders" (Marilynn Winbush)

Act Two: "God Could Give Me Anything" (Jai Oscar St. John, Sheila Ellis, Cleavant Derricks); "But Never Jam Today" (reprise) (Company, Lynne Thigpen); "I Like to Win" (Marilynn Winbush); "And They All Call the Hatter Mad" (Lynne Thigpen); "Jumping from Rock to Rock" (Jeffrey Anderson-Gunter, Marilynn Winbush, Company); "They" (Jai Oscar St. John, Sheila Ellis, Cleavant Derricks); "Long Live the Queen" (reprise) (Company); "I've Got My Orders" (Marilynn Winbush, Company)

Over a period of sixteen years, Vinnette Carroll presented at least five musical adaptations of the works of another Carroll (Lewis). But for all her efforts, the shows never quite got off the ground and of the two most visible adaptations, one (***Alice***) closed prior to Broadway and the other (*But Never Jam Today*) lasted just one week in New York.

The first of Carroll's *Alice* musicals was developed in collaboration with Anita McShane (who coproduced the current version) in an Actors' Studio production in 1962; from there, the work was presented on April 23, 1969, for one performance at the New York City Center (with a score by Gershon Kingsley, choreography by Talley Beatty, and a cast that included Marie Thomas as Alice and Sherman Hemsley as The Mad Hatter and The Seven of Spades). As ***Alice*** (and with a score by Micki Grant), the musical's pre-Broadway tryout opened at the Forrest Theatre, Philadelphia, Pennsylvania, on May 31, 1978, for an anticipated summer's run before moving on to New York; but poor reviews and lack of business forced an early closing in mid-June (for more information about ***Alice*** and other musicals based the *Alice* stories, see entry for ***Alice***).

Two months after ***Alice***'s closing, Carroll produced *But Never Jam Today* in workshop at the Urban Arts Corps Theatre in August 1978 for twelve performances with Marilynn Winbush, Cleavon Derricks, Clinton Derricks-Carroll (Carroll's adopted son), and Reginald Vel Johnson. A year later the current *But Never Jam Today* opened on Broadway with a book by Carroll and Bob Larimer, lyrics by Larimer, and music by Larimer, Alan Keys, H. B. Barnum, and Donald Johnston; the production included many of the cast members who had appeared in the August 1978 mounting.

Richard Eder in the *New York Times* noted that while the musical included characters and episodes from Lewis B. Carroll's original novels, Vinnette Carroll's adaptation was "a rabbit hole's away from the spirit and the humor" of the originals. In order to reach her dreams, Alice has to travel on a board game from Square One to Square Eight, and Eder said the show itself never got beyond Square Three. Alice's ordeals were "shared by the audience," and the story "haphazardly hopscotches its way across Wonderland." Douglas Watt in the *New York Daily News* said the entire evening lacked imagination, and he found the book, lyrics, and music "stultifying" with choreography that reinforced the "pervasive level of mediocrity." He also thought the set resembled "a sort of chic Coney Island bathhouse."

Edwin Wilson in the *Wall Street Journal* complained that the show lacked "sparkle and inventiveness," and Clive Barnes in the *New York Post* noted that "one man's jam is another man's jelly" and said the "insufferably cute" book was full of "radical cheek" which came across as "a singularly charmless kiddie show." While Joel Siegel on WABCTV7 thought the score was "wonderful" and in concert format would be a hit, the book got "curiouser and curiouser" and it sometimes seemed the dialogue had "never been north of 110th Street."

GILDA RADNER LIVE FROM NEW YORK

Theatre: Winter Garden Theatre
Opening Date: August 2, 1979; *Closing Date*: September 22, 1979
Performances: 52
Lyrics and *Music*: See below for credits.
Skits: Anne Beatts, Lorne Michaels, Marilyn Suzanne Miller, Don Novello, Michael O'Donoghue, Gilda Radner, Paul Shaffer, Rosie Shuster, Alan Zwiebel
Direction: Lorne Michaels; *Producers*: Ron Delsener and Lorne Michaels (Barbara Burns, Associate Producer); *Choreography*: Patricia Birch; *Scenery*: Eugene Lee and Akira Yoshimura; *Costumes*: Franne Lee and Karen Roston; *Lighting*: Roger Morgan; *Musical Direction*: Howard Shore
Cast: *Gilda Radner*, Diana Grasselli, Myriam Valle, and Maria Vidal (of Desmond Child and Rouge), Bob Christianson, Don Novello, Paul Shaffer, Nils Nichols, The Candy Slice Group (John Caruso, Paul Shaffer, Howard Shore, and G. E. Smith)
The revue was presented in two acts.

Gilda Radner was a popular comedian on NBC's *Saturday Night Live*, and in 1975 had appeared in the Off-Broadway revue *National Lampoon Show* (besides Radner, the cast of that production included John Belushi, Bill Murray, and Harold Ramis). Like Bruce Forsyth's stint at the Winter Garden Theatre earlier in the season, the critics felt Radner's choice of venue was too large and would have been better served in a more intimate setting. Further, the critics said her material (which here was in the nature of an uncensored episode of *Saturday Night Live*) worked better on television, and some of the skits lost their way within the confines of the large auditorium. Since her material didn't translate well to the stage as independent comedy, the evening was best enjoyed only if one was familiar with her television work. One or two critics hoped Radner would return in a vehicle equal to her talents, but her only other Broadway appearance was in Jean Kerr's 1980 comedy *Lunch Hour* which didn't make much of an impression and lasted for just 262 performances. Radner's career was cut short by illness, and she died in 1989.

The evening included a handful of songs: Radner's well-received opening number "Let's Talk Dirty to the Animals" (lyric and music by Michael O'Donoghue); "I Love to Be Unhappy" (lyric and music by Gilda Radner and Paul Shaffer); "Goodbye, Saccharine" (lyric and music by Hardwick, Marilyn Suzanne Miller, and Paul Shaffer); "If You Look Close" (lyric and music by Gilda Rader and Paul Shaffer); "Gimme Mick" (lyric and music by Gilda Radner and Paul Shaffer); "Honey (Touch Me with Your Clothes On)" (lyric and music by Gilda Radner and Paul Shaffer); and a special "piano recital" and sing-along of "The Way We Were" (1973 film *The Way We Were*; lyric by Marilyn and Alan Bergman, music by Marvin Hamlisch).

Radner offered a parade of her popular television personas, including the unpleasant and self-obsessed teenager Judy Miller, the past-her-prime Jewish princess and former rock star Rhona Weiss, the adenoidal Lisa Loopner, the deaf and eternally confused teacher Emily Litella, and the pushy television newscaster Roseanne Roseannadanna.

Also from *Saturday Night Live* was Don Novello, who appeared in three sequences in his television persona of Father Guido Sarducci, who is supposedly the rock music critic and gossip columnist for the "unofficial" Vatican newspaper *L'Osservatore Romano*. Novello had created the character in nightclubs, and it became part of his standard repertoire on the late-night television series. The critics felt his monologues were the highlights of the evening, and they particularly enjoyed "Pay for Your Sins" in which the priest explains that for each day we live God deposits $14.50 into a heavenly bank account for us. When we die, God charges us for our sins by withdrawing the appropriate amount; because God requires $100,000 to forgive a murder, that could be a bit of a problem, but an act of masturbation costs just a quarter (but the good father notes that those quarters certainly add up).

Mel Gussow in the *New York Times* said Radner was an "original," but her show was a "disappointment." He noted that "diehard Radnerians" would probably be "thoroughly entertained," but otherwise the evening lacked the "lunacy" of *Saturday Night Live*. He also mentioned that the Winter Garden was a "cavernous space for such a small-scale entertainment." Don Nelson in the *New York Daily News* said the evening never quite matched Radner's "splendid" opening number "Let's Talk Dirty to the Animals," and he felt her special brand of television humor didn't "translate" well to the stage.

Edwin Wilson in the *Wall Street Journal* said most of the evening was "extended TV fare" and he noted that "what might get by on the TV tube tends to go down the tubes on Broadway." But Radner had "genuine" talent and he wondered "what marvels she might accomplish if she appeared in a Broadway show worthy of her talents." Clive Barnes in the *New York Post* found the revue "outrageously funny" and said Radner's characterizations were "shrewdly observed and impeccably presented," and Howard Kissel in *Women's Wear Daily* said Radner was "an extremely engaging and talented comedienne" who gave her fan base her "greatest hits" but needed to find her own voice in order "to sustain an evening of theatre."

John Beaufort in the *Christian Science Monitor* felt the large Winter Garden stage wasn't the appropriate venue for Radner's Broadway debut because "the overall effect is a diminution rather than an enhancement of the Radner persona," and David Ansen in *Newsweek* said the revue was an "amiable, if unsurprising, entertainment" and he praised Don Novello as "the sharpest wit of the evening."

As *Gilda Radner Live*, the cast album was released by Warner Brothers Records (LP # HS-3320), and was later issued on CD by Rhino Flashback. As *Gilda Live*, a 1980 film version of the revue was directed by Mike Nichols and released by Broadway Entertainment and Warner Brothers.

NAUGHTY MARIETTA

Theatre: New York State Theatre
Opening Date: August 30, 1979; *Closing Date*: September 2, 1979
Performances: 6
Book: New book by Jack Eddleman, based on the adaptation by Frederick S. Roffman from the original book by Rida Johnson Young
Lyrics: Rida Johnson Young; additional lyrics by Frederick S. Roffman
Music: Victor Herbert
Direction: Jack Eddleman; *Producer*: The New York City Opera Company; *Choreography*: Graciela Daniele; *Scenery*: Oliver Smith; *Costumes*: Patricia Zipprodt; *Lighting*: Ken Billington; *Choral Direction*: Lloyd Walser; *Musical Direction*: John Mauceri
Cast: Elizabeth Hynes (Marietta d'Altena), Howard Hensel (Captain Richard Warrington), Alan Titus (Etienne Grandet), Susanne Marsee (Adah Le Clercq), Lara Teeter (Private Silas Slick), Dana Krueger (Lizette), James Billings (Acting Governor Grandet), David Gately (Florenze), Don Yule (Sergeant Harry Blake), Harlan Foss (Rudolfo), Taras Kalba (Pirate), Michael Rubino (Pirate), Edward Zimmerman (Town Crier), Susan Delery-Whedon (Flower Girl), Sally Lambert (Flower Girl, Felice), Cindy Lynn Aaronson (Nanette), Leslie Luxemburg (Fanchon), Barry Carl (Knife Grinder, Turk), George Bohachevsky (Flower Vendor), Louis Perry (Bird Vendor), Robert Brubaker (Fruit Vendor), Harris Davis (Sugar Cane Vendor), Don Carlo (Indian), Jose Bourbon (Pierrot), Toni-Ann Gardella (Graziella), Glenn Rowan (Major-Domo), Esperanza Galan (Spanish Dancer); San Domingo Ladies: Toni-Ann Gardella, Candace Itow, and Rebeka Pradera; Quadroon Waiters: Taras Kalba, Michael Rubino, Rafael Romero, and Jose Bourbon; Mervin Crook (Man at Auction); Ensemble: The New York City Opera Company Chorus and Dancers
The operetta was presented in two acts.
The action takes place in Louisiana in 1803, on the island of Barataria at the mouth of the Mississippi River and in New Orleans.

In August 1978, the New York City Opera Company had presented a new version of Victor Herbert's 1910 operetta *Naughty Marietta*. The production hadn't gone over well, and according to Raymond Erickson in the *New York Times*, Beverly Sills (who had become the company's new general director shortly after the revival closed) asked Jack Eddleman to "start over from scratch and give me a hit!" So Eddleman readapted the book (for the 1978 revival, Rida Johnson Young's original book had been adapted by Frederick S. Roffman), and also directed the new production.

In reviewing the current revival, Harold C. Schonberg in the *New York Times* noted there were major cast changes, the book had been "tightened," and there were "fewer of the longueurs" from last year. But he cautioned that the operetta didn't "speed along" and said the work lacked "musical substance." The score's famous songs were "cloying" and "the very soul and substance of Muzak." Further, the music "lacked backbone" and was "pulverizingly genteel." The new adaptation offered "more fun," and while last season's cast treated the work as if it were *Parsifal*, there was thankfully "a little give and take" in the new adaptation. Last year there were "embarrassed titters" in the audience, and now there was "affectionate laughter and jeering." But for all that, he wondered if the revival had been "worth all the effort."

For more information about the operetta, the 1978 production, and a list of musical numbers, see entry for the August 1978 revival.

THE MERRY WIDOW

Theatre: New York State Theatre
Opening Date: September 5, 1979; *Closing Date*: September 9, 1979
Performances: 7 (in repertory)
Libretto and *Lyrics*: Victor M. Leon and Leo Stein; English adaptation and dialogue by Ursula Eggers and Joseph D. Rugeris and English lyrics by Sheldon Harnick
Music: Franz Lehar
Direction: Tito Capobianco; *Producer*: The New York City Opera Company; *Choreography*: Jessica Redel; *Scenery* and *Costumes*: Carl Toms; *Lighting*: Ken Billington; *Musical Direction*: Imre Pallo
Cast: David Rae Smith (Baron Mirko Zeta), Marianna Christos (Valencienne), Alan Titus (Count Danilo Danilovitch), Diana Soviero (Anna Glawari), Bruce Reed (Camille de Rosillon), Harlan Foss (Vicomte Cas-

cada), Alan Kays (Raoul St. Brioche), Herbert Hunsberger (Bogdanovitch), Jane Shaulis (Sylviane, Dodo), William Ledbetter (Kromov), Penny Orloff (Olga, Jou-Jou), Louis Perry (Pritchitch), Susan Delery-Whedon (Praskovia, Clo-Clo), James Billings (Njegus), Candace Itow (Lolo), Toni-Ann Gardella (Frou-Frou), Raven Wilkinson (Margot); Members of Petrovenian and Parisian Society, Dancers, Servants, and Waiters: The New York City Opera Company Chorus and Dancers
The operetta was presented in three acts.
The action takes place in Paris during the early 1900s.

The New York City Opera Company had most recently produced Franz Lehar's operetta *The Merry Widow* a year earlier. For more information about the operetta and its recent New York revivals, see entries for the 1974, 1976, April 1978, and September 1978 productions.

Allen Hughes in the *New York Times* praised Imre Pallo's "authoritative and supple" conducting and said the "opulent" décor offered "the kind of eye-filling grandeur" that was "just right" for operetta. But he had occasional reservations about the two leads. He had hoped to be "entranced" by Diana Soviero, but reported she'd often "look sidewise and down at the stage floor." And he suspected "crisper diction" and a "steelier voice than her extraordinarily pretty one" would have been helpful. As for Alan Titus, he sometimes tried too hard "for operatic effect in a work not made for it."

PETER PAN, OR THE BOY WHO WOULDN'T GROW UP

"A Musical Production of the Play by Sir James M. Barrie"

Theatre: Lunt-Fontanne Theatre
Opening Date: September 6, 1979; *Closing Date*: January 4, 1981
Performances: 551
Book: (*Note*: The book for the musical has never been officially credited; some sources incorrectly cite James M. Barrie, who died seventeen years before the musical was produced.)
Lyrics: Carolyn Leigh
Music: Mark Charlap
Additional Lyrics: Betty Comden and Adolph Green
Additional Music: Jule Styne
Based on the 1904 play *Peter Pan*, or *The Boy Who Wouldn't Grow Up* by James M. Barrie.
Direction and *Choreography*: Rob Iscove; *Producers*: Zev Bufman and James M. Nederlander in association with Jack Molthen, Spencer Tandy, and J. Ronald Horowitz; *Scenery*: Peter Wolf; *Costumes*: Bill Hargate; *Lighting*: Thomas Skelton; *Musical Direction*: Jack Lee
Cast: Jonathan Ward (Michael), James Cook (Nana), Maggy Gorrill (Liza, Ostrich), Marsha Kramer (Wendy, Jane), Alexander Winter (John), Beth Fowler (Mrs. Darling), George Rose (Mr. Darling, Captain Hook), *Sandy Duncan* (Peter Pan), Jim Wolfe (Lion), Richard Loreto (Turtle), Robert Brubach (Kangaroo), Chris Farr (Slightly), Michael Estes (Curly), Rusty Jacobs (First Twin), Joey Abbott (Second Twin), Carl Tramon (Tootles), Dennis Courtney (Nibs), Guy Stroman (Noodler), Arnold Soboloff (Smee), Kevin McCready (Crocodile), Maria Pogee (Tiger Lily), Jon Vandertholen (Starkey), Trey Wilson (Cecco), Steven Yuhasz (Mullins), Gary Daniel (Jukes), Neva Rae Powers (Wendy Grown Up); Pirates: William Carmichael, James Cook, Gary Daniel, Dianna Hughes, Guy Stroman, Jon Vandertholen, Trey Wilson, Steven Yuhasz; Indians: Robert Brubach, Maggy Gorrill, Sharon-Ann Hill, Richard Lareto, C. J. McCaffrey, Kevin McCready, David Storey, Jim Wolfe; Trees: C. J. McCaffrey, Kevin McCready, David Storey
The musical was presented in three acts.
The action takes place early in the twentieth century, first in London and then in Neverland.

Musical Numbers

(*Note*: * = songs by Leigh and Charlap; ** = songs by Comden, Green, and Styne.)
Act One: "Tender Shepherd" (*) (Beth Fowler, Marsha Kramer, Alexander Winter, Jonathan Ward); "I've Got to Crow" (*) (Sandy Duncan); "Neverland) (**) (Sandy Duncan); "I'm Flying" (*) (Sandy Duncan, Marsha Kramer, Alexander Winter, Jonathan Ward)

Act Two: "Morning in Neverland" (**) (Animals, The Lost Boys); "Pirate Song" (George Rose, Pirates); "A Princely Scheme" (aka "Hook's Tango") (*) (George Rose, Pirates); "Indians!" (Maria Pogee, Indians); "Wendy" (**) (Sandy Duncan, Boys); "Another Princely Scheme" (George Rose, Pirates); "I Won't Grow Up" (Sandy Duncan, Boys); "Mysterious Lady" (**) (Sandy Duncan, George Rose, Company); "Ugg-a-Wugg" (**) (Sandy Duncan, Maria Pogee, Children, Indians); "Distant Melody" (**) (Marsha Kramer)

Act Three: "Hook's Waltz" (**) (George Rose, Pirates); "The Battle" (Sandy Duncan, George Rose, Company); "I've Got to Crow" (reprise) (Sandy Duncan, Company); "Happily Ever After" (**) (Sandy Duncan, Tinkerbell); "Tender Shepherd" (reprise) (Marsha Kramer, Alexander Winter, Jonathan Ward); "I Won't Grow Up" (reprise) (The Darling Family, The Lost Boys); "Neverland" (reprise) (Sandy Duncan)

The hit revival told the familiar story of Peter Pan (Sandy Duncan), the boy who never grew up and lives in magical Neverland with the Lost Boys. He sometimes secretly visits the Darling Family's home in London in order to hear Wendy (Marsha Kramer) read stories to her young brothers, and one night returns there to retrieve his lost shadow. When he's discovered by Wendy, he invites her and her brothers to visit Neverland, and (with the help of some pixie dust) they're soon flying off to the wondrous land of Indians, fairies, mermaids, strange animals, and Captain Hook (George Rose) and his band of pirates. But eventually the Darling children realize they must return home and resume the business of growing up. But not Peter Pan, who will remain in Neverland and stay forever young.

Walter Kerr in the *New York Times* said the program credited "Flying by Foy," but that was "nonsense" because the "flying is by Duncan, and it's the most abandoned I've ever seen"; Douglas Watt in the *New York Daily News* found her "a smashing Peter Pan to behold" and noted she "flies like a dream" (and she saved her greatest effect for the finale, when she took her curtain call by flying into the auditorium and over the heads of the audience); and John Beaufort in the *Christian Science Monitor* found Duncan "among the nimblest in the long line of Peter Pans" and noted she was "slight of figure but commanding of spirit."

Jack Kroll in *Newsweek* commented that one of the "charms" of Duncan's performance was the "hint that Peter's refusal to grow up is a predicament as well as a blessing," and Gerald Clarke in *Time* said her performance was "so right that it is easy to forget how wrong it could be, and the show's success is chiefly hers."

Dennis Cunningham on WCBSTV2 said George Rose was "a comic festival unto himself," but Clarke complained that Rose "overshot his mark" with "campy mannerisms" and as a result his "almost effeminate" Hook was "modeled less on [Cyril] Ritchard and more on Hermione Gingold."

Marilyn Stasio in the *New York Post* found the revival "endlessly enchanting," but Howard Kissel in *Women's Wear Daily* said it was "enjoyable but not really satisfying" (and he reported that while Rob Iscove was the director and choreographer of record, Ron Field had unofficially taken over these duties). Joel Siegel on WABCTV7 said Duncan was "absolutely superb" and "at *least* Mary Martin's equal" and while *Peter Pan* was not a "great" musical, the production made it a "great show."

During the revival's tryout, Todd Porter (John) and Christina Kumi Kimball (Liza and Tiger Lily) were succeeded by Alexander Winter and Maggy Gorrill.

The musical first opened at the Winter Garden Theatre on October 20, 1954, for 152 performances with Mary Martin (Peter Pan) and Cyril Ritchard (Mr. Darling and Captain Hook). The relatively short run is misleading: the production was a virtual sell-out at every performance and the limited engagement was extended from sixteen to nineteen weeks. And because the producers had signed a contract with NBC to televise the musical during the spring of 1955, the legendary television version was shown live (and in color) on March 7, just a few days after the Broadway closing. As part of the network's *Producers' Showcase* series, the musical was seen by some sixty-five million viewers (or about 64,768,048 more than the approximate 231,952 who saw the production on Broadway). A second live production was shown on January 9, 1956, and this was followed by a third live presentation on December 8, 1960. The 1955 and 1956 telecasts exist only in black-and-white, and the 1960 version remains the only one in color (this version was re-telecast in 1963, 1966, 1973, 1989, and 1990, and was later released on DVD by GoodTimes Video).

Besides the current production, the musical has been revived on Broadway four times with Cathy Rigby in mostly limited-engagement bookings: on December 13, 1990 (Lunt-Fontanne Theatre, 45 performances); on January 5, 1992 (Minskoff Theatre, 48 performances); on November 23, 1998 (Marquis Theatre, 48 performances); and on April 7, 1999 (Gershwin Theatre, 168 performances). The 1999 revival was taped and shown on the Arts and Entertainment Network in 2000 and was issued on DVD by Hart Sharp Video.

The 1954 cast album was issued by RCA Victor (LP # LOC-1019/LSO-1019E) and the CD was released by RCA/BMG (# 3762-2-RG). In 1997, Jay Records released an album with Cathy Rigby (CD # CDJAY-1280), and other recordings include a 1976 Hong Kong production sung in Cantonese (HMI Records CD # 103) and a 1991 Paris cast album (Carrerre Records CD # 9031-76251-2).

On December 4, 2014, the musical was telecast by NBC with Allison Williams (Peter Pan) and Christopher Walken (Captain Hook). Although this politically corrected version omitted "Ugg-a-Wugg," Alessandra Stanley in the *New York Times* noted that "near-naked [Indian] men gyrating like Chippendales dancers weren't necessarily any more culturally sensitive." Five songs were added for the telecast: Leigh and Charlap's "When I Went Home," which had been cut during the 1954 tryout; the offending "Ugg-a-Wugg" became "True Blood Brothers," with a new lyric by Adolph Green's daughter Amanda Green, who also wrote new lyrics for three songs from other Comden, Green, and Styne musicals, "A Wonderful World without Peter" (heard as "Something's Always Happening on the River" from the 1958 play with music *Say, Darling*) and "Only Pretend" and "Vengeance" (heard as "I Know about Love" and "Ambition" in the 1960 Broadway musical *Do Re Mi*). The soundtrack was released by Broadway Records, and the DVD by Universal/NBC.

Awards

Tony Award Nominations: Best Revival (*Peter Pan*); Best Leading Actress in a Musical (Sandy Duncan)

EVITA

Theatre: Broadway Theatre
Opening Date: September 25, 1979; *Closing Date*: June 25, 1983
Performances: 1,567
Book and *Lyrics*: Tim Rice
Music: Andrew Lloyd Webber
Direction: Harold Prince; *Producers*: Robert Stigwood in association with David Land (R. Tyler Gatchell Jr., and Peter Neufeld, Executive Producers); *Choreography*: Larry Fuller; *Scenery* and *Costumes*: Timothy O'Brien and Tazeena Firth; *Lighting*: David Hersey; *Musical Direction*: Rene Wiegert
Cast: Patti LuPone (Eva), Terri Klausner (Eva [Wednesday and Saturday matinees]), Mandy Patinkin (Che), Bob Gunton (Peron), Jane Ohringer (Peron's Mistress), Mark Syers (Magaldi); Company—The People of Argentina: Dennis Birchall, Peppi Borza, Tom Carder, Robin Cleaver, Andy DeGange, Mark East, Teri Gill, Carlos Gorbea, Pat Gorman, Rex David Hays, Terri Klausner, Michael Lichtefeld, Carol Lugenbeal, Paula Lynn, Morgan MacKay, Peter Marinos, Sal Mistretta, Jack Neubeck, Marcia O'Brien, Nancy Opel, Davia Sacks, James Sbano, David Staller, Michelle Stubbs, Robert Tanna, Clarence Teeters, Susan Terry, Phillip Tracy, David Vosburgh, Mark Waldrop, Sandra Wheeler, Brad Witsger, John Leslie Wolfe, Nancy Wood, John Yost; Children: Megan Forste, Bridget Francis, Nicole Francis, Michael Pastryk, Christopher Wooten
The musical was presented in two acts.
The action takes place mostly in Argentina during the period 1934–1952.

Musical Numbers

Act One: "A Cinema in Buenos Aires, July 26, 1952" (Company); "Requiem for Evita" (Company); "Oh, What a Circus" (Mandy Patinkin, Company); "On This Night of a Thousand Stars" (Mark Syers); "Eva, Beware of the City" (Mark Syers, Patti LuPone, Family); "Buenos Aires" (Patti LuPone, Dancers); "Goodnight and Thank You" (Mandy Patinkin, Patti LuPone, Lovers); "The Art of the Possible" (Bob Gunton, Patti LuPone, Colonels); "Charity Concert" (Company); "I'd Be Surprisingly Good for You" (Patti LuPone, Bob Gunton); "Another Suitcase in Another Hall" (Jane Ohringer); "Peron's Latest Flame" (Mandy Patinkin, Patti LuPone, Company); "A New Argentina" (Patti LuPone, Bob Gunton, Mandy Patinkin, Company)
Act Two: Entr'Acte (Orchestra); "On the Balcony of the Casa Rosada" (Bob Gunton, Mandy Patinkin, Company); "Don't Cry for Me, Argentina" (Patti LuPone); "High Flying, Adored" (Mandy Patinkin, Patti

LuPone); "Rainbow High" (Patti LuPone, Dressers); "Rainbow Tour" (Mandy Patinkin, Patti LuPone, Bob Gunton, Peronists); "The Actress Hasn't Learned (the Lines You'd Like to Hear)" (Patti LuPone, Mandy Patinkin, Company); "And the Money Kept Rolling In (and Out)" (Mandy Patinkin, Company); "Santa Evita" (Children, Workers); "Waltz for Eva and Che" (Patti LuPone, Mandy Patinkin); "She Is a Diamond" (Bob Gunton, Officers); "Dice Are Rolling" (Bob Gunton, Patti LuPone); "Eva's Final Broadcast" (Patti LuPone, Mandy Patinkin); "Montage" (Company); "Lament" (Patti LuPone, Mandy Patinkin)

The British import *Evita* was clearly the season's event musical, and with 1,567 performances was its longest-running show. The work won seven Tony Awards (including Best Musical), enjoyed one of the few hit Broadway songs of the era ("Don't Cry for Me, Argentina"), and established Patti LuPone as the foremost musical theatre star of the era.

Based on the life of Eva Peron (1919–1952), the sung-through musical by Tim Rice and Andrew Lloyd Webber centered on the ambitious Argentine actress and radio performer Eva Duarte. A poor "backstreet girl," she captured the fancy of the country's popular general Juan Peron, and upon their marriage and his election to the presidency they ruled the country. Because of her background, Eva was never accepted by the Argentine military or by the country's social set, and was generally snubbed by royalty and governments during her "rainbow tour" of Europe. However, the poor (the shirtless ones, or descamisados) embraced her as a symbol of upward mobility, and while her foundation for the poor has been ridiculed as a sham from which she and Peron skimmed millions, the foundation apparently spent a fortune on such social issues as poverty and equal rights for women. But Eva and Peron's world came to an end when she was diagnosed with cancer and died in 1952 at the age of thirty-three. He remained in power for three more years; after his exile to Spain, he returned to Argentina and was again elected president, but he never recaptured the popularity of his years with Eva.

Like Rice and Webber's ***Jesus Christ Superstar***, the musical was first a concept album. It was released by MCA Records in 1976 on a two-LP set (# MCA2-11003) and later issued on a two-CD set by MCA (# MCAD2-11541) with Julie Covington (Eva), Paul Jones (Peron), and C. T. (Colm) Wilkinson (Che); one song from the album ("The Lady's Got Potential") wasn't carried over for the stage version, which premiered at the Prince Edward Theatre on June 21, 1978, for 3,176 performances with Elaine Page (Eva), Joss Ackland (Peron), and David Essex (Che).

The musical had many strengths and some structural weaknesses, but the overpoweringly theatrical nature of the production won the day, and Harold Prince's brilliant direction transformed the material into compelling musical theatre.

The libretto's major problem was that it reported rather than dramatized events, and as a result it seemed that a second *Evita* musical was taking place offstage and the one presented in view of the audience was a reporter's version of Eva's life and times. And while Rice's lyrics tried for cleverness with puns and colloquialisms, they sometimes came across as sophomoric. But the character of Eva was carefully crafted as an enigmatic and complicated woman who was both villain and saint, and so the creation was an ingenious one that blended a hard, cold, and grasping figure with one who was also soft and vulnerable.

The musical daringly began with the announcement of Eva's death and her subsequent funeral, and there was a carefully wrought circular structure to the score. During the funeral scene, an unseen Eva briefly sings a snippet of "Don't Cry for Me, Argentina" to the millions who attend her funeral, and then later at the height of her and Peron's political power she again sings the number, this time on the balcony of the presidential palace Casa Rosada as the masses below watch and cheer her. Moreover, an early scene found her hairdressers, beauty consultants, and fashion designers extolling her "Eyes! Hair! Mouth! Figure!" as they prepare her for the "Rainbow Tour," and at the end of the musical, and with the same music, her morticians exclaim over her "eyes, hair, face, image" as they prepare to embalm her.

Rice and Webber also created some fictional friction between Eva and Che (Guevara). In real life, the two never met, but in the musical he was a sardonic narrator of the events and he shadowed Eva as her long-lost conscience. After an introductory choral sequence, it was Che who was given the musical's first full-fledged song with his ironic description of Eva's funeral ("Oh, What a Circus"), and the number was one of many in which Rice created an early first-act "commentary" song for a (usually) male figure; ***Superstar*** had earlier offered "Heaven on Their Minds" for Judas, and *Blondel* (1983), *Chess* (1986, London; 1988, New York), and *Aida* (2000) followed suit with similar ones.

The richly melodic score was one of Webber's finest, and he and Rice went off in fascinating tangents, such as the surreal "Waltz for Eva and Che"; the pounding soldiers' lament "Peron's Latest Flame" (in their dark glasses and military finery, the soldiers stomped out their contempt for Eva, and Larry Fuller's march-like dance was one of the choreographic highlights of the era); Che's ambivalent ode to Eva, "High Flying, Adored"; Eva's exultant "Rainbow High"; and the blistering choral sequence "A New Argentina." And of course there was the ubiquitous "Don't Cry for Me, Argentina," Eva's powerful moment before the crowds at the Casa Rosada. As mentioned, this was one of the era's few theatre songs to find wide popularity, and it's all the more surprising because even in context the lyric is oblique and abstract with a touch of the dadaesque about it. *Evita* may well be the only musical to emerge with a stream-of-consciousness hit song. The score's weakest and most extraneous number is "Another Suitcase in Another Hall" for one of Peron's discarded mistresses, a number that virtually demands to be cut but nonetheless always shows up in revivals and even made its way into the film version.

Walter Kerr in the *New York Times* complained that the story was told "second-hand" from Che's viewpoint, and thus the evening was an "emotional limbo" in which he felt he was reading "endless footnotes" without benefit of the text. As for the score, it sometimes seemed "as though Max Steiner had arranged it for Carmen Miranda," but there was nonetheless an array of waltzes, polkas, and marches that "keep us alert for tricky tempo-shifts." He praised Patti LuPone ("ice water plainly runs in her veins," and she moved with "rattlesnake vitality") and scenic designers Timothy O'Brien and Tazeena Firth, who created a world of "placards, banners, torches and bodies" to depict political rallies and inaugurations. (There was also creative use of a catwalk-like bridge, which was most effective when it represented the balcony of the Casa Rosada where Eva sings "Don't Cry for Me, Argentina" to the masses.)

Edwin Wilson in the *Wall Street Journal* said the mise en scène was the musical's most important aspect because the physical production was "dazzling"; he praised the "frightening crescendo" of "A New Argentina" with its shirtless peasants carrying posters and torches, and he noted that "The Art of the Possible" provided a "deadly version" of musical chairs in which Peron and his rival generals vie for the last standing chair of politics and power. Prince also made effective use of newspaper projections and newsreel films. But Wilson commented that the authors wanted to both glamorize and denounce Eva, and as a result the evening was "hopelessly muddled."

Douglas Watt in the *New York Daily News* said *Evita* was a "dud." The musical looked "exceedingly smart" and offered many "clever staging touches," but was "spectacularly vulgar" as well as "dispiriting and even pointless." John Beaufort in the *Christian Science Monitor* suggested that for all the "striking" visuals and "nervous theatrical energy," there was "a lack of dramatic substance," and Howard Kissel in *Women's Wear Daily* found the musical more "banal" than ***Superstar*** with its "characterless" music and "predictable" material, but he admired Prince's staging and the show's scenic design.

Jack Kroll in *Newsweek* reported that on opening night someone asked Arthur Miller what he thought of *Evita*, and the playwright replied that he had a "good time" but wished there had been "more content." Kroll felt that despite the show's "theatrical fireworks," the evening was "a very soft show about a very tough cookie." T. E. Kalem in *Time* said *Evita* was "a spectacular eye-catcher" but "seldom gets a grip on a playgoer's feelings." The score was for the most part "ingratiatingly melodic" but seemed "composed by the British equivalent of ASCAP anonymous" and the lyrics too often fell back on "straw-clutching rhymes." But he praised Larry Fuller's "army platoon in full regalia" and their "absurdist parody of close-order drill," said Prince directed with "brilliant precision at a crackling tempo" and noted that Prince hurled "the dramatic thunderbolts of the evening." Kalem pointed out that in the political rally sequences Prince "engulfs players and playgoers alike in a demagogic inferno."

Clive Barnes in the *New York Post* found *Evita* "a stunning, exhilarating experience, especially if you don't think about it too much." LuPone and Mandy Patinkin gave "dazzling" performances and "rarely if ever" had he seen "a more excitingly staged Broadway musical," one which "will deservedly become a classic Broadway memory." But he noted the show's content was "hollow" because the audience was expected "to deplore Evita's morals but adore her circuses."

There are over three dozen recordings of the score, but the essential ones are the above-cited studio cast album as well as the original London and Broadway cast recordings. The London production was released by MCA (CD # 3527) and the Broadway cast album was issued by MCA on a two-LP and a two-CD set (LP # MCA-2-11007 and CD # MCAD2-11007). And lest we forget, there was also *Disco Evita* (Polygram CD # 314-537-473-2) which includes seven numbers from the musical as well as a song titled "Eva's Theme: Lady Woman" (by Boris Midney), with all vocals performed by Festival. The script of the musical was published in hardback by Drama Book Specialists in 1978.

The impressive 1996 film version was released by Universal Pictures; directed by Alan Parker and with a screenplay by Parker and Oliver Stone, the film starred Madonna (Eva), Jonathan Pryce (Peron), and Antonio Banderas (Che), and included a new song, "You Must Love Me," which won the Academy Award for Best Song. The film was released on DVD by Cinergi Pictures Entertainment, Inc., and Buena Vista Pictures (# 13849), and the two-CD soundtrack album was issued by Warner Brothers Records (# 946346).

The musical was revived on Broadway at the Marquis Theatre on April 5, 2012, for 337 performances with Elena Roger (Eva), Michael Cerveris (Peron), and Ricky Martin (Che); the production included "You Must Love Me," and the cast album was released by Sony on a two-CD set (which included bonus material of Roger singing "Don't Cry for Me, Argentina" in Spanish).

Fourteen years earlier, Jerome Lawrence and Robert E. Lee's Broadway drama *Diamond Orchid* looked at the story of Eva and Juan Peron (here they were called Paulita and Jorge Salvador Brazo). The play opened at Henry Miller's Theatre on February 10, 1965, for five performances, and the leading roles were played by Jennifer West and Mario Alcalde.

Awards

Tony Awards and Nominations: Best Musical (***Evita***); Best Leading Actress in a Musical (**Patti LuPone**); Best Featured Actor in a Musical (Bob Gunton); Best Featured Actor in a Musical (**Mandy Patinkin**); Best Director of a Musical (**Hal Prince**); Best Book (**Tim Rice**); Best Score (lyrics by **Tim Rice** and music by **Andrew Lloyd Webber**); Best Scenic Designer (Timothy O'Brien and Tazeena Firth); Best Costume Designer (Timothy O'Brien and Tazeena Firth); Best Lighting Designer (**David Hersey**); Best Choreographer (Larry Fuller)
New York Drama Critics' Circle Award: Best Musical (1979–1980) (***Evita***)

THE 1940'S RADIO HOUR

"A New Musical"

Theatre: St. James Theatre
Opening Date: October 7, 1979; *Closing Date*: January 6, 1980
Performances: 105
Play: Walton Jones
Lyrics and *Music*: See list of musical numbers for lyricist and composer credits.
Direction: Walton Jones; *Producers*: Jujamcyn Productions, Joseph P. Harris, Ira Bernstein, and Roger Berlind; *Choreography*: Thommie Walsh; *Scenery*: David Gropman; *Costumes*: William Ivey Long; *Lighting*: Tharon Musser; *Musical Direction*: Stanley Lebowsky
Cast: Arny Freeman (Pops Bailey), John Sloman (Stanley), Josef Sommer (Clifton A. Feddington), Stanley Lebowsky (Zoot Doubleman), Jack Hallett (Wally Fergusson), Merwin Goldsmith (Lou Cohn), Jeff Keller (Johnny Cantone), Crissy Wilzak (Ginger Brooks), Kathy Andrini (Connie Miller), Stephen James (B. J. Gibson), Joe Grifasi (Neal Tilden), Mary-Cleere Haran (Ann Collier), Dee Dee Bridgewater (Geneva Lee Browne), John Doolittle (Biff Baker). Jo Speros (Darla); *Orchestra*: Stanley Lebowsky (Zoot Doubleman), Maurice Mark (Neeley "Flap" Kovacs), Jane Ira Bloom (Bonnie Cavanaugh), Billy Butler (Custis Jones), Ray Chanfeld (Gus Bracken), Dennis Elliott (Scoops Millikan), Josh Edwards (Moe "Lockjaw" Ambrose), John Doolittle (Biff Baker), Joe Petrizzo (Fritz Canigliaro), Dennis Anderson (Charlie "Kid Lips" Snyder), J. D. Parran (Ned "Woof" Bennett), Mel Rodnon (Totts Schoenfeld), Rick Centalonza (Red Bradford), Jon Goldman (Bob "Bobo" Lewis), Ron Tooley (Buzz Cranshaw), Bruce Samuels (Phil Bentley), Lloyd Michaels (Pieface Minelli)
The musical was presented in one act.
The action takes place in New York City on December 21, 1942, at about 8 P.M.

Musical Numbers

Note: The program didn't include a list of musical numbers; the following is taken from the published script.
"Chattanooga Choo-Choo" (1941 film *Sun Valley Serenade*; lyric by Mack Gordon, music by Harry Warren) (Josef Sommer, Kathy Andrini, Company); "Pepsi Cola" (musical advertisement) (Kathy Andrini, Stephen

James, Company); "Daddy" (lyric and music by Bobby Troupe) (Kathy Andrini, Band); "(Our) Love Is Here to Stay" (1938 film *The Goldwyn Follies*; lyric by Ira Gershwin, music by George Gershwin) (Jeff Keller); "That Old Black Magic" (1942 film *Star-Spangled Rhythm*; lyric by Johnny Mercer, music by Harold Arlen) (Mary-Cleere Haran); "Ain't She Sweet" (lyric by Jack Yellen, music by Milton Ager) (John Doolittle, Company); "How About You" (1942 film *Babes on Broadway*; lyric by Ralph Freed, music by Burton Lane) (Stephen James, Kathy Andrini); "Blue Moon" (with a different lyric, the song was written as "Prayer" and was intended for the 1934 film *Hollywood Party*; it was later revised but unused as "Manhattan Melodrama" aka "It's Just That Kind of Play" for the 1934 film *Manhattan Melodrama*, and was heard in that film as "The Bad in Every Man"; as an independent song not introduced in a musical or film, the number became popular as "Blue Moon"; lyric by Lorenz Hart, music by Richard Rodgers) (Joe Grifasi); "Chiquita Banana" (musical advertisement) (Girls); "Rose of the Rio Grande" (lyric by Edgar Leslie, music by Harry Warren and Ross Gorman) (Dee Dee Bridgewater, Men); "I'll Never Smile Again" (1941 film *Las Vegas Nights*; lyric and music by Ruth Lowe) (Joe Grifasi, Stephen James, Mary-Cleere Haran, Crissy Wilzak, Kathy Andrini, Jeff Keller); "The Boogie-Woogie Bugle Boy from Company 'B'" (1941 film *Buck Privates*; lyric and music by Don Raye and Hughie Prince) (Stephen James, Kathy Andrini, Crissy Wilzak); "Blues in the Night" (1941 film *Blues in the Night*; lyric by Johnny Mercer, music by Harold Arlen) (Crissy Wilzak, Men); "Jingle Bells" (with Glenn Miller arrangements) (Kathy Andrini, Crissy Wilzak, Stephen James, Mary-Cleere Haran, Jack Hallett, Company); "I Got It Bad (and That Ain't Good)" (*Jump for Joy*, 1941; lyric by Paul Francis Webster, music by Duke Ellington) (Dee Dee Bridgewater); "At Last" (1942 film *Orchestra Wives*) (lyric by Mack Gordon, music by Harry Warren) (Stephen James); "Little Brown Jug" (lyric and music by Joseph Winner; with Glenn Miller arrangements) (Band); "Have Yourself a Merry Little Christmas" (1944 film *Meet Me in St. Louis*; lyric and music by Hugh Martin and Ralph Blane) (Mary-Cleere Haran); "Strike Up the Band" (*Strike Up the Band*, 1930; lyric by Ira Gershwin, music by George Gershwin) (Company); "I'll Be Seeing You" (*Right This Way*, 1938; lyric by Irving Kahal, music by Sammy Fain) (Mary-Cleere Haran, Jeff Keller, Company); "The Mutual Manhattan Variety Cavalcade Theme" (music by Stanley Lebowsky) (Band)

Walton Jones's *The 1940's Radio Hour* was a facsimile of a supposedly typical radio show from 1942. The fictional "The Mutual Manhattan Variety Cavalcade" airs weekly on Mondays—direct from the WOV Broadcast Studios in the Algonquin Room on the ground floor of the Hotel Astor in New York City. It's December 21, it's a cold and snowy night outside, and inside the technical staff and performers are getting ready for the weekly broadcast. Among the radio-land population are Frank Sinatra–type Johnny Cantone (Jeff Keller), four thrushes (Kathy Andrini, Mary-Cleere Haran, Crissy Wilzak, and Dee Dee Bridgewater), the announcer Clifton A. Feddington (Josef Sommer), the comic (Joe Grifasi), the band trumpeter who is about to go into the army (Stephen James), the stage manager (Merwin Goldsmith), the stage doorman (Arny Freeman), and other regulars. During the course of the broadcast the songs and patter are interrupted for advertisements ("You mean there's a nice-smelling soap a girl can depend on to protect her against offending?"), and because there's a studio audience (that is, the audience attending *The 1940's Radio Hour*), there's also an applause sign.

The intimate show was pleasant and mild-mannered, and worked quite well in a small venue like Washington, D.C.'s Kreeger Theatre at Arena Stage almost a year earlier. But like so many intimate shows of the era, it opted for a large house (the St. James Theatre) when it moved on to Broadway. Clearly, the St. James was the wrong choice for such a cozy musical, and so the show lasted just three months in New York. One suspects that an Off-Broadway production would have enjoyed a long and profitable run.

Walter Kerr in the *New York Times* noted that when the musical was "good" it was "really very good" and "when it is bad you know what it is." He praised the broadcast itself, but felt the early part of the evening that introduced the characters was slow-going. These were "hand-me-down people" who said "highly guessable things" (and he groaned over such dialogue as, "Can you loan me twenty bucks?" "I could. I won't, but I sure could"). Edwin Wilson in the *Wall Street Journal* echoed Kerr's sentiments, and wished Jones's book had "stuck to the broadcast"; but the various "lapses" didn't "break the overall spell" and he said that "from today's perspective, many people might feel [the world of the 1942 broadcast] was not a bad place to be."

Douglas Watt in the *New York Daily News* said if the cavalcade show was still on the air, he'd "tune in every week." The evening was a "lively, tuneful, goofy and colorful toy" with "unimportant" dialogue but a "totally exhilarating hour of singing, dancing and funny commercials." John Beaufort in the *Christian Science Monitor* noted that the applause signs were "wholly unnecessary with the super-enthusiastic first-night audience." And Jack Kroll in *Newsweek* felt the evening's tone wavered "from sweet to sly to silly" but overall had a "real feeling for the pre-TV days when your ears were a receiving set for a whole world that opened inside your imagination like a flower of sound."

Clive Barnes in the *New York Post* said the musical was "fairly slender" but that Jones had captured the atmosphere of the war years "extraordinarily well." He noted the performances were "most engaging" and the old songs "splendidly memorable," but suggested the show might have been "more fun" in a cabaret setting.

The 1940's Radio Hour was first produced by the Ensemble Studio Theatre in New York during 1974 (where it was apparently produced as *The 1940's Radio Hour Christmas Show*), and then by the Yale Repertory Theatre on December 28, 1977, for sixteen performances (in what *Best Plays* reported as a world premiere). The Arena Stage production opened on November 3, 1978, and included Crissy Wilzak, Jeff Keller, Stephen James, Joe Grifasi, John Doolittle, and Jack Hallett, all of whom were seen in the Broadway version a year later. For Arena, the role of Clifton A. Feddington was played by Timothy Jerome. For New York, musical director Stanley Lebowsky portrayed Zoot Doubleman, the musical conductor for the broadcast (and of course Lebowsky was the musical director of the musical itself). Lebowsky was the composer of ***Gantry***, and in the 1950s wrote the music for the hit song "The Wayward Wind."

The programs for the Arena Stage and Broadway productions included special inserts of the program for the radio broadcast itself (the program biography for "Ginger Brooks" notes that she "became an overnight success as the only singing waitress and stacker at Romeo's Spaghetti House" . . . and, by the way, "Ginger's favorite color is red"). It appears the producers of "The Mutual Manhattan Variety Cavalcade" must have had some genuine Hollywood pull. "Have Yourself a Merry Little Christmas" was written for the MGM film *Meet Me in St. Louis*, which had its world premiere on November 22, 1944, and yet the song was heard on the variety hour some twenty-three months earlier!

Although not included in the published script, the song "You're Driving Me Crazy (What Did I Do?)" (lyric and music by Walter Donaldson) was heard in the Broadway production; and "Rosie the Riveter" (lyric and music by Redd Evans and John Jacob Loeb) was cut during previews.

The script was published in paperback by Samuel French in 1981.

SUGAR BABIES

"The Burlesque Musical"

Theatre: Mark Hellinger Theatre
Opening Date: October 8, 1979; *Closing Date*: August 28, 1982
Performances: 1,208
Sketches: Ralph C. Allen (based on traditional burlesque material)
Lyrics: Dorothy Fields and Al Dubin
Music: Jimmy McHugh
Additional Lyrics and *Music*: Arthur Malvin, and Jay Livingston and Ray Evans (*Note*: See song list for specific credits.)
Direction and *Choreography*: Ernest Flatt (production supervised by Ernest Flatt and sketches directed by Rudy Tronto); *Producers*: Terry Allen Cramer and Harry Rigby in association with Columbia Pictures (Thomas Walton Associates and Frank Montalvo, Associate Producers); *Scenery* and *Costumes*: Raoul Pene du Bois; *Lighting*: Gilbert V. Hemsley Jr.; *Musical Direction*: Glen Roven
Cast: *Mickey Rooney* (Mickey), Scot Stewart (Scot), Ann Jillian (Jillian), Tom Boyd (Tom), Peter Leeds (Peter), Jack Fletcher (Jack), Jimmy Mathews (Jimmy), *Ann Miller* (Ann), Sid Stone (Sid); Bob Williams and Louie; The Sugar Babies: Laura Booth, Christine Busini, Diane Duncan, Chris Elia, Debbie Gornay, Barbara Hanks, Jeri Kansas, Barbara Mandra, Robin Manus, Faye Fujisaki Mar, Linda Ravinsky, Michele Rogers, Rose Scudder, Patti Watson; The Gaiety Quartet: Jonathan Aronson, Eddie Pruett, Michael Radigan, Jeff Veazey
The revue was presented in two acts.

Musical Numbers

Act One: Overture (Orchestra); *A Memory of Burlesque*—"A Good Old Burlesque Show" (lyric by Arthur Malvin, music by Jimmy McHugh) (Mickey Rooney, Friends); *Welcome to the Gaiety*—"Let Me Be Your

Sugar Baby" (lyric and music by Arthur Malvin) (Peter Leeds, Jack Fletcher, The Sugar Babies); "Meet Me 'Round the Corner" (sketch) (Jimmy Mathews, Scot Stewart, Peter Leeds, Mickey Rooney, Rose Scudder, Chris Elia, Michele Rogers, Ann Jillian); *Travelin'*— "In Louisiana" (lyric by Arthur Malvin, music by Jimmy McHugh); "I Feel a Song Comin' On" (1935 film *Every Night at Eight*; lyric by Dorothy Fields and George Oppenheimer, music by Jimmy McHugh); and "Goin' Back to New Orleans" (lyric and music by Arthur Malvin) (Ann Miller, The Sugar Babies, The Gaiety Quartet); "The Broken Arms Hotel" (sketch) (Jack Fletcher, Tom Boyd, Mickey Rooney, Jimmy Mathews, Rose Scudder); *Feathered Fantasy* (*Salute to Sally Rand*)—"Sally" (lyric by Arthur Malvin, music by Jimmy McHugh) (Scot Stewart, Barbara Hanks, The Sugar Babies); The Pitchman (Sid Stone); *Ellis Island Lament*—"Immigration Rose" (lyric by Eugene West and Irwin Dash, music by Jimmy McHugh) (Mickey Rooney, The Gaiety Quartet); "Scenes from Domestic Life" (sketch) (Ann Jillian, Jimmy Mathews, Jack Fletcher, Peter Leeds, Tom Boyd, Scot Stewart, Robin Manus, Laura Booth, Debbie Gornay); *Torch Song* (*After Bobby Clark*)—"Don't Blame Me" (*Clowns in Clover*, 1932 [closed during its pre-Broadway tryout]; lyric by Dorothy Fields, music by Jimmy McHugh) (Ann Miller, Eddie Pruett); "Orientale" (Christine Busini; introduced by Jack Fletcher); "The Little Red Schoolhouse" (sketch) (Ann Miller, Rose Scudder, Diane Duncan, Jimmy Mathews, Mickey Rooney); *The New Candy-Coated Craze*—"The Sugar Baby Bounce" (lyric and music by Jay Livingston and Ray Evans) (Ann Jillian, Chris Elia, Linda Ravinsky); *Special Added Attraction*: *Madame Rentz and Her All-Female Minstrels Featuring The Countess Francine*—(Introduction: Jack Fletcher)/*Song*: "Down at the Gaiety Burlesque" and "Mr. Banjo Man" (lyrics and music by Arthur Malvin) (Ann Miller, Mickey Rooney, Jeff Veazey, The Sugar Babies)

Act Two: "Candy Butcher" (Sid Stone, The Gaiety Quartet); *Girls and Garters*—"I'm Keeping Myself Available for You" (lyric by Arthur Melvin, music by Jimmy McHugh) and "Exactly Like You" (*International Revue*, 1930; lyric by Dorothy Fields, music by Jimmy McHugh) (Ann Jillian, The Sugar Babies); "Justice Will Out" (sketch) (Tom Boyd, Peter Leeds, Mickey Rooney, Ann Miller); *In a Greek Garden* (*Salute to Rosita Royce*)—"Warm and Willing" (lyric by Jay Livingston, music by Jimmy McHugh) (Ann Jillian); "Presenting Madame Alla Gazaza" (Peter Leeds, Sid Stone, Ann Miller, Jeff Veazey, Mickey Rooney, Jimmy Mathews, Jack Fletcher, Eddie Pruett, Ann Jillian, Jonathan Aronson, Chris Elia); *Tropical Madness*—"Cuban Love Song" (1931 film *The Cuban Love Song*; lyric by Dorothy Fields, music by Jimmy McHugh and Herbert Stothart) (Scot Stewart and Michele Rogers); "Cautionary Tales" (sketch) (Rose Scudder, Jimmy Mathews, Eddie Pruett, Michael Radigan, Jeri Kansas, Jack Fletcher, Peter Leeds, Tom Boyd, Sid Stone); *Jimmy McHugh Medley*—"Every Day Another Tune (lyric and music by Arthur Melvin); "I Can't Give You Anything but Love, Baby" (*Blackbirds of 1928*; lyric by Dorothy Fields); "I'm Shooting High" (1935 film *King of Burlesque*; lyric by Ted Koehler); "When You and I Were Young Maggie Blues" (lyric and music by Harold "Jack" Frost, George Washington Johnson, J. A. Butterfield, and Jimmy McHugh); and "On the Sunny Side of the Street" (*International Revue*, 1930; lyric by Dorothy Fields) (Mickey Rooney, Ann Miller); Presenting Bob Williams and Louie; *Old Glory*—"You Can't Blame Your Uncle Sammy" (lyric by Al Dubin and Irwin Dash, music by Jimmy McHugh) (Company)

Sugar Babies was a deliriously joyful salute to old-time burlesque as well as a tribute to composer Jimmy McHugh, and it starred two Hollywood legends of the MGM years, Mickey Rooney and Ann Miller. It came along a few days after the premiere of ***Evita*** and a month after the opening of the ***Peter Pan*** revival, and with these three hits the new season was off to a flying start.

Gorgeously decked out in scenery and costumes by Raoul Pene du Bois, the revue included a number of classic burlesque sketches ("Meet Me 'Round the Corner," "The Little Red Schoolhouse"), nods to burlesque queens of yore (Little Egypt and Sally Rand), a bevy of standards by Jimmy McHugh, Bob Williams's classic routine with his lazy dog Louie, plus pitchmen, candy butchers, and pulchritudinous chorus girls. No one was surprised when Ann Miller showed she could out-tap 'em all, but she raised eyebrows with her crisp singing voice in the great Merman tradition of brassy Broadway belting.

Mickey Rooney was in his glory as the naughty boy of burlesque, and nothing on Broadway topped his drag routine as the dowdy, run-down "countess" (Francine in the show, Hortense in the published script) who wears a loud flowered slit-skirt dress of shocking pinks and baby blues (costume designer Raoul Pene du Bois had come up with some delicious horrors for Ethel Merman to wear in *Panama Hattie* [1940], but even Hattie might have deemed Mickey's outfit a trifle tacky), a frowzy blonde wig, and high heels worn with white rolled-down socks. To the accompaniment of sentimental music, the countess recalls the sad saga of the men in her life: On her wedding night, the groom asked if he was her first, and she replied, "*Why does everybody ask me that?*" When she entered a bar with her pet duck, someone asked, "Where did you get that pig?" She replied, "It's not a pig; it's a duck." And the person informed her, "*I was talking to the duck.*" When someone from her past asked what she was up to, she replied, "*Fifty dollars.*" And the countess was particularly rueful about the army colonel who fell in love with her and held her close, closer, and even closer . . . "*and then he went off in his uniform and I never saw him again.*" Rooney's monologue as the countess kept topping itself with corny lines, outrageous puns, and risqué humor, and it may have been the most inspired moment of his long career.

Walter Kerr in the *New York Times* said the evening was a "Rooney occasion," and the "indefatigable" performer was "exactly as talented" as when at the age of three or four he "rammed a cigar into his mouth" and "made a star of himself." And Miller was in "stunning shape," tapped "as though there'd been no yesterday," and sang with "a voice as penetrating as a noon whistle." He concluded that he had "a grand time, thank you."

John Beaufort in the *Christian Science Monitor* noted that in his Broadway debut Rooney proved he was a great comic in the tradition of Sid Caesar, Bobby Clark, Bert Lahr, and Jimmy Durante. He was the "consummate entertainer," and Miller's voice had "shattering impact" and her dances aimed "for the speed of light." The headline of T. E. Kalem's review in *Time* saluted "Mighty Mick on Broadway," and he noted that Miller's "taps are tops" and said the patriotic finale sent playgoers home "on a wave of euphoria." Jack Kroll in *Newsweek* said Rooney was "as much Mr. Show Business as anyone from Century City to Shubert Alley," and Miller "fills the air with a star-shower of taps" and sang "in the clarion tradition of Ethel Merman." He also noted that her "astonishing jet-black sculptured coiffure" was like a "tonsorial badge of honor."

Edwin Wilson in the *Wall Street Journal* said the revue was a "fast-paced entertainment" with "more corn than was harvested in Iowa in the fall" and if all the risqué one-liners "were laid end to end they would stretch the length of the Orpheum circuit." Clive Barnes in the *New York Post* praised the "wonderfully slick" and "very nostalgic" revue, and noted that "no expense" had been "spared" in this "homage to a classical American theatrical form."

During the tryout, the following were deleted: the songs "Wouldn't You Like to Taste My Pear" (lyric by Arthur Malvin, music by Jimmy McHugh), "I'm in the Mood for Love" (1935 film *Every Night at Eight*; lyric by Dorothy Fields, music by Jimmy McHugh), and "I Just Want to Be a Song and Dance Man" (lyric by Harold Adamson, music by Jimmy McHugh) and the sketch "The World's Greatest Female Sharpshooter" (which may have morphed into "The World's Greatest Knife Thrower" for the national tour). During the Broadway run, "I Want a Girl (Just Like the Girl That Married Dear Old Dad)" (lyric by William Dillon, music by Harry von Tilzer) was added to the score. When Bob Williams and Louie left the production, the sketch "Bon Appetit" was added, and then later a juggling sequence by Michael Allen Davis was substituted. The sketch "Justice Will Out" seems to have undergone at least two title changes ("The Court of Last Retort" and "Irish Justice") during the course of the revue's tryout, Broadway run, and national tour.

The script was published in paperback by Samuel French in 1983. The cast album was released by Broadway Entertainment Records (LP # BE-8302-R); for the album, Jane Summerhays sang the Ann Jillian role, and the album includes: "Immigration Rose," which was cut during the Broadway run; "I'm in the Mood for Love" and "I Just Want to Be a Song and Dance Man," both of which had been cut during the tryout; and "The City Song" (lyric and music by Mickey Rooney), which was added during the Broadway run. The audiocassette release of the cast album (# BE—8302-C) also includes: "The Little Red School House," "The Sugar Baby Bounce," "The Song of the Auctioneer" (lyric and music by Leroy Van Dyke; added during the Broadway run), "Cuban Love Song," and two numbers apparently added during the Broadway run ("Father, Dear, Father, Dear" and "The Boss Upstairs"). The CD was released by Varese Sarabande (# VSD-5453).

At different times during the Broadway run, Miller was joined by Joey Bishop, and then later by Rip Taylor; and Rooney was joined by Helen Gallagher. There were various national tours of the production; one starred Rooney and Miller; another Carol Channing and Robert Morse; and another Eddie Bracken and J. P. Morgan (later in the tour, Bracken costarred with Mimi Hines and Phil Ford). The tours included salutes to Ed Wynn ("A Very Moving Love Story") and Sophie Tucker, and the latter tribute included "I'm the Last of the Red Hot Mamas" (lyric by Jack Yellen, music by Milton Ager), "Papa, Don't Go Out Tonight" (lyric by Jack Yellen, music by Milton Ager), and "Some of These Days" (lyric and music by Sheldon Brooks). Other songs added for the tour were: "A Good Old Mammy Song" (lyric and music by Irwin Levine and L. Russel Brown), "I Can't Believe That You're in Love with Me" (lyric by Clarence Gaskill, music by Jimmy McHugh), and

"Trouble in Paradise" (lyric and music by Michael Martin Brown); and the sketch "Our Divine Diva" ("Direct from the Met") was also added.

The London production opened at the Savoy Theatre on September 13, 1988, with Rooney and Miller.

Awards

Tony Award Nominations: Best Musical (*Sugar Babies*); Best Leading Actor in a Musical (Mickey Rooney); Best Leading Actress in a Musical (Ann Miller); Best Director of a Musical (Ernest Flatt and Rudy Tronto); Best Book (Ralph G. Allen and Terry Rigby); Best Score (lyrics and music by Arthur Malvin); Best Costume Designer (Raoul Pene du Bois); Best Choreographer (Ernest Flatt)

THE MOST HAPPY FELLA

Theatre: Majestic Theatre
Opening Date: October 11, 1979; *Closing Date*: November 25, 1979
Performances: 52
Book, *Lyrics*, and *Music*: Frank Loesser
Based on the 1924 play *They Knew What They Wanted* by Sidney Howard.
Direction: Jack O'Brien; *Producers*: Sherwin M. Goldman; A Sherwin M. Goldman Production in association with the Michigan Opera Theatre (David DiChiera, General Director) and Emhan, Inc.; *Choreography*: Graciela Daniele; *Scenery*: Douglas W. Schmidt; *Costumes*: Nancy Potts; *Lighting*: Gilbert V. Hemsley Jr.; *Musical Direction*: Andrew Meltzer
Cast: Bill Hastings (The Cashier, The Brakeman), Louisa Flaningam (Cleo), Sharon Daniels (Amy aka Rosabella), Linda Michele (Amy aka Rosabella [for Wednesday and Saturday matinees]); Waitresses: Karen Giombetti, Tina Paul, D'Arcy Phifer, and Smith Wordes; Tim Flavin (Busboy), Dan O'Sullivan (The Postman), Giorgio Tozzi (Tony), Frederick Burchinal (Tony [for Wednesday and Saturday matinees]), Adrienne Leonetti (Marie), Steven Alex-Cole (Max), Dennis Warning (Herman), Dean Badolato (Clem), David Miles (Jake), Kevin Wilson (Al), Stephen Dubov (Sheriff), Richard Muenz (Joe aka Joey), Gene Varrone (Giuseppe), Darren Nimnicht (Pasquale), Franco Spoto (Ciccio), Joe McGrath (The Doctor), Lawrence Asher (The Priest); The Neighbors' Ladies: Melanie Helton, Dee Etta Rowe, Jane Warsaw, and Sally Williams; Michael Capes (The Bus Driver); All the Neighbors and All the Neighbors' Neighbors: Steven Alex-Cole, Lawrence Asher, Dean Badolato, Michael Capes, Richard Croft, Stephen DuBov, Tim Flavin, Karen Giombetti, Bill Hastings, D. Michael Heath, Melanie Helton, David Miles, Tina Paul, D'Arcy Phifer, Patrice Pickering, Candace Rogers, Dee Etta Rowe, Bonnie Simmons, Jane Warsaw, Richard White, Carla Wilkins, Sally Williams, Kevin Wilson, Smith Wordes
The musical was presented in two acts.
The action takes place in San Francisco and Napa Valley in 1927.

Musical Numbers

Act One: Overture (Orchestra); "Ooh! My Feet!" (Louisa Flaningam); "I Know How It Is" (Louisa Flaningam, Sharon Daniels); "House and Garden" (Sharon, Daniels, Louisa Flaningam); "Seven Million Crumbs" (Louisa Flaningam); "I Don't Know" (Sharon Daniels); "Maybe He's Kind of Crazy" (Sharon Daniels, Louisa Flaningam); "Somebody, Somewhere" (Sharon Daniels); "The Most Happy Fella" (Giorgio Tozzi, Neighbors); "A Long Time Ago" (Adrienne Leonetti, Giorgio Tozzi); "Standing on the Corner" (Dennis Warning, Dean Badolato, David Miles, Kevin Wilson); "Joey, Joey, Joey" (Richard Muenz); "Soon You Gonna Leave Me, Joe" (Giorgio Tozzi);"Rosabella" (Giorgio Tozzi); "Abbondanza" (Gene Varrone, Darren Nimnicht, Franco Spoto); "Plenty Bambini" (Giorgio Tozzi); "Sposalizio" (Neighbors); "Special Delivery!" (Dan O'Sullivan); "Benevenuta" (Gene Varrone, Darren Nimnicht, Franco Spoto, Richard Muenz); "Aren't You Glad?" (Sharon Daniels); "No Home, No Job" (Sharon Daniels); "Eyes Like a Stranger" (Adrienne Leonetti); "Don't Cry" (Richard Muenz, Sharon Daniels)

Act Two: Prelude (Orchestra); "Fresno Beauties" (Workers); "Cold and Dead" (Sharon Daniels, Richard Muenz); "Love and Kindness" (Joe McGrath); "Happy to Make Your Acquaintance" (Sharon Daniels, Giorgio Tozzi, Louisa Flaningam); "I Don't Like This Dame" (Adrienne Leonetti, Louisa Flaningam); "Big D" (Louisa Flaningam, Dennis Warning, Neighbors); "How Beautiful the Days" (Giorgio Tozzi, Sharon Daniels, Adrienne Leonetti, Richard Muenz); "Young People" (Adrienne Leonetti, Giorgio Tozzi, Young Neighbors); "Warm All Over" (Sharon Daniels); "Old People Gotta" (Giorgio Tozzi); "I Like Everybody" (Dennis Warning, Louisa Flaningam); "I Love Him" (Sharon Daniels); "I Know How It Is" (Louisa Flaningam); "Like a Woman Loves a Man" (Sharon Daniels); "My Heart Is So Full of You" (Giorgio Tozzi, Sharon Daniels); "Hoedown" (Giorgio Tozzi, Sharon Daniels, Neighbors); "Mamma, Mamma" (Giorgio Tozzi); "Abbondanza" (reprise) (Gene Varrone, Darren Nimnicht, Franco Spoto); "Goodbye, Darlin'" (Louisa Flaningam, Dennis Warning); "I Like Everybody" (reprise) (Dennis Warning, Louisa Flaningam); "Song of a Summer Night" (Joe McGrath, Neighbors); "Please Let Me Tell You" (Sharon Daniels); "Tell Tony and Rosabella Goodbye for Me" (Richard Muenz); "She Gonna Come Home wit' Me" (Giorgio Tozzi); "Nobody's Ever Gonna Love You" (Giorgio Tozzi, Adrienne Leonetti, Louisa Flaningam); "I Made a Fist!" (Dennis Warning, Louisa Flaningam); Finale (Company)

The current revival of Frank Loesser's *The Most Happy Fella* was the third of five for the richly melodic work that was based on Sidney Howard's 1924 Pulitzer Prize-winning drama *They Knew What They Wanted.* Vineyard-owner Tony (Giorgio Tozzi) is a lonely middle-aged man who courts a young waitress Amy (Sharon Daniels) by mail. He calls her Rosabella, and although he once saw her in a restaurant, she never noticed him and assumes from his letters that he's young and handsome because he enclosed a photo of his hired hand Joe (Richard Muenz). When Amy discovers the truth, she goes ahead with the marriage to Tony but goes to bed with Joe on her wedding night. She becomes pregnant by him, and Joe takes off for the wide open spaces without ever knowing he's the father of her child. Tony discovers she's pregnant and banishes her from his home, but soon realizes that he loves her and must forgive her: after all, her mistake was one of the head, not of the heart.

The nearly sung-through musical premiered at the Imperial Theatre on May 3, 1956, and played for 678 performances. The rich score offered a wealth of soaring melody, including Tony and Rosabella's explosively joyous "My Heart Is So Full of You"; the shimmering choral number "Song of a Summer Night"; Joe's haunting "Joey, Joey, Joey"; the gorgeous quartet "How Beautiful the Days"; Rosabella's yearning "Somebody, Somewhere"; Tony's swirling and exultant "Rosabella"; and the lovely ballads "Don't Cry" and "Warm All Over." There was also the virile barbershop quartet-styled "Standing on the Corner" and the "Italian" crowd-pleasers "Abbondanza" and "Sposalizio."

Some of the critics were in a bit of a grouchy mood, and with many cool reviews the musical didn't attract audiences and played for less than seven weeks. Mel Gussow in the *New York Times* said the book's structure was "shaky" with a "predictable" outcome; he also noted that as Tony's jealous sister Marie, Adrienne Leonetti came from "the furrowed-brow school of acting" with her Medea-like approach to the role, and Louisa Flaningam (as Cleo, Amy's waitress friend) was "more Annie Oakley than Ado Annie." Clive Barnes in the *New York Post* stated the "bad opera" was mostly a mix of "poor Puccini and inferior diet-cola," and if the music was "disappointing" the lyrics were "insupportably banal."

Douglas Watt in the *New York Daily News* suggested the dramatic parts of the musical were the least appealing in terms of entertainment value, and when the work opted for "19th century operatic devices" the effect was "almost invariably stale." But the work "demands to be heard at regular intervals" and even with its problems *The Most Happy Fella* was "superior to the average Broadway musical." Howard Kissel in *Women's Wear Daily* said the "first-class" revival had "awkward and old-fashioned" plot construction, but Loesser's "emotionally overpowering" score was a "triumph" with one "of the most rapturous [scores] ever conceived for Broadway."

John Beaufort in the *Christian Science Monitor* said he could "scarcely imagine a more luxuriously voiced" Tony than Giorgio Tozzi's interpretation, and Sharon Daniels's Amy was one of "melting vocalism and manner." He also noted that Loesser's score was "a rich tapestry" of songs, arias, recitatives, and choral numbers. T. E. Kalem in *Time* praised the "opulent" score and said the unamplified voices brought "vocal witchcraft" to the production; and an unsigned review in *Newsweek* (probably by Jack Kroll) said Loesser's score was a "melodic cornucopia" that made the current Broadway scene seem "brittle and anemic" in comparison. He mentioned there were "creaks" in the plot and he wondered why Loesser seemed to forget about

Joe during the last half of the musical, but even so *The Most Happy Fella* was "one of the brightest ornaments from the golden age of the Broadway musical."

The first revival was presented by the New York City Center Light Opera Company on February 10, 1959, for 16 performances; the company also presented the musical at City Center on May 11, 1966, for 15 performances as part of a seasonal salute to musicals by Loesser. The musical was later produced by the New York City Opera Company at the New York State Theatre on October 19, 1991, for ten performances and then on March 7, 2006, with Paul Sorvino in the title role. On February 13, 1992, an intimate version with a two-piano orchestra opened at the Booth Theatre for 229 showings (Loesser had earlier adapted the score for two pianos, and the result was a surprisingly delightful experiment).

The original London production opened at the Coliseum on April 21, 1960, for 288 performances, and the current revival was seen on public television in March 1980.

The 1956 cast album was released on three LPs by Columbia Records (LP # OL-5120-22; later issued on a two-CD set by Sony Broadway # S2K-48010); a three-CD studio cast recording of the score was released by Jay Records (# CDJAY3-1306) with Richard Muenz reprising his role of Joe from the current revival, and the album includes a number of deleted songs written for the original production, including "I'll Buy Everybody a Beer," "Eyes Like a Stranger" (which was reinstated for the current production), and "House and Garden" (which was reinstated for the preview performances of the current production and was probably heard throughout the run). The cast album of the London production was later released by Sepia Records (# 1154) and includes bonus tracks of eight pop recordings of the score.

The script was published in the October 1958 issue of *Theatre Arts*, which is also an interesting issue because its cover features a photo of Barry Sullivan in costume from a scene in the 1958 musical *Goldilocks* (Sullivan assumed the role after Ben Gazzara dropped out, and soon Sullivan himself was succeeded by Don Ameche).

During the many years when Lucy and Ricky Ricardo lived in New York, they occasionally attended the theatre (Lucy and Ethel memorably disrupted a performance of the fictional drama *Over the Teacups*), and one time Lucy, Ricky, Ethel, and Fred went to a Broadway musical, and that musical was *The Most Happy Fella* (Desilu Productions was a silent partner in the production's investment, and selections from the cast album were heard during the episode). Before seeing the show, Fred said he didn't know anything about the plot, but given the show's title it was clear the story was about a bachelor.

Awards

Tony Award Nomination: Best Leading Actor in a Musical (Giorgio Tozzi)

STREET SCENE

Theatre: New York State Theatre
Opening Date: October 13, 1979; *Closing Date*: November 10, 1979
Performances: 5 (in repertory)
Book: Elmer Rice
Lyrics: Langston Hughes and Elmer Rice
Music: Kurt Weill
Based on the 1929 play *Street Scene* by Elmer Rice.
Direction: Jack O'Brien (Stephen Willems, Stage Director); *Producer*: The New York City Opera Company (Beverly Sills, General Director; John S. White, Managing Director); *Choreography*: Patricia Birch; *Scenery*: Paul Sylbert; *Costumes*: Nancy Potts; *Lighting*: Gilbert V. Hemsley Jr.; *Choral Direction*: Lloyd Walser; *Musical Director*: John Mauceri
Cast: Martha Thigpen (Greta Fiorentino), Diane Curry (Emma Jones), Rosemarie Freni (Olga Olsen), Ralph Bassett (Carl Olsen), Marie Young (Neighborhood Woman), Carol Rosenfeld (Shirley Kaplan), Leo Postrel (Abraham Kaplan), Kay Schoenfeld (Salvation Army Girl), Cindy Lynn Aaronson (Salvation Army Girl), Arthur Woodley (Henry Davis), Timothy Eaton (Willie Maurrant), Eileen Schauler (Anna Maurrant), Alan Kays (Sam Kaplan), Norman Large (Daniel Buchanan), Lila Herbert (Mrs. Buchanan), William Chapman

(Frank Maurrant), Robert Paul (George Jones), William Ledbetter (Steve Sankey), Jonathan Green (Lippo Fiorentino), Sally Lambert (Mrs. Hildebrand), Kathleen Hegierski (Jenny Hildebrand), Denise Adoff (Graduate), Vanessa Williams (Graduate), Matthew McGrath (Charlie Hildebrand), Dela Bartolini (Mary Hildebrand), Kimara Lovelace (Grace Davis), Catherine Malfitano (Rose Maurrant), Harlan Foss (Harry Easter), Bronwyn Thomas (Mae Jones), Reed Jones (Dick McGann), Bill Herndon (Vincent Jones), Don Carlo (Doctor Wilson), Edward Zimmerman (Officer Murphy), Robert Brubaker (Milkman), Anne Cawlo (Joan), Alizon Hull (Myrtle), Harris Davis (Workman), John Henry Thomas (Eddie), Suzy Block (Sally), Raymond Whitney (Joe), Richard Nelson (Strawberry Seller, Policeman), Susan Delery-Whedon (Corn Seller), Don Yule (James Henry), Irwin Densen (Fred Cullen), Merle Schmidt (Old Clothes Man), Frank Tippie (Man, Furniture Mover), Barry Carl (Man), Herbert Hunsberger (Man), Mark Mattaliano (Grocery Boy), Louis Perry (Ambulance Driver), Susan Egan (Music Student), James Sergi (Intern), Marie Young (Nursemaid), Rita Metzger (Nuresmaid), Don Henderson (Policeman), Harriet Greene and Merle Schmidt (Middle-Aged Couple); Off-Stage Voices: Vanessa Williams, Anne Cawlo, and Lila Herbert

The musical was presented in two acts.

The action takes place on the stoop and front sidewalk of a New York City tenement during a period of twenty-four hours in June.

The New York City Opera Company's current production of Kurt Weill's *Street Scene* was its seventh revival of the 1947 Broadway musical which had most recently been presented a year earlier with most of the same principals. After the current showing, the company brought back the work one more time in 1990. For the song listing and more information about the musical, see entry for the October 1978 revival.

Peter G. Davis in the *New York Times* said the production was "not to be missed" and noted that the more he saw the musical the more he was "touched by the richness and variety of its musical inspiration, the direct honesty of its sentiments and the sheer skill that creates such a vital piece of musical theatre." Davis said John Mauceri conducted "with sensitivity and assurance," and while the critic had some quibbles with some of the leading performances he nonetheless felt that Eileen Schauler had a "moving intensity," William Chapman showed "dramatic forcefulness," and Catherine Malfitano's soprano was "lovely."

During the current run, the October 27, 1979, performance was telecast live for public television.

SNOW WHITE AND THE SEVEN DWARFS

Theatre: Radio City Music Hall

Opening Date: October 18, 1979; *Closing Date*: November 18, 1979

Performances: 38 (*Note*: The production resumed on January 11, 1980, and closed on March 8, 1980, after sixty-eight more performances, for a seasonal total of 106 showings.)

Book: Joe Cook

Stage Lyrics: Joe Cook; *Film Lyrics*: Larry Morey

Stage Music: Jay Blackton; *Film Music*: Frank Churchill

Based on the 1938 Walt Disney film *Snow White and the Seven Dwarfs*.

Direction and *Choreography*: Frank Wagner; *Producer*: Radio City Music Hall Productions, Inc., and Robert F. Jani, Producer; *Scenery*: John William Keck; *Costumes*: Frank Spencer; *Mask Designs* and *Animal Costumes*: Joe Stephen; *Lighting*: Ken Billington; *Musical Direction*: Don Smith

Cast: David Pursley (Chamberlain), Thomas Ruisinger (King), Anne Francine (Queen), Mary Jo Salerno (Snow White), Charles Hall (Mirror, Witch), Yolande Bavan (Luna), Heidi Coe (Greta), Richard Bowne (Prince Charming), Lauren Lipson (Mother), Bruce Sherman (Huntsman); The Seven Dwarfs: Don Potter (Doc), Richard Day (Happy), Benny Freigh (Grumpy), Louis Carry (Sneezy), Jay Edward Allen (Bashful), Jerry Riley (Sleepy), Michael E. King (Dopey); Singers: Ronald Brown, Kenneth Kantor, Peter Costanza, David Dusing, Clifford Fearl, G. Jan Jones, Patricia Landi, Lauren Lipson, Linda Motashami, Dawn Parrish, Caryl Tenney; Dancers: Conni Brazleton, Beth Buker, Mary-Pat Carey, John Cashman, Danny Clark, Heidi Coe, Joan Cooper, Jay Coronel, Christopher Daniels, Ron Dunham, Alfred Gonzales, Martha Goodman, Jennifer Hammond, Norb Joerder, Janet Marie Jones, David Lee, Kim Leslie, Malcolm Perry, Michael Ragan, Patricia Register, Roger Rouillier, Jerry Sarnat, Hope Sogawa, Reisa Sperling, Thomas J. Stanton, Cassie Stein, Lynn Williford, Kim Wollen

The musical was presented in one act.

The action takes place once upon a time in a faraway land.

Musical Numbers

Note: * = songs by Cook and Blackton; ** = songs by Morey and Churchill

Overture (Orchestra); "Welcome to the Kingdom" (*) (Company); "Queen's Presentation" (*) (Company); "I'm Wishing" (**) (Mary Jo Salerno, Heidi Coe, Villagers); "One Song" (**) (Richard Bowne); "With a Smile and a Song" (**) (Mary Jo Salerno, Animals); "Whistle While You Work" (**) (Mary Jo Salerno, Animals); "Heigh-Ho" (**) (The Seven Dwarfs); "Bluddle-Iddle-Um-Dum" ("The Washing Song") (**) (The Seven Dwarfs); "Will I Ever See Her Again" (*) (Richard Bowne); "The Dwarfs' Yodel Song" ("The Silly Song") (**) (Mary Jo Salerno, The Seven Dwarfs, Animals); "Someday My Prince Will Come" (**) (Mary Jo Salerno); "Heigh-Ho" (reprise) (The Seven Dwarfs); "Here's the Happy Ending" (*) (Company)

For a few years during the 1970s, there was fear that the Radio City Music Hall would meet the wrecker's ball, but fortunately the iconic movie palace was saved, and beginning with the 1979–1980 season the theatre's new management team began producing a series of revue-like programs (including the venue's annual Christmas show) along with a very occasional book musical, such as the current *Snow White and the Seven Dwarfs* (see Appendix I for a list of the Music Hall's programs for the entire 1979–1980 season).

Based on Walt Disney's classic 1938 cartoon film, *Snow White* retained most of the movie's songs by Larry Morey and Frank Churchill (and a few new ones by Joe Cook and Jay Blackton) and followed the film's story line (with a few embellishments). The familiar fairy tale told of the beautiful Snow White (Mary Jo Salerno) who is doomed to a living death inside a glass coffin when her evil stepmother the queen (Anne Francine) gives her a poisoned apple to eat. But a kiss from Prince Charming (Richard Bowne) awakens the sleeping beauty and all ends well. And there were of course the seven dwarfs and the animal characters around, too.

John Corry in the *New York Times* noted that the "spectacle" offered "imaginative things," including anthropomorphic animals and trees (the latter were fluorescent), scenery that flew in from the wings or descended from the flies, and even some stage business in the aisles of the auditorium (there was also thunder, lightning, and rain, and, yes, Prince Charming made his entrance on a white steed). But Corry felt the romance didn't "reach" the second balcony and the show's "magic moments" tended to "drift off into space" because the venue was a "cavern" ("possibly the world's most interesting cavern," he added). Just in case we didn't get it, he called the theatre a "cavern" for a total of seven times.

Howard Kissel in *Women's Wear Daily* said the evening had "plenty of theatrical hocus-pocus to make it a treat for the kids" and the performances had "great charm," including Anne Francine, who was "deliciously wicked" as the vain and evil queen; Loren Craft in the *New York Daily News* noted the production had "more color than a box of crayons" and Francine was "good being bad"; Marilyn Stasio in the *New York Post* praised John William Keck's "truly spectacular" scenery and Ken Billington's "operatically intense lighting" which was especially striking when it added to the "splendor and terror" of the queen's transformation into a witch; John Beaufort in the *Christian Science Monitor* mentioned that Frank Spencer's costumes were "opulent" and Billington's lighting designs ranged "from the spooky to the dazzling"; and Joel Siegel on WABCTV7 praised the "breathtaking special effects" and concluded that the show provided "a wonderful, magical time."

The cast album was released by Buena Vista Records (LP # 5009).

For the national tour, the musical was presented in two acts, with the intermission following "Will I Ever See Her Again."

A lavish children's musical on the scale of *Snow White* was unusual for the era, but beginning in the mid-1990s children's musicals seemed to take over Broadway with the Disney blockbusters *Beauty and the Beast* and *The Lion King*. From there, the floodgates opened and Disney offered an array of stage musicals based on their films (*Tarzan*, *Mary Poppins*, *The Little Mermaid*, *Newsies*, *Aladdin*, and, as of the writing, *The Hunchback of Notre Dame* is apparently around the corner). Other producers got into the act with musicals aimed at children and teenage girls (*Legally Blonde*, *Xanadu*, *Shrek*, Rodgers and Hammerstein's *Cinderella*, and *Matilda*).

A KURT WEILL CABARET

"His Broadway and Berlin Songs"

Theatre: Bijou Theatre
Opening Date: November 5, 1979; *Closing Date*: June 1, 1980
Performances: 72
Lyrics: See song list for specific credits.
Music: Kurt Weill
Direction: Production "supervised" by Billie McBride and Herb Vogler; *Producer*: An Arthur Shafman International, Ltd. Presentation
Cast: *Martha Schlamme, Alvin Epstein*; Steven Blier (Piano)
The revue was presented in one act.

Musical Numbers

His Berlin Songs: "Moritat" ("Ballad of Mack the Knife") (*The Threepenny Opera*, 1928; original German lyric by Bertolt Brecht, English lyric by Marc Blitzstein) (Alvin Epstein); "Barbara-Song" (*The Threepenny Opera*, 1928; original German lyric by Bertolt Brecht, English lyric by Marc Blitzstein) (Martha Schlamme); "Alabama-Song" (*The Rise and Fall of the City of Mahagonny*, 1930; original English lyric by Bertolt Brecht) (Martha Schlamme, Alvin Epstein); Duet: "Herr Jakob Schmidt" (*The Rise and Fall of the City of Mahagonny*, 1930; the original German lyric by Bertolt Brecht may have been performed) (Martha Schlamme, Alvin Epstein); "Ballad of Sexual Slavery" (*The Threepenny Opera*, 1928; original German lyric by Bertolt Brecht, English lyric by George Tabori) (Alvin Epstein); "Ballad of the Pimp and the Whore" (*The Threepenny Opera*, 1928; original German lyric by Bertolt Brecht, English lyric by Marc Blitzstein) (Martha Schlamme, Alvin Epstein); "Pirate Jenny" (*The Threepenny Opera*, 1928; original German lyric by Bertolt Brecht, English lyric by Marc Blitzstein) (Martha Schlamme); "Kanonen-Song" (aka "Army Song" and "Recruitment Song") (*The Threepenny Opera*, 1928; original German lyric by Bertolt Brecht, English lyric by Marc Blitzstein) (Alvin Epstein); "Soldatenweib" ("Ballad of the Soldier's Wife") (original German lyric by Bertolt Brecht; written and composed in 1946, this song was the final collaboration between Brecht and Weill) (Martha Schlamme); "Eating" ("Essen") (*The Rise and Fall of the City of Mahagonny*, 1928; original lyric by Bertolt Brecht, English lyric by Arnold Weinstein) (Martha Schlamme, Alvin Epstein)
His Broadway Songs: "That's Him" (*One Touch of Venus*, 1943; lyric by Ogden Nash) (Martha Schlamme, Alvin Epstein); "September Song" (*Knickerbocker Holiday*, 1938; lyric by Maxwell Anderson) (Alvin Epstein); "The Saga of Jenny" (*Lady in the Dark*, 1941; lyric by Ira Gershwin) (Martha Schlamme, Alvin Epstein)
Back to Berlin: "Bilbao Song" (*Happy End*, 1929; the original German lyric by Bertolt Brecht may have been performed) (Martha Schlamme); "Sailor's Tango" (*Happy End*, 1929; original German lyric by Bertolt Brecht, English lyric by Will Holt) (Alvin Epstein); "Surabaya Johnny" (*Happy End*, 1929; the original German lyric by Bertolt Brecht may have been performed) (Martha Schlamme); "The Life That We Lead" (*The Rise and Fall of the City of Mahagonny*, 1930; original German lyric by Bertolt Brecht, English lyric by Will Holt) (Martha Schlamme, Alvin Epstein)
. . . *And Others* (*Note*: The program didn't identify songs in this sequence.)

The perennial composer-tribute revue *A Kurt Weill Cabaret* played its current on-and-off New York engagement over a period of seven months for a total of seventy-two performances. The concert-like evening starred Martha Schlamme and Alvin Epstein and opened on November 5, 1979. It offered an irregular series of performances in repertory with the mime show *Mummenshanz* and also sometimes played late-evening performances, and closed on November 25 after ten showings. It reopened on December 26, again in repertory with *Mummenshanz* and again with a schedule that incorporated late-evening performances, and closed on March 4, 1980, after thirty showings. It started a regular schedule of showings beginning on May 6, and closed on June 1 after thirty-two performances.

Musical tributes to Weill were something of a cottage industry, and Schlamme sang in seven of them. She and Will Holt starred in *The World of Kurt Weill in Song* (1963), which after *A Party with Betty Comden and*

Adolph Green (1958) is the second composer/lyricist-tribute revue presented in New York (after the flood-gates opened and the new genre became institutionalized with an average of two produced each season on Broadway, Off Broadway, or Off Off Broadway (as of this writing, approximately one hundred such revues have opened since 1958). *World* opened Off Broadway at The Howff Theatre on June 6, 1963, for 245 performances (its cast recording was titled *A Kurt Weill Cabaret*), and the following year a second edition followed on May 12, 1964, at the Jan Hus Playhouse for 164 performances, again with Schlamme and Holt.

In 1969, Schlamme and Epstein appeared in another Weill evening called *Whores, Wars & Tin Pan Alley*. In 1976, the first of four productions of *A Kurt Weill Cabaret* opened (with Holt and Dolly Jonah), and after the current 1979 production (in which Epstein replaced Leonard Frey during previews) Schlamme and Epstein also appeared in the 1981 and 1984 revivals. Schlamme was also in the 1979 revue *A Woman without a Man Is . . .*, which included songs by Weill.

Other Kurt Weill tributes seen Off Broadway are: *Berlin to Broadway with Kurt Weill* (1972 and 2000); *Julie Wilson: From Weill to Sondheim* (1987); *Stranger Here Myself* (1988; with Angelina Reaux); *The World of Kurt Weill* (*not* a version of the earlier *The World of Kurt Weill in Song*; 1992; Juliette Koka); and *Here Lies Jenny* (2004; Bebe Neuwirth). There were also a few Off-Broadway productions that included songs by Weill: *Brecht by Brecht* (1962; a reading of selections from Brecht's writings that included a few songs); *An Evening with Wolfgang Roth* (1977); and *An Evening with Ekkehard Schall* (1985). The 2007 Broadway production *LoveMusik* (with Michael Cerveris and Donna Murphy) explored Weill and Lotte Lenya's relationship; the text was based on their letters and the evening included some thirty songs composed by Weill.

In reviewing the current production of *A Kurt Weill Cabaret*, Richard F. Shepard in the *New York Times* said the revue was "an hour and a half of charm and first-rate professionalism" and was "as pleasant an evening of song as you will hear this season." Schlamme and Epstein made an "attractive pair" and they had "honed their performance to the proverbial fine edge."

STRIDER

"A Play with Music"

Theatre: Helen Hayes Theatre
Opening Date: November 21, 1979; *Closing Date*: May 18, 1980
Performances: 214
Play: Mark Rozovsky; English adaptation by Robert Kalfin and Steve Brown (based on a translation by Tamara Bering Sunguroff)
Lyrics: Uri Riashentsev; English lyrics by Steve Brown
Music: Mark Rozovsky and S. Vetkin; music adapted by and new music composed by Norman L. Berman
Based on the 1886 short story "Kholstomer: The Story of a Horse" by Leo Tolstoy.
Direction: Robert Kalfin and Lynne Gannaway; *Producers*: Arthur Whitelaw and Miriam Bienstock in association with Lita Starr (A Chelsea Theatre Production); *Scenery*: Wolfgang Roth; *Costumes*: Andrew B. Marlay; *Lighting*: Bobby Monk; *Musical Direction*: Norman L. Berman
Cast: Roger DeKoven (Vaska, Mr. Willingstone), Gordon Gould (Prince Serpuhofsky), Ronnie Newman (General, Announcer), Pamela Burrell (Viazapurikha, Mathieu, Marie), *Gerald Hiken* (Strider), Katherine-Mary Brown (Actor), Jeannine Khoutieff (Actor), Vicki Van Grack (Actor), Skip Lawing (Groom), Nina Dova (Gypsy), Benjamin Hendrickson (Count Bobrinsky, Darling, The Lieutenant), Igors Gavon (Feofan, Fritz), Vincent A. Feraudo (Bet Taker), Charles Walker (Vendor), John Brownlee (Actor), Nancy Kawalek (Actor), Karen Trott (Gypsy), Tad Ingram (Actor), Steven Blane (Gypsy)
The play with music was presented in two acts.
The action takes place in Russia during the latter part of the nineteenth century.

Musical Numbers

Note: The program didn't list musical numbers; the following information is taken from the published script (some titles are best-guesses).

Act One: Overture (Gypsy Orchestra); "It's Time to Take Out the Nags!" (Roger DeKoven, Benjamin Hendrickson); "Mortal" (Chorus); "Song of the Herd" (Herd); "Conversation of Strider and the Herd" (Gerald

Hiken, Herd); "Duet" (Pamela Burrell, Gerald Hiken); "Darling's Romance" (Benjamin Hendrickson); "Oh, Cruel and Hard of Heart Is Man" (Herd); "Serpuhovsky's Song" (Gordon Gould); "Along the Blacksmith's Alley" (Gerald Hiken, Igors Gavon, Gordon Gould)

Act Two: "It's Time to Take Out the Nags!" (reprise) (Roger DeKoven); "Serpuhovsky's Romance" (Gordon Gould, Gypsies); "Oh, Hard Is Life for Man and Horse" (reprise) (Herd); Ending Sequence (Company)

Based on Leo Tolstoy's 1886 short story "Kholstomer: The Story of a Horse," *Strider*'s title character (played by Gerald Hiken) was a piebald horse that had a sometimes happy but ultimately sad existence, and the story was framed by his last moments when his throat is about to be slit because he's deemed useless by his owners. Strider's life paralleled man's own journey (and the play contrasted the lives of Strider and his onetime owner Prince Serpuhofsky), and the work was also a political allegory of Russia during the late nineteenth century (Hiken's Strider was costumed like a Russian serf). In some ways, Tolstoy's story was reminiscent of Anna Sewell's earlier *Black Beauty* (1877), which also looked at the proud and later unhappy days of a horse's life.

In their reviews of the earlier Off-Broadway production (which had opened the previous May; see below), the critics were mixed in their assessment of the evening. Mel Gussow in the *New York Times* praised Hiken's Harpo Marx–like horse, and noted that not since Zero Mostel's *Rhinoceros* had "an actor been so magnificently transmogrified." He also liked Benjamin Hendrickson, whose horse character pranced and preened "like a spoof of Nureyev." He said the music was "lively, all-purpose gypsy," but the lyrics "sometimes seem as if they had not quite made it out of Russia." Clive Barnes in the *New York Post* noted that Strider's life was one of "unexpected triumph and undeserved despair" and Hiken's performance was "superb" and "magnificent." T. E. Kalem in *Time* also saw some of Harpo Marx in Hiken's interpretation of the ultimately tragic Strider, and said that "to praise" Hiken was "too faint a thing to do" because you could only believe in his characterization "if you have ever been moved to laughter, truth and tears."

But John Beaufort in the *Christian Science Monitor* felt the evening tended to be "tedious and didactic," and as a result "a little bit of *Strider* goes a long way"; Christopher Sharp in *Women's Wear Daily* said the play wasn't a waste of time but wasn't "exactly thrilling"; and although Douglas Watt in the *New York Daily News* was also reminded of Harpo Marx in Hiken's performance, he mentioned that the evening was "wearing."

The play had been successful in Russia, and *Strider* was the first Russian play to be produced in New York under the then-new United States and Soviet Union Copyright Agreement.

As *Strider: The Story of a Horse*, the play had opened Off-Broadway at the Chelsea Theatre Center on May 31, 1979, for 189 performances.

The script was published in paperback by Samuel French, in 1981, and includes the lyric of "Live Long Enough," a new song that hadn't been heard in the Russian and Off-Broadway productions. The song was added for the Broadway edition a few months into its run, and was sung by Strider (and an offstage chorus) toward the end of the second act when his former owner Prince Serpuhovsky fails to recognize the "poor wreck" of his former horse.

Awards

Tony Award Nominations: Best Leading Actor in a Play (Gerald Hiken); Best Featured Actress in a Play (Pamela Burrell)

KING OF SCHNORRERS

"A New Musical"

Theatre: Playhouse Theatre
Opening Date: November 28, 1979; *Closing Date*: January 13, 1980
Performances: 63
Book, Lyrics, and *Music*: Judd Woldin; additional lyrics by Amy Seidman, Susan Birkenhead, and Herb Martin
Based on the 1894 novella *The King of Schnorrers* by Israel Zangwill.

Direction and *Choreography*: Grover Dale; *Producers*: Eric Krebs and Sam Landis (Linda Canavan, Associate Producer); *Scenery*: Ed Wittstein; *Costumes*: Patricia Adshead; *Lighting*: Richard Nelson; *Musical Direction*: Robert Billig

Cast: Thomas Lee Sinclair (Rodriguez, President), Ralph Bruneau (Harry Tinker), Jerry Mayer (Mendel, Butler, Furtado, Treasurer), Angelina Reaux (Sadie, Housekeeper), Paul Binotto (Aaron, Wilkinson, Cosmetician), Ed Dixon (Isaac, Belasco, Chancellor), Rick McElhiney (Greenbaum), Lloyd Battista (Da Costa), Sophie Schwab (Deborah Da Costa), John Dossett (David Ben Yonkel)

The musical was presented in two acts.

The action takes place during 1791 in the East End of London.

Musical Numbers

Act One: "Hail to the King" (Lloyd Battista, Thomas Lee Sinclair, Street Peddlers); "Chutzpah" (lyric for chorus by Amy Seidman) (Lloyd Battista, Thomas Lee Sinclair, Quartet); "I'm Only a Woman" (Sophie Schwab); "Just for Me" (John Dossett, Ralph Bruneau); "I Have Not Lived in Vain" (Ed Dixon); "The Fine Art of Schnorring" (Lloyd Battista); "Tell Me" (lyric by Susan Birkenhead) (Sophie Schwab); "What Do You Do?" (John Dossett); "It's Over" (lyric by Herb Martin) (Street Peddlers)

Act Two: "Murder" (Ralph Bruneau, Peddlers); "Dead" (John Dossett, Jerry Mayer); "Chutzpah" (reprise) (Company); "Guided by Love" (Sophie Schwab); "Tell Me" (reprise) (Sophie Schwab, John Dossett); "Sephardic Lullaby" (Paul Binotto); "Each of Us" (Company); Finale (Company)

King of Schnorrers had a convoluted history, and the current production was the third of four versions of the material; to further add to the confusion, the musical underwent three different title changes, and even one of the three titles had a slight variation of spelling. As *Pettycoat Lane*, the show premiered at the George Street Playhouse in New Brunswick, New Jersey, in January 1979; from there, it was seen Off Broadway as *King of Schnorrers* at the Harold Clurman Theatre, where it opened on October 9, 1979, for thirty performances. The current Broadway production (also as *King of Schnorrers*) played for six weeks, and then as *Petticoat Lane* the script was published in paperback by Samuel French, Inc., in 1981. And as *Tatterdemalion* the musical was seen Off Broadway at the Douglas Fairbanks Theatre on October 27, 1985, for twenty-five showings.

A note in the program for the Off-Broadway production stated that while the word "schnorrer" translates as "beggar," the word bore "little resemblance to a mendicant. He is first of all a professional who, through his generous receipt of your charity, allows you to fulfill your religious obligations to help the unfortunate," and while he "does not ask alms, he claims them, never hesitating to use his extensive knowledge of the Scriptures to berate the non-generous."

The thin plot centered on the cunning and proud Da Costa (Lloyd Battista), who is King of the Schnorrers and is virtual royalty among the Sephardic Jews in the London of 1791. His daughter Deborah (Sophie Schwab) falls in love with cabinet maker David (John Dossett), but the haughty Da Costa feels the lowly David is undeserving of her. The young man then devises a scheme to trick the trickster, and by evening's end he wins Deborah.

At least three of the critics felt the musical strayed too deep into *Fantasticks* territory, and one or two also noted similarities to *Fiddler on the Roof*. As a result, the evening was predictable, and like so many shows of the period the reviewers thought the musical belonged in a much smaller venue.

Mel Gussow in the *New York Times* said the "amiable little" musical had book, lyrics, and music that were "middling," but noted that director and choreographer Grover Dale's "most artful" stroke was a dance of clothes in which a wardrobe came to life "with sleeves and shoes moving in rhythm as if activated by an unseen puppeteer." He concluded that Dale and the performers "enriched" the production but couldn't "transform the familiar, home-spun material."

Dennis Cunningham on WCBSTV2 felt the "small and charming little enterprise" had "misguided delusions of grandeur" and should have remained Off Broadway, and Joel Siegel on WABCTV7 said the "whimsical" musical ("with loud echoes of *The Fantasticks*") made a "mistake" by transferring to Broadway where its "intimacy" got lost (he said to see the show "only if you can schnorr yourself the tickets").

In reviewing the earlier Off-Broadway production, Patricia O'Haire in the *New York Daily News* found the music "pleasant," the performances "nice," and the costumes "quite imaginative." But it was all "too predictable," and she concluded that the evening's "main appeal" was Dale's "bright, smart and engaging" direction. Marilyn Stasio in the *New York Post* complained that the subplot about the young lovers bogged down the story, and noted that Deborah's "independent" character was contradicted by her "gooey love-song lyrics." The cast "staggered under the relentless cuteness of it all" and the show couldn't overcome its "thin" material. Christopher Sharp in *Women's Wear Daily* said the plot revolved around a single joke, but even so the show could "waste an audience's time with a certain charm."

Soon after the Broadway opening, the first scene was revised; the song "Hail to the King" was cut, and two ("Petticoat Lane" and "It's Better to Give Than Receive") which had been heard in the Off-Broadway production were reinstated.

The Off Broadway version featured Philip Casnoff, who was succeeded by John Dossett for Broadway. Five songs from Off Broadway were omitted for Broadway ("A Man Is Meant to Reason," "It's a Living," "Try Me," "Petticoat Lane," and "It's Better to Give Than Receive"), but as mentioned above the last two were reinstated after the Broadway opening. Similarly, the new song ("Hail to the King") added for Broadway was eventually cut. At some point during the Broadway run (but not on opening night), "Just for Me," which had been heard during the Off-Broadway production, was added. For *Tatterdemalion*, six new songs were added: "Ours," "Born to Schnorr," "Blood Lines," "An Ordinary Man," "Well Done, Da Costa," and "Leave the Thinking to Men"(the latter with lyric by Susan Birkenhead); songs that had been heard in earlier productions of the work but weren't used in *Tatterdemalion* were: "Sephardic Lullaby," "It's Better to Give Than Receive," "It's a Living," "The Fine Art of Schnorring," "What Do You Do?," "Just for Me," "Hail to the King," "Try Me," and "Guided by Love."

BETTE! DIVINE MADNESS

Theatre: Majestic Theatre
Opening Date: December 5, 1979; *Closing Date*: January 6, 1980
Performances: 40
Special Material: Bette Midler, Jerry Blatt, and Bruce Vilanch
Direction: Bette Midler and Jerry Blatt; *Producers*: Ron Delsener; *Choreography*: Marla Blakey (Toni Basil, Additional Choreography); *Lighting*: Chipmonck (aka E. H. Beresford Monck); *Musical Direction*: Tony Berg and Randy Kerber, Co-Musical Directors
Cast: *Bette Midler*, The Staggering Harlettes (Franny Eisenberg, Linda Hart, and Paulette McWilliams), Shabba-Doo (aka Adolfo "Shabba-Doo" Quinones); Background Vocals: Carl Hall
The concert was presented in two acts.

Bette! Divine Madness was Bette Midler's third Broadway visit of the decade (for more information, see ***Bette Midler*** and ***Bette Midler's Clams on the Half-Shell Revue***). The current concert featured her backup girl trio the Harlettes as well as dancer Shabba-Doo, and the evening included a number of favorites in her repertoire such as "The Boogie-Woogie Bugle Boy from Company 'B'" (1941 film *Buck Privates*; lyric and music by Don Raye and Hughie Prince), "Chapel of Love" (lyric and music by Jeff Barry, Ellie Greenwich, and Phil Spector), and "Do You Wanna Dance?" (lyric and music by Bobby Freeman) as well as her hit title song from her recent 1979 film *The Rose* (lyric and music by Amanda McBroom). There were of course the usual Sophie Tucker jokes ("Sophie's choices") and Midler's mermaid Dolores Delago ("the toast of Chicago") made an appearance (when out of water, Dolores gets around on a wheelchair).

Robert Palmer in the *New York Times* said the evening's message was "pop culture as trash," and noted Midler was "such a pro at faking emotions that it's difficult to catch much feeling from her singing, even when she seems to mean it" and that she tended "to reduce everything she gets her hands on to showbiz tinsel." But she had "lots of lung power and an underwhelming amount of taste," she had "talent," and her performance of "pure entertainment" suggested "that something more meaningful might be taking place."

As *Divine Madness*, the 1980 film version was taken from a live performance at the Pasadena Civic Auditorium; directed by Michael Ritchie and released by Warner Brothers, the ads proclaimed that Midler was "A National Treasure Chest," and, indeed, the film's logo showed Midler sitting in Lincoln's place at the Lincoln Memorial, and on the record and video releases she replaced Jefferson as one of the presidents at Mount Rushmore. The film was released on DVD by Warner Home Video, and the soundtrack was issued on LP by Atlantic/Q Records and on CD by Rhino Atlantic.

OKLAHOMA!

Theatre: Palace Theatre
Opening Date: December 13, 1979; *Closing Date*: August 24, 1980
Performances: 293
Book and *Lyrics*: Oscar Hammerstein II
Music: Richard Rodgers
Based on the 1931 play *Green Grow the Lilacs* by Lynn Riggs.
Direction: William Hammerstein; *Producers*: Zev Bufman and James M. Nederlander in association with Donald C. Carter; *Choreography*: Agnes de Mille (choreography re-created by Gemze de Lappe); *Scenery*: Michael J. Hotopp and Paul de Pass; *Costumes*: Bill Hargate; *Lighting*: Thomas Skelton; *Musical Direction*: Jay Blackton
Cast: *Mary Wickes* (Aunt Eller), *Laurence Guittard* (Curly), *Christine Andreas* (Laurey), Robert Ray (Ike Skidmore), Stephen Crain (Slim), Harry Groener (Will Parker), Martin Vidnovic (Jud Fry), Christine Ebersole (Ado Annie Carnes), Bruce Adler (Ali Hakim), Martha Traverse (Gertie Cummings), Philip Rash (Andrew Carnes), Nick Jolley (Cord Elam); Singers: Sydney Anderson, Stephen Crain, Lorraine Foreman, Nick Jolley, John Kildahl, Jessica Molaskey, Joel T. Myers, Philip Rash, Robert Ray, Martha Traverse, M. Lynne Wieneke; Dancers: Eric Aaron, Brian Bullard, Phillip Candler, Judy Epstein, David Evans, Tonda Hannum, Louise Hickey, Kristina Koebel, Leslie Morris, Michael Page, Patti Ross, Kevin Ryan, Anthony Santiago, Ilene Strickler, Robert Sullivan, Susan Whelan
The musical was presented in two acts.
The action takes place in the Indian Territory (now Oklahoma) just after the turn of the twentieth century.

Musical Numbers

Act One: "Oh, What a Beautiful Mornin'" (Laurence Guittard); "The Surrey with the Fringe on Top" (Laurence Guittard, Christine Andreas, Mary Wickes); "Kansas City" (Harry Groener, Mary Wickes, Boys); "I Cain't Say No" (Christine Ebersole); "Many a New Day" (Christine Andreas, Girls); "It's a Scandal! It's a Outrage!" (Bruce Adler, Boys); "People Will Say We're in Love" (Laurence Guittard, Christine Andreas); "Pore Jud Is Dead" (Laurence Guittard, Martin Vidnovic); "Lonely Room" (Martin Vidnovic); "Out of My Dreams" (Christine Andreas, Girls); "Laurey Makes Up Her Mind" (ballet) (Laurey: Louise Hickey; Curly: David Evans; Jud: Anthony Santiago; The Child: Judy Epstein; Jud's Postcards: Patti Ross, Ilene Strickler, and Susan Whelan; Laurey's Friends: Sydney Anderson, Tonda Hannum, Kristina Koebel, Leslie Morris, and Martha Traverse; Cowboys: Eric Aaron, Brian Bullard, Phillip Candler, Joel T. Myers, Michael Page, Kevin Ryan, and Robert Sullivan)
Act Two: "The Farmer and the Cowman" (Philip Rash, Mary Wickes, Robert Ray, Harry Groener, Laurence Guittard, Christine Ebersole, Ensemble); "All er Nothin'" (Christine Ebersole, Harry Groener, Two Dancing Girls); "People Will Say We're in Love" (reprise) (Laurence Guittard, Christine Andreas); "Oklahoma" (Laurence Guittard, Christine Andreas, Mary Wickes, Robert Ray, Stephen Crain, Philip Rash, Nick Jolley, Ensemble); "Oh, What a Beautiful Mornin'" (reprise) (Christine Andreas, Laurence Guittard, Ensemble); Finale (Company)

Happily, the revival of *Oklahoma!* was not a radical reinterpretation of Oscar Hammerstein II and Richard Rodgers's evergreen. The corn was still as high as an elephant's eye and the wavin' wheat still smelled sweet, but here was a slightly darker *Oklahoma!*, especially in the performances of Christine Andreas (Laurey) and Martin Vidnovic (Jud). Andreas's Laurey was more brooding than usual, and this time around the ballet "Laurey Makes Up Her Mind" really seemed to be about something. A choice between Curly or Jud? Normally, there's no contest, and clearly in the real world Jud wouldn't stand a chance with Laurey. But with the casting of Vidnovic there was now a Jud we'd never before seen: a romantic-looking stallion who makes Curly seem somewhat coltish. Vidnovic's striking interpretation was charged with frustrated sexual energy, and it was clear from his performance that when Jud was alone in his shack he did more than just look at the racy French postcards nailed to the wall above his bunk. He was handsome and attractive, and it was understandable why Laurey might consider going to the picnic with him. Heretofore, and like *Carousel*'s Jigger, Jud had always seemed a somewhat intrusive but necessary secondary-character plot device. But here Jud was a presence, and Vidnovic's beautifully and achingly performed "Lonely Room" made this generally forgotten song from the score a powerful and memorable statement of Jud's outsider status.

The critics praised the score, and Vidnovic received rave reviews, but there were a few quibbles about the book, criticisms that went all the way back to the original production: in his seasonal summary of the 1942–1943 season, George Jean Nathan noted that after the late second-act title song sequence, there was some "extension of the action" that "loses the audience"; John Anderson in the *New York Journal-American* suggested that the long first act needed tightening; and Wilella Waldorf in the *New York Post* found the opening scene "mild" and "somewhat monotonous" with everyone "warbling" in front of the farm house (she noted that life on the old farm was apt to grow a bit "tiresome").

For the current revival, T. E. Kalem in *Time* found the book "creaky" with dialogue which resembled "subtitles from a silent movie," and Howard Kissel in *Women's Wear Daily* said the show suffered from "often dated material." But Clive Barnes in the *New York Post* exclaimed that *Oklahoma!* was a show "to freshen your heart" in this "spanking new production," and Douglas Watt in the *New York Daily News* said that William Hammerstein (Oscar's son) had "brightly and lovingly" directed the classic.

Walter Kerr in the *New York Times* praised Andreas. Her Laurey had "a real streak of the potential wanton" which justified her "wild curiosity" about Jud, whom Vidnovic played as "a festering promise somewhere west of Eden." He found Mary Wickes "dandy," said Harry Groener was the show's "unexpected discovery," and noted that Laurence Guittard and Christine Ebersole were "perfectly acceptable" but "not more than that." He also mentioned that the show seemed about twenty minutes too long and suggested some "snipping" was needed in the "anticlimactic scenes."

Kalem said Vidnovic brought "a Freudian depth of characterization and richly textured voice" to a "thankless role"; Kissel said he was "compelling"; Barnes said he was "impressively malevolent"; John Beaufort in the *Christian Science Monitor* reported that he received a "deserved opening-night ovation"; and Jack Kroll in *Newsweek* said his performance was the "real power" in the production with his interpretation of "a dark, troubled underground man filled with desperate desires and perverted yearnings."

Watt found Guittard an "ideal" Curly; Barnes said he was one of the "best" Curlys he'd ever seen and noted that Andreas's Laurey was "startlingly pretty and exquisitely sung"; and Edwin Wilson in the *Wall Street Journal* found her "one of the best Laureys ever."

Beaufort reported that after the finale, there was a "sentimental impromptu" in which Oklahoma's Governor George Nigh presented Christine Ebersole with a feathered Indian headdress, and the onstage ceremony included four members from the original 1943 production (Alfred Drake, Joan Roberts, Joseph Buloff, and Howard Da Sylva) as well as choreographer Agnes de Mille. (Incidentally, Jay Blackton, who was the musical director for the original production, performed similar duties for the revival.)

Oklahoma! premiered at the St. James Theatre on March 30, 1943, for a then record-breaking run of 2,212 performances. Including the current production, the musical has been revived in New York nine times: a return engagement by the national touring company opened at the Broadway Theatre on May 29, 1951, for seventy-two performances, and was followed by five productions at City Center by the New York City Center Light Opera Company on August 31, 1953 (forty performances), March 19, 1958 (fifteen performances), February 27, 1963, and a return engagement on May 15, 1963 (a total of thirty performances), and December 15, 1965 (twenty-four performances). The musical was next produced by the Music Theatre of Lincoln Center at the New York State Theatre on June 23, 1969, for eighty-eight performances, and after the current production, the work was most recently seen on Broadway at the Gershwin Theatre on March 21, 2002, for 388 performances.

The current revival was recorded by RCA Victor Records (LP # CBL1-3572). The 1943 cast album was issued on a 78 RPM set by Decca Records (later reissued on LP # DL-8000, and most recently released on CD by MCA Classics Records # MCAD-10798, which includes both an alternate take and a complete version of "Pore Jud Is Dead"). The script was published in hardback by Random House in 1943, and was also included in the company's 1959 hardback collection *Six Plays by Rodgers and Hammerstein*; and in 2010 the script was published by Applause Theatre & Cinema Books. The script was also published in the 2014 hardback collection *American Musicals* by the Library of Congress, which includes the scripts of fifteen other musicals. All the lyrics for the used, cut, and unused songs are included in the collection *The Complete Lyrics of Oscar Hammerstein II*. Max Wilk's *Ok! The Story of "Oklahoma!"* was published in hardback by Grove Press in 1993 (and was republished in paperback by Applause Books in 2002).

The musical was first produced in London at the Drury Lane on April 29, 1947, for 1,548 performances. The 1955 film version was filmed twice, for both the Todd-AO and CinemaScope processes; the Todd-AO road show release was distributed by Magda Theatre Corporation, and RKO Radio Pictures distributed the CinemaScope version. The home video releases have been issued by Twentieth Century-Fox, and a recent two-DVD set (# 0-24543-20843-3) includes both the Todd-AO and CinemaScope versions. A 1998 London revival was released on DVD by Image Entertainment (# ID1055700KDVD), and a Japanese production by the Takarazuka company was issued on DVD (Takarazuka Creative Arts Co. Ltd. # TCAD-149).

Two weeks after the opening of the current revival, Richard Rodgers died at the age of seventy-seven.

Awards

Tony Award Nominations: Best Leading Actress in a Musical (Christine Andreas); Best Featured Actor in a Musical (Harry Groener)

COMIN' UPTOWN

"A NEW MUSICAL"

Theatre: Winter Garden Theatre
Opening Date: December 20, 1979; *Closing Date*: January 27, 1980
Performances: 45
Book: Philip Rose and Peter Udell
Lyrics: Peter Udell
Music: Garry Sherman
Based on Charles Dickens's 1843 novella *A Christmas Carol.*
Direction: Philip Rose; *Producers*: Ridgely Bullock and Albert W. Selden in association with Columbia Pictures (Leslie K. Bullock, Associate Producer); *Choreography*: Michael Peters (Frances Lee Morgan, Associate Choreographer); *Scenery*: Robin Wagner; *Costumes*: Ann Emonts; *Lighting*: Gilbert V. Hemsley Jr.; *Musical Direction*: Howard Roberts
Cast: Trio—Deborah Lynn Bridges, Deborah Burrell, and Jenifer Lewis; Gregory Hines (Scrooge), John Russell (Bob Cratchit, Deacon), Larry Marshall (Tenants' Representative, Christmas Past), Saundra McClain (Mary, Christmas Present), Robert Jackson (Minister, Christmas Future), Tiger Haynes (Marley), Loretta Devine (Young Mary), Duane Davis (Young Scrooge), Vernal Polson (Young Scrooge's Assistant), Ned Wright (Reverend Byrd), Esther Marrow (Gospel Singer), Virginia McKinzie (Mrs. Cratchit, Deacon's Wife), Shirley Black-Brown (Cratchit Daughter), Allison R. Manson (Cratchit Daughter), Carol Lynn Maillard (Martha Cratchit), Kevin Babb (Tiny Tim); Harlem Residents: Kevin Babb, Shirley Black-Brown, Deborah Lynn Bridges, Deborah Burrell, Roslyn Burrough, Barbara Christopher, Duane Davis, Ronald Dunham, Milton Grayson, Linda James, Kevin Jeff, Jenifer Lewis, Carol Lynn Maillard, Allison R. Manson, Esther Marrow, Frances Lee Morgan, Raymond Patterson, Vernal Polson, Glori Sauve, Eric Sawyer, Kiki Shepard, Faruma Williams, Ned Wright
The musical was presented in two acts.
The action takes place in Harlem during Christmases present, past, and future.

Musical Numbers

Act One: "Christmas Is Comin' Uptown"(Christmas Shoppers, Trio, Gregory Hines); "Somebody's Gotta Be the Heavy" (Gregory Hines); "Christmas Is Comin' Uptown" (reprise) (Christmas Shoppers); "Now I Lay Me Down to Sleep" (Gregory Hines); "Get Your Act Together" (Tiger Haynes); "Lifeline" (Larry Marshall, Trio); "What Better Time for Love" (Gregory Hines, Loretta Devine); "It Won't Be Long" (Esther Marrow, Congregation); "What I'm Gonna Do for You" (Gregory Hines); "What Better Time for Love" (reprise) (Loretta Devine); "Get Down, Brother, Get Down" (Saundra McClain, The Presents [Trio]); "Sing a Christmas Song" (Carolers); "Sing a Christmas Song" (reprise) (The Cratchit Family, Carolers); "What

Better Time for Love" (reprise) (Kevin Babb, The Cratchit Family); "Have I Finally Found My Heart?" (Gregory Hines)

Act Two: "Nobody Really Do" (Robert Jackson, Trio); "Goin', Gone" (Robert Jackson); "Get Down, Brother, Get Down" (reprise) (The Cratchit Family, Mourners); "One Way Ticket to Hell" (Trio); "Nobody Really Do" (reprise) (Robert Jackson, Trio); "Born Again" (reprise) (Gregory Hines); "Born Again" (reprise) (Gregory Hines, Company)

The Wiz was a black urban update of *The Wizard of Oz*, ***Alice*** and ***But Never Jam Today*** looked at Lewis Carroll from the black perspective, and ***Timbuktu!*** was a reimagined *Kismet* turned into a black fantasy set in the fabled ancient city, and so the creators of *Comin' Uptown* no doubt hoped that an updated black version of Charles Dickens's *A Christmas Carol* was just the recipe for a hip hit black musical set in contemporary Harlem that featured Scrooge (Gregory Hines) as a slum landlord. Added to the mix were gospel singers (just as many 1940s musicals and revues offered the de rigueur South American number, throughout the 1970s and well into the next decade, it seemed every other musical had the requisite gospel sequence), knowing humor (when Scrooge has Christmas dinner sent to the Cratchits, the meal consists of Chinese take-out and Jewish deli food because these are the only shops open on Christmas Day), and songs with such dreary and clichéd titles as "Somebody's Gotta Be the Heavy," "Get Your Act Together," and "Get Down, Brother, Get Down."

Comin' Uptown opened just in time for Christmas, but never saw Groundhog's Day. It played for little more than five weeks and lost its huge capitalization (of reportedly $1.4 million). Most of the critics weren't amused, the audiences didn't come, and the producers couldn't parlay the evening into a ***Wiz***ardly hit. But even if the show had been a masterpiece, it had one major factor going against it: the holiday story. In the era of *Comin' Uptown*, holiday musicals never found a foothold on Broadway turf. Shows like *Subways Are for Sleeping* (1961), *She Loves Me* (1963), and *Promises, Promises* (1968) used the holidays as background for their plots and even served up a Christmas song or two, but the musicals themselves weren't about the holidays and weren't based on Christmas classics.

Although Meredith Willson's *Here's Love* (1963) was based on the beloved 1947 film *Miracle on 34th Street*, it floundered after a season on Broadway, lost money, and never attained classic holiday status (as *It's Beginning to Look a Lot Like Christmas* it occasionally surfaces in regional theatre at holiday time [Willson borrowed his 1951 classic holiday song and interpolated it into the score of *Here's Love*]). And two musicals with lyrics by Sheldon Harnick, Michel Legrand's 1981 adaptation of Dickens (produced as *Penny by Penny* and *A Christmas Carol*) with Richard Kiley as Scrooge, and Joe Raposo's 1986 *A Wonderful Life* (based on the 1946 film *It's a Wonderful Life*), never made much of an impression. The former briefly toured, and the latter is occasionally revived in regional theatre, but neither braved the holiday snows of Broadway.

Decades later, producers figured it out. Christmas-themed musicals were best suited for limited-run engagements during the holiday season, and their brief annual national tours centered on December bookings for New York. As a result, *White Christmas* (in 2008 and 2009), *Elf* (2010 and 2011), and *A Christmas Story* (2012) paid visits to Broadway during the Christmas season, and for eleven seasons Madison Square Garden's Paramount Theatre produced its own lavish *A Christmas Carol* (lyrics by Lynn Ahrens, music by Alan Menken) from 1994 to 2003.

The critics were mostly disappointed with *Comin' Uptown*. They found the book, lyrics, and music mostly pedestrian and felt the show never quite settled down and told its story. It was overproduced with lavish décor, and its book stumbled: the Cratchits didn't make an appearance for the first seventy minutes of the first act, and when Scrooge saw a mere glimpse of Tiny Tim he was transformed from grouch to good guy. Further, Hines was one of the most dazzling dancers of the era, but the show ignored his talents for most of the evening and gave him little in the way of dancing. It was only in the musical's final scenes that he was allowed to let loose (with the show-stopping "Born Again"). As a result, the musical has all but disappeared; its later most visible moment occurred in the early 1990s when during one Christmas season Saks devoted its holiday-themed store-front window displays to Broadway musicals with Christmas motifs, and so *Comin' Uptown* (along with such shows as *Subways Are for Sleeping*) was featured.

Richard Eder in the *New York Times* mentioned that with all the revivals in recent years, many felt "we'd be better off with new musicals at any price." But in the case of *Comin' Uptown*, "the price was too high" because the show was "careless and costly, elaborate and enervating." The songs were "mainly conventional" and lacked "emotional resonance," and the book never established a real relationship between Scrooge and the Cratchits, including Tiny Tim. Douglas Watt in the *New York Daily News* said the lavishly appointed musical was a "ponderous bore" with "completely undistinguished" songs, and it was only in the musical's final moments that Hines came "fully into his own" as he leaped and tapped to "Born Again."

Christopher Sharp in *Women's Wear Daily* said Hines was "the only reason" why the new musical had any entertainment value, and if his readers wanted to see the star's "outstanding performance" they'd better rush "before this production says 'Sayonara.'" Edwin Wilson in the *Wall Street Journal* said the book and songs were "all too predictable," but what the show lacked in "finesse" it made up in "exuberance."

Clive Barnes in the *New York Post* said "Hurricane Gregory" was probably "the best tap dancer in the world since Bill Robinson" and "Born Again" was a chance to see the "great performer in almost shattering action." But the book was "as pedestrian as a tortoise," the lyrics were "scarcely more nifty," and the music was "not unduly distinguished." John Beaufort in the *Christian Science Monitor* liked the "generously upbeat and outgoing entertainment," and T. E. Kalem in *Time* said the evening was "a high-gloss package that should brighten everybody's holiday." He noted that his "highest praise" went to scenic designer Robin Wagner, who gave "special luster to this Christmas present from Harlem" and who was the "unseen star" of such recent musicals as ***On the Twentieth Century*** and ***Ballroom***.

As *Christmas Is Comin' Uptown*, the script was published in paperback by Samuel French in 1982.

THE BABES IN TOYLAND

"A Musical Fantasy for the 80's" / "A Musical Extravaganza"

Theatre: Felt Forum
Opening Date: December 21 1979; *Closing Date*: January 1, 1980
Performances: 16
Book: Glenn McDonough; book adapted by Ellis Weiner
Lyrics: Glenn McDonough; new lyrics by Shelly Markham and Annette Liesten
Music: Victor Herbert; new music by Shelly Markham and Annette Liesten
Direction: Munson Hicks; *Producers*: Barry and Fran Weissler; *Choreography*: Tony Stevens; *Scenery* and *Costumes*: Michael J. Hotopp and Paul de Pass; *Lighting*: Associated Theatrical Designers; *Musical Direction*: Bob Christianson
Cast: Mark Holleran (Tom, Vendor # 2), Roger Lawson (Sugarbear, Vendor # 1), Michael Calkins (Horace, Vendor # 3); The Puppets: Mona Finston, Edward T. Jacobs, Robert Hancock, Lynn Hippen, Steve Mathews, and Alan F. Seiffert; Dan Kruger (Promoter, Old King Cole), Edward T. Jacobs (Haystack), Ken Bonafons (Grandfather), Debbie McLeod (Mary), S. Barkley Murray (Mother Goose), C. A. Hutton (Barnaby), Alan F. Seiffert (Jack Be Nimble, Drummer Boy), Lynn Hippen (The Old Woman in the Shoe); The Children in the Shoe: Mona Finston and Steve Mathews; Ken Bonafons and Alan F. Seiffert (Humpty Dumpty); Robert Hancock (The Wall, Computer Bob), Shari Watson (Little Bo Peep); The Ladies of the Grand Ballet: S. Barkley Murray, Edward T. Jacobs, and Shari Watson; The Shrouds: S. Barkley Murray and Alan F. Seiffert; The Toy Soldiers: Mona Finston, Robert Hancock, Lynn Hippen, Dan Kruger, Steve Mathews, S. Barkley Murray, Alan F. Seiffert; Puppeteers: Mona Finston, Robert Hancock, Lynn Hippen, Steve Mathews, Alan F. Seiffert
The musical was presented in two acts.
The action takes place in Toyland during the present time.

Musical Numbers

Act One: "Big Baby" (Mark Holleran, Roger Lawson, Michael Calkins, Debbie McLeod, Mona Finston, Edward T. Jacobs, Robert Hancock, Lynn Hippen, Steve Mathews, Dan Kruger); "It's a Sweet Life" (Mark Holleran, Roger Lawson, Michael Calkins, Debbie McLeod); "Something Must Be Done" (Mark Holleran, Roger Lawson, Michael Calkins, Debbie McLeod, Dan Kruger, Ken Bonafons, Alan F. Seiffert, Robert Hancock, S. Barkley Murray, Lynn Hippen, Mona Finston, Steve Mathews); "Don't Cry, Bo Peep" (Mark Holleran, Roger Lawson, Michael Calkins, Debbie McLeod); "Step Out in Front" (Mark Holleran, Roger Lawson, Michael Calkins, Debbie McLeod); "Dream Toyland" (Ken Bonafons, S. Barkley Murray, Edward T. Jacobs, Shari Watson, Roger Lawson, Mark Holleran, Michael Calkins, Nursery Rhyme Characters, Toyland Visitors)

Act Two: "The Two of Us" (Mark Holleran, Debbie McLeod); "The March of the Wooden Soldiers" (Mona Finston, Robert Hancock, Lynn Hippen, Dan Kruger, Steve Mathews, S. Barkley Murray, Alan F. Sieffert); "Disco Toyland" (Company)

The Babes in Toyland (which was advertised as "A Musical Fantasy for the 80s") was an updated version of Victor Herbert and Glenn McDonough's hit Broadway musical *Babes in Toyland*, which opened on October 13, 1903, at the Majestic Theatre for 192 performances. Among the evergreens from Herbert's score are two Christmas perennials, "Toyland" and "The March of the Wooden Soldiers." The current version was a limited engagement that played at Madison Square Garden's Felt Forum. It's uncertain if the revival was under a Broadway or Off-Broadway contract; *Theatre World 1979–1980* classified the musical as an Off-Broadway production, but *Best Plays* didn't commit itself and just mentioned the show in passing as "a special holiday attraction for children."

The new plot focused on the musical trio The Babes (Mark Holleran [Tom], Roger Lawson [Sugarbear], and Michael Calkins [Horace]), who are performing a cross-country tour; along the way they meet Mary (Debbie McLeod), and the trio soon becomes a quartet. The foursome is really a fivesome because Sugarbear's shaggy dog, Haystack (Edward T. Jacobs), always tags along. When The Babes come upon Toyland, they discover the town and its fairy-tale characters are in despair because the evil outsider Barnaby (C. A. Hutton) has taken over Mother Goose's Tunnel of Love and is converting it into his House of Horrors where his robot-like computer will mass-produce plastic versions of the beloved characters in Toyland. But good wins the day, Barnaby is ousted, and, since we are still in the 1970s, everyone celebrates at the Disco Toyland.

Richard F. Shepard in the *New York Times* said the show was "quite nice for the season" and was a "sunny and funny" entertainment that was "visually colorful and aurally pleasing" (but he noted the prerecorded sound was "squishy" and had a "seashell echo"). He described the score as a combination of "soft rock, disco, traditional sweet pop" and familiar Victor Herbert.

The cast album was released by Dream Music Company (LP # BIT-91550) and produced by Barry and Fran Weissler (who also produced the musical). The album had limited distribution and seems to have been sold only in the venues where the musical played. The cast album includes the song "Bare Facts," which wasn't listed in the show's souvenir program.

The Babes in Toyland premiered on November 2, 1979, at the American Shakespeare Theatre in Stratford, Connecticut, and the souvenir program indicated that after the New York run the musical would play in such cities as Boston, Atlanta, and Philadelphia. The program asked, "Where will it all end?" And it answered its own question with "Not until there's a Babe in every borough."

For two weeks during December 1979, New York theatergoers had the opportunity to see a more traditional revival of *Babes in Toyland* as well as *The Babes in Toyland*. The former was produced by the Light Opera of Manhattan at the Eastside Playhouse on November 28, 1979, for thirty-five performances; for this version, McDonough's original book was revised by William Mount-Burke and Alice Hammerstein Mathias (the latter also wrote new lyrics for the production).

DADDY GOODNESS

"A Musical Fable"

The musical opened on August 16, 1979, at the Forrest Theatre, Philadelphia, Pennsylvania, and then opened on September 13, 1979, at the National Theatre, Washington, D.C., where it permanently closed on October 7, 1979.

Book: Ron Miller and Shaunielle Perry

Lyrics: Ron Miller

Music: Ken Hirsch

Based on the 1968 play *Daddy Goodness* by Richard Wright and Louis Sapin.

Direction: Israel Hicks; *Producers*: Ashton Springer with Motown in association with Marty Markinson, Joseph Harris, and Donald Tick; *Choreography*: Louis Johnson; *Scenery*: Santo Loquasto; *Costumes*: Bernard Johnson; *Lighting*: Jennifer Tipton; *Musical Direction*: Lea Richardson

Cast: Rod Perry (Sam), *Freda Payne* (Lottie), Arthur French (Jeremiah), *Clifton Davis* (Thomas), Clebert Ford (Pastor Weeks), Sandra Reaves-Phillips (Annie, Mary), Carol-Jean Lewis (Ethel), *Ted Ross* (Daddy Goodness), Dan Strayhorn (Luke), Raymond Bazemore (Postman), Clyde Williams (Willis), Brenda J. Davis (Mother), Stefanie Showell (Daughter), Ned Wright (Doctor Pruitt), Roslyn Burrough (Mrs. Perkins), Ann Duquesnay (Night Club Singer), Dwayne Phelps and Brenda Garratt (Night Club Dancers); Ensemble: Vikki Baltimore, Raymond Bazemore, Roslyn Burrough, Brenda J. Davis, Gary Easterling, Brenda Garratt, Charles "C. B." Murray, Dwayne Phelps, M. W. Reid, Wynonna Smith, Nancy-Suzanne, Clyde Williams

The musical was presented in two acts.

The action takes place during the recent past in a country town in Louisiana in "sweet summer."

Musical Numbers

Act One: "Goodness Don't Come Easy When You're Bad" (Rod Perry, Freda Payne, Arthur French); "I Got Religion" (Ted Ross, Clifton Davis); "Spread Joy" (Carol-Jean Lewis, Townspeople); "Big Business" (Clifton Davis, Carol-Jean Lewis, Sandra Reaves-Phillips, Workers); "Hungry" (Rod Perry, Freda Payne); "Lottie's Purification" (Freda Payne, Ted Ross, Workers); "We'll Let the People Decide" (Clebert Ford, Ted Ross); "One More Step" (Dan Strayhorn, Congregation); "People Make Me Cry" (Ted Ross)

Act Two: "One More Step" (reprise) (Clifton Davis, Workers); "True Love Is the Mother of Us All" (Freda Payne); "Outside o' That You're Doin' Fine" (Ned Wright, Clifton Davis); "I Don't Want to Do It Alone No More" (Ann Duquesnay); "Daddy's Decision" (Ted Ross); "Don't Touch That Dial" (Carol-Jean Lewis, Company); "People Make Me Cry" (reprise) (Ted Ross); "You're Home" (Rod Perry, Freda Payne); Finale (Company)

Daddy Goodness was a self-described fable that spoofed religion, and most of its leading characters were cynical charlatans. When it seems that Daddy Goodness (Ted Ross) has died, his best friend Sam (Rod Perry) takes his body to the cemetery in a wheelbarrow which is promptly struck by lightning. Daddy Goodness rises—but not from the dead. He was just dead drunk. Huckster Thomas (Clifton Davis) sees an opportunity here, and so quickly promotes Daddy Goodness's "resurrection" as a modern-day miracle and founds a new religion to celebrate the occasion. As the church grows, so do the financial contributions and soon Thomas and his cohorts are rolling in money. But Daddy Goodness repents of his sins and disowns the scoundrels who have bilked the innocent of their money.

There were clearly satiric opportunities in the storyline, but because the musical failed to capitalize on them the evening was obvious and tiresome. The score was for the most part similarly lacking, and only the sassy opening number "Goodness Don't Come Easy When You're Bad" had sparkle. Otherwise, "Hungry" was an overwrought ballad, "We'll Let the People Decide" was a would-be dramatic duet that fell flat, and, worst of all, was Daddy Goodness's lugubrious soliloquy "People Make Me Cry," one of the dreariest theatre songs of the era.

Ernest Schier in the *Philadelphia Evening Bulletin* said the musical was "large and unwieldy" without one "redeeming" character. Further, the show's "views of black morality and black enterprise are demeaning."

As the tryout progressed from Philadelphia to Washington, D.C., the following songs were cut: "Spread Joy," "True Love Is the Mother of Us All," and "Outside o' That You're Doin' Fine."

Freda Payne recorded "Hungry" for her album *Hot* (Capitol Records LP # ST-12003).

Appendix A: Chronology (by Season)

The following is a seasonal chronology of the 285 productions discussed in this book. Musicals that closed during their pre-Broadway engagements or during New York preview performances are marked with an asterisk (*) and are listed alphabetically at the end of the season in which they were produced.

1970

Charles Aznavour
Gantry
Georgy
Operation Sidewinder
Purlie
Blood Red Roses
Minnie's Boys
Look to the Lilies
Applause
Cry for Us All
The Boy Friend
Park
Company

1970–1971

Bob and Ray: The Two and Only
The Rothschilds
Story Theatre
Light, Lively and Yiddish
The President's Daughter
Two by Two
The Me Nobody Knows
Lovely Ladies, Kind Gentlemen
Soon
Ari
No, No, Nanette
Oh! Calcutta!
Follies
Johnny Johnson
70, Girls, 70
Metamorphoses
Frank Merriwell, or *Honor Challenged*
Earl of Ruston
**Lolita, My Love*
**Prettybelle*

1971–1972

You're a Good Man, Charlie Brown
Jesus Christ Superstar
Aint Supposed to Die a Natural Death
To Live Another Summer, to Pass Another Winter
On the Town
The Grass Harp
Only Fools Are Sad
Two Gentlemen of Verona
Wild and Wonderful
Inner City
Anne of Green Gables
The Sign in Sidney Brustein's Window
Grease
The Selling of the President
A Funny Thing Happened on the Way to the Forum
Sugar
That's Entertainment
Lost in the Stars
Dont Bother Me, I Cant Cope
Different Times
Tommy
Hard Job Being God
Dont Play Us Cheap

Heathen!
**Candide*
**ClownAround*
**W.C.*

1972–1973

Man of La Mancha
Mass
Jacques Brel Is Alive and Well and Living in Paris
From Israel with Love
Dude, or *The Highway Life*
Hurry, Harry
Pacific Paradise
Mother Earth
Pippin
Lysistrata
Dear Oscar
Ambassador
Via Galactica
Purlie
The Grand Music Hall of Israel
Tricks
Shelter
A Little Night Music
Irene
Seesaw
Cyrano
Nash at Nine
Smith
**Comedy*
**Halloween*
**Mary C. Brown and the Hollywood Sign*

1973–1974

The Desert Song
Raisin
Molly
Gigi
Good Evening
Bette Midler
The Pajama Game
The Beggar's Opera
An Evening with Josephine Baker
Liza
Lorelei, or *Gentlemen Still Prefer Blondes*
Rainbow Jones
Sextet
Over Here!
Candide
The Consul
Music! Music!
Words and Music
Sammy
Ride the Winds
The Magic Show
**Brainchild*
**Gone with the Wind*
**Rachael Lily Rosenbloom and Don't You* Ever *Forget It!*
**A Song for Cyrano*
**The Student Prince*

1974–1975

The Merry Widow
Die Fledermaus
Gypsy
Mack & Mabel
Charles Aznavour on Broadway
The Big Winner
In Concert: Andy Williams with Michel Legrand
Tony Bennett and Lena Horne Sing
Anthony Newley/Henry Mancini
Mourning Pictures
Johnny Mathis
Sgt. Pepper's Lonely Hearts Club Band on the Road
Eddy Arnold
The 5th Dimension
Raphael in Concert
Where's Charley?
Good News
The Wiz
Black Picture Show
Shenandoah
Man on the Moon
Dance with Me
The Night That Made America Famous
Goodtime Charley
The Lieutenant
The Rocky Horror Show
Seals and Crofts
Doctor Jazz
A Letter for Queen Victoria
The Consul
Bette Midler's Clams on the Half-Shell Revue
Rodgers and Hart
**I Got a Song*
**Miss Moffat*

1975–1976

Chicago
A Chorus Line
Die Fledermaus

The Robber Bridegroom
The 5th Season
Treemonisha
Me and Bessie
Hello, Dolly!
A Musical Jubilee
Boccaccio
Very Good Eddie
Home Sweet Homer
Pacific Overtures
Rockabye Hamlet
Bubbling Brown Sugar
My Fair Lady
Monty Python Live!
Shirley MacLaine
Rex
So Long, 174th Street
Threepenny Opera
1600 Pennsylvania Avenue
Something's Afoot
**The Baker's Wife*
**Sing America Sing*
**Truckload*

1976–1977

An Evening with Diana Ross
Godspell
The Merry Widow
Pal Joey
Let My People Come
Guys and Dolls
Die Fledermaus
Debbie
Going Up
La Belle Helene
Oh! Calcutta!
Porgy and Bess
Siamsa
The Robber Bridegroom
Don't Step on My Olive Branch
The Saint of Bleecker Street
Bing Crosby on Broadway
Music Is
Barry Manilow on Broadway
Your Arms Too Short to Box with God
Fiddler on the Roof
Ipi-Tombi
A Party with Betty Comden and Adolph Green
Piaf . . . A Remembrance
I Love My Wife
Side by Side by Sondheim
Annie
The King and I
Happy End
Toller Cranston's The Ice Show
**Hellzapoppin*

1977–1978

Beatlemania
Die Fledermaus
Man of La Mancha
Estrada
Comedy with Music
Cleo on Broadway
Hair
The Act
Jesus Christ Superstar
Lou Rawls on Broadway
Elvis The Legend Lives
On the Twentieth Century
Timbuktu!
Hello, Dolly!
Dancin'
A History of the American Film
The Merry Widow
The Saint of Bleecker Street
Ain't Misbehavin'
Angel
Runaways
Working
**Alice*
**Barbary Coast*
**The Last Minstrel Show*
**Nefertiti*
**The Prince of Grand Street*
**Spotlight*

1978–1979

The American Dance Machine
The Best Little Whorehouse in Texas
Stop the World I Want to Get Off
Naughty Marietta
The Merry Widow
Eubie!
King of Hearts
Street Scene
Gorey Stories
Platinum
IceDancing
Ballroom
A Broadway Musical
Monteith and Rand
The Grand Tour
Sarava

They're Playing Our Song
Whoopee!
Coquelico
Sweeney Todd, the Demon Barber of Fleet Street
Spokesong, or *The Common Wheel*
Zoot Suit
Carmelina
My Old Friends
The Utter Glory of Morrissey Hall
Up in One
I Remember Mama
**Back Country*
**Home Again, Home Again*
**Oh, Kay!*

1979

The Madwoman of Central Park West
Bruce Forsyth on Broadway!
Got Tu Go Disco
Broadway Opry '79
Every Good Boy Deserves Favour
But Never Jam Today
Gilda Radner Live from New York
Naughty Marietta
The Merry Widow
Peter Pan, or *The Boy Who Wouldn't Grow Up*
Evita
The 1940's Radio Hour
Sugar Babies
The Most Happy Fella
Street Scene
Snow White and the Seven Dwarfs
A Kurt Weill Cabaret
Strider
King of Schnorrers
Bette! Divine Madness
Oklahoma!
Comin' Uptown
The Babes in Toyland
**Daddy Goodness*

Appendix B: Chronology (by Classification)

Each one of the following 285 productions discussed in this book is listed chronologically within its specific classification. For more information about a show, see Appendix A, "Chronology (by Season)," as well as the specific entry for a particular production.

Some productions were revived more than once during the decade, and so their titles are followed by the particular year in which they were produced.

Many of the musicals that opened during the decade were revue-like in format and eschewed a traditional book with plot and characters. As a result, some shows don't neatly fit into a particular classification. For example, *Blood Red Roses* had a revue-like structure but could technically be classified as a book musical; on the other hand, *Aint Supposed to Die a Natural Death*, *Inner City*, and a few other productions created an overall mood and atmosphere to convey a particular outlook and philosophy about their subject matter but are probably best defined as revues or as revue-like musicals rather than as book musicals.

I've placed each production into the category that I believe best defines it, but many shows fall into a gray area, and some might technically fall under two classifications. For example, *Gone with the Wind* is an import (from Japan and Great Britain) that closed during its pre-Broadway tryout and thus was never seen in New York. While it's both an import *and* a pre-Broadway closing, I opted to classify it as an out-of-town closing.

BOOK MUSICALS WITH NEW MUSIC (84)

The following book musicals offered new lyrics and music.

Gantry
Georgy
Purlie
Blood Red Roses
Minnie's Boys
Look to the Lilies
Applause
Cry for Us All (during part of tryout, the production was titled *Who to Love*)
Park
Company
The Rothschilds
The President's Daughter
Two by Two
Lovely Ladies, Kind Gentlemen
Soon
Ari
Follies

70, Girls, 70
Frank Merriwell, or *Honor Challenged*
Earl of Ruston
Jesus Christ Superstar
The Grass Harp
Wild and Wonderful
Grease
Sugar
Different Times
Dont Play Us Cheap
Heathen!
Mass
Dude, or *The Highway Life*
Hurry, Harry
Pippin
Lysistrata
Dear Oscar
Via Galactica
Tricks
Shelter
A Little Night Music
Seesaw
Cyrano
Smith
Raisin
Molly
Rainbow Jones (during part of tryout, the production was titled *R.J.*)
Sextet
Over Here!
Ride the Winds
The Magic Show
Mack & Mabel
The Big Winner
The Wiz
Shenandoah
Man on the Moon
Goodtime Charley
The Lieutenant
Doctor Jazz
Chicago
The 5th Season
Boccaccio
Home Sweet Homer (during most of tryout, the production was titled *Odyssey*)
Pacific Overtures
Rex
So Long, 174th Street
1600 Pennsylvania Avenue
Something's Afoot
Music Is
I Love My Wife
Annie
The Act (during part of tryout, the production was titled *Shine It On*)
On the Twentieth Century
Angel

King of Hearts
Platinum
Ballroom
A Broadway Musical
The Grand Tour
Sarava
They're Playing Our Song
Sweeney Todd, the Demon Barber of Fleet Street
Carmelina
The Utter Glory of Morrissey Hall
I Remember Mama
Got Tu Go Disco
Comin' Uptown

BOOK MUSICALS WITH PREEXISTING MUSIC (3)

Gigi and *Snow White and the Seven Dwarfs* included songs from their earlier film versions as well as new songs especially written for their stage productions.

Gigi
The 1940's Radio Hour
Snow White and the Seven Dwarfs

OPERAS (1)

Treemonisha

PLAYS WITH INCIDENTAL SONGS (6)

The productions in this category are probably best defined as plays that included songs and incidental music.

Operation Sidewinder
The Sign in Sidney Brustein's Window
The Selling of the President
Mourning Pictures
Black Picture Show
Zoot Suit

REVUES (26)

Sugar Babies is clearly a revue, but many of the productions listed in this category (such as *Aint Supposed to Die a Natural Death*, *Bubbling Brown Sugar*, and *A History of the American Film*) aren't quite traditional revues. They don't completely fit into the category of a book musical and are perhaps best described as revue-like in nature.

Story Theatre
Light, Lively and Yiddish
Metamorphoses
Aint Supposed to Die a Natural Death
Inner City

That's Entertainment
Hard Job Being God
Mother Earth
Nash at Nine
Music! Music!
Sgt. Pepper's Lonely Hearts Club Band on the Road
Me and Bessie
Rodgers and Hart
A Musical Jubilee
Bubbling Brown Sugar
Your Arms Too Short to Box with God
Piaf . . . A Remembrance
Beatlemania
Elvis the Legend Lives
A History of the American Film
Working
Eubie!
Gorey Stories
Broadway Opry '79
Sugar Babies
A Kurt Weill Cabaret

PERSONALITY REVUES (32)

Personality revues are often more in the nature of concert-like personal appearances by well-known performers. Sometimes these revues included other entertainers, but it's clear each production was designed to showcase the special skills and talents of its specific headliner.

Charles Aznavour
Bob and Ray: The Two and Only (Bob Elliott and Ray Goulding)
Bette Midler
An Evening with Josephine Baker
Liza (Minnelli)
Words and Music (Sammy Cahn)
Sammy (Davis Jr.)
Charles Aznavour on Broadway
In Concert: Andy Williams with Michel Legrand
Tony Bennett and Lena Horne Sing
Anthony Newley/Henry Mancini
Johnny Mathis
Eddy Arnold
The 5th Dimension
Raphael in Concert (Miguel Raphael Martos Sanchez)
The Night That Made America Famous (Harry Chapin)
Seals and Crofts (Jim Seals and Dash Crofts)
Bette Midler's Clams on the Half-Shell Revue
Monty Python Live!
Shirley MacLaine
An Evening with Diana Ross
Debbie (Reynolds)
Bing Crosby on Broadway
Barry Manilow on Broadway
Comedy with Music (Victor Borge)

Cleo on Broadway (Cleo Laine)
Lou Rawls on Broadway
Monteith and Rand (John Monteith and Suzanne Rand)
Up in One (Peter Allen)
Bruce Forsyth on Broadway!
Gilda Radner Live from New York
Bette! Divine Madness (Bette Davis)

ICE REVUES (2)

Toller Cranston's The Ice Show
IceDancing

DANCE MUSICALS AND REVUES (3)

Tommy (story ballet with music from the album *Tommy*)
Dancin' (dance revue with mostly preexisting music)
The American Dance Machine (dance revue with preexisting music)

REVUES AND MUSICALS THAT ORIGINATED OFF BROADWAY OR OFF OFF BROADWAY (20)

The Me Nobody Knows (revue)
Oh! Calcutta! (1971) (revue)
You're a Good Man, Charlie Brown (revue)
Two Gentlemen of Verona (book musical with new music)
Don't Bother Me, I Cant Cope (revue)
Jacques Brel Is Alive and Well and Living in Paris (revue)
Dance with Me (book musical with preexisting music)
A Chorus Line (book musical with new music)
The Robber Bridegroom (1975; book musical with new music)
Godspell (revue)
Let My People Come (revue)
The Robber Bridegroom (1976; book musical with new music)
Ain't Misbehavin' (revue)
Runaways (revue)
The Best Little Whorehouse in Texas (book musical with new music)
My Old Friends (book musical with new music)
The Madwoman of Central Park West (personality revue; previously produced as *My Mother Was a Fortune-Teller*)
King of Schnorrers (book musical with new music)
Oh! Calcutta! (1976) (revue)
But Never Jam Today (book musical with new music)

IMPORTS (22)

To Live Another Summer, to Pass Another Winter (revue)
Only Fools Are Sad (revue; previously produced as *Once There Was a Hassid*)
Anne of Green Gables (book musical)
From Israel with Love (revue)

Pacific Paradise (revue)
Ambassador (book musical)
The Grand Music Hall of Israel (revue)
Good Evening (revue; previously produced as *Behind the Fridge*)
The Rocky Horror Show (book musical)
A Letter for Queen Victoria (book musical)
Rockabye Hamlet (book musical; previously produced as *Kronberg: 1582*, and later as *Something's Rockin' in Denmark!*)
Siamsa (revue)
Don't Step on My Olive Branch (revue)
Ipi-Tombi (revue)
Side by Side by Sondheim (revue with preexisting music)
Happy End (book musical)
Estrada (revue)
Coquelico (revue)
Spokesong, or *The Common Wheel* (play with incidental songs)
Every Good Boy Deserves Favour (play with incidental music)
Evita (book musical)
Strider (play with incidental songs; an import that had previously been produced Off Broadway)

REVIVALS (56)

In some cases, the revivals listed in this category were radically revised (such as *The Babes in Toyland*) or are ones that were altered from the original productions (*No, No, Nanette*, *Irene*, *Whoopee!*, and others).

The Boy Friend (book musical)
No, No, Nanette (book musical)
Johnny Johnson (book musical)
On the Town (book musical)
A Funny Thing Happened on the Way to the Forum (book musical)
Lost in the Stars (book musical)
Man of La Mancha (1972; book musical)
Irene (book musical)
The Desert Song (book musical)
The Pajama Game (book musical)
The Beggar's Opera (book musical)
Lorelei, or *Gentlemen Still Prefer Blondes* (book musical; revised version of *Gentlemen Prefer Blondes*)
Candide (1974; book musical)
The Consul (1974; opera)
The Merry Widow (1974; operetta)
Die Fledermaus (1974; operetta)
Gypsy (book musical)
Where's Charley? (book musical)
Good News (book musical)
The Consul (1975; opera)
Die Fledermaus (1975; operetta)
Hello, Dolly! (1975; book musical)
Very Good Eddie (book musical)
My Fair Lady (book musical)
Threepenny Opera (book musical)
The Merry Widow (1976; operetta)
Pal Joey (book musical)
Guys and Dolls (book musical)

Die Fledermaus (1976; operetta)
Going Up (book musical)
La Belle Helene (operetta)
Porgy and Bess (opera)
The Saint of Bleecker Street (1976; opera)
Fiddler on the Roof (book musical)
A Party with Betty Comden and Adolph Green (personality revue)
The King and I (book musical)
Die Fledermaus (1977; operetta)
Man of La Mancha (1977; book musical)
Hair (book musical)
Jesus Christ Superstar (1977; book musical)
Timbuktu! (book musical; revised version of *Kismet*)
Hello, Dolly! (1978; book musical)
The Merry Widow (April 1978; operetta)
The Saint of Bleecker Street (1978; opera)
Stop the World I Want to Get Off (book musical)
Naughty Marietta (1978; operetta)
The Merry Widow (September 1978; operetta)
Street Scene (1978; book musical)
Whoopee! (book musical)
Naughty Marietta (1979; operetta)
The Merry Widow (1979; operetta)
Peter Pan, or *The Boy Who Wouldn't Grow Up* (book musical)
The Most Happy Fella (book musical)
Street Scene (1979; book musical)
Oklahoma! (book musical)
The Babes in Toyland (book musical; revised version of *Babes in Toyland*)

RETURN ENGAGEMENTS (1)

In contrast to a revival, the traditional return engagement is usually a limited booking of a musical's touring company. Because the run isn't open-ended, the Broadway engagement is usually another stop on the road tour, most often at the beginning or the end of the tour.

Purlie (1972) (book musical)

PRE-BROADWAY CLOSINGS (29)

Lolita, My Love (book musical with new music)
Prettybelle (book musical with new music)
Candide (1971 revival; book musical)
ClownAround (revue)
W.C. (book musical with new music)
Comedy (book musical with new music)
Halloween (book musical with new music)
Mary C. Brown and the Hollywood Sign (book musical with new music)
Brainchild (book musical with new music)
Gone with the Wind (import; book musical)
Rachael Lily Rosenbloom and Don't You Ever *Forget It!* (book musical with new music)
A Song for Cyrano (revival; book musical)
The Student Prince (revival; operetta)

I Got a Song (revue with preexisting music)
Miss Moffat (book musical with new music)
The Baker's Wife (book musical with new music)
Sing America Sing (revue with mostly preexisting music)
Truckload (book musical with new music)
Hellzapoppin (basically a revival in name only; revue with new music)
Alice (book musical with new music)
Barbary Coast (book musical with new music)
The Last Minstrel Show (book musical with new and preexisting music)
Nefertiti (book musical with new music)
The Prince of Grand Street (book musical with new music)
Spotlight (book musical with new music)
Back Country (book musical with new music)
Home Again, Home Again (book musical with new music)
Oh, Kay! (revival; book musical)
Daddy Goodness (book musical with new music)

Appendix C: Discography

The following two lists are of cast recordings, studio cast recordings, or recordings that were released in song collections. The first list represents those musicals that were initially produced in the 1970s, and the second reflects those that were produced prior to 1970 but were revived during the decade.

For specific information about these recordings, see entries for particular shows. The criterion for inclusion in these lists is that the recordings were officially on sale to the public at one time or another. Demo recordings are not included unless they were later released for sale.

Note that while there weren't full-length cast recordings of some productions (such as *Blood Red Roses*, *Daddy Goodness*, *Home Sweet Homer*, and *Sarava*), a song or two from these shows were sometimes included in collections of show or popular music albums. These productions are included in the following lists, and more information about a specific recording can be found in the show's entry.

RECORDINGS OF MUSICALS THAT FIRST OPENED IN THE 1970S

The Act
Ain't Misbehavin'
Aint Supposed to Die a Natural Death
Ambassador
Angel
Annie
Applause
The Baker's Wife
Ballroom
The Best Little Whorehouse in Texas
Bette! Divine Madness (recorded as *Divine Madness*)
Blood Red Roses
Bob and Ray: The Two and Only
Brainchild
Bubbling Brown Sugar
Carmelina
Chicago
A Chorus Line
ClownAround
Company
Cry for Us All
Cyrano
Daddy Goodness
Different Times
Doctor Jazz
Dont Bother Me, I Cant Cope
Dont Play Us Cheap
Dude, or The Highway Life
Earl of Ruston
Eubie!
Every Good Boy Deserves Favour
Evita
Follies
Gantry
Gigi
Gilda Radner Live from New York (recorded as *Gilda Radner Live*)
Godspell
Good Evening
Goodtime Charley
The Grand Tour
The Grass Harp
Grease
Hard Job Being God
Heathen! (recorded as *Aloha*)
Home Again, Home Again
Home Sweet Homer

I Love My Wife
I Remember Mama
Inner City
Ipi-Tombi
Jesus Christ Superstar (based on recordings originally released in 1969 and 1970)
King of Hearts
Let My People Come
The Lieutenant
A Little Night Music
Lolita, My Love
Look to the Lilies
Mack & Mabel
The Madwoman of Central Park West
The Magic Show
Man on the Moon
Mary C. Brown and the Hollywood Sign
Mass
Me and Bessie
The Me Nobody Knows
Minnie's Boys
Miss Moffat
Molly
Mother Earth
Nefertiti
Only Fools Are Sad
On the Twentieth Century
Operation Sidewinder
Over Here!
Pacific Overtures
Pippin
Platinum
Prettybelle
The Prince of Grand Street
Purlie
Raisin
Rex
The Robber Bridegroom
Rockabye Hamlet
Runaways
Sarava
Seesaw
70, Girls, 70
Sgt. Pepper's Lonely Hearts Club Band on the Road (based on the 1967 recording *Sgt. Pepper's Lonely Hearts Club Band*)
Shelter
Shenandoah
Siamsa
Side by Side by Sondheim
1600 Pennsylvania Avenue (recorded as *A White House Cantata*)
Snow White and the Seven Dwarfs
So Long, 174th Street
Story Theatre
Sugar
Sweeney Todd, the Demon Barber of Fleet Street
They're Playing Our Song
Timbuktu! (recorded as *Timbuktu!* and based on the 1953 musical *Kismet*, which has been recorded numerous times)
To Live Another Summer, to Pass Another Winter
Tommy (based on the 1969 recording)
Treemonisha
Two by Two
Two Gentlemen of Verona
The Utter Glory of Morrissey Hall
Via Galactica
W.C.
The Wiz
Working
Your Arms Too Short to Box with God
Zoot Suit

RECORDINGS OF MUSICALS PRODUCED IN NEW YORK DURING THE 1970S BUT ORIGINALLY PRODUCED BEFORE 1970

Anne of Green Gables
The Babes in Toyland (originally produced as *Babes in Toyland*)
The Beggar's Opera
The Boy Friend
Candide
The Consul
The Desert Song
Die Fledermaus
Fiddler on the Roof
A Funny Thing Happened on the Way to the Forum
Going Up
Gone with the Wind (originally produced as *Scarlett* and *Gone with the Wind*)
Good News
Guys and Dolls
Gypsy
Hair
Happy End
Hello, Dolly!
Irene
Johnny Johnson

The King and I
A Kurt Weill Cabaret (an early version of the revue was produced as *The World of Kurt Weill in Song*)
La Belle Helene
Lost in the Stars
Man of La Mancha
The Merry Widow
The Most Happy Fella
My Fair Lady
Naughty Marietta
No, No, Nanette
Oh! Calcutta!
Oh, Kay!
Oklahoma!
On the Town
The Pajama Game
Pal Joey
A Party with Betty Comden and Adolph Green
Peter Pan
Porgy and Bess
The Saint of Bleecker Street
Stop the World I Want to Get Off
Street Scene
The Student Prince
Threepenny Opera
Very Good Eddie
Where's Charley?
Whoopee!
You're a Good Man, Charlie Brown

Appendix D: Filmography

The following are two lists of film, television, home video, and radio versions of musicals discussed in this book. The first list represents those musicals that had their New York premieres during the 1970s, and the second those that were first produced prior to 1970 but were revived during the decade. In some cases, a musical was the subject of a documentary-style television show, and these are also included below. For more information, see entry for specific musical.

FILM VERSIONS OF MUSICALS THAT OPENED IN THE 1970S

Ain't Misbehavin'
The American Dance Machine
Anne of Green Gables
Annie
Applause
The Best Little Whorehouse in Texas
Bette! Divine Madness (film released as *Divine Madness*)
The Big Winner
Chicago
A Chorus Line
Company
Dont Play Us Cheap
Every Good Boy Deserves Favour
Evita
Follies
Gilda Radner Live from New York (film released as *Gilda Live*)
Godspell
Good Evening (released as *Behind the Fridge*)
The Grass Harp (television documentary)
Grease
Jesus Christ Superstar
A Little Night Music
The Magic Show
The Me Nobody Knows
Pacific Overtures (film; also television documentary)
Pippin
Purlie
Rockabye Hamlet
The Rocky Horror Show (film released as *The Rocky Horror Picture Show*)
The Saint of Bleecker Street
Something's Afoot
Sweeney Todd, the Demon Barber of Fleet Street
Tommy
Treemonisha
The Wiz
Working
Zoot Suit

FILM VERSIONS OF MUSICALS THAT WERE REVIVED DURING THE 1970S

The Babes in Toyland (as *Babes in Toyland*)
The Beggar's Opera
The Boy Friend
Candide
The Consul
The Desert Song
Die Fledermaus
Fiddler on the Roof
A Funny Thing Happened on the Way to the Forum
Gentlemen Prefer Blondes (revived as *Lorelei*, or *Gentlemen Still Prefer Blondes*)
Going Up
Good News
Guys and Dolls
Gypsy
Hair
Hello, Dolly!
Irene
Jacques Brel Is Alive and Well and Living in Paris
The King and I
Kismet (revived as *Timbuktu!*)
Lost in the Stars
Man of La Mancha
The Merry Widow
The Most Happy Fella
My Fair Lady
Naughty Marietta
No, No, Nanette
Oh! Calcutta!
Oh, Kay!
Oklahoma!
On the Town
The Pajama Game
Pal Joey
Peter Pan
Porgy and Bess
The Saint of Bleecker Street
Stop the World I Want to Get Off
Street Scene
The Student Prince
Threepenny Opera
Where's Charley?
Whoopee!
You're a Good Man, Charlie Brown

Appendix E: Gilbert and Sullivan Operettas

The following is a chronological list of all operettas by W. S. Gilbert and Arthur Sullivan that were revived on Broadway during the period January 1, 1970–December 31, 1979. After each title, the opening date, number of performances, name of theatre, and name of producer(s) are given.

Of the fourteen major works by Gilbert and Sullivan, the decade saw four produced in New York: *The Mikado*, or *The Town of Titipu*; *H.M.S. Pinafore*, or *The Lass That Loved a Sailor*; *The Pirates of Penzance*, or *Love and Duty*; and *Iolanthe*, or *The Peer and the Peri*.

The Mikado (March 17, 1974, five performances; New York State Theatre; The New York City Opera Company)

The Mikado (September 1, 1974, six performances; New York State Theatre; The New York City Opera Company)

The Mikado (March 9, 1975, three performances; New York State Theatre; The New York City Opera Company)

H.M.S. Pinafore (September 27, 1975, five performances; New York State Theatre; The New York City Opera Company)

H.M.S. Pinafore (February 22, 1976, four performances; New York State Theatre; The New York City Opera Company)

The Mikado (May 5, 1976, ten performances; Uris Theatre; James M. Nederlander by arrangement with the D'Oyly Carte Opera Trust, Ltd., and Dame Bridget D'Oyly Carte)

The Pirates of Penzance (May 6, 1976, eight performances; Uris Theatre; James M. Nederlander by arrangement with the D'Oyly Carte Opera Trust, Ltd., and Dame Bridget D'Oyly Carte)

H.M.S. Pinafore (May 16, 1976, four performances; Uris Theatre; James M. Nederlander by arrangement with the D'Oyly Carte Opera Trust, Ltd., and Dame Bridget D'Oyly Carte)

H.M.S. Pinafore (September 3, 1976, four performances; New York State Theatre; The New York City Opera Company)

The Pirates of Penzance (March 26, 1977, four performances; New York State Theatre; The New York City Opera Company)

The Pirates of Penzance (October 29, 1977, two performances; New York State Theatre; The New York City Opera Company)

Iolanthe (July 17, 1978, two performances; New York State Theatre; James and Joseph Nederlander in association with the City Center of Music and Drama, Inc., and in association with the D'Oyly Carte Opera Trust, Ltd., and Dame Bridget D'Oyly Carte by arrangement with Barclays Bank International)

The Mikado (July 18, 1978, three performances; New York State Theatre; James and Joseph Nederlander in association with the City Center of Music and Drama, Inc., and in association with the D'Oyly Carte Opera Trust, Ltd., and Dame Bridget D'Oyly Carte by arrangement with Barclays Bank International)

H.M.S. Pinafore (July 21, 1978, three performances; New York State Theatre; James and Joseph Nederlander in association with the City Center of Music and Drama, Inc., and in association with the D'Oyly Carte Opera Trust, Ltd., and Dame Bridget D'Oyly Carte by arrangement with Barclays Bank International)

The Pirates of Penzance (July 24, 1978, two performances; New York State Theatre; James and Joseph Nederlander in association with the City Center of Music and Drama, Inc., and in association with the D'Oyly Carte Opera Trust, Ltd., and Dame Bridget D'Oyly Carte by arrangement with Barclays Bank International)

Appendix F: Other Productions

The following selected productions played on Broadway (or in the New York City metropolitan area) during the 1970s and utilized songs, sketches, dances, or background music.

1970

Gloria and Esperanza

By Julie Bovasso (ANTA Theatre, February 4, 1970, four performances)
The drama included choreography by Raymond Bussey; the production's assistant choreographer was William Pierce.

1970–1971

The Good Woman of Setzuan

By Bertolt Brecht (translation by Ralph Manheim) (Vivian Beaumont Theatre, November 5, 1970, forty-six performances)
The revival included songs by Herbert Pilhofer and John Lewin, and background music by Pilhofer.

The Playboy of the Western World

By John Millington Synge (Vivian Beaumont Theatre, January 7, 1971, fifty-two performances)
The revival included music by John Duffy, all of which was based on traditional Irish folk songs.

A Midsummer Night's Dream

By William Shakespeare (Billy Rose Theatre, January 20, 1971, sixty-two performances)
The revival included background music by Richard Peaslee ("with the Actors and Felix Mendelssohn").

Lenny

By Julian Barry (Brooks Atkinson Theatre, May 26, 1971, 455 performances)
The play included incidental music by Tom O'Horgan, who directed the production.

1971–1972

The Black Light Theatre of Prague

Text by Jiri Srnec and Frantisek Kratochvil (City Center, September 27, 1971, ten performances)
The evening of magic and mime included music by Jiri Srnec.

Mary Stuart

By Friedrich Schiller (translation by Stephen Spender) (Vivian Beaumont Theatre, November 11, 1971, forty-four performances)
The revival included background music by Stanley Silverman.

Narrow Road to the Deep North

By Edward Bond (Vivian Beaumont Theatre, January 6, 1972, forty-four performances)
The play included background music by Stanley Silverman.

Twigs

By George Furth (Broadhurst Theatre, November 14, 1972, 289 performances)
The evening of four one-act plays (*Emily*, *Celia*, *Dorothy*, and *Ma*) included the song "Hollywood and Vine" (lyric by Stephen Sondheim and George Furth, music by Stephen Sondheim) for *Celia*. The play was published in hardback by Samuel French in an undated edition that includes the complete lyric of the song. The lyric is also included in Stephen Sondheim's collection *Look, I Made a Hat: Collected Lyrics (1981–2011) with Attendant Comments, Amplifications, Dogmas, Harangues, Digressions, Anecdotes and Miscellany*.
Twigs was filmed for television and telecast on CBS on March 6, 1975, with Carol Burnett in the leading roles.

Sticks and Bones

By David Rabe (John Golden Theatre, March 1, 1972, 366 performances)
The play included the song "Baby, When I Find You" (lyric by David Rabe, music by Galt MacDermot).

1972–1973

Much Ado About Nothing

By William Shakespeare (Winter Garden Theatre, November 11, 1972, 136 performances)
The revival included incidental songs by Peter Link and two ragtime numbers by Scott Joplin; the production was choreographed by Donald Saddler.
Link's contributions were: "Meet You 'Hind the Barn," "Ballad for a Summer Evening," "Hogwash," "Light of Love," "Jimmie," "Goodbye, Fred," and "Marcella." The rags by Joplin were "Maple Leaf Rag" and "Smoker Rag."
The production was filmed for television and was telecast on February 2, 1973; the DVD was released by Kultur Video.

The Creation of the World and Other Business

By Arthur Miller (Shubert Theatre, November 30, 1972, twenty performances)
The play included incidental music by Stanley Silverman.

1973–1974

The Good Doctor

By Neil Simon (Eugene O'Neill Theatre, November 27, 1973, 208 performances)
The production included an introductory concert to set the tone and atmosphere of the evening, which included the following sequences: "Oop Tymbali," "Good Doctor Opus # 1," "Trans Siberian Railroad," "Father and Son," "Good Doctor Opus # 2," "Morning Dance," "Dance for the Gathering I," and "Dance for the Gathering II." The concert and background music were by Peter Link, and the songs were by Neil Simon (lyrics) and Link (music).

Measure for Measure

By William Shakespeare (Billy Rose Theatre, December 26, 1973, seven performances)
The revival included background music by Virgil Thomson.

Ulysses in Nighttown

By Marjorie Barkentin (Winter Garden Theatre, March 10, 1974, sixty-nine performances)
The revival included background music by Peter Link; Swen Swenson created the staging for the dance sequences.

Jumpers

By Tom Stoppard (Billy Rose Theatre, April 22, 1974, forty-eight performances)
The play included the song "Beyond My Reach" (lyric by Mort Goode, music by Claus Ogerman); the production also included lyrics by Tom Stoppard. Dennis Nahat created both the choreography and the tumbling sequences.

Turtlenecks/The One-Night Stand

By Bruce Jay Friedman and Jacques Levy (closed during its pre-Broadway tryout; as *Turtlenecks*, the production opened on August 6, 1973, at the Fisher Theatre, Detroit, Michigan, and closed on September 22, 1973, at the Forrest Theatre, Philadelphia, Pennsylvania, where it was titled *The One-Night Stand*)
The play included incidental music by Stanley Walden.
Not to be confused with *One Night Stand*, the musical with book and lyrics by Herb Gardiner and music by Jule Styne, which played eight preview performances at the Nederlander Theatre for the period October 20–October 25, 1980, before permanently closing there prior to its official Broadway opening.

1974–1975

Love for Love

By William Congreve (Helen Hayes Theatre, November 11, 1974, twenty-four performances)
Directed by Harold Prince, the revival included incidental music by Paul Gemignani as well as songs with lyrics by Hugh Wheeler and music by Gemignani.

The Member of the Wedding

By Carson McCullers (Helen Hayes Theatre, January 2, 1975, twelve performances)
The revival included incidental music by Charles Strouse.

1975–1976

The Lady from the Sea

By Henrik Ibsen (translation by Michael Meyer) (Circle in the Square Theatre, March 18, 1976, seventy-seven performances)
The revival included incidental music by Richard Peaslee.

Trelawny of the "Wells"

By Arthur Wing Pinero (Vivian Beaumont Theatre, October 15, 1975, forty-seven performances)
The revival included incidental music by Peter Link.

Hamlet

By William Shakespeare (Vivian Beaumont Theatre, December 17, 1975, forty-seven performances)
The revival included incidental music by John Morris.

Yentl

By Leah Napolin and Isaac Bashevis Singer (Eugene O'Neill Theatre, October 23, 1975, 224 performances)
The revival included incidental music by Mel Marvin.

The Royal Family

By George S. Kaufman and Edna Ferber (Helen Hayes Theatre, December 30, 1975, 232 performances)
The revival included incidental music by Claibe Richardson.

Legend

By Samuel Taylor (Ethel Barrymore Theatre, May 13, 1976, five performances)
The comedy included music by Dan Goggin. The "original Broadway soundtrack" album was released by Theatre Archives Records (LP # TA-7801) and includes background music heard in the production (including the sequence "The Stagecoach Robbery" which was deleted prior to opening night).

1976–1977

The Cherry Orchard

By Anton Chekhov (translation by Jean-Claude van Itallie) (Vivian Beaumont Theatre, February 17, 1977, sixty-two performances).
The revival included incidental music by Elizabeth Swados.

Agamemnon

By Aeschylus ("conceived" by Andrei Serban and Elizabeth Swados with a text that used parts of the original Greek as well as Edith Hamilton's translation) (Vivian Beaumont Theatre, May 18, 1977, thirty-eight performances)
The revival included incidental music by Elizabeth Swados.

Lily Tomlin in "Appearing Nitely"

By Jane Wagner and Lily Tomlin (Biltmore Theatre, March 24, 1977, eighty-four performances)
The evening consisted of sketches and included incidental music by Jerry Frankel.

Vieux Carre

By Tennessee Williams (St. James Theatre, May 11, 1977, seven performances)
The evening consisted of two playlets and included incidental music by Galt MacDermot.

1977–1978

The Effect of Gamma Rays on Man-in-the-Moon Marigolds

By Paul Zindel (Biltmore Theatre, March 4, 1978, sixteen performances)
The revival included incidental music by Richard Peaslee.

Stages

By Stuart Ostrow (Belasco Theatre, March 19, 1978, one performance)
The play included incidental music by Stanley Silverman.

1978–1979

Taxi Tales

By Leonard Melfi (Century Theatre, December 28, 1978, six performances)
The evening of short one-act plays included the song "Taxi," lyric and music by Jonathan Hogan.

Tip-Toes

Book by Guy Bolton and Fred Thompson, lyrics by Ira Gershwin, and music by George Gershwin (Brooklyn Academy of Music, March 24, 1979, for nineteen performances)

The musical was first produced on December 28, 1925, at the Liberty Theatre for 194 performances. The revival's cast included Georgia Engel, Russ Thacker, and Bob Gunton. A studio cast recording of the score (with Emily Loesser, Lewis J. Stadlen, Lee Wilkof, and Mark Baker) was released on a two-CD set by New World Records (# 80598-2), which also included a studio cast recording of the Gershwins' 1925 musical *Tell Me More.*

1979

Rise and Fall of the City of Mahagonny

Libretto by Bertolt Brecht and music by Kurt Weill (English adaptation by David Drew and Michael Geliot) (Metropolitan Opera House, November 16, 1979, eleven performances)

This production of *Mahagonny* marked its Met premiere. It was later produced there in 1981 (seven performances), 1984 (seven performances), and 1995 (five performances). The full-length version of the opera was first produced as *Aufstieg und Fall der Stadt Mahagonny* on March 9, 1930, in Leipzig, Germany, at the Neues Theatre, and the work premiered in New York on April 28, 1970, at the Anderson Theatre for eight performances in an English translation by Arnold Weinstein (the cast included Barbara Harris, Frank Porretta, and Estelle Parsons).

Bent

By Martin Sherman (New Apollo Theatre, December 2, 1979, 240 performances)

The drama included incidental music by Stanley Silverman.

Note: During the decade, the following operas had their New York premieres. In chronological order, they are: Kurt Weill's *Rise and Fall of the City of Mahagonny* (1970; the opera was also produced by the Metropolitan Opera in 1979 [see above]), Lee Hoiby's *Summer and Smoke* (1972), Carlisle Floyd's *Markheim* (1973), Robert Wilson's *The Life and Times of Joseph Stalin* (1973), Philip Glass's *Einstein on the Beach* (1976), Thomas Pasatieri's *Washington Square* (1977), Dominick Argento's *Miss Havisham's Fire* (1979), and Dominick Argento's *Postcard from Morocco* (1979). These works are discussed in my reference book *Off-Broadway Musicals, 1910–2007: Casts, Credits, Songs, Critical Reception and Performance Data of More Than 1,800 Shows* (2010).

Appendix G: Black-Themed Revues and Musicals

The following is an alphabetical list of revues and musicals discussed in this book that have subject matter predominantly dealing with American and/or African black culture in theme, plot, and character. These include book musicals exclusively about blacks and written and composed by blacks (*Dont Play Us Cheap*); book musicals exclusively about blacks and written and composed by both blacks and whites (*The Wiz*); musicals about blacks written by whites (*Porgy and Bess*); revue-like musicals that deal with black themes and issues (*Aint Supposed to Die a Natural Death*); book musicals that include white and black casts and deal with racial issues (*A Broadway Musical, 1600 Pennsylvania Avenue*); black composer tribute revues with black casts (*Ain't Misbehavin', Eubie!*); personality revues with black performers (*An Evening with Josephine Baker, Johnny Mathis*); black versions of white musicals (*Guys and Dolls*); and predominantly white musicals that include major black characters (*Gone with the Wind*, the 1973 revival of *The Pajama Game*).

A Broadway Musical
Ain't Misbehavin'
Aint Supposed to Die a Natural Death
Alice
Black Picture Show
Bubbling Brown Sugar
But Never Jam Today
Cleo on Broadway
Comin' Uptown
Daddy Goodness
Doctor Jazz
Dont Bother Me, I Cant Cope
Dont Play Us Cheap
Eubie!
An Evening with Diana Ross
An Evening with Josephine Baker
The 5th Dimension
Gone with the Wind
Got Tu Go Disco
Guys and Dolls
Hello, Dolly! (1975)
Inner City
Johnny Mathis
The Last Minstrel Show
Look to the Lilies
Lost in the Stars
Lou Rawls on Broadway
Me and Bessie
The Me Nobody Knows
Miss Moffat
My Old Friends
The Pajama Game
Porgy and Bess
Prettybelle
Purlie
Raisin
Rockabye Hamlet
Runaways
Sammy
Shenandoah
1600 Pennsylvania Avenue
Stop the World I Want to Get Off
Timbuktu!
Tony Bennett and Lena Horne Sing
Treemonisha
Two Gentlemen of Verona
The Wiz
Your Arms Too Short to Box with God

Appendix H: Jewish-Themed Revues and Musicals

The following is an alphabetical list of revues and musicals discussed in this book that have subject matter predominantly Jewish in theme, plot, and character.

Ari
The Big Winner
Don't Step on My Olive Branch
Fiddler on the Roof
The 5th Season
From Israel with Love
The Grand Music Hall of Israel
The Grand Tour
Hard Job Being God
King of Schnorrers
Light, Lively and Yiddish
Only Fools Are Sad
The President's Daughter
The Prince of Grand Street
The Rothschilds
To Live Another Summer, to Pass Another Winter
Two by Two

Appendix I: Radio City Music Hall Productions

During the 1979–1980 season, Radio City Music Hall Productions, Inc., offered four presentations, one of which (*Snow White and the Seven Dwarfs*) was a new book musical based on the 1937 Walt Disney film.

Snow White and the Seven Dwarfs (October 18, 1979; 106 performances) (See entry in text for more information.)
The Magnificent Christmas Spectacular (November 25, 1979; ninety-one performances)

(Later in the season, *It's Spring: The Glory of Easter* opened on March 14, 1980, for fifty-six performances, and *A Rockette Spectacular* opened on May 4, 1980, for eighty-nine performances.)

Appendix J: Published Scripts

The following are alphabetical lists of published scripts for the musicals discussed in this book. The first represents productions that premiered in the 1970s, and the second those shows produced prior to 1970 but revived during the decade.

The criterion for these lists is that the scripts were officially on sale to the public at one time or another; entries in this book occasionally refer to unpublished scripts, but these aren't included in the appendix. For more information about a specific script, see the show's entry for name of publisher and publication date.

SCRIPTS OF MUSICALS FIRST PRODUCED IN THE 1970S

The Act
Angel
Applause
Ballroom
The Best Little Whorehouse in Texas
Black Picture Show
Bubbling Brown Sugar
Chicago
A Chorus Line
Comin' Uptown (published as *Christmas Is Comin' Uptown*)
Company
Cyrano
Dont Bother Me, I Cant Cope
Every Good Boy Deserves Favour
Evita
Follies
Frank Merriwell, or *Honor Challenged*
Goodtime Charley
Gorey Stories
The Grand Tour
The Grass Harp
Grease
A History of the American Film
Jesus Christ Superstar
A Letter for Queen Victoria
A Little Night Music
Look to the Lilies
Lovely Ladies, Kind Gentlemen
Mack & Mabel
Mass
The Me Nobody Knows
Minnie's Boys
My Old Friends
The 1940's Radio Hour
On the Twentieth Century
Operation Sidewinder
Over Here!
Pacific Overtures
Park
Pippin
Purlie
Rainbow Jones
Raisin
The Robber Bridegroom
The Rocky Horror Show
The Rothschilds
Runaways
Seesaw
Shelter
Shenandoah
Smith
Something's Afoot
Story Theatre
Strider
Sugar Babies

Sweeney Todd, the Demon Barber of Fleet Street
They're Playing Our Song
Tommy
Treemonisha
Tricks
Two Gentlemen of Verona
The Utter Glory of Morrissey Hall
The Wiz

SCRIPTS OF MUSICALS PRODUCED PRIOR TO 1970 BUT PRESENTED IN NEW YORK DURING THE 1970S

Anne of Green Gables
The Beggar's Opera
The Boy Friend
Candide
The Consul
The Desert Song
Die Fledermaus
Fiddler on the Roof
A Funny Thing Happened on the Way to the Forum
Good News
Guys and Dolls
Gypsy
Hair
Happy End
Hello, Dolly!
Johnny Johnson
Jacques Brel Is Alive and Well and Living in Paris
The King and I
Kismet (produced as *Timbuktu!*)
La Belle Helene
Lost in the Stars
Man of La Mancha
The Merry Widow
My Fair Lady
Oh! Calcutta!
Oklahoma!
On the Town
The Pajama Game
Pal Joey
Porgy and Bess
The Saint of Bleecker Street
Street Scene
Threepenny Opera
Where's Charley?
You're a Good Man, Charlie Brown

Appendix K: Theatres

For the productions discussed in this book, the New York theatres where they played are listed in alphabetical order. Following each theatre's name is a chronological list of the shows that played there (for those shows that had more than one production during the decade, the entry is identified by year).

Many productions transferred to other theatres, and entries are so noted. If a show transferred once, the notation "transfer" follows the title; if a show transferred more than once, notations such as "second transfer" and "third transfer" are given.

ALVIN THEATRE

Company
Tricks
Molly
Shenandoah
Annie

AMBASSADOR THEATRE

The Boy Friend
Story Theatre
Metamorphoses
Aint Supposed to Die a Natural Death (transfer)
Me and Bessie
Godspell (second transfer)
Eubie!
Dancin' (transfer)

ANTA THEATRE

Purlie (1970; second transfer)
Different Times
A Letter for Queen Victoria
Bubbling Brown Sugar
A History of the American Film
Whoopee!
Annie (first transfer)

BEACON THEATRE

Sgt. Pepper's Lonely Hearts Club Band on the Road

BELASCO THEATRE

Light, Lively and Yiddish
Oh! Calcutta! (1971)
Mother Earth
The Rocky Horror Show
Ain't Misbehavin' (second transfer)

BILLY ROSE THEATRE

The President's Daughter
Earl of Ruston
Heathen!
Purlie (1972)
The Beggar's Opera

BIJOU THEATRE

Sextet
Ride the Winds
A Kurt Weill Cabaret

BILTMORE THEATRE

The Robber Bridegroom (1976)
Hair
Up in One

BOOTH THEATRE

Very Good Eddie
Gorey Stories
Monteith and Rand

BROADHURST THEATRE

Cry for Us All
70, Girls, 70
Grease (first transfer)
Rachael Lily Rosenbloom and Don't You Ever *Forget It!*
Godspell
Dancin'

BROADWAY THEATRE

Purlie (1970)
Dude, or *The Highway Life*
Candide (1974)
The Wiz (transfer)
Guys and Dolls
Sarava (transfer)
Evita

BROOKS ATKINSON THEATRE

Lysistrata

CENTURY THEATRE

The American Dance Machine

CIRCLE IN THE SQUARE THEATRE

Where's Charley?
Pal Joey
Spokesong, or *The Common Wheel*

CITY CENTER 55TH STREET THEATRE

Anne of Green Gables
Tommy
Music! Music!
The Merry Widow (1974)
Monty Python Live!

CORT THEATRE

The Magic Show

EDEN THEATRE

Grease
Smith
The Big Winner
The 5th Season

EDISON THEATRE

Johnny Johnson
Only Fools Are Sad
That's Entertainment
Dont Bother Me, I Cant Cope (transfer)
Hard Job Being God
Boccaccio
Me and Bessie (transfer)
Oh! Calcutta! (1976)

ETHEL BARRYMORE THEATRE

Aint Supposed to Die a Natural Death
Inner City
Dont Play Us Cheap
The Night That Made America Famous
I Love My Wife

EUGENE O'NEILL THEATRE

Annie (second transfer)

FELT FORUM

The Grand Music Hall of Israel
The Babes in Toyland

46TH STREET THEATRE

No, No, Nanette
Raisin
Chicago
Working
The Best Little Whorehouse in Texas

GEORGE ABBOTT THEATRE

Gantry

HARKNESS THEATRE

The Robber Bridegroom (1975)
So Long, 174th Street
Ipi-Tombi

HELEN HAYES THEATRE

The Me Nobody Knows
To Live Another Summer, to Pass Another Winter
Nash at Nine
Rodgers & Hart
Strider

IMPERIAL THEATRE

Minnie's Boys
Two by Two
On the Town
Lost in the Stars
Pippin
Comedy with Music
They're Playing Our Song

JOHN GOLDEN THEATRE

Blood Red Roses
Park
Bob and Ray: The Two and Only
You're a Good Man, Charlie Brown
Shelter
Words and Music
Going Up

LITTLE THEATRE

Man on the Moon
A Party with Betty Comden and Adolph Green (transfer)

LONGACRE THEATRE

Frank Merriwell, or *Honor Challenged*
The Sign in Sidney Brustein's Window
Jesus Christ Superstar (1977)
Ain't Misbehavin'
But Never Jam Today

LUNT-FONTANNE THEATRE

Look to the Lilies
The Rothschilds
A Funny Thing Happened on the Way to the Forum
Ambassador
The Pajama Game
Raisin (transfer)
Rex
Hello, Dolly! (1978)
A Broadway Musical
Peter Pan, or *The Boy Who Wouldn't Grow Up*

LYCEUM THEATRE

The Me Nobody Knows (transfer)
Wild and Wonderful
Mourning Pictures
The Lieutenant
Something's Afoot
Your Arms Too Short to Box with God

MAJESTIC THEATRE

Lovely Ladies, Kind Gentlemen
Grease (third transfer)
Sugar
A Little Night Music (transfer)
Mack & Mabel
The Wiz
Estrada
The Act
Ballroom

I Remember Mama
The Most Happy Fella
Bette! Divine Madness

MARK HELLINGER THEATRE

Ari
Jesus Christ Superstar (1971)
Seesaw (transfer)
Shenandoah (transfer)
1600 Pennsylvania Avenue
Lou Rawls on Broadway
Timbuktu!
Platinum
Sarava
The Utter Glory of Morrissey Hall
Sugar Babies

MARTIN BECK THEATRE

The Grass Harp
Happy End

MAYFAIR THEATRE

Dance with Me

METROPOLITAN OPERA HOUSE

Mass
Every Good Boy Deserves Favour

MINSKOFF THEATRE

Irene
Pippin (transfer)
Charles Aznavour on Broadway
Tony Bennett and Lena Horne Sing
Bette Midler's Clams on the Half-Shell Revue
Hello, Dolly! (1975)
Rockabye Hamlet
Debbie
Cleo on Broadway
Angel
King of Hearts
IceDancing
Got Tu Go Disco

MOROSCO THEATRE

Let My People Come
A Party with Betty Comden and Adolph Green
Side by Side by Sondheim (transfer)

MUSIC BOX THEATRE

Charles Aznavour
Rainbow Jones
Side by Side by Sondheim

NEW YORK STATE THEATRE

The Consul (1974)
Die Fledermaus (1974)
The Consul (1975)
Die Fledermaus (1975)
Die Fledermaus (1976)
La Belle Helene
The Saint of Bleecker Street (1976)
Die Fledermaus (1977)
The Merry Widow (April 1978)
The Saint of Bleecker Street (1978)
Stop the World I Want to Get Off
Naughty Marietta (1978)
The Merry Widow (September 1978)
Street Scene (1978)
Naughty Marietta (1979)
The Merry Widow (1979)
Street Scene (1979)

PALACE THEATRE

Applause
From Israel with Love
Pacific Paradise
Cyrano
Bette Midler
An Evening with Josephine Baker
Lorelei, or *Gentlemen Still Prefer Blondes*
Eddy Arnold
Goodtime Charley
Treemonisha (transfer)
Home Sweet Homer
Shirley MacLaine
An Evening with Diana Ross
Siamsa
Toller Cranston's The Ice Show.
Man of La Mancha (1977)
Elvis The Legend Lives

The Grand Tour
Oklahoma!

PLAYHOUSE THEATRE

Dont Bother Me, I Cant Cope
Dear Oscar
Don't Step on My Olive Branch
Piaf . . . A Remembrance
King of Schnorrers

PLYMOUTH THEATRE

Good Evening
Godspell (first transfer)
Runaways
Ain't Misbehavin' (transfer)

RADIO CITY MUSIC HALL

Snow White and the Seven Dwarfs

RITZ THEATRE

Soon
Hurry, Harry

ROYALE THEATRE

Grease (second transfer)
Jacques Brel Is Alive and Well and Living in Paris
Good News

ST. JAMES THEATRE

Two Gentlemen of Verona
A Musical Jubilee
My Fair Lady
Music Is
On the Twentieth Century
Carmelina
Broadway Opry '79
The 1940's Radio Hour

SHUBERT THEATRE

The Selling of the President
A Little Night Music
Over Here!
A Chorus Line

22 STEPS THEATRE

Coquelico
My Old Friends
The Madwoman of Central Park West

URIS THEATRE

Via Galactica
Seesaw
The Desert Song
Gigi
Sammy
In Concert: Andy Williams with Michel Legrand
Anthony Newley/Henry Mancini
Johnny Mathis
The 5th Dimension
Raphael in Concert
Seals and Crofts
Treemonisha
The Merry Widow (1976)
Porgy and Bess
Bing Crosby on Broadway
Barry Manilow on Broadway
The King and I
Annie (third transfer)
Sweeney Todd, the Demon Barber of Fleet Street

VIVIAN BEAUMONT THEATRE

Operation Sidewinder
Man of La Mancha (1972)
Black Picture Show
Threepenny Opera

WINTER GARDEN THEATRE

Georgy
Purlie (1970; first transfer)
Follies
Liza
Gypsy
Doctor Jazz
Pacific Overtures
Fiddler on the Roof
Beatlemania
Zoot Suit
Bruce Forsyth on Broadway!
Gilda Radner Live from New York
Comin' Uptown

Bibliography

For the productions discussed in this book, I used source materials such as programs, souvenir programs, flyers, window cards (posters), sheet music, published and unpublished scripts (including preproduction and rehearsal scripts), and recordings (including demonstration, or demo, recordings). In addition, many reference books were helpful in providing both information and reality checks, and these are listed below.

Asch, Amy, ed. *The Complete Lyrics of Oscar Hammerstein II.* New York: Alfred A. Knopf, 2008.

Best Plays. As of this writing, the most recent edition of the venerable series is Jenkins, Jeffrey Eric, ed., *The Best Plays Theatre Yearbook of 2007–2008.* New York: Limelight Editions, 2009.

Bloom, Ken. *American Song: The Complete Musical Theatre Companion*, 2nd ed. New York: Schirmer Books, 1996.

Gilvey, John Anthony. *Before the Parade Passes By: Gower Champion and the Glorious American Musical.* New York: St. Martin's Press, 2005.

Green, Stanley, ed. *Rodgers and Hammerstein Fact Book: A Record of Their Works Together and with Other Collaborators.* New York: The Lynn Farnol Group, 1980.

Hart, Dorothy, and Robert Kimball, eds. *The Complete Lyrics of Lorenz Hart.* New York: Alfred A. Knopf, 1986.

Kimball, Robert, ed. *The Complete Lyrics of Frank Loesser.* New York: Alfred A. Knopf, 2003.

Leonard, William Torbert. *Broadway Bound: A Guide to Shows That Died Aborning.* Metuchen, NJ: The Scarecrow Press, 1983.

Nathan, George Jean. *The Theatre Book of the Year 1942–1943.* New York: Alfred A. Knopf, 1943.

Norton, Richard C. *A Chronology of American Musical Theatre* (3 vols.). New York: Oxford University Press, 2002.

Sondheim, Stephen. *Finishing the Hat: Collected Lyrics (1954–1981) with Attendant Comments, Principles, Heresies, Grudges, Whines and Anecdotes.* New York: Alfred A. Knopf, 2010.

Sondheim, Stephen. *Look, I Made a Hat: Collected Lyrics (1981–2011) with Attendant Comments, Amplifications, Dogmas, Harangues, Digressions, Anecdotes and Miscellany.* New York: Alfred A. Knopf, 2011.

Suskin, Steven. *More Opening Nights on Broadway.* New York: Schirmer Books, 1997.

Suskin, Steven. *Show Tunes: The Songs, Shows, and Careers of Broadway's Major Composers* (3rd ed.). New York: Oxford University Press, 2000.

Theatre World. As of this writing, the most recent edition of this important annual is *Theatre World, Volume 68, 2011–2012* (Ben Hodges and Scott Denny, editors; Milwaukee, WI: Theatre World Media, 2013).

Wlaschin, Ken. *Gian Carlo Menotti on Screen: Opera, Dance and Choral Works on Film, Television and Video.* Jefferson, NC: McFarland & Company, Inc., 1999.

Note: Virtually all the brief newspaper quotes in this book come from the annual series *New York Theatre Critics' Reviews.* Each volume includes the complete newspaper reviews of all plays and musicals (along with the names of the critics and the newspapers) to open on Broadway during a calendar year (for example, the 1975 volume includes reviews of all the shows that opened on Broadway [as well as a few Off-Broadway productions] during calendar year 1975, and not during the traditional theatre seasons of 1974–1975 or 1975–1976).

Index

About the Author

Dan Dietz was a Woodrow Wilson Fellow at the University of Virginia, and the subject of his graduate thesis was the poetry of Hart Crane. He taught English and the history of modern drama at Western Carolina University, and then later served with the U.S. Government Accountability Office and the U.S. Education Department. He is the author of *Off-Broadway Musicals, 1910–2007: Casts, Credits, Songs, Critical Reception and Performance Data of More Than 1,800 Shows* (2010), which was selected as one of the outstanding reference sources of 2011 by the American Library Association. He is also the author of *The Complete Book of 1940s Broadway Musicals* (2015), *The Complete Book of 1950s Broadway Musicals* (2014), and *The Complete Book of 1960s Broadway Musicals* (2014) (all published by Rowman & Littlefield). *The Complete Book of 1960s Broadway Musicals* was chosen by Booklist Online as an Editors' Choice for Reference Sources of books published in 2014.